Readings on the Rhetoric of Social Protest

Third Edition

Readings
on the Rhetoric
of Social Protest

Charles E. Morris III
Syracuse University

Stephen Howard Browne
The Pennsylvania State University

Strata Publishing, Inc.
State College, Pennsylvania

9 8 7 6 5 4 3 2 1

Published by:
Strata Publishing, Inc.
P.O. Box 1303
State College, PA 16804
USA
telephone: 814-234-8545
fax: 814-238-7222
web site: http://www.stratapub.com

Text and cover design by WhiteOak Creative.

Photo on front cover and pages ii, 5, and 147, "Fragment of the Berlin wall,"
© iStockphoto.com/CrazyD.

Credits and acknowledgments appear on pages vii–xiii and on this page by reference.

The URLs in this book were accurate as of the date cited or the date of publication. The authors and Strata do not guarantee the accuracy of information provided in websites listed.

Library of Congress Cataloging-in-Publication Data

Readings on the rhetoric of social protest / [edited by] Charles E. Morris III, Syracuse University, Stephen Howard Browne, The Pennsylvania State University. -- [Third edition].
     pages cm
 Includes bibliographical references and index.
 ISBN 978-1-891136-30-6 (pbk. : alk. paper)
 1. Social movements. 2. Persuasion (Rhetoric) I. Morris, Charles E., II. Browne, Stephen H.
 HM881.R43 2013
 303.48'4--dc23
                         2012051666

ISBN 978-1-891136-30-6

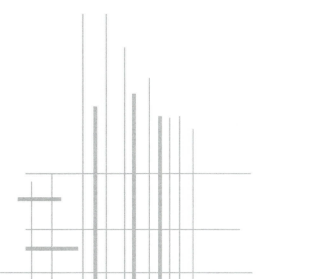
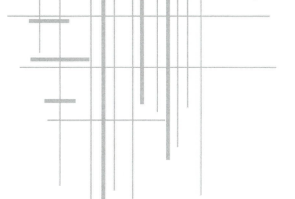

For Scott Rose and Margaret Michels

CREDITS AND ACKNOWLEDGMENTS

Leland M. Griffin, "The Rhetoric of Historical Movements," *Quarterly Journal of Speech* 38 (April 1952): 184–188, copyright © National Communication Association, reprinted by permission of (Taylor & Francis Ltd, http://www.tandfonline.com) on behalf of National Communication Association.

Franklyn S. Haiman, "The Rhetoric of the Streets: Some Legal and Ethical Considerations," *Quarterly Journal of Speech* 53 (April 1967): 99–114, copyright © National Communication Association, reprinted by permission of (Taylor & Francis Ltd, http://www.tandfonline.com) on behalf of National Communication Association.

Robert L. Scott and Donald K. Smith, "The Rhetoric of Confrontation," *Quarterly Journal of Speech* 55 (February 1969): 1–8, copyright © National Communication Association, reprinted by permission of (Taylor & Francis Ltd, http://www.tandfonline.com) on behalf of National Communication Association.

Herbert W. Simons, "Requirements, Problems, and Strategies: A Theory of Persuasion for Social Movements," *Quarterly Journal of Speech* 56 (February 1970): 1–11, copyright © National Communication Association, reprinted by permission of (Taylor & Francis Ltd, http://www.tandfonline.com) on behalf of National Communication Association.

Richard B. Gregg, "The Ego-Function of the Rhetoric of Protest," *Philosophy and Rhetoric* 4:1 (Spring 1971): 71–91. Copyright 1971 by The Pennsylvania State University. Reproduced by permission of The Pennsylvania State University Press.

Theodore Otto Windt, Jr., "The Diatribe: Last Resort for Protest," *Quarterly Journal of Speech* 58 (February 1972): 1–14, copyright © National Communication Association, reprinted by permission of (Taylor & Francis Ltd, http://www.tandfonline.com) on behalf of National Communication Association.

Karlyn Kohrs Campbell, "The Rhetoric of Women's Liberation: An Oxymoron," *Quarterly Journal of Speech* 59 (February 1973): 74–86, copyright © National Communication Association, reprinted by permission of (Taylor & Francis Ltd, http://www.tandfonline.com) on behalf of National Communication Association.

Robert S. Cathcart, "Movements: Confrontation as Rhetorical Form," *Southern Speech Communication Journal* 43 (Spring 1978): 233–247. Reproduced with the permission of Southern States Communication Association.

Robert Cox and Christina R. Foust, "Social Movement Rhetoric," republished with permission of SAGE Publications, Inc., from *The SAGE Handbook of Rhetorical Studies,* ed. Andrea A. Lunsford, Kirt H. Wilson, and Rosa A. Eberly, 2009; permission conveyed through Copyright Clearance Center, Inc.

Michael Calvin McGee, "'Social Movement': Phenomenon or Meaning?" *Central States Speech Journal* 31 (Winter 1980): 233–244. Reproduced with the permission of the Central States Communication Association.

David Zarefsky, "A Skeptical View of Movement Studies," *Central States Speech Journal* 31 (Winter 1980): 245–254. Reproduced with the permission of the Central States Communication Association.

Stephen E. Lucas, "Coming to Terms with Movement Studies," *Central States Speech Journal* 31 (Winter 1980): 255–266. Reproduced with the permission of the Central States Communication Association.

James R. Andrews, "History and Theory in the Study of the Rhetoric of Social Movements," *Central States Speech Journal* 31 (Winter 1980): 274–281. Reproduced with the permission of the Central States Communication Association.

Charles J. Stewart, "A Functional Approach to the Rhetoric of Social Movements," *Central States Speech Journal* 31 (Winter 1980): 298–305. Reproduced with the permission of the Central States Communication Association.

Stephen Hartnett, "Lincoln and Douglas Meet the Abolitionist David Walker as Prisoners Debate Slavery: Empowering Education, Applied Communication, and Social Justice," *Journal of Applied Communication Research* 26 (May 1998): 232–253, copyright © National Communication Association, reprinted by permission of (Taylor & Francis Ltd, http://www.tandfonline.com) on behalf of National Communication Association.

Daniel C. Brouwer, "ACT-ing UP in Congressional Hearings," reprinted by permission from *Counterpublics and the State* edited by Robert Asen and Daniel C. Brouwer, the State University of New York Press © 2001, State University of New York. All rights reserved.

Kevin Michael DeLuca and Jennifer Peeples, "From Public Sphere to Public Screen: Democracy, Activism, and the 'Violence' of Seattle," *Critical Studies in Media Communication* 19 (June 2002): 125–151, copyright © National Communication Association, reprinted by permission of (Taylor & Francis Ltd, http://www.tandfonline.com) on behalf of National Communication Association.

Phaedra C. Pezzullo, "Resisting 'National Breast Cancer Awareness Month': The Rhetoric of Counterpublics and Their Cultural Performances," *Quarterly Journal of Speech* 89 (November 2003): 345–365, copyright © National Communication Association, reprinted by permission of (Taylor & Francis Ltd, http://www.tandfonline.com) on behalf of National Communication Association.

Darrel Enck-Wanzer, "Trashing the System: Social Movement, Intersectional Rhetoric, and Collective Agency in the Young Lords Organization's Garbage Offensive," *Quarterly Journal of Speech* 92 (May 2006): 174–201, copyright © National Communication Association, reprinted by permission of (Taylor & Francis Ltd, http://www.tandfonline.com) on behalf of National Communication Association.

With kind permission from Springer Science+Business Media: *Qualitative Sociology,* "The Place of Framing: Multiple Audiences and Antiwar Protests near Fort Bragg," 29, 2006, 485–505, Michael T. Heaney and Fabio Rojas, © Springer Science + Business Media, Inc. 2006.

CONTENTS

PREFACE

The third edition of *Readings on the Rhetoric of Social Protest*, like the preceding editions, is designed for instructors and students in courses that study social protest from a rhetorical perspective. On the basis of our own teaching experiences and many conversations with a diverse community of colleagues who have similar teaching goals, we agreed that we wanted a book that would offer ready access to a rich but dispersed literature on the subject in a single volume; highlight key theoretical, historical, and critical developments; and provide a basis upon which students could extend their own explorations and insights.

We have benefited greatly from colleagues who used the book and provided valuable feedback that confirmed our belief in the volume's classroom utility, deepened our perspectives, and suggested ways in which it might be enriched to serve instructors and students more fully. Our new selections and commentary reflect a desire to meet current pedagogical needs and account for recent scholarly developments. As in previous editions, our purpose is to offer some of the best work in the discipline and allied fields, and to bring it together in a cogent, clear, and productive format. We believe that instructors and students will find in these pages a wide range of provocative issues, intriguing personalities, inventional resources, and suggestive lines of scholarly inquiry.

The rhetorical analysis of social protest is as diverse as the voices, texts, meanings, bodies, images, and performances it seeks to explain. Instructors and students are confronted with a potentially bewildering array of approaches, topics, critical objects, and questions. What, precisely, is rhetorical about protest, dissent, resistance, movement? How do we go about identifying, analyzing, and evaluating rhetorical action for social change and in opposition to established institutions and cultural norms? Why is it important to study such action? What are the proper objects of our study? What can we learn about protest and rhetoric generally from attention to specific case studies? This collection of readings provides a map of sorts, first to assist students into the field and then into those more specific areas that have demarcated the scholarship. We have also sought through our selections

to allow for free exploration across several domains, as well as for structural reconfigurations to fit the goals of particular courses. The chapter introductions acquaint students with leading authors, issues, and movements, and encourage readers to observe points of similarity and difference, note key developments, and consider prospects for further study.

ORGANIZATION OF THE BOOK

The readings are arranged in two major sections, "Origins and Trajectories" and "Critical Touchstones," reflecting two generations of scholarly approaches within the discipline. The first generation of scholarship engaged with and struggled over definitions of "social movement," object domain, methodologies, and theoretical perspectives. Some of its questions about the means and ends of protest are returning to prominence in the second generation, which has so far focused attention on critical analysis of individual rhetorical acts and performances, or on constellations of them, usually within particular movements or protest groups. This work, too, is theoretically sophisticated and productive, but it critically centers the object of analysis, the historically specific experiences, and the engagements of protest rhetoric to a greater degree than its predecessors. Students will also discover contemporary scholars returning to fundamental issues and questions that animated their forebears and that generate connections and points of departure across the two major sections of the book.

In each section, we have organized essays into chapters that address common themes, issues, and audiences. Each chapter is arranged in chronological order to suggest an unfolding series of conceptual concerns, allowing students to identify patterns and transformations and to develop an increasingly sharpened and sophisticated approach to the subject.

Section I: Origins and Trajectories
The essays in the first section explicitly create and debate the rhetorical nature, purpose, and functions of social movements.

Chapter 1, "Theoretical Foundations and New Directions," presents essays that speak directly to the ways that social protest movements may be conceptualized as an area of rhetorical inquiry. The stress, accordingly, tends toward definition, jurisdiction, and scope. Students are encouraged to consider the characteristics that define social movements as rhetorical phenomena, the types of rhetoric at work in social protest and how they are manifested, the ethical and psychological dimensions of such rhetoric, the dynamics of social and political action, and the contexts that enable and constrain resistance and movement.

Chapter 2, "Competing Perspectives," includes essays that take a critical view of the precepts established in the first chapter. These essays emphasize some of the limits that the first generation of movement scholars imposed and offer alternatives and priorities for advancing scholarly inquiry. They stress, in particular, the interplay of history and theory, and bring into sharp relief such questions as whether movements are best understood with reference to the former or the latter. Students are encouraged to identify and differentiate among scholarly approaches and assumptions.

Section II: Critical Touchstones

To illustrate the possibilities of social movement criticism, the second section offers a selection of critical touchstones, or case studies, that take up a rich variety of historical and contemporary movement for social reform and radical transformation. Collectively, these essays offer a means of conceptualizing social protest rhetoric in broad terms, beyond the contextual and strategic particularities of a single movement—spanning movements, time, space, texts, affects, and bodies. In grouping the essays into four thematic chapters, we hope to encourage comparative analysis and theory building, from a multiplicity of scholarly perspectives and cases linked by a designated conceptual focal point or rhetorical issue, helping students to deepen their analyses of protest rhetoric within an individual movement.

Chapter 3, "Tactics for External Audiences," offers essays that examine how rhetoric is directed from a movement outward to expose oppression, unsettle the norms and policies enabling that oppression, and persuade others—the state, institutions, media, potential recruits,

bystanders, and the general public—to embrace the movement's transformative ideals and agenda. What rhetorical situations do protest rhetors confront? What tactical means, both conventional and innovative, are available, preferred, and selected in specific historical circumstances, to appeal to and confront complex audiences of opponents, allies, and other agents of influence? Within the framework of social protest, in short, what are the available means of persuasion?

Chapter 4, "Tactics for Internal Audiences," addresses similar questions about how movement rhetoric is directed inward, toward members and sympathizers, for purposes of recruitment, mobilization, conflict resolution, and entrenchment. How is rhetoric used to entice potential members? Craft a coherent and sustaining vision and identity? Invigorate the movement in times of frustration and fatigue? Resolve conflicts among members? Adapt collective goals and maintain unity to shifting circumstances? Adapt strategy across time and circumstance? Build coalitions with other protest groups and movements?

Chapter 5, "Tactics of Control," considers the rhetorical responses from those against whom a movement has mobilized, or from others who perceive the movement as a threat. These essays explore how opponents of social movements—such as individuals writing hate mail, countermovements, and mainstream media reflecting the hegemonic society—work rhetorically to undermine, contain, or domesticate protest discourse. What are the available rhetorical means of controlling protest rhetoric? How do power arrangements shape those responses? How do those responses change movement strategy? Can we understand protest rhetoric and its oppositional counterpart as interdependent?

Chapter 6, "Tactical Modifications," considers the influence of time on social protest rhetoric. Given that social transformation never occurs overnight, how do changing circumstances, shifting demographics and dynamics of membership and opposition, and cultural change itself shape rhetorical tactics for the duration of the movement? How do developments over time exhaust favored tactics or inspire new tactics? How does protest rhetoric succeed or fail according to its long-range tactical vision and capacity for modification?

Our chapter divisions reflect our assessment of concerns and interests that occur in many movements and that are prominently featured in the study of social protest rhetoric. No doubt other conceptual configurations will come to mind. Our object is neither to endorse any one approach to the study of social protest nor to privilege a particular movement or movements, but to highlight the diversity and directions of current scholarship, providing a wide range of examples that indicate the theoretical, historical, and critical assumptions and practices that drive scholars' work on social protest rhetoric. Over all, the goal with this section—as in the book as a whole—is to draw attention to patterns that range across categories, topics, and methods.

As editors, we have made every effort to reproduce the essays exactly as they appeared in their original publication. Exceptions include the correction of minor typographical errors and the insertion of "[*sic*]" to indicate accuracy where the original phrasing was unusual. All unitalicized appearances of "[sic]" are in the original essay. In addition, footnotes have been moved to the end of each essay.

The **Selected Bibliography** is designed to serve several purposes. Students can link and extend their projects to existing work in many fields on many different movements; explore key issues related to the rhetorical study of protest in greater detail, depth, and scope; and find models of scholarly writing for their own projects. For each movement, we list references to primary materials, historical contexts, and critical analysis from among the best scholarship of academic fields studying social protest.

The bibliography has been updated and expanded in this edition to include five new movements that are transforming our world as we speak: Arab Spring/Arab Awakening, Latina/o movements, Occupy, Prison Reform and Death Penalty Abolitionism, and the Tea Party. For some of these movements the research is only just emerging, so the sources listed here are only a beginning; they are likely to be richly supplemented over the next several years.

Readings on the Rhetoric of Social Protest provides instructors and students access to a long and productive tradition of rhetorical scholarship. Our hope is that this collection may introduce students to this tradition and cutting edge work and provide inspiration for scholarly investigation of their own.

FEATURES OF THE NEW EDITION

In light of feedback to the organization of the second edition, the general structure of the book and the number of essays remains the same. To keep pace with developing scholarship and the array of diverse and significant movements that students might engage, however, we have replaced some selections with newer works, especially in Section II.

With two exceptions, the readings in Section I, "Origins and Trajectories" remain the same. To Chapter 1, we have moved Karlyn Kohrs Campbell's canonical 1973 essay "The Rhetoric of Women's Liberation: An Oxymoron," a foundational theoretical work that we now believe should have been in this Chapter 1 all along. In the same chapter, we have added Robert Cox and Christina Foust's "Social Movement Rhetoric," a disciplinary genealogy and analysis of social protest scholarship that maps work in allied fields—past, present, and future—and therefore constitutes an important new beginning to envisioning and teaching social movements.

In Section II, "Critical Touchstones," in response to teachers who used the second edition, we have added more scholarship on contemporary movements. Although this edition still includes exemplary studies in movements from the nineteenth century through the 1960s, which are important to the history, theory, and criticism of social protest, we recognize that they are increasingly remote to today's students and scholars. Newer selections reflect current interests, perspectives, and touchstones regarding "new social movements" and "new communication technologies" that constitute and facilitate social action in rapidly changing global contexts —rendering some new movements not so new, and perhaps not movements, tomorrow.

That said, we emphasize that our goal was *not* to represent every social movement, nor to favor any particular movement, but rather to represent a wide array of social movements. We also hoped to highlight a variety of meaningful approaches and applications for the rhetorical case study of social protest, selected for their diversity as well as their theoretical and critical contributions to this area of study.

ACKNOWLEDGMENTS

For a period of more than a year during 2009 and 2010, we were not certain that this volume would be published, in our opinion owing to what theorists and polemicists call "academic capitalism." It was a demoralizing time. However, having one's book on social protest rhetoric stalled on the verge of production has a way of stirring the activist spirit within one, and bringing forth the voice of dissent that is surging in one's throat. After months of negotiation with powers-that-be, and an exhilarating speech and floor debate in San Francisco on behalf of this volume and similar projects, we were back in business. Born of struggle, then, this third edition of *Readings on the Rhetoric of Social Protest* is particularly meaningful to us. The aftertaste of struggle sometimes can be very sweet indeed.

Our gratitude, then, always abundant, is all the more deeply heartfelt because numerous colleagues and friends generously lent their expert advice and copious suggestions, voiced their solidarity, and shared their political skill so that this volume would come to be. We thank so very much Angela Aguayo, Southern Illinois University; Robert Asen, University of Wisconsin–Madison; Diana Ashe, University of North Carolina at Wilmington; Kevin Ayotte, California State University, Fresno; Jason Edward Black, University of Alabama; Carole Blair, University of North Carolina; Jennifer Borda, University of New Hampshire; Dan Brouwer, Arizona State University; Carl Burgchardt, Colorado State University; Kevin Carragee, Suffolk University; Karma Chávez, University of Wisconsin–Madison; Jim Cherney, Wayne State University; Dana Cloud, University of Texas at Austin; Terri Cornwell, Liberty University; Tasha Dubriwny, Texas A & M University; Jeremy Engels, Penn State University; Cara Finnegan, University of Illinois; Christina Foust, University of Denver; Barbara Oney Garvey, Hanover College; Chuck Goehring, San Diego State University; Greg Goodale, Northeastern University; David Henry, University of Nevada, Las Vegas; Dale Herbeck, Northeastern University; Kristin Hoerl, Butler University; Diane Hope, Rochester Institute of Technology; Davis Houck, Florida State University; Carl T. Hyden, Morgan State University; Spoma Jovanovic, University of North Carolina at Greensboro; Brendan T. Kendall, Clemson University; Jeffrey Kurtz, Denison University; Randall A. Lake, University of Southern California; John Lucaites, Indiana University; Kristy Maddux, University of Maryland; Jimmie Manning, Northern Kentucky University; Matthew May, North Carolina State University; Bryan Mack-McCann, Wayne State University; Sara McKinnon, University of Wisconsin–Madison; Tom Nakayama, Northeastern University; Lester Olson, University of Pittsburgh; Susan Owen, University of Puget Sound; Catherine H. Palczewski, University of Northern Iowa; Jennifer Peeples, Utah State University; Phaedra Pezzullo, Indiana University; Kendall R. Phillips, Syracuse University; Michele Ramsey, Penn State University Berks; Erin J. Rand, Syracuse University; Angela Ray, Northwestern University; Valerie Renegar, Southwestern University; Spencer Schaffner, University of Illinois at Urbana-Champaign; Shannon Scott, Seattle Pacific University; Brant Short, Northern Arizona University; Signatories of the 2010 NCA Resolution on Copyright Fees; Stacey K. Sowards, University of Texas at El Paso; Belinda Stillion Southard, University of Georgia; Ted Striphas, Indiana University; Karen Taylor, University of Alaska Fairbanks; Robert Terrill, Indiana University; Mari Boor Tonn, University of Richmond; Phillip Voight, Gustavus Adolphus College; Darrel Wanzer, University of Iowa; Jason Warren, George Mason University; and Richard West, Emerson College.

For the day-to-day and the above-and-beyond during this book's long matriculation, Chuck expresses special thanks and love to Dan, Rob, Tom, Dale, Pam, Jason, Karma, Sara, Phaedra, Ted, Michele, Mary Kate, Shea, Katie, Andrew, Austin, the fabulous "regulars" on Facebook, and Jackson and Cooper.

We could not have finished this volume without the marvelous Scott Rose, who listened sympathetically to seemingly ceaseless discussion of copyright politics and offered his wealth of support. Scott also skillfully handled, with patience and aplomb, the tedious and frustrating but invaluable work of proofreading much of this manuscript in its messiest post-scanning phase. Cheers, Mr. Rose!

Kathleen Domenig and Brian Henry are now old friends and longstanding collaborators. This volume no doubt proved to be daunting for them, too, but they never flinched and always believed in the value of this project. Their engaging shop talk, hilarious banter, deep commitment to scholarship and pedagogy, and consummate professionalism are gifts for which we feel fortunate, and their courageous and creative venture, Strata, Inc., is a gift to the field.

We dedicate our work on this volume to Scott Rose and Margaret Michels, our partners and mainstays, with love and endless thanks for everything.

Introduction

Why study the rhetoric of social protest? For one answer, we need only turn to the past, for there, in the unfolding dramas of history, can be found a remarkable range of voices striving to make the world over again. But of course such voices are not of the past only. Our own exhilarating and vexing age—the age of Facebook and Twitter, Occupy and Arab Spring—is being shaped decisively by people coming together, debating, designing, and otherwise mobilizing and deploying material and symbolic resources for social change. Scholars from across the humanities and social sciences are paying close attention to the contexts, cultures, modalities, and performances of protest. Of central importance to this wide and diverse expanse of disciplinary and interdisciplinary study are the contributions of scholars studying protest rhetoric, whose work we have selected and here present.

Although their aims, methods, objects, and conclusions vary widely, these authors share several assumptions that unite them in a common enterprise. In the first place, they recognize that rhetoric is not set off from or opposed to reality, but constitutes a reality of its own. Students of rhetoric in movements and social protest understand that *words are deeds*, that language has force and effect in the world. To study the rhetoric of social protest is to study how symbols—words, signs, images, music, bodies—operate to shape our perceptions of reality and invite us to act accordingly. Moreover, contemporary scholarship has also suggested how nonlinguistic and nonsymbolic presences and absences contribute to material conditions and lived experience. Bodies in pain or pleasure, speeches delivered at a rally, protest marches, movement encampments, letters to the editor, teach-ins, self-immolations, media sound bites, documentaries, manifestos, image events on the public screen, tweets and status updates, cell phone and YouTube videos, and many other rhetorical practices are seen as types of symbolic

and material action, which is very much in evidence all around us.

In the second place, our authors understand social movements to be definitively *rhetorical:* that is, movements for reform and radical transformation are intrinsically bound up with the interruption, intervention, alteration, negotiation, and implications of representations and meanings; with voice and image and performance, affects and emotions, norms and policies. The rhetorical dimensions and manifestations of any given protest or movement will of course differ from those of others. Some protests and movements fail, others prosper; and the very terms of success, effects, and effectivity are variously interpreted and much debated. Whatever their resources and strategies, whatever their aims and effects, movements are by their nature rhetorical. Why? Because, as the following essays suggest, they organize and perform the symbolic and the material to persuasive ends; they address unsettled issues of public importance; and they seek change not through violence or coercion but through force of argument and appeal. Now, symbols, bodies, persuasion, contingency, materiality, public life, argument, and appeal are concepts definitive of rhetoric itself; thus when we discover the rhetorical dynamics of a particular movement, we are really finding something out about rhetoric in general.

Proceeding from these assumptions, the essays offer differing and compelling statements on the definition, function, scope, performance, and consequences of social movements, and on the means and modalities by which they are given rhetorical expression. We have organized these studies on the rhetoric of social protest according to two distinct avenues of inquiry: first, theoretical statements that founded study in this field, scholarly debates that advanced those perspectives, and cutting-edge theoretical and methodological trajectories; and, second, rich historical case studies that have applied, complicated, challenged, and extended such theory by exploring the lived rhetorical experiences of protestors and movements.

Section I, "Origins and Trajectories," consists of two chapters. The essays in these chapters suggest what may be gained from approaching the rhetoric of protest and social movements from various *theoretical perspectives*. We do not use the term "theoretical perspectives" to mean sets of grand abstractions but, rather, ways of seeing in the most fundamental terms what movements *are*.

The essays in Chapter 1, "Theoretical Foundations and New Directions," ask, and begin to answer, such questions as: How do we know a social movement when we see it? What are its distinguishing features? On what basis can we generalize the qualities that seem to define certain social movements as similar to others? How are social movements different from each other? What, precisely, is rhetorical about social movements? What object or objects of study are of special interest to the rhetorical scholar? How should the rhetorical scholar go about analyzing and evaluating the rhetorical phenomena of social protest?

Chapter 2, "Competing Perspectives," contains an important set of essays that probe and challenge the assumptions, implications, and execution of movement scholarship as it had previously been practiced. These readings, however, should not be interpreted as dismissing earlier work. Instead, they signal a crucial stage in the development of all good scholarship, where settled opinion is reassessed, criticized, and opened up to greater avenues of insight. To that end, several prominent historians, critics, and theorists of rhetoric revisit the claims of earlier work and find that its promises were not born out convincingly. Most of these critics, themselves accomplished students of social movements, are not skeptical about the potential or worth of the subject; they seek, rather, to reevaluate and correct perceived shortcomings in the formation of issues, in the restrictiveness of certain approaches, and

in the balance between historical recovery and the critical interpretation of movement activity. Taken together, these competing perspectives help us situate the study of rhetorical movements historically as well as critically, clarify basic terms of agreement and difference, and target areas for continued growth and enhanced understanding of the subject.

Section I represents scholars' efforts to provide broad perspectives on the relationship between rhetoric and social movements. In locating important questions and issues central to this relationship, the essays in these chapters give us a variety of theoretical vantage points from which to begin study of a specific movement.

Section II, "Critical Touchstones," follows the trajectory of the field, from the point at which many rhetorical critics became anxious to apply and test theoretical foundations and competing perspectives forged by the pioneering scholarship, through the subsequent decades in which such critics deepened and diversified the analysis of rhetorical practices within historically specific cases of social protest. Over time, these scholars have illuminated various rhetorical dimensions of individual movements, while contributing to the larger study of social protest and rhetoric in general. Critical analyses have dominated the rhetorical study of social movements since 1980.

With this substantial and enduring turn in scholarship, the issues raised by previous essays no longer stand on hypothetical grounds; instead they are made manifest in the lived strategic and performative experiences of protesters, and in their myriad audiences. One exciting component of the critical approaches featured in Section II is the attention to historical detail. Case studies focus on the scope, form, function, performance, media, and evolution of specific social movements, within their specific historical circumstances and over time, in much greater depth than do works predominantly focused on theory. More exciting, especially for rhetorical scholars, is that case studies provide a "street-level" encounter with protest rhetoric itself. Having encountered and engaged actual rhetoric, we often return to theory, to the general questions of movements and rhetoric, with fresh eyes and new insights.

The essays in Chapter 3, "Tactics for External Audiences," consider the persuasive means of publicizing, dramatizing, justifying, confronting, and advocating a particular protest cause. How does a performance in a prison class, or testimony delivered before a congressional subcommittee, or a melodramatic narrative, or an image event of anarchic violence, or piling trash at intersections of an urban barrio, or baring the scar of a missing breast and a mastectomy, or strategic deployments of space in a military town or a campus bathroom, work rhetorically to awaken, engage, attack, and sometimes convert targeted individuals, institutions, and the general populace into recognition of the problems that compelled protestors to seek redress and transformation?

Chapter 4, "Tactics for Internal Audiences," contains works that focus on the rhetoric deployed to mobilize people and resources for the movement, nurture relationships, maintain morale and commitment during the long and arduous campaign, develop and negotiate strategy, and build coalitions between social movement organizations. What personae, voices, symbols, arguments, and rituals rouse and attract potential members to join and participate in a social movement, sacrifice on its behalf, and stay involved? In response, we encounter here, among several fascinating objects of study, tribal rituals, a manifesto, civil disobedience, performances of militant motherhood, Supreme Court arguments, and an unlikely collaboration against racism and homophobia in Arizona.

In studying the rhetoric of social protest, we also discover that protestors are not the only ones crafting strategies and performing them. Oppressors fight back, sometimes rhetorically, sometimes legally, and sometimes violently. The state, various political and cultural institutions, and the mainstream media ignore, co-opt,

discredit, or silence protestors. These are a few of the examples we witness in studies collected in Chapter 5, "Tactics of Control."

Finally, essays in Chapter 6, "Tactical Modifications," reveal that time and timing are crucial elements of study in understanding social protest. Historical circumstances change during the lifespan of a social movement, creating shifting contingencies, opportunities, and constraints that protestors must account for and adapt to if they hope to achieve their goals. Those goals, the vision of the movement, also alter and evolve over time. Given these vicissitudes, what strategic adjustments do protestors make to strike a timely blow, manage unforeseen difficulties, recruit new members, maintain or renew outside interest in the movement, reinvigorate those dedicated to the cause, and transform the vision and/or collective identity of the movement?

In order to stimulate critical reflection on all these important issues in the rhetoric of social protest, we have collected exemplary studies of a wide array of significant movements in United States history, including the animal rights, woman suffrage, labor, antipoverty, antiwar, civil rights, Black and Red and Latino/a power, gay and women's liberation, pro-life/choice, prisoner rights, AIDS activism, environmentalism, disability rights, queer and gender rights, and antiglobalization movements. This diverse sampling of protest rhetoric, in a sense, invites us into the fray; we experience tactical choices as they were drawn from a limited reservoir at portentous and everyday moments in our history. In experiencing the situated history of protest discourse we also learn much about the choices protesters make in its wake, and perhaps chart for ourselves a blueprint for future persuasive action on behalf of social change.

Section I

Origins and Trajectories

Chapter 1

Theoretical Foundations and New Directions

The first set of essays suggests what may be gained from approaching the rhetoric of protest and social movements from various theoretical perspectives. That is, scholars offer diverse explanations about what a movement is, what comprises and constitutes it, what it does, and how it does it. Scholars also offer diverse explanations about how we should go about the business of analyzing movement—definitionally, historically, critically, comparatively—and whether participation should also be our business.

We begin our first section with Leland M. Griffin, who is widely considered to have pioneered the study of movements from a rhetorical perspective. In "The Rhetoric of Historical Movements" (1952), he proposes broadening the rhetorical critic's traditional emphasis on speakers to include larger and more complex sets of rhetorical phenomena. For students interested in the study of historical movements, questions of focus, scope, method, and criteria immediately present themselves, and here Griffin offers some useful answers. The "student's goal," he concludes, "is to discover . . . the rhetorical patterns inherent in the movement selected for investigation."

The tumultuous 1960s prompted a great deal of reflection on the sources, character, and limits of social protest. Students of rhetoric, in particular, were forced to reexamine conventional principles. In "The Rhetoric of the Streets: Some Legal and Ethical Considerations" (1967), Franklyn S. Haiman, a prominent scholar of free speech, seeks to make sense of what he calls the "rhetoric of the streets" and asks what legal and ethical concerns are posed by "the new rhetoric." Is such rhetoric destructive of organized society? Ought it to be allowed under certain circumstances? And even if such activity is protected by the First Amendment, Haiman asks, "Is the activity ethical?"

Social protest during the 1960s extended well beyond the public speeches usually associated with classical rhetorical criticism. Robert L. Scott and Donald K. Smith, in "The Rhetoric of Confrontation" (1969), are especially concerned with "the rhetoric of confrontation" and the revolutionary potential implied by such activity. To study confrontation in this sense, they argue, is to study an "inherently symbolic" process, and thus to seek an explanation for why people act in this way, what power dynamics are at work in social protest, and what the implications of such protest are for social relations. In view of the new problems posed by the rhetoric of confrontation, they, like Griffin and Haiman, call for a reevaluation of traditional models and theories of rhetoric.

In his essay "Requirements, Problems, and Strategies: A Theory of Persuasion for Social Movements" (1970), Herbert W. Simons answers the call by stressing the distinctive challenges that movement leaders face when they attempt to mobilize dissent. Most, if not all, movements contain predictable requirements and problems, he says, which in turn suggest strategies available to leaders for their resolution. Simons, borrowing from findings in sociology, maps out these challenges and argues that "the rhetoric of a movement must *follow*, in a general way, from the very nature of movements." A movement leader, in turn, is to be tested by his or her "capacity to fulfill the requirements of his [or her] movement by resolving or reducing rhetorical problems."

The rhetoric of social protest, whatever form it takes, has typically been thought of as outward-directed. That is, it seeks to alter the status quo by persuading or forcing others to change their attitudes, beliefs, and actions. In his provocative and influential essay "The

Ego-Function of the Rhetoric of Protest" (1971), however, Richard B. Gregg argues that a good deal of such rhetoric is actually inward-directed. Where Simons draws from sociological theory, Gregg applies certain psychological insights into the nature of ego functions to suggest that protest messages help constitute, maintain, and defend advantageous conceptions of the self. Gregg identifies several ways in which the self-addressed nature of such rhetoric contains, as well, certain tactical advantages.

Once scholars began to study more diverse forms of symbol usage, new questions emerged as to the nature, scope, and function of certain types of confrontational rhetoric. The strident and frequently outlandish language of many 1960s protest movements, for example, prompted many to wonder just how effective such rhetoric might be. Was it productive or counterproductive? By what criteria are we to evaluate such questions? An essay by Theodore Otto Windt, Jr., "The Diatribe: Last Resort for Protest" (1972), offers a compelling case study in one type of confrontational speech. Locating the diatribe within a long tradition of social criticism, Windt concludes that, effective or not, it is often a "last resort" when traditional rhetorical strategies are no longer seen as viable.

Karlyn Kohrs Campbell further destabilizes traditional conceptions of social protest in her exploration of "The Rhetoric of Women's Liberation: An Oxymoron" (1973). Although the women's liberation movement is indebted to Black Power and the New Left, Campbell claims it created a new "genre" of protest rhetoric, distinctive for interdependent substantive and stylistic qualities that coalesced to reject "certain traditional concepts of the rhetorical process—as persuasion of the many by an expert or leader," and traditional concepts of audiences. Feminists of the "second wave" sought by means of an "'anti-rhetorical' style" known as "consciousness-raising" to transform women's self-perception and identity in relation to

contexts of power, and to simultaneously "violate the reality structure," namely the sexism and misogyny dominating the psychosocial culture, through "attack metaphors" and "symbolic reversals." Campbell here offers rich rhetorical perspective on movement mobilization and the challenges of ideological constraint.

Rhetorical movements may differ drastically in motive, types of rhetoric deployed, and effect, but they hold certain definitive elements in common. Chief among these, Robert S. Cathcart argues in "Movements: Confrontation as Rhetorical Form" (1978), is "form," a key instance of which he calls "confrontational form." In particular, movements stage ritualized conflict, a kind of "enactment that dramatizes the symbolic separation of the individual from the existing order." Cathcart's controversial essay poses this sense of confrontation against a sense of it as merely an instrument to be used. As a type of ritual enactment, confrontation is best understood as a means to "consummate" one's departure from the existing order and identification within the new movement.

Finally, success in studying the rhetoric of social protest would seem to be facilitated not only by engaging the roots of this domain of inquiry, but also its genealogy, current trajectories, research gaps, and future directions. Robert Cox and Christina R. Foust, in their essay "Social Movement Rhetoric" (2009), provide just this invaluable orientation. They trace the study from its early emphases on the discourse of movement leaders, the rhetoric of the streets, the rhetorical functions of a movement, and the dramatism of protest; through the 1980s debates over definition and methodology; and forward into current scholarship. Their survey of these contemporary explorations of counterpublics, nonlinguistic and extralinguistic material performances and modalities such as bodies and images, resistant acts unconnected to formal movements, and changing global contexts altering what democracy and dissent might mean and entail, reveals scholars reconfiguring how we think about protest agents, audiences, effects, and rhetoric itself through a diverse array of cutting-edge theories and methodologies. Cox and Foust close with areas of study that, lamentably, have been neglected in rhetorical studies, especially non-Western protest modalities and contexts.

As these essays suggest, to inquire into the theoretical foundation of movement study is to ask questions of the most basic kind. However diverse they may be, movements of social protest share certain properties, enough at least to warrant certain generalizations as to their sources, structures, and relationships to other forms of organized resistance. Movements, in other words, are not isolated and unique phenomena. But if this is so, how do we go about establishing such generalizations? One approach, evident in several essays in this chapter, is to press the question of the source or ground of movement rhetoric. From what do movements originate, and in what ways do their rhetoric take from this source? Each essay answers this question differently; some, like Griffin's and Simons's essays, suggest that movements are responses to specific historical circumstances, and that the rhetoric that promotes (and frequently undermines) them ought to be examined accordingly. Gregg, who sees evidence of certain psychological needs in the motives and actions of movement adherents, advances a rather different view. Cox and Foust chart current scholarship that questions the very terms of democracy, culture, and public engagement seemingly taken for granted in these foundational essays. However variant their accounts, these scholars are similarly interested in understanding what motivates people to gather and express their dissatisfaction with the world around them, and how they go about it.

To ask after the theoretical foundations and new directions of rhetorical movements is to ask, in addition, about the province of rhetoric itself. One tradition of rhetoric—though by no means the only tradition—assumes that rhetorical analysis is best suited to the exploration of how speakers use language to persuade audiences to enlightened choice. There is merit to this approach, of course, but virtually all our authors seek to expand the range of rhetorical action well beyond this model. In theory and in manifest practice, they argue, rhetoric describes a broad range of symbolic and material activity, encompassing not only speeches by movement leaders but bodily intervention, images, street theater, marches, posters, songs, streaming video, documentaries, indeed all the means of persuasion imaginable and necessary for organized protest and individual activist performances. Rhetorical movements, they insist, cannot be adequately studied without a heightened sense of the *media* through which protest is given voice, effect, and circulation. It is no small part of the legacy of movement studies, theoretically considered, that our understanding of what gets to count as rhetorical has been permanently altered and is ever changing.

To think theoretically about rhetorical movements is to examine, finally, the interplay of voices within and among organized protests. Students of the subject are especially concerned to identify the ways in which certain kinds of movements—for example, radical and conservative—share some properties but differ in other important respects. What characterizes the rhetoric of reform that sets it apart from the rhetoric of reactionary or radical movements? The question is a subset of a broader theoretical interest in rhetorical form, especially as that form appears to cohere in movements generally. Cathcart, in particular, has offered a compelling and controversial answer to this question, but the issue cuts to the heart of all studies in movement rhetoric. Ultimately, it leads us to wonder whether there is something intrinsic about the nature of movements that distinguishes its rhetoric from other modes of symbolic and material suasory performance.

The Rhetoric of Historical Movements
Leland M. Griffin

When the student undertakes the rhetorical pursuit of an individual orator, he enters a scholarly bailiwick whose boundaries are clearly demarked. Convenient temporal limits for the study are set by the orator's vital dates; the speaker himself supplies the point of focus, the thread of his life a motif, and his career, analyzed and evaluated in all its ramifications from "early speech training" to climactic utterances, provides the matter of the study. Techniques of analysis and appraisal in the biographical approach have become conventionalized, and the central problem for those concerned with research in this area, for the moment at least, would appear to be one of objective rather than of method. Many useful biographical studies have been produced, many more will be, and a fund of information about orators will eventually be accumulated.

Nevertheless, the belief has taken increasing hold that approaches to the study of public address other than the biographical ought to be encouraged. The recommendation has been made,[1] for example, that we pay somewhat less attention to the single speaker and more to speakers—that we turn our attention from the individual "great orator" and undertake research into such selected acts and atmospheres of public address as would permit the study of a multiplicity of speakers, speeches, audiences, and occasions. For the student who would move in this direction, at least four approaches would seem to be available: the period study; the regional, or regional-period study; the case study, or more properly, the collection of case studies confined to a specific theme and time; and the movement study, concerned with the survey of public address, in historical movements. Of the four approaches listed, the one last mentioned has received perhaps the least attention. As with the other approaches, various questions concerning critical method and objective will confront the student who undertakes the rhetorical study of

a movement. This paper undertakes to set forth some questions and suggest some answers.

I

A first question which may confront the student: *what should be the point of focus in the movement study?*

Let us say that an historical movement has occurred when, at some time in the past: 1. men have become dissatisfied with some aspect of their environment; 2. they desire change—social, economic, political, religious, intellectual, or otherwise—and desiring change, they make efforts to alter their environment; 3. eventually, their efforts result in some degree of success or failure; the desired change is, or is not, effected; and we may say that the historical movement has come to its termination.

As students of rhetoric our concern is obviously with those efforts which attempt to effectuate change, not through the forces of wealth or arms, but through the force of persuasion. In the term *historical movement*, then, *movement* is for us the significant word; and in particular, that part of the connotative baggage of the word which implies change conveys the quality of dynamism. For as the historical movement, looked upon as a sustained process of social inference, is dynamic, and has its beginning, its progression, and its termination, so the rhetorical component of the movement is dynamic, and has its inception, its development, and its consummation. The student's task is to isolate the rhetorical movement within the matrix of the historical movement: the rhetorical movement is the focus of his study. It is to be isolated, analyzed, evaluated, and described, so that he can say, for the particular historical movement which he investigates: this was the pattern of public discussion, the configuration of discourse, the physiognomy of persuasion, peculiar to the movement.

presence of the propagandist, and the various devices of propaganda, in the theoretical atmosphere of the times. The principle demonstrates, one might add, that a need exists for further background studies in the development of theories of rhetoric and public opinion, and in the history of the teaching of rhetoric as well—studies such as those completed by Guthrie, Utterback, and Perrin; and a need for a body of period and regional-period studies which will give us specific demonstrations of the integration of theory and practice.

V

A fifth question: *how should the student go about the process of synthesis involved in reporting the movement?*

The general method of presenting the material, I believe, should be that of the literary historian rather than that of the statistician. That is, we should strive for movement studies which will preserve the idiom in which the movement was actually expressed. The movement, then, will not be completely atomized; rather it will be so presented as to convey the quality of dynamism, the sense of action, chronologically; and even chapters essentially topical will be chronological in development.

The inherent difficulty arising from the necessity for the researcher to treat speakers, speeches, and audiences analytically, while at the same time he endeavors to present the movement synthetically, in a broad, chronological manner, may be resolved by a method of turning the movement on a spit, as it were, by piercing it now from one angle, now from another, as the movement spirals to its consummation. Thus, by centering on a significant series of debates, or a convention, or a political rally, of 1830; by centering on an important editorial, pamphlet, or book of 1831; by centering on an effective drama, satire, or sermon of 1832, he may accomplish the business of pushing the movement forward, and of piercing it from many angles. By threading the careers of selected speakers through the course of his study, the writer will achieve a sense of unity. In short, he will make use of the techniques of the case study and of the biographical study.

Obviously the writer will reinforce and enliven the study with ample quotation from the discourse; he will make full use of memoirs, letters, and other contemporary documents to give the study flesh and blood.

It is equally obvious that the introductory chapters of the study will be devoted to backgrounds—to the historical background and the rhetorical background of the movement; that the body of the study will be devoted to description, analysis, and criticism of the inception, development, and consummation phases of the rhetorical movement; that the final chapters will serve to reset the rhetorical movement in the matrix of the historical movement, the historical movement itself in the times; and that it will summarize the rhetorical pattern peculiar to the movement and present other pertinent conclusions.

VI

The reply to questions concerning primary objective in any particular movement study should now be apparent: essentially, the student's goal is to *discover*, in a wide sense of the term, the rhetorical pattern inherent in the movement selected for investigation.

But as the historical movement becomes a discrete field for research in public address, as studies employing the movement approach accumulate, certain broader results may become manifest. From the identification of a number of rhetorical patterns, we may discover the various configurations of public discussion, whether rhetorical patterns repeat themselves when like movements occur in the intervals of time, whether a consistent set of forms may be said to exist. We may learn something more about orators—even about the great orators—whom we may come to see from a new perspective, since they rarely speak except within the framework of a movement; and we may come to a more acute appreciation of the significance of the historically insignificant speaker, the minor orator who, we may find, is often the true fountainhead of the moving flood of ideas and words. By seeing numbers of men in an act and atmosphere of discourse, we may indeed produce fresh transcripts of particular moments of the past. We may come closer to discovering the degree of validity in our fundamental assumption: that rhetoric has had and does have a vital function as a shaping agent in human affairs. And finally, we may arrive at generalizations useful to those anticipated writers of the comprehensive histories of public address—histories that might well be conceived in terms of movements rather than of individuals.

Notes

1 Specifically, by Herbert A. Wichelns in "The Study of Public Address," a paper read at the 1946 conference of the Speech Association of America.

The Rhetoric of the Streets: Some Legal and Ethical Considerations

Franklyn S. Haiman

One hears considerable criticism these days of the tactics employed by contemporary protest groups—by the Vietnam war dissenters, the civil rights movement, or students demanding a greater share in campus decision-making. Many such challenges come from those in our society, presumably in a majority, who oppose some or all of the views of these protest groups and who might be expected to divert a portion of their hostility toward the methods used rather than the goals sought.

But when one finds those who profess neutrality or friendship toward the goals of the dissenters also expressing doubt about the methods they employ, it is time to attempt a serious assessment of the situation. For, indeed, many objective observers of the contemporary "rhetoric" of the streets do have misgivings about its propriety and even its legality. The term "rhetoric" as used here is put in quotation marks because only by the broadest of definition do some of the activities to be discussed fall into what has traditionally been called the province of rhetoric. If rhetoric means only verbal communication, we are clearly dealing here with matters outside that boundary. If, however, we take Aristotle's phrase to mean literally "all the available means of persuasion," then we do have here a problem in rhetorical criticism.

Regardless of terminology, our society today is confronted with a wide range of activities unfamiliar to those accustomed to thinking of protest in terms of a Faneuil Hall rally or a Bughouse Square soapbox orator. With respect to the Vietnam war we have witnessed everything from vigils, sit-ins at draft boards, and picket signs accusing the President of murder, to the burning of draft cards and self-immolation. On campuses across the country we have seen mass rallies doused by the hoses of firemen, sit-ins at administration buildings, and boycotts or threatened boycotts of classes.

The civil rights movement has generated perhaps the widest range of new forms. Invented to protest racial discrimination by restaurants, the sit-in has been extended to churches, libraries, real estate offices, and boards of education. The mass rally, an old form in itself, has been expanded to new locations and new dimensions—before the jailhouse, in the middle of the street, or through the center of the nation's capitol city. Slogans and folk songs have assumed a new importance. Picketing, another older form, has also gone to new locations—before pavilions at the World's Fair or into a Chicago residential area to protest in front of the mayor's home. Mass marches through hostile territory—like Selma, Alabama, or all-white neighborhoods of Chicago—have attracted national attention. Going limp when arrested, obstructing the flow of traffic, and lying down in front of bulldozers on school construction sites have probably been the most extreme of the new forms—short, of course, of those employed in Harlem, Rochester, Cleveland, and Watts.

In attempting to review the major lines of criticism directed at this new array of rhetorical expressions, one finds that he can group them into three broad areas. The first line of criticism asserts that insofar as the contemporary rhetoric of the streets violates the law it produces a climate of anarchy from which, in the end, no one can gain. It is argued that to engage in the obstruction of traffic or to trespass on the property of others because one believes that his cause is good is to take the law into one's own hands and to create a society in which everyone's rights are threatened. The wanton looting and shooting which have erupted in some of our cities are alleged to be evidence of the ultimate end to which all of this leads. It is said that civil disobedience, even for the highest of motives, cannot be condoned in a society where legal channels—courts, legislatures, and the public forum—are available for the expression of grievances. One cannot condone civil disobedience for the "good guys" without allowing it for the "bad guys"; for who is to distinguish good motives from evil ones? Justice must be impartial and even-handed.

A second category of criticism is directed at those aspects of the new rhetoric, admittedly legal and even appropriate under some circumstances, but alleged to violate the proposition that, in an orderly society, there must be prescribed times, places, and manners for protest. Critics point out that two of the leading spokesmen for the libertarian view regarding freedom of speech, philosopher Alexander Meiklejohn and Supreme Court Justice Hugo Black, have themselves supported this principle,[1] and that much of the current rhetoric of the streets exceeds the bounds of permissible time, place, and manner.

More specifically, they argue that protest is not justified if it constitutes an invasion of the privacy of others.[2] A prime example often cited is the series of marches of August, 1965, led by Negro comedian Dick Gregory to and around the home of Mayor Richard J. Daley in Chicago's Bridgeport section, an area of modest middle-class homes. Critics have condemned this and all other instances of picketing or parading in residential areas on the ground that "a man's home is his castle" and that such an intrusion was an invasion of the mayor's privacy, as well as that of his family and neighbors. Professor Alfred Kamin, of Loyola University Law School in Chicago, makes an impressively documented presentation of the legal arguments for this point of view which he summarizes: "The thesis of this article is simple. . . . In the constitutional

value scale, the quiet enjoyment and privacy of residential premises—even of the privately owned homes of public officials—merits a higher priority than freedom of speech."[3] Kamin draws support for his thesis primarily from court decisions in the area of labor-management disputes, which appear to reject any right of workers to carry their grievances to the doorsteps of their employers' homes, and from the substantial number of states (nine, to be exact) which have enacted statutory bans on residential picketing.

A slightly different rationale for objecting to the time, place, or manner of expressing deviant views was that used by Federal District Judge Samuel Perry in an injunction handed down in Chicago in September, 1966. Judge Perry enjoined the American Nazi Party and its leader, George Lincoln Rockwell, from demonstrating within one-half mile of any Jewish house of worship on any Jewish holy day, if clothed in Nazi garb or displaying Nazi symbols. He argued that such demonstrations would constitute an interference with the exercise of religious freedom by Jews attending their synagogues—a right which, unlike that of privacy, is explicitly recognized by the First Amendment.

Protests have also been challenged on the grounds that, under certain circumstances, they may place an undue strain upon the community's resources or may conflict with other community interests. One of the most current and significant illustrations of this rationale, found in an injunction issued by the Circuit Court of Cook County, Illinois, in August, 1966, limited the scope of marches then being conducted by the Chicago Freedom Movement under the leadership of Martin Luther King. This injunction, still in force, is of the utmost interest to the development of the law regarding freedom of speech, for it is a carefully drawn and relatively qualified ban which could well stand up on appeal to higher courts. It does not enjoin the marches entirely, but provides only that there shall not be more than one such march in Chicago per day, that only one neighborhood at a time may be the target, that no more than 500 persons may march, and that marches shall be confined to daylight times other than the rush hours. The basic justification for these limitations, argued before the Court on behalf of Chicago Police Superintendent O. W. Wilson, was that the police department could not simultaneously discharge its obligation to protect the marchers from the activities of hostile counter-demonstrators and fulfill its responsibilities to protect the safety and welfare of the community. Wilson charged that, at the height of the marches, when hundreds of policemen were diverted to the protection of demonstrators, crime rates had risen in other areas of the city.[4] He also suggested that the morale of the police department suffered severely during this period and that the financial costs to the city were exorbitant. How much effort, critics ask, can a city government reasonably be expected to make to protect dissenters from counter-violence, especially when the majority of taxpayers and voters may share the attitudes of those counter-demonstrators?

Finally, the time, place, or manner issue is sometimes argued on the basis of an "innocent bystander" theory[,] which says that protest is permissible only so long as it is confined so as to affect the legitimate targets of the protest but not to inconvenience others. Hence one might concede that the mayor, as a public official, is a fair target for protest even when he is at home, but that his family and neighbors, the "innocent bystanders," should not have to be subjected to the same harassment. Similarly, the man who cannot get to work on time because of the congestion caused by a march, or the student who cannot study because of the turmoil created by campus demonstrations or boycotts of classes, may assert that their rights as innocent bystanders should take precedence over the free speech claims of the protesters. An analogy is sometimes made here to the secondary boycott in labor-management relations—an activity which is regarded as impermissible because of its harmful effects on those who are only tangentially related to the dispute.

The third major category of criticism directed at the contemporary rhetoric of the streets concerns objections which may be the most difficult and most profound from the point of view of the rhetorical critic. At the core of these objections is the proposition that the new rhetoric exceeds the bounds of rational discourse which teachers of rhetoric value so highly and are dedicated to promote; that the new rhetoric is "persuasion" by a strategy of power and coercion rather than by reason and democratic decision-making. This line of thought has been expressed in at least two different ways.

In an article in this journal, Professor Leland Griffin coined the phrase "body rhetoric" to express the thesis that much of the new rhetoric is not persuasion at all, at least as rhetoricians are accustomed to defining that term, but instead constitutes the "holding of a gun at the head" of those to whom the protests are directed.[5] Pickets at a mayor's home or college students sitting in at an administration building are simply throwing their weight around, says the critic, until the authorities give them what they want. If the Chicago Freedom Movement marchers are only interested in communicating a message, then why (given mass media coverage) cannot the same point be made with 500 marchers in one neighborhood as with 5,000 marchers in six neighborhoods simultaneously? To such critics the intention of the marchers seems not to be simply to *communicate* grievances, but to throw the city into such chaos that it will be *forced* to meet their demands.

Even the greatest champions of free speech have expressed doubts about such demonstrations. Justice Hugo Black has said:

> The First and Fourteenth Amendments, I think, take away from government, state and federal, all power to restrict freedom of speech, press, and assembly *where people have a right to be, for such purposes.* This does not mean, however, that these amendments also grant a constitutional right to engage in the conduct of picketing or patrolling, whether on publicly owned streets or on privately owned property . . . . Were the law otherwise, people on the streets, in their homes and anywhere else could be compelled to listen against their will to speakers they did not want to hear. Picketing, though it may be utilized to communicate ideas, is not speech, and therefore is not of itself protected by the First Amendment.[6]

A majority of the United States Supreme Court, speaking through Justice Arthur Goldberg in the same case, proclaimed: "We emphatically reject the notion . . . that the First and Fourteenth Amendments afford the same kind of freedom to those who would communicate ideas by conduct such as patrolling, marching, and picketing on streets and highways as these amendments afford to those who communicate ideas by pure speech."[7]

The second line of criticism related to the general issue of rationality of discourse raises the age-old question of the new rhetoric's resort to emotional appeals. The focus here is on the popularity among contemporary protest movements of sloganeering, folksinging, draft-card burning, and other modes of communication that appear designed to elicit signal responses.[8] Catchphrases such as "Black Power," picket signs reading "Hey, Hey, LBJ, How Many Kids Have You Killed Today?" the joining of hands and the singing of "We Shall Overcome," the speeches of Mario Savio, and the folksongs of Joan Baez and Pete Seeger are all cited as evidence of this tendency.

This is the outline of a rather formidable brief challenging the contemporary rhetoric of the streets. The challenge has been posed in both legal and ethical terms, and it raises, in substance, two kinds of questions about the new rhetoric: (1) Is the particular activity in question protected, or should it be, by the First Amendment? and (2) Even if legal, is the activity ethical? Let's turn now to the case for the defense.

Regarding the question of disobedience, civil or otherwise, to the law, one must concede that such activity does have an undermining effect on established authority and tends toward an anarchic social climate. Justice must be administered without discrimination either for or against the dissenter; if he breaks the law he must be punished. Yet, having recognized this, I would note some important qualifications often overlooked.

Many who currently advocate and practice civil disobedience do not expect nor ask for exemption from punishment. They are keenly aware that a lawless society cannot survive, but they are willing to pay whatever penalties the civil law may exact in order to obey what they regard as a higher law, be it the law of their religion or their conscience, which requires them to protest what they view as some injustice in their society. They seek no special privileges, but rather hope that their willingness to suffer penalties for

their convictions may communicate a message to the consciences of others and thus pave the way for social change. One can admire the courage and sympathize with the goals of such persons and still recognize, as they do, that they must be punished for their actions. One might go even further to suggest that such civil disobedience merits support, though not exemption from punishment, so long as it does no physical harm to others. Sharper distinctions may need to be made, for example, between the *inconvenience* resulting from the tying up of traffic to a World's Fair and the *physical danger* of a Watts riot. Indeed, a riot is not *civil* disobedience at all, and rioters are usually an entirely different group of people from the kind who engage in conscientious disobedience.

Critics of civil disobedience also need to be reminded that some kinds of law-breaking are, paradoxically, quite legal. Again, finer distinctions are needed. So-called civil disobedience, which involves the violation of a law believed by the protesters to be unconstitutional and later found by the courts to be unconstitutional, may be exempt from punishment. One may, under some circumstances, with both legal and moral justification, disobey a local or state law in order to obey a higher civil law, *i.e.*, the United States Constitution. Granted, one cannot embark on such a course lightly; for it is the United States Supreme Court, not the individual citizen, that, in our system, must ultimately decide whether a law is or is not constitutional. But if one is willing to run the risk of losing that decision (thereby paying the penalty, of course), he is fully justified in such a violation.

Many Supreme Court decisions, particularly those involving the First Amendment, support this position. One landmark case, in 1938, reversed the conviction of a member of the Jehovah's Witnesses who had been arrested and fined for distributing religious literature in Griffin, Georgia, under a city ordinance which the Court found to be an unconstitutional infringement on the freedom of speech and press.[9] More recently, in 1965, a Baltimore, Maryland, theatre manager who had deliberately flaunted the state's movie censorship statute because he thought it unconstitutional and was arrested and convicted in the lower courts, saw his conviction overturned by the Supreme Court, which agreed that the law violated the First Amendment.[10] Then, of course, there have been the long line of sit-in cases from the South, some of which have been decided on narrower grounds than the First Amendment, and some of which have involved refusal to obey police orders rather than laws, but all of which have been norm-breaking activities that provoked sanctions at the local level which were later reversed by the United States Supreme Court.[11]

One cautionary note must be appended here. The Supreme Court has, on occasion, taken the attitude that if a citizen believes a law or local administrative rule to be unconstitutional he must exhaust all possible administrative and judicial remedies before proceeding to its violation.[12] This position has not been sufficiently elaborated to make clear precisely how much effort a citizen must make to seek legal remedies before resorting to disobedience. This appears to depend somewhat on the particular circumstances of the law and violation in question. But, despite these qualifications, it is clear that dissenters have no obligation to conform indefinitely to statutes and ordinances that conflict with the Constitution. If this be deleterious to established authority, then established authority had better be brought into conformity with the law.

But what of *un*civil disobedience? Can anything be said in defense of Watts and of angry voices in the streets which sometimes seem to be calling for violence? Certainly not within the framework of a democratic society, where only peaceful change can be accepted. But should we not be somewhat troubled by the awareness that, despite the destruction to property, despite the loss of lives, despite the backlash of public opinion, these outbreaks have precipitated significant reforms that previously had been notably slow in coming? It would seem that even the "rhetoric of the riot," mindless and indiscriminate as it may be, has its positive function in contemporary America. What moral can be drawn from this, short of abandoning the conviction that a civilized society is preferable to the law of the jungle? Perhaps simply that if the channels for peaceful protest and reform become so clogged that they appear to be (and, in fact, may be) inaccessible to some segments of the population, then the Jeffersonian doctrine that "the tree of liberty must be refreshed from time to time, with the blood of patriots and tyrants" may become more appropriate to the situation than more civilized rules of the game.

The problems associated with the time, place, and manner of protest must now be addressed together with the possibility that countervailing interests such as privacy, convenience, or the safety and welfare of the community may justify some curtailments of the rhetoric of the streets. One can hardly quarrel with the general thesis, supported by Meiklejohn and Black, that there is no constitutional right to protest whenever, wherever, and however one chooses. There must be, as Professor Harry Kalven has so aptly put it, a "Robert's Rules of Order for use of the public forum of the streets," for it is an "unbeatable proposition that you cannot have two parades on the same corner at the same time."[13] The real questions in this area are not questions about the correctness of the *principle*, but rather about the reasonableness and equity of its *application* to particular conflict situations. We must look beneath the pat phrases such as "innocent bystander" and "invasion of privacy," or the surface reasonableness of the Chicago Freedom Movement injunction, to do some honest weighing of the competing interests at stake.

The "innocent bystander" theory is the first which requires closer scrutiny. As was indicated earlier, an analogy is often made here to the illegality of secondary boycotts in labor-management relations. But serious questions can be raised about the validity of applying this theory to political and social protest movements. The grievances involved in labor-management disputes are essentially grievances held by one private party, or group of private parties, against the actions or policies of another private party, whereas the grievances involved in most protest movements are directed to the body politic as a whole and are redressable only by public policy or action. Thus it is arguable that on issues such as civil rights and the Vietnam war there is no such thing as an innocent bystander. Every citizen who supports the status quo, either actively or by passive acquiescence, is a legitimate target for the communications of the dissenter.

Furthermore, an examination of particular cases may reveal important shortcomings in the innocent bystander theory. The marches to Mayor Daley's home in the summer of 1965 provide a good example. Just how "innocent" were the "bystanders" in this case, the neighbors? After all, the message being communicated by the demonstrators concerned racial discrimination, and it was no accident (in view of either the motivations or effects of the march) that the mayor happened to live in an all-white neighborhood of the city, which has, over the years, been known for its resistance to the "intrusion" of Negro homeowners from adjacent areas. Although Mayor Daley was ostensibly the primary target of communication, the protesters certainly perceived his neighbors as legitimate recipients of their message. How often, in other instances where the innocent bystander theory is invoked, may the circumstances be similar?

But some would hold that even the mayor, although admittedly not an innocent bystander, should have the right to a private life, free from the harassments of political and social turmoil. What of this right to privacy as an alleged countervailing interest to freedom of speech? What of Kamin's case for the banning of protest from all residential areas? What of the fact that even Zechariah Chafee, one of the most respected proponents of freedom of speech, has been troubled over matters related to this issue?[14]

One can hardly deny that allowing for the expression of dissent in residential areas does indeed impinge on other important rights and privileges. The question, I think, is what price a society is willing to pay to insure that the messages of minority groups are not screened out of the consciences of those to whom they are addressed. For once the principle is invoked that listeners may be granted some immunity from messages they think they would rather not hear, or which cause them annoyance, a Pandora's box of circumstances is opened in which the right of free speech could be effectively nullified. Also, difficult problems arise in defining a residential area. Would not a prohibition against demonstrations in such areas turn out to mean that those who can afford to live in neighborhoods zoned exclusively for single-family dwellings would be protected, while those who live on a street with a shopping area, a gas station, a real estate office, or a public building would have no more protection than if they resided in an office building in the heart of the downtown center?

Perhaps appropriately, the United States Supreme Court, at least at this point in its development of a theory of free speech, has been unwilling to weight the scales in the manner suggested by Chafee and Kamin. On the contrary, there are cases which make clear the Court's view that the right to privacy, emotionally appealing as it may be, must not be purchased at major cost to the First Amendment.

An early precedent in this area was provided in 1943, in a case involving a city ordinance which prohibited the door-to-door distribution of handbills. A member of the Jehovah's Witnesses was arrested, convicted, and fined for circulating a leaflet announcing a religious meeting. Although the prosecution argued, in justification of the ordinance, that this was an industrial town in which many men worked a night shift and slept during the day, the Supreme Court ruled that "door to door distribution of circulars is essential to the poorly financed causes of little people."[15] The Court indicated that a householder may post a notice on his door that he does not wish his door-bell rung and may enforce such a wish through the laws of trespass, but it held that a blanket prohibition of door-to-door soliciting by the city is unconstitutional. This position was reaffirmed in 1951, by implication, when the Supreme Court *upheld* a municipal ordinance prohibiting door-to-door solicitation for commercial magazines *only* because of the commercial element involved.[16] Had the solicitation been for political or religious causes, the Court presumably would have reached a different conclusion.

To be sure, these cases have involved only single solicitors, and a different posture might be taken by the Supreme Court if a case involving large numbers of marchers in a residential area goes up on appeal. But perhaps offsetting the numbers factor will be the consideration that marchers do not ordinarily ring door-bells and seldom walk on private property. If they remain on the public sidewalks and streets, the possible issue of trespass cannot intrude, and the Court will have to deal simply with the clash between an alleged right of residential privacy and freedom of speech.

Closely related to the right-to-privacy and innocent-bystander arguments is the assertion that the contemporary rhetoric of the streets sometimes creates inconvenience for other persons. This claim need not detain us long. Dissent is always an inconvenience to those who like the status quo, sometimes maddeningly so. But, again, a Jeffersonian epigram may give perspective—reminding us that it is "timid men who prefer the calm of despotism to the turbulent sea of liberty." One is tempted to be skeptical about those who complain so loudly over the congestion or annoyance generated by a civil rights march, but who do not raise similar objections to the St. Patrick's Day parade or the Saturday afternoon football crowds. Or, as Harry Kalven puts it, in suggesting that the "equal protection" clause of the Constitution may have some bearing on this problem: "Everyone at some time or other loves a parade whatever its effects on traffic and other uses of public streets. Municipalities pressed by concern with the protest movement may be inhibited in any rush to flat nondiscriminatory prohibitions by the difficulty of distinguishing between the parades we like and others. Equal protection may, therefore, require freedom for the parades we hate."[17]

Much more serious than the inconvenience argument is the claim set forth in the Chicago Freedom Movement case that unless protest marches are restricted in size and scope, dangerous consequences, such as a rise in the crime rate, may ensue for the city. How many police, critics query, can the government reasonably be expected to divert to the maintenance of order at locations where dissenters choose to aggravate hostile audiences? Or, put in another form, how large a hostile audience can dissenters reasonably expect the police to contain? The answer I am inclined to give is "Everything it takes including, if necessary, calling out the National Guard."

How can such an extreme position be defended? Simply on the grounds that to take any *other* course of action is to issue an invitation to hostile audiences to veto the right of dissent whenever they desire to do so. Only by the firmest display of the government's intention to use all the power at its disposal to protect the constitutional rights of dissenters will hecklers be discouraged from taking the law into their own hands. To be sure, the temporary costs may seem astronomical, but they may be nothing compared to the costs that could be suffered in the long run through any other course. This principle was clear to our national government when it posted an army on the campus of the University of Mississippi to insure that one man, James Meredith, was granted his rights to enter and to remain at that institution. Its reverse was equally clear in Little Rock, Arkansas, when Governor Orval Faubus let it be known (either out of conviction or desire) that the state's police power could not cope with those who wished to block the entry of Negro children to Central High School.

One can agree with this principle and still take the position that limitations on the time, place, and manner of protest designed to make the task of the police more manageable, are legitimate so long as they do not interfere substantially with the right of protesters to communicate their messages. This, in essence, is the rationale for the limited kind of injunction issued against the Chicago Freedom Movement marches; and, as evidence of good faith, the police superintendent could point to the rather formidable effort his department had put forth to protect the marches which had already taken place and which had aroused hundreds of hostile counter-demonstrators to potential and actual violence. But, again, one must look more closely at the specific facts of the situation to determine just how reasonable such limitations are.

Is it reasonable, for example, to confine protest marches to daylight hours? From the police department's viewpoint it is much simpler to control the behavior of crowds in daylight than in the dark. From the viewpoint of marchers who have to work for a living during the day, and who can protest only after-hours, it appears to be an effective deprivation of the right to communicate their grievances (except on Sundays!).

Is it reasonable to limit marches to no more than 500 persons? From the police department's viewpoint, yes; for the same message can be communicated by 500 as by 5,000, and at much less strain to community resources. From the viewpoint of the marchers, as well as from the theory of Marshall McLuhan, the medium of 5,000 marchers does *not* communicate the same message as 500. Furthermore, what of the constitutional rights to free speech of the potential 501st marcher? Who is to decide which 500 gets to march and which group does not?

Is it reasonable to limit marches to one neighborhood of the city per day? From the police department's viewpoint, certainly; for with little difficulty enough police can be assigned to one area to insure the maintenance of peace and order. From the viewpoint of the marchers, however, such a limit assumes a degree of coordination and unanimity among the parties enjoined that is rather presumptuous. To tell Mr. Albert Raby that he and his associates cannot march on the northwest side of the city because the Reverend Martin Luther King and his friends are marching that day on the southeast side not only presumes a conspiracy of planning between the two, but, more important, raises important constitutional issues of equal protection of the law. If the injunction against the Chicago Freedom Movement remains on the books and becomes, as it well might, a national precedent, I believe that a significant erosion of the First Amendment will have occurred.

I turn next to Judge Perry's injunction against the Nazis, and its thesis that to allow Mr. Rockwell and his dozen-or-so goons to parade in Nazi garb in front of Jewish synagogues is to interfere with the right of Jews to exercise their religious freedom. The issue was *not* that Rockwell would disrupt services by throwing rocks through the synagogue windows or by broadcasting from a sound truck on the street in front; it was *not* that his pickets would obstruct the free flow of pedestrians on their way to and from their house of worship; it was *not* that they would do anything but peacefully and quietly parade with hated symbols (which might provoke *others* to violence), and *this* is what was alleged would be such an interference with the exercise of religious freedom that it justified the denial of Rockwell's freedom of speech. When making people angry or offending their sensibilities becomes a basis for shutting off communication because they happen to be on their way to pray, one can only marvel at the rationalizations a society will invent to justify suppression of the deviant.

One final issue in the time, place, and manner category asks whether certain areas within the public domain can legitimately be declared off-limits from the rest of the public forum. The most frequently proposed site for such an exception is the courthouse, on the theory that

the right to a fair trial, unencumbered by the pressures on judge and jury that might accrue from demonstrators gathered on the courthouse grounds, justifies carving this exception from the free speech realm. Indeed, laws are already on the books at all levels of government providing for just such an exception. But now the question is being raised as to whether other sites should be similarly exempt. The most recent case of importance, decided by the Supreme Court on November 14 of last year, found a narrow majority taking the position that not only was a Tallahassee, Florida, jailhouse entitled to such exemption, but even suggesting that the state may declare other public property out of bounds to protest, so long as it does so on a non-discriminatory basis.[18] The facts in this case were relatively simple, as described by Justice Black in the majority opinion:

> Disturbed and upset by the arrest of their schoolmates . . . a large number of Florida A. & M. students . . . decided to march down to the county jail . . . . A group of around 200 marched from the school and arrived at the jail singing and clapping. They went directly to the jail door entrance where they were met by a deputy sheriff . . . . He asked them to move back, claiming they were blocking the entrance . . . . They moved back part of the way, where they stood or sat, singing, clapping and dancing, on the jail driveway and on an adjacent area upon the jail premises.

There is then some difference of opinion about what happened. The majority asserts that "even after their partial retreat, the demonstrators continued to block vehicular passage over this driveway up to the entrance of the jail." After being warned by the sheriff to leave or face arrest, and after refusing to depart, they were arrested, and later convicted for trespass. The minority opinion, written by Justice William O. Douglas[,] asserts:

> The evidence is uncontradicted that the petitioners' conduct did not upset the jailhouse routine; things went on as they normally would. None of the group entered the jail. Indeed, they moved back from the

entrance as they were instructed. There was no shoving, no pushing, no disorder . . . the entrance to the jail was not blocked . . . . If there was congestion, the solution was a further request to move to lawns or parking areas, not complete ejection and arrest.

Although this disputed emphasis in the factual situation may have had some bearing on the Court's decision, the difference between majority and minority went to more fundamental matters. The majority, in effect, seemed to be returning partially to a theory of law that had been propounded in 1897, in a case involving the use of the Boston Commons as a public forum, but which appeared to have been a dead letter since the famous *Hague v. C.I.O.* decision in 1939. In 1897, the Court had taken the position that the government has the same power to regulate the use of public property as an individual owner has to regulate the use of his private property, and that the government of Boston was fully within its rights to control the use of the Commons as it saw fit.[19] But in 1939, Justice Owen Roberts, in announcing the *Hague* decision of the Court, had said in a much-quoted passage: "Wherever the title of street and parks may rest, they have immemorially been held in trust for the use of the public and time out of mind, have been used for purposes of assembly, communicating thoughts between citizens, and discussing public questions. Such use of the streets and public places has from ancient times, been a part of the privileges, immunities, rights, and liberties of citizens."[20]

The *Hague v. C.I.O.* philosophy seemed to prevail in all cases bearing on this issue that went to the Supreme Court after 1939. As recently as 1963, reversing the conviction of 187 Negro students who had gathered for a demonstration on the state capitol grounds at Columbia, South Carolina, an eight to one majority had declared: "The circumstances in this case reflect an exercise of these basic constitutional rights in their most pristine and classic form. The petitioners felt aggrieved by laws of South Carolina . . . . They peaceably assembled at the site of the State Government and there peaceably expressed their grievances."[21]

But now, in the *Adderley* case, a majority of the Court says, as in 1897, "The State, no less than a private owner of property, has power to preserve the property under its control for the use to which it is lawfully dedicated." This statement is reconciled with the *Edwards* decision as follows: "In *Edwards,* the demonstrators went to the South Carolina Capitol grounds to protest. In this case they went to the jail. Traditionally, state capitol grounds are open to the public. Jails, built for security purposes, are not." Here the majority seems to be taking a slightly modified Boston Commons position. The state may decide which public areas are appropriate for speech and which are not, so long as the uses to which these areas are "traditionally" and "lawfully dedicated" are taken into account.

Justice Douglas, speaking for the minority, did not think the matter so simple: "The jailhouse, like an executive mansion, a legislative chamber, a courthouse, or the statehouse itself . . . is one of the seats of government whether it be the Tower of London, the Bastille, or a small county jail. And when it houses political prisoners or those whom many think are unjustly held, it is an obvious center for protest." There are other complexities as well. What of the frequent situation at small county seats, for example, or towns and villages, where the legislative chamber, executive offices, courtroom, and jail are all housed in the same building? Are the surrounding sidewalks, driveways, and lawns to be off-limits or not?

There are even difficulties, as Professor Kalven has pointed out, with laws such as the simple prohibition of courthouse picketing, which was one of the issues in *Cox v. Louisiana* in 1965. There, Justice Goldberg had said for the Supreme Court: "There can be no question that a State has a legitimate interest in protecting its judicial system from the pressures which picketing near a courthouse might create." But Kalven asks of this ruling: "Would this same protest have been permissible if moved a few blocks away? Could one, for example, distribute leaflets highly critical of the Court near the courthouse? Is there pressure and intimidation in the protest in front of the courthouse that ceases to be present when it is in front of the state house? Or is the principle that it is all right to intimidate legislatures but not courts?"[22]

I must admit to sharing some of the ambivalence which has apparently plagued the Supreme

Court concerning this last question. Perhaps the right to a fair trial is undermined by crowds on the courthouse steps, just as it may be undermined by an unfettered freedom of the press to publicize pre-trial allegations of guilt. And perhaps some carefully drawn measures are needed to protect the conduct of a trial from such distortions. But when extensions of this line of thought lead to decisions such as the one that was made in *Adderley,* I am inclined to join with Justice Douglas' dissent:

> There may be some instances in which assemblies and petitions for redress of grievances are not consistent with other necessary purposes of public property . . . . No one, for example, would suggest that the Senate gallery is the proper place for a vociferous protest rally . . . . But this is quite different than saying that all public places are off-limits to people with grievances . . . by allowing these orderly and civilized protests against injustice to be suppressed, we only increase the forces of frustration which the conditions of second-class citizenship are generating amongst us.

The category of criticism of contemporary protest movements which asserts that their rhetoric exceeds the bounds of rational discourse must, finally, be addressed. The first charge here was that the "body rhetoric" employed is a *physically* coercive tactic which has little to do with the exercise of freedom of *speech.* To deal intelligently with this charge a distinction must be made between demonstrations which do *not* directly obstruct the functioning of an institution or society and those which do physically interfere with a normal flow of activity. I have already dealt with the latter type of protest in discussing civil disobedience, and wish here to address the issue solely in the context of admittedly legal and peaceful uses of the protesters' bodies to "bear witness" to their cause.

The difficulty people have in focusing exclusively on that issue and keeping it from being blurred with the other is itself instructive, for so often the reaction that is generated by the mass physical bearing of witness creates situations that deteriorate into physical disruption. Thus a march which begins as a peaceful parade of 1,000 through the streets of Chicago soon turns into a potential race riot requiring the intervention of hundreds of policemen. But let us be clear, as so few people seem to be, about what has changed this peaceful parade into such a potentially dangerous activity that the mere threat to march is perceived as a coercive weapon. The change has been wrought *by the hostile audience* which, rather than contenting itself to stay at home and ignore the demonstrators, chooses to go out on the streets to confront them. There is nothing *inherently* coercive about one dissenter, or one hundred, or one thousand, walking peaceably down a street or gathering to sing in front of a building. Their activity is endowed with coercive potential only if others go forth to do battle with them, or feel too guilty and fearful to leave them alone.

The logic of this seems so compelling that it is difficult to understand why it is so seldom perceived. It was apparently not perceived in the summer of 1966 by the mayor and police superintendent of Chicago who repeatedly suggested, in their public pronouncements on television and in the press, that the marchers, although admittedly within their legal rights, were holding a gun at the head of the city and should, for the sake of the general welfare, cease and desist. To be sure, a few appeals were also made to the white residents of affected neighborhoods to stay at home and ignore the marchers, but the burden of guilt and the call for maximum restraint were placed squarely on the shoulders of the Freedom Movement. Only Roman Catholic Archbishop John P. Cody seemed to analyze the problem more clearly, but even he ended up with essentially the same appeal:

> In the past several weeks, civil rights groups have been conducting marches and demonstrations in all-white neighborhoods of our community. Their purpose has been to draw the attention of the citizenry to the plight of minority groups, many of whose members are financially capable of buying or renting better homes but impeded from so doing by what can only be called a conspiracy of fear, suspicion and bigotry.
>
> The right of such groups to march and demonstrate is in itself beyond question . . . . Those who seek to deny

this right by either threats or violence are clearly in violation of the law and morally blameworthy.

This being said, it now appears that a new dimension has been added to the marches and demonstrations in the Chicago area. Because of the shameful reaction of some to the exercise of a basic freedom of our land, representatives of government, the police, and many other responsible groups are convinced that if the marches and demonstrations continue in the manner in which they have been proceeding, the result will very likely be serious injury to many persons and perhaps even the loss of lives.

In view of all this, it would seem that the leaders of the civil rights movement are themselves confronted by a serious moral obligation, namely that they prayerfully reconsider the methods now being employed to achieve their altogether just and laudable purposes. They have not been guilty of violence and lawlessness. Others have. But the action of these others are now a circumstance which they must take into account in assessing their activities.

It is truly sad, indeed, deplorable, that citizens should ever have to be asked to suspend the exercise of their rights because of the evil-doing of others. However, in my opinion and in the opinion of many men of good will, such is the situation in which we now find ourselves.[23]

The United States Supreme Court, in its latest dealings with the "body rhetoric" issue in *Cox v. Louisiana*, has attempted, as we noted earlier, to fashion a distinction between "pure speech" and "conduct" such as patrolling, picketing, or marching, which may be the *vehicle* for speech but is not, according to Justice Goldberg's majority opinion, entitled to so wide a range of constitutional protection as speech itself. This opinion may well return to haunt the Court as having enunciated a distinction impossible to defend and maintain. For as Justice John Harlan wrote in 1961, in a concurring opinion in a decision to overturn the sit-in convictions of a group of Negroes at a Southern lunchcounter: "Such a demonstration in the circumstances . . . is as

much a part of the free trade in ideas . . . as is verbal expression more commonly thought of as speech. It, like speech, appeals to good sense and to the power of reason as applied through public discussion . . . just as much as, if not more than, a public oration delivered from a soapbox at a street corner. This Court has never limited the right to speak . . . to mere verbal expression."[24]

Harry Kalven, too, in one of his typically keen analyses, has suggested: "The Court's neat dichotomy of 'speech pure' and 'speech plus' will not work. For it leaves us without an intelligible rationale. For one thing the exercise of constitutional rights in their 'most pristine and classic form' in *Edwards* has become an exercise in 'speech plus'. . . . If it is oral, it is noise and may interrupt someone else; if it is written, it may be litter. Indeed this is why the leaflet cases were an appropriate model . . . the leaflets were not simply litter, they were litter with ideas."[25]

Having said all I have in defense of "body rhetoric," let me indicate an important qualification. One would have to be naive to believe that the leaders of contemporary protest groups are unaware of the power potential of their demonstrations (even if that power is conferred upon them by the fearful or hostile audience) or that they are unwilling to exploit such situations to their own advantage. Some have been quite frank about it. For example, Professor Griffin calls attention to Bayard Rustin's comments:

> We need to go into the streets all over the country and to make a mountain of creative social confusion until the power structure is altered. We need in every community a group of loving troublemakers, who will disrupt the ability of the government to operate until it finally turns its back on the Dixiecrats and embraces progress.[26]

I have little doubt that the leaders of the Chicago Freedom Movement hoped that their marches would so distress the key people in the city's power structure that they would be forced to the bargaining table—which, indeed, they were—prepared to make substantial concessions. Such tactics are certainly no part of rational discourse, although they may establish the preconditions for it.

Furthermore, one cannot deny that slogan-eering, folksinging, and draft-card burning fall into a category of persuasion that hardly passes muster by the standards of rational discourse, which this author and many others who have written on the ethics of persuasion have pro-posed. This is not to suggest that these activities are illegal, which is quite another question. Here I would support, for example, the position taken by the American Civil Liberties Union that public draft-card burning is an act of symbolic communication entitled to the protections of the First Amendment.

But on what *ethical* basis can these strate-gies of physical and psychological manipula-tion, insofar as this may be what they are, be defended? Their only justification, in my view, is that the norms of the democratic process may be inapplicable to the situations in which these strategies are employed. To be more explicit:

> When one person or a few people in a group or society possess all the guns, muscles, or money, and the others are relatively weak and helpless, optimum conditions do not exist for discussion, mutual influence, and democracy. Discussion in such circumstances occurs only at the sufferance of the powerful; and generous as these persons may sometimes be, they are not likely voluntarily to abdicate their power when vital interests are at stake . . . . The most solid and enduring basis for democracy exists when the participants possess relative equality of power. Discussion is assured only when those desiring discussion—usually those who are dissatisfied with the present state of affairs—have sufficient power to make those in control of the situation listen to them.[27]

It is not easy to determine, in any given setting, the degree to which the democratic process, and hence the opportunities for reasoned discourse, are indeed available; and the situation may be perceived quite differently from various vantage points. Perhaps the best one can do is to avoid the blithe presumption that the channels of rational communication are open to any and all who wish to make use of them and attempt,

instead, a careful assessment of the power structure of the situation. To whatever extent one finds an imbalance of power and a concomi-tant unwillingness on the part of the holders of power to engage in genuine dialogue, he may be less harsh in his judgment of those who seek to redress the balance through non-rational strategies of persuasion.

What I am suggesting here is not a lowering of the standards to be espoused for the ideal conduct of public discussion and debate. On the contrary, every effort should be made to help create the conditions under which the achieve-ment of those standards becomes a possibility. But we will not attain those conditions by clos-ing our eyes to the realities of the world about us and condemning out of hand the contemporary rhetoric of the streets.

Notes

[1] "When self-governing men demand freedom of speech they are not saying that every individual has an unalienable right to speak whenever, wherever, however he chooses . . . . The common sense of any reasonable society would deny the existence of that unqualified right. No one, for example, may, without consent of nurse or doctor, rise up in a sickroom to argue for his principles or his candidate." Alexander Meiklejohn, *Political Freedom* (New York, 1960), p. 25.

"Such an argument has as its major unarticulated premise the assumption that people who want to propagandize protests or views have a constitutional right to do so whenever and however and wherever they please. That concept of constitutional law was vigorously and forthrightly rejected in . . . *Cox v. Louisiana*. . . . We reject it again." Justice Hugo Black, speaking for a majority of the Supreme Court on November 14, 1966, in *Adderley v. Florida*.

[2] Although the "right to privacy" is nowhere mentioned in the U.S. Constitution or Bill of Rights, it has gained increasing recognition by legal scholars and the courts as a privilege worthy of some constitutional protection. This development reached its high-water mark in 1965, when the Supreme Court invalidated Connecticut's ban on the dissemination of birth control information. In the majority opinion written by Justice William O. Douglas the Court relied upon a right of privacy which it found

implied in the First, Third, Fourth, and Ninth Amendments as the primary basis for striking down the Connecticut law. *Griswold v. Connecticut,* 381 US 479.

3 Alfred Kamin, "Residential Picketing and the First Amendment," *Northwestern University Law Review,* LXI (May–June 1966), 182.

4 Paragraph 24 of complaint in *Wilson v. King, et. al.,* Case #66 Ch 4938 in Chancery in Circuit Court of Cook County.

5 Leland Griffin, "The Rhetorical Structure of the 'New Left' Movement: Part I," *QJS,* 1 (April 1964), 127.

6 *Cox v. Louisiana,* 379 US 536 (1965), 578.

7 *Ibid.,* 555.

8 Alfred Kamin also puts picketing in this category: "The picket line elicits conditioned responses . . . a primitive and unsophisticated illustration of McLuhan's dictum, 'The medium is the message.'" "Residential Picketing," 198–199.

9 *Lovell v. Griffin,* 303 US 444.

10 *Freedman v. Maryland,* 380 US 51.

11 See *Garner v. Louisiana,* 368 US 157 (1961); *Shuttlesworth v. Birmingham,* 373 US 262 (1963); *Peterson v. Greenville,* 373 US 244 (1963); *Lombard v. Louisiana,* 373 US 267 (1963); *Barr v. City of Columbia,* 378 US 146 (1964); *Robinson v. Florida,* 378 US 153 (1964); *Griffin v. Maryland,* 378 US 130 (1964); *Bouie v. City of Columbia,* 378 US 347 (1964); *Bell v. Maryland,* 378 US 226 (1964); *Hamm v. City of Little Rock,* 379 US 306 (1964); and *Brown v. Louisiana,* 383 US 131 (1966).

12 See *Poulos v. New Hampshire,* 345 US 395 (1953).

13 Harry Kalven, Jr., "The Concept of the Public Forum: *Cox v. Louisiana,*" *The Supreme Court Review,* 1965, pp. 25–26.

14 "Great as is the value of exposing citizens to novel views, home is one place where a man ought to be able to shut himself up in his own ideas if he desires. . . . A doorbell cannot be disregarded like a handbill. It takes several minutes to ascertain the purpose of a propagandist and at least several more to get rid of him. . . . A man's house is his castle, and what is more important his wife's castle. A housewife may fairly claim some protection from being obliged to leave off bathing the baby and rush down to the door, only to be asked to listen to a sermon or a political speech . . . . Freedom of the home is as important as freedom of speech." Zechariah Chafee, *Free Speech in the United States* (Cambridge, 1948), pp. 406–407.

15 *Martin v. Struthers,* 319 US 141, 146.

16 *Brevard v. City of Alexandria,* 341 US 622.

17 "The Concept of the Public Forum," p. 30.

18 *Adderley v. Florida.*

19 *Davis v. Massachusetts,* 167 US 43.

20 *Hague v. C.I.O.,* 307 US 496, 515.

21 *Edwards v. South Carolina,* 372 US 229.

22 "The Concept of the Public Forum," pp. 30–31.

23 From the statement of Archbishop John P. Cody, *Chicago Daily News,* August 10, 1966.

24 *Garner v. Louisiana,* 368 US 157, 201–202.

25 "The Concept of the Public Forum," p. 23.

26 Bayard Rustin, "The Meaning of the March on Washington," *Liberation,* VIII (October 1963), 13.

27 Dean C. Barnlund and Franklyn S. Haiman, *The Dynamics of Discussion* (Boston, 1960), p. 12.

The Rhetoric of Confrontation
Robert L. Scott and Donald K. Smith

"Confront" is a simple enough verb meaning to stand or to come in front of. Like many simple words, however, it has been used in diverse contexts for varied purposes and has developed complex meanings. Among these the most interesting, and perhaps the strongest, is the sense of standing in front of as a barrier or a threat. This sense is especially apparent in the noun "confrontation."

Repeatedly in his book *Essays in the Public Philosophy,* Walter Lippmann uses the word "confrontation" in the sense of face-to-face coming together of spokesmen for disparate views. Confrontation, as he saw it then, was the guarantee of open communication and fruitful dissent. But Lippmann's book was copyrighted in 1955. Today, his phrase "because the purpose of the confrontation is to discern truth" sounds a bit archaic. If so, the remainder of his sentence, "there are rules of evidence and parliamentary procedure, there are codes of fair dealing and fair comment, by which a loyal man will consider himself bound when he exercises the right to publish opinion,"[1] seems absolutely irrelevant to the notion of "confrontation" as we live with it in marches, sit-ins, demonstrations, and discourse featuring disruption, obscenity, and threats.

Although certainly some use the word "confrontation" moderately, we shall be concerned here with the radical and revolutionary suggestion which the word carries more and more frequently. Even obviously moderate circumstances today gain some of the revolutionary overtones when the word is applied, as it might be[,] for example, in announcing a church study group as the "confrontation of sacred and secular morality."

Acts of confrontation are currently at hand in such profusion that no one will lack evidence to prove or disprove the generalizations we make.[2]

Confrontation crackles menacingly from every issue in our country (Black Power and Student Power, as examples), hemisphere (Castroism, for example), and globe (Radical Nationalism everywhere). But primary to every confrontation in any setting, radical or moderate, is the impulse to confront. From what roots does that impulse spring?

RADICAL DIVISION

Radical confrontation reflects a dramatic sense of division. The old language of the "haves" and the "have-nots" scarcely indicates the basis of the division, nor its depth. The old language evokes the history of staid, well-controlled concern on the part of those who have, for those who have not. It suggests that remedy can come from traditional means—the use of some part of the wealth and talent of those who have to ease the burden of those who have not, and perhaps open opportunities for some of them to enter the mainstream of traditional values and institutions. It recalls the missionary spirit of the voluntary associations of those who have—the legislative charity of the New Deal, the Fair Deal, the Welfare State, and the whole spectrum of international development missions.

A benevolent tone characterizes the old rhetoric of social welfare. The tone assumes that all men seek and should increasingly have more of the available wealth, or education, or security, or culture, or opportunities. The values of those who "have" are celebrated as the goals to which all should aspire, and effective social policy becomes a series of acts to extend opportunity to share in those values. If those who have can provide for others more of their own perquisites—more of the right to vote, or to find employment, or to go to college, or to consume goods—then progress is assured.

Although the terms "have" and "have not" are still accurate enough descriptions of the conditions that divide people and groups, their evocation of a traditional past hides the depth and radical nature of current divisions. Those on the "have not" side of the division, or at least some of their theorists and leaders, no longer accept designation as an inert mass hoping to receive what they lack through action by the "haves." Neither do they accept any assumption that what they wish is membership in the institutions of those who have, or an opportunity to learn and join their value system. Rather the "have nots" picture themselves as radically divided from traditional society, questioning not simply the limitations of its benevolence but more fundamentally its purposes and modes of operation. Whether they experience deprivation as poverty, or lack of political power, or disaffection from traditional values, the "have not" leaders and theorists challenge existing institutions. This radical challenge, and its accompanying disposition toward confrontation, marks the vague attitudinal web that links revolutionaries in emerging nations to Black Power advocates in America or to students and intellectuals of the New Left. Three statements will illustrate the similar disposition of men who serve rather different causes in varied circumstances.

For Frantz Fanon, Algerian revolutionary and author of *The Wretched of the Earth*, the symbol of deprivation is the term "colonisation," and the end of confrontation is "decolonisation": "In decolonisation there is therefore the need of a complete calling in question of the colonial situation. If we wish to describe it precisely, we might find it in the well-known words 'The last shall be first and the first last.' Decolonisation is the putting into practice of this statement. That is why, if we try to describe it, all decolonisation is successful."[3]

For Black Power advocate Stokely Carmichael, the enemy is white racism, which is to be confronted, not joined: "Our concern for black power addresses itself directly to this problem, the necessity to reclaim our history and our identity from the cultural terrorism and depredation of self-justifying white guilt. To do this we shall have to struggle for the right to create our own terms through which to define ourselves and our relationship to the society, and to have these terms recognized. This is the first necessity of a free people, and the first right that any oppressor must suspend."[4]

For students in the New Left, the enemy to be confronted is simply "the establishment," or often in the United States, "technocracy." As student Frederick Richman sees the division:

> The world in which the older generation grew up, and which the political systems support, is no longer one which youth can accept. In a world of rampaging technology, racial turmoil, and poverty, they see a President whose program is constituted largely of finishing touches to the New Deal, and a Congress unwilling to accept even that. In a time when personal freedom is of increasing concern, they see a republic operated by an immense bureaucratic structure, geared more to cold war adventures than to domestic needs, stifling individual initiative along with that of states and cities. Finally, they see a political system obsessed with stability and loyalty instead of with social justice.[5]

Those have-nots who confront established power do not seek to share; they demand to supplant.

They must demand to supplant for they live in a Manichean world. Fanon, who features the term, argues that the settler (we may translate "settler" into other words, e.g., racist, establishment, or power structure) is responsible for the situation in which he must now suffer: "The colonial world is a Manichean world."[6] Those who rule and take the fruit of the system as their due create an equation that identifies themselves with the force of good (order, civilization, progress) which struggles with evil (chaos, the primitive, retrogression). In such a circumstance,

established authority often crusades to eliminate the vessels of evil by direct action; but often its leaders work benignly and energetically to transform the others into worthy copies of themselves. At best, the process of transformation is slow, during which time the mass of the others must be carefully held apart to keep them from contaminating the system. Only a few can cross the great gulf to be numbered among the good. Claiming to recognize the reality of this process, which is always masked under exalted labels, black radicals in America cry that the traditional goal of integration masks and preserves racism. In an analogous posture, Students for a Democratic Society picture their educational system as a vast machine to recruit servants for a traditional society, perpetuating all of the injustices of that society.

Whether the force of "good" works energetically and directly or indirectly and somewhat benignly, those without caste must strive to supplant such holders of power. Forced to accept a Manichean struggle, they must reverse the equation, not simply to gain food, land, power, or whatever, but to survive. Reversing the equation will deny the justice of the system that has dehumanized them.

The process of supplanting will be violent for it is born of a violent system. To complete the long quotation introduced above from Fanon: "The naked truth of decolonisation evokes for us the searing bullets and bloodstained knives which emanate from it. For if the last shall be first, this will only come to pass after a murderous and decisive struggle between the two protagonists. That affirmed intention to place the last at the head of things . . . can only triumph if we use all means to turn the scale, including, of course, that of violence."[7]

As Eric Hoffer concludes in his study of mass movements, those who make revolutions are apt to see themselves as spoiled, degraded, and without hope as things exist. But they locate the genesis of their degradation in things, in others, in the world as it is organized around them.[8]

THE RITE OF THE KILL

The enemy is obvious, and it is he who has set the scene upon which the actors must play out the roles determined by the cleavage of exploitation.

The situation shrieks kill-or-be-killed. "From here on in, if we must die anyway, we will die fighting back and we will not die alone," Malcolm X wrote in his "Appeal to African Heads of State." "We intend to see that our racist oppressors also get a taste of death."[9]

Judgments like "the oppressor" cannot be made without concomitant judgments. If there are those who oppress, there are those who are oppressed. This much seems obvious, but beneath that surface is the accusation that those oppressed have been something less than men ought to be. If one stresses the cunning, tenacious brutality of the oppressor, he suggests that the oppressed has been less than wise, alert, and strong. If one feels the heritage of injustice, then he senses the ignominy of his patrimony. The blighted self must be killed in striking the enemy. By the act of overcoming his enemy, he who supplants demonstrates his own worthiness, effacing the mark, whatever it may be—immaturity, weakness, subhumanity—that his enemy has set upon his brow.

To satisfy the rite that destroys the evil self in the act of destroying the enemy that has made the self evil, the radical may work out the rite of kill symbolically.[10] Harassing, embarrassing, and disarming the enemy may suffice, especially if he is finally led to admit his impotence in the face of the superior will of the revolutionary. Symbolic destruction of some manifestation of evil is well illustrated by the outbursts on campuses across America directed toward Dow Chemical. As far as we know[,] in every confrontation of authority centering around the presence on the campus of a recruiter from Dow Chemical, the demonstrators early announced their intention of paralyzing the process until the recruiter agrees on behalf of the company to contaminate the scene no further with his presence.

Michael Novak, a Stanford University professor, pictures student disruption as a tactic to remove the mask of respectability worn by the establishment and kept in place both by the centralized control of communication processes and the traditional canons of free speech.

> The balance of power in the formation of public opinion has been altered by the advent of television. The society of independent, rational individuals envisaged

by John Stuart Mill does not exist. The fate of all is bound up with the interpretation of events given by the mass media, by the image projected, and by the political power which results. . . . In a society with respect for its political institutions, officials have only to act with decorum and energy in order to benefit by such respect and to have their views established as true until proven false . . . .

> What, then, does freedom of speech mean in a technological society? How can one defend oneself against McCarthyism on the one hand and official newspeak on the other? The solution of the students has been to violate the taboos of decorum and thus embrace Vice President Humphrey, the CIA, Dow Chemical, and other enemies in an ugly scene, hoping that the unpopularity of the radicals will rub off on those embraced. They want to make the heretofore bland and respectable wear that tag which most alarms American sensibilities: "controversial."[11]

Student Stephen Saltonstall of Yale University views coercive disruption as the obvious tactic by which "a small concentrated minority" group can bring society to heel and proposes use of this tactic by students to "destroy the university's capability to prop up our political institutions. By stalemating America's intellectual establishment," he continues, "we may be able to paralyze the political establishment as well." Saltonstall's specific recommendations are far-ranging: "A small, disciplined group of shock troops could pack classes, break up drills, and harass army professors. . . . Students could infiltrate the office staffs of the electronic accelerators and foreign policy institutes and hamper their efficiency. The introduction of a small quantity of LSD in only five or six government department coffee-urns might be a highly effective tactic. Students should prevent their universities from being used as forums for government apologists. Public figures like Humphrey and McNamara, when they appear, should be subject to intimidation and humiliation."[12]

Some who confront the oppressive authority seek to transform its representatives as well as themselves, working to wipe out the Manichean world. Such a stance is typical of the strongly Christian representatives of the Civil Rights Movement in this country. But those who advocate killing the enemy or degrading him symbolically act out more simply and more directly the dynamics dictated by the sense of radical division.

CONFRONTATION AS A TOTALISTIC STRATEGY

Part of the attraction of confrontation is the strong sense of success, so strong that it may be a can't-lose strategy. After all in the Christian text Fanon cites ironically, "The last *shall* be first." The last shall be first precisely because he is last. The feeling is that one has nowhere to go but up, that he has nothing to lose, that after having suffered being down so long, he deserves to move up. Aside from the innate logic of the situation, four reasons for success seem apparent. In them we can imagine the radical voice speaking.

a. *We are already dead.* In the world as it is, we do not count. We make no difference. We are not persons. "Baby, it don't mean shit if I burn in a rebellion, because my life ain't worth shit. Dig?"[13] There is no mistaking that idiom, nor the sense behind it. Some radicals take oaths, changing their names, considering themselves as dead, without families, until the revolution succeeds. It is difficult to cow a dead orphan.

b. *We can be reborn.* Having accepted the evaluation of what is, agreeing to be the most worthless of things, we can be reborn. We have nothing to hang on to. No old identity to stop us from identifying with a new world, no matter how horrifying the prospect may seem at the outset; and a new world will certainly be born of the fire we shall create. You, the enemy, on the other hand, must cling to what is, must seek to stamp out the flames, and at best can only end sorrowing at a world that cannot remain the same. Eventually you will be consumed.

c. *We have the stomach for the fight; you don't.* Having created the Manichean world, having degraded humanity, you are overwhelmed by guilt. The sense of guilt stops your hand, for what you would kill is the world you have made. Every blow you strike is suicide and you know it. At best, you can fight only delaying actions. We can strike to kill for the old world is not ours but one

in which we are already dead, in which killing injures us not, but provides us with the chance of rebirth.

d. *We are united and understand.* We are united in a sense of a past dead and a present that is valuable only to turn into a future free of your degrading domination. We have accepted our past as past by willing our future. Since you must cling to the past, you have no future and cannot even understand.

CONFRONTATION AS A NON-TOTALISTIC TACTIC

Radical and revolutionary confrontation worries and bleeds the enemy to death or it engulfs and annihilates him. The logic of the situation that calls it forth bids it be total. But undoubtedly confrontation is brought about by those who feel only division, not radical division. For these the forces of good and evil pop in and out of focus, now clearly perceived, now not; now identified with this manifestation of established power and now that. These radicals may stop short of revolution because they have motives that turn them into politicians who at some point will make practical moves rather than toss every possible compromise and accommodation into the flaming jaws that would destroy the old order.

Student activists in the New Left vacillate in their demands between calls for "destruction" of universities as they are now known and tactical discussions of ways of "getting into the system" to make it more responsive to student goals.[14]

Drift toward non-totalistic goals seems consistent with both the general affluence of this group and its position as a small minority in a large student population generally committed to establishment goals and values. It may also reflect a latent response to the embarrassment of affluent students, beneficiaries of the establishment, who claim the language and motivations of the truly deprived.[15]

Similarly, the perception of confrontation as a tactic for prying apart and thus remodeling the machines of established power seems evident in many adherents of the Black Power movement. In many ways, the power Stokely Carmichael and Charles V. Hamilton forecast in their book is quite conventional, drawing analogies from past, thoroughly American experiences.[16]

Finally, one should observe the possible use of confrontation as a tactic for achieving attention and an importance not readily attainable through decorum. In retiring temporarily from his task of writing a regular newspaper column, Howard K. Smith complained bitterly of a press which inflated Stokely Carmichael from a "nobody who . . . had achieved nothing and represented no one" into "a factor to be reckoned with."[17] But Carmichael knows, from bitter experience, the art of confrontation. Martin Luther King writes of meeting a group of small boys while touring Watts after the riot. "We won!" they shouted joyously. King says his group asked them, "How can you say you won when thirty-four Negroes are dead, your community is destroyed, and whites are using the riot as an excuse for inaction?" The reply was, "We won because we made them pay attention to us."[18]

Without doubt, for many the act of confrontation itself, the march, sit-in, or altercation with the police is enough. It is consummatory. Through it the radical acts out his drama of self-assertion and writes in smeary, wordless language all over the establishment, "we know you for what you are. And you know that we know." Justifying the sense of rightness and, perhaps, firing a sense of guilt in the other is the hopeful outcome of the many coy confrontations of some shy radicals.[19]

CONFRONTATION AND RHETORICAL THEORY

We have talked of the *rhetoric* of confrontation, not merely confrontation, because this action, as diverse as its manifestations may be, is inherently symbolic. The act carries a message. It dissolves the lines between marches, sit-ins, demonstrations, acts of physical violence, and aggressive discourse. In this way it informs us of the essential nature of discourse itself as human action.

The rhetoric of confrontation also poses new problems for rhetorical theory. Since the time of Aristotle, academic rhetorics have been for the most part instruments of established society, presupposing the "goods" of order, civility, reason, decorum, and civil or theocratic law. Challenges to the sufficiency of this theory and its presuppositions have been few, and largely proposed either by elusive theologians such as

Kierkegaard or Buber, or by manifestly unsavory revolutionaries such as Hitler, whose degraded theories of discourse seemed to flow naturally from degraded values and paranoid ambitions.

But the contemporary rhetoric of confrontation is argued by theorists whose aspirations for a better world are not easily dismissed, and whose passion for action equals or exceeds their passion for theory. Even if the presuppositions of civility and rationality underlying the old rhetoric are sound, they can no longer be treated as self-evident.[20] A rhetorical theory suitable to our age must take into account the charge that civility and decorum serve as masks for the preservation of injustice, that they condemn the dispossessed to non-being, and that as transmitted in a technological society they become the instrumentalities of power for those who "have."

A broader base for rhetorical theory is also needed if only as a means of bringing up to date the traditional status of rhetoric as a theory of managing public symbolic transactions. The managerial advice implicit in current theories of debate and discussion scarcely contemplates the possibility that respectable people should confront disruption of reasonable or customary actions, obscenity, threats of violence, and the like. Yet the response mechanisms turned to by those whose presuppositions could not contemplate confrontation often seem to complete the action sought by those who confront, or to confirm their subjective sense of division from the establishment. The use of force to get students out of halls consecrated to university administration or out of holes dedicated to construction projects seems to confirm the radical analysis that the establishment serves itself rather than justice. In this sense, the confronter who prompts violence in the language or behavior of another has found his collaborator. "Show us how ugly you really are," he says, and the enemy with dogs and cattle prods, or police billies and mace, complies. How can administrators ignore the insurgency of those committed to jamming the machinery of whatever enterprise is supposed to be ongoing? Those who would confront have learned a brutal art, practiced sometimes awkwardly and sometimes skillfully, which demands response. But that art may provoke the response that confirms its presuppositions, gratifies the adherents of those presuppositions, and turns the power-enforced victory of the establishment into a symbolic victory for its opponents.

As specialists interested in communication, we who profess the field of rhetoric need to read the rhetoric of confrontation, seek understanding of its presuppositions, tactics, and purposes, and seek placement of its claim against a just accounting of the presuppositions and claims of our tradition. Often as we read and reflect we shall see only grotesque, childish posturings that vaguely act out the deeper drama rooted in radical division. But even so, we shall understand more, act more wisely, and teach more usefully if we open ourselves to the fundamental meaning of radical confrontation.

Notes

1 (New York, 1955), p. 128.

2 Readers will find our generalizations more or less in harmony with other discussions of radical rhetoric which have appeared in the *QJS* recently, e.g., Parke G. Burgess, "The Rhetoric of Black Power: A Moral Demand?" LIV (April 1968), 122–133; Leland M. Griffin, "The Rhetorical Structure of the 'New Left' Movement: Part I," L (April 1964), 113–135; and Franklyn S. Haiman, "The Rhetoric of the Streets: Some Legal and Ethical Considerations," LIII (April 1967), 99–114.

These writers sense a corporate wholeness in the messages and methods of various men. An attempt to explain the combination of message and method which forms the wholeness gives rise in each case to a *rhetoric*. All these efforts seem to us impulses to examine the sufficiency of our traditional concepts in dealing with phenomena which are becoming characteristic of contemporary dissent. In seeing rhetoric as an amalgam of meaning and method, these writers break with a tradition that takes rhetoric to be amoral techniques of manipulating a message to fit various contexts.

Rhetoric has always been response-oriented, that is, the rationale of practical discourse, discourse designed to gain response for specific ends. But these writers see response differently. For them, the response of audiences is an integral part of the message-method that makes the rhetoric. Thus, rhetoric is shifted from a focus of reaction to one of interaction or transaction. (See especially Burgess, 132–133; Griffin, 121; and Haiman, 113.)

Although we believe we share the sense of *rhetoric* which permeates these essays, we claim to analyze a fundamental level of meaning which underlies them.

3 Tr. Constance Farrington (New York, 1963), p. 30.

4 "Toward Black Liberation," *Massachusetts Review,* VII (Autumn 1966), 639–640.

5 "The Disenfranchised Majority," *Students and Society,* report on a conference, Vol. 1, No. 1; an occasional paper published by the Center for the Study of Democratic Institutions (Santa Barbara, Calif., 1967), p. 4.

6 Fanon, p. 33. The book is replete with references to "Manicheanism."

7 *Ibid.,* p. 30.

8 *The True Believer* (New York, 1951), pp. 19–20 and *passim.*

9 *Malcolm X Speaks,* ed. George Breitman (New York, 1966), p. 77.

10 See Fanon, p. 73.

11 "An End of Ideology?" *Commonweal,* LXXXVII (March 8, 1968), 681–682.

12 "Toward a Strategy of Disruption," from *Students and Society,* p. 29.

13 Quoted by Jack Newfield, "The Biggest Lab in the Nation," *Life,* LXIV (March 8, 1968), 87.

14 *Students and Society.* A full reading of the conference proceedings reveals clearly this split among the most vocal and militant of New Left students.

15 For an analysis of the structure and characteristics of the student left, see Richard E. Peterson, "The Student Left in American Higher Education," *Daedalus,* XCVII (Winter 1968), 293–317.

16 *Black Power: The Politics of Liberation in America* (New York, 1967), see especially Chap. 5.

17 "Great Age of Journalism Gone?" *Minneapolis Star,* February 19, 1968, p. 5B.

18 *Where Do We Go From Here: Chaos or Community?* (New York, 1967), p. 112.

19 See Norman Mailer, "The Steps of the Pentagon," *Harper's Magazine,* CCXXXVI (March 1968), 47–142 [published in book form as *Armies of the Night* (New York 1968)]. It may seem difficult to believe but Mailer, who calls himself a "right radical," fits our adjectives, coy and shy.

20 Herein lies a major problem for rhetorical theory. In a sense Haiman's essay (note 2) is a defense of these values accepting the responsibility implied by his analysis which shows a significant case made by the very existence of "A Rhetoric of the Streets" which demands a rebuttal. Burgess' essay (note 2) sees Black Power as a unique method of forcing conventional thought to take seriously its own criterion of rationality.

Requirements, Problems, and Strategies:
A Theory of Persuasion for Social Movements
Herbert W. Simons

Given the usual problems of estimating the effects of a single speech, of assessing the factors that may have produced those effects, and of evaluating the speech in light of the speaker's intent,[1] it is not surprising that few rhetoricians have undertaken the much more difficult task of analyzing the role of persuasion in social movements.[2] When one advances to the movement as a unit of study, these problems are magnified and others are introduced. As any number of currently unemployed college presidents can attest, it is frequently impossible to separate detractors from supporters of a social movement, let alone to discern rhetorical intentions,[3] to distinguish between rhetorical acts and coercive acts,[4] or to estimate the effects of messages on the many audiences to which they must inevitably be addressed. Actions that may succeed with one audience (e.g., solidification of the membership) may alienate others (e.g., provocation of a backlash).[5] For similar reasons, actions that may seem productive over the short run may fail over the long run (the reverse is also true).[6]

Add to these problems of analysis the sheer magnitude of the unit of study: a time span that may extend through several stages[7] for a decade or longer; a host of varied and often unconventional symbols and media;[8] not one leader and one following but several of each (themselves frequently divided into competing factions).[9] Designed for microscopic analysis of particular speeches, the standard tools of rhetorical criticism are ill-suited for unravelling the complexity of discourse in social movements or for capturing its grand flow. Hence it is with good cause that the major contributor to the development of an appropriate methodology has himself cautioned the uninitiated against study of any but the most minute social movements, and then only in the light cast by historical perspective.[10]

Professor Griffin has prescribed a relativistic and essentially clinical process for identifying and evaluating "the pattern of public discussion, the configuration of discourse, the physiognomy of persuasion, peculiar to a movement."[11] Yet the analyst could probably fulfill and even go beyond Griffin's definition of his task if only he could draw more heavily on theory.[12] No theory of persuasion in social movements can as yet be applied predictively to particular cases or tested rigorously through an analysis of such cases. But theory can nevertheless be illuminative. In addition to suggesting categories for descriptive analysis (a skeletal typology of stages, leaders, media, audiences, etc. has already been provided by Griffin),[13] it can indicate—admittedly in general terms—the requirements that rhetoric must fulfill in social movements, the means available to accomplish these requirements, and the kinds of problems that impede accomplishment. By enumerating rhetorical requirements, theory identifies the ends in light of which rhetorical strategies and tactics may be evaluated. By suggesting parameters and directions to the rhetorical critic, theory places him in a better position to bring his own sensitivity and imagination to bear on analyses of particular movements.

This paper is aimed, in preliminary fashion, at providing a leader-centered conception of persuasion in social movements.[14] Rooted in sociological theory, it assumes that the rhetoric of a movement must *follow*, in a general way, from the very nature of social movements. Any movement, it is argued, must fulfill the same functional requirements as more formal collectivities. These imperatives constitute *rhetorical requirements* for the leadership of a movement. Conflicts among requirements create *rhetorical problems* which in turn affect decisions on *rhetorical strategy. The primary rhetorical test of the leader—and, indirectly, of the strategies he employs—is his capacity to fulfill the requirements of his movement by resolving or reducing rhetorical problems.*

A social movement may be defined, combining concepts offered by Smelser and by Turner and Killian, as an uninstitutionalized collectivity that mobilizes for action to implement a program for the reconstitution of social norms or values.[15] Movements should be distinguished, as such, from panics, crazes, booms, fads, and hostile outbursts, as well as from the actions of recognized labor unions, government agencies, business organizations, and other institutionalized decision-making bodies.

The focus of this paper is on reformist and revolutionary movements. Blumer distinguished these "specific" social movements from "general["] social movements (amorphous social trends) and from "expressive" social movements, of which religious cults are a prototype.[16] Although geared to specific social movements (and especially to contemporary cases), the theory is applicable with somewhat less consistency to general and expressive movements, perhaps neglected by Blumer's classification scheme, as secessionist movements and movements aimed at the restoration or protection of laws, rules, and/or agencies.[17]

In the pages that follow, examination is made of the necessary functions of reformist and revolutionary rhetoric and of the types of problems that arise from inherently conflicting demands. Presentation of the theory next proceeds to a consideration of alternative strategies of adaptation: the tactics and styles appropriate to each and their respective advantages and disadvantages.

RHETORICAL REQUIREMENTS

Sociological theorists have inferred the functional imperatives of formal organizations from an analysis of their structural characteristics.[18] A social movement is not a formal social structure, but it nevertheless is obligated to fulfill parallel functions.[19] Like the heads of private corporations or government agencies, the leaders of social movements must meet a number of rhetorical requirements, arranged below under three broad headings.

1. *They must attract, maintain, and mold workers (i.e., followers) into an efficiently organized unit.* The survival and effectiveness of any movement are dependent on adherence to its program, loyalty to its leadership, a collective willingness and capacity to work, energy mobilization, and member satisfaction. A hierarchy of authority and division of labor must be established in which members are persuaded to take orders, to perform menial tasks, and to forego social pleasures. Funds must be raised, literature printed and distributed, local chapters organized, etc.[20]

2. *They must secure adoption of their product by the larger structure* (i.e., the external system, the established order). The product of any movement is its ideology, particularly its program for change.[21] Reformist and revolutionary rhetorics both seize on conditions of real deprivation or on sharp discrepancies between conditions and expectations—the reformist urging change or repair of particular laws, customs, or practices, the revolutionary insisting that a new order and a vast regeneration of values are necessary to smite the agents of the old and to provide happiness, harmony, and stability.[22]

3. *They must react to resistance generated by the larger structure.* The established order may be "too kind" to the movement or it may be too restrictive. It may steal the movement's thunder by anticipating its demands and acting on some of them, by appointing a commission to "study the problem," or by bribing or coopting personnel. On the other hand, it may threaten, harass, or socially ostracize the membership, refuse to recognize or negotiate with the movement, or deny it access to the mass media.[23] The leadership of a social movement must constantly adjust to backlash reactions and pseudosupportive reactions as well as to overreactions by officials on which it may capitalize.

Social movements are severely restricted from fulfilling these requirements by dint of their informal compositions and their positions in relation to the larger society. By comparison to the heads of most formal organizations, the leaders of social movements can expect minimal internal control and maximal external resistance. Whereas business corporations may induce productivity through tangible rewards and punishments, social movements, as voluntary collectivities, must rely on ideological and social commitments from their members. At best, the movement's leadership controls an organized core of the movement (frequently mistaken for the movement itself) but exerts relatively little influence over a relatively larger number of sympathizers on its periphery.[24] Existing outside the larger society's conceptions of justice and reality, moreover, movements threaten and are threatened by the society's sanctions and taboos: its laws, its maxims, its customs governing manners, decorum, and taste, its insignia of authority, etc.

Although organizational efficiency and adaptation to pressures from the external system are clearly prerequisite to promotion of a movement's ideology, in other respects the various internal and external requirements of a movement are incompatible. *Shorn of the controls that characterize formal organizations, yet required to perform the same internal functions, harassed from without, yet obligated to adapt to the external system, the leader of a social movement must constantly balance inherently conflicting demands on his position and on the movement he represents.*

RHETORICAL PROBLEMS

Unless it is understood that the leader is subjected to incompatible demands, a great many of his rhetorical acts must seem counterproductive. An agitator exhorts his following to revolutionary fervor and then propounds conservative solutions to the evils he has depicted.[25] Another leader deliberately disavows the very program he seeks to achieve.[26] A third leader encourages his supporters to carry Viet Cong flags or to "raze the Pentagon" or to heckle another spokesman for the movement, despite advance knowledge that these acts will fragment the movement and invite bitter reactions from outsiders.[27]

On the other hand, the disintegration of a movement may be traced to its failure to meet one or more of the demands incumbent upon it. To deal with pressures from the external system, a movement may lose sight of its ideological values and become preoccupied with power for its own sake.[28] Careful, by contrast, to remain consistent with its values, the movement may forsake those strategies and tactics that are necessary to implement its program.[29] To attract membership support from persons with dissimilar views, the movement may dilute its ideology, become bogged down with peripheral issues or abandon all substantive concerns and exist solely to provide membership satisfactions.[30]

Short of causing disintegration, the existence of crosspressures enormously complicates the role of the leader, frequently posing difficult choices between ethical and expediential considerations. The following are illustrative of these dilemmas and of other rhetorical problems created by conflicting demands.

1. When George Wallace vowed, after losing a local election, that he would never again be "out-niggered," he was referring to a phenomenon that has its counterpart on the left as well. Turner and Killian have suggested that strong identification by members with the goals of a movement —however necessary to achieve *esprit de corps*— may foster the conviction that any means are justified and breed impatience with time-consuming tactics. The use of violence and other questionable means may be prompted further by restrictions on legitimate avenues of expression, imposed by the larger structure. Countering these pressures may require that the leader mask the movement's objectives, deny the use of tactics that are socially taboo, promise what he cannot deliver, exaggerate the strength of the movement, etc. A vicious cycle develops in which militant tactics invite further suppression, which spurs the movement on to more extreme methods. Lest the moderate leader object to extremist tactics, he may become a leader without a following.[31]

2. The leader may also need to distort, conceal, exaggerate, etc., in addressing his own supporters. To gain intellectual respectability within and/or outside the movement, ideological statements should be built on a logical framework and appear consistent with verifiable evidence.[32] Yet mass support is more apt to be secured when ideological statements are presented as "generalized beliefs," over-simplified conceptions of social problems, and magical, "if-only" beliefs about solutions.[33] Statements of ideology must provide definition of that which is ambiguous in the social situation, give structure to anxiety and a tangible target for hostility, foster in-group feelings, and articulate wish-fulfillment beliefs about the movement's power to succeed.[34] Hence the use of "god words" and "devil words"[35] as well as "stereotypes, smooth and graphic phrases and folk arguments."[36]

Among isolated individuals, those anxiety, hostility, and wish-fulfillment beliefs that are socially taboo are likely to be repressed or inhibited. They are expres[s]ed unconsciously or if consciously, only to one's self, or if expressed to others, said more to expunge feelings than to share them.[37] What is largely expressive for the isolated individual is rhetorical for the movement's leadership. Particularly in militant movements, the leader wins and maintains adherents by saying to them what they cannot say to others or even to themselves. A major rhetorical process, then, consists of legitimizing privately held feelings by providing social support and rationalizations for those feelings.

Apart from placing a strain on the ideological values of the movement and its leaders, the deliberate use of myths, deceptions, etc. creates practical problems. When outsiders discover that the size of the membership has been exaggerated or when followers learn that they are far from united, the leader must invent rationalizations for his deceptions through a new rhetoric of justification or apology. Worst of all, the leadership may come to believe its own falsehoods. As Kenneth Keniston has noted, "Movement groups . . . tend to develop strong barriers on their outside boundaries, which impede communication and movement outside the group; they frequently exhibit an 'anti-empirical' inability to use facts in order to counter emotion-based distortions and impressions; interaction within the group often has a quality of 'surreality.'"[38]

3. Pressures for organizational efficiency are incompatible with membership needs. An energized membership is the strength of any movement and its *esprit de corps* is essential to goal implementation. Yet morale cannot be secured through abdications of leadership. Members may feel the need to participate in decision-making, to undertake pet projects on their own initiatives, to "put down" leaders or other followers, to obstruct meetings by socializing, or to disobey directives. The leadership cannot ignore these needs; yet it cannot accede to all of them either. The problem is especially acute in movements that distrust authority and value participatory democracy. During the hectic days of Vietnam Summer, according to Keniston, the secretarial staff of the central office demanded and received equal status and responsibilities with a seasoned political staff. As a result, experienced organizers were forced to perform menial chores while the former clerical workers advised local projects.[39]

4. The leaders of social movements face discrepancies between role expectations and role definitions. The leader must appear to be what he cannot be. Expected to be consistent, for example, he must nevertheless be prepared to renounce previously championed positions. Expected to be sincere and spontaneous, he must handle dilemmas with consummate manipulative skill. When, in one year, Malcolm X broke with Elijah Muhammad, shifted positions on integration and participation in civil rights demonstrations, and confessed his uncertainties on other issues, he inevitably alienated some followers and invited charges of weakness and inconsistency from his enemies.[40] When Allard Lowenstein politicked with student groups in behalf of Sen. Eugene McCarthy, he had to seem as unlike a "pol" as possible.[41]

5. The leader must adapt to several audiences simultaneously. In an age of mass media, rhetorical utterances addressed to one audience are likely to reach others. Outsiders include those who are sympathetic, indifferent, and opposed. As shall later be argued, another key variable is the extent to which those in the larger structure are susceptible to threats of force. Within the movement interfactional conflicts invariably develop over questions of value, strategy, tactics, or implementation. Purists and pragmatists clash over the merits of compromise. Academics and activists debate the necessity of long-range planning. Others enter the movement with personal grievances or vested interests. Pre-existing groups, known to have divergent ideological positions, are nevertheless invited to join or affiliate with the movement because of the power they can wield.[42]

6. Movements require a diversity of leadership types with whom any one leader must both compete and cooperate.[43] Theoreticians, agitators, and propagandists must launch the movement; political and bureaucratic types must carry it forward. Ideological differences among the leadership must also be expected insofar as the leadership reflects internal divisions among the following. Finally, there may

well be cleavages among those vested with positions of legitimate authority, those charismatic figures who have personal followings, those who have special competencies, and those who have private sources of funds or influence outside the movement. Much of the leader's persuasive skill is exhibited in private interactions with other leaders.

RHETORICAL STRATEGIES

From the foregoing discussion it should be quite clear that the leader of a social movement must thread his way through an intricate web of conflicting demands. How he adapts strategies to demands constitutes a primary basis for evaluating his rhetorical output. Along a continuum from the sweet and reasonable to the violently revolutionary, one may identify *moderate, intermediate,* and *militant* types of strategies, each with its own appropriate tactics and styles.

Little needs to be said about the strategy of the moderate. His is the pattern of peaceful persuasion rhetoricians know best and characteristically prescribe, the embodiment of reason, civility, and decorum in human interaction. Dressed in the garb of respectability and exhibiting Ivy League earnestness and midwestern charm, the moderate gets angry but does not shout, issues pamphlets but never manifestos, inveighs against social mores but always in the value language of the social order. His "devil" is a condition or a set of behaviors or an outcast group; never the persons he is seeking to influence. They, rather, are part of his "we" group, united if only by lip-service adherence to his symbols. In textbook terms, the moderate adapts to the listener's needs, wants, and values; speaks his language, adjusts to his frame of reference; reduces the psychological distance between his movement and the larger structure. Roy Wilkins exemplified the approach when he argued that the "prime, continuing racial policy looking toward eradication of inequities must be one of winning friends and influencing people among the white majority."[44]

If moderates assume or pretend to assume an ultimate identity of interests between the movement and the larger structure, militants act on the assumption of a fundamental clash of interests. If moderates employ rhetoric as an alternative to force, militants use rhetoric as an expression, an instrument, and an act of force. So contradictory are the rhetorical conceptions of moderate and militant strategists that it strains the imagination to believe that both may work. Yet the decisive changes wrought by militant rhetorics in recent years gives credence to the view that the traditionally prescribed pattern is not the only viable alternative.

The core characteristic of militant strategists is that they seek to change the actions of their primary targets as a precondition for changes in attitudes.[45] By means of direct action techniques and verbal polemics, militants threaten, harass, cajole, disrupt, provoke, intimidate, coerce. Hostility is also expressed in dress, manners, dialect, gestures, in-group slogans, and ceremonies.[46] Although the aim of pressure tactics may be to punish directly (e.g., strikes, boycotts), more frequently they are forms of "body rhetoric," designed to dramatize issues, enlist additional sympathizers, and delegitimatize the established order.[47] The targets of sit-ins, sleep-ins, and other confrontational activities are invited to participate in a drama of self-exposure. Should they reject militant demands, they may be forced to unmask themselves through punitive countermeasures, thus helping to complete the rhetorical act.[48] Confrontation, according to Scott and Smith, "dissolves the line between marches, sit-ins, demonstrations, acts of physical violence, and aggressive discourse. In this way it informs us of the essential nature of discourse itself as human action."[49]

Militant and moderate strategies are antithetical, yet each has highly desirable characteristics. Decisions to employ "intermediate" strategies may be viewed as efforts to obtain the following advantages of each while still avoiding their respective disadvantages. Once again, the following dilemmas derive from conflicting rhetorical requirements.

1. Militant tactics confer visibility on a movement; moderate tactics gain entry into decision centers. Because of their ethos of respectability moderates are invited to participate in public deliberations (hearings, conferences, negotiating sessions, etc.), even after militants have occasioned those deliberations by prolonged

and self-debilitating acts of protest. On the other hand, the militant has readier access to the masses. Robert C. Weaver has lamented that "today, a publicized spokesman may be the individual who can devise the most militant cry and the leader one who can articulate the most far-out position."[50]

2. For different reasons, militants and moderates must both be ambivalent about "successes" and "failures." Militants thrive on injustice and ineptitude by the larger structure. Should the enemy fail to implement the movement's demands, the militant is vindicated ideologically, yet frustrated programmatically. Should some of the demands be met, he is in the paradoxical position of having to condemn them as palliatives. The moderate, by contrast, requires tangible evidence that the larger structure is tractable in order to hold followers in line; yet "too much" success belies the movement's reason for being.

3. Militant supporters are easily energized; moderate supporters are more easily controlled. Having aroused their following the leaders of a militant movement frequently become victims of their own creation, Robespierres and Dantons who can no longer contain energies within prescribed limits or guarantee their own tenure.[51] On the other hand, moderate leaders frequently claim that their supporters are apathetic. As Turner and Killian have pointed out: "To the degree to which a movement incorporates only major sacred values its power will be diffused by a large body of conspicuous lip-service adherents who cannot be depended upon for the work of the movement."[52]

4. Militants are effective with "power-vulnerables"; moderates are effective with "power-invulnerables"; neither is effective with both.

As the writer has argued in an earlier article, a distinction needs to be made between two objects of influence.[53] Persons most vulnerable to pressure tactics are the leaders of public and quasi-public institutions: elected and appointed government officials who may be removed from office or given an unfavorable press; church and university leaders who are obliged to apply "high-minded" standards in dealing with protests; executives of large corporations whose businesses are susceptible to loss of income and who are publicly committed to an ethic of social responsibility.

"Power-invulnerables" are those who have little or nothing to lose by publicly voicing their prejudices and acting on their self-concerns. With respect to the movement for black equality:

> They are the mass of white Americans who are largely unaffected by rent strikes and boycotts and who have so far defended their neighborhood sanctuaries or have physically and psychologically withdrawn to the suburbs. The average American may fear riots but he can escape from them. He may or may not approve of boycotts and demonstrations but in either case he is largely unaffected by them. He is subject to legislation but in most cases until now he has been able to circumvent it. Only through communications aimed at a change in his attitudes or through carefully formulated and tightly enforced government policies can his actions be appreciably modified.[54]

By reducing the psychological distance between the movement and the external structure, the moderate is likely to win sympathizers, even among "power-vulnerables." But as those in positions of power allocate priorities (they, too, are subjected to conflicting demands), they are unlikely to translate sympathy into action unless pressured to do so. Should the leader of a movement strike militant postures, he is likely to actuate "power-vulnerables" but at the same time prompt backlash groups to apply their own pressure tactics.

Where the movement and the larger structure are already polarized, the dilemma is magnified. However much he may wish to plead reasonably, wresting changes from those in public positions requires that the leader build a sizable power base. And to secure massive internal support, the leader must at least *seem* militant.

So the leader of a social movement may attempt to avoid or resolve the aforementioned dilemmas by employing "intermediate" strategies, admittedly a catchall term for those efforts that combine militant and moderate patterns of influence. The leader may alternate between carrot and stick or speak softly in private and stridently at mass gatherings. He may form broadly based coalitions that submerge ideological differences or utilize spokesmen with similar values but contrasting styles. Truly the exemplar of oxymoronic postures, he may stand as a "conservative radical" or a "radical conservative," espousing militant demands in the value language of the established order or militant slogans in behalf of moderate proposals. In defense of militancy, he may portray himself as a brakeman, a finger in the dike holding back an angry tide. In defense of more moderate tactics, he may hold back an angry tide without loss of reputation, as Jerry Rubin and Abbie Hoffman did in urging nonviolence on their "yippie" following during the Democratic Convention in Chicago: "We are a revolutionary new community and we must protect our community . . . . We, not they, will decide when the battle begins. . . . We are not going into their jails and we aren't going to shed our blood. We're too important for that. We've got too much work to do."[55]

Intermediacy can be a dangerous game. Calculated to energize supporters, win over neutrals, pressure power-vulnerables, and mollify the opposition, it may end up antagonizing everyone. The well-turned phrase may easily appear as a devilish trick, the rationale as a rationalization, the tactful comment as an artless dodge. To the extent that strategies of intermediacy require studied ambiguity, insincerity, and even distortion, perhaps the leader's greatest danger is that others may find out what he really thinks.

Still, some strategists manage to reconcile differences between militant and moderate approaches and not simply to maneuver around them. They seem able to convince the established order that bad tasting medicine is good for it and seem capable, too, of mobilizing a diverse collectivity within the movement.

The key, it would appear, is the leader's capacity to embody a higher wisdom, a more profound sense of justice; to stand above inconsistencies by articulating overarching principles. Few will contest the claim that Martin Luther King, Jr.[,] epitomized the approach. Attracting both militants and moderates to his movement, King could win respect, even from his enemies, by reconciling the seemingly irreconcilable. The heart of the case for intermediacy was succinctly stated by King himself in a speech which

Professor Robert Scott has analyzed: "What is needed is a realization that power without love is reckless and abusive and love without power is sentimental and anemic. Power at its best is love implementing the demands of justice, and justice at its best is power correcting everything that stands against love."[56]

Viewed broadly, the great contemporary movements all seem to require combinations of militant and moderate strategies. Tom Hayden can be counted upon to dramatize the Vietnam issue; Arthur Schlesinger, to plead forcefully within inner circles. Threats of confrontation may prompt school boards to finance the building of new facilities in ghetto areas, but it may take reasonableness and civility to get experienced teachers to volunteer for work in those facilities. Demands by revolutionary student groups for total transformations of university structures may impel administrators to heed quasi-militant demands for a redistribution of university power. Support for the cause by moderate groups may confer respectability on the movement. Thus, however much they may war amongst themselves, militants and moderates each perform essential functions.

Summary

This paper has attempted to provide a broad framework within which persuasion in social movements, particularly reformist and revolutionary movements, may be analyzed. Derived in large measure from sociological theory and from an examination of contemporary cases, it has examined rhetorical processes from the perspective of the leader of a movement: the requirements he must fulfill, the problems he faces, the strategies he may adopt to meet those requirements.

What emerges most sharply from the foregoing discussion are the extraordinary rhetorical dilemmas confronting those who would lead social movements. Movements are as susceptible to fragmentation from within as they are to suppression from without. Impelled to fulfill the same internal and external requirements as the heads of most formal organizations, their leaders can expect greater resistance to their efforts from both insiders and outsiders.

The needs of individual members are frequently incompatible with organizational imperatives; appeals addressed to the intelligentsia of a movement incompatible with appeals addressed to the masses; the values for which the movement stands incompatible with tactical necessities. In the face of these and other problems, the leader may adopt the traditionally prescribed tactics and style of the moderate or those of his more militant counterpart. Yet the choice between moderate and militant strategies introduces still other dilemmas. The great leaders (and the great movements) seem capable of combining these seemingly antithetical strategies without inconsistency by justifying their use with appeals to higher principles.

Notes

1 See, for example, Lester Thonssen and A. Craig Baird, *Speech Criticism* (New York, 1948), ch. 17.

2 For the decade prior to the writing of his text, Professor Edwin Black found only three such studies reported in *QJS* or *Speech Monographs*. See his *Rhetorical Criticism: A Study in Method* (New York, 1965), pp. 22–23.

3 For a discussion of the problem of discerning intent, see Rudolf Heberle, *Social Movements* (New York, 1951), pp. 94–95. According to Lang and Lang, "the ideology presented to the mass of followers is a 'mask' for the real beliefs of the inner core. Its 'real' ideology is hidden from all but the initiated." See Kurt Lang and Gladys Engel Lang, *Collective Dynamics* (New York, 1961), p. 539.

4 To understand the rhetoric of a militant movement requires an analysis of force as the backdrop against which communication frequently takes place and similarly requires an analysis of communication, not as an alternative to force, but as an instrument of force. Four recent articles in *QJS* have dealt with the problem and the questions of ethics raised by it. See Parke G. Burgess, "The Rhetoric of Black Power: A Moral Demand?" *QJS*, LIV (April 1968), 122–133; Franklyn S. Haiman, "The Rhetoric of the Streets: Some Legal and Ethical Considerations," *QJS*, LIII (April 1967), 99–114; James R. Andrews, "Confrontation at Columbia: A Case Study in Coercive Rhetoric," *QJS*, LV (February 1969), 9–16; and Robert L. Scott and Donald K. Smith, "The Rhetoric of Confrontation," *QJS*, LV (February 1969), 1–8.

5 One variant of the problem is discussed by Wayne E. Brockriede and Robert L. Scott, "Stokely Carmichael: Two Speeches on Black Power," *Central States Speech Journal*, XIX (Spring 1968), 3–13.

6 The problems of estimating long-range effects are nicely illustrated in Howard H. Martin's appraisal of the effects of the antiwar "teach-ins." See "Rhetoric of Academic Protest," *Central States Speech Journal*, XVII (Spring 1966), 244–250.

7 For a classic typology of stages, see Carl A. Dawson and Warner E. Gettys, *An Introduction to Sociology*, rev. ed. (New York, 1935), ch. 19.

8 For an intriguing analysis of nonobvious symbols, see Hugh D. Duncan, *Communication and Social Order* (New York, 1962).

9 For example, during its hey-day, the civil rights movement encompassed SNCC, CORE, and the NAACP, each of which was torn by internal fragmentation.

10 Leland M. Griffin, "The Rhetoric of Historical Movements," *QJS*, XXXVIII (April 1952), 184–188.

11 *Ibid.*, 185.

12 Griffin has suggested that the development of theory must await further research. Yet there is reason to believe, here as elsewhere, that theory and research must develop apace of each other. As Black has argued (p. 22), the researcher can do little without a framework for analysis.

13 Griffin, 185–187.

14 Consistent with Scott and Smith's view of rhetoric as *managed* public discourse (p. 8), the paper focuses on the intentional symbolic acts of those who lead social movements. Emphasis on more spontaneous acts of communication (rumor, milling, social contagion, etc. by non-leaders) has been provided by those who have stressed the primitive features of social movements. The "classic" is Gustave Le Bon, *The Crowd: A Study of the Popular Mind* (London, 1897).

15 Neil J. Smelser, *Theory of Collective Behavior* (New York, 1962), pp. 110 and 129–130 and Ralph H. Turner and Lewis M. Killian, *Collective Behavior* (Englewood Cliffs, N.J., 1957), p. 308.

16 Herbert Blumer, "Social Movements," in *New Outline of the Principles of Sociology*, ed. A. M. Lee (New York, 1946), pp. 200, 202, and 214.

17 Any classification of social movements must have arbitrary features. For other categorizations, see Lang and Lang, pp. 497–505.

18 See, for example, Chester I. Barnard, *The Functions of the Executive* (Cambridge, Mass., 1938) and Robert K. Merton, *Social Theory and Social Structure* (Glencoe, Ill., 1949).

19 According to Lang and Lang (p. 493), it is the quasi-structural character of social movements that distinguishes them from formal organizations

on the one hand and spontaneous mass behavior on the other. Although claiming to stress the nonstructural aspects of social movements, Lang and Lang have provided the most adequate account of their structural imperatives. See pp. 495–496 and 531–537. See also C. Wendell King, *Social Movements in the United States* (New York, 1956).

20 See *From Max Weber: Essays in Sociology,* ed. H. H. Gerth and C. Wright Mills (New York, 1946); Barnard; Peter M. Blau, *The Dynamics of Bureaucracy* (Chicago, 1955); and Philip Selznick, *TVA and the Grass Roots* (Berkeley and Los Angeles, 1949).

21 Blumer, pp. 210–211.

22 See Smelser, pp. 109–110 and 121–122.

23 *Ibid.,* 282–286.

24 Lang and Lang, p. 495.

25 See Christopher Lasch on Stokely Carmichael, "The Trouble with Black Power," *New York Review of Books,* X (February 29, 1968), 4–14.

26 According to Turner and Killian (p. 337) this is the usual case for revolutionary movements. They are forced to retain several identities. The same should also be true of retrogressive movements. See, for example, Henry Kraus, *The Many and the Few* (Los Angeles, 1947).

27 See Norman Mailer, "The Steps of the Pentagon," *Harper's Magazine,* CCXXXVI (March 1968), 47–142. Mailer described the disruptive effects of Yippie leaders on "straights."

28 The "iron law of oligarchy" may be overstated, but it is not without merit. See Turner and Killian, p. 372.

29 Norman Mailer and others have ascribed just this failure to Eugene McCarthy. See "Miami Beach and the Siege of Chicago," *Harper's Magazine,* CCXXXVII (November 1968), 41–130. Cf. pp. 77 and 93.

30 See, for example, Sheldon L. Messinger, "Organizational Transformation: A Case Study of a Declining Social Movement," *American Sociological Review,* XX (February 1955), 3–10.

31 Turner and Killian, p. 373.

32 Blumer, p. 210.

33 Smelser, p. 82.

34 The writer has inferred these rhetorical functions from Smelser's thorough analysis of the belief components common to all forms of collective behavior and to social movements in particular (pp. 79–130, 292–296, and 348–352). For comparable statements of these leadership requirements, see Eric Hoffer, *The True Believer* (New York, 1951).

35 See Leland M. Griffin's use of the terms. "The Rhetorical Structure of the 'New Left' Movement: Part I," *QJS,* L (April 1964), 113–135. According to Eric Hoffer (p. 89), "mass movements can rise and spread without belief in a God, but never without belief in a devil."

36 Blumer, p. 210.

37 For a discussion of such nonrhetorical speech functions, see, for example, Jon Eisenson, J. Jeffery Auer and John V. Irwin, *The Psychology of Communication,* rev. ed. (New York, 1963), pp. 20–29.

38 *Young Radicals: Notes on Committed Youth* (New York, 1968), p. 159.

39 *Ibid.,* pp. 160–161.

40 See *The Autobiography of Malcolm X* (New York, 1965).

41 See David Halberstam, "The Man Who Ran Against Lyndon Johnson," *Harper's Magazine,* CCXXXVII (December 1968), 47–66.

42 For a discussion of other intramovement divisions, see Smelser, pp. 302–306 and 361–364.

43 Like Margaret Sanger or Martin Luther King, Jr., the same leader may encompass all or almost all of the necessary roles. This is rare, however. See Turner and Killian, pp. 472–476.

44 "What Now?—One Negro Leader's Answer," *New York Times Magazine,* August 16, 1964, p. 11.

45 Considerable experimental evidence suggests that where actions and attitudes are discrepant, the latter are more likely to change. See Ralph L. Rosnow and Edward J. Robinson, *Experiments in Persuasion* (New York, 1967), pp. 297–308.

46 In the "black power" movement, for example, what may actually be most frightening to whites are its nonprogrammatic symbols: faded levis, "hang loose" manners, clenched fist salutes, the "honkie" epithet, "soul" and "brother" identifications, the ritual handshake, etc. For an excellent analysis of nonverbal symbolism among black militants, see Ulf Hannerz, "The Rhetoric of Soul: Identification in Negro Society," *Race,* IX (April 1968), 453–465.

47 See, for example, John R. Searle, "A Foolproof Scenario for Student Revolts," *New York Times Magazine,* December 29, 1968, pp. 4–5 and 12–15; Daniel Walker, *Rights in Conflict* (New York, 1968), chs. 2 and 3; and Herbert W. Simons, "Confrontation as a Pattern of Persuasion in University Settings," *Central States Speech Journal,* XX (Fall 1969), 163–169.

48 See Scott and Smith, 8.

49 *Ibid.,* 7.

50 *Philadelphia Bulletin,* March 2, 1966, p. 3. See also Paul L. Fisher and Ralph L. Lowenstein, *Race and the News Media* (New York, 1967).

51 Walker, pp. 49–51.

52 Turner and Killian, p. 337.

[53] Herbert W. Simons, "Patterns of Persuasion in the Civil Rights Struggle," *Today's Speech,* XV (February, 1967), 25–27.

[54] *Ibid.,* 26.

[55] Quoted in Walker, pp. 136–137.

[56] Quoted in Robert L. Scott, "Black Power Bends Martin Luther King," *Speaker and Gavel,* V (March 1968), 84.

The Ego-Function of the Rhetoric of Protest
Richard B. Gregg

In recent years rhetorical analysts have been concerned with the problem of understanding and accounting for the rhetoric of protest. Their studies examine a variety of rhetorical dimensions; we have seen explorations of the nature of "coercive" as opposed to "persuasive" rhetoric, examinations of the legality of acts of protest and confrontation, descriptions of the rhetorical strategies of certain protest movements, essays on the psycho-symbolic aspects of confrontation, analyses of the rhetorical tensions of moderate and extremist political leaders, and discussions of the potential meanings underlying such current idiomatic expressions as "Black Power."[1] I hope to augment understanding by suggesting that an analysis of the rhetoric of contemporary protest reveals certain prominent patterns and that an examination of those patterns leads to the conclusion that we are witnessing on the public stage a rhetorical function which has been largely ignored in rhetorical study. Specifically, I refer to a particular *ego-function* of rhetoric.

The thesis of this paper will be developed in the following way: first, I shall take cognizance of the rhetorical transaction as it is usually viewed by rhetorical analysts. Once we establish the essential features of the communicative act typically labeled "rhetorical," we can more clearly delineate peculiar characteristics of contemporary protest rhetoric which seem to abrogate the kind of public discussion we have always approved of. Next, I shall broaden the analysis by granting that a person may choose to address himself, and that regardless of his reasons for such behavior, this primary transaction of self with self may properly be designated "rhetorical." At this point, I hope to clarify the concept, "ego-function," as it is used in the analytical portion of the paper. I shall then examine the patterns of protest rhetoric which demonstrate the ego-function of discourse and, finally, reflect on some of the results and effects of such discourse.

I

Typically, when we refer to a rhetorical transaction, we have in mind a situation wherein a speaker undertakes to produce a message for the purpose of affecting the perceptions, beliefs, attitudes, and behaviors of a listener or group of listeners. The end goals of such discourse are seen as pragmatic in some sense, and the speaker is successful insofar as he can maneuver his listener to assent to the point of view, claims, or actions proposed by the speaker. This point of view operates on the basic assumption that when people communicate with each other, they somehow physically or symbolically face toward each other. And if the act of communication is to be successful, there must be a mutual willingness and commitment to interact. Carroll C. Arnold, in his discussion of the qualities of oral rhetoric, describes several distinctive features of rhetoric viewed in this perspective:

A. A speaker and some listeners are *knowingly engaged* in a mutual, working relationship of considerable intellectual and psychological interdependence. [As Arnold explains it, in this relationship the listener, insofar as he allows the relationship to continue, concedes to his speaker the privilege of *trying* to direct his perceptions of reality.]

B. Speaker and listener know, or think they know, that each will behave according to his own purposes and has the right to so behave. Because of this knowledge, speakers will sometimes seek to conceal their aims and grounds for choice but on other occasions will make their intentions and principles of choice unmistakably clear.

C. Speaker and listener are knowingly engaged in a relationship wherein the listener's immediate definitions of "sufficient reasons" are the coin of exchange. Having chosen to exert influence through speech, the speaker entered, as it were, into a special bargain with his sovereign listeners. He accepted as determining—for each moment of relationship—his listeners' standards of "sufficiency."[2]

Let us examine the particular restraints which are inherent in this perspective. There is a continuum of openness and mutual interaction joining the parties involved. In every case, some kind of identification is required in order for communication to be effective. The communicator who wishes to get his listener to concur in an attitude or agree to a position or undertake an action must somehow establish an identification between attitudes and beliefs already held by the listener and the particular proposals of the communicator. The continuum of identification we are talking about runs the gamut from the case of a communicator who conceals his real motives as he manipulates those symbolic strategies which will be most effective with his listeners to the kind of ideal argumentative situation described by Johnstone and Natanson in which all values and strategies are laid bare by the parties involved so that one's self is uniquely open to an examination of one's basic perceptions and presuppositions.[3] In every instance along this continuum, the communicator is attempting to draw his listener closer to him, and to do so he must, through appearance or reality, identify intellectually and emotionally with his target audience.

The rhetoric of protest would "logically" seem to be aimed at those in power or positions of authority who appear responsible for the conditions being protested. The usual view of rhetorical communication expects the entreaties, appeals, arguments, and exhortations of those asking for change to speak somehow to the basic reasoning and feeling capacities of those in authority. But contemporary public protest does not make this kind of appeal. Rather than raise a few specific issues which might be dealt with by programmatic changes or legislation, spokesmen for protest movements thrust forward a host of issues or demands. In many cases the demands go beyond the power of the authorities to act; it somehow seems unreasonable to expect the president of a Pennsylvania university to be able to grant amnesty to Bobby Seale. And when authority figures try to respond to individual issues, they find protest leaders moving to a perspective which includes the total social, political, and economic scene, demanding sweeping revolutionary change. The escalation of demands, in fact the very couching of wishes in terms of demands, appears to those in positions of power, reacting to the rhetoric, to foreclose meaningful discussion. Opportunities for dialogue become further limited as protestors, at moments of confrontation reduce their verbalization to slogans, epithets, and chants, and rely upon obscene gestures and sheer body force to make their points. Protestors appear to reject opportunities for identification, refuse to make the kinds of appeals which might gain them a receptive audience, and in fact, flaunt and make a mockery of the values and ways of behaving which are so meaningful to the "establishment." Rhetoric, as we usually understand it, seems to flee the scene, leaving in its place coercion, threat, and intimidation.

We can better understand what is happening if we realize that the stance taken by the more radical protestors in the latter part of the 1960's was one facing deliberately away from those persons, actions, and things grouped together and identified in the construct, "establishment." The rhetoric which comes from one holding such a stance directs itself to the "establishment" only indirectly, if at all, and programmatic concerns become incidental to more personal functions. I shall argue that the primary appeal of the rhetoric of protest is to the protestors themselves, who feel the need for psychological refurbishing and affirmation. Spokesmen for protest movements also become surrogates for others who share their intimate feelings of inadequacy. The rhetoric is basically self-directed, not other-directed in the usual sense of that term, and thus it can be said to be fulfilling an ego-function. We must now clarify the concept, "ego-function."

Recently, Don Burks proposed that "just as there is an internal or self-dialectic so there is self-persuasion, and as internal dialectic is analogous to dialectic with others, so self-persuasion is analogous to persuasion of others."[4] Burks suggests that rhetorical discourse can be pictured on a continuum having as its extremes the directing of appeals and arguments toward others and the directing of appeals and arguments to one's self. Burks' thesis encourages a useful expansion of the concept of rhetoric, and I believe the rhetoric of contemporary protest can be more fully accounted for by considering how it operates as "self-addressed" discourse. Burks identifies an aspect of the ego-function of rhetoric I shall focus on: the act of communication wherein one's self is his primary audience and where others identify with the rhetoric insofar as they share similar ego-concerns.

A second aspect of the ego-function of rhetoric has to do with *constituting* self-hood through expression; that is, with establishing, defining, and affirming one's self-hood as one engages in a rhetorical act.[5] The idea here refers to self-persuasion in a peculiar way, for what is at stake is not the nature of the rhetorical claims or the sense and probity of appeals and arguments for their own sakes, but just the fact that the rhetoric must be verbalized in order for one's self-hood to be realized. Rhetoric, in this sense, takes on the aspects of both act and appeal, the two occurring simultaneously. Perhaps it is more accurate to say that rhetoric is part of act, and the adoption of a particular rhetorical stance is self-confirming and enhancing.

One remark made earlier bears repeating. We must be aware that at the same time an individual is engaged in a rhetorical act for the primary purpose of establishing his own identity to himself, he may also, acting as surrogate, aid in the establishment of identities for others. Sometimes interacting affirmations accomplish the ego-identification of a number of selves.

What I am proposing is that an examination of the rhetoric of protest—to be specific, the rhetoric of Black Power, the student rebellion, and the Women's Liberation Movement—reveals the above aspects of ego-function to be conjoined and that this feature of this rhetoric is responsible for much of the emotional consternation and response it arouses. I do not claim that the ego-function of rhetoric I am going to talk about is new. It has always been present in rhetorical acts. I am suggesting that we have not considered it sufficiently before, essentially because it has not been forced upon our attention in so pronounced a manner as in our own time.

When discussing the status of one's ego, there are three general conditions we may refer to. There is the condition of ego-forming and building, the stage where various kinds of activities affirm the being and boundaries of personhood. Once the ego is fairly well established, there is the ever-continuing process of ego-maintenance, the repeated reaffirmation of one's self-hood, and one may argue along with the Existentialists that in an evolutionary sense one's ego is constantly undergoing modification. But changes at this stage are incremental, not revolutionary, and are undergirded by a basic stability. Finally, just as ego can be established and affirmed, so it can be denied and destroyed, traumatically or by slow attrition.

The process of ego establishment has been viewed in a number of perspectives. We know that the relationship between infant and parents is crucial to the establishment of ego. From the standpoint of communication, we understand that physical stroking imparts early feelings of security to the infant, and that as he matures he will replace physical stroking as a means of affirmation. Before too many years, the peer group will play a significant role in the affirmation of self-hood. Throughout all these interactions a person constructs an order; he weighs, evaluates, and orients toward goals so that a symbolic hierarchy is established in which he locates himself. Unless this process of ego-establishment is specifically focused on, it will be overlooked in the day-to-day events of one's existence. But when the search for identity of ego takes place on the public stage, when large numbers of individuals are engaged in a struggle to achieve affirmation, and when the drama of the struggle is intensified by media coverage, the social scene becomes streaked with exacerbating tensions. In such a scene, the rhetorical act exhibits a number of peculiar characteristics relating to ego-function.

II

One of the most notable components of the protest rhetoric of recent years is the number of allusions to self-hood. Such allusions spring from three different postures. There appears to be a strong need to recognize and proclaim that one's ego is somehow ignored, or damaged, or disenfranchised. A second posture, following logically from the first, proclaims, extols, and describes in exaggerated fashion the strengths and virtues of the ego sought after. A third posture, operating on the psychological principle of victimage, decries and attacks the ignorance or malicious qualities of an enemy: a foreign ego which stands in dislogistic juxtaposition to the desired ego.

The spokesmen for Black Power in the 1960's took some pains to point out to their black brothers that they had succumbed to and been emasculated by white society. For example, Stokely Carmichael, speaking to students at Morgan State in 1967,[6] refers to the shame blacks feel about themselves. "You need to stop being ashamed of being black and come on home," he says. Later in the speech he exhorts, "We have to learn to love and respect ourselves. That's where it should begin. That's where it must begin. Because if we don't love us, ain't nobody going to love us." Throughout the speech Carmichael deplores the fact that blacks allowed whites to define status and existence for them, rather than resolutely and forthrightly declaring their own black self-hood. For too many years, says Carmichael, blacks tried to gain respectability and status (or we might say self-hood) by imitating whites, i.e., by establishing black fraternities and sororities which catered to light-skinned "Negroes" when admission to white social organizations was denied.

> Can you begin to get the guts to develop a criteria for beauty for black people? That your nose is boss; your lips are thick, you are black and you are beautiful? Can you begin to do it so that you are not ashamed of your hair and you don't cut it to the scalp so that naps won't show? Girls, are you ready? Obviously it is your responsibility to begin to define the criteria for black people about their beauty. Because you are running around with your Nadinola cream. Your campus, the black campuses of this country, are becoming infested with wigs and Mustangs and you are to blame for it. You are to blame for it.[7]

There is a clear element of self-deprecation in Carmichael's remarks, which effects impact because of negative self-imagery perceived by many blacks. There is obviously a chink in the ego armor of one who resigns himself to repeated seduction or emasculation by others. The theme of a great deal of black rhetoric in the 1960's held that blacks had been stripped of their heritage and culture and therefore suffered because of their lack of self-identification.

Sometimes, the charge that the black ego lacked strength was left at the implicative stage. At other times it was clearly expressed:

> You haven't got a revolution that doesn't involve bloodshed. And you're afraid to bleed. I said, you're afraid to bleed.
> As long as the white man sent you to Korea, you bled. He sent you to Germany, you bled. He sent you to the South Pacific to fight the Japanese, you bled. You bleed for white people, but when it comes to seeing your own churches being bombed and little black girls murdered, you haven't got any blood. You bleed when the white man says bleed; you bite when the white man says bite; and you bark when the white man says bark. I hate to say this about us, but it's true.[8]

The rhetoric of black revolution does not place sole blame for the black condition on the weaknesses of the black race. By far the greatest culprits are the white man and his society; and it is "Whitey" who must ultimately pay a price for his immoral treatment of blacks. Again, Malcolm X:

. . . the black man in America has been colonized mentally, his mind has been destroyed. And today, even though he goes to college, he comes out and still doesn't even know he is a black man. He is ashamed of what he is, because his culture has been destroyed, his identity has been destroyed, he has been made to hate his black skin, he has been made to hate the texture of his hair, he has been made to hate the features that God gave him.[9]

There are many more examples of rhetoric from black revolutionary leaders revealing images of negative self-hood which must be exorcised by blacks and replaced by qualities of strength, self-love, determination, and action. Black spokesmen seem to be pointing out that the struggles to achieve acceptance into white society by trying to imitate whites, adopting white standards and accepting the roles whites force them into, have aimed at chimerical goals and resulted in degradation. The perception that choosing to play "Whitey's" game is a mistake leads black spokesmen to eulogize blackness and exhort blacks to discover the positive qualities of their unique blackness.

The rhetoric of student revolution takes up the question of selfhood in terms of depersonalization and castigation of "the system" or "the power structure" for perpetrating numerous acts of suppression. Revolutionary notions spring from a set of images picturing various institutional and bureaucratic structures of society operating to homogenize the spirits of those touched by them, treating individuals as objects, and causing the loss of individual identity. The relatively programmatic "Port Huron Statement" states it thus:

We regard *men* as infinitely precious and possessed of unfulfilled capacities for reason, freedom, and love. In affirming these principles we are aware of countering perhaps the dominant conceptions of man in the twentieth century: that he is a thing to be manipulated and that he is inherently incapable of directing his own affairs. We oppose depersonalization that reduces human beings to the status of things.[10]

Mario Savio, sitting in at Sproul Hall on the Berkeley campus, further delineated the ego problems of students as he described his perception of their alienated plight and the pressures of "the system" which demanded a sacrifice of self-hood:

Many students here at the University, many people in society, are wandering aimlessly about. Strangers in their own lives, there is no place for them. They are people who have not learned to compromise, who for example have come to the University to learn to question, to grow, to learn—all the standard things that sound like clichés because no one takes them seriously. And they find at one point or another that for them to become part of society—very often they must compromise those principles which were most dear to them. They must suppress the most creative impulses they have, this is a prior condition for being part of the system. The university is well structured, well tooled, to turn out people with all the sharp edges worn off—the well-rounded person. The university is well equipped to produce that sort of person, and this means that the best among the people who enter must for four years wander aimlessly much of the time questioning why they are on campus at all, doubting whether there is any point in what they are doing, and looking toward a very bleak existence afterward in a game in which all of the rules have been made up—rules which one cannot really amend.[11]

Here is as good an expression of helplessness as one can find from a student revolutionary. To be aware that one has an ego, to know of the existence of one's self-hood, there must be not only a feeling of being noticed, of being attended to, but a perception of being able to control at least a portion of the situations in which one finds himself. The perception that totally impersonal forces direct the destinies of the individual leads many to feelings of emptiness and despair.

A few years later, the rhetoric of student revolution took on a more ominously personal tone. A few days after the student occupation of

Harvard's University Hall, Nick Gagarin, executive editor of the *Crimson,* wrote:

> We all agonize over the fate of the oppressed people of South Vietnam, and the oppressed people of Black America, and the oppressed people of Roxbury. But the realization that lies just around the corner is that we too are an oppressed people. Any radical movement at Harvard should base itself on our own needs—the needs of the oppressed student class.[12]

If one feels oppressed, he implies that there is an oppressor—someone responsible for the oppression. Oppression is a stronger and somehow more personal term than "depersonalization." Yet there is also a tension in the call for personal ego-affirmation and counterattack against such impersonal perceptual constructs as "the system" and "the establishment." There are, necessarily, difficulties involved when one struggles to establish his self-concept, his personhood, over against impersonal things. One does better if he chooses to identify with and against other *persons,* and we shall shortly see the ambiguity arising from student protestors' difficulties in identifying personalized "enemies."

Spokeswomen for the Women's Liberation Movement reveal the same concern for their egos that is found in the rhetoric of Black Power and in the student rebellion. To be a typical, domiciled woman is to be stripped of identity. As Nanette Rainone says, "The guy on the assembly line doesn't want to be a woman. It's not that the work at home is worse than at the factory. It's that he realizes it's nothingness, total nothingness."[13] American womanhood is seen by Lib followers as misrepresented by the false imagery of television. Jo Freeman declares that genuine women have been rendered invisible. "I look at the T.V. screen and the ads, and there is this person who's either sexy or shrill, and that's what's called a woman. I'm not that person, nor is any one of my friends. But you never see any of us."[14] The heart of the matter seems to be that women are reduced to sexual receptacles, objects, or toys to be enjoyed at the whims of men. Dana Densmore, a spokeswoman for the Feminine Liberation Movement, makes the point as she addresses "liberal" men:

> No thanks, Mr. Smug Liberal, I've tried your delicious masochistic sex and it nauseates me to think about it. I'm a person, not a delectable little screwing machine equipped with subroutines for cocktail-mixing and souffle-making and listening enchanted to all the pompous drivel you pour out to impress me.[15]

In a recent article in *Esquire,* Sally Kempton described her early feelings about herself in relation to her sexual role and to men as feelings in tune with the imagery of the 1950's: ". . . Marilyn Monroe was the feminine archetype of the period, and Marilyn Monroe was sexy because of her childishness. It is not much of a step from seeing oneself as a child in relation to men to seeing oneself as their victim; obviously a child does not control its environment, obviously a child is powerless before adults."[16] Kempton lands squarely on woman's negative self-image when describing her necessity to eschew self-love in order to get along in traditional society.

> Self-love is indeed a handicap to a being whose primary function is supportive, for how is a woman adequately to support another ego when her self-love demands the primacy of her own? Women learn in many ways to suppress their selfishness, and by doing so they suppress also their self-esteem. If most men hold women in contempt it is no greater than the contempt in which women hold themselves. Self-love depressed becomes self-loathing. Men are brought up to command, women to seduce; to admit the necessity of seduction is to admit that one has not the strength to command. It is in fact to accept one's own objecthood, to internalize one's oppression.[17]

So there we have it. In all three instances of protest rhetoric, the Woman's Lib Movement, the student revolution, and the rhetoric of Black Power, we see reflections of intense feelings of self-deprecation and ego-deprivation.

In each case the rhetoric contains statements which express a sense of guilt about inadequacy, stronger perhaps among blacks and women than among students, but present by implication even among the latter. It is not my purpose to explore the psychological realities of, or reasons for, the explicit or implicit statements of personal concern, inadequacy, ineptitude, and guilt, though this subject deserves extended study. My object is to show that these are present in contemporary protest rhetoric. It is enough for my purpose to point out that protest spokesmen and followers do choose even to proclaim their perceptions of ego-deprivation and their need for self-affirmation.

III

The acknowledgements just summarized place those who share the perceptions in symbolically defensive positions from which they must extricate themselves before they can realize more positive identities. One way of extrication is to locate what one perceives as the persons, behaviors, actions, or conditions which cause or contribute to feelings of inadequacy, then to take a positive stand against them. In the protest movements we are examining, the struggle for a resurrected self seems to be aided by locating other selves, establishing personality typologies among them, and using these as targets for arrows of scorn, ridicule, condemnation, and charges of character defect. This rhetorical identification of personalized enemies enhances establishment of self-hood in several ways. By identifying against an other, one may delineate his own position—locate himself by contrast. By painting the enemy in dark hued imagery of vice, corruption, evil, and weakness, one may more easily convince himself of his own superior virtue and thereby gain a symbolic victory of ego-enhancement. The rhetoric of attack becomes at the same time a rhetoric of ego-building, and the very act of assuming such a rhetorical stance becomes self-persuasive and confirmatory.

We need not take long to establish that the rhetoric of all three protest movements we are examining contains clear images of the enemy. Black spokesmen are eloquent in their elaboration of suppression by the white man. Political

and economic exploitation is enlarged upon, but inevitably, "Whitey's" moral character is scrutinized and found wanting. Floyd McKissick, for instance, explained to his audience at a national conference on Black Power that white supremacy and white fear of blacks stems from deep-seated feelings of inferiority. "Whitey" is neurotic, psychotic, and determined to maintain his position even if it means extermination of all blacks: "Yes. The Man has the capacity to neglect, to destroy, to shoot, to kill—if his victim is not white. He has the capacity for genocide."[18] Carmichael wrote in a SNCC pamphlet that Blacks must undertake to condemn the white system, for whites are morally incapable of self-condemnation.[19]

An element of ambiguity enters the rhetoric of student protest where the purpose becomes that of identifying the enemy. For example, at the November 1965 peace march on Washington, past SDS President Carl Ogelsby identified such personages as Lyndon Johnson, McGeorge Bundy, bank presidents, beardless liberals, Kermit Roosevelt, Ellsworth Bunker, Jr., Adolph Berle, Averill Harriman, and Joseph Farland as representatives of those perpetuating suppression. But Ogelsby went on to declare that these men could not be called evil. Rather, they were "divided from their compassion by the institutional system that inherits us all."[20] The ambiguity here is that when one perceives a construct such as "the system" as the cause of evil, he is forced to a basic and total condemnation. Yet "the system" or "the establishment" does not present a localized or personalized enemy. Consequently, spokesmen for student rebellion often denounced individuals in positions of authority in a way which charged them with responsibility for a monolithic system and implied that they had the ability to make sweeping changes unilaterally. On April 22, 1968, Mark Rudd sent a letter to Columbia University's president of the moment, Grayson Kirk. It contained language placing responsibility in a more personal manner than Ogelby's:

> You might want to know what is wrong with this society, since after all, you live in a very tight self-created world. We can point to the war in Vietnam as an example of the unimaginable wars of aggression you are

prepared to fight to maintain your control over your empire. . . . We can point to your using us as cannon fodder to fight your war. We can point out your mansion window to the ghetto below you've helped to create through your racist University policies, through your unfair labor practices, through your city government and your police.[21]

After such events as those at the Chicago Democratic Convention and at Kent State, the student revolutionaries' rhetoric became yet more personal as cops were labelled "pigs" and government officials referred to as "imperialists" and "warmongers." Such terminology seems intended to reduce those labelled to a subhuman or de-personalized status, and this is precisely what makes the attack so personal to those who are targets of the labelling.

Spokeswomen for Women's Liberation pick out the chauvinistically dominated male society as their revolutionary target, and men, quite naturally, become the enemy. Says Kempton:

> For insofar as a woman lives by the standards of the world, she lives according to the standards set by men. Men have laid down the rules and definitions by which the world is run, and one of the objects of their definitions is women. Men define intelligence, men define usefulness, men tell us what is beautiful, men even tell us what is womanly.[22]

The manifesto for SCUM (Society for Cutting Up Men) rhetorically creates the ultimate negative male image: ". . . the male is a biological accident . . . an incomplete female, a walking abortion . . . . To be male is to be deficient, emotionally limited; maleness is a deficiency disease and males are emotionally crippled."[23] The images of the enemy of all three protest movements are clearly drawn in a rhetorical way which enhances the ego images of protest followers.

IV

As the result of attacking enemies, protestors appear to experience and express feelings of ego-enhancement, ego-affirmation, and even ego-superiority. For blacks, the continued repetition of the theme, "Black is beautiful," coupled with the charge, "White is inferior," will lead to a hoped for redefinition of the black man, cast in a more favorable image. Black spokesmen have made a point of enumerating special strengths of blacks, ranging from McKissick's observation that blacks because of their oppression experienced a "privileged perception" of reality not enjoyed by the white man,[24] to Malcolm X's proclamation that America is a great and rich nation because the forefathers of contemporary blacks, the slaves, made it rich through their strenuous exertions without compensation.[25]

For students, there is less public pronunciation of ego-affirmation than of a private, communal sharing of ego-well-being in participation and in the excitement, dangers, and crusading joys of participating in a movement which encourages the rhetorical stance of self-stroking. I return to the words of Nick Gagarin, reflecting on his feelings while occupying a university building: "What was most euphoric was us and what we were to each other. For those few hours we WERE brothers and sisters. We did reach out and hold onto each other . . . . You had to realize—whatever your politics and whatever your tactics—that we were very beautiful in University Hall, we were very human, we were very together. . . ."[26]

Here is a clear expression of the discovery and enjoyment of group self-hood; it becomes easily transposed to a feeling of individual ego-satisfaction. A clearer expression of individual self-hood is recorded by Wayne Booth, who quotes a student allegedly finding himself by virtue of participating in a sit-in: "Until I went into that building . . . I wasn't even alive; I didn't know what life was about. Something permanent happened to me in there; I'll never be the same."[27]

For many students, political protest can become the covering activity that conveys a sense of importance, power, exhilaration, and danger, all feelings related to self-affirmation and expression.

The rhetoric of the Women's Lib movement, with the symbolic and personal interaction that takes place wherever Lib members gather to explore their status, seems to achieve positive ego-affects similar to those experienced by students who identify in adversity. Poetess Susan Sands reports her personal experience while attending the November 1969 Congress to Unite Women:

> It was so very inspiring and yet so strange that Friday evening, the first night of the congress, when all these women came together, everyone opening up to one another for the first time . . . . First women came to express their theories, give voice to their complaints. But by the time the congress was over, a beautiful feeling of unity existed.[28]

The spirit of ego-affirmation is strong and it is catching. Helen Dudar, who wrote a special report for *Newsweek* on Women's Lib, ends with personal ruminations about her emotional and attitudinal state following an interview with a follower of the Lib movement:

> I came home that night with the first of many anxiety-produced pains in the stomach and head. Superiority is precisely what I had felt and enjoyed and it was going to be hard to give up. That was an important discovery. One of the rare and real rewards of reporting is learning about yourself. Grateful though I am for the education, it hasn't done much for the mental stress. Women's Lib questions everything; and while intellectually I approve of that, emotionally I am unstrung by a lot of it.
>
> Never mind. The ambivalence is gone; the distance is gone. What is left is a sense of pride and kinship with all those women who have been asking all the hard questions.[29]

The content of the rhetoric we have examined reveals a central concern of protest movements. The concern expressed publicly is nonetheless a personal concern, often seeking affirmation of individual identity through group unity. The thrust of protest rhetoric is disturbing precisely because it is so blatantly personal and because it reflects a stance which seems to thwart the idealized kind of problem discussion we like to see on the public stage.

Style becomes very important in a rhetorical stance dictated by a concern for self. (Style, as I use the term here, is all inclusive. It refers to style of behaving, style of dress, style of speaking, style of total identification.) Blacks extol their freedom of body movement, students proclaim the virtues of their pot-smoking reveries, Women's Lib followers will undertake the chivalrous actions of men themselves. Blacks proudly wear their Afro hairdos, students make a quasi-religious symbol of hair, and women's lib members dramatically cast off their bras and forego make-up. And all three protest movements harangue the enemy with obscenities, take delight in the linguistic unmasking of the proclaimed values of what they label "the establishment," and construct a privileged language all their own. Style is so terribly important because it relates so directly to self-hood. One's style is what one is, in a publicly demonstrable sense.

What is most directly at stake in contemporary public rhetoric is precisely life-style, or self-hood. In our present polarized society, to attack the life style of "the establishment" helps in the identification of one's own style. To defend one's life style publicly is, by implication, to attack the life styles of others who adhere to dissimilar styles. For those engaging in protest, to attempt to argue, convince, or plead in the style of "the establishment" is to be "co-opted" by "the establishment." I am emphasizing a point made by Edwin Black in his recent analysis of a portion of the discourse of the Radical Right. He concludes that we find in such rhetoric enticements not simply to believe something but to *be* something,[30] and Parke Burgess, when discussing the rhetoric of moral conflict, says:

> The strategies and motives of any rhetoric . . . represents an invitation to a life-style, an invitation to adopt a pattern of strategies and motives, verbal and nonverbal, that determine how men and women will function together in culture.[31]

Blacks have repeatedly referred to linguistic style when they have disavowed white definitions of beauty, strength, and virtue and exhorted their black audiences to redefine themselves. Mark Rudd acknowledges linguistic style in a slightly different vein when he says: "'Up against the wall, motherfucker' defines the terms. It puts the administration and the interests they represent on one side, leftist students and the interests of humanity on the other."[32] Women's Lib spokesmen are also cognizant of the definitive qualities of linguistic style. Recall Sally Kempton's warning, quoted above, about the dangers of allowing men to define women's existence. All of this points to a need for stylistic distance from the opposition in order to enhance one's self-hood. If one perceives that the linguistic devices of others are factors that reduce self-concept, it becomes imperative to reject those linguistic devices.

V

What can we now say about the rhetoric of protest? We can say that one of the major aspects of protest rhetoric is its concern for the ego. The concern is revealed both in the way the symbolic motif of personal confrontation is developed in rhetoric and in the emphasis on style. The particular stance from which the rhetoric springs, and which the rhetoric reinforces, yields the following advantages to protestors:

1. It encourages the maintenance of distance from an adversary. The results here are several-fold: the perceived adversary becomes a symbolic enemy, helpful in the process of purging the ills of self and in the process of identifying self by identifying against others; it also helps secure the self against the possibility of being co-opted by others. At the same time, it enhances self-identification by beckoning to kindred spirits who may provide the essential friendly "other" for self-establishment.
2. It aids in the protestor's definition of situation, and definition helps give one symbolic control. The reflexive aspect of protest rhetoric, in this sense, cannot be overestimated. Symbolic reconstruction of situation, which recasts the exigencies

and individuals, with whom one cannot or does not want to cope, into images of "enemyness," allows one to reject them, flaunt them, strike out against them, and so gain some initiative of action.
3. The establishment of distance, referred to above, will generate attention and perhaps fear, or even grudging respect from the adversary. As Erving Goffman says, "The image that one status grouping is able to maintain in the eyes of an audience of other status groupings will depend upon the performer's capacity to restrict communicative contact with the audience."[33] As we have seen, protest rhetoric seems purposely to ignore the styles of communication that might result in meaningful communication with the establishment.
4. In a perverse kind of way, protest rhetoric and protest behavior can force the kind of counter-reaction which is ego-gratifying to some individuals. The exhilaration obtained from calling the "power structure": "fascists," "repressive," and "violent" is one thing. To experience the cracking of heads, to see the blood, to face the wall of bayonets, or to receive some milder kind of "bust" from the "establishment" is proof for some that their views of reality, their perspectives which focus toward the establishment of self-hood are correct. The victory so obtained is symbolic, but nonetheless psychologically valid and important.

Counter-reaction is occurring, both physically and rhetorically. There are various motives for such physical reprisals as the moving of police to campuses or calling in the National Guard, ranging from sheer psychological frustration to attempts to save lives and property perceived to be threatened. But one factor which cannot be overlooked is the threat to self-hood felt by those who identify themselves and their ways of life with the institutions, mores, and folkways which are condemned by protestors.

It is easy to understand how individuals perceiving themselves, their life styles, their values threatened by an intensifying rhetoric of counter-identification become frightened by behaviors which disrupt their hitherto predictable world and sense the need to reassert themselves and to defend their own ego-identifications. Such persons would find comfort in knowing that they were not alone and powerless and insignificant in the face of what they view to be threatening situations. For such persons Richard Nixon's eulogistic references to the "Silent Majority" and the "quiet American" provide identifying labels. Mayor Richard Daley becomes a useful surrogate self; but perhaps Spiro Agnew best typifies the identifications of the "Silent American." As Arthur Schlesinger, Jr.[,] pointed out, "It is cultural politics, and not public policy, which is the Vice-President's bag. He has emerged as hero, or villain, not in the battle of programs but in the battle of life styles."[34] Agnew takes self-proclaimed pride in such things as incentive, respect for law, and patriotism. He inveighs against the enemy: the "glib activist element who would tell us our values are lies," the "arrogant ones" who are "asking us to repudiate principles that have made this country great. Their course is one of applause for our enemies and condemnation for our leaders." Agnew calls for a "positive polarization" against "kooks," "demagogues," "cynics," "learned idiocy," and the "radical or criminal left," against the whole "effete corps of impudent snobs" "with their masochistic tendencies." Tit for tat, style for style, Agnew holds his own with the protestors. And the Silent American feels better. The hardhat Joe Kelly, whose profile appeared in the *New York Times Magazine* of June 28, 1970,[35] is energized and reaffirmed by the rhetorical stance of those who oppose protest movements.

VI

There are distinctive patterns in contemporary rhetoric which reflect a newly prominent personal stance. The peculiar characteristics and effects of this stance have not commonly received attention from students of rhetoric. Historically much of rhetorical and philosophical analysis and criticism tends to set "rhetorical discourse" within moral ideals which presuppose the principles of "rational" discussion. Such critical perspectives grant approbative notice to discourse which appears to coincide with the demands and constraints of "rationality" and disregard or deprecate discourse which falls outside these domains. My proposition is that analytical views which presuppose that "communicative intent" and "reasoning together" or even "feeling together" exhaust the primary goals of men's and women's serious discourse do not yield either useful or plausible descriptive and critical accounts of much current discourse. A chorus of "protest rhetoric" cannot be ignored; it is present, and its critical disclosure is required.

I hope this essay illustrates that consideration of the ego-functions of rhetoric can produce fruitful understandings of rhetorical transactions. Precisely *how* these understandings are best obtained and *why* ego-rewarding rhetoric seems "cacophonous" to others are topics that richly deserve the attention of philosophical rhetoricians and philosophers of rhetoric.

Notes

[1] The following studies are examples of the kinds of analysis referred to: James R. Andrews, "Confrontation at Columbia: A Case Study in Coercive Rhetoric," *QJS*, LV (February, 1969), 9–16; and "The Rhetoric of Coercion and Persuasion: The Reform Bill of 1832," *QJS*, LVI (April, 1970), 187–195; Franklyn Haiman, "The Rhetoric of the Streets: Some Legal and Ethical Considerations," *QJS*, LIII (April, 1967), 99–114; Arthur L. Smith, *Rhetoric of Black Revolution* (Boston, 1969); Herbert R. Simons, "Patterns of Persuasion in the Civil Rights Struggle," *Today's Speech*, XV (February, 1967) 25–27, and "Requirements, Problems, and Strategies: A Theory of Persuasion for Social Movements," *QJS*, LVI (February, 1970), 1–11; Robert L. Scott and Donald K. Smith, "The Rhetoric of Confrontation," *QJS*, LV (February, 1969), 1–8; Robert L. Scott and Wayne Brockriede, *The Rhetoric of Black Power* (New York, 1969); Parke G. Burgess, "The Rhetoric of Black Power: A Moral Demand?" *QJS*, LIV (April, 1968), 122–133; Robert D. Brooks, "Black Power: The

Dimensions of a Slogan," *Western Speech,* XXXIV (Spring, 1970), 108–114; Richard B. Gregg, A. Jackson McCormack, and Douglas J. Pedersen, "The Rhetoric of Black Power: A Street-Level Interpretation," *QJS,* LV (April 1969), 151–160.

2 Carroll C. Arnold, "Oral Rhetoric, Rhetoric, and Literature," *Philosophy and Rhetoric,* 1 (Fall, 1968), 202–204.

3 For example, see Henry W. Johnstone, Jr., "Some Reflections on Argumentation" and Maurice Natanson, "The Claims of Immediacy," both in *Philosophy, Rhetoric and Argumentation* (University Park, Pennsylvania, 1965), ed. by Maurice Natanson and Henry W. Johnstone, Jr.

4 Don M. Burks, "Persuasion, Self-Persuasion, and Rhetorical Discourse," *Philosophy and Rhetoric,* 3 (Spring, 1970), 109–119. I do not see Burks' conceptualization in any way negating the dimensions of commitment and openness described by Arnold, cited above. Rather, when thinking of self-rhetoric, one simply needs to transpose the dimensions discussed by Arnold into the terms of an intra-personal transaction. Thus, one opens himself, in some fashion, to self-examination, to appeals and arguments to self, and even to rationalization and self-deception.

5 The term "constitutive," as I use it here, corresponds with Sesonske's discussion of constitutive speech. Alexander Sesonske, "Saying, Being, and Freedom of Speech," *Philosophy and Rhetoric,* 1 (January, 1968), 25–37. Sesonske points out that ". . . speech may be constitutive not merely in the sense of providing one way, among others, in which a certain state or character trait may be realized, but may be *necessary* for the occurrence of some traits of personality or character. That is, it is not merely that in talking a certain way one is being a person of a certain sort, but also that one cannot be a person of some sorts unless he talks in a certain way."

6 The text of the speech appears in *The Rhetoric of the Civil Rights Movement,* ed. by Haig A. and Hamida Bosmajian (New York, 1969), pp. 109–125.

7 *Ibid.,* p. 121.

8 Malcolm X, "Message to the Grass Roots," in *Malcolm X Speaks,* ed. by George Breitman (New York, 1965), p. 7.

9 These remarks were made by Malcolm X during a debate with James Farmer at Cornell University on March 7, 1962. The transcript appears in *The Rhetoric of the Civil Rights Movement, op. cit.,* pp. 59–87. The particular quotation cited appears on page 74.

10 "From the Port Huron Statement," in *The New Student Left,* ed. by Mitchell Cohen and Dennis Hale (Boston, 1967), p. 12.

11 Mario Savio, "An End to History," in *The New Student Left,* p. 252.

12 This statement comes from an editorial entitled "Non-Politics on the Battlefront," which appeared in the Harvard *Crimson.* Part of the editorial is reprinted in Steven Kelman, *Push Comes to Shove* (Boston, 1970), pp. 162–163.

13 *Newsweek,* March 23, 1970, p. 71.

14 *Ibid.,* p. 71.

15 Quoted in Julie Ellis, *Revolt of the Second Sex* (New York, 1970), p. 53.

16 Sally Kempton, "Cutting Loose," *Esquire,* July, 1970, p. 54.

17 *Ibid.,* p. 55.

18 Floyd McKissick, "Speech at the National Conference on Black Power," in *The Rhetoric of the Civil Rights Movement, op. cit.,* p. 130.

19 *The Rhetoric of the Civil Rights Movement, op. cit.,* p. 130.

20 Carl Ogelsby, "Let Us Shape the Future," in *The New Student Left, op. cit.,* pp. 312–321.

21 Jerry L. Avorn, *et al., Up Against the Ivy Wall* (New York, 1969), pp. 25–26.

22 Sally Kempton, *op. cit.,* p. 55.

23 Quoted in *Revolt of the Second Sex, op. cit.,* p. 65.

24 *The Rhetoric of the Civil Rights Movement, op. cit.,* p. 127.

25 Malcolm X, "The Ballot or the Bullet," in *Malcolm X Speaks, op. cit.,* p. 32.

26 Quoted in Steven Kelman, *op. cit.,* p. 162.

27 Wayne C. Booth, "The Scope of Rhetoric Today," paper presented at the Wingspread Conference, National Project on Rhetoric, January 26, 1970.

28 Ellis, *op. cit.,* pp. 44, 45.

29 *Newsweek, op. cit.,* p. 78.

30 Edwin Black, "The Second Persona," *QJS,* LVI (April, 1970), 119.

31 Parke Burgess, "The Rhetoric of Moral Conflict: Two Critical Dimensions," *QJS,* LVI (April, 1970), 120.

32 Mark Rudd, "Symbols of the Revolution," in Jerry L. Avorn, *et al., Up Against the Ivy Wall, op. cit.*

33 Erving Goffman, *The Presentation of Self in Everyday Life* (New York, 1959), p. 241.

34 Arthur Schlesinger, Jr., "The Amazing Success Story of Spiro Who?" *The New York Times Magazine* (July 26, 1970), p. 5.

35 Richard Rogin, "Joe Kelly Has Reached His Boiling Point," *The New York Times Magazine* (June 28, 1970) pp. 12–24.

The Diatribe: Last Resort for Protest
Theodore Otto Windt, Jr.

Describing the rhetorical mood of World War II, Everett Lee Hunt observed, "We do not hope fondly, nor pray fervently. We turn from words to things. Instead of teaching war aims we teach mathematics and physics. And there is no proof that the boys do not fight just as well."[1]

Ironically, the protest against the war in Vietnam aroused fond hopes and fervent prayers as protesters turned from things to words. Lacking the instruments of power available to those conducting the war, demonstrators had to rely on public opinion fashioned through speeches, signs, flags, lectures, teach-ins and whatever other methods could be improvised. Lacking access to television and newspapers, they had to create forums and devise means for attracting publicity. In working toward these ends, they created rhetorical forms and committed symbolic acts which sometimes seemed at odds with their goals and which often outraged both proponents and opponents of the war. My purpose in this essay is to examine several aspects of the rhetoric used by some protesters, especially the Yippies, that at first glance seem counterproductive: obscenities, strident moralism, and the "counter-culture" life-style.

1

When President Johnson's policy in Vietnam evolved into bombing North Vietnam and sending hundreds of thousands of American troops to South Vietnam, young people opposed to the war grew desperate. They invented simplistic slogans such as "Hey! Hey! LBJ! How many kids did you kill today?" While respectable critics continued a rational rhetoric of protest and Senators held hearings to determine the accuracy of claims by the administration, some young people used obscenities to describe their outrage and frustrations about the war. Indeed, obscenities became common place. A writer in *Rat,* an underground newspaper, wrote: "What

difference can there be between shoving liberty up the ass of Vietnam and giving America love in the same way? (When you're up against a wall the gun may loom larger than the man and a penis without human context loses the power of creation.)"[2] These profanities shocked even those supporting the peace movement. Why this language? Why alienate your audience? Why deliberately offend potential supporters?

The question of obscenities weighed almost as heavily on some sympathetic minds as did the fact that protesters insisted on the absolute righteousness of their cause. As Noam Chomsky's essays exemplify, gradually the issue changed from politics to morality. Lionel Abel aptly pointed out that Chomsky attempted no political assessment of Vietnam, but concentrated on moral judgments.[3] In a widely quoted section Chomsky wrote:

> By entering the arena of argument and counter-argument, of technical feasibility and tactics, of footnotes and citations, by accepting the presumption of legitimacy of debate on certain issues, one has already lost one's humanity.
> . . . .
> There may have been a time when American policy in Vietnam was a debatable matter. This time is long past. *It is no more debatable than . . . the Russian suppression of Hungarian freedom.* The war is simply an obscenity, a depraved act by weak and miserable men . . .[4]

This attack on political debate is the intellectual counterpart of those who shouted down spokesmen for the war when they appeared on campuses. Again, practical questions arise. Why take a position that clearly violates freedom of speech? How can the claim to moral superiority be reconciled with obscenities? Beyond these speculative questions, do not obscenities and the refusal to debate or listen render spokesmen against the war vulnerable to attacks on questions unrelated to the war? Do not these become counter-productive politically and rhetorically?

Compounding these problems, some protesters insisted on living and flaunting a new life-style. In so doing they extended the scope of protest beyond politics to American culture. Some adopted hippie garb; others imitated the revolutionary dress of Castro. Che Guevara and W. C. Fields became folk heroes. "Counter-culture" people ridiculed and then deserted the affluent, middle-class families from which they came. They established communes and lived communally. Each act seemed to backfire in the anti-war movement: each provided a rhetorical aid to supporters of the war, created an embarrassment to opponents of the war.

These activities converge in the rhetoric and antics of the Youth International Party, the Yippies. Moreover, the Yippies added frivolity and jest—"put-ons"—which amazed, confounded, and perplexed both friends and foes. Observing their activities at the Democratic convention in Chicago in 1968 at which time they nominated Pigasus for President and adopted the slogan: "Why take half a hog when you can have the whole hog?" a bewildered Theodore H. White concluded that their nickname, "Crazies," aptly described them. He thought they were sad, naïve people and that they appealed only to groups willing to exploit them: "The police; television; and those calculating organizers who can manipulate them as a skirmish line into the forefront of confrontation . . ."[5] These sentiments, echoed by journalists and scholars, became the conventional wisdom about such protesters.

If the anti-war movement's only source of power lay in public opinion, how are we to understand these acts that seem not only absurd but counterproductive as well? To gain perspective we may hark back to the archetypal moral protesters, the Cynics of Greece, and to the diatribe, their distinctive rhetorical form.[6] In so doing I intend to establish the following ideas: (1) a long historical tradition lies behind this rhetoric and life-style; (2) the rhetorical strategies and symbolic acts were a product of circumstances and moral commitments; and (3) perceiving circumstances as they did, neither the Cynics nor the Yippies could use traditional strategies for protest.

2

Oswald Spengler once wrote that no culture has so adored another as we have adored ancient Greece. This romantic idealization has found eloquent expression in, among others, Edith Hamilton: "For a hundred years Athens was a city where the great spiritual forces that war in men's minds flowed along together in peace; law and freedom, truth and religion . . . there was a truce to their eternal warfare, and the result was the balance and clarity, the harmony and completeness, the word Greek has come to stand for."[7]

Few societies are perfect, and the ideals envisioned by man are seldom practiced by men. So it was with Greece. The Greeks produced great poets and philosophers, but they reviled Euripides, persecuted Anaxagoras, Protagoras, and Aristotle. Socrates drank hemlock. Nor were all Greeks seekers-after-truth or devoted to country. Herbert Muller wrote that some tyrants betrayed their native land, and soldiers often fought against their own country. The common citizens were "mercenary, jealous, and suspicious of one another."[8]

"Harmony and completeness," "law and freedom" hardly reigned after Periclean Athens. In the late fifth century Athenian land troops bogged down in a land war in the distant, small country of Sicily, committed unspeakable atrocities, and eventually were defeated by an inferior force. Athens was conquered first by Macedonia and later by Rome. At the beginning of the fourth century Athens was dissolving under the weight of its own arrogance. The fabric of its society was rent with internal dissension.

This human side of Athenians and this political-cultural climate must be understood if we are to understand the Cynics. They were products of the Hellenistic age, "a time when old standards had been discarded, and the individual was left to the mercy of capricious but irresistible forces."[9]

Diogenes and the Cynics. Cynics began to appear in the fourth century in Athens, but did not flourish as a sect until the second century.

Diogenes of Sinope (413–327 B.C.) was the most renowned although Hegisias of Sinope and Crates of Thebes also gained some repute. Despite the claim that Antisthenes, a Socratic, formed the Cynic tradition and the fact that Cynicism developed as a school two hundred years after the death of Diogenes, Diogenes emerged as patron saint of the movement even as his ideas were distorted through legend.[10]

Diogenes, an intellectual not too unlike Socrates in his influence on followers, cut an unconventional swath in Athenian society. Some called him a "Socrates gone mad."[11] He walked barefoot in the snow,[12] slept in abandoned tubs, and was known to have lighted a lamp in broad daylight announcing "I am looking for a man."[13] Once he went into the theatre after the festival and upon meeting those coming out stated, "This is what I practise doing all my life."[14] Furthermore, Cynics as a sect "never washed, never had their hair cut, wrapped themselves in rags and lived on alms like beggars . . . ."[15] Diogenes and his followers broke with society, lived as strangers under the protection of laws they despised, and offended fellow-citizens by gross rudeness and shameless indecencies.

Diogenes believed in absolute humanism; that is, as Diogenes Laertius related, "allowing convention no such authority as he allowed to natural right, and asserting that the manner of life he lived was the same as that of Heracles when he preferred liberty to everything."[16] "The antithesis between nature and convention seems to have originated with Hippias,"[17] but Diogenes made it the cornerstone of his doctrine of natural rights and the motivating force in his way of living. To live by men's conventions is to embrace the death of person; to defy society is to embrace life. The choice is clear-cut. One can have no truck with customs regardless of the disguises they wear: laws, civil authority, political institutions, social mores. In taking this position Diogenes divorced himself from the normal flow of society by rejecting both the civic and the civilized life.

Diogenes's view of the world was pessimistic and misanthropic. Once, upon seeing the officials of the temple leading a thief away, he was reported to have said, "The great thieves are leading away the little thief."[18] He argued that money was the "mother-city of all evils."[19] Thus, he took to begging. On one occasion he begged alms from a statue. When asked why he acted so absurdly, he replied that he hoped "To get practice in being refused."[20] Appropriately, the dog became his symbol. When asked why people called him a dog, he answered: "I fawn on those who give me anything, I yelp at those who refuse, and I set my teeth in rascals."[21] When he died, Athenians raised a marble statue of a dog over his grave.

Cynicism. Diogenes Laertius observed of the Cynics: "They are content . . . to do away with the subjects of Logic and Physics and to devote their whole attention to Ethics."[22] For Cynics every question is an ethical question. Each problem, they contended, when stripped of its veneer of self-interest reveals a fundamental moral issue. However, they seemed more interested in public ethics than private morality. This moralistic posture restricted the options open to them in rhetoric and pointed directly to a particular life-style.

Commitments begat a way of living that many found disturbing. Diogenes Laertius wrote: "They also hold that we should live frugally, eating food for nourishment only and wearing a single garment. Wealth and fame and high birth they despise. Some at all events are vegetarians and drink cold water only and are content with any kind of shelter or tub, like Diogenes, who use[d] to say it was the privilege of gods to need nothing and of god-like men to want but little."[23] The bizarre acts of Cynics served symbolic purposes. First, they took their beliefs out of the abstract and made them part of their lives. They did what they professed, especially when it came to money. They recognized that to earn money meant to accept conventional means for getting money, and beyond that, to adopt conventional modes of living. According to Diogenes, any compromise with society is a compromise of ethics. He apparently made a clear distinction between humanity and society. The former is natural and good; the latter is unnatural and corrupt. Thus, Farrand Sayre concluded, "Disregard of honor and reputation ... was developed into open defiance of public opinion by shamelessness...."[24]

Second, the Cynics did not possess power and by all accounts did not seek political influence. They were cultural critics, not politicians. To confirm their beliefs they committed symbolic acts, and these acts flowed directly from their beliefs. To prove their commitment to natural man and their condemnation of conventions, they lived on subsistence level and represented a standard with which most of us are unfamiliar—that of the minimum.[25] They rejected the striving-achieving ethic upon which Athens, like so many other societies, was built. They resorted to begging and to renouncing the luxuries life affords. Each act symbolically reinforced the commitment to a different way of living, even as it repudiated the conventional way in which men live.

Often they carried their beliefs to extremes. When accused of acting lewdly (apparently Diogenes masturbated in public), he replied that he wished it "were as easy to banish hunger by rubbing the belly."[26] In addition, Diogenes found no impropriety in stealing from the temple.[27] To steal from the temple or another corrupt institution is to commit no crime, for society's institutions are immoral. The critic must interject that Cynics probably would have been sorely offended had someone stolen from them because then the thief would have been stealing from the wrong people: the natural man, the good community of man. Such an act surely would have been considered immoral just as stealing from those protecting society would be considered just. Each of these acts had meaning to Cynics. Each was intended to shock sensibilities, to scandalize by profaning societal customs, to challenge what existential theologians describe as man's pre-understanding about how one should talk and respond to ideas and actions.[28] Furthermore, Cynics argued that each act was natural: something everyone would do were he not inhibited by corrupt societal customs, or something everyone would be able to do were conventional institutions replaced by the community of natural men.

The Cynics were the first to celebrate the universal brotherhood of mankind.[29] Living outside society they contended they served a higher purpose—the human community which knows no race, creed, or nationality. Thus, they renounced marriage, parental rights to children, and citizenship. The natural community of man transcends these ethereal claims and binds together man with woman, friend with foe, nation with nation in the quest for individual freedom and equality. Their life-style represented an alternative way of living which others—depressed by the compromises that politics and politeness demand—could embrace as an escape from the repression of Society to the freedom of Cynicism. Conversely, Cynics established counter-conventions, surely as rigid as those they denounced, that functioned symbolically as a protest against society's norms.

The Cynics were critics of conventions, gadflies of popular culture, censors of men who did not act upon their beliefs. Moralistic to the point of misanthropy, they gave expediency little place in their lives or thought. Every action, they believed, should be guided by moral principles founded upon a belief in absolute humanism. Most men make distinctions between moral problems and political problems, between professional responsibilities and personal commitments. The Cynics denied, even condemned, these distinctions as artificial, as products of societal conditioning which had corrupted man's mind and sense of right. The Cynics would not admit that any institution had any legitimate authority unless it was based on the natural rights of man, in other words, on the noble savage.[30]

The diatribe. The Cynics' moralistic posture led to a dilemma. If society is *a priori* immoral, how is a Cynic to live within it without compromising himself? Conversely, if man can be redeemed, does not the Cynic have a duty to lead the way? The answers to these questions led to two distinct rhetorical strategies.

Some Cynics apparently decided the only thing to do in an immoral society was to withdraw into private contemplation, neither to accept nor to ask anything from others and thereby preserve their personal purity. One can see the rhetorical import of silence and withdrawal. They are symbolic acts; both affirm and legitimize private commitments, thus enhancing the *ethos* of the Cynic. Moreover, few can resist the curiosity to ask why one has withdrawn and why one remains silent. To ask these questions sincerely is to abolish habitual presuppositions about the Cynic and thereby to establish a new common ground the Cynic can use to voice his criticism of society.

Others did not withdraw, and they decidedly were not silent. Some wrote satires, thus retreating into literary life. Others sought civic salvation by wandering about the country delivering diatribes to whomever would listen. Unlike professional speakers, they did not aim at persuasion by traditional means. Audiences would have to experience the totality of their wrongs, much as contemporary existentialists believe man will not realize his condition until he has experienced existential shock. Thus, Cynics sought to dramatize their criticism of society through the diatribe, an extemporaneous sermon used for these occasions. Its invention was based "on themes drawn from their own doctrines—usually on paradoxes which would attract a crowd; and they illustrated and decorated them with anecdotes, character-sketches, fables, dialogues against imaginary opponents, topical references, parodies of serious poetry, obscene jokes, and slang phrases."[31]

To describe the diatribe is to describe a series of analogies which when taken together may add up to our understanding of it. The diatribe is the rhetorical version of the philosophic dialogue and bears a resemblance to the dialogue roughly similar to the relationship between conventional speeches and philosophic disquisitions.[32] It is an attempt to criticize, to entertain, to shock and to convey impressions of public figures, all in one. Bion, a Cynic, supposedly developed it as a distinct rhetorical genre. We have sufficient information about what Cynics believed and a few fragments, some of which I have quoted from Diogenes, to reconstruct an outline of its major features.

The diatribe is to conventional speeches what Alice's adventures in Wonderland are to conventional life. Logic is inverted; assumptions are reversed; the unexpected is not unusual. Most speeches are given to persuade by drawing upon the beliefs of the audience as resources for proofs. The speaker tries to appeal to reason, emotion, conventional beliefs or attitudes, or conscience by not offending traditional beliefs or feelings. He attempts to establish his *ethos* by reflecting the *ethos* of his audience. In other words, he seeks identification with his constituency.

Cynics rejected these strategies as compromises with an immoral society. Man's conscience, his logic and emotions, his perspectives and attitudes have been corrupted by immoral institutions. To reflect the *ethos* of society is to reflect civic corruption. Man must be cleansed of unclean expectations and thoughts. To this end, Cynics attacked basic societal values to which conventional speakers would customarily appeal. The diatribe, then, is moral dramaturgy intended to assault sensibilities, to turn thought upside-down, to turn social mores inside-out, to commit in language the very same barbarisms one condemns in society.

A major purpose of the diatribe is shock, which serves two ends. First, it gathers an audience when orthodox speeches will not. Diogenes Laertius recorded the following incident: "When one day he [Diogenes] was gravely discoursing and nobody attended to him, he began whistling, and as people clustered about him, he reproached them with coming in all seriousness to hear nonsense, but slowly and contemptuously when the theme was serious."[33] Whistling was unusual, unexpected, logically meaningless. Given the Greeks' sense of decorum it might have been considered shocking. Yet, whistling served a rhetorical purpose.

Beyond attracting attention, shock also functions as the first step toward rearranging perspectives. People seldom become concerned about problems until they are shocked. The diatribe is intended both to satirize fundamental values and expectations by dramatizing the chasm that exists between ideals and practices, between language and actions, between illusions and actualities. By bizarre uses of language and through symbolic acts, Cynics challenged the traditional form of rhetorical and cultural transactions and ridiculed basic values.

Through the diatribe Cynics parodied the rhetorical situation. The themes they treated were personal freedom, personal courage, personal purity. Dignified topics, indeed. Yet the style, marked by obscenity and slang, was far from dignified. Instead of reflecting the *ethos* of an audience, Cynics scorned it by dressing as they did and by acting as they did.

Opposed to conventional morality, Cynics proposed a counter-morality. Issues should be argued in terms of how they would affect the community of man for better or worse regardless of political or economic consequences. What contributes to greater freedom from society's restrictions is good; what reinforces societal conventions or institutions is evil. The right of man to live his natural life without interference from society forms the basis for this morality.

The diatribe is to rhetoric what satire is to literature. Each attempts to reduce conventional beliefs to the ridiculous, thereby making those who support orthodoxy seem contemptible, hypocritical, or stupid. Each seeks laughter, but not for its own sake. Rather, laughter serves as a cleansing force to purge pre-conceptions about ideas, to redeem ignored causes, to deflate pomposity, to challenge conventional assumptions, to confront the human consequences of ideas and policies. Exaggeration, parody, puns, incongruity, and burlesque typify each. If the listener is to respond appropriately, he must realize what the Cynic or satirist intends. One does not respond to Sophocles as he responds to Aristophanes. So too with speakers. One has to change one's expectations in order to see the diatribe as part of a larger movement to redirect man's perspectives, to reconstruct mankind's aspirations.

But the diatribe is a distinct genre. Satire may be one of the methods used to achieve an effect. Furthermore, the satirist does not have to act or provide symbolic proofs for what he believes. The Cynic must act to legitimize his speeches. Thus, preposterous acts become part of the legitimizing process for this rhetoric, proof positive the Cynic means what he says. These acts also leave him open to *ad hominem* charges, logically irrelevant to issues at hand, but rhetorically potent in destroying his *ethos*.

The major weakness of the diatribe is that it is limited in effectiveness. Once attention has been gained and criticism voiced, the diatribe diminishes in usefulness. People demand serious remedies, seriously treated. Moral dramaturgy must give way to conventional rhetorical forms.

Criticism of Cynics. Critics have dealt harshly with Cynics. Two major criticisms have been raised; W. W. Tarn summarizes: "It (Cynicism) was not a philosophy like those of the four schools with a body of doctrine; it was a way of life, a mode of thought, and was entirely negative; you were to discard everything on which civilization had been built up, and often enough, unless you were a Crates or a Demona, you ended by finding nothing at the bottom but mere animalism. It never *constructed* anything, anything which affected men otherwise than as individuals . . . ."[34] These criticisms have merit, but miss the point. If Cynicism is not a philosophy because it does not have a "body of doctrine," then the pre-Socratics—especially Heraclitus—must be banished from the canons of philosophic inquiry for the same reason. Defending themselves, Cynics would reply that to judge them by conventional standards is to admit that one is so bound up in conventions that one cannot entertain new ideas or possibilities.

To say Cynics are totally negative is to echo a charge made against them throughout the centuries. True, the major thrust is negative, a misanthropic criticism of customs. But for Cynics this assault is essential if men are ever to see how much their lives are controlled by society's mores. They would contend that each criticism they make contains the ideas about what ought to be, even if those ideas remain unstated. That Cynics treat men as individuals, they would claim, is precisely how men ought to be treated.

The major weakness of Cynicism is not nihilism, but romanticism. Cynicism is founded on two major assumptions: (1) social institutions and mores are *a priori* corrupt; and (2) natural man, freed from societal restrictions, is *a priori* good. From these two assumptions the diatribe, absurd acts, and conclusions logically and consistently flow. But neither assumption will stand the scrutiny of history or reason.

What, then, are we to say about Cynicism? Tarn is essentially correct when he says it is not philosophic. It is a rhetorical movement, a standing protest against the hypocrisy and corruption that attends civic life. The diatribe, limited though it may be, is intended to illuminate and to purge corruption when other methods fail. It is the rhetoric and life-style of the outsider who finds himself alienated from civic life and who discovers a morality, an extremely romantic morality, in personal experience to replace that founded on tradition. He opposes the compartmentalization of life into neat pigeonholes that allows man to act one way on one occasion and a contradictory way on another. Instead, Cynics celebrate the unity of life. We live, they proclaimed, in a universe, not a multiverse. Thought, language, and action are intimately related. Without language there is no thought. And language conditions thought. But each is empty of real content if men do not act upon what they believe. In this sense, Cynics were the first existentialists, more in the mold, however, of Ionesco than Sartre.

3

Donald R. Dudley concluded his book on Cynicism by suggesting that we shall probably never see their kind again. His judgment was premature. The tradition was resurrected as a cult by the Beat Generation of the nineteen-fifties and by Ken Kesey's Merry Pranksters in the early nineteen-sixties. Jerry Rubin and Abbie Hoffman, who formed the Yippies, turned Cynicism into part of the mass movement protesting contemporary American myths and mores.

The war in Vietnam proved the crucible for this resurrection on a mass basis. Many young people opposed the war. This opposition was not merely intellectual; it was painfully existential. At the outset of the anti-war movement protesters relied on traditional forms for protest: speeches, essays, peaceful demonstrations. These failed to change policy. The war grew, and they grew weary of traditional forms. Frustrations increased as death tolls rose.

In the eyes of many young people, Joseph Heller's *Catch 22* had become a terrifying reality. Even as President Johnson approved of dissent, he also denounced dissenters as "Nervous Nellies" and accused them of speaking from paranoid frustrations and even cowardice.[35] Protesters

could say they objected to the war on moral grounds, only to learn that this would not protect them from the draft. Some sought refuge in the Nuremburg principle that stated that private men have a responsibility to act against governments that violate political morality. But the refuge was hardly a sanctuary. The very government that sanctioned that principle—indeed, enforced it at the Nazi trials—was the same government that would jail protesters for acting against its policies in Vietnam. According to many protesters, each of these acts added up to a consuming hypocrisy in American life. Recognition of this corruption led to a realization that new rhetorical strategies would have to be developed if lives were to be saved, if the civic fabric that held together man with man were to be mended. But first, they had to understand why they had failed when they had protested through conventional channels using conventional means.

First, language. The administration had attempted to placate people into supporting the war by a Newspeak which turned people into "personnel," horrible deaths into weekly statistics, defeats into victories and a repressive military dictatorship into a democratic government with "free elections." Each concrete event—whether favorable or unfavorable to the U.S. Government—was transformed into an example that proved an abstract principle, belief, or assumption. The existential theory of objectification certainly found verification in this rhetoric.

The original protesters used the prevailing language of American politics and seemingly (to them) lost their cause. Jerry Rubin described their problem in a speech in Cincinnati, Ohio: "When they control the words, they control everything, and they got the words controlled. They got 'war' meaning 'peace'; they got 'fuck' being a bad word[;] they got 'napalm' being a good word—they got 'decency' that to me is indecent. The whole thing is like backwards, and we gotta turn it around."[36] A new language had to be created to express new ideas, new perspectives, new attitudes. But what language?

They realized that their second mistake lay in their belief that reasoned, academic discourse in the tradition of pragmatic liberalism would be respected and would change Johnson's Vietnam policy. Instead, the administration deserted pragmatic language about Vietnam and resorted to the rhetoric of anti-communist ideology to justify its policy. Furthermore, the President ignored arguments against the war even as he patronized dissent, a doubly cruel blow. Finally, the teach-in lost force as it became commonplace. Protesters realized that new forums and new forms would have to be created if the momentum of the anti-war movement were to be sustained. But what new forums and what new forms? And how should they be created?

Providing answers to these questions led to divisions within the anti-war movement. Most continued traditional methods for protest and began looking toward the 1968 election as a means for ending American participation in the war. These people sought to work within the system by changing leaders. They treated Vietnam as a policy to be reversed, even as they admitted greater issues were involved, by using conventional resources of political and rhetorical power.

Others viewed the war as an illustration of a higher principle, a symptom of a disease in the body politic. But they disagreed among themselves about what truth could be drawn from the example, what surgery was needed on the patient. Thus, some became pacifists opposed to all wars; others embraced Marxism or Anarchism as an alternative to capitalistic welfare-statism; some joined the Weatherpeople and went underground in hopes of overthrowing the American government; still others formed the Yippies. Frequently, they fought among themselves as vigorously as they fought with supporters of the war.

Yippies as Cynics. Yippies rejected the ideological solutions to American problems that Marxists, Anarchists, Weatherpeople and others advocated. They based their beliefs on absolute humanism: "There are no ideological requirements to be a yippie. Write your own slogan. Protest your own issue. Each man his own yippie."[37] This individualism marked them as a unique faction within the anti-war movement. Yet, they did hold a loosely-knit set of beliefs that fall into the tradition of Cynicism.

Yippies contended that man is not free because he has been conditioned and defiled by corrupt institutions. Men who believe in these institutions initiate and perpetuate wars, racism, and oppression through conventions they have established. Yippies sought freedom from oppressive conventions and societal restrictions. "Free is the essence of Yippie!"[38] Like the Cynics of Greece, they cherished personal freedom. Unlike other factions within the peace coalition that sought to transform institutions to fit ideological concerns, Yippies sought to do away with institutions altogether. Furthermore, unlike some militants who resorted to violence, Yippies generally relied on ridicule and "put-ons." At the march on the Pentagon, they joined devout worshippers in chanting Hari Krishna and intoned sustained sounds of "Ommmmmmm" as attempts to exorcize the evil "vibrations" arising from that military establishment.

They also rejected the work-ethic and advocated "ripping off" conventional institutions. Man should be freed from the drudgery of work so he can celebrate life, be creative, and enjoy sex. In their eyes each of these activities is a natural function that has been suppressed by corrupt customs. Thus, public sexual acts serve as political-rhetorical metaphors signaling liberation from conventions even as they protest conventions. Underlying these acts is a firm belief that while sex is natural and creative, war is unnatural and destructive. To commit public sexual acts is to attempt to shock people into recognizing that the very same customs that suppress sex sustain wars. Until those customs are discarded and the institutions that perpetuate them are destroyed, man will feel guilty about sex and will continue to make wars.

Mixed with these general beliefs are specific political demands: disarmament, an immediate end to the war in Vietnam, community control, and so on.[39] This grab-bag of cultural criticism, political demands, and ridiculous antics has led to attacks on Yippies from all sides. The Left denounced them as acid-heads, freaks, and hippies who are diverting energies from the revolution. Hippies denounced them as Marxists in disguise who use rock music, dope, and psychedelics to seduce "flower people" into political action.[40] In fact, both are mistaken.

Yippies are the heirs of Cynicism which they have transformed into a rhetorical movement intended to change civic life in America. They seek to change perspective rather than impose ideologies on people. "Yippies believe there can be no social revolution without a head revolution and no head revolution without a social revolution."[41] Jerry Rubin and Abbie Hoffman are America's hip version of Diogenes of Sinope.

The diatribe of the Yippies. Jerry Rubin's book, *Do It!*, provides an excellent example of Cynical rhetoric. Rubin not only indulges in diatribes, he also comments on the purposes of his strategies. The theme of the book is the need to liberate man from oppressive institutions. Therefore, Rubin ridicules both traditional politics and the ideological politics of the Right and New Left as mirror-images of one another. Each still supports political institutions. They disagree about what the content of those institutions ought to be. Thus, one chapter in the book is entitled: "George Wallace is Bobby Kennedy in Drag."

Do It! is loosely strung together as the author jumps from topic to topic recounting the evils of society. It is filled with devices traditionally assigned to diatribes which evoke laughter, repulsion, and, oddly enough, reflection. However, the hallmark of this rhetoric is obscenity. Photographs of nudes present natural man or woman to the reader. Profanities are repeated page after page. These serve to undermine any language of good manners or polite forms by making public that which previously had been confined to locker-rooms. They are used to shock. Rubin states that the "more people you alienate, the more people you reach. If you don't alienate people, you're not reaching them."[42]

Beyond the need to shock, Yippies use obscenities to mark the hypocrisy of society, a hypocrisy symbolized by those who support the war without pangs of conscience, but who, were they to see a person walk nude through the streets, would rise up in moral indignation. By shouting and writing profanities, they name the war "The Great Obscenity" and thus wave the bloody shirt of misplaced values in the faces of business-as-usual Americans, classes-as-usual academics.

Symbolic acts. The diatribe cannot be considered apart from the antics of the Yippies, for each is a part of the rhetorical process. Here a distinction must be made between those in government and those outside. For a man in power to confirm his rhetoric, he must enact policies which are reasonably consistent with positions he has taken. Otherwise, his credibility may be questioned. For a man out of power, he must invent symbolic acts which confirm his beliefs, or he is open to the charge of hypocrisy. Thus, the antics of the Yippies are not only symbolic protests, but also symbolic confirmations of their ideas that enhance *ethos* among supporters.

Refusing to live within conventional society, Yippies adopted unconventional dress—Indian costumes, Revolutionary War uniforms, Santa Claus suits—as marks of identification for their movement and as means of attracting coverage by the media. Rubin and Hoffman dressed in court justice robes and challenged Attorney General John Mitchell to a boxing match. They wore their hair long and sometimes took off their clothes in public. Rubin summarized the intention of these acts: "We're living TV commercials for the revolution. We're walking picket signs. Every response to long-hairs creates a moral crisis for straights. We force adults to bring all their repressions to the surface, to expose their real feelings."[43] To produce this moral crisis they profaned traditional symbols that the majority considers sacred. They attempted to arouse emotions by forcing the public to experience secular (and in some cases, religious) sacrilege.

Desecration of the American flag and waving the Viet Cong flag become major symbolic acts in this process. Tom Wolfe has Ken Kesey, a novelist and Cynic, explain the rhetorical purposes of desecrating traditional symbols [Kesey seizes an American flag and grinds his foot on it]: "[D]on't just describe an emotion, but arouse it, make them experience it, by manipulating the symbol of the emotion, and sometimes we have to come into awareness through the back door."[44] Much of the rhetoric of the Cynics and Yippies is an attempt to change the house of society by stealing in through the back door. These absurd acts—sexual and otherwise—were attempts to manipulate symbols by repudiating and profaning their traditional, conventional meanings, thus producing horror among people who had never examined their reasons for responding as they had toward these symbols.

This strategy culminates in the Cynical tradition of the wonderland "politics of experience." Don't argue about corrupt ideas, ridicule them. Don't placate degenerate emotions, produce them, bring them to the surface. Don't merely criticize society, create a counter-society. Do it!

Effects. The effects of the diatribe are mixed. Even as Yippies assaulted traditional myths, they created myths about themselves which did not attract a wide following.

The bizarre antics of Yippies gained them a forum on television, a necessity for protest. Jerry Rubin and Abbie Hoffman became instant electronic celebrities. Yet, when they used profanities or carried symbolic acts too far, they lost access to media. The public in general did not react positively to them. Though no survey has been taken to ascertain the public's response to Yippies, in particular, there have been studies of reactions to "protesters." In 1968 the Survey Research Center of the University of Michigan found that nearly seventy-five percent of the people reacted negatively to protesters. Among those who favored complete withdrawal from Vietnam, as many as fifty-three percent reacted negatively.[45] We can assume with some degree of safety that the percentages would have been higher in reaction to Yippies.

On the other hand, the Yippies and other extreme groups among the anti-war movement contributed to making political critics of the war who worked within the system respectable. In contrast to the obscenity-shouting Yippies and the popular image of the bomb-hurling Weatherpeople, Senators Fulbright, Kennedy, Church and McGovern seemed to the American public models of responsible criticism. Just as Stokely Carmichael legitimized the moderate, non-violent posture of Martin Luther King, Jr., so too, the violent acts of the Weatherpeople and the absurd acts of the Yippies contributed to acceptance of traditional criticism of the war and enhanced the *ethos* of those critics who held positions of power.

4

The rhetorical mood of the Vietnam war has been frenzied and fervent. Unlike the first and second World Wars, the Vietnam war seems not to be fought for a higher, moral purpose. Critics do not believe that it will "make the world safe for democracy" or preserve the "arsenal of democracy." Critics see it as a dirty war fought for obscure purposes, at best, or evil ends, at worst. In opposing the war they had, as Thomas Mann once observed, two choices: to take a position that is either ironic or radical.

Yippies chose an extreme form of irony, the diatribe. They revived, probably unknowingly, the Cynical tradition to protest a war and a society that supported that war. In so doing they alienated from their cause as many, if not more, than they drew to it.

Yippies rejected the civic society and did everything within their power to identify themselves as outcasts. Yet, irony has a way of turning upon those who use it. In one sense, the Yippie movement is a mirror-image of those who conducted the war. The administration claimed it had the duty to use any means necessary to preserve democracy and freedom, even the defense of Vietnam and the use of napalm on civilians. Many within the anti-war movement, including the Yippies, claimed the same right: the duty to use any means necessary to stop the war. Ideology replaced reflection. Morality transcended politics.

Notes

1 Everett Lee Hunt, "The Rhetorical Mood of World War II," *QJS*, 29 (Feb. 1943), 4–5.

2 Quoted in Stephen Spender, *The Year of the Young Rebels* (1968; rpt. New York: Vintage Books, 1969), p. 8. Profanities used in speeches were seldom broadcast or published in reporting protest rallies. We can understand the reluctance of newspapers to print them and of television stations to broadcast them.

However, many of us who attended anti-war rallies recall the vehemence with which speakers used obscenities to describe their outrage at the war. I remember vividly a young man who developed his ideas quite reasonably until he reached the climax of his speech. Then, everything he attacked he called "shit." The policy was shit. The leaders supported the war were shit. People who supported the war were shit. The effect was striking and drew repeated applause and cheers.

3 Lionel Abel, "The Position of Noam Chomsky," *Commentary,* 47 (May 1969), 35–44. The

distinction between politics and morality is, at best, difficult to draw. Every politician contends he takes positions for moral reasons. There is, I believe, one major distinction, and Chomsky's essays point to it.

Chomsky denies that the issue of American intervention in Vietnam is debatable. He believes our policy is wrong; the war is immoral. There is nothing more to be said on that subject. Even to debate the issue is to suggest, regardless of how significant the suggestion may be, that there is another side to the issue. The question is not debatable. This is a moral stance.

Our political processes are based on a contrary assumption: every question is open to debate within *legal* limits. Only whether we ought to debate is not debatable. This stance is considered the hallmark of democratic politics. (Cf.: "SAA Credo for Responsible Communication in a Free Society," adopted August 20, 1963.) Those who speak from these assumptions create a political-legal rhetoric.

The conflict between these two stances can be seen in this example: is the following question debatable—"Was the systematic extermination of six million Jews by the Nazis justified?" From a strictly political-legal position, one would have to answer that debate is justified, even though one may find it personally objectionable. Chomsky would deny that this is a legitimately debatable question. He would argue that only the unreasonable and inhumane would debate such a question.

4 Noam Chomsky, *American Power and the New Mandarins* (New York: Pantheon Books, 1969), p. 9. Emphasis added. Though Chomsky shares a moral position with Yippies and Cynics, he should not have this book classified as a diatribe. It is a lamentation. Chomsky has a perspective and purpose more akin to Old Testament prophets than Greek Cynics.

5 Theodore H. White, *The Making of the President 1968* (New York: Atheneum, 1969), p. 286.

6 On the use of archetype or generic forms as tools of rhetorical analysis, see Hermann G. Stelzner, "The Quest Story and Nixon's November 3, 1969 Address," *QJS*, 57 (April 1971), 163–172. My approach differs somewhat from his. Mr. Stelzner uses a *literary* genre to interpret a political speech. He seems more interested in interpreting Mr. Nixon's self-image than in describing the circumstances that produced the speech, or in analyzing the arguments used by the President, or in evaluating the effects the address produced. I am trying to establish distinct *rhetorical* genres to interpret rhetorical acts.

7 Edith Hamilton, *The Greek Way to Western Civilization* (1942; rpt. New York: Mentor Books, 1948), p. 190.

8 Herbert Muller, *The Uses of the Past* (1952; rpt. New York: Mentor Books, 1954), p. 114.

9 Donald R. Dudley, *A History of Cynicism* (London: Methuen, 1937) pp. ix–x.

10 Cf. Farrand Sayre, *Diogenes of Sinope: A Study of Greek Cynicism* (Baltimore: J. H. Furst Company, 1938), pp. 99–129.

11 Diogenes Laertius, *Lives of Eminent Philosophers*, trans. R. D. Hicks (New York: G. P. Putnam's Sons, 1925), II, vi, 54, p. 55.

12 *Ibid.*, vi, 34, p. 35.

13 *Ibid.*, vi, p. 43. The insertion of "honest" into this statement probably occurred around the seventh century. "Courageous" would have been more appropriate as it would have been consistent with Greek style and Diogenes' thinking.

14 *Ibid.*, vi, 64, p. 67.

15 H. I. Marrou, *A History of Education in Antiquity*, trans. George Lamb (1956; rpt. New York: Mentor Books, 1964), p. 282.

16 Diogenes Laertius, vi, 71, p. 73.

17 Everett Lee Hunt, "Plato and Aristotle on Rhetoric and Rhetoricians," *Historical Studies of Rhetoric and Rhetoricians*, ed. Raymond F. Howes (Ithaca, New York: Cornell University Press, 1961), p. 24.

18 Diogenes Laertius, vi, 45, p. 47.

19 *Ibid.*, vi, 50, p. 53.

20 *Ibid.*, vi, 49, p. 51.

21 *Ibid.*, vi, 60, p. 63.

22 *Ibid.*, vi, 103, p. 107.

23 *Ibid.*, vi, 104, p. 109.

24 Farrand Sayre, *The Greek Cynics* (Baltimore: J. H. Furst Company, 1948), p. 17.

25 Dudley, p. x.

26 Diogenes Laertius, vi, 69, p. 71.

27 *Ibid.*, vi, 73, p. 7.

28 John MacQuarrie, *The Scope of DeMythologizing: Bultmann and His Critics* (1960; rpt. New York: Harper Torchbooks, 1966), pp. 45–53.

29 This conclusion is debatable. Cf.: W. W. Tarn, "Alexander, Cynics and Stoics," *American Journal of Philology*, 60 (Jan. 1939), pp. 41–70.

30 This affirmation of the natural rights of man may be taken as the original commitment to what later became known as the romantic school of political thought. Rousseau developed the idea into a full-scale political, literary and educational philosophy.

31 Gilbert Highet, *The Classical Tradition* (1949; rpt. New York: Galaxy Books, 1957), p. 304.

32 Dudley, p. 111.

33 Diogenes Laertius, vi, 28, p. 29.

34 W. W. Tarn, 42.

35 *The New York Times,* Late City Ed., 18 May, 1966, p. 8, cols. 1–3.

36 Jerry Rubin, "Do It!" *The Conspiracy,* ed. Peter and Deborah Babcox and Bob Abels (1969; rpt. New York: Dell Books, 1969), p. 214.

37 Jerry Rubin, *Do It!* (1970; rpt. New York: Ballantine Books, 1970), p. 84.

38 Free [Abbie Hoffman], *Revolution for the Hell of It* (1968; rpt. New York: Pocket Books, 1970), p. 153.

39 Free, pp. 173–174.

40 Rubin, p. 83.

41 *Ibid.,* p. 84.

42 *Ibid.,* p. 127.

43 *Ibid.,* p. 95.

44 Tom Wolfe, *The Electric Kool-Aid Acid Test* (1968; rpt. New York: Bantam Books, 1969), p. 166.

45 Philip E. Converse and Howard Schuman, "'Silent Majorities' and the Vietnam War," *Scientific American,* 222 (June 1970), 24. For a more detailed study of the public's reaction to protest against the war, see Milton J. Rosenberg, Sidney Verba, and Philip E. Converse, *Vietnam and the Silent Majority: The Dove's Guide* (New York: Harper & Row, 1970).

The Rhetoric of Women's Liberation: An Oxymoron
Karlyn Kohrs Campbell

Whatever the phrase "women's liberation" means, it cannot, as yet, be used to refer to a cohesive historical political movement. No clearly defined program or set of policies unifies the small, frequently transitory groups that compose it, nor is there much evidence of organizational unity and cooperation.[1] At this point in time, it has produced only minor changes in American society,[2] although it has made the issues with which it is associated major topics of concern and controversy. As some liberation advocates admit, it is a "state of mind" rather than a movement. Its major manifestation has been rhetorical, and as such, it merits rhetorical analysis.

Because any attempt to define a rhetorical movement or genre is beset by difficulties, and because of the unusual status of women's liberation I have briefly described, I wish to state explicitly two presuppositions informing what follows. First, I reject historical and socio-psychological definitions of movements as the basis for rhetorical criticism on the grounds that they do not, in fact, isolate a genre of *rhetoric* or a distinctive body of *rhetorical* acts.[3] The criteria defining a rhetorical movement must be rhetorical; in Aristotelian terminology, such criteria might arise from the relatively distinctive use or interpretation of the canons and modes of proof. However, rather than employing any codified critical scheme, I propose to treat two general categories—substance and style. In my judgment,

the rhetoric of women's liberation (or any other body of discourses) merits *separate* critical treatment if, and only if, the symbolic acts of which it is composed can be shown to be distinctive on both substantive and stylistic grounds. Second, I presume that the style and substance of a genre of rhetoric are interdependent.[4] Stylistic choices are deeply influenced by subject-matter and context,[5] and issues are formulated and shaped by stylistic strategies.[6] The central argument of this essay is that the rhetoric of women's liberation is a distinctive genre because it evinces unique *rhetorical* qualities that are a fusion of substantive and stylistic features.

DISTINCTIVE SUBSTANTIVE FEATURES

At first glance, demands for legal, economic, and social equality for women would seem to be a reiteration, in a slightly modified form, of arguments already familiar from the protest rhetoric of students and blacks. However, on closer examination, the fact that equality is being demanded *for women* alters the rhetorical picture drastically. Feminist advocacy unearths tensions woven deep into the fabric of our society and provokes an unusually intense and profound "rhetoric of moral conflict."[7] The sex role requirements for women contradict the dominant values of American culture—self-reliance, achievement, and independence.[8] Unlike most other groups, the social status of women is defined primarily by birth, and their social position is at odds with fundamental democratic values.[9] In fact, insofar as the role of rhetor entails qualities of self-reliance, self-confidence, and independence, *its very assumption is a violation of the female role.* Consequently, feminist rhetoric is substantively unique by definition, because no matter how traditional its argumentation, how justificatory its form, how discursive its method, or how scholarly its style, it attacks the entire psycho-social reality, the most fundamental values, of the cultural context in which it occurs. As illustration, consider the apparently moderate, reformist demands by feminists for legal, economic, and social equality—demands ostensibly based on the shared value of equality. (As presented here, each of these demands is a condensed version of arguments from highly traditional discourses by contemporary liberationists.)

The demand for legal equality arises out of a conflict in values. Women are not equal to men in the sight of the law. In 1874, the Supreme Court ruled that "some citizens could be denied rights which others had," specifically, that "the 'equal protection' clause of the Fourteenth Amendment did not give women equal rights with men," and reaffirmed this decision in 1961, stating that "the Fourteenth Amendment prohibits any arbitrary class legislation, except that based on sex."[10] The legal inferiority of women is most apparent in marriage laws. The core of these laws is that spouses have reciprocal—not equal—rights and duties. The husband must maintain the wife and children, but the amount of support beyond subsistence is at his discretion. In return, the wife is legally required to do the domestic chores, provide marital companionship, and sexual consortium but has no claim for direct compensation for any of the services rendered. Fundamentally, marriage is a property relationship. In the nine community property states, the husband is considered the head of the "community," and so long as he is capable of managing it, the wife, acting alone, cannot contract debts chargeable to it. In Texas and Nevada, the husband can even dispose of the property without his wife's consent, property that includes the income of a working wife. The forty-one common law states do not recognize the economic contribution of a wife who works

only in the home. She has no right to an allowance, wages, or income of any sort, nor can she claim joint ownership upon divorce. In addition, every married woman's surname is legally that of her husband, and no court will uphold her right to go by another name.[11]

It seems to me that any audience of such argumentation confronts a moral dilemma. The listener must either admit that this is not a society based on the value of equality or make the overt assertion that women are special or inferior beings who merit discriminatory treatment.[12]

The argument for economic equality follows a similar pattern. Based on median income, it is a greater economic disadvantage to be female than to be black or poorly educated (of course, any combination of these spells economic disaster). Although half of the states have equal pay laws, dual pay scales are the rule. These cannot be justified economically because, married or single, the majority of women who work do so out of economic necessity, and some forty percent of families with incomes below the poverty level are headed by women. Occupationally, women are proportionately more disadvantaged today than they were in 1940, and the gap between male and female income steadily increases.[13] It might seem that these data merely indicate a discrepancy between law and practice—at least the value is embodied in some laws—although separating values and behavior is somewhat problematic. However, both law and practice have made women economically unequal. For example, so long as the law, as well as common practice, gives the husband a right to the domestic services of his wife, a woman must perform the equivalent of two jobs in order to hold one outside the home.[14] Once again, the audience of such argumentation confronts a moral dilemma.

The most overt challenge to cultural values appears in the demand for social or sexual equality, that we dispense forever with the notion that "men are male *humans* whereas women are human *females*,"[15] a notion enshrined in the familiar phrase, "I now pronounce you *man* and wife." An obvious reason for abolishing such distinctions is that they lead to cultural values for men as men and women as wives. Success for men is defined as instrumental, productive labor in the outside world whereas "wives" are confined to "woman's place"—child care and domestic labor in the home.[16] As long as these concepts determine "masculinity" and "femininity," the woman who strives for the kind of success defined as the exclusive domain of the male is inhibited by norms prescribing her "role" and must pay a heavy price for her deviance. Those who have done research on achievement motivation in women conclude that: "Even when legal and educational barriers to achievement are removed, the motive to avoid success will continue to inhibit women from doing 'too well'—thereby risking the possibility of being socially rejected as 'unfeminine' or 'castrating'"[17] and "The girl who maintains qualities of independence and active striving (achievement-orientation) necessary for intellectual mastery defies the conventions of sex appropriate behavior and must pay a price, *a price in anxiety*."[18] As long as education and socialization cause women to be "unsexed" by success whereas men are "unsexed" by failure, women cannot compete on equal terms or develop their individual potentials. No values, however, are more deeply engrained than those defining "masculinity" and "femininity." The fundamental conflict in values is evident.

Once their consequences and implications are understood, these apparently moderate, reformist demands are rightly seen as revolutionary and radical in the extreme. They threaten the institutions of marriage and the family and norms governing child-rearing and male-female roles. To meet them would require major, even revolutionary, social change.[19] It should be emphasized, however, that these arguments are drawn from discourses that could not be termed confrontative, alienating, or radical in any ordinary sense. In form, style, structure, and supporting materials, they would meet the demands of the strictest Aristotelian critic. Yet they are substantively unique, inevitably radical, because they attack the fundamental values underlying this culture. The option to be moderate and reformist is simply not available to women's liberation advocates.

DISTINCTIVE STYLISTIC FEATURES

As a rhetoric of intense moral conflict, it would be surprising indeed if distinctive stylistic features did not appear as strategic adaptations to a difficult rhetorical situation.[20] I propose to treat "stylistic features" rather broadly, electing to view women's liberation as a persuasive campaign. In addition to the linguistic features usually considered, the stylistic features of a persuasive campaign include, in my view, characteristic modes of rhetorical interaction, typical ways of structuring the relationships among participants in a rhetorical transaction, and emphasis on particular forms of argument, proof, and evidence. The rhetoric of women's liberation is distinctive stylistically in rejecting certain traditional concepts of the rhetorical process—as persuasion of the many by an expert or leader, as adjustment or adaptation to audience norms, and as directed toward inducing acceptance of a specific program or a commitment to group action. This rather "anti-rhetorical" style is chosen on substantive grounds because rhetorical transactions with these features encourage submissiveness and passivity in the audience[21]— qualities at odds with a fundamental goal of feminist advocacy—self-determination. The paradigm that highlights the distinctive stylistic features of women's liberation is "consciousness raising," a mode of interaction or a type of rhetorical transaction uniquely adapted to the rhetorical problem of feminist advocacy.

The rhetorical problem may be summarized as follows: women are divided from one another by almost all the usual sources of identification —age, education, income, ethnic origin, even geography. In addition, counter-persuasive forces are pervasive and potent—nearly all spend their lives in close proximity to and under the control of males—fathers, husbands, employers, etc. Women also have very negative self-concepts, so negative, in fact, that it is difficult to view them as an audience, i.e., persons who see themselves as potential agents of change. When asked to select adjectives to describe themselves, they select such terms as "uncertain, anxious, nervous, hasty, careless, fearful, dull, childish, helpless, sorry, timid, clumsy, stupid, silly, and domestic . . . understanding, tender, sympathetic, pure, generous, affectionate, loving, moral, kind, grateful, and patient."[22] If a persuasive campaign directed to this audience is to be effective, it must transcend alienation to create "sisterhood," modify self-concepts to create a sense of autonomy, and speak to women in terms of private, concrete, individual experience, because women have little, if any, publicly shared experience. The substantive problem of the absence of shared values remains: when women become part of an audience for liberation rhetoric, they violate the norms governing sex appropriate behavior.

In its paradigmatic form, "consciousness raising" involves meetings of small, leaderless groups in which each person is encouraged to express her personal feelings and experiences. There is no leader, rhetor, or expert. All participate and lead; all are considered expert. The goal is to make the personal political: to create awareness (through shared experiences) that what were thought to be personal deficiencies and individual problems are common and shared, a result of their position as women. The participants seek to understand and interpret their lives as women, but there is no "message," no "party line." Individuals are encouraged to dissent, to find their own truths. If action is suggested, no group commitment is made; each must decide whether, and if so which, action is suitable for her.[23] The stylistic features heightened in this kind of transaction are characteristic of the rhetoric as a whole: affirmation of the affective, of the validity of personal experience, of the necessity for self-exposure and self-criticism, of the value of dialogue, and of the goal of autonomous, individual decision making. These stylistic features are very similar to those Maurice Natanson has described as characteristic of ["]genuine argumentation":

> What is at issue, really, in the risking of the self in genuine argument is the immediacy of the self's world of feeling, attitude, and the total subtle range of its affective and conative sensibility. . . . I open myself to the viable possibility that the consequence of an argument may be to make me *see* something of the structure of my immediate world . . . the personal and immediate domain of individual experience. . . .
>
> . . . feeling is a way of meaning as much as thinking is a way of formulating. Privacy is a means of establishing a world, and what

genuine argument to persuade does is to publicize that privacy. The metaphor leads us to suggest that risking the self in argument is inviting a stranger to the interior familiarity of our home . . . .[24]

Even a cursory reading of the numerous anthologies of women's liberation rhetoric will serve to confirm that the stylistic features I have indicated are characteristic. Particularly salient examples include Elizabeth Janeway's *Man's World, Woman's Place,* "The Demise of the Dancing Dog,"[25] "The Politics of Housework,"[26] *A Room of One's Own,*[27] and "Cutting Loose."[28] The conclusion of the last essay cited will serve as a model:

> The true dramatic conclusion of this narrative should be the dissolution of my marriage; there is a part of me which believes that you cannot fight a sexist system while acknowledging your need for the love of a man. . . . But in the end my husband and I did not divorce. . . . Instead I raged against him for many months and joined the Woman's Liberation Movement, and thought a great deal about myself, and about whether my problems were truly all women's problems, and decided that some of them were and that some of them were not. My sexual rage was the most powerful single emotion of my life, and the feminist analysis has become for me, as I think it will for most women of my generation, as significant an intellectual tool as Marxism was for generations of radicals. But it does not answer every question. . . . I would be lying if I said that my anger had taught me how to live. But my life has changed because of it. I think I am becoming in many small ways a woman who takes no shit. I am no longer submissive, no longer seductive. . . .
>
> My husband and I have to some degree worked out our differences. . . . But my hatred lies within me and between us, not wholly a personal hatred, but not entirely political either. And I wonder always whether it is possible to define myself as a feminist revolutionary and still remain in any sense a

wife. There are moments when I still worry that he will leave me, that he will come to need a woman less preoccupied with her own rights, and when I worry about that I also fear that no man will ever love me again, that no man could ever love a woman who is angry. And that fear is a great source of trouble to me, for it means that in certain fundamental ways I have not changed at all.

I would like to be cold and clear and selfish, to demand satisfaction for my needs, to compel respect rather than affection. And yet there are moments, and perhaps there always will be, when I fall back upon the old cop-outs. . . . Why should I work when my husband can support me, why should I be a human being when I can get away with being a child?

Women's liberation is finally only personal. It is hard to fight an enemy who has outposts in your head.[29]

This essay, the other works I have cited here, and the bulk of women's liberation rhetoric stand at the farthest remove from traditional models of rhetorical discourse, judged by the stylistic features I have discussed. This author, Sally Kempton, invites us into the interiority of her self, disclosing the inner dynamics of her feelings and the specific form that the problem of liberation takes in her life. In a rhetorically atypical fashion, she honors her feelings of fear, anger, hatred, and need for love and admits both her own ambivalence and the limits of her own experience as a norm for others. She is self-conscious and self-critical, cognizant of the inconsistencies in her life and of the temptation to "cop out," aware of both the psychic security and the psychic destruction inherent in the female role. She is tentatively describing and affirming the beginnings of a new identity and, in so doing, sets up a dialogue with other women in a similar position that permits the essay to perform the ego-functions that Richard Gregg has described.[30] The essay asks for the participation of the reader, not only in sharing the author's life as an example of the problems of growing up female in this society, but in a general process of self-scrutiny in which each person looks at the

dynamics of the problems of liberation in her own life. The goal of the work is a process, not a particular belief or policy; she explicitly states that her problems are not those of all women and that a feminist analysis is not a blueprint for living. Most importantly, however, the essay exemplifies "risking the self" in its most poignant sense. The Sally Kempton we meet in the essay has been masochistic, manipulative, an exploiter of the female role and of men, weak, murderous, vengeful and castrating, lazy and selfish. The risk involved in such brutal honesty is that she will be rejected as neurotic, bitchy, crazy, in short, as not being a "good" woman, and more importantly, as *not like us*. The risk may lead to alienation or to sisterhood. By example, she asks other women to confront themselves, recognize their own ambivalence, and face their own participation and collaboration in the roles and processes that have such devastating effects on both men and women. Although an essay, this work has all the distinctive stylistic features of the "consciousness raising" paradigm.

Although the distinctive stylistic features of women's liberation are most apparent in the small group processes of consciousness raising, they are not confined to small group interactions. The features I have listed are equally present in essays, speeches, and other discourses completely divorced from the small group setting. In addition, I would argue that although these stylistic features show certain affinities for qualities associated with psychotherapeutic interaction, they are rhetorical rather than expressive and public and political rather than private and personal. The presumption of most psychotherapy is that the origins of and solutions to one's problems are personal;[31] the feminist analysis presumes that it is the social structure and the definition of the female role that generate the problems that individual women experience in their personal lives. As a consequence, solutions must be structural, not merely personal, and analysis must move from personal experience and feeling to illuminate a common condition that all women experience and share.

Finally, women's liberation rhetoric is characterized by the use of confrontative, non-adjustive strategies designed to "violate the reality structure."[32] These strategies not only attack the psycho-social reality of the culture, but violate the norms of decorum, morality, and "femininity" of the women addressed. Essays on frigidity and orgasm,[33] essays by prostitutes and lesbians,[34] personal accounts of promiscuity and masochism,[35] and essays attacking romantic love and urging man-hating as a necessary stage in liberation[36] "violate the reality structure" by close analysis of tabooed subjects, by treating "social outcasts" as "sisters" and credible sources, and by attacking areas of belief with great mythic power. Two specific linguistic techniques, "attack metaphors" and symbolic reversals also seem to be characteristic. "Attack metaphors" mix matrices in order to reveal the "nonconscious ideology"[37] of sexism in language and belief, or they attempt to shock through a kind of "perspective by incongruity."[38] Some examples are: "Was Lurleen Wallace *Governess* of Alabama?" A drawing of Rodin's "Thinker" as a female. "Trust in God; She will provide."[39] "Prostitutes are the only honest women because they charge for their services, rather than submitting to a marriage contract which forces them to work for life without pay."[40] "If you think you are emancipated, you might consider the idea of tasting your menstrual blood—if it makes you sick, you've got a long way to go, baby."[41] Or this analogy:

> Suppose that a white male college student decided to room or set up a bachelor apartment with a black male friend. Surely the typical white student would not blithely assume that his black roommate was to handle all the domestic chores. Nor would his conscience allow him to do so even in the unlikely event that his roommate would say: "No, that's okay. I like doing housework. I'd be happy to do it. . . ." But change this hypothetical black roommate to a female marriage partner, and somehow the student's conscience goes to sleep.[42]

Symbolic reversals transform devil terms society has applied to women into god terms and always exploit the power and fear lurking in these terms as potential sources of strength. "The Bitch Manifesto" argues that liberated women are bitches—aggressive, confident, strong.[43] W.I.T.C.H., the Women's International Terrorist Conspiracy from Hell, says, in effect, "You think we're dangerous, creatures of the devil, witches? You're right! And we're going to hex you!"[44] Some feminists have argued that the lesbian is the paradigm of the liberated female;[45] others have described an androgynous role.[46] This type of reversal has, of course, appeared in other protest rhetorics, particularly in the affirmation that "black is beautiful!" But systematic reversals of traditional female roles, given the mystique associated with concepts of wife, mother, and loving sex partner, make these reversals especially disturbing and poignant. Quite evidently, they are attempts at the radical affirmation of new identities for women.[47]

The distinctive stylistic features of women's liberation rhetoric are a result of strategic adaptation to an acute rhetorical problem. Women's liberation is characterized by rhetorical interactions that emphasize affective proofs and personal testimony, participation and dialogue, self-revelation and self-criticism, the goal of autonomous decision making through self-persuasion, and the strategic use of techniques for "violating the reality structure." I conclude that, on stylistic grounds, women's liberation is a separate genre of rhetoric.

THE INTERDEPENDENCE OF SUBSTANTIVE AND STYLISTIC FEATURES

The rhetorical acts I have treated in the preceding section, particularly as illustrated by the excerpt from an essay by Sally Kempton, may seem to be a far cry from the works cited earlier demanding legal, economic, and social equality. However, I believe that all of these rhetorical acts are integral parts of a single genre, a conclusion I shall defend by examining the interdependent character of the substantive and stylistic features of the various discourses already discussed.

Essays such as that of Sally Kempton are the necessary counterparts of works articulating demands for equality. In fact, such discourses spell out the meaning and consequences of present conditions of inequity and the implications of equality in concrete, personal, affective terms. They complete the genre and are essential to its success as a persuasive campaign. In the first section, I argued that demands for equality for women "attack the entire psycho-social reality." That phrase may conceal the fact that such an attack is an attack on the *self* and on the roles and relationships in which women, and men too, have found their identities traditionally. The effect of such an argument is described by Natanson, "When an argument hurts me, cuts me, or cleanses and liberates me it is not because a particular stratum or segment of my world view is shaken up or jarred free but because *I* am wounded or enlivened—*I* in my particularity, and that means in my existential immediacy: feelings, pride, love, and sullenness, the world of my actuality as I live it."[48] The only effective response to the sensation of being threatened existentially is a rhetorical act that treats the personal, emotional, and concrete directly and explicitly, that is dialogic and participatory, that speaks from personal experience to personal experience. Consequently, the rhetoric of women's liberation includes numerous essays discussing the personal experiences of women in many differing circumstances—black women, welfare mothers, older women, factory workers, high school girls, journalists, unwed mothers, lawyers, secretaries, and so forth. Each attempts to describe concretely the personal experience of inequality in a particular situation and/or what liberation might mean in a particular case. Rhetorically, these essays function to translate public demands into personal experience and to treat threats and fears in concrete, affective terms.

Conversely, more traditional discourses arguing for equality are an essential counterpart to these more personal statements. As a process, consciousness raising requires that the personal be transcended by moving toward the structural, that the individual be transcended by moving toward the political. The works treating legal, economic, and social inequality provide the structural analyses and empirical data that permit women to generalize from their individual experiences to the conditions of women in this society. Unless such transcendence occurs, there is no persuasive campaign, no rhetoric in any public sense, only the very limited realm of therapeutic, small group interaction.

The interrelationship between the personal and the political is central to a conception of women's liberation as a genre of rhetoric. All of the issues of women's liberation are simultaneously personal and political. Ultimately, this interrelationship rests on the caste status of women, the basis of the moral conflict this rhetoric generates and intensifies. Feminists believe that sharing personal experience is liberating, i.e., raises consciousness, because all women, whatever their differences in age, education, income, etc., share a common condition, a radical form of "consubstantiality" that is the genesis of the peculiar kind of identification they call "sisterhood." Some unusual rhetorical transactions seem to confirm this analysis. "Speak-outs" on rape, abortion, and orgasm are mass meetings in which women share extremely personal and very negatively valued experiences. These events are difficult to explain without postulating a radical form of identification that permits such painful self-revelation. Similarly, "self-help clinics" in which women learn how to examine their cervixes and look at the cervixes of other women for purposes of comparison seem to require extreme identification and trust. Feminists would argue that "sisterhood is powerful" because it grows out of the recognition of pervasive, common experience of special caste status, the most radical and profound basis for cooperation and identification.

This feminist analysis also serves to explain the persuasive intent in "violating the reality structure." From this point of view, women in American society are always in a vortex of contradiction and paradox. On the one hand, they have been, for the most part, effectively socialized into traditional roles and values, as research into their achievement motivation and self-images confirms. On the other hand, "femininity" is in direct conflict with the most fundamental values of this society—a fact which makes women extremely vulnerable to attacks on the "reality structure." Hence, they argue, violations of norms may shock initially, but ultimately they will be recognized as articulating the contradictions inherent in "the female role." The violation of these norms is obvious in discourses such as that of Sally Kempton; it is merely less obvious in seemingly traditional and moderate works.

Conclusion

I conclude, then, that women's liberation is a unified, separate genre of rhetoric with distinctive substantive-stylistic features. Perhaps it is the only genuinely *radical* rhetoric on the contemporary American scene. Only the oxymoron, the figure of paradox and contradiction, can be its metaphor. Never is the paradoxical character of women's liberation more apparent than when it is compared to conventional or familiar definitions of rhetoric, analyses of rhetorical situations, and descriptions of rhetorical movements.

Traditional or familiar definitions of persuasion do not satisfactorily account for the rhetoric of women's liberation. In relation to such definitions, feminist advocacy wavers between the rhetorical and the non-rhetorical, the persuasive and the non-persuasive. Rhetoric is usually defined as dealing with public issues, structural analyses, and social action, yet women's liberation emphasizes acts concerned with personal exigences and private, concrete experience, and its goal is frequently limited to particular, autonomous action by individuals. The view that persuasion is an enthymematic adaptation to audience norms and values is confounded by rhetoric which seeks to persuade by "violating the reality structure" of those toward whom it is directed.

Nor are available analyses of rhetorical situations satisfactory when applied to the rhetoric of women's liberation. Parke Burgess' valuable and provocative discussion of certain rhetorical situations as consisting of two or more sets of conflicting moral demands[49] and Thomas Olbricht's insightful distinction between rhetorical acts occurring in the context of a shared value and those occurring in its absence[50] do not adequately explicate the situation in which feminists find themselves. And the reason is simply that the rhetoric of women's liberation appeals to *what are said to be* shared moral values, but forces recognition that those values are *not*

shared, thereby creating the most intense of moral conflicts. Lloyd Bitzer's more specific analysis of the rhetorical situation as consisting of "one controlling exigence which functions as the organizing principle" (an exigence being "an imperfection marked by urgency" that "is capable of positive modification"), an audience made up "only of those persons who are capable of being influenced by discourse and of being mediators of change," and of constraints that can limit "decision and action needed to modify the exigence"[51]—this more specific analysis is also unsatisfactory. In women's liberation there are dual and conflicting exigences not solely of the public sort, and thus women's liberation rhetoric is a dialectic between discourses that deal with public, structural problems and the particularly significant statements of personal experience and feeling which extend beyond the traditional boundaries of rhetorical acts. A public exigence is, of course, present, but what is unavoidable and characteristic of this rhetoric is the accompanying and conflicting personal exigence. The concept of the audience does not account for a situation in which the audience must be *created under the special conditions* surrounding women's liberation. Lastly, the notion of constraints seems inadequate to a genre in which to act as a mediator of change, either as rhetor or audience member, is itself the most significant constraint inhibiting decision or action—a constraint that requires the violation of cultural norms and risks alienation no matter how traditional or reformist the rhetorical appeal may be.

And, similarly, nearly all descriptions of rhetorical movements prove unsatisfactory. Leland Griffin's early essay on the rhetoric of historical movements creates three important problems: he defines movements as occurring "at some time in the past"; he says members of movements "make efforts to alter their environment"; and he advises the student of rhetoric to focus on "the pattern of public discussion."[52] The first problem is that the critic is prevented from examining a contemporary movement and is forced to make sharp chronological distinctions between earlier efforts for liberation and contemporary feminist advocacy; the second problem is that once again the critic's attention is diverted from efforts to change the self, highly significant in the liberation movement, and shifted toward efforts to change the environment; and the third is a related deflection of critical concern from personal, consciousness-raising processes to public discussion. Herbert Simons' view of "a leader-centered conception of persuasion in social movements" defines a movement "as an un-institutionalized collectivity that mobilizes for action to implement a program for the reconstitution of social norms or values."[53] As I have pointed out, leader-centered theories cannot be applied profitably to the feminist movement. Further, women's liberation is not characterized by a *program* that mobil[i]zes feminist advocates to reconstitute social norms and values. Dan Hahn and Ruth Gonchar's idea of a movement as "socially shared activities and beliefs directed toward the demand for change in some aspect of the social order"[54] is unsuitable because it overlooks the extremely important elements of the personal exigence that require change in the self. There are, however, two recent statements describing rhetorical movements that are appropriate for women's liberation. Griffin's later essay describing a dramatistic framework for the development of movements has been applied insightfully to the inception period of contemporary women's liberation.[55] What makes this description applicable is that it recognizes a variety of symbolic acts, the role of drama and conflict, and the essentially moral or value-related character of rhetorical movements.[56] Also, Robert Cathcart's formulation, again a dramatistic one, is appropriate because it emphasizes *dialectical enjoinment in the moral arena*" and the *dialectical tension growing out of moral conflict.[*"]*[57]

And so I choose the oxymoron as a label, a metaphor, for the rhetoric of women's liberation. It is a genre without a rhetor, a rhetoric in search of an audience, that transforms traditional argumentation into confrontation, that "persuades" by "violating the reality structure" but that presumes a consubstantiality so radical that it permits the most intimate of identifications. It is a "movement" that eschews leadership, organizational cohesion, and the transactions typical of mass persuasion. Finally, of course, women's liberation is baffling because it has no

program, because there is no clear answer to the recurring question, "What do women want?" On one level, the answer is simple; they want what every person wants—dignity, respect, the right to self-determination, to develop their potentials as individuals. But on another level, there is no answer—not even in feminist rhetoric. While there are legal and legislative changes on which most feminists agree (although the hierarchy of priorities differs), whatever liberation is, it will be something different for each woman as liberty is something different for each person. What each woman shares, however, is the paradox of having "to fight an enemy who has outposts in your head."

Notes

[1] A partial list of the numerous groups involved in women's liberation and an analysis of them is available in Julie Ellis, *Revolt of the Second Sex* (New York: Lancer Books, 1970), pp. 21–81. A similar list and an analysis emphasizing disunity, leadership problems, and policy conflicts is found in Edythe Cudlipp, *Understanding Women's Liberation* (New York: Paperback Library, 1971), pp. 129–170, 214–220. As she indicates, more radical groups have expelled members for the tendency to attract personal media attention, used "counters" to prevent domination of meetings by more articulate members, and rejected programs, specific policies, and coherent group action (pp. 146–147, 166, 214–215). The most optimistic estimate of the size of the movement is made by Charlotte Bunch-Weeks who says there are "perhaps 100,000 women in over 400 cities." ("A Broom of One's Own: Notes on the Women's Liberation Program," *The New Women*, ed. Joanne Cooke, Charlotte Bunch-Weeks and Robin Morgan [1970; rpt. Greenwich, Conn.: Fawcett Publications, 1971], p. 186.) Even if true, this compares unfavorably with the conservative League of Women Voters with 160,000 members (Cudlipp, p. 42) and the National Council of Women representing organizations with some 23 million members whose leadership has taken an extremely anti-liberationist stance. (See Lacey Fesburgh, "Traditional Groups Prefer to Ignore Women's Lib," *New York Times*, 26 Aug. 1970, p. 44.)

[2] Ti-Grace Atkinson said: "There is no movement. Movement means going some place, and the

movement is not going anywhere. It hasn't accomplished anything." Gloria Steinem concurred: "In terms of real power—economic and political—we are still just beginning. But the consciousness, the awareness—that will never be the same." ("Women's Liberation Revisited," *Time,* 20 Mar. 1972, pp. 30, 31.) Polls do not seem to indicate marked attitude changes among American women. (See, for example, *Good Housekeeping,* Mar. 1971, pp. 34–38, and Carol Tavris, "Woman and Man," *Psychology Today,* Mar. 1972, pp. 57–64, 82–85.)

3 An excellent critique of both historical and socio-psychological definition of movements as the basis for rhetorical criticism has been made by Robert S. Cathcart in "New Approaches to the Study of Movements: Defining Movements Rhetorically," *Western Speech,* 36 (Spr. 1972), 82–88.

4 A particularly apt illustration of this point of view is Richard Hofstadter's "The Paranoid Style in American Politics," *The Paranoid Style in American Politics and Other Essays* (New York: Knopf, 1965), pp. 3–40. Similarly, the exhortative and argumentative genres developed by Edwin Black are defined on both substantive and stylistic grounds in *Rhetorical Criticism: A Study in Method* (New York: Macmillan, 1965), pp. 132–177.

5 The interrelationship of moral demands and strategic choices is argued by Parke G. Burgess in "The Rhetoric of Moral Conflict: Two Critical Dimensions," *QJS,* 56 (Apr. 1970), 120–130.

6 The notion that style is a token of ideology is the central concept in Edwin Black's "The Second Persona," *QJS,* 56 (Apr. 1970), 109–119.

7 See Burgess, *op. cit.* and "The Rhetoric of Black Power: A Moral Demand?" *QJS,* 54 (Apr. 1968), 122–133.

8 See Matina S. Horner, "Femininity and Successful Achievement: A Basic Inconsistency," *Roles Women Play: Readings toward Women's Liberation,* ed. Michele Hoffnung Garskof (Belmont, Calif.: Brooks/Cole, 1971), pp. 105–108.

9 "Woman's role, looked at from this point of view, is archaic. This is not necessarily a bad thing, but it does make woman's position rather peculiar: it is a survival. In the old world, where one was born into a class and a region and often into an occupation, the fact that one was also sex-typed simply added one more attribute to those which every child learned he or she possessed. Now to be told, in Erik Erikson's words, that one is 'never not-a-woman' comes as rather more of a shock. This is especially true for American women because of the way in which the American ethos has honored the ideas of liberty and individual choice . . . woman's

traditional role *in itself* is opposed to a significant aspect of our culture. It is more than restricting, because it involves women in the kind of conflict with their surroundings that no decision and no action open to them can be trusted to resolve." (Elizabeth Janeway, *Man's World, Woman's Place: A Study in Social Mythology* [New York: William Morrow, 1971], p. 99.)

10 Jo Freeman, "The Building of the Gilded Cage," *The Second Wave,* I (Spr. 1971), 33.

11 *Ibid.,* 8–9.

12 Judicial opinions upholding discriminatory legislation make this quite evident. "That woman's physical structure and the performance of maternal functions place her at a disadvantage in the struggle for subsistence is obvious . . . the physical well-being of woman becomes an object of public interest and care in order to preserve the strength and vigor of the race . . . looking at it from the viewpoint of the effort to maintain an independent position in life, she is not upon an equality . . . she is properly placed in a class by herself . . . . The reason . . . rests in the inherent difference between the two sexes, and in the different functions in life which they perform." (*Muller v. Oregon,* 208 U.S. 412 [1908], at 421–423.) This and similar judicial opinions are cited by Diane B. Schulder, "Does the Law Oppress Women?" *Sisterhood is Powerful,* ed. Robin Morgan (New York: Vintage Books, 1970), pp. 139–157.

13 Ellis, pp. 103–111. See also Caroline Bird, with Sara Welles Briller, *Born Female: The High Cost of Keeping Women Down* (1968; rpt. New York: Pocket Books, 1971), particularly pp. 61–83.

14 "The Chase Manhattan Bank estimated a U.S. woman's hours spent at housework at 99.6 per week." (Juliet Mitchell, "Women: The Longest Revolution [excerpt]," *Liberation Now!* ed. Deborah Babcox and Madeline Belkin [New York: Dell, 1971], p. 250.) See also Ann Crittenden Scott, "The Value of Housework," *Ms.,* July 1972, pp. 56–59.

15 Aileen S. Kraditor, *Up From the Pedestal: Selected Writings in the History of American Feminism* (Chicago: Quadrangle Books, 1968), p. 24.

16 The concepts underlying "woman's place" serve to explain the position that women hold outside the home in the economic sphere: "Are there any principles that explain the meanderings of the sex boundaries? One is the idea that women should work inside and men outside. Another earmarks service work for women and profit-making for men. Other rules reserve work with machinery, work carrying prestige, and the top job to men.

Most sex boundaries can be explained on the basis of one or another of these three rules." (Bird, p. 72.)

[17] Horner, p. 121.

[18] From E. E. Maccoby, "Woman's Intellect," *The Potential of Woman,* ed. S. M. Farber and R. H. L. Wilson (New York: McGraw-Hill, 1963), pp. 24–39; cited in Horner, p. 106.

[19] In the economic sphere alone, such changes would be far-reaching. "Equal access to jobs outside the home, while one of the pre-conditions for women's liberation, will not in itself be sufficient to give equality for women. . . . Society must begin to take responsibility for children; the economic dependence of women and children on the husband-father must be ended. The other work that goes on in the home must also be changed— communal eating places and laundries for example. When such work is moved into the public sector, then the material basis for discrimination against women will be gone." (Margaret Benston, "The Political Economy of Women's Liberation," *Roles Women Play,* pp. 200–201.)

[20] The individual elements described here did not originate with women's liberation. Consciousness raising has its roots in the "witnessing" of American revivalism and was an important persuasive strategy in the revolution on mainland China. Both the ancient Cynics and the modern Yippies have used violations of the reality structure as persuasive techniques (see Theodore Otto Windt, Jr., "The Diatribe: Last Resort for Protest," *QJS,* 58 [Feb. 1972], 1–14), and this notion is central to the purposes of agit-prop theatre, demonstrations, and acts of civil disobedience. Concepts of leaderless persuasion appear in Yippie documents and in the unstructured character of sensitivity groups. Finally, the idea that contradiction and alienation lead to altered consciousness and revolution has its origins in Marxian theory. It is the combination of these elements in women's liberation that is distinctive stylistically. As in a metaphor, the separate elements may be familiar; it is the fusion that is original.

[21] The most explicit statement of the notion that audiences are "feminine" and rhetors or orators are "masculine" appears in the rhetorical theory of Adolf Hitler and the National Socialist Party in Germany. See Kenneth Burke, "The Rhetoric of Hitler's 'Battle,'" *The Philosophy of Literary Form* (1941; rpt. New York: Vintage Books, 1957), p. 167.

[22] Jo Freeman, "The Social Construction of the Second Sex," *Roles Women Play,* p. 124.

[23] The nature of consciousness raising is described in Susan Brownmiller, "Sisterhood is Powerful" and June Arnold, "Consciousness-Raising," *Women's Liberation: Blueprint for the Future,* ed. Stookie Stambler (New York: Ace Books, 1970), pp. 141–161; Charlotte Bunch-Weeks, pp. 185–197; Carole Hanisch, "The Personal is Political," Kathie Sarachild, "A Program for Feminist 'Consciousness Raising,'" Irene Peslikis, "Resistances to Consciousness," Jennifer Gardner, "False Consciousness," and Pamela Kearon, "Man-Hating," in *Notes from the Second Year: Women's Liberation, Major Writings of the Radical Feminists,* ed. Shulamith Firestone and Anne Koedt (New York: By the Editors, 1970), pp. 76–86.

[24] Maurice Natanson, "The Claims of Immediacy," *Philosophy, Rhetoric and Argumentation,* ed. Maurice Natanson and Henry W. Johnstone, Jr. (University Park: Pennsylvania State Univ. Press, 1965), pp. 15, 16.

[25] Cynthia Ozick, "The Demise of the Dancing Dog," *The New Women,* pp. 23–42.

[26] Redstockings, "The Politics of Housework," *Liberation Now!,* pp. 110–115. Note that in this, as in other cases, authorship is assigned to a group rather than an individual.

[27] Virginia Woolf, *A Room of One's Own* (New York: Harbinger, 1929).

[28] Sally Kempton, "Cutting Loose," *Liberation Now!,* pp. 39–55. This essay was originally published in *Esquire,* July 1970, pp. 53–57.

[29] *Ibid.,* pp. 54–55.

[30] Richard B. Gregg, "The Ego-Function of the Rhetoric of Protest," *Philosophy & Rhetoric,* 4 (Spr. 1971), 71–91. The essay is discussed specifically on pp. 80–81.

[31] Granted, there are humanistic or existential psychological theorists who argue that social or outer reality must be changed fully as often as psychic or inner reality. See, for example, Thomas S. Szasz, *The Myth of Mental Illness* (1961; rpt. New York: Dell, 1961), R. D. Laing and A. Esterson, *Sanity, Madness, and the Family* (1964; rpt. New York: Basic Books, 1971), and William H. Grier and Price M. Cobbs, *Black Rage* (New York: Basic Books, 1968). However, the vast majority of psychological approaches assumes that the social order is, at least relatively, unalterable and that it is the personal realm that must be changed. See, for example, Sigmund Freud, *A General Introduction to Psychoanalysis,* trans. Joan Riviere (1924; rpt. New York: Washington Square Press, 1960), Wilhelm Stekel, *Technique of Analytical Psychotherapy,* trans. Eden and Cedar Paul (London: William Brown, 1950), Carl A. Whitaker and Thomas P. Malone,

The Roots of Psychotherapy (New York: Blakiston, 1953), and Carl R. Rogers, *Client-Centered Therapy* (Boston: Houghton Mifflin, 1951).

32 This phrase originates with the loose coalition of radical groups called the Female Liberation Movement (Ellis, p. 55). See also Pamela Kearon, "Power as a Function of the Group," *Notes from the Second Year,* pp. 108–110.

33 See, for example, Anne Koedt, "The Myth of the Vaginal Orgasm," *Liberation Now!,* pp. 311–320; Susan Lydon, "The Politics of Orgasm," and Mary Jane Sherfey, M.D., "A Theory on Female Sexuality," *Sisterhood is Powerful,* pp. 197–205, 220–230.

34 See, for example, Radicalesbians, "The Woman-Identified Woman," *Liberation Now!,* pp. 287–293; Ellen Strong, "The Hooker," Gene Damon, "The Least of These: The Minority Whose Screams Haven't Yet Been Heard," and Martha Shelley, "Notes of a Radical Lesbian," *Sisterhood is Powerful,* pp. 289–311; Del Martin and Phyllis Lyon, "The Realities of Lesbianism," *The New Women,* pp. 99–109.

35 Sally Kempton's essay is perhaps the most vivid example of this type. See also Judith Ann, "The Secretarial Proletariat," and Zoe Moss, "It Hurts to be Alive and Obsolete: The Aging Woman," *Sisterhood is Powerful,* pp. 86–100, 170–175.

36 See Shulamith Firestone, "Love," and Pamela Kearon, "Man-Hating," *Notes from the Second Year,* pp. 16–27, 83–86.

37 This term originates with Sandra L. Bem and Daryl J. Bem, "Training the Woman to Know Her Place: The Power of a Nonconscious Ideology," *Roles Women Play,* pp. 84–96.

38 This phrase originates with Kenneth Burke and is the title of Part II of *Permanence and Change,* 2nd rev. ed. (Indianapolis: Bobbs-Merrill, 1965).

39 Emmeline G. Pankhurst, cited by Ellis, p. 19.

40 Ti-Grace Atkinson, cited by Charles Winick and Paul M. Kinsie, "Prostitutes," *Psychology Today,* Feb. 1972, p. 57.

41 Germaine Greer, *The Female Eunuch* (New York: McGraw-Hill, 1970), p. 42.

42 Bem and Bem, pp. 94–95.

43 Joreen, "The Bitch Manifesto," *Notes from the Second Year,* pp. 5–9.

44 "WITCH Documents," *Sisterhood is Powerful,* pp. 538–553.

45 See, for example, Martha Shelley, "Notes of a Radical Lesbian," *Sisterhood is Powerful,* pp. 306–311. Paralleling this are the negative views of some radical groups toward heterosexual love and marriage. See "The Feminists: A Political Organization to Annihilate Sex Roles," *Notes from the Second Year,* pp. 114–118.

46 See, for example, Caroline Bird, "On Being Born Female," *Vital Speeches of the Day,* 15 Nov. 1968, pp, 88–91. This argument is also made negatively by denying that, as yet, there is any satisfactory basis for determining what differences, if any, there are between males and females. See, for example, Naomi Weisstein, "Psychology Constructs the Female, or the Fantasy Life of the Male Psychologist," *Roles Women Play,* pp. 68–83.

47 Elizabeth Janeway makes a very telling critique of many of these attempts. She argues that the roles of shrew, witch, and bitch are simple reversals of the positively valued and socially accepted roles of women. The shrew is the negative counterpart of the public role of the wife whose function is to charm and to evince honor and respect for her husband before others; the witch is the negative role of the good mother—capricious, unresponsive, and threatening; the bitch is the reversal of the private role of wife—instead of being comforting, loving, and serious, she is selfish, teasing, emasculating. The point she is making is that these are not new, creative roles, merely reversals of existing, socially defined roles. (pp. 119–123, 126–127, 199–201.)

48 Natanson, pp. 15–16.

49 Parke G. Burgess, "The Rhetoric of Moral Conflict: Two Critical Dimensions."

50 Thomas H. Olbricht, "The Self as a Philosophical Ground of Rhetoric," *Pennsylvania Speech Annual,* 21 (Sept. 1964), 28–36.

51 Lloyd F. Bitzer, "The Rhetorical Situation," *Philosophy & Rhetoric,* 1 (Jan. 1968), 6–8.

52 Leland M. Griffin, "The Rhetoric of Historical Movements," *QJS,* 38 (Apr. 1952), 184–185.

53 Herbert W. Simons, "Requirements, Problems, and Strategies: A Theory of Persuasion for Social Movements," *QJS,* 56 (Feb. 1970), 3.

54 Dan F. Hahn and Ruth M. Gonchar, "Studying Social Movements: A Rhetorical Methodology," *Speech Teacher,* 20 (Jan. 1971), 44, cited from Joseph R. Gusfield, ed., *Protest, Reform, and Revolt: A Reader in Social Movements* (New York: Wiley, 1970), p. 2.

55 Brenda Robinson Hancock, "Affirmation by Negation in the Women's Liberation Movement," *QJS,* 58 (Oct. 1972), 264–271.

56 Leland M. Griffin, "A Dramatistic Theory of the Rhetoric of Movements," *Critical Responses to Kenneth Burke,* ed. William H. Rueckert (Minneapolis: Univ. of Minnesota Press, 1969), p. 456.

57 Robert S. Cathcart, p. 87.

Movements: Confrontation as Rhetorical Form
Robert S. Cathcart

"Every movement . . . has form. It is a progress from *pathema* through *poiema* to *mathema:* from a 'suffering, misfortune, passive condition, state of mind,' through 'a deed, doing, action, act,' to an 'adequate idea; the thing learned.'. . . To study a movement is to study a drama, an act of transformation, an act that ends in transcendence, the achievement of salvation. And hence to study a movement is to study its form."[1]

This statement will serve as a beginning point for the contentions I advance. I assume that few would quarrel with the notion that a movement has form, and most rhetorical scholars accept the idea that a movement is primarily a symbolic or rhetorical act.[2] But, having said that movements are rhetorical acts, I have not said much more than the sociologists who say that movements are collective acts seeking social change. To understand movements as rhetorical acts constrained by a particular rhetorical form requires that we know something about how this form is exhibited, what are the forces that shape it and in turn are shaped by it, how it does its work, and the reasons for its existence as form.

In an earlier essay I argued that "Movements are carried forward through language, both verbal and non-verbal, in strategic [ways] that bring about identification of the individual with the movement. . . . [M]ovement is a form related to a rationale and a purpose . . . one which gives substance to its rationale and purpose."[3]

It was my purpose then to establish the notion that movements are essentially rhetorical transactions of a *special type,* distinguishable by the peculiar reciprocal rhetorical acts set off between the movement on the one hand and the established system or controlling agency on the other. I argued, "It is this *reciprocity* or *dialectical enjoinment in the moral arena* which defines movements and distinguishes them from other dramatistic forms."[4] I concluded, this "particular dialectic . . . becomes the *necessary ingredient* which produces the rhetorical form that we

have come to recognize as a political or social movement."[5]

Since the appearance of that essay a number of articles on the rhetoric of movements have expressed disagreement with my position. The disagreements have centered mainly around the contentions that either my definition was incomplete, or too narrow and restrictive to be of practical use to rhetoricians studying movements.[6] That it was incomplete must be granted. That it was too narrow depends on whether one seeks definitions which will cast the widest net, allowing a multitude of acts to be claimed as movements, or definitions that will so focus our vision that we can more exactly distinguish amongst various similar appearing rhetorical acts. I for one think there is much merit in pursuing definitions which allow us to sort out rhetorical transactions that in the general socio-political milieu appear to be quite similar but which have at base a particular rhetorical form which brings forth a unique set of rhetorical strategies.

With that in mind, I will argue that a movement can be identified by its *confrontational form.* More specifically, I will argue that movements are a kind of ritual conflict whose most distinguishing form is *confrontation.* Unfortunately, the word "confrontation" is loosely applied to a wide variety of acts and enactments such as "confronting the morning newspaper" or "confronting the elements," as well as "confronting the police" or "confronting the system." Also, when applied in socio-political conflict it carries the notion of violence and the negation of reason. Despite such common usage and mis-usage, I find the concept, *confrontation,* to have a symbolic significance which, when traced to its conceptual underpinnings, is quite revealing of those collective behaviors referred to as "movements."

In this essay I will use confrontation to mean that form of human behavior labeled "agonistics," i.e. pertaining to ritual conflicts. Confrontation is symbolic display acted out when one is in the throes of agon. It is a highly dramatistic form; for every ritual has a moral aspect, expressing, mobilizing social relationships, confining or altering relationships, maintaining a reciprocal and mutual balancing system. Agonistic ritual is redressive. It is a means of reaffirming loyalties, testing and changing them or offering new ones to replace old loyalties, always expressed in a kind of muted symbolic display designed to elicit a symbolic response which changes attitudes and values without major and unlimited conflict. Confrontation as an agonistic ritual is not a prelude to revolution or warfare but is a ritual enactment that dramatizes the symbolic separation of the individual from the existing order.[7]

I note that others in the field of rhetoric like Scott, Burgess, Simons, Andrews, and Bailey have found "confrontation" to be worthy of examination in its own right, or at least as an adjunct to communication.[8] They have pointed out that, contrary to popular notions, confrontation is not anti-communication but rather is an extension of communication in situations where confronters have exhausted the normal (i.e., accepted) means of communication with those in power.[9] Further, they consider confrontation to be a communicative form directly associated with movements. Their examination of confrontation has, however, been limited to its *instrumental role*—to its use as a tactic for gaining an audience or opening channels to carry the primary message.[10] In addition, some of these studies have implied that confrontation is a somewhat questionable or exceedingly desperate form of communication.[11]

Without denying confrontation's widespread and important instrumental function, I wish to present confrontation as a *consummatory form essential to a movement.* To do so it is necessary first to re-examine the question, What is it we are seeing and describing when we talk about *a movement?* Most rhetorical scholars have answered this in part by using sociological descriptions; for example, the object referred to as a movement is "an uninstitutionalized collectivity that mobilizes for action to implement a program for the reconstitution of social norms and values."[12] In addition, there has been a general acceptance of the idea that there are various or distinctive types of movements such

as reform movements, radical movements, etc. This view of movements as types has also been drawn from the literature of the sociologists of collective behavior. Accordingly, what we seem to be seeing when we observe a movement is a group of people, not identified by institutional membership, who act together to produce change; and this "acting together" can be distinguished by how militantly or aggressively the group performs, and by whether the goal of the group is change in social norms, hierarchical change, or a reordering of values. It generally is argued that, depending on the group's goals and methods, there will be produced a distinctive *form* of rhetoric.

I find it difficult to accept such a construct or definition of movements, not because I want to be a purist about the word "movement" but because such a definition fails, in my opinion, to help us distinguish between two fundamentally different forms of rhetoric—one which I shall call *managerial* and the other I shall call *confrontational.* To put it another way, it can be very useful to our understanding of sociopolitical activities if we can distinguish between those rhetorical acts which by their form uphold and re-enforce the established order or system and those which reject the system, its hierarchy and its values. Needless to say, the great bulk of communication in any society must of necessity fall into the former category. As Scott, Bevilacqua and others have pointed out, almost all Aristotelian rhetorics are *managerial* in form.[13] They are designed to keep the existing system viable: they do not question underlying epistemology and group ethic. On the other hand, *confrontational* rhetoric occurs only in special and limited circumstances, such as periods of societal breakdown or when moral underpinnings are called into question.

It is this confrontational aspect—the questioning of the basic values and societal norms—that makes true movements a real threat that cannot be explained away as a temporary malfunction of the system or as the conspiratorial work of a handful of fanatics. Though some individuals may have felt threatened when former Black Panther leader Bobby Seale ran for the office of Mayor of Oakland, California, many more felt a great sense of relief. And, rightly so, because no matter how radical his campaign platform the form of his rhetoric as *office seeker* was supportive of the system. It was an overt act of faith in the legitimacy of the established order. On the other hand, no member of the established order could mistake the threat to the whole system when Seale and other Black Panthers confronted the Oakland police and the California State Assembly with rifles and shotguns in hand, for the Panthers were saying symbolically that they rejected the laws and codes of the "white establishment" and were placing themselves outside or apart from the existing white racist hierarchy. To know that the latter was confrontational and not managerial communication, one has only to examine the reciprocating rhetorical acts which came forth from all levels of the existing system. Almost all, including many blacks, condemned the act as a step toward anarchy or toward a suicidal racial war perpetuated by black devils of destruction. In other words, almost all perceived of it as a rhetorical act emanating from *outside the system.*

Using this notion of confrontational rhetoric as the counterpart of managerial rhetoric, I find that many of the so-called "types" of movements described in recent literature do not appear to be movements at all, but rather adjustments to the existing order. A closer look at those activities labeled "reform" movements reveals a rhetorical form which is managerial rather than confrontational. Their rhetoric is primarily concerned with adjusting the existing order, not rejecting it. The reformist campaign stays inside the value structures of its existing order and speaks with the same vocabularies of motive as do the conservative elements in the order. The reform must not seem to be a threat to the very existence of the established order, or the reformers may be forced out of the common value system. The reform movement uses a managerial rhetoric because to some degree it must have a *modus vivendi* with those in power if it is to exist.

To place reform movements on a continuum with radical movements by the claim that they are inherently the same kind of act—just less militant or aggressive—is to misconstrue the uses of "identification" and "consubstantiation" in a rhetorical setting.[14] I find Griffin to be instructive on how to recognize the managerial form

of identification and consubstantiation underlying reform movement rhetoric: "Though men, in any system, are inevitably divided, 'identification is compensatory to division.' And through identification with a common condition or 'substance,' men achieve an understanding (a sense of unity, identity, or consubstantiality). Any system that endures implies an adequate understanding, a dynamic understanding . . . . It is the understanding essential to the ultimate achievement of integration. . . . For it provides the basis for communication. . . . Men agree on meaning, value, and desire; and hence they gladly submit to a code of control, obey the commandments."[15] What we see when a "reform" movement or "status" movement, etc., is viewed through the Burkean prism is a rhetorical form which recognizes the division but accepts "the common substance." Such movements produce a rhetoric that embraces the values of the system, accepts that the order has a code of control which must not be destroyed, while at the same time striving to gain acceptance of that which will perfect (or restore to perfection) the system. Such a rhetoric is essentially managerial.

Furthermore, I believe that those who would have an activity that seeks corrective change in the system labeled "a movement" make the mistake of assuming that either there will be no alienation or agitation within a well-ordered system, or that movements are the only means of redress or alteration in the established order. As I pointed out in my earlier essay,

> We must be aware that when we talk of society, or the establishment, or the system, we are talking about a dynamic, ever[-]changing *collection of groups*. In one sense every group activity within society is a movement but in another and more important sense the ever-evolving, changing society is the *status quo*. What the rhetorical critic of movements must be concerned with then is not definitions [of movements] . . . which describe the dynamic *status quo*, i.e., the [activities] which give it its dynamism, but definitions which describe those collective behaviors which cannot be accommodated within the normal [motion] of the *status quo*.[16]

What most so-called reform movements have in common is the basic acceptance of the system as *the* system, along with its moral imperatives and ethical code. The rhetorical form produced by such groups is characterized by consubstantiating motives which are ground for the strategies for improving or perfecting the order. Examples of this are the Populist call for more direct representation in government and more control over (and therefore more rightful rewards for) one's own labors, and the Civil Rights call of the 1960's for "Freedom Now," meaning the wider distribution and more even application of the justice and equality basic to the established system. Even so-called "status" or "transcendent" movements, with their striving for the moral improvement of individuals, are at base claiming that more perfect individuals will improve the existing order and make it function better morally.

Further, I believe that a careful examination of the rhetoric of such collectives, reform movements and the like, will reveal that their strategies of identification and consubstantiation are formed out of what Burke calls "the mystery" or the "keeping of the secret." It is Burke's position that "mystery arises at that point where different kinds of beings are in communication."[17] In any good rightful system men accept the mystery and strive to keep the secret; that is, preserve the hierarchy.[18] Within such rhetoric, identification with agency and purpose is always present. It is necessarily so because what we have is the rhetoric of piety, the essence of which is to establish what properly goes with what. To Burke, the rhetoric of piety is "a system builder, a desire to round things out, to fit experiences together as a unified whole."[19] It is the rhetoric of piety—the keeping of the secret—that is characteristic of most reform activities, and it is that which keeps the rhetoric in bounds—that which limits its agitation and dictates its strategies. This keeping of the secret governs also the *counter rhetoric* produced, which *defines the acts of the group seeking change as "reforms" rather than revolution.*

There is, I believe, another kind of collective behavior which is perceived of (or reacted to) as "radical" or "revolutionary." Its form is *confrontational*. It contains the rhetoric of "corrosion" and "impiety."[20] The dramatic enactment of this rhetoric reveals persons who have become so alienated that they reject "the mystery" and cease to identify with the prevailing hierarchy. They find themselves in a scene of confrontation where they stand alone, divided from the existing order; and inevitably they dream of a new order where there will be salvation and redemption. Once again, Griffin's description of this act is informative. He says such persons are "moved by an impious dream of a mythic new order—inspired with a new purpose . . . they are moved to act: moved . . . to rise up and cry *No* to the existing order—and prophesy the coming of the new. And thus movements begin."[21]

This confrontation I consider to be "consummatory"—the essential form of a movement, *because up to the point of confrontation it is impossible to know that a radical or true movement exists.* That is, without confrontation the movement rhetoric cannot be distinguished from the rhetoric of the collective seeking change and improvement, but not replacement of the existing order. It is the confrontational form that *produces dialectical enjoinment in the moral arena.* For, in every political order there are those who are alienated and who seek change within the hierarchy, and there will always be those who seek power and control over events and groups—those who want a greater "share of the pie" and those who want to improve the existing order for its own sake. Inevitably these persons will form collectives and utilize a rhetoric that petitions, that recruits, that even threatens dire consequences. What distinguishes these collectives from radical or true movements is that *they do not confront the system.* Rather, they maintain the mystery; i.e., keep the secret that the existing order is a true order, one that is in continual movement toward perfection and in which communication through identification and consubstantiation is possible. No matter how contentious the change seekers may become, there is an understood code of control—an identity, a consubstantiality which places limits on the kinds of rhetorical acts that may be performed. In short, there is a dramatization at this level that is rhetorically different from the dramatic enactment of those who confront the system.

For a movement to be perceived as something other than the evolving status quo or the legitimate action of system change agents there must be created a drama or agonistic ritual which forces a response from the establishment commensurate with the moral evil perceived by movement members. The confrontation ritual is enacted by the juxtaposing of two human forces or two agents, one standing for the erroneous or evil system and the other upholding the new perfect order. These two agents must be brought into ritual conflict through confrontation in order for both to recognize that this is no ordinary reform or realignment of the established order.

The rhetoric of a movement is a rhetoric of re-ordering rather than of reforming. As Burke points out, every order implies hierarchy—what goes with what, what is more, what is less, what is necessary, etc. Hierarchy includes what is *not* proper, *not* useful, *not* valuable; thus "the negative." Man, the seeker after perfection, recognizes the negative and becomes aware of his own guilt. And to remove guilt he must seek redemption either through striving to perfect the hierarchy (i.e., established order) or by recognizing the evil of the erroneous system, confessing to his own victimage (mortification) and confronting the evil system with a new, more perfect order (redemption).

Through confrontation the seekers of change (the victims) experience a conversion wherein they recognize their own guilt, transcend the faulty order and acquire a new perspective. This "symbolic rejection of the existing order is a purgative act of transformation and transcendence. It affirms the commitment of the converted to the movement—to the new understanding . . . and hence it endows them with a new condition 'substance'—with a new identity, a new unity, a new motive."[22]

The enactment of confrontation gives a movement its identity, its substance and its form. No movement for radical change can be taken seriously without acts of confrontation. The system co-opts all actions which do not question the basic order, and transforms them into system messages. Confrontational rhetoric shouts "Stop!" at the system, saying, "You cannot go on assuming you are the true and correct order; you must see yourself as the evil thing you are."

An excellent example of the rhetoric of confrontation can be found in the act of the "Catonsville 9" wherein nine Catholic priests and lay workers used napalm to burn the selective service files at Catonsville, Maryland[,] in 1968. According to Charles Wilkinson, who has made a rhetorical study of this incident as part of the Catholic Anti-War Movement in the United States,[23] "The rhetoric of guilt is employed by nine 'American Citizens' and 'Catholic Christians' burdened with a collective sense of guilt for their country as a war-waging empire and for the church as an accomplice in those wars. Here, the rhetoric is clearly directed to themselves as well as to the masses which comprise the status quo of both church and state. . . . Most immediately it addressed the Nine themselves since they also required the rhetorics of its languaging process to enable them to act as they did."[24] The words of the Nine in their mimeographed press release reveal the nature of the confrontation—the rejection of the mystery, the victimage, and the dream of a new order:

> We, American citizens, have worked with the poor in the ghetto and abroad. In the course of our Christian ministry we have watched our country produce more victims than an army of us could console or restore. . . . All of us identify with the victims of American oppression all over the world. We use napalm on these records because napalm has burned people to death in Vietnam, Guatemala and Peru; and because it may be used on America's ghettos. We destroy these draft records not only because they exploit our young men, but because these records represent misplaced power, concentrated in the ruling class of America. . . .
>
> We are Catholic Christians who take the Gospel of our Faith seriously . . . we confront the Catholic Church, other Christian bodies and the synagogues of America with their silence and cowardice in the face of our country's crimes.[25]

The incident at Catonsville was a confrontation, and as such it forced a dialectical enjoinment in the moral arena between the perpetrators and the established order.

No individual can be *of* the movement without an act which recognizes one's own guilt or complicity with the system and which commits the individual to the *new* order. As Scott and Smith point out in their study of the rhetoric of confrontation, confrontation symbolizes the rite of the kill: "The situation [confrontation] shrieks kill-or-be-killed. . . . The blighted self must be killed in striking the enemy. By the act of overcoming his enemy, he who supplants demonstrates his own worthiness, effacing the mark, whatever it may be—maturity, weakness, sub-humanity—that his enemy has set upon his brow. . . . To satisfy the rite that destroys the evil self in the act of destroying the enemy that has made the self evil, the radical may work out the rite of the kill symbolically."[26]

Brenda Robinson Hancock demonstrates how this act of confrontation as guilt and redemption is essential to the Women's Liberation Movement. In her article, "Affirmation by Negation in the Women's Liberation Movement," she points out that, "Lashing out at the enemy can serve to release women's own guilt feelings in a liberating catharsis. A frequent refrain in feminist rhetoric is that no revolution can occur unless women recognize their oppressed status; such recognition implies they have somehow participated in the oppression, at least by submitting to it. Many women have actually prided themselves on their duplicity—their ability to play at ignorance and helplessness, for example. Guilt from recognizing one's own acquiescent role in the oppression must be turned outward toward the oppressor."[27]

Robinson provides an analysis of an essay by Robin Morgan, "Goodbye to All That," which she considers exemplary of this aspect of the movement, and she finds that "Morgan's statement rings with the eloquence of all the previous no's combined, with a spirit not tentative but angry and final. The enemy is established. The victimage is complete. There is no entreaty to denounce male chauvinism; she rejects it outright." She concludes: "Morgan's essay illustrates that the process of negating the existing order and naming the enemy is important not only in isolating the movement's victim, but also in giving women identity as the *antithesis* of men."[28]

Here we see the use of confrontational rhetoric as a "totalistic strategy," to use the words of Scott and Smith.[29] The members of the movement through confrontation draw the line that excludes themselves from the existing order and creates their total dependence on the movement. It is the point from which there is no turning back. Confrontation is a proclamation. It proclaims through the movement, "We are already dead but we are reborn." It says, "We are united in the movement and we understand you for what you are, and you know that we understand."

Confrontation as rhetoric is not an act of violence per se; nor is it a method of warfare. Rather, it is a symbolic enactment which dramatizes the complete alienation of the confronter. As a rhetorical act it is more consummatory than instrumental. It takes a form which prevents the receiver from construing its meaning as an expression of personal dissatisfaction or as a prod toward more rapid response to grievances. Confrontation demands a response that goes beyond the actions of the confrontation itself. It is a dramatization created by the forced juxtaposing of two agents, one standing for the evil, erroneous system and the other upholding the new or "perfect" order. These two agents must be brought into conflict through confrontation in order for both to recognize that what is called for is a moral response appropriate to the moral accusation communicated by the act of confrontation.

It is the act of confrontation that causes the establishment to reveal itself for what it is. The establishment, when confronted, must respond not to the particular enactment but to the challenge to its legitimacy. If it responds with full fury and might to crush the confronters, it violates the mystery and reveals the secret that it maintains power, not through moral righteousness but through its power to kill, actually or symbolically, those who challenge it. Invariably, the response of the establishment spokesmen will reveal whether or not there has been an actual confrontation. The response to confrontation is always characterized by polarization and radical division. Grievances are not recognized as such in confrontation; they are portrayed as trumped-up charges to fool the public and hide the conspiracy. The leadership of the movement is not recognized, for it has no legitimacy, and to confer with it would be tantamount to doing business with the devil. The response of the establishment to confronters is to treat them as moral lepers: to isolate them and pin the anarchist label on them. Such response fuels the confrontation and points the way for the movement. Now the secret has been revealed—the mystery violated—and the struggle can be seen as a true moral battle for power and for the legitimate right to define the true order.

Confrontation serves, also, to identify the membership of the movement. Movements are rag-tag organizations at best, continually plagued by problems of organization, recruitment and mobilization. Acts of confrontation demand a personal commitment beyond simply agreeing with the goals of the movement or recognizing that there are wrongs to be righted. To engage in confrontation requires that the individual admit complicity with the oppressors and to publicly confess guilt, while at the same time redeeming oneself. Many a follower of a movement stops short of confrontation, hoping to keep up a protest without either denying the system or the self. Witness, for example, the role of many liberals during the Vietnam antiwar movement. Acts of confrontation, however, are acts of acting together. They are public statements of conversion which, when coupled with the establishment response, formally commit the individual to the movement, making such individuals dependent on the movement for whatever legitimacy they are to have. Without the act of confrontation a movement would not be able to identify its true believers.

There remains much to be discovered about confrontation and the rhetoric of movements. Confrontation as a rhetorical act may be as important in its own way as the rhetorical act of identification. I believe a Burkean philosophy of rhetoric allows for, even requires, a rhetoric of confrontation if we are to fully understand the role of man as symbol maker and user.

Notes

1 Leland M. Griffin, "A Dramatistic Theory of the Rhetoric of Movements," *Critical Responses to Kenneth Burke,* ed. William H. Rueckert (Minneapolis: Univ. of Minnesota Press, 1969), 461–62. Within this statement Griffin is quoting from Kenneth Burke's *A Grammar of Motives,* pp. x–xvi, 38–43, 376; *Counter-Statement,* pp. 48, 128, 213–14; and *The Philosophy of Literary Form,* p. 76.

2 See Leland M. Griffin, "The Rhetoric of Historical Movements," *Quarterly Journal of Speech,* 38 (1952), 181–85; Edwin Black, *Rhetorical Criticism* (New York: The Macmillan Co., 1965); Herbert Simons, "Requirements, Problems and Strategies: A Theory of Persuasion for Social Movements," *Quarterly Journal of Speech,* 56 (1970), 1–11; Dan F. Hahn and Ruth Gonchar, "Studying Social Movements: A Rhetorical Methodology," *The Speech Teacher,* 20 (1971), 44–52; Charles A. Wilkinson, "A Rhetorical Definition of Movements," *The Central States Speech Journal,* 27 (1976), 88–94; Ralph R. Smith and Russel R. Windes, "The Rhetoric of Mobilization: Implications for the Study of Movements," *The Southern Speech Communication Journal,* 42 (1976), 1–19.

3 Robert S. Cathcart, "New Approaches to the Study of Movements: Defining Movements Rhetorically," *Western Speech,* 36 (Spring 1972), 86. This point is supported in part by William Bruce Cameron, *Modern Social Movements* (New York: Random House, 1966), 174.

4 Cathcart, "New Approaches to the Study of Movements: Defining Movements Rhetorically," p. 87.

5 Cathcart, "New Approaches to the Study of Movements: Defining Movements Rhetorically," p. 88.

6 Wilkinson (p. 90) states, "Unfortunately, Cathcart's article, though quite intentionally, ends where it should begin." And, Smith and Windes (p. 142) observe, "Change to a more restricted usage can have negative consequences." Also, Ralph R. Smith and Russel R. Windes ("The Innovational Movement: A Rhetorical Theory," *Quarterly Journal of Speech,* 61 [1975], 142) state, "While Cathcart properly limits the definition of rhetorical movements to the features of discourse, his approach does not distinguish between movements and other classes of rhetorical acts."

7 H. L. Nieburg, "Agonistics—Rituals of Conflict," *The Annals of the American Academy of Political and Social Science,* 391 (1970), 56–73.

8 Robert L. Scott and Donald K. Smith, "The Rhetoric of Confrontation," *Quarterly Journal of Speech,* 55 (1969), 1–8; James R. Andrews, "Confrontation at Columbia: A Case Study in Coercive Rhetoric," *Quarterly Journal of*

Speech, 55 (1969), 9–16; Herbert W. Simons, "Confrontation as a Pattern of Persuasion in University Settings" (Unpublished paper, Temple Univ., 1969); Harry A. Bailey, Jr., "Confrontation as an Extension of Communication," *Militancy and Anti-Communication*, ed. Donn W. Parson and Wil A. Linkugel (Lawrence, Kansas: House of Usher, 1969), pp. 11–26; and Parke G. Burgess, "The Rhetoric of Moral Conflict: Two Critical Dimensions," *Quarterly Journal of Speech*, 56 (1970), 120–30.

9 See, for example, Bailey, "Confrontation as an Extension of Communication" (p. 24): "It [confrontation] is generally a signal that the usual and established methods of securing policy are not sufficient."

10 See Bailey (p. 24): "Confrontation . . . is that which is designed to bring about bargaining not non-negotiable demands." See also, Andrews (p. 16): "It may be that in an examination of the means of protest and not necessarily in an inherent worthiness of their goals . . . the rhetorical critic could reach judgments concerning the essential nature of confrontation." Scott and Smith (p. 7), however, treat confrontation as both instrumental and consummatory: "One should observe the possible use of confrontation as a tactic for achieving attention and an importance not readily attainable through decorum." And, "Without doubt, for many the act of confrontation itself, the march, the sit-in, or altercation with police is enough. It is consummatory."

11 An example is the statement by William Bruce Cameron, "Some Causes and Effects of Campus Confrontations," in *Militancy and Anti-Communication* (p. 35): "Confrontation precludes disproof because it does not permit a rational examination of the issues. Often the very people who claim to be most concerned about examining the issues stage confrontations in such a way that no serious examination could possibly take place."

12 Simons, p. 3.

13 Robert L. Scott, "A Synoptic View of Systems of Western Rhetoric," *Quarterly Journal of Speech*, 61 (1975), 445–46; Vincent Bevilacqua, "Philosophical Origins of George Campbell's *Philosophy of Rhetoric*," *Speech Monographs*, 32 (1965), 7.

14 For an explanation of "identification" and "consubstantiation" as in gratiation see Kenneth Burke, *A Rhetoric of Motives* (New York: George Braziller, Inc., 1955), pp. 19–29, 55–69, and Kenneth Burke, "Rhetoric—Old and New," *The Journal of General Education*, 5 (1951), 203.

15 Griffin, *Critical Responses to Kenneth Burke*, p. 458.

16 Cathcart, pp. 85–86.

17 Burke, *A Rhetoric of Motives*, p. 115.

18 Griffin, *Critical Responses to Kenneth Burke*, p. 459.

19 Burke, *Permanence and Change* (Rev. ed., Los Altos, Calif.: Hermes Publications, 1954), 69–75.

20 Burke, *The Rhetoric of Religion* (Berkeley: Univ. of California Press, 1970), pp. 215–22.

21 Griffin, *Critical Responses to Kenneth Burke*, p. 460.

22 Griffin, *Critical Responses to Kenneth Burke*, p. 465.

23 Charles Wilkinson, "The Rhetoric of Movements: Definition and Methodological Approach, Applied to the Catholic Anti-War Movement in the United States," Diss. Northwestern Univ. 1974.

24 Charles Wilkinson, "The Rhetorical Criticism of Movements: A Process Analysis of the Catonsville Nine Incident" (Unpublished paper, Northwestern University, 1977), p. 9.

25 Charles Wilkinson, "The Rhetorical Criticism of Movements: A Process Analysis of the Catonsville Nine Incident," p. 16.

26 Scott and Smith, p. 4. In this passage the authors draw upon the ideas of Franz Fanon as expressed in *The Wretched of the Earth*.

27 Brenda Robinson Hancock, "Affirmation by Negation in the Women's Liberation Movement," *Quarterly Journal of Speech*, 58 (1972), 266.

28 Hancock, p. 267.

29 Scott and Smith, p. 6.

Social Movement Rhetoric

Robert Cox and Christina R. Foust

Since 1952, when Leland M. Griffin called on critics to "isolate the *rhetorical* movement" in historical movements, rhetorical study of movements has proved to be both a heuristic and episodic endeavor. In their approach to such studies, critics also have begun to blur the lines between the rhetoric of a discrete "movement" and broader scholarship in public discourse studies. Gaonkar (2002) observed that as scholars have come to view discourse as an "immensely rich and complex" object of analysis, the demand has risen "for a flexible critical practice no longer governed by a single monolithic theoretical perspective" (p. 411).

We believe that a similar critical flexibility has come to characterize recent study of oppositional rhetorics and the discrete acts or practices of movements. Through analysis of "counterpublics" (Asen, 2000; Asen & Brouwer, 2001) and resistant bodies and images (DeLuca, 1999a, 1999b; DeLuca & Peeples, 2002; Harold & DeLuca, 2005), social movement rhetoric (SMR) scholars have offered new protocols for engaging the discourse of those challenging dominant norms and institutions. At the same time, critics are bringing new, more nuanced perspectives to traditional movement texts (e.g., Dr. King's "Letter" from the Birmingham jail) as well as to key figures and discursive practices in the civil rights, women's, and other social movements.[1]

Throughout its growth, the study of movements has broadened rhetorical theory and criticism by bringing uninstitutionalized, nonnormative, and incongruous voices into conversation with public discourse scholarship. We share this desire to inquire broadly into the sources of social transformations as well as the need for critical reflexivity. We have therefore reviewed the major trajectories in SMR scholarship to suggest areas of congruence as well as departures. We survey these developments in five sections: (1) early studies of SMR; (2) rethinking the figure of "social movements": "New Social Movements" (NSM) and counterpublics; (3) performing resistance: bodies, images, and public screens; (4) democracy, representation, and new modalities of social dissent; and (5) continuing challenges for the study of SMR. Since understandings of theory and critical practice emerge most clearly in engagements with discourse, we have attempted to illustrate these major areas through the work of scholars most closely associated with each period or practice.

EARLY STUDIES OF SOCIAL MOVEMENT RHETORIC

Early SMR scholars distanced themselves from the "great orator" tradition of public address, seeking instead to understand a multiplicity of voices urging changes beyond the judgment of single audiences. Moreover, the vibrant, sometimes confrontational rhetoric of the 1960s occasioned critics to question the fecundity and ethics of traditional theory and to deepen their conceptions of movement discourse. By the 1970s, critics had fashioned a conceptual vocabulary assigning rhetoric a central role in social change. Through rhetorical appeals, leaders could balance competing demands placed on their movements and potentially affect wider change. Influenced by the work of Kenneth Burke, other critics theorized SMR as it took place within dialectical struggles with dominant norms and institutions. By the 1980s, diverse characterizations of movement rhetoric in early studies would give rise to spirited debates on the nature and relevance of the "social movement" figure itself.

Griffin (1952) is widely credited with the first attempt to characterize the rhetoric of movements as a distinct area for rhetorical scholarship. He challenged public address scholars to forego the "clearly demarked" and "conventionalized" study of great orators (p. 184) in favor of analyzing "the pattern of public discussion, the configuration of discourse, the physiognomy of persuasion" (p. 185) peculiar to a movement. He located such patterns within larger historical movements, or concerted efforts to change the "social, economic, political, religious," (p. 184) or other conditions that people deemed unsatisfying. Anticipating his later Burkean approach (see Griffin, 1969), he encouraged critics to trace this *rhetorical* "pattern" as the movement proceeded through its phases of development, from "a period of inception" through "rhetorical crisis" to "a period of "consummation" (Griffin, 1952, p. 186). Nevertheless, the sit-ins, marches, and "confrontational" rhetoric occurring in the 1960s would severely strain Griffin's framework, occasioning critics to rethink neo-Aristotelian standards of rhetoric, reason, and persuasion.

The "Rhetoric of the Streets": 1960s Movement Studies

By the late 1960s, both the message and means of street protests that were associated with struggles for civil rights, Black Power, feminism, peace, and campus democracy shook the foundations of "reasonable" public speech. Skeptics denounced a "climate of anarchy," which they attributed to the "rhetoric of the streets," including draft-card burnings, boycotts, traffic blockades, campus sit-ins, mass marches through segregated neighborhoods, and obscene chants protesting the Vietnam war (Haiman, 1967, p. 100). The new rhetoric exceeded "the bounds of permissible time, place, and manner" (p. 100) and the traditional province of rhetoric as "verbal communication" (p. 99). Most important for rhetorical critics, some charged that the new rhetoric constituted "'persuasion' by a strategy of power and coercion rather than by reason and democratic decision-making" (p. 102).

In a defense of the "Rhetoric of the Streets," Haiman (1967) offered a justification of agitators' "body rhetoric" as a First Amendment right and an understandable tactic that dramatized the injustice of a law and, in the case of riots, catalyzed the process of institutional reform. Rather than dismissing outright such protests as irrational, he argued that critics should "avoid the blithe presumption that the channels of rational communication are open to any and all who wish to make use of them and attempt, instead, a careful assessment of the power structure of the situation" (p. 114). He thus inaugurated a call for alternative theories of movement rhetorics capable of explaining new modalities of protest and the exigencies inspiring them.

Haiman's call was not always echoed by other critics. Andrews (1969), for example, criticized the militant rhetoric and actions of Students for a Democratic Society. The group had seized an administrative building at Columbia University in May 1968 to protest construction of a gymnasium that affected a nearby Harlem neighborhood. Yet, the activists' "physical rhetoric of resistance," Andrews argued, was "coercive" since it limited the audience's choices, and thus fell beyond the canons of rhetoric conceived as "persuasion" (p. 9).

Others such as Burgess (1968) stressed the urgency of re-interpreting the apparently threatening expression of such groups. The confrontational rhetoric of "Black Power," he argued, was not "a call to arms but a call for justice, a call uttered outside law and order," because the institutions that created and enforced order were "racist" (p. 123). Critics who judged such rhetoric through the standards of reasonableness and the inherent morality of democratic institutions were

bound to dismiss Black Power as a *coercive* threat. By failing to engage Black Power rhetoric on its own terms, critics could perpetuate a racist status quo under the guises of order, calm, and "business as usual" (p. 130).

Others also took up the challenge posed by the 1960s rhetoric of the streets, questioning the traditional view of rhetoric as a set of "amoral techniques of manipulating a message to fit various contexts" (Scott & Smith, 1969, p. 2, fn. 2). The most provocative response was Scott and Smith's (1969) assertion that Black Power advocates and leaders of the New Left rejected the common notion that their protests were cries for inclusion within the status quo and its institutions. Radical leaders did not represent "an inert mass hoping to receive what they lack[ed] through action by the 'haves'" (p. 2). In an attempt to understand such rhetoric on its own terms rather than as a cry for "recognition," they urged critics to explore the ways in which unorthodox dissent represented a powerful challenge to dominant norms. They argued, moreover, that confrontation challenged not only the "establishment" but academic rhetorics that "have been for the most part instruments of established society, presupposing the 'goods' of order, civility, reason, decorum, and civil or theocratic law" (p. 7).

Critics who engaged the radical, material, and symbolic acts of 1960s protests more often than not read these sympathetically by locating their emergence within conditions of social and economic injustice. Early SMR critics also adopted a self-consciously critical stance toward rhetorical theory itself. As Scott and Smith (1969) pointedly insisted,

> A rhetorical theory suitable to our age must take into account the charge that civility and decorum serve as masks for the preservation of injustice, that they condemn the dispossessed to non-being, and that as transmitted in a technological society they become the instrumentalities of power for those who "have." (p. 8)

Following the work of early SMR critics, two major perspectives emerged that identified social movements as grand undertakings employing an array of strategic choices and rhetorical styles: (1) a leader-centered approach inspired by new sociological theories that identified core "functions" of movements, and (2) a Burkean approach that viewed movements as "dramatistic" forms.

The Rhetorical "Functions" of Movements

Simons (1970) laid the foundation for the functional approach to SMR, arguing that the standard tools of rhetorical criticism were "ill-suited for unraveling the complexity of discourse in social movements or for capturing its grand flow" (p. 2). Simons viewed movements as organizations, not unlike corporations or state agencies, whose leaders faced certain "rhetorical requirements": to "*attract and mold workers* (i.e., followers) *into an efficiently organized unit,*" to "*secure adoption of their product by the larger structure* (i.e., the external system, the established order)," and to "*react to resistance generated by the larger structure*" (pp. 3–4). Stewart (1980) reworked Simons's assumptions, as a "functional approach," positioning rhetoric "as the primary *agency* through which social movements perform necessary *functions* that enable them to come into existence, to meet opposition, and, perhaps, to succeed in bringing about (or resisting) change" (p. 299).

Though the functional approach treated social movements as organizations, it characterized them as "uninstitutionalized collectivit[ies]" (Simons, 1970, p. 3). As such, leaders faced very difficult rhetorical situations given their movements' status as "outsiders." As Simons noted,

> Shorn of the controls that characterize formal organizations, yet required to perform the same internal functions, harassed from without, yet obligated to adapt to the external system, the leader of a social movement must constantly balance inherently conflicting demands on his [or her] position and on the movement he [or she] represents. (p. 4)

The basis of the functional approach, in Simons's view, was the ability of the leader to craft "strategies" that fulfilled "the requirements of the movement by resolving or reducing rhetorical problems" (p. 2).

The functional approach represented a significant departure from the hermeneutic approach urged by critics of the 1960s radical rhetoric. Unlike Burgess (1968, 1970), Scott and Smith (1969), Gregg (1971), Windt (1972), Campbell (1973), and others who sought to understand movements in their own rights, the functional approach seemed like social science, seeking theories which would advance "generalizations" about movement rhetoric (Stewart, 1980, p. 298), and end critics' "preoccup[ation] with explicating the events . . . the people . . . and the strategies . . . that have captured headlines and intruded upon our world" (p. 298). Though functional critics did not claim an ability to predict a movement's course, their approach prioritized efforts to *classify* movement advocates and/or their discourse according to taxonomies of "militant," "moderate," or "intermediate" strategies (Simons, 1970), or as "revivalistic" or "innovative" movements (Stewart, 1980). Thus, while the functional approach provided a vocabulary distinctive to the rhetorical study of movements, it tended to decenter "specific events, speeches, and strategies" (Stewart, 1980, p. 298) in favor of the social movement figure itself. This orientation later proved somewhat limiting since, as we suggest below, the notion of a discrete "movement" would be increasingly questioned.

Movements as Dramatistic Form

Departing from the functional approach, other scholars, influenced by Kenneth Burke, proposed to view social movements as a dialectical form or *movement* in the social arena. Griffin (1969) offered the earliest statement of this approach by extending Burke's idea of the "negative" or conflict as impetus for the "dramatistic" transformations that movements experience. Like the functional critics, Griffin envisioned a grand theory, though it would be based in a view of language itself: As a result of their symbol-creating nature, humans, "moved by the impious dream of a mythic new Order," inevitably experience conflict ("Guilt") and thus are moved "to rise up and cry *No* to the existing order" (p. 460). For Griffin, then, "to study a movement is to study a progress, a rhetorical striving"

(p. 461). This rhetorical striving was "a progress from *pathema* through *poiema* to *mathema*: from a 'suffering, misfortune, passive condition, state of mind,' through 'a deed, doing, action, act,' to an 'adequate idea; the thing learned'" (p. 461, quoting Burke, 1945, pp. 38–43). In Griffin's view, to study a movement was "to study a drama, an Act of transformation, an Act that ends in transcendence, the achievement of salvation" (p. 462).

The attempt to identify the *rhetorical* form of movements led to efforts by others—similarly influenced by Burke—to specify this form as a distinctive act and therefore the focus of rhetorical study. Chief among these was Cathcart (1972, 1978), who proposed that movements are distinguished by reciprocal acts set off between the movement and the established order, a "*dialectical enjoinment in the moral arena* [italics added]" (1972, p. 87). For Cathcart (1978), this reciprocity was constituted by a radical break with societal norms, "a kind of ritual conflict whose most distinguishing form is *confrontation*" (p. 235). Whereas scholars such as Andrews (1969), Burgess (1968), Scott and Smith (1969), and Simons (1970) had looked at confrontation as an *instrumental* act—a tactic to open channels of communication—Cathcart (1978) now proposed confrontation "as a *consummatory form essential to a movement*" (p. 237). That is, confrontational rhetoric ensures the agonistic ritual that a radical break from the established order calls forth. The rhetoric of such movements thus differs from the neo-Aristotelian "managerial rhetorics" of reform or status-quo movements since those, while disagreeing with a practice or policy, stay "within the value structures of its existing order" and speak "with the same vocabularies of motive as do the conservative elements in the order" (p. 239).

Cathcart's insistence on a dialectical view drew immediate criticism. Critics charged that it was an incomplete account (Wilkinson, 1976), and a "more restrictive usage" having potentially "negative consequences" for rhetorical study of movements (Smith & Windes, 1975, p. 142). Whether for these reasons, or because the fires of social controversies had begun to lessen in the United States by the 1980s, the search for

sweeping accounts of the rhetoric of movements ceased by the end of the decade.

CONTESTING THE FIGURE OF "SOCIAL MOVEMENTS": NEW SOCIAL MOVEMENTS AND THE DISCOURSE OF COUNTERPUBLICS

The tensions among the diverse theoretical assumptions in early SMR scholarship became heightened during the 1970s and were fully articulated in the 1980s. Forums such as the *Central States Speech Journal* (*CSSJ*) featured debates about the nature of movements and methodological approaches to the study of their rhetorics. Some skeptics questioned the self-evident figure of a "social movement" itself (McGee, 1980; Sillars, 1980). Others remained committed to views of movements as already-constituted entities with specific rhetorical demands on their leaders (Simons, 1980; Simons, Mechling, & Schreier, 1984; Stewart, 1980). Still others lamented the obsession with theory and urged a return to historical and critical studies of specific movements and texts (Andrews, 1980; Lucas, 1980; Zarefsky, 1980).

The impetus for debates over the study of SMR came from both pedagogical and methodological concerns. Though Griffin (1980) notably praised the pluralistic study of social movements, others argued that "the lack of consistent methodology" confused students and failed to foster uniquely *rhetorical* scholarship (Hahn & Gonchar, 1971, p. 44). As a consequence of these and other concerns, contributors to special issues of *CSSJ* in 1980 and 1983 addressed a number of pivotal questions: How should theorists conceive of the relationship between rhetoric and its object—the social movement? Are movements identifiable phenomena whose life and success depend on rhetoric? Should scholarship emphasize theory building or historical and critical analysis? Should critics conceive of movements as born of, and engaged in, oppositional struggles with rhetorically defined "enemies?"

A principal focus in these debates was an assumption of early SMR scholars that movements were already-constituted entities, with empirical identities, stages of development, strategies, and so on. Against this, McGee (1980) insisted movements are not observable, knowable "things"; instead, the concept "movement" is "a set of meanings" (p. 233), an *analogy*, "comparing the flow of social facts to physical movements" (pp. 236–237). Positing that movements exist prior to rhetoric, McGee charged, reduces rhetoric to a "passive, reactive . . . facilitator of change, subordinate to and determined by an objective phenomenon" (p. 242). Alternatively, critics should explore "changes in patterns of discourse *directly*" (p. 243), echoing Griffin's (1952) call to analyze changes in the "pattern of public discussion" (p. 185).

In a similar vein, Zarefsky (1980) charged that studies that sought "generalizable claims about patterns of persuasion characteristic of movements as a class" rested on the false premise that "movements comprise a distinct rhetorical genre" (p. 246). For example, movements are not inherently *out*groups, since they are sometimes "sponsored and financed by government" (p. 246). As a result, he believed that a key premise of the dramatistic model was not above reproach: "Only in a situation of actual revolution . . . could one say that there is no common ground among participants in a controversy" (p. 247) sharing at least some cultural ground with the "enemy." Instead of disputes about conceptual models, Zarefsky argued that the primary contribution of SMR scholarship is historical: Critics should explore how "our understanding of history will be enhanced by attention to [a movement's] rhetorical dimension" (p. 253). Andrews (1980), too, argued that critics should avoid "the imposition of consistency at the expense of complexity" (p. 281) and urged more historical case studies to counter the generalizations of theory-driven criticism.

However, the social movement figure was not without its defenders. Simons (1980) argued that SMR scholarship would suffer if the views of McGee and Zarefsky were "widely accepted, since they transgressed the commonly accepted understanding of movements as recognizable in their struggles for change" (p. 307). Rather than bicker over terminology, scholars should focus on locating the "invariant characteristics" of

movements (p. 314). Likewise, Stewart (1983) objected, "regardless of what we call them, [movements] have been major forces for change and resistance to change in American history" (p. 77). McGee (1983), however, sharply delineated the functional and critical viewpoints, arguing that the former reflected "the sterile, preposterous world of logical positivism" (p. 75). Rhetorical critics were not "technicians" (p. 76); instead, urging an "interpretive, critical theory," he proposed that they focus on the movement of human consciousness evident in rhetorical discourse (p. 74).

In many ways, McGee's position reflected the wider "critical turn" occurring in the humanities. Movement scholars in sociology, cultural studies, and rhetoric turned increasingly to the study of marginal voices within (and against) dominant publics. In doing so, they employed a range of critical and interpretive theories beyond the taxonomies of the functional model. Some scholars would find alliances with critics of theorist Jürgen Habermas's concept of a liberal public sphere. Critical studies of "new" social movements and the discourse of "counterpublics" would become dominant trajectories in SMR scholarship.

Rhetoric and New Social Movements

In spite of the vigorous debates in the 1980s, the study of SMR waned during the decade. Lucas (1988) found such scholarship to be "moribund"; it was difficult, he noted, even "to find a glimmer of interest in confrontation as a rhetorical strategy" (p. 243). Although some disputed Lucas's assessment, it was clear that "concern with synthesizing issues of 'definition, form, methodology, and meaning' [had] moved from center stage" (Henry & Jensen, 1991, quoting Griffin, 1980, p. 232). Nevertheless, two developments outside of communication studies would begin to influence SMR scholarship: "New Social Movement" theorists' interest in the role of discourse and a corresponding interest in theorizing "counterpublics" as a mode of critical resistance.

The emergence of so-called New Social Movement (NSM) theory came as social theorists attempted to understand movements that foregrounded issues of identity and a "politics of recognition," in lieu of, or alongside, a "politics of redistribution" (Fraser, 1997b).[2] Originating in European social theory (Habermas, 1981; Melucci, 1985; Offe, 1985), NSM proponents offered a competing model to the rational-actor approach of "resource mobilization" theory (McCarthy & Zald, 1977) to account for the movements emerging in the 1960s and 1970s (civil rights, feminism, gay and lesbian struggles, ecology, etc.). In rhetorical studies, for example, Darsey's (1991) analysis of "gay liberation rhetoric" in the late 1970s and 1980s attempted to understand the construction of a movement's interests from the discourse of those within the movement itself.

A central insight in NSM theory was the constitutive role of culture, particularly discourse, in the activities and interests of oppositional groups. As Palczewski (2001) observed, instead of seeing a movement as a "unity, to which one attributes goals, choices, interests, decisions," NSM scholars insisted that these features be viewed "as results instead of as points of departure" (p. 166; quoting Melucci, 1985, p. 793). This approach provided considerable impetus for the conceptual shift urged by McGee (1980, 1983), foregrounding the *rhetoric* of social movements rather than a *social movement's* rhetoric.

Though NSM scholarship was relatively limited within the rhetorical study of movements, its focus on the constitutive nature of discourse has been advanced in another thread of rhetorical scholarship: the study of publics and "counterpublic" discourse. Viewing social movements as counterpublics invited critics to appreciate the ability of movements "to function outside the dominant public as a site of critical oppositional force" (Palczewski, 2001, p. 165). As a result, Brouwer (2006) argued that the emergence of counterpublic theory "reinvigorated the study of social movements by shifting the terrain of such studies" (p. 204).

Counterpublics and Social Movement Rhetoric

The term *counterpublic* emerged initially in reaction to Habermas's (1962/1989) description of the bourgeois public sphere as a realm of "common" interests and a socially accessible sphere of rational-critical debate able to mediate state authority. Negt and Kluge (1993), Landes (1988), and others objected that alternative "counterpublics," whose participants did not share the attributes of a unified, bourgeois public sphere, existed alongside this public in the life of workers and women's roles in the literary salons of the 18th century.

The work of two social theorists, in particular, appeared to be influential as rhetorical scholars elaborated an understanding of "counterpublic" discourse in constituting multiple publics. In using the term *subaltern counterpublics,* Fraser (1992) called attention to "parallel discursive arenas where members of subordinated social groups invent and circulate counterdiscourses to formulate oppositional interpretations of their identities, interests, and needs" (p. 123). In addition, Felski (1989) noted that, unlike the idealistic traits of Habermas's bourgeois public sphere—notably, a bracketing of specific interests, and an assumption of "universal" interests—the discursive labor of counterpublics is "directed toward an affirmation of specificity in relation to gender, race, ethnicity, age, sexual preference, and so on" (p. 166).

Importantly, the affirmation of specific interests in counterpublic theory is not exclusively inward, toward a collective solidarity. For both Fraser and Felski, the recognition of a dialectic of withdrawal and engagement with dominant publics is critical. Fraser argued that counterpublics retain a *publicist* orientation: They "aspire to disseminate [their] discourse to ever widening arenas" (p. 124). As such, counterpublics have a dual character: "They function as spaces of withdrawal and regroupment; on the other hand, they also function as bases and training grounds for agitational activities directed toward wider publics" (p. 124). Thus, in both instances, the discursive practices of counterpublics *matter;* that is, they enable construction of interests inwardly and "agitational activities" toward public audiences.

For many scholars of SMR, the dialectical character of counterpublics signaled a productive focus in recognizing not only the achievement of marginal groups in articulating the bases of their exclusion but also their oppositional or counterpublicist orientation as they challenged those norms or discourses sustaining their exclusion.[3] Brouwer (2006) commented that, for rhetorical scholars, who are "prone to thinking in terms of agonistics, eristics, conflict, dissent, argument, controversy, or social movement," the "counter-public's origins in oppositionality render it familiar and potentially productive" (p. 198).

Indeed, by the early 21st century, rhetorical critics had begun to deploy the concept of "counterpublic" in wide-ranging studies of oppositional rhetorics. Among these were studies of the antisuffrage movement (Maddux, 2004); government censorship of the black press in the early 20th century (Squires, 2001); struggles for recognition and redress by HIV/AIDS groups (Brouwer, 2001; 2005) and women with breast cancer (Pezzullo, 2003a); opposition to the state (Asen and Brouwer, 2001); and efforts by some to constitute virtual or "cyber-counterpublics" (McDorman, 2001; Palczewski, 2001).

Still, the term *counterpublic* has not always been used consistently. Asen and Brouwer (2001) have pointed out that "scholars sometimes write about counterpublics with a frustrating vagueness" (p. 8). And Brouwer (2006) has noted that scholars have yet to "systematically interrogate differences between *counterpublics and social movements* [italics added]" (p. 204). In some cases, the term appears to be used simply for "movement" or as a synonym for "new social movements," while in other cases, "counter-public" signals the internal, reflexive discourse of a group's turn away from dominant publics to focus inward. Influenced perhaps by Warner's (2002a) view that counterpublics are "structured by alternative dispositions or protocols" (p. 56), some have associated counterpublics with their *non*public phase of withdrawal. For example, Maddux (2004) has argued that the evolution of the antisuffrage movement into an antiradical movement in 1917 represented a change "from social movement organizing to counterpublic discursive space" (p. 302). Whereas movements are defined by persuasion directed at external audiences (in Maddux's view), counter-publics are marked by an "internal discursive exchange" (p. 302), and are "further delineated by what Warner calls the 'reflexive circulation of discourse'" (pp. 302–303, quoting Warner, 2002b, p. 420). Others such as Brouwer (2001)

invoke *counterpublic* precisely to capture the "oscillation" of groups such as ACT-UP, "between protected enclaves . . . [and] broader surroundings in which they can test those ideas against the reigning reality'" (p. 89, quoting Mansbridge, 1996, p. 57).

In an attempt to clarify, Asen (2000) and Asen and Brouwer (2001) have posed the question of what is specifically "*counter*" (and significant) about the discourse of *counter*publics? Warning against the danger of simple classificatory schemas—the identification of counterpublics along lines of group identity, topics, or spheres as ontological markers—they proposed to foreground "counter" as a *qualifier* of "public," yielding "a rich and varied set of conceptual understandings" (Asen & Brouwer, 2001, p. 9). The point appears to be that the category of counterpublic is not meant to be ontologically stable or even distinct from "movement," itself a discursive achievement. Rather, "counterpublic" is seen as an analytic category that invites attention to the particular achievements of self-reflexive discourse as it aids in binding identifications and inventing the vocabularies of an opposition. For SMR critics, developments in counterpublic theory thus invited a "move toward multiplicity, the move to loosen borders" (Asen & Brouwer, 2001, p. 17).

In an important sense, critical study of NSMs and counterpublics appears to extend McGee's (1980; 1983) call to decenter the "movement" figure. In counterpublic studies, scholars have departed from leader-centered approaches and the assumption that movements are preconstituted entities. Instead, many critics turned to the self-initiated rhetorical acts of particular activists, street performers, antiapartheid theologians, HIV/AIDS 'zine writers, and others who, through their discursive inventions, position themselves in opposition to dominant publics. Still, as Brouwer (2006) reminds SMR scholars, the "precise contours" of counterpublics "have yet to be thoroughly elaborated" (p. 204). The same might be said of two other major trajectories in recent SMR scholarship—a critical, "performative turn" in understanding the body and its communicability; and emerging studies of "democracy" and new modalities of social protest in global society.

PERFORMING RESISTANCE: BODIES, IMAGES, AND PUBLIC SCREENS

Throughout the 1980s and 1990s, poststructuralist social theory became increasingly influential in scholarly conversations about rhetoric. Theoretical orientations debated by the early SMR scholars faded from research agendas as discourse fragmented and new modalities of protest and communication technologies eclipsed the traditional oration in cultural significance. Instead, SMR critics and rhetorical scholars generally explored texts as they denaturalized ideology, displaced metanarratives, and disrupted cultural authority, often through pastiche and playfulness. For instance, Blair, Jeppeson, and Pucci (1991) adopted a "postmodern" perspective in reading the Vietnam Veterans Memorial as resisting "a single, signature style" (p. 266) and embodying dissent amidst other memorials in Washington, D.C., through its "refusal of unities or universals" (p. 267).

A similar, postmodern perspective encouraged rhetorical critics to attend to the malleability and "polysemy" of texts (Ceccarelli, 1998) and ways in which modernist approaches privileged rationality and propositional rhetorics at the expense of other ways of knowing and acting in the world. Some found alliance with scholars in performance studies who urged recognition of the extrasymbolic, material character of human expression and the embodied and fluid nature of identity (Butler, 1990). Indeed, performance and rhetorical scholars have influenced each other's work in a growing body of scholarship on resistance and social change (e.g., Cohen-Cruz, 1998; Fuoss, 1997; Haedicke & Nellhaus, 2001; Kershaw, 1999; Pezzullo, 2003a, 2003b). Though not always identified with discrete "movements," two related areas have emerged that reflect a "performative turn": studies of bodies and material rhetoric and studies of visual rhetorics and images of the body in resistance.

Performance, Bodies, and Material Rhetoric

Like earlier critics of the "rhetoric of the streets," recent critics of social protest have argued that received frameworks are unable to explain the irrational (or a-rational), material, and embodied appearance of resistance as a public practice. Although rhetoric, since ancient times, has been a "bodily art" (Hawhee, 2004), its corporeal dimensions have been largely deemphasized over the centuries. However, by approaching resistance as *performance* or as *performed*, an emerging group of critics believe they are better able to understand material and corporeal acts of dissent through their own logics or grammars. Furthermore, by foregrounding rhetorical *acts of resistance*, rather than the *social movement* figure, performance-based criticism has drawn closer to the hermeneutic objectives of some early SMR scholars.

An important marker of such studies is Fuoss's (1997) analysis of depression-era labor strikes as cultural performances. These events, he argued, were "heightened occasions" (p. 173) that were both strategic and excessive. Strikers scheduled, publicized, and sequenced their performances; they acknowledged the temporal and spatial contexts that established a stage for their events and constrained their ability to meet political ends. Yet such performances exceeded rhetors' strategic efforts for change, encouraging playfulness and escapism for those involved. By treating resistance (strikes, in this case) as a performance, SMR critics began to read "effects" beyond the strategic goals typically associated with social movements, considering instead the "liminal" state between instrumentality and aesthetics (Bruner, 2005, p. 140).

One site of resistance that has received much attention from both rhetorical and performance critics has been the growing antiglobalization or "global justice" movement against the neoliberal expansion of capital. For example, Bruner (2005) observed that protests at meetings of international capital (World Bank, International Monetary Fund, etc.) often become sites of resistance in which aspects of the "carnivalesque" occur. By carnivalesque, Bruner was referring to the historical experience of festivals that provided common people with opportunities to critique authority and hierarchy, as well as experiment with identities and alternative possibilities for communal life. Bruner argued that the carnivalesque involves an embracing of the "fictive" (e.g., the wearing of masks, reversal of binaries, suspension of rank, and other hierarchies) in which the fluidity and "betweenness" of such play may (at times) prove powerful vis-à-vis the "humorless" logic of corrupt states. "The humorless state has a very difficult time dealing with absurdity, symbolic protest, and the curious blending of the fictive and the real," such as when environmentalists performed as sea turtles at the 1999 Seattle protests against the World Trade Organization (WTO) (p. 148). Such suspension of the "real," Bruner argued, enables "a temporary retextualizing of social formations that expose their 'fictive' foundations" (p. 139).

Though not treating resistance as a cultural performance, other scholars have used performance theory to create a more holistic methodology for appreciating acts of resistance beyond their linguistic components. For instance, Feldman's (1991) rich study of the Irish Republic Army (IRA) introduced the notion of a "biosymbolic complex" wherein the human body and its material practices, formations of space, and symbolic narratives intertwine to form a complicated rhetorical palette. Feldman's work with IRA prisoners suggested that the human body itself—not simply the significations that emanate from and surround it in the form of words, clothing, and artifacts—may become a wellspring of resistance.

Similarly, Pezzullo (2003a) foregrounded the display, movements, and disruptions of bodies in her analysis of the San Francisco–based Toxic Links Coalition (TLC) "tour" of agencies and institutions associated with environmental causes of cancer. (TLC is an alliance of women with cancer, cancer survivors, and other health and environmental groups.) By focusing on street performances of participants, Pezzullo attended to "the ways in which the body, affect, and desire disrupt the normative discursive logics of publics" (p. 351, quoting Deem, 2002, p. 448). The assumptions of performativity in work such as Feldman's and Pezzullo's invite critics to explore the rhetorical significance of the body and materiality as these interact with counterpublic narratives or as they stand as rhetorics on their own terms.

Moreover, the nature of some protests themselves has invited rhetorical critics to privilege the non- or extrasymbolic dimensions of protest. DeLuca (1999b), for example, has argued that

radical groups such as Earth First!, ACT UP, and Queer Nation "slight formal modes of public argument" and envision the ends of activism beyond "the conventional goals of electoral, legislative, legal, and material gains" (p. 9). Opel and Pompper's (2003) *Representing Resistance* featured studies of antiglobalization protests that foreground the performative or rhetorical body as a key site of resistance. For example, Vanderford (2003) described the actions of the Italian collective Ya Basta! as it ironically appropriated consumer culture to oppose neoliberal trade ideologies. The group transformed recycled trash and other artifacts such as "rubber duckie" inner tubes into symbolic armor to wear at protests. The appearance of activists standing down armed police, protected only by children's flotation devices, aided the public in understanding "on which side lay reason, and who started the violence" (p. 17). Like Bruner, Vanderford argued that "the laughter of carnival overcomes the seriousness of official culture as grotesque and blasphemous bodies displace reverence and dogmatism" (pp. 17–18).

Importantly, such critics insist that bodies are not, in any simple way, "determined or limited by verbal frames. . . . [They] exceed the protocols of deliberative reasoning" (DeLuca, 1999b, p. 12). Extending this critique to an assumption of earlier theory, DeLuca has argued that our understanding of the body cannot be limited to how it serves certain movement "functions": For instance, to treat bodily spectacles (e.g., Julia "Butterfly" Hill's living in an ancient redwood tree for three years) as simply "getting attention" diminishes the rhetorical power of the body. Alternatively, he proposed that critics understand the effects of "body rhetoric" in new ways. For instance, the body may materialize or challenge a dominant proposition. Protestors also "translate" their bodies into new signs of identification, such as when a tree sitter "'becomes' the tree" (p. 13). Finally, DeLuca argued that embodied presence may be "a direct response" to authority, a "NO" that impedes authority's ability to act with legitimacy (p. 17).

This last interpretation of the body points to an important, but potentially confounding, assumption in recent scholarship on resistance: The human body is both symbolic and extrasymbolic, "enmeshed in a turbulent stream of multiple and conflictual discourses that shape what [it] mean[s] in particular contexts" (DeLuca, 1999b, p. 12) and presenting a "force" that makes it both "a sublime and contested site" (p. 17). Put differently, some critics have assumed that the body both represents strategic, linguistic persuasion and exceeds symbolic action through its bare material presence. In the 1960s, this tension between the body as symbolic and the body as material framed the debates over the "rhetoric of the streets," as rhetorical critics questioned whether Black Power or students' corporeal protest was "coercion" or "persuasion."

As rhetorical critics increasingly focus on the body in resistance, difficult questions remain: Is the *physical presence* of protestors "enough" to count as resistance? If we attempt to assess body rhetoric through the grammar of linguistic signs, do we reduce its corporeal power? Finally, can critics craft a conceptual vocabulary that respects the body as both *physis* and *nomos,* as material and symbolic? Similar questions might also be asked of the growing study of visual rhetorics and of mediated images of resistant bodies.

Image Events, Visual Rhetoric, and Public Screens

Like recent criticism of the body in resistance, studies of visual rhetoric depart from traditional interpretive frameworks in accounting for the impact of visually mediated rhetorics. While the former approaches its object of analysis by foregrounding the human body as it performs in concrete space, recent work in visual rhetoric foregrounds the *mediation* of bodies, in photographs, televised or hyperlinked images of resistance. We acknowledge that this distinction appears somewhat arbitrary; the emphasis, however, partly reflects a rupture in some critics' understanding of contemporary media culture as a basis for understanding the significance of visual resistance. For DeLuca and Peeples (2002), for example, antiglobalization protests in 1999 dramatized a new sociopolitical world in which multinational corporations "eclips[e] the nation-state" and where television screens represent "the contemporary shape of the public sphere" (p. 126).

In this environment, DeLuca and Peeples argued, new conceptual resources become necessary to interpret newer forms of resistance. In particular, the Habermasian concept of the public sphere, grounded in visions of 18th-century salon conversations, privileged face-to-face communication and embodied voices. As a result, they contended, public sphere scholarship "ignores the social and technological transformations of the 20th century" (p. 131). The advent of television and the Internet has "fundamentally transformed the media matrix that constitutes our social milieu, producing new forms of social organization and new modes of perception" (p. 131). New media, for example, flatten hierarchies and rely on "remediation" (the presence of one medium in another), while "disseminating" a distracting amount of information (p. 132).

Given these shifts, critics face new challenges in appreciating contemporary forms of resistance: "TV places a premium on images over words, emotions over rationality, speed over reflection, distraction over deliberation, slogans over arguments, the glance over the gaze, appearance over truth" (p. 133). With the *public screen,* critics are invited to appreciate, rather than dismiss, ways in which a resistant act "both participates in and punctures the habit of distraction characteristic of the contemporary mode of perception" (p. 145). Like the human body that may exceed and interrupt dominant discourses, images of resistance may "interrupt the flow . . . give pause . . . by making the mundane malevolent, the familiar fantastic" (p. 145).

Separately, DeLuca (1999a) has suggested that a particular form of rhetorical logic is gaining currency within the new media milieu, what he terms "image events." Such events work by "reducing a complex set of issues to [visual] symbols that break people's comfortable equilibrium" (p. 3); they are "mind bombs," that, quoting Manes (1990, p. 77), "work to expand 'the universe of thinkable thoughts'" (p. 6). Image events—such as images of Greenpeace activists steering rubber rafts between whaling ships and whales—are typically invented through and with television, privileging the visual over the linguistic, and deconstructive logics over propositional logics. DeLuca noted that, in earlier studies, visually mediated events "have tended not to be recognized as rhetorical acts working for social movement" (p. 58). That, however, is not the case in recent scholarship.

Like performance-oriented criticism of the body in resistance, a number of critics have attempted to account for the extra-linguistic impacts of visual rhetoric within or surrounding the social movement context. For instance, Harold and DeLuca (2005) revisited the "haunting images" of Emmett Till, the black Chicago teenager who was brutally murdered while visiting his uncle in Money, Mississippi, in 1955. The Till case is remembered as a catalyst for the civil rights movement and remains in America's consciousness, in no small part, because of the photographs of Till's corpse and open-casket funeral: "The dissemination and reception of this image—of the severely mutilated face of a child—illustrates the rhetorical and political force of images in general and of the body specifically" (p. 266).

Echoing scholarship on the body, Harold and DeLuca argued that the image of Till's corpse "temporarily provokes a physical response that temporarily precedes and exceeds 'sense'" (p. 275). His corpse and its image provided "graphic testimony to the brutal race hatred in the 1950s South in a way that written text could never have done." (p. 274). It provided a point of articulation for Southern and Northern blacks, and sympathetic whites; the images galvanized a movement. Harold and DeLuca's analysis, we suggest, points to an emerging line of interpretation regarding rhetoric's impact: "We would not suggest that the experience of viewing this body is easily described as an unproblematic *recognition* of one's self (and hence, one's vulnerability) in the corpse, but more of an inability to ignore the witnessing as an event—a rhetorical event that requires a response" (p. 280). In addition to "galvanizing" a movement, the body and its image prompts a form of subjectivity: such rhetoric moves people to witness.

In short, a major trajectory of recent scholarship has begun to explore acts of social protest within a performative context as corporeal, material, and, at times, as mediated resistance. However, we believe that questions remain as

scholars continue this line of research: How do individual acts of resistance, such as image events, relate to movements more broadly, if not through functionalist vocabularies of "requirements" or the reconciling of competing "demands" of the movement? What are the effects of material, corporeal performances and mediated visual rhetoric? Are critics unduly isolating such acts of resistance from their discursive contexts or the "social movement" figure itself?

In an important sense, the relationship of discrete acts to broader movements raises questions more generally about the "possibilities of alternative terrains of practice, power, and politics" that increasingly define the experiences of cultural and mediated life in democracy (Best, 2005, p. 232). And, it is here, we believe, that a final, promising line of SMR scholarship is emerging.

DEMOCRACY, REPRESENTATION, AND NEW MODALITIES OF DISSENT

In addition to recent shifts in methods and the objects of study (e.g., bodies, images), there also has emerged scholarship that is rethinking democracy and the role of "representation" via new modalities of dissent within democracies. Much of the impetus for this scholarship derives from Hardt and Negri's (2000) provocative critique of representation in the altered logics of global society. In their ambitious work *Empire*, they argued the global rise of a post-Fordist economy of "knowledge, information, communication, and affects" (p. 407) is leading to a form of "imperial" sovereignty, which infiltrates and infuses all realms of human life. Within this postmodern milieu, "the economic, political, and cultural increasingly overlap and invest one another" (p. xiii). In their subsequent work, *Multitude,* Hardt and Negri (2004) contend that only nonmodernist forms of resistance, or movements "whose constitution and action is based not on identity or unity" (p. 100), may effectively resist imperial sovereignty.

What implications do Hardt and Negri's theses have for the study of SMR? One that has only begun to be fleshed out, we believe, lies in their claim that resistance does not gain its power from traditional modes of representation —what they sometimes refer to as "mediation"— such as appeals to the nation-state, public sphere, or "identity" (Greene, 2004). Hardt and Negri (2000) propose, alternatively, that a new revolution will begin as the "multitude" (their figure of collective resistance) recovers a kind of *immanence* within *Empire:* "Through the cooperation, the collective existence, and the communicative networks that are formed and reformed within the multitude . . . the multitude reveals labor as the fundamental creative activity that . . . goes beyond any obstacle imposed on it and constantly re-creates the world" (pp. 401–402). Greene (2004) similarly argues that "human innovation and invention" (p. 170), particularly *rhetoric,* powers resistance.

Hardt and Negri's questioning of the "modern legacy of mediation" underwriting traditional ideas of citizenship (Greene, 2004, p. 170) has opened new inquiry into the modalities of social protest occurring in democracies. Neoliberal orderings of democracies, particularly, are viewed as disempowering for citizenship and critical publicity. Institutions such as the World Bank and WTO, for example, seek "not to expand sites of public deliberation, and not to strengthen local democratic processes, but to accelerate the privatization of state-held assets ranging from telecommunications to mining to energy to water" (Bruner, 2003, p. 694). As the relationships among citizens, nation-states, and channels of dissent undergo change, SMR scholars have begun to broaden the scope of their inquiry by exploring alternative theories of democracy and their implications for social change.

At the forefront of such theories have been efforts to understand the move by contemporary protestors away from modes of representation and the traditional mediations of nation, political party, and identity, and towards new channels through which actors organize and speak. These new communication technologies (NCTs) tend to be more experiential, drawing on "everyday" forms and modes of democratic practices. In particular, NCTs work together to form "the base and the basis for" the activism by antiglobalization and other progressive movements (Kahn & Kellner, 2005, p. 88). For example, the digitized worlds of the blogosphere and Internet, as well as

the expanding array of mobile technologies such as cell phones and PDAs (personal data assistants) have helped to globalize local issues, form alliances, coordinate resistant actions, and circulate oppositional discourses (Kahn & Kellner, 2005; Russell, 2005).

Interestingly, as Stengrim (2005) suggests of the international Web network of independent media or "Indymedia," the grassroots use of NCTs performatively resists corporate globalization while it enables activists to dissent. Through "a multiplicity of subversive gestures that promote political activism, forward political critique, and take over the vehicles by which knowledge is produced and transferred" (p. 294), Indymedia challenges a growing, corporate monopoly of global media. Although critics should be wary of viewing NCTs as a panacea of democracy, Kahn and Kellner (2005) suggest that the evolving "technoculture make[s] possible . . . a refocusing of politics on everyday life" (p. 93).

Interestingly, contemporary activists not only employ new modalities to communicate and organize; their uses reflect the loose, hyperlinked, and immanent logics implicit in this networked environment (Pickard, 2006). Antiglobalization activists, for example, rely upon the communicative fabric and logics of hyperlinks: "Networks are open structures, able to expand without limits, integrating new nodes as long as they are able to communicate within the network, namely as long as they share the same communication codes" (Castells, 1996, p. 470; quoted in Pickard, 2006, p. 319). The important difference for SMR scholars is that network structures diverge from the traditional forms of activism that rely on organization and long-lasting relationships (e.g., top-down or "leader-followers" movement structures). Networks ally, instead, with the fractured, fleeting, distracting environment of DeLuca and Peeples's (2002) "public screen."

In addition to rethinking movement organizing and modes of resistance, some SMR scholars are beginning to rethink "democracy." For instance, in considering the "globalization movement," Best (2005) shifts from a reliance on "New Social Movement" theories for evaluating movements. These, she argues, do not necessarily "further the necessary conditions of democracy, especially in relation to their constitution of public life and public space" (p. 215). Instead, she suggests, critics must first understand "the contemporary experiences and practice of democracy," itself (p. 215). Democracy, she proposes, is not so much the constitution of a *sphere*, but an "assemblage of modes of material and discursive organizing designed to grant popular power" (p. 215).

Like Kahn and Kellner, Best (2005) believes a theorization of democracy must begin with the "everyday" practices that make "democracy . . . a way of life" (p. 215, quoting Carey, 1997, p. 233). People increasingly experience democracy through the mediation of NCTs: "Democracy has evolved into an electronic/digital and visceral compound, lived and practiced through individual and collective levels of experience interwoven with mediated resources" (p. 221). Thus, while critics have chastised contemporary movements for failing to "provide for . . . the formation of public space" (p. 223), Best interprets the loosely organized, spectacular protests of the globalization movement as pushing toward democracy-as-practice, rather than democracy-as-space or sphere.

What might these new approaches hold for the study of movement rhetoric? For Best, theories of the everyday and cultural aspects of democracy offer "a map for scrutinizing new routes of power that traverse the daily, individualized, and highly mediated modes of contemporary democratic citizenship, a map [also] for subjecting these pathways of power to more specific and potentially constructive critique and reconstruction" (p. 232). In an important sense, scrutiny of such "new routes of power" invite renewed reflection regarding what constitutes "social movement rhetoric," and what are its relevant agents, modalities, and effects that may be related to social change.

CONTINUING STUDY OF SOCIAL MOVEMENT RHETORIC

In the last four decades, the study of SMR has broadened considerably, both in its modes of analysis and objects of study. The most obvious development has been the steady move from broad or a priori theories of the rhetoric of movements to a "critical pluralism" (Gaonkar, 2002, p. 410) that characterizes public discourse studies more broadly. This move has broadened critics' understanding of complex texts that enable both opponents and supporters of a dominant order to contest or bolster the discursive terms of power. To use Gaonkar's description, rhetorical critics now see the "object domain" of movement or resistance studies—whether a speech to supporters of a bus boycott, dissemination of a photograph, or a street performance—"as immensely rich and complex and almost coextensive with 'discourse' and 'discursivity' that calls for a flexible critical practice" (p. 411).

As SMR study has gained flexibility, the idea of a discrete "social movement" has become somewhat problematic. While not quite abandoning the reference, many critics increasingly are bracketing a focus on large collectivities in favor of specific texts, performative acts, or discursive interventions. In so doing, critics have expanded the field of rhetorical analysis and the conceptual or theoretical categories that inform their understanding of social change. Among the important changes characterizing the study of SMR over the last four decades have been the following:

1. A shift from an emphasis on SMR to the *rhetorical acts* or practices related to movements and their opponents. The distinction speaks to the interest of many critics in reading concrete practices in their own right, rather than as signs of a larger movement's "functions" (e.g., "getting attention").

2. An expanded understanding of the *audience(s)* and/or *objectives* of oppositional rhetorics, recognizing the multiple intentions or constitutive forces at work. Such multiple objectives include not only confronting state institutions or reforming laws, but also challenging discursive norms that themselves sustain dominance. In addition, counterpublic theories have invited attention to the arenas in which marginal groups "invent and circulate counterdiscourses to formulate oppositional interpretations of their [own]

identities, interests, and needs" (Fraser, 1992, p. 123).

3. A rethinking of the concept of *rhetoric* itself, beyond the binary of "reason" versus "coercion" that concerned early SMR scholars. This has led to a wider recognition of the linguistic and *non-* or *extra*linguistic modalities of social protest, including material, bodily, visual, and NCT-mediated rhetorics.

4. An embrace of *plural, critical modes of analysis,* drawing from a wide range of conceptual and theoretical perspectives appropriate to the varied linguistic and extralinguistic forms of dissent.

5. An implicit shift in theorizing the efficacy or *effect* of the rhetorical acts of movements. Because this latter development raises a number of questions for continuing study of movement rhetoric, we return to it below.

We expect the study of SMR will continue to broaden its scope and modes of analysis as groups make use of new communication technologies and other "new routes of power" (Best, 2005). As these studies unfold, we note two challenges for SMR scholars: (1) a more systematic analysis of non-Western movements and perspectives, and (2) an effort to theorize more explicitly the *effects* of social movement or "resistant" rhetorics.

Non-Western Movements and Perspectives

Despite recent interest in "Indymedia" networks and the global justice movement (Best, 2005; Bruner, 2005; Opel & Pompper, 2003; Stengrim, 2005), rhetorical critics have paid slight attention to social movements in other regions of the world. Neither Simons, Mechling, and Schreier's (1984) extensive review of SMR studies nor Morris and Browne's (2006) recently updated collection includes studies of movements in non-Western cultures. The reason may not be hard to discern. Apart from the Chartist and early British peace movements (Andrews, 1967a, 1967b, 1973), the principal focus of SMR critics in the past four decades has been U.S. movements.[4] Similarly, critics have been slow to appreciate non-Western perspectives for the

study of movement discourse. Carabas (2003), for example, noted that rhetorical scholarship on counterpublics "use[s] mostly Western concepts and employ the tools of liberal democracy as the default mode of thinking about the relationship between the state and marginalized communities" (p. 170).[5]

The failure largely to include non-Western case studies and perspectives remains a challenge for the study of SMR. This is particularly relevant in light of controversies surrounding the effects of economic globalization in many Third World nations. For example, Doyle (2005) noted the "profound difference" between U.S. and Philippine environmental movements in his study of resistance in the Philippines against multinational mining companies. The latter, he observed, were "more revolutionary," pursuing radically different strategies of resistance against multinational corporate behaviors (p. 50). Relatedly, Keck and Sikkink (1998) have drawn attention to the emergence of transnational networks of advocates that coordinate their work on human rights, environment, violence against women, and others concerns. Although some communication scholars (Dempsey, 2007; Garrido & Halavais, 2003; Kowal, 2002) have begun to examine this mode, SMR critics—with the exception of antiglobalization networks—have largely ignored such alliances.

Theorizing "Effect" in SMR Studies

Social movements arise ostensibly to affect change—whether to reform unjust laws, throw off an oppressive regime, or rewrite discursive or normative practices. It was inevitable, therefore, that SMR critics would face questions of *efficacy:* How do the rhetorical acts of movements "matter"? In some ways, however, the question of efficacy remains the white elephant in the room as scholars often ignore the conceptual ambiguities in the vocabulary and categories for assessing the consequential nature of movement and, particularly, "resistant" rhetoric. As a result, a number of questions remain: In what ways are the linguistic and extralinguistic acts of activists related to changes (if any) in law, policy, prevailing discourses, activists' identities, or interests? If historical events are overdetermined or the result of multiple and complex causes, can SMR scholars speak intelligibly about "effects" at all? What are the conceptual or theoretical challenges in specifying *rhetorical* effects, instead of external policy or historical effects?

Early SMR scholars seldom raised questions about the conceptual bases for an assessment of "effects." For example, Griffin (1952) set the tone when he invited critics to evaluate the "effectiveness" of a movement's rhetoric simply in terms of "the ends projected by the speakers and writers" and "the theories of rhetoric and public opinion indigenous to the times" (p. 187). In a similar vein, Simons (1970) proposed that the "primary rhetorical test" of a leader and of the strategies chosen was their ability to fulfill the movement's "functional requirements" by resolving or reducing the dilemmas or conflicts among these functions (p. 2).

Early assessments of effect assumed a *strategic* context in which movements or their leaders were seen as achieving or failing to achieve state or other institutional outcomes (civil rights legislation, campus reform, etc.). Yet few, if any, critics provided an account of how rhetorical acts or utterances were articulated to these external events. In their survey of rhetorical studies of movements from 1968 to 1977, Simons et al. (1984) found that although these studies "had little difficulty pronouncing judgments of success or failure, they did not always indicate clearly what they meant by these terms" (p. 845). Perhaps recognizing the complex processes in such outcomes, they observed that "the rhetoric of social movements may sometimes be a necessary condition for social change, but it is never a sufficient condition" (p. 836).

By the 1990s and early 2000s, critics had largely abandoned broad claims about the "effects" of a movement's rhetoric. Instead, SMR critics turned to descriptions of "resistance" or characterized particular discursive acts or performances as "resistant," "destabilizing," "transgressive," or some other attribute. DeLuca (1999b), for example, noted that, within the context of homophobia, "by their very presence at a protest the [gay rights] activists are enacting a defiant rhetoric of resistance" (p. 17). And, in describing street performances protesting a festival's honoring of Andrew Jackson, Schriver and Nudd (2002) explained: "By infiltrating the parade we hoped to destabilize the spectacle of whitewashed history" (p. 213). Although long

a theme in cultural theory and media studies (Scott, 1990; Williams, 1977), references to "resistance" and its variants now began to appear in rhetorical and performative accounts of movements (Houston & Kramarae, 1991; Jordan, 2003; Kennedy, 1999; Opel & Pompper, 2003; Sanger, 1995). While this move may promise a more nuanced understanding, few critics have offered an account of actual processes of influence of a "resistant" act. Among the more promising, we believe, is Harold and DeLuca's (2005) account of the "rhetorical force" occasioned by the dissemination and reception of the images of the mutilated corpse of Emmett Till (see above).

Nevertheless, the move to describe oppositional acts or texts as "resistant" or "destabilizing" assumes a theory of effectivity still largely absent from SMR scholarship. As a result, key questions remain for critics: How is "resistance" related to power? In praising "resistant acts" are SMR critics "'settling' for cultural raids" (Cloud, 2001, p. 244) while larger systems of dominance remain in place? In what ways are acts of "resistance" articulated to wider discursive codes and/or changes in material or political conditions?

Conclusion

As we have seen in this chapter, the scholarship of SMR has developed into a diverse, critically flexible literature driven by the (often) unorthodox voices of social change. As such, SMR scholars have pushed the understanding of rhetoric and public discourse beyond its rational, propositional, and linguistic roots. Through their analyses, rhetoric and public discourse scholars have developed the vocabularies and critical methods offering students and other scholars a means to understand some of the relevant sources of social change. These approaches have shifted the critic's focus from discrete social movement figures to discursive fields (see Wilson, 2005) and arenas (e.g., counterpublics), diverse channels of mediation (e.g., the body, visual images, and NCTs), and performances of democracy in and through which social change occurs. In the end, we believe, a robust theory of the efficacy or impact of rhetorical acts in oppositional struggles holds the greatest promise for continued development and contribution of SMR scholarship. For beyond simple accounts of "resistance" lies the possibility of understanding the relationships among discursive acts, power, and the sources of social and political transformation.

Notes

[1] See the special issues devoted to rhetorical analyses of Dr. King's "Letter" from Birmingham jail (*Rhetoric & Public Affairs, 7*(1), 2004) and the 50th anniversary of the murder of Emmett Till and Rosa Parks' refusal to give up her seat on a Montgomery bus (*Rhetoric & Public Affairs, 8*(2), 2005).

[2] Despite the heuristic of Fraser's observation and rise of new struggles around gender, race, sexuality, and other concerns of "recognition," the claim that such movements were "merely cultural," not having economic or material implications, drew sharp criticism, most notably from Judith Butler (1997) (for a response, see Fraser, 1997).

[3] Some rhetorical scholars had called attention earlier to the discursive achievement of marginal groups in articulating their own interests or identities. See, particularly, Gregg's (1971) thesis of an "ego-function" of protest rhetorics, and Lake's (1983, 1991) studies of the "ritual self-address" of Native American rhetorics.

[4] Notable exceptions include Doxtader's (2001) analysis of the civil and theological uses of "reconciliation" as forms of resistance against apartheid in South Africa; Fabj's (1993, 1998) studies of the defiance of Italian women against the Mafia and the rhetoric of the Mothers of Plaza De Mayo, in Buenos Aires, Argentina; and Cloud's (2001) thesis that the economy and nation state remain as important sites of struggle in the 1998 revolt in Indonesia.

[5] One important exception is the study of ethnic protests within the U.S. that draw on rhetorical traditions reflecting the cultural or national heritage of these groups (Dicochea, 2004; Hammerback, Jensen, & Gutiérrez, 1985; Lake, 1983, 1991; Wong, 1992). For example, Hammerback and Jensen (1994) draw on traditions of the "proclamation" in Mexican social upheavals to assess Chicano protests and organizing by farm workers in the U.S. in the 1960s and 1970s.

References

Andrews, J. R. (1967a). The ethos of pacifism: The problem of image in the British peace movement. *Quarterly Journal of Speech, 53*, 28–33.

Andrews, J. R. (1967b). Piety and pragmatism: Rhetorical aspects of the early British peace movement. *Communication Monographs, 34*, 423–436.

Andrews, J. R. (1969). Confrontation at Columbia: A case study in coercive rhetoric. *Quarterly Journal of Speech, 55*, 9–16.

Andrews, J. R. (1973). The passionate negation: The chartist movement in rhetorical perspective. *Quarterly Journal of Speech, 59*, 198–208.

Andrews, J. R. (1980). History and theory in the study of the rhetoric of social movements. *Central States Speech Journal, 31*, 274–281.

Asen, R. (2000). Seeking the "counter" in counterpublics. *Communication Theory, 10*, 424–446.

Asen, R., & Brouwer, D. C. (2001). *Counterpublics and the state.* Albany: State University of New York Press.

Best, K. (2005). Rethinking the globalization movement: Toward a cultural theory of contemporary democracy and communication. *Communication and Critical/Cultural Studies, 2*, 214–237.

Blair, C., Jeppeson, M. S., & Pucci, E., Jr. (1991). Public memorializing in postmodernity: The Vietnam Veterans Memorial as prototype. *Quarterly Journal of Speech, 77*, 263–288.

Brouwer, D. C. (2001). ACT-ing UP in congressional hearings. In R. Asen & D. C. Brouwer (eds.), *Counterpublics and the state* (pp. 87–109). Albany: State University of New York Press.

Brouwer, D. C. (2005). Counterpublicity and corporeality in HIV/AIDS zines. *Critical Studies in Media Communication, 22*, 351–371.

Brouwer, D. C. (2006). Communication as counterpublic. In G. J. Shepherd, J. St. John, & T. Striphas (Eds.), *Communication as . . . Perspectives on theory* (pp. 195–208). Thousand Oaks, CA: Sage.

Bruner, M. L. (2003). Global governance and the critical public. *Rhetoric & Public Affairs, 6*, 687–708.

Bruner, M. L. (2005). Carnivalesque protest and the humorless state. *Text and Performance Quarterly, 25*, 136–155.

Burgess, P. G. (1968). The rhetoric of black power: A moral demand? *Quarterly Journal of Speech, 54*, 122–133.

Burgess, P. G. (1970). The rhetoric of moral conflict: Two critical dimensions. *Quarterly Journal of Speech, 56*, 120–130.

Butler, J. (1990). *Gender trouble: Feminism and the subversion of identity.* New York: Routledge.

Butler, J. (1997). Merely cultural. *Social Text, 52–53*, 265–277.

Campbell, K. K. (1973). The Rhetoric of Women's Liberation: An Oxymoron. *Quarterly Journal of Speech 59*, 74–86.

Carabas, T. (2003). Review of *Counterpublics and the state*. *Southern Communication Journal, 68*, 169–170.

Castells, M. (1996). *The rise of network society.* Malden, MA: Blackwell.

Cathcart, R. S. (1972). New approaches to the study of movements: Defining movements rhetorically. *Western Speech, 36*, 82–88.

Cathcart, R. S. (1978). Movements: Confrontation as rhetorical form. *Southern Speech Communication Journal, 43*, 233–247.

Ceccarelli, L. (1998). Polysemy: Multiple meanings in rhetorical criticism. *Quarterly Journal of Speech, 84*, 395–406.

Cloud, D. L. (2001). Doing away with Suharto—and the twin myths of globalization and new social movements. In R. Asen & D. C. Brouwer (eds.), *Counterpublics and the state* (pp. 235–263). Albany: State University of New York Press.

Cohen-Cruz, J. (Ed.). (1998). *Radical street performance: An international anthology.* London: Routledge.

Darsey, J. (1991). From "Gay is good" to the scourge of AIDS: The evolution of gay liberation rhetoric, 1977–1990. *Communication Studies, 42*, 43–66.

Deem, M. (2002). Stranger sociability, public hope, and the limits of political transformation. *Quarterly Journal of Speech, 88*, pp. 444–454.

DeLuca, K. M. (1999a). *Image politics: The new rhetoric of environmental activism.* New York: Guilford Press.

DeLuca, K. M. (1999b, Summer). Unruly arguments: The body rhetoric of Earth First!, Act Up, and Queer Nation. *Argumentation and Advocacy, 36*, 9–21.

DeLuca, K. M., & Peeples, J. (2002). From public sphere to public screen: Democracy, activism, and the "violence" of Seattle. *Critical Studies in Media Communication, 19(2)*, 125–151.

Dempsey, S. E. (2007). Towards a critical organizational approach to civil society contexts: A case study of the difficulties of transnational advocacy. In B. J. Allen, L. A. Flores, & M. P. Orbe (Eds.), *The international and intercultural communication annual: Communicating within/across organizations* (Vol. 30, pp. 317–339). Washington, DC: National Communication Association.

Dicochea, P. R. (2004). Chicana critical rhetoric: Recrafting *la causa* in Chicana movement discourse, 1970–1979. *Frontiers: A Journal of Women Studies, 25*, pp. 77–92.

Doxtader, E. (2001). In the name of reconciliation: The faith and works of counterpublicity. In R. Asen and D. C. Brouwer (eds.), *Counterpublics and the state* (pp. 59–85). Albany: State University of New York Press.

Doyle, T. (2005). *Environmental movements in majority and minority worlds.* New Brunswick, NJ: Rutgers University Press.

Fabj, V. (1993). Motherhood as political voice: The rhetoric of the mothers of Plaza De Mayo. *Communication Studies, 44*, 1–18.

Fabj, V. (1998). Intolerance, forgiveness, and promise in the rhetoric of conversion: Italian women defy the Mafia. *Quarterly Journal of Speech, 84*, 190–208.

Feldman, A. (1991). *Formations of violence. The narrative of the body and political terror in Northern Ireland.* Chicago: University of Chicago Press.

Felski, R. (1989). *Beyond feminist aesthetics: Feminist literature and social change.* Cambridge: Harvard University Press.

Fraser, N. (1992). Rethinking the public sphere: A contribution to the critique of actually existing democracy. In C. Calhoun (Ed.), *Habermas and the public sphere* (pp. 109–142). Cambridge: MIT Press.

Fraser, N. (1997a). Heterosexism, misrecognition, and capitalism: A response to Judith Butler. *Social Text, 52/53*, 279–289.

Fraser, N. (1997b). *Justice interruptus: Critical reflections on the "post-socialist" condition.* New York: Routledge.

Fuoss, K. (1997). *Striking performances/Performing strikes.* Jackson: University Press of Mississippi.

Gaonkar, D. P. (2002). Introduction [The Forum: Public and counterpublics]. *Quarterly Journal of Speech, 88*, 410–412.

Garrido, M., & Halavais, A. (2003). Mapping networks of support for the Zapatista movement: Applying social network analysis to study contemporary social movements. In M. McCaughey & M. Ayers (Eds.), *Cyberactivism: Critical practices and theories of online activism* (pp. 165–184). New York: Routledge.

Greene, R. (2004). The concept of global citizenship in Michael Hardt and Antonio Negri's Empire: A challenge to three ideas of rhetorical mediation. In G. A. Hauser & A. Grim (Eds.), *Rhetorical democracy: Discursive practices of civic engagement* (pp. 165–171). Mahwah, NJ: Lawrence Erlbaum.

Gregg, R. B. (1971). The ego-function of the rhetoric of protest. *Philosophy and Rhetoric, 4*, 71–91.

Griffin, L. M. (1952). The rhetoric of historical movements. *Quarterly Journal of Speech, 38*, 184–188.

Griffin, L. M. (1969). A dramatistic theory of the Rhetoric of movements. In W. H. Rueckert (Ed.),

Critical responses to Kenneth Burke, 1922–1966 (pp. 456–478). Minneapolis: University of Minnesota Press.

Griffin, L. M. (1980). On studying movements. *Central States Speech Journal, 31,* 225–232.

Habermas, J. (1981). New social movements. *Telos,* 94, 33–37.

Habermas, J. (1989). *The structural transformation of the public sphere* (T. Burger, Trans.). Cambridge, MA: MIT Press. (Original work published 1962)

Haedicke, S. C., & Nellhaus, T. (Eds.). (2001). *Performing democracy: International perspectives on urban community-based performance.* Ann Arbor, MI: University of Michigan Press.

Hahn, D. F., & Gonchar, R. M. (1971). Studying social movements: A rhetorical methodology. *Speech Teacher, 20*(1), 44–52.

Haiman, F. S. (1967). The rhetoric of the streets: Some legal and ethical considerations. *Quarterly Journal of Speech, 53,* 99–114.

Hammerback, J. C., & Jensen, R. J. (1994). Ethnic heritage as rhetorical legacy: The plan of Delano. *Quarterly Journal of Speech, 80,* 53–70.

Hammerback, J. C., Jensen, R. J., & Gutiérrez, J. A. (1985). *A war of words: Chicano protest of the 1960s and 1970s.* Westport, CT: Greenwood Press.

Hardt, M., & Negri, A. (2000). *Empire.* Cambridge, MA: Harvard University Press.

Hardt, M. & Negri, A. (2004). *Multitude: War and democracy in the age of empire.* New York: Penguin.

Harold, C., & DeLuca, K. M. (2005). Behold the corpse: Violent images and the case of Emmett Till. *Rhetoric & Public Affairs, 8,* 263–286.

Hawhee, D. (2004). *Bodily arts: Rhetoric and athletics in ancient Greece.* Austin: University of Texas Press.

Henry, D., & Jensen, R. J. (1991). Social movement criticism and the renaissance of public address. *Communication Studies, 42,* 83–93.

Houston, M., & Kramarae, C. (1991). Speaking from silence: Methods of silencing and of resistance. *Discourse and Society, 2,* 387–399.

Jordan, J. W. (2003). Sabotage or performed compliance? Rhetorics of resistance in temp worker discourse. *Quarterly Journal of Speech, 89,* 19–40.

Kahn, R., & Kellner, D. (2005). Oppositional politics and the internet: A critical/reconstructive approach. *Cultural Politics: An International Journal, 1,* 75–100.

Keck, M. E., & Sikkink, K. (1998). *Activists beyond borders: Advocacy networks in international politics.* Ithaca, NY: Cornell University Press.

Kennedy, K. (1999). Cynic rhetoric: The ethics and tactics of resistance. *Rhetoric Review, 18,* 26–45.

Kershaw, B. (1999). *The radical in performance: Between Brecht and Baudrillard.* London: Routledge.

Kowal, D. (2002). Digitizing and globalizing indigenous voices: The Zapatista movement. In G. Elmer (Ed.), *Critical Perspectives on the Internet* (pp. 105–126). Lanham, MD: Rowman Littlefield.

Lake, R. A. (1983). Enacting red power: The consummatory function in Native American protest rhetoric. *Quarterly Journal of Speech, 69,* 127–142.

Lake, R. A. (1991). Between myth and history: Enacting time in Native American protest rhetoric. *Quarterly Journal of Speech, 77,* 123–151.

Landes, J. (1988). *Women and the public sphere in the age of the French revolution.* Ithaca, NY: Cornell University Press.

Lucas, S. E. (1980). Coming to terms with movement studies. *Central States Communication Journal, 31,* 255–266.

Lucas, S. E. (1988). The renaissance of American public address: Text and context in rhetorical criticism. *Quarterly Journal of Speech, 75,* 241–260.

Maddux, K. (2004). When patriots protest: The anti-suffrage discursive transformation of 1917. *Rhetoric & Public Affairs, 7,* 283–310.

Manes, C. (1990). *Green rage: Radical environmentalism, and the unmaking of civilization.* Boston: Little, Brown.

Mansbridge, J. (1996). Using power/fighting power. In S. Benhabib (Ed.), *Democracy and difference: Contesting the boundaries of the political* (pp. 46–66). Princeton, N.J.: Princeton University Press.

McCarthy, J. D., & Zald, M. (1977). Resource mobilization and social movements: A partial theory. *American Journal of Sociology, 82,* 1212–1241.

McDorman, T. F. (2001). Crafting a virtual counterpublic: Right-to-die advocates on the Internet. In R. Asen & D. C. Brouwer (eds.), *Counterpublics and the state* (pp. 187–209). Albany: State University of New York Press.

McGee, M. C. (1980). "Social movement": Phenomenon or meaning? *Central States Speech Journal, 31,* 233–244.

McGee, M. C. (1983). Social movement as meaning. *Central States Speech Journal, 34,* 74–77.

Melucci, A. 1985. The symbolic challenge of contemporary movements. *Social Research 52,* 789–815.

Morris, C. E., III, & Browne, S. H. (2006). *Readings on the rhetoric of social protest* (2nd ed.). State College, PA: Strata.

Negt, O., & Kluge, A. (1993). *Public sphere and experience: Towards analysis of the bourgeois and proletarian public sphere* (P. Labanyi, J. O. Daniel, & A. Oksiloff, Trans.). Minnesota: University of Minnesota Press. (Original work published 1972)

Offe, C. (1985). New social movements: Challenging the boundaries of institutional politics. *Social Research, 52,* 817–868.

Opel, A., & Pompper, D. (Eds.). (2003). *Representing resistance: Media, civil disobedience, and the global justice movement.* Westport, CT: Praeger.

Palczewski, C. H. (2001). Cyber-movements, new social movements, and counter-publics. In D. Brouwer & R. Asen (Eds.), *Counterpublics and the state* (pp. 161–186. New York: State University of New York Press.

Pezzullo, P. C. (2003a). Resisting "National Breast Cancer Awareness Month": The rhetoric of counterpublics and their cultural performances. *Quarterly Journal of Speech, 89,* 345–365.

Pezzullo, P. C. (2003b). Touring "cancer alley," Louisiana: Performances of community and memory for environmental justice. *Text and Performance Quarterly, 23,* 226–252.

Pickard, V. W. (2006). United yet autonomous: Indymedia and the struggle to sustain a radical democratic network. *Media, Culture, & Society, 28,* 315–336.

Russell, A. (2005). Myth and the Zapatista movement: Exploring a network identity. *New Media & Society, 17,* 559–577.

Sanger, K. L. (1995). Slave resistance and rhetorical self-definition: Spirituals as a strategy. *Western Journal of Communication, 59,* 177–192.

Schriver, K., & Nudd, D. M. (2002). Mickee Faust Club's performative protest events. *Text & Performance Quarterly, 22,* pp. 196–216.

Scott, J. C. (1990). *Domination and the acts of resistance: Hidden transcripts.* New Haven, CT: Yale University Press.

Scott, R. L., & Smith, D. K. (1969). The rhetoric of confrontation. *Quarterly Journal of Speech, 55,* 1–8.

Sillars, M. O. (1980). Defining movements rhetorically: Casting the widest net. *Southern Speech Communication Journal, 46,* 17–32.

Simons, H. W. (1970). Requirements, problems, and strategies: A theory of persuasion for social movements. *Quarterly Journal of Speech, 56,* 1–11.

Simons, H. W. (1980). On terms, definitions, and theoretical distinctiveness: Comments on papers by McGee and Zarefsky. *Central States Speech Journal, 31,* 306–315.

Simons, H. W., Mechling, E. W., & Schreier, H. N. (1984). The functions of human communication in mobilizing for action from the bottom up: The rhetoric of social movements. In C. C. Arnold

& J. W. Bowers (Eds.), *Handbook of rhetoric and communication theory* (pp. 792–867). Boston: Allyn and Bacon.

Smith, R. R., & Windes, R. R. (1975). The innovational movement: A rhetorical theory. *Quarterly Journal of Speech, 61,* 140–153.

Squires, C. (2001). The black press and the state. In R. Asen & D. C. Brouwer (Eds.), *Counterpublics and the state* (pp. 111–136). Albany: State University of New York Press.

Stengrim, L. A. (2005). Negotiating postmodern democracy, political activism, and knowledge production: Indymedia's grassroots and e-savvy answer to media oligopoly. *Communication and Critical/Cultural Studies, 2,* 281–304.

Stewart, C. J. (1980). A functional approach to the rhetoric of social movements. *Central States Speech Journal, 31,* 298–305.

Stewart, C. J. (1983). A functional perspective on the study of social movements. *Central States Speech Journal, 34,* 77–80.

Vanderford, A. (2003). Ya Basta!—A mountain of bodies that advances, seeking the least harm possible to itself. In A. Opel & D. Pompper (Eds.), *Representing resistance: Media, civil disobedience, and the global justice movement* (pp. 16–26). Westport, CT: Praeger.

Warner, M. (2002a). *Publics and Counterpublics.* New York: Zone Books.

Warner, M. (2002b). Publics and counterpublics (abbreviated version). *Quarterly Journal of Speech, 88,* 413–425.

Wilkinson, C. A. (1976). A rhetorical definition of movements. *Central States Speech Journal, 27,* 88–94.

Williams, R. (1977). *Marxism and literature.* Oxford, UK: Oxford University Press.

Wilson, K. H. (2005). Interpreting the discursive field of the Montgomery bus boycott: Martin Luther King Jr.'s Holt Street address. *Rhetoric & Public Affairs, 8,* 299–326.

Windt, T. O., Jr. (1972). The diatribe: Last resort for protest. *Quarterly Journal of Speech, 72,* 1–14.

Wong, K. (1992). A fitting rhetorical response: Asian American social protest of the 1960s and 1970s. In J. C. Hammerback & P. M. Fitts (Eds.), *Conference in rhetorical criticism, 1990–1991: Addresses of the conference and commended papers* (pp. 12–19). Hayward, CA: California State University.

Zarefsky, D. (1990). A skeptical view of movement studies. *Central States Speech Journal, 31,* 245–254.

Chapter 2

Competing Perspectives

The essays in the previous chapter represent some of the most original, forceful, and influential statements on social protest and movements. Most of them were published during a period of considerable ferment within and outside the academy. It should come as no surprise, then, that theirs were hardly the last words on the subject. For all their rich yield, movement studies by the 1980s were coming under increasing scrutiny. Some of their influential expression comprises this volume's second chapter.

In 1980, leading scholars published a set of essays in a special issue of *The Central States Speech Journal*. Their aim was to address the issues they considered most significant to the prospects of movement studies. Among the most pointed critiques is Michael Calvin McGee's essay, "'Social Movement': Phenomenon or Meaning?" McGee argues that rhetorical critics were operating under confused assumptions about the very nature of their subject. Do movements exist objectively in the world (as "phenomena"), he asks, or are they really subjective ascriptions about human activity measurable only by changes in discourse formations ("meaning")? McGee is very clear about his own position: "the whole notion of 'movement,'" he contends, "is mythical, a trick-of-the-mind which must be understood *as an illusion* and not as a fact."

Where McGee looked to further theoretical work as a way of advancing movement studies, several members of the special symposium argued that such studies are best conceptualized as historical inquiry. In "A Skeptical View of Movement Studies," for example, David Zarefsky suggests that rhetorical movements did not constitute a unique domain of collective action, nor was there anything inherently rhetorical about all movements. Rather, Zarefsky notes, "history has many dimensions," and "like

other phenomena, a historical movement can be studied from different points of view; the rhetorical historian complements the efforts of other scholars who examine the political dimensions, or the economic, or the cultural." Movement studies that stress the rhetorical dimensions of such activity, he claims, are best undertaken as "fundamentally a contribution to history."

A good deal of effort over the past several decades had been devoted to conceptualizing the nature, scope, and function of rhetorical movements. Certainly there was justification for some of this work, but for some scholars it came at the cost of more grounded exploration of actual instances of social protest. In "Coming to Terms with Movement Studies," a sharply reasoned rebuttal of McGee's position, Stephen E. Lucas argues that the disjunctions drawn between movements as "phenomena" or "meaning" are unfounded, the result of excessive theorizing and not enough historical labor. "What we need," Lucas insists, "is less controversy about definitions, orientations, and presuppositions and more research." This research will prove more useful, he notes, to the extent that it charts changes in discourse that respond to shifting situational demands and asks why movements unfold as they do.

Like Zarefsky and Lucas, James R. Andrews sees the future of movement studies as an essentially historical enterprise. In "History and Theory in the Study of the Rhetoric of Social Movements," he argues that the tendency to theorize too readily from particular cases encourages students to reason from unwarranted presuppositions and to make ungrounded generalizations about the necessarily particular features of these cases. Consistent with his stress on specific historical phenomena, Andrews offers a brief case study of the English radical "Orator" Hunt as a way of demonstrating his argument. "The rhetorical historian's independence of theory," he suggests, "must come through his or her willingness to examine the process of rhetorical influence without preconceived theoretical notions of how that process must have worked in particular cases."

But is it not possible to theorize reasonably about the nature of rhetorical movements as such? Are there not, as Simons argues above, distinctive features that seem to characterize movements across individual cases? While Zarefsky, Lucas, and Andrews limit theoretical generalizations to a certain circumscribed role, they also emphasize the need to study movements as rooted in their distinctive matrix of rhetorical, situational, and cultural

possibilities. By contrast, in "A Functional Approach to the Rhetoric of Social Movements," Charles J. Stewart argues that we stress such specifics at our peril and thus lose sight of the macroscopic dimensions of rhetorical movements. Stewart offers, as a corrective, a "functional" approach that "views rhetoric not as art, artifact, or the manipulation of techniques for specific effects but as the agency through which social movements perform essential functions." Far from being merely isolated, singular phenomena, he explains, movements may be generally studied by the functions they employ, including the ways in which they transform perceptions of history and society, prescribe and mobilize action, and work to sustain themselves.

"Social Movement": Phenomenon or Meaning?
Michael Calvin McGee

The problem before me is determining whether or not the rhetoric of social movements constitutes a distinctive theoretical domain. I want to say "of course," but I cannot: Like dramaturgists with the concept "script," and psychohistorians with the concept "fantasy," social theorists have failed to shoulder the burden of defending the empirical relevance and/or utility of one of their most basic concepts, "social movement."[1] Since I would not like being read as arguing definitions, as many do, I intend to demonstrate that when I say "Social movement is a set of meanings and not a phenomenon," my reference is to a significant error of conceptualization. I believe that the rhetoric of social movements may become a distinctive theoretical domain, but only as a theory of human consciousness. The second part of this essay is an elaboration of that conviction.

I

As I understand the process of theory-building, if it is to achieve the status "theory," any prose must reliably describe, explain, and predict something directly or inferentially in human experience.[2] There is no doubt that "social movement(s)" exist in human experience, but there is serious disagreement about *how* they exist.[3] The critical problem for theorists is determining whether "social movement" is *directly* or *inferentially* in human experience. If a thing is directly in experience, it is a "phenomenon"; if it is inferentially in experience, it is an interpretation, a "set of meanings."

Descriptions, explanations, and predictions of phenomena are theories of *things* "out there" which present themselves equally to all human beings. In the social world, then, institutions and organizations such as the U.S. Congress and Standard Oil Corporation are phenomena present to each of us regardless of our political views or personal experience with them. Descriptions, explanations, and predictions of meaning, on the other hand, are theories of *consciousness*, of human agreements as to the significance, salience, utility and morality of phenomena. Thus, in the social world, policies and ideologies such as "containment" and "imperialism" are sets of meanings inferentially held by the whole or a significant part of society.

Theories of things, of course, can take consciousness into account, and theories of consciousness can explain the rise, fall or persistence of phenomena. For example, Whyte's classic study of American business organizations suggests convincingly that the reward system forces human beings to display the signs of a particular consciousness, whereas Horkheimer's equally classic study of "authority" shows persuasively that interactions in the nuclear family explain the emergence of totalitarian states and institutions.[4] The problem is not connecting phenomena and meanings, therefore, but rather deciding which explains what.

If I witness the phenomenon "man speaking," and if I am curious about the content of what is being said, a conceptual choice between at least two alternatives[5] looms before me: (a) I can decide that the phenomenon "comes first" and say that "speaking" and "content" are properties, components, or manifestations of the whole phenomenon. I hear "man speaking" claiming to be "reasonable," and I agree that what I hear is "reasonable." I am not thus far in error, but if I go further in regarding a *quality* of "speaking" ("reasonable") as if it were a property of the phenomenon itself ("reason"), I have made a mistake. I have rediscovered a formally correct but empirically irrelevant 18th-century notion, "faculty psychology."[6] (b) On the other hand, I can decide that sets of meanings "come first" and argue that "speaking" and "content" are signifiers, articulation, or material manifestations of a particular consciousness which I recognize as more or less common. I hear "man speaking" claim that "Standard Oil is a cancer on American democracy" and interpret the words as indicating that "man speaking" does not like "Standard Oil" and that, in his view, policies toward "Standard Oil" should function much as treatments for a deadly disease function. Again, I am not thus far in error, but if I go further and view a phenomenon ("Standard Oil") as if it necessarily implied one specific set of meanings (one's policy toward things metaphorically regarded as "cancerous"), I have made a fundamental mistake reciprocating

the error which produced faculty psychology.[7] The error in both cases is that I have confused phenomena and interpretations.

Most writers on the subject, particularly those working under the influence of American empirical sociology, treat social movements as if they were phenomenal. Smelser, for example, chooses the term "collective behavior" as a synthesis of "collective outbursts" (panics, crazes, and hostile outbursts) and "collective movements" (a collective effort to modify norms and values). Having suggested that perceptions of collective behavior are "spontaneous and fickle," that episodes of collective behavior "cannot be controlled experimentally," and that case studies of collective behavior cannot be demonstrated to be typical, he asks the question, "To what kinds of phenomena does this term refer?" Smelser has, in my judgment, answered his question before he begins. "Collective behavior," as he uses the term, cannot possibly refer to phenomena; rather, his disclaimers suggest that if we have a subject of study at all, it is *meaning*. Yet Smelser continues by associating collective behavior with particular situations which are "determinants" of belief and attitude. Specifically refusing materialist, symbolist, and psychological descriptions of the human consciousness, Smelser proceeds to identify the phenomenal situation in which collective behavior occurs with the collective behavior itself. By the time he has identified "movements," he seems to be talking strictly about political organizations and assumes that there is a correspondence between one's membership in an organization and one's universe of attitudes and beliefs.[8]

In communication studies, too, "social movements" are treated as phenomenal. Indeed, Simons has suggested that there is now a "near consensus" as to the identity of "movement," that "social movement" is now part of "conventional scholarly parlance," and that securing paradigmatic agreement as to "conceptual geography" is no longer a problem. Simons' "near consensus" appears to be an agreement that differences in the usage of "movement" reflect differences in "disciplinary perspective rather than differences in the phenomena." In the mold of American empirical sociology, Simons objectivates "social movement" by giving the alleged phenomenon an almost organic presence: "Any student of movements must come to grips with the mix of elements that comprise movements of whatever sort: *their* structural and functional characteristics; *their* origins in society and culture; *their* evolution over time; the resources *they* mobilize and deploy; the power wielded against *them;* the ideas that *animate them;* the symbolic acts and artifacts that embody those ideas; and the intended and unintended effects that movements produce" (italics mine). So clear is Simons' treatment of "social movements" as if "they" were phenomena that he consistently commits the pathetic fallacy and comes dangerously close to the organic metaphor Nisbet so roundly condemns.[9]

"Social movement(s)" are not phenomena *as a matter of fact,* and creating a theory from such a conception is to create the sociological or rhetorical equivalent of "faculty psychology." In one sense, developing this argument is easy, for all that need be demonstrated is the widely-recognized ambiguity of the alleged phenomenon we are to call "movement(s)."[10] If I speak of "Civil Rights Movement," "Labor Movement," or "Feminist Movement," I am referring either to a series of behaviors or to a political organization which I could designate in several ways. Thus, when I see angry picketers blocking the entrance to a factory, I might conceptualize my experience with the agency of one or another of the following signifiers, each with its own nuance: (a) "campaign," (b) "agitation," (c) "rebellion," (d) "organization," (e) "cabal," (f) "revolution," (g) "protest," (h) "sociopathic outburst," (i) "demonstration," (j) "alienation," (k) "petitioning for redress of grievances," (l) "symbolic action and/ or transcendence," (m) "instrumental behavior," (n) "subversion," (o) "industrial sabotage," or (p) "social movement." Each choice represents an attitudinal/stylistic alternative with the power to express an individuated ordering of social reality and to dictate the nature of any generalization I might subsequently offer. Each term, in other words, is a *meaning*, a conclusion one comes to about the phenomenon being witnessed. Of course, one is not only entitled to such conclusions, but also generally encouraged to seek them. No error is involved in seeing a parade of picketers as a "social movement." The mistake is

treating the meaning as if it were itself a phenomenon: The objective, empirical phenome[n]on of human beings angrily parading in front of a fence stays the same despite my choice of one term or another to characterize and conceptualize it. When I operate as a theorist by fiat of definition, therefore, insisting that there are "determinants" or "defining characteristics" which make the phenomenal episode "social movement" and nothing else, I am either politicizing my theory or imputing motives to human actors by fiat of definition only. In the first case, I would accept the claim of human actors that their activity is a "social movement," and that claim might not be theoretically motivated, but merely a ploy to gain power by controlling the perceptions of potential adherents and opponents. In the other case, I would consider the claims, or lack of claims, of social actors irrelevant. I would infer "determinants" or "defining characteristics" from the episode which make my meaning seem to characterize and motivate participating social actors. Neither tactic is, in my judgment, theoretically justifiable. "Movements" are not phenomena, nor does the concept "movement" explain a phenomenon empirically; rather, "movement" is an analogue comparing the flow of social facts to physical movement. It is an interpretation of phenomenal data controlled less by what happens in the real world than by what a particular user of the analogue wants to see in the real world. If I were to distinguish "social movement(s)" from the other sixteen interpretive alternatives listed above, I would say on the basis of our experience with major "movements" of this century—communism, fascism, unionism, and egalitarianism—that the term "social movement(s)" causes us to order social and historical facts such that we can maintain the illusion of "morality," "purpose," and "destiny" in largely self-aggrandizing collective behavior.[11]

My conclusion, of course, depends on recognizing that "movement" is neither a neolog nor a univocal neutral term. That is, I presume that consciousness of "movement" is in the public mind and therefore in ordinary language and that the etymology and currency of the term in two intellectual traditions makes the proposition "movement is a phenomenon" an arguable claim, not simply an operational definition. And that is the rub, for the claim that "movement is a phenomenon" rests historically and presently on the theorist's prerogative to attach any label to any phenomenon in any context which sensibly suits the purpose of theorizing. There is no test which we may use to "prove" a descriptor, since definitions are by nature arbitrary understandings meant to facilitate thinking rather than be the subject of dispute. But we should take care that such understandings do not actually cloud and disrupt thinking. If the function of a definition is to confuse a perspective toward a fact with the fact itself, the exercise is not truly definitional, but conceptual.

Though the line between "concept" and "definition" is subtle, it has been drawn often and with profit.[12] In fact, there are *tests* of conceptualization, mechanisms which we can use to demonstrate the utility or descriptiveness of one way of conceiving sensible facts as opposed to another. Mathematical modeling, for example, can show us unintentional errors of causation in generalizations made by researchers who, blinded by the specificity of their work, can come to reasonable but empirically irrelevant interpretations of their data.[13] When one realizes that the sentence "Movement is a phenomenon" is more an argumentative claim than an operational definition, the intellectual history of the problem "movement" performs the same function as mathematical modeling. That is, by reconstructing the debate which seems to end in the proposition "Movement is a phenomenon," we can understand the intentional origins of the variant conceptions of "movement" and, therefore, some of the theoretical consequences of choosing to believe the proposition. When I survey the history of the concept "movement," then, I mean not to suggest that there is an aura of "legitimacy" in earlier characterizations of "movement," but rather that the history of the concept reveals the pragmatic and ideal pitfalls awaiting those who make ill-advised conceptual choices.[14]

The analogue "movement" first came into the English language in 1828 as a transliteration of the French idiom *dans le mouvement,* with specific reference to "Oxford" and "Labor" movements. The French idiom called up images of lemming-like behavior. To refer to Cardinal Newman's theology and Feargus O'Connor's

agitation as "movement" was journalistically to organize curious behaviors into a scenario which could be used politically both to oppose and to tolerate the activity of fringe social groups.[15] It so happened that the term was chosen by intellectuals at a time when learning was marked by an emerging historical consciousness, an awareness of the ways prior human activity constrain immediate choice. "Movement" was thus seen as "historical." The "swim" human beings find themselves caught up in is the product of an "historical order," a causal sequencing of events, characters, episodes which is "movement" from past to present. Hegel, Carlyle, Marx, Comte, and Von Ranke suggested that the past contained evidence of human destiny which in time would lead to formulary "laws of history." Thinkers influenced by Marx, Comte[,] and Von Ranke attempted to adapt empirical methods developed in the natural sciences to create a "science of history" and thus used the past as a data base for theory construction.[16] Other writers used Hegel and Carlyle as models for an enterprise which consisted of rewriting history to conform to traditional patterns of Western moral beliefs. Goldwyn Smith, for example, saw "true" history as "the embodiment of pure morality and true religion."[17] The tension between these ideas of "movement" created a century-long debate. The question, however, was not about "movement," for everyone was then agreed that history "moves" in directions which can be known. The issue was materialism versus idealism: The dispute was over *what* 'moves' in history—the material things which are our physical environment or the human ideas which mediate and interpret the facts of our experience?

As Richard Weaver explains, the "historicism" of such figures as Marx and Carlyle came under rigorous attack from writers acquainted with Vienna positivism.[18] The critique has been more methodological than conceptual, however. The question *"What* 'moves' in history?" was considered illegitimate because it was "paratheoretical," not because "movement" is an inappropriate metaphor for human collective behavior.[19] Marx could not prove that "the dialectic" actually existed in history, the argument went, and in the absence of positive proof, we should believe instead that it was invented rather than discovered by Marx and imposed on rather, than derived from history. Hence, the classic "problem of mediation" or "fallacy of imputation" was posed.[20] A failure of method, of course, can always be corrected in the romantically rational world of the positivist. "Movement" was a useful concept which needed only specification and translation in terms of verifiably observable human activity. Thus, in specific response to historicist theses, the argument "Movement is a phenomenon" was advanced. In the United States, there is a linear, unobstructed development of this viewpoint from La Piere to Heberle to Smelser and other contemporaries.[21] Only recently has what Lichtheim called "the conservative sterility of academic positivism" become apparent to Americans who ponder "movement" sociologically. Simons is not alone in drawing from German phenomenology alternatives to the rigid methodological catechism of positivism.[22] But however much I applaud such advances, I also worry that the critique remains at the level of methodology rather than conception. I believe, in other words, that Simons et al. reject positivism in the study of "movement" while retaining the co[u]nterproductive positivist first premise, that "Movement is a phenomenon."

When we think of it as a thrust in an argument rather than as an operational definition, the proposition "Movement is a phenomenon" illustrates three logical fallacies: (a) it is a *tu quoque;* (b) it is an unwarranted *reductio;* and (c) it works by affirming a consequent rather than by establishing a condition.

(a) Positivists and pragmatists intended to reject both Marxist and Idealist historicism on the ground that interpretations of the past could not be replicated, that "movement" was an analogy only and not provable with the facts of history. But as Polanyi and Ziman both have argued, the difference between historicism and even theoretical physics is in this respect a difference of degree, not of kind.[23] There is always a problem of mediation. Because "movement" is not by any claim purely empirical, our very recognition of something so conventional as "Labor Movement" depends on an interpretation rather than data. However closely we define a particular "movement," the existence of the term in ordinary language increases the

probability that it is an *a priori* label pressed from the mind either of the theorist or of the political activist onto the social events witnessed. This is not to say that earlier historicist usages are to be preferred; rather, if it was a fallacy for Marx to confuse discovery and invention, it is also a fallacy for Simons to confuse discovery and invention.

(b) Further, beyond the annoying inelegance of *tu quoque,* the proposition "Movement is a phenomenon" seems to be an unwarranted *reductio.* There is a "swim of things" which catches each of us in the impulse to demonstrate how secure we can be in the comfortable confines of collectivity. The "swim of things" is an urge, a drive to make collective behavior more comfortable and human existence therefore more "meaningful." Hegel, Marx, Carlyle, and Von Ranke posed a set of questions directly related to the experience, not of particular facts, but of a *zeitgeist:* How are "meaning" and "pattern" perceived in human social life? Where does this "swim" originate, and where does it go? Do such concepts as "progress" and "human destiny" have any capital? Such questions necessarily are begged by sociological conceptions because the expressed need to define an interpretive analogy as an empirical fact requires us to translate human fear and hope into human behavior and social fact. We cannot even use the *word* directly when we write theories: Thus, in the conceptual system Simons et al. suggest, "social movement" seems to mean little more than "organization," "industry," and/or "sector."[24] There is nothing in such operational translations about human consciousness of "movement": All the questions inspired by the nineteenth-century analogy disappear in the study of what are conceived to be *things.* Put another way, Simons et al. do not *require* either the concept "movement" or the concept "rhetoric"; they say nothing about the human condition which could not be said with the term "organizational communication," and they say nothing at all about the *meaning* of collective life, about "progress" and "human destiny."

(c) Finally, the claim "Movement is a phenomenon" works only by affirming the consequent. A "Civil Rights Movement," for example, comes to be recognized, even to *exist* as "movement," not because a writer carefully compared "organization" or "behavior" to well-thought-out theoretical models of "movement," but rather because a group of alienated individuals chose to define the nature and direction of their political behavior with the analogue "movement." Nor it is difficult to explain such choice, for it is no accident that a sociological conception of "movement" first appears in a context of determinism. In the terms of nineteenth-century social theory, a "movement" is always and inevitably successful because it is propelled by history itself. No matter what we do, no matter how we attempt to alter historical forces, the "movement" drones on in 4-4 time, never impeded for more than a trice. It is *this* meaning which survived the demise of historicism, *this* meaning which is an indispensable part of communist, fascist, unionist and egalitarian ideologies. A politician, even in the United States, would have to be a fool to call an attempt to use the brute power of an aroused collectivity anything other than "movement." Thus, if we agree that an organization calling itself "Hitler Youth Movement" *in fact* is an empirical specification of the concept "movement," we thereby grant an aura of academic or theoretical legitimacy to a patently rhetorical ploy. Put in logical form, we would be saying "If social movement existed empirically, surely people in fact would organize themselves into groups called 'movements.' Since people have organized themselves into groups they call 'movements,' then social movement exists empirically and can be studied objectively." That tactic, characteristically employed by such lights of American empirical sociology as Smelser and Bell, affirms a consequent.[25]

If we choose to believe that "Movement is a phenomenon," I conclude, the product of our work will always be theoretically suspect and as empirically irrelevant as Simons et al. observe "objectivist" sociological theory to be.[26] We could justify our most fundamental concepts against competing Marxian and structuralist alternatives only by claiming as a weakness in our competitors' logic of assumptions that we ourselves make. We would always be hard-pressed to transcend specificity, unable to answer the abidingly interesting questions originally posed with the concept "movement." And we would be obliged to ground operational methods in formal and informal logical fallacies, thereby opening ourselves not only to the charge that we are sloppy scientists, but even to the suggestion that our procedures tend to foster a political loading of allegedly descriptive theoretical constructs.[27]

II

What are the alternatives? Assuming that we have no more wish to associate ourselves with the homilies of orthodox Marxism than to drink the bitter residues of positivism, I believe that we should encourage Zarefsky, Hyde and Smith, Carleton, Frentz and Farrell, McGuire, and others in developing concepts of communication in general and "movement" in particular which focus on the problems of meaning and interpretation.[28] That is, if the study of "movement" is ever to become a "distinctive theoretical domain," I believe that it must be as a "hermeneutic" theory, not as a purely "behavioral" or "phenomenal" theory. I would like to seek an account of human consciousness, not an account of human organizational behavior. Both technical and practical perceptions of "movement" suggest that human beings *want* to see their environment described as an ordered progression of mutually salient episodes. The possibility that life is nothing more than a cosmic joke, a random and entropic set of essentially irrelevant experiences, is so unflattering that we tend to dismiss it summarily. Whether one is caught up in political agitation, fascinated by the appearance of pattern and meaning in history, or desirous of being no more than a detached witness to endemic social change, "movement" is our fondest wish, our dream, a reason to continue living in human society, for it contains an affirmation of human significance. A consciousness is presumed by the concept "movement" which *requires* meaning, order[,] and pattern in human experience even when these regularities must be manufactured. A theory of movement, therefore, must determine the identity and meaning of the consciousness which inspires us, as citizens and as scholars, to seek and see "movement" when we look at historical and social facts. Is it useful to think of the fact of change or the attempt to change as "movement"? What function does such a characterization have in the human mind? What relationship does consciousness of "movement" bear to human collective behavior? To what extent are such visions merely manipulative delusions? In my mind, these should be the primary and abiding questions of a theory of social movement.

A theory of movement answering such questions would represent a total reconceptualization of current procedures, a basic alteration of figure and ground relationships between "movements" and human communication. In nineteenth-century historicism, "movement" was not a phenomenon, but it was thought to be objective. So "movement" was ground or context, and human communication, when it was thought of at all, was considered to exist as a figure within the "movement." Similarly, those who accept the sociological proposition that "Movement is a phenomenon" see an objective thing, sometimes an organization or institution, sometimes a more gelatinous "situation" with objective "constraints" which allegedly imprison or circumscribe intentional communication.[29] In either case, the "rhetoric of social movements" is passive, reactive, a facilitator of change, subordinate to and determined by an objective phenomenon. When I envision an alternative theory of movement, however, I see "movement" existing as a figure or meaning within the ground/context of human communication. "Movement" is a meaning within a term, an organizing analogue of social facts which can be objectivated only in linguistic usage. Because it is the expression of those who need, seek[,] and see "progress" or "destiny," the whole notion of "movement" is mythical, a trick-of-the-mind which must be understood *as an illusion* and not as a fact. I believe, therefore, that the appropriate models for our scientific study of "movement" are treatises in critical science. I mean to recommend the work of such as Habermas, Feuer, Gouldner, Eco, and Foucault on the problem of consciousness generally and the problem of ideology specifically. In my mind, these *are* the conceptually legitimate studies of "movement(s)."[30]

I agree in principle with Zarefsky and Sillars that rather than trying to create a theory about the use of communication in social movements, we probably are better off exploiting the uniqueness of our subject matter by making a rhetorical theory *of* movement.[31] That is, the impulse to see "movement" in certain changes and not in others is recorded in attempts to make such perception general through the rhetorical community. A survey of any nation's rhetoric should clearly indicate that normative descriptions for common phenomena have or have not changed. When people use new words—or obviously attribute new meaning to old words—we can assume that consciousness of their environment has "moved" by measure of the difference in descriptors themselves or in meanings. We will not say that "movement" exists or has occurred until we can demonstrate by a survey of public discourse that descriptors of the environment have changed *in common usage* in such a way as to make "movement" an arguably acceptable term useful in formulating the chain of facts we believe to have constituted a real change. The primary objective of a theorist working under such constraint is to *prove* rather than *presume* the existence of "movement(s)." I have argued elsewhere for one alternative in such proof: Because there is a basic vocabulary of normative terms in any social-political system, and because those terms exhibit both diachronic and synchronic structures, we can prove "movement" by observing changes in the "ideographic" structures of social norm-systems.[32] Since one can produce the rhetorical artifacts which document this evolution of meanings, technical use of the concept "movement" seems legitimate. The rhetorical artifacts which warrant claims of "movement" also give us a concrete object of study, for we can point to changes in patterns of discourse *directly,* in a way conceptually impossible if we conceive of "movement" as existing apart from consciousness and/or independent of the discourse which communicates consciousness.

Lucas has characterized the two orientations contrasted here as a reconcilable disagreement between "historical" and "sociological" conceptions of "movement." At first I was comfortable with this synthesis, I think, because I have more sympathy for the 19th-century historicist than for the 20th-century positivist. Upon reflection, however, I cannot agree that my approach is "historical"; rather, it is communicational or rhetorical and as far from last century's historicism as Herbert Simons is from Emile Durkheim. Further, I cannot agree that Simons and I are "looking at approximately the same phenomenon," for I see no phenomenon at all, but only a series of words with meanings to be discovered and verified. If it could be established that "social movement(s)" were *both* phenomena and a set of meanings, there would be a difference of perspective, with Simons opting to see the phenomenon "coming first" in an explanation of belief and attitude and I preferring to see a pattern of consciousness "coming first" in an explanation of episodes and behaviors. But until I see convincing arguments to the contrary, I continue to believe that "social movement" is not a phenomenon *as a matter of fact.* I cannot escape the conviction that there is an egregious mistake in sociological theory now being borrowed and perpetuated by communication theorists. "Social movement" ought not to be a *premise* with which we *begin* research, defining what we want to see and, lo and behold, finding it. Rather, "social movement" ought to be a *conclusion,* a carefully considered and well-argued inference that changes in human consciousness are of such a nature that "social movement" has occurred, or that the rhetorical activity of a group of human beings would produce "social movement" if it were effective. Theoretical descriptions of "social movement(s)," in other words, ought to make questions of consciousness "come first," focusing on the fact of collectivity and not on the accident of an allegedly pre-existing phenomenon. To believe otherwise, I think, is quite simply to embrace an unfortunately conventional error.

Notes

1 For a much more detailed defense of the claim that conceptual failures currently hamper the development of all social and political sciences, see W. Lance Bennett, *The Political Mind and the Political Environment: An Investigation of Public Opinion and Political Consciousness* (Lexington, MA: Lexington Books, 1975), especially pp. 4–25, 80–103, 110–11. See also Gareth Stedman Jones, "From Historical Sociology to Theoretical History," *British Journal of Sociology,* 27 (1976), 295–305.

2 In my view, theory must (a) formally advance a generalization which (b) resolves a mystery apt to be confronted in daily experience. The truth-claim advanced (c) must be demonstrably reliable when it is measured against (d) some, but no particular, clearly articulated epistemic standard. A *complete* theory provides (e) a conceptually clear and formal *description* of the object of theorizing, (f) an *explanation* of the origin and salience of the object, and (g) criteria useful in *prediction* of probable outcome in future encounters with like objects.

3 See Anthony Giddens, *Central Problems in Social Theory: Action, Structure and Contradiction in Social Analysis* (Berkeley: Univ. of California Press, 1979), especially pp. 165–233; Michel Foucault, *The Archaeology of Knowledge,* trans. Alan M. Sheridan-Smith (1969; Eng. trans. New York: Harper, 1972); J. G. A. Pocock, *Politics, Language and Time* (New York: Atheneum, 1973); Rosalind Coward and John Ellis, *Language and Materialism: Developments in Semiology and the Theory of the Subject* (London: Routledge & Kegan Paul, 1977).

4 See William H. Whyte, Jr., *The Organization Man* (New York: Simon & Schuster, 1956); Max Horkheimer, *Critical Theory: Selected Essays,* trans. Matthew J. O'Connell et al. (New York: Seabury, 1972), pp. 47–128.

5 A conceivable third alternative would require us to recognize the "speaking" and "content" as identities and as themselves the object of study, "coming first" in the attempt to explain phenomena as the grounding of signification (the "ultimate signified") and in the attempt to understand human consciousness "imprisoned" in its material manifestation, language. See Maurice Merleau-Ponty, *Signs,* trans. Richard C. McCleary (1960; Eng. trans. Evanston: Northwestern Univ. Press, 1964); Jacques Lacan, *Écrits, A Selection,* trans. Alan M. Sheridan-Smith (New York: W. W. Norton, 1977); and Fredric Jameson, *The Prison-House of Language* (Princeton: Princeton Univ. Press, 1972).

6 See Gary Lynn Cronkhite, "Logic, Emotion, and the Paradigm of Persuasion," *Quarterly Journal of Speech,* 50 (1964), 13–18.

7 See Hayden White, *Metahistory: The Historical Imagination in Nineteenth-Century Europe* (Baltimore: The Johns Hopkins Univ. Press, 1973), pp. 22–29.

8 Though he cautions the reader that he is using "collective behavior" in a highly technical sense, Smelser [is] using a persuasive definition. He wishes to argue that such behaviors as panics, crazes, hostile outbursts, and "movements" are distinct *in kind* from ordinary social behaviors. But this remains an assertion in his theory, for he fails

to confront the sense in which *all* social behavior is collective behavior, distinct from what he wishes to *call* "collective" only in interpretive judgments an observer might make about the rationality, the utility, or the morality of the behavior. See Neil J. Smelser, *Theory of Collective Behavior* (New York: Free Press, 1962), pp. 2–21.

[9] Herbert W. Simons, Elizabeth Mechling, and Howard N. Schr[e]ier, "Functions of Communication in Mobilizing for Collective Action From the Bottom Up: The Rhetoric of Social Movements," in *Handbook of Rhetorical and Communication Theory,* ed. Carroll C. Arnold and John Waite Bowers (Boston: Allyn & Bacon), in press. See also, Herbert W. Simons, "Commentary on Zarefsky's Paper," Working Papers of Seminar on Rhetoric and Social Movements, Speech Communication Association, San Antonio[,] TX, November 1979; p. 6: "The term 'social movement' and the definition of that construct typically provided by sociologists have become part of conventional scholarly parlance. Given that there is near-consensus, and given that general agreement on terms and definitions enables a scholarly community to move on to other profitable issues, I believe that we should accept the sociological conception unless very good reasons can be provided to the contrary. Thus far I have not heard those good reasons." Cf. Robert A. Nisbet, *Social Change and History* (London: Oxford Univ. Press, 1969), especially pp. 251–67.

[10] I have yet to read a book on "social movement(s)" conceived as a phenomenon which did *not* assert the difficulty of distinguishing forms of "mass phenomena." Typically, writers survey the English language for terms which journalists have or might use to describe unusual mass behaviors. Such terms are then organized, usually orthogonally, with some variation of "size" (genus/species, e.g.) on one axis and some variation of degree of organization (formal/informal, e.g.) on the other. After fifty years of research and development, the continued need to define *a priori* (and *then* proceed to ask "To what kinds of phenomena does this term refer?") seems to bespeak such conceptual confusion that one wonders if it might not be the case that "collective behavior flows from sources beyond empirical explanation."

[11] See Jean-Paul Sartre, *Critique of Dialectical Reason: A Theory of Practical Ensembles,* trans. Alan Sheridan-Smith, ed. Jonathon Ree (London: NLB, 1976), pp. 256–341. Something of the dilemma of intellectuals at once desiring "scientific" theory and to avoid Mannheim's paradox (the choice between

politicizing theory and imputing motives[)] is captured in J. A. Hall, "The Roles and Influence of Political Intellectuals: Tawney vs. Sidney Webb," *British Journal of Sociology,* 28 (1977), 351–62). In my mind the clear alternative is to abandon phenomenal or behavioral empiricism in favor of symbolic or "hermeneutic" empiricism.

[12] See, for example, Alfred Schutz, *The Phenomenology of the Social World,* trans. George Walsh and Frederick Lehnert (Evanston: Northwestern Univ. Press, 1967), pp. 215–50; Roger Poole, *Towards Deep Subjectivity* (New York: Harper & Row, 1972), pp. 44–77.

[13] See, e.g., Dean Hewes, "Finite Stochastic Modeling of Communication Processes," *Human Communication Research,* 1 (1975), 271–83; Joseph N. Cappella, "Talk-Silence Sequences in Informal Conversations I," *Human Communication Research,* 6 (1979), 8–14.

[14] Within what I understand to be Cappella's meaning, I am suggesting that we regard the sentence "Movement is a phenomenon" as an "intentional communication" at least figuratively "uttered" in a conversation begun about the year 1828. See Joseph N. Cappella, "The Functional Prerequisites of Intentional Communicative Systems," *Philosophy & Rhetoric,* 5 (1972), 231–47.

[15] See Herbert Marcuse, "Repressive Tolerance," in Robert Paul Wolff, Barrington Moore, Jr., and Herbert Marcuse, *A Critique of Pure Tolerance* (Boston: Beacon, 1969), pp. 81–123.

[16] See Howard Becker and Harry Elmer Barnes, *Social Thought from Lore to Science,* 3rd ed., 3 vols. (New York: Dover, 1961), 2:560–787.

[17] Goldwyn Smith, *Lectures on the Study of History* (Toronto: Univ. of Toronto Press, 1873), p. 44. See also, Benedetto Croce, *History as the Story of Liberty,* trans. Sy[l]via Sprigge (London: Allen & Unwin, 1941).

[18] See Richard Weaver, *The Ethics of Rhetoric* (Chicago: Henry Regnery, 1953), pp. 211–32; and Richard Weaver, "Concealed Rhetoric in Scientistic Sociology," Richard L. Johannesen, Rennard Strickland and Ralph T. Eubanks, eds., *Language is Sermonic: Richard M. Weaver on the Nature of Rhetoric* (Baton Rouge: Louisiana St. Univ. Press, 1970), pp. 139–58.

[19] See Karl R. Popper, *The Poverty of Historicism,* 3rd ed. (1961; rpt. New York: Harper & Row, 1964); M. M. Bober, *Karl Marx's Interpretation of History,* 2nd ed. (1948; rpt. New York: Norton, 1965).

[20] See Willard A. Mullins, "Truth and Ideology: Reflections on Mannheim's Paradox," *History and Theory,* 4 (1966): 164–95; Martin Seliger,

The Marxist Conception of Ideology: A Critique (Cambridge: Cambridge Univ. Press, 1977), pp. 129–201; Douglas Kellner, "Ideology, Marxism and Advanced Cap[i]talism," *Socialist Review,* 8 (1978), 37–66.

21 See, for example, Richard T. La Piere, *Collective Behavior* (New York: McGraw-Hill, 1934); Rudolf Heberle, *Social Movements* (New York: Appleton Century-Crofts, 1951); Smelser; Nisbet; John A. Rex, "The Spread of the Pathology of Natural Science to the Social Sciences," *The Sociological Review,* Monograph 16 (1970), 143–62.

22 George Lichtheim, "Sartre, Marxism, and History," *History and Theory,* 2 (1963), 229. With just the hint of contradicting their earlier conceptual base, Simons et al. borrow from Peter Berger's *Sacred Canopy* the notion that human beings in collectivity have the capacity to dictate the conditions of "objectivity," that we "socially construct" reality and then externalize and reprocess our objectivated conceptions. Berger follows Luckmann, Schutz, and others in rejecting any argument which holds that the "out there" world is anything other than *the embodiment of meaning.* Simons sees in this model a synthesis of the "objectivist" and "interactionist" views of movement, but as far as I can tell, Berger's is an unambiguous statement of the interactionist view, and a rejection of what Simons calls "objectivism." Simons confuses "objectivism" and the standard "interactionist" term "objectivation." Though there is always a dialectical relationship between the individual and the objectivated social world, Berger (pp. 60–61) reminds us that "It is important to keep in mind that the objectivity of the institutional world, however massive it may appear to the individual, is a humanly produced, constructed objectivity." The hint of contradiction, of course, is magnified in Simon's exchange with Zarefsky. There Simons argued strongly for the *exclusion* of "institutionalized movements" from our conception "social movement," but according to Berger and Luckmann, *the only thing which can be objectivated is precisely a social institution!* Contrast Simons, Mechling and Schreier, pp. 48–59 with Peter L. Berger and Thomas Luckmann, *The Social Construction of Reality* (New York: Anchor Books, 1967), pp. 60–61, 104–28; and Alfred Schutz and Thomas Luckmann, *The Structure of the Life-World,* trans. Richard M. Zaner and H. Tristram Engelhardt, Jr. (Evanston: Northwestern Univ. Press, 1973), pp. 261–304.

23 See Michael Polanyi, *Personal Knowledge,* corrected ed. (Chicago: Univ. of Chicago Press, 1962), pp. 3–17, 132–202; and John Ziman, *Public Knowledge* (Cambridge: Cambridge Univ. Press, 1968), pp. 13–29, 77–101.

24 See Simons, Mechling and Schreier, especially pp. 3–7.

25 Smelser rejects out of hand the possibility that "collective behavior flows from sources beyond empirical explanation," defines "collective behavior" eccentrically and technically as an *a priori* construct, and proceeds to adduce examples and to find phenomena which fit his prior distinctions. As Dolbeare and Dolbeare indicate, Daniel Bell worked the same alchemy with the construct "ideology." See Smelser, pp. 1–21; Daniel Bell, *The End of Ideology* (Glencoe, IL: Free Press, 1960); Kenneth M. Dolbeare and Patricia Dolbeare, *American Ideologies* (Chicago: Markham, 1971), pp. 1–21.

26 See Simons, Mechling and Schreier, p. 50, where they develop this argument.

27 The concrete human behaviors one would like to perceive as "revolutionary" or part of a "movement" are clearly distinguishable from ordinary criminal behavior only by the value judgment that something inherent in the society legitimates sociopathic conduct. What might seem a simple operational labeling in theory, therefore, could be in practice a stamp of legitimacy (even of approval) for erstwhile criminal behavior, transforming, for example, the "Bader-Meinhoff Gang" of terrorists into an incipient "revolutionary movement" of crusaders against oppression.

28 See David Zarefsky, "President Johnson's War on Poverty: The Rhetoric of Three 'Establishment' Movements," *Communication Monographs,* 44 (1977), 352–73; Michael J. Hyde and Craig R. Smith, "Hermeneutics and Rhetoric: A Seen but Unobserved Relationship," *Quarterly Journal of Speech,* 65 (1979), 347–63; Walter M. Carleton, "What is Rhetorical Knowledge? A Response to Farrell—And More," *Quarterly Journal of Speech,* 64 (1978), 313–28; Michael McGuire, "Mythic Rhetoric in *Mein Kampf:* A Structuralist Critique," *Quarterly Journal of Speech,* 63 (1977), 1–13; Thomas B. Farrell and Thomas S. Frentz, "Communication and Meaning: A Language-Action Synthesis," *Philosophy & Rhetoric,* 12 (1979), 215–55.

29 This is evident in Simons, "Reply to Zarefsky," p. 4: "I view my own approach as highly consonant with Bitzerian situational theory. I argue, in his terms, that a given *class* of situational exigences and constraints will impel and constrain

movement rhetors in particular ways. For example, a militant movement organization will typically be more constrained by agents of social control then, say, an established philanthropic organization; and its rhetoric will thus differ as well." Simons' reference is to Lloyd F. Bitzer, "The Rhetorical Situation," *Philosophy & Rhetoric,* 1 (1968), 1–14. Bitzer's is a causal theory with the causes presupposed: Communication and its situation are *covariant* with each other, but they are *codeterminant* only with "exigence."

30 See, for example, Michel Foucault, *The Archaeology of Knowledge,* trans. Alan M. Sheridan-Smith (1969; Eng. trans. rpt. New York: Harper & Row, 1976); Umberto Eco, *A Theory of Semiotics* (Bloomington: Indiana Univ. Press, 1976); Lewis Feuer, *Ideology and the Ideologists* (New York:

Harper & Row, 1975); Alvin Gouldner, *The Dialectic of Ideology and Technology* (New York: Seabury, 1976); Jürgen Habermas, *Communication and the Evolution of Society,* trans. Thomas McCarthy (Boston: Beacon, 1975).

31 See David Zarefsky, "On Distinctions without Differences: Do Social Movements Have a Unique Rhetorical Form?" Working Papers of the Seminar on Rhetoric and Social Movements, Speech Communication Association, San Antonio[,] TX, November 1979; and Malcolm O. Sillars, "Defining Movements Rhetorically: Casting the Widest Net," *Southern Speech Communication Journal,* in press.

32 See "The 'Ideograph': A Link Between Rhetoric and Ideology," *Quarterly Journal of Speech,* 66 (1980), 1–16.

A Skeptical View of Movement Studies
David Zarefsky

Rhetorical scholars have approached the study of social movements from two distinct points of view. The first is *historical;* the scholar seeks to make claims about the movement's development and its relation to other events. The historically-oriented scholar takes the phrase, "the rhetoric of movements," to mean that movements exist as historical phenomena and that they employ rhetoric. Their rhetoric should be studied so that we will know more about the use of persuasion in efforts to mobilize for or to resist social change.

The second perspective for movement studies is *theoretical;* the scholar seeks to make generalizable claims about patterns of persuasion characteristic of movements as a class. To the theoretically-oriented scholar, the phrase, "the rhetoric of movements," marks out a distinct domain of rhetorical behavior. Movements are characterized by recurrent rhetorical patterns not found in other instances of persuasion. Otherwise, there would be no need to identify movements as a separate category. From this perspective, individual movements serve as case studies to test general propositions which

not only explain persuasion in the past but also permit predictions about the future.

The argument of this essay is that theoretically-oriented studies of social movements, since they depend upon establishing the uniqueness of movement rhetoric, have not been very productive. By contrast, essentially historical studies are rich in potential value and ought to be pursued.

THE EMERGENCE OF THE UNIQUENESS ISSUE

When Griffin first recommended that rhetorical scholars examine movements,[1] he was responding to what were then the predominant modes of rhetorical criticism: biographies of individual orators and analyses of the effects of individual speeches. Griffin was convinced that great orators and orations, however significant, were not the whole stuff of which a history of public address should be formed. He thought instead that a comprehensive history of persuasion "might well be conceived in terms of movements rather than individuals."[2] As a result, he urged that rhetorical scholars round out the history of public address by investigating the role of persuasion in sustained efforts to bring about or to retard social change.

Griffin did not distinguish "movements" from "campaigns" or other instances of rhetorical behavior having cumulative effects over time. Indeed, since his immediate motive was to enrich the study of the history of public address, it was desirable that his definition of "movement" be quite broad. In that way, studies of "a multiplicity of speakers, speeches, audiences, and occasions"[3] would be encouraged. In the past twenty-five years there have been numerous studies—of *pro* and *anti*-movements, insurgent and elitist movements, successful and unsuccessful movements, historical and contemporary movements. As the studies have accumulated, scholars began to ask what the rhetorical dimensions of these movements have in common and whether any features set them apart from other cases of persuasion. The profusion of studies makes the uniqueness issue salient. The issue, in short, is whether movements comprise a distinct rhetorical genre, either in the sense that they have a unique form or in the sense that they arise in a unique type of situation. If so, then the foundation can be laid for a rhetorical theory specific to movements. If not, then attempts to develop such a theory are likely to be unproductive. To settle the issue, one must examine theoretically-based studies of movements.

THEORETICAL STUDIES: DISTINCTIVENESS BY DEFINITION

One theoretical approach to movement studies is to *define* movements as different from other kinds of persuasion. This approach is well represented by the work of Cathcart.[4] Noting that most sociological theories of movements stress their status as uninstitutionalized collectives, Cathcart inquires whether unique rhetorical behavior is manifest in efforts to direct change occurring outside established institutional boundaries. He concludes that the "establishment" response to such efforts at social change is the key variable. If the "establishment" regards the protest as illegitimate and focuses on that issue, it creates what Cathcart calls a state of

dialectical enjoinment. Accordingly, Cathcart *defines* movements as a rhetorical form featuring a dialectic between the established order and those who question its moral legitimacy.

The first question that must be asked about Cathcart's definition is: Does the dialectic which he describes occur only between "establishments" and "uninstitutionalized collectivities?" If the answer is no, then we cannot say that a movement has a unique rhetorical form. And the answer to this question is no, as a counterexample should demonstrate.

In my study of President Lyndon Johnson's War on Poverty,[5] I found a series of collective efforts to obtain change which, far from being uninstitutionalized, were sponsored and financed by government. Yet the same dialectical pattern emerged. The "challenging *pro* movement" confronted the "power structure" and charged that it was illegitimate because it had sold out to political machines. Political leaders responded that it was wrong for the War on Poverty to use public funds to organize attacks on public officials and focused on that issue. *Both* sets of forces were supported by the political "establishment," yet the state of dialectical tension which Cathcart describes was present. This is not a unique example. The juvenile delinquency projects during the Kennedy Administration followed much the same pattern.[6] So do self-help organizations funded through public or private philanthropy but which define their mission in opposition to the charity "establishment."[7] So too does any controversy in which government regulators decry excessive business profits as illegitimate or immoral, only to encounter the response that the government's intervention in the economy is itself inappropriate. A creative imagination, no doubt, easily could suggest other instances in which the dialectical enjoinment Cathcart describes can be found *within* the boundaries of established institutions.

It might be argued that instances such as these do not really illustrate dialectical enjoinment because there is a large fund of common beliefs which these groups share. By the very fact of their institutionalized status, they subscribe to the legitimacy and norms of the established order. They may draw on these norms for premises on which they would agree; this agreement, in turn, makes it possible for them to communicate directly with one another. They need not engage in what Cathcart calls an "agonistic ritual" to attract the attention of a wider public to their cause.

Such a rejoinder, however, is really beside the point. For the groups in practice appeal not to each other but to a broader public. Certainly they behave as if they were engaged in an agonistic ritual. If rhetorical behavior is taken at face value, then these efforts clearly satisfy Cathcart's standard for movements even though they do not come from uninstitutionalized collectives. Alternatively, if one looks "beneath the surface" and relies on external data to determine whether there "really" is dialectical enjoinment, one would be unlikely ever to find such a state. Only in a situation of actual revolution, if then, could one say that there is no common ground among participants in a controversy. Because of this dilemma, Cathcart's definition is either too narrow, permitting no case of true dialectical enjoinment, or too broad, including far more rhetorical behavior than is unique to uninstitutionalized collectives.

Cathcart's attempt at distinctiveness by definition might still be salvaged if the form which he calls "movement" is distinct from other patterns of persuasion. Hence, a second question must be posed: Whether in institutionalized or uninstitutionalized groups, is the form of "dialectical enjoinment" different from other rhetorical forms? An affirmative answer would identify essential distinguishing features; a negative answer would deny the essential differences between "movement" and some other rhetorical pattern.

Again the answer is negative. Cathcart's concept of "dialectical enjoinment" is essentially the same as "*stasis* in place."[8] This *stasis* develops when the heart of a controversy involves the appropriate forum, or place, to consider the dispute. The procedural *stasis* preempts the substantive ones; when the question of place is raised, the dispute must focus on that issue. Whether the courts or the legislature is the appropriate place to discuss sex discrimination takes precedence over whether it is a problem and what should be done about it. Likewise, deciding whether Congress or a constitutional convention should determine the Federal budget takes precedence over what the size of the budget should be. And a claim that appealing to the professor, not lodging a formal protest with the dean, is the appropriate way to redress an academic grievance preempts consideration of the merits of the grievance. When Cathcart maintains that the "control agents and general public perceive that the collective is acting outside the system and . . . choose to respond to this aspect rather than the grievance,"[9] he suggests that the "establishment" says in effect, "You do not have standing to discuss your grievances"—a charge which focuses subsequent discussion on the question of place.

Since *stasis* in place is preemptive, one might expect disputants to raise this issue if they think they can succeed without addressing the substantive questions. The behavior Cathcart sees as defining a movement may be undertaken as a strategy. Rhetors may define their adversaries (or themselves) as inside or outside institutional norms, not as a reflection of objective differences in ideology, but in order to serve the purpose of widening or narrowing the scope of conflict.[10] For this reason, recourse to *stasis* in place can be a universally available choice, regardless of the rhetorical situation. Of course, one could identify this haggling over place as "movement" if he or she wished, but there would be no gain. The term would be used in such a different way from its sociological roots as to invite confusion. It would not say anything new about the behavior being examined. And it would not establish "movements" as a rhetorical genre in a way that would facilitate what Simons calls "a social science of rhetorical choice, one that delimits strategic and stylistic options in the face of situational and purposive constraints."[11]

Beneath the two questions raised lurks a more fundamental one: Is the distinction between acting "inside" and "outside" the system valid?[12] In answering this question, we may be misled if we too quickly accept the self-reports of actors who describe themselves as a "movement" because they are outside the system. "Movement" is a "persuasive definition";[13] it attaches to one's actions the connotations of motion, determinism, future-orientation, and sympathy for the underdog. As Jimmy Carter demonstrated in 1976, there may be strategic reasons for defining oneself as "outside the system." Those out of power may so define themselves in order to raise the stakes, enhance the drama of the situation, and impart a sense of destiny. Those in power may so characterize themselves to distinguish themselves from their predecessors, to imply that they cannot be co-opted, or to attract attention. Consequently, the distinction which rhetors make so easily will give the critic a very hard time. Confrontations provoked by militant foes of nuclear power, for instance, are as much a part of "the system" as are Congressional debates. Indeed, the essence of a democratic polity is that it is open to a multiplicity of speakers and modes of advocacy. The only actors who might truly fall "outside" the system are those who renounce advocacy in favor of terrorism or revolution—and Cathcart's definition does not necessarily distinguish even these acts from agonistic ritual.

For the previously developed reasons, Cathcart's definition fails to establish the distinctiveness of "movements" as a rhetorical form.[14] If movements are not unique, then there is no basis for constructing a rhetorical theory specific to them. Propositions which describe or explain social movements might easily apply to other rhetorical behavior as well.

THEORETICAL STUDIES: DISTINCTIVENESS BY SITUATION

A second group of scholars also have argued that movements have distinct rhetorical features although the reasoning is quite different from Cathcart's. Rather than *defining* movements as a rhetorical form, they accept the definitions offered by sociologists. Various usages may be found, but the term *movement* generally is taken to designate collective action conducted outside the framework of established institutions to achieve major social change.[15] Behavior which satisfies these criteria is distinguished from that which does not. As the sociologist finds that movements differ from other organizations in structure and function, so rhetorical scholars adopting this approach believe that movements differ in the type of rhetorical situation to which

they must respond. A distinctive constellation of rhetorical problems confronts a movement and requires a distinctive pattern of response.

This position is well represented by the work of Herbert W. Simons, who argues that social movements face unique rhetorical requirements, confront unique rhetorical problems, and must generate unique rhetorical strategies.[16] Since the requirements and problems define the situation and produce the strategic response, the test of Simons' argument is twofold: (1) Do the requirements and problems he identifies as unique to social movements also characterize other forms of persuasion? (2) If so, do they generate unique strategic choices? If the first question is answered affirmatively or the second question negatively, Simons' position would seem flawed—in the first case because there would be no difference in situation and in the second case because the situational difference would not constrain strategic choice.

On what grounds might situations be argued to be unique? From Simons' more recent writing, two distinguishing features can be inferred. First, unlike campaigns, movements are not presumed to be legitimate. Hence, they must struggle for access to the means of communication. Second, movements have fewer means to reward and punish their followers; consequently, they have a more difficult task of maintaining internal control. Both of these claims, however, seem to be based on stereotypes and do not apply uniquely to movements.

Whether one has legitimacy and effective access to communication media depends more on the rhetorical situation than on one's membership in a sociological category. The recent experience of President Jimmy Carter provides an instructive example. During the summer of 1979 (well before Iran and Afghanistan), the President found himself in an anomalous situation: his standing in public opinion polls had fallen so low that his leadership was not taken seriously. As a result, he had difficulty alerting the American public to the problems inherent in continued reliance on imported oil. Although he could hold press conferences or deliver major addresses, he could not induce his audience to pay attention to his message. It was necessary for him to stage spectacles to attract attention: first, the dramatic cancellation of a scheduled address, then the retreat to Camp David, and finally, the sojourn on the *Delta Queen*. The rhetorical requirement was the need to be taken seriously; the problem was that the President's credibility was in doubt; and his strategy apparently was the staging of a spectacle.

To be sure, an insurgent protest group cannot go to Camp David; nor can its leaders attract publicity by taking a riverboat cruise. But they too can stage spectacles—by holding protest marches, by disrupting traffic, or by "sitting in" at a public building. Simons would seem compelled to assume that the two situations are markedly different. But are they really? The requirements and problems are the same. The persuader's objective depends on the support of a wider audience, one that must be created through publicity, and yet effective publicity cannot be assured because the persuader's credibility is in question. The strategy is the same—to stage a spectacle to gain attention which can be exploited for one's cause. The difference is one of *tactics*.[17] On the basis of this example, then, it seems that the first alleged difference between movements and other rhetorical ventures would need to be attenuated: movements select different tactics in executing the same strategies which respond to the same requirements and problems that face other persuaders. And even this limited version of the hypothesis needs to be tested rather than assumed. After all, any persuader will employ a potentially large repertoire of tactics, so that one's behavior does not become too predictable. And it may well be, for example, that the President's cancellation of the speech and the insurgents postponement of a scheduled march are both examples of a more general tactic which is shared by both insurgent and elite rhetors. Until this alternative formulation is carefully explored, the first alleged difference between movements and other rhetorical behavior is difficult to accept.

As for the second point, that movements have fewer means to reward or punish their participants, that too seems to depend on the situation. A political administration with low ratings in the polls will have a difficult time enforcing its will upon Congress, the bureaucracy, or the citizenry at large. A long-term campaign, such as the effort to rebuild major cities for the 21st century, will encounter difficulty sustaining support of people who will not themselves benefit from achievement of the goal. Gamson maintains that this problem is faced by philanthropic organizations as well as social movements, since "support cannot be explained by personal interest."[18]

On the other hand, to say that a social movement has few means of reward or punishment is to ignore the fact that social movements usually are composed of *organizations*, which by virtue of the levels of status and hierarchy implicit in formal structure have means of control. Moreover, if a social movement stands in opposition to a weak "establishment," its means of control may be derived from its own perceived legitimacy. In short, both movements and "establishments" may be in a strong or weak position. The nature of the situation, rather than their institutionalized or noninstitutionalized status, will determine their means of social control. Neither of the generalizations inferred from Simons' writing supports the claim that social movements confront unique rhetorical requirements or problems, or employ unique strategies.

In short, Simons' argument that social movements face unique rhetorical situations seems deficient. Through counter-examples, I have tried to suggest that other collectives face similar rhetorical requirements and problems, and generate similar strategies. One might respond that, despite individual cases of similarity, the *constellation* of problems facing movements poses unique rhetorical demands. This argument, in fact, seems to embody Simons' position. But the reply begs the question. It may be true that movements face a unique constellation of *problems*, but it does not follow that the constellation poses unique *rhetorical demands* or generates unique *rhetorical strategies*. The case of the Johnson Administration's War on Poverty may help to clarify this point.[19] The War on Poverty did not satisfy the sociological definition of a social movement, yet it displayed a similar rhetorical pattern. In responding to this argument, Simons, Mechling, and Schreier identify a number of differences between the War on Poverty and insurgent movements:

governments have more material resources, insurgents must mobilize largely by ideological appeals, insurgents encounter different types of resistance, and protest depends on publicity.[20] But unless these differences produce in the social movement a distinct pattern of rhetorical behavior, there seems to be no insight gained by identifying the situation as unique. And it is questionable whether any distinct rhetorical pattern results. Greater material resources will not necessarily give a government legitimacy in a specific rhetorical situation. Nearly any large-scale campaign will employ ideological appeals; even the President of the United States felt compelled to dramatize the energy issue and to portray it as a "crisis of confidence." While types of resistance may vary from one group to another, the resulting rhetorical situation may well be the same. The statement that protest requires publicity is true regardless of the protest's source. In general, the fact that Simons and his colleagues note these differences, yet fail to show that they produce a unique rhetorical pattern, represents *support* for the position I have advanced.

To summarize, even if social movements differ from other collectives in the problem they face, this difference does not appear to represent a rhetorical constraint. The rhetorical choices of movement rhetors appear quite similar to those of advocates in seemingly quite dissimilar situations. Without a significant difference in constraints or choices, theorists have a shaky basis for regarding "movement" as a rhetorically significant construct about which unique propositions can be offered and tested.

THE PROPER ROLE OF MOVEMENT STUDIES

I have argued that extant theory of "the rhetoric of social movements" fails to establish satisfactorily that there is such a thing. However much the sociologist might gain from distinguishing between movements and campaigns, it is not clear that there are inherently significant rhetorical differences. And, if not, then "the rhetoric of social movements" does not constitute a distinct theoretical domain.

What implications result from such a conclusion? It does not follow that students of movement rhetoric have wasted their time. Indeed, if the insights derived from the study of movements are applicable to persuasive campaigns generally, they may have accomplished more than they realize. It is noteworthy, for instance, that the stages and features which Griffin observed in social movements can be found in persuasive ventures ranging from public policy analysis to psychotherapy.[21] If movement scholars actually have contributed to theories of collective rhetorical behavior generally, then rather than bemoan the loss of "social movements" as a distinct category, we should rejoice at the gain.

Instead of abandoning the study of movements, then, we need to be clearer about what sorts of knowledge claims our study will produce. The primary benefits of movement studies are not theoretical but historical. The historical scholar of social movement rhetoric takes, as given, instances of collective behavior which the sociologist labels a "movement" and then examines their rhetorical dimensions. When Griffin advised studying the rhetorical component within a historical movement, he recognized that history has many dimensions. Like any other phenomenon, a historical movement can be studied from different points of view; the rhetorical historian complements the efforts of other scholars who examine the political dimensions, or the economic, or the cultural.

The movement study, then, is fundamentally a contribution to history. And significant contributions certainly have been made. For example, Griffin's own studies of the Antimasonic movement of the 1830's and the "New Left" of the 1960's have provided valuable insight into the dynamics of those social forces.[22] Andrews' study of the Chartist movement in England facilitates understanding of the turbulence surrounding early 19th-century proposals for reform.[23] And Lucas' recent study of pre-Revolutionary rhetoric in Philadelphia helps one to explain the development of a revolutionary mentality in America during the years preceding independence.[24] These examples are hardly exhaustive.

Without denigrating the theoretical insight offered by any of these studies, it seems safe to say that they reveal more about the events examined than they do about movement rhetoric in general. Distinguishing movements from other species of rhetoric was not their purpose, nor was theory construction their primary objective. Like most historical studies, they presuppose theories of history and of rhetoric. They also yield hypotheses, axioms, and some of the data from which more general theories may be built. But the reason to study the movement's rhetoric is not that a distinct class of rhetoric thereby will be identified. Instead, the reason is that the movement either had or failed to have historical significance, and that our understanding of history will be enhanced by attention to its rhetorical dimension. Such a gain in understanding, after all, is the benefit which the rhetorical historian seems best equipped to provide.

In addition to the historical role of movement studies, "movement" itself may be a useful notion as a metaphor. Rhetorical behavior of various kinds might be studied productively by examining it through the perspective which this metaphor provides. In this way, we may be able to see the acts in a different light and thereby enhance our critical understanding and appreciation. Examining the War on Poverty as a movement, for example, may illumine an otherwise hidden aspect of its nature. In like manner, Griffin describes a study in progress which uses the notion of "movement" to interpret the assassination of President Kennedy.[25] And Simons, Chesebro, and Orr analyzed the 1972 Presidential campaign from the "movement" perspective.[26] Such studies indicate that "movement" may be heuristically useful as a metaphor even if indistinct as a theoretical construct.

Finally, the difficulties surrounding the notion of "movement" as a distinct rhetorical form may prompt us to reexamine other classifications of rhetorical acts. Our usual practice has been to differentiate by subject area: political campaigns, advertising, religious conversions, legal argument, and the like.[27] Sometimes we have distinguished on the basis of the objectives sought so that we have a rhetoric of innovation, of preservation, of reform, of revolution, and of restoration. Sometimes we have distinguished according

to whether or not the campaign is an insurgent effort. What is true of movement studies may be true of other types as well: that we have created constructs and rhetorical categories prematurely, and on an *a priori* basis rather than as the outgrowth of historical research. The merit of a skeptical view of "movement studies" should be to alert us to just this danger. Instead of imprisoning ourselves in our own assumptions and arbitrarily limiting the force of our generalizations, we will ask whether the distinctiveness of a situational type has been established. We will insist that uniqueness be shown by reference to cases, troublesome cases as well as obvious ones. And we thereby will enable critics to contribute more productively to the development of potent theories of rhetorical practice. Reflection on current trends in movement studies should suggest possibilities as well as pitfalls.

Notes

[1] Leland M. Griffin, "The Rhetoric of Historical Movements," *Quarterly Journal of Speech*, 38 (1952), 184–88.

[2] Griffin, p. 188.

[3] Griffin, p. 184.

[4] See Robert S. Cathcart, "New Approaches to the Study of Movements: Defining Movements Rhetorically," *Western Speech*, 36 (1972), 82–88; "Movements: Confrontation as Rhetorical Form," *Southern Speech Communication Journal*, 43 (1978), 233–47; "Defining Social Movements Rhetorically: A Second Look," paper presented at the Eastern Communication Association Convention, Philadelphia, May 1979.

[5] David Zarefsky, "President Johnson's War on Poverty: The Rhetoric of Three 'Establishment' Movements," *Communication Monographs*, 43 (1977), 352–73.

[6] See John E. Moore, "Controlling Delinquency: Executive, Congressional, and Juvenile, 1961–64," *Congress and Urban Problems*, ed. Frederic N. Cleveland (Washington: Brookings Institution, 1968), pp. 110–72.

[7] I am indebted to David Droge who is examining epilepsy self-help groups in a dissertation in progress, Northwestern University.

[8] See S. Hultzén, "*Status* in Deliberative Analysis," *The Rhetorical Idiom*, ed. Donald C. Bryant (1958; rpt. New York: Russell and Russell, 1966), pp. 97–123.

[9] Cathcart, "Second Look."

10 See E. E. Schattschneider, *The Semisovereign People* (New York: Holt, Rinehart and Winston, 1960), pp. 16–18.

11 Herbert W. Simons, "'Genre-alizing' about Rhetoric: A Scientific Approach," *Form and Genre: Shaping Rhetorical Action,* ed. Karlyn Kohrs Campbell and Kathleen Hall Jamieson (Falls Church, Va.: Speech Communication Association, 1977), p. 33.

12 Cathcart appears to use the terms "establishment," "system," and "established agencies of change" interchangeably. In his 1978 essay, he distinguishes between "rhetorical acts which by their form uphold and reinforce the established order or system and those which reject the system, its hierarchy and its values." Cathcart, "Movements: Confrontation as Rhetorical Form," p. 237.

13 The term, "persuasive definition," is taken from Charles L. Stevenson, *Ethics and Language* (New Haven: Yale University Press, 1944), pp. 206–26.

14 For criticisms of Cathcart on other grounds, see Charles A. Wilkinson, "A Rhetorical Definition of Movements," *Central States Speech Journal,* 27 (1976), 90; Ralph R. Smith and Russel R. Windes, "The Innovational Movement: A Rhetorical Theory," *Quarterly Journal of Speech,* 61 (1975), 142; Dan F. Hahn and Ruth M. Gonchar, "Social Movement Theory: A Dead End," *Communication Quarterly,* 28 (1980), 60–64.

15 For typical definitions of "social movement," see Joseph R. Gusfield, ed., *Protest, Reform, and Revolt: A Reader in Social Movements* (New York: Wiley, 1970), p. 2; Barry McLaughlin, *Studies in Social Movements* (New York: Free Press, 1969), p. 4; Herbert Blumer, "Elementary Collective Behavior," in *New Outline of the Principles of Sociology,* ed. Alfred McClung Lee (New York: Barnes and Noble, 1949), p. 199; Neil J. Smelser, *Theory of Collective Behavior* (New York: Free Press, 1962), pp. 110, 129–30; Ralph H. Turner and Lewis M. Killian, *Collective Behavior* (Englewood Cliffs, N.J.: Prentice-Hall, 1957), p. 308. It is possible to overstate this consensus. For example, Ash characterizes the American Revolution and New Deal as social movements and suggests that the most successful movements are organized by elites. See Roberta Ash, *Social Movements in America* (Chicago: Markham, 1972).

16 "Requirements, Problems, and Strategies: A Theory of Persuasion for Social Movements," *Quarterly Journal of Speech,* 56 (1970), 1–11.

17 In one sense, the rhetorical problems facing the President and the protesters seem quite different. After all, Carter did not need to obtain access to the media, whereas acquiring access is one problem confronting a movement. Upon closer analysis, however, this difference seems illusory. *Effective* access is the key. If the President appears on television and the public does not listen or take him seriously, he is no better off than are protesters who do not receive television coverage in the first place.

18 William A. Gamson, *The Strategy of Social Protest* (Homewood, Ill.: Dorsey, 1975), p. 61.

19 Zarefsky, "President Johnson's War on Poverty."

20 Herbert W. Simons, Elizabeth Mechling, and Howard N. Schreier, "Functions of Communication in Mobilizing for Collective Action from the Bottom Up: The Rhetoric of Social Movements," *Handbook of Rhetorical and Communication Theory,* ed. Carroll C. Arnold and John Waite Bowers (Boston: Allyn and Bacon), in press.

21 See James A. Jones, "Federal Efforts to Solve Contemporary Social Problems," *Handbook on the Study of Social Problems,* ed. Erwin O. Smigel (Chicago: Rand McNally, 1971), p. 560; Jerome D. Frank, *Persuasion and Healing,* rev. ed. (Baltimore: Johns Hopkins Press, 1973), pp. 85–105.

22 Leland M. Griffin, "The Rhetorical Structure of the Antimasonic Movement," *The Rhetorical Idiom,* ed. Donald C. Bryant (1958; rpt. New York: Russell and Russell, 1966), pp. 145–59; "The Rhetorical Structure of the 'New Left' Movement: Part I," *Quarterly Journal of Speech,* 50 (1964), 113–35.

23 James R. Andrews, "The Passionate Negation: The Chartist Movement in Rhetorical Perspective," *Quarterly Journal of Speech,* 59 (1973), 196–208.

24 Stephen E. Lucas, *Portents of Rebellion: Rhetoric and Revolution in Philadelphia, 1765–76* (Philadelphia: Temple University Press, 1976).

25 Leland M. Griffin, "Encounter at Dallas: Imaginary Movements and the Rhetoric of Assassination," position paper for the Speech Communication Association Seminar on Movements, San Antonio, November 1979.

26 Herbert W. Simons, James W. Chesebro, and C. Jack Orr, "A Movement Perspective on the 1972 Presidential Campaign," *Quarterly Journal of Speech,* 59 (1973), 168–79.

27 See the chapters on persuasion in the family, in marketing, in bargaining and negotiation, in legal trials, and in political campaigns in Michael E. Roloff and Gerald R. Miller, ed., *Persuasion: New Directions in Theory and Research* (Beverly Hills, California: Sage Publications, 1980).

Coming to Terms with Movement Studies
Stephen E. Lucas

We have reached the end of the first generation of movement studies by rhetorical scholars.
Although few such studies existed prior to 1965,
better than two hundred have been published in
the past fifteen years.[1] Yet our understanding of
the rhetoric of social movements remains essentially epiphanic. Despite the insights, provocative
ideas, and heuristic values of many individual
books and essays, we have yet to develop much
systematic research or theory-building about
how rhetoric functions in the inception, progress,
and culmination of social movements. Moreover, we have become increasingly bogged down
in debate over focus and terminology. To review
and assess this debate is one cardinal aim of this
essay. The other is to recommend priorities for
scholarship in the rhetoric of social movements.

I

Almost any study of rhetorical communication
is concerned with movement in the broadest and
most literal sense of the term—especially studies
that deal with more than a single discourse:
biographical studies engage the movement of
thought, action, and expression in the career
of one man or woman; period studies treat the
movement of ideas and attitudes as revealed
in and shaped by the public rhetoric circulated
in society during a finite span of time; stylistic
analyses of the evolution and significance
of archetypal figures take up the movement of
particular modes of expression over time; genre
studies that seek to chart the development of
forms of public address attend to the movement
of recognizable patterns of discourse across time.
Situational studies also deal with movement, for
rhetorical situations are dynamic configurations
of thought and action that are constantly in
motion as they come into being, evolve, mature,
pass out of being, and give rise to other situations.
Even formalistic studies of individual rhetorical
texts must give heed to movement because rhetorical discourses are not inert entities that are
perceived whole by audiences, but are temporally

emergent symbolic acts that unfold sequentially
through time.

Yet we do not consider all such analyses to
be movement studies.[2] The phrase "movement
studies" has customarily been used by rhetoricians to designate investigations of the persuasive
efforts of a fairly large number of people working
together to alter or supplant some portion of the
existing culture or social order, usually by non-
institutionalized means.[3] In the past few years,
however, this approach—derived principally
from sociological concepts and orientations—
has been criticized by rhetoricians seeking
alternatives.

One particularly arresting critique comes from
Michael C. McGee, who disdains almost every
current construction of the concept of movement. "Empirical sociologists, social psycholo-
gists, and most contemporary rhetoricians,"
he charges, "seem to be studying 'movement'
only by a stretch of the imagination." In his
essay "In Search of 'The People': A Rhetorical
Alternative," he asserts that "movement" ought
to be thought of in its "traditional" sense, as "the
historical movement of ideas" over time. In this
volume, McGee disavows his previous notion
of "historical movement" in favor of "a hermeneutic theory of movement." "Social movement,"
he contends, "is a set of meanings and not a
phenomenon." In his view, "the whole notion
of 'movement' is mythical, a trick-of-the-mind
which must be understood *as an illusion* and not
as a fact." A defensible theory of "movement"
should therefore be constructed "as a theory
of meaning, not as a theory of phenomena, an
account of human consciousness, not an account
of human organizational behavior." Rather
than trying to create "a theory about the use of
communication *in* social movements," he says, we
would be better off "exploiting the uniqueness of
our subject matter by making a rhetorical theory
of movement."[4]

McGee's central concern is not the rhetoric
of *individual* social movements, but rhetoric as
a factor in the *general process* of social movement

(change). He directs attention to the role of rhetoric in the long-term development of social identities, cultural meanings, political norms, and the like. This is a valuable orientation, for it recognizes that public communication is a puissant force in the creation, fortification, and decay of those basic, enduring ideas and values that LeBon called "the generalized beliefs" constituting "the real framework of civilization."[5]

The usefulness of McGee's orientation, however, should not camouflage the serious flaws in his critique of social movement theory. For one thing, that critique is based largely on a series of straw men, the most important of which is the proposition, "movement is a phenomenon." McGee attributes this proposition to American empirical sociologists and to various rhetorical theorists who have drawn from their work. But the attribution is at best oversimplified. Although many sociologists and rhetoricians do believe that "movement is a phenomenon," they also believe that it is a particular kind of phenomenon—one closely related to what McGee calls "consciousness." It is a mistake to imply that the vast majority of contemporary scholars claim that social movements exist "apart from consciousness and independent of the discourse which communicates that consciousness."[6] Virtually all rhetoricians and most sociologists who deal with the subject appear to recognize that explicating a social movement requires, among other things, an account of the perceptions, opinions, beliefs, attitudes, and values—of the "consciousness"—of people involved with the movement.[7]

Not only is the general proposition "movement is a phenomenon" a straw man, so too are various of the positions McGee associates with it. Take, for example, his claim that "the argument 'Movement is a phenomenon' works only by affirming the consequent." In the course of supporting this claim, McGee states:

> By agreeing that an organization calling itself "Hitler Youth Movement" *in fact* is an empirical specification of the concept "movement," theorists would be granting an aura of factual legitimacy to a patently rhetorical ploy. Put in logical form, we would be saying "If social movements existed empirically, surely people in fact would organize themselves into groups they call 'movements.' Since people have organized themselves into groups they call 'movements,' then social movement exists empirically and can be studied objectively." That tactic . . . affirms a consequent.

So it may. But McGee does not demonstrate that there is a substantial group of sociologists or rhetoricians who actually adopt the tactic.[8] Indeed, the tactic is so preposterous that it is difficult to imagine serious scholars employing it.

The same is true of McGee's claim that it is a mistake for theorists to insist, by fiat of definition, that a group of people angrily parading in front of a factory can be classified as "'social movement' and nothing else."[9] Such insistence is doubtless mistaken. But so is McGee's implication that it is typical of prevailing sociological and rhetorical approaches to social movements. McGee does not cite any theorists who actually adopt the position he criticizes. Nor can I think of any who do. Indeed, it is difficult to imagine any student of social movements classifying a single incident such as a group of people parading in front of a factory as a social movement at all, much less claiming that such an incident could not be classified as anything but a social movement. McGee is again refuting a straw man that holds no discernible resemblance to the positions actually espoused by the people he indicts.

A second major flaw in McGee's critique is that, to a large extent, it is not specific to movement theory but could be leveled at almost any concept expressed in ordinary language. McGee's essay is informed throughout by the observation that words and their referents are not identical, that "the objective, empirical phenomenon" remains the same "despite my choice of one term or another to characterize and conceptualize it." With this truism there can be no quarrel. Nor can there be great quarrel with the claim that "however closely we define a particular 'movement,' the existence of the term in ordinary language increases the probability that it is an *a priori* label pressed from the mind either of the theorist or of the political activist onto the social events witnessed." But neither of these statements makes a special indictment of the utility of "social movement" as a descriptive label or theoretical construct, or of the proposition that "movement is a phenomenon." When examined closely, much of McGee's critique of social movement theory reduces to the commonplace observation that the term *movement* "is an interpretation of phenomenal data controlled less by what happens in the real world than by what a particular user of the analogue wants to see in the real world."[10]

In addition, the central question of McGee's essay presupposes a false dichotomy between phenomena and meaning, between objective conditions and subjective reality. Subjective reality does not exist independently of social forces, events, and institutions, but is intricately interconnected with them, both influencing their nature, direction, and impress, and in turn being influenced by them. Social movements are both phenomena and meaning. They exist in the phenomenal world, but they are phenomena about which we form perceptions, interpretations, and judgments.[11] They are in this respect no different from most other phenomena. To ask whether social movements are "phenomena or meaning" is a misleading question that ignores the complex and symbiotic relationship between the world "out there" and the ways we perceive that world and invest it with order, meaning, and evaluative shadings.[12]

Finally, it should be noted that McGee intermixes two different constructions of the term "movement" throughout his essay. At times, he uses "movement" in the broad sense—to refer to large social trends, drifts, or currents. In this usage, "social movement" might be read as meaning something akin to "social change." At other times, he uses "movement" to refer to particular social movements. Both usages are legitimate. The problem is that McGee does not distinguish clearly between them and, at times, appears to use them interchangeably. He does not take account of the fact that although the general process of movement/change in society and the operations of specific social movements are doubtless related, they are not identical. The former is a transcendent process of which the latter may compose one facet. Moreover, when McGee does use "movement" discretely, it is, as often as not, to refer to social movement/change in general. But this is not the way the term has been used in prevailing scholarship about social movements. In short, much of McGee's analysis of "movement theory" is concerned, not with particular social movements, but with the broad process of movement/change in society. As a result, it does not meet head-on the concepts and issues which have been at the center of either rhetorical or sociological scholarship about social movements.

The problems of McGee's critique notwithstanding, there is considerable attraction in his call for a rhetorical theory of movement. But even should such a theory be developed, there is no reason why McGee's approach need supplant either existing terminology about collective behavior or continued study of the rhetoric of social movements—especially since the rhetoric of social movements is often a potent force in the general process of social movement/change.

The call for a rhetorical theory of movement has much in common with the concept of "rhetorical movement." Efforts to formulate such a concept may be traced back most clearly to Robert Cathcart's essay "New Approaches to the Study of Movements: Defining Movements Rhetorically."[13] Cathcart assailed existing historical and socio-psychological definitions of movement as "*ill-suited* to the formulation of an adequate theory of the rhetoric of movements" because they do not realize that "movements are essentially rhetorical in nature." What was needed, he said, was a rhetorical definition of movements that "could make us masters of our own house rather than slaves to the historians and social scientists." Borrowing heavily from Leland M. Griffin's 1969 "Dramatistic Theory of the Rhetoric of Movements,"[14] Cathcart identified "*dialectical enjoinment in the moral arena*" as "the *necessary ingredient* which produces the rhetorical form that we have come to recognize as a political or social movement." Unfortunately, Cathcart's examination of the regnant definitions of social movements was cursory. Nor did he seek to develop more than the beginning of an alternative definition.

Charles Wilkinson later refined and extended Cathcart's partial definition to provide a more fully developed conception of rhetorical movement. Like Cathcart, Wilkinson affirmed that "all movements are essentially rhetorical," and his thinking likewise relied heavily upon the premises and vocabulary of Burkeian dramatism. He defined rhetorical movements as *"languaging strategies by which a significantly vocal part of an established society, experiencing together a sustained dialectical tension growing out of moral (ethical) conflict, agitate to induce cooperation in others, either directly or indirectly, thereby affecting the status quo."* One virtue of this definition, Wilkinson claimed, was that it demarcated the rhetorician's object of study, "thus setting him apart from either or both historian and sociologist."[15]

Although Cathcart and Wilkinson have advanced the major attempts formally to define "rhetorical movement," the phrase has been widely used, albeit most often casually, cryptically, and inexactly. In her essay on the rhetoric of women's liberation, for example, Campbell rejects out of hand historical and socio-psychological definitions of movements as the basis for rhetorical criticism. "The criteria defining a rhetorical movement," she holds, "must be rhetorical." But what she means by "rhetorical movement" is not clear. At one point she appears to use the term to refer to the rhetoric of a social movement; at another she seems to think of it as "a persuasive campaign"; at yet another she all but equates it with "genre."[16] Bormann also finds the notion of rhetorical movement attractive, although his use of it is couched in the peculiar language of fantasy theme analysis. "A rhetorical movement," he states, "contains small group fantasy chains, public fantasy events, and a rhetorical vision in a complex and reciprocal set of relationships." One result of propagating a rhetorical vision is the emergence of "a rhetorical movement." What that might be, however, Bormann does not explain.[17] In his essay on the rhetoric surrounding the war on poverty program, Zarefsky points out serious problems in previous definitions of "rhetorical movement" and calls for "a definition which identifies the rhetorical situations to be called movements." Although Zarefsky does not provide such a definition, he does suggest that "rhetorical movements" may best be thought of as synonymous with "persuasive campaigns" in general.[18]

Obviously, if the concept "rhetorical movement" is to acquire utility for either theory or research, it must receive more thorough and systematic explication. At present, it offers no evident advantages over the more sharply defined "social movement." Equally important, the premise underlying the notion of "rhetorical movement"—that movements are essentially rhetorical in nature—has yet to be demonstrated, or even adequately elucidated, although it has been asserted so repeatedly and so insistently that one would think it had been. It will not do to adduce *a priori* premises about the nature of man as a symbol-using animal or about the general importance of rhetoric in society and then to move blithely from those premises to the conclusion that social movements in particular are essentially rhetorical in nature. The claim that social movements are essentially rhetorical is an empirical claim that requires empirical confirmation.[19] Nor will it do to say that "movements as he [the rhetorical analyst] studies them are in their *essence* rhetorical,"[20] for such statements are really about the scholarly interests of rhetoricians and not about the nature of social movements. After all, movements are doubtless essentially historical for the historian and essentially social for the sociologist.[21]

But even if the claim that movements are essentially rhetorical in nature were adequately enucleated and authoritatively established, it would not necessarily follow that "social movements" should be discarded in favor of "rhetorical movements"—especially since, as Zarefsky has suggested, the latter may most profitably be seen as a larger category of which social movements compose only one subset.[22]

Advocates of "rhetorical movement" have too hastily discounted the utility for rhetorical scholarship of sociological orientations to social movements. Although sociologists "generally feel more comfortable studying social structure and behavior than studying symbols and belief systems,"[23] there is little in current sociological thinking that is inherently hostile to studying movements from a rhetorical perspective. Indeed, there is much to encourage such study. For one thing, some sociologists have dealt insightfully with matters germane to the rhetoric of social movements, including rumor as an element in collective behavior, the determinants of social movement strategies, the influence of countermovement activities upon movement development, channels of communication as a factor in the growth and maintenance of social movements, the public perception of protest, how movements "manage" the available "resources" to realize their objectives, the ways movement leaders use verbal and nonverbal symbols to define and sell their ideology and to stimulate followers to action.[24]

More important, many sociologists now appear to agree that the ultimate success of social movements depends upon their ability to challenge persuasively prevailing thoughts, beliefs, attitudes, and values. The *outcome* of a successful social movement is usually alteration in some area of established social relations, Herbert Blumer explains, but the essential *process* of a movement is one "in which attention has to be gained, interests awakened, grievances exploited, ideas implanted, doubts dispelled, feelings aroused, new objects created, and new perspectives developed."[25] To say that a social movement has taken place is to say that there have occurred changes of some magnitude in the "feelings, resentments, worries, fears, concerns, and hopes of large numbers of people."[26] Discontent, many sociologists now recognize, is a psychological phenomenon. In the words of John Wilson, "the origins of social unrest cannot be fully described until the meaning which actors themselves attach to the situation has been discovered."[27] "Collective behavior is not only collective action," Turner and Killian state, "it is also collaboration in creating an accepted version of reality."[28] It is today a basic tenet among sociologists that social movements are energized by a powerful set of beliefs regarding what is wrong with things as they are and what should be done about them. It is widely acknowledged that to study the rise and progress of social movements is, among other things, to study the processes through which beliefs are generated, articulated, promulgated, and come to be accepted (or rejected) by groups in society.

Social movements are complex phenomena that invite interrogation from a number of perspectives. Sociological and rhetorical perspectives are best seen as complementary. To date, students of communication have illuminated many aspects of social movements, including the rhetorical structure of social movements,

the rhetorical problems confronting movement leaders, the rhetorical strategies employed to surmount these problems, the psycho-symbolic features of movement discourse, the legal and ethical dimensions of movement rhetoric, and the generic features of the rhetoric of movements. Rhetoricians can continue to investigate these and other aspects of movement rhetoric without either denigrating the value of sociological studies or inventing neologisms.[29]

Ultimately, the most important test of any scholarly concept is whether it allows us better to describe, analyze, and interpret the phenomena with which it purports to deal. Thus far, the concept "rhetorical movement" has not stood up to this test. It is much easier to announce objectives and principles than to apply them fruitfully in criticism and easier to adumbrate new approaches to rhetorical analysis than to put them into practice.[30] It is also much simpler to call for new theories than to develop them. What we need is less controversy about definitions, orientations, and presuppositions and more research.

This is not to say that such controversy should be eschewed. But as pluralism is the watchword in other areas of rhetorical scholarship, so should it be here as well. There is no reason why some analysts cannot study persuasive campaigns in general, others the broad process of social movement/change, and still others the rhetoric of social movements. All three approaches take as their subjects differing, albeit related, phenomena. The value of each will ultimately depend, not upon ringing assertions of its superiority, nor upon its claim to be the special property of any academic discipline, but upon the quality and significance of the studies conducted in its name. With this in mind, I should like briefly to suggest some directions for future scholarship in the rhetoric of social movements.

II

The place to begin is by noting that rhetorical analysts too often fail to come to terms with the intrinsically kinetic nature of movement rhetoric. As I have observed elsewhere, a social movement is not a material object that exists only in a given place and at a given time, but is a progression of human behavior which must be understood in temporal as well as in spatial terms.[31] Neither a movement nor its discourse are static. My point is not that the discourse of a movement unfolds chronologically; that is self-evident. Nor is my contention that movements proceed through various stages that are accompanied by permutations in rhetoric; this has long been recognized. Charting the temporal progression of discourse is only the beginning step in understanding the rhetoric of a social movement. More vital are the further steps of 1) explicating the cumulative metamorphosis of discourse in response to emerging exigencies imposed from within and without the movement and 2) assaying how that metamorphosis functions. The passage of a social movement through the stages of inception, crisis and consummation is less important than the ways rhetoric helps to propel the movement from stage to stage or to retard its evolution. To demonstrate that the rhetoric of a movement is different at moment C from what it was at moment B, and different at moment B from what it was at moment A, is only propaedeutic to the crucial tasks of explaining why the discourse evolved as it did and of assessing how that evolution influenced the nature, direction, intensity, and outcome of the movement.

But rhetoric is not all that "moves" in a social movement. Social movements arise out of and are shaped by the dynamic interaction of multifarious and effervescent forces. For present purposes, I shall focus on three: objective material conditions, rhetorical discourse, and the perceptions, attitudes, and values—the "consciousness"—held by the members. None of these forces "moves" independently of the others. Scholars who wish to explicate how rhetoric functions in social movements need to deal with all three forces and the interconnections among them. Understanding as they do that rhetoric is "a vital . . . shaping agent in human affairs,"[32] rhetoricians frequently beg the question when it comes to demonstrating how rhetoric actually shapes human affairs. Too often, they adopt a sort of rhetorical determinism that oversimplifies the complex linkages between rhetorical communication and important contextual variables—institutional arrangements, socioeconomic structures, technological developments,

demographic patterns, environmental conditions, channels of communication, and the like. The role of rhetoric in social movements cannot be explained either by looking solely at the formal properties of movement discourse or by applying *a priori* premises about the importance of rhetoric in the construction of social reality, but only by careful investigation of the interplay between discourse and the other factors that condition the process of social movements.

Such investigation can go forward most profitably in two ways. One is by explicitly theory-oriented studies that advance carefully drawn, substantive hypotheses about the rhetoric of social movements and then explore those hypotheses precisely and systematically.[33] Another is by essentially atheoretical case studies that analyze the rhetoric of individual movements from the inside out. At present, the need for such case studies appears to be more pressing than that for theory-oriented studies because the most telling deficiency for the generation of theory about movement rhetoric is the absence of sufficient knowledge about the role of rhetoric in particular movements. Such knowledge will provide a crucial foundation for mature, empirically-grounded theory.

Among the kinds of case studies that need to be undertaken, perhaps foremost are ones that deal exactingly, not just with some facet or another of movement rhetoric, but with the rhetoric of individual movements from inception through culmination. One advantage of such a comprehensive approach is that it compels the analyst to treat the movement and its discourse as temporal processes, rather than as static entities. Another is that it encourages the analyst to engage the full body of movement rhetoric, rather than to focus just on one set of historically prominent addresses or on the discourse of a conspicuous leader. A study of the rhetoric of Samuel Adams, or of the Boston Massacre orations, for instance, is not a study of the American revolutionary movement. A third advantage of the comprehensive approach is that it allows one to see the rhetoric of a social movement in its full complexity. Although we have a large number of individual studies dealing with particular aspects of movement rhetoric, we do not have a good sense of the significance of those aspects vis à vis one another. For example, it is important to know that the rhetorical activities of protest movements may fulfill for participants.[34] But it is equally important to understand the relationships among this ego-function and other functions performed by movement rhetoric. One avenue to such understanding is through intensive, comprehensive study of the discourse of individual movements.

Such study is admittedly most feasible with historical movements. Although the great surge of interest in current rhetorical transactions has yielded substantial dividends, the decidedly contemporary orientation of the great bulk of movement studies leads one to question the extent to which our general understanding of the rhetoric of social movements is skewed by an excessive reliance on movements of the past two decades.[35] Of course, contributions to our knowledge of rhetorical behavior are defined less by the artifacts or acts we examine than by the questions we ask about them and the answers we provide. Still, looking at certain kinds of phenomena precludes asking certain kinds of questions. It is idle, for example, to seek to investigate the long-range rhetorical consequences of a contemporary social movement. Moreover, a certain kind of myopia is almost inescapable in studies of contemporary phenomena. The perspective afforded by the passage of time is an asset not to be lightly dismissed, particularly since there are numerous historical movements that would richly reward rhetorical scrutiny. The turbulence of the 1960's notwithstanding, the first half of the nineteenth century remains the period of greatest and most intense social ferment in American history. From the election of Jefferson to the onset of the Civil War, America witnessed a remarkable variety of social movements, including several waves of religious revivalism, powerful crusades against Masonry, Catholicism, immigrants, and slavery, and concerted efforts in behalf of utopian communalism, temperance, women's rights, and southern sectionalism. Imaginative and resourceful analysis of the discourse of such historical movements would not only be valuable in its own right, but would appreciably enrich our developing theoretical understanding of movement rhetoric in general.

By the same token, we could profit greatly by developing a body of substantive studies dealing with the rhetoric of social movements in Europe, Asia, and Africa. Rhetorical scholars have heretofore confined themselves almost exclusively to investigating movements indigenous to America or Great Britain. Yet the social, political, and religious values and institutions, as well as the rhetorical traditions and praxes, of Anglo-America are not necessarily those of other Western nations and are most certainly not those of non-Occidental nations. We should know much more than we do about the rhetoric of such movements as the French, Russian, and Chinese revolutions, the millenarian quests of medieval Europe, and the anti-colonial crusades of the developing Third World nations. In studying the discourse of such movements, it will be crucial to keep in mind that the standards of rhetoric as they have developed in the West for the past 2,000 years are unique "expressions of Western culture, applicable within the context of Western cultural values." Should we seek to deal with the rhetoric of non-Western nations solely "in terms that have proved appropriate in the West, the results would be biased, inadequate, and misleading."[36] Rhetoricians who study Continental or Third World social movements will face the formidable task of mastering cultures and languages different from their own. But until such study is undertaken in earnest, our understanding of the rhetoric of social movements will remain partial and parochial.

Finally, we ought not to overlook the rhetoric of those forces that arise in opposition to social movements. Countermovement groups may be spearheaded by private citizens or by public authorities. In either case, their activities—rhetorical and nonrhetorical—almost always compose a crucial variable in the development of social movements. Once a movement has evoked active opposition, it evolves through a series of events and counterevents, assertions and counterassertions, strategies and counterstrategies. We cannot explicate adequately the rhetoric of a movement until we take into account the exigencies it was designed to surmount. Among such exigencies are those imposed by the rhetoric of hostile forces outside the movement. Although that rhetoric may be, strictly speaking, extrinsic to a movement, it is crucial to comprehending the functional attributes of movement discourse. Moreover, the rhetoric of countermovement advocates is a subject that merits serious inquiry in and of itself. Like other scholars, rhetoricians have generally been more interested in studying social change than social maintenance. We need to learn much more about the symbolic processes of social control, and investigating countermovement rhetoric in defense of established ideas and institutions is one route to such learning.

"What should we be doing?" and "How should we do it?" are perennial questions for any area of scholarship. By posing them in this essay, my aim has not been so much to criticize what has been done in the past as to suggest ways of improving what is to be done in the future. We should now be ready to put at rest disputes over definition, focus, and terminology and to get on with the task of building a more substantial sophisticated body of research in all areas of movement studies.

Notes

1 These are reviewed by Herbert Simons, Elizabeth Mechling, and Howard Schreier, "Functions of Communication in Mobilizing for Collective Action from the Bottom Up: The Rhetoric of Social Movements," *Handbook of Rhetorical and Communication Theory*, eds. Carroll C. Arnold and John Waite Bowers (Boston: Allyn and Bacon), in press. All quotations from this essay are from the pre-publication manuscript.

2 For a contrary view see Malcolm Sillars, "Defining Movements Rhetorically: Casting the Widest Net," *Southern Speech Communication Journal*, 46 (1980), 17–32.

3 This definition of "social movements" is an amalgam of those offered by Wm. Bruce Cameron, *Modern Social Movements* (New York: Random House, 1966), p. 7, and John Wilson, *Introduction to Social Movements* (New York: Basic Books, 1973), p. 8.

4 *Quarterly Journal of Speech*, 61 (1975), 235n; "'Social Movement': Phenomenon or Meaning?" *Central States Speech Journal* (this issue), 1, 15–17 [from original ms.].

5 Gustave LeBon, *The Crowd: A Study of the Popular Mind* (1895; rpt. New York: Viking, 1960), p. 142. My characterization of McGee's overriding interest in the general process of social movement/change is based not only upon his essay for this volume, but also upon other of his writings, especially

"The 'Ideograph': A Link between Rhetoric and Ideology," *Quarterly Journal of Speech*, 66 (1980), 1–16; "The Origins of 'Liberty': A Feminization of Power," *Communication Monographs*, 47 (1980), 23–45; and "In Search of 'The People.'"

6 McGee, "'Social Movement'," p. 18 [from ms.].

7 This point receives fuller treatment later in my essay.

8 McGee, "'Social Movement'," pp. 13–14 [from ms.]. To be sure, McGee claims that the tactic is "characteristically employed by such lights of American empirical sociology as Smelser and Bell," but he does not actually quote either as saying anything that closely resembles the hypothetical statement he condemns as affirming a consequent. Nor can I find any such statement in the works by Bell and Smelser cited by McGee in footnote 25. Moreover, I cannot find in the pages of Dolbeare and Dolbeare's *American Ideologies* cited by McGee an indictment of Bell that corresponds with McGee's. Indeed, Bell is not mentioned by name anywhere in those pages, except on page 20, as a bibliographical entry. To make such a serious indictment of Smelser, Bell, and, by implication, other leading students of social movements requires something more concrete than a hypothetical scenario.

9 McGee, "'Social Movement'," p. 6 [from ms.].

10 Ibid., pp. 6, 12, 7 [from ms.]. A further caveat might be entered here. McGee implies that ordinary language cannot be used precisely and that the term "movement" is invariably used sloppily and inexactly. Neither implication is correct. Indeed, much of the energy of contemporary scholarship is devoted to using ordinary language in increasingly precise ways, and not without success. Moreover, contrary to McGee's suggestion, the term "movement" is not always "the expression of those who need, seek and see 'progress' or 'destiny'" (p. 17) [from ms.]. It is used impartially by scholars to designate a certain type of collective behavior. McGee need not agree with that usage, but he errs in attributing the motivations of interested political agents to everyone who uses the term "movement."

11 And, of course, part of that process of perception, interpretation, and judgment includes the very act of deciding which phenomena are properly to be labeled "social movements."

12 Early in his essay, McGee appears to recognize the problems of divorcing objective phenomena from meaning. By the end, however, he appears to revert to a hard-and-fast distinction between social movements as phenomena and as meanings attached to phenomena. This is most evident in his statement that, as far as social movements are concerned, he sees "no phenomenon at all, only

a series of words with meanings to be discovered and verified" (p. 19) [from ms.]. In so stating, McGee also intimates that discourse itself does not exist as an objective phenomenon. But this is a very curious position indeed. Would it not be preferable to say that rhetorical documents exist as objective phenomena, but that the meanings attached to those documents are matters of social construction?

13 *Western Speech*, 36 (1972), 82–88. Also see Cathcart's "Movements: Confrontation as Rhetorical Form," *Southern Speech Communication Journal*, 43 (1978), 233–47, as well as his essay in this issue.

14 In *Critical Responses to Kenneth Burke*, ed. William H. Rueckert (Minneapolis: University of Minnesota Press, 1969), pp. 456–78.

15 Charles Wilkinson, "A Rhetorical Definition of Movements," *Central States Speech Journal*, 27 (1976), 88–94.

16 Karlyn Kohrs Campbell, "The Rhetoric of Women's Liberation: An Oxymoron," *Quarterly Journal of Speech*, 59 (1973), 74–86.

17 Ernest G. Bormann, "Fantasy and Rhetorical Vision: The Rhetorical Criticism of Social Reality," *Quarterly Journal of Speech*, 58 (1972), 399.

18 David Zarefsky, "President Johnson's War on Poverty: The Rhetoric of Three 'Establishment' Movements," *Communication Monographs*, 44 (1977), 371–72.

19 It should be noted that my aim here is not to deny that social movements are essentially rhetorical (they may be), but to stress that the claim cannot be accepted until it is demonstrated and not simply asserted.

20 Zarefsky, p. 371.

21 Wilkinson recognizes this much, but his efforts to answer the question, "What is the essence of movements *qua* movement?" are overly facile and partly circular. Note, for example, his claim that "because of the nature of man, of language, and of movements themselves, all movements are essentially rhetorical, having historical, sociological, and other components defined according to the accidents of time, place, and circumstance" ("Rhetorical Definition," p. 92).

22 Zarefsky, p. 372.

23 Gary T. Marx and James L. Wood, "Strands of Theory and Research in Collective Behavior," in *Annual Review of Sociology*, ed. Alex Inkeles, James Coleman, and Neil Smelser (Palo Alto: Annual Review, Inc., 1975), p. 382.

24 See, for example, Gordon W. Allport and Leo Postman, *The Psychology of Rumor* (New York: Henry Holt, 1947); Ralph H. Turner, "Determinants of Social Movement Strategies," in *Human Nature and Collective Behavior: Papers in Honor of Herbert Blumer*, ed. Tomatsu Shibutani (Englewood Cliffs: Prentice-Hall, 1970), pp. 145–64; Neil J. Smelser, *Theory of Collective Behavior* (New York: Free Press, 1963); Ralph H. Turner, "The Public Perception of Protest," *American Sociological Review*, 34 (1969), 815–31; Anthony Oberschall, *Social Conflict and Social Movements* (Englewood Cliffs: Prentice-Hall, 1973); William A. Gamson, *The Strategy of Social Protest* (Homewood: Dorsey, 1975); Hugh Dalziel Duncan, *Communication and Social Order* (New York: Oxford University Press, 1968); Clifford Geertz, "Ideology as a Cultural System," in *Ideology and Discontent*, ed. David E. Apter (Glencoe: Free Press, 1964), pp. 47–76; Leo Lowenthal and Norbert Guterman, *Prophets of Deceit: A Study of the Techniques of the American Agitator* (New York: Harper and Row, 1949). For detailed reviews of the sociological literature on social movements consult Marx and Wood, "Strands of Theory and Research"; Stanley Milgram and Hans Toch, "Collective Behavior: Crowds and Social Movements," in *Handbook of Social Psychology*, 2nd ed., ed. Gardner Lindzey and Elliott Aronson (Reading: Addison-Wesley, 1968–69), IV, 507–610.

25 "Collective Behavior," in *Review of Sociology: Analysis of a Decade*, ed. Joseph B. Gittler (New York: Wiley and Sons, 1957), p. 148.

26 Milgram and Toch, "Collective Behavior," p. 585.

27 Wilson, p. 68.

28 Ralph H. Turner and Lewis M. Killian, *Collective Behavior*, 2nd ed. (Englewood Cliffs: Prentice-Hall, 1972), p. 249.

29 Cf. Simons, Mechling, and Schreier, "Mobilizing for Collective Action," 13.

30 Donald C. Bryant, "Of Style: Buffon and Rhetorical Criticism," in *Essays on Rhetorical Criticism*, ed. Thomas R. Nilsen (New York: Random House, 1968), p. 53.

31 Stephen E. Lucas, *Portents of Rebellion: Rhetoric and Revolution in Philadelphia, 1765–76* (Philadelphia: Temple University Press, 1976), p. xx.

32 Leland M. Griffin, "The Rhetoric of Historical Movements," *Quarterly Journal of Speech*, 38 (1952), 188.

33 Nor, contrary to David Zarefsky's claim, must such studies be predicated upon the assumption that movements comprise a distinct rhetorical genre, "A Skeptical View of Movement Studies," *Central States Speech Journal* [this issue]. It is one thing to identify a phenomenon and to ask what it is and

how it functions; it is quite another to ask whether the phenomenon is unique. Although the latter is doubtless an important question concerning the rhetoric of social movements, it does not have to be answered affirmatively in order to construct generalizations of a theoretical order about the nature and functions of the rhetoric employed in social movements.

34 Richard B. Gregg, "The Ego-Function of the Rhetoric of Protest," *Philosophy and Rhetoric*, 4 (1971), 71–91.

35 The categorization of "movement-related" studies by Simons, Mechling, and Schreier ("Mobilizing for Collective Action," note 11) appears to indicate that studies of historical movements have predominated over analyses of contemporary movements. But some of the historical studies they list can be classified as "movement studies," or even as "movement-related," only by a stretch of the imagination. Two cases in point are Michael McGuire's essays "Rhetoric, Philosophy and the Volk: Johann Gottlieb Fichte's *Addresses to the German Nation*," *Quarterly Journal of Speech*, 62 (1976), 135–44, and "Mythic Rhetoric in *Mein Kampf*: A Structuralist Critique," *Quarterly Journal of Speech*, 63 (1977), 1–13.

36 Robert T. Oliver, *Communication and Culture in Ancient India and China* (Syracuse: Syracuse University Press, 1971), p. 3.

History and Theory in the Study of the Rhetoric of Social Movements
James R. Andrews

Discussing Leland Griffin's seminal essay, "The Rhetoric of Historical Movements," Edwin Black observed that Griffin, by "suggesting a reconstitution of the subject matter of rhetorical criticism from the individual speaker or the individual speech to the persuasive movement," had "opened a new and exciting prospect to rhetorical criticism."[1] In the thirty years since Griffin's essay was published, the study of social movements by rhetorical scholars has become extensive and serious. But there has also been something of a revolution in rhetorical criticism in recent years. As Black has put it[,] "There is less uniformity in the techniques of rhetorical criticism and in the sorts of subjects deemed appropriate to it, less agreement on its proper role or its ideal condition, more contention, more experiment, more confusion, more vitality."[2] What is true of criticism in general is also true of the study of the rhetoric of social movements in particular.

One aim of this symposium is to systematize what we know and to focus future research. The goal of this paper is to contribute to these efforts by offering and discussing the following propositions. First, theory must be grounded in and related to the history of movement rhetoric. Second, theory can enrich historical investigation by suggesting lines of inquiry and patterns of interpretation. Third, historical investigation can identify complexities that have the potential for confounding or enhancing theory construction. Fourth, historical investigation which is free of the constraints of theory validation or extension may, in the long run, provide more useful data for theory construction.

THEORY AND HISTORY

The exciting, and frustrating, characteristic of a movement is that it *moves*, and what makes it move, in large measure, is the way language is manipulated to control or interpret events. In this sense, rhetoric makes moving possible—moving in all directions, pushing, shoving, lurching forward and falling backward as the movement encounters its environment. Growing out of the environment, intruding into the environment, reacting to the environment, and becoming a part of the environment, the social movement is simultaneously a rhetorical response and a rhetorical stimulus.

Out of this jumble of events, some sense must be made by those who experience them. Any set of human actions is likely to be perceived differently when experienced from the way they are perceived, recollected, or reconstructed. "The historian's choice of significant incidents," Wedgwood once observed, "is often different from that of contemporaries."[3] What rhetoric, itself, does is to define and interpret the significance of human activity for those engaged in the activity.

Theorists seek to explain how rhetoric performs this defining and interpreting function predictably in social movements in general. But a theory of the rhetoric of social movements can best be generated when it is grounded in the history of movement rhetoric.[4] To be sure, few theoretical arguments about the rhetoric of social movements ignore history altogether. The quality of such arguments, however, is much improved when based on a developed and detailed historical case study rather than a few selected examples that provoke the theorist's imagination.

Although theory often grows out of basic historical research, it is also true that theory can stimulate and offer direction to historians. The investigation of real cases can be aided when rhetorical scholars are stimulated to look for consistent patterns that have been observed and generalized. At the least, theoretical categories can direct historical inquiry. The work of Campbell on the women's movement, Gregg on modern protest rhetoric, and my own study of the role of coercion and persuasion in the student protest at Columbia are but a few examples of studies that have been shaped, or at least stimulated, by theoretical perspectives.[5]

The examination of historical cases and the construction of theory, then, are inextricably bound together. Historical investigation is the data base, as it were, for theory; theory, for its part, can enrich the historian's inventional process. At the same time, historical inquiry is necessarily atheoretical in a fundamental way.

Butterfield, in his indictment of the Whig interpretation of history, warned historians against precisely what theorists must do—generalize the predictability of human behavior. It is not for the historian, Butterfield asserted, "to stress and magnify the similarities between one age and another. . . . Rather, it is his work to destroy those very analogies which we imagine to exist."[6] Although scholars in all fields

recognize the immense complexity of human behavior, historians have long been particularly suspicious of theory. As Plumb has argued, for example, particular constructions of the meaning of the past have been used in order to exert social control.[7] The rhetorical historian's independence of theory must come through his or her willingness to examine the process of rhetorical influence without preconceived theoretical notions of how that process must have worked in particular cases. Smith and Windes, in their critique of current movement theory, argue, for example, that theorists' particular focus on radical segments of movement rhetoric has distorted, or at least limited, a broader understanding of movement rhetoric. Now their point may well be arguable, but it certainly suggests that the historical/critical process could certainly be skewed significantly if the historian began his or her investigation with the preconception of how rhetoric operated in all movements.[8]

The historian, by asking the question, how did rhetoric function in a particular social movement, may uncover complexities of or deviations from current theory, and may consequently generate data enriching the development of theory. Essentially, atheoretical historical studies provide less tainted information with which theorists can subsequently deal. These propositions may be further explicated by brief reference to the rhetoric of one historical movement.

HENRY HUNT AND THE MOVEMENT FOR POLITICAL REFORM

For radicals during the Regency period, the most common established way of communicating with Parliament was by means of petitions. Petitions, when presented in the House of Commons, always occasioned a speech by a supporter of the petition and rarely provoked extended debate. But more important, particularly for the unrepresented working class, was the process of preparing and presenting the petitions and the speechmaking called forth by the mass meetings at which petitions were approved. These mass meetings provided a way of expressing feelings and attitudes for those who had few other ways of doing so; from them emerged a truly radical rhetoric shaped by situational factors that denied the masses both direct access to the power structure and a means of voicing their discontent.[9]

Radical speakers who addressed the petition meetings faced several interrelated problems: to speak meaningfully to the crowds attending, to avoid provoking the local magistrates to take immediate punitive action, to goad the upper classes into concessions without frightening them into repression, and to maintain the image of the peaceable constitutionalist employing lawful and traditionally sanctioned means of reform.[10] Naturally, no one succeeded in solving all of these difficulties, but the radical speaker who came closest was Henry Hunt, "impudent, active, vulgar; in almost all respects the best mob orator of the day."[11] His rhetoric mixed ominous allusions to the day when "men would demand their rights ... or die nobly in the struggle," with denunciations of "the children of corruption, who fattened on the vitals of the country."[12]

Henry Hunt was a powerful—and flamboyant—orator, in both language and delivery, and addressed the cheering multitudes with consummate skill.[13] E. P. Thompson observed that the "very frustrations of a popular movement, in which thousands of powerless men were pitted against an armed establishment, were released in hyperbole; and Hunt, as the orator of the great reform assemblies, knew how to touch these responses."[14] Touching the mob, however, was not regarded in better quarters as a worthy thing to do. As Lord Castlereagh frostily remarked, "I am grown as popular in 1821 as unpopular formerly, and, of the two, unpopularity is the more convenient and gentleman-like."[15] Hunt was and still is regarded as a demagogue. Even the generally sympathetic Thompson concludes that "Hunt voiced, not principle or even well-formulated Radical strategy, but the emotions of the moment. Striving always to say whatever would provoke the loudest cheer, he was not the leader but the captive of the least stable portion of the crowd."[16]

This view of Hunt, however, overlooks the important role of the agitator in movement rhetoric. The emotions he expressed were real and salient to the working class. As Wendell Phillips, another great agitator, once observed, "The great mass of people can never be made to stay and argue a long question. . . . They must be made to feel it through the hides of their idols."[17]

Representative in form and content of Hunt's rhetoric was a speech he delivered at a mass meeting held at Spa Fields on November 15, 1816.[18] Hunt's speech addressed two audiences in a distinctive way.

First, he issued a warning to the upper classes. The threat to the powerful is unmistakable even if implicit enough to avoid the charge of out-and-out incitement. Physical force was to give way to the petitioning process, but such force *was* surely justifiable as a last resort. The address to the Prince Regent called upon him to recommend to Parliament that it "listen, before it is *too late,* to those repeated prayers of the People."[19]

Second, Hunt took great pains to convince the working class to perceive itself positively. There was an image of the labouring class, held and propagated by the ruling class, that cast the "lower orders" in an unsavory role. Charles Kingsley was later to observe that "young men believed ... that the masses were their natural enemies," and that they would have to be prepared to fight to save their property from being pillaged and their sisters from being ravished.[20] David Giddies, in attacking a bill to set up parish schools for the poor, told the House of Commons in 1807 that educating the "labouring classes of the poor" was a measure "pregnant with mischief." Education would undermine the role that Giddies clearly saw as the proper role of the lower classes: being "good servants in agriculture, and other laborious employments, to which their rank in society has destined them."[21] Canning, as Hunt alleged, was pleased to refer to "the swinish multitude."[22] The image of the labouring class was seen in vivid relief when contrasted with the middle class. The workers were consistently distinguished from the "respectable" elements of society. And it was the "middling classes" that Sir James Mackintosh believed "possess the largest share of sense and virtue."[23] Political cartoonists, always especially savage no matter what side they were on, caricatured the lower classes and their radical leaders. In July, 1819, a cartoon, "The Smithfield Parliament: i.e., universal suffrage—the new speaker addressing the members," shows Hunt with the head of an ass speaking to an audience of cattle, sheep, pigs, and donkeys. "I shall be ambitious, indeed," the Hunt depiction says, "if I thought my bray would be heard by the immense and respectable multitude I have the honour to address." The audience of domestic animals applaud, murmur approval, and shout, "here here!—bravo!"[24]

To undermine such caricatures, Hunt redefined the images of both the working class and the ruling class by exalting the former and exerating [*sic*] the latter. Taxation, he said, was at the heart of all distress. The people were being taxed unmercifully to retire a debt resulting from fighting a war to suppress liberty (the war against Napoleonic France) and from maintaining an army in France to uphold the tyrannical Bourbons against the wishes of the French people, to keep a standing army at home to awe Englishmen, and to provide a plethora of pensions and sinecures for the family, friends, and political supporters of the ruling class. The solution, said Hunt, was to provide representation of the people in the House of Commons, which would then put an end to corruption. Such an argument cast the lower classes as the producers of taxes and as the useful portion of society.[25]

The deference of servant to master and the conviction that one's station in life was not only inferior but inescapable, worked against self-respect for the lower classes. In his speech, Hunt combined argument with style to portray a much different kind of contrast between the classes. He used stylistic elements to establish a vision of the "oppressors" as vile parasites who bore down upon the workers. The metaphor portrayed England's rulers as loathsome scavengers, the "children of corruption" who "fatten on the vitals of the country." Those who "devoured" the people's earnings "gorged and fattened on the spoils of an oppressed nation." Obviously, such men were hardly to be deferred to, admired, or, ultimately, obeyed.

To establish group consciousness, Hunt relied largely on contrast. He juxtaposed "the borough-mongering faction, who thought of nothing but oppressing the people," against a positive image of the "people" themselves. The people, according

to Hunt, suffered and were yet patient and brave through their sufferings. Taxed on his "loaf," his "pot of beer," and his "bushel of salt," forced by taxes to pay double for "his soap, candles, sugar, tea, and other articles," the labourer was a "miserable victim." The "People of England" might be "hungry" and "naked," they might be an "unhappy and starving People," but they were "industrious and patient" nonetheless. The contrast was clear. There were the oppressors and the victims; those taxed on the necessities of life and those profligates who spent the tax; the plunderers and the plundered; the industrious People of England and the scavengers who exploited them. The patient victim would seem to be justified in throwing off the yoke, but violence, Hunt recognized, would be "folly." Nevertheless, the right to make demands was unquestionable.

Admittedly, this illustration is not the full analysis and description of the rhetoric of a movement alluded to in the first section of this paper. It is the merest distillation of a much more intensive study. But as an example, it may serve to highlight the major points advanced earlier in this paper.

THEORETICAL IMPLICATIONS AND FURTHER RESEARCH

Simons and his colleagues have offered a definition of social movements as "sustained efforts by non-institutionalized collectives to mobilize resources, resist counter-pressures and exert external influence in behalf of a cause."[26] To the student of rhetoric, the crucial consideration is precisely how these "sustained efforts" translate into rhetorical behaviors.

A collective must first be conscious of itself. Any movement must deal somehow with social perceptions of reality by using rhetoric to alter, shape, and extend the ways in which the world is seen by those living in it. If one were to look carefully at the rhetorical response to societal problems in the early stages of a movement, he/she might provide data for hypotheses that delineates a strategy generalizable to what might be called the "collectivization" stage. Looking at the rhetoric of radical reformers like Henry Hunt, theorists interested in the formation of coalitions might discern ways in which the vilification of authority plays a positive role in social movements. Thompson tends to see the "demagogic element" as encouraging "the wholly unconstructive rhetoric of denunciation."[27] But was Hunt's denunciation so obviously illogical? On the contrary, it played a vital role in shaping the lower classes' perception of themselves. From the historical-rhetorical analysis, then, a possible hypothesis emerges: Groups must define themselves in a positive manner before they can truly become a collective, and rhetorical strategies such as denunciation may further the prerequisite group consciousness. Some theorists would not find this a particularly novel idea, but the rhetoric of Henry Hunt does provide data with which one can deal.

Other theorists may wish to examine the rhetoric of British reformers from a social knowledge perspective since "the over-arching function of social knowledge," according to Farrell, "is to transform the society into a community."[28] The efforts of radicals to deal with the conflicting audiences might well be examined with an eye to discovering how radicals attempted to establish for these audiences a "personal relationship to other actors in the social world." A fuller understanding of the rhetorical problems faced by reformers might be reached by exploring Farrell's contention that both advocates and audiences "will—of necessity—presume a kind of knowledge which depends upon our direct or indirect experiences of collective 'others,' and which applies an interest to these others which is generalizable."

Still other theorists might find in the discourse of men like Henry Hunt clues to the nature and function of ideographs in social movements. In a recent study, McGee suggested the more careful study of what he termed the "ideograph" based on the argument "that the ideology of a community is established by the usage of such terms in specifically rhetorical discourse, for such use as constitute excuses for specific beliefs and behaviors made by those who executed the history of which they were a part."[29] The study of nineteenth-century reformist rhetoric, particularly that stream of which Hunt is a representative, would seem to be a particularly fruitful area in which to search for the ideograph

in action, since, according to McGee, "an ideograph is an ordinary language term found in political discourse. It is a high-order abstraction representing collective commitment to a particular but equivocal and ill-defined normative goal. It warrants the use of power, it excuses behavior and belief which might otherwise be perceived as eccentric or antisocial, and guides behavior and belief into channels easily recognized by a community as acceptable and laudable."[30]

It might also be that the particular forms of language used by reformists of all stripes could provide a basis for useful theoretical constructions. As Jensen, who recently studied the use of metaphor in British debates on the American revolution, observed that, "a complex, abstract, fluid reality may be made inappropriately into a simple, concrete, and static 'reality' through the metaphor."[31] Simons and his colleagues, citing Lucas on radical Whig rhetoric in pre-Revolutionary Philadelphia, conclude that one of the long-term effects that movements have on the forms of rhetoric used by later groups is that its "style of discourse may also set a precedent."[32] Both the enemies of reform who were apt to describe the masses as the "swinish multitude" and the radicals who saw those in power as the "children of corruption" offer highly suggestive lines of inquiry and masses of data for those scholars who seek to explicate the rhetorical power of metaphor.[33]

In these instances, and in others that could be adduced, it is clear that theory and history can interact to the mutual enrichment of both. Given the data generated by an historical study, theorists are provided with more evidence against which to test their constructs. In turn, theoretical constructs may suggest useful lines of inquiry for historical study as well as offering explanations for what otherwise might be puzzling.

There is, of course, a caveat. Propositions that assert the independence of rhetoric and theory should suggest that over-reliance on theoretical constructs can lead to intellectual myopia. There is great danger, for example, if the historian conceives his/her task simply as a search for ideographs, or as a means of establishing the ways in which any group has created its own self-image. Clearly, this argument is made by Smith and Windes. They assert that, "first, students of public address may give inordinate attention to collective persuasive action in which the establishment-conflict pattern can be discerned, ignoring important collective acts which cannot be interpreted through a dialectic of radical division. Second, the nature of collective acts might be distorted in order to pick the mold of the establishment-conflict pattern."[34] Their solution is to identify different kinds of movements that call forth different rhetorical patterns. But even this has certain inherent difficulties for the historian/critic. They recognize that "all movements may employ one or more" of the strategies they describe as particularly characteristic of "innovational movements" and argue that "a consistent and necessary pattern of usage" is the key to determining the "innovational movement." The pitfall the historian must avoid in discerning patterns of historical events is the imposition of consistency at the expense of complexity. Smith and Windes allege, for example, that "the innovational movement is distinct from the establishment-conflict movement in that the latter calls for a reconstruction of society's values, its perceptions of worth and its class arrangements; whereas the former acts with the expectation that the changes it demands will not disturb the symbols and constraints of existing values or modify the social hierarchy."[35] I would submit that the movement for political reform in England in the early nineteenth century, while it encompassed diverse groups and demonstrably divergent goals, could not be neatly described by such a distinction since the *interaction* of the various elements of the movement can only be understood when one realizes that both sets of perceptions and demands described by Smith and Windes were operating simultaneously within what can most logically be conceived of as one movement.[36]

As the present generation of scholars undertakes careful and systematic study of the rhetoric of social movements, an understanding of both the interdependence and the independence of theory and history must be made clear. For historians, the explanation of rhetorical behavior in given situations is paramount. For theorists, the nature and functions of movement rhetoric in general is of the highest priority.

As R. H. Tawney observed, "all branches of history present enigmas, which only labour can unravel."[37] By recognizing the distinctive nature of their scholarly labors, rhetorical historians and rhetorical theorists can engage in research productive of a deeper understanding of the rhetoric of social movements.

Notes

[1] *Rhetorical Criticism: A Study in Method* (New York: Macmillan, 1965), p. 22. The reference is to Leland M. Griffin, "The Rhetoric of Historical Movements," *Quarterly Journal of Speech*, 38 (1952), 184–88.

[2] Edwin Black, *Rhetorical Criticism: A Study in Method* (1965; rpt. Madison, Wisconsin: University of Wisconsin Press, 1978), pp. ix–x.

[3] C. V. Wedgwood, *The King's War: 1641–1647* (London, Collins Fontana, 1958), p. 11.

[4] Griffin's seminal essay, for example, grew out of his careful study of the Anti-Masonic movement. Leland Milburn Griffin, "The Antimasonic Persuasion: A Study of Public Address in the American Antimasonic Movement, 1826–1838," Diss. Cornell University 1950. More recently, Smith and Windes' statement on "innovational movements" emerged from their investigation of the Sunday School movement in nineteenth-century America. Ralph R. Smith and Russel R. Windes, "The Innovational Movement: A Rhetorical Theory," *Quarterly Journal of Speech*, 61 (1975), 140–53.

[5] Karlyn Kohrs Campbell, "The Rhetoric of Women's Liberation: An Oxymoron," *Quarterly Journal of Speech*, 59 (1973), 74–86; Richard B. Gregg, "The Ego-Function of the Rhetoric of Protest," *Philosophy and Rhetoric*, 4 (1971), 71–91; James R. Andrews, "Confrontation at Columbia: A Case Study in Coercive Rhetoric," *Quarterly Journal of Speech*, 55 (1969), 9–16.

[6] Herbert Butterfield, *The Whig Interpretation of History* (Harmondsworth, Middlesex: Penguin Books, 1973), p. 17.

[7] J. H. Plumb, *The Death of the Past* (Boston: Houghton Mifflin, 1971).

[8] Smith and Windes, p. 142.

[9] The fact that there was distress among the lower classes is exceedingly well-documented in almost any history of the period. For examples of contemporary accounts that detail different aspects of the problem, see the following Parliamentary papers: *Second Report from the*

Select Committee on the State of Education Among the Lower Orders in the Metropolis 1816 (427) iv; *Select Committee on Criminal Commitments and Convictions (2nd Report) 1828* (545) vi; *Report of the Select Committee on Factory Children's Labour* [the Sadler Report], Vol. xv, 1831–1832; *First Report of the Commissioners Appointed to Collect Information in the Manufacturing Districts Relative to the Employment of Children in Factories . . . : with Minutes of Evidence and Reports of District Commissioners 1833* (450) xx. See also, Thomas Babington Macaulay's speech in the House of Commons, March 19, 1832: *Parliamentary Debates, Third Series,* XI (1832), 454–55; Samuel Bamford, *Passages in the Life of a Radical* (London: Heywood, 1941).

[10] For a discussion of a contemporary radical leader's problems, some of which directly parallel those faced in the nineteenth century, see Herbert W. Simons, "Requirements, Problems, and Strategies: A Theory of Persuasion for Social Movements," *Quarterly Journal of Speech,* 56 (1970), 1–11.

[11] Cited by Henry Jephson, *The Platform: Its Rise and Progress,* 2 vols. (London: Macmillan, 1892), pp. 1, 383.

[12] Cited by E. P. Thompson, *The Making of the English Working Class* (New York: Vintage Books, 1963), p. 630, n.: *Examiner,* 17 November 1816, p. 730.

[13] Henry Hunt, known as "Orator" Hunt, was born in Wiltshire in 1773, the son of a prosperous farmer. He was generally acknowledged as the leading radical spokesman for parliamentary reform after the Napoleonic Wars. He was returned for the popular borough of Preston and sat in the House of Commons in 1830–33. He faulted the Reform Bill of 1832 on the grounds that it was much too restricted, giving no political power to the working classes. For an account of his speaking in 1819, see Charles W. Lomas, "Orator Hunt at Peterloo and Smithfield," *Quarterly Journal of Speech,* 48 (1962), 400–05.

[14] Thompson, p. 623.

[15] Cited by R. H. White, *Waterloo to Peterloo* (London: William Heinemann, 1957), p. 78.

[16] Thompson, p. 630.

[17] Cited by Mary G. McEdwards, "Agitative Rhetoric: Its Nature and Effect," *Western Speech,* 32 (1968), 38.

[18] The particular address offered at this meeting was to the Prince Regent; it was in all essentials similar to petitions presented to Parliament.

[19] All excerpts of Hunt's speech are from the *Examiner,* 17 November 1816, pp. 730–732.

[20] Cited by George Rude, *The Crowd in History 1780–1848* (New York: John Wiley, 1964), p. 182.

[21] *Parliamentary Debates,* First Series, IX (1807), p. 798.

[22] Jephson, 11, p. 385.

[23] Cited by John Cannon, *Parliamentary Reform 1640–1832* (Cambridge: Cambridge University Press, 1973), p. 176.

[24] Thomas Wright, *England Under the House of Hanover,* 2 vols. (1848; rpt. Port Washington, N.Y.: Kennikat Press, 1971), [p.] 11, 457.

[25] Indeed, when Hunt returned to London in 1822 after his incarceration in Ilchester Gaol, he was greeted by "The Committee of the Useful Classes," Thompson, p. 775.

[26] Herbert W. Simons, Elizabeth Mechling, and Howard N. Schreier, "Mobilizing for Collective Action from the Bottom Up: The Rhetoric of Social Movements," in *Handbook of Rhetorical and Communication Theory,* eds. Carroll C. Arnold and John Waite Bowers (Boston: Allyn and Bacon), in press.

[27] Thompson, p. 623.

[28] Thomas B. Farrell, "Knowledge, Consensus, and Rhetorical Theory," *Quarterly Journal of Speech,* 62 (1976), 11.

[29] Michael Calvin McGee, "The 'Ideograph': A Link Between Rhetoric and Ideology," *Quarterly Journal of Speech,* 66 (1980), 1–16.

[30] McGee, p. 15.

[31] J. Vernon Jensen, "British Voices on the Eve of the American Revolution: Trapped by the Family Metaphor," *Quarterly Journal of Speech,* 63 (1977), 43.

[32] Simons, Mechling, and Schreier, pp. 133–34.

[33] See, for example, Michael M. Osborn and Douglas Ehninger, "The Metaphor in Public Address," *Speech Monographs,* 29 (1962), 223–34; Michael M. Osborn, "The Evolution of the Theory of Metaphor in Rhetoric," *Western Speech,* 31 (1967), 121–31; Michael Osborn, "Archetypal Metaphor in Rhetoric: The Light-Dark Family," *Quarterly Journal of Speech,* 53 (1967), 115–26; William E. Rickert, "Winston Churchill's Archetypal Metaphors: A Mythopoetic Translation of World War II," *Central States Speech Journal,* 28 (1977), 106–12.

[34] Smith and Windes, p. 142.

[35] Ibid., p. 144.

[36] See James R. Andrews, "The Rhetoric of Coercion and Persuasion: The Reform Bill of 1832," *Quarterly Journal of Speech,* 61 (1970), 187–95.

[37] *The Radical Tradition* (Harmondsworth, Middlesex: Penguin Books, 1966), p. 199.

A Functional Approach to the Rhetoric of Social Movements

Charles J. Stewart

Leland M. Griffin concluded his pioneering essay, "The Rhetoric of Historical Movements," by envisioning a time when "from the identification of a number of rhetorical patterns, we may discover the various configurations of public discussion, whether rhetorical patterns repeat themselves when like movements occur in the intervals of time, whether a consistent set of forms may be said to exist."[1] Although scholars have produced many studies since Griffin's essay, little progress has been made toward the goals of understanding the nature of social movement rhetoric and of constructing generalizations that apply to different movements in different periods.[2]

Several factors have contributed to our failure. First, we have been preoccupied with explicating the events (Selma, Columbia University, Wounded Knee), the people (Martin Luther King, Jr., Stokely Carmichael, Jerry Rubin), and the strategies (civil disobedience, confrontation, obscenity) that have captured headlines and intruded upon our world.[3] Second, we have employed microscopic approaches that substantially limit studies in proportion to the amount of rhetoric that social movements produce.[4] Many studies have offered valuable insights into specific events, speeches, and strategies, but they have contributed little to generalizations about the rhetoric of social movements. Third, social movements have proved to be elusive phenomena that vary in purpose, size, structure, membership, stages of development, and degree of change desired.[5]

An approach that seems most promising for making significant strides toward Griffin's vision is one viewing rhetoric as the primary *agency* through which social movements perform necessary *functions* that enable them to come into existence, to meet opposition, and, perhaps, to succeed in bringing about (or resisting) change. Functions are indispensable processes that contribute to the furtherance or maintenance of social movements.[6] A functional approach views rhetoric not as art, artifact, or the manipulation of techniques for specific effects but as the agency through which social movements perform essential functions. It is macroscopic in application, treating rhetorical efforts with broad brushstrokes, and thus is more capable than traditional microscopic approaches of contributing to our understanding of the immense rhetorical canvasses produced by a bewildering array of social movements.

The notion of a *functional* approach to the study of social movement rhetoric has appeared in several essays. For example, Richard B. Gregg explored the ego-function of protest rhetoric.[7] Dale G. Leathers observed that the rhetorical strategy of the John Birch Society "was highly functional for the maintenance of in-group solidarity."[8] And Michael McGee concluded his essay, "In Search of 'The People': A Rhetorical Alternative," by suggesting that the "analysis of rhetorical documents should not turn inward, to an appreciation of persuasive, manipulative techniques, but outward to *functions* of rhetoric."[9]

Herbert W. Simons and Bruce E. Gronbeck have provided both theoretical bases for a functional approach and lists of functions that might serve as guides for the study of social movement rhetoric. In his effort to provide a "leader-centered conception of persuasion in social movements," Simons wrote that social movements "must fulfill the same functional requirements as more formal collectivities. These imperatives constitute *rhetorical requirements* for the leadership of a movement."[10] He discussed these functions or requirements under three broad headings:

1. They must attract, maintain, and mold workers (i.e., followers) into an efficiently organized unit.
2. They must secure adoption of their product by the larger structure (i.e., the external system, the established order).
3. They must react to resistance generated by the larger structure.

In a more recent essay, Simons et al. reiterated the value of a functional approach to the rhetoric of social movements, discussed three broad rhetorical functions (mobilization, exercise of external influence, and resistance to counterinfluence), and identified functions instrumental to accomplishment of these tasks:

1. Justifying the movement's mission to its constituents and to third parties
2. Infusing the mission with a sense of urgency
3. Acquiring material and nonmaterial resources
4. Organizing activists into a disciplined and cohesive unit
5. Gratifying constituents' personal needs
6. Selling to or imposing upon the movement's targets its program for action
7. Discrediting oppositions
8. Countering efforts at social control.[11]

In "The Rhetoric of Social-Institutional Change: Black Action at Michigan," Bruce E. Gronbeck discussed social-psychological, political-institutional, philosophical-ideological, and rhetorical forces operant in times of social-institutional change, and concluded: "Rhetorical forces function as a set of skills able to create, sustain, and terminate movements by uniting the other forces." The rhetorical analyst, according to Gronbeck, should ask three questions: (1) What functions are fulfilled by rhetorical discourse? (2) With what substance are these functions fulfilled? (3) And, in what form does that substance appear? Gronbeck listed six rhetorical functions and applied them to the Black Action Movement at the University of Michigan in the spring of 1970:

1. Defining: Somebody or some group takes the first step. A problem is defined and a solution is urged.
2. Legitimizing: Legitimizers can lend positive authority, a regional or national presence to a budding movement.
3. In-gathering: The movement builds a power base, a group of adherents ready to talk, march, and fight for the cause.
4. Pressuring: The movement also mounts a campaign urging reform or revolution.
5. Compromising: After direct confrontation, usually some sort of compromise must be worked out.
6. Satisfying: Leaders must be able to return to the masses of their movement, proclaiming victory, even if only partial gains have been made.[12]

Each of these functions is identified with a particular stage of social movement development as prescribed by Griffin: defining and legitimizing with the inception phase, in-gathering and pressuring with the rhetorical crisis phase, and compromising and satisfying with the consummation phase.[13]

Building on the foundations laid by previous writers, I delineate the following scheme of general and specific functions that rhetorical analysis may employ in systematic studies of social movement rhetoric:

1. Transforming Perceptions of History
   a. Altering perceptions of the past
   b. Altering perceptions of the present
   c. Altering perceptions of the future
2. Transforming Perceptions of Society
   a. Altering perceptions of the opposition
   b. Altering self-perceptions
3. Prescribing Courses of Action
   a. Prescribing what must be done
   b. Prescribing who must accomplish the task
   c. Prescribing how the task must be accomplished
4. Mobilizing for Action
   a. Organizing and uniting the discontented
   b. Gaining sympathy and support from opinion leaders or legitimizers
   c. Pressuring the opposition
5. Sustaining the Social Movement
   a. Justifying setbacks and delays
   b. Maintaining viability of the movement
   c. Maintaining visibility of the movement[14]

Several caveats are in order before details of the model are presented. First, social movements are conceived of as organized, uninstitutionalized, and expansive collectivities that mobilize for action to bring about or to resist programs for change primarily through rhetoric and that are countered by established orders.[15] The term *rhetoric* is used in this essay to denote the process by which a social movement seeks through the manipulation of verbal and nonverbal symbols to affect the perceptions of target audiences and thus to bring about changes in their ways of thinking, feeling, and/or acting. By my view, rhetoric is the primary *agency* available to social movements for satisfying a variety of functions. Moreover, it is pervasive even when a movement attempts to bargain or to coerce.[16]

Second, while I believe that the functions listed above are essential to the existence and success of social movements, I do not claim that these functions are unique. Social movements differ from institutionalized collectivities, not so much in terms of the functions their rhetoric must perform, as in terms of the constraints placed upon the fulfillment of these functions. As others have noted, the uninstitutionalized nature of social movements greatly limits their power to reward or punish and hence their strategic options.[17]

Third, while all social movements are required to perform the preceding functions, depending on the fundamental nature of their programs for change, some functions will assume greater prominence than others. *Innovative* social movements seek limited replacement (reform) or total replacement (revolutionary) of existing norms, values, and power distributions with new ones. *Revivalistic* social movements seek limited replacement or total replacement of existing norms, values, and power distributions with ones from a venerable, idealized past. *Resistance* social movements seek to block changes in norms, values, and power distributions.

Finally, the functional scheme presented in this essay is not developed chronologically or in conjunction with a series of progressive stages. Social movements are expansive collectivities that may contain many campaigns and a variety of organizations. Each campaign (e.g., the Montgomery bus boycott, the march on Selma, the 1963 demonstration at the Lincoln Memorial) and each social movement organization (e.g., the Southern Christian Leadership Conference, the Student Nonviolent Coordinating Committee, the Black Panthers) may progress through a lifecycle such as inception, rhetorical crisis, and consummation, but the lifecycles of campaigns and organizations may not coincide with one another or with the movement as a whole. Social movements are unlikely to perform any function once and then proceed to another task. Some functions may dominate the rhetoric of a movement at a given time, yet most demand attention on a continual basis.

A FUNCTIONAL SCHEME FOR ANALYZING THE RHETORIC OF SOCIAL MOVEMENTS

1. Transforming Perceptions of History

Target audiences, especially when a social movement is in its infancy, may be unaware of a problem, may refuse to believe that a problem exists, may believe that the problem does not require drastic action, and may be optimistic about the future. A variety of established orders (schools, governments, courts, labor unions, social and professional groups, religious organizations, and the mass media) foster and reinforce these perceptions. Social movements must alter the ways audiences perceive the past, the present, and the future to convince them that an intolerable situation exists and that it warrants urgent action.[18]

These specific functions are often interrelated in a social movement's rhetoric. A revivalistic movement may view the past as a paradise lost, one worth resurrecting at any cost. The future, a return to an idealized past, may be portrayed as a perfect point in time or a perfect place.[19] A resistance movement may contend that society has progressed to a high state and see efforts by social movements and the established order as threatening to return society to a primitive past or to transport it into a future devoid of all that is sacred.[20] An innovative movement may portray the present as a result of or a continuation of an intolerable past and argue that the future will be bright only if the movement is successful.[21]

Social movements may find it necessary to revise their versions of history as they age, meet with successes and failures, and adapt to changing situations.[22]

2. Transforming Perceptions of Society

Social movements must attempt to alter target audiences' perceptions of the opposition, that opposition being all individuals and groups that movements feel are opposing societal changes necessary to alleviate intolerable conditions or to prevent intolerable conditions from developing. The rhetorical task is to strip such opponents of their legitimacy. Some rhetorical efforts portray the opposition as powerful, demonical, conspiratorial forces while others ridicule the opposition as pathetic, disorganized, impotent obstructions. Although conspiracy and devil appeals are prominent in the rhetoric of many movements, we do not know if these appeals are more common and vitriolic in particular types of social movements or how they change as movements encounter varying situations.

Social movements must attempt to alter the self-perceptions of target audiences so that supporters and potential supporters come to believe in their self-worth and ability to bring about urgent change. Efforts such as replacing old labels attached to groups by their oppressors are designed to instill feelings of pride and power, to help audiences discover themselves as substantial human beings, and to encourage them to question social relationships and coalitions. Social movements often hope that self-discovery may result in a new "personal identity" and in the realization of "a people."[23] Self-discovery is an important means of creating "we-they" distinctions and a basis of group identification through a sense of shared fate.[24] "We," the "people," may come to represent all that is good while "they," the "oppressors," represent all that is evil.

3. Prescribing Courses of Action

Social movements must explain *what* should be done.[25] This function comprises the social movement's list of demands and solutions that will alleviate a condition, prevent undesired changes, or bring on the millennium or utopia.[26] Each movement must explain, defend, and sell its program for change. Problems develop when a number of organizations within a social movement prescribe different demands and solutions. Changing social situations, efforts by established orders to negate or to co-opt a movement's demands and solutions, and the necessity to address a variety of target audiences also may require alterations in explanations and content of demands and solutions. As John Wilson has noted, "When new sensitivities are created by social events and collectives, ideologies, to be accepted, must cater to these new sensitivities."[27] Efforts to adapt to new sensitivities, however, always expose social movement leaders and groups to charges of revisionism by movement purists.

Social movements must prescribe *who* ought to do the job. For one thing, in order to establish legitimacy, each social movement must convince audiences that only an uninstitutionalized collectivity is willing and able to bring about or to resist change. For another, social movement rhetoric may espouse specific types of organization and leadership or specific organizations and leaders best suited to solving urgent problems. Some social movements establish membership limitations to create elites capable of dealing with "unsolvable" conditions and the omnipotent forces that have produced them. "We-they" distinctions may be as prevalent within a social movement as they are between the social movement and its opposition. One movement faction may declare open warfare against another faction it deems ideologically deviant or inferior in membership. Samuel Gompers did not conceal his pleasure over the demise of the Knights of Labor, a union of unskilled workers that he considered to be an unnatural form of labor organization.[28]

Social movements must propose and defend *how* the job is to be done, that is, which strategies, tactics, and communication channels are most appropriate and potentially most effective.[29] A revolutionary resistance movement may have a wide range of tactical choices but a narrow range of channels. A reform movement may have access to many channels but be limited to moderate, socially acceptable tactics. No movement can rely on the same means of change for long. Followers of the media become bored with them, and established orders learn how to deal with strategies and tactics rather quickly. A social movement may splinter into factions over differing views on how the job must be done, and some movement members may be more committed to means than to ends. Tactics such as strikes and boycotts often affect "innocent people" and may provoke "backlashes" that are fostered by established orders. Thus, movements must defend their actions and changes in actions to both members and non-members.

4. Mobilizing for Action

It is not enough for a social movement to present its views on history, society, and courses of action. It must also mobilize target audiences into performing appropriate actions.[30] It must unite and organize discontented factions and arouse them to perform a variety of actions. Some actions are self-change oriented: believers need to purify themselves before they can change others. Some are aimed at gaining control of agencies of influence: voting officials in or out of office, purchasing or creating communication media, or gaining control of corporations through stock proxies.[31] Other actions seek to gain the attention, sympathy, and support of opinion leaders, or to apply pressure on opponents, to gain recognition, concessions, or capitulation from antagonists. But whatever their aim, social movements need years of untiring efforts by large numbers of people to gain or prevent change. They must convince followers that victory is near, or at least inevitable, if all is done correctly, if followers remain steadfast in their commitment, and if unity is maintained. Movements must create and maintain what Eric Hoffer refers to as an "extravagant hope" within the membership.[32]

5. Sustaining the Movement

Since social movements usually last for years and experience changing social circumstances, they must perform functions that sustain them. They may have to explain and justify apparent setbacks, why they appear to be making few meaningful gains, why agreements with established orders have not been implemented or have been ineffective, and why they have not reached a goal by a target date. The variety of audiences social movements address may perceive progress, victories, agreements, and priority of goals differently. Internal and external opponents capitalize on delays and setbacks to proclaim superiority over a movement or its organization.

Social movements must wage a continual battle to remain viable. More rhetorical energy may be expended on fund raising, membership drives, acquisition of materials and property, and maintenance of movement communication media than on selling ideologies to target audiences and pressuring the opposition. Reinforcing commitment of members and satisfying membership gratifications limit a movement's ability to perform other functions. Ironically, a movement may become too successful. Growth in membership and geographical sphere of influence and creeping institutionalization may seriously reduce the informality of structure and the feeling of urgency that attracted people to the movement.[33] Thus, a serious decline in membership and commitment may occur when success seems near.

Social movements must remain visible. "Out of sight, out of mind" is an appropriate adage. Social movements, the media, and target audiences have insatiable appetites for rhetorical happenings, but few social movements have adequate leadership, membership, energy, and funds to satisfy these appetites over long periods while fending off counter efforts by opponents. Old events that drag on receive little attention and produce serious drains on a movement's resources. Social movements often resort to rhetorical events such as ceremonies, annual meetings, and anniversary celebrations to remain visible to both members and nonmembers.

Conclusions

A functional approach appears to be the best vehicle by which scholars may approach Leland Griffin's vision of discovering "rhetorical patterns" or a "consistent set of forms" in the rhetoric of social movements. The journey will be neither simple nor quick, and, undoubtedly, the functional scheme presented will undergo refinement as our knowledge and experience grow.

As functional studies accumulate, we should be able to piece together the rhetorical puzzle of social movements and to formulate answers to several questions. How are essential functions performed by: (1) Different types of social movements—innovative, revivalistic, resistance? (2) Social movements demanding differing degrees of change? (3) Social movements that encounter changing situations? (4) Social movements that confront different types and degrees of opposition? (5) Social movements as they experience successes and failures or growth and decline? (6) Differing factions within social movements? (7) Social movements that face conflicting demands? (8) Social movements as they age and approach termination because of failure or institutionalization?

Notes

1 *Quarterly Journal of Speech*, 38 (1952), 188.

2 For an excellent review, see Herbert W. Simons, Elizabeth Mechling, and Howard Schreier, "Functions of Communication in Mobilizing for Collective Action from the Bottom Up: The Rhetoric of Social Movements," in *Handbook on Rhetorical and Communication Theory*, ed. Carroll C. Arnold and John W. Bowers (Boston: Allyn and Bacon), in press.

3 See James R. Andrews, "Confrontation at Columbia: A Case Study of Coercive Rhetoric," *Quarterly Journal of Speech*, 55 (1969), 9–16; Thomas W. Benson and Bonnie M. D. Johnson, "The Rhetoric of Resistance: Confrontation with the Warmakers, Washington, D.C., October 1967," *Today's Speech*, 16 (1968), 35–42; Wayne E. Brockriede and Robert L. Scott, "Stokely Carmichael: Two Speeches on Black Power," *Central States Speech Journal*, 19 (1968), 3–13; Donald K. Smith, "Martin Luther King, Jr.: In the Beginning at Montgomery," *Southern Speech Journal*, 34 (1968), 8–17; Robert L. Scott and Donald K. Smith, "The Rhetoric of Confrontation," *Quarterly Journal of Speech*, 55 (1969), 1–8; Mary G. McEdwards, "Agitative Rhetoric: Its Nature and Effect," *Western Speech*, 32 (1968), 36–43.

4 See Finley C. Campbell, "Voices of Thunder, Voices of Rage: A Symbolic Analysis of a Selection from Malcolm X's 'Message to the Grass Roots,'" *Speech Teacher*, 19 (1970), 101–10; Bernard J. Brommel, "The Pacifist Speechmaking of Eugene V. Debs," *Quarterly Journal of Speech*, 52 (1966), 146–54.

5 See William B. Cameron, *Modern Social Movements* (New York: Random House, 1966); Leland M. Griffin, "A Dramatistic Theory of the Rhetoric of Movements," *Critical Responses to Kenneth Burke*, ed. William Rueckert (Minneapolis: University of Minnesota Press, 1969); Roberta Ash, *Social Movements in America* (Chicago: Markham, 1972); C. A. Dawson and W. E. Gettys, *Introduction to*

Sociology (New York: Ronald Press, 1935); Rudolph Heberle, *Social Movements: An Introduction to Political Sociology* (New York: Appleton-Century-Crofts, 1951).

6 This definition was developed from a discussion of the meaning of the term function in Robert K. Merton, *Social Theory and Social Structure*, 2d ed. (Glencoe, Ill.: The Free Press, 1957) pp. 19–25.

7 "The Ego-Function of the Rhetoric of Protest," *Philosophy and Rhetoric*, 4 (1971), 71–91.

8 "The Rhetorical Strategy of the New Right Movement," unpublished paper presented at the annual convention of the Speech Communication Association, 1972.

9 *Quarterly Journal of Speech*, 61 (1975), 248.

10 "Requirements, Problems, and Strategies: A Theory of Persuasion for Social Movements," *Quarterly Journal of Speech*, 56 (1970), 1–11.

11 Simons, Mechling, and Schreier.

12 In *Explorations in Rhetorical Criticism*, ed. Gerald Mohrmann, Charles Stewart, and Donovan Ochs (University Park, Pa.: Pennsylvania State University Press, 1973), pp. 96–113.

13 Leland M. Griffin, "The Rhetoric of Historical Movements," 186; Griffin, "A Dramatistic Theory of the Rhetoric of Movements," 456–478. The notion of a natural progression of strategies from normal discursive means to extreme forms of confrontation is developed in John W. Bowers and Donovan J. Ochs, *The Rhetoric of Agitation and Control* (Reading, Mass.: Addison-Wesley, 1971), pp. 16–38.

14 This scheme of functions is being developed in conjunction with Craig Allen Smith of Memphis State University. For other discussions of essential functions, see Ralph H. Turner and Lewis Killian, *Collective Behavior*, 2nd ed. (Englewood Cliffs, N.J.: Prentice-Hall, 1972), 245–425; John Wilson, *Introduction to Social Movements* (New York: Basic Books, 1973); Hans Toch, *The Social Psychology of Social Movements* (New York: Bobbs-Merrill, 1965); Gary B. Rush and R. Serge Denisoff, *Social and Political Movements* (New York: Appleton-Century-Crofts, 1971).

15 This definition is based on ones in Cameron, *Modern Social Movements*, 7; Wilson, *Introduction to Social Movements*, 8; Simons, "Requirements, Problems, and Strategies," 3; Charles A. Wilkinson, "A Rhetorical Definition of Movements," *Central States Speech Journal*, 27 (1976), 91.

16 See Herbert W. Simons, *Persuasion: Understanding, Practice, and Analysis* (Reading, Mass.: Addison-Wesley, 1976), pp. 43–44, 250–86; Herbert W. Simons, "Persuasion in Social Conflicts: A Critique

of Prevailing Conceptions and a Framework for Future Research," *Speech Monographs,* 39 (1972), 227–47; Parke G. Burgess, "Crisis Rhetoric: Coercion vs. Force," *Quarterly Journal of Speech,* 59 (1973), 69; James R. Andrews, "The Rhetoric of Coercion and Persuasion: The Reform Bill of 1832," *Quarterly Journal of Speech,* 56 (1970), 195.

17 See Michael Lipsky, "Protest as a Political Resource," *The American Political Science Review,* 52 (1968[)], 1144–1148, 1157–1158; James Q. Wilson, "The Strategy of Protest: Problems of Negro Civic Action," *Journal of Conflict Resolution,* 3 (1961), 291–303; Robert Dahl, "The Analysis of Influence in Local Communities," in *Social Science and Community Action,* ed. Charles R. Adrian (East Lansing: Michigan State University Press, 1960); Herbert W. Simons, "Requirements, Problems, and Strategies," 1–11.

18 See Ernest G. Bormann, "Fantasy and Rhetorical Vision: The Rhetorical Criticism of Social Reality," *Quarterly Journal of Speech,* 58 (1972), 396–407; Richard B. Gregg, "A Phenomenologically Oriented Approach to Rhetorical Criticism," *Central States Speech Journal,* 17 (1966), 83–90; Bruce Fireman and William A. Gamson, "Utilitarian Logic in the Resource Mobilization Perspective," in *The Dynamics of Social Movements,* ed. Mayer N. Zald and John D. McCarthy (Cambridge, Mass.: Winthrop, 1979), pp. 27–31.

19 See E. J. Hobsbawn, *Primitive Rebels,* 2nd ed. (New York: Praeger, 1963); Melvin J. Lasky, *Utopia and Revolution* (Chicago: University of Chicago Press, 1976); Wilson, *Introduction to Social Movements;* Carl Wayne Hensley, "Rhetorical Vision and the Persuasion of a Historical Movement: The Disciples of Christ in Nineteenth[-]Century American Culture," *Quarterly Journal of Speech,* 61 (1975), 250–64.

20 See Martha Solomon, "The Rhetoric of STOP ERA: Fatalistic Reaffirmation," *Southern Speech Communication Journal,* 44 (1978), 42–59; Philip C. Wander, "The John Birch and the Martin Luther King Symbols in The Radical Right," *Western Speech,* 35 (1971), 4–14.

21 See Karlyn Kohrs Campbell, "The Rhetoric of Radical Black Nationalism: A Case Study of Self-Conscious Criticism," *Central States Speech Journal,* 22 (1971), 151–160; Karlyn Kohrs Campbell, "The Rhetoric of Women's Liberation: An Oxymoron," *Quarterly Journal of Speech,* 59 (1973), 74–86.

22 See Parke G. Burgess, "The Rhetoric of Black Power: A Moral Demand?" *Quarterly Journal of Speech,* 54 (1968), 122–133; and Robert L. Heath, "Dialectical Confrontation: A Strategy of Black Radicalism," *Central States Speech Journal,* 24 (1973), 168–177.

23 McGee, pp. 235–49; Campbell, pp. 74–86; Brockriede and Scott, pp. 3–13.

24 Aaron Gresson, III, "Phenomenology and the Rhetoric of Identification—A Neglected Dimension of Coalition Communication Inquiry," *Communication Quarterly,* 26 (1978), 14–23.

25 For an excellent discussion of social movement efforts to prescribe courses of action, see Wilson, pp. 89–134.

26 See Barbara A. Larson, "Samuel Davies and the Rhetoric of the New Light," *Speech Monographs,* 38 (1971), 207–16; Richard J. Ilkka, "Rhetorical Dramatization in the Development of American Communism," *Quarterly Journal of Speech,* 63 (1977), 414–20.

27 Wilson, pp. 91–97.

28 Samuel Gompers, "Address to the Machinists Convention," *American Federationist,* 8 (1901), 251.

29 See Leland M. Griffin, "The Rhetorical Structure of the 'New Left' Movement: Part I," *Quarterly Journal of Speech,* 50 (1964), 114–27; Malcolm O. Sillars, "The Rhetoric of the Petition in Boots," *Speech Monographs,* 39 (1972), 92–104.

30 See Ralph R. Smith and Russel R. Windes, "The Rhetoric of Mobilization: Implications for the Study of Movements," *Southern Speech Communication Journal,* 42 (1976), 1–19.

31 Saul D. Alinsky, *Rules for Radicals: A Pragmatic Primer for Realistic Radicals* (New York: Vintage, 1972), 165–83.

32 Eric Hoffer, *The True Believer* (New York: Harper and Row, 1951), p. 18.

33 Mayer N. Zald and Roberta Ash, "Social Movement Organizations: Growth, Decay and Change," *Social Forces,* 44 (1966), 327–41.

Section II

Critical Touchstones

Chapter 3

Tactics for External Audiences

Social movements do not arise in a vacuum. They are situated in time and place, and thus take their distinctive form in the immediate historical contexts from which they develop. The rhetoric fueling such movements may, accordingly, be seen in large part as a response to prevailing social norms, practices, and constraints. To understand movement discourse in this way is to be especially attentive to the situational factors that provoke protest, shape relations between movement actors and their audiences, and determine the persuasive resources available to them. Even the most idealistic social movements are bound by the realities of the world as it is given; for success to be possible, movements must be alive to external circumstances.

The essays in this chapter illustrate ways in which movement activists adapt strategically to the situations they confront, and examine how rhetoric is directed from the movement outward. By stressing "external audiences," we mean to highlight the process through which movements negotiate certain relationships with their audiences, opponents, media, and publics. Movement leaders, spokespersons, and members, these studies show, frequently find it necessary to alter conventional relationships between speaker and audience in some significant way. This realignment may take the form of explicit confrontation, adoption of new modes of depiction and new genres of discourse, or mobilization of "counterpublics" to get the voices of protest heard more clearly. The authors thus teach us that movements, to be effective, must be closely attuned to the shifting demands of the situations they confront. They must also strategically address both those they wish to persuade and those most likely to resist their efforts.

We usually think of the classroom as the space in which we *learn about* activism and social movements, rather than as a site in and through which we can *engage in* the work of social justice. Stephen Hartnett seeks to alter such habitual practice in "Lincoln and Douglas Meet the Abolitionist David Walker as Prisoners Debate Slavery: Empowering Education, Applied Communication, and Social Justice" (1998). Recounting his experience in the Indiana Prison System, Hartnett expounds on the means by which "practicing empowerment pedagogy" transformed the prison classroom into a "workshop for democracy" by teaching history, critical analysis, public speaking, and debating skills. The project afforded the means by which students could critically engage the history of slavery and racism in the United States, relate those legacies to contemporary prison issues and contexts, and find their voices in rhetorical performance, thus contributing to their hopeful transformation into "self-reflexive beings with agency" or responsible citizens. Hartnett argues that this activist pedagogy extended into the larger prison culture as students engaged fellow inmates, and as their work circulated in the larger public sphere.

The selection and deployment of strategic actions are never predetermined, are often freighted with meanings and emotions, and are always consequential for movement identity, vision, and success. In "ACT-ing UP in Congressional Hearings" (2001), Daniel C. Brouwer examines the militant, direct-action organization ACT UP's strategic "oscillation" between multiple, even seemingly contradictory, publics and counterpublics for the sake of advancing the struggle against the HIV/AIDS epidemic. Brouwer observes the ironic context in which ACT UP's signature activist mode of confrontational disruption, including direct condemnation of the U.S. government, resulted in access to Congressional hearings. Despite deep ambivalence and heated disagreement among ACT UP activists, members served as witnesses five times in congressional hearings on AIDS issues. Brouwer argues that oscillation between sites and spheres of protest, both inside and outside normative political channels, created opportunities to inform legislators and shape the rhetorical resources of policy deliberation, generated counterpublicity, and increased access to "strong" publics. The risks of cooptation or disidentification existed, as ACT UP activists attested, but the strategic advantages of rhetorical diversity in performance modalities brought heightened visibility and meaningful policy changes.

The relationship between movement tactics and participatory democracy is dramatically reconfigured in Kevin Michael DeLuca and Jennifer Peeples's essay "From Public Sphere to Public Screen: Democracy, Activism, and the 'Violence' of Seattle" (2002). In explaining the 1999 protests against the World Trade Organization, the authors argue that scholars' nostalgic embrace of public sphere theory, with its norms of face-to-face interaction, consensus, openness, dialogue, rationality, and civility, prevents an understanding of "the new topography of political activity" in the twentieth and twenty-first centuries. By contrast, DeLuca and Peeples conceptualize the "public screen," on which activists perform "image events" that generate the publicity necessary to shape public opinion and to hold corporations and government accountable for their actions. In Seattle, the authors contend, activists tactically used "symbolic violence" and "uncivil disobedience" to expand media coverage, provoking substantive debate and galvanizing an international prodemocratic globalization movement.

Phaedra C. Pezzullo applies and advances public sphere theory differently in "Resisting 'National Breast Cancer Awareness Month': The Rhetoric of Counterpublics and their Cultural Performances" (2003). Drawing

on performance theory and engaging in ethnographic participant observation, Pezzullo seeks to explicate the "cultural performances" of counterpublics, "rhetoric of the streets" that often goes unrecorded and unanalyzed. Pezzullo's case study concerns the Toxic Links Coalition's "Stop Cancer Where It Starts" tour. TLC exposes "greenwashing" and "pinkwashing"—discourses that appear to support the environment and women while camouflaging practices that in fact harm them—perpetrated by the popular campaign known as National Breast Cancer Awareness Month. Through its lunch hour tour, which includes various "embodied" protest rhetorics, TLC targets sponsors of NBCAM, such as the pharmaceutical company AstraZeneca, for masking their complicity in the environmental causes of the disease that they claim to fight, profiting from the "entire cycle of cancer," and focusing on detection instead of prevention.

The stench of historical garbage in El Barrio of East Harlem stirs the intersectional imagination of Darrel Enck-Wanzer in "Trashing the System: Social Movement, Intersectional Rhetoric, and Collective Agency in the Young Lords Organization's Garbage Offensive" (2006). The mounting, noxious trash that the nascent Young Lords Organization first started cleaning up, then deployed in a "moment of antagonism" by blocking streets with it and burning it, rhetorically functioned both instrumentally and constitutively to generate critique and movement against/within "the system." Enck-Wanzer adapts the concept of intersectionality to reconfigure how rhetorical scholars analyze protest rhetoric in relation to rhetorical norms, insisting that the field's longstanding text-centric focus should give way to a perspective that accounts for the equal, simultaneous, and mutually shaping rhetorical forms of <bodies-words-images>. Enck-Wanzer's study crosses the sections of this volume by illustrating how protest action that is ostensibly directed at an external audience, such as the state, concomitantly and constitutively calls a people, community, and movement into being through the internal rhetoric of mobilization.

Michael T. Heaney and Fabio Rojas, in "The Place of Framing: Multiple Audiences and Antiwar Protests near Fort Bragg" (2006), draw on ethnographic fieldwork in Fayetteville, North Carolina, to examine the complex strategic and symbolic relationship between place and framing in the antiwar movement. Heaney and Rojas focus on the March 2005 antiwar protests in Fayetteville on the second anniversary of the Iraq War. Needing to reconstitute itself after the reelection of George W. Bush, a coalition of antiwar organizations selected the home of Fort Bragg—a Republican city with a long history of military life and peace activism, and a longer history still of racism—as a strategic site to advance "support the troops," a new frame that activists co-opted from mainstream discourse so as to advantageously "harness the hegemony." Heaney and Rojas analyze the complicated and contentious interactions among national antiwar coalition leaders, regional groups, and especially local activists, veterans, military families, counterprotestors, and the media, that resulted from this particular combination of place and frame. Fayetteville both strategically enabled and constrained antiwar rhetorical vision and performance in opposition to the War on Terror.

Melodrama as a means of protest has an undeservedly bad reputation, according to Steven Schwarze's essay "Environmental Melodrama" (2006). Against the assumptions and critiques claiming that melodrama—the morally and emotionally charged conflict between polarized opposing forces—is reductionistic and distorting, Schwarze offers a compelling case for reconsidering melodrama as a "productive inventional resource for countering the ideological simplifications of dominant public discourses and prying spheres of controversy open to a wider range of voices." Drawing on examples from the environmental and global justice movement, with a particularly detailed analysis of the controversy over asbestos in Libby, Montana, Schwarze conceptualizes and illustrates five key productive rhetorical functions of melodrama. Schwarze closes the essay with an insightful consideration of *kairos,* or rhetorical timing, asking when melodrama might function most effectively for movements. According to his analysis, melodrama works best during the nascence of a cause and for those whose voices have been silenced.

Perhaps the last place we might expect to encounter social movement action is in the public bathroom, but that is precisely where PISSAR (People in Search of Safe and Accessible Restrooms), a university student and staff coalition of "disability and genderqueer activists," did its activist business. Isaac West, in "PISSAR's Critically Queer and Disabled Politics" (2010), draws on this case at the University of California to urge rhetoric scholars of social movements to take space more seriously, and to understand it as a dynamic site of regulative normativities and identities (gender, sexuality, ability), stigma, and shame, as well as a site of potential resistance by bodies that might produce such spaces differently. The public bathroom offers a particularly ripe location for such spatial activism because of its attendant cultural anxieties and its invidious, pervasive manifestation of ableism, transphobia, and sexism. PISSAR ironically comprised a coalition of groups that historically harbored mutual suspicions and evasions because of the politics of stigma and shame. The solidarity forged and perspective gained through its "patrols"— measuring dimensions of stalls and toilet paper dispensers, stocking tampons, installing diaper changing stations, and creating gender-neutrality safety—was negotiated spatially through activists' own embodied anxieties about themselves and each other in order to achieve "consubstantiality" and meaningful transformation on campus.

Lincoln and Douglas Meet the Abolitionist David Walker as Prisoners Debate Slavery:
Empowering Education, Applied Communication, and Social Justice
Stephen Hartnett

Jason Sample has gigantic, overwhelming hands; huge, the-size-of-baseball-mitt hands.[1] *Greetings with Jason entail losing my small, smashable self in his enormous, enveloping restraint. It didn't take us long to realize that while our energy is equal, our strength is not. "Hey, bro, how's the drive?" "Jason, giant-man, how ya doing?" Our high-five fades into a hand shake in a joyous yet safely choreographed dance: I swing my arm upward, greeting Jason with all my might; he cradles my hand gently, trying his best not to knock me down or snap my limbs in his enthusiasm. An intense, combative student haunted by deep political convictions, I shudder to think of Jason as an angry young man enflamed with too much drink.*

Jason has spent the week pulling the overnight shift in the dairy factory,[2] *pumping iron, and working through Foucault's (1977)* Discipline and Punish: The Birth of the Prison, *and he's eager to talk about it, so before my jacket is off, before my book-bag hits the desk, he's peppering me with observations, questions, and comparisons: "So, look, not to diss Foucault, but I think he's got it all wrong about the, 'Hey Slim, yeah, tomorrow night, right'. Sorry man, uh, so, yeah, Foucault and this panopticon business: you gotta realize they don't need a technology of surveillance when they've got snitches, right? I mean they're everywhere; damn man, the whole joint hops on the say-so of snitches. See? I don't know, that kinda bugged me. So how you doing? Everything cool?"*

Yes, everything is cool: it's another night of college in the Correctional Industrial Facility, a squeaky clean, hospital-bright-fluorescent-white, plopped down in the middle of a cornfield, video cameras hanging from the wall, guards stationed at every door, drug dogs roaming the yard, double rows of razor wire outside the 4" slatted window, medium-security prison in Pendleton, Indiana.[3] *And, for*

better or worse, Jason and me and the guys in Speech Communication 310 are gonna spend the next three hours thinking about something else, someplace else—through the empowering alchemy of education, we're gonna slip through these walls into the realm of freedom.

Assuming that the miraculous diversity of the United States of America baffles any attempt to arrive at a unified, homogenous sense of "social justice" (see Laclau & Mouffe, 1985; Trend, 1996), it seems prudent to agree that "social justice" cannot amount to a strictly set program of demands and blueprints for change, but rather, to an open-ended and literally infinite process of articulating needs and aspirations within a democratically organized social space. This thesis has received ample attention in the brilliant, historically-based work of (among others) Bercovitch (1993) and Morone (1990); scholars of applied communication may be more familiar with this notion of social justice as a democratic unfolding of ever-changing demands via Cheney's (1995) award-winning essay, where he observed that "democracy [is] a self-critical, self-regenerating, and self-correcting process, as opposed to a conception that emphasizes a specific type of structural arrangement" (p. 183). Social justice, then, while clearly requiring certain material standards of equal capacity for achievement (such as those outlined by Bernts, d'Anjou, & Houtman, 1992; Brenkert, 1991; Sen, 1992; Vermunt & Tornblom, 1996) is just as importantly concerned with creating *a heuristic social space* in which citizens engage in public activities that literally re-create the possibilities of future public action. Indeed, the pursuit of social justice is inextricably enmeshed within the educational process of enabling citizens not only to communicate, but to communicate in democratic, empowering forums that encourage future conversations. As Dewey (1916) put it so eloquently, "The aim of education is to enable individuals to continue their education; the object and reward of learning is continued capacity for growth" (p. 100).

When approached from this heuristic standpoint as those activities that engage in both the pursuit of specific, short-term goals of social justice *and* the more general, long-term and self-renewing teaching of the skills necessary to debate what is or is not social justice, applied communication may be framed productively as both the study of *and* construction of democratic public space that is simultaneously political *and* pedagogical. This essay accordingly proceeds under the assumption that fusing traditional and "postmodern" pedagogical practices with basic public speaking skills and materials committed to challenging the status quo is an excellent means of linking empowering education, applied communication, and the pursuit of social justice (see Aronowitz & Giroux, 1991; Becker, 1994; L. Davis & Mirabella, 1990; Shor, 1992; Simon, 1992). I take this to be the driving *ethos,* but not necessarily the *praxis* of much recent work in the field of communication. The caveat here, concerning the difference between *ethos* and *praxis*—what Conquergood (1995) analyzed as the dialectic of rigor and relevance—reflects the fact that engaged scholars not only need to approach issues of social justice as *sites of research,* but as sites of research *and* engagement with disadvantaged communities. Indeed, as Frey, Pearce, Pollock, Artz, & Murphy (1996) argued, an empowering applied communication of social justice requires a "sensibility" that "foregrounds ethical concerns," engages in "structural analyses" of the social causes of ethical problems, "adopts an activist orientation," and, as an expression of "solidarity," seeks "identification with others" (p. 111). Some remarkable examples of work that has pursued this four-tiered social justice "sensibility" are Brown (1992), Cheney (1995), Conquergood (1994), Schmitz, Rogers, Phillips, & Paschal (1995), and Strine (1992), as each of these essays, illustrating the social justice imperative articulated by Frey et al. (1996), engaged in research "not only *about* but *for* and *in the*

interests of the people with whom" the research is conducted (p. 117).

In an attempt to contribute to the body of work merging the possibilities of scholarly research *and* political engagement, this essay offers a case study of what I envision as an empowering applied communication of social justice. Indeed, while my work over the past seven years as a scholar has focused primarily on the historical legacy of slavery and its current re-institutionalization in the form of what I call the *correctional-industrial-complex,*[4] much of my energy as a teacher and activist has focused on the possibilities of prison pedagogy and prison-based political activism. To demonstrate how I have attempted to fuse these agendas with the pragmatic, *praxis*-oriented concerns of applied communication, I engage below in the following three steps. First, I discuss a prison project in which student/prisoners re-staged the 1858 Lincoln/Douglas debates as a more fully representative three-way debate including Lincoln, Douglas, and the black abolitionist, David Walker. Second, I outline some "outreach" strategies that extended the energy of the classroom into the larger site of the prison itself, so that even those prisoners who were not enrolled in the college program became participants in the empowering dialogues established in the classroom. Third, I describe some of the outreach strategies that proved effective in launching the empowering educational practices of the classroom into the even larger setting of the loose community comprised of prison-rights activists, politically engaged scholars, and friends and families of prisoners. Throughout these three sections, I interweave materials regarding the political economy of the correctional-industrial-complex and discussions of the theoretical underpinnings linking applied communication, social justice, and progressive pedagogy. My hope is that by situating the prison classroom as a site for rethinking our national history, for generating informed debate on controversial political subjects, and for serving as a launching pad for more traditionally public, democratic forms of community-based activity, we might begin to approach applied communication as the pursuit of social justice.

LINCOLN V. DOUGLAS V. WALKER IN PRISON DEBATE: A CASE STUDY OF APPLIED COMMUNICATION, EMPOWERING EDUCATION, AND THE PURSUIT OF SOCIAL JUSTICE

The maximum-security Indiana Reformatory and the medium-security Correctional Industrial Facility are both located in the lovely village of Pendleton, IN, and are situated next door to one another, with the two prisons separated only by the Wildwind Country Club golf course. Drawing on six years of experience teaching a variety of Speech Communication courses for Ball State University in both of these prisons, the Lincoln v. Douglas v. Walker debate of April 24, 1996, was staged in lieu of a traditional final exam for Speech Communication 310: Historical Forms of Public Address. I taught a class similar to this, entitled Contemporary and Historical Forms of Public Address, in the Fall of 1994, and divided the course into three roughly equal sections on antebellum slavery, civil rights, and contemporary prison issues. Partially because both other professors and I address these latter two subjects in other courses, and I imagine partially because much of the material from the first section was so new to them, students—in both anonymous class evaluations and personal conversations—indicated overwhelmingly that they would like to study more antebellum materials. Hence, when offered the chance to teach Speech Communication 310 again in the spring of 1996, I took the students' advice and built the entire course around the questions of slavery, racism, and antebellum politics. Thus, at the foundational level of organizing the class subject matter, I followed both students' urgings and Worth's (1993) suggestion that "postmodern pedagogy" needs to encourage "a more critically interactive role to students" (p. 6).

Having followed students' suggestions on building the class around exclusively antebellum materials, I then divided the class into three sections: sections one and two each included four weeks of reading and discussion, one week of review, and culminated in students writing traditional research essays on the assigned materials.[5] While students were deeply interested

in the topic of study, they, like most undergraduates, did not possess the cultural capital to suggest a comprehensive array of materials. Hence, I attempted to balance readings between context-providing secondary materials regarding the political economy of slavery, manifest destiny, and the crises leading up to the Civil War (including Foner, 1941/1968; Freehling, 1990; Genovese, 1961; Hartnett, 1997 [then in draft]; Hietala, 1985) and primary materials that demonstrate different forms of public address (including Foster's, 1855/1990, rambunctious New York tour-guides and newspaper essays; R. J. Walker's, 1844/1971, massively influential pamphlet on Texas annexation; D. Walker's, 1829/1992, equally influential abolitionist manifesto; and the complete text of the 1858 Lincoln/Douglas debates, 1993). The goal of these first two sections, then, following traditional pedagogical methodology, was to provide students with a sweeping overview of the key historical movements of the period, an introduction to some of the period's important primary documents, and a critical vocabulary to begin analyzing the period in a sophisticated, nuanced manner.

Following Branham's (1995) observation that "in [the prison] environment of near-total control and regimentation, speech and debate activities are rare and significant acts of self-determination and resistance" (p. 118), and utilizing the fact that the Speech Communication Department of Ball State University had, for years, been emphasizing public speaking skills in its classes at the Correctional Industrial Facility (with multiple sections taught each semester by myself and my colleague, Jon Rutter), it seemed both pedagogically empowering and practically feasible to consider concluding the course with a performative/investigative presentation in which the students could shape a semester's worth of learning into a public debate. The third section of the course, therefore, was devoted to two weeks of small group workshops in which we examined different debate tactics, research agendas, and rhetorical strategies, one week of practice runs, and then the final, culminating debate. Thus, in week fourteen of the semester, we staged a debate (with invited guards, administrators, other prisoners, members of the press, and visitors from the "free world") in which three teams addressed the question of slavery. One team played the role of Lincoln, and was responsible for representing the newly formed Republican Party; one team played the role of Douglas, and was responsible for representing the States' Rights position of the Democratic Party; and one team played the role of David Walker, and was responsible for representing the abolitionist movement. All three teams were interracial, and, while allowed spontaneous in-character rebuttals and cross-examinations, and autobiographical answers to audience questions, were required to structure their presentations primarily with the actual words of their respective historical figures.

As the incumbent Senator and recognized elder statesmen of the period, Douglas was given the opening slot. Greg Velasquez began the debate, stalking ominously around the podium in fancy high-top basketball shoes,[6] hyper-active hands slashing the air as he railed against Lincoln's hypocrisy and detailed in chronological fashion how the Republican Party destroyed the old two-party balance between the Whigs and the Democrats, thus leaving the nation adrift in dangerous political flux. In a fine adoption of the vernacular of the period, Greg concluded his opening attack on both the "Black Republicans" (Lincoln) and the "fanatical abolitionists" (Walker) by repeating Chief Justice Roger Taney's infamous 1857 Dred Scot decision that the Declaration of Independence "did not and will not speak for the Negroes, because *they're not our kin.*" In keeping with the rowdy nature of the original debates, Greg's teammates and friends hooted their approval while the Lincoln and Walker teams hissed in dismay. The Lincoln team then offered its opening remarks, with Greg Bergfeld, the articulate, methodical college-in-prison student coordinator for our program, a grandfather, and yet another prisoner serving a first-time non-violent drug charge[7] (not to mention a straight "A" student) attacking the intentional vagueness of Douglas' States' Rights doctrine as but a charade for the Democrats' expansionist "do nothingism" on slavery. Then, in the second half of the Lincoln team's opening comments, after a playful tag-team switcheroo, Sol (Solomon Richardson), a

long-timer on the verge of release, playing out his remaining "down time" by writing endless letters in a flowing, elegant script, and a renewed devotion to running (*"Man, used to be when I was on, I'd do 50 laps 'round the rec. yard without even thinking; hell, now, 25 and I'm whooped"*), derided the incendiary tone of Walker's jeremiad and, in another astute use of historically accurate vernacular, made even more bitter by the words slipping rhythmically from the mouth of a black man, warned "Do not be fooollled by this Black radical. Oh no. I assure you, fellow citizens, that Mr. Walker is pulling the wooooolll from his head over ooouuur eyes." *The crowd erupted in applause.*

At this early juncture in the debate, our guests already appeared stunned to realize both how powerfully racism dominated the political discourse of the period *and* how sharp, knowledgeable, and persuasive *prisoners* could be, as guards gasped, friends beamed with new-found respect, and one fellow professor whispered in my ear, "We could never pull this off on campus." Simultaneously, as Bergfeld and Sol returned triumphantly to the Lincoln team's table, it appeared that the rest of the debaters, witnessing the remarkable effect their classmates were having on the crowd, suddenly recognized the transformative power of informed public debate, and threw themselves into the effort with even more fully evocative and playful energy. The Walker team subsequently began its opening comments with D. J. (David Johnson) at the podium, standing tall and confident in his prison-issued pressed-denim shirt, buttoned as always all the way to the top button, serial number stamped across the breast pocket full of pens and pencils, by making the wonderfully performative gesture of thanking the audience for enabling his "not altogether unexpected resurrection." (The debates took place in 1858, whereas Walker was lynched in 1830. The students, fully versed in Walker's millennial religious beliefs, found the reference funny; the audience did not appear to pick up on the joke, yet D.J.'s infectious smile and the laughter of his classmates carried the moment nonetheless.) D.J. then proceeded in rich biblical language, excoriating both Douglas and Lincoln for their profligate moral compromises, before turning the podium over to Jason Sample, who, in a characteristically thundering final proclamation, announced (again, in historically accurate vernacular) that the moral treachery of both Douglas and Lincoln had produced "a bastard Constitution that is but a blood-soaked rag." This incendiary claim, coupled with Jason's vocal crescendo and his *very* large hands smashing down upon the podium, concluded the opening round with the audience hooting wild approval, while the teams, in historically inaccurate form, I'm afraid, exchanged celebratory high fives. And so it went, through the positioning twenty-minute opening remarks, the biting ten-minute rejoinders, a frenzied ten-minute recess to gather notes and thoughts, a round of impassioned ten-minute closing remarks, and twenty minutes of questions and answers with the audience.

It would be difficult to describe the debate in more detail without filling another fifteen pages with the rhetorical minutia of antebellum politics, yet I can say this: the debaters received a standing ovation from their peers, the invited guests, the prison's supportive Education Director, Mr. Charles Jones, and even the select men and women in attendance paid to serve as their captors. As one reporter covering the event for a local non-profit paper wrote in her story, "The teams declaimed their views with wit and wisdom, while those assembled booed, hissed, and applauded according to their inclination" (C. R. Jones, 1996, p. 3). The debate therefore, enabled us to stage an empowering *counterpublic*, in which a marginalized and viciously stereotyped group of men were able to construct the shape and texture of their own voices while engaging in thoughtful, serious political debate (on the theory of counterpublics, see Fraser, 1990; for a remarkable example of a performative counterpublic, see Maguire & Mohtar, 1994). Indeed, the students found that by combining rigorous research with the public presentation of their ideas in a structured yet playful democratic forum, they were—*for some of them for the first time in their lives*—empowered to speak as authoritative, concerned citizens. As Greg Velasquez wrote in his post-debate review:

> I thought the debate was fantastic! It's amazing how slavery to this day is "taboo"

in some sense: people are still frightened to talk about it. I must admit I was one. But you'll be happy to know that we all used considerable time outside of class discussing the issues. I think it helped bring a sort of peace and serenity among us.

I would like to believe that this "peace and serenity" is at least partially the result of practicing empowering education. Indeed, it appears that Greg and his classmates' hard-earned ability to situate more fully their current predicament within the larger historical trajectory of racism and disciplinary culture literally enabled them to comprehend their lives in a more fully conscious, politically articulate manner. The success of the debate and the tone of Greg's letter confirm that the empowering strategies outlined above worked to accomplish three of the primary goals of the class: 1) to enable students to analyze how ruling elites have historically used racial tropes to disguise their own cultural, political, and economic agendas; 2) to provide students with a new perspective on U.S. slavery and racism, and thus a strong historical grounding for analyzing their own current situation within the correctional-industrial-complex; and 3) to empower students to produce informed and articulate speech acts that placed them in the mainstream of democratic discourse. In terms of communication, then, these three goals, following Frey et al. (1996), sought to "enfranchise" the student/prisoners "in the production of speech acts, episodes, relationships, and enunciative positions" that could both identify "the grammars that oppress or underwrite relationships of domination" (p. 112), and reconstruct these speech acts in empowering, democracy-enhancing public debate (for an elegant elaboration of these ideas, see Farrell, 1993).

To make the connections among these three goals more obvious for our debate audience, I began my "professor's preface" to the debate by observing that while Alabama Prison Commissioner Ron Jones has recently reinstated "chain gangs" that labor for 12-hour shifts breaking rocks ("Alabama to Make Prisoners," 1995; Bragg, 1995), the Mississippi Department of Corrections has returned to dressing prisoners in traditional striped uniforms in order to "humiliate them" (Bragg, 1995, p. A9). I argued that these examples suggested that the correctional-industrial-complex has begun to return to the performative disciplinary routines of Reconstruction's leased convict system (see Hartnett, in press-a; Novak, 1978; Sellin, 1976), hence returning to the institutionalized racism of the Jim Crow period. This argument was expanded when Greg Bergfeld, in response to a question from the audience about the historical importance of slavery to contemporary prisoners, suggested that we are witnessing the rebirth of the semiotics of an extreme and punitive racial segregation in tandem with arrest rates that would appear to be recreating the worst aspects of America's troubled history with racial issues.[8] Indeed, to update Bergfeld's claim with recent statistics, whereas the Bureau of Justice Statistics (1997b) estimated that 4.4% of all white men "will be admitted to prison during their lifetime," 16% of all Hispanic men and a whopping 28.5% of all black men will go to prison (p. 1). In answer to another audience member's question, Sol responded with a comparison between slavery and contemporary arrest rates. Based on his research for our class on the Rhetoric of Crime (in which Bergfeld, D.J., and other debaters were enrolled), Sol noted that the incarceration rate for young black men is "six times the rate for whites" ("More Inmates," 1994, p. 8), and that the incarceration rate for black men in the United States in 1991 was 3,109 per 100,000, while in apartheid South Africa, it was 729 per 100,000 (Mauer, 1992, p. 24, Table 2). Bergfeld's and Sol's points were clear: from their perspective as emerging historians, students of criminology, critics of the politics of communication, *and prisoners,* the shadow of slavery is much closer than one might imagine.

This may seem like a disappointing, even frightening realization, yet by approaching the questions of slavery, racism, communication, and disciplinary culture in this manner, students quickly realized that categories of "race" and versions of "democracy" are but the expedient rhetorical constructions of temporary alliances formed among various politico-economic groups, and that slavery (again, like our own crisis of prisons) therefore was not a "conspiracy" or a universally accepted form of domination, but

rather, a complicated politico-economic and cultural system both supported and contested by competing political factions. This fact became most obvious when the Lincoln and Douglas teams, mimicking the historical tendency of white supremacy in general, joined forces to marginalize Walker's abolitionist rhetoric as too extreme and too dangerous to be considered seriously. Perhaps a second reason, then, why the debate enabled Greg V. and his classmates to achieve a sense of "peace and serenity" is that it enabled them to realize that ideologies are not inexplicable instances of "false consciousness" or mass stupidity, but rather, the necessary conceptual apparati and explanatory narratives that give shape and meaning to real-life practices. This realization suggests that ideologies are subject to transformation, and that life is less reified and deterministic than a cynical perspective might suggest, and, therefore, more open to informed intervention. In short, by constructing the Lincoln/Walker/Douglas debate as a combination of historical, cross-cultural, and oppositional materials, and by then celebrating the empowering skills of giving voice to one's concerns via basic public speaking skills, students were encouraged to realize that they, like their historical predecessor, possess political agency, and that the world of democratic politics—although structured heavily by (among others) racist, sexist, and classist agendas—is nonetheless remarkably open, *even to prisoners,* for critical interventions by organized and articulate activists. In short, *engaging applied communication as the pursuit of social justice turned the classroom into a workshop for democracy* (along these lines, see the excellent essays by Conquergood, 1993; Sprague, 1993; Strine, 1993).

By means of comparison with traditional prison pedagogy, it is interesting to note that of the considerable body of literature on teaching college in prisons, much of it argues that: 1) students/prisoners are behaviorally disturbed (Kiser, 1987); 2) the overpowering atmosphere of prison is inimical to higher education (Cheatwood, 1988; Collins, 1988a); or 3) the project of prison education is irredeemably compromised from the start by a paralyzing "accommodative" stance toward "the overall penitentiary ethos" (Collins, 1988b, p. 101).

There is no question that the prison setting may be a detriment to learning, and that teaching in prisons wraps the educator in a series of complicated ethical and political questions (for example, if I am paid to teach in prison—which I was in Indiana, whereas my current work in California is on a volunteer basis—does that make me but an idealistic cog in the machinery of the correctional-industrial-complex?), yet the data demonstrate persuasively that prisons may very well become our new community colleges for poor (and especially black) men; hence, it is crucially important that we teach prisoners. For example, the state of California's budget for fiscal year 1996/97, for the first time ever, appropriated more money for prisons (9.4% of the budget, up from 2% in 1980) than for the University of California and California State University systems combined (8.7% of the budget, down from 12.6% in 1980) (Connolly, McDermid, Schiraldi, & Macallair, 1996). Furthermore, since 1980, the state of California has slashed the budget's percentage of educational spending by roughly 25%, while raising prison spending (as a percentage of the overall budget) by roughly 500% (see Butterfield, 1995). One of the results of such dramatic redistribution of resources is that while, between 1984 and 1994, the state fired 8,082 university and college employees, the California Department of Corrections hired 25,864 new guards to police 112,000 new prisoners (Connolly, McDermid, Schiraldi, & Macallair, 1996). An even more ominous result of this process is that in the state of California, *black men in prison* (41,434) *outnumber black men in college* (10,474) *by a ratio of almost four-to-one* (Connolly, McDermid, Schiraldi, & Macallair, 1996). California is not alone in this shocking fact, as nationally "the 583,000 black men incarcerated in prisons and jails are more than the 537,000 [black men] enrolled in higher education" ("More Inmates," 1994, p. 8). Despite these figures, the 1994 Omnibus Crime Bill denied prisoner access to Pell Grants, thus making it even more difficult for incarcerated men and women to pursue educational opportunities.[9] Without sounding hyperbolic, then, the data demonstrate that *we are teaching an entire generation of young black men that they are neither students, nor citizens, but criminals.* Given this troubling context, teaching in prisons, teaching prisoners about the historical legacy of slavery, and working with prisoners to help them construct their own communication strategies for articulating how this legacy affects contemporary prison issues are crucially important tasks.

The idea behind the Lincoln v. Douglas v. Walker debate, then, was to construct a pedagogy of empowering education that assumed three standards: 1) empowering education should be focused, *in the best tradition of applied communication,* on public engagements with local communities rooted in concrete communicative situations; 2) such activist engagements with local communities should be based, *in the best tradition of academic rigor,* on vigorous scholarship; and 3) these academically rigorous yet locally tested engagements with specific communicative situations should, *in the best tradition of struggling for social justice,* be critically self-reflexive regarding the role of education and communication in both sustaining and recreating democratic public culture. The question, then, given these criteria, is how to proceed from the classroom to the community, from empowering education and applied communication to social justice.

APPLIED COMMUNICATION AS A MEANS OF EXTENDING THE CLASSROOM, PART ONE: EMPOWERING EDUCATION AS OUTREACH WITHIN THE PRISON

A common complaint within prison education literature is that the peculiar environment of prisons compromises the mission of higher education. For example, R. Jones (1991) argued that college-in-prison programs suffer from what he called "the invisibility thesis": "The context of learning permits no clearly defined boundaries between 'the campus' and the social world which participants inhabit and therefore fails to suggest the institutional transfer of authority requisite to credible identity formation" (p. 9). However, instead of allowing the complexities of the prison environment to infringe on the goals and practices of the classroom, teachers may just as well use the classroom as a launching pad from which to engage the rest of the prison. Indeed, if prison educators accept the notion that college-in-prison programs are embedded within a prison environment from which they cannot escape, and within which they are deeply implicated at all times, then one of the most radical goals for teachers who wish to engage in empowering education in prisons is to extend the energy of the classroom into the larger community of the prison itself—literally, to use each specific course as an outreach program that attempts to bring new materials, ideas, and intellectual and political energies into the prison.

One step in working towards an empowering education of applied communication that strives to achieve social justice via outreach activities is to consider Freire's (1970/1994) seminal study, *Pedagogy of the Oppressed,* where he defined "problem-posing education" (in terms that clearly echo the fundamental premises of "applied communication"; see Eadie, 1990, 1994; Seibold, 1995) as a form of activist pedagogy in which students and teachers strive collectively for "the emergence of consciousness" as *critical interventions in reality* (pp. 60, 62). This is a crucial concept for those who wish to practice empowering education in prison classrooms, for the very nature of prison is to isolate "offenders" from society, thereby denying them any sense of themselves as responsible citizens with productive obligations to their communities. Emphasizing problem-posing situations that enable prisoners to engage critically in their social world (whether it is the prison itself or the community from which they came—more on this below) is, therefore, a crucial first step towards the self-constructive process Freire calls "becoming" (p. 65; see also Tootoonchi, 1993). Indeed, a key component of Freire's theory of empowering education is his insistence that learning is an open-ended pursuit of the as-yet incomplete self/community. Specifically, Freire argued that one of the hallmark tendencies of the "oppressed" is that they are denied political agency via the state-sponsored abandonment (and even repression) of their intellectual abilities; hence, for the oppressed, fulfilling their potential as students is simultaneously and unavoidably a step towards the fulfillment of their potential as self-reflexive political beings with agency. This explains

Freire's claim that "problem-posing education is revolutionary futurity...it is prophetic and hopeful" (p. 65).

The Lincoln/Douglas/Walker debate provides an example of how Freire's notion of "problem-posing education" enabled students to link applied communication practices with the dual imperatives of struggling for social justice via "outreach" activities while engaging simultaneously in the dialogues that point toward their own "revolutionary futurity." For example, prior to the actual debate, we spent two weeks in small group research and debate workshops, and then one week in loose, ragged rehearsal. The workshops were particularly heated, with much arguing about the ground rules of the debate, but with even more concern voiced about how the prison would respond, during the next three weeks and after, to rumors that college students were arguing in favor of slavery. Hence, the class agreed that each debater would take it upon himself to explain to anyone who would listen that the class was *playing these roles* in order to understand more fully the historical groundings of slavery, racism, and the correctional-industrial-complex. In the process of making these controversy-diffusing explanatory appeals to their fellow prisoners, class participants soon found themselves besieged by cell-mates interested in engaging in the dialogue initiated in our classroom. Indeed, the debate teams soon found themselves both loaning out books, essays, and class notes to their non-collegiate bunk-mates and friends *and* receiving materials, ideas, and constant advice from concerned parties. Obviously, the outright controversy of staging a debate on slavery was more than enough to launch the assignment out of the classroom and into a prison-wide consideration of the subject.

This may seem like a provocative, perhaps even dangerous, strategy, yet in initiating the debate, and by saturating the classroom (and hence, at least part of the prison) with information on the subject, the project achieved a dramatic goal: specifically, it enabled both the classroom students and the larger population of non-classroom prisoners to address the political economy of slavery from an informed perspective that countered both popular misconceptions and the silence-as-usual that surrounds issues of racism.[10] By then culminating the project with a public presentation, we created a situation in which the classroom evolved into something more like an unofficial cultural center in which rigorous intellectual activity and engaged political action merged in the form of a public, democratic exchange of ideas, information, and sources for future study and activism. Indeed, as one student (who has asked to remain anonymous) wrote in his post-debate review, "I think we have set a fine example of men coming together in peaceful teams trying to find solutions to the problems of slavery, racism, and prisons."

As an exercise in applied communication *praxis*, then, each of the debate teams learned quickly that dogma on any side of the issue led inevitably (within the classroom) to breakdowns in communication, (within the prison) to hard feelings and possibly dangerous scapegoating, and, ultimately (in U.S. history), to mass violence. Hence, the debate workshops focused attention on the absolute necessity of sound research, prudent dialogue, and the ability to function as a productive member of a collective team. In this sense, the project—like all ventures in applied communication should be—became an exercise in recognizing that productive democratic debate is inherently dependent on rigorous scholarship, nuanced rhetoric, and healthy doses of humor, spontaneity, and mutually reciprocal graciousness. The Lincoln/Douglas/Walker debate, then, even in its generative, formative workshop period, enabled students to engage in what Aronowitz and Giroux (1993) referred to as "the pedagogy of possibility" (p. 46). While they did not use the term "applied communication," Aronowitz and Giroux (1993) elaborated some possibilities of social justice–based applied communication, when they argued that transformative, empowering education combines "critical reflection and action" as a means of socializing students into the world of democratic politics, and that such a "pedagogy of possibility" must "help students develop a deep and abiding faith in the struggle to overcome injustices and to change themselves" (p. 46). Furthermore, in a passage that clearly emphasized the importance of applied communication, Aronowitz and Giroux argued that this pedagogy of possibility must demonstrate a "commitment to expanding

dialogue and exchange across lines of cultural difference *as part of a wider attempt to deepen and develop democratic public life*," [italics added] so as to "make despair unconvincing and hope practical" (pp. 51, 46). By enabling students to engage in precisely this kind of dialogue-expanding and hope-reviving process of reaching out to their fellow prisoners, the Lincoln/Douglas/Walker debate demonstrated the productive possibilities of merging applied communication practices with the "pedagogy of possibility."

It is important to add that at the time this debate was staged, I had been teaching in the Correctional Industrial Facility for six years, and felt comfortable that the classroom assignment would not generate violence in the prison itself. My confidence was based on two premises. First, I believed that because the debate was framed as a problem-posing task, as a concrete example of the requisite mode of flexible-perspective research that underlies all legitimate historical inquiry and political advocacy, the students could persuade their fellow prisoners that what we were engaging in was a necessary form of political critique. Second, because I had worked previously with some students in the class, including Greg Bergfeld, D.J., Sol, Jason, and others, in as many as three classes a semester for as many as three years, I was convinced that they were sophisticated enough intellectually, and secure enough physically (in terms of the hard-core realities of prison power dynamics) to engage the project in a productive, safe, and even playful manner. As the opening section of this essay described, and as I had anticipated, the remarkable students at the Correctional Industrial Facility handled the problem-posing task with grace and feverish energy, generating lively classroom discussion, working through stacks of research materials, and providing a context for non-collegiate prisoners to engage in important historical debates. By culminating the class in a lively and well-attended public performance, the students guaranteed that a prison in Indiana, *their community*, was—for at least a few weeks—on fire with informed and passionate debate regarding the relationships among slavery, racism, communication, and disciplinary culture.

To summarize this second section, it has been my experience that prisoners desperately desire a hopeful sense of a future in which their post-incarceration lives will be fulfilling. Recognizing this need for what Freire (1970/1994) called "revolutionary futurity" suggests that empowering education may be based productively on specific and concrete problem-posing tasks that encourage the advancement of students not only as potential scholars and intellectuals, but also as social beings whose *telos* is enlightened and engaged civic responsibility. One of the most obvious difficulties with pursuing this strategy is that many prisoners are deeply skeptical regarding attempts to socialize them into the culture of democracy. This skepticism is a rational response to lingering perceptions of the dubious role of education (or the lack thereof) in U.S. history. For example, our abolitionist team cited David Walker (1829/1992) claiming that "[i]t is a notorious fact, that the major part of the white Americans, have, ever since we have been among them, tried to keep us ignorant, and make us believe that God made us and our children to be slaves to them and theirs" (p. 33). For many prisoners, this link among slavery, ignorance, and "education" that is little more than training for subservience to "the man" is a ghost that haunts and compromises the desire to learn. Indeed, given the historically co-optive role played by the U.S. status-quo educational system (see Aronowitz & Giroux, 1993; Kelly, 1995), and considering the hellish conditions of life behind bars, it is not surprising that "So What?" is one of the questions voiced most commonly in prison-based college classrooms. Goldin and Thomas's (1984) research with prisoners in Illinois corroborates this claim, as they concluded that "students are especially critical of the apparent irrelevance of education programs to the 'real life' needs inmates will have upon release" (p. 126).

Skepticism of the role of specific educational assignments (and even of education in general) is thus a perfectly understandable perspective for prisoners. It is, therefore, crucial that prison-based educators provide their students with clear-cut assignments that encourage them both to engage in the requisite academic materials of the chosen course *and* to put that learning into action/practice as an empowering "critical intervention into reality." Ideally, such dual-agenda projects enable students to link the specific pedagogic function of completing an assignment or course of study with the larger political function of generating a new sense of the self-as-agent. The goal of problem-posing pedagogy, then, is to demonstrate to students that pursuing rigorous educational goals leads inevitably to self and community empowerment (along these lines, see Duguid, 1988; Elias, 1994; hooks, 1994). The positive response of students, their fellow prisoners, prison administrators, and even some of the prison guards, suggests that the Lincoln/Douglas/Walker debate approached these goals, both as a classroom-specific example of "problem-posing" pedagogy and as an example of how the pedagogy of possibility may serve as the context for dialogue-expanding outreach activities.

APPLIED COMMUNICATION AS A MEANS OF EXTENDING THE CLASSROOM, PART TWO: EMPOWERING EDUCATION AS OUTREACH TO THE COMMUNITY

Extending the empowering pedagogy of the classroom ideally transcends the prison itself, reaching into the larger community of prison-rights activists, engaged scholars, and the families and friends of prisoners. Staging public debates is one obvious strategy, but an important feature of the Lincoln/Douglas/Walker debate—in addition to serving as a context for bringing both guests and press into the prison—was the twenty-minute question-and-answer session that concluded the debate, in which the previously in-character debaters stepped back from their roles as Lincoln, Douglas, or Walker, and, speaking autobiographically, answered questions regarding their experiences with researching the material, staging the debate, and interacting with other prisoners concerning the complicated historical, cultural, and political questions raised by the debate. As informed "experts" fielding questions from fellow citizens, the prisoners came to recognize the implicit link between education and citizenship; just as importantly in terms of outreach strategies, the question-and-answer session allowed the audience to hear the "voices" of the debaters in a more immediate, personal way. Given the rampant scapegoating of "Lock 'em Up" hysteria, the personal stories conveyed in the question-and-answer session's dialogue amounted to a radically humanizing moment in which "free" citizens found themselves confronted by the intelligence, humor, and rich possibility of a group of men who had existed previously for them solely as stereotypes. One can only hope that this new consciousness regarding the humanity of prisoners will reverberate through the social lives of our debate guests, thus enabling the lessons of the debate to reach out into communities beyond the walls of the prison.

Another outreach strategy is to encourage students to rewrite preliminary drafts of their classroom work, which the student and instructor can then edit together; the instructor can then type up the material on his or her computer (the students with whom I work do not have access to typewriters, let alone personal computers) and submit it to one of the burgeoning group of prison-rights and/or progressive, grassroots community magazines.[11] There are three goals of this simple strategy: 1) to extend the research methods and academic energy of the classroom to an even larger, more public audience; 2) to enable students/prisoners to recognize that they have meaningful choices regarding the sources of their news; and 3) to demonstrate by example that even a group as disempowered as prisoners may play active roles—via their mastery of sound research skill and argumentation techniques—in dynamic public debates.[12] Ideally then, extending the energy of the classroom into a more public forum provides students with an introduction to the cultural practices of democracy (along these lines, see Anderson, 1996). As Giroux (1992) suggested, such empowering educational and outreach strategies strive "to provide students and audiences with the competencies needed to develop and experience a pluralistic conception of citizenship and community that dignifies democracy" (p. 245).

For example, Robert Kelly (1997), a shy, deeply religious man enrolled in our Rhetoric of Crime course, became so angered by the swelling public debate regarding prisoners working for private corporations in prison that he drafted a letter to the respected alternative newsmagazine, *In These Times*. In his exuberant personal correspondence to me announcing both the letter's publication and his imminent return to freedom, his lovely wife, and his old neighborhood in Gary, IN, Robert wrote that seeing his ideas in print confirmed for him "the indispensable virtue of speaking out." A more explicitly political tone, in terms of linking the possibilities of empowering education, applied communication practices, and the pursuit of social justice, was established by "Trotsky" (1993b) (this prisoner's *nom de guerre*), where, in one of his many remarkable articles drafted originally as part of an assignment for one of our classes in the Indiana Reformatory, he argued:

> Informing ourselves and the public is the first step in creating radical change. We are doing that right now; *Human Rights Held Hostage* [see note 11] is designed to keep us informed about what is taking place in Indiana's prisons. But there is more that we can do, whether we're in prison or on the streets: we need to spread information like fire, write to individuals, newspapers, and other prison journals. Sharing our experiences and thoughts through these outlets can only lead to organization, education, and the breaking down of our marginalization (p. 9).

Trotsky, a brilliant, passionate, desperately giving young man who had been imprisoned since he was fifteen, "with less than a ninth-grade education," having already "attempted suicide, being turned away from the love and support of my family and friends, and basically giving up on life" ("Trotsky," 1993a, p. 10), found empowering education a pathway not only to personal redemption, but to forging new bonds, as an author and organizer, with outside communities. Tragically, Trotsky, suffering from leukemia, poor prison health services, and a variety of other severe prison-related deprivations, died in prison before he turned 21.

Encouraging students/prisoners to participate as both readers of and contributing authors and artists to community magazines, therefore—assuming they survive the calamities of prison—provides them with the much-needed opportunity to forge what Duguid (1992) called the "social engagements" that enable them to begin the process of "re-engaging with society by gathering commitments and allegiances which imply a new kind of life" (p. 42). Thus, by extending the empowering educational and applied communication strategies of the classroom into the community, the classroom becomes a workshop for democracy that provides students/prisoners with an excellent opportunity to begin the long process of reintegrating themselves into their communities not as "ex-cons," or future troublemakers, but rather, like Robert Kelly, as creative and productive citizens (in addition to the student/prisoner examples of Trotsky, 1993a, 1993b, and R. Kelly, 1997; also see Bari, 1993, 1994a, 1994b; Wise 1995). Indeed, pursuing such empowering education as the practice of democracy and social justice points to what Wartenberg (1990) defined as transformative power: "the use of power that seeks to bring about its own obsolescence by means of the empowerment of the subordinate agent" (p. 184). Put simply, the goal of such transformative power is to engage students in problem-posing projects that enable them to realize their own potential as creative and competent social agents who, by pursuing their own engagements in democratic culture, mature into teachers and activists in their own right, regardless of their initial relationship to the teachers who prompted or structured the beginning stages of the process (also see Sprague, 1993). As Melvin Jones, an elderly San Quentin prisoner whose academic work has been hampered by the prison's refusal to provide him with decent reading glasses, explained in his course review for our class, entitled "Philosophical, Criminological, and Literary Thoughts on the Curious Relationships among Law, Justice, Property, and Democracy" (Communication 61, Spring, 1997):

> This class taught me that my concerns are legitimate, but that my frustration does not have to be an anchor, but a catapult to do more to help myself and my people. . . . The invigorating part is that I am angry and refuse to accept things as they are.

One can only hope that Melvin's frustrations continue to grow, and that he will, upon his release, catapult himself into the process of struggling for social justice within his local community.

A third strategy for extending the empowering pedagogy of the classroom via outreach projects is for educators to follow through on the advice proposed by Aronowitz and Giroux (1991) that "teachers as transformative intellectuals need to become a movement marked by an active involvement in oppositional spheres" (p. 51). This is where the project of merging empowering education, applied communication practices, and the fight for social justice comes full circle, for just as I have argued that empowering education in prisons needs to be problem-posing and geared towards the socialization of students/prisoners as active and informed citizens taking part in the democratic process, so teachers too need to engage in this same process, so that we too attack specific political problems via our participation in oppositional movements that are public, democratic, and historically progressive (for further examples of this work, see Hartnett, in press-b, and Spacks, 1997). In short, this means that those of us who strive to teach empowering education and applied communication need to recognize that *our obligations as citizens do not end in the classroom;* we too must shoulder the democratic responsibility of participating in the public search for social justice.

In closing, it is appropriate to return to Dewey's (1916) argument that democracy and education are inextricably linked, and that democracy, like education, must strive to enable and celebrate our collective "continued capacity for growth" (p. 100). The applied communication practices described above strive to support this "capacity for growth" by recognizing that the production of informed public debate is a crucial element in both the formation of empowered, responsible citizens *and* the reproduction of democracy itself. Indeed, Kris Wise (1995), one of the many young poets using his "down time" in the Correctional Industrial Facility as a means of creating a new, responsible, utopian self immersed in community, celebrates the possibilities of such empowering education and applied communication when, as part of his end-of-the-semester review of his role in an oral presentation staged for a class on Interpersonal Communication, he wrote:

> I want no more of
> Life that knows only death. In love
> I trust. The sacred field of reverence
> is all I need. To be
> found in who I am becoming. Willingly
> excited by imperfection. Forgiven
> the misery of existence: Awakened
> to the adventures that may now occur. (p. 27)

Endnotes

[1] Throughout this essay the names of students/ prisoners, unless otherwise noted, are genuine. At the end of all of my prison classes, students are asked to write essays analyzing their growth throughout the semester, discussing their impressions of the impact of education on their lives, and detailing their wishes for future courses. The assignment includes explicit directions for indicating whether prisoners' responses may be cited in public discourse, and whether their names may be used. Anonymous references, therefore, indicate a student response in which the author agreed to share his words yet wished to remain anonymous. All references to published works by students/prisoners are cited in the references.

[2] Like Jason, hundreds of thousands of prisoners labor in prison industries operated by federal, state, and private organizations. At the federal level, this captive labor falls under the jurisdiction of Federal Prison Industries Incorporated, the Federal Bureau of Prisons' manufacturing consortium known by the confusing acronym of UNICOR. While paying inmate laborers entry-level wages of 23 cents per hour, UNICOR boasts gross annual sales of over $250 million (DiIulio, 1991). Raymond Luc Levasseur (1993), an inmate at the "supermax" in Marion, IL, notes that during the Korean War, fully 80% of UNICOR products were sold to the Department of Defense. Levasseur claims that UNICOR materials produced in the infamous maximum-security Federal Prison in Lexington, KY., have recently fulfilled Defense Department contracts totaling up to $12 million. Hence, prison laborers are forced to produce materials that support the imperial ambitions of a nation in which they cannot vote.

At the state level, one example of prison labor is the $1.2 million per year "Prison Blues" program, in which the Oregon Department of Corrections employs prison laborers to produce a "Prison Blues" line of clothing (for public sale primarily in Asia, but also in the U.S.), with projected yearly sales of over $1.2 million. Despite these profits, prisoners reportedly earn real wages (their $8 per hour wage minus state-imposed restitution fees and room and board) of $1.80 an hour (Wright, 1994).

In terms of the complicated ethical, political, and juridical issues regarding the use of prison labor for private corporations, see the arguments in M. Davis (1995), Erlich (1995), Greenburg (1994), Parenti (1996), Shichor (1996), and Wright (1994).

[3] Whereas the *correctional-industrial-complex* (defined in endnote 4) is a sweeping, critical term of analysis, the Correctional Industrial Facility is a specific, medium-security prison in Pendleton, IN.

[4] The term "correctional-industrial-complex"—much like its predecessor, the military-industrial-complex—refers to the interlocking interests of State-sponsored correctional and policing organizations, privately owned industrial corporations, and the multiple groups of political players who profit from the manipulation of the tropes of racism, fear of crime, and law and order. The premier discussions of this concept are Christie (1993), Lilly and Knepper (1993), Rasmussen and Benson (1994), and Reeves and Campbell (1994). In terms of establishing the clout of this correctional-industrial-complex, it is important to note that U.S. prisons and jails currently house over 1.6 million "offenders" (Bureau of Justice Statistics [BJS], 1997a), and that the total population of citizens under some form of State-sponsored disciplinary institution (including prisons, jails, probation, and parole) for the year 1995 (the most recent year for which figures are available) was 5,129,700 (BJS, 1996, p. 540, table 6.1). In fact, over 14.5 million U.S. Americans were arrested in 1995 alone (BJS, 1996, p. 394, table 4.1). Hence, regardless of one's political perspective on how or why this is happening, the startling fact is that the U.S. both arrests and imprisons more of its citizens than any other nation on the face of the planet. *We are, therefore, becoming a "democratic" police state in which imprisoning "deviant" citizens is a major growth industry fueling a correctional-industrial-complex.*

By means of example, consider the logic of this correctional-industrial-complex as it functions in the state of Indiana, where the 1996

State budget allocated $35 million to hire new prison guards and state troopers and to build new mental hospitals, and another $11 million for the architectural design (but not building) of a new 1,000-bed prison (Macintyre, 1995). This means that the State of Indiana plans to spend close to $46 million for new penal programs (in addition to existing budgetary allocations), while simultaneously cutting prisoner counseling, prisoner health care, transitional programs, and other rehabilitative programs (for a stunning exposé of this process, see Hamm, 1992; also see Hartnett, 1994).

The unprecedented acceleration of resources directed into the correctional-industrial-complex—estimated by The National Council on Crime and Delinquency, in 1994, to reach, including state and federal expenditures on prisons over the next ten years, $351 billion ("NCCD Analysis Finds," 1994)—is made even more confusing by the fact that while imprisonment rates have doubled since 1980 (BJS, 1993b, 1993c), the BJS (1993a) reported that "the level of violent crime in 1992 did not differ significantly from the number measured in 1981. . . . Approximately 6.6 million violent crimes occurred in both 1981 and 1992" (p. 1). Additionally, while pro-incarceration ideologues trumpet the impending doom of skyrocketing murder rates, the fact is that the 1993 homicide rate of 9.3 per 100,000 citizens is actually less than the corresponding 1973 figure of 9.4 per 100,000 (Lusane, 1994). Hence, despite the fact that there is no corresponding escalation of violent crime, the correctional-industrial-complex has embarked on the most accelerated imprisonment binge in U. S. history.

We are thus witnessing the production of a *correctional-industrial-complex* in which society's already limited resources and funds are redistributed significantly away from social justice–based forms of spending, such as education, housing, and health care, in favor of what The American Friends Service Committee characterized as a prison-based "fortress economy" (Lichtenstein, 1990). Without intending to sound hyperbolic, it seems important to argue that the correctional-industrial-complex represents a fundamental assault on the premises and future possibilities of democracy.

5 In terms of what such "traditional" essays entailed, students were required to outline briefly the major historical and political trends of the period as described in our secondary materials, to engage in a detailed critique of one of the major ideologies buried within these trends (such as modernity, liberalism, capitalism, or mass democracy), and, based on our primary materials, to explicate three of the dominant rhetorical tropes used to construct this ideology. Students therefore were required to demonstrate their ability to analyze how communication is structured by rhetorical tropes, political ideologies, and historical contexts.

6 Greg's high-tech sneakers—like many other consumer items, from things as mundane as toothpaste and deodorant to expensive goods like televisions and radios—had to be purchased through the prison-run "commissary," essentially a prison-run store in which prisoners pay inflated prices for consumer products. Nationally, such commissaries enable the correctional-industrial-complex to supply prison profiteers with a ready mass of consumers locked into State-guaranteed markets. For example, an anonymous Campbell's Soup spokesperson celebrated the fact that prisons amount to "the nation's fastest growing food market" (Lilly & Knepper, 1993, p. 158), totaling over $1 billion per year in contracts. This means that corporations with contracts with the correctional-industrial-complex have a vested interest in escalating imprisonment rates, accelerating prison construction, and increasing funding for "law and order" strategies. As an anonymous prison profiteer interviewed by Greenberg (1994) observed, "The more crooks you have the better business is for us" (p. 15).

7 Like Greg, a majority of the newly incarcerated prisoners in the United States are charged with non-violent crimes. In fact, the Sentencing Project reported that "of the 155% increase in new court commitments to State prisons from 1980–1992, 16% were violent offenders, while drug, property, and public order offenders accounted for 84%" (cited in "More Inmates," 1994, p. 8). In terms of Federal prisons, the Department of Justice reported that 60% of the prison population is made up of "drug offenders," meaning prisoners, again like Greg, with "minimal or no prior criminal history *whose offense did not involve sophisticated criminal activity and whose behavior was non-violent*" [italics added] (Office of the Deputy Attorney General, 1994, pp. 106, 101).

8 One reviewer questioned whether or not Bergfeld would actually use the term "semiotics," yet based on his (and his classmates') previous work in courses offered by my colleague Jon Rutter and I on critical theory, nonverbal communication, persuasion, argumentation, and one class that we team-taught on film criticism, Greg and his

classmates were well versed in the theories of Roland Barthes, John Berger, and a host of other scholars working in the field of semiotics.

[9] It is unfortunate that the Congressional (and public) debate regarding prisoner access to Pell Grants not only ignored multiple studies that suggested that educational programs both reduce recidivism (BJS, 1989) and make prisons less violent, more manageable institutions (Taylor, 1992), but was based on a misrepresentation of the historically democratizing function of Pell Grants (Hartnett, 1995; Taylor, 1994). Specifically, Pell Grants are not a misguided and tax-wasting liberal handout to criminals, but rather, one of the primary tools in the U.S. for providing post-secondary educational opportunities for the poor. In fact, prior to passage of the Omnibus Crime Bill [*Public Law 103-322: Violent Crime Control and Law Enforcement Act of 1994*, passed 13 September, 1994], any academically eligible student from a family of four with an average yearly income of less than $25,000 was authorized to receive Pell Grant money to help pay for college. Contrary to popular misunderstandings, prisoners who receive Pell Grants do not take money out of the pockets of law-abiding, financially needy students, as Pell Grants are awarded on an "entitlement basis" (which means that poor, would-be students do not compete against each other for the money; one is either eligible or not). Furthermore, of the 4 million Pell Grants, totaling $6.4 billion, awarded in 1994, 27,700 prisoners received grants worth $41 million, which amounts to considerably less than 1% of the national Pell Grant budget (Phillips, 1994). In the two prisons in Indiana where I worked during the 1994–95 academic year, students were eligible for $1,150 per semester, times two semesters. With approximately 300 full-time students enrolled, this Pell Grant total came close to $690,000. Compared to the $46 million that the State of Indiana plans to spend on locking up more criminals, $690,000 for educational programs seems like a wise investment.

An even more insidious aspect of the Crime Bill's assault on the historic function of Pell Grants is that while it seeks to deny inmates the possibility of attaining a college education, and thus one of the most effective opportunities to "rehabilitate" themselves, the bill simultaneously pledges $200 million for the creation of a nation-wide scholarship fund for college-age students who agree to serve as law-enforcement officers (Lewis, 1994). What this amounts to, then—in a move that clearly mimics the politico-economic

trajectory of the Reagan/Bush era (see M. Davis, 1986; Galbraith, 1992; Kolko, 1988)—is a massive redistribution of wealth away from the "undesirable" underclasses and into the hands of students who are willing to support status-quo politics. (For overviews of the Crime Bill, see Benekos & Merlo (1995), Johnston & Holmes (1994), and Lusane (1994).

[10] One of the primary goals of the class and the debate was to enable students to comprehend the strategies by which *ideologies are produced.* Popular misconceptions about prison, prisoners, crime, racism, and drugs, for example, are generally the result of complicated and overlapping corporate, media, and political strategies that serve the needs of ruling elites. This is not the place for an extended argument regarding the critical theory of ideology; for analyses of how popular misconceptions regarding the relationships among crime, drugs, and racism are produced by and for the benefit of ruling elites, see Bertram, Blachman, Sharpe, & Andreas (1996), Christie (1993), Hartnett (1996, in press-a), Leps (1992), Reeves and Campbell (1994), and Reiman (1990).

[11] See *The Prison News Service* (Box 5052, Station A, Toronto, Ontario, Canada, M5W 1W4), recently renamed *Bulldozer: Walkin' Steel* (published by the Committee to End the Marion Lockdown; P.O. Box 578172, Chicago, IL 60657-8172); *Lip* (1400 West Devon #243, Chicago, IL 60660); *The Community Times* (P.O. Box 3125, W. Lafayette, IN 47906); the newsletters published by The Prison Action Committee (Suite 1060, 542 South Dearborn, Chicago, IL 60605), The Crossroads Support Network (3021 West 63rd Street, Chicago, IL 60629), and The Indianapolis Peace and Justice Center (3808 N. Meridian St., Room 203, Indianapolis, IN 46208); on the West Coast, see *Prison Focus* (2489 Mission St. #28, San Francisco, CA 94110). For a complete listing of sources, contact The Prison Activist Resource Center (P.O. Box 3201, Berkeley, CA 94703). Although only published regularly for two years, from January 1993 through the Autumn of 1994, *Human Rights Held Hostage,* which covered prison issues nationally but focused especially on Indiana and Illinois prisons, provided a remarkable outlet for prisoner-authored essays, drawings, and poems.

[12] Rideau and Wikberg's (1993) anthology is an excellent example of how prisoners may engage in the kinds of progressive-pedagogy-as-outreach strategies discussed here, as the prisoner-authored essays collected in this text were written originally for *The Angolite,* the magazine edited by Rideau

and Wikberg from the maximum-security prison in Angola, LA. For more information about this magazine, contact *The Angolite: The Prison Newsmagazine,* Louisiana State Penitentiary, Angola, LA 70712.

References

Alabama to make prisoners break rocks. (1995, July 29). *New York Times,* p. A5.

Anderson, S. (1996). Ethnography as advocacy: Enabling the voices of women prisoners. In P. Spacks (Ed.), *Advocacy in the classroom: Problems and possibilities* (pp. 408–421). New York: St. Martin's Press.

Aronowitz, S., & Giroux, H. (1993). *Education still under siege* (2nd ed.). Westport, CT: Bergin & Garvey.

Aronowitz, S., & Giroux, H. (1991). *Postmodern education: Politics, culture, and social criticism.* Minneapolis: University of Minnesota Press.

Bari, A. (1993). Political repression in Indiana: The M.C.C. prototype. *Prison News Service, 40,* 3.

Bari, A. (1994a). If not us, who? If not now, when? *Prison News Service, 46,* 16–17.

Bari, A. (1994b). If not us, who? If not now, when? Part two. *Prison News Service, 47,* 12–13.

Becker, C. (Ed.). (1994). *The subversive imagination: Artists, society, and social responsibility.* New York: Routledge.

Benekos, P., & Merlo, A. (1995). Three strikes and you're out! The political sentencing game. *Federal Probation, 59,* 3–9.

Bercovitch, S. (1993). *The rites of assent: Transformations in the symbolic construction of America.* New York: Routledge.

Bernts, T., d'Anjou, L., & Houtman, D. (1992). Citizenship and social justice. *Social Justice Research, 5,* 195–212.

Bertram, E., Blachman, M., Sharpe, K., & Andreas, P. (1996). *Drug war politics: The price of denial.* Berkeley: University of California Press.

Bragg, R. (1995, March 26). Chain gangs to return to roads of Alabama. *New York Times,* p. A9.

Branham, R. (1995). "I was gone on debating": Malcolm X's prison debates and public confrontations. *Argumentation and Advocacy, 31,* 117–137.

Brenkert, G. (1991). *Political freedom.* London: Routledge.

Brown, W. (1992). Culture and AIDS education: Reaching high-risk heterosexuals in Asian-American communities. *Journal of Applied Communication Research, 20,* 275–291.

Bureau of Justice Statistics. (1989). *Special report: Recidivism of prisoners released in 1983.* Washington, DC: Department of Justice.

Bureau of Justice Statistics. (1993a). *Jail inmates 1992.* Washington, DC: Department of Justice.

Bureau of Justice Statistics. (1993b). *Prisoners in 1992.* Washington, DC: Department of Justice.

Bureau of Justice Statistics. (1993c). *National crime victimization survey report: Criminal victimization 1992.* Washington, DC: Department of Justice.

Bureau of Justice Statistics. (1996). *Sourcebook of criminal justice statistics 1995.* Washington, DC: Department of Justice.

Bureau of Justice Statistics. (1997a). *Prison and jail inmates at midyear 1996.* Washington, DC: Department of Justice.

Bureau of Justice Statistics. (1997b). *Lifetime likelihood of going to state or federal prison.* Washington, DC: Department of Justice.

Butterfield, F. (1995a, April 12). Prison-building binge in CA casts shadow on higher education. *The New York Times,* p. A11.

Butterfield, F. (1995b, May 23). Major crimes fall for third year, but experts don't see trend. *The New York Times,* p. C19.

Cheatwood, D. (1988). The impact of the prison environment on the incarcerated learner. *Journal of Correctional Education, 39,* 184–186.

Cheney, G. (1995). Democracy in the workplace: Theory and practice from the perspective of communication. *Journal of Applied Communication Research, 23,* 167–200.

Christie, N. (1993). *Crime control as industry: Towards gulags, Western style* (2nd ed.). London: Routledge.

Collins, M. (1988a). Towards a distinctive vocation for prison educators: Some key concerns and relevant strategies. *Journal of Correctional Education, 39,* 24–28.

Collins, M. (1988b). Prison education: A substantive metaphor for adult education practice. *Adult Education Quarterly, 38,* 101–110.

Connolly, K., McDermid, L., Schiraldi, V., & Macallair, D. (1996). *From classrooms to cell blocks: How prison building affects higher education and African American enrollment.* San Francisco: Center on Juvenile & Criminal Justice.

Conquergood, D. (1993). Storied worlds and the work of teaching. *Communication Education, 42,* 337–348.

Conquergood, D. (1994). Homeboys and hoods: Gang communication and cultural spaces. In L. Frey (Ed.), *Group communication in context: Studies of natural groups* (pp. 23–55). Hillsdale, NJ: Lawrence Erlbaum.

Conquergood, D. (1995). Between rigor and relevance: Rethinking applied communication. In K. N. Cissna (Ed.), *Applied communication in the 21st century* (pp. 79–96). Mahwah, NJ: Lawrence Erlbaum.

Davis, L., & Mirabella, M. B. (Eds.). (1990). *Left politics and the literary profession.* New York: Columbia University Press.

Davis, M. (1986). *Prisoners of the American dream: Politics and economy in the history of the US working class.* London: Verso.

Davis, M. (1995, February 20). Hell factories in the field: A prison-industrial complex. *The Nation,* pp. 229–234.

Dewey, J. (1916) Democracy and education: An introduction to the philosophy of education. New York: Macmillan.

DiIulio, J. (1991). *No escape: The future of American corrections.* New York: Basic Books.

Duguid, S. (1988). To inform their discretion: Prison education and empowerment. *Journal of Correctional Education, 39,* 174–181.

Duguid, S. (1992). Becoming interested in other things: The impact of education in prison. *Journal of Correctional Education, 43,* 38–44.

Eadie, W. (1990). Being applied: Communication research comes of age. *Journal of Applied Communication Research 18,* 1–6.

Eadie, W. (1994). On having an agenda. *Journal of Applied Communication Research, 22,* 81–85.

Elias, R. (1994). Declaring peace on crime. *The Humanist, 54,* 7–11.

Erlich, R. (1995). Workin' for the man: Prison labor. *Covert Action Quarterly, 54,* 58–63.

Farrell, T. (1993). *Norms of rhetorical culture.* New Haven, CT: Yale University Press.

Foner, P. (1968). *Business and slavery: The New York merchants and the irrepressible conflict.* New York: Russell and Russell. (Original work published 1941)

Foster, G. (1990). New York by gaslight. In S. Blumin (Ed.), *New York by gaslight and other urban sketches by George Foster* (pp. 70–197). Berkeley: University of California Press. (Original work published 1850)

Foucault, M. (1977). *Discipline and punish: The birth of prison* (A. Sheridan, Trans.). New York: Pantheon Books.

Fraser, N. (1990). Rethinking the public sphere. *Social Text, 25/26,* 56–80.

Freehling, W. (1990). *The road to disunion: Secessionists at bay, 1776–1854.* Oxford, England: Oxford University Press.

Freire, P. (1994). *Pedagogy of the oppressed.* (M. B. Ramos, Trans.). New York: Continuum. (Original work published 1970)

Frey, L., Pearce, W. B., Pollock, M. A., Artz, L., & Murphy, B. A. O. (1996). Looking for justice in all the wrong places: On a communication approach to social justice. *Communication Studies, 47,* 110–127.

Galbraith, J. K. (1992). *The culture of contentment.* New York: Houghton Mifflin.

Genovese, E. (1961). *The political economy of slavery.* New York: Vintage Books.

Giroux, H. (1992). *Border crossings: Cultural workers and the politics of education.* New York: Routledge.

Goldin, C., & Thomas, J. (1984). Adult education in correctional settings: Symbol or substance? *Adult Education Quarterly, 34,* 123–134.

Greenberg, J. (Reporter). (1994, August 3). Building and maintaining prisons is a growth industry. *All Things Considered.* Washington, DC: National Public Radio.

Hamm, M. (1992). Searching for a heartbeat: Correctional treatment and the war on drugs. *Journal of Correctional Education, 43,* 74–81.

Hartnett, S. (1994, April 20). Getting at real rehabilitation. *Nuvo,* p. 10.

Hartnett, S. (1995, April 17). Cell block grants. *In These Times,* pp. 6–7.

Hartnett, S. (1996). Imperial ideologies: Media hysteria, racism, and the addiction to the war on drugs. *Journal of Communication, 45*(2), 161–169.

Hartnett, S. (1997). Senator Robert Walker's 1844 letter on Texas annexation: The rhetorical 'logic' of imperialism. *American Studies, 38,* 27–54.

Hartnett, S. (in press-a). Prisons, profit, crime, and social control: A hermeneutic of the production of violence. In M. Nagel (Ed.), *Race, class, and community.* New York: Humanities Press.

Hartnett, S. (in press-b). Democracy is difficult: Merging prison pedagogy and prison-based politics. In S. Dailey (Ed.), *The future of performance studies: The next millennium.* Annandale, VA: The National Communication Association.

Hietala, T. (1985). *Manifest design: Anxious aggrandizement in late Jacksonian America.* Ithaca, NY: Cornell University Press.

hooks, b. (1994). *Teaching to transgress: Education as the practice of freedom.* London: Routledge.

Johnston, D., & Holmes, S. (1994, September 14). Experts doubt effectiveness of crime bill. *The New York Times,* pp. A1, 12.

Jones, C. R. (1996, May). Prisoner/students invite *IPJC* to Lincoln/Douglas/Walker debate. *Indianapolis Peace and Justice Newsletter,* p. 3.

Jones, R. (1991). Mass education and the legitimation of prison higher education. In R. Blair (Ed.), *Corrections and higher education monograph* (pp. 7–11). Richmond: Eastern Kentucky University.

Kelly, E. (1995). *Education, democracy, and public knowledge.* Boulder, CO: Westview Press.

Kelly, R. (1997, May 12). Prison profiteering. *In These Times,* 5.

Kiser, G. (1987). Disciplinary problems among inmate college students. *Federal Probation, 51,* 42–48.

Kolko, J. (1988). *Restructuring the world economy.* New York: Pantheon Books.

Laclau, E., & Mouffe, C. (1985). *Hegemony and socialist strategy: Towards a radical democratic politics.* London: Verso.

Leps, M. C. (1992). *Apprehending the criminal: The production of deviance in nineteenth-century discourse.* Durham, NC: Duke University Press.

Levasseur, R. L. (1993) Armed and dangerous. *Prison News Service, 42,* 9.

Lewis, N. (1994, August 27). President foresees safer U.S. *The New York Times,* p. A6.

Lichtenstein, A. (1990). *The fortress economy: The economic role of the U.S. prison system.* Philadelphia: American Friends Service Committee.

Lilly, J. R., & Knepper, P. (1993). The corrections-commercial complex. *Crime & Delinquency, 39,* 150–166.

Lincoln, A., & Douglas, S. (1993). *The Lincoln-Douglas debates: The first complete, unexpurgated text* (H. Holzer, Ed.). New York: Harper Perennial.

Lusane, C. (1994). Congratulations! It's a crime bill. *Covert Action Quarterly, 50,* 14–22.

Macintyre, L. (1995, March 31). Senate committee OKs more money than Bayh requested. *The Indianapolis Star,* p. B7.

Maguire, M., & Mohtar, L. (1994). Performance and the celebration of a subaltern counterpublic. *Text and Performance Quarterly, 14,* 238–252.

Mauer, M. (1992). Americans behind bars: A comparison of international rates of incarceration. In W. Churchill & J. J. Vander Wall (Eds.), *Cages of steel: The politics of imprisonment in the U.S.* (pp. 22–37). Washington, DC: Maisonneuve Press.

More inmates in the U.S. than ever before. (1994, September 13). *The New York Times,* p. A8.

Morone, J. (1990). *The democratic wish: Popular participation and the limits of American government.* New York: Basic Books.

NCCD analysis finds. (1994). *Corrections Digest, 25,* 1–4.

Novak, D. (1978). *The wheel of servitude: Black forced labor after slavery.* Lexington: University of Kentucky Press.

Office of the Deputy Attorney General and the Bureau of Prisons. (1994, February 16). U.S. Department of Justice: An analysis of non-violent drug offenders with minimal criminal histories. *The Criminal Law Reporter, 54,* Text no. 8.

Parenti, C. (1996, January 29). Making prison pay: Business finds the cheapest labor of all. *The Nation,* 11–14.

Phillips, L. (1994, April 14). Crime bill may close book on inmates grants. *USA Today,* p. A3.

Rasmussen, D., & Benson, B. (1994). *The economic anatomy of a drug war: Criminal justice in the commons.* London: Rowman & Littlefield.

Reeves, J., & Campbell, R. (1994). *Cracked coverage: Television news, the anti-cocaine crusade, and the Reagan legacy.* Durham, NC: Duke University Press.

Reiman, R. (1990). *The rich get richer and the poor get prison: Ideology, class, and criminal justice* (3rd ed.). New York: Macmillan.

Rideau, W., & Wikberg, R. (Eds.). (1993). *Life sentences: Rage and survival behind bars.* New York: Times Books.

Schmitz, J., Rogers, E., Phillips, K., & Paschal, D. (1995). The public electronic network (PEN) and the homeless in Santa Monica. *Journal of Applied Communication Research, 23,* 26–43.

Seibold, D. (1995). *Theoria* and *praxis:* Means and ends in applied communication research. In K. N. Cissna (Ed.), *Applied communication in the 21st century* (pp. 23–38). Mahwah, NJ: Lawrence Erlbaum.

Sellin, J. T. (1976). *Slavery and the penal system.* New York: Elsevier.

Sen, A. (1992). *Inequality reexamined.* Cambridge, MA: Harvard University Press.

Shichor, D. (1995). *Punishment for profit: Private prisons/public concerns.* Thousand Oaks, CA: Sage.

Shor, I. (1992). *Empowering education: Critical teaching for social change.* Chicago: University of Chicago Press.

Simon, R. (1992). *Teaching against the grain: Texts for a pedagogy of possibility.* New York: Bergin & Garvey.

Spacks, P. (Ed.). (1997). *Advocacy in the classroom: Problems and possibilities.* New York: St. Martin's Press.

Sprague, J. (1993). Why teaching works: The transformative power of pedagogical communication. *Communication Education, 43,* 349–366.

Strine, M. S. (1992). Understanding "how things work": Sexual harassment and academic culture. *Journal of Applied Communication Research, 20,* 391–400.

Strine, M. S. (1993). Of boundaries, borders, and contact zones: Author(iz)ing pedagogical practices. *Communication Education, 43,* 367–376.

Taylor, J. (1992). Post-secondary correctional education: An evaluation of effectiveness and efficiency. *Journal of Correctional Education, 43,* 132–141.

Taylor, J. (1994). Pell Grants for prisoners. In M. Williford (Ed.), *Higher education in prison: A contradiction in terms?* (pp. 167–172). Phoenix, AZ: American Council on Education.

Tootoonchi, A. (1993). College education in prisons: The inmates' perspective. *Federal Probation, 57,* 34–40.

Trend, D. (Ed.). (1997). *Radical democracy: Identity, citizenship, and the state.* New York: Routledge.

Trotsky (1993a). Marginalization. *Human Rights Held Hostage, 5,* 8–9.

Trotsky (1993b). Open letter from Pendleton lockdown. *Prison News Service, 42,* 10.

Vermunt, R., & Tornblom, K. (1996). Introduction: Distributive and procedural justice. *Social Justice Research, 9,* 305–310.

Walker, D. (1992). *Appeal to the colored citizens of the world, but in particular, and very expressly, to those of the United States of America.* New York: Hill & Wang. (Original work published 1829)

Walker, R. J. (1971). Letter of Mr. Walker, of Mississippi, relative to the annexation of Texas. In F. Merk, *Fruits of propaganda in the Tyler administration* (pp. 221–252). Cambridge, MA: Harvard University Press. (Original work published 1844)

Wartenberg, T. (1990). *The forms of power: From domination to transformation.* Philadelphia: Temple University Press.

Wise, K. (1995). Time to change. *Kombat, 12,* 27.

Worth, F. (1993). Postmodern pedagogy in the multicultural classroom: For inappropriate teachers and imperfect spectators. *Cultural Critique, 25,* 5–32.

Wright, P. (1994, July/August). Slaves of the state. *Z Magazine,* 24–26.

ACT-ing UP in Congressional Hearings

Daniel C. Brouwer

On March 10, 1987, playwright and AIDS activist Larry Kramer presented a fiery speech in New York City criticizing not only the city and federal governments' inexcusably poor responses to the AIDS epidemic but also the queer community's own play-by-the-rules approach to the epidemic. Building on the awakened anger of his audience, Kramer challenged them: "Do we want to start a new organization devoted solely to political action?" (quoted in Crimp & Rolston 1990, 27). An overwhelming number of people responded affirmatively, and on 12 March 1987, the first chapter of the AIDS Coalition to Unleash Power (ACT UP) was formed in New York City.[1] Only twelve days later, ACT UP members staged their first demonstration on Wall Street, protesting what they perceived as an overly cozy relationship between the federal Food and Drug Administration (FDA) and the pharmaceutical company, Burroughs Wellcome, maker of azidothymidine (AZT).[2] An effigy was burned, traffic was snarled, and arrests were made. More importantly, ACT UP gained national attention through coverage of the demonstration, and the FDA soon after changed its policy in question.

A sudden emergence as a potentially volatile force with which to reckon and a growing presence in the national mediascape characterize the first several years of ACT UP's existence. That first Wall Street demonstration set the tone: ACT UP came to be known as an activist group that employed disruptive, unruly, and often highly performative modes of protest in public spaces. Establishing a precedent later followed by such queer activist groups as Queer Nation and Lesbian Avengers, ACT UP often invaded seemingly apolitical or restricted sites (Gamson 1989, 86).[3] In fact, to the casual observer, these kinds of public demonstrations—heckling the president, disrupting a service at St. Patrick's Cathedral in New York City, interrupting trading at the New York Stock Exchange—have come to stand in for all of the group's political activity. But this casual observation is reductive, for ACT UP is remarkable for its employment of a wide variety of sites for its activist energies. While much scholarly and popular attention has been granted to the group's unruly public performances, in this essay I cast my gaze away from these more familiar public demonstrations and instead examine members' less-well-known participation in the state-sponsored forum of U.S. congressional hearings. While ACT UP participation in congressional hearings is infrequent and spans a period of only two and a half years, scholarly examination of these hearings provides an opportunity to examine counterpublic and state interactions under conditions regulated by, and thus ostensibly favorable to, the state; in such a forum, what can and what do these activists make of their participation?

A mutual unease between ACT UP members and federal officials charges the hearings: on the one hand, ACT UP fears for co-optation by virtue of merely appearing in the forum; on the other hand, the threat of a disruptive violation of the discursive norms of the hearings might rightly set the representatives on edge. I argue that textual evidence from witnesses' testimony shows that ACT UP members hold a profoundly ambivalent view about their participation. There is a cautious recognition among ACT UP members of the potential benefits of "oscillation" between such distinct sites as the group's relatively enclaved organizational, committee, and affinity group meetings, public demonstrations "in the streets," and state-sponsored congressional hearings. But there also exists a strong current of frustration with the highly choreographed nature of the hearings, as well as a concern that participation in the hearings is inevitably an exercise in co-optation. In addition, I argue that ACT UP members' participation instigates a critical publicity and provides a mechanism by which members gain access to stronger publics; in this way, what might be gained in the near future becomes more important than the results of the immediate discursive exchange between representatives and activists.

By way of building support for these arguments, I first briefly note practices of counterpublicity by ACT UP. Second, I provide a brief history of the interactions between ACT UP and institutions and representatives of the federal government, which leads to a narrowing of my focus on the congressional hearing as a particular site of discursive activity. Locating the hearings within the theoretical rubric of public sphere studies, I argue that the hearings constitute a "weak" public nested within the strong procedural public of Congress. Having established this foundation, in the fourth section I amplify key

themes of the testimony of ACT UP members. Finally, I note the ways in which textual evidence from the hearings and extratextual evidence about the organization help us to understand reasons for members' participation in this forum.

ACT UP AND COUNTERPUBLICITY

Initiated by Rita Felski (1989) and catalyzed into theoretical currency by Nancy Fraser (1992), the category of the "counterpublic" illuminates the workings of marginal peoples. Felski defines a counterpublic as an "oppositional discursive space" (1989, 155) and counterpublic spheres as "critical oppositional forces within the society of late capitalism" (166). For Felski, a counterpublic sphere is "counter" because it is *partial*—partial because it consciously and unapologetically concerns itself with the emancipation of particular identities/groups rather than orienting itself to the goal of universal human emancipation endemic to some liberal political theory (167). Yet, a counterpublic sphere is "public" because it directs its discourse outward into society. Fraser's explanation of the dual character of subaltern counterpublics—as "spaces of withdrawal and regroupment" on the one hand, and as "bases and training grounds for agitational activities directed toward wider publics" (124) on the other hand—emphasizes the publicist orientation of the counterpublic. Amplifying the dangers of overemphasis on withdrawal and regroupment, Jane Mansbridge (1996) joins Felski and Fraser in positing an imperative that links counterpublics to other public arenas. "For participation to help people understand their interests better," Mansbridge argues, people may find it necessary "to oscillate between protected enclaves . . . and more hostile but also broader surroundings in which they can test those ideas against the reigning reality" (57).

Oscillation guarantees neither short-range nor long-range victories for activists, but without it counterpublics forego the possibilities of their critical and expansive work. In the case of ACT UP, I argue that members' oscillations between spheres and fora revitalize public discourse.[4] In the "bases and training grounds" (Fraser 1992, 124) of organizational meetings, committee meetings, caucus meetings, and affinity group meetings, members choose enemies, suggest alliances, propose direct actions, debate means and ends, praise and condemn each other, articulate visions of justice, and engage in a multitude of other activities that foster the creation and refinement of oppositional discourses that are counter to dominant and mainstream discourses about AIDS. Activists employ those oppositional discourses during their appearances in the wider publics of talk shows, community meetings, medical symposia, and "the streets."

Reference to specific acts of *counterpublicity* (see Doxtader elsewhere in this volume) by ACT UP members verifies their success not only in expanding discursive space but also in gaining material victories. As an activist group committed to direct action, the group's appearances in wider publics often take the form of public demonstrations: targets of the group's ire are legion and include local, state, and federal governments; private industry; and religious figures and institutions. Demonstrations at the New York Stock Exchange in 1987, 1988, and 1989 dramatized the culpability of the nation's private sector in the AIDS crisis. Just weeks after the 1987 demonstration (the organization's first), the Food and Drug Administration announced that it would speed up the approval process for anti-HIV drugs. Similarly, one result of the 1989 Wall Street demonstration (involving activist invasion and interruption of the floor of the New York Stock Exchange) was Burroughs Wellcome's subsequent decision to reduce the price of AZT by 20 percent. A 10 December 1989 protest against the incursions of New York City's John Cardinal O'Connor into the city's political arena involved a massive demonstration outside St. Patrick's Cathedral as well as a disruption of the Mass services inside the Cathedral. While most accounts portrayed the actions as anti-Catholic and disrespectful of the freedom of religious worship, in the view of many ACT UP activists the actions signaled their willingness to use whatever means necessary, excepting physical violence, to achieve their goals and served notice to future targets. More recently, in the spring and summer of 1999, activists pestered Vice-President and presidential candidate Albert Gore along his campaign trail, disrupting his speeches and accusing him of malignant neglect in his seeming unwillingness to encourage pharmaceutical companies

to release anti-HIV drugs at affordable rates to African countries. Under pressure from activists and political leaders here and abroad, the Clinton Administration chose Al Gore to deliver the first ever health-focused address before the United Nations Security Council on 10 January 2000. Such acts of counterpublicity demonstrate how ACT UP members' oscillation toward wider publics expands discursive space and wins material gains.

ACT UP's participation in congressional hearings is another example of the group's oscillation between spheres of activity. In the next two sections, I provide a very brief description of ACT UP's activities on a federal level and then locate the forum of the congressional hearing within the rubric of public sphere theory.

ACT UP AND THE STATE

While federal officials and institutions were early and frequent targets of the group's anger, the group made efforts to intertwine itself with federal officials and federal institutions through deliberation and negotiation. Archival records (ACT UP/New York Records, box 29) indicate that during the 11 January 1987 ACT UP general meeting, House Representative Theodore Weiss (D, NY) spoke to the membership and fielded questions. Further evidence of the group's willingness to work earnestly with Congress appears in a 1990 document by the Congressional Action Working Group in which the Group announces its purpose "to work with Congress in formulating a Congressional Agenda for action to end the AIDS crisis" (n.p.). And a flier in the fall of 1992 announces the revitalization of a congressional working group "to create specific legislative proposals, and use direct action to force Congress to implement them" (n.p.).

In addition to these efforts at earnest collaboration, ACT UP activists also mounted lively demonstrations staged at federal institutions such as the White House and at venues where federal officials like then-President Ronald Reagan and then–Food and Drug Administration chief Frank Young appeared.[5] One of the most pivotal events to accelerate the entrée of ACT UP into fora at the federal level was the 11 October 1988 demonstration at the Food and Drug Administration (FDA) headquarters in Rockville, Maryland. Organized by a national coalition of AIDS activist groups, the protest drew nearly one thousand demonstrators in an effort to "seize control of the FDA." Two key factors contributed greatly to the unarguable success of the demonstration: first, ACT UP members had reached a compelling level of competency with regard to medical knowledge and research protocol as a result of their rigorous autodidacticism; second, the demonstration was meticulously plotted and campaigned, a process that included the development of a press kit distributed to the media and to the FDA (Crimp and Rolston 1990, 76). While technically the demonstrators did not infiltrate and seize control of the FDA, they did interrupt the business of the day, managed to place graphics and banners on the entrance to the building, and staged numerous activist performances before a large media contingent. Shortly after the demonstration, the FDA met activist demands by making significant changes to its AIDS drug research and distribution policies. Over the next year, ACT UP members benefited from a marked increase in federal officials' and pharmaceutical company representatives' willingness to listen to and invite them to participate in discussions about research.

Crimp and Rolston (1990) proclaim the FDA demonstration to be "unquestionably the most significant demonstration of the AIDS activist movement's first two years" (76), in large part because it propelled activists into more fora, including congressional hearings, at the federal level. Indeed, the first ACT UP–affiliated activist testified at a congressional hearing just six months after the demonstration. Like Crimp and Rolston, I argue that well-timed and well-plotted demonstrations serve a critical function: although as discursive phenomena they are profoundly antideliberative, ironically the demonstrations help activists gain access to previously restricted fora, such as hearings.[6]

SITUATING CONGRESSIONAL HEARINGS AS PUBLICS

Recent work by Jürgen Habermas, particularly his discourse theory of democracy elaborated in *Between Facts and Norms* (1996), provides a way

of recognizing the United States Congress as a state-sponsored procedural public. Habermas joins Fraser (1992) in recognizing the multivariate interwranglings of state and civic bodies in parliamentary and representative democratic governments.[7] His discourse theory distinguishes between constitutionally guaranteed, decision-oriented *procedural* publics that serve as "contexts of justification" (307) and as safety mechanisms for social cohesion, and informal, opinion-forming *general* publics that serve as "contexts of discovery" (307). Especially during House and Senate floor debate, the function of Congress as a procedural public becomes clear. Thus, similar to Fraser's description of sovereign parliaments as "a public sphere *within* the state" (134), we can describe the floors of Congress as a public nested within the state.

The various House and Senate committees and subcommittees play extraordinary roles in the functioning of the federal government. Indeed, Woodrow Wilson's famous utterance in 1895 that "Congress in its committee rooms is Congress at work" (1925, 79) holds true today. Joseph Bessette (1994), writing about the quality and character of deliberative democracy in the history of the United States, claims that "by design it is in committees and subcommittees that the most detailed and extensive policy deliberation occurs within Congress" (156). Essential to the ability of committees to craft public policy are hearings. Hearings conducted by various House and Senate committees function as "contexts of discovery" in which citizens, experts, academics, and elected representatives (not mutually exclusive identities) participate in discursive wrangling designed to elicit information and arguments, to publicize issues, and to mobilize support for specific policies. And while Bessette concedes that hearings sometimes serve nondeliberative functions such as enhancing a representative's public profile or embarrassing the presidential administration, still he argues that they are "eminently suited for investigating the merits of pending proposals" (156).

Witnesses at congressional hearings provide arguments, statistics, personal narratives, and other data that not only aid committee members in formulating and revising the language of their bills but also provide members with rhetorical resources during their discursive performances on the floors.[8] In this way, "hearings serve the rhetorical function of invention for committee members" (Rives 1967). In addition, hearings participate in a critical publicity. Habermas's (1996) insistence that legislative branches of constitutional governments keep "institutionalized opinion- and will-formation open to the informal circulation of general political communication" (183) betrays his hope that a critical publicity can emerge from publics. In congressional hearings, critical publicity operates on three levels. On one level, during the immediate, face-to-face interactions between witnesses and state representatives, witnesses can "publicize" their "criticism" of the state. On another level, as noted above, the likelihood exists that representatives will transport and translate portions of witness testimony to the House or Senate floor. On a third level, because of the presence of media representatives, witnesses are almost guaranteed that their testimony will be disseminated to wider, mediated audiences.[9] As I argue later, ACT UP members exploit these levels of critical publicity to help them advance their critique of the state.

Despite these possibilities to inflect significantly the nation's discourse about public policy, obstacles exist for witnesses who serve as activists for social change. A significant impediment to deliberation in the hearings is the fact that state representatives determine and enforce norms of discourse. In the forum of the congressional hearing, status inequities between state officials and civilian and professional witnesses mean that state officials dictate the format of the hearings, the content of the hearings, and to some extent the modes of expression (Davis 1981). Witnesses do not have the power to dictate the overarching course of the hearing, to challenge the rules or norms of the setting, to engage in (excessively) non-normative modes of expression without the threat of expulsion, or to engage in extended cross-examination with other witnesses or with representatives.[10] (The architecture of hearing rooms, where seating for members of Congress is elevated, conveys this inequity.) Another obstacle is the fact that hearings function as a "weak" public, an arena whose discursive activities are oriented to opinion-formation, in contrast to "strong" publics wherein both opinion-formation and decision-making activities occur (Fraser 1992, 134). As such, activist witnesses do not directly participate, through voting, in the final determination of policy proposals.

In summary, hearings constitute a "weak" public—preparatory and interstitial, occurring after an agenda has been set but before decision-making has begun—nested within the strong, procedural public of Congress. With these understandings of the nature of the forum—its possibilities and limitations—I now turn my attention to elaboration of the qualities of testimony among the ACT UP activists.

IN THEIR OWN WORDS: TESTIMONY OF ACT UP MEMBERS IN CONGRESSIONAL HEARINGS

ACT UP members are not the first individuals affected by AIDS to offer testimony at congressional hearings. The precedent of having people with AIDS testify before Congress was established in August 1983, when such individuals participated in hearings held to evaluate the "Federal Government's Response to AIDS." In 1985, another round of hearings to evaluate the federal government's response to AIDS was held, and this round included testimony from people with AIDS as well as advocates from AIDS-related organizations (not mutually exclusive categories). In short, a precedent had been set for having people with AIDS (PWAs) and AIDS activists offer testimony four years before the formation of ACT UP and five years before members of the group began testifying before Congress.

A review of Congressional Information Service (CIS) indexes from 1987 through 2000 indicates that during the nearly fifteen years of ACT UP's existence, five individuals explicitly affiliated with ACT UP have testified. The first to testify, Iris L. Long, PhD, the founder of ACT UP/NY's Treatment and Data Committee, did so on April 28, 1988, on the issues of development, testing, and availability of therapeutic drugs for AIDS. Two other witnesses, Martin Delaney and Jim Eigo, testified on behalf of ACT UP at the 10 July 1989 hearing, on the issue of parallel-track research designs for clinical drug development. On 21 March 1990, Jim Davis from ACT UP/NY testified on the housing needs of people with AIDS. Later that year, Tony Davis, a member of ACT UP/NY's Treatment and Data Committee, testified before a House subcommittee convened to discuss drug availability and research for opportunistic infections.[11]

ACT UP members' testimony is notably different from the testimony of the PWAs who had testified before them, especially with regard to topic and style of address. This is so, I argue, for three distinct reasons: first, ACT UP members and PWAs are specifically requested by congressional representatives to speak about different aspects of AIDS; second, ACT UP members and PWAs often view their political relationship with the federal government from different perspectives; and third, none of the ACT UP members identifies as seropositive or AIDS-diagnosed. While most ACT UP–ers express some sense of frustration or anger with the federal government, most do so in restrained and reasonable tones. Except for one person, these witnesses express their dissent and agitation respectfully. All adhere to a loose five- to seven-minute time frame for their opening statements and answer questions earnestly, and all but one avoid interruptions or diversions in the course of the deliberations. Finally, all ACT UP witnesses avoid the more unruly types of behavior typical at their demonstrations—shouting slogans, shouting others down, chaining oneself to heavy, immovable objects—and thus avoid being ejected from the hearings.

ACT UP members' remarks that most illuminate counterpublic participation in this state-sponsored forum coalesce around five distinct themes: expertise, dialogue, surveillance, access to strong publics, and use of multiple fora. The struggles and successes of AIDS activists to enter the privileged realm of medical expertise are well documented, and in ACT UP testimony we find assertive confirmations of the expertise of people with AIDS and AIDS activists.[12] Iris Long, for example, calls for the government to submit its protocols for placebo-based studies to "a panel of expert AIDS patient advocates" (House 1988, 194) and notes that the Reagan-appointed Presidential Commission on HIV had included among its recommendations an ACT UP–authored proposal for an electronic registry of all clinical drug trials in the New York City area (195). Nearly two years later, in what must

have registered as a fit of humorous presumption to the representatives present, Jim Davis kindly offers the services of ACT UP expertise: "The People with AIDS Housing Committee of ACT UP New York is available to consult with any Member of Congress on this or any future legislation regarding housing for people living with AIDS" (House 1990a, 76). Related to the theme of expertise is the theme of dialogue; Long's model of dialogue in which activists set agendas, present them to the public and to government officials, and debate as rough equals with officials (House 1988, 193) begins to resemble Habermas's (1996) account of the long road from "general publics" to procedural publics (314).

The theme of surveillance arises as ACT UP members reverse the putative spying relations between counterpublics and states. In the hearings, both Jim Eigo and Long announce to federal officials and wider audiences (via media publicity about the hearings) that it is the federal government that is under surveillance by ACT UP. "ACT UP was the first organization to monitor the status of the AIDS treatment program of NIAID [National Institute of Allergic and Infectious Diseases]" (House 1988, 193), Long notes. The irony of her assertion is that it is typically government (federal, state, or local) that monitors people with AIDS both epidemiologically and politically. Indeed, in addition to the ostensibly benign data gathering of the Centers for Disease Control and Prevention, Federal Bureau of Investigations officers (as well as local police officers) have been known to infiltrate chapter meetings (Bull 1991; Osborne 1993). Aware that it is being watched, the group watches back. Iterating the group's commitment to future publication of federal misdirection or inaction, Long's reversal of the direction of scrutiny posits ACT UP as a savvy watchdog.

The fourth theme of access to strong publics asserts the significance of oscillation to the group. On 20 July 1989, testimony by Martin Delaney on behalf of Project Inform and ACT UP/San Francisco is most notable for its explicit commentary on the difference between "weak" and "strong" publics and its criticism of the government for excluding PWAs and AIDS activists from stronger, decision-making publics or bodies. Delaney holds out hope for productive dialogue by noting a "good spirit of collaboration currently between activists and regulators" (House 1989, 27) despite previous vilification and frustration. Still, Delaney laments that few inroads have been made in gaining PWAs and AIDS activists greater access to opinion-forming *and* decision-making bodies. Straining at the boundaries of his earlier acknowledgment of "a spirit of collaboration," Delaney concludes his testimony with a demand and a threat:

> We feel it's time for the voice of patients to be given first authority here. We've waited for 8 years, patients have cooperated, and we're increasingly dissatisfied with the results. Fortunately, this frustration comes at a time when there do appear to be signs of real progress on the horizon, but so far, it's only rhetoric, not the results, and we believe it's Congress' duty to regularly check in and put some accountability into the system. If we fail to do that, I think you're going to see the greatest explosion of community unrest here since the Vietnam War. (30)

Bracketing the unfortunate characterization of rhetoric as mere words divorced from the realm of action, we find in Delaney's unveiled threat a significant shift in strategy. A frustration derived in part from continued exclusions from strong publics shall, if left unaddressed, foment radical activity in multiple general publics.

This threat and a similar assertion by Tony Davis in 1990 serve to alert federal officials that AIDS activists will not be mollified by occasional participation in congressional hearings; rather, they will, to turn to the fifth theme, continue to employ multiple arenas for the accomplishment of their agendas. Speaking at hearings to discuss drug availability and research for opportunistic infections on 1 August 1990, Davis gives equal emphasis to ACT UP's participation both within the politically sanctioned forum of the hearing and outside of that political avenue via demonstrations and protests. Toward the beginning of his testimony, Davis reviews the past two years of the Treatment and Data Committee's activities.

> We have met with researchers, clinicians, and pharmaceutical companies. We have lobbied and demonstrated against the lack of interest in treatments for opportunistic

infections. In the last 6 months, AIDS activists from across the nation have mounted demonstrations at the Centers for Disease Control in Atlanta and the National Institutes of Health in Bethesda. (House 1990b, 26)

In this review, Davis clarifies the broad range of communicative avenues and communicative styles of which ACT UP is capable and in which it is willing to engage. Not so subtly, Davis warns that even when they finally gain entry to the fora to which they have demanded access, activists will neither evacuate previously employed fora nor inhabit the new fora as polite guests. ACT UP's refusal to allow Secretary of Health and Human Services Louis Sullivan to present the closing address at the Sixth International AIDS Conference in San Francisco in July of 1990 verifies these points.[13]

In their testimony, ACT UP members address an immediate audience comprised of other witnesses and federal officials; to the federal officials present, they direct accusations and warn of continued scrutiny and dissent in general publics. However, they exploit the principle of publicity that inheres in the forum in order to gain wider audiences for their denunciations of federal inaction and injustice. Furthermore, they explicitly thematize and critique the conditions and limitations of the very forum in which they have agreed to participate.

Of equal significance to the particular ways in which they use the forum is the basic fact *that* they use forum. An alternative, politically viable response to an invitation to appear at the hearings would be refusal: to refuse an invitation would dramatize one's profound lack of faith in the forum. Instead, activists not only accept but also seek out invitations to hearings. At this juncture, I explore in more detail the political stakes involved in participation in the hearings by way of arriving at a more thorough and nuanced account of their presence.

THE PROMISES AND PITFALLS OF PARTICIPATION

As I noted earlier, ACT UP is remarkable in its successful endeavor to seek out and use a vast array of arenas and fora. Some of those fora, like congressional hearings, are extant sluices and canals of the political system; as such, they are imagined in a radical political worldview as "inside." Deemed the radical wing of the AIDS social movement since its formation in 1987, ACT UP has garnered, not surprisingly, both praise and condemnation from other AIDS activists for their pointed, disruptive, performative public demonstrations and for their occasional refusal to work through the standard, liberal channels for amelioration. But it should be noted that early in its history, largely as a result of its persistence, the group gained entry to fora from which it had previously been excluded.

A tension between working inside the system and outside of the system has concerned the group since its earliest days (Cohen 1997, 98; Golden 1992).[14] Handelman (1990) writes about this tension as it has been manifested in ACT UP meetings: "Frequently, the meetings wallow in virulent disagreement over side issues. Is ACT UP co-opted by being granted a seat on a government panel?" (85). More specifically, Handelman quotes ACT UP member Jim Eigo in direct reference to the tension between radical and liberal tactics:

> He [Eigo] disagrees with those who would rather ACT UP remain a radical street organization and never have any members on government panels. "You're only co-opted if you're forced to mute your criticisms," he says. "I just see it as direct action of a different sort." (89)

Eigo's own participation in 20 July 1989 House subcommittee hearings shows him refusing to mute his criticism: in addition to his warning about surveillance and critical publicity, he more than any of the other ACT UP witnesses amplifies moral and ethical criticism of federal practices. Emphasizing the urgency of getting drugs to those whose health is precarious, Eigo asserts that "people whose only alternative is death or deterioration cannot ethically be asked to wait for bureaucratic niceties" (House 1989, 39) required in placebo studies. And against those physicians who complain about the daunting task of conducting efficient research on a parallel-track model, Eigo argues that their opposition to a "humanitarian plan to ease my community's

suffering, saying it might prevent them from doing a job they've been unable to do thus far, is a measure of the distance they stand from my community" (41). Eigo's critics within the group might discern in his position a political naiveté, a brazen faith in the power of individuals to resist deep structures of power and discipline. To these critics, the well-being of the group depends critically on maintaining its staunch outsider status. Indeed, as chapters in numerous cities have disbanded and as the media presence of the group has diminished from the mid-1990s on, many (including Larry Kramer) argue that rapid and excessive moves to insider politics have enervated the group (Farber 1995).[15]

Besides the political threat of cooptation through participation in a state-sponsored forum, AIDS activists risk the emotional threat of disidentification. In addressing a body that does not necessarily respect you and in abiding by that body's norms of discourse, the sacrifices can be great. Cindy Patton (1997) notes these sacrifices when she writes about the oscillation of queer activists: "Sometimes we must make sense to government agents, but we shouldn't confuse this reeling moment of apparently transparent communication with a true recognition of queer presence by forces who generally oppose us" (209).[16] Although Patton writes more broadly of queer activism, her warning against a facile assumption that invitation or permission to address the state is an authentic acknowledgment of respect holds for radical AIDS activists, many of whom are queer.

Despite these stakes and activists' keen awareness of them, ACT UP members' participation in congressional hearings over a two-and-a-half-year period can be explained in large part by the multiple benefits accrued and potentially accruable to the group through oscillation. In my reading, there are several possible benefits of oscillation, each of which is borne out of the testimony discussed in the previous section. First, participation in the hearings gains the group wide, national publicity, thus enhancing the group's credibility to elected officials and to the nation at large. Indeed, the fact that the immediate audience is not necessarily the most significant audience to activists who testify is an important rhetorical feature of the encounter. Elected representatives and invited witnesses alike frequently indicate that they are speaking past or beyond those who are immediately present and are addressing instead a wider, mediated audience. When news of activists' participation in the hearings reaches members of this mediated audience, the activists' discourse is legitimized by virtue of being invited by the state.

Similarly, the hearings provide yet another forum for recognition and repetition of the group's messages in local, regional, or national media. However, as I mentioned earlier, the group neither ceases its participation in other fora nor sacrifices its prerogative to be dissatisfied. Although group members do not "act up" (in the colloquial sense) at the hearings, Martin Delaney and Tony Davis exploit their presence at the hearings to express their displeasure with the nature of the hearing as a forum and to broadcast threats and warnings about future activist interventions.

Another significant reason for ACT UP's oscillation is the fact that implementation of the group's recommendations, particularly their calls for new protocols for drug trials, is dependent upon federal resources, notably federal money. Until—that is, *unless*—activists, researchers, and health care providers can gain enough funds through private sources, dependence upon the state will remain inextricable. Tony Davis admits as much in his testimony when he says "although we AIDS activists have been and will continue to be critics of NIAID [National Institute of Allergy and Infectious Diseases], we do recognize the fact that Congress must provide the funding to enable NIAID to keep pace with research opportunities" (House 1990b, 27). Furthermore, activists recognize that through appeals to the state they can put more pressure on private industry, particularly pharmaceutical companies. Profoundly skeptical of pharmaceutical companies' concern for anything other than profits, ACT UP members frequently demonstrated against the companies in order to compel them to reduce drug prices and to commence a more vigorous research regimen, but they also called on the state to regulate the profit-driven industry. As Eric Sawyer succinctly noted at a 1993 demonstration: "The [pharmaceutical] industry can't regulate itself. The federal

government is going to have to step in" (quoted in Sanchez and Wheeler 1993, A1). In order to have their demands met, AIDS activists cannot afford to repudiate the state as an interlocutor, nor can PWAs stop being clients of a welfare state simply because that is what they prefer. Not surprisingly, inextricable dependence on the state foments a profound ambivalence among PWAs and activists. Lauren Berlant (1997) explains:

> Disidentification with U.S. nationality is not, at this moment, even a theoretical option for queer citizens: as long as PWAs (People with AIDS) require state support, as long as the official nation invests its identity in the pseudoright to police nonnormative sexual representations and sexual practices, the lesbian, gay, feminist, and queer communities in the United States do not have the privilege to disregard national identity. We are compelled, then, to read America's lips. (150)

And when marginal individuals like PWAs and AIDS activists do address the nation in a state-sponsored forum such as hearings, Berlant discerns "acts of strange intimacy between subaltern peoples and those who have benefited by their subordination" (222–223).

Finally, oscillation benefits ACT UP because it enables the group to push for access to strong publics. As Cohen (1997) argues, "activist pressure in the form of demonstrations made opportunities to sit down with policy makers more available, and activists took eager advantage of them" (98).[17] During (but especially after) the two-year period of ACT UP testimony, various agencies of the federal health complex invited members of ACT UP and other activist organizations to participate as observers or as voting members of treatment and prevention committees. Of particular significance was the decision by National Institutes of Health (NIH) leaders to permit full activist participation in AIDS Clinical Trial Groups (ACTGs). This decision, made in early 1991 just a few months after the last ACT UP member testified at a hearing, was particularly bold, for it recognized PWAs and activists as possessors of a kind of medical expertise. Furthermore, it provided PWAs with the opportunity to discuss the viability of treatment options before release and to question researchers and direct the course of discussion. Most importantly, the decision extended equal voting power to PWAs and activists (d'Adesky 1991, 158). In short, the ACTGs were the first federal, "strong" procedural public to which activists gained access—access that participation in the "weak" procedural publics of congressional hearings facilitated.

Conclusion

On 1 October 1991, at the U.S. Capitol, members of ACT UP demonstrated both outside and inside of the building. As 300 protesters stood on the Capitol steps shouting and chanting in a legal demonstration sanctioned by an official permit, one demonstrator inside the building interrupted the flow of Senate floor debate by shouting from the public gallery (Associated Press 1991).[18] The events of this day synecdochically represent the long-term political strategy of many members of ACT UP: this strategy seeks to work inside and outside of extant channels of political activity simultaneously. I have argued that as a group ACT UP holds a profoundly ambivalent attitude toward the Congressional hearing forum. Although ACT UP members participate in this forum at the state's invitation, they remain skeptical of the efficacy of both the forum *in toto* and their own participation in the forum. However, these activists use the forum of the hearings to strive to gain greater access to "stronger" procedural publics where they can be involved in decision-making as well as opinion-forming endeavors. Furthermore, because the very nature of the forum guarantees dispersal of ACT UP discourses to wider audiences, and because the discourses that members produce, however strident, still bear the mark of state tolerance, the benefits of oscillation are too compelling for activists to ignore.

The case of ACT UP participation in congressional hearings informs and revises studies in the public sphere in at least two ways. First, it demonstrates that when counterpublics stand in an antagonistic relationship with a state, activists' alliances with a few politically sympathetic elected officials can set in motion

an impressive penetration of the state. At the federal level, Theodore Weiss of New York and Henry Waxman of California have proven to be these sympaticos, convening hearings in the early 1980s the main purpose of which was to give expression to the federal government's poor response to AIDS. Before the formation of ACT UP in 1987, these and other members of Congress invited people with AIDS and AIDS activists to testify and to scrutinize and critique the federal government. At hearings chaired by these representatives, oppositional discourse was neither squelched nor contained, for the chairmen pursue lines of questioning with the witnesses, and the presence of media representatives guarantees wider publicity. When ACT UP formed, activists in the organization were able to exploit extant, amicable relations with state representatives in order to gain their access to hearings. Second, we find that counterpublic agents can be as strategic as states in the employment or exploitation of specific fora. Whereas states have often been accused of extending fora to dissidents and marginals for the purpose of strategic dilution of political opposition, the testimony of ACT UP members in congressional hearings betrays a calculating orientation. I do not mean to say that activists sought to deceive elected officials. Rather, the strategic orientation inheres in the exploitation of their participation as a tool for further penetration of the state. As strategic acts, ACT UP members' appearances before the state are far from mythic notions of the citizen's trip to Washington, DC. In an important sense, hearing testimony functions as a ritual of citizenship. But the relationship that activists presume with their government is a far cry from grateful supplication. As autodidactic medical experts and as accomplished veterans of civil disobedience, ACT UP activists approach the state as critics and reformers.

Notes

[1] Kramer is often incorrectly named the sole founder of ACT UP/New York. While his March 10 speech was an extraordinary catalyst for the formation of the group, and while his was an especially vibrant voice in the group for almost two years, Kramer should be recognized as one of several cofounders of the group. Other cofounders

include Maxine Wolfe, Bradley Ball, Eric Sawyer, and Michelangelo Signorile. Members chose the name of the group at the 19 March 1987 meeting.

2 AZT, also known as azidothymidine or zidovudine, was the first anti-HIV drug released by the federal Food and Drug Administration. The drug was originally developed in 1964 as a possible cancer treatment, was shelved when proven ineffective, and was retested in the mid-1980s as a possible anti-HIV treatment. Burroughs Wellcome obtained the patent and marketed the drug as Retrovir.

3 These tactics are hardly new to oppositional politics; indeed, ACT UP members, some of whom participated in social movements in the 1960s and 1970s, owe a great debt to the spirit and the practices of earlier politics. ACT UP was the first organization to mobilize these tactics in the fight against AIDS.

4 Valeria Fabj and Matthew Sobnosky argue that ACT UP's dismantling of technical, public, and private sphere boundaries serves to rejuvenate the public sphere. Against Jürgen Habermas, who interprets the inclusion of private interests into the public sphere as detrimental and damaging to the public sphere (Habermas 1989, 132, 198), Fabj and Sobnosky (1995) interpret ACT UP's "translat[ion of] private concerns of people with AIDS into public issues" (172) as an enhancement to the development of AIDS public health policies and the practice of medical AIDS research. Following Fabj and Sobnosky, I have argued that through oscillation activists succeeded in both challenging and expanding notions of "expertise," in democratizing health care formulation and provision, and in reconfiguring boundaries between private, public, and technical spheres (Brouwer 2000).

5 Accounting for the quantity and quality of all ACT UP activities oriented toward the nation and the federal government is far beyond the scope and means of this study. However, brief mention of a few salient activities is warranted. A protest at the U.S. Capitol building in September 1990 resulted in the disruption of federal proceedings. In that protest, ACT UP members disrupted a Senate Judiciary Committee hearing on the nomination of Judge David Souter for the Supreme Court; protestors' shouts denounced the harm to women that Souter's anti-abortion views would occasion ("Souter Day 1" 1990). Thousands of demonstrators at the April 1993 March on Washington for Lesbian and Gay Rights linked arms and encircled the Capitol to dramatize a demand for more spending on AIDS research; one organizer of the demonstration asked demonstrators to stand with their backs facing the Capitol in a symbolic reversal of congressional betrayal against people with AIDS (Sanchez and Miller 1993, A1). More recent instances of ACT UP 'presence' in or around Congress include ACT UP/New York's Eric Sawyer criticizing the low level of U.S. funding for global AIDS at a state department briefing on World AIDS Day, 1 December 1997, and the pronouncement of a brief eulogy for Steve Michael, founder of ACT UP/Washington [D.C.], by Eleanor Norton Holmes on 3 June 1998.

6 Here, I am corroborated by ACT UP member Mark Smith (quoted in Weinraub 1991, E1), and scholar Peter Cohen (1997, 98, 100–101). However, contrary views—that unruly civil disobedience forestalls, if not corrodes, possibilities for discussion and debate between ACT UP members and officials and researchers—are more numerous. For popular accounts of this argument, see Cotton (1990); Leo (1990, 1992); and Labash (1996). The threat of such an unrecoverable loss of an audience as the aftermath of disruption was made manifest in 1990 when, during the closing address of the Sixth Annual International AIDS Conference, ACT UP protesters prevented Secretary of Human Health and Services Louis Sullivan from speaking by shouting him down; later that day, Sullivan announced, "I will not in any way work with those individuals" (quoted in Zonana 1990, A3).

7 Habermas's early configuration of the relationship between the state, civil society, and the private sphere called for a strict, normative demarcation of those entities. Criticism of this demarcation has been ample. Fraser (1992), for example, points to the existence of parliamentary forms of government and their unsettling of strict demarcations between state and civil society as evidence of the inadequacy of that model. To a significant degree, Habermas has revised his theories in recognition of such criticism (see, e.g. Habermas 1996).

8 A brief description of the procurement and management of witnesses is warranted: Both majority and minority party committee members invite witnesses to testify. Interested parties who have not been invited to testify may request the opportunity. When the testimony of a particular witness is deemed crucial but that witness rejects an invitation to testify, committees are accorded the power to compel the witness to testify through a subpoena. Witnesses are required to submit in advance a written copy of their testimony, and

both the written and spoken testimony appear in published transcripts of committee hearings (Goehlert and Martin 1989, 15).

9 Miller (1978) and Keefer (1993) express skepticism about the critical role of publicity generated by congressional hearings. Miller notes that committees sometimes establish hostile relations with media representatives (658). Meanwhile, Keefer argues that media's efforts to generate participation actually hinder citizen participation in public policy processes (421). Despite this skepticism, I strive to show through textual and extratextual data that ACT UP witnesses successfully exploit the possibilities for critical publicity at the hearings.

10 A pointed critique of these rules of discourse comes from Martin Delaney, founder of Project Inform in San Francisco, during 20 July 1989 hearings on revising federal research practices: "I came here today with great frustration because, as I say, we have been through so many other commissions, Congress people and meetings over the last few years, that we feel after awhile our words are going on deaf ears here. On many occasions when we get through this process, no matter what we say, Dr. Fauci and Dr. Young come up after us and have the last word and there's never an opportunity to cross examine them from our point of view" (House 167)

11 No ACT UP–affiliated witnesses are listed in the CIS Index after 1990. All four of the hearings at which ACT UP members appear were convened by House committees: Government Operations; Banking, Finance, and Urban Affairs; and Energy and Commerce.

12 Some of the most important work on AIDS and expertise is by Patton (1990), Treichler (1991), and Epstein (1995, 1996). For studies that foreground the communicative dimensions of AIDS expertise, see Brashers and Jackson (1991) and Fabj and Sobnosky (1995).

13 In 1988, at the Fourth International AIDS Conference in Montréal, ACT UP famously stormed the main stage of the conference, demanding, among other things, a greater role in planning and administrating the conference. The next year and ever since, ACT UP members have played key roles in the conferences. The apparent irony that emerges in a comparison of the 1988 and 1990 conferences derives from juxtaposing the group's demand for gaining access and being allowed to participate with their disruption of a public address and their refusal to allow Louis Sullivan to participate.

14 Research through the ACT UP/NY archives at the New York Public Library corroborates this claim. A review of minutes of the meetings from March 1987 through December 1994 indicates that frequent debates, some of them virulent, occur between members over the ideological purity and efficacy of insider versus outsider politics. Minutes of the meetings do not, however, indicate debate over participation in congressional hearings. For example, in May of 1988, minutes of the meeting indicate that "Iris Long reported about a congressional hearing where she and others testified," but there is no indication of discussion or debate. Of course, this could be attributed to the weariness or inattention of the note-taker.

15 To members of ACT UP/Paris during a speech in 1995, ACT UP/New York cofounder Larry Kramer advocated the following: "If you have a choice of being on the inside or being on the outside, stay on the outside. . . . You must be very careful not to become researchers who take the place of researchers, or doctors who take the place of doctors. Remain activists" (quoted in Tinmouth 1995/1996, 52).

16 The term *queer* is not unproblematic. Throughout this essay, I have been using the term broadly to refer to theories and practices that are critical of and resistant to the normative, in a way similar to Michael Warner's description of queer as "an aggressive impulse of generalization . . . [that] rejects a minoritizing logic of toleration or simple political interest-representation in favor of a more thorough resistance to regimes of the normal" (1993, xxvi). In this sense, *queer* refers neither exclusively nor inherently to same-sex erotics and sexuality.

17 Provocatively, Cohen (1997) describes ACT UP street activism as "bourgeois militancy" (105), and he links male ACT UP activists' eagerness to work on the inside to class style and class privilege.

18 For accounts of this demonstration, see Associated Press (1991), Wilgoren (1991), and Foerstel (1991).

References

ACT UP/New York Records. Manuscripts and Archives Division. New York Public Library.

Associated Press. 1991. AIDS protesters arrested at Capitol, 1 October. http://web.lexis-nexis.com (10 December 1998).

Berlant, Lauren. 1997. *The queen of America goes to Washington City: Essays on sex and citizenship.* Durham, NC: Duke University Press.

Bessette, Joseph M. 1994. *The mild voice of reason: Deliberative democracy and American national government.* Chicago: University of Chicago Press.

Brashers, Dale, and Sally Jackson. 1991. "Politically-savvy sick people": Public penetration of the technical sphere. In *Argument in controversy: Proceedings of the seventh SCA/AFA conference on argumentation,* edited by Donn Parson. Annandale, VA: Speech Communication Association.

Brouwer, Daniel C. 2000. Representations of gay men with HIV/AIDS across scenes of social controversy: A contribution to studies in the public sphere. Ph.D. diss., Northwestern University.

Bull, Chris. 1991. Spy allegations pit Pennsylvania police against activists. *Advocate,* 26 February, 22.

Cohen, Peter. 1997. 'All they needed': AIDS, consumption, and the politics of class. *Journal of the History of Sexuality* 8:86–115.

Cotton, Paul. 1990. Scientifically astute activists seek common ground with clinicians on testing new AIDS drugs. *Journal of the American Medical Association* 264:666–669.

Crimp, Douglas, and Adam Rolston. 1990. *AIDS demographics.* Seattle, WA: Bay Press.

d'Adesky, Anne-Christine. 1991. Empowerment or co-optation? *Nation,* 11 February, 252:158.

Davis, Kristine M. 1981. A description and analysis of the legislative committee hearing. *Western Journal of Speech Communication* 45:88–106.

Epstein, Steven. 1995. The construction of lay expertise: AIDS activism and the forging of credibility in the reform of clinical trials. *Science, Technology, & Human Values* 20:408–437.

———. 1996. *Impure science: AIDS, activism, and the politics of knowledge.* Berkeley: University of California Press.

Fabj, Valeria, and Matthew J. Sobnosky. 1995. AIDS activism and the rejuvenation of the public sphere. *Argumentation and Advocacy* 31:163–184.

Felski, Rita. 1989. *Beyond feminist aesthetics: Feminist literature and social change.* Cambridge, MA: Harvard University Press.

Foerstel, Karen. 1991. Hill AIDS protest brings 74 arrests and a foul smell. *Roll Call,* 3 October.

Fraser, Nancy. 1992. Rethinking the public sphere: A contribution to the critique of actually existing democracy. In *Habermas and the public sphere,* edited by Craig Calhoun. Cambridge, MA: Massachusetts Institute of Technology Press.

Gamson, Joshua. 1989. Silence, death, and the invisible enemy: AIDS activism and social movement 'newness.' *Social Problems* 36:351–367.

Goehlert, Robert U., and Fenton S. Martin. 1989. The legislative process and how to trace it. In *Congress and law-making: Researching the legislative process.* 2d ed. Santa Barbara, CA: ABC-CLIO.

Golden, Mark. 1992. ACT UP redux. *QW,* 11 October, 22–25.

Habermas, Jürgen. 1989. *The structural transformation of the public sphere: An inquiry into a category of bourgeois society.* Translated by Thomas Burger and Frederick Lawrence. Cambridge, MA: Massachusetts Institute of Technology Press.

———. 1996. *Between facts and norms: Contributions to a discourse theory of law and democracy.* Translated by William Rehg. Cambridge, MA: Massachusetts Institute of Technology Press.

Handelman, David. 1990. ACT UP in anger. *Rolling Stone,* 8 March, 80–82, 85–86, 89–90, 116–117.

Keefer, Joseph D. 1993. The news media's failure to facilitate citizen participation in the Congressional policymaking process. *Journalism Quarterly* 70:412–424.

Labash, Matt. 1996. ACT-UP vs. PETA: Clash of the titans. *Weekly Standard,* 8–15 July, 28.

Leo, John. 1990. When activism becomes gangsterism. *U.S. News & World Report,* 5 February, 18.

———. 1992. The politics of intimidation. *U.S. News & World Report,* 6 April, 24.

Mansbridge, Jane. 1996. Using power/fighting power. In *Democracy and difference: Contesting the boundaries of the political,* edited by Seyla Benhabib. Princeton, NJ: Princeton University Press.

Miller, Susan H. 1978. Congressional committee hearings and the media: Rules of the game. *Journalism Quarterly* 55:657–663.

Osborne, Duncan. 1993. ACT UP and the FBI. *Advocate,* 29 June, 60–61.

Patton, Cindy. 1990. *Inventing AIDS.* New York: Routledge.

———. 1997. *Fatal advice.* Durham, NC: Duke University Press.

Rives, Stanley G. 1967. Congressional hearings: A modern adaptation of dialectic. *Journal of the American Forensic Association* 4:41–46.

Sanchez, Rene, and Bill Miller. 1993. Gay activists carry protests to Capitol and White House; demonstrations focus on AIDS, rights for lesbians. *Washington Post,* 25 April, A1.

Sanchez, Rene, and Linda Wheeler. 1993. On the march, in joy and pain; gay activists begin gathering amid celebrations and protests. *Washington Post,* 24 April, A1.

Souter day 1: 'Silent on abortion,' backs privacy rights. 1990. *Abortion Report,* 14 September.

Tinmouth, David. 1995/1996. POZ honors. *POZ,* December/January, 45–53.

Treichler, Paula. 1991. How to have theory in an epidemic: The evolution of AIDS treatment activism. In *Technoculture*, edited by Constance Penley and Andrew Ross. Minneapolis: University of Minnesota Press.

U.S. House. 1988. Subcommittee on Human Resources and Intergovernmental Relations of the Committee on Government Operations. *Therapeutic drugs for AIDS: Development, testing, and availability.* 100th Cong., 2d sess. 28 and 29 April.

———. 1989. Subcommittee on Health and the Environment of the Committee on Energy and Commerce. *AIDS issues (Part 2).* 101st Cong., 1st sess. 20 July and 18 September.

———. 1990a. Subcommittee on Housing and Community Development of the Committee on Banking, Finance and Urban Affairs. *Housing needs of persons with Acquired Immune Deficiency Syndrome (AIDS).* 101st Cong., 2d sess. 21 March.

———. 1990b. Subcommittee on Human Resources and Intergovernmental Relations of the Committee on Government Operations. *Drugs for opportunistic infections in persons with HIV disease.* 101st Cong., 2d sess. 1 August.

Warner, Michael. 1993. Introduction. In *Fear of a queer planet: Queer politics and social theory*, edited by Michael Warner. Minneapolis: University of Minnesota Press.

Weinraub, Judith. 1991. AIDS activists' routes of pain; from all walks of life, marching on a disease. *Washington Post,* 1 October, E1.

Wilgoren, Debbi. 1991. 74 AIDS activists arrested in Capitol protests. *Washington Post,* 2 October, A24.

Wilson, Woodrow. 1925. *Congressional government.* Boston, MA: Houghton Mifflin.

Zonona, Victor. F. 1990. Did AIDS protest go too far? Conference: ACT UP draws fire and praise after activists shouted down a cabinet official in San Francisco. *Los Angeles Times,* 2 July, A3.

From Public Sphere to Public Screen:
Democracy, Activism, and the "Violence" of Seattle

Kevin Michael DeLuca and Jennifer Peeples

From November 30 to December 3, Seattle, high-tech capital of the present future, became the site of a contested New World Order as the forces of global capital, meeting under cover of the anonymous acronym WTO (World Trade Organization), were surprised by a cacophonous cadre of international grassroots activists in a pitched battle over visions of the future. Images flashed worldwide—crowds of thousands clogging the commercial center of Seattle and stranding WTO delegates in the mass of humanity; sea turtles and hard hats linking arms and marching together; black-clad anarchists trashing the material manifestations of corporate global dominance: Starbucks, Nike Town, McDonald's; shaken government officials decrying the outbreak of participatory citizenship; black-booted sci-fi stormtroopers marching in goose step and restoring order via tear gas, rubber bullets, and concussion grenades.

Seattle and subsequent fair trade and democratic globalization protests[1] around the world are striking crystallizations of a complex confluence of social, economic, technological, environmental, and political processes. These protests illustrate contemporary public acts of global citizenry that suggest new conditions for the possibility of participatory democracy in a corporate-controlled mass-mediated world. Chief among these new conditions are transformed economic/political and technological realities.

First, the activists recognize transnational corporations as the dominant powers of the new millennium. Seattle protesters pointedly smashed the windows of "Nike Town." Although corporations have been important players for some time, they are now clearly the dominant political, social, economic, and environmental forces on the planet, eclipsing the nation-state (Hardt and Negri, 2000; Friedman, 1999; and Greider, 1997). There are numerous indicators of this change in sovereignty. The wealth of a number of companies exceeds that of many nations. For example, as of 1999 Microsoft's market value was equivalent to the gross domestic product of Spain, GE's to Thailand, Wal-Mart's to Argentina, and Hewlett-Packard's to Greece (Morgenson, 2000). The laws of countries are struck down if they impede free trade ("Behind the Hubbub in Seattle," 1999; "Messages for the W.T.O.," 1999). In the United States the defense industry de facto sets budget priorities and military policy, so that the collapse of the Soviet Union hardly impacts defense spending and citizens are left to wonder whatever happened to the "peace dividend" (Center for Defense Information, www.cdi.org).

Corporate control of our democratic government's policies is evident on many other issues. With respect to environmental issues, strong pro-environmental sentiments among the general populace (Dunlap, 2000) are trumped by corporate prerogatives, with the lobbyists of industry dictating environmental legislation. In a recent example, Enron founder Kenneth Lay had private meetings with the Bush Administration to help formulate an energy policy with extensive environmental implications (Slocum, 2001; Milbank and Kessler, 2002; Rich, 2002). Even science, reputedly the last redoubt of objectivity and pure knowledge, is funded and circumscribed by corporate desire. Swiss pharmaceutical giant and biotech pioneer Novartis literally underwrites the University of California, Berkeley Department of Plant and Microbial Biology. UCal, Berkeley also has the BankAmerica Dean of the Haas School of Business. The controversial mining company Freeport McMoran funds a chair in environmental studies at Tulane University. Conservative media mogul Walter Annenberg bankrolls the Annenberg Schools of Communication at the University of Pennsylvania and University of Southern California. University of Pennsylvania's Center for Bioethics is sponsored by Monsanto, de Code Genetics, Millennium Pharmaceuticals, Pfizer, and Geron Corporation (Press and Washburn, 2000; Gelbspan, 1997; Elliott, 2001). In short, from environmental regulation on the local and global level to university research agendas, corporate interests are inextricably entwined in "public" activities, a process that sociologist Boggs terms "corporate colonization"—the "increased corporate penetration into

virtually every corner of modern American life" (2000, p. 9).

Second, global democratization and fair trade activists recognize the TV screen as the contemporary shape of the public sphere and the image event designed for mass media dissemination as an important contemporary form of citizen participation. Aside from writing letters to political representatives, attending public forums, and voting, the activists acknowledge the imperative to appear on the television screen alongside the staged image events of governments and corporations. In the case of Seattle, the protesters realized the need to contest the WTO meeting as a crowning image event for President Clinton and free trade. In staging a competing image event, the activists enacted what has become a fact among media scholars: "A media culture has emerged in which images, sounds, and spectacles help produce the fabric of everyday life, dominating leisure time, shaping political views and social behavior, and providing the materials out of which people forge their very identities" (Kellner, 1995, p. 1).

In recognizing the dominance of corporations and new technologies, the activists acknowledge the change in sovereignty on the world stage and enact a transformation of citizen participation. The purpose of this essay will be to discuss and delineate those changes and their consequences for the public sphere and participatory democracy. More specifically, this essay will introduce the "public screen" as a necessary supplement to the metaphor of the public sphere for understanding today's political scene. The concept of the public screen enables scholars to account for the technological and cultural changes of the 20th century, changes that have transformed the rules and roles of participatory democracy. Our introduction of the public screen is an act infused with hope. The writings of many critics of public discourse are wracked with despair over the state of contemporary politics and culture. Boggs's judgment is typical: "As the twenty-first century dawns, American politics is in an increasingly pathetic condition. . . . Measured by virtually any set of criteria, the political system is in a (potentially terminal) state of entropy. . . . the deterioration of the public sphere has potentially devastating consequences for citizen empowerment and social change, not to mention the more general health of the political domain itself" (2000, pp. 1, vii). Decline is not the only possible narrative. Viewing contemporary public discourse through the prism of the public screen provokes a consideration of the emergence of new forms of participatory democracy. In what follows, we present an overview and criticism of the public sphere, introduce the characteristics of the public screen, and then treat the "violent" Seattle protests as a case study of participatory politics on the public screen.

FROM PUBLIC SPHERE TO PUBLIC SCREEN

The public sphere is ubiquitous in contemporary social theory. The most cursory of searches turns up a plethora of titles trumpeting its presence: *The Black Public Sphere; Masses, Classes, and the Public Sphere; America's Congress: Actions in the Public Sphere, James Madison through Newt Gingrich; Uncivil Rites: American Fiction, Religion, and the Public Sphere; The Public Sphere in Muslim Societies; Hindu Public Sphere; Spaces of their Own: Women's Public Sphere in Transnational China; From Handel to Hendrix: The Composer in the Public Sphere;* and *Necro Citizenship: Death, Eroticism, and the Public Sphere in the Nineteenth-Century United States.* Despite this bewildering array of permutations, the initial conceptualization of the public sphere had a certain focused coherence. Inaugurated by Jürgen Habermas's *Structural Transformation of the Public Sphere,* ideally the public sphere denotes a social space wherein private citizens gather as a public body with the rights of assembly, association, and expression in order to form public opinion.[2] The public sphere mediates between civil society and the state, with the expression of public opinion working to both legitimate and check the power of the state. This public opinion is decidedly rational: "the critical judgment of a public making use of its reason" (Habermas, 1989, p. 24). The public sphere assumes open access, the bracketing of social inequalities, rational discussion, focus on common issues, face-to-face conversation as the privileged medium, and the ability to achieve consensus. It is important to remember that Habermas's book was an historical study of the rise of the bourgeois public sphere and its decline in late capitalist society. Habermas laments the passing of the bourgeoisie public sphere and the rise of mass media spectacles, a turn of events he sees as the disintegration or refeudalization of the public sphere—a return to the spectacle of the Middle Ages. He argues that the activity of the public sphere has been replaced with consumerism: "Rational-critical debate had a tendency to be replaced by consumption, and the web of public communication unraveled into acts of individuated reception, however uniform in mode" (1989, p. 163).

Despite its unfortunate historical fate, the public sphere has become a vital concept for social theory, with two takes predominating: uncritical acceptance and critical acceptance. The former position involves the taking-for-granted of an unexamined public sphere and importing it uncritically for contemporary social theory (as is suggested by its promiscuous use in the above list of titles). The latter position is of more interest to us. It involves the curious dynamic of subjecting the public sphere to scathing criticisms, but then declaring it to be absolutely necessary. Michael Schudson, for example, who suggests that at least in America there has never been a public sphere, nevertheless concludes, "I find the concept of a public sphere indispensable as a model of what a good society should achieve. It seems to me a central notion for social or political theory" (1992, p. 160). The position, then, is that Habermas's conceptualization and history of the public sphere has many flaws, foremost among them his privileging of dialogue and fetishization of a procedural rationality at the heart of the public sphere. These flaws produce an exclusionary and impoverished normative ideal that shuns much of the richness and turbulence of the sense-making process; still, the concept of the public sphere remains essential. As Nancy Fraser argues in a 33-page essay detailing the flaws of the public sphere, "something like Habermas's idea of the public sphere is indispensable to critical social theory and democratic political practice" (1992, p. 111). Kendall Phillips reenacts this dynamic, making a compelling argument that the public sphere's privileging of consensus silences dissent and condemns resistance, yet insisting that "a whole-sale rejection of the public sphere or consensus seems little better than blind faith in the exemplar and its foundation" (1996, p. 233; for useful criticisms of the public sphere, see Curran, 1991; Eley, 1992; McLaughlin, 1993; Pateman, 1988; Peters, 1993; and Ryan, 1992).

Still, is it wise to retain the concept of the public sphere for a televisual world characterized by image and spectacle? Habermas suggests not, finding "the world fashioned by the mass media is a public sphere in appearance only" (1989, p. 171). Although not advocating wholesale rejection, we think the public sphere needs a supplement. Before introducing the public screen, we want to elaborate on our reasons for supplementing the concept of the public sphere.

Our reservations revolve around the power of terms to shape and confine thinking. Certainly, the public sphere evokes echoes of ancient Greece. In so many ways, the small city-state of Athens has stunted the Western imagination, especially with respect to what constitutes political activity and citizenship. In evoking ancient Athens, the public sphere evokes a particular vision of politics. The Athenian agora models our metaphoric marketplace of ideas, an open and diverse (though not in terms of class and gender) space of multiple activities, including trade, laws, entertainment, and politics. As cultural historian Richard Sennett notes, it was a space of "sword-swallowers, jugglers, beggars, parasites, and fishmongers ... [and] philosophers. . . . The evolution of Athenian democracy shaped the surfaces and the volume of the agora, for the movement possible in simultaneous space served participatory democracy well. By strolling from group to group, a person could find out what was happening in the city and discuss it" (1994, pp. 54–55).

The Pynx, Athens' theater of democracy, calls forth our attachments to the New England town meeting on the village square or the public forum. A sloped, bowl-shaped theater, literally "a place for seeing," the architecture of the Pynx amplified the one voice addressing a seated, captive audience (the structure functioned as a stone microphone, if you will). It was a democratic space in that any citizen could answer the herald's call, "Who wishes to speak?", yet unlike in the agora, the theater amplified the power of the voice of the speaker. "Yet the Pynx, whose clear design emphasized the seriousness of attending to words, put the people literally in a vulnerable position. Rhetoric constituted the techniques for generating verbal heat. This body-art deployed 'tropes,' or figures of speech, in such a way that a mass of people could become aroused" (Sennett, 1994, pp. 66, 63).

Despite the significant differences in methods and purposes of the agora and Pynx, we want to underline that they both privilege words in the form of embodied voices. Contemporary techno-industrial culture shares that privileging. When people imagine the ideal public sphere as the seat of civic life, the soul of participatory democracy, whether it be the marketplace of ideas wherein multiple knots of private conversations in coffee houses and salons add up to a public, or town meetings wherein anyone can say his or her piece, the public sphere is imagined as a place of embodied voices, of people talking to each other, of conversation. This is a deep impulse and a beautiful dream and it is endemic to our vision of the public sphere, of democracy, of even communication itself. This is evident in our televised presidential election town meetings, wherein the "live" audience in the room makes the event authentic, real. John Dewey imagined the primordial act of communication as two people sitting on a log, face-to-face, talking. As Habermas puts it, "A portion of the public sphere comes into being in every conversation in which private individuals assemble to form a public body" (1974, p. 49). Even the postmodern prophet of simulacra, Jean Baudrillard, falls under the spell of bodily presence. In remarking on the 1968 protests in France, he critiques the mass media as transmission systems at a distance and praises posters and notices printed on walls as immediate and thus the "real revolutionary media ... everything that was an immediate inscription, given and returned, spoken and answered, mobile in the same space and time, reciprocal and antagonistic" (1972/1981, p. 176). Baudrillard's emphasis on immediacy, the spoken and answered, idealizes the face-to-face encounter and privileges such speech as authentic. The Baudrillard example is compelling in that he discusses written forms of communication as if they were spoken. Posters and notices are "spoken and answered." They are better than mass media because they are not distant but immediate, like speech. Similarly, although the public sphere includes written forms of communication, embodied conversation functions as the ideal baseline. Yet the dream of the public sphere as the engagement of embodied voices, democracy via dialogue, cloisters us, for perforce its vision compels us to see the contemporary landscape of mass communication as a nightmare.

If envisioning a public sphere of embodied voices makes sense within the Western imaginary, Jacques Derrida and John Peters gift us with a second seeing of our situation. Much of Derrida's work traces and deconstructs the privileging of face-to-face speech in the history of Western thought, what he terms a "logocentrism which is also a phonocentrism: absolute proximity of voice and being, of voice and the meaning of being, of voice and the ideality of meaning" (1976, pp. 11–12). Peters, in his history of communication as "a registry of modern longings" (1999, p. 2), traces and critiques a similar history of the privileging of presence, of "the dream of communication as the mutual communion of souls" (1999, p. 1; see also Schudson, 1997). As Peters notes, "dialogue has attained something of a holy status. It is held up as the summit of human encounter, the essence of liberal education, and the medium of participatory democracy" (1999, p. 33). Both Derrida and Peters offer dissemination as the primordial form of communication, the first turn before dialogue. Their point, an insight highlighted in an age of mass communication, is that communication/transmission/reception/meaning/understanding/communion may never happen, "that a letter can always not arrive at its destination, and therefore it never arrives. And this is really how it is, it is not a misfortune, that's life, living life" (Derrida, 1987, p. 33). In counterpoint to a public sphere underwritten by consensus through communication or communion via conversation, dissemination reminds us that all forms of communication are founded on the risk of not communicating.

Taking dissemination rather than dialogue as characteristic of contemporary communication practices, then, necessarily alters the trajectory of our thinking about politics and society. The public screen is an accounting that starts from the premise of dissemination, of broadcasting. Communication as characterized by dissemination is the endless proliferation and scattering of emissions without the guarantee of productive exchanges. Peters cites the parables of Jesus as the paradigmatic example of dissemination in order to suggest that dissemination offers a model of communication that is more democratic, open, public, equitable, receiver-oriented, and in tune with humanity's multiple communication practices (1999, pp. 35, 5 1–59, 267–68). As Peters concludes,

> Dialogue still reigns supreme in the imagination of many as to what good communication might be, but dissemination represents a saner choice for our fundamental term. Dissemination is far friendlier to the weirdly diverse practices we signifying animals engage in and to our bumbling attempts to meet others with some fairness and kindness. Open scatter is more fundamental than coupled sharing; it is the stuff from which, on rare, splendid occasions, dialogue may arise. Dissemination is not wreckage; it is our lot. (1999, p. 62)

In short, although an historically and culturally understandable desire, the fondness for bodily presence and face-to-face conversations ignores the social and technological transformations of the 20th century that have constructed an altogether different cultural context, a techno-epistemic break. The preceding few pages were meant to suggest the limitations of the public sphere as a guiding metaphor for social theory because it holds static notions of the public arena, appropriate political activity, and democratic citizenship, thus ignoring current social and technological conditions. Further, as a normative ideal, the public sphere promotes as unquestioned universal goods several deeply problematic notions: consensus, openness, dialogue, rationality, and civility/decorum. As a supplement, we want to introduce the public screen as a metaphor for thinking about the places of politics and the possibilities of citizenship in our present moment.

Remediation, Hypermediacy, and Images

The public screen. Such a concept takes technology seriously. It recognizes that most, and the most important, public discussions take place via "screens"—television, computer, and the front page of newspapers. Further, it suggests that we cannot simply adopt the term "public sphere" and all it entails, a term indebted to orality and print, for the current screen age. The new term takes seriously the work of media theorists suggesting that new technologies introduce new forms of social organization and new modes of perception.

Our starting premise, then, is that television and the Internet in concert have fundamentally transformed the media matrix that constitutes our social milieu, producing new forms of social organization and new modes of perception. As art historian W. J. T. Mitchell suggests, "The difference between a culture of reading and a culture of spectatorship, for instance, is not *only* a formal issue; it has implications for the very forms that sociability and subjectivity take, for the kinds of individuals and institutions formed by a culture" (1995, p. 3). These implications can be extrapolated both forward to the Internet and back to the avalanche of communication technologies of the 19th and 20th centuries, especially photography, telegraph, telephone, radio, and film.

These technologies have intensified the speed of communication and obliterated space as a barrier to communication (Kern, 1983; Carey, 1989). They physically shrink the world while simultaneously mentally expanding it, producing a vast expansion of geographical consciousness. Thoreau's caustic comments about the telegraph have come true. We know and care when Princess Di has a car crash. Texas may not have much to say to Maine, but it is transmitted nevertheless. Further, segregated space is breached, flattening multiple forms of hierarchy (Meyrowitz, 1985). As media scholar Ian Angus explains, "Media of communication constitute

primal scenes, a complex of which defines the culture of a given place and time, an Epoch of Being" (2000, p. 190).

This quotation warrants elaboration. Angus is stating that at any historical moment a plurality of media coexist and interact. This point, suggested by McLuhan's observation that "the 'content' of any medium is always another medium" (1964, p. 23), is usefully extended by Bolter and Grusin's discussions of remediation and hypermediacy. Remediation is "the representation of one medium in another" (1999, p. 45) and examples include computer games like *Myst* or *Doom* that remediate photography and film or web sites that remediate television. Importantly, Bolter and Grusin argue that remediation is not a linear process and that "older media can also remediate newer ones" (1999, p. 55). For example, newspapers like *USA Today* remediate both television and the Windows layout of computer screens. Remediation is closely linked to the logic of hypermediacy: "contemporary hypermediacy offers a heterogenous space, in which representation is conceived not as a window on to the world, but rather as 'windowed' itself—with windows that open on to other representations or other media. The logic of hypermediacy multiplies the signs of mediation" (Bolter and Grusin, 1999, p. 34).

The notions of remediation and hypermediacy are crucial to our discussion of the public screen, for when we discuss the public screen primarily through television and newspaper examples, it is with three understandings. First, TV is never simply TV, but a medium immersed in the process of remediations among multiple media. Second, the public screen is a scene of hypermediacy. Third, at a meta-level, remediation provides a frame for conceptualizing the relation between the public sphere and the public screen. The latter neither simply succeeds the former nor are they utterly distinct arenas. Rather, the public screen and the public sphere exist in a dialectic of remediation. To herald the emergence of the public screen is not to announce the death of the public sphere, though it may suggest its eclipse.

Angus, in making the now common observation that media do not merely transmit information and represent reality but fundamentally constitute it, goes one step further. Yes, media produce culture, but they are also the primal scene upon which culture is produced and enacted. In other words, in techno-industrial culture media become the ground of Being. To push this point, media are not mere means of communicating in a public sphere or on a public screen; media produce the public sphere and public screen as primal scenes of Being. Particular configurations of media institute the scene or open the spaces from which epistemologies and ontologies emerge.

Today's scene is predominantly a visual one. TV trades in a discourse dominated by images not words, a visual rhetoric. In our television culture, we are experiencing a shift from Rorty's "linguistic turn" to what Mitchell terms a "pictorial turn" (1995, p. 11). TV's imagistic discourse has become so dominant that even newspapers can do no better than imitate TV, moving to shorter stories and color graphics. The epitome of this trend is the national newspaper, *USA Today,* but even the grey *New York Times* now prints color photographs on the front page. If we take remediation seriously, Susan Sontag's observations on photography are also illuminating with respect to the ceaseless circulation of images in our media matrix: "Industrial societies turn their citizens into image-junkies. . . . turn experience itself into a way of seeing. . . . an event has come to mean, precisely, something worth photographing," something that has appeared on the public screen (1977, pp. 24, 18–19). Baudrillard pushes this point: "Photography brings the world into action (acts out the world, is the world's act) and the world steps into the photographic act (acts out photography, is photography's act)" (2000, p. 3). These comments are suggestive for thinking about a public discourse of images. John Hartley's provocative analysis of the politics of pictures more explicitly gets at the transition from public sphere to public screen. Hartley suggests that there is no real public, but, rather that the public is the product of publicity, of pictures. The public's fictional status, however, should not be "taken as a disqualification from but as a demonstration of the social power (even truth) of fictions" (Hartley, 1992, p. 84). Images, then, are important not because they represent reality but create it: "They are the place where collective social action, individual identity and

symbolic imagination meet—the nexus between culture and politics" (Hartley, 1992, p. 3).

Transforming Publicity

So what do these technological transformations portend for democracy? Advocates of the public sphere often criticize the contemporary political imagescape by evoking the fullness of the public sphere ideal and a past golden age. Michael Schudson cites a representative example:

> Christopher Lasch, for instance, bemoans "the transformation of politics from a central component of popular culture into a spectator sport." What once existed but has been lost, in Lasch's view, is "the opportunity to exercise the virtues associated with deliberation and participation in public debate." What we are seeing is "the atrophy of these virtues in the common people— judgment, prudence, eloquence, courage, self-reliance, resourcefulness, common sense." (1992, p. 142)

Of course, Lasch's position suggests that our fall from grace could be rectified by a collective act of will. Studying media suggests not. New technologies have transformed our social context, generating new forms of social organization and new modes of perception. TV places a premium on images over words, emotions over rationality, speed over reflection, distraction over deliberation, slogans over arguments, the glance over the gaze, appearance over truth, the present over the past.

Yet even theorists aware of the structural transformations introduced by technologies fall into Lasch's reactionary pose. Kathleen Hall Jamieson, after skillfully explaining how TV has rendered traditional public address obsolete, concludes that we need more occasions for traditional public address (1988, pp. 238–255). Neil Postman, in his book *Amusing Ourselves to Death* (1985), understands the new context but tips his hand with his title and frames his discussion in terms of the loss of the pre-TV golden age of the Lincoln-Douglas debates [Schudson nicely explodes that myth (1992)].

These critics base their critiques on the assumption of an idealized public sphere predicated on rationality, face-to-face talk, consensus, equality, contemplation, and the bracketing of power relations. Such a frame unnecessarily limits understanding of the possibilities of participatory politics in a mass-mediated society. Technological and social changes have produced the public screen. For a cultural critic, the key response to the structural transformations of our moment is neither to adopt a moral pose nor to express yearnings for a mythical past, but to explore what is happening and what is possible under current conditions. If embodied gatherings of culturally homogenous, equal citizens engaged in rational dialogue with the goal of consensus is no longer a dominant mode of political activity, what constitutes politics today? One answer is the public screen. Groups perform image events (DeLuca, 1999) for dissemination via corporate-owned mass media that display an unceasing flow of images and entertainment. Although today's televisual public screen is not the liberal public sphere of which Habermas dreams, wherein a rational public through deliberative discussion achieves public opinion, neither is it the medieval public sphere of representative publicity that Habermas fears, a site where rulers stage their status in the form of spectacles before the ruled. Rather, on today's public screen corporations and states stage spectacles (advertising and photo ops) certifying their status before the people/public *and* activists participate through the performance of image events, employing the consequent publicity as a social medium for forming public opinion and holding corporations and states accountable. Critique through spectacle, not critique versus spectacle. Greenpeace's image fare against Soviet and Japanese whalers (DeLuca, 1999), college students' shantytown campaign against corporate and institutional investment in apartheid South Africa (Williams, 1986), and ACT UP's in-your-face activism against AIDS indifference (DeParle, 1990) attest to the possibilities of such practices.

Note that the public screen contains a shift in the function of public opinion. In Habermas's public sphere, public opinion is designed to criticize and control the power of the state. As already argued, in the present historical moment

corporations have eclipsed nation-states in many respects as the dominant players on the world scene. For Habermas, the rise of corporations has corrupted the public sphere:

> "Public opinion" takes on a different meaning depending on whether it is brought into play as a critical authority in connection with the normative mandate that the exercise of political and social power be subject to publicity or as the object to be molded in connection with a staged display of, and manipulative propagation of, publicity in the service of persons and institutions, consumer goods, and programs. (1989, p. 236)

Although not disagreeing with Habermas's account, we think it is only partial and neglects the opportunities the public screen engenders for citizens to hold corporations accountable. The publicity activists generate via the public screen is just as often directed toward corporations as toward governments. Given the importance of image on the public screen, even powerful corporations are vulnerable to image-fare and must be protective of their public image (for examples, see Beder, 1997; Greider, 1992). A compelling recent example has been the campaign against sweatshop labor. Activists, many of them college students, have used the public screen to generate public opinion against the use of sweatshop labor by global corporations, including Nike, Wal-Mart, and the GAP (Gourevitch, 2001; the major groups in this effort are United Students Against Sweatshops, the National Labor Committee, the Fair Labor Association, and the Worker Rights Consortium).

Image Events in a Time of Distraction

The public screen is a constant current of images and words, a ceaseless circulation abetted by the technologies of television, film, photography, and the Internet. These technologies' speed, stream of images, and global reach create an ahistorical, contextless flow of jarring juxtapositions. The public screen promotes a mode of perception that could best be characterized as "distraction."

The public sphere, in privileging rational argument, assumed a mode of perception characterized by concentration, attention, and focus. German social theorists contemplating the effects of film, radio, photography, and urbanism recognized the emergence of a new mode of perception. Horkheimer and Adorno lamented the effects of film,

> Real life is becoming indistinguishable from the movies. The sound film, far surpassing the theater of illusion, leaves no room for imagination or reflection on the part of the audience, who is unable to respond within the structure of the film. . . . They are so designed that quickness, powers of observation, and experience are undeniably needed to apprehend them at all; yet sustained thought is out of the question if the spectator is not to miss the relentless rush of facts. (1972, pp. 126–127)

Observing the state of middle-class Germany amidst the new technologies and the culture industry in the 1920s and 30s, Siegfried Kracauer wrote of people living in a state of distraction: "Society does not stop the urge to live amid glamour and distraction, but encourages it wherever and however it can" (1998, pp. 89).

Eschewing mere judgment, Walter Benjamin sought to understand distraction as the mode of perception most appropriate to the technologically transformed conditions of the 20th century. Benjamin conceived of the audience as "a collectivity in a state of distraction" and asserted that "the tasks which face the human apparatus of perception at the turning points of history cannot be solved by optical means, that is, by contemplation, alone. They are mastered gradually by habit, under the guidance of tactile appropriation" (1968, pp. 232, 233). Benjamin is suggesting that the focused gaze has been displaced by the distracted look of the optical unconscious, the glance of habit, which is tactile in the sense that one is not an observer gazing from a critical distance, but an actor immersed in a sea of imagery, a self pressed upon by the play of images and driven to distraction to survive. The self utilizes "a way of looking

and experiencing the world in which the eye does not act to hold external objects in a firm contemplative gaze, but only notices them in passing and while also keeping a series of other objects in view" (Latham, 1999, p. 463; see also Abbas, 1996).

The key point is that these theorists understand distraction not as a lack of attention but as a necessary form of perception when immersed in the technologically induced torrent of images and information that constitutes public discourse in the 20th and 21st centuries. Speed and images, singly and in concert, annihilate contemplation. Although distraction and the glance are antithetical to the public sphere and were read negatively by theorists such as Horkheimer, Adorno, and Kracauer as signs of the decline of civilization, the dialectic of Enlightenment, we suggest that they be read not morally but analytically as signs of the emergence of a new space for discourse, the public screen, that entails different forms of intelligence and knowledge.

Given that in modern industrial society people "directly know only tiny regions of social life" and that of "all the institutions of daily life, the media specialize in orchestrating everyday consciousness. . . . They name the world's parts, they certify reality as reality" (Gitlin, 1980, pp. 1–2), the public screen is an unavoidable place of politics. As Gronbeck bluntly puts it, "The telespectacle, for better or worse, is the center of public politics, of the public sphere. . . . we must recognize that the conversation of the culture is centered not in the *New York Review of Books* but in the television experience" (1995, p. 235). Citizens who want to appear on the public screen, who want to act on the stage of participatory democracy, face three major conditions that both constrain and enable their actions: 1) private ownership/monopoly of the public screen, 2) Infotainment conventions that filter what counts as news, and 3) the need to communicate in the discourse of images.

These are formidable constraints; yet they are also rich opportunities. Yes, ownership often restricts content that is against the interests of the transnational corporations that own and advertise on the media. Yes, the fact that private companies driven by profits own the media restricts access for citizens and most activist groups that simply cannot afford to buy time (McChesney, 1999). Yes, the visual bias of TV works against those deploying traditional, word-based forms of argument. Still, there are opportunities. First, the need for media companies to be competitive and attract audiences opens up the public screen to stories beyond the narrow ideological interests of transnational capital. Further, although certain news conventions work against activist groups, others, most notably the emphasis on the new, drama, conflict, objectivity, and compelling visuals, open up the public screen. Finally, TV amplifies voices, enabling one person (Dr. Kevorkian) or small groups to communicate to millions via the public screen.

This understanding of mass media has translated into a practice of staging image events for dissemination. In a book written shortly before Greenpeace's first image event, early Greenpeace Director Robert Hunter argued that the mass media provide a delivery system for image events that explode "in the public's consciousness to transform the way people view their world" (1971, p. 22). As fellow activist Paul Watson elaborated, "The more dramatic you can make it, the more controversial it is, the more publicity you will get. . . . The drama translates into exposure. Then you tie the message into that exposure and fire it into the brains of millions of people in the process" (quoted in Scarce, 1990, p. 104).

Greenpeace is an early example of a group lacking organization, resources, and a large membership deploying dramatic visuals and an understanding of the public screen to achieve astonishing successes. The fair trade/democratic globalization protests provide a contemporary opportunity to study the possibilities and consequences of the public screen. The Seattle WTO protests provide a particularly rich example, in part because the public screen is more developed and complex than it was in the 1970s and in part because Seattle was a contested image event wherein several groups competed over its meaning: the Clinton Administration, corporate sponsors, peaceful protesters, uncivil disobedience activists, and anarchists. Further, a key component of Seattle was violence (in various forms), a type of "communication" *a priori* ruled out of the public sphere. In part, then, our analysis will focus on violence and how it works on the public screen.

THE BATTLE IN SEATTLE: THE USES OF VIOLENCE

There are so many legal precautions against violence, and our upbringing is directed towards so weakening our tendencies toward violence, that we are instinctively inclined to think that any act of violence is a manifestation of a return to barbarism. . . . almost uninterruptedly since the eighteenth century, economists have been in favour of strong central authorities, and have troubled little about political liberties. It may be questioned whether there is not a little stupidity in the admiration of our contemporaries for gentle methods.

—Georges Sorel, *Reflections on Violence*

Violence is never an appropriate way to settle differences. I know that the violence comes from a tiny segment who through such actions detract from those who have come there to constructively protest. The World Trade Organization has sought in recent years to expand its contacts with people from all segments of society. Our efforts at transparency have not been perfect. More work needs to be done. But progress in this area can only be made through constructive dialogue.

—Mike Moore, Director-General, World Trade Organization

A little broken glass in the streets of Seattle has transformed the World Trade Organization into a popular icon for the unregulated globalization that tramples human values on every continent, among rich and poor alike.

—William Greider, "The Battle Beyond Seattle"

When thinking about the WTO in Seattle, we must first recognize that it was designed by the Clinton Administration as an image event. As politicians and their advisers clearly understand, with the advent of television, dramatic visuals have become required fare. For example, when then-President Bush wanted to announce clean air legislation he traveled to Arizona to use the Grand Canyon as a visual backdrop. Seattle, export capital of the U.S., was consciously chosen as the scene for Clinton's triumphant procession. Success was scripted, with Clinton as the star in the heroic tale of free-trade prosperity. The title of the production was to be the "Clinton Round," the sequel to the founding "Uruguay Round" in 1995. Corporate sponsorship was secured, with companies such as General Motors, Boeing, and Microsoft paying as much as $250,000 for access to heads of state, ministers, and delegates during the conference (Lean, 1999). Seeing the stage set, however, a diverse range of activists decided it would be the perfect opportunity to launch their issues onto the public screen.

In an example of the hypermediacy of the public screen, the plan for Seattle was clearly laid out on the internet and in alternative newspapers, handbills, and flyers circulating in Seattle for weeks before November 30th.[3] Organizers anticipated that tens of thousands of people would converge on downtown Seattle and "transform it into a festival of resistance with mass nonviolent direct action, marches, street theater, music and celebration" ("Resist the World Trade Organization" handbill).[4] Even with extensive discussions of nonviolent tactics, organizers expected violence—from the police. The rules of enactment were explicitly laid out. In their "colorful festival" of civil and uncivil disobedience, the protesters would provide the provocation and the violence would come from the police.[5] As anyone with a television or access to a newspaper during those few days in 1999 will readily agree, the protest did not turn out exactly as planned. The festival of color was punctuated with black-clad anarchists and the nonviolent direct action was upstaged by images of smashed windows, burning trash bins, and brutal interactions with the police.

Both establishment voices and non-violent activists denounced the violence, especially the symbolic violence of the anarchists. (By symbolic violence, we mean acts directed toward property, not people, and designed to attract media attention.) The dominant response lamented the violence as drowning out the message of the nonviolent protesters. An editorial in the *Seattle Times* opined, "It took thousands of peaceful protesters to shut down the opening ceremonies of the World Trade Organization. It took only a few hundred punks, vandals, and self-proclaimed anarchists to turn downtown Seattle from a festive Christmas scene to a dump" ("WTO Seattle becomes a playpen for vandals," 1999, B4). Activist Cathy Ahern complained, "I am so disappointed how this turned out. We had weeks of training how to do this correctly. It was supposed to be peaceful. . . . It's been completely destroyed. Our message is not going to get out and I'm so mad" (as quoted in Postman, Broom and Davila, 1999, p. A13). Arlie Schardt, president of Environmental Media Services, concurred, "I just think it's tragic that all the news here is about a handful of anarchists and not the tens of thousands of activists who conducted model marches" (as quoted in Cooper, 1999, A2). Such criticisms fail to consider important elements of politics and social change on a global and televisual public screen. The WTO protests are an instructive example of the productive possibilities of violence on today's public screen.

By definition, the news is about what is new, what is out of the ordinary. The news is attracted to disturbers of order and deviation from the routine. As the news adage goes, "if it bleeds, it leads" (Kerbel, 2000). Aside from bloodshed, nothing fits these parameters more precisely than symbolic protest violence and uncivil disobedience. In Seattle, such acts served to highlight the lack of citizen access and input in the WTO decision-making process. These acts also encouraged the police response of tear gas and concussion grenades that made for some of the most compelling images coming from the WTO protest. The symbolic violence and uncivil disobedience worked together in a nuanced fashion. The nonviolent protesters served to provoke the police at least as much as the anarchists did. Indeed, police violence against nonviolent protesters performing uncivil disobedience started before the anarchists acted. We suspect that the anarchists' symbolic violence justified intense media coverage of the police violence because media framing often portrayed the police violence as a response to the anarchists. In other words, the presence of the anarchists allowed the media to provide some sort of explanation, however inadequate, of a police force out of control. Police violence against activists at the IMF/World Bank protest in Washington, D.C. the following spring went largely unreported. The event also lacked symbolic anarchist violence. In Seattle, then, symbolic violence and uncivil disobedience in concert produced compelling images that functioned as the dramatic leads for substantive discussions of the issues provoking the protests.

Since the civil rights and antiwar protests of the 1960s, activists have learned the lessons of images. They understood Seattle as an occasion not for warfare but for imagefare. The protesters' chants of "The whole world is watching" clearly echo the 1960s. The whole world did watch— not because thirty thousand protesters gathered in one location, but because uncivil disobedience and symbolically violent tactics effectively disrupted the WTO, shut down Seattle, provoked police violence, and staged the images the media feed upon. An analysis of media coverage of the WTO protests reveals such tactics as necessary ingredients for compelling the whole world to watch.

TV Screens

Analysis of the television evening news coverage for the first day of violence, November 30, suggests the productive role of violence in social protest on the public screen. Combined coverage time on CNN, ABC, CBS, and NBC increased by 26% from Monday's coverage and the placement of the story improved from the third, fourth, or fifth story to the lead or second story. The opening images were clearly ones of violence and conflict: protesters smashing a Starbucks; police in sci-fi riot gear shooting tear gas canisters and concussion grenades; police roughing up protesters. Other images did get through, though: thousands in the labor march; environmentalists in sea turtle costumes; protesters nonviolently blocking streets. Significantly, the protesters' criticisms of the WTO received an impressively extensive and sympathetic airing— the claim that the WTO is an undemocratic

organization with a pro-corporate agenda that in practice overrules national labor, environmental, and human rights laws was broadcast to an international audience. In addition to the power of the images themselves, this airing happened in two ways. First, among the images of violence were interspersed quotations from the protesters. On NBC, for example, dramatic images of violence yielded to a female protester declaring, "We're just normal people who are tired of the exploitation of the multi-national corporations through out the world." Second, the "breaking news" stories focusing on violent images were invariably followed by background stories focusing on the issues that make the WTO controversial. ABC reporter Deborah Wong concluded one such story: "For these protesters, this single organization, the WTO, has come to symbolize just about all that is wrong in the modern world. So in this global economy, where bigger is better and only the fittest survive, these people complain they have less and less control over their jobs and the laws which protect their communities." Such background stories sought out the perspectives of protesters. On ABC, a female protester remarked, "There is a general dissatisfaction here with corporate culture, absolutely, and we're not going to have that slammed down our throats." CBS interviewed unemployed Mary Fleure of the United Steelworkers of America, who explained, "We're just being swallowed up by corporate greed. We can't compete. I can't feed my family."

To think that the WTO protests would have been lead stories and would have received such extensive airtime without symbolic violence (there was difficult competition from mass graves in Mexico) is to neglect the dynamics of the news media. Far from discrediting or drowning out the message of the WTO protesters, the symbolic violence generated extensive media coverage and an airing of the issues. Comparing television coverage in Seattle with succeeding protests in Washington, D.C. and Qatar is suggestive.

The pattern of TV evening news coverage reveals that although the major networks (CNN, ABC, CBS, NBC) expected a significant story in Seattle, they did not anticipate the extent of the protests and the outbreaks of both anarchist and police violence. The Sunday and Monday nights preceding the opening day of the WTO meetings received 10:40 and 13:10 minutes of airtime, respectively. Tuesday, the first day of protests and violence, saw an increase in coverage to 17 minutes and the WTO was the lead or second story on all four networks. On Wednesday, when the extent of Tuesday's "mayhem" became clear, coverage reached 28:30 and the WTO protests were the lead story on all four networks. On Thursday, the WTO remained the top story on three of the four networks and garnered 16:40 minutes of coverage. On these nights, most reports followed the two-part structure already illustrated in the analysis of the Tuesday coverage: an opening story with a focus on the violence followed by a background story to cover the substantive issues of the protesters.

After Seattle, the next major globalization event was the World Bank/International Monetary Fund (WB/IMF) spring meetings in Washington, D.C. The coverage pattern was almost the reverse of that in Seattle and suggests the crucial role of violence in garnering time on the public screen. On the Saturday and Sunday preceding the Monday opening, the WB/IMF protests were the lead story on six of the seven broadcasts (NBC did not have a Sunday evening broadcast) and received 10 and 13:20 minutes of coverage, respectively. Coverage peaked on Monday with the opening of the meetings. Although receiving 17:30 minutes of coverage, the WB/IMF protests were not the lead story on any network. Notably, due to a variety of factors, there was no active anarchist presence and much less police violence. Although the meetings and protests continued on Tuesday, there was no coverage at all that evening. Apparently, without violence or the threat of violence, the protests were not even worthy of coverage despite the significance of the issues being discussed. This pattern has repeated itself at other globalization events and protests. The most recent round of WTO meetings were held November 9–14, 2001. Doha, Qatar was purposefully chosen as the site in order to reduce the likelihood of protests and violence. That goal was achieved, as there were just small protests and no violence. Consequently, there was absolutely no TV evening news coverage by the four major networks.

Although these three events included varying contextual factors, the results are very suggestive. In the Seattle and Washington, D.C. cases, preliminary coverage was modest. When violence broke out in Seattle, coverage escalated. When dramatic violence did not occur in DC, coverage disappeared. In Qatar, where violence was ruled out *a priori* by the choice of venue, television coverage was nonexistent. Clearly, then, the symbolic violence and police violence did not detract from more substantive coverage of the protesters' issues. On the contrary, without such violence or its threat, TV news coverage quickly evaporated.

Newspaper Screens

Interestingly, *The New York Times* in their lead editorial comes to the same mistaken conclusion as the peaceful protesters: "The violence and property destruction diverted attention from the basic point the demonstrators sought to make—the need to reform the W.T.O.'s procedures and values" ("Messages for the W.T.O.," 1999, p. A30). The editorial, in its remaining six paragraphs, details the grievances of the nonviolent protesters, argues for the need to respond substantively, and concludes: "vital issues affecting the health and prosperity of the planet deserve a visibly fair hearing" (p. A30). This editorial serves as a microcosm of the newspaper coverage generally: the violence serves as a dramatic lead that opens into expansive and extensive coverage of the issues surrounding the WTO protests.

As was true for television, images played a dominant role in the print media coverage of the WTO protests. Headline stories were accompanied by quarter-page images (some as large as ten and a half inches across) of police and protesters facing off in teargas-fogged streets. From November 28th, 1999 to December 2nd, 1999, *The New York Times, Washington Post, Los Angeles Times,* and *USA Today* ran sixty-five images of the WTO convention and related protests in downtown Seattle. Of those sixty-five images, the vast majority, forty-one, were uncivil disobedience shots. Eight were of peaceful protests. Ten of the pictures documented the negotiations of the delegates, the proceedings taking place in the convention, and the address of President Clinton. Three images were of the anarchists and their actions. This emphasis on images supports notions of remediation and hypermediacy—viewers witness the events in Seattle through the public screens of both their televisions and newspapers.

Prior to the anarchists' symbolic violence, the uncivil disobedience, and the violent police response of Tuesday November 30th, newspaper coverage was fairly limited (thirteen images and twenty-four articles). Judging by the number of articles covering the WTO convention (three on the 28th, 12 on the 29th, and 9 on the 30th), the newspapers' interest in the protest was beginning to wane by the morning of the 30th until the violence in the streets shifted the coverage dramatically. The aggressive direct action protests and symbolic violence (which intensified the police response) catapulted the protests into national headlines. For the first time, on December 1st all four newspapers ran front-page images of the convention, each opting to display pictures of the violent interaction between police and protesters. Fifteen of the images that accompanied the eighteen articles covering the WTO were of acts of uncivil disobedience or of the violent police response. Two images were of the anarchists and their actions. Two images were of the convention proceedings. Although violence was a focus of the photographs and the lead stories, the papers reported criticisms of the WTO and the predominantly peaceful character of the protests was emphasized. This trend continued on December 2nd with the four newspapers running a noteworthy sixteen images of uncivil disobedience. If we are thinking of the newspapers through the metaphor of the public screen, then the front page becomes particularly important. Out of thirteen front-page images during the days of protest, eight were of uncivil disobedience, two were of peaceful protest, two were of the convention proceedings, and one was of an anarchist.

This attention to the conflict outside of the conference not only increased scrutiny of the action of the protesters and police, but also increased coverage of the WTO in general. For example, *The New York Times* ran two articles on the WTO on November 28th, four on the 29th, four on the 30th, seven articles, editorials and letters to the editor on December 1st, and a remarkable fourteen documents on December 2nd. The shocking close-up of a woman's bleeding face on A1 in the *L.A. Times* directs readers to A18 where another image of protesting in the streets draws readers' attention to the column, "WTO: What's at Issue?" The column lists and briefly explains the major issues facing the trade ministers in Seattle: agriculture, Uruguay round assessment, anti-dumping measures, labor and environment, WTO reform, intellectual property and China (Iritani, 1999). *The New York Times* makes a similar move on the 1st, creating a chart listing "Who's Protesting and What They Object To" in the first column and "What They Want" in the second ("Behind the Hubbub in Seattle," 1999). The article focuses solely on the issues of worker, environmental, and consumer groups. A similar dynamic was at work in the *Washington Post* and *USA Today*. "This weird jamboree" inspired *USA Today* to detail the issues of unions, environmentalists, steel workers, food-safety advocates, and poor countries ("Cover Story: This weird jamboree," Cox and Jones, 1999, p. 1A). Far from stealing the limelight from the legitimate protesters, the compelling images of violence and disruption increased the news hole and drew more attention to the issues.

This increase in coverage can be compared to the coverage of the WB/IMF protests in Washington, D.C. the following spring. Police cracked down on activists before the start of the conference by closing down protest headquarters and making preemptive arrests. These preventive strikes by the Washington, D.C. police curtailed most of the symbolic violence and direct action seen on the streets of Seattle. Backing our claim that the violence in the streets of Seattle actually produced more media coverage, the reporting on the WB/IMF conference did not spike as it did in Seattle. For example, in *The New York Times* coverage remained modest as the conference went on: three articles April 15th, six on the 16th, six on the 17th, six on the 18th, and three on the 19th.

In even starker contrast to the protest in Seattle was the recent WTO meeting in Qatar, where the protesters who did attend were reduced to handing out anti-globalization pamphlets. The entire WTO-Qatar coverage in *The New York Times* from November 10th to November 15th[,] 2001 was less than that of December 2nd, 1999 alone (thirteen documents). None of the articles graced the front page of the newspaper and nearly half the documents (six) were in the C section of the paper. The *Los Angeles Times* gave the talks even less attention, with a mere six articles covering the convention. This again reinforces our claim that the World Trade Organization and its far-reaching agreements fall below the level of consciousness of most media organizations in the absence of the compelling images constructed through the symbolic violence and uncivil disobedience that marked the convention in Seattle. As we found in the television coverage, such protest actions did not detract from the message. On the contrary, they increased the visibility and extensiveness of newspaper coverage of the protesters' criticisms of the WTO.

Screen Effects

The WTO protests accomplished much. On an immediate level, ordinary citizens excluded from the meetings managed through protest to affect those meetings and contribute to their failure. As European Union trade commissioner Pascal Lamy admitted, "What's happening outside is having an effect on the negotiations" (quoted in Sanger and Kahn, 1999, p. A14). At a more general level, on the difficult terrain of a corporate-dominated public screen, thousands of global citizens managed to turn a summit dedicated to streamlining the world for corporate profits into an unruly "forum" on human rights, environmental standards, and social justice in the emerging new world. In exposing the often arcane issues of trade policy to the glare of the media, the protests provoked a debate over free trade versus fair trade. Public discussions about trade are now considering environmental concerns as well as profit concerns, human rights as well as property rights. Indeed, President Clinton was moved to echo many protester concerns in his speech to the WTO. Clinton called for economic justice, worker rights, human rights, environmental protections, and an open and accessible WTO (1999). This public discussion has continued. *The American Prospect*'s recent

special issues on globalization and its critics, *The Face of Globalism* (Summer 2001) and *Globalism and the World's Poor* (Winter 2002), are examples of some of the fallout of Seattle.

On a global level, the Seattle protests have sparked an international pro-democratic globalization movement that has staged protests in Washington, D.C., Prague, Quebec City, Salzburg, Genoa and other cities around the world. A front page story in the *Washington Post* prior to the WB/IMF meetings opened: "The last time opponents of global capitalism confronted the ranks of domestic law enforcement—in Seattle, Nov. 30 to Dec. 3—the results were clouds of tear gas, volleys of rubber bullets and the makings of a mass protest movement whose energy and appeal have surprised even some of its organizers. Round 2 is scheduled for April 16 and 17 in Washington." Though the article dismisses the anarchists as "vandals" and "looters" "running amok," it also admits that they have changed the topography of the political terrain: "Last year, as every year, a demonstration was called during the IMF and World Bank spring meetings in Washington. Twenty-five people showed up." A veteran critic of the World Bank and IMF remarks, "Something has changed. We may fancy ourselves good organizers, but I don't think we could have planned for this" (Montgomery and Santana, 2000, pp. 1, 5).

In provoking an international maelstrom over globalization, activists have accomplished a substantial political achievement. The activists in Seattle and since have been able to link sweatshops, union-busting, human rights violations, environmental degradation, and poverty as consequences of corporate globalization. In short, they have unified farm and environmental and union and anti-colonial groups into a voice that has effectively named corporate globalization as a problem and site of struggle, not an inexorable natural process. The activists have punctured the claims of corporate globalization to universality and to inevitability by giving voice to those left out.

Finally, the symbolic violence and uncivil disobedience of protesters exposed the violence of the state and transnational capital as the allegedly progressive haven of Seattle cracked down with a show of force worthy of 1960s Birmingham or Los Angeles. The trashing of civil liberties, not Starbucks, may be the lasting image of Seattle. Violence often helps foment activism and form community (Browne, 1996). In addition to exposing the violence of the state on behalf of corporate interests in Seattle, in challenging the WTO the protesters have sparked a conversation about the violence of global corporations in their daily practices. A smashed Nike storefront dims in comparison to the violence of sweatshop labor around the world. Yes, violence is disturbing. But for people excluded by governmental structures and corporate power, symbolic protest violence is an effective way to make it onto the public screen and speak to that power. Such symbolic protest violence is often a necessary prerequisite to highlight the nonviolent elements of a movement that might otherwise be marginalized in the daily struggle for media coverage. In the "Battle for Seattle," symbolic violence helped make real the protest chant "Whose world? Our world! Whose streets? Our streets!"

Dense Surfaces: Contemplating Image Events

As the preceding content analysis suggests, the symbolic violence and the uncivil disobedience fulfilled the function of gaining the attention of the distracted media. Counter to charges by peaceful protesters, then, such image events did not drown out their message, but enabled it to be played more extensively and in greater depth. Media coverage of this issue was not a zero-sum game. Uncivil disobedience and the anarchists' actions expanded the totality of coverage. If we take image events seriously as visual discourse, however, we cannot simply reduce them to the function of gaining attention for the "real" rhetoric of words. It is our claim that image events are a central mode of public discourse both for conventional electoral politics (Dahlgren, 1995; Donovan and Scherer, 1992; Gronbeck, 1995; Jamieson, 1988; Postman, 1985) and alternative grassroots politics in an era dominated by a commercial, televisual, electronic public screen (Szasz, 1995; DeLuca, 1999). We must consider image events, then, as visual

philosophical-rhetorical fragments, mind bombs that expand the universe of thinkable thoughts.

Image events are dense surfaces meant to provoke in an instant the shock of the familiar made strange. They suggest a Benjaminian sense of time, where any moment can open up on eternity, any moment can be the moment that changes everything, the moment that redeems the past and the future. And it is all there on the surface. In a familiar city, Seattle, home of the Mariners, computer geeks, airplanes, rain, and coffee, a familiar place, Starbucks, the national neighborhood coffee shop, is shattered by a hammer, everyday object and sign of national industriousness. The familiar made strange, the shock of recognition that the familiar is not necessarily innocuous, the hint of the "banality of evil." The chain of targets reinforces the message: Nike Town, Old Navy, McDonalds, Banana Republic, Planet Hollywood (for a detailed explanation of the choice of targets, see Hawken, 2000).

This is made clear in the intentions of the anarchists. Though intentionality cannot dictate meaning or effect, it can help us glimpse possible surfaces of the multi-faceted image event. In a 13-minute *60 Minutes II* report on "The New Anarchists," reporter Scott Pelley frames the story with these opening words: "Who were those masked men and women in Seattle? Those violent demonstrators who attacked down town, toppled a police chief, and wrecked the Clinton Administration's cherished trade conference?" The story itself consists mostly of stunning video of the protests (shot by the anarchists) and of interviews during which the anarchists explain their positions. After images of people in black shattering storefronts, the reporter asks, "What is the point?" An anarchist responds, "Economic incentive to not hold meetings like that at all. Psychological incentive to reconsider the kind of society we live in that fills our world with Starbucks and McDonalds." The psychological impact is emphasized again in the words of an anarchist that close the story: "You stare at a television and you see logos and you're in a daze and these symbols pop up everywhere in your life. When that is shattered, it breaks a spell and we're trying to get people to wake up before it's too late."

These comments display an acute appreciation of the public screen and image events. The anarchists' image event of shattering windows obeys the rules of the public screen. It both participates in and punctures the habit of distraction characteristic of the contemporary mode of perception. It participates in order to be aired—it is brief, visual, dramatic, and emotional. It punctures to punctuate, to interrupt the flow, to give pause. It punctures by making the mundane malevolent, the familiar fantastic.

CHARTING THE PUBLIC SCREEN

The point of this essay has been to explore the constraints and opportunities of the public screen, a current place for participatory democracy. It is incumbent upon activists, academics, indeed, all citizens of the world, to understand the new topography of political activity. Under contemporary conditions, the public screen is the essential supplement to the public sphere. In comparison to the rationality, embodied conversations, consensus, and civility of the public sphere, the public screen highlights dissemination, images, hypermediacy, spectacular publicity, cacophony, distraction, and dissent. We have focused on the image event as one practice of the public screen because it highlights the public screen as an alternative venue for participatory politics and public opinion formation that offers a striking contrast to the public sphere. Our account, however, is not an exhaustive treatment of the public screen. This is true even with respect to Seattle.

The public screen includes the pundits on talking head TV, whose political discourse is molded as much by the requirements of the public screen as by the rationality of the public sphere. It includes the staged campaigns of electoral politics, managed by contemporary wizards of Oz such as Michael Deaver, Lee Atwater, and James Carville. It includes sitcoms and other entertainment TV, where national "discussions" on race, class, feminism, and sexual identity take place on *Cosby, Roseanne, Ally McBeal,* and *Ellen.* It includes films that deliver the definitive verdict for public memory on such key moments as the Holocaust (*Schindler's List*), World War II

(*Saving Private Ryan*), the Kennedy assassination (*JFK*), and the 60s (*Forrest Gump*).

The public screen includes the advertising and public relations of corporations, arguably the dominant discourses of our time (Ewen, 1996; Beder, 1997). This statement rings truer when one considers how the structure of newspapers in the United States is built around advertising and public relations. Newspapers (as well as TV news) are financially dependent on advertising, with the news hole dependent on the amount of advertising. Consequently, as a rule advertising comprises at least 50% of page space in most newspapers. Though not as visually obvious, public relations releases comprise much of the news in newspapers and television. For instance, one study found that more than half of the *Wall Street Journal*'s news stories were based on news releases (Beder, 1997, pp. 112–113, 116–117). The enormous expenditures of corporations on advertising and public relations are evidence of the importance corporations attribute to the public screen. McDonald's and Coke, owners of two of the most recognizable icons in the world today (rivaling the Christian cross), annually spend over $1 billion and $800 million, respectively, on advertising alone (Farley and Cohen, 2001, p. 26). It is worth noting that advertising and public relations become dominant discourses with the advent of 20th century mass communication technologies—the very same technologies that Habermas argues contribute to the decline of the public sphere.

Even the conversation of book culture is centered not in the *New York Review of Books* but on the public screen, as acclaimed novelist Barbara Kingsolver laments while on book tour:

> Can modern literary success really come
> down to this, an author's TV persona? In a
> word, yes. . . . but what criteria that could
> possibly fit in a fifty-eight-second TV spot
> will guide them to an informed choice? The
> quality of a book's prose means nothing in
> this race. What will win it a mass audience is
> the author's ability to travel, dazzle, stake out
> name recognition, hold up under pressure,
> look good, and be witty—qualities unrelated,
> in fact, to good writing, and a lifestyle that is

writing's pure nemesis. . . . Where would we be now if our whole literary tradition were built upon approximately the same precepts as the Miss America competition? Who would win: Eudora Welty or Vanna White? (1995, pp. 163–164).

This essay is an opening sketch in a needed exploration of the conditions of possibility for rhetoric, politics, and participatory democracy in the techno-industrial corporate-controlled culture that bestrides the planet. As Kingsolver's dismay displays, measuring contemporary discourse by the criteria of an idealized public sphere and romanticized past merely produces despair and nostalgia. Such dismay and nostalgia are characteristic reactions of critics of the contemporary "corrupted" public sphere, which always falls short of an imagined golden past, a Lake Wobegon polis. A public sphere orientation inevitably finds current discourse wanting.

Thinking about rhetoric, politics, and culture through the prism of the public screen, however, enables a seeing of the world anew. Pro-democratic globalization protests, TV sitcoms, Hollywood films, advertising, and public relations do not represent lack, multiple signs of the decline of civilization. Instead, thought through the metaphor of the public screen, such practices are productive of new modes of intelligence, knowledge, politics, rhetoric, in short, new modes of being in the world. It is not a simple seeing, however. The descriptor "new" is not attached with a moral meaning of "good" or "bad"; rather, "new" is an analytical term marking the emergence of difference. Similarly, the concept "public screen" is neither working within a moral economy nor positing a normative ideal, but is opening a space for retheorizing the places of the political. The public screen images a complex world of opportunities and dangers. This complexity is evident in the very term "public screen." In the move from public sphere to public screen, retaining the term "public" is problematic. The airwaves in the United States are by law the property of the public, but they are leased in such a way that media companies own them for all intents and purposes. The Walt Disney Co. need not grant us a soapbox from which to air our views. Although the airwaves

are privately controlled territory, they now function as the sites of public space, much the way a shopping mall does in the stead of the town square. Clearly, in many ways this is unfortunate for democracy (McChesney, 1999; Boggs, 2000). In addition, both theoretically and practically the very distinction between public and private has eroded. Still, the public screen, though privately controlled, is public. The complexity of the public screen warrants neither bemoaning a lost past nor celebrating a technological utopia. The charge for critics is not to decry a lacking present or embrace a naive future. The charge for critics is to chart the topography of this new world.

Notes

1 Our choices of the terms "fair trade" and "democratic globalization" to describe the protests is a political and intellectual move designed to work against the labeling of such protests in the mass media as "anti-globalization" or "anti-trade." Such media labels are the first step to dismissing the protesters as Luddites, Nativists, simpletons, or unruly college kids who simply are against things and do not understand the realities of the world. Our terms recognize the specificity of the protests, the comprehensiveness of the critique, and the global nature of this activist movement.

2 Although Habermas is credited with the term public sphere, concern over the public has a long history that can be traced at least to Aristotle. The 1st Amendment of the United States can be read as a theory of the role of the public in a democracy (Jhally, 1989). In the first half of the 20th Century, John Dewey, Walter Lippmann, and Hannah Arendt were important theorists of the public in a mass-mediated democracy.

3 The following analysis focuses on television and newspaper coverage. This is largely a practical decision. Internet information is notoriously ephemeral. Sites that had extensive WTO protest coverage now have, at most, abbreviated archives (zmag.org; indymedia.org). Since we argue that the public screen and its technologies are characterized by hypermediacy and remediation, the ephemeralness of internet material is not analytically decisive.

4 The organizations responsible for planning the direct action and printing the literature were all identified as cosponsors: Direct Action Network, Global Exchange, Rainforest Action Network, Ruckus Society, Project Underground, National Lawyer's

Guild, Green Party (Seattle), Earth First! (Seattle), Adbusters, Center for Campus Organizing, Committee in Solidarity with the People of El Salvador, 50 Years is Enough, Industrial Workers of the World, and Mexico Solidarity Network.

[5] Uncivil disobedience includes such tactics as verbal harassment and blocking streets and buildings in the hopes of provoking a response and creating an image event and is in contrast to peaceful protests like marches. Besides being more disorderly, it is also qualitatively different from the respectful civil disobedience espoused by Martin Luther King Jr., though the latter is often designed to provoke a violent response. King's civil disobedience was founded on love of one's opponents and predicated on the belief that one's opponents were fundamentally good and could be converted from their erroneous practices. Democratic globalization activists are motivated by the irreconcilable conflicts between the goals of capitalist corporate globalism and the values of democracy, fair trade, and environmental sustainability.

Bibliography

Abbas, A. (1996). Cultural studies in a postculture. In C. Nelson and D. Gaonkar (Eds.), *Disciplinarity and dissent in cultural studies* (pp. 289–312). New York: Routledge.

Angus, I. (2000). *Primal scenes of communication.* Albany: SUNY.

Baudrillard, J. (1972/1981). *For a critique of the political economy of the sign.* U.S.A.: Telos.

Baudrillard, J. (2000). Photography, or the writing of light. *Ctheory.Net* (pp. 1–6).

Beder, S. (1997). *Global spin.* White River Junction, VT: Chelsea Green.

Behind the hubbub in Seattle. (Dec. 1, 1999). *The New York Times*, p. A14.

Benjamin, W. (1968). The work of art in the age of mechanical reproduction. In H. Arendt (Ed.), *Illuminations* (pp. 217–252). New York: Schocken.

Boggs, C. (2000). *The end of politics: Corporate power and the decline of the public sphere.* New York: Guilford.

Bolter, J. & Grusin, R. (1999). *Remediation.* Cambridge: MIT.

Browne, S. (1996). Encountering Angelina Grimké: Violence, identity, and the creation of radical community. *Quarterly Journal of Speech, 82,* 55–74.

Carey, J. (1989). *Communication as culture.* Boston: Unwin Hyman.

Clinton, W. (1999, Dec 2). Clinton's words: Open the meetings. *The New York Times,* A15.

Cooper, H. (1999, Dec. 2). Waves of protests disrupt WTO meeting. *The Wall Street Journal,* A2.

Cox, J. & Jones, D. (1999, Dec 2). Cover story: This weird jamboree. *USA Today,* pp. A1–2.

Curran, J. (1991). Rethinking the media as a public sphere. In P. Dahlgren & C. Sparks (Eds.), *Communication and citizenship.* London: Routledge.

Dahlgren, P. (1995). *Television and the public sphere: Citizenship, democracy, and the media.* London: Sage.

DeLuca, K. (1999). *Image politics: The new rhetoric of environmental activism.* New York: The Guilford Press.

DeParle, J. (1990, Jan 3). Rude, rash, effective, ACT-UP shifts AIDS policy. *The New York Times,* p. B1.

Derrida, J. (1974/1976). *Of grammatology.* Baltimore: The John Hopkins University Press.

Derrida, J. (1981). *Positions.* Chicago, IL: University of Chicago Press.

Derrida, J. (1987). *The post card.* Chicago: University of Chicago.

Donovan, R. & Scherer, R. (1992). *Unsilent revolution: Television news and American public life.* Cambridge: Cambridge University.

Dunlap, R. (2000, April 18). Americans have positive image of the environmental movement. *The Gallup Organization,* www.gallup.com/poll/releases/pr000418.asp.

Eley, G. (1992). Nations, publics, and political cultures: Placing Habermas in the nineteenth century. In C. Calhoun (Ed.), *Habermas and the public sphere* (pp. 289–339). Cambridge, MA: MIT Press.

Elliott, C. (2001). Pharma buys a conscience. *The American Prospect,* 12 (17), pp. 16–20.

Ewen, S. (1996). *PR! A social history of spin.* New York: Basic Books.

Farley, T. and D. Cohen. (2001 December). Fixing a fat nation. *The Washington Monthly,* pp. 23–29.

Fraser, N. (1992). Rethinking the public sphere: A contribution to the critique of actually existing democracy. In C. Calhoun (Ed.), *Habermas and the public sphere* (pp. 109–142). Cambridge, MA: MIT Press.

Friedman, T. (1999). *The Lexus and the olive tree.* New York: Farrar, Straus, Giroux.

Gelbspan, R. (1997). *The heat is on.* Reading, MA: Addison-Wesley.

Gitlin, T. (1980). *The whole world is watching.* Berkeley: University of California.

Gourevitch, A. (2001, June 29). No justice, no contract: The Worker Rights Consortium leads the fight against sweatshops. *The American Prospect Online.*

Greider, W. (1992). *Who will tell the people*. New York: Simon and Schuster.

Greider, W. (1997). *One world, ready or not: The manic logic of global capitalism*. New York: Simon and Schuster.

Greider, W. (1999, December 27). The battle beyond Seattle. *The Nation*, 269 (22), 5–6.

Gronbeck, B. E. (1995). Rhetoric, ethics, and telespectacles in the post-everything age. In R. H. Brown (Ed.), *Postmodern representations: Truth, power, and mimesis in the human sciences and public culture*. United States: University of Illinois Press.

Habermas, J. (1974). The public sphere: An encyclopedia article (1964). *New German Critique, 1*, 49–55.

Habermas, J. (1989). *The structural transformation of the public sphere*. Cambridge: MIT.

Habermas, J. (1994). Further reflections on the public sphere. In C. Calhoun (Ed.), *Habermas and the public sphere* (pp. 421–461). Cambridge, Massachusetts: The MIT Press.

Hardt, M. & Negri, A. (2000). *Empire*. Cambridge: Harvard University.

Hartley, J. (1992). *The politics of pictures*. New York: Routledge.

Hawken, P. (2000, February 16). *The WTO: Inside, outside, all around the world*. (www.co-Intelligence.org/WTOHawken.html).

Horkheimer, M. & Adorno, T. (1972). *Dialectic of enlightenment*. New York: Herder.

Hunter, R. (1971). *The storming of the mind*. Garden City, NY: Doubleday.

Iritani, E. (1999, December 1). WTO: What's at issue? *Los Angeles Times*, p. A18.

Jamieson, K. H. (1988). *Eloquence in an electronic age*. New York: Oxford University Press.

Jhally, S. (1989). The political economy of culture. In I. Angus & S. Jhally (Eds.), *Cultural politics in contemporary America*. New York: Routledge.

Kellner, D. (1995). *Media culture*. New York: Routledge.

Kerbel, M. (2000). *If it bleeds, it leads*. Boulder, CO: Westview.

Kern, S. (1983). *The culture of time and space: 1880–1918*. Cambridge, MA: Harvard University Press.

Kingsolver, B. (1996). *High tide in Tucson*. New York: Harper.

Kracauer, S. (1998). *The salaried masses: Duty and distraction in Weimar Germany*. New York: Verso.

Latham, A. (1999). The power of distraction: distraction, tactility, and habit in the work of Walter Benjamin. *Environment and Planning D: Society and space, 17*, 451–473.

Lean, G. (1999, Aug 22). Gates offers ministers for sale at world trade conference. *The Independent*, p. 1.

McChesney, R. (1999). *Rich media, poor democracy*. New York: New Press.

McLaughlin, L. (1993). Feminism, the public sphere, media, and democracy. *Media, culture and society, 15*, 599–620.

McLuhan, M. (1964). *Understanding media: The extension of man*. New York: McGraw-Hill.

Messages for the W.T.O. (1999, December 2). *The New York Times*, p. A30.

Meyrowitz, J. (1985). *No sense of place*. New York: Oxford University.

Milbank, D. & Kessler, G. (2002, January 18). Enron's influence reached deep into Administration. *Washington Post*, p. A1.

Mitchell, W. (1995). *Picture theory*. Chicago: University of Chicago.

Montgomery, D. and Santana, A. (2000, April 2). D.C. gets ready for World Bank, IMF Meetings. *Washington Post*, A1.

Moore, M. (1999, November 30) Director-General's press statement. *World Trade Organization Web Site* [On-Line]. Available: *http://www.wto.org/wto/new/press157.htm*.

Morgenson, G. (1999, December 26). A company worth more than Spain? *The New York Times*, Section 3, p. 1.

Pateman, C. (1988). The fraternal social contract. In J. Keane (Ed.), *Civil society and the state: New European perspectives* (pp. 101–27). London: Verso.

Peters, J. (1999). *Speaking into the air*. Chicago: University of Chicago.

Peters, J. D. (1993). Distrust of representation: Habermas on the public sphere. *Media, Culture and Society, 15*, 541–571.

Phillips, K. (1996), The spaces of public dissension: Reconsidering the public sphere. *Communication Monographs, 63*, 231–248.

Postman, D., Broom, J., and Davila, F. (December 1, 1999) Some protesters tried to stop violence. *The Seattle Times*, p. A13.

Postman, N. (1985). *Amusing ourselves to death: Public discourse in the age of show business*. New York: Viking.

Press, E. & Washburn, J. (2000). The kept university. *The Atlantic Monthly, 285:3*, 39–54.

Rich, F. (2002, January 19). The United States of Enron. *The New York Times*, A19.

Ryan, M. (1992). Gender and public access: Women's politics in nineteenth-century America. In C. Calhoun (Ed.), *Habermas and the public sphere* (pp. 259–288). Cambridge, MA: MIT Press.

Sanger, D. & Kahn, J. (1999, December 1). A chaotic intersection of tear gas and trade talks. *The New York Times*, A14.

Scarce, R. (1990). *Eco-warriors: Understanding the radical environmental movement.* Chicago, IL: Noble Press.

Schudson, M. (1992). Was there ever a public sphere? If so, when? Reflections on the American case. In C. Calhoun (Ed.), *Habermas and the public sphere* (pp. 143–163). Cambridge, MA: MIT Press.

Schudson, M. (1997). Why conversation is not the soul of democracy. *Critical Studies in Mass Communication, 14 (4)*, 297–309.

Sennett, R. (1994). *Flesh and stone: The body and the city in western civilization.* New York: W. W. Norton.

Slocum, T. (2001). Blind Faith: How deregulation and Enron's influence over government looted billions from Americans. *Public Citizen, www.citizen.org,* pp. 1–28.

Sontag, S. (1977). *On photography.* New York: Farrar, Straus, and Giroux.

Szasz, A. (1995). *Ecopopulism.* Minneapolis: University of Minnesota [Press].

Williams, L. (1986, February 2). Pressure rises on colleges to withdraw South Africa interests. *The New York Times,* p. 14.

WTO Seattle becomes a playpen for vandals. (1999, Dec. 1). *The Seattle Times,* p. B4.

Resisting "National Breast Cancer Awareness Month": The Rhetoric of Counterpublics and Their Cultural Performances

Phaedra C. Pezzullo

Many of us have known someone with breast cancer or have survived breast cancer. For U.S. women, breast cancer is the most frequently diagnosed form of cancer,[1] accounting for approximately one-third of all new cancer cases in women.[2] In addition to the more than two million current U.S. breast cancer survivors, the Y-ME National Breast Cancer Organization claims that, "this year, breast cancer will be newly diagnosed every three minutes, and a woman will die from breast cancer every 13 minutes."[3] In response to this epidemic, breast cancer activism has increased rapidly since the mid-1980s to form the breast cancer movement.[4] Amid growing publicity, research funds, and attention to breast cancer in the past two decades, identifying the causes of breast cancer remains a top priority for the movement.

Although much of our knowledge about breast cancer, and cancer generally, is fraught with uncertainty, it is generally accepted that at least some people have developed cancers owing to environmental pollution.[5] Assuming for the sake of argument that the skeptical estimate of "two percent ... put forth by those who dismiss environmental carcinogens" is minimally accurate, Sandra Steingraber comments:

Two percent means that 10,940 people in the United States die each year from environmentally caused cancers. This is more than the number of women who die each year from hereditary breast cancer—an issue that has launched multi-million dollar research initiatives.[6] This is more than the number of children and teenagers killed each year by firearms—an issue that is considered a matter of national shame. It is more than three times the number of non-smokers estimated to die each year of lung cancer caused by exposure to secondhand smoke—a problem so serious it warranted sweeping changes in laws governing air quality in public spaces. It is the annual equivalent of wiping out a small city. It is thirty funerals every day.[7]

Further, Steingraber emphasizes, "none of these 10,940 Americans will die quick painless deaths. They will be amputated, irradiated, and dosed with chemotherapy."[8] Despite the staggering number of lives represented, cancer advocates continue to encounter significant obstacles when attempting to bring environmentally-related carcinogens into the foreground of U.S. public dialogue.

Ironically, one of these impediments may be the success of the U.S. environmental movement.[9] Polls consistently suggest that the majority of people in the U.S. consider themselves to be environmentalists.[10] The government has institutionalized many laws and a federal agency dedicated to environmental protection.[11] Some even estimate that "more Americans now recycle than vote for president."[12] Further, "green" advertising has become one of the fastest growing advertising trends for industries ranging from gasoline to plastics.[13] The popularity of environmental discourse, however, has made it increasingly difficult for the public to discriminate between talk about being green and action taken to stop environmentally destructive practices.

To address this problem of obfuscation, environmentalists have named the phenomenon of disingenuous environmental appearances "greenwashing." For the purposes of this essay, greenwashing refers not only to "greening" the appearances of products and commodity consumption, but also to the deliberate disavowal of environmental effects. In relation to environmental causes of cancer, thus, greenwashing has become a critical term used to identify when a person, group, or institution purports to care about environmental health (both human and nonhuman) yet does something that perpetuates the production and distribution of environmental carcinogens.

Discourses about breast cancer warrant a closer examination of greenwashing and illustrate the ways in which dominant institutions and figures engage in what might appropriately be called "pinkwashing," by which I mean talk about women that does not necessarily empower women.[14] Karen Fitts, for example, argues that although

> physicians often presume cosmetic concerns are primary to newly diagnosed women, many patients look instead to high rates of incidence (one in eight women), the ordeal of treatment (slash, burn, and poison), and that the number of breast cancer deaths per year (50,000) has not diminished in fifty years.[15]

In other words, Fitts claims that cultural and medical discourses often promote the business of "saving breasts, not lives."[16] Indeed, although cosmetic issues are important to many women,

how one looks is usually relatively unimportant compared to reducing the lethal effects of cancer and the debilitating ordeal of treatment. As in arguments regarding greenwashing, a tension exists between the appearance of caring for women and practices that improve women's lives. I argue, therefore, that public debates over breast cancer are currently constrained in ways that are inextricably linked to environmental and gendered discourses.[17] In this essay, I investigate one perhaps unexpected example of greenwashing and pinkwashing that currently frames public discourses about breast cancer: National Breast Cancer Awareness Month (NBCAM).

Designated the month of October, NBCAM is filled with activities from wearing pink ribbons to organizing fundraising marathons to sponsoring public service announcements on television. This month-long, multi-pronged campaign has provided opportunities for numerous organizations and individuals to galvanize public attention and raise awareness about breast cancer detection, legislation, and experiences. Because opposition to NBCAM is rarely heard, the discourse promoted by NBCAM arguably has become institutionalized as hegemonic "common sense"[18] in the current approach to breast cancer in the U.S.

In this essay, I examine how one coalition of activists is attempting to reveal the gap between the appearance of, and the practices enabled by, NBCAM or, in the words of one advocate, "to rip off the mask of polluter-sponsored Breast Cancer Awareness Month."[19] Specifically, I analyze the San Francisco–based Toxic Links Coalition's (TLC) annual "Stop Cancer Where It Starts" tour. This campaign is constituted primarily by a cultural performance of noncommercial advocacy tours. Adapting the rhetoric of the traditional "toxic tour" (when environmental justice advocates travel to and through communities that have been toxically polluted), the tour takes TLC's grievances to the doorsteps of the institutions that it believes are responsible for producing and enabling toxic pollution. Over the years, TLC has developed its tour to target corporations, non-profits, government agencies, and public relations firms, all of which arguably are powerful actors who frame public opinion and the dominant discourse about breast cancer.

As an examination of how one group of people and related institutions challenge the way another group of people and related institutions have dominated public discourse, this essay hopes to contribute to the ongoing interdisciplinary dialogues about public spheres. Rhetorical scholarship on public spheres has explored the efficacy of what feminist theorists Rita Felski and Nancy Fraser have named "counterpublics," understood as arenas for resisting dominant spheres of public life.[20] Central to this research have been such questions as: What is "counter"? What is "public"? Which theories of multiple spheres can account for the efficacy of efforts to resist existing hegemonic power relations?[21] This essay focuses on the related but often overlooked question: How can we study the creation and maintenance of "actually existing"[22] public spheres and counterpublics? Answering this question, I believe, may guide public sphere scholars to consider how expanding our approaches to studying public spheres may enable us to theorize further the discourses produced by counterpublics.

Using the specific social controversy of pinkwashing environmental contributions to breast cancer, I demonstrate the limits of a binary conceptualization of publics and counterpublics by illustrating how a public discourse such as the one promoted by NBCAM can foster both conservative and progressive political ends for the breast cancer movement. I interpret the people who organized and/or enacted TLC's tour as a counterpublic that invited/challenged those who observed to engage and, ideally, to join them. In other words, the tour performed a discourse that attempted to interpellate people into an identification with TLC, a counterpublic, so more people might strengthen the impact of their discourse. By analyzing TLC's advocacy tour as the cultural performance of a counterpublic, I foreground the non-verbal activities that are involved in negotiating public life, including physical, visual, emotional, and aural dimensions.

This essay develops in three sections. First, I review public sphere scholarship and discuss the importance of studying counterpublics, the possibilities of such arenas, and the usefulness of drawing on participant observation to study the cultural performances that constitute them.

Second, I examine NBCAM's influence on public dialogue about cancer and TLC's response as concrete examples of the form and function of the cultural performances of a "feminist counterpublic," which, as defined by Bonnie J. Dow and Mari Boor Tonn, offers the "potential to function as a critique of patriarchal modes of reasoning as well as to offer an empowering alternative."[23] Third, I analyze one of TLC's tours as a cultural performance that attempted rhetorically to invent a space for resisting the discourse promoted by NBCAM. I conclude by theorizing about the shifting and overlapping boundaries between counterpublics in a social movement and by foregrounding the ways in which participant observation studies may help us to grasp more fully the complexity of their performances.

PUBLIC SPHERES

The translation into English of Jürgen Habermas's *The Structural Transformation of the Public Sphere*[24] reinvigorated a robust interdisciplinary dialogue among U.S. scholars about the "ideal" and the historical public sphere.[25] In describing the ideal public sphere, Habermas writes:

> The bourgeois public sphere may be conceived above all as the sphere of private people come together as a public to engage [public authorities] in a debate over the general rules governing relations in the basically privatized but publicly relevant sphere of commodity exchange and social labor.[26]

"The importance of the public sphere," Craig Calhoun notes, "lies in its potential as a mode of social integration."[27] In other words, as Nancy Fraser argues, a public sphere "designates a theater in modern societies in which political participation is enacted through the medium of talk" (emphasis added).[28] Gerard Hauser emphasizes that a "public" involves activities that "are often local, are often in venues other than institutionalized forums, are always issue specific, and seldom involve the entire populace."[29]

For the purposes of this essay, I limit my review of public sphere literature to those works directly related to discussions of what constitutes a counterpublic, how we have studied them, and why this work is particularly relevant to struggles for social and environmental justice. Subsequently, I elaborate on the utility of participant observation studies for studying the theater of engaged, creative activities that are performed by counterpublics. In doing so, I emphasize the usefulness of performance theory to studies of public sphere activities that include but are not limited to talk.

Finding Counterpublics

Critics of Habermas's *Structural Transformation* have been skeptical about the ideal type of public sphere that he initially described: a singular, overarching public sphere in which all citizens potentially would be able to negotiate decisions of collective concern. In Calhoun's anthology on the public sphere, for example, many scholars argue "for a notion of multiple, sometimes overlapping or contending, public spheres," especially in light of the various contesting social groups initially ignored by Habermas, such as women and social movements.[30] In response, Calhoun claims: "It seems to me a loss simply to say that there are many public spheres . . . . It might be productive rather to think of the public sphere as involving a field of discursive connections . . . a network."[31] This argument (although using different vocabulary) subsequently has found support from most public sphere scholars. Charles Taylor, for example, argues for the utility of the concept of "nested public spheres," Seyla Benhabib for a "plurality of modes of association," and Gerard Hauser for a "reticulate structure."[32] This suggests a general consensus that public sphere scholars need to theorize the complex relations among multiple public spheres more fully.

Some scholars, particularly those invested in feminist politics, have argued that when we theorize relations among publics, we need to pay attention to power relations and to the various types of publics that form in one's society. Felski, for instance, claims that "the experience of discrimination, oppression, and cultural dislocation provides the impetus for the development of a self-consciously oppositional identity," namely a "feminist counter-public sphere."[33] The hegemony of patriarchal policies and practices often motivates feminists to respond collectively in the hope of altering the conditions and practices of gender-based oppression. Similarly influenced by the experiences of women, Fraser draws upon the second wave of the feminist movement to expand on the concept of counterpublics, which she defines as "parallel discursive arenas where members of subordinated social groups invent and circulate counterdiscourses to formulate oppositional interpretations of their identities, interests, and needs."[34] Constitutive of a public's "counter" status, therefore, is the rhetorical invention of a discourse that challenges an already existing discourse that has been enabling the oppression of a particular social group.

Given the popularity and compelling nature of Felski's and Fraser's arguments, recent public sphere scholarship has attempted to clarify and to expand the concept of a counterpublic. Notably, in "Seeking the 'Counter' in Counterpublics," Robert Asen claims:

> Consent versus dissent, public versus counter—fixing these terms as binary oppositions restricts theory and criticism. The movement towards multiplicity in public sphere theory belies such binaries. Theorists and critics would do well to seek out relations among publics, counterpublics, and spheres *as advocates in the "actually existing" public sphere construct these relationships through discursive engagement* (emphasis added).[35]

In other words, Asen suggests that in theorizing relations among publics and counterpublics, we must be careful not to oversimplify the aforementioned power relations. Indeed, many social theorists long have argued that binary oppositions (such as black/white, man/woman) can be limiting. Lisa Cartwright additionally cautions: "The terms counterpublic or countercultures suggest oppositionality, when in fact many alternative publics are forged around the increasingly fragmented special interests that constitute the global market."[36] Thus, when public dialogues reflect a multi-faceted negotiation of power, it is particularly important to recognize the complexity of various public spheres without reducing conflicts to mere binaries.

Furthermore, Asen's argument suggests the importance of considering how discursive engagements constitute relationships among publics and counterpublics. In order to emphasize the importance of both the linguistic (talk) and the non-linguistic (non-verbal gestures, visual images, and so on) in public life, I choose to refer to both as "discourse" in my analysis of NBCAM's and TLC's rhetoric.[37] In what follows, I ask: how might the discourse promoted by NBCAM be perceived as a "counter" perspective to patriarchal discourses? Conversely, if NBCAM fosters an oppressive discourse about breast cancer, how might TLC define its discourse in opposition to that dominance? In order to account for the discursive and non-discursive facets of these discourses, I argue that theories of performance are useful.

Studying Cultural Performances

"Moved to the level of performance," Hauser argues, "rhetoric opens inventional spaces: places where ideas, relationships, emotional bonds, and courses of action can be experienced in novel, sometimes transformative, ways."[38] Performance, in this sense, influences the capacity of rhetoric to become a persuasive practice. It is the activity that constitutes public discourse.

Cultural performances, as characterized by Kirk W. Fuoss, have seven aspects. They are temporally framed, spatially framed, programmed (that is, they follow an order of activities), communal, "heightened occasions" involving display, reflexive and reflective, and scheduled, publicized events.[39] When enacted for rhetorical ends, a dialectical relationship exists between cultural performances and public spheres: publics both produce and are produced by cultural performances.[40] As Dwight Conquergood observes, it is

> through cultural performances [that] many people both construct and participate in 'public' life. Particularly for the poor and marginalized who are denied access to middle-class 'public' forums, cultural performance becomes the venue for 'public discussion' of vital issues central to their communities, as well as an arena for gaining visibility and staging identity.[41]

Analysis of such arenas, Hauser claims, "requires capturing their activity," their performances, to some degree.[42] Thus far, most public sphere studies have involved textual analysis of secondary sources such as newspapers, magazines, congressional transcripts, and websites to capture the arguments and implications of various public spheres. In this essay, however, I hope to demonstrate that participant observation can be used in a way that might complement and/or extend the rich work that has been offered by prior studies of public spheres. Although Michael Warner has argued that a public does not require copresence,[43] this does not preclude the possibility that copresence may be illustrative when studying publics; thus, I believe it is worth considering when and why participant observation of a public might make a difference.

Conquergood has argued that "Nancy Fraser's concept of 'subaltern counterpublics' is very useful" in appreciating the role of cultural performances for counterpublics, yet he also reminds us that

> discourse . . . is not always and exclusively verbal: Issues and attitudes are expressed and contested in dance, music, gesture, food, ritual, artifact, symbolic action, as well as words . . . . [I]nvestigated historically within their political contexts, [cultural performances] . . . are profoundly deliberative occasions.[44]

One motive for public sphere scholars to conduct participant observation, therefore, is the opportunity to witness and record discourses that are left out of traditional written records—the cultural performances that often are altered or excluded when translated into written words.[45] Some studies of non-linguistic facets of cultural performances in public life related to textual analysis exist,[46] but the attentiveness and access to such factors enabled by the use of participant observation and the study of performance theory offer the possibility of additional approaches to this research.

Participant observation also offers an opportunity to study public discourse that is not yet recorded, a situation in which textual analysis is impossible. This is particularly important for those of us invested in counterpublic or subaltern studies. By definition, the discourses of counterpublics (for lack of a better term) are not represented significantly in mainstream culture owing to their marginalized status and/or because the perspectives expressed are what Raymond Williams calls "emergent."[47] A rhetorical model for studying public spheres, Hauser suggests, "reveals rather than conceals the emergence of publics as a process."[48] To capture a sense of the emergent process, participant observation is an attractive alternative because, as Richard Bauman argues, "[u]ltimately, the relative proportion and interplay of authority and creativity, the readymade and the emergent, must be determined empirically, in the close study of performance itself."[49] By conducting participant observation, public sphere scholars may affirm the importance of cultural performances unrecognized by mainstream culture and, in the process of interpretation, offer a record of them.

Performance is relevant to public sphere studies as a critical perspective that informs our ways of knowing and what we desire to know. As Conquergood contends,

> [t]he performance paradigm privileges particular, participatory, dynamic, intimate, precarious, embodied experience grounded in historical process, contingency, and ideology. Another way of saying it is that performance-centered research takes as both its subject matter and method the experiencing body situated in time, place, and history.[50]

Through its attentiveness to bodies, performance theory enables us to account for the role of nonverbal activities in shaping public discourse. Melissa Deem adds that "[b]y allowing for the radical potentialities of the rhetorical, new understandings can be developed of the ways in which the body, affect, and desire disrupt the normative discursive logics of publics."[51]

In order to explore the counterhegemonic potential of counterpublic performance, I now turn to the ways in which NBCAM and TLC have articulated their discourses about breast cancer, with the larger goal of illuminating their relationship to one another.

Breast Cancer Activism

Mary Douglas and Aaron Wildavsky have argued that "more is at stake in the debate on the causes of cancer than mere hypotheses. Whole empires of industry and of government depend on the answers."[52] To enhance appreciation of some of the stakes in this debate, I identify and consider the institutional justifications for establishing NBCAM and TLC, which will permit a more informed assessment of NBCAM and TLC as rhetorical interventions in public life.

NBCAM

October was designated National Breast Cancer Awareness Month (NBCAM) in 1984 by Zeneca, a subsidiary of Imperial Chemical Industries Limited. Zeneca is an international pharmaceutical company that has merged and demerged since 1912 with such chemical corporations as DuPont, Imperial Chemical Industries Limited (ICI), Merck, and Astra.[53] Now called AstraZeneca, it is one of the world's top three pharmaceutical companies.[54] As one journalist characterizes the scope of the company,

> It's a case of have passport, will travel. AstraZeneca is quoted on the UK and Swedish stock exchanges. Its global corporate headquarters are in London. Group R&D [Research and Development] is directed from Sodertajle in Sweden and it has a strong presence in the all-important U.S. market. Plus sales and marketing operations in more than 100 countries; manufacturing facilities in 19 countries and six major research centres.[55]

Global in its reach, it is no surprise to discover that AstraZeneca's profits are in the billions.[56]

AstraZeneca explains its motivation for marketing breast cancer detection on the NBCAM website:

> Prior to their merger with Astra in June 1999, Zeneca, Inc. conducted an in-house breast cancer screening program, beginning in 1989 .... In 1996, the company analyzed the total direct healthcare and lost productivity costs of screening, referrals, and initial management of malignancies.

The total cost of implementing the in-house screening program was $400,000. Without the program, total direct costs would have been almost $1.5 million (if the cancers were discovered at later, more advanced stages). Therefore, the calculated savings with the program were $1.1 million. AstraZeneca has published the Breast Cancer HealthSite Guide to assist other companies—large and small—in developing a workplace screening program.[57]

(Astra)Zeneca's initial justification for NBCAM was one of basic accounting, not a critique of how women's healthcare has been assessed or implemented nor a desire to prevent women from developing breast cancer; instead, it was cost-effective for a company to detect cancer in its employees during the disease's earlier stages. Hence, in NBCAM's message, "early detection is your best protection," the "you" addressed was and continues to be not the broad public of "women," but female employees of self-interested companies. "Your best protection," in other words, could be interpreted as an attempt to constitute a public in response to employers' interest in profit and productivity.

Since its original screening program, AstraZeneca has added that the health of women is also a motivating factor. A 2001 company press release quoted David Brennan, President and Chief Executive Officer, AstraZeneca L.P., U.S., as saying: "The most important advantage of worksite programs is their ability to save lives."[58] Indeed, the medical community generally agrees that early cancer detection in adults over 50 increases a person's chances of survival compared to detection at a later stage.

The sponsor list of NBCAM has grown to include the American Academy of Family Physicians, American Cancer Society, American College of Obstetricians and Gynecologists, American College of Radiology, American Medical Women's Association, American Society of Clinical Oncology, Breast Cancer Resource Committee, Cancer-Care, Inc., Cancer Research Foundation of America, Centers for Disease Control and Prevention, The Susan G. Komen Breast Cancer Foundation, National Alliance of Breast Cancer Organizations, National Cancer Institute, National Medical Association, Oncology Nursing Society, and Y-ME National Breast Cancer Organization.[59] Presumably, the growing sponsor list of NBCAM suggests the popularity of AstraZeneca's stance on breast cancer, a combination of the corporate cost-effectiveness of providing breast cancer screening and the medical fact that early detection increases the chance of a person living with cancer surviving for a longer period of time.

Although neither of these factors directly reflects feminist critiques of patriarchy, one result of NBCAM could be saving women's lives—a goal that unquestionably would be a feminist value. Furthermore, this diverse list of groups suggests that the activities involved in NBCAM offer possibilities for a wider range of purposes and agendas than mammograms. In addition, as NBCAM has grown exponentially, more people than ever before have begun to talk about breast cancer, a feminist accomplishment in itself.

Again, increased awareness motivates more women to be screened for cancer which, in turn, may save lives and helps those with cancer feel less isolated. These positive effects of NBCAM are a good reason for the symbolic pink ribbon of breast cancer awareness to resurface every October in countless venues, from television commercials and award ceremonies of the stars to U.S. postage stamps and lapel pins. In this sense, NBCAM creates and sustains a counterhegemonic discourse in relation to previous silence on the subject. At a minimum it counters indifference, which Briankle G. Chang reminds us is the "enemy of communication."[60]

Besides, every step matters, right? Who cares if "Checks for the Cure" only donates five percent of each purchase to breast cancer research? Or if KitchenAid only donates $50 for each *pink* Stand Mixer sold in the month of October? Or if it costs more money to mail a NBCAM Yoplait yogurt lid to the company than it will donate ($0.10/lid)?

These corporate charity practices are not unique to NBCAM; corporations will not abandon their desire to earn profits. If they are driven by their bottom line, isn't some percentage of the profits, however small, the most for which we can ask? With so many corporations involved, these small steps seem to add up. Although cause-related marketing is "used to consolidate existing markets, capture new ones, and increase corporate profit," as Samantha King argues in her study of breast cancer corporate philanthropy, it may be also "posited, in part, as a response to the consumer's desire for an ethical, meaningful, community-oriented life."[61]

The question remains: why would anyone want to resist NBCAM? Without belittling the life-altering possibilities enabled by early detection, TLC offers an answer that counters the common sense of NBCAM by asking why we have not done more to stop the sources of environmentally-linked cancers, particularly breast cancer. To appreciate more fully the politics which inform such a counterdiscourse, I now turn briefly to the origins of TLC.

TLC

The San Francisco Bay Area of California has the highest rate of breast cancer of any area in a Western country.[62] A predominantly African American community in the Bay Area, Bayview/ Hunter's Point has the highest breast cancer rate in the U.S. for women under 40.[63] Partly in response to these findings, the Toxic Links Coalition (TLC) was founded in the Bay Area in 1994 by representatives of groups such as Breast Cancer Action, Greenpeace, West County Toxics Coalition, and the Women's Cancer Resource Center.[64] TLC describes itself as

> a growing alliance of community groups, women with cancer and cancer survivors, healthcare and environmental justice organizations, silicone survivors, women with endometriosis, and other reproductive disorders, and concerned individuals working together to educate our communities about the links between environmental toxins and the decline in public health.[65]

TLC's primary effort has been to reclaim the breast cancer debate from corporations such as AstraZeneca. In other words, TLC is attempting to recast NBCAM as the prevailing public response to breast cancer and to challenge its dominance by creating a counterdiscourse. According to Greenaction, a member

of TLC, the objection to NBCAM is at least two-fold. First, TLC disapproves of the initial sponsor of NBCAM. AstraZeneca, TLC argues, "profits by first producing many of the toxins implicated in the breast cancer epidemic and then by selling the drugs used to treat the disease."[66] To clarify, in addition to sponsoring NBCAM, AstraZeneca is "the manufacturer of the world's best selling cancer drug (Nolvadex, or tamoxifen citrate, with sales of $470 million per year) . . . and does a $300 million annual business in the carcinogenic herbicide actochlor."[67] At one point, the corporation was the third largest producer of pesticides in the U.S.[68] Thus, AstraZeneca has profited from the entire cancer cycle from cause to detection to treatment.[69] Although the last two activities might appear to have positive implications for women, TLC argues that combining the three warrants a closer examination of AstraZeneca's intentions.

Second, TLC wants to shift public discourse about breast cancer from promoting mammograms to "what might be causing breast cancer"[70] or "to the environmental causes of cancer."[71] In other words, TLC objects to framing cancer discourse in terms of the singular focus of detection and, instead, wants to foreground the question of prevention. For this reason, TLC emphasizes the importance of stopping the production of carcinogenic, toxic chemicals.

To do this, TLC both has renamed and, thus, reframed the month of October as Cancer Industry Awareness Month (instead of NBCAM) in large part by sponsoring annual "Stop Cancer Where It Starts" tours. These are one-hour walking tours protesting the institutions that have contributed to environmentally-caused cancers by producing dangerous chemicals or by covering up hazardous chemical exposures to the public. Since 1994, the size of the tour has ranged from approximately 100 to 400 participants.[72] Although a predominately European American group tends to participate, the speakers represent a range of ethnic backgrounds, including African American and Asian American activists. Both women and men are scheduled as speakers and attend as participants in this cultural performance. DiChiro notes: "The tour is always held on a workday during lunch time for maximum visibility and to accommodate working people willing to relinquish their lunch hour."[73] This time of the day exposes a broad audience to these activities, from the increased foot traffic on the sidewalks to the congested and, therefore, slowed vehicle traffic on the roads.

Evidence that TLC's discourse about environmentally-linked breast cancer has reached a wider audience may be found in the local television news reportage, in newspaper coverage, and in a mural that has traveled around the U.S. as a public art advocacy piece.[74] Additionally, in 2000, TLC "persuaded the cities of San Francisco and Berkeley, as well as the County of Marin, to pass resolutions naming October 'Stop Cancer Where It Starts Month.'"[75]

Articles and TV news clips of TLC's tours, however, include only brief glimpses of its campaign and tactics. To examine the discursive and nondiscursive dimensions of this campaign, I attended the October 3, 2001, tour as a participant-observer, interviewed tour participants, and explored secondary accounts of the tours.[76] Although each tour differs, focusing on one tour offers the opportunity to provide a more detailed and textured account of the activities of TLC than exists, for example, in secondary sources.

Stop Cancer Where It Starts

There were five "stops" on the TLC tour I attended: Pacific Gas and Electric (for running a polluting power plant in Hunter's Point and refusing to clean up the toxins or compensate for residents' health problems at Daly City's Midway Village), Bechtel (for engineering and building nuclear power plants and raising the price of water in San Francisco), Chevron (for operating an oil refinery in Richmond, CA, that pollutes local communities with toxins and for their international environmentally racist practices), the American Cancer Society (for downplaying environmental causes of cancer and not taking a stance on any environmental legislation), and Solem & Associates (for providing public relations services to the aforementioned businesses).[77] Each stop included one to four speakers from the coalition groups and included women and men of varied age, race, ethnicity, class, and health (some had survived cancer and some had not been diagnosed with cancer).

On October 3, 2001, approximately 100 people traveled to what is known as the financial district of downtown San Francisco in order to walk several blocks on this "toxic tour."[78] As the tour moved from business to business, stopping traffic, tour participants walked across streets and redirected countless people who were walking on the sidewalks as part of their everyday routines. The tour created an inventive, spontaneous, persuasive, and risky mobile theater for cultural performance by communicating physically, visually, emotionally, corporeally, and aurally.

Visually, numerous signs on wooden sticks displayed campaign messages: "TOXINS in our world = CANCER in our bodies"; "HEALTH BEFORE CORPORATE WEALTH"; "STOP CANCER WHERE IT STARTS"; "ENVIRONMENTAL JUSTICE NOW." There were signs for each specific site that targeted specific green- and pinkwashing campaigns (for example, "$OLEM & A$$OC.: *LIARS* FOR HIRE"). We walked behind a large banner held by two to four people that displayed the TLC symbol (a hand with the following design in its palm: a circle and slash, symbolizing "no," over a barrel with a skull and crossbones label, spilling liquid) and stated: "TOXIC LINKS COALITION: UNITED FOR HEALTH AND ENVIRONMENTAL JUSTICE."

Tour participants were asked to donate a dollar for a pin that displays the iconic breast cancer awareness pink ribbon unpredictably looping downward into a rope that reflects an upside down, yet symmetrical noose with the words: "fight the CANCER INDUSTRY LINKS COALITION." Choosing to link the popular symbol of the increasingly institutionalized pink ribbon with the insidious image of a noose performs a powerful rhetorical juxtaposition: silky ribbons are transformed into knotted ropes, implying that women are not just dying but are being purposefully killed. This image signifies the wash of a public awareness campaign gone awry. In other words, the symbol articulates the campaign that purports to be doing something about breast cancer, NBCAM, to death,[79] which prompts the question, "Is it true?" Perhaps NBCAM isn't perfect, but is it killing women just as publicly and certainly as a hanging would?

The performative power of eye-catching signs and costumes was constitutive of TLC's attempts critically to interrupt taken-for-granted practices on the days of their tours.[80] Several participants dramatized the tour's message by creatively embodying alternative personae. Two participants, calling themselves the Queen and King of Cancer, wore torn costume ball outfits with crowns (declaring their titles) attached to their wigs. To heighten their deadly looks, they painted their faces white with large black circles around their eyes and dark lipstick. The King's facial "skin" was peeling off his face, contributing to his aura of deterioration. Another participant strutted about on stilts. With a flowing white outfit, she moved high above us, like a haunting ghost. One woman, with the assistance of two others who helped her carry the weight, stepped into a papier-mâché puppet costume, approximately ten feet high and twenty feet wide, of a purple woman with an exposed mastectomy scar on the left side of her chest and two large hands that displayed the TLC symbol's design in their palms. Although these individuals did not speak with words on the tour, their dramatic personae invited spontaneous rhetorical engagements that enacted TLC's message, particularly on the walks between stops.

Employing inventive visual resources is a tactic with a long history in most social movements.[81] Constructing such "image events," as Kevin Michael DeLuca has argued in regard to U.S. environmental and environmental justice movements, is an opportunity to "deconstruct and articulate identities, ideologies, consciousnesses, communities, publics, and cultures in our modern industrial civilization."[82]

In their study of ACT UP, Adrienne Christiansen and Jeremy Hanson argue that the exigencies of AIDS and the constraints of AIDS rhetoric have motivated activists to draw on the comic frame as a response. Appreciating ACT UP's tactical responses within this context, they claim, "should help us better understand and interpret the motives and actions of similarly angry, alienated, and dispossessed groups."[83] This may explain the actions of cancer activists who also face incredible tragedy and who have chosen to respond comically by touring and wearing costumes. Recognizing the role of such creative activities seems vital to assessing the transformative potential of counterpublic discourse.

Just before the tour began, a shiny black sport utility vehicle pulled up to the sidewalk. Some of us had begun to move, attempting to obey the police order to allow people to walk into the PG&E building, when the passenger and driver emerged. Immediately my attention was drawn to the driver, who wore a wide[-]brimmed red hat with a black flower and a matching red dress. I then looked at the passenger. To my surprise, she was placing a gas mask on her face. By this time the driver had walked in front of the police line, unbuttoned her dress, pulled out her right arm, and exposed her mastectomy scar. As the tour crowd cheered, the two began posing for photographs. The police could not stop or detain the woman in red for indecent exposure because although it is illegal to bare a woman's breast in public, she had exposed no breast.

RavenLight, as I later learned was the driver's name, explained to me that she had participated in every previous TLC tour, although she wasn't part of TLC, in order to lend her body to such events. She also noted that she consistently stood a bit apart in order to attract attention and to allow the groups who had planned these events their space "if they weren't comfortable" with her exposed mastectomy scar.[84] Indeed, my observation of how drivers and pedestrians reacted to the tour was that those who caught sight of RavenLight's exposed body typically stared and sometimes quickly looked back once or twice before moving away. Not having time to question them, I cannot know what these observers felt. Disgust? Intrigue? Shock? Admiration? Clearly, however, they found the image of RavenLight, a survivor of breast cancer, difficult to ignore and perhaps even more difficult to forget.[85]

Continuing on the tour, we walked up a steep San Francisco street and RavenLight turned to the side to look for oncoming traffic. A woman who looked to be under 30—perhaps only because she wore pigtails—stepped between RavenLight and me. When she saw RavenLight's chest, she gasped. We stopped. RavenLight glanced back in the woman's direction. The young woman then reached one hand out in the direction of RavenLight's exposed scar as she brought her other hand to her own chest, which was covered with a T-shirt that sank to her touch. Her eyes filled with tears and she said, "Sister—you are so brave." RavenLight smiled, and they hugged. In that moment, all three of us, the woman in red who risked contact, the woman in pigtails who risked reaching out to communicate, and the observer who risked sharing that intimate exchange, felt present.

What is productive about these feelings of presence is that RavenLight evoked strong and sensual reactions from others. Her body's performance of an alternative discourse suggests that if we wish to transform politics, we need to expose our physical, emotional, and political scars. We need to wonder why we feel compelled to look and/or to look away. In terms of TLC's political campaign, we need to consider the costs of our production of toxins. We need to examine the reasons why a breast cannot be present in our body politic until it is absent. By extension, we need to ask, what is the place of women in our body politic? RavenLight's body bespeaks alternative possibilities—about women, cancer, and "progress."[86] My participant observation of this embodied cultural performance offered me the means to engage the way that some activists, borrowing words from DeLuca, "have challenged and changed the meanings of the world not through good reasons but through vulnerable bodies, not through rational arguments but through bodies at risk."[87]

For feminists, raising questions regarding "bodies that matter"[88] often reflects a desire to dispute patriarchal assumptions about sex, gender, and sexuality. Elizabeth Grosz summarizes the relevance of this project in terms of the historical articulation of women to corporeality and men to disembodiment:

> Patriarchal oppression . . . justifies itself, at least in part, by connecting women much more closely than men to the body and, through this identification, restricting women's social and economic roles to (pseudo) biological terms. Relying on essentialism, naturalism, and biologism . . . women are somehow [perceived as] more biological, more corporeal, more natural than men.[89]

Because technical, political, and popular discourses have historically tended to relegate women to bodies in a derogatory sense (as non-intellectual, utilitarian extensions of heterosexual men's desires and reproductive needs), engaging the politics of the body and embodiment enables feminists to challenge a range of oppressive practices (such as thinking that reifies a mind/body split, suppression or denial of female agency, and spatial politics of gendered labor). Resisting such patterns fosters conversations about re-imagining these dynamics, such as exploring the performativity of gender, re-examining holistic approaches to medicine, and challenging spatial boundaries that limit female mobility.

Sharon Crowley claims that contemporary women are indebted to second-wave feminists for delineating just how "the personal is political." Further, she argues, "negatively charged cultural constructions of women's bodies as both dangerous and fragile have forced women to become highly conscious of their bodies—the space they occupy in a room, on the street, in a crowd."[90] In other words, the lived experiences of many women arguably lead to a certain level of self-reflexivity and self-consciousness about corporeality. In the case of RavenLight, her conscious exposure of her scar, in ways both playful and defiant, performs an embodied rhetoric that pushes witnesses to confront what is dangerous to and fragile in the body politic.

In addition to physically, visually, and emotionally performing TLC's message, the tour also turned public spaces into a theater of sound. The speakers used a microphone, enabling their voices to be heard by tour participants and those passing by. Participants blew whistles, clapped, hissed, laughed, shouted, and repeatedly chanted TLC's message, "Stop cancer where it starts." Walking amid the skyscrapers and traffic of downtown San Francisco, those of us on the tour frequently saw people peering down at us from their office windows to see/hear what all the noise was about.

The speakers detailed and elaborated on NBCAM's reactive focus on cancer. In these public performances, the interconnectedness of domination—environmental, gendered, racial, and economic—was articulated as the motivation for TLC's anti-NBCAM campaign. Excerpts from the welcome speech of Barbara Brenner from Breast Cancer Action are illustrative:

I want to tell you why I'm here and why I hope you're here. I'm here because a woman is diagnosed with breast cancer every three minutes in this country. I'm here because thirty years ago a woman's risk of breast cancer was one in twenty—and today it's one in eight. I'm here because this year in the United States alone, 238,000 women will hear the words: 'You have breast cancer.' And I'm here because just continuing to diagnose ever-increasing cases of breast cancer is simply unacceptable. What we need, what we demand, and what we will not rest until we get is true cancer prevention.

Beginning with statistics that affirm the increasingly large number of women who are diagnosed with breast cancer every year, Brenner established the exigence for her and for this tour: a lack of true cancer prevention in the ongoing public dialogue about breast cancer. She also reinforced the goal of the tour: shifting from the discourse of awareness promoted by NBCAM to a discourse of prevention that addresses environmental causes. As she puts it, "we will not rest" until prevention (not awareness) becomes the goal.

Brenner then articulated what TLC believes is necessary to address prevention:

I'm here because it's time, it's way past time for people concerned about cancer to start making connections. Connections between increasing incidents of many kinds of cancer—including my own kind of cancer, breast cancer—and equally scary, childhood cancers and what we as a society do to our air, our water, and our food supplies. Connections between what PG&E does to our poorest communities like Hunter's Point and Midway Village while claiming to look out for our interests in this so-called power crisis. Connections between the pharmaceutical companies that make millions on breast cancer drugs and the message you hear every October that mammograms are the answer to the cancer problem.

Brenner used what has come to be called a feminine style of speaking by referring to her personal experience with breast cancer and by identifying with others' political struggles with childhood cancers, poverty, racial injustice (the references to Hunter's Point and Midway Village), and corporate profits.[91] She reinforced the feminist belief in the fundamental connection between the personal and the political.

In focusing on the theme of connections, Brenner also highlighted the wash of NBCAM's discourse by articulating the inconsistencies between what we are told and the costs of such discourses. The appearance of NBCAM as a relatively popular discourse about breast cancer, her words suggest, may obfuscate the continued environmental degradation that causes breast cancer. This feminist rhetorical tactic of making connections is further evident in the name—the Toxic *Links* Coalition. By articulating experiences of environmental injustice with the profits of public institutions that support NBCAM, Brenner and TLC are able to suggest a critique of the discourse promoted by NBCAM as a strategy of green- and pinkwashing.[92]

Brenner concluded her speech by defining the tour as an act of resistance and issuing a call to action:

The pressure for that type of prevention starts here, in the streets, in front of PG&E and Bechtel and Chevron and the American Cancer Society and Solem & Associates, their PR firm. And we're having a huge impact. A few years ago, Chevron began sponsoring the Race for the Cure. When are we going to see the Race for the Cause? . . . So, take this tour today with hope in your hearts, with the knowledge that you are making a huge difference, and with a commitment to staying involved after it's over. Stop Cancer Where It Starts. Thank you.

Brenner's address characterized the tour as the starting place for pressure, the opportunity to make a huge impact, and a promise to build a growing community with a future commitment to staying involved. She encouraged other people to join her—to invoke a familiar cultural cliché—not just in talking the talk, but in walking the walk. She reiterated that the goal of the tour is not to promote a cure, but to begin stopping the cause. Subsequent speeches on the tour addressed some combination of the general themes Brenner outlined and the specifics prompted by each stop. When the tour participants stood in front of Chevron, for example, Henry Clark from the West County Toxics Coalition reiterated the lack of corporate accountability for causing health complications in his community:

> Although to this very day, Chevron denies any type of responsibility at all for any of the health problems in our community [boos from the crowd], we know that's a lie. They will want to blame people's lifestyles; they want to blame every other reason but those tons and tons of chemical poisons that are being spewed into our community like daily dioxins or methalyne chloride or the 127,000 tons of chemicals that were being spewed from their hazardous waste incinerator there at the Chevron-Arco Chemical Company in our community before we got it shut down and got it dismantled a few years ago. [Audience cheers].

Similar to Brenner's tactic of making connections, Clark linked corporate pollution to public health problems. Despite Chevron's denial of accountability, Clark suggested that his community was not fooled by this "lie." According to Michael R. Riech's study of chemical disasters, the prevalence of corporate denial and community resistance to this response is common: "Private companies use administrative action to avoid or delay litigation, reduce negative publicity, and minimize the company's overall liability."[93] Industry attempts to contain or privatize the conflict, in other words, while communities such as Clark's hope to do just the opposite by expanding or socializing the conflict.

Appropriately, Clark subsequently expanded his local struggle to the global scene:

> Chevron said that they wanted to be a "good neighbor," and we're going to hold them accountable to being a good neighbor; but, being a good neighbor is more than just talk. Being a good neighbor is taking some action and listening to the community's concerns and demands and reducing those chemicals that are being released into our community and investing some of those profits into pollution prevention and compensating people for the health damages and the destruction that has occurred in our community over the years. That would be the test of a real good neighbor. [Audience cheers.] And not only being a good neighbor to us in Richmond—because we're going to hold them accountable—but, to being a good neighbor to our brothers and sisters internationally where Chevron has their operations at—be that in . . . Ecuador or be that in South Africa or wherever it's at. The bottom line, Chevron, is this here: is that you can't give no lip service to us in Richmond—talking about being a good neighbor and you're poisoning and polluting our brothers and sisters in other parts of the world—because this is one struggle, this is one fight, and we're going to hold you accountable wherever you are.

Drawing on the corporate appropriation of the phrase "good neighbor," Clark reappropriated the term by defining what such a role would entail (taking some action). Similarly, at the end of his speech, Clark directly addressed the corporation ("you"), appropriated the corporate term usually reserved for evaluating economic gains ("the bottom line"), and redefined the grounds for assessing the bottom line as accountability. Additionally, his argument, like others presented that day, made connections. It broadened the tour's struggle to the international level insofar as the neighborhood TLC was defending was every neighborhood.

The role of the public relations industry in promoting green- and pinkwashing by enabling corporate denial of accountability for the causes of breast cancer was highlighted at the last tour stop. Standing in front of the public relations firm of Solem & Associates, Judith Brady, one of the founders of TLC and the editor of

One in Three: Women with Cancer Confront an Epidemic,[94] talked about the ways that PR has fostered a corporate-dominated discourse about breast cancer.

> *Brady:* Maybe you're wondering why we're here in front of this innocuous looking office building—
> *Anonymous voice:* Tell us why we're here!!
> *Brady:* We're here in front of the offices of a public relations agency by the name of Solem & Associates—
> *Audience:* Boo!!! Hssssssssss . . .
> *Brady:* So, let me tell you what their job is. Their job is to make sure that you think in such a way that other companies such as Chevron can profit. It's kind of a no-brainer. If people really knew what Chevron did, would they support it?
> *Audience:* No!
> *Brady:* If people really knew how PG&E was ripping us off; would they support it?
> *Audience:* No!
> *Brady:* If people really knew how dangerous nuclear power is, would Bechtel still exist?
> *Audience:* No!
> *Brady:* You know how come they still exist? Because of people like Solem & Associates. This PR agency has among its clients PG&E, Bechtel, and Chevron. One of their favorite gimmicks is to create what we call an astroturf organization. They create phony grassroots groups, and it is through those phony groups that they give their live voice to the public. They've done it many times . . . . In terms of PG&E, these folks here, Solem & Associates, have a very unsavory history. In 1994, they created a phony group called "Citizens for Economic Security" in Alameda, across the Bay, when Alameda was trying to municipalize its own gas lines. Watch for it. You can bet they will do it here. And they also have knee-jerk names with words like "freedom" and "security" and stuff like that. You can imagine we're going to find groups like "San Franciscans for Utility Freedom" or "Californians for Dependable Power" or "Citizens for Free Enterprise"—something like that. And through that, through those groups, they will tell their lies.

The theme of deception ran throughout Brady's interactive speech. Environmentalists such as Brady have taken to calling PR front groups "astroturf" (versus grassroots groups) to symbolize their lack of public support or roots. As Brady's speech points out, greenwashing strategies provide "the appearance of public support and citizen advocacy" while making no attempt to engage people in dialogue that will foster just change.[95]

Although the tour is the primary cultural performance through which TLC attempts to influence public debate, observers and participants were handed fliers containing information about how to become more involved with each group in the coalition. In addition, each speaker reinforced the need for participants and observers to do more after the tour. Accordingly, the tour was a cultural performance whose implicit rhetorical structures, as Richard Schechner has explained, lead to overt social dramas, which lead to implicit social processes, which lead to manifest stage performances, which lead back to implicit rhetorical structures, and so on.[96] As Victor Turner has argued, this circular pattern between the overt and the implicit, the social and the stage, helps us to appreciate that any cultural performance is part of a larger context.[97] These fluid, dynamic activities that constitute public life are what open inventional spaces to create new discourses and, therefore, alter relationships among publics and counterpublics.

Conclusion

Breast cancer is an epidemic that currently risks the lives of too many women. NBCAM brings this situation to public attention each year. Although NBCAM initially may have been inspired by profits, it has exceeded (Astra) Zeneca's original intentions. NBCAM has raised public awareness of breast cancer. It is no small accomplishment to find Americans talking about cancer and breasts in public forums without facing silence or snickering. These cultural shifts in public opinion and public discourse can be attributed, at least in part, to NBCAM. Therefore, NBCAM cannot be reduced to "the dominant public discourse" because it has fostered a public dialogue that runs counter to the hegemonic frame that marginalizes the significance of breast cancer. As Dow and Tonn explain, a feminist or counterpublic may be identified on the basis of its twofold potential for critique and for empowerment.[98] NBCAM has met these criteria by criticizing previous silences and inactions about breast cancer and by empowering women by offering them a means to resist prevailing attitudes. Both NBCAM's and TLC's claims to further the breast cancer movement, therefore, arguably have been legitimate, albeit with different goals and activities.

Yet identifying the counterhegemonic potential of NBCAM as a part of the breast cancer movement does not preclude the possibility of reading TLC's tour as a counterpublic response to NBCAM. As Robert Asen and Daniel Brouwer argue, "exclusion from prominent channels of political discourse and a corresponding lack of political power . . . is neither fixed nor total."[99] Like most social movements, breast cancer activism consists of multiple critiques and actions. Reducing public spheres and counterpublics to facile binaries, as stated earlier, often essentializes and/or is inaccurate and, hence, unproductive. Additional study of subaltern or emerging counterpublics would benefit from highlighting the ways in which power is articulated and rearticulated in specific contexts.

Further, this analysis of NBCAM and the TLC tour suggests that conflating a social movement with a single public, counter or otherwise, oversimplifies, at least in some instances. Some social movements, especially broadly based movements such as environmentalism or feminism, are made up of varied groups and forms of activism that reflect multiple identities, concerns, and opinions. That variety should be an integral part of assumptions underlying future studies of publics and how they are related to social movements as distinct, yet linked cultural formations.

My fieldwork with TLC suggests that using participant observation techniques enables rhetorical critics to explore the messy complexities of public life and the power negotiations involving emergent discourses and counterpublics. As a critical tool, participant observation compels critics to travel to public spaces to feel, to observe, and to participate in cultural performances firsthand. It also helps critics to consider the rhetorical force of counterpublics and of cultural performances, and to consider that the ways in which we interact with and engage specific publics can influence our judgments. It reminds us that publics are not phenomena that exist "out there," involving other people and affecting bodies other than our own.

More than a visual or psychological argument, TLC's tour created an affective and embodied theater for rhetorical engagement. In my account of these interactions, I have attempted to illustrate the ways that TLC's toxic tour performed reversed hegemonic attitudes about breast cancer. Instead of asking why anyone would want to resist NBCAM, TLC asks why anyone would not. Instead of romanticizing detection, TLC reminds us of how horrifying the moment is when someone hears those three words, "You have cancer." Instead of focusing on what cannot be changed, such as heredity, TLC asks, what can we change?

TLC's campaign is based on resistance to NBCAM insofar as its prevalence has limited public deliberation through focusing on breast cancer detection).[100] By linking toxins and cancer, health and wealth, environmental justice and feminism, TLC has offered a potentially persuasive counterdiscourse to NBCAM's response to the U.S. breast cancer epidemic. Prior to my exposure to TLC's campaign, I did not question National Breast Cancer Awareness Month, and I suspect that I am not alone. TLC's cultural performances prompt those exposed to consider more carefully the causes of breast cancer and to ask what else a month dedicated to fighting breast cancer could become.

Notes

1 Sandra Steingraber, *Living Downstream: A Scientist's Personal Investigation of Cancer and the Environment* (NY: Random House, 1997), 47.

2 American Cancer Society, *Cancer Facts and Figures 2001* (NY: American Cancer Society, Inc., 2001), 11. In comparison, approximately 1,500 new breast cancer cases were estimated to be diagnosed in men in 2001, and it is estimated that 553,400 people in the U.S. would die from cancer and 1,268,000 new cancer cases would be discovered in 2001 alone (10, 7, 6). Proctor approximates that for every U.S. citizen alive, "one in three will contract the disease and one in five will die from it." Robert N. Proctor, *Cancer Wars: How Politics*

Shape What We Know and Don't Know About Cancer (NY: Basic Books, 1995), 1.

3 Y-ME National Breast Cancer Organization, 2001, available from http://www.y-me.org/cancerInfo/cancerInfo.html.

4 Klawiter, "Racing for the Cure, Walking Women, and Toxic Touring: Mapping Cultures of Action Within the Bay Area Terrain of Breast Cancer," *Social Problems* 461 (1999): 104.

5 Not surprisingly, some still claim that "studies have never shown a clear association between environmental toxins and elevated rates of the disease." See Barron H. Lerner, *The Breast Cancer Wars: Hope, Fear, and the Pursuit of a Cure in Twentieth-Century America* (Oxford: Oxford University Press, 2001), 267. Another disturbing trend, according to Yadlon, has been to attribute the cause of cancer to women who have not "made the 'proper' dietary and reproductive choices," that is, who have not been "skinny women and good mothers." Susan Yadlon, "Skinny Women and Good Mothers: The Rhetoric of Risk, Control, and Culpability in the Production of Knowledge About Breast Cancer," *Feminist Studies* 23 (1997): 645–6.

6 Some rhetoricians have written about the problematic assumptions made in studies of hereditary breast cancer[.] See, for example, Celeste Michelle Condit, Deirdre Moira Condit, and Paul J. Achter, "Human Equality, Affirmative Action, and Genetic Models of Human Variation," *Rhetoric and Public Affairs* 4 (2001): 92–4.

7 Steingraber, "The Social Production of Cancer: A Walk Upstream," in *Reclaiming the Environmental Debate: The Politics of Health in a Toxic Culture,* ed. Richard Hofrichter (Cambridge, MA: MIT Press, 2000), 31.

8 Steingraber, "The Social Production of Cancer," 31.

9 By most estimates, the environmental movement is considered a success. See, for example, Riley E. Dunlap and Angela G. Mertig, *American Environmentalism: The U.S. Environmental Movement, 1970–1990* (New York: Taylor & Francis, 1992); Joe Miller, "Earth Day at 30: Greener, Cleaner and Growing," *The News and Observer,* Raleigh, North Carolina, 21 April 2000, p. E1; Jonathan Rauch, "There's Smog in the Air, But It Isn't All Pollution," *The Washington Post,* 30 April 2000, p. B01.

10 See Glen Martin, "Earth Day Report Card—We Still Care, Sort Of," *The San Francisco Chronicle,* 22 April 2000, p. A1; L. J. Shrum, John A. McCarty, and Tina M. Lowrey, "Buyer Characteristics of the Green Consumer and Their Implications for Advertising Strategy," *Journal of Advertising* 24 (September 1995): 71.

11 Richard N. L. Andrews, *Managing the Environment, Managing Ourselves: A History of American Environmental Policy* (New Haven, CT: Yale University Press, 1999).

12 Marcy Darnovsky, "Green Living in a Toxic World: The Pitfalls and Promises of Everyday Environmentalism," in *Reclaiming the Environmental Debate: The Politics of Health in a Toxic Culture,* ed. Richard Hofrichter (Cambridge, MA: MIT Press, 2000), 219.

13 For evidence of its increasing popularity, see the special issue on green advertising in the *Journal of Advertising* (24 September 1995): 21–31.

14 Although I had not seen the term "pinkwashing" before, many feminists have criticized the ways in which corporate appropriations of feminist symbols, slogans, and discourses broaden the gap between talking about women and improving the lives of women. See, for example, Yadlon, 1997; Karen Fitts, "The Pathology and Erotics of Breast Cancer," *Discourse* 21 (1999): 3–20; Audre Lorde, *The Cancer Journals: Special Edition* (San Francisco, CA: Aunt Lute Books, 1997). Mark Dowie offers a brief but particularly poignant example of the appropriation of "female emancipation" for PR purposes. See John Stauber and Sheldon Rampton, *Toxic Sludge is Good for You!: Lies, Damn Lies and the Public Relations Industry* (Monroe, ME: Common Courage Press, 1995), 1.

15 Fitts, 4.

16 Fitts, 9. This trend to contemplate breasts more than cancer in breast cancer discourses often lends itself to the sexualization of the disease. In an article pointed out to me by John Delicath, Lurie notes: "The cover of the February 8, 2002 issue of *Time* magazine features a naked, airbrushed, very thin woman with blond hair, shown from the waist up, standing sideways, covering her breasts with one arm while the other is awkwardly bent upward. She is staring off into space with a completely disengaged expression, like a mannequin, or a blow-up doll." She concludes, "One can't help but wonder if breast cancer gets so much coverage because of the first word in the disease, not the second." Karen Lurie, February 27, 2002, "Making cancer sexy," available from http://www.alternet.org.

17 Some may be inclined to label a study of environmental and feminist arguments and practices a study of "ecofeminism," but TLC does not use this label.

18 By hegemonic "common sense," I refer to Antonio Gramsci, who defines it as historically constructed yet taken-for-granted societal beliefs. See *Selections from the Prison Notebooks,* trans. and ed. Quintin

Hoare and Geoffrey Nowell Smith (New York: International Publishers, 1997/1971), 323–42.

19 Bradley Angel, "Stop Cancer Where It Starts" tour speech, taped by author, San Francisco, CA, 3 October 2001.

20 Rita Felski, *Beyond Feminist Aesthetics: Feminist Literature and Social Change* (Cambridge, MA: Harvard University Press, 1989); Nancy Fraser, "Rethinking the Public Sphere: A Contribution to the Critique of Actually Existing Democracy," in *Habermas and the Public Sphere,* ed. Craig Calhoun (Cambridge, MA: MIT Press, 1992), 109–42.

21 See Gerard A. Hauser, *Vernacular Voices: The Rhetoric of Publics and Public Spheres* (Columbia: University of South Carolina Press, 1999); Robert Asen, "Seeking the 'Counter' in Counterpublics," *Communication Theory* 10 (2000): 424–46; Robert Asen and Daniel C. Brouwer [eds.], *Counterpublics and the State* (New York: State University of New York Press, 2001).

22 I borrow this phrase from Asen.

23 Bonnie J. Dow and Mari Boor Tonn, "'Feminine Style' and Political Judgment in the Rhetoric of Ann Richards," *Quarterly Journal of Speech* 79 (1993): 300.

24 Jürgen Habermas, *The Structural Transformation of the Public Sphere: An Inquiry into a Category of Bourgeois Society,* trans. Thomas Burger (Cambridge, MA: MIT Press, 1962/1989).

25 G. Thomas Goodnight and David B. Hingstman, "Studies in the Public Sphere," *Quarterly Journal of Speech* 83 (1997): 351–99.

26 Habermas, 27.

27 Craig Calhoun, *Habermas and the Public Sphere* (Cambridge, MA: MIT Press, 1992), 6.

28 Fraser, 2.

29 Hauser, 32.

30 Calhoun, 37.

31 Calhoun, 37.

32 Hauser, *Vernacular Voices;* Seyla Benhabib, "Toward a Deliberative Model of Democratic Legitimacy," in *Democracy and Difference: Contesting the Boundaries of the Political,* ed. Seyla Benhabib (Princeton, NJ: Princeton University Press, 1996), 67–94; Charles Taylor, *Philosophical Arguments* (Cambridge, MA: Harvard University Press, 1995).

33 Felski, 167.

34 Fraser, 123.

35 Asen, 444–5.

36 Lisa Cartwright, "Community and the Public Body in Breast Cancer Media Activism," *Cultural Studies* 12 (1998): 121.

37 I use the term "discourse" in this paper; I am referring to what Ernesto Laclau and Chantal Mouffe have defined as "the entire material density of the multifarious institutions, rituals and practices through which a discursive formation is structured." In *Hegemony and Socialist Strategy: Towards a Radical Democratic Politics* (London: Verso, 1985), 109.

38 Hauser, 33.

39 Kirk T. Fuoss, *Striking Performances/Performing Strikes* (Jackson, MS: University Press of Mississippi, 1997), 173–4.

40 This argument parallels Kirk T. Fuoss's claim regarding the relationship between cultural performances and community. See "'Community' Contested, Imagined, and Performed: Cultural Performances, Contestation, and Community in an Organized-Labor Social Drama," *Text and Performance Quarterly* 15 (1995): 79–98.

41 Dwight Conquergood, "Rethinking Ethnography: Towards a Critical Cultural Politics," *Communication Monographs* 58 (1991): 189.

42 Hauser, 33.

43 Michael Warner, "Publics and Counterpublics (abbreviated version)," *Quarterly Journal of Speech* 88 (2002): 415.

44 Conquergood, 189.

45 Conquergood's argument refers to ethnography; however, it may be applied to participant observation. Although Conquergood suggested the usefulness of an ethnographic approach to rhetorical studies of cultural performances a decade ago, to my knowledge, public sphere studies have not responded. By developing a case for the usefulness of participant observation, this essay hopes to encourage all forms of participant observation, including ethnography. See Dwight Conquergood, "Rethinking Ethnography," and "Ethnography, Rhetoric, and Performance," *Quarterly Journal of Speech* 78 (1992): 80–97.

46 See, for example, Adrienne E. Christiansen and Jeremy J. Hanson, "Comedy as Cure for Tragedy: ACT UP and the Rhetoric of AIDS," *Quarterly Journal of Speech* 82 (1996): 157–70; Kevin Michael DeLuca, *Image Politics: The New Rhetoric of Environmental Activism* (New York: Guilford Press, 1999); Karen Foss and Kathy L. Domenici, "Haunting Argentina: Synecdoche in the Protests of the Mothers of Plaza de Mayo," *Quarterly Journal of Speech* 87 (2001): 237–58.

47 I thank Steve Schwarze for suggesting this theoretical link and Ted Striphas for locating the sources. See Raymond Williams, "Base and Superstructure in Marxist Cultural Theory," *New Left Review* 82 (1973): 3–16; Raymond Williams, *Marxism and Literature* (Oxford: Oxford University Press, 1977).

48 Hauser, 49.

[49] Richard Bauman, "Performance," in *Folklore, Cultural Performances, and Popular Entertainments: A Communications-Centered Handbook,* ed. Richard Bauman (New York: Oxford University Press, 1992), 42–3.

[50] Conquergood, "Rethinking Ethnography," 187.

[51] Melissa Deem, "Stranger Sociability, Public Hope and the Limits of Political Transformation," *Quarterly Journal of Speech* 88 (2002): 448.

[52] Mary Douglas and Aaron Wildavsky, *Risk and Culture: An Essay on the Selection of Technological and Environmental Dangers* (Berkeley: University of California Press, 1982), 58.

[53] AstraZeneca (2001), "AstraZeneca U.S. History," available from http://www.astrazeneca-us.com/about/history.asp.

[54] "Corporate Profile: The Arranged Marriage," *The [UK] Independent,* 24 February 1999, p. 5; N. Pandya, "Jobs & Money: Jobs: Company Vitae: AstraZeneca which this week held its AGM and posted first quarter profits of £694m—up 12%," *The [UK] Guardian,* 28 April 2001, p. 23.

[55] Pandya, 23.

[56] Pandya, 23.

[57] Breast Cancer Awareness Month (2001), "Help Promote NBCAM," available from http://www.nbcam.org/promote_healthsite.cfm.

[58] AstraZeneca (2001), "New Survey Finds Few Employers Provide On-Site Breast Cancer Screening," available from http://www.astrazeneca-us.com/news/article.asp?file=2001102701.htm.

[59] National Breast Cancer Awareness Month (2001), "NBCAM Board of Sponsors," available from http://www.nbcam.org/board.cfm.

[60] Briankle G. Chang, *Deconstructing Communication: Representation, Subject and Economics of Exchange* (Minneapolis, MN: MN Press, 1996), 56. I first read this poignant statement in Ronald Walter Greene's "Rhetorical Pedagogy as a Postal System: Circulating Subjects through Michael Warner's 'Publics and Counterpublics,'" *Quarterly Journal of Speech* 88 (2002): 434–43.

[61] Samantha King, "An All-Consuming Cause: Breast Cancer, Corporate Philanthropy, and the Market for Generosity," *Social Text* 194 (2001): 115–43.

[62] Zillah R. Eisenstein, *Manmade Breast Cancers* (Ithaca, NY: Cornell University Press, 2001), 96.

[63] K. Nyasha, "For Women Under 40, Hunters Point Breast Cancer Rate Highest in U.S.," *Bayview Newspaper,* 28 September 2001, available from http://www.greenaction.org/hunterspoint/press/sfbayview09281.shtml. "A report from the city's Department of Public Health said that between 1988 and 1992, 60 black women in Bayview–Hunters Point ['San Francisco's forgotten southeast corner'] were found to have breast cancer—and 41 percent of them were under age 50. In the rest of San Francisco, only 22 percent would be expected to fall in that age group. The study also found elevated rates of cervical cancer but lower-than-expected rates of prostate cancer and non-Hodgkin's lymphoma among black men." In C. Johnson, "Disputed S.F. Power Plant Expected to Get 1st OK Neighbors Worry About Health Issues," *The San Francisco Chronicle,* 4 March 1996, p. A13. "Bayview–Hunters Point has two Superfund sites, areas in which federal funds pay for toxic cleanups, and more than 100 other identified toxic waste spots . . . . [A] task force found that all six schools in Bayview–Hunters Point had asthma rates that averaged between 15 and 20 percent. That's the highest rate in the city, and four times higher than the state average." In J. B. Johnson, "Bayview Holding Breath on Plants; If Bid is Best, S.F. Would Buy and Shutter 2 PG&E Stations," *The San Francisco Chronicle,* 8 June 1998, p. A15.

[64] For more information about the beginnings of the coalition, see Klawiter.

[65] Toxics Links Coalition (2001), "Toxic Links Coalition Home Page," available from http://homeflash.net/~dlscism/toxiclinks/home_text.html.

[66] Toxic Links Coalition, 1.

[67] Proctor, 255, 266.

[68] Judith Brady, 10 November 1999, "Cancer Industry Tour," available from http://www.sfbg.com/News/34/06/6other.html.

[69] Similarly, "GE and DuPont, rivals for the leads in Superfund toxic sites, sell more than $100 million worth of mammography machines every year (GE) and much of the film used in those machines (DuPont)." Proctor, 257.

[70] Greenaction (2001), "Action Alert: Stop Cancer Where It Starts!" available from http://www.greenaction.org/cancer/pr100301.shtml.

[71] Toxic Links Coalition, videotape from "Stop Cancer Industry" tour, San Francisco, CA, 1997. The author thanks Judith Brady for lending her sole copy for the author's research.

[72] Until 2001, according to TLC activists I interviewed, the number attending steadily grew. In 2001, the numbers were slightly smaller. Although the cause was uncertain, many assumed the drop in attendance was occasioned by the events of 9/11.

[73] Giovann DiChiro, "Bearing Witness or Taking Action?: Toxic Tourism and Environmental

Justice," in *Reclaiming the Environmental Debate: The Politics of Health in a Toxic Culture,* ed. Richard Hofrichter (Cambridge, MA: MIT Press, 2000), 281.

74 See S. Rubenstein, "S.F. Rally Against High Cancer Rates in Bayview–Hunters Point," *The San Francisco Chronicle,* 22 September 1995, p. A21; Syracuse Cultural Peace Workers, *Peace Calendar* (Syracuse, NY: Syracuse Cultural Workers, 2002); *Who Holds the Mirror?: The Mural, Oral Histories, and Pedagogy of The Breast Cancer Oral History Action Project* (Berkeley: BCOHAP, 1998); Mary Ann Swissler, "Touring the Breast-Cancer Industry," *Progressive* 61 (December 1997), 14.

75 Toxic Links Coalition (2001), pamphlet.

76 After I participated in a tour, I provided TLC with a videotape. I subsequently discovered that TLC had a tape of a previous tour, which was incomplete.

77 The American Cancer Society was not a planned stop, but "it was on the way," and one activist was prepared to address it.

78 TLC annually obtains a permit from local police to demonstrate in public.

79 By "articulation," I refer to what Stuart Hall defines as "the form of the connection that can make a unity of two different elements, under certain conditions . . . . a linkage which is not necessary, determined, absolute, and essential for all time." Lawrence Grossberg, "On Postmodernism and Articulation: An Interview with Stuart Hall," in *Stuart Hall: Critical Dialogues in Cultural Studies,* ed. David Morley and Kuang-Hsing Chen (New York: Routledge, 1996), 141. Ernesto Laclau and Chantal Mouffe (1985) note that when articulations occur, the elements themselves are modified as a result; *Hegemony and Socialist Strategy: Towards a Radical Democratic Politics,* 2nd ed. (London: Verso, 2001), 105.

80 This language is borrowed from Thomas B. Farrell's claim that "rhetoric, despite its traditional and quite justifiable association with the preservation of cultural truisms, may also perform an act of *critical interruption* where taken-for-granted practices of a culture are concerned" (emphasis added). In *Norms of Rhetorical Culture* (New Haven: Yale University Press, 1993), 258. See also Phaedra C. Pezzullo, "Performing Critical Interruptions: Rhetorical Invention and Narratives of the Environmental Justice Movement," *Western Journal of Communication* 64 (2001): 1–25.

81 Kevin Michael DeLuca, "Unruly Arguments: The Body Rhetoric of Earth First!, ACT UP, and Queer Nation," *Argumentation and Advocacy* 36 (1999): 9–21. Recall that Depression-era labor strikers used mock performances; see Fuoss, 1997. Also recall that early preservationists and conservationists drew on images and political theater; see Roderick Nash, *Wilderness and the American Mind,* 3rd ed. (New Haven: Yale University Press, 1967/1982).

82 DeLuca, 17.

83 Christiansen and Hanson, 16.

84 RavenLight, interview by author, San Francisco, CA, 3 October 2001.

85 The politics of displaying mastectomy scars is beyond the scope of this project. For a feminist analysis of the cultural politics of such displays, see Lurie, Fitts, and Cartwright.

86 In explaining her choice of tactics, RavenLight states: "Wouldn't you think that if one in eight people had one arm or one leg, we'd ask what's going on? I'm too angry to die. I bare my de-breast in a fierce political stance. Breast cancer has been hidden under heavy layers of shame, guilt, and puffs of cotton stuffed inside empty bras for too many decades. I choose to use my body to put a face on this hideous disease." *Who Holds the Mirror?* 14–15.

87 "Unruly Arguments," 11.

88 This phrase is borrowed from Judith Butler's book, *Bodies that Matter: On the Discursive Limits of "Sex"* (London: Routledge, 1993).

89 Elizabeth Grosz, *Volatile Bodies: Toward a Corporeal Feminism* (Bloomington: Indiana University Press, 1994), 14.

90 Sharon Crowley, "Afterword: The Material of Rhetoric," in *Rhetorical Bodies,* ed. Jack Selzer and Sharon Crowley (Madison: University of Wisconsin Press, 1999), 358.

91 In her work on "feminine style," Karlyn Kohrs Campbell has suggested that women's historical experiences led to a tendency to display certain characteristics when speaking, such as using personal tone and experiences[.] Given Campbell's non-essentialist appreciation for the historical roots of this pattern, it is important to recognize that this mode of engagement is not determined by biology. See *Man Cannot Speak For Her: A Critical Study of Early Feminist Rhetoric* (New York: Greenwood Press, 1989).

92 TLC's rhetoric reflects contemporary theoretical discussions of "articulation," which Stuart Hall defines as "to utter, to speak forth, to be articulate" and "the form of the connection that can make a unity of two different elements, under certain conditions . . . . a linkage which is not necessary,

determined, absolute, and essential for all time." In Grossberg, 141. Laclau and Mouffe, 105, also note that when this articulation occurs, the elements themselves are modified as a result.

93 Michael R. Reich, *Toxic Politics: Responding to Chemical Disasters* (Ithaca, NY: Cornell University Press, 1991), 186 and passim.

94 Judy Brady, *1 in 3: Women with Cancer Confront an Epidemic* (Pittsburgh, PA: Cleis Press, 1991).

95 Stauber and Rampton, 82.

96 Richard Schechner, *Performance Theory* (London: Routledge, 1988).

97 Victor Turner, *From Ritual to Theatre: The Human Seriousness of Play* (New York: Performing Arts Journal Press, 1982).

98 Dow and Tonn.

99 Asen and Brouwer, 2001, 2–3.

100 For a discussion of the "antecedent rhetorical conditions" of public spheres, see Gerard Hauser, "Prisoners of Conscience and the Counterpublic Sphere of Prison Writing: The Stones that Start the Avalanche," in *Counterpublics and the State,* ed. Robert Asen and Daniel C. Brouwer (Albany, NY: State University of New York Press, 2001), 36.

Trashing the System:
Social Movement, Intersectional Rhetoric, and Collective Agency in the Young Lords Organization's Garbage Offensive
Darrel Enck-Wanzer

The colonized man [sic] who writes for his people ought to use the past with the intention of opening the future, as an invitation to action and a basis for hope.[1]

[W]e need to develop critical theories of Latino politics. Arguably, the main task for such a theoretical practice should be to devise, from within the movements and/or in collaboration with them, an analysis of the achievements, virtues, potentials, and limits of Latino politic while producing (in theory and practice) Latino radical political discourses.[2]

The setting is New York City in 1969; more specifically, the setting is East Harlem (also known as Spanish Harlem or El Barrio), a predominantly Puerto Rican section of New York City. Economic conditions are lean: jobs are hard to come by (especially if you do not speak English) and those jobs you can find involve hard physical labor and little pay. For those fortunate enough to find work, more than one job is often needed to support a family. The benefits of "Great Society" social programs that aimed to improve the economic conditions are lost in the messy bureaucratic web spun by the state in conjunction with local Puerto Rican–run professional organizations.[3] Politically, the community is disparaged as "docile," and the role of political activism is monopolized by professionals, "experts," and elites.[4] By most accounts, life for the working class Puerto Rican in El Barrio leaves much to be desired.[5] It is within this context that the Young Lords Organization

(hereafter YLO) emerged and sought change. The first order of business for the Lords was to devise a way to get word out to the people of El Barrio that they had formed and were seeking radical transformations in the immediate community and beyond. After a combination of careful deliberation, community investigation, and pure happenstance, the nascent YLO launched their first political offensive to advance social movement: the "garbage offensive."

The garbage offensive emerged in late June/early July 1969, when El Barrio was dirty and the city sanitation department was ignoring the needs of the neighborhood. To address the problem, the YLO (a small group at this time, composed of a handful of members) began quite simply by arriving every Sunday to clean up the garbage. On July 27, one day after officially becoming the New York chapter of the Young Lords Organization, and two weeks after starting to clean the streets, the first point of social discord surfaced when some members attempted unsuccessfully to procure new supplies (brooms, cans, etc.) from the local sanitation department. It was at this point that the YLO came face to face with the bureaucracy of the liberal capitalist system and subsequently advanced a revolt in El Barrio. The YLO, together with a variety of community members who had been helping them pick up garbage, took heaped trash collections and placed them in several busy intersections, blocking significantly the traffic coming into and going out of Manhattan. The tactical placement of garbage peaked on August 17 when hundreds of Barrio Boricuas expanded their rebellion to include overturning cars, lighting fire to the trash, and assaulting police property.[6] The Sunday garbage offensives continued until September 2, with Lords and other community members engaged actively in dissent. YLO Minister of Information, Pablo "Yorúba" Guzmán, recounts, "We would hit and run, block to block, talking and spreading politics as we went, dodging the slow-moving pigs sent to crush any beginning Boricua movement for freedom. The garbage offensive united us through struggle."[7]

In examining the burgeoning rhetoric of the YLO's garbage offensive, I argue that the long-standing constraint on agency to which they were responding—the exigence creating a need to be "united . . . through struggle"—demanded an inventive rhetoric that was decolonizing both in its aim and in its form. In terms of aim or function, the YLO asserted a form of independence; they demanded, through their words and actions, freedom from an oppressive "system" that had subjugated Puerto Ricans for half of a millennium.[8] With regard to form, the YLO declined the opportunity to mimic the form of the oppressor's rhetoric and reforms (e.g., leader-centered rhetorics, public speeches, or legal changes). The YLO, to the contrary, engaged in an *intersectional rhetoric* that refused to privilege or be disciplined by single rhetorical forms (e.g., verbal, visual, or embodied forms). If, as John Louis Lucaites has argued, "every rhetorical performance enacts and contains a theory of its own agency—of its own possibilities—as it structures and enacts relationships between speaker and audience, self and other, action and structure," then the *form* of the YLO's rhetoric is

a critical component for addressing this broader problematic of agency.[9] By encouraging diverse discursive forms to intersect to produce a movement rhetoric qualitatively different from others at the time, the YLO constructed a collective agency challenging the status quo and, in some ways, foreshadowed more contemporary movement discourses.[10] Examining the YLO's garbage offensive, then, presents rhetorical scholars with an opportunity to revise our collective and growing understanding of how marginalized groups craft power through rhetoric.

As an interrogation of how one radical political organization sought to define a new social imaginary and delineate a space for social movement, this essay hopes to contribute to ongoing disciplinary dialogues about social movement tactics and rhetoric. Early rhetorical scholarship focused on social movement identifies importantly the ways in which rhetorical agents go beyond speech to accomplish their persuasive goals. Leland M. Griffin's 1964 essay on the emerging "New Left" movement, for example, notes how "body rhetoric" (bodies used as symbolic modes of influence) instigates new modes of appeal, thus altering the trajectory of verbal arguments.[11] Similarly, James R. Andrews's study of "coercive rhetoric" at Columbia University notes that the *actions* of protestors, while "non-persuasive" (i.e., not symbols intended to influence), point to a need to examine "the means of protest" in order to better understand the rhetoric of social dissent.[12] And Herbert W. Simons expands our conceptualization of body rhetoric by suggesting that it is "designed to dramatize issues, enlist additional sympathizers, and delegitimize the established order."[13] While what these scholars and others studying diverse forms of dissent say is agreeable, they do not explicate fully the rhetorical effectivity of body rhetoric in conjunction with other rhetorical forms—especially in the context of a need to constitute new forms of agency in the face of lived colonial oppression. As an addition to the disciplinary social movement dialogue, this essay asks: How can a movement articulate a sense of agency through a rhetoric that employs bodies, images, and speech in ways that do not privilege one over the others? Answering this question may prompt rhetorical scholars interested in social movement to question dominant assumptions about agency and its relationship to rhetorical form.

Using the YLO's garbage offensive as a focal point, this essay demonstrates the need to explore more fully the relationship between agency and rhetorical form by illustrating the ways in which the YLO defines a space for social movement in El Barrio through a formally *intersectional rhetoric*. What is meant by "intersectional rhetoric," here, is a rhetoric that places multiple rhetorical forms (in this case, speech, embodiment, and image) on relatively equal footing, is not leader-centered, and draws from a number of diverse discursive political or rhetorical conventions. The garbage offensive is interpreted here as an attempt by the YLO to lay bare the internal inconsistencies of "the system" and establish an anti-colonial sense of agency for the people of El Barrio partially through use of the popular Puerto Rican tradition of *jaibería,* which is a form of subversive complicity.

This essay develops over three sections. The first section offers a critical review of social movement scholarship in rhetorical studies paying particular attention to (a) the ways in which that scholarship incorporates attentiveness to non-verbal rhetorical forms, (b) the importance of developing further such an attentiveness, and (c) the relevance of eliding the metaphor of the "text" in order to examine intersecting rhetorical forms and the resulting implications for anti-colonial agencies. The second section examines the garbage offensive as an example of intersectional rhetoric that provided an alternative to (at the time) dominant activist discourses that privileged single rhetorical forms (often speech or writing) produced by charismatic leaders. The final section offers an extended conclusion that expands on the relevance of intersectional rhetoric as a heuristic for the critique of social movement discourse that emerges organically from an organization attempting to constitute a space for collective agency beyond the dominant colonial imaginary.

SOCIAL MOVEMENTS, OLD AND NEW

The rhetorical study of social movements has a long and rich history in our field, of which others offer more comprehensive reviews than space

allows in this forum.[14] Agreeing, by and large, with Michael Calvin McGee and Kevin DeLuca, it is assumed here that the rhetorical significance of a "movement" lies not in the discourse that comes out of a specific *group;* as McGee suggests, that is to put the cart before the horse because it presupposes movements as phenomena—as entities that speak.[15] Rather, "movement" is a measurement of the discourse itself; to talk about social movement is to talk about the ways in which a discourse represents a shift away from or challenge to a dominant social imaginary as evident in narratives, ideographs, and other rhetorics.[16] This essay is focused on *what* movement scholars look at when they are examining the rhetoric of social movement.

In the first essay written on social movement in rhetorical studies, Griffin lays out a set of practices and goals for analyzing movements. In "The Rhetoric of Historical Movements," Griffin goads critics to "judge the discourse in terms of the theories of rhetoric and public opinion indigenous to the times"—a charge important to keep in mind when critiquing the rhetoric of marginalized groups who may be operating within rhetorical and political traditions different from those within which the critic is living.[17] Bernadette Calafell and Fernando Delgado make a similar point more recently, arguing that critics should deal with and "accept the text on its terms."[18] Furthermore, in their analysis of one of the key texts of the farm workers' movement ("The Plan of Delano") and the rhetoric of Caesar Chavez, John Hammerback and Richard Jensen repeat this sentiment by arguing that understanding the rhetoric of the Plan of Delano and the farm workers' movement requires an understanding of the rhetorical history of "plans" as a distinct rhetorical genre operative in Mexican political discourse.[19] Significantly, this scholarship points to a need to consider *forms* and histories of rhetoric that may fall outside the traditional purview of U.S. rhetorical studies. Griffin concludes his original essay arguing that "essentially, the student's goal is to *discover,* in a wide sense of the term, the rhetorical pattern inherent in the movement selected for investigation."[20]

One direction in which the "discovery" of rhetorical patterns directed scholars was toward more holistic engagements of specific protests and the structures of persuasion and coercion in social movements. In an early essay on the "New Left" movement, Griffin remarks on the importance of "direct action tactics," a "physical rhetoric of resistance," and "'body' rhetoric" as forms that serve to alter the dramatistic scene and open up the possibilities for persuasive discourse.[21] Andrews notes similarly the relevance of such non-verbal forms in enacting "coercive rhetorics" that bolster the "stories" and "hyperbolic description" of protesters at Columbia in 1968.[22] Scott and Smith suggest the same in claiming, "The act carries a message," which is to situate confrontation within a dramatistic frame and recognize that "symbolic action" is more than just the words someone speaks.[23] Herbert W. Simons also seems to be in agreement, arguing that "militant tactics," including embodied rhetorics, "confer visibility on a movement" and dramatize the scene in ways words alone might not make possible.[24] Finally, scholars like Franklyn S. Haiman and Parke G. Burgess acknowledge the importance of embodiment in the "rhetoric of the streets," a label they give the protest phenomenon active in the 1960s.[25] While vital entry-points into the discussion, all of these accounts seem to face four main limitations with respect to dealing effectively with an embodied and intersectional rhetoric like the YLO's garbage offensive.

First, despite explicit recognitions to the contrary, all have a *verbal bias* that directs them to be concerned first and foremost with the *words* protestors speak and write. For example, Andrews seems genuinely interested in the rhetorical functions of body rhetoric, but that interest is limited to the ways in which embodiment bolsters or accents the protesters' linguistic tactics, arguments, stories, labels, descriptions, etc.[26] In other words, he does not take up embodied discourses on their own terms, as rhetorics themselves. In Griffin's analysis of the New Left, body rhetoric occupies only part of one page in a rather lengthy essay devoted mostly to tracing the New Left's ideological evolution in its *written* works. Scott and Smith face a similar outcome in recognizing the importance of the body in something like the rhetoric of Black Power, but then spend most of their

critical energies devoted to offering an account of the language of confrontation emerging principally from Franz Fanon.[27] McGee, too, rarely acknowledged the importance of extra-linguistic rhetorics, choosing instead to focus on changes in words and their meanings.[28] In being most concerned with written or spoken words, scholars of rhetoric and social movement do not devote enough critical attention to embodiment or visuality—an interpretive move that makes it difficult to evaluate a robust connection between form and agency in the YLO's garbage offensive.

Second, although rhetorical scholars focusing on social movement have documented the key role non-verbal rhetorics play in confrontation and the rhetoric of the streets, that role is often reduced to an *instrumentality* that enables or facilitates verbal rhetorics. Griffin, for example, considers body rhetoric one possibility in an early stage of social movement development when a non-rational, non-democratic scene invites non-rational, non-democratic acts. This, however, is one stop along a movement's evolution, eventually giving way to "the decision to speak openly ('overtly,' unambiguously)."[29] For Andrews, body rhetoric heightens the coerciveness of speech. While he agrees with Scott and Smith that it can be "consummatory," Andrews never explicates the tactical functioning of body rhetoric. John Bowers, Donovan Ochs, and Richard Jensen place themselves in a similar position when they deny the rhetoricity of consummatory acts and insist on the instrumental function of any rhetoric, especially nonverbal agitation tactics.[30] For Simons, "militants use rhetoric as an expression, an instrument, and an act of force." Furthermore, by conferring "visibility," embodied rhetorics open spaces for "moderate tactics" to "gain entry into decision centers."[31]

While certainly true in some instances, reducing non-verbal rhetoric to such an instrumental role fails to consider what the rhetoric itself is up to—what cultural or social work it is accomplishing. Even DeLuca (who, ironically, is often quite critical of Simons) seems to mirror Simons by arguing that staged, embodied "image events" alter public consciousness through their instrumental usefulness in getting a message out (for example with the 1999 Seattle WTO protest images serving "as a dramatic lead that opens into expansive and extensive coverage of the issues surrounding the WTO protests").[32] Alberto Melucci would agree that a focus on the instrumentality of any movement activities risks missing the point of the movement:

> Contemporary movements operate as signs, in the sense that they translate their actions into symbolic challenges to the dominant codes. . . . In this respect, collective action is a *form* whose models of organization and solidarity deliver a message to the rest of society. Collective action . . . raises questions that transcend the logic of instrumental effectiveness and decision-making by anonymous and impersonal organizations of power.[33]

Hence, reducing embodiment to instrumental utility is problematic because it obscures the ways in which rhetorical and organizational *form* may be constitutive and central to a movement's political and social objectives rather than a means to an end.

Third, rhetorical social movement scholarship is too often *leader-centered* to be fully applicable to a study of an organization like the YLO, which did not have a clear leader. Simons offers an early justification for "a leader-centered conception of persuasion in social movements" in arguing that the "primary rhetorical test of the leader—and, indirectly, of the strategies he [sic] employs—is his capacity to fulfill the requirements of his movement by resolving or reducing the rhetorical problems."[34] Others who write on social movement tend to focus on particular leaders, even if they do not offer an explicitly leader-centered "theory" of movements. For example, virtually all of the scholarship on 1960s/1970s Chicano movement rhetoric (most of which was written by Hammerback and Jensen) examines the words of particular charismatic leaders.[35] The majority of scholarship on Black Power is also focused on leaders' rhetoric.[36] To be clear, this is not necessarily a problem. In many of these instances, it makes perfect sense to focus on leaders and their rhetoric because, in those instances, leaders were central to a movement both in terms of producing messages and

being visible to audiences. Stokely Carmichael, for example, was clearly a charismatic leader who made Black Power palatable to countless people. Malcolm X was, similarly, a brilliant rhetorician and worthy of a great deal of critical ink. The problem, instead, is that leader-centered studies do not equip a critic to examine the rhetoric of a group that saw itself first and foremost as a *collective* and resisted internally the tendencies for leaders to emerge. Furthermore, they risk glossing over the issue at stake: the YLO rhetoric's form and content assembled an anti-colonial collective agency that came before consideration of even the group's leadership position within a broader Puerto Rican movement.

In contemporary scholarship, critics have become particularly adept at engaging different rhetorical "texts" of social movement. Hammerback and Jensen's groundbreaking work on the Chicano movement and Fernando Delgado's exploration of the ideographs of the Chicano "plans" and their ideological valences are two prime examples that illustrate rhetorical engagements of verbal (written and spoken) "texts" of the Chicano rights/power movement.[37] My fourth critique of social movement literatures, however, is that many of the aforementioned studies run the risk of *reifying or fetishizing the "text"* (even if "text" is not words on a page or in a speech) in a way that misses the radical fragmentation of late-modern movement rhetorics.[38] I hope not to be misunderstood, here. Rhetorical scholarship has done a marvelous job adapting itself to changing circumstances and "textual" forms. For example, recent years have seen an explosion of valuable scholarship on so-called "visual rhetoric" addressing topics ranging from the discursive and ideological functions of "iconic" photographs, to the roles of images in the construction of identities, and the rhetorical function of the visual in spurring and advancing social movement(s).[39] Notwithstanding such advancements, the *metaphor* of the "text" may hinder considering fully the possibilities of movement discourses—like the YLO's—that operate differently "in the streets," because "text" restricts our critical attention to certain aspects of rhetoric while obscuring other aspects.

To state it directly, the problem is that most critical rhetorical heuristics for examining movement discourse *do not account for the confluence of forms in a radically fragmented vernacular rhetoric* like that of the YLO garbage offensive. As Dwight Conquergood argues, "The verbal/visual bias of Western regimes of knowledge blinds researchers to meanings that are expressed forcefully through ... what de Certeau called 'the elocutionary experience of fugitive communication. ...'"[40] This focus also blocks critics from interrogating the ways in which different discursive *forms* (e.g., speech, performance, and image) combine to build a unique intersectional rhetorical vision. To adopt an aphorism from critical race feminists' work on the intersectionality of oppression: the movement that takes place at the intersection of these different discursive forms is greater than the sum of its parts.[41] In other words, coming to a discourse with the assumption that *different forms intersect with each other equally* will help us to see something differently than if we assume that the primary social work is being done by *either* verbal, visual, or embodied forms.

By highlighting this limitation of contemporary social movement research, I wish to draw our attention to how our *critical heuristics* for engaging marginalized discourses (heuristics rooted in a different system of speech making) may be unfit to groups like the YLO. Some scholars attempt valiantly to adapt to new forms, but as Kent Ono and John Sloop write with respect to "vernacular discourses,"

> Rhetoricians cannot take the tools they have now and blithely apply them to the study of cultures. Rather, new methods, approaches, orientations, even attitudes, toward cultures need to be created. ... [C]ritical rhetoric must be reconceived in light of the vernacular discourse that challenges approaches founded within Western notions of domination, freedom, and power.[42]

Scott and Smith frame the task similarly, writing,

> As specialists interested in communication, we who profess the field of rhetoric need

to read the rhetoric of confrontation, seek understanding of its presuppositions, tactics, and purposes, and seek placement of its claim against a just accounting of the presuppositions and claims of our tradition.[43]

While one might rightly object both to the notion from Scott and Smith that we "read" the rhetoric of confrontation and to the notion from Ono and Sloop that we start anew, it is important to try to shift our critical optics (at least slightly) about street movement rhetoric so that we might see beyond how <bodies *plus* words>/function, and begin seeing how <bodies-words-images>/intersect to form (an)other rhetoric of resistance that is qualitatively different than a critic might have assumed.

The importance of this challenge to our disciplinary heuristics is particularly pronounced in the instance of the YLO's garbage offensive. If the garbage offensive is approached as a "text" to be "read" and as guided principally by one rhetorical form or another, then we risk losing sight of the important connection between rhetorical form/movement tactics and the constitution of an anti-colonial Nuyorican agency. Just as examining the *content* of the YLO's discourse is relevant to understanding how they constitute Nuyorican agency, so too is examining the *form* of that discourse critical to seeing how they challenge agency in the diaspora. In what follows, I demonstrate how the YLO's garbage offensive functions as an intersectional rhetoric and why a critical heuristic attuned to the intersection of forms is necessary for seeing such rhetoric's constitutive effects on agency. This analysis is guided by two primary assumptions: First, the act of resistance in the garbage offensive should not be reduced to an instrumentality; doing so risks overlooking the constitutive effects of their performance.[44] Second, focusing solely or separately (that is, apart from visual and verbal) on the embodied performance aspects of the situation traps us conceptually and critically in a related but different way by denying the intersectionality of rhetorical forms constitutive of this resistance and of the agency of "the people" of El Barrio.

TRASHING THE SYSTEM: ARTICULATING AGENCY THROUGH THE GARBAGE OFFENSIVE'S (RE)CLAIMING OF SPACE

Two days after the climactic moment of the garbage offensive, the *New York Times* offered an account of the scene in El Barrio on August 17, 1969:

> Against a backdrop of decaying tenements, a low-income housing project, and the Penn Central tracks that carry commuters to the suburbs, a purple-bereted youth told yesterday why his group, the Young Lords Organization, had sparked a garbage-dumping protest in East Harlem on Sunday.
>
> During the protest, residents of the area around Park Avenue and 110th Street joined in heaping and burning garbage at several intersections. . . .
>
> In claiming credit for the protests, a group of Young Lords said yesterday that they had acted to show the people of El Barrio, East Harlem's Puerto Rican Slum, that such activity was necessary to get city action to meet community needs.[45]

In an article that originally appeared in the *Village Voice* over 25 years after the garbage offensive introduced New York City to the YLO, Pablo Guzmán recounts, with exhilaration and a more personal tone, the climax of the scene on August 17, 1969:

> I had never done anything like this before. Twelve other guys, one woman, myself, and a small handful of people who, until moments before had been spectators, were about to set a barricade of garbage on fire. Garbage in the ghetto sense: rusted refrigerators from empty lots, the untowed carcasses of abandoned vehicles, mattresses, furniture, and appliances off the sidewalk as well as the stuff normally found in what few trash cans the city saw fit to place in *El Barrio*.[46]

This was an important (even critical) moment for the young Boricuas leading the YLO in their first

protest. The moment represented a turning point, not just for the Lords—signaling their entrance into the New York political landscape—but also for the community members who had been living in squalor due to the City's unwillingness to provide services to them equal to those offered the affluent white citizens down the street.[47] All of this, however, is to get us ahead of ourselves. In order to obtain a better sense of the situation in which the Lords emerged and the ethos of their response, we have to journey back several weeks before this turning point.

The YLO's story begins in January 1969, when a group of Puerto Rican college students gathered as a kind of consciousness-raising measure to understand the situation of their brothers and sisters in the El Barrio. By one former Lords' own admission, "the intentions of these people were good, but vague."[48] As months passed, different people entered and left the group, which became known as the Sociedad de Albizu Campos (SAC).[49] In May 1969, the group began to clarify its mission with the help of several key members. First, Guzmán (who would become Minister of Information and one of the most visible and vocal members of the group) came to New York and joined the discussions. Next, David Perez (a political radical from Puerto Rico who came to New York via Chicago) met up with Guzmán and the SAC. On their first night spent talking together, they came to an agreement that the SAC needed to stop meeting and start acting. A couple of weeks later (on June 7, 1969) they found their model for activism: the Young Lords Organization, a street gang "turned political" in Chicago.[50] At this point, the members of the SAC developed coalitions with some of the other activist Puerto Rican groups from El Barrio and the Lower East Side, and after a series of mergers, a unified group—the New York Young Lords—received an official charter from the Chicago organization on July 26, 1969.[51]

In the beginning, the Lords were filled with revolutionary desires—they wanted nothing short of a different world, an almost utopian world in which their people (and all "the people") could coexist peacefully and equally. The older members of the group (the ones who had some college education and had founded the

SAC before the Lords) were especially well read. "Toiling at our studies," recounts former Young Lord Miguel "Mickey" Melendez, "we developed a good sense of what the people needed and how to proceed in order to succeed in political struggles . . . or so we thought."[52] They were academic revolutionaries at the beginning, having read "Che, Fidel, Fanon, Marx, Lenin, Jefferson, The Bill of Rights, Declaration, Constitution— [they] read everything."[53] Quickly, however, the Lords learned that these different theoretical perspectives offered little solace to the (poor and often uneducated) people in El Barrio, as most people simply did not see the relevance of such theories in practice. Therefore, the activists decided they would have to go to the people to figure out what they needed if it was not Che's revolution. Said Juan Gonzalez, "We must go to them . . . to the masses. . . . They may know something we don't. So first, we must go to the people of El Barrio."[54]

And go to the people they did, donning their grassroots activist/ethnographic researcher hats and venturing out into El Barrio.[55] Coming across some men playing dominoes (a common pastime for Nuyorican men at the time), the young radicals inquired as to what these men thought was the biggest problem facing their community. Said one older man of El Barrio, "Don't you see the garbage all throughout the streets? It is overflowing the entire area with smelly odor . . . everywhere! Don't you smell it? It's horrible!"[56] This opinion was reaffirmed later in the day when they came across a group of doñas (older, presumably married women): "Look at the garbage!' said one of the doñas. 'It smells! For how long do we have to take this . . . ?' the vehemence of their outrage was surprising to us only because we failed to recognize the obvious."[57] Standing amidst the stench, they realized promptly that the all-pervading garbage indeed was an important, if not the most important, issue that they had to address.

Garbage, though, cannot be easily textualized. In fact, the whole garbage offensive event presents significant difficulties in terms of textualization. Unlike the speeches delivered in the mainstream civil rights movement or the discrete "image events" for contemporary radical environmentalists, there is no single static "text" to which

we can turn to critique. Even in their newspaper, *Palante,* and their book, *Palante: Young Lords Party,* the Lords declined the opportunity to offer up a sustained "text" of the event.[58] As Conquergood suggests, "Subordinate people do not have the privilege of explicitness, the luxury of transparency, the presumptive norm of clear and direct communication, free and open debate on a level playing field that the privileged classes take for granted."[59] This creates a methodological problem because we are now *forced* to *make* sense of the event by stringing together the many utterances of different members of the Lords. The critic must be (perhaps as s/he always must be) a *bricoleur,* assembling "texts" and defining the bounds of a fragmented rhetoric.[60] Once we do this, we have a very moving and powerful story about the material and symbolic conditions under which the YLO lived and operated. Their situation—environmentally, politically, economically—was one marked by filth and decay. The images of these decrepit conditions were re-presented through words depicting/describing a sensory explosion by drawing attention to the physical (omni)presence of the garbage.

Seeing garbage as a key issue began structuring the narratives and experiences of the Lords. For example, one early issue of their newspaper, *Palante,* states,

> East Harlem is known as El Barrio—New York's worst Puerto Rican slum. . . . There is glass sprinkled everywhere, vacant lots filled with rubble, burnt out buildings on nearly every block, and people packed together in the polluted summer heat. . . . There is also the smell of garbage, coming in an incredible variety of flavors and strengths.[61]

Furthermore, in another early issue of *Palante,* Felipe Luciano (the chairperson of the organization) wrote,

> They've treated us like dogs for too long. When our people came here in the 1940's, they told us New York was a land of milk and honey. And what happened? Our men can't find work. . . . Our women are forced to become prostitutes. Our young people get hooked on drugs. And they won't even

give us brooms to sweep up the rubbish in our streets.[62]

This return to the centrality of garbage is indicative of the broader dialogues occurring at the time.

As such, garbage was experienced and constructed, verbally and visually, as a central material problem in its own right. It was the proverbial slap in the face in light of all the other conditions faced by the people of El Barrio. Garbage represented both evidence of the state's disrespectful and malicious attitude toward the community and proof of "the system's" incapability to deal with its own intemperance. Visual imagery works, here, on several interrelated levels. First, there is a raw, very material sense of visuality that must be considered. The YLO and members of the community *experienced* the rotting and rusting garbage of El Barrio on a daily basis—a factor that is important to consider when reading critically the offensive. Why is this an important element? This relatively unmediated, multisensory, and markedly visual experience provided a physical manifestation of the frustrations the people felt about the system. It also *showed* them, prior to the assistance of the Lords' verbal interventions, the failure of the system to take into account its own excesses.

The result of this experience was a moment of what Ernesto Laclau and Chantal Mouffe call *antagonism*. "[F]ar from being an objective relation," according to Laclau and Mouffe, antagonism "is a relation wherein the limits of every objectivity are shown. . . . [It is] a witness of the impossibility of final suture."[63] Moments of antagonism, then, are moments when the apparent fixity and completeness of an ideological fantasy or social imaginary (i.e., liberal capitalism) are disrupted. Such a moment forced them to question why a supposed democracy guided by principles of fairness and equality would treat its citizens so differently. Why would the garbage trucks drive through El Barrio to pick up trash in Manhattan, but rarely stop to pick up the same trash in the Nuyorican neighborhood? Such a question became an impetus to act.

Reflecting back one year after the YLO organized, Guzmán recounts the decision to act: "We decided that the first issue we could organize people around was the filth in the streets and lots, since it was clearly visible. . . . For the two Sundays before the Tompkins Square rally, we cleaned 110th Street in El Barrio, rapping while we went."[64] The act of cleaning may not seem all that radical; however, the Lords' actions early in the garbage offensive are important rhetorically in several ways. In one piece of photographic evidence from the garbage offensive, for example, we see Guzmán sweeping up the street. In contrast to the way in which Puerto Ricans had been defined by scholars and government officials as "docile" and inactive, Guzmán's sweeping is instructive of an active life in opposition to racist docility—"it participates in the transfer and continuity of knowledge," especially in the context of the verbal messages and lore surrounding the event.[65] As indicated above, Lords like Guzmán, David Perez, and Juan Gonzalez were not from El Barrio, but rather were college-educated, working- to middle-class Puerto Ricans and looked the part: they regularly clothed themselves middle-class, usually wearing button-up oxfords, and looked more like the kind of people Barrio residents would work *for* than have working for them. When they were seen sweeping up the street, their bodies serve as a critique of labor hierarchies and inequality through their presence in action in El Barrio. Just by *being* there—on and with the streets—the Lords performed resistance by reclaiming and redrawing their own public space and articulating Barrio citizenship with the *vita activa*. "This brought the college people and the street people together, 'cause when street people saw college people pushing brooms and getting dirty, that blew their minds."[66] Exploding such a "mind bomb" was a critical step in changing fundamentally the consciousness of Barrio people to get them to imagine a world beyond inaction.[67]

On Saturday, July 26, 1969 (after sweeping the streets for two weeks), the group received their official charter to become the New York (or, more accurately, East Coast) chapter of the "Young Lords Organization" and held a rally at Tompkins Square to announce their existence and state their agenda. The next day, they went about cleaning the streets; this time, however, they reached another turning point. Recalls Guzmán, "On Sunday, July 27, we needed more brooms for all the community people who were with us. We went to a garbage (sanitation) office nearby and were given a racist runaround."[68] The precise details of what happened at this point are unclear. Some stories claim that Guzmán punched a sanitation official and stole some supplies. Other stories portray a scene wherein they were sent to another office and denied supplies there, too. Whatever happened, Melendez's assessment seems to hold consistent: "The only choice we had was confrontational politics";[69] and by "confrontational politics," Melendez really means direct-action protests, which were repeated nearly every Sunday up to August 17—the biggest protest of them all.

Fed up with the apparently contradictory and inherently racist actions of "the system," the Young Lords sought to rectify the situation. First, they began blocking off streets with the trash they had collected. Lexington, Madison, and Third Avenues were blocked at 110, 111, 115, 118, and 120th Streets. After they noticed people in cars and buses moving the trash out of the way, they got a little more insistent and began lighting fire to the trash. "Fires were set to cars, bottles were thrown, and the people proved for all time that the spirit of the people is always greater than the man's pigs."[70] This moment of antagonism served as a moment of radical possibility—it opened up the available means of persuasion and action so as to make meaningful social movement probable; as such, the people had challenged "the system" and made clear that "the system" was neither invincible nor contained. In the end, Felipe Luciano triumphantly asserted, "We're building our own community. Don't fuck with us. It's as simple as that."[71]

Guzmán details similarly the ways in which this guerrilla offensive was part of both short- and long-term struggles:

> The handful of us who were there employed basic techniques of urban guerrilla warfare: flexibility, mobility, surprise, and escape. By involving our people directly in revolution and participation (Thousands [sic] of spics blocked streets and fought cops that

summer), we made many LORDS and won friends to the struggle.[72]

Note that for Guzmán, the garbage offensive was not *principally* about cleaning up the streets, although that was important; the garbage offensive was always about more than just trash—it was about *guerrillismo,* constituting Lords, building a community, and constructing a place and space for literal and social movement in El Barrio.[73]

It may be tempting, however, to read the garbage offensive as a political tool. This is the interpretation preferred by historian Johanna Fernandez in the only sustained analysis of the garbage offensive.[74] Declining to acknowledge the interpretive move she makes in analyzing the garbage offensive, Fernandez presents a matter-of-fact assessment of the offensive from a social services perspective. Fernandez advances a causal argument about the effect and success of the garbage offensive based on a reading of secondary sources from the time period. In her assessment, the garbage offensive was only about picking up the trash and it was a success because the city sanitation department began picking up trash in El Barrio. Missing the fact that the sanitation department quickly went back to irregular trash collection (which can be verified by looking at subsequent issues of *Palante*), Fernandez overlooks the *political* implications of the garbage offensive. One of her sources would agree. Carl Davidson, writing for the *Guardian* in 1970, observed, "City sanitation officials were forced to meet with the community three times and promise to remedy the situation, but with few results so far.... However, the actions had the effect of establishing the presence of the Young Lords in the community."[75]

Mickey Melendez offers a similarly instrumental read of the garbage offensive, but directs his attention to politics. He argues,

> An "offensive" has no value in itself; it is a political tool. It is a resource in the political education of the masses. What we intended to do was to show the people a path toward a high level of political consciousness, to understand the power that lies in the hands and the souls of the working people.[76]

We can imagine Melendez's position as, in a sense, a standard rhetorical account of what the YLO was attempting in their resistance. Bowers, Ochs, and Jensen likely might agree that the offensive was rhetorical insofar as it was a symbolic act designed to achieve an instrumental goal.[77] Likewise, while Melendez's account goes beyond the idea that the offensive was *merely* about getting the trash picked up, the offensive retains a kind of instrumental quality. The offensive, in Melendez's reading, was a *tool*—an instrument like a compass helping people get their bearings straight. Like the way that a compass directs people toward their destination, the offensive pointed people to an *awareness of politics*. It showed people that their political voice could be acknowledged in an era where quite the contrary seemed the case.

The political consciousness of which Melendez speaks, though, does not suggest a fundamental shift in the way "the people" saw the role of the political or themselves within a political system. Rather, the offensive swept people up in the fervor of the moment, helping them understand that politics and resistance were possible. Yet this perspective does not seem to go far enough. While it is certainly the case that there is an instrumental element in any offensive, *reducing* the garbage offensive to instrumentality misses the possibility that the act of protest itself has a constitutive effect on the people involved and those who bear witness to it.

One feasible way to move beyond this instrumental focus on the garbage offensive is to interpret it as an embodied act of decolonization. This attitude is best exhibited by Agustín Laó, who argues that the garbage offensive engaged in a "Spatial Politics of recasting the colonized streets through direct action [that] is grounded in the common sense of cleanliness ('we are poor but clean'), and the performative power and polyvalence of the symbolism of cleansing."[78] Furthermore, Laó suggests, "[t]his great sweeping-out became an act of decolonization, a form of humanizing the living space, a way of giving back dignity to our place, by taking it back.["]79 Notice that Laó does not really *reduce* the offensive to pure instrumentality; rather, he seems to be cognizant of the ways in which the *form* of the protest has significant

implications. His attentiveness to the "spatial politics" of the offensive is particularly significant because it makes the focal point the *performance* of cleansing and/in protest, suggesting that the *act itself* has important political/identity-constituting implications that come prior to any benefits accrued as a *result* of the protest (that is, as a result of the offensive's instrumentality). Laó's interpretation is incisive; but he seems hesitant to expand or extend the theoretical importance of this move.

Taking a cue from Laó and radicalizing Melendez's point about political consciousness, a more productive engagement of the garbage offensive would understand it as a rhetorical performance of trashing "the system." To begin unpacking this metaphor, we might return once more to retrospective remarks made by Guzmán, who writes,

> We hoped to show that our object as a nation should not merely be to petition a foreign government (amerikkka) to clean the streets, but also to move on that government for allowing garbage to pile up in the first place. By *questioning this system's basic level of sanitation,* our people would then begin to question drug traffic, urban renewal, sterilization, etc., until the whole corrupt machine could be exposed for the greedy monster it is.[80]

One of the central devil figures for the YLO (as it was for many radical groups of the era) was "the system."[81] Drawing primarily from Herbert Marcuse's *One Dimensional Man,* "the system" represents the (more or less) monolithic, assimilating machine that is able to keep the dominant group dominant and ensure that resistance can never be truly successful. The system keeps the rich rich, the poor poor, and maintains that inequality without critical reflection.

The italicized portion of Guzmán's quotation seems particularly incisive because it offers a triple meaning that could be overlooked easily, but demonstrates nicely the performative aspect argued by Laó. First, there is a literal/material read of the fragment: literally, the activities of the garbage offensive served the purpose of questioning the cleanliness of their material environment. This was certainly part of the offensive's effect, given the immediate concerns they had about the "squalor of the barrio."[82] Second, there is an initial symbolic reading of the fragment: through the garbage offensive, they were questioning the cleanliness of the system, suggesting that "this system" is dirty, corrupt, and drenched in the garbage water of inequality. Finally, there is another, more Marcusean symbolic read of the fragment: through the offensive, they were questioning the sanitizing force of the system; that is, they questioned the system's capacity to clean up politics and eradicate opposition. Reading the apostrophe, then, as possessing the tools and agency to clean demonstrates a different performative critique lacking in both Melendez and Laó's interpretations.

All of this is helpful analysis, but to realize its fuller impact and glean more out of the garbage offensive (rhetorically, materially, and politically) we must be attentive to not only the instrumental and performative nature of the event, but the material resources and the locally global moves the YLO was proffering vis-á-vis "the system." It is to this end that we ought to look at how different elements of the situation fit together to form a remarkable normative claim about how "the people" of El Barrio *should* act politically—that is, a claim (of sorts) about the ethos of their agency. Here we could understand garbage to be functioning as a synecdoche for the excesses of liberal capitalism; the sanitation department's refusal to assist functions as a sign of capitalism's failure to cope with those excesses. Through an intersectional rhetoric, the garbage offensive incited a moment of antagonism in which the literal and symbolic excesses of the liberal capitalist "system" were called into question, opening up a space for the YLO to begin advancing social movement amongst "the people" of El Barrio.

Thought of in this manner, we have to take into account the ways that the raw, stinky materiality of the garbage functioned as a *part* of a larger *whole* (the system) that is made to *show* the people the excesses of the liberal capitalist system. This is painfully obvious in the descriptions of the garbage offered by the YLO—and made even more poignant in images they circulated (e.g., images of kids playing—a game of

tag, or possibly king of the hill—atop a sea of garbage). Such images serve to make present, through a remembering and re-visioning of trash, the material scope of the problem. Additionally, in the stories about their exchanges with the sanitation department, the Lords make the department's refusal to assist (either before, during, or after the YLO's intervention) a sign of "the system's" failure to cope with its own immoderation.

When we combine this symbolic-materialist reading with the kind of performative interpretation Laó offers, we end up with the point that the YLO was able to call into question the logic of "the system" in such a way as to open up a discursive space. Within this space, a kind of social movement is advanced. The YLO's performance of resistance, through an intersectional rhetoric, altered fundamentally people's consciousness about their relationship to "the system" and the possibilities for their futures. The space made possible new significations and practices of an anti-colonial agency that was intimately tied to both the YLO's *message* and the *form* that "message" took. As such, it is in the intersectional rhetorical act of making the garbage do something and its twin of doing something with the garbage (and the words and images invoking garbage) that we more fully understand the greatest strengths of the offensive. The ways in which bodies get positioned vis-á-vis the system in the garbage offensive are a critical component of this intersectional rhetoric. Just as words and images seem to advance an argument about the relationship between the people, the system, and the environment, so too do bodies enact a similar message of dissent. By *(en)acting* this significant critique of the system, the YLO articulated a fundamentally *political* social imaginary that altered the Latino political landscape in New York for years to come.[83]

Despite the apparent constitutive benefits of the garbage offensive, there remains a looming question about the offensive: Why does any of this matter given that the garbage offensive "failed" to achieve its instrumental goal of getting El Barrio cleaned up? This is certainly a noteworthy question, and one that raises another question: How can we interpret the YLO as challenging the system when their explicit demand was a reformist one for the sanitation department to pick up the trash (a clear reliance on a component of the very system they were critiquing)? These are important challenges for which reasonable answers can be offered; however, my first question is a bit of a red herring. While the practical goal of any rhetoric may be to persuade people to act in one way or another, instrumental "success" may not be the best criterion on which to base our judgments.[84] Rather, we would do well to remember that rhetorics serve constitutive functions that articulate a "people" and imbue them with certain qualities, capacities, and ideals.[85] Thought of as a moment of constitution, the garbage offensive should be understood as a success because the performance of an intersectional rhetoric of resistance challenged the constraints of the system on sociopolitical agency. Specifically, the Lords were able to both translate a language of revolutionary consciousness into the language of the people (the residents of El Barrio) and provide a set of practical resources for *enacting* that consciousness. By enlisting the people of El Barrio in this initial struggle, the Lords both created a revolutionary, even radical, democratic discursive space and defined an ethos of radicalism that escaped the tentacles of the system.[86]

The fact that the Young Lords sought ultimately to use the system, however, does not undercut this constitutive success. While it may seem paradoxical (or contradictory) for them to make such a move—and it may, indeed, be paradoxical—the Young Lords' demands on the system were performed in the spirit of *jaibería*. In *Puerto Rican Jam: Rethinking Colonialism and Nationalism*, Ramón Grosfoguel, Frances Negrón-Muntaner, and Chloé S. Georas turn to what they call "the popular tradition of *jaibería*" to articulate a space for oppositional agency amongst Puerto Ricans struggling for radical democracy. Defined, in Puerto Rican usage, as "collective practices of nonconfrontation and evasion . . . , of taking dominant discourse literally in order to subvert it for one's purpose, of doing whatever one sees fit not as a head-on collision . . . but a bit under the table,"[87] *jaibería* is "a form of complicitous critique or subversive complicity"[88] that can result in the extreme adoption of dominant/ruling ideologies, beliefs,

or actions in order to demonstrate their shortcomings and instigate movement.

Although they did not always adopt such an attitude, it is exactly this strategy that the Young Lords deployed in advancing their demands in the garbage offensive. They could have rejected the system outright; instead they adopted a different relation to the system by demanding a leveling equality (the literal promise of liberalism) vis-á-vis garbage collection. Rather than simply continuing to pick up all of the garbage themselves, the YLO demanded that the sanitation department assist in various ways. The subversion, however, lies in their knowing full well that New York City's sanitation officials were unwilling and incapable of meeting their demands. In making demands that could not be fulfilled, the YLO's apparent complicity functioned as a critique and rupturing of the system's racist/classist underpinnings.

This reliance on the system is also a key difference between the Young Lords and other anti-colonial groups in the U.S. at the time. Seen from a post-colonial vantage with an emphasis on national independence, such reliance on the state would be read merely as complicity with oppression—as the further perpetuation of a "colonial mentality."[89] The YLO case, though, problematizes that analysis by challenging the lines between "us" and "them" in a Manichean struggle. As such, their ultimate reliance and insistence on the system served as a "complicitous critique" undermining the system's legitimacy when it could not meet the YLO's demands. In this sense, the YLO's failure in getting the sanitation department to pick up trash regularly was a success for the Lords because it both furthered their critique and demonstrated another way in which resistance could occur.

POSTSCRIPT: SOCIAL MOVEMENT CRITIQUE AND THE YOUNG LORDS

In the end, it is the breadth and subversive quality of the Young Lords' intersectional rhetoric that makes the garbage offensive such a unique and radical instance of resistance, and such a difficult scenario for critics of social movement rhetoric to evaluate. The YLO refused to comply with the formal norms of (the) Anglo rhetorical tradition(s); thus the shortcomings of extant approaches cannot (or at least, do not) account for an intersectional rhetoric like that of the YLO. In the sense I am using it, "intersectional rhetoric" can be a descriptive label for a phenomenon that appeared in the Young Lords' rhetoric of movement breaking out of a *formally* one-dimensional Marcusean system. "Intersectional rhetoric" is a *kind* of rhetoric wherein one form of discourse is not privileged over another; rather, diverse forms intersect organically to create something challenging to rhetorical norms. Intersectional rhetoric, then, is more than <words +/images +/bodies> because those different forms can be present without intersecting and challenging norms of textual boundedness. Instead, intersectional rhetoric is better represented as three intersecting lines. In their intersection, one is not privileged over another; they are not ordered hierarchically. In so challenging rhetorical norms, intersectional rhetoric also functions in a hybrid political space, exhibiting a kind of incredulity toward the political traditions (e.g., U.S. liberal democracy) with which rhetorical traditions are bound. Incredulity does not necessarily mean that they reject those traditions; instead, intersectional rhetoric pushes the boundaries of traditions and encourages a hybridization or mixing of ideas. Furthermore, this difference in form represents a distinctive stylization of power compared to what we find in the speeches of Malcolm X or the writings of the New Left, for example. The intersection of images, words, and actions from an entire community of individuals formally mimics an articulation of collective agency that finds strength in the articulation of a "people" rather than any particular person. While collective agency may not be unique to the YLO, the way in which the YLO accomplished the task through an intersectional rhetoric is previously under-explored in the social movement literature.

With this, however, comes a need to challenge our disciplinary conceptions of "rhetoric," "texts," and "movement" to test the bounds of text-centric critique within our scholarship. By enacting an intersectional *sensibility* (in the way the object of critique is assembled, the limits of "rhetoric" rethought, and ideological movement reconsidered), this essay attempts to create the space for some movement of its own—movement away from a scholarly enterprise marked by expectations of formal and textual boundedness. The analogy to "intersectionality" in critical race scholarship mentioned earlier is relevant here. If bound by categories such as "race," "gender," or "class," we see racism *or* sexism *or* classism; but we do not see racist-sexism, sexist-racism, racist-sexist-classism, etc. Similarly, when bound by "textual" categories, we have difficulty making sense of the ways in which word and body combine to create something qualitatively distinct from words or bodies considered separately. As conceived here, "intersectional rhetoric" is both a label for a kind of discourse and a marker for a critical attitude necessary to examine such rhetorics. This is where status quo approaches to social movement probably fall short of the task. While someone like McGee, through his focus on "ideographs," does well to problematize the "texts" of social movement, he remains concerned only with the verbal—a byproduct of disciplinary constraints and/on his choice of object. Likewise, DeLuca, Scott and Smith, Simons, and others have done well to call into question our preoccupation with the verbal; but in so doing they risk treating "image events" or "body rhetoric" as discrete "texts" or only instrumental stylizations.

To back up for a moment, though, perhaps this critique of McGee, DeLuca, Scott and Smith, Simons, Bowers, Ochs, and Jensen et al. belies my own desire to take rhetors up "on their own terms." We must recognize that McGee's concern is with mainstream rhetorics of social control that most readily manifested themselves in the form of ideographs circulating in public, verbal argument. Correspondingly, DeLuca is concerned primarily with discourses that are also, in many ways, "mainstream" in the ways in which they circulate in dominant, corporately owned news media. In both instances, then, we are dealing with historically contingent rhetorical forms of social movement—arguably an older one with McGee's and a more contemporary one with DeLuca's. Additionally, both McGee and DeLuca examine movement rhetorics that have a particular socio-spatial positionality; both examine dominant or circulatory dominant (by virtue of their dissemination in mass media) rhetorics. In taking such foci, McGee and DeLuca are convincing and both have advanced compelling critiques of their subject matter, but their approaches should not be the final word in a methodologically progressive rhetorical formulation of social movement critique. While the work of all of these scholars has had, in the words of Ono and Sloop, "broad 'historical' impact," it has often done so "without the additional examination of texts that have profound effect on vernacular communities and have widespread effects on *communitas*."[90] What might be suggested here is that, although most rhetorical critics offer appropriate and productive heuristics for engaging the discourses they engage, they may only offer an initial starting point from which to critique the YLO or any number of other "movement" rhetors.

Furthermore, while we cannot deny the *possibility* of a primarily instrumental political offensive, the *desirability* of interpreting this instance only (or even predominantly) through such a lens is challenged when we begin to recognize what this ignores. As Kenneth Burke argues, while symbols may be used as tools, instrumentality is not their principle purpose (they are a form of action, he says); similarly, this essay suggests that the intersectional rhetoric of the YLO's garbage offensive represents a way of acting in the world and, in the process, serves to constitute that world by delineating a material place (El Barrio) and discursive space (*political* Nuyoricans in El Barrio) for this altered public consciousness.[91] Diana Taylor writes, in a manner reminiscent of Burke's theorization of the scene-act ratio, that

> [T]he place allows us to think about the possibilities of the action. But action also defines place. If, as Certeau suggests, "space is practiced place," then there is no such thing as place, for no place is free of history and social practice.[92]

The rhetorical constitution of such a space affords the YLO the opportunity to challenge prior constructions of Barrio Boricuas and invent a new, radical democratic political consciousness that played in the hybrid space between U.S. American and Puerto Rican, domestic and foreign, etc. In her engagement of Chicana feminist writing, Lisa Flores suggests,

> Creating space means rejecting the dichotomy of either at the margins or in the center and replacing that perspective with one that allows for Chicana feminists to be at their own center intellectually, spiritually, emotionally, and ultimately physically. The desire for space is the need for both a physical location and an intellectual one.[93]

Similarly, the YLO invented an intellectual, political, and physical space in which radical democratic resistance through "community control" could be envisioned and, in some cases, realized.

Importantly, the YLO articulated this radical democratic space at the intersections of various rhetorical forms rather than through dominant modalities. For Laclau, "a radical democratic society is one in which a plurality of public spaces, constituted around specific issues and demands . . . , instills in its members a civic sense which is a central ingredient of their identity as individuals." Laclau continues, "Not only is antagonism not excluded from a democratic society, it is the very condition of its institution."[94] In this way, the YLO exploited an antagonism in "the system" and, through their intersectional rhetorical performance, constituted a radically democratic space. Their rhetorical performances functioned, Taylor would likely agree, "as vital acts of transfer, transmitting social knowledge, memory, and a sense of identity through reiterated, or what Richard Schechner has called 'twice-behaved behavior.'"[95] Quite significantly, the way in which the YLO accomplished this task was through an *intersectional* rhetoric that our critical heuristics must be fine-tuned to notice more clearly. The status quo models of envisioning "texts" and privileging discrete rhetorical forms are insufficient to this task. In the words of Conquergood, "The hegemony of textualism needs to be exposed and undermined."[96]

Considering the different aspects of the garbage offensive together, I hope the case of the YLO has made clear that looking at just one facet (i.e., words, images, or bodies), or at these characteristics discretely or instrumentally, only provides a partial view of the significance of the garbage offensive. When we consider the verbal, visual, and corporeal forms of discourse and how they come together, however, we see an *intersectional* rhetoric that articulates a particular anti-colonial sensibility for acting in the world. We also see an intersectional *rhetoric* that resists hegemonic norms for appropriate protest rhetoric because it refuses to recognize the singularity or boundedness of any solitary rhetorical form.

Such a critical attitude may also help to explicate meaning from other movement rhetorics that emerge after the mainstream civil rights movements, which were similarly intersectional and lacked clear leaders. The question of how other movements—perhaps environmental, feminist, GLBT, and critical race movements—articulate unique agencies in the absence of charismatic leaders, speeches, and access to mass dissemination may also be addressed through an attentiveness to the intersection of rhetorical forms because "every rhetorical performance enacts and contains a theory of its own agency."[97] But addressing these questions in different contexts is a challenge to our research and our critical perspectives. This is the lesson we must learn from the YLO garbage offensive: status quo theories of rhetorical movement efficacy obscure the full experience of Other rhetorics; it is by expanding our critical heuristics that we can best begin moving beyond a restrictive boundedness in our own disciplinary spaces. Hopefully other scholars of rhetoric and social movement will take up this call to examine the unique work done at the intersection of rhetorical forms. In this sense, the garbage offensive can stand out as a moment of radical possibility both for the people of El Barrio and for rhetoricians today.

Notes

1 Frantz Fanon, *The Wretched of the Earth* (New York: Grove, 1963), 232.

2 Agustín Laó-Montes, "Niuyol: Urban Regime, Latino Social Movements, Ideologies of Latinidad," in *Mambo Montage: The Latinization of New York,* ed. Agustín Laó-Montes and Arlene M. Dávila (New York: Columbia University Press, 2001), 141–42.

3 See Antonia Pantoja, "Puerto Ricans in New York: A Historical and Community Development

Perspective," *Centro Journal* 2, no. 5 (1989): 21–31; Carlos Rodríguez-Fraticelli and Amílcar Tirado, "Notes Towards a History of Puerto Rican Community Organizations in New York City," *Centro Journal* 2, no. 6 (1989): 35–47.

4 For an account of the narrative and an attendant critique of docility, see Juan Flores, *Divided Borders: Essays on Puerto Rican Identity* (Houston, TX: Arte Publico Press, 1992), 13–60.

5 The History Taskforce of the Center for Puerto Rican Studies offers an explanation of the economic conditions of Puerto Ricans on the Island and in New York (and the relationship between the two) in History Task Force Centro de Estudios Puertorriqueños, *Labor Migration under Capitalism: The Puerto Rican Experience* (New York: Monthly Review Press, 1979).

6 While "Nuyorican" tends to be a term descriptive of a population (people of Puerto Rican descent who live in New York City), "Boricua" encompasses the description and adds a political edge. Derived from the original Arawak/Taino name of Puerto Rico (Borinquen, meaning Land of the Brave Lords), the term "Boricua" has been adopted as a politically charged, culturally nationalist term for Puerto Ricans. Being similar to the movement from African American to "Black," or Mexican American to "Chicano," "Boricua" historicizes the Puerto Rican colonial experience through a shift in signifier. I will, however, switch more or less freely between "Boricua," "Nuyorican," and "Puerto Rican" in this essay.

7 Pablo "Yoruba" Guzmán, "One Year of Struggle," *Palante,* July 17, 1970, 12–13.

8 For good introductory texts on Puerto Rican history, see James L. Deitz, *Economic History of Puerto Rico: Institutional Change and Capitalist Development* (Princeton: Princeton University Press, 1986); History Task Force Centro de Estudios Puertorriqueños, *Labor Migration;* Manuel Maldonado-Denis, *Puerto Rico: A Socio-Historic Interpretation,* trans. Elena Vialo (New York: Vintage Books, 1972); Kelvin A. Santiago-Valles, *"Subject People" and Colonial Discourses: Economic Transformation and Social Disorder in Puerto Rico, 1898–1947* (Albany: State University of New York Press, 1994); José Trías Monge, *Puerto Rico: The Trials of the Oldest Colony in the World* (New Haven: Yale University Press, 1997).

9 Quoted in Cheryl Geisler, "How Ought We to Understand the Concept of Rhetorical Agency," *Rhetoric Society Quarterly* 34, no. 3 (2004): 13.

10 I am thinking of different social movement organizations that do not operate principally through speech or writing. This might include

different feminist, GLBT, or environmental movement organizations.

11 Leland M. Griffin, "The Rhetorical Structure of the 'New Left' Movement: Part I," *Quarterly Journal of Speech* 50 (1964): 127.

12 James R. Andrews, "Confrontation at Columbia: A Case Study in Coercive Rhetoric," *Quarterly Journal of Speech* 55 (1969): 16.

13 Herbert W. Simons, "Requirements, Problems, and Strategies: A Theory of Persuasion for Social Movements," *Quarterly Journal of Speech* 56 (1970): 8.

14 For a comprehensive history, see Charles E. Morris III and Stephen H. Browne, eds., *Readings on the Rhetoric of Social Protest* (State College, PA: Strata Publishing, 2001). For a history critical of dominant trajectories, see Kevin DeLuca, *Image Politics: The New Rhetoric of Environmental Activism* (New York: Guilford, 1999).

15 Michael Calvin McGee, "'Social Movement': Phenomenon or Meaning?" *Central States Speech Journal* 31 (1980): 233.

16 "Social imaginaries" combine attentiveness to the explicit political doctrines (e.g., liberal democracy and socialism), social habits/practices (e.g., voting and protest), and symbolic systems (e.g., myths, narratives, and images) in a manner that highlights the "ways of understanding the social." They "become social entities themselves, mediating collective life." To put it differently, "social imaginary" is one way to talk about the hegemonic structuration of the social in manners that informs and is informed by political discourse and *habitus*. See Dilip Parameshwar Gaonkar, "Toward New Imaginaries: An Introduction," *Public Culture* 14 (2002): 4. On contemporary discussions of the social imaginary, see Benjamin Lee and Edward LiPuma, "Cultures of Circulation: The Imaginations of Modernity," *Public Culture* 14 (2002): 191–213; Charles Taylor, "Modern Social Imaginaries," *Public Culture* 14 (2002): 91–124; Charles Taylor, *Modern Social Imaginaries, Public Planet Books* (Durham, NC: Duke University Press, 2004).

17 Leland M. Griffin, "The Rhetoric of Historical Movements," *Quarterly Journal of Speech* 38 (1952): 187.

18 Bernadette Marie Calafell and Fernando P. Delgado, "Reading Latina/o Images: Interrogating *Americanos*," *Critical Studies in Media Communication* 21 (2004): 18. See also Kent A. Ono and John M. Sloop, "The Critique of Vernacular Discourse," *Communication Monographs* 62 (1995): 19–46; Fernando P. Delgado, "When

the Silenced Speak: The Textualization and Complications of Latina/o Identity," *Western Journal of Communication* 62 (1998): 420–38.

19 John C. Hammerback and Richard J. Jensen, "Ethnic Heritage as Rhetorical Legacy: The Plan of Delano," *Quarterly Journal of Speech* 80 (1994): 53–70.

20 Griffin, "Historical Movements," 188.

21 Griffin, "'New Left' Movement," 127.

22 Andrews, "Confrontation," 10 and 12–13.

23 Robert L. Scott and Donald K. Smith, "The Rhetoric of Confrontation," *Quarterly Journal of Speech* 55 (1969): 7.

24 Simons, "Requirements," 8.

25 Franklyn S. Haiman, "The Rhetoric of the Streets: Some Legal and Ethical Considerations," *Quarterly Journal of Speech* 53 (1967): 99–114; Parke G. Burgess, "The Rhetoric of Black Power: A Moral Demand?," *Quarterly Journal of Speech* 54 (1968): 122–33; Franklyn S. Haiman, "Nonverbal Communication and the First Amendment: The Rhetoric of the Streets Revisited," *Quarterly Journal of Speech* 68 (1982), 371–83.

26 Andrews, "Confrontation," 12–14.

27 In another work, co-authored with Wayne Brockriede, Scott again recognizes the importance of non-verbal rhetoric, but proceeds to focus only on the verbal because there is "much more difficulty in giving a decent account of nonverbal elements than of verbal." See Robert Lee Scott and Wayne Brockriede, *The Rhetoric of Black Power* (New York: Harper & Row, 1969), 2.

28 McGee, "'Social Movement'," 243. See McGee's Van Zelst Lecture for an example of his focusing on extra-linguistic rhetoricity. Even there, however, McGee's attention is on "performativity" generally, not on specific examples of body rhetoric in action. Michael Calvin McGee, "On Feminized Liberty" (paper presented at the Van Zelst Lecture, Evanston, IL, May 1985).

29 Griffin, "'New Left' Movement," 127.

30 John W. Bowers, Donovan J. Ochs, and Richard J. Jensen, *The Rhetoric of Agitation and Control*, 2nd ed. (Prospect Heights, IL: Waveland, 1993), 1–2. A good example is in Bowers et al.'s initial discussion of nonviolent resistance in the early mainstream civil rights movement. Suggesting that agitators use "their bodies as symbols of their extremely strong convictions about laws and customs" places bodies in a subservient position to the "convictions" that are expressed verbally (40). Of all the specific agitation tactics they identify, only five (of the nearly 30, by my counting) do not incorporate the verbal; but all five are to be evaluated for

their instrumentality vis-á-vis verbally motivated strategies.

31 Simons, "Requirements," 8.

32 Kevin DeLuca and Jennifer Peeples, "From Public Sphere to Public Screen: Democracy, Activism, and the 'Violence' of Seattle," *Critical Studies in Media Communication* 19 (2002): 141. The charge of instrumentalism is one that DeLuca and Peeples explicitly deny but, nevertheless, may fall victim to given statements like the one quoted.

33 Alberto Melucci, John Keane, and Paul Mier, *Nomads of the Present: Social Movements and Individual Needs in Contemporary Society* (London: Hutchinson Radius, 1989), 12.

34 Simons, "Requirements," 2–3. Simons has developed this leader-centered theory further in subsequent publications.

35 John C. Hammerback and Richard J. Jensen, "The Rhetorical Worlds of César Chávez and Reies Tijerina," *Western Journal of Speech Communication* 44 (1980): 166–76; Richard J. Jensen and John C. Hammerback, "Radical Nationalism among Chicanos: The Rhetoric of José Angel Gutiérrez," *Western Journal of Speech Communication* 44 (1980): 191–202; Richard J. Jensen and John C. Hammerback, "'No Revolutions without Poets': The Rhetoric of Rodolfo 'Corky' Gonzales," *Western Journal of Speech Communication* 46 (1982): 72–91; John C. Hammerback, Richard J. Jensen, and José Angel Gutiérrez, *A War of Words: Chicano Protest in the 1960s and 1970s* (Westport, CT: Greenwood Press, 1985); John C. Hammerback, "Jose Antonio's Rhetoric of Fascism," *Southern Communication Journal* 59 (1994): 181–95; Hammerback and Jensen, "Ethnic Heritage," 53–70; Ruby Ann Fernandez and Richard J. Jensen, "Reies Lopez Tijerina's 'the Land Grant Question': Creating History through Metaphors," *Howard Journal of Communication* 6 (1995): 129–45; John C. Hammerback and Richard J. Jensen, *The Rhetorical Career of César Chávez,* 1st ed. (College Station: Texas A & M University Press, 1998).

36 See, for example, Victoria J. Gallagher, "Black Power in Berkeley: Postmodern Constructions in the Rhetoric of Stokely Carmichael," *Quarterly Journal of Speech* 87 (2001): 144–57; Scott and Brockriede, *The Rhetoric of Black Power;* Charles J. Stewart, "The Evolution of a Revolution: Stokely Carmichael and the Rhetoric of Black Power," *Quarterly Journal of Speech* 83 (1997): 429–46. An exception to this is Parke Burgess's essay on Black Power. See Burgess, "The Rhetoric of Black Power: A Moral Demand?" 122–33.

37 On Hammerback and Jensen, see Hammerback and Jensen, "Rhetorical Worlds," 166–76; Jensen and Hammerback, "Radical Nationalism," 191–202; Jensen and Hammerback, "No Revolutions," 72–91; Hammerback, Jensen, and Gutiérrez, *War of Words;* Hammerback, "Jose Antonio," 181–95; Hammerback and Jensen, "Ethnic Heritage," 53–70; Fernandez and Jensen, "Land Grant," 129–45; Hammerback and Jensen, *The Rhetorical Career of César Chávez.* On Delgado, see Fernando Pedro Delgado, "Chicano Movement Rhetoric: An Ideographic Interpretation," *Communication Quarterly* 43 (1995): 446–54; Fernando Pedro Delgado, "Chicano Ideology Revised: Rap Music and the (Re)Articulation of Chicanismo," *Western Journal of Communication* 62 (1998): 93–113; Delgado, "Silenced Speak," 420–38; Fernando Delgado, "The Rhetoric of Fidel Castro: Ideographs in the Service of Revolutionaries," *Howard Journal of Communication* 10 (1999): 1–14; Calafell and Delgado, "Reading Latina/o Images," 1–21.

38 Michael Calvin McGee, "Text, Context, and the Fragmentation of Contemporary Culture," *Western Journal of Speech Communication* 54 (1990): 274–89; Raymie E. McKerrow, "Critical Rhetoric: Theory and Praxis," *Communication Monographs* 56 (1989): 91–111.

39 For example, DeLuca, *Image Politics;* Kevin DeLuca, "Unruly Arguments: The Body Rhetoric of Earth First!, ACT UP, and Queer Nation," *Argumentation and Advocacy* 36 (1999): 9–21; Kevin DeLuca, "Articulation Theory: A Discursive Grounding for Rhetorical Practice," *Philosophy and Rhetoric* 32 (1999): 334–48; Kevin Michael Deluca and Anne Teresa Demo, "Imaging Nature: Watkins, Yosemite, and the Birth of Environmentalism," *Critical Studies in Media Communication* 17 (2000): 241–60; DeLuca and Peeples, "Seattle," 125–51; Janis L. Edwards and Carol K. Winkler, "Representative Form and the Visual Ideograph: The Iwo Jima in Editorial Cartoons," *Quarterly Journal of Speech* 83 (1997): 289–310; Cara A. Finnegan, "The Naturalistic Enthymeme and Visual Argument: Photographic Representation in the 'Skull Controversy'," *Argumentation and Advocacy* 37 (2001): 133–50; Cara A. Finnegan, *Picturing Poverty: Print Culture and F.S.A. Photographs* (Washington, DC: Smithsonian Institution Press, 2003), Cara A. Finnegan and Jiyeon Kang, "'Sighting' the Public: Iconoclasm and Public Sphere Theory," *Quarterly Journal of Speech* 90 (2004): 377–402; Robert Hariman and John Louis Lucaites, "Dissent and Emotional

Management in a Liberal-Democratic Society: The Kent State Iconic Photograph," *Rhetoric Society Quarterly* 31 (2001): 5–32; John Louis Lucaites, "Visualizing 'the People': Individualism and Collectivism in *Let Us Now Praise Famous Men*," *Quarterly Journal of Speech* 83 (1997): 269–89; John Louis Lucaites and Robert Hariman, "Visual Rhetoric, Photojournalism, and Democratic Political Culture," *Rhetoric Review* 20 (2001): 37–42.

40 Dwight Conquergood, "Performance Studies: Interventions and Radical Research," *The Drama Review* 46 (2002): 146.

41 For an excellent example of this attitude, see Kimberlé Crenshaw, "Demarginalizing the Intersection of Race and Sex: A Black Feminist Critique of Antidiscrimination Doctrine, Feminist Theory, and Antiracist Politics," in *Feminist Legal Theory: Readings in Law and Gender*, ed. Katharine T. Bartlett and Rosanne Kennedy (Boulder, CO: Westview, 1991), 57–80. Crenshaw writes, "Because the intersectional experience is greater than the sum of racism and sexism, any analysis that does not take intersectionality into account cannot sufficiently address the particular manner in which Black women are subordinated" (58). See, also, Kimberlé Crenshaw, "Mapping the Margins: Intersectionality, Identity Politics, and Violence against Women of Color," *Stanford Law Review* 43 (1991): 1241–99; Angela Harris, "Race and Essentialism in Feminist Legal Theory," in *Feminist Legal Theory: Readings in Law and Gender*, ed. Katharine T. Bartlett and Rosanne Kennedy (Boulder, CO: Westview, 1991), 201–34; Cheryl I. Harris, "Critical Race Studies: An Introduction," *UCLA Law Review* 49 (2002): 1215–39.

42 Ono and Sloop, "Vernacular Discourse," 40.

43 Scott and Smith, "Confrontation," 8.

44 Ronald Walter Greene, "The Aesthetic Turn and the Rhetorical Perspective on Argumentation," *Argumentation and Advocacy* 35 (1998): 19–29. The division between "influence" and "constitutive" models of persuasion and identification are set up in the first couple of pages and extended throughout the essay.

45 Joseph P. Fried, "East Harlem Youths Explain Garbage-Dumping Demonstration," *New York Times*, August 19, 1969, 86.

46 Pablo Guzmán, "La Vida Pura: A Lord of the Barrio," in *The Puerto Rican Movement: Voices from the Diaspora*, ed. Andrés Torres and José E. Velázquez (Philadelphia: Temple University Press, 1998), 155.

47 Sadly, a trip to New York City today verifies the same tendency, even if it is not as pronounced.

Affluent, predominantly white areas like much of the Manhattan borough are blessed with regular, efficient garbage collection. East Harlem, still overwhelmingly Latino (including people of Mexican and Dominican descent, in addition to the Puerto Rican majority) continues to face less regular garbage collection and street cleanings. The police presence, on the other hand, is much more visible on 106th and Madison (East Harlem) than on 50th and Madison (a wealthy business center in Manhattan).

48 Young Lords Party and Michael Abramson, *Palante: Young Lords Party*, 1st ed. (New York: McGraw-Hill, 1971), 8.

49 "Sociedad de Albizu Campos" translates as the "Albizu Campos Society." Pedro Albizu Campos was the Harvard-educated co-founder and leader of the Puerto Rican Nationalist Party in the 1930s.

50 Unless otherwise noted, as in this sentence, all references to the Young Lords will refer to the New York Young Lords, who are the focus of this study. I limit my focus to the New York group because they were the most explicitly political group, had the greatest effect on Nuyorican radicalism, and were the only group involved in the garbage offensive.

51 Young Lords Party and Abramson, *Palante*, n. p. and 73–74. The New York group eventually split from Chicago in 1970 because they felt Chicago "hadn't overcome being a gang." The Young Lords *Organization* then became the Young Lords *Party*—a name and mission they retained until changing into a different, decidedly Maoist organization in 1972. See Guzmán, "La Vida Pura," 157, 67–68.

52 Miguel Melendez, *We Took the Streets: Fighting for Latino Rights with the Young Lords* (New York: St. Martins, 2003), 93. This kind of quasi-intellectualism bears some similarity to the SDS, which makes sense both because of the YLO's temporal proximity to SDS and Juan Gonzalez's involvement with SDS at Columbia after Mark Rudd ascended to national leadership. For another account of such intellectualism, see Todd Gitlin, *The Sixties: Years of Hope, Days of Rage*, rev. trade ed. (New York: Bantam Books, 1993).

53 Guzmán in Young Lords Party and Abramson, *Palante*, 74.

54 Quoted in Melendez, *We Took the Streets*, 94.

55 This means of going out into the community taps into a tradition of "community organizing" at least as old as Saul Alinsky's work in the 1930s. Although not published until after the "garbage offensive," see Saul David Alinsky, *Rules for Radicals: A Practical Primer for Realistic Radicals*,

1st ed. (New York: Random House, 1971). This tactic was certainly similar to those used by SNCC in the South and SDS in New York and New Jersey in the 1960s (Juan Gonzalez, as mentioned in a previous footnote, had been active in SDS leadership at Columbia before helping form the Lords).

56 Quoted in Melendez, *We Took the Streets,* 95.

57 Melendez, *We Took the Streets,* 96.

58 The closest they come is in volume 1, no. 4, where there are several small news pieces about the garbage offensive. Even here, however, the narrative remains fragmented, disjointed, and (by nature of there being several pieces) repetitive. *Palante* was originally sold on street corners and subway stations in El Barrio, the Bronx, and the Lower Eastside. It was eventually sold at newsstands throughout New York City in addition to the more interactive means of distribution.

59 Conquergood, "Performance Studies," 146.

60 See McGee, "Fragmentation," 274–89. Also see DeLuca, *Image Politics,* 147–55.

61 "El Barrio and the YLO Say No More Garbage in Our Community," *Palante* 1, no. 4 (1969): 19.

62 Quoted in Matthew Gandy, *Concrete and Clay: Reworking Nature in New York City, Urban and Industrial Environments* (Cambridge, MA: MIT Press, 2002), 165–66.

63 Ernesto Laclau and Chantal Mouffe, *Hegemony and Socialist Strategy: Towards a Radical Democratic Practice* (London: Verso, 1985), 125.

64 Guzmán, "One Year," 12.

65 Diana Taylor, *The Archive and the Repertoire: Performing Cultural Memory in the Americas* (Durham, NC: Duke University Press, 2003), 5. For an account of the narrative and an attendant critique of docility, see Flores, *Divided Borders,* 13–60.

66 Guzmán quoted in Young Lords Party and Abramson, *Palante,* 75.

67 DeLuca uses "mind bomb" to reference the explosive psychological effect image events have on collective consciousness. For an introduction to the term, see DeLuca, *Image Politics,* 1–22.

68 Guzmán, "One Year," 12.

69 Melendez, *We Took the Streets,* 105.

70 Ministry of Information, "Pigs Oink in Fear as YLO and the People March Thru the Streets," *Palante* 1, no. 4 (1969): 17.

71 Quoted in "El Barrio and the YLO Say No More Garbage in Our Community," *Palante* 1, no. 4 (1969): 19.

72 Guzmán, "One Year," 12.

73 One might object to my use of "space" in this essay given that the rhetorical scholarship on social movement(s) does not point to a similar construction. While this is mostly true, DeLuca is an exception. For DeLuca, "space" is aligned with the strategic practices of those in power (e.g., legislative and legal space) and "suggests an impersonal geometrical region known through the rationalized, objective methods of science" (76). He suggests a need to focus on "place" which is "a particular locality of which a person has an intimate knowledge derived from passionate attachment and caring inhabitation" (76). I understand his desire to focus on "place" rather than "space" (especially given the definitional game he plays), but his division between the two relies on a false dichotomy. While the advances of social movement certainly emanate from particular *places,* social movement (even if scholars like McGee and DeLuca do not explain it this way) seems to be directed at the (re)formulation of cultural or discursive *spaces* in which terrains or fields of intelligibility are constructed and reconstructed. In this sense, to talk about the Young Lords as constructing a space is meant to draw attention to two things: first, the Lords redefine the barrioscape to make it an acceptable location for contestation and dissent; second, and more importantly, the Lords help to constitute a "people" who could, contrary to popular and academic characterizations, *be political* (an agential change). My position seems, moreover, to be more in line with Michel de Certeau's explanation of space as "practiced place." See Michel de Certeau, *The Practice of Everyday Life* (Berkeley: University of California Press, 1984), 117.

74 Johanna Fernandez, "Between Social Service Reform and Revolutionary Politics: The Young Lords, Late Sixties Radicalism, and Community Organizing in New York City," in *Freedom North: Black Freedom Struggles Outside the South, 1940–1980,* ed. Jeanne F. Theoharis and Komozi Woodward (New York: Palgrave Macmillan, 2003), 255–85.

75 Carl Davidson, "Young Lords Organize in New York," *Guardian,* October 18, 1969, 6.

76 Melendez, *We Took the Streets,* 109. I am not oversimplifying Melendez's account, here. This is as far as his read of the purpose and significance of the garbage offensive goes.

77 Bowers, Ochs, and Jensen, *Agitation,* 1–17.

78 Agustín Laó, "Resources of Hope: Imagining the Young Lords and the Politics of Memory," *CENTRO: Journal of the Center for Puerto Rican Studies* 7, no. 1 (1995): 37.

79 Laó, "Resources of Hope," 37.

80 Guzmán, "One Year," 12, emphasis added.

81 A survey of the primary literature on Black Power, the Black Panther Party, Students for a Democratic Society, and others makes this evident. See Max Elbaum, *Revolution in the Air: Sixties Radicals Turn to Lenin, Mao and Che* (London; New York: Verso, 2002). By "devil figure," I allude to Richard Weaver's notion of an ultimate term that carries a negative force. A "devil term" is the dialectical counterpart to a "god term," which Weaver defines as "that expression about which all other expressions are ranked as subordinate and serving dominations and powers" (212). See Richard M. Weaver, *The Ethics of Rhetoric* (Davis, CA: Hermagoras Press, 1985).

82 Iris Morales, "*¡Palante, Siempre Palante!* The Young Lords," in *The Puerto Rican Movement: Voices from the Diaspora*, ed. Andrés Torres and José E. Velázquez (Philadelphia: Temple University Press, 1998), 213.

83 Marta Moreno, speaking of the Young Lords, reminds us of the importance of "this group of young men and women of color who made significant impact on history. Inequalities in the areas of culture, education, prison reform, housing and health care came under their careful scrutiny and systematic attack. Significant changes directly resulted from their efforts." See Marta Moreno, "The Young Lords Party, 1969 1975; 'Publisher's Page,'" *Caribe* 7, no. 4 (1983): 2. It is ironic that, given the importance of the Lords recognized by Puerto Rican scholars, there is so little written about them. Writing broadly about scholarly attention to Puerto Rican movement(s), Andrés Torres argues, "The historical record on this experience is almost nonexistent. Even within the 'social movements' and 'diversity' literature, we find barely a mention of the Puerto Rican contribution to the insurgency that changed the United States." See Andrés Torres, "Introduction: Political Radicalism in the Diaspora—the Puerto Rican Experience," in *The Puerto Rican Movement: Voices from the Diaspora*, ed. Andrés Torres and José E. Velázquez (Philadelphia: Temple University Press, 1998), 1.

84 This, in part, is what led Edwin Black to critique neo-Aristotelian critics; it is certainly part of Maurice Charland's motivation behind his work on Quebec. See Edwin Black, *Rhetorical Criticism: A Study in Method* (Madison: University of Wisconsin Press, 1965); Maurice Charland, "Constitutive Rhetoric: The Case of the Peuple Québécois," *Quarterly Journal of Speech* 73 (1987): 133–50.

85 See Charland, "Constitutive Rhetoric," 133–50. See also McGee, "On Feminized Liberty," 1–31; Michael C. McGee, "In Search of 'the People': A Rhetorical Alternative," *Quarterly Journal of Speech* 61 (1975): 235–49; Michael Calvin McGee, "The 'Ideograph': A Link between Rhetoric and Ideology," *Quarterly Journal of Speech* 66 (1980): 1–16; Barbara A. Biesecker, "Rethinking the Rhetorical Situation from within the Thematic of *Différence*," in *Contemporary Rhetorical Theory: A Reader*, ed. John Louis Lucaites, Celeste Michelle Condit, and Sally Caudill (New York: Guilford, 1999), 232–46; Greene, "Aesthetic Turn," 19–29.

86 José Esteban Muñoz makes a similar point vis-á-vis the constitutive potential of Latina/o performances today. He writes, "The performance praxis of US Latina/os assists the minoritarian citizen-subject in the process of denaturalizing the United States' universalizing 'national affect' fiction as it asserts ontological validity and affective difference." See José Esteban Muñoz, "Feeling Brown: Ethnicity and Affect in Ricardo Bracho's *The Sweetest Hangover (and Other STDs)*," *Theatre Journal* 52 (2000): 72.

87 Ramón Grosfoguel, Frances Negrón-Muntaner, and Chloé S. Georas, "Beyond Nationalist and Colonialist Discourses: The *Jaiba* Politics of the Puerto Rican Ethno-Nation," in *Puerto Rican Jam: Rethinking Colonialism and Nationalism*, ed. Frances Negrón-Muntaner and Ramón Grosfoguel (Minneapolis: University of Minnesota Press, 1997), 30–31.

88 Negrón-Muntaner and Grosfoguel, *Puerto Rican Jam*, 31.

89 For an analysis of Puerto Ricans' modern colonial status, see Ramón Grosfoguel, *Colonial Subjects: Puerto Ricans in a Global Perspective* (Berkeley: University of California Press, 2003), 4–5.

90 Ono and Sloop, "Vernacular Discourse," 20.

91 Kenneth Burke, "Definition of Man," in *Language as Symbolic Action: Essays on Life, Literature, and Method* (Berkeley: University of California Press, 1966), 3–24.

92 Taylor, *The Archive and the Repertoire*, 29.

93 Lisa A. Flores, "Creating Discursive Space through a Rhetoric of Difference: Chicana Feminists Craft a Homeland," *Quarterly Journal of Speech* 82 (1996): 153, footnote 8.

94 Ernesto Laclau, *Emancipation(S)* (London: Verso, 1996), 121.

95 Taylor, *The Archive and the Repertoire*, 2–3.

96 Conquergood, "Performance Studies," 147.

97 Lucaites, quoted in Geisler, "Rhetorical Agency," 13.

The Place of Framing:
Multiple Audiences and Antiwar Protests near Fort Bragg
Michael T. Heaney and Fabio Rojas

ABBREVIATIONS

FPWJ	Fayetteville Peace with Justice
ISO	International Socialist Organization
IVAW	Iraq Veterans Against the War
MFSO	Military Families Speak Out
NCPJC	North Carolina Peace and Justice Coalition
OVMF	organizations of veterans and military families
PFADP	People of Faith Against the Death Penalty
UFPJ	United for Peace and Justice
VFP	Veterans for Peace

A small crowd gathered downtown at 9 AM on Saturday, March 19, 2005, in the parking lot not far from the Airborne and Special Operations Museum in Fayetteville, North Carolina. By 11 AM, the crowd had swelled to about 4,000 people, many of whom carried hand-held signs with messages like "Support My Dad, Not the War" and "War Targets People of Color." The crowd began to march, led by protesters carrying a large banner stating "REAL support for the troops; BRING THEM HOME NOW." Contingents from organizations representing veterans and military families followed the lead banner. A wide range of progressive, radical, and antiwar contingents trailed behind them, along with unaffiliated people from the surrounding area and neighboring states. A small group of about 40 counterprotesters stood along the parade route, which ended in Rowan Park, holding signs with messages like "God bless our president; God bless our troops" and "Straight girls ❤ men in uniform."

The Fayetteville antiwar rally was, in many ways, like thousands of rallies held around the globe since the United States announced plans to invade Iraq (Cortright, 2004; Walgrave &

Verhulst, 2004). But the location, timing, and strategy behind this rally made it stand out. March 19, 2005, was the second anniversary of the Iraq War's start and the first significant milestone for the American antiwar movement since President George W. Bush's reelection. Prominent antiwar activists saw the second anniversary as an opportunity to refocus the movement in the wake of the election. The national leaders of United for Peace and Justice (UFPJ)—the nation's broadest coalition of antiwar organizations—sought to extend the framing of the movement, in part, as an effort to "support the troops," as had been attempted by some activists opposed to the Gulf War in 1991. If the antiwar movement could capitalize on broad public support for men and women in uniform, then it could partially "harness the hegemony" of supporters of the war (especially the Bush Administration and other Republicans), who relied heavily on invocations of patriotism and public fears of terrorism to dominate the discourse about Iraq (Maney, Woehrle, & Coy, 2005; see also Gramsci, 1992). Through the tactic of rallying near Fort Bragg—one of the Army's largest military installations—and in North Carolina—one of the "red states" won by Bush in 2000 and 2004, movement leaders intended to amplify the "support the troops" frame, attract new adherents among veterans and military families, and demonstrate strength in a Republican stronghold.

The Fayetteville antiwar rally is a significant example of an effort by social movement leaders using place as a symbol in a framing strategy. The strategic use of Fort Bragg changed the politics of the rally in ways that were beyond the full control of movement leaders. Some local residents of Fayetteville claimed a privileged voice within the coalition sponsoring the rally, which suppressed the expression of alternative framings pertaining to the "right of resistance" of the Iraqi people and the historical legacy of racism in the American South. At the same time, prowar activists challenged the use of Fort Bragg by antiwar activists. Even President Bush joined the fray by traveling to Fort Bragg to give a foreign policy address on June 28, 2005 (Stevenson, 2005). The use of Fort Bragg as a symbol by antiwar movement leaders made it more readily available to other actors, thus clearing new ground for framing disputes over the Iraq War.

While much is known about place and framing separately in shaping social movements, less research illuminates how they interact with one another. One important question about the interaction between place and framing is: Under what conditions can social movement leaders use place effectively to frame political activity? We argue that places have multivalent meanings because multiple audiences of the social movement understand a place's significance differently. As a result, movement actors and their opponents are rarely able to control exclusively the meaning of a place in a framing dispute. Rather, the interaction of multiple actors determines the meaning of place for the movement and its targeted audiences. In the case of the Fayetteville antiwar rally, we examine the interaction of five groups: national antiwar leaders, the local community, competing factions within the antiwar movement, counterprotesters espousing a prowar position, and the Bush Administration. We contend that, in 2005, an alliance among national antiwar leaders, local activists in Fayetteville, and veterans organizations collaborated successfully to project a frame of antiwar protests near Fort Bragg as supportive of the troops and military families. The use of Fayetteville as a place allowed actors outside the movement to dispute the symbolism of the place. By 2006 the original antiwar alliance had broken down such that the Fayetteville protests were less successful in projecting the "support the troops" frame.

PLACE AND FRAMING IN SOCIAL MOVEMENTS

The interface between framing and the place of social movement activity is examined by various scholars, most notably Ferree, Gamson, Gerhards, and Rucht (2002), McAdam (1996), Miller (2000), and Sewell (2001). The theoretical objective of this article is to offer a more extensive explanation of the processes that connect place and framing. We note that the invocation of place by one set of actors expands the scope of a conflict, thus altering the political balance of forces among contending actors (Schattschneider, 1960). The ability of social movement actors to project their desired frames depends on the new balance. In this section, we highlight key ideas about framing, place, and conflict to explain how the multiple meanings of a place affect social movement framing.

Theories of Movement Framing and Discourse

According to Goffman (1974, pp. 10–11), a "frame" establishes a "definition of a situation . . . in accordance with the principles of organization that govern events . . . and our subjective involvement in them." Frames have the potential to render "what would otherwise be a meaningless aspect of a scene into something that is meaningful . . . and provide background for understanding events" (Goffman, 1974, pp. 21–22). Framing—the process of manipulating frames—is a vital tactic at the disposal of social movement leaders who seek to mobilize their constituents for collective action (Gamson, 1988, 1992). Framing strategies include "bridging" (connecting two ideologically congruent but disconnected frames), "amplification" (clarifying or emphasizing existing beliefs or values), "extension" (broadening a frame to include interests that were previously peripheral to the movement), and "transformation" (replacing old understandings and meanings with new ones; Snow, Rochford, Worden, & Benford, 1986, pp. 467–476). Successful framing has the potential to alter the beliefs and values that individuals hold when making decisions (Tversky & Kahneman, 1981), the decisions themselves (Riker, 1986), and ultimately the outcomes of contentious politics (Mansbridge, 1986).

Frames do not exist in a predefined form before the beginning of a conflict, but emerge dynamically through strategic interactions among leaders, activists, and opponents (Oliver

& Johnston, 2000; Snow, 2004; Snow & Benford, 1992; Westby, 2002). During this process, activists draw widely upon the discursive repertoires available to them while forming new repertoires of collective action (Auyero, 2004; Ellingson, 1995; Fine, 1995; Steinberg, 1998, 1999; Tilly, 1978, p. 151). One possible tactic in this struggle is for weaker actors to borrow from the hegemonic discourses of stronger actors in an effort to co-opt powerful symbols, stories, and frames for their own ends. Maney *et al.* (2005) argue that peace movement organizations frequently attempt to harness the hegemony of opponents to counter threats to civil liberties and democracy. However, not all peace movement organizations adhere to this strategy, especially those with "oppositional identities rooted in consciousness of structural inequalities," preferring instead to challenge the hegemony of opponents (Maney *et al.*, 2005, p. 375).

Adherents to a movement or a countermovement may have substantial disagreements about which frames are most appropriate and effective. Framing disputes may be fundamentally tactical in nature. Within a coalition, participants may fear that the use of a particular frame will direct attention away from their issues or concerns (Babb, 1996; Benford, 1993), overextend the movement in a way that dilutes its strength (Snow & Benford, 1988, p. 206), or create backlash by the opposition (Zald & Useem, 1987; McVeigh, Myers, & Sikkink, 2004; Meyer & Staggenborg, 1996). Participants in a countermovement may fear that a particular frame will allow the movement to convey its false messages effectively or otherwise mislead the public (Evans, 1997). Alternatively, framing disputes may be deeply substantive in nature. In the case of Maney *et al.*'s (2005) study of peace movement organizations, some of these groups prefer frames that challenge hegemony (rather than harness it), not because these frames would be more successful in mobilizing public opinion to end a war, but because their organizational identities are wholly inconsistent with hegemonic frameworks.

Places are symbols in the discursive repertoires of movements that are readily accessible during framing disputes. The influence of place on the dynamics of social movements thus

matters directly to framing. In the next section, we consider the emerging literature on place and its implications for interpreting framing disputes.

Place, Space, and Geography in Social Movements

While scholars often incorporate place into their accounts of contentious politics (e.g., Garrow, 1978; Gould, 1995; Zhao, 2001), there have been recent calls to more prominently feature geography in social movement theory. Miller (2000, p. 3) argues that "[a] more geographically sensitive conceptualization of social movements is necessary if social movements are to be understood in their full complexity and variability." Though progress has been made toward this end (see especially Jacobson, 2002; Miller & Martin, 2003; Sewell, 2001), critics charge that the connection between place and contentious politics remains undertheorized (Tilly, 2003, p. 203).

Movement researchers and geographers focus on the roles that space and place play in movement activities. First, recruitment studies establish that physical proximity to movement activists increases the chance that a person will join a movement. Zhao's (2001) study of the 1989 Chinese democracy movement shows that students were more likely to join the movement if their roommate was in the movement, a process resulting in clustering of student activists in specific dormitories. Gould's (1995) research on the 1871 Paris commune reveals a similar process at work. Persons were more prone to join the revolt against the French state if their friends and neighbors did so. This propensity suggests that the neighborhood is an important unit of analysis in the study of urban conflict (Gould, 1995). Similarly, Miller's (2000) analysis of the nuclear freeze movement demonstrates that neighborhoods have powerful channeling effects. He finds that access to anti-nuclear politics in Boston was influenced by a person's residential neighborhood. Local institutions mattered, since activists were more likely to work through a university group if they lived close to MIT or Harvard or to start working with anti–defense contractor groups if they lived in a zone with many contractors. Places are not only relevant to activists, but also to state actors that seek to stymie activism. McCarthy and McPhail (2006) document how police rely on the public forum doctrine systematically to dislocate protesters from the formal targets of the protest. This body of research helps to demarcate the conditions under which place affords (or limits) opportunities to participants in contentious politics.

In addition to serving as a context for action and a facilitator of participation, places may be manipulated symbolically by social movement leaders. Sewell (2001, pp. 64–66) observes that social movement leaders sometimes attempt to harness the symbolic value of place to influence the opinions of outside observers. For example, the 1963 March on Washington gathered in front of the Lincoln Memorial in order to connect symbolically the goals of the Civil Rights Movement with Abraham Lincoln's emancipation of the slaves. The result was to transform forever the meaning of the Washington Mall, which is now widely understood as a place where aggrieved populations can gather to register their discontent with social, economic, or political conditions (Sewell, 2001, p. 65). Similarly, McAdam (1996, p. 348) contends that when Martin Luther King, Jr., selected Birmingham as a place to march in 1963, the decision was calculated to provoke violence, attract media attention, and increase public awareness of racial injustice. Thus, place helped to frame the civil rights movement as a struggle of peaceful activists against an unjust social system in the South. A limitation of the symbolism-of-place accounts presented by Sewell (2001) and McAdam (1996) is that they focus on the work of one actor in establishing the meaning of a place. While we do not dispute that there may be moments in history when one leader exerts unilateral influence, we think it is more generally true that the invocation of place sparks a mobilization of myriad actors who seek to lay claim to the proper interpretation of place.

Multivalent Meanings and the Scope of Conflict

Like most symbols, places have multivalent meanings—they mean different things to different people (Klatch, 1988). A place may hold one meaning for local residents, another for minority groups, and still another for national politicians. These meanings are constructed over time through the histories that different groups share with the events they participate in at that place (Nepstad, 2004). If differences in meaning correlate with variations in geographic scale, then invocation of place as a symbol will mobilize different types of audiences at the local, regional, or national levels; which scales are most relevant is part of a socially constructed process (Brenner, 2004; Miller, 2000).

Place has the potential to broaden the conflict because invoking the symbolism of place draws new audiences to a conflict. An expanded scope of conflict is of great significance because, as Schattschneider (1960, p. 2, emphasis in original) argues, "the outcome of every conflict is determined by the *extent* to which the audience becomes involved in it." Activists generally call upon place as a symbol because they believe that the expanded scope is to their advantage. However, the intervention of new participants in the conflict disrupts the balance of forces and changes the nature of the conflict (Schattschneider, 1960, pp. 2–5). Once the scope of conflict adjusts, new forces may then have the upper hand (Kollman, 1998). We highlight that the existence or absence of alliances among participants at different geographic scales may prove decisive in this discursive struggle.

Consistent with these arguments, we make three claims about the conditions under which social movement leaders use place effectively when framing political activity:

1. *Instability of the scope of conflict* makes it exceptionally difficult for any one set of actors to control exclusively the meaning of a place in a framing dispute. As Schattschneider (1960, p. 5) explains, the balance of forces in a conflict is not stable until everyone has become involved in it. The multivalent meanings of place are established through the dynamic interaction of multiple audiences. Activists are mindful of these interactions and, thus, attempt to craft their claims in ways that appeal to multiple audiences, both proximate and distant.

2. *Invocation of symbols visibly associated with a place* enhances the effectiveness of actors in using place to project a frame. Different

symbols resonate more or less with varied audiences, so which symbols are projected in conjunction with a place influences the how the place's significance is viewed by observers. Activists are especially attentive to how media are likely (or unlikely) to represent their symbolic gestures (Koopmans, 2004; Koopmans & Olzak, 2004).

3. *Mobilized participants in the local community* occupy a privileged place in establishing the meaning of a place in a framing dispute. Members of the local community may claim privileges in establishing the meaning of a place vis-á-vis the outsiders who have temporarily invaded their space.[1] Even if they do not genuinely speak for a cross-section of the local community, outside audiences tend to give greater credence (within limits) to mobilized local participants in a conflict (Naples, 2002). This condition highlights the dual relationship between place and framing: framing may employ place to its own ends, but place may enable or constrain framing in response. The relevance of the local community partially explains why "a framing that may be highly effective in one place may be completely ineffective in other places" (Miller, 2000, p. 23).

In the ethnography that follows, we examine the use of Fayetteville by prominent antiwar leaders as a place to project the "support the troops" frame in 2005 and 2006. First, we explain why Fayetteville was selected by national and local leaders as the site of major protest, mindful of the multiple meanings of the place and the diverse audiences attentive to their activities. Their goal was to broaden the scope of conflict in a way that would effectively extend the frame of the antiwar movement as supportive of the troops. Second, we discuss the participation of active duty soldiers, veterans, and military families as symbols appropriately representative of Fayetteville as a place. Third, we highlight the privilege of activists from the local community in the coalition supporting the Fayetteville rally vis-à-vis other antiwar activists. Fourth, we note the challenge to the antiwar movement's

symbolic use of Fayetteville by prowar counter-protesters. Fifth, we report on the breakdown of the strategy to use Fayetteville to project the "support the troops" frame during 2006. At the same time, we call attention to the effect of mobilizations in Fayetteville on the increased institutionalization of the North Carolina peace movement.

ETHNOGRAPHIC FIELDWORK

As part of a larger research project, we attended numerous large-scale antiwar protest events in the Midwest, Northeast, and Washington, DC, during the 2002–2006 period. As the second anniversary of the Iraq War approached, we received e-mails from activist listservers, noticed postings on antiwar Web pages, and had conversations with informants leading us to conclude that the rally in Fayetteville on March 19, 2005, merited special attention. Our perception was that the antiwar movement had slipped into a period of confusion after John Kerry's loss in the 2004 Presidential election. Prominent leaders expressed a desire to use the second anniversary to reframe the movement, thus providing an opportunity for us to gain on-the-ground insight into the strategic behavior and tactics of a movement self-consciously at a turning point. We were especially interested in the decision by UFPJ[2] to direct resources and attention to a military town in North Carolina, since doing so was a considerable departure from its regular tactic of staging massive rallies in large cities.

Our fieldwork involved four visits to North Carolina over a one-year period. The first visit was on the weekend of March 18–20, 2005. In addition to attending the rally on Saturday, March 19, we networked informally with leaders of the event in a public hospitality space, attended the affiliated hip-hop concert on Friday, March 18, and participated in the cosponsored conferences on March 20. The second visit on the weekend of April 1–3, 2005, was to attend an informal retreat sponsored by the leaders of the North Carolina Peace and Justice Coalition (NCPJC). In conjunction with the retreat, which was intended to assess the success of the March 18–20 weekend, we attended the annual banquet of Black Workers for Justice on April 2.

The third visit was on June 28 and 29, 2005, in conjunction with President Bush's visit to Fort Bragg for the purpose of a nationally televised address on the Iraq War. The fourth visit was the weekend of March 17–19, 2006, on the occasion of the third anniversary of the war. In addition to these four visits, we shadowed the North Carolina contingent at the nationwide antiwar gathering in Washington, DC, during September 24–26, 2005.

During our visits, we produced written and audio field notes and took photographs. We conducted in-depth interviews with fifteen leaders (including two counterprotest leaders), fifty-two short interviews with rank-and-file activists, Fayetteville residents, and counter-protesters, and disseminated a brief survey which was completed by 108 participants at the March 19, 2005, rally and 145 participants at the March 18, 2006, rally. We reviewed a videotape of the 2005 weekend produced by Atlanta Indymedia, as well as media accounts of the events. While this article draws primarily upon our observations and interviews during our five field visits, we used the additional sources of information to check our recollections of events.

HARNESSING THE SYMBOLISM OF FAYETTEVILLE

The multivalent meanings of Fayetteville resonate with audiences that are supportive of and opposed to the Iraq War. As the home of Fort Bragg, as well as a historical center of peace activism and racial oppression, Fayetteville simultaneously represents war, patriotism, peace, and southern racism in the eyes of diverse audiences. This section considers how these meanings led national and local antiwar activists to converge on Fayetteville as the site of a major antiwar rally in 2005.

Fayetteville has been home to Fort Bragg since the middle of World War I, when it was established as a permanent location for year-round artillery practice by the army (Office of the Command Historian, 2005). Since that time, the fort has become a center for airborne and special forces, and a source of economic, political, and psychological dependence for the city's population of 121,015 people (49% white,

42% black, 9% other or multi-racial; U.S. Census Bureau, 2005).

Along with a tradition of service and pride, an oppositional consciousness has evolved in Fayetteville as social activists have attempted to harness hegemony by co-opting the symbolism of Fort Bragg for their own ends. During the Vietnam War era, organizations like GI's United Against the War in Indochina and Concerned Officers Against the War sponsored contentious marches down Hay Street and into Rowan Park (Lutz, 2001, pp. 140–141). In the midst of conflicts with the town's population, the local Quaker House, which provided information, encouragement, and support to conscientious objectors, was burned to the ground in a suspicious fire on May 20, 1970 (Lutz, 2001, p. 165).

Although the 1980s and 1990s were quiet times for the peace movement in Fayetteville, citizens maintained an activist community. In late 2000, activists from the reincarnated Quaker House established a chapter of People of Faith Against the Death Penalty (PFADP). On September 4, 2001, PFADP successfully prompted the city council to pass a resolution in favor of a North Carolina death penalty moratorium. In the aftermath of the September 11 attacks, PFADP sought ways to remain active on issues tied to the "culture of violence," leading them to found an organization called Fayetteville Peace with Justice (FPWJ) in November 2001.

When declaration of a "War on Terror" shifted the nation's attention toward foreign affairs, FPWJ joined the emerging statewide antiwar network. FPWJ leaders participated in a November 2002 rally in the state capital of Raleigh that drew many of North Carolina's key activists. Having participated in the Raleigh event and built relationships broadly across North Carolina, FPWJ members proposed a statewide event in Fayetteville on the Iraq War's first anniversary. Army veteran Lou Plummer, a member of FPWJ, put out a call to action in February 2004 that resulted in a rally on March 20, 2004, that drew about 1,100 people to Fayetteville. This was the largest peace rally in the city since the Vietnam War. By highlighting the involvement in the rally by military veterans, their families, and the families of those on active duty, FPWJ established that Fort Bragg could be used counter-hegemonically as a symbol by the antiwar movement, even in the post-911 era.

Several leading antiwar activists described the national antiwar movement as "demoralized" in the aftermath of the President Bush's 2004 reelection. However, FPWJ activists sensed that they had only begun to tap into the symbolism of Fort Bragg, so they quickly began to organize a repeat performance of the rally in Fayetteville. With a successful precedent and an already established network of activists, efforts were undertaken to produce an event with a broader reach and visibility. Consistent with our first claim, this strategy expanded the scope of conflict around Fort Bragg. FPWJ renewed its invitation for others to join with military families and veterans, thus seeking to harness the symbolic legitimacy of these individuals' past and present military involvement when holding a protest near Fort Bragg (consistent with our second claim).

On November 20, 2004, the first of several planning meetings was held in Fayetteville in preparation for the second-anniversary event. Consistent with our third claim, members of FPWJ invoked the fact that the initial invitation came from Fayetteville to augment their authority throughout the planning process. Although the coalition behind the rally would eventually span beyond North Carolina, notions of appropriateness by activists in the local community occupied a privileged place in the discussions and weighed heavily in the choices of tactics.

While local community activists called attention to the potential resonance of a larger event in Fayetteville, it was principally national antiwar movement leaders in UFPJ who seized the opportunity to use a rally near Fort Bragg as part of a larger framing strategy. For them, staging a widely visible rally in Fayetteville was one tactic to attract the attention of the media and to transform the way other attentive audiences viewed the antiwar movement. At the same time, national antiwar leaders could not simply have chosen any town with a fort to stage a successful rally. The participation of local community members in the planning process gave activists legitimacy that enabled institutional access to meetings halls, parks, and streets that would not

have been as easily available otherwise (certainly not without extensive legal assistance).

North Carolina activists began to reach out for broad support once the decision to hold the rally was finalized. Bryan Proffitt of Hip Hop Against Racist War, a North Carolina resident on the UFPJ national steering committee, authored a proposal for UFPJ to support a weekend-long event (March 18–20) as an expansion of the single-day event the previous year. In addition to a rally in Rowan Park on Saturday, March 19, the proposal called for a hip-hop concert on Friday, a Southern Organizers Conference on Sunday, and financial and logistical support from UFPJ's national office. This support would enable the coalition of activists in North Carolina—now identifying itself as the North Carolina Peace and Justice Coalition (NCPJC)—to increase its resources and institutionalize its efforts. The actual events of the weekend followed Proffitt's original proposal almost to the letter, with the only exception being the absence of a celebrity speaker, such as filmmaker Michael Moore or Congresswoman Cynthia McKinney.

Proponents of the Fayetteville rally tapped the multivalent meanings of Fayetteville in making their appeals for support. For example, activists at the local and national levels stressed that rallying in Fayetteville demonstrated a symbolic commitment to organizing in the South. Proffitt's proposal emphasized the strategic importance of the South to the antiwar movement:

> Many national organizations pay lip-service to their understanding of the South's significance, but few commit the resources necessary to help Southern organizers do our work. This has to change, and UFPJ has an opportunity to be at the center of a process of building a Southern network, and a Southern movement, to replace war and occupation with justice and self-determination (Proffitt, 2004, p. 1).

Proffitt's proposal went on to detail the ways in which place ought to be a critical element in UFPJ's strategy; Fayetteville's symbolic value was not only due to its proximity to Fort Bragg, but also due to its location in the heart of a de-unionized land of immigrant labor, rural evangelical Republicanism, and the unmistakable legacies of racism and the decimation of native peoples (Proffitt, 2004). This sentiment was echoed by UFPJ's national representative, Hany Khalil, when he spoke to the First National Convention of Iraq Veterans Against the War (IVAW) on March 20, 2005:

> United for Peace and Justice decided to support this rally... because we know that organizing in the South is the key for the peace movement; for the future of the progressive movement in this country. And we know that building with veterans and military families is essential to those tasks as well. And I think that the work that people have done over the past few months has helped to show all those people out there who said that there was such a thing as blue states and red states, and that wrote off the South, that that was completely wrong.

Staging a major rally in Fayetteville was both symbolic of, and a vital opportunity for, expanding the reach of antiwar and progressive movements in the South.

Antiwar activists recognized that the successful use of Fayetteville as a place depended not only on the choice of the city itself, but also on the invocation of appropriate symbols associated with the place (consistent with our second claim). Key activists recognized that the symbolic importance of organizing in Fayetteville was tied to who delivered the message for the antiwar movement. They were mindful that the place of the rally could attract a different kind of adherent to the movement, thus augmenting the authority of the "support the troops" frame (see also Druckman, 2001). By choosing tactics that emphasized the role of organizations of military families and veterans, organizers believed that they could begin to shape public opinion. As NCPJC staff member Andrew Pearson explained:

> There was a very clear recognition that, at least for the public and the media, what we were doing would be irrelevant if it didn't have a stronger ethos in who was

delivering the message. And who better to express antiwar sentiment and actually resonate with people at this point in the antiwar movement than people who were experiencing it directly? ... We learned on February 15, 2003 [the date of the "Global Day of Action"] that no matter how many millions of everyday people you get in the streets, the administration can still do what they want, but that when you get people from the inside, Pentagon officials, CIA people, GIs, vets, military families, people who are really integral to making the war happen resist, then there is a real power and a real chance to stop or prevent those kinds of conflicts and occupations.

UFPJ supported the rally by supplying $5,000 of seed money, sharing its mailing lists, offering logistical support, and giving prominent attention to Fayetteville on its web page. UFPJ did not give the same level of attention on its web page to other rallies. For example, UFPJ sponsored a bus from New York (the location of its organizational headquarters) to Fayetteville, rather than directly support a large rally in Central Park organized by Troops Out Now! UFPJ's tactic of highlighting one place—Fayetteville—for national attention was coupled with efforts to deemphasize numerically larger events held in other locales. These tactics helped to legitimize Fayetteville's rally as the "national" protest event on March 19 and directed the attention of the antiwar movement to it.

With UFPJ's leadership, the scope of attention to the Fayetteville rally broadened to audiences that had not been involved in the conceptualization or planning of the rally. Other antiwar organizations quickly recognized the significance of the Fayetteville protest. For example, the principal organizations responsible for sponsoring antiwar events in Washington, DC, over the past several years (the DC Antiwar Network, Code Pink, and International ANSWER) cancelled their planned protests in Washington in order to send buses to Fayetteville. (Notably, each of these organizations is known for challenging—rather than harnessing—hegemony.) As a result, the Washington, DC, area did not host a major protest event the weekend of March 19. Instead, small prayer vigils were held by Quaker organizations near the Capitol building and in Clarendon, Virginia.[3] The national mobilization effort made Fayetteville one of a few cities to host a larger protest on the war's second anniversary than on the first.

A wide variety of national, international, and independent media—including television, radio, print, and Internet publications—reported on the Fayetteville rally. For example, a basic search of newspapers using Pro-Quest identified twelve distinct articles that covered the rally, including the *New York Times, Washington Post, USA Today, Atlanta Journal-Constitution,* and *San Francisco Chronicle,* but not including the widespread attention paid by left-leaning independent media outlets (such as *Democracy Now!*). Some of these articles explained the event explicitly as part of a strategy of the movement to amplify the "support the troops" frame (e.g., Basu, 2005; Finer, 2005). A truly astonishing aspect of all these articles is that Fayetteville is mentioned side-by-side with New York, London, and San Francisco. The fact that a relatively small city in the middle of rural North Carolina is juxtaposed with the great cities of the world is strong evidence that movement leaders were effective in using the rally to amplify the "support the troops" frame. Some of this attention may have been due to media expectations that a conflict might erupt with a protest so close to a military base (Gitlin, 1980). Regardless of whether every observer of the protest interpreted it as supportive of the troops, the increased attention to the rally no doubt amplified the intended frame. This symbolic use of place as a central tactic in a framing strategy is analogous to its use during the civil rights movement, as detailed by McAdam (1996) and Sewell (2001).

VETERANS AND MILITARY FAMILIES TAKE CENTER STAGE

Staging an antiwar rally near Fort Bragg required organizers to strike a delicate balance. While they wished to project the notion that the rally was supportive of the troops and military families, they were mindful that their plans might be interpreted by some observers as opposition to the troops themselves. This sensitivity stemmed from the awareness that multiple audiences are observing the activities of the movement, as we note in our first claim. Thus, the physical presence and participation of individuals representing organizations of veterans and military families (which hereafter are called OVMFs) was seen as vital to projecting a pro-troops frame. The OVMFs were perceived as being the appropriate actors to harness the hegemony of the War on Terror since it is difficult or impossible for war proponents to label them as "disloyal" or "unpatriotic," as is done more easily to members of other groups. The perceived necessity of OVMFs in the rally privileged their role vis-á-vis other constituencies within NCPJC, including (but not limited to) Quakers, peace activists, African Americans, civil libertarians, women, and socialists. The concerns and tactics of OVMFs came to dominate an event ostensibly planned to "support the troops."

The multivalent meanings of Fayetteville encouraged OVMF involvement. Fayetteville resonated with these groups not only because of the desire to project the "support the troops" frame, but because of the significance of Fort Bragg in the history of the military and of resistance to the military. Mary Barr of Gainesville, Florida, a member of Veterans for Peace (VFP) and the GI Rights Hotline, noted that Fayetteville was significant to her because of the historic role Quaker House had played as the first safe house for conscientious objectors during the Vietnam War. Today, Quaker House is one of the national headquarters for the GI Rights Hotline. Jerry McRaith of Rice Lake, Wisconsin, President of the Northwoods Chapter of VFP, told us that he came to Fayetteville in order to support other veterans' organizations, especially IVAW and Military Families Speak Out (MFSO) and to observe the reaction of local people to the protest. For McRaith, place facilitated both the expression of solidarity and the testing of movement tactics.

In conjunction with the OVMFs, the organizers of the rally used three principal tactics to amplify the extended frame. First, the parade to Rowan Park was led by the OVMFs. Second, the choice of speakers for the stage in Rowan Park was weighted toward members of the OVMFs.

Third, IVAW and MFSO held their national meetings in Fayetteville on the day following the rally.

Representatives of the OVMFs marched in the front of the parade to Rowan Park, carrying banners to declare the presence of each organization.[4] A few contingents of non-OVMFs, such as the Campus Antiwar Network, the Women's International League for Peace and Freedom, and the North Carolina Council of Churches, carried banners in the parade, but they followed significantly behind the OVMFs. The order and visual appearance of the parade conveyed a clear hierarchy with the OVMFs at the apex. We think it is significant that this is the only protest we attended during the 2002–2006 period that unambiguously placed OVMFs at the top of a multi-organizational hierarchy. Photographs of other events did not show OVMFs leading large antiwar marches.

The appearance of veterans in the parade helped create visual images and sounds consistent with the place. Many veterans wore combat uniforms and participated in an elaborate series of "sound off" leader-response calls, consistent with the repertoire of their military training. We counted nineteen distinct calls by marching veterans. A typical call was: "We're the veterans against the war. We know what we're marching for. Two years ago we went to war. Now what are we fighting for?" Veterans' dress and chants conveyed a coherence lacked by most other groups in the parade, which leaders hoped would orient the coverage by news media. Their efforts to frame news coverage were largely successful (in this particular news cycle, at least). For example, National Public Radio broadcast the veterans' "sound off" calls in its coverage of the event (Marshall-Genzer, 2005).

On the main stage in Rowan Park, sixty percent of the scheduled speakers (24 out of 40) were either veterans or members of military families. Of the remaining sixteen speakers, four were conscientious objectors, three were family members of victims of terrorist attacks or war violence, and nine represented civic, religious, or political organizations unaffiliated with the military, such as the Muslim-American Public Affairs Council, the International Solidarity Movement, and the Coalition of Immokalee Workers. Only one speaker, Rann Bar-On of the International Solidarity Movement, did not address the plight of soldiers, veterans, military families, or innocent American civilians who have been victimized in the War on Terror or the Iraq War.[5]

While all of the OVMFs were prominent at the rally, many of the activists were fond of saying that "the Iraq veterans are the rock stars of the peace movement." One of the more widely discussed speeches was given by Michael Hoffman, a co-founder of IVAW, who was honorably discharged from the Marine Corps. After taking the stage to a standing ovation, Hoffman used his platform, in part, to call for support for better veterans' benefits:

> When we joined the military, we signed a contract. But a contract works two ways. We said we would be willing to fight and die for our government. The government said they would take care of us after we do fight, and they are welching on that promise right now. We are here in Fayetteville now to say that we will stand by the troops, that we will support them, that we will fight for the benefits that we earned, that we were promised, and you will help us fight for that.

Another speaker representing the OVMFs was Cindy Sheehan, co-founder of Gold Star Families for Peace, whose son Casey was killed in Iraq. Sheehan garnered worldwide attention a few months later in August 2005 when she camped outside of President Bush's ranch in Crawford, Texas, demanding to know the "noble cause" for which her son died.

The fact that IVAW and MFSO elected to hold their annual meetings in Fayetteville on March 20 solidified the rally on March 19 as an event endorsed by veterans and military families. The conferences afforded these organizations a critical opportunity to unite, support one another, and reflect on their place in the contemporary antiwar movement. In a remarkably candid speech that opened the IVAW conference, Vietnam veteran David Cline, National President of VFP, reacted to the strategic position occupied by the veterans' organizations by borrowing a metaphor from military combat:

One of the things that I've learned is that when the shit gets heavy and they call you unpatriotic, love to get a veteran out in front, because it is hard to criticize you. And I don't mind running cover for anybody; that's being a point man. But being a point man means that you're part of the crew. And you have to be listened to at the table and treated justly.

He continued by considering the balance that veterans should strike in this role:

We can't allow ourselves to be put into a position of being window dressing for the peace movement. Now, there's two sides to this, because not only is there a danger of just being window dressing, but there's also a danger of thinking that the movement should just be in support of or behind military families and veterans. See the only way we're going to get a broad-based social movement in this country is to organize all the people that are concerned around their real issues.

Cline's further comments conveyed that OVMFs held the balance of power in the antiwar movement at the moment and the potential to exert sway over its strategies and tactics. While the OVMFs were drawn into the rally because of their symbolic consonance with Fort Bragg (consistent with our second claim), requesting their participation ultimately yielded power to these groups over the rally's agenda and staging.

THE LOCAL COMMUNITY WITHIN THE COALITION

The national scope of the 2005 antiwar rally brought a diverse cadre of activists to Fayetteville. Although solidarity with the troops and OVMFs drew many of these visitors, others came with agendas pertaining to the injustices of capitalism, southern racism, homophobia, religious freedom for Muslims, the Israeli-Palestinian conflict, and many other issues. Some activists sought to use the rally as an opportunity to project these alternative agendas. However, consistent with our third claim, activists from the local community

exerted privileges in the planning and execution of the rally that prevented alternative frames from dominating the discourse surrounding the event. Instead, an alliance among local activists, national antiwar leaders, and the OVMFs kept the event focused on supporting the troops.

The objection of key actors within FPWJ and NCPJC to airing alternative frames was more tactical than substantive in nature. In private, the many rank-and-file activists in NCPJC were more readily drawn into discussions concerning "white privilege in the South," sexism, or homophobia than they were into conversations about the Iraq War. For example, the most widely discussed stage event was the performance by the Cuntry Kings, a self-proclaimed group of "Drag Kings," that presented a skit criticizing the military's discrimination on the basis of sexual orientation. Debates about sexuality were a central part of activists' discursive repertoires, nurtured during their concurrent careers in other social movements. But, during NCPJC discourses, activists saw the "support the troops" frame as more appropriate and effective *in this place* than the alternatives. Even some self-identified socialists could agree that it would not be strategically productive for the rally to be framed as having been "sponsored by socialists."

Alternative framings were rejected principally because the state-level actors in NCPJC listened closely to the FWPJ members' objections [to] these frames. In particular, the sponsorship of conferences by the OVMFs was viewed as grounds for sensitivity. Local leaders such as Lou Plummer spoke for the OVMFs in the NCPJC meetings, declaring what types of plans would or would not be palatable in Fayetteville. For example, the authority of the local community was invoked to stymie discussion of an event that might take place closer to the gates of Fort Bragg, or on Hay Street, as occurred during the Vietnam War. Activists did not push to march through the center of town, but accepted a parade route through a quiet, residential area, in part to avoid confrontations with local people. These decisions resulted, in part, because the proximity of local activists made them essential to securing permits and negotiating with police and, in part, out of a desire not to alienate the OVMFs and pro-military residents of the local area.

The core leadership of NCPJC acquiesced to the desire of local activists to keep the rally focused on the hegemony-harnessing frame of supporting the troops. However, other elements of the NCPJC coalition resisted this decision, preferring instead to challenge hegemony. Especially salient was the question of whether NCPJC should support the "right of resistance" of the Iraqi people against the American occupation. While a defense of the "right of resistance" is common at rallies sponsored by sectarian movement organizations like International ANSWER, such claims are especially incendiary in a town where the families of injured and killed soldiers live. When representatives of the ISO on the NCPJC Steering Committee raised the prospect of affirming the "right of resistance," they were quickly rebuffed by core coalition leaders and FPWJ representatives.

The "right of resistance" was only one of several issues on which ISO representatives were criticized by others in NCPJC as drawing upon a discursive repertoire that was inappropriate within the local community. During the planning process, ISO-FPWJ disputes materialized in discussions about who would speak on the stage. During the evaluation process, credit or blame for different aspects of the weekend depended on adherence to what was appropriate in Fayetteville. At evaluation sessions, we witnessed two tense confrontations between representatives of ISO and FPWJ, one on March 20 and one on April 2. The end result was that core coalition leaders asked ISO representatives not to participate in further NCPJC meetings or events.

Despite the efforts by coalition leaders to suppress alternative framings, their tactics were not entirely successful. Numerous FPWJ activists were irate when the *Fayetteville Observer* pictured a contingent from the International Socialist Organization (ISO) on the front page, rather than a contingent of veterans (Williams, 2005). Regardless of the efforts of movement leaders, local news media exploited the symbols of the rally in the ways that seemed appropriate to them. This outcome illustrates our first claim that no one set of actors can control exclusively the meaning of a place and demonstrates the limits of what a movement can accomplish by symbolic manipulation.

Privileges of the local community advantaged proponents of the "support the troops" frame in dialogues with critics of the military present at the rally and conference. We spoke at length with Efia Nwangaza, a civil rights attorney and former member of the Student Nonviolent Coordinating Committee, who served on UFPJ's national steering committee as a representative of Not in Our Name, an organization focused on resistance to the U.S. government's war on terrorism. She was also one of the facilitators of the Southern Organizers Gathering on March 20. During the interview, Nwangaza challenged the pro-troops frame of the weekend. She noted that the speakers on Saturday focused "almost exclusively on U.S. losses" and with a few exceptions "did not acknowledge the humanity of the Iraqi people." Of the weekend, she complained that:

> There was too much deference to the military. People formerly in the military have to be accountable for their participation in the military. Why were they in the military in the first place? The United States military does not have a history of largesse. It has a history of imperialism.

Rather than extending the frame of the antiwar movement to support the troops, Nwangaza proposed a frame "transformation" in which the antiwar movement promoted justice for all peoples, regardless of race or nationality. Consistent with our second claim, Nwangaza invoked the former slave market in downtown Fayetteville as a counterhegemonic symbol associated with the place to advance a race-based critique of the military. To Nwangaza, Fayetteville vividly symbolized historical racism. Local activists responded by arguing that the prevailing logic of Fayetteville is that because the individuals who serve in the military put their lives on the line for the country, and because their families and community make considerable emotional and economic sacrifices when soldiers go to war, civilians who come to military communities must show special deference and respect to the military during their visits.

NCPJC rejected racism, homophobia, and the right of resistance in framing disputes because of their perceived need to pacify multiple audiences simultaneously, especially OVMFs, local activists, and the local community more broadly. These frames were more visible at rallies elsewhere which were not perceived to be subject to the same constraint. Rallies held the same weekend in San Francisco, Chicago, and New York more openly stressed these relatively radical frames in advertisements, hand-held signs, and staged speeches.[6] First, the liberal-leaning local communities in each of these places are—or are perceived to be—more tolerant of counter-hegemonic frames. Second, the wishes of the OVMFs were not a constraint in these places, since they were not central players in these protest coalitions. Third, none of the sponsors of these events made place a part of the framing strategy. In the case of Fayetteville, place significantly constrained the use of alternative frames. This comparison suggests that on a more general level (and consistent with our first claim), the choice of frames depends on the particular set of audiences that protest sponsors seek to reach with their frame.

COUNTERING ANTIWAR PROTESTERS

By invoking Fayetteville and Fort Bragg as part of their framing strategy, antiwar activists provoked the involvement of people who understood these places as symbolic of patriotism and conservative values (consistent with our first claim). For them, protesting so close to a military installation was evidence of disrespect for—rather than support of—the troops. Disputes over the "support the troops" frame were most explicit when the March 19 parade encountered about 40 counterprotesters on the left side of the road, in a section marked off by police tape. Arguments between marchers and counterprotesters frequently touched on the meaning of place. The counterprotest sponsor was Free Republic, an Internet-based conservative discussion forum created by Jim Robinson in 1996. The counterprotesters challenged the view that the protest was supported by veterans and military families. Instead, they targeted the groups present whose organizational identities were rooted in oppositional consciousnesses. One of the counterprotesters, a middle-aged white female, had a bull horn:

The veterans and the men and women who have family members who were killed are being used as pawns by leftist groups. . . . There are no pro-America groups who are marching with Madea Benjamin. There are no pro-America groups who are marching with Brian Becker and ANSWER and the International Socialist Organization, the Workers World Party, United for Peace and Justice, the biggest leftist Marxists in the country. They all hate America. You are dancing in the blood of dead American soldiers. You give these people money and the money is sent to Iraq to blow up more American soldiers. Madea Benjamin and Code Pink are not peace-loving. They want more Americans dead. The more Americans that Code Pink sees dead, the more they celebrate.

At this point, a crowd of drumming protesters passed, chanting, "Support the troops for real. Bring them home now." The counterprotesters passed the bull horn to a middle-aged white male:

Hey don't lie to these people. . . . You don't give a damn about the war. You're using the war as an excuse to push socialism. We hear you over there yelling "Money for jobs and money for education.". . . But what do you want? You are using the war as an excuse. You would rather we lose the war. The more American soldiers die, the more you can push your agenda. You're not interested in the life of American troops.

These arguments were typical of counterframing strategies in which political opponents seize movement claims and frames and try to alter their policy implications (Naples, 2002).

A primary goal of the counterprotesters was to communicate that the protesters were not symbolically representative of Fayetteville or Fort Bragg. First, very literally, the protesters were not "from here." They were bussed in from somewhere else; most likely, New York City.[7] Second, the protesters did not "belong here" because they did not hold the values appropriate in this place. They are socialist and anti-American. They did not really support the troops and, in fact, were likely to bring them harm. One counterprotester, a middle-aged white man, told us:

> Some of these people's mother and father helped kill some of my friends in Vietnam doing the same garbage that these people here are doing. I've got a son and a son-in-law overseas. And they're trying to kill them too.

Third, the fact that the protesters came to Fayetteville, as opposed to going somewhere else, proves that they are against the troops. A young white female recommend that, "if they're against the war, they should go to where the decisions are made in Washington, DC. Since they're here, they must be against the soldiers." Although not part of the counterprotest, Brad Trogdon, a white Fayetteville resident, shared a similar sentiment:

> I really think it was disgusting because Fayetteville is probably the largest military town in North Carolina. Fort Bragg is probably the largest military base in the country.[8] For you to have protests—now I understand that all people have their First Amendment rights . . . However, I think that when you have a show like that it is so totally disrespectful to the troops who are over there fighting to give them that right . . . and more so to the families of the people still left behind over here.

President Bush seized the last word on Fort Bragg in 2005 when he came to town to give a televised address to the nation on June 28. His presence reflected the expanded scope of conflict brought about by the rally and can be viewed as an attempt to reassert hegemony over the use of the fort as a symbol in the War on Terror. North Carolina activists interpreted the President's choice of place for his speech as a reaction to their rally on March 19. Bridgette Burge—a member of the inner circle of NCJPC—wrote to us in a personal e-mail on June 28 that "President Bush is headed to Fort Bragg today for a pep-rally. We see it as a victory of our framing efforts and strategic use of place. This administration is reacting to our framing! Brilliant."[9]

We traveled to Fayetteville on the day of the President's speech. Members of FPWJ staged a small vigil of about fifty people at the Market House in the town center, with Chuck Fager of Quaker House serving as the principal organizer. Several of the participants we interviewed objected that the President's speech was "using the troops as a prop" to support his "failed policies." Interestingly, the March 19 rally can be seen in exactly the same light: the use of the troops as a prop, a symbol, with a politically loaded, specific meaning. Regardless of whether the President's speech at Fort Bragg was, in fact, scheduled to react to the Fayetteville antiwar rally, we view the dialogue among activists as an archetypal example of our first claim: A place cannot be owned or controlled by any one set of actors in contentious politics. Instead, place becomes a touchstone through which divergent audiences compete for advantage in a framing dispute.

ONE YEAR LATER

We revisited Fayetteville one year later for the third anniversary of the war. NCPJC organized a rally on March 18, 2006. Many of the same activists—dogged still by counterprotesters from Free Republic—worked behind the scenes as the contingent paraded from downtown into Rowan Park. Veterans groups were largely absent, yielding a much different look and sound for the march. Media accounts estimated that approximately one thousand people turned out. According to our survey, only a few marchers (8.27%) came from outside North Carolina, in contrast to the approximately 38.89% that we estimate made the journey from another state the previous year.

We noticed significantly less police surveillance in 2006 than we had in 2005, and the tension between police and organizers was markedly less palpable than it had been. Likewise, disagreements among internal participants seemed nonexistent in 2006, in contrast to how they had boiled above the surface in 2005. Members of the ISO were visibly absent from the program and all other aspects of the event. The Southern Organizers Gathering at the Rainbow Room on Sunday morning consisted of a progressively dwindling small group from Fayetteville and the surrounding local areas. The scope of conflict had obviously narrowed.

Without UFPJ directing media attention to the rally in 2006, it escaped significant news coverage. Our Pro-Quest search identified only one article (from a Raleigh newspaper) that covered the Fayetteville rally (Stock, 2006). While news coverage alone does not establish conclusively that a movement's frames are received by intended audiences or not, it is a fair indicator of the likelihood. We think that the significant differences in coverage between the two rallies is strong evidence of the relative success of the 2005 rally in projecting its intended frame in comparison with the 2006 rally.

The relative absence of contention and excitement at the 2006 rally solidified, for us, the tremendous significance of what had happened in Fayetteville the year before. In 2005, national antiwar leaders had self-consciously turned to Fayetteville as part of a grand framing strategy. They did not use Fayetteville or Fort Bragg freely and without constraint—they faced resistance from the local community, factions within the movement, and an organized counterprotest. Nonetheless, it was the alliance among national leaders in UFPJ, local activists, and OVMFs that injected broad significance into the Fayetteville rally in 2005. Their strategy amplified one of the multivalent meanings of Fayetteville in the eyes of multiple audiences attentive to these events.

National antiwar leaders saw 2006 as a year to reframe the movement in light of the Bush Administration's bungling of emergency aid during Hurricane Katrina. Many of the veterans organizations that had been such a vital force during the 2005 Fayetteville rally instead joined the "Veterans Gulf March" from Mobile to New Orleans (March 14–19, 2006), which focused on the theme "Every bomb dropped in Iraq explodes over the Gulf Coast" (Veterans Gulf March, 2006). In this case, place was part of a "bridging" strategy that attempted to amplify the connection between the frames "social needs" and "wasteful war." In keeping with the framing strategy of national leaders, the NCPJC organizers pointed to the New Orleans rally when speaking to the press during their own rally

(Stock, 2006). This switch in focus to New Orleans highlights the efforts of movement leaders to alter how place serves as a symbolic backdrop for a movement.

Although the 2005 rally near Fort Bragg was but a moment in history, it was also a moment with lasting consequences for its hosts in Fayetteville and in North Carolina. Many participants from the Fayetteville rally went to Washington on September 24, 2005, with 40 of them staying in town to lobby Congress on Monday the 26th. Lobby day coordinator Tamara Tal told us that "March 19 helped to unify us and give us focus. It inspired us to keep working together." During the lobby day in Congress, we noticed that the North Carolina contingent was among the most organized groups, with perhaps only the New York contingent maintaining a similarly high level of focus. On April 22–23, 2006, NCPJC held a statewide convention "to formalize a 3 year old network of antiwar, peace, and justice activists and organizations into a strong, democratic, statewide, powerful and accountable Coalition" (NCPJC, 2006). It formally agreed on points of unity and elected a steering committee (to supplant governance by the previous "interim" steering committee). This move expanded NCJPC's organizational capacity and allowed it to respond rapidly to events of the spring and summer of 2006, such as widespread discontent over congressional efforts to crack down on immigration.

The inner circle of NCPJC tentatively decided not to organize a fourth anniversary march near Fort Bragg in 2007. They have accepted that the symbolic power of Fort Bragg for the antiwar movement has faded, at least for the moment. Yet the ability of North Carolina activists to stage three successive rallies in Fayetteville helped to provide the impetus that made greater institutionalization of the movement possible.

Conclusion: Place and Movement Tactics

The meaning of place is multivalent within social movements. Places neither have inherent meanings that can be invoked freely by any participant in a discourse, nor do the inhabitants of a place have exclusive control over the significance of where they live. Rather, places become resonant symbols through negotiation and interaction among multiple audiences. Actors within coalitions and countermovements use place differently in these discourses, sometimes preferring to use place to harness the hegemony of opponents, while other times choosing to challenge the hegemony of opponents. As the scope of conflict broadens, competing audiences construct the relevant graphic geographic scale: a place alternatively becomes representative of a local population, a region, and a nation's history. In analyzing these dynamics, our ethnography contributes to scholarly understandings of place in social movements by clarifying the processes through which frames, tactics, and audiences interrelate during contentious politics.

Political actors regularly invoke geographic places as part of their framing tactics. Beyond the Fayetteville rallies, Martin Luther King, Jr.'s marches on Washington, Selma, and Birmingham, Cindy Sheehan's vigil in Crawford, the Veterans' Gulf March, and the 2004 Republican National Convention all reflect the strategic use of place. Political actors rarely find, however, that their tactics work precisely as planned. Rather, the multivalent meanings of a place interest new audiences in the conflict, widening its scope. If leaders fail to align key audiences according to the intended frame, the result may be the opposite of what was planned. The reaction of mobilized participants within the local community may be especially influential in affecting the outcomes of these framing disputes.

Our ethnography specifies that place is often a critical part of the discursive opportunity structure that allows social movement actors to shape public opinion (Snow, 2004). In doing so, we fulfill, in part, Miller's (2000, p. xv) call for "analysis of local mobilizing efforts and their interactions with broader-scale processes." We identify and explain the processes that govern these interactions: the changing scope of conflict among multiple audiences, the successful and unsuccessful invocation of visibly associated symbols, and the privileged position of local participants in the conflict. In doing so, our analysis jointly enhances theories of place and theories of framing in contentious politics.

Fayetteville alternatively stands for patriotism, militarism, resistance to militarism, the South, or racism, depending on whom you ask. Especially in 2005, antiwar activists were able to channel the symbolism of place to frame the antiwar movement as mobilized in part to "support the troops." One limitation of our account is that we arrived on the scene once the frames and the key players had been well defined. As a result, we see less clearly than we would like the role of place in the initial filtering of competing frames. Further research could fruitfully explore this filtering process, perhaps focusing more on the routine—rather than contentious—stage of framing. Such investigations could prove to be an opportunity to connect more clearly discussions of identity formation, emotions, and resource mobilization with frame construction.

Notes

[1] The collective identity formation process, which establishes who is or is not a "member" of the community in question and what constitutes a "locality," also may prove to be a contested aspect of the place-based framing dispute (Miller, 2000, p. 20; see also Martin & Miller, 2003, p. 148).

[2] A list of abbreviations is provided at the beginning of the article.

[3] We hired two observers to attend these events and conduct surveys of the participants. Our observers confirmed media accounts that these vigils did not resemble the massive protests that have been commonplace in Washington since George W. Bush became President.

[4] The OVMFs carrying banners were IVAW, MFSO, VFP, Vietnam Veterans Against the War, and Gold Star Families for Peace.

[5] Bar-On was arrested later in the day for crossing the police perimeter in symbolic defiance of the wall separating the Palestinians and Israelis in Israel. He was the only person arrested at the event.

[6] We hired graduate students in each of these places to conduct surveys and observe the events. These reports, along with Web searches we conducted, provide the evidence for this point.

[7] A survey conducted by NCPJC of 806 participants sheds some light on this issue. About 63.28% of the respondents came from North Carolina and about 36.72% from out of state, including 3.6% from New York. Assuming 4000 people in attendance, that would be 2,531 "local" participants

and 1,469 from out of state, including 144 New Yorkers. So while the majority of participants were North Carolinians, well over a thousand people came from someplace else, including the equivalent of three busloads of New Yorkers.

[8] In fact, the nation's largest military base is Fort Hood, which is near Killeen, Texas.

[9] Burge's precise choice of words in this e-mail is almost certainly influenced by her exposure to an early draft of our paper. We had decided that our ethnographic fieldwork was finished by this point (although it turned out not to be), so we shared our draft with members of the inner circle of NCPJC, from whom we solicited feedback. Even though her choice of words is likely influenced by us, we nonetheless believe that the general sentiment that the President was reacting to them would have been felt by the activists.

References

Auyero, J. (2004). When everyday life, routine politics, and protest meet. *Theory and Society, 33,* 417–441.

Babb, S. (1996). "A true American system of finance": Frame resonance in the U.S. labor movement, 1866 to 1886. *American Sociological Review, 61,* 1033–1052.

Basu, M. (2005). Military wife becomes war protester. *Atlanta Journal-Constitution.* March 19.

Benford, R. D. (1993). Frame disputes within the nuclear disarmament movement. *Social Forces, 71,* 677–701.

Brenner, N. (2004). *New state spaces.* New York: Oxford University Press.

Cortright, D. (2004). *A peaceful superpower.* Goshen, Indiana: Fourth Freedom Forum.

Druckman, J. N. (2001). On the limits of framing effects. *Journal of Politics, 63,* 1041–1066.

Ellingson, S. (1995). Understanding the dialectic of discourse and collective action. *American Journal of Sociology, 101,* 100–144.

Evans, J. H. (1997). Multi-organizational fields and social movement organization frame content. *Sociological Inquiry, 67,* 451–469.

Ferree, M. M., Gamson, W. W., Gerhards, J., & Rucht, D. (2002). *Shaping abortion discourse.* Cambridge, UK: Cambridge University Press.

Fine, G. A. (1995). Public narration and group culture. In H. Johnston and B. Klandermans (Eds.), *Social movements and culture* (pp. 127–143). Minneapolis: University of Minnesota Press.

Finer, J. (2005). Iraq War opponents stage protest near Fort Bragg. *Washington Post.* March 20.

Gamson, W. A. (1988). Political discourse and collective action. *International Social Movement Research, 1,* 219–244.

Gamson, W. A. (1992). *Talking politics.* New York: Cambridge University Press.

Garrow, D. J. (1978). *Protest at Selma.* New Haven: Yale University Press.

Gitlin, T. (1980). *The whole world is watching.* Berkeley: University of California Press.

Goffman, E. (1974). *Frame analysis.* New York: Harper and Row.

Gould, R. V. (1995). *Insurgent identities.* Chicago: University of Chicago Press.

Gramsci, A. (1992). *Prison notebooks.* New York: Columbia University Press.

Jacobson, D. (2002). *Place and belonging in America.* Baltimore: Johns Hopkins University Press.

Klatch, R. E. (1988). Of meanings and masters. *Polity, 21,* 137–154.

Kollman, K. (1998). *Outside lobbying.* Princeton: Princeton University Press.

Koopmans, R. (2004). Movements and media. *Theory and Society, 33,* 367–391.

Koopmans, R., & Olzak, S. (2004). Discursive opportunities and the evolution of right-wing violence in Germany. *American Journal of Sociology, 110,* 198–230.

Lutz, C. (2001). *Homefront.* Boston: Beacon Press.

McAdam, D. (1996). The framing function of movement tactics. In D. McAdam, J. D. McCarthy, & M. N. Zald (Eds.), *Comparative perspectives on social movements* (pp. 338–356). New York: Cambridge University Press.

McCarthy, J. D., & McPhail, C. (2006). Places of protest. *Mobilization, 11,* 229–247.

McVeigh, R., Myers, D. J., & Sikkink, D. (2004). Corn, Klansmen, and Coolidge. *Social Forces, 83,* 653–690.

Maney, G. M., Woehrle, L. M., & Coy, P. G. (2005). Harnessing and challenging hegemony. *Sociological Perspectives, 38,* 357–381.

Mansbridge, J. J. (1986). *Why we lost the ERA.* Chicago: University of Chicago Press.

Marshall-Genzer, N. (2005). *Army base is site of protests marking war anniversary. Weekend Edition, March 20, 2005.* Washington, DC: National Public Radio.

Martin, D. G., & Miller, B. A. (2003). Space and contentious politics. *Mobilization, 8,* 143–156.

Meyer, D. S., & Staggenborg, S. (1996). Movements, countermovements, and the structure of political opportunity. *American Journal of Sociology, 101,* 1628–1660.

Miller, B. A. (2000). *Geography and social movements.* Minneapolis: University of Minnesota Press.

Miller, B. A., & Martin, D. G. (Eds.) (2003). Special issue: Space, place, and contentious politics. *Mobilization, 8*, 143–232.

Naples, N. (2002). From "beloved community" to family values. In D. Meyer, N. Whittier, & B. Robnett (Eds.), *Social movements: Identity, culture, and the state* (pp. 226–246). New York: Oxford University Press.

NCPJC. (2006). *April 2006 statewide convention.* http://www.ncpeacejustice.org/

Nepstad, S. E. (2004). Persistent resistance. *Social Problems, 51*, 43–60.

Office of the Command Historian. (2005). *Fort Bragg history.* http://www.bragg.army.mil/

Oliver, P. E., & Johnston, H. (2000). What a good idea! *Mobilization, 4*, 37–54.

Proffitt, B. (2004). *Fayetteville proposal to UFPJ.* Raleigh: NCPJC.

Riker, W. H. (1986). *The art of political manipulation.* New Haven: Yale University Press.

Schattschneider, E. E. (1960). *The semisovereign people.* Orlando: Harcourt Brace.

Sewell Jr., W. H. (2001). Space in contentious politics. In R. R. Aminzade, J. A. Goldstone, D. McAdam, E. J. Perry, W. H. Sewell Jr., S. Tarrow, & C. Tilly (Eds.), *Silence and voice in the study of contentious politics* (pp. 51–88). Cambridge: Cambridge University Press.

Snow, D. A. (2004). Framing processes, ideology, and discursive fields. In D. A. Snow, S. A. Soule, & H. Kriesi (Eds.), *The Blackwell companion to social movements* (pp. 380–412). Malden, MA: Blackwell Publishing.

Snow, D. A., & Benford, R. D. (1988). Ideology, frame resonance, and participant mobilization. *International Social Movement Research, 1*, 197–217.

Snow, D. A., & Benford, R. D. (1992). Master frames and cycles of protest. In A. D. Morris & C. M. Mueller (Eds.), *Frontiers in social movement theory* (pp. 133–155). New Haven, CT: Yale University Press.

Snow, D. A., Rochford, E. B., Worden, S. K., & Benford, R. D. (1986). Frame alignment processes, micromobilization, and movement participation. *American Sociological Review, 51*, 464–481.

Steinberg, M. W. (1998). Tilting the frame. *Theory and Society, 27*, 845–872.

Steinberg, M. W. (1999). The talk and back talk of collective action. *American Journal of Sociology, 105*, 736–780.

Stevenson, R. (2005). Bush to tell why he sees a "clear path to victory." *New York Times.* June 28.

Stock, S. (2006). After 3 years, peace march is about ending war—now. *Raleigh News and Observer.* March 20.

Tilly, C. (1978). *From mobilization to revolution.* Reading, MA: Addison-Wesley.

Tilly, C. (2003). Contention over space and place. *Mobilization, 8*, 221–226.

Tversky, A., & Kahneman, D. (1981). The framing of decisions and the psychology of choice. *Science, 211*, 453–458.

U.S. Census Bureau. (2005). *United States Census 2000.* http://www.census.gov/

Veterans Gulf March. (2006). *Veterans march to New Orleans.* http://www.vetgulfmarch.org/

Walgrave, S., & Verhulst, J. (2004). *Who takes to which streets?* Paper presented at the conference of the European Consortium for Political Research, Uppsala, Sweden.

Westby, D. L. (2002). Strategic imperative, ideology, and frame. *Mobilization, 7*, 287–304.

Williams, A. (2005). Thousands protest war. *Fayetteville Observer.* March 20.

Zald, M. N., & Useem, B. (1987). Movement and countermovement interaction. In M. N. Zald & J. D. McCarthy (Eds.), *Social movements in organizational society* (pp. 247–271). New Brunswick, NJ: Transaction Publishers.

Zhao, D. (2001). *The power of Tiananmen.* Chicago: University of Chicago Press.

Environmental Melodrama

Steven Schwarze

Melodrama is a recurrent rhetorical form in environmental controversies. From local land management to global warming, from resource extraction to toxic contamination, environmental issues often get constituted within a melodramatic frame. As it generates stark, polarizing distinctions between social actors and infuses those distinctions with moral gravity and pathos, melodrama offers environmental advocates a powerful resource for rhetorical invention. Arguably, melodrama's ubiquity in environmental controversy stems from its capacity to provide a coherent, synthetic response to several of the persistent rhetorical obstacles facing environmental advocates. It can transform ambiguous and unrecognized environmental conditions into public problems; it can call attention to how distorted notions of the public interest conceal environmental degradation; and, it can overcome public indifference to environmental problems by amplifying their moral and emotional dimensions. To the extent that melodrama serves these purposes, it presents itself as an enticing rhetorical strategy for environmental advocates.

The attractiveness of the melodramatic frame as a mode of engaging recurrent rhetorical obstacles makes this rhetorical phenomenon worthy of theoretical explication and critical analysis. Yet contemporary rhetorical scholarship has paid little theoretical attention to melodrama, a deficiency that has led to consistently negative critical judgments of the form. Theoretically, the few discussions of melodrama within rhetorical studies interpret the form by focusing on its tendency to reify and simplify public controversies.[1] Ironically, this perspective simplifies melodrama, mistaking one of its dimensions—polarization—for the larger rhetorical action of that frame. In fact, the multiple appeals of melodrama can work together to complicate and transform public issues, not just reduce them to simplistic formulations. A richer theory of melodrama would account for both transformative and reifying possibilities of the form. As a matter of rhetorical theory, then, melodrama clearly merits further scrutiny.

Moreover, the reduction of melodrama to polarization risks diminishing the range of critical judgments of the form and its uses. The narrow focus on melodrama's capacity for polarization encourages blanket negative judgments of the form itself, foreclosing the possibility of situated rhetorical assessments. Such wholesale judgments of the melodramatic frame are not surprising, given the discipline's embrace of Kenneth Burke and the valorization of the comic frame as a superior mode of engagement with public controversies.[2] Even critical readings

of Burke affirm his negative judgment of melodrama based on its polarizing tendency. Gregory Desilet, for example, endorses Burke's indictment of melodrama or "factional tragedy" found in *Attitudes Toward History*. "Burke rightly sees that this brand of melodramatic catharsis fuels the narrowness of moral indignation, serving to perfect divisions between people rather than minimize them."[3] While Desilet (and Burke) is right to caution us about the danger of perfecting division, I would urge caution about the implicit assumption that division is always or necessarily a problem to be minimized. In some situations, clarifying and enabling division may be beneficial, and melodrama can offer a potentially fitting rhetorical response to those situations. A broader theoretical conception of melodrama would explain how its combination of appeals can generate *productive* forms of polarization that recast the line between identification and division in beneficial ways. Consequently, such a conception of melodrama would facilitate a full range of critical judgments that are sensitive to specific rhetorical contexts.

In response to these deficiencies, this essay advances a concept of melodrama as a complex and integrated rhetorical form. In doing so, it seeks to elevate the status of melodrama to that of comedy and tragedy as a central concept in rhetorical theory; it intends to make a wider range of critical responses to melodrama more readily available; and it attempts to provoke reflection on the grounds for judgment in rhetorical criticism. While I contextualize this argument within the realm of environmental controversy, the essay addresses issues regarding identification, polarization, and moral and emotional appeals that persist for all rhetorical scholars.

PRIVILEGING COMEDY, DENIGRATING MELODRAMA

Melodrama stands as a relatively neglected but potentially productive category for interpreting the framing of public controversies. While this neglect may be explained by the negative connotations that adhere to popular conceptions of melodrama,[4] it also may be a consequence of the Burkean terministic screen that influences rhetorical studies. Burke's comic and tragic frames are core concepts in rhetorical criticism, and several scholars of environmental rhetoric have adopted his broader dramatistic perspective.[5] But continued reliance on Burke's frames may deflect our attention from alternate frames in public controversy. Burke himself refers only briefly to melodrama, as a subset of tragedy;[6] for scholars of public controversy, however, the concept merits greater attention, since its features make it a particularly appealing option for those engaged in communication about virtually any public issue. As literary theorist Robert Bechtold Heilman has claimed, the realm of melodrama is the realm of competition and rivalry, and therefore melodrama often constitutes "the special conflicts produced by public situations: this or that group fights to compel a community or nation to adopt a program or pattern of life."[7] In this light, melodrama would seem to be a useful resource for scholars wishing to understand the dynamics of public controversy.

However, melodrama has received surprisingly scant attention within rhetorical studies. Michael Osborn and John Bakke's essay about narratives of the Memphis sanitation strike of 1968 is one of the few articles that attempts to theorize melodrama as a concept for interpreting public discourse. They affirm Heilman's observation about the centrality of melodrama in constituting public controversy, asserting "an inevitable thesis: melodrama is the most rhetorical mode of narrative."[8] However, Osborn and Bakke's analysis of the Memphis narratives ultimately yields a broad indictment of melodrama on grounds shared by many critics of environmental rhetoric—its moralism, its pathos, and its simplification of complex situations. In their words, "A vision of the world that expresses itself through moral absolutes, appeals to feeling, simplicity, rigidity, and stereotypes may offer boundless opportunity for error if not inhumanity."[9] Near the end of the essay, Osborn and Bakke support these criticisms with reference to the rhetorical action of melodrama. They assert that melodrama draws sharp distinctions between opposing forces, making resolutions difficult to negotiate; it personalizes problems, deflecting attention from systemic issues; it invites simple solutions, denying the complexity of controversial situations; and

finally, it blinds us to the capacity for change among others and failure among ourselves.[10] While these claims will be addressed later in this essay, of primary importance here is their normative judgment of melodrama as rhetorical form. Ultimately, Osborn and Bakke contend that the polarizing tendency of melodrama threatens the "circles" or relationships that constitute a community: "Rhetorical melodramas are dangerous because they drive these circles apart and diminish the sense of shared communal life".[11]

Osborn and Bakke's desire for social unity is shared by scholars who praise Burke's comic frame. For these scholars, social unification is assumed to be the *telos* of rhetoric, and the comic frame is viewed as unique in its capacity to enable unification in divisive situations. For example, A. Cheree Carlson endorses the comic frame's establishment of a clown who functions to promote a community's engagement with its errors and mistakes. "When the clown is punished, dialogue can begin, eventually leading to a rapprochement."[12] Similarly, Adrienne Christiansen and Jeremy Hanson support Burke's preference for the comic frame "because the rhetor who speaks from the comic frame assumes that humans eventually will recognize their shared social identifications and will respond in a moral manner."[13] For these critics, the comic frame is valuable precisely because it forsakes the divisiveness of the tragic frame in favor of unification within a reformed social order.

Certainly, unification can be a desirable goal, but a desire for unification in all situations may be misplaced. Promoting division and drawing sharp moral distinctions can be a fitting response to situations in which identification and consensus have obscured recognition of damaging material conditions and social injustices.[14] So, while use of the comic frame can be an appropriate rhetorical strategy in some situations, scholars must be wary of making judgments about the comic frame—or any other frame, for that matter—as an *inherently* superior form for public discourse. Carlson, for example, on one hand judges the comic frame to be "the most humane frame for understanding and acting in society;"[15] on the other hand, she recognizes elsewhere that the comic frame may not always be the best strategy for promoting social change. "Naturally, some social orders are so rigid that there may be no wedge for accommodation at first, thus in some cases a movement must either abandon the charitable mode or be prepared to wage a forty year struggle much as Gandhi pursued in India."[16] William Lewis, too, has argued that comedy can be an insufficient mode of engaging questions of social justice because "it subordinates the pain of social life and the felt reality of conflicts to visions of integration that somehow reconcile the vital tensions of politics and society."[17] In some instances, then, the integrative action of comedy may be less appropriate than melodrama's dynamics of division.

Given the infinite variability of uses and contexts, it is questionable to privilege rhetorical frames apart from their deployment in specific contexts. Christiansen and Hanson's study of ACT UP reveals the difficulty of moving from situated rhetorical judgments to broader generalizations about frames. They make a convincing case that ACT UP's rhetoric exemplifies "an appropriate and sensible use of the comic frame;" in particular, they document how comic rhetoric was an especially fitting counterpoint to the dominant tragic discourse surrounding AIDS in the 1980s.[18] From this case, they cautiously conclude "that there may be *recurring social conditions* for which rhetoric in the comic frame may be the only sensible response. Although there may be more, Burke (1959) suggests several of those conditions: When society deals with 'anguish, injustice, disease and death.'"[19] Their tentativeness in making these claims is appropriate. After all, the comic frame may be invoked effectively or ineffectively, and other frames might be equally or more sensible in particular contexts. As this essay will suggest, melodramatic rhetoric also can be a wise response to these very conditions of anguish, injustice, disease and death.

By displacing unification as the primary *telos* of rhetoric and resisting decontextualized judgments of frames, we can begin to give melodramatic rhetoric fair critical consideration. This consideration is rooted in a broader assumption that should guide rhetorical criticism: the question of division—and its compensatory counterpart, identification—should remain an open one. The critical concern surrounding melodrama should not be *that* it generates conflict and division; rather, it should lie in *how* melodrama constitutes particular conflicts and *whether* it promotes divisions (and identifications) that are beneficial in particular circumstances. As Burke reminds us, the line between identification and division is always a matter of rhetorical contestation.

> (P)ut identification and division ambiguously together, so that you cannot know for certain just where one ends and the other begins, and you have the characteristic invitation to rhetoric.... When two men collaborate in an enterprise to which they contribute different kinds of services and from which they derive different amounts and kinds of profit, who is to say, once and for all, just where "cooperation" ends and one partner's "exploitation" of the other begins? The wavering line between the two cannot be "scientifically" identified; rival rhetoricians can draw it at different places, and their persuasiveness varies with the resources each has at his command.[20]

Arguably, melodrama is one of the resources available for drawing this line. And if we agree that the line between identification and division is not a matter of scientific certainty but of normative judgment, then the rhetorical resources used to draw that line must be judged flexibly, with an eye toward their timeliness and appropriateness to the situation. I turn below to examples of environmental melodrama that fit this flexible rule, both to provide counterpoint to negative assessments of melodrama within rhetorical studies and to provide further support for the argument that rhetorical frames must be evaluated on a case-by-case basis.

CONCEPTUALIZING MELODRAMA

As mentioned above, fair consideration of melodrama also requires a sufficiently complex theoretical account of the concept. Initially, melodrama's contribution to the rhetorical lexicon can be clarified through its relationship to comedy and tragedy. Melodrama can be distinguished from tragedy according to the locus of conflict that orients each frame. Upon first glance, melodrama and tragedy appear to share the characteristic of examining conflicts that lead to pain and suffering. But as Heilman argues, tragedy focuses on conflicts *within* individuals, whereas melodrama and comedy are staged around conflicts *between* individuals and some external opponent. "In tragedy, the bad guy is within; in melodrama, he is the external adversary that one is lined up against; in comedy, he turns out to be not so bad after all or else lives on peripherally, a steady ingredient in life but not a serious danger that demands combative action and makes life impossible."[21] Importantly, tragedy is not a blanket term for all narratives of devastation. Tragedy and melodrama should be distinguished by the location of conflict; melodrama constitutes *social and political conflict* rather than personal, inner conflict.

Further, melodrama's orientation to conflict differs from that of comedy. Whereas comedy mediates and mitigates conflict, melodrama clarifies conflict through *polarization.* Consequently, melodrama and comedy imply different trajectories of political action. Heilman captures the relationship between melodrama and comedy in this way:

> Melodrama and comedy, then, share a large common ground: they are both ways of meeting the world—the many-sided, inconsistent, imperfect world, occasionally gratifying or fulfilling, often frustrating, and perhaps still more often seeming punishably unregenerate. Melodrama would do something about it, comedy would strive for ways of coming to terms with it. Melodrama would take arms, comedy accept. Melodrama is for victory or defeat, comedy for compromises.[22]

Thus, while comedy seeks to reconcile conflict via compromises, melodrama sharpens conflict through a bipolar positioning of characters and forces. This constitution of conflict leads Jeffrey D. Mason to argue that "the essential action of melodrama is to polarize its constituents, whatever they may be—male and female, East and West, civilization and wilderness, and, most typically, good and evil."[23]

Indeed, as Mason suggests, melodramatic polarization is *moralistic* in character. According to Peter Brooks, the moralistic tone is a vestige of melodrama's emergence during the French Revolution. As the traditional bases for moral order were overthrown, melodrama helped fill the void by staging new visions of moral order. The moral impetus of early melodrama, Brooks suggests, is even consistent with traditional rhetorical practices of the time.

> Like the oratory of the Revolution, melodrama from its inception takes as its concern and raison d'etre the location, expression, and imposition of basic ethical and psychic truths. It says them over and over in clear language, it rehearses their conflicts and combats, it reenacts the menace of evil and the eventual triumph of morality made operative and evident.[24]

In a post-traditional world, a world without clear moral frameworks, melodrama attempts to give voice to what Brooks calls the 'moral occult,' the domain of spiritual values that is implicit within but hidden by the material world, "and which demands to be uncovered, registered, articulated."[25] Melodrama, then, frames conflict not as a mere difference of opinion, but as evidence of fundamental moral clash.

Finally, melodrama's moral polarization is shored up by a structure of feeling Heilman refers to as *monopathy.* Stark moral oppositions and the location of conflict between rather than within social actors encourage a unitary emotional identification with victors or victims, whether celebrating the former or sympathizing with the latter. This "oneness of feeling," as Heilman defines it, provides audiences both with a respite from their personal inner struggles and a motive force for collective action. "The oneness within makes it easier to contribute to, and in turn is reinforced by, the oneness without, the union of the like-minded: the satisfaction of being on a moral bandwagon, of being 'with it,' of feeling 'solidarity,' of cooperating in a crusade or a quest for salvation; or the reassurance of fellowship in the face of disaster."[26] Monopathy, in other words, begets identification with those who are on the side of virtue or who have been victimized by villains.

These four features—a focus on socio-political conflict, polarization of characters and positions, a moral framing of public issues, and development of monopathy—comprise the rhetorical action of melodrama. While other rhetorical forms also may produce these outcomes, in melodrama they work in concert to constitute a coherent perspective on the world. This position is consistent with Osborn and Bakke's view that "melodrama interprets as it personalizes events and provides their moral and emotional coherence."[27] Within environmental controversies, the coherence offered by melodrama typically serves an oppositional political stance and mode of public address. At one level, melodrama constitutes opposition; its *telos* is precisely to configure conflict and then generate solidarity and motivate action among those who might engage one side of the conflict. On another level, the use of melodrama by environmental activists in particular is oppositional in a political sense; it critically interrupts dominant modes of argument and appeal that obscure threats to the quality and future of life on the planet.[28] The next section explains how melodrama can intervene as an oppositional force in environmental controversies.

ILLUSTRATING MELODRAMA

The subsequent explanation of the rhetorical action of melodrama includes brief examples of several environmental controversies, but it returns persistently to a case in which the melodramatic frame is a pervasive feature in public discourse: asbestos exposure in Libby, Montana. In Libby, over 200 people have died from asbestos-related diseases and over 1000 people currently reveal evidence of lung abnormalities consistent with exposure to asbestos. These exposures are the result of the mining and milling of asbestos-contaminated vermiculite near Libby for most of the twentieth century, as well as widespread distribution of the mine's products throughout the community. Mine workers,

their families, and community members with no connection to the mine ultimately became the endpoint of multiple pathways of exposure to various amphibole forms of asbestos. Although the W. R. Grace Company stopped mining in 1990, residents continued to face significant environmental exposure to asbestos throughout the community. In addition to contamination near abandoned processing facilities, vermiculite products were used as insulation in many Libby homes (as well as 15 to 35 million homes in the US alone), as soil conditioner in residents' gardens, and as fill material for the school skating rink and running track. Newspaper accounts in November 1999 began to reveal some of these conditions, as well as evidence that company, state, and federal officials knew of the asbestos hazard in Libby and did little to prevent it. Soon afterward, federal environmental and public health officials sent emergency teams to investigate conditions in Libby, and later expanded the scope of their investigation to hundreds of facilities across North America that processed Libby vermiculite. The entire town of Libby eventually was put on the Environmental Protection Agency's (EPA) National Priorities List for cleanup under Superfund legislation, and in February 2005 seven former and current W. R. Grace employees were indicted for knowing endangerment, obstruction of justice, violation of the Clean Air Act and other alleged crimes related to the Libby operation.

Since 1999, a tremendous amount of public discourse—including public advocacy, resident testimony, journalistic accounts, documentary film, and photojournalism—has emerged to characterize and address the asbestos problem in Libby and the scope of its effects. Melodrama is the overarching frame in this discourse. Across the genres mentioned above, a consistent narrative draws clear lines of conflict between victimized residents and W. R. Grace (the company that operated the mine from 1963 until its closure), highlights the sense of moral violation and social injustice, and encourages monopathic identification with local activists and exposure victims. I will refer to the public discourse surrounding the Libby situation in order to support five arguments about the rhetorical action of melodrama.

First, *melodrama can situate conflict on the social and political plane, clarifying issues of power that are obscured by privatizing rhetoric.* In contrast to discourses that frame environmental issues as matters of personal decision-making or action, melodrama can effectively place the fault line of environmentalism between the producers of significant environmental damage and those who suffer its effects. While melodramatic rhetoric may rely heavily on the testimony of personal experience and the depiction of individual persons, it positions those elements in conflict with other forces to evoke the power relationships at play in a particular situation. In more general terms, melodrama constitutes ecological conditions and socio-political relations as fundamentally imbricated.

In Libby, the asbestos situation came to light through stories that W. R. Grace had exploited the community by knowingly exposing residents to asbestos and hiding that knowledge from the community. Initial newspaper coverage of the situation focused on the role W. R. Grace managers had played in downplaying hazards and attributing health problems to the high incidence of smoking among workers.[29] Through such attributions, the company effectively privatized those health problems. But over time, evidence amassed suggesting that the company and the community's interests were not the same. Journalists revealed company memos showing that mine managers knew workers were getting sick from asbestos; W. R. Grace thwarted EPA efforts to clean up contamination, and in April 2001 the company filed for Chapter 11 bankruptcy protection, which stayed all civil actions against the company. Public discourse depicted the company's managers as nefarious, and residents deciphered the company's interests as being opposed to the interests of its workers. For example, at an August 2001 public meeting in Libby attended by Governor Judy Martz, activist Gayla Benefield made the case for Superfund designation in this way.

> This is a corporation whose philosophy was based in putting profit over human lives. This is a company that we welcomed into our state and community in 1963 thinking that they were our friend. This

is a corporation that has devastated our community. This is the corporation that you [Governor Martz] may feel deserves another chance?[30]

This framing of W. R. Grace as a company opposed to the community is reinforced by emotional vignettes and testimony from Libby residents who were unknowingly exposed or otherwise affected by asbestos. The series of newspaper articles that broke the Libby story, Andrew Schneider's "Uncivil Action," offers a melodramatic frame by juxtaposing articles about the company's knowledge of the hazard with articles filled with emotional stories about the deaths of innocent victims.[31] The implicit moral framework provided by that juxtaposition—innocent victims harmed by a powerful, deceptive corporation—further crafts a clear division between residents in the community and the corporation. Thus, the appeals of melodrama work together to reconstitute the dominant community understanding of the problem, expanding its scope from a private problem of "just a few old miners" to a community-wide problem caused by the agents of a callous corporation and requiring political action.

This melodramatic depiction of opposed socio-political forces is pervasive in environmental controversy, especially as it arrays these forces using victim/villain and David/Goliath character types.[32] In the Love Canal controversy, for example, Lois Gibbs and her neighbors targeted the Governor of New York and state health officials as prominent public obstacles to relocation of Niagara Falls residents who were threatened by buried toxic waste.[33] More broadly, corporate boycotts often villainize a particular organization or industry by demonstrating how their actions victimize unsuspecting citizens. Such tactics allow advocates to define an obscure or unrecognized situation and provide a clear understanding of the entities that exercise power in that situation.

This emphasis on melodrama's constitution of socio-political conflict comes into tension with the assumption that melodrama's personification of villains "may divert our attention from underlying conditions that require systemic change and may drain our rhetoric of genuine social critique."[34] This is true in some instances; within the sphere of environmental controversy, Terence Check argues that public scapegoating of Exxon in the aftermath of the Valdez oil spill "worked to deflect attention from systemic issues concerning oil production and consumption."[35] Yet the personification of villains also can point precisely at a system's pressure points and provide the motive force for sustaining social critique. As a rhetorical process, personification can work via synecdoche to signify systemic failure. By focusing attention on public officials, residents in the Love Canal controversy symbolized the inertia of bureaucracy and provided a clear target for public advocacy and activism. Similarly, the personification of organizations as agents in environmental campaigns against corporations hardly blunts social critique; it can generate socio-political conflict by bringing environmental practices and regulatory enforcement under scrutiny. Further, criticism can be sustained as corporate logos and symbols provide easily recognized resources for oppositional iconography.[36] Through symbolic reversal, advocates can tap into powerful mass identifications to generate indignation at environmental and human exploitation perpetrated by corporations.

Within a melodramatic frame, reliance on sharply opposed characters need not blunt the possibility of political critique. Simplified characterizations can initiate critique by providing a clear and recognizable entry point—a prominent government official, a well-known corporation, a widely circulated logo or slogan—for broader discussions of environmental problems among wider audiences. While the extent of critique will vary from one situation to the next, the crucial point here is that melodrama offers a strategy for criticizing and resisting the potentially depoliticizing effects of environmental discourses that focus on personal habits, private actions, or consumption dilemmas.[37]

Second, *melodrama can reconfigure social relationships and articulate interests that have been obscured by universalizing and singularizing rhetorics.* In contrast to discourses that homogenize or singularize the interests of a population,[38] melodrama's polarizing tendencies can facilitate the disclosure of opposed interests and enable the formation of new social and political

relationships on the basis of those interests. This extends the previous argument about melodrama's capacity to articulate conditions as matters of social concern and public contestation; melodrama can give particular form and direction to that contestation. Specifically, as melodrama polarizes, it can encourage reconsideration of the allegiances and shared substance that might normally lead audiences to accept a certain set of social and political arrangements. In doing so, melodrama can be part of a critical rhetoric that questions assertions of a single or universally shared public interest.

Libby provides a powerful example of how melodramatic rhetoric can reformulate distorted notions of the public interest. For several decades, identification between community members and the companies that owned the mine, Zonolite and later W. R. Grace, was strong. Journalistic reports and documentary films amply illustrate how residents perceived W. R. Grace as a good citizen and how mine workers perceived their jobs as the best in the community.[39] But as evidence of the company's knowledge and the extent of asbestos-related disease emerged, a new discourse about the company also emerged. As illustrated above, the circulation of emotional stories illustrating the scope and nature of asbestos disease in Libby, contextualized by evidence that the company knew miners were getting sick at alarming rates, tied moral and emotional appeals together to call into question W. R. Grace's role in the community. Residents spoke of how the company had violated their trust, and it led some residents to see W. R. Grace as a barrier to fulfilling [the] community's need for an effective clean-up. In other words, the melodramatic rhetoric depicting the community's health and W. R. Grace's awareness of health problems illustrated how the interests of the company were not isomorphic with those of the community, even though those interests had been articulated and accepted as such for several decades.

In that situation, redrawing the line between identification and division was necessary for residents to acknowledge the problem and address its aftermath effectively. Melodramatic rhetoric about past and present events in Libby generated a healthy skepticism about W. R. Grace's clean-up efforts and provisions to pay for medical care for Libby residents diagnosed with asbestos-related illnesses.[40] Both Libby residents and EPA officials came to see that W. R. Grace's interests in maximizing profits had persistently undermined their claims about helping the community. In this instance, melodrama effectively redefined the characters in the situation; instead of being viewed as a pillar of the community or a partner in cleanup, the company rightfully came to be seen as an enemy of the people and their health.

The melodrama surrounding Libby performed two important rhetorical interventions. First, it helped break the identification between community residents and the company. No longer were residents quietly trustful of W. R. Grace's actions; they closely scrutinized the company's early clean-up efforts, found asbestos-contaminated vermiculite remaining at clean-up sites, and displayed vermiculite at public meetings to dramatize W. R. Grace's ineptitude and disregard for the community.[41] Second, breaking this identification allowed public health to be articulated as a significant public interest. Whereas Grace had consistently downplayed threats for decades and sustained a perception of asbestos as merely a "nuisance dust," and whereas workers had accepted health problems as the price of having a good job with a good company, now concerns about public health came to the foreground. After decades of denial and a discourse that put a "good job" ahead of environmental and health concerns, the connection between W. R. Grace's dissembling and the pervasive health problems in Libby no longer could be ignored. The melodramatic depiction of the company's actions not only showed how the interest of community health had been systematically repressed; it also facilitated its return.

Other environmental controversies, especially those with a salient public health dimension, illustrate how the polarization of characters or groups can work to reformulate notions of the public interest. For example, at the national level, opponents of a proposed trust fund for compensating asbestos victims highlight the history of deceit and denial by asbestos companies in order to generate public skepticism about claims that the proposal is truly in the interest of victims.

Even the Environmental Working Group's heavily documented website on "asbestos litigation reform," a resource filled with graphs, charts, and copious citations from scientific and medical journals, relies heavily on moral labeling and an evocative emotion-laden picture of an asbestos victim to frame their overall message about asbestos companies:

> This site takes the visitor behind closed doors at asbestos companies and their insurers via internal documents showing that company after company was willing to let workers suffer and die long after it was clear that asbestos was killing them. It is precisely the callous behavior evidenced by these documents that is at the core of all asbestos litigation.[42]

Using very different means, the Toxic Links Coalition also draws attention to conflicts between private and public interests with regard to environmental causes of cancer.[43] Their street performances invoke moral outrage and monopathic identification with cancer victims to generate resistance to industries that contribute to these cancers. By exposing the duplicitous rhetorical strategies companies use to deflect attention from the production and dissemination of carcinogens, advocates attempt to show how these organizations' actions do not necessarily coincide with the public interest.

The tendency of melodrama to polarize the social landscape, then, can serve to enrich public understanding of the interests at stake in environmental controversies. It can help audiences resist rhetorical appeals to the public interest that cloak environmentally degrading practices and ultimately serve narrow private interests. In doing so, the polarization of melodrama can constitute new lines of conflict, allowing new issues and alternative grounds for political judgment to emerge.

Third, by identifying perpetrators and crafting public interests, *melodrama can remoralize situations that have been demoralized by inaccuracy, displaying concerns that have been obscured by the reassuring rhetoric of technical reason.* In contrast to discourses that define environmental issues in strictly scientific terms and reassure citizens about technological control of natural phenomena, melodrama can foreground the moral dimension of all human actions and thus offer a new basis for challenging those that contribute to ecological degradation. Melodrama's capacity to articulate moral concerns makes the frame an especially attractive option when scientific, technological, and bureaucratic discourses are blocking meaningful participation in public affairs and restricting discussion to technical spheres of controversy.

The distinctively melodramatic frame typically interprets polarized, socio-political conflicts in moral terms. Conflicts are not simply about competing interests; the pursuit of these interests leads to *moral* wrongs, injustices that cannot be rectified through political compromises or minor adjustments to existing practices. In environmental controversies, melodrama often advances this position by disclosing foreknowledge of environmental hazards to suggest deception and inaction on the part of government agencies and corporations. In the Libby situation, Schneider's initial articles and testimony from local residents at a public meeting in December 1999 juxtaposed technical claims about the safety of the mine with the verbal and bodily testimony of asbestos victims.[44] Schneider's articles, for example, revealed that company officials not only knew of the possibility of asbestos-related health hazards as early as 1956, but had been keeping track of workers' health status through an annual lung x-ray program. The juxtaposition of this evidence with residents hooked to oxygen tanks implies that officials knew what was happening to their fellow citizens but refused to warn residents or take action. Combined with residents' repeated claims that they were reassured that the dust was not asbestos and was not harmful, this narrative of deception and inaction taps into the victim/villain motif and further reinforces a moral framing of the situation.

Similarly, Bill Moyers' PBS documentary on the vinyl chloride industry, *Trade Secrets*, shuttles between images of confidential company memos describing toxic workplace exposure in scientific language and episodes of workers on hospital beds or widows tearily recalling their spouse's suffering.[45] These melodramatic juxtapositions offer a clear moral framework for interpreting the actions of company decision-makers. They characterize officials as knowledgeable about toxic hazards in scientific terms, but utterly indifferent to the human suffering that resulted from those hazards. As with the rhetoric surrounding Libby, the melodramatic frame here mobilizes *ethos*—particularly, questions of moral character—to call into question the invocation of narrow forms of *logos*. Melodrama puts the inaccuracy of scientific language on display and highlights its potential moral blindspots.

Melodrama, then, partakes in the rhetoric of moral confrontation.[46] To the extent that melodrama combines polarization and moral claims, it frames situations as confrontations between the virtuous and the villainous, and encourages audiences to take sides in such confrontations in order to repair the moral order. While it can be argued that the moralizing tendency of melodrama hinders the possibility for pragmatic compromise, this begs the question of whether compromise is always an appropriate rhetorical purpose or objective. As Jonathan Lange has shown, radical environmental groups often view compromise as an underlying cause of, not a solution to, ecological degradation.[47] In turn, these groups' confrontational rhetoric breaks from the pattern of compromises sought by mainstream environmentalism in order to reveal the shortcomings of past compromises. By renaming situations in moral terms, melodrama enables advocates to question the appropriateness of calls for compromise that ignore the history of moral slights committed by parties to the compromise. Melodrama, then, can function to reconstitute the parameters of controversy by positioning advocates and interpellating audiences in a stance opposed to the amoral and immoral actions of political adversaries.

Fourth, sustaining this oppositional stance takes considerable energy, but melodrama can provide that energy. Specifically, *melodrama can encourage a unity of feeling, offering a basis for identification that has been obscured by emotionally dissipating and dispassionate rhetorics.* In contrast to environmental discourses that promote equal degrees of concern for competing viewpoints—whether through appeals to "balance"[48] that encourage seemingly rational tradeoffs and compromises, or through the trope of "uncertainty" that intends to weaken motivation and forestall action[49]— melodrama offers monopathy, a "singleness of feeling" that strengthens identification with one party to a controversy. Like the other appeals of melodrama, monopathy can oppose dominant discourses by giving voice to their strategic silences. In doing so, it provides a rallying point and source of identification for those whose voices have been excised from the dominant social and political order.[50]

The monopathy of the public discourse surrounding Libby reinforces the aspects of polarization and moral framing described above. Newspaper reports and public testimony increasingly display the anger that residents direct at W. R. Grace, and as they depict entire families who suffer from asbestos disease, they elicit pity for innocent victims. Photojournalistic essays, too, promote sympathy for the victims by persistently revealing symbols of death: hearses, coffins and white crosses with victims' names that are installed at the Libby cemetery every Memorial Day weekend.[51] But monopathic identification is not purely about victimage; book and film treatments of the events in Libby place local activists Gayla Benefield and Les Skramstad in the role of heroes in the story, who struggle mightily against government bureaucracy, corporate deception and community silence to bring the problem to light.[52] Conversely, those sources tend to downplay the voices of residents who believe that their fellow citizens knew of the asbestos hazards or were in some way responsible for their plight. Overall, the public discourse surrounding Libby promotes monopathic identification with Libby residents affected by asbestos disease, and generally blocks identification with company officials and those in the community who appear to oppose the heroic Benefield and Skramstad.

Broader environmental discourses further illustrate the two components implicit in the notion of monopathy. From one angle, stress on the *singleness* of feeling can counter the dissipation of energy and feeling by tempered, moderate rhetoric. For example, the rhetoric of cost-benefit analysis dissipates concerns about human and environmental well-being to the extent that it

characterizes these concerns as needing to be "balanced" with the regulatory costs incurred by polluting companies. The related rhetorical frame of "jobs versus the environment" also dissipates concerns about ecological degradation by encouraging audiences to divide their allegiances. These kinds of rhetoric exploit our split subjectivities, encouraging us to perceive political choices as necessary and inevitable "tradeoffs" between monetary wealth and a healthy planet, even though such tradeoffs often perpetuate damage both to economic systems and the ecological systems on which the former depend. As a form of oppositional rhetoric, melodrama attempts to restore the energy dissipated through these balancing acts and tradeoffs. It consolidates and channels that energy so that muted voices may be heard loud and clear. In its most powerful manifestations, it can displace the ideological privileging of balance, revealing how presumably even-handed and rational discourses of regulation can diminish citizen voices and consistently fail to enhance the quality of life on the planet.[53]

From another angle, stress on the singleness of *feeling* foregrounds emotion as a crucial mode of meaning-making and appeal. The emergence of emotional appeals in environmental controversy signifies not a lack of rationality, but rationality's lack—that is, the inability of technical rationality to fully constitute the *meaning* of a recalcitrant material reality. Whether it is the inability of an EIS (Environmental Impact Statement) to convey the spirit of an endangered species or a wild place, or the suspicious claims of a company with a track record of deception, the limitations of technical rhetoric can lead advocates to invoke emotional appeals as a supplement. Together with a moral framing of conflict, the emotional supplement provided by melodrama can enrich the idioms of environmental conflicts and help to situate them in public rather than technical spheres of controversy.[54] Emotional appeals can then serve to promote identification with the victims of environmental degradation, especially among those who may have little specific knowledge of a particular environmental situation but sympathize with those in positions of pain, suffering and exploitation. Sympathetic depiction of victims in Libby is mirrored in other toxic exposure situations such as Chernobyl and Bhopal. Emotional appeal also can extend identification beyond the boundaries of the human. The depiction of oil-soaked birds after the Exxon Valdez crash encouraged sympathy for innocent victims and brought the "costs" of oil dependence home to audiences. Across these cases, we see how the emotionally charged characterization of environmental victims can elicit feelings of pity, grief and anger that encourage audiences to take the side of those victims.

The foregoing arguments lead to a fifth and final claim: *melodrama has the capacity to complicate and transform, not merely simplify and reify, public controversies.* In contrast to assertions that melodrama oversimplifies and reifies conflict, the examples in this essay demonstrate that melodrama also can be a transformative rhetorical force, one that can compose nascent conflicts and shift the parameters of ongoing controversies. This observation becomes available once we discern the potential of *polarization* within melodramatic form. While polarization may oversimplify and harden some conflicts, in others it interacts with the other resources of melodramatic form in ways that invent new issues, identities, audiences and grounds for judgment.

Melodrama's transformative potential is obscured by the conventional wisdom that such rhetoric oversimplifies and reifies conflict. For example, in their assessment of the "costs" of melodrama, Osborn and Bakke assert that the form "actuates the rhetorical temptation to oversimplify and distort people and events to facilitate choice.... It reduces the complexity and disorder of life-as-lived to simple, coherent explanations of opposed interests."[55] Then, these polarized characterizations are reified through the moral and emotional appeals of melodrama; in their view, the form "rigidifies the positions in conflict, fixing them in opposed moral certainties, and making negotiation and concession quite difficult."[56] However, this view reduces the rhetorical action of polarization to the facilitation of choice based on a false dilemma.[57] Such a view interprets polarization merely as an *instrumental* tactic for persuasion within a relatively fixed field of controversy, rather than considering how it might operate as part of an overall

constitutive rhetoric that seeks to generate the very parameters and objects of controversy.[58]

The public discourse surrounding Libby illustrates how melodrama can invent and transform public controversy, not merely simplify and reify existing positions. In Libby claims of moral rupture and emotional trauma within the community articulated a new understanding of social relations. As critical publicity deepened, previously strong identifications with W. R. Grace began to crumble. Also, the melodramatic framing of an innocent population victimized by a knowing victimizer transformed a set of unremarkable, taken-for-granted illnesses into an unparalleled environmental health disaster perpetrated by knowing corporate agents. As a result, the Libby melodrama focused the attention of public agencies on W. R. Grace, setting into motion a nation-wide investigation of hundreds of vermiculite processing facilities and raising awareness of the hazards of Zonolite insulation in homes across North America. In other words, the melodrama of Libby *invented* public controversy, both locally and nationally. It restored public health as a significant issue in Libby, it placed asbestos back on the environmental and public health agenda in the United States, and it prodded EPA and other agencies to take action on the ground and fundamentally reconsider asbestos policy.

Consider, too, how melodrama complicated understanding of public health and environmental conditions in Libby. Prior to late 1999, those conditions were oversimplified to the point that virtually no public discourse circulated about them. As morally and emotionally charged stories emerged about the devastating impact of asbestos disease on entire families, it became clear that the health problem was not limited to miners. Consequently, the Agency for Toxic Substances and Disease Registry undertook one of the largest public health screenings in the United States to determine the scope of asbestos disease in the Libby area. Multiple federal agencies engaged in new studies to discern how Libby asbestos differed from other, more common forms of asbestos. In this context, melodramatic rhetoric about families harmed by asbestos hardly deflected attention from scientific aspects of the issue. If anything, such stories forced new scientific inquiry into the properties of asbestos and the public health ramifications of exposure to asbestos-contaminated vermiculite. Thus, the melodramatic frame that constituted the asbestos hazard in Libby arguably complicated a deeply oversimplified situation, giving form and meaning to a disparate set of material conditions.

Beyond Libby, the global justice movement's opposition to neoliberal trade policies further illustrates how melodrama can invent and transform public controversy. Movement rhetoric is melodramatic to the extent that it constitutes controversy over global trade as a political struggle pitting powerful corporations and trade institutions against the interests of ordinary citizens; generates moral outrage over human rights violations, cultural imperialism, and environmental degradation that flow from global trade; and encourages sympathetic identification with victims as well as heroes of political struggle.[59] This rhetoric attempts to destabilize a public discourse limited to high-level disputes over the mechanics of global trade and force issues of ecological sustainability, labor rights and democratic participation onto the public agenda.[60] Within this expanded set of issues, advocates contest what counts as "the middle course" and interrogate whose version of "progress" ultimately warrants decisions. In addition, by nurturing moral outrage and generating sympathy for victims, melodrama can transform isolated local troubles into broader regional, national or international problems. Much of the campus rhetoric about sweatshops, university investments and purchasing practices illustrates how melodramatic rhetoric can effect transformations in audiences, issues and grounds for judgment.

These examples demonstrate that melodrama need not oversimplify or reify public controversy. Melodrama can expand the possibilities of controversy by bringing new issues to public attention, soliciting support from far-flung and previously inactive audiences, and complicating the grounds for public judgment. Controversy certainly can become rigid when identities and issues are already well-defined, and melodrama merely rehearses them. But when conflicts have yet to be articulated and practices are taken-for-granted, a melodramatic frame can recast their "substance" through political, moral and emotional appeals in order to generate new forms of consubstantiality that could muster opposition to the established order. Admittedly, this may delay resolution of issues, but not because it reifies conflict; instead, melodrama defers resolution as it seeks an equally important end: democratization and enrichment of the domain of controversy.

ASSESSING MELODRAMA: IMPLICATIONS FOR RHETORICAL PRACTICE AND SCHOLARSHIP

For environmental advocates, melodrama provides a rhetorical framework that can articulate multiple concerns that are hidden, ignored, or repressed in a culture that operates according to a simplistic calculus of "progress" and "economic growth." It can bring emotion into the foreground, complicating public discourse that takes a purely scientific and technical approach to environmental problems. It can polarize situations so that victims of environmental degradation might have a voice, complicating public discourse systematically dominated by producers of that degradation. And it forces moral questions onto the agenda, complicating public discourse that focuses on technical matters to the exclusion of issues of right and wrong. To the extent it synthesizes these oppositional rhetorical actions, melodrama presents itself as a productive inventional resource for countering the ideological simplifications of dominant public discourses and prying spheres of controversy open to a wider range of voices.

Given the arguments in this essay, practicing advocates as well as rhetorical theorists and critics should attempt to discern conditions under which melodrama is more or less likely to be a productive rhetorical choice. By this, I mean to ask when melodrama would have the most potential for the transformative possibilities I have described, and when it would be less likely to enrich public discourse. The examples in this essay point toward the conclusion that melodrama may have greater potential to generate productive outcomes when issues are nascent and when voices have been muted or excluded from the rhetorical field. For emerging or relatively unrecognized public issues, melodrama can provide those issues a discernible outline along easily recognizable moral and emotional contours, facilitating broad identification among diverse audiences. In fact, melodrama may find its richest rhetorical possibilities when the initial bonds of identification between victims and audiences are relatively weak. This may seem counterintuitive, but the cases of Libby and global justice rhetoric point in this direction. When bonds are strong, melodramatic rhetoric may do little more than reinforce existing identities and perspectives on a controversy; but when audiences are encouraged to empathize with unknown or far-flung victims, there is a much greater possibility for *transformed* perceptions of public problems. Arguably, it was this potential for broad public support of Libby's residents, along with the sense that government agencies were complicit with past injustices, which pressured government officials to take the situation in Libby seriously.

Conversely, melodrama appears less likely to be a productive choice when controversies are well-defined, issues have been thoroughly articulated, and a full range of stakeholders has identified possible means for resolution. These conditions suggest a relatively advanced stage of conflict, and here the potential of melodrama is constrained. Since it maps easily onto already polarized situations, melodrama can reify conflict; and if participants generally agree to seek compromise, they are likely to dismiss the moral and emotional appeals of melodrama as distractions from pragmatic resolution. Melodrama may help tip the undecided to one side, but it is less likely to realize its transformative potential when the poles of conflict are well established.[61]

This initial attempt to theorize melodrama, then, suggests that melodrama may be a more productive rhetorical choice for inventing and transforming controversy than resolving it. However, these assertions about when melodrama "works" are speculative and rooted primarily in the analysis of a single case. Further research by rhetoricians working in other contexts would contribute to enhanced understanding of conditions that are more or less favorable for melodramatic intervention. Still, the recurrence of the melodramatic frame at various levels of environmental controversy presents an especially rich field of inquiry for environmental communication scholars in particular.

For rhetorical scholars, the concept of melodrama I have advanced facilitates improved theoretical comprehension and critical judgment in several ways. First, treating melodrama as an integrated rhetorical form enhances accurate identification of frames and encourages more careful analysis of frames, consistent with Carlson's argument that critics "must examine carefully the tactics of a group before judging whether its strategy...rises from the comic frame." This essay points to the fact that rhetorical tactics can migrate easily between different frames. For example, the scapegoating tactic so central to the tragic frame also appears in melodrama as advocates identify villains and polarize competing positions. Similarly, while other scholars have identified perspective by incongruity[62] and juxtaposition[63] as useful tactics within a comic frame, these also emerge in melodramatic rhetoric, especially as they position moral and emotional appeals alongside dominant discourses that displace those concerns. Because of the easy migration of tactics and appeals between frames, critics must attend to multiple tactics and their interaction in the process of rhetorical analysis. An integrated conception of melodrama's appeals encourages such attention.

Second, this conception of melodrama enables observation of the frame's *transformative* possibilities. These possibilities are largely ignored by melodrama's critics, who dwell on polarization to highlight how melodrama reifies and oversimplifies public controversy. If we consider that the moral, monopathic and sociopolitical appeals of melodrama can reconfigure patterns of identification and generate new topics of controversy, then melodrama must be seen as more than a mere instrument of reification. Likewise, formal manifestations of apparent simplicity—diametrically opposed interests, stark moral conflicts, narrow monopathic appeals— are taken by some critics as incontrovertible signs of oversimplification,[64] yet this may belie how the rhetorical *action* of melodrama can actually complicate public understanding by enhancing perception of largely unrecognized issues and challenging the simplicity of dominant discourses. Melodrama's individual appeals may seem simple, but together they can generate rhetorical action that complicates the realm of public controversy.

Third, this study consequently discourages the use of simplicity and complexity as criteria for judgments of frames *per se*, apart from a frame's use in particular circumstances. While some melodramas may respond to a complex situation with simplifications that stifle alternative voices and foreclose options, the examples of environmental melodrama noted in this essay operate conversely: they respond to oversimplified situations in order to complicate public discourse. They invoke seemingly simple storylines about environmental issues in order to amplify muted voices, expand the range of issues relevant to public decision-making, and invent new possibilities for creating a sustainable and healthy environment. The charge of simplification loses force as we interpret how a particular melodramatic framing interacts with other available meanings to enrich, rather than eviscerate, the quality of public discourse. Rather than criticize a frame for being simple or praising it for being complex, it is preferable to assess how and toward what ends that frame simplifies and complicates in a specific situation.

Fourth and finally, this theorization of melodrama and the implications I have drawn underscore the relevance of *kairos* as principle for critical judgment and rhetorical practice. For criticism, this conclusion interrupts the valorization of the comic frame in the discipline. Rather than privilege one frame as inherently superior to others, the basis for critical judgment is better cast in terms of *kairos:* to what extent does a particular rhetorical intervention operate as a timely and opportune response to contingent circumstances and particular audiences? This sophistic principle allows critics to acknowledge the typical strengths and limitations of a particular frame, but also encourages critics to rethink what might count as a strength

or a fault in relation to specific situations. For practice, even Burke, the consummate champion of comedy, recognized that there are always choices—in particular, political choices—to be made between competing frames: "The choice must be weighed with reference to the results we would obtain, and to the resistances involved."[65] Given the stakes of our environmental challenges and the mighty economic, political, and cultural resistance to addressing those challenges in a significant way, it is not surprising that contemporary advocates see melodrama as a timely and appropriate rhetorical strategy for addressing environmental issues.

Notes

[1] This interpretation is most apparent in Michael Osborn and John Bakke, "The Melodramas of Memphis: Contending Narratives during the Sanitation Strike of 1968," *Southern Communication Journal* 63 (Spring 1998): 220–234; see also Carl Burgchardt, "Discovering Rhetorical Imprints: La Follette, 'Iago,' and the Melodramatic Scenario," *Quarterly Journal of Speech* 71.4 (November 1985), especially pp. 449–452. For a more recent essay that rehearses the "dangerous ramifications" of melodrama in the context of national identity, see Elisabeth Anker, "Villains, Victims, and Heroes: Melodrama, Media, and September 11," *Journal of Communication* (March 2005): 22–37.

[2] A. Cheree Carlson, "Gandhi and the Comic Frame: 'Ad Bellum Purificandum,'" *Quarterly Journal of Speech* 72 (1986): 446–455; and "Limitations on the Comic Frame: Some Witty Women of the Nineteenth Century," *Quarterly Journal of Speech* 74 (1988): 310–322; Adrienne E. Christiansen and Jeremy J. Hanson, "Comedy as Cure for Tragedy: ACT UP and the Rhetoric of AIDS," *Quarterly Journal of Speech* 82 (May 1996): 157–170; Anne Teresa Demo, "The Guerilla Girls' Comic Politics of Subversion," *Women's Studies in Communication* 23 (Spring 2000): 133–156; Gregory Desilet, "Nietzsche Contra Burke: The Melodrama in Dramatism," *Quarterly Journal of Speech* 75 (1989): 65–83; Brian L. Ott and Eric Aoki, "The Politics of Negotiating Public Tragedy: Media Framing of the Matthew Shepard Murder," *Rhetoric and Public Affairs* 5.3 (Fall 2002): 483–505; Kimberly A. Powell, "The Association of Southern Women for the Prevention of Lynching: Strategies of a

Movement in the Comic Frame," *Communication Quarterly* 43 (Winter 1995): 86–99; Caitlin Wills Toker, "Debating 'What Ought To Be': The Comic Frame and Public Moral Argument," *Western Journal of Communication* 66 (Winter 2002): 53–83.

3 Desilet, "Nietzsche," 76.

4 For one analysis of melodrama in contemporary popular culture, see Daniel Mendelsohn, "The Melodramatic Moment," *The New York Times,* March 23, 2003. Available at http://www.nytimes.com.

5 Terence Check, "Condemning a Corporation: Exxon as Scapegoat," In *Proceedings of the Fourth Biennial Conference on Communication and Environment,* ed. Susan L. Senecah (Syracuse, NY: SUNY College of Environmental Science and Forestry, 1997), 133–144; Mark Meister and Phyllis Japp, "Sustainable Development and the Global Economy: Rhetorical Implications for Improving the Quality of Life," *Communication Research* 25 (August 1998): 399–422; Tarla Rai Peterson, *Sharing the Earth: The Rhetoric of Sustainable Development* (Columbia, SC: University of South Carolina Press, 1997); Toker, "Debating."

6 Kenneth Burke, *Attitudes Toward History* (Berkeley: University of California Press, 1935), 41.

7 Robert Bechtold Heilman, *The Iceman, the Arsonist, and the Troubled Agent: Tragedy and Melodrama on the Modern Stage* (Seattle: University of Washington Press, 1973), 49.

8 Osborn and Bakke, "Melodramas," 223.

9 Osborn and Bakke, "Melodramas," 224.

10 Osborn and Bakke, "Melodramas," 230.

11 Osborn and Bakke, "Melodramas," 232.

12 Carlson, "Limitations," 312.

13 Christiansen and Hanson, "Comedy," 160.

14 Steve Schwarze, "Juxtaposition in Environmental Health Rhetoric: Exposing Asbestos Contamination in Libby, Montana," *Rhetoric and Public Affairs* 6.2 (Summer 2003): 313–336.

15 Carlson, "Gandhi," 448.

16 Carlson, "Limitations," 319.

17 William Lewis, "Of Innocence, Exclusion, and the Burning of Flags: The Romantic Realism of the Law," *Southern Communication Journal* 60.1 (1994): 4–21.

18 Christiansen and Hansen, "Comedy as a Cure for Tragedy," 158.

19 Christiansen and Hanson, "Comedy as a Cure for Tragedy," 169.

20 Kenneth Burke, *A Rhetoric of Motives* (Berkeley: University of California Press, 1950), 25.

21 Robert Bechtold Heilman, *The Ways of the World: Comedy and Society* (Seattle: University of Washington Press, 1978), 94–95.

22 Heilman, *Ways of the World,* 96.

23 Jeffrey D. Mason, *Melodrama and the Myth of America* (Bloomington, IN: Indiana University Press, 1993): 16.

24 Peter Brooks, *The Melodramatic Imagination* (New York: Columbia University Press, 1984/1976): 15.

25 Brooks, *Melodramatic Imagination,* 20–21.

26 Heilman, *Iceman,* 52.

27 Osborn and Bakke, "Melodramas," 224.

28 Phaedra C. Pezzullo, "Performing Critical Interruptions: Stories, Rhetorical Invention, and the Environmental Justice Movement," *Western Journal of Communication* 65 (2001): 1–25.

29 Andrew Schneider, "A Town Left to Die," *Seattle Post-Intelligencer,* November 18, 1999. Available at http://seattlepi.nwsource.com/uncivilaction/lib18.shtml.

30 David F. Latham, "Libby presents united front to governor," *The Montanian,* August 15, 2001, pg. 8. One month later, at a field hearing in Libby that included EPA director Christine Todd Whitman and Montana's congressional delegation, speakers were calling the actions of W. R. Grace "criminal" and one suggested that they be charged with homicide.

31 Available at http://seattlepi.nwsource.com/uncivilaction/. (The title of the series plays off the book and movie "A Civil Action," which recounted the toxic contamination situation in Woburn, Massachusetts—also involving W. R. Grace.) In addition, the documentary film *Dust to Dust* visually performs this juxtaposition by showing document as well as extensive footage of Margaret Vatland (Gayla Benefield's mother) on her deathbed, coughing and gasping for air as a result of asbestosis that she contracted through exposure to her husband's work clothes. This footage helps develop monopathic identification with victims and with Benefield. Michael Brown Productions, *Dust to Dust: A Documentary Feature,* dir. Michael Brown, 2002.

32 Lawrence Buell, "Toxic Discourse," *Critical Inquiry* 24 (1998).

33 Lois Gibbs, *Love Canal: The Story Continues . . .* (Gabriola Island, Canada: New Society Publishers, 1998).

34 Osborn and Bakke, "Melodramas," 229.

35 Check, "Condemning," 134.

36 For one recent study, see Christine Harold, "Pranking Rhetoric: 'Culture Jamming' as Media

Activism," *Critical Studies in Media Communication* 21.3 (September 2004): 189–211.

37 For contrasting perspectives on the politics of green consumerist discourses, see M. Jimmie Killingsworth and Jacqueline S. Palmer, "Liberal and Pragmatic Trends in the Discourse of Green Consumerism," in *The Symbolic Earth: Discourse and Our Creation of the Environment*, eds. James G. Cantrill and Christine L. Oravec (Lexington, KY: The University Press of Kentucky, 1996) and Timothy Luke, "Green Consumerism: Ecology and the Ruse of Recycling," in *Ecocritique: Contesting The Politics of Nature, Economy and Culture* (Minneapolis: University of Minnesota Press, 1997).

38 For a discussion of discourses that rhetorically homogenize and singularize interests, see Celeste Michelle Condit, "Hegemony in a Mass-Mediated Society: Concordance about Reproductive Technologies," *Critical Studies in Mass Communication* 11.3 (September 1994): 205–230.

39 This sense of community, especially among mine workers, is depicted vividly in the beginning of *Dust to Dust*. The idyllic descriptions and depictions of social unity against the backdrop of the rugged, pristine beauty of northwest Montana sets up a powerful contrast to the rest of the film's portrayal of the mine's devastating effects on the community's well-being. Lawrence Buell argues that these motifs of "pastoral betrayal" and an "Eden lost" to pollution are typical in the rhetoric of toxic contamination; here, they heighten the sense of villainy and moral rupture characteristic of melodrama. Buell, "Toxic Discourse," 639–665.

40 Upon W. R. Grace's announcement in January 2000 that they would pay for medical bills, former miner Les Skramstad reflected, "In the past, everything that Grace has touched involving health problems at the mine has wound up hurting the miner and his family. Many people need the medical help that (Grace is) offering, but you can understand why some are frightened about the company being involved." Andrew Schneider, "Grace to pick up medical bills in tainted town," *Seattle Post-Intelligencer,* January 22, 2000. Available at http://seattlepi.nwsource.com/uncivilaction /libb221.shtml. Subsequently, victims have seen several unannounced cutbacks to the insurance coverage provided by Grace.

41 At the August 2001 public meeting, "Skramstad presented to Martz a quart-size jar of asbestos-contaminated vermiculite that he said he scooped up [at] the export plant after W. R. Grace & Co.

had supposedly cleaned the area. 'I didn't do any excavating, all I did was look under a piece of plywood. I could have gotten a five-gallon bucket but I thought this would do.'" David F. Latham, "Libby presents united front to governor," *The Montanian,* August 15, 2001, pg. 1.

42 http://www.ewg.org/reports/asbestos/facts/index .php.

43 Phaedra Pezzullo, "Resisting 'National Breast Cancer Awareness Month': The Rhetoric of Counterpublics and their Cultural Performances," *Quarterly Journal of Speech* 89.4 (November 2003): 345–365.

44 Schwarze, "Juxtaposition."

45 *Trade Secrets: A Moyers Report.* Public Affairs Television, Inc., 2001.

46 Brant Short, "Earth First! and the Rhetoric of Moral Confrontation," *Communication Studies* 42.2 (Summer 1991): 172–188.

47 Jonathan I. Lange, "Refusal to Compromise: The Case of Earth First!," *Western Journal of Speech Communication* 54 (1990): 473–494; see also Short, "Earth First!"

48 Robert Patterson and Ronald Lee, "The Environmental Rhetoric of 'Balance': A Case Study of Regulatory Discourse and the Colonization of the Public," *Technical Communication Quarterly* 6.1 (Winter 1997): 25–40.

49 Robert Cox, *Environmental Communication and the Public Sphere* (Thousand Oaks, CA: Sage Publications, 2006): 344–346.

50 "One of the strengths of the [environmental] movement has been its ability to build on the frustrations and rage of people who see their quality of life threatened by technological systems and perceive themselves as victims." Fischer, *Citizens,* 111.

51 See Brian Plonka's "Living and Dying in Libby," which won First Place in the Issue Reporting Picture Story category of the 2002 Pictures of the Year International competition. Images available at http://www.poy.org/59/16/1601plonb01.html.

52 However, their heroism is bolstered by victimage, too. Both Benefield and Skramstad have asbestos disease, and such disease is pervasive in their families. Benefield has dozens of relatives who are affected; Skramstad's commonplace, echoed across multiple texts and in his own testimony, is that it was bad enough that he has asbestos disease but absolutely wrong that he "had to bring it home to his wife and kids."

53 Patterson and Lee, "The Environmental Rhetoric of 'Balance.'"

54 G. Thomas Goodnight, "The Personal, Technical, and Public Spheres of Argument: A Speculative Inquiry into the Art of Public Deliberation," *Journal of the American Forensics Association* 18.4 (Spring 1982): 214–227.

55 Osborn and Bakke, "Melodramas," 230.

56 Osborn and Bakke, "Melodramas," 231.

57 This position is consistent with other rhetorical scholarship on polarization, which explains polarization as a tactic that invites audiences to "abandon the middle course" and take sides on some issue. William D. Harpine, "Bryan's 'A Cross of Gold:' The Rhetoric of Polarization at the 1896 Democratic Convention," *Quarterly Journal of Speech* 87.3 (August 2001): 295.

58 This instrumental view is explicit in one classic statement in the rhetoric of social movements, Bowers, Ochs and Jensen's *The Rhetoric of Agitation and Control*. By defining rhetoric as the rationale of "instrumental, symbolic behavior," the constitutive potential of agitation is obscured. Polarization is again treated simply as a means "to force a conscious choice between agitation and control." John W. Bowers, Donovan J. Ochs, and Richard J. Jensen, *The Rhetoric of Agitation and Control*, 2nd ed. (Prospect Heights, IL: Waveland Press, 1993), 34. In contrast, Charles Stewart's study of Stokely Carmichael's rhetoric illustrates how polarization not only offers audiences stark choices, but also can recast social identities and constitute moral issues. Charles Stewart, "The Evolution of a Revolution: Stokely Carmichael and the Rhetoric of Black Power," *Quarterly Journal of Speech* 83.4 (November 1997): 429–446.

59 For example, one "Citizen's Guide" to the World Trade Organization produced in the run-up to the 1999 Seattle meeting describes how "corporate interests trample workers" in a trade dispute over bananas. The guide insinuated that "huge campaign donations by Chiquita CEO Carl Lindner" influenced the US to argue for trade sanctions against Europe on account of their preference for Caribbean bananas over those grown in Central America (where Chiquita owns plantations). The guide positions this affluent CEO's interests at odds with the livelihood of indigenous farmers. Quoting unnamed Caribbean womens' groups, the guide explains how the European market provided "thousands of families in the sub-region of the Windward Islands a measure of security and has afforded us dignity and self-reliance. The loss of this security through a sudden change in market opportunities would leave us without resources to build a future for our families and our countries.'" Working Group on the WTO/MAI, "A Citizen's Guide to the World Trade Organization," July 1999. Available at http://depts.washington.edu /wtohist/documents/citizens_guide.pdf.

60 Communication scholars are giving increasing attention to how discourses circulating around globalization are problematizing agenda issues, social identities, and the very forums of public participation; respectively, see Kevin Michael DeLuca and Jennifer Peeples, "From Public Sphere to Public Screen: Democracy, Activism, and the 'Violence' of Seattle," *Critical Studies in Media Communication* 19.2 (June 2002): 125–151; Raka Shome and Radha S. Hegde, "Culture, Communication, and the Challenge of Globalization," *Critical Studies in Media Communication* 19.2 (June 2002): 172–189; and J. Robert Cox, "'Free Trade' and the Eclipse of Civil Society: Barriers to Transparency and Public Participation in NAFTA and the Free Trade Area of the Americas," In *Proceedings of the Sixth Biennial Conference on Communication and Environment*, eds. Marie-France Aepli, Stephen P. Depoe, and John W. Delicath (Cincinnati, OH: Center for Environmental Communication Studies, 2001), 172–181.

61 Jonathan Lange and Mark Moore's studies of the spotted owl controversy in the Pacific Northwest are instructive here. Melodramatic rhetoric surely reified the existing conflict between loggers and environmentalists. It is questionable whether any rhetoric could have ameliorated this conflict successfully, but as Moore suggests, advocates might have reclaimed the symbol of the owl to generate new modes of consubstantiality. Jonathan I. Lange, "The Logic of Competing Information Campaigns: Conflict over Old Growth and the Spotted Owl," *Communication Monographs* 60.3 (September 1993): 239–257; Mark P. Moore, "Constructing Irreconcilable Conflict: The Function of Synecdoche in the Spotted Owl Controversy," *Communication Monographs* 60.3 (September 1993): 258–274.

62 Toker, "Debating."

63 Powell, "Association of Southern Women."

64 This is clearly the case throughout Osborn and Bakke's delineation of the distinct traits of melodramatic characters; among other things, such characters are *"incredibly simple representations of humanity."* This observation quickly leads them to flatly assert, "Indeed, melodrama denies complexity" (222).

65 Burke, *Attitudes*, 5.

PISSAR's Critically Queer and Disabled Politics
Isaac West

One of the most exciting and productive sites for queer coalitional politics may be, ironically enough, the linkage between the everyday concerns of lesbians, gays, bisexuals, transpeople, (LGBTs) and people with disabilities.[1] I write "ironically enough" because many members of these communities, save those who live at the intersections of these identities, have labored to untangle the negative articulations of one with the other.[2] LGBT advocates have invested considerable time and energy in countering the medicalization and pathologization of their identities and desires, a struggle that continues today with campaigns against religiously based reparative therapies and the continued classification of transgender identifications as "gender identity disorder." As for people with disabilities, in ways different yet similar to LGBTs, they have been figured as asexual beings or hypersexual deviants. Therefore, to link the interests of people with disabilities and LGBTs may seem counter-intuitive, regressive, and politically risky. Yet, in a liberal-democratic polity that only sometimes tolerates LGBTs and people with disabilities, the continued vitality and vibrancy of LGBT, queer, and disability politics is dependent largely upon the ability of these advocates to develop forms of coalitional politics that articulate their modalities of domination to the interests of other similarly situated groups. In a context where queer liberalism, a potentially oxymoronic strategy of uncritical inclusion, prevails over queer politics, the recognition, promotion, and adaptation of alternative strategies for resisting the suffocating grip of "hetero/homo-corporo-normativities" is urgently needed.[3]

Narrowing down the larger topic of LGBT and/or queer coalitional politics to transgender advocacy actions, my interest here is how transpeople and people with disabilities have found common cause through their shared experiences. Despite the obvious differences between transpeople and people with disabilities, generally speaking they negotiate a number of similar

issues in their daily lives, and their explicit articulation may prove useful in forging political alliances. These common experiences include: difficulties, if not outright discrimination, in: securing an education, job, and/or housing; demonization and/or condemnation by religious officials; violence from perpetrators of hate crimes; and familial and social rejection, and shame.[4] To this list I would add another issue which may at first glance seem trivial, yet, upon further consideration, is crucial for the living of meaningful lives: safe and accessible bathrooms.

Public bathrooms are far from a trivial concern given that face-to-face publicity is enabled and constrained in important ways by the availability of safe and accessible public bathrooms. First, the location and condition of public bathrooms provide explicit physical markers about the gendered and abled expectations of the bodies in that area. The differences between the lines for the men's and women's bathrooms, as well as the use of bathrooms designated for people with disabilities by people without disabilities, speak volumes about the infusion of cultural norms into architecture. Second, as critical geographers Rob Kitchin and Robin Law note, an individual's inability to find safe and accessible public bathrooms subjects them to "'the bladder's leash,' restricting how long they are able to stay in a place and thus constraining their participation."[5] The "bladder's leash" not only limits the amount of time that a person can spend in a public location, it can prevent someone from even attempting to participate in these publics. As a result, people with disabilities and transpeople must be uniquely mindful of the accommodations available in places such as restaurants, stores, airports, schools, and their places of employment.

Instead of atomizing the differences between people with disabilities and transpeople, and further participating in the dissimulation of the interdependent circuitries authorizing the able-bodied and bigendered normativities underwriting the regulation of public places, I suggest these struggles are two sides of the same coin in that members of these identity groups want to be free from their bladder's leashes, both of which are ultimately tethered to the pole of an idealized, mythic, and normative body. Thus, in the spirit of promoting and developing radical democratic coalitional politics interested in challenging intersecting modalities of domination, in this essay I explore how these seemingly disparate groups have articulated, negotiated, and managed their differences while practicing a coalitional politics that questions the safety and accessibility of public bathrooms.

This argument unfolds in the following manner. The following section makes a case for taking more seriously the mutually constitutive and rhetorical relationship between place, space, and identity. Communication scholars often treat place and space as the site of rhetorical practice, noting it as a material constraint without exploring the interpenetrating rhetorical relationship between individuals in place and space. In lieu of this two-dimensional flattening of place and space, one that treats them as inert and extra-discursive material realities, I mobilize these concepts as three-dimensional and dynamic elements integrally linked to the rhetorical production of identity and agency. More specifically, the examination of public bathrooms offers insight into the gendered and abled logics actively undergirding these seemingly banal places. Communication critics can offer interventions into these cultural practices by attending to the identity work negotiated in/through the materiality and performativity of these spaces.

The next section analyzes the actions of People in Search of Safe and Accessible Restrooms (PISSAR), a genderqueer and disability coalition composed of college students and staff dedicated to providing safe and accessible bathrooms.[6] With the goal of demonstrating the productive potential of coalitional politics informed by critical queerness and disability, I explore the inventional resources created by the interaction of genderqueer and disabled bodies in campus bathrooms. The members of PISSAR addressed multiple forms of shame directed at them, including the internalized shame of their own bodies, the shame associated with bathroom activities and politics, and the potential sources of shame created by the articulation of their stigmatized identities together. By surveying and actually meeting in campus bathrooms, PISSAR negotiated a spatially based consubstantiality of shame to challenge the homo/hetero-corporo-normativity of public places and spaces. In the concluding section, I suggest that in their recognition of public bathrooms as a site of performative identity formation, PISSAR exemplifies a provocative model for theorizing and practicing critically queer politics outside of the hegemonic and increasingly ineffective logics of gay white male shame that guide much of contemporary GLBT and queer politics. To justify these conclusions, I first turn to a discussion of the relationship between rhetoric, place, space, and identity.

THE RHETORICITY OF PLACE, SPACE, AND IDENTITY

In the context of this essay, the concepts "space" and "place" are informed by Michel de Certeau's simple yet provocative maxim: "space is a practiced place."[7] Place and space, in Certeau's formulations of the terms, are given meaning by the practices employed in them creating a relationship between place and strategy, and space and tactics. The association of place with strategy signifies how locations are "circumscribed as *proper* and thus serve as the basis for generating relations with an exterior distinct from it."[8] To clarify, in an attempt to dictate the proper set of actions and relationships between members of a polity, the "strong" use strategies, or the recourse to naturalized hierarchies outside of the immediate physical relationship, to create places to manage the maneuvering of the "weak."[9] Public bathrooms, then, are places in that they are designed and provided for a limited number of functions (urinating, defecating, changing a diaper, vomiting, washing our hands, fixing our hair and/or makeup, gaining our composure, and brushing our teeth), they are divided by the sexes through an appeal to a naturalized system of biological separation, and they are regulated and surveilled by the law to enforce these taken-as-given differences.

Of course, public bathrooms are used for a number of purposes unintended by their owners—some people fuck and suck in them, others use them to buy and use drugs, and individuals who are homeless may use them for hygienic purposes or as a respite from the elements and the violence directed toward them. In these ways, the place of the public bathroom becomes a space. To complete the explanation of the dialectical pairing, as opposed to places and strategies, spaces are associated with tactics or "calculated actions" that "play on and with a terrain imposed on it and organized by the law of a foreign power."[10] Remembering Certeau's interest in the rhetorical conditions of contingency and probability, those interested in turning places into spaces:

> must accept the chance offerings of the moment . . . and make use of the cracks that particular conjunctions open in the surveillance of the proprietary powers.
> It poaches in them. It creates surprises in them. It can be where it is least expected. It is a guileful ruse. In short, a tactic is an art of the weak.[11]

The spatiality of resistance, inherently wedded to timing, relies on fugitive power relations, and these relations create the conditions to reimagine the material worlds we inhabit. Steven Pile reminds us that while "spaces of resistance are multiple, dynamic, and weak (in their effectiveness, but also because resistance is also dangerous)," they are "only ever in part controlled by the practices of domination."[12] Therefore, challenges to cultural hegemonies are located primarily in the alterations of quotidian routines, and in spatializing the understanding of resistance, we can, as Pile and Michael Keith urge us to do, draw "attention not only to the myriad spaces of political struggles, but also to the politics of the everyday space, through which political identities constantly flow and fix."[13] This conceptualization of space and place, along with strategies and tactics, assists us in understanding the complex interaction between space, identity, and agency.

As should be clear, the concomitant construction of identity and space is inherently communicative, and it deserves further theorization. Communication critics are especially well-attuned at thinking through the constitutive symbolic conditions of a culture. However, these critiques tend to isolate and privilege symbolic action over the spaces in which they are enacted and, thus, we seldom take up the task of understanding their co-production.[14] Considerations of place and time are often taught as instrumental and normative guides to the proper response to or experience of a given exigency. The purchase of this epistemological certainty exacts a high opportunity cost in that its faith in the determining relationship between place/occasion and the rhetorical act comes at the expense of thinking in more complex ways about the constitutive nature of space *and* communication. In the words of communication scholar Raka Shome, critics interested in intervening in cultural formations must forego the notion that space is "a mere setting or an innocent background in, over, or across which cultural activities and practices are seen to be occurring," opting instead for a perspective that acknowledges "the role that space plays in the (re)production of social power."[15] The implication of this move, according to Shome, is that we must account for the symbolicity of space as it "functions as a technology—a means and a medium—of power that is socially constituted through material relations that enable the communication of specific politics" while making others more difficult.[16]

Certeau's perspective assists us in understanding Shome's attention to the contextualized agentic effectivities of space and identity. While drawing attention to the spatial dimensions of power relations, Shome simultaneously problematizes acontextual understandings of identity to prevent the importation of stable subjectivities into the dynamic operations of space and identity.[17] As a result, agency is found in the localized interaction between subjects and the spaces in which they operate, which is to say in the performativity of identity and space. Nothing is guaranteed in advance as subjects necessarily work in between the constraining and enabling conditions found in the contingent and the probable, whether they recognize it or not.

With that said, the regulation of place presents formidable obstacles to practices of resistance, and critical attention must be paid to the contextualized nature of this dialectic. As Michel Foucault provocatively suggested "a whole history remains to be written of *spaces*— which would at the same time be the history of *powers* (both these terms in the plural)— from the great strategies of geo-politics to the little tactics of the habitat."[18] In a lecture first presented in 1967, Foucault was particularly interested in the secularization of Western societies and the attendant spatial effectivities of these cultural transformations. Ever concerned with the dispersion and dissimulation of power relations, he postulated space was in a period of partial desanctification, meaning that as the unilateral exercise of power and hence the determination of subjectivity had transferred from the centralized location of the church to the exercise of power from innumerable points, resistant subjects increasingly challenged the naturalness and centrally controlled meanings of places. The complete desanctification of places remains incomplete, however, because our cultural logics are arranged around "oppositions that remain inviolable, that our institutions and practices have not yet dared to break down," including those spaces and places defined by the split between public and private matters.[19]

Cultural geographer David Sibley locates the limits of desanctification in micropolitical and biopolitical exercises of power. Sibley argues that in spite of the continual undoing of places into spaces, "there seems to me to be a continuing need for ritual practices to maintain the sanctity of space in a secular society . . . Today, however, the guardians of sacred spaces are more likely to be security guards, parents or judges rather than priests."[20] In the case of public bathrooms, they are treated by many as places of gender regulation as they are policed in both the figurative and literal senses of the word.[21] Transpeople often face the possibility of being treated as gender transgressors for using the "wrong" bathroom. In response to a survey taken by the San Francisco Human Rights Commission, transpeople documented the negative reaction to their use of public restrooms. The stories ranged from having security guards harass them to losing jobs to "[getting] the shit kicked out of me for using the 'wrong bathroom.'" One respondent wrote

that they "almost got killed."[22] "The bathroom problem," according to Judith Halberstam, "illustrates in remarkably clear ways the flourishing existence of gender binarism despite rumors of its demise."[23] In spite of increasingly fluid notions of gender, the binary logic of sex remains the dominant ideology of corporeal legibility, a legibility defined primarily by visual c(l)ues. Ironically enough, then, Halberstam contends, "gender's very flexibility and seeming fluidity is precisely what allows dimorphic gender to hold sway" as the "definitional boundaries of male and female are so elastic, there are very few people in any given public space who are completely unreadable in terms of their gender."[24] In turn, these codes of cultural legibility authorize the biopolitical practice of gender policing, thereby allowing anxious individuals to punish those who trouble the stability of sexual and gender categories. Thus, even with the malleability of gender codes, "the transphobic imagination," according to Richard Juang, allows the bathroom to "become an extension of a genital narcissism (which could be expressed, roughly, as 'my body is how sex should be defined for all other bodies' and 'the presence of other kinds of body violates the sex of my own body')."[25]

Anxieties about public bathrooms are heightened by the fact that, in using the bathroom, we perform a private act in a public place with strangers. Moreover, using the bathroom leaves us vulnerable. We are in compromised positions that limit our lines of sight, be it because of a stall or a urinal. We expose parts of our bodies that are otherwise hidden from view— parts of our bodies that we typically don't want strangers to see. We pass fluids and objects that make a mess, can be noisy, and smell. In order to allay some of our anxieties, we invoke state-based protections to ensure that public bathrooms are places regulated by a variety of legal technologies. Transgender individuals are especially prone to this violence because of the naturalized assumptions about bodies, genders, and sexuality. Kath Browne explains how transgender transgressions of public bathrooms are especially threatening "in part because the leakiness of bodies cannot be associated with the fluid possibilities of sexed bodies" for "where bodies are revealed as unstable and porous, flowing between the sexes may be more threatening; where one border (bodily) is contravened others (man/woman) may be more intensely protected."[26]

Of course, women's and men's restrooms are policed in similar yet different ways. According to Patricia Cooper and Ruth Oldenziel, for women, more than men, the bathroom is a space "where they take care of their bodies and where they might remove themselves from public scrutiny or surveillance, exercise some authority, or forge bonds of solidarity."[27] Public bathrooms for women are areas where non-excretory activities are more likely to take place—women may, among other things, go to the bathroom in groups to have private conversations, reapply makeup and fix their hair, or regroup after a confrontation. In contrast, men's public restrooms involve what Halberstam terms "an architecture of surveillance" where each man stands at his urinal and looks straight ahead at the wall for fear he might be spotted sizing up the competition; talking at the urinals or between stalls is reserved only for the closest of friends and only when other men are not around. However, Halberstam continues, it is also a space for "homosocial interaction and of homoerotic interaction." Halberstam summarizes the distinction between men's and women's bathrooms in the following manner: while men's bathrooms "tend to operate as a highly charged sexual space in which sexual interactions are both encouraged and punished, women's rest rooms tend to operate as an arena for enforcement of gender conformity."[28] For transpeople, then, pissing and shitting always carries with it the chance for legal and physical violence.

Taken together, the works of the preceding theorists are useful heuristics for understanding the spatio-temporal modalities of power as well as the need to focus on the actions of specific bodies in particular spaces. As Tim Cresswell astutely notes, "the geographical ordering of society is founded on a multitude of acts of boundary making—of territorialization— whose ambiguity is to simultaneously open up the possibilities for transgression."[29] Attention to the communicative acts associated with space-making practices helps to bridge the practico-theoretical aporias identified by geographers in resistance scholarship. For example,

Doreen Massey reads Certeau as offering too strict an opposition and distinction between place and time, privileging the latter while negating the dynamism of the former, which has the inadvertent effect of stabilizing the meaning of space and obscuring its constitutive political potential.[30] Massey interrogates this dualism as one complicit with feminizing space and masculinizing time, and thus connected to larger logics underwriting the naturalization of gender ideologies.[31] Similarly, Lise Nelson identifies the lack of spatial consideration in many invocations of performativity (a Butlerian concept indebted to Foucault), operative primarily in representational critique, as a limiting condition to effective political intervention.[32] With these criticisms in mind, I would like to suggest that a reinvigorated reading of Certeau and Foucault, one that mobilizes their work in relation to contextualized communicative acts in a spatio-temporal context, especially that of quotidian practices such as those associated with public bathrooms, addresses the concerns of geography scholars who are rightly worried about acontextualized understandings of space and identity. If we take seriously the notion, like Robyn Longhurst, that "bodies are also always in a state of becoming with places,"[33] and that practices of resistance are inaugurated by the fluidity of both bodies and places/spaces, we can comprehend more fully, as Lynn Stewart suggests, how "space [is] a *product* of the human body" where the "ability to *produce* space, rather than just to *conceive* space, is the means by which people can take back power in their everyday lives."[34] Accordingly, the histories of power, space, and place that remain to be written must be sensitive to the gender, racial, and able-bodied discourses (to name only a few categories of analysis) that animate these spaces. Using their perspectives to inform my reading of PISSAR's actions, I turn to such behavior to demonstrate how the performativity of identity is informed by and simultaneously informs spatial politics.

PISSAR PATROLS AND POLITICS

The students and staff that formed PISSAR met at the 2003 University of California Students of Color Conference hosted on the University of

California–Santa Barbara (UCSB) campus. In a case of serendipitous scheduling, the conveners slated the transgender and disability caucuses at the same time in adjacent rooms. However, as each group noticed they had attracted only a few attendees, the two caucuses merged together to share their concerns about the campus. In the course of the meeting, the disability caucus disclosed their intention to survey the accessibility of campus bathrooms. Understanding the possible convergence of their interests, the disability caucus asked the transgender caucus if they would be interested in jointly undertaking the project. Given that transgender students are especially vulnerable to harassment and violence in and around public bathrooms, the members of the transgender caucus eagerly accepted the invitation.[35] In one recollection of the event, "everyone in the room suddenly began talking about the possibilities of a genderqueer/disability coalition, and PISSAR was born."[36] The choice of the name PISSAR was not merely an extension of the group's playful attitude; it also embraced and projected a queer attitude to challenge euphemistic discussions of bathrooms that impede the interrogation of what they termed "pee privilege."[37] Members of the group described the name as a "tool" that drew attention to the fact that all of us need to piss and shit and "warned" others that they were "about to talk about something 'crude.'"[38]

PISSAR soon discovered that another campus group with a blunt name meant to call attention to bodily functions was similarly interested in bathroom politics. "Aunt Flo and the Plug Patrol" had been voluntarily stocking tampon and pad machines on campus after the university failed to hire a new company to supply them. Stocking over 200 bathrooms on campus with tampons and pads bought from a wholesaler, Aunt Flo and the Plug Patrol made about $100 a month in profits which they funneled to student groups on campus.[39] Understanding the intimate connections of the gendered politics of bathrooms, PISSAR allied themselves with Aunt Flo and the Plug Patrol to make the campus a safe place to piss, shit, and bleed.[40] Aunt Flo and the Plug Patrol provided PISSAR with start-up funds to purchase the materials needed for their "PISSAR patrols" including gloves, tape

measures, clipboards, and their signature bright yellow t-shirts with spray-painted stenciling: "PISSAR" on the front and "FREE 2 PEE" on the back. In return, PISSAR included information about tampon and pad machines on their checklist. When constructing their checklist, a member of PISSAR raised the issue of changing tables and they added this consideration to their list. As a result of this attitudinizing frame, one that in their own words "refuse[d] to accept a narrow definition of 'queer' that denie[d] the complexities of our bodies,"[41] PISSAR broadly defined themselves in their mission statement as a group dedicated to making the campus a space where "people with all sorts of bodies and all sorts of genders should be free to pee, free to shit, free to bleed, free to share a stall with an attendant or change a baby's diaper."[42]

PISSAR's actions invite further investigation given their practice of radical democratic politics concerned with bodies and identities in space. More specifically, PISSAR enacted critically queer and disabled politics designed to counter the shame and stigma attached to their bodies. By directly confronting stigma and shame in the place of its inscription, PISSAR transformed campus bathrooms into a space of coalitional politics. PISSAR provides valuable lessons for LGBT, queer, and disabled advocates about how to challenge their own and others' attitudes about the safety and accessibility of campus bathrooms.

Consubstantial Spaces of Shame

PISSAR's members negotiated three interdependent levels of shame. First, they had to overcome the shame associated with the assertion that public bathrooms are a politically important issue. Of course, the disabled and genderqueer members faced similar yet different obstacles in overcoming this shame. Among the obstacles they shared, public bathrooms are easily branded as an unimportant or fringe concern when compared with "real" political issues such as access to medical care, equal employment, and housing opportunities, and lobbying for partnership rights. In addition, the disabled members had to contend with the mistaken perception that the Americans with Disabilities Act had already resolved the issue of bathroom accessibility. Like other protected classes before them, the disabled have felt the pain of formal equality's double-edged sword, repeatedly confronting those who assure them that they are treated equally in spite of their experiences to the contrary. Unlike the disabled, genderqueers are generally not afforded legal access to discourses of equality and must turn to their supposedly natural allies: gays, lesbians, and bisexuals. However, among other reasons, gays, lesbians, and bisexuals are often hesitant to lend their time and energy to bathroom politics as they do not want to associate themselves with the shameful subject of public sex in bathrooms.[43]

On a more personal level, PISSAR members dealt with a second source of shame when they confronted their feelings about their own bodies. The trans-identified members of the group harbored varying degrees of "internalized shame" generated by their "visible queerness" and "genderqueerness."[44] In a visual economy that tolerates LGBTs as long as they seamlessly assimilate or operate within "acceptable stereotypes of gay appearance," the trans members felt the gravitational pull of the politics of respectability practiced by a number of LGBTs.[45] When LGBTs align themselves with or adopt normative cultural markers of sex, gender, and sexuality, they further marginalize those who operate outside these dominant logics. As a result, the genderqueer-identified members reported a general sense of internalized shame that was compounded by the need to discuss their unique needs, as well as the private topic of bodily functions. According to PISSAR, this is an exceptionally difficult task as "we're trained from an early age not to talk publicly about what happens in the bathroom; we don't even have *language* for what happens in there; many of us still rely on the euphemisms our parents used when we were three."[46] In this way, the genderqueer members had to embrace their doubly stigmatized difference by publicly articulating themselves as pissing and shitting trans bodies.

The disabled members similarly negotiated their identities over and against the corporeal normativities and the discursive propriety associated with public bathrooms. As for the pressure to minimize their differences from the nondisabled, the members stated, "In striving to assimilate to nondisabled norms, many of us gloss over the need for the assistance some of us have in using the bathroom."[47] In a culture defined by ableist norms that can project shame onto disabled bodies, people with disabilities have an incentive to minimize their differences to prevent further stigmatization. For PISSAR's disabled members, these normalizing regimes are compounded by the fact that "particularly in mixed company (that is, in the presence of nondisabled folks), we are reluctant to talk about the odd ways we piss and shit." In the absence of these frank discussions, they felt that "this reticence has hindered our bathroom politics, often making it difficult for us to demand bathrooms that meet all of our needs."[48] These needs, identified on PISSAR's checklist, included: signs denoting the accessibility of the bathroom, stall doors wide enough for wheelchairs, toilets mounted at an accessible height with a generous amount of space around them, the presence of grab bars, accessible toilet paper dispensers, and sinks, soap dispensers, and mirrors placed at an accessible height.[49] Hence, like the genderqueer members, the disabled members had to place their own bodies at risk by publicly marking their difference as pissing and shitting beings.

Finally, the members had a third level of shame to deal with in relation to the mutual articulation of their struggles. In trumpeting PISSAR's coalition-building efforts, I do not mean to suggest that it was an easy endeavor. In the only published history of PISSAR, the members suggested that the shame and stigma associated with queerness and disability proved to be formidable obstacles in their alliance:

> our shame isn't always directed outward, toward the society and institutions that helped create it. It often drives a wedge between communities that might otherwise work together. And it is *precisely* this kind of embodied shame—the shame that we feel in our bodies and the shame that arises out of the experience and appearance of our bodies—that drives the divisions between queer and disability communities. PISSAR initially had trouble bridging this gap, in that some of our straight disabled members

worried about the political (read: queer) implications of our bathroom-mapping work.[50]

As this quote evidences, instead of reading the hesitation of the straight-identified disabled members of PISSAR as markers of their fear or hatred of gender-transgressors, they might be better understood within the context of the shame produced by the nefarious intersections of compulsory heterosexuality and disability. As suggested by Alison Kafer, a queer feminist with disabilities who was a member of PISSAR, "compulsory heterosexuality accrues a particular urgency among some segments of the disability community" as "many have wanted to appear 'normal,' 'natural,' and 'healthy' in other aspects of their lives." Therefore, it should come as no surprise that "the larger culture's heterosexism and homophobia are thus reproduced within the disability community."[51] At the same time, the nondisabled genderqueer members of the group had to interrogate their ableist assumptions to overcome the divisions engendered by their desires to "distance themselves from disabled people in an effort to assert their own normalcy and health."[52] Thus, the members of PISSAR encountered what Kenneth Burke would call the "characteristic invitation to rhetoric" in that they needed to bridge the symbolic divisions generated by these interpenetrating discursive constellations of shame.[53]

These internalized and projected discourses of shame produced division, yet they also contained the seeds of identification through the rhetorical construction of consubstantiality. Breaking down Burke's vocabulary, consubstantiality is achieved when the interests of two distinct individuals are articulated together through "common sensations, concepts, images, ideas, [and] attitudes," or what Burke would term the substance of rhetoric.[54] Importantly, especially for those interested in the politics of identity, consubstantiality requires constant renewal, for even as consubstantiality is an *"acting-together,"* it is a temporary identification between those who are "joined and separate, at once a distinct substance and consubstantial with another."[55] Consubstantiality, then, is a fragile union, one in need of continual rhetorical renewal, as it negotiates the competing motives of the concerned parties. As an important addendum to Burke's work, we must consider how the spatial locations of consubstantiality constrain and enable the potential for identification. Contextualizing this discussion in PISSAR's spatial politics engages the problematic, while also demonstrating the possibilities of reanimating shame as a productive discursive element of critically queer and disabled politics.

CRITICAL QUEERNESS AND DISABILITY

According to the members of PISSAR, the act of coming together in the campus bathrooms and "repeatedly talking openly about people's need for a safe space to pee helps us break through some of the embodied shame and recognize our common needs."[56] When the disabled members patrolled with the genderqueer members, many of them reported a greater understanding of the fear and anxiety generated by sex-specific bathrooms. In one memorable case of consubstantiality, the members of PISSAR recounted the evolution of a straight-identified disabled man's attitudes toward gender-neutral bathrooms. Once skeptical and dismissive of the need to accommodate genderqueer students and staff, after going out on a few patrols he was able to link his own struggles with his trans counterparts through the language of accessibility.[57] This is not to say that he understood these accessibility issues as equal to one another. Instead, as they state, he was able to "make the connection between disability oppression and genderqueer oppression" which then created favorable conditions for his continued participation in coalitional politics.

Likewise, after the trans members of the group worked together with their disabled colleagues, they understood the spatial dynamics of campus bathrooms in a way that fostered connections between them. Using their checklist, the nondisabled together with the disabled members measured the width, height, and overall accessibility of numerous parts of the bathroom. As they describe it, the checklist operated as a "consciousness-raising tool" among their own members. Several trans/genderqueer members did not understand how inaccessible the campus bathrooms were for many of the disabled students on campus. For one nondisabled member, "going through the PISSAR checklist caused her to view the entire built world through different eyes."[58] "Rather than focusing on the alleged failures and hardships of disabled bodies," the PISSAR members directed their attention to "the failures and omissions of the built environment—a too-narrow door, a too-high dispenser."[59] By reframing the issue as one of the architectural privileging of "the 'normal' body and its needs," the nondisabled members of PISSAR could start to understand how they and the disabled were both working against corporeal normativities. As they described it, "this switch in focus from the inability of the body to the inaccessibility of the space makes room for activism" between groups that may not initially notice their shared sources of struggle.[60] The nondisabled members realized that ability, like sex, is a naturalized, as opposed to a natural, condition, and the accommodation of ability is a choice that could be made differently to better account for bodies of different sizes, shapes, and mobility.

In this way, PISSAR, unlike many LGBT and queer advocates before them, effectively addressed *both* the shame and stigma directed at their bodies to bolster their coalition. Michael Warner demands that queer coalitions attend to the interrelated and divisive pressures of stigma and shame; otherwise, these coalitions will inevitably incorporate themselves into and thus strengthen, rather than weaken, the social hierarchies that authorize the violence directed at LGBTs. Drawing upon Erving Goffman's work, Warner explains the relationship between stigma and shame as one of identity (stigma) and acts (shame).[61] Unfortunately, too many LGBTs, in Warner's words, have dealt with "ambivalence of belonging to a stigmatized group" by "embrac[ing] the identity but disavow[ing] the act," meaning that LGBTs, with their rainbow flags and Human Rights Campaign bumper stickers, latch onto pride in their identity as *the* countervailing affect to the shame directed at their sexual and corporeal practices.[62] However, LGBT investment in pride in their identity

often involves a distancing of themselves from the shameful acts that define their identities, which then manifests itself in divisions between "normal" and "deviant" LGBTs. As a result, Warner suggests, the "incoherence and weakness" of LGBT politics are rooted in the decision to "challenge the stigma on identity, but only by reinforcing the shame of sex" and thereby choosing to "articulate the politics of identity rather than become a broader movement targeting the politics of sexual shame."[63] In response to these normalizing pressures, Warner offers an ethics of queer life that embraces shame and abjection as that which binds together and hence should guide queer politics: "Queers can be abusive, insulting, and vile toward one another but because abjection is understood to be the shared condition, they also know how to communicate through such camaraderie a moving and unexpected form of generosity." Warner further states, "no one is beneath its reach, not because it prides itself on generosity, but because it prides itself on nothing. The rule is: Get over yourself . . . At its best, this ethic cuts against every form of hierarchy you could bring into the room."[64] PISSAR's simultaneous challenging of the stigma and shame of disabled and trans pissing and shitting bodies provides an instructive example for how we can initiate coalitional politics that trouble the sexual and corporeal normativities of public spaces.

By articulating their coalitional work in the particular space of campus bathrooms, PISSAR avoided the potential pitfalls associated with single-issue identity politics, namely allowing the differences between similarly situated individuals to overwhelm their synergistic merger. When crafting their mission statement, the members of PISSAR, composed primarily of graduate students with an interest in queer and/or disability studies, explicitly stated their commitment to "multi-identity organizing" as well as "working in tandem with other interest groups on campus and elsewhere."[65] Explicitly identifying themselves elsewhere as a queer organization, they further clarified their investment in a "*queer* queerness" that "encompasses both sexually and medically queer bodies, that embraces a diversity of appearances and disabilities and needs." PISSAR translated this critical attitude into their checklist which they described as "a manifesto of sorts" that "models *queer* coalition-building by incorporating disability, genderqueer, childcare, and menstruation issues into one document, refusing single-issue analysis."[66]

PISSAR, a self-described "coalition group of disability and genderqueer activists," may be best understood then as the fusion of critically queer and disabled politics. First advanced by Butler, the concept of critical queerness is meant to highlight the fact that queer, as a category of identity and site of cultural agency, must "remain that which is, in the present, never fully owned, but always and only redeployed, twisted, queered from a prior usage and in the direction of urgent and expanding political purposes."[67] Seeing it as a necessary precondition for the radical democratization of queer politics, Butler asks us to resist the temptation to circumscribe queerness by embracing and "affirm[ing] the contingency of the term: to let it be vanquished by those who are excluded by the term but who justifiably expect representation by it" and "to let it take on meanings that cannot now be anticipated by a younger generation whose political vocabulary may well carry a very different set of investments."[68] Embracing a critically queer attitude, PISSAR's mobilization of queerness refused to define it narrowly along identical lines of sexuality, choosing instead to inaugurate an interrogation of the bigendered and abled normativities associated with public bathrooms.

Of course, assigning temporal and spatial fluidity and contingency to queerness is not meant to render it a completely empty signifier. Rather, the emphasis here is on resisting the stable noun form of "queer" in favor of its usage as a contextual adjective and active verb.[69] Crip theorist (crip theory is to disability studies what queer theory is to LGBT studies) Robert McRuer further differentiates between virtual and critical queerness, a distinction based on the actions of the queer subject. As McRuer argues, "a virtually queer identity" can be "experienced by anyone who fail[s] to perform heterosexuality without contradiction and incoherence (i.e., everyone)" while a "critically queer perspective [would] presumably mobilize the inevitable failure to approximate the norm, collectively 'working the weakness in the norm.'"[70] McRuer's interest in

these terms rests primarily in their translation to disability contexts to differentiate between living a disabled life (virtual disability) and acts where disabled individuals and groups "have resisted the demands of compulsory able-bodiedness and have demanded access to a newly imagined and newly configured public sphere where full participation is not contingent on an able body" (critical disability).[71] These distinctions prevent the all-too-easy equivocations made in the declarations that everyone is queer, and, if they live long enough, disabled—a move meant to universalize these identities while simultaneously neutralizing their radical potential to unsettle unquestioned institutional, corporeal, and spatial normativities.

In this particular case, PISSAR's attention to the material effectivities of the spatial normativities that failed to account for disabled and gender-transgressive bodies provided the inventional resources necessary to animate a critically queer and disabled politics. Composed primarily of educators, the members of PISSAR identified their activism as "a teaching model in and of itself" by "combin[ing] education with social change," and we would be well served by further investigating how they embodied a critical corrective that challenges the devaluation or ignorance of material space in radical democratic theory.[72] As outlined above, I understand critical queerness and critical disability to be radical democratic projects. With that said, as critical geographer Michael Brown rightly notes, the theorization of radical democracy generally "lacks any sort of geographical imagination" as it often fails "to consider that citizens are always engaging in politics in actual locations."[73] Like Shome, Brown finds the use of spatial metaphors (e.g. "creating space" for a practice or group) especially irksome as it risks "import[ing] fixed, essentialized notions of space into the geographical imagination of political theory (to the extent that it actually has one)."[74] Figurative or discursive space alone could not solve the issue of safe and accessible campus bathrooms. Therefore, out of logistical and political necessity, PISSAR's enactment of radical democracy had to take place in the actual space of the campus bathrooms.

The PISSAR patrols provide a potent rejoinder to those who dismiss queer and disability studies' potential for praxis. Situated on a university campus and composed largely of graduate students with an interest in queer and/or disability studies, PISSAR actively articulated their theoretical training to their political activities. In their description of the PISSAR patrols, one group of members framed the connections in the following way: "Because the bathroom is our site, and the body in search of a bathroom is our motivation, we recognized early on the need to be concerned with the body and theory together. PISSAR's work is an attempt at embodying theory, at theorizing from the body."[75] PISSAR patrol members armed with rubber gloves and tape measures utilized a checklist that covered disability accessibility and gender safety issues as well as the accessibility and supply of tampons and pads, and the presence of a changing table. Fully aware of the risks associated with their actions, yet still wanting to gather the necessary information in an "unapologetically public way," PISSAR established guidelines to reduce the risk of harassment and violence, including working during the day in groups of three, at least one person would wear PISSAR's bright yellow t-shirt to raise awareness of the group while also establishing a justification for their spatial transgression, and, finally, making an effort to include persons of varying gender identities.[76] By coming together and working together in bathrooms, the different members of PISSAR placed their own bodies at risk while also experiencing the discomfort and anxieties experienced by others. In this way, PISSAR members enacted a radical democratic politics that utilized space as a generative locus for critically queer and disabled politics built upon the appropriation of shame.

Pissing Off Power

At the conclusion of their patrols, PISSAR confirmed their suspicion that their campus bathrooms presented serious obstacles for disabled and trans students and staff. With regard to disabled accessibility, PISSAR reported that of the "approximately 50 single-stall restrooms identified by UCSB as both accessible *and* gender-neutral . . . a majority of restrooms (including those at Health Services) [were] not fully wheelchair accessible and up to ADA

codes."[77] PISSAR also found the gender-neutral bathrooms to be riddled with problems as "many 'gender-neutral' bathrooms were incorrectly marked with poor signage, and most [were] functioning as de facto men's rooms because of their placement directly next to specifically marked women's rooms;" these bathrooms were far from safe in that they created "embarrassing and dangerous" situations for genderqueers.[78] Armed with these results, PISSAR met with university administrators, including the chancellor of the University of California system, to demand a solution to these problems. In response to PISSAR's arguments, the Transgender Law and Policy Institute reported UCSB recently "converted 17 single-occupancy restrooms from gendered to gender-neutral and are investigating the feasibility of converting an additional 17."[79] In addition, all future major construction on the UCSB campus will include gender-neutral bathrooms.[80]

In the end, PISSAR seems to have been a temporary coalition, one that withered away once their rhetorical exigencies were addressed by the university administration. Their website is defunct, and many of the members have moved on to other campuses. However, they undoubtedly learned valuable lessons about how to participate in coalitional politics.

RECONSIDERING TIME, SPACE, AND RESISTANCE

PISSAR's particular practice of coalitional politics, one motivated by the overcoming of stigma and shame and emphasizing the rhetoricity of place, space, and identity, brings to light three important issues about the effectivities of critically queer and disabled politics. First, public bathrooms reflect cultural biases that erect potential barriers for individuals who prefer to participate in public life. For genderqueers and people with disabilities, the seemingly natural system of sexual segregation creates limiting and dangerous places hostile to extended public engagement. Rather than accept these conditions as unfortunate realities, PISSAR used their bodies and voices to remind us that these architectural choices are precisely that—choices to conform to hetero-corporo-normativities and therein accommodate the mythic norms of sex, gender, and able-bodiedness. More importantly, PISSAR called attention to other ways of arranging, marking, constructing, and equipping public bathrooms to lessen the already incredible stigma and shame associated with pissing and shitting in public. While the disabled have some avenues of legal recourse to address issues of accessibility, assuming of course that they can afford the legal representation needed to initiate such challenges, trans people generally do not enjoy comparable legal status as a protected class. If legal scholar Lisa Mottet is correct in her assertion that the courts will generally treat bathroom access for transpeople "as just a minor inconvenience that they do not want to micromanage," we will need to continue this work in venues outside of the courts.[81] It is my hope that this essay makes a compelling case for why all of us should be willing to examine our own pee privilege and thus support efforts like PISSAR's in the name of securing safe and accessible spaces for everyone to piss and shit in peace.

PISSAR's embodied politics raise a second set of issues concerning the rhetorical undoing of place, space, and identity. Rhetorical scholars often treat the space/place of rhetoric's enactment as an inert material reality that serves as an innocent backdrop to the reception of the spoken word. Or, on the other end of the spectrum, the occasion is seen as a determining factor in how the rhetor responds to the rhetorical situation. What I would like to suggest is that neither of these perspectives fully captures the ways place/space relate to the rhetorical production of identity and agency. PISSAR's activism, including the choice to meet in their members' campus bathrooms to confront their shared and different forms of shame, demonstrates Certeau's principle that space is a practiced place where individuals can challenge the power relations meant to exclude them from creating publics more hospitable to their needs. Also, in line with Foucault's theorization of space, PISSAR's embodied resistance to the hetero-corporo-normativities governing public places reminds us that spaces are given meaning through the contestation of identity in those spaces.

Finally, PISSAR's negotiation of stigma and shame provides an instructive example of the kinds of correctives needed to energize critically queer politics and resist the normalizing pressures of liberalism. LGBT investment in pride as the antidote to sexual shame often results in the normalization of LGBT politics. However, instead of trying to rid ourselves of shame, might we mobilize it instead as the nodal point for a broader-based critique that refracts social processes and projections of shame? As Eve Sedgwick eloquently argues, shame cannot be quarantined as stigmatized individuals and groups cannot escape the "permanent, structuring fact of identity" performed by shame, but they can, as Sedgwick suggests, explore the "powerfully productive and powerfully social metamorphic possibilities" of its affect.[82] PISSAR's explicit articulation of the needs of genderqueer and disabled bodies negotiated, through the idioms of shame, spatially based identifications as a necessary component of political coalition.

PISSAR's explicit declaration of their intentions to animate a "queer queerness" that addressed the various ways in which bodies are disciplined and regulated in public bathrooms provides a useful model for countering the logics of shame that dominate GLBT and queer politics. Queer studies and activism, on Halberstam's reading, must divest itself from "white gay male identity politics," motivated by white gay male shame, "that focuses its libidinal and other energies on simply rebuilding the self that shame dismantled rather than taking apart the social processes that project shame onto queer subjects in the first place."[83] She continues: "If queer studies is to survive gay shame, and it will, we all need to move far beyond the limited scope of white gay male concerns and interests." Echoing Butler's commentary on critical queerness, Halberstam suggests that queer theorists and activists must be willing to learn from and adopt the intersectional critiques forwarded by those steeped in feminist, ethnic studies, and I would add crip theory/disability studies to the list.[84] Critically queer groups such as PISSAR that define themselves broadly as coalitions countering related forms of domination provide a provocative model for thinking outside of the logics of gay white male shame. And in a rhetor-ical culture where normalcy is the dominant trope, this is an urgent task indeed.

Notes

1 I consciously employ "people with disabilities" and "disability" over other terms because these are the terms preferred by the majority, if not all, of the authors I cite. As with all identity categories, we must be attentive to linguistic self-determination and the cultural-political work performed by these identity markers. Unfortunately, according to Simi Linton, many terms meant to mark the agency of those with disabilities (such as "differently abled" or "physically challenged") "convey the boosterism and do-gooder mentality endemic to the paternalistic agencies that control many disabled people's lives." *Claiming Disability: Knowledge and Identity* (New York: New York University Press, 1998), 14.

2 As Robert McRuer explains, LGBTs and people with disabilities often serve as metaphors for the other through "conflation and stereotype: people with disabilities are often understood as somehow queer (as paradoxical stereotypes of the asexual or oversexual person with disabilities would suggest), while queers are often understood as somehow disabled (as an ongoing medicalization of identity, similar to what people with disabilities more generally encounter, would suggest)." "Compulsory Able-Bodiedness and Queer/Disabled Existence," in *Disability Studies: Enabling the Humanities,* ed. Sharon Snyder, Brenda Jo Brueggemann, and Rosemarie Garland-Thomson (New York: Modern Language Association of America, 2002), 94.

3 For more on the anxieties generated by queer liberalism, see David Eng, Judith Halberstam, and José Esteban Muñoz, "What's Queer About Queer Studies Now?," *Social Text* 23 (2005): 1–17. Like Santiago Solis, I use "hetero-corporo-normativity" to highlight the interrelated logics of able-bodiedness and heterosexuality. "Snow White and the Seven 'Dwarfs'—Queercripped," *Hypatia* 22 (2007): 129. I add "homo" to this term to mark the potential for sexual minorities to participate in these normativities.

4 This list is adapted from one generated by Carrie Sandahl, "Queering the Crip or Cripping the Queer? Intersections of Queer and Crip Identities in Solo Autobiographical Performances," *GLQ* 9 (2003): 26. There are, of course, important differences between these two populations. As

Ellen Samuels notes, the commonalities are strained when issues such as visibility and coming out are factored into the analogy for there are a number of disabilities that are not optically obvious. "My Body, My Closet: Invisible Disability and the Limits of Coming-out Discourse," *GLQ* 9 (2003): 233–55. Thus, while many of the disability issues discussed here involve physical impediments created by human-designed architecture, I understand "disability" as a category of identification that encompasses more than physical impairment.

5 Rob Kitchin and Robin Law, "The Socio-Spatial Construction of (In)Accessible Public Toilets," *Urban Studies* 38 (2001): 289.

6 "Genderqueer" often refers to individuals who refuse traditional sexual and gender markers such as "woman" or "man," and the attendant gender expectation with these categories.

7 Michel de Certeau, *The Practice of Everyday Life,* trans. Steven Rendall (Berkeley, CA: University of California Press, 1984), 117.

8 Ibid., xix.

9 Ibid., 36.

10 Ibid., 35.

11 Certeau, *Everyday Life,* 35.

12 Steve Pile, "Introduction: Opposition, Political Identities and Spaces of Resistance," in *Geographies of Resistance,* ed. Steve Pile and Michael Keith (London: Routledge, 1997), 16.

13 Steve Pile and Michael Keith, "Preface," in *Geographies of Resistance,* ed. Steve Pile and Michael Keith (London: Routledge), xi.

14 While not considered in the text, two strands of inquiry in communication studies are notable exceptions to this rule. First, numerous essays have dealt with the connection of memory, identity, and place/space in venues such as museums and memorial sites. Second, critics concerned with counterpublics have taken up the issues of rhetoric and space in a sustained fashion. Most notably, Phaedra Pezzullo's ethnographic study of toxic tours poignantly captures the transformative possibilities of cultural performances in the spaces of corporate pollution. *Toxic Tourism: Rhetorics of Pollution, Travel, and Environmental Justice* (Tuscaloosa: University of Alabama Press, 2007). My essay complements this work by attending to the mundane production of identity in the unremarkable spaces of everyday life.

15 Raka Shome, "Space Matters: The Power and Practice of Space," *Communication Theory* 13 (2003): 40.

16 Ibid., 40.

[17] Ibid., 43.

[18] Michel Foucault, *Power/Knowledge: Selected Interviews & Other Writings, 1972–1977* (New York: Pantheon Books, 1980), 149.

[19] Michel Foucault, "Of Other Spaces," *Diacritics* 16 (1986): 23.

[20] David Sibley, *Geographies of Exclusion: Society and Difference in the West* (London: Routledge, 1995), 72.

[21] Ruth Holliday and John Hassard, "Contested Bodies: An Introduction," in *Contested Bodies,* ed. Ruth Holliday and John Hassard (London: Routledge, 2001), 13.

[22] Jodie Marksamer and Dylan Vade, *Gender Neutral Bathroom Survey* (San Francisco: San Francisco Human Rights Commission, 2002), n.p.

[23] Judith Halberstam, *Female Masculinity* (Durham, NC: Duke University Press, 1998), 22.

[24] Ibid., 20.

[25] Richard M. Juang, "Transgendering the Politics of Recognition," in *Transgender Rights,* ed. Paisley Currah, Richard Juang, and Shannon Price Minter (Minneapolis: University of Minnesota Press, 2006), 247.

[26] Kath Browne, "Genderism and the Bathroom Problem: (Re)Materialising Sexed Sites, (Re)Creating Sexed Bodies," *Gender, Place and Culture* 11 (2004): 338.

[27] Patricia Cooper and Ruth Oldenziel, "Cherished Classifications: Bathrooms and the Construction of Gender/Race on the Pennsylvania Railroad During World War II," *Feminist Studies* 25 (1999): 15.

[28] Halberstam, *Female Masculinity,* 24.

[29] Tim Cresswell, *In Place/Out of Place: Geography, Ideology, and Transgression* (Minneapolis: University of Minnesota Press, 1996), 149.

[30] Doreen Massey, "Entanglements of Power: Reflections," in *Entanglements of Power: Geographies of Domination/Resistance* (London: Routledge, 2000), 282. See also, Massey, *For Space* (London: Sage, 2005), 25–30, 45–8.

[31] [Doreen] Massey, *Space, Place, and Gender* (Minneapolis: University of Minnesota Press, 1994), 7.

[32] Lise Nelson, "Bodies (and Spaces) Do Matter: The Limits of Performativity," *Gender, Place and Culture* 6 (1999): 331–53.

[33] Robyn Longhurst, *Bodies: Exploring Fluid Boundaries* (London: Routledge, 2001), 5.

[34] Lynn Stewart, "Bodies, Visions, and Spatial Politics: A Review Essay on Henri Lefebvre's *The Production of Space," Environment and Planning D: Society and Space* 13 (1995): 610.

[35] Brett Genny Beemyn, "Making Campuses More Inclusive of Transgender Students," *Journal of Gay & Lesbian Issues in Education* 3 (2005): 81–2.

[36] Simone Chess, Alison Kafer, Jessi Quizar, and Mattie Udora Richardson, "Calling all Bathroom Revolutionaries," in *That's Revolting: Queer Strategies for Resisting Assimilation,* ed. Mattilda [Bernstein Sycamore] (Brooklyn, NY: Soft Skull Press, 2004), 190.

[37] Ibid., 189.

[38] Ibid., 192.

[39] Twyla Ilyne Johnson, "Aunt Flo Faces Unending Flow," *Daily Nexus,* January 23, 2003, http://www.dailynexus.com/article.php?a=4255 (accessed June 15, 2007).

[40] Chess et al., "Calling all Bathroom," 191.

[41] Chess et al., "Calling all Bathroom," 193.

[42] "PISSAR Mission and Goals," http://www.uweb.ucsb.edu/~schess/organizations/pissar/mission.html (accessed June 15, 2007).

[43] Chess et al., "Calling all Bathroom," 194.

[44] Ibid., 194.

[45] Ibid., 193.

[46] Ibid., 193.

[47] Ibid., 194.

[48] Ibid., 194.

[49] "PISSAR Patrol Checklist," http://www.uweb.ucsb.edu/~schess/organizations/pissar/checklist.htm (accessed June 15, 2007).

[50] Chess et al., "Calling all Bathroom," 196.

[51] Alison Kafer, "Compulsory Bodies: Reflections on Heterosexuality and Able-Bodiedness," *Journal of Women's History* 15, (2003): 82–3.

[52] Chess et al., "Calling all Bathroom," 197.

[53] Kenneth Burke, *A Rhetoric of Motives* (Berkeley: University of California Press, 1950), 25.

[54] Ibid., 21.

[55] Ibid., 21.

[56] Chess, et al., "Calling all Bathroom," 197.

[57] Ibid., 201.

[58] Ibid., 201.

[59] Ibid., 200.

[60] Ibid., 200.

[61] Michael Warner, *The Trouble with Normal: Sex, Politics, and the Ethics of Queer Life* (Cambridge, MA: Harvard University Press, 1999), 28.

[62] Ibid., 33.

[63] Ibid., 31.

[64] Ibid., 35.

[65] "PISSAR Mission and Goals."

[66] Chess et al., "Calling all Bathrooms," 197.

[67] Judith Butler, *Bodies That Matter: On the Discursive Limits Of "Sex"* (New York: Routledge, 1993), 228.

[68] Ibid., 230.

69 Janet Jakobsen, "Queer Is? Queer Does? Normativity and the Problem of Resistance," *GLQ* 4 (1998): 511–36.

70 Robert McRuer, *Crip Theory: Cultural Signs of Queerness and Disability* (New York: New York University Press, 2006), 30.

71 Ibid., 30.

72 "PISSAR Mission and Goals."

73 Michael Brown, *Replacing Citizenship: AIDS Activism & Radical Democracy* (New York: Guilford Press, 1997), 15, 14.

74 Ibid., 184.

75 Chess et al., "Calling all Bathrooms," 192.

76 Ibid., 191, 201.

77 "Minutes from Eucalyptus Meeting," July 23, 2003 http://www.uweb.ucsb.edu/~schess/organizations /pissar/Eucalyptus%20Meeting.htm (accessed June 15, 2007).

78 Ibid.

79 Transgender Law and Policy Institute, "College/ Universities and K-12 Schools," http://www .transgenderlaw.org/college/index.htm (accessed June 15, 2007).

80 Patricia Leigh Brown, "A Quest for a Restroom That's Neither Men's Room Nor Women's Room," *New York Times*, March 4, 2005, http://www.nytimes.com/2005/03/04/national /04bathroom.html?ex=1184212800&en=80c1b6e9 9582ed3c&ei=5070 (accessed June 15, 2007).

81 Lisa Mottet, "Access to Gender-Appropriate Bathrooms: A Frustrating Diversion on the Path to Transgender Equality," *Georgetown Journal of Gender and the Law* 4 (2003): 744.

82 Eve Kosofsky Sedgwick, "Queer Performativity: Henry James's *The Art of the Novel*." *GLQ* 1 (1993): 14.

83 Judith Halberstam, "Shame and White Gay Masculinity," *Social Text* 23 (2005): 220, 224.

84 Ibid., 224.

Chapter 4

Tactics for Internal Audiences

Because movements seek to alter the status quo, they must employ rhetoric in such a way that their message gets heard and acted upon. Consequently, their messages must be targeted to external audiences in strategic and sometimes novel ways. But the success of any movement depends on the solidarity of its members— the enduring strength of their commitment, investment, and performance. Creating and maintaining that solidarity may be the most pressing challenge that movements confront: members sometimes tire under the strain of opposition, commitments waver, other pressures intervene, conflict arises, or apathy sets in. For that matter, the very act of joining a movement presupposes a sense of identity that may not initially exist and must be created, deepened, nurtured, and sustained.

The following essays address rhetorical tactics directed to internal audiences. How do movements recruit members and sustain collective commitment? How do intragroup dynamics shape a sense of personal identity, shared and reciprocal emotions, and visions of worldmaking? How can members be kept from faltering in the face of strong opposition— especially violence or incarceration? In adapting too much to the demands of external audiences, a movement may lose internal identity or ideological purity. At times, the stress in the formation of group identity may limit the will of movement actors to attack directly the forces of opposition or oppression. The choices are never easy. A misstep either way could weaken the movement. Material sacrifices take their toll.

In "Enacting Red Power: The Consummatory Function in Native American Protest Rhetoric" (1983), Randall A. Lake contends that scholars have misunderstood the many so-called rhetorical "failures" of the American Indian Movement. AIM's confrontational protest rejected white culture by adopting traditional tribal language and ritual. Such tactics consistently failed to persuade whites, thus appearing to be strategically ill-conceived. Lake argues, however, that the primary audience was not white, but red. "The key to understanding how Native American protest rhetoric functions," Lake concludes, "is to understand what the Red Power movement wants. . . . The overriding militant aim is to regenerate traditional Indian religious beliefs and to restore the ancient ways of life." AIM's protest discourse can be seen as "ritual self-address" achieving "consummation"—the calling into being or perfection of the movement—by symbolically expressing traditional tribal beliefs.

What if the strategic goal is not to preserve but instead to radically alter communal identity, not only for the sake of self-worth but for the very lives of its members? Bonnie J. Dow addresses this question in "AIDS, Perspective by Incongruity, and Gay Identity in Larry Kramer's '1,112 and Counting'" (1994). By 1983, the exponential proliferation of AIDS could be attributed substantially to homophobic silence and neglect by various medical and governmental institutions. However, as activist Larry Kramer insisted, the gay community also contributed to its own destruction through denial, disbelief, and complacency regarding sexual behavior that was at the core of its cultural and political identity. In order to survive, gay men needed new priorities, new subject positions. Kramer sought this radical transformation, Dow contends, through "perspective by incongruity," which "de-naturalizes a given set of meanings or values and questions their adequacy for explaining or directing experience." Kramer's polemic exploded indifference through the shock of accumulating statistics, rage against lethal discriminatory practices, and guilt about gay complicity and hypocrisy, creating an opportunity for "genuine argument," the "existential disruption" that achieves open reflection, redefinition of self, and communal action.

A movement's capacity and will to reflect and act often depends on the rhetorical style of its leaders. Driven to explain the charismatic appeal of Labor leader "Mother" Jones, Mari Boor Tonn, in "Militant Motherhood: Labor's Mary Harris 'Mother' Jones" (1996), focuses on the convergence of militancy and femininity in Jones's rhetoric of mobilization and maintenance. Mother Jones succeeded by assuming the role of matriarch for the labor movement. The maternal "nurturing" component of her rhetoric empowered her severely oppressed audiences by embracing and comforting them, instilling in them the confidence to defend themselves. But as all mothers know, nurturing is not enough. Growth must be spurred by the equal presence of the militant persona, confronting those who threaten a mother's constituency and challenging her "children" to mobilize and fight. Jones's "militant face," Tonn concludes, tells us much about the "feminist style" and gender politics in social movement discourse.

In "Inventing Citizens, Imagining Gender Justice: The Suffrage Rhetoric of Virginia and Francis Minor" (2007), Angela G. Ray and Cindy Koenig Richards examine the benefits to movement culture that may still accrue from a failed external strategy. Disputes about how to respond strategically to ongoing gender discrimination split the woman suffrage movement into two organizations in 1869. Members of the newly formed National Women's Suffrage Association believed in direct action and launched an audacious campaign called the "New Departure," founded on the premise that women's rights already existed and should be exercised rather than petitioning for their creation. Many women, including most famously Susan B. Anthony, attempted to register and vote. The refusal to allow Virginia Minor to register as a voter in St. Louis in 1872 led to a lawsuit, *Minor v. Happersett,* ultimately decided unanimously against women's or universal suffrage by the U.S. Supreme Court in 1875. Ray and Koenig Richards explain that

the Minors engaged in a "hermeneutic strategy," that is, a subversive "simple" reading of the Constitution that depicted women's right to vote as always having been self-evidently inscribed, but misunderstood and misapplied because of cultural and political gender bias. The courts were not persuaded, but even in this strategic failure the Minors succeeded in creating a new "symbolic citizen," gender and race neutral in principle, that spurred the imagination and mobilization of scores of women, who were now armed with a logic to justify and animate their struggle against gender inequality.

The where and with whom of protest discourse are relocated and repositioned by Karma R. Chávez in "Counter-Public Enclaves and Understanding the Function of Rhetoric in Social Movement Coalition-Building" (2011). Chávez's study responds to the paucity of analysis regarding the "internal rhetoric" or behind-the-scenes engagements that produce the public protest discourse and performance that most rhetoric scholars of social movements study. Scholars have also paid scant attention to the coalition politics, interactions, and collaborations most often forged outside of the public sphere. Enclaves constitute significant sites of rhetorical invention and bridging, the vital work of which is largely unknown even when it results in public protest action. Chávez conducted field work participant observation and interviews with two groups in Tucson, Arizona: Wingspan, a GLBT community center, and *Coalición de Derechos Humanos,* a grassroots, migrants rights organization. Though the constituencies did not unanimously embrace each other, activists in both movements worked to create solidarity through interpretations of the broader public scapegoating, discrimination, and violence manifested through politics, media, and law enforcement. Such meaning making, Chávez argues, provided members of both movements perspective on their parallel oppression, the ground of "coalitional subjectivities," repertoires of argument, affective affinities, and strength in mobilization when they did, singly or in tandem, go public.

Enacting Red Power:
The Consummatory Function in Native American Protest Rhetoric
Randall A. Lake

In the late 1960s and the 1970s, particularly the period from 1968 to 1974, the "Red Power" movement received national attention. The names and events associated with the movement are familiar: Vernon and Clyde Bellecourt; Leonard Peltier; Dennis Banks and Russell Means; the American Indian Movement (AIM); Alcatraz; the Trail of Broken Treaties; Wounded Knee; the Trail of Self-Determination; the Longest Walk. Yet despite the publicity, the movement has had little success in convincing white society to redress Indian grievances.

Most commentators attribute this failure to the use of protest strategies that are unpersuasive, and indeed repellant, to whites. Rhetorical critics have observed that white society does not take Red Power nearly as seriously as the movement takes itself. In general, these critics note, militant rhetoric serves only to reinforce in whites nonserious, stereotypic "Wild West" images of Indian protestors and their cause. One critic, for example, observes that the notion of Red Power first was advanced as a tongue-in-cheek parody of Black Power, and argues that this is symptomatic of the Indians' inability to establish their movement as a "serious social force."[1] Another critic suggests that the militant rhetoric at the 1973 siege of Wounded Knee, South Dakota, created a comic, and therefore counterproductive, image of the militant struggle: "The AIM rhetorical vision of young, brave Native Americans willing to die to bring justice to their people was not the drama that the American people took seriously. Instead, the image the media portrayed of hot-headed, irresponsible young Indians who decked themselves out in war-paint and feathers to stage a 'pathetic drama' for media attention became the prevalent believable reality."[2] Indian actions at Wounded Knee "emerged as a parody of themselves—a reaction based on the white man's matinee stereotype of how Indians act, instead of a creative response to a present-day situation."[3] The 1972 militant

occupation of the federal Bureau of Indian Affairs (BIA) headquarters was a "symbolic attempt to change attitudes," but it "accomplished very little for the Indian cause."[4] The BIA occupation was "a rhetorical and, as a consequence, a political failure."[5]

The common assumption, that militant Indian rhetoric attempts to change white attitudes, is widespread. In reaction to the vandalism occasioned by the BIA occupation, for instance, the *Washington Evening Star* opined: "Through the years there has been a deep reservoir of public sympathy for the American Indians, but it is bound to be diminished by the atrocious spectacle staged here in recent days. It could be dried up almost totally if there are more such dangerous and destructive capers by Indian extremists."[6] Historian Wilcomb Washburn of the Smithsonian Institution believes "Indian radicals have hindered efforts in behalf of the Indians and that ultimately Indian Power depends not on number of guns, but on the support of whites."[7]

Many Indians, however, reject this assumption. One woman wrote to the *Kansas City Star*: "Our power (which is increasing) has never, I repeat, never depended on the support of the white people or any other group except ourselves, various Indian groups, especially the A.I.M. and beautiful people like Russell Means and Dennis Banks."[8] The claim implies that militant Indian rhetoric is more appropriately viewed from a perspective which examines its significance for Indians themselves.

This essay argues for this alternative perspective. The claim is that the judgments of failure so often leveled against Native American protest rhetoric are problematic because they misanalyze this rhetoric's primary audience. Most Red Power rhetoric is directed at movement members and other Indians for purposes of gathering the like-minded, and is addressed only secondarily to the white establishment. For the Indian audience, Red Power rhetoric is persuasive insofar as it serves consummatory purposes prescribed by traditional Indian religious/cultural precepts. White audiences, which do not share these precepts, remain unconvinced and even alienated; nevertheless, consummatory strategies are necessary and effective techniques of Indian self-address. I establish this claim in four steps. First, the role of tradition in AIM demands is examined. Second, the manner in which traditional religious belief and experience restrict the ability of language to persuade whites is discussed. Third, consistent with traditional tribal beliefs which give language a ritual function, militant Indian rhetoric is examined as a form of ritual self-address. Finally, militant rhetoric is shown to enact movement demands and thereby successfully to fulfill its consummatory function.

In brief, AIM may have been judged a failure only because its rhetoric is expected to do something which it is not intended to do.[9] This essay seeks to reveal heretofore unacknowledged features of AIM rhetoric and thereby to illuminate and clarify our understanding of the role of consummatory motives in protest rhetoric.

I

The key to understanding how Native American protest rhetoric functions is to understand what the Red Power movement wants.[10] The ideology from which their demands spring also constrains the manner in which these demands may be voiced. The overriding militant aim is to regenerate traditional Indian religious beliefs and to restore the ancient ways of life.

Contending that "in every way the process of Western Civilization commits a genocide toward all living things,"[11] militant Indian rhetors flatly reject assimilation into white society, advocating instead a return to traditional tribal values.[12] Russell Means, co-founder of AIM, explains that, in 1970, the organization took a "long look" at itself: "We looked Indian, we dressed Indian, but we didn't know *why* we were Indians. We decided to go back to seek out the old people and find out. We returned to traditional Indian religion and its values and concepts. We found out that Indian spirituality among traditional people

is what rules every aspect of their lives. Based upon our traditional religion, we then devised a short-range plan of action for the American Indian Movement."[13] Clyde Bellecourt, another co-founder, proclaimed that the Longest Walk, which wound its way from San Francisco to Washington, D.C., in 1978, was dedicated to "the millions of Indian people who gave their lives that we might be given the opportunity to gather here to create, to build, to bring back the Old Ways, the ways of survival."[14]

This general concern to recover tradition is manifested in several specific movement demands.[15] One of these is the demand that a viable land base for the tribes be restored in accordance with treaties which typically granted Indians large sections of the continent "for as long as the river flows and the grass grows." Point Ten of the "Twenty Points" of the Trail of Broken Treaties caravan calls for "land reform and restoration of a 110-million acre native land base," sets priorities for recovery, advocates "consolidation of Indians' land, water, natural and economic resources," and demands "termination of leases and condemnation of non-Indian land title."[16] A rough measure of the importance of this issue is the number of land claims before Congress; in the East alone, about twenty claims, involving eleven million acres from Maine to Louisiana, were under consideration in 1978.[17] Indians often reject monetary settlements offered by the Indian Claims Commission in lieu of land return.[18]

The demand for land restoration is motivated by two concerns. The first is economic: many Indians wish to take advantage of the potentially huge value of the mineral resources on disputed lands.[19] The second is spiritual: militants see a land base as a prerequisite to cultural renewal. Vine Deloria, Jr., Native America's foremost intellectual, puts the matter bluntly: "No movement can sustain itself, no people can continue, no government can function, and no religion can become a reality except it be bound to a land area of its own.... So-called *power* movements are primarily the urge of peoples to find their homeland and to channel their psychic energies through their land into social and economic reality."[20] Traditional Indian religious beliefs and social customs were related intimately to tribal existence on the land and, as urban Indians testify, it is extraordinarily difficult to sustain the Old Ways in an alien environment.[21] This helps explain a pronounced activist preoccupation with ecological issues and the preservation of the land. For, given the dependence of traditional Indian existence—physically, culturally, and spiritually—upon nature, destruction or loss of nature means the end of the Indian as well.[22]

In short, restoration of a tribal land base is necessary for the restoration of the tribes themselves, their cultures, and their religions. AIM efforts to recover the Black Hills are efforts "to save the spiritual center of their nation."[23] In this way, the general militant concern with the recovery of tradition is manifested in a specific movement demand.

Similar motives underlie the activist demand for Indian "self-determination," a fundamental, many-faceted concern since 1960, when the National Indian Youth Council first began to agitate for Indian interests.[24] First and foremost, militants demand that the tribes be recognized as legally sovereign nations. Such recognition would require that the Federal government return to treaty-making as the appropriate means of conducting business with the tribes (a procedure abandoned by Congress in 1871), and that Congressional and judicial guarantees of a treaty relationship, with automatic relief for violations, be established.[25] Second, militants desire to restore traditional tribal forms of self-government. In 1934, each tribe was given the option to adopt a BIA-written tribal constitution, thereafter to be governed by a duly-elected tribal council on the familiar Western democratic model. Virtually all tribes voted to do so. However, to many militants, these tribal councils are white institutions, and some of the most bitter conflicts in Indian country have focused on alleged corruption and other improprieties on the part of these "duly-elected" officials.[26] Hence, militants urge that the 1934 provision be repealed and traditional tribal governance be reinstated.[27] Soon after the end of the siege of Wounded Knee, one AIM leader advised: "We've tried this government and it's failed. It's degraded our people and caused the ills that have fallen upon us. So we can see that the only way to regain what we've lost, regain our relationship with the Mother Earth, is to go back to the system of government that's done so well for us for so long."[28]

Third, militant Indians demand that the BIA be abolished and that control over energy contract negotiations and social and economic development programs be returned to the tribes.[29] Activists resent the missionary approach which has permeated BIA policies and the implication that a white bureaucracy knows better what is best for Indians than do Indians themselves.[30] Investigators have noted a progressive widening in the scope of BIA duties from "the management of all Indian Affairs" to "the management of all the affairs of Indians,"[31] commenting: "Although the normal expectation in American society is that a private individual or group may do anything unless it is specifically prevented by the government, it might be said that the normal expectation on the reservation is that the Indians may not do anything unless it is specifically permitted by the government."[32] Russell Means complains: "We were supposed to be sovereign, independent peoples. Now we have over 4,000 laws that govern *us* that do not govern *you*. And then you get into over 20,000 more rules and regulations from the different agencies of government, government agencies that control us."[33]

The specific demands for self-determination share an underlying militant desire to control their own destinies. As *Akwesasne Notes*, the foremost Native American newspaper, editorializes: "All of these issues are intertwined. To develop economic self-reliance, (or even economic independence,) a people must exercise sovereignty. To exercise sovereignty, the Native nations must achieve economic self-reliance. To do any of these things, they must control all elements of their own lives."[34]

Again, a primary motive for sovereignty is spiritual. Leaders realize that religious and cultural renewal is impossible without self-determination. According to AIM, three enemies of Indian people block the restoration of tradition: the Christian church, which subverts traditional religions; the public schools, which undermine traditional languages and cultures; and the Federal government, which perpetuates tribal dependency and precludes the assertion of traditional Indian self-reliance.[35] In opposing these forces, AIM sees itself as "the spiritual rebirth of our nation."[36] "The American Indian Movement," declares Vernon Bellecourt, "is basically a religious movement which is first of all based on traditionalism."[37]

II

This traditional ideology renders problematic the assumption that Native American protest rhetoric is addressed to whites. For, as some observers have noted, confrontational strategies are inconsistent with certain traditional Indian religious and cultural precepts. Edward Streb observes: "The Indian radical, believing that the use of white artifacts threatens his heritage, is likely to reject or, at best, half-heartedly apply what he considers 'non-Indian' confrontational techniques. The Indian is faced with a serious dilemma; he must either surrender his identity and use the 'white man's methods of persuasion,' or forego such methods, postpone his cultural annihilation, but fail in his quest for 'Red Power.'"[38] Not all rhetorical modes are open to Indians if they are to remain Indians. If one assumes that activist demands are genuine, that militant Indian rhetors are serious about recovering the Old Ways, then the Old Ways may shape the manner in which these demands legitimately may be voiced. Put another way, the Red Power movement's ideology contains assumptions about the conditions under which its members speak, and thereby restricts the process of persuasion. Two restrictions concerning the nature of human action and the capacities of language suggest that Native American protest rhetoric, when seen from its own metaphysical viewpoint, is not addressed primarily to whites.[39]

The first restriction is that neither humans nor language is considered a primary agency of change. The proposition that language is instrumental assumes that language symbols can influence the beliefs, attitudes, and behaviors of others, and assumes, moreover, that this influence is not restricted deterministically to confirming the raw sense experiences of either speaker or listener. These assumptions have so permeated communication and rhetorical theory as to be taken for granted. The thesis of symbolic interactionism, for example, is that language permits humans to transcend sense experience and create meanings.[40] These assumptions may be culturally bounded, however. The ability of language to exert such influence is circumscribed in Indian metaphysics, wherein the experiential character of all knowledge is emphasized.[41] The role of Peyote, an hallucinogenic plant and the basic spiritual tool of the Native American Church, is illustrative. A maxim of the Church is "The only way to find out about Peyote is to take it and learn from Peyote yourself."[42] A Commanche member is quoted as saying, "The white man talks *about* Jesus; we talk *to* Jesus."[43] Such data prompt J. S. Slotkin to conclude that "the Peyotist, epistemologically speaking, is an individualist and empiricist; he believes only what he himself has experienced."[44] Vine Deloria, Jr., argues that *all* Indian religions are fundamentally experiential.[45]

When belief is dependent upon experience, the persuasive capacities of language are reduced sharply. This limitation is illustrated by the linguistic conventions of certain tribes. A Wintu, for example, "never says starkly *this is;* if he speaks of reality which is not within his own restricting experience, he does not affirm it, he only implies it."[46]

These linguistic limitations restrict the human ability to influence others. One Indian activist writes: "Since it is not of the instructions of human beings to try to force the will of one upon another, or to try to force another people to change, it is not for us to force the white people to become what they truly are to be."[47] This relatively passive attitude toward others can be seen in the day-to-day operations of modern activist "warrior societies," particularly during the siege of Wounded Knee where, it was said, there was no discipline except self-discipline.[48] In short, because language is experientially confined, humans are not meant to act aggressively upon each other.

Yet, even if language were not so restricted, its use in addressing white audiences would remain problematic. A second restriction concerns Indian perceptions of the way whites historically have misused language when dealing with the tribes.

The communicative capacities of language presume a minimum degree of integrity in the symbol system used. Without some conventions requiring continuity in the meaning of words over time and fidelity to fact (i.e., truth-telling), communication would be impossible. This is particularly true of oral cultures because "in a society without written languages, without signed agreements, and without licenses a man's word had to be his bond. There was no other. If men lied, tribal society would not function."[49]

Unfortunately, Indians allege, the invention of written language has caused "a blind worship of written history, of books, of the written word, that has denuded the spoken word of its power and sacredness."[50] In fact, they argue, "writing systems have served largely through history to enslave men rather than to serve any useful religious, spiritual or esthetic purpose, since the original use of writing was to write down lists of slaves and to keep an account of what you had in your warehouse."[51] Thus, the written word has destroyed the sanctity of the spoken word, a condition manifested, Indians claim, in the proverbial "forked tongue" of white people. In 1787, a Delaware chief charged: "There is no faith to be placed in their words . . . They will say to an Indian, 'My friend; my brother.' They will take him by the hand, and, at the same moment, destroy him."[52]

Such mistrust continues. Militants view the words of whites, from the Declaration of Independence and the Constitution to the promises of the BIA, as everywhere belied by their actions.[53] Ralph Ware, an Oklahoma Kiowa, comments acerbically: "I can see what our tribal chairman went through a long, long time ago. These white people are so foxy and so smart with words. They're liars, really. They use candy and money. They steal too. And if you're with them long enough, they smell bad."[54] In short, communication is jeopardized because whites have destroyed the sanctity of the word.

In fact, discourse addressed to whites is not merely ineffectual; it is dangerous as well. Because such address requires contact with whites, it risks the contamination of Indian culture and reverence for the truth by the corrupting influence of white culture and its lies. Thus, some militant Indians advocate complete withdrawal from contact with whites in order best to safeguard tribal traditions.[55]

In sum, both the inherent limitations of language as a tool of influence and white abuse of this tool render militant attempts to persuade whites problematic. As a result, as noted at the outset of this section, AIM might appear to be confronted with a serious dilemma. However, the dilemma is a false one. For while movement ideology proscribes the address of white audiences, it also generates a consummatory alternative which both respects traditional religious precepts and enables the movement to achieve a measure of success by addressing Indians themselves.

III

Because traditional Indian religious precepts restrict the scope of human action, an alternative agency is necessary to account for the genesis of phenomena. According to these same precepts, this agency is Power, or supernatural force, described as "what works to effect everything which is beyond the ordinary power of men, outside the common processes of nature; it is present in the atmosphere of life, attaches itself to persons and to things, and is manifested by results which can only be ascribed to its operation."[56] The beliefs of the Sioux (the tribal background of most AIM leaders) are representative. To them: "All life is *wakan* [holy]. So also is everything which exhibits power, whether in action, as the winds and drifting clouds, or in passive endurance, as the boulder by the wayside. For even the commonest sticks and stones have a spiritual essence which must be reverenced as a manifestation of the all-pervading mysterious power that fills the universe."[57] All things—animals, birds, plants, rocks, water, celestial bodies, meteorological phenomena—potentially have Power, and the final arbiter of its existence in any given case is personal experience.[58] Thus supernatural force, found among the beliefs of most "primitive" peoples across the globe,[59] in the largest sense is "the animating principle of the universe."[60]

When viewed as a rhetorical resource, Power adds to language a consummatory capacity. Because one can acquire Power for one's own use and learn from it how to live, Power is, epistemologically, a source of knowledge which is experienced.[61] The hunting tribes historically depended upon individual acquisition of Power via the dream or vision quest.[62] In both, Power, incarnated in some animal, bird, or other being, appears to the individual and performs certain actions or creates certain images which become the means by which it may be recalled later. For example, Power may sing a song which one then must repeat each time one attempts to invoke this Power in the future.[63] The planting tribes, whose existence was regularized by the growing season, deemphasized personal acquisition of Power and relied instead upon elaborate tribal cer[e]monies.[64] Yet the role of Power in both cases remains the same. Once Power is encountered, a link with the supernatural has been established which may be drawn upon in the natural world, through ceremonial reenactment, for purposes of protecting, healing, ensuring a successful hunt or harvest, and so on.

Thus supernatural Power is the principal instrument of mediation between one human and another, and between humans and their natural environment. Language is instrumental largely in the sense that it can invoke the supernatural. Discourse may be addressed, but its audience is Power, not other humans. And Power is addressed through ritual, through the proper recitation of songs, prayers, and dance. The proper ritual, correctly performed, invokes the auspices of the supernatural, which then performs as bidden. "The ritual details are important not because they [perform] in themselves but because once the proper procedure has been carried out the power . . . is expected to recognize its own songs and prayers and to honor its pledges to act at the individual's bidding."[65] Moreover, the wrong word used in a ceremony produces failure and even disaster.[66]

In brief, the principal resources of language are magical.[67] Thought (the inner form of speech) and speech (which imposes the power of thought on the external world) are the two basic components of ritual creation and restoration.[68] Speech is directly efficacious in modifying reality by the invocation of Power. Ritual language thus is not descriptive, but performative. "Ritual language does not describe how things are; it determines how they will be. Ritual language is not impotent; it is powerful. It commands, compels, organizes, transforms, and restores. It disperses evil, reverses disorder, neutralizes pain, overcomes fear, eliminates illness, relieves anxiety,

and restores order, health, and well-being."[69] Language, in other words, not only classifies experience but also controls it.[70] Without ritual language, humans are greatly reduced in stature and their control of the independently existent world around them is greatly impaired; they become "the acted upon rather than the actor, the created rather than the creator, the object rather than the subject."[71] Ritual language as agency, then, is essential for human status as agent.

Power reveals the patterns for ritual language, and typically these are the patterns used for generations. In fact, according to much Indian mythology, the patterns are those used primordially by supreme beings in calling the universe into existence.[72] Hence, ritual language repeats the original creation and thereby effectively enacts tradition.[73] The past is made present through speech.

The significance of ritual discourse to militant Indian protest rhetoric is corroborated by the widespread Native American concern to preserve traditional tribal languages. Perhaps the most eloquent voice on behalf of this concern is that of Gayle High Pine, who argues that words identify the manner in which humans are related to all other elements in the world. "Languages," she writes, "were given to us as a way of knowing the Creation. Words describe the way in which our relatives of the Creation relate to our lives. Words tie the world together in an intricate network of relationships."[74] "A nation's language sets a basic relationship to the Creation and its parts."[75] The purpose of language is that of "reuniting ourselves with our natural ways . . . relearning how to experience the world in the true spirit-knowledge of our ancestors."[76] Different languages identify different relationships, and so contain different instructions for living. High Pine continues: "Each language has its own life, its own spirit, and its instructions are to shape and carry our thoughts in the sacred paths given to its nation."[77] "There is a reason and purpose in different peoples having their own language and way of life. These are the means of identifying each other, of seeing the world in a natural way, and of causing your life to follow natural ways."[78] In sum, she notes, possessing a language "gives the people of a nation a shared world and makes them of one seeing and feeling and one shared relationship with all the beings about them—it is this which has made the people of a nation of one spirit, binding together free individuals as one."[79]

Thus, the plea for the preservation of native languages is, in fact, a plea for preserving the integrity of native worldviews because discourse is epistemic, i.e., the carrier of the knowledge of tradition and its instructions for living. As High Pine suggests: "If the language is kept that strong, the spiritual ways can once again grow strong—but not the other way around."[80] Moreover, the loss of native languages means the loss of their unique ritual power and, thereby, the capacity to implement these instructions. High Pine warns: "But a language that is allowed to die is gone forever. And all that depends on that language die [sic] with it. Even ceremonies that are conducted in English cannot regain their true complete strength compared to their original form."[81] To abandon native languages, therefore, is to abandon both knowledge of the proper way of life and the Power necessary to live it, in a kind of epistemological and ontological suicide.

If one assumes that Red Power rhetoric is addressed to white audiences, this concern for native languages will seem misplaced and even counterproductive. After all, the active efforts of Indians themselves are much more important for the survival of these languages than are any white efforts. In fact, while a given native language could not be used to address members of other tribes, for whom the language is incomprehensible, no native language could be used to address whites, who do not even share the worldview which makes the ritual dimension of these languages possible. In this respect, native languages are inherently divisive, separating one native nation from another and, even more, separating all native nations from prospective white audiences.[82] However, among Indians who acknowledge the ritual dimension, the preservation of native languages literally becomes "a matter of life or death . . . a matter of the people being able to be strong and to fight and to win," and the "last chance for survival."[83]

In sum, the application of traditional Native American spiritual beliefs to the Red Power movement, which avowedly is grounded in and wishes to recapture this tradition, yields a view of language which incorporates a necessary consummatory dimension. Militant rhetoric exemplifies this view of language and functions as ritual discourse addressed primarily to those who share the worldview which generates this rhetorical mode, i.e., Indians themselves.

Perhaps the exemplary "representative anecdote" for this view of language is the common militant characterization of white society as a disease, usually cancer, alcoholism, or rabies.[84] In Indian metaphysics, disease is a malevolent manifestation of Power which can be cured only through the efforts of a more potent, beneficent Power.[85] The disease metaphor thus illustrates the ritual dimension of language in the respect that disease is not an object of persuasion. A cure is not effected by cajoling the illness to leave the body. Rather, health is restored when the disease is removed forcibly and cast aside by the correct enactment of a prescribed ritual. So it is with the disease of white society, which is not to be persuaded to leave Indians alone, free to maintain healthy, active traditional societies. Instead, health can be restored only when white society's pernicious influences are exorcised through the ritual enactment of tradition.[86]

IV

The principle of ritual enactment assists in the interpretation of the Red Power movement's symbolic actions. Among militants certain ancient practices are commonly advocated and practiced, including: home birthing; food growing habits; the wearing of medicine pouches and the painting of faces as if preparing for battle; reliance on the vision experience for guidance in dealing with whites; pipe-smoking and purification in the sweat lodge; revival of the Sun Dance; and use of traditional tribal names, e.g., Dene (Navajo), Lakota (Sioux), and Hau de no sau nee (Iroquois).[87] Considered symbolically, these acts, merely by being taken, in effect enact tradition, and thereby defeat threats from white society. Clyde Bellecourt acknowledges this process, claiming that the paramilitary threat to Indians posed by the FBI "parallels their efforts to destroy Martin Luther King, to destroy Malcolm X, to destroy the Black Panther Party, and to destroy the Black Civil Rights Movement in this country. *But we have been able to overcome that through these sacred pipes, the sacred drum, and the ceremonies.*[88]

Similarly, militant Indians symbolically enact their demands for land and sovereignty. The strategy of occupation has been a prominent militant tactic. In November, 1969, young Indians landed on Alcatraz Island and began an occupation which lasted nineteen months.[89] The tactic soon spread, and at least thirty-four other incidents occurred through 1978, including occupations at such geographically diverse sites as the national and a variety of regional offices of the BIA; Mount Rushmore; Gresham, Wisconsin; Moss Lake, New York; Shiprock, New Mexico; and of course Wounded Knee, South Dakota.[90]

The sit-in is a common instrumental, confrontational strategy of protestors of all kinds. From the perspective of Indian metaphysics, it also uniquely and magically enacts the demand for land return. And certain occupations are especially noteworthy for their geographical importance to Indians. As noted above, the occupation of Mount Rushmore assumes added meaning because the Black Hills are the spiritual center of the Sioux religion.[91]

Similarly, Wounded Knee, nothing more than a tiny, isolated bit of South Dakota prairie to most whites, has great historical significance for Indians. For, in 1890, on the same site, the Seventh Cavalry of the U.S. Army massacred nearly 300 Sioux men, women, and children who had gathered for a tribal ceremony, in what is generally acknowledged as the final battle of the Indian wars.[92] Thus, for militants, the 1973 occupation recaptured pre-massacre history, and served symbolic notice that the "Indian problem" was not yet resolved. As Means proclaimed during the siege: "The white man says that the 1890 massacre was the end of the wars with the Indian, that it was the end of the Indian, the end of the Ghost Dance. Yet here we are at war, we're still Indians, and we're Ghost Dancing again. And the spirits of Big Foot and his people are all around us."[93] Through occupation, the past is made present.

Finally, the modern militant demand for sovereignty also is enacted in several ways, including: the establishment of Survival Schools as alternatives to white education; the comparison of the militant struggle against whites with the efforts of ostensibly sovereign Third World nations to cast off the yoke of colonialist oppression; the performative declaration, made at Wounded Knee, that an Independent Oglala Nation had been constituted; and the common performative utterances which serve to divide Indian from white, such as the claim, "We have never participated in America. Our people have never joined America."[94] Each of these strategies implicitly treats Native Americans as independent entities of stature equal to that of other recognized "nations," including the United States, and thereby enacts the demand for sovereignty.

These examples are suggestive of the way in which a consummatory rhetoric functions in the Red Power movement, i.e., by ritually enacting both Indian tradition in general and movement demands in particular. The actions described achieve their purposes simply by being; they are, thus, ends in themselves for those who acknowledge the ritual dimension of symbolic acts.[95]

V

This essay has examined the tension between a Native American worldview and the putative constraints that are placed on protest rhetoric directed to the American government and public. Failure to acknowledge this worldview leads to the condemnation of Native American protest rhetoric for alienating white audiences, but overlooks the manner in which ritual militant rhetoric literally enacts "Red Power." Thus, this analysis illustrates the misleading results which can be produced when a majority culture critical perspective is imposed on minority culture discourse.

The thesis that minority protest rhetoric can be examined profitably and made meaningful through nontraditional analysis certainly is not original. Since Robert L. Scott and Donald K. Smith noted the inherent biases in neo-Aristotelian criticism toward decorum, civility, reason, and "the Establishment," numerous theoretical studies in the rhetoric of confrontation have appeared.[96] The New Left, black nationalism, and feminism have been popular subjects for treatment.[97] In a general way, this essay supports these studies. In a more detailed way, it suggests certain refinements in earlier findings.

Richard Gregg's seminal essay also discusses the consummatory motive in protest rhetoric, calling it an "ego-function."[98] While the foregoing analysis of AIM supports Gregg's view in most respects, it also suggests one refinement. The claim that Red Power rhetoric is primarily a form of ritual self-address corroborates Gregg's general thesis that "the primary appeal of the rhetoric of protest is to the protestors themselves, who feel the need for psychological refurbishing and affirmation."[99] In the case of the American Indian Movement, however, this felt need appears to be not only or merely psychological, but the demands of an entire *weltanschauung*. Aaron Gresson has so extended Gregg's work, describing a typical "epistemological imbalance" between protestor and society, and Native American protest discourse resembles in many ways what Gresson calls the "rhetoric of creation."[100]

Similarly, Robert Cathcart writes of the ritual, consummatory aspects of movement rhetoric. The foregoing analysis of AIM raises two questions about this description. First, Cathcart argues that a necessary part of the ritual is a "conversion" in which the protestors recognize their own guilt and complicity with the corrupt establishment, and then transcend this faulty order and acquire a new perspective.[101] However, many Indian militants deny that they have ever been a part of our society or that they are in any sense guilty of sustaining it.[102] The notion that the exorcism of complicity must be a part of the ritual is problematic, and perhaps is an unnecessary aspect of Cathcart's account.

More fundamentally, by making confrontation *the* consummatory purpose of a movement, Cathcart's description appears overly restrictive.[103] What of a movement for separatism? Many Indian activists claim: "We are not radicals. We are not trying to revolutionize society. If society would leave us alone, we would leave it alone."[104] In fact, since the Trail of Self-Determination marched to Washington, D.C., in 1975–1976, very few visible Indian-white confrontations have arisen. What "began as a small band of urban, politically minded

reformers has been transformed into a pervasive, decentralized spiritual movement woven into the fabric of traditional Indian culture."[105] However, if one believes that confrontation is the defining consummatory purpose of a movement, then one must conclude that such decentralization demonstrates that the movement is failing, while, in actuality, it may better illustrate the movement's final success: provoking the spiritual rebirth of Indian culture.

Admittedly, this is "success" of a peculiar kind. Withdrawal from whites may succeed in bringing about the separatism desired by Indian militants, but it thereby also perpetuates the conditions of life which white assistance could ameliorate. Enactment does not eliminate the realities of abject poverty, poor health, low educational achievement, and premature death.[106] Realistically, the support of both whites and Indians may be required if the Red Power movement is to achieve all its goals, a situation which many Indians acknowledge. Yet where the process of gaining white support threatens traditional Indian culture, militant Indians have chosen tradition, and the ritual self-address which enacts it, in the belief that the Old Ways offer the only real hope for the long-term betterment of the Indian condition, even though "it's going to be a process that most of us won't even be around to see."[107]

Perhaps this strategic choice is understandable given the relatively bleak short-run prospects for improvement. The disparity between the sheerly political power of Indian militants and the supernatural Power of their world-view is striking. Given their miniscule political clout, attempts to persuade the white establishment may be fruitless, and consummatory self-address that enacts movement demands may be the most promising mode of discourse available to Native Americans. Ritual language is certainly the rhetorical mode which best respects and protects their "Indianness."

Notes

1 Edward Streb, "The Alcatraz Occupation, '69–'71: A Perceived Parody of Power Movements" (paper presented at the Central States Speech Association Convention, Milwaukee, Wisconsin, April, 1974), p. 5.

[2] Tracey Bernstein Weiss, "Media Speaks with Forked Tongue: The Unsuccessful Rhetoric of Wounded Knee" (paper presented at the Speech Communication Association Convention, Houston, Texas, December, 1975), p. 9.

[3] Joyce Frost, "A Rhetorical Analysis of Wounded Knee II, 1973: A Conflict Perspective" (paper presented at the Central States Speech Association Convention, Milwaukee, Wisconsin, April, 1974), p. 12.

[4] Donovan J. Ochs, "A Fallen Fortress: BIA, 1972" (paper presented at the Central States Speech Association Convention, Milwaukee, Wisconsin, April, 1974), p. 6.

[5] John F. Cragan, "Rhetorical Strategy: A Dramatistic Interpretation and Application," *Central States Speech Journal*, 26 (1975), 11.

[6] Quoted in *Trail of Broken Treaties: B.I.A. I'm Not Your Indian Anymore* (2nd ed.; Rooseveltown, N.Y.: *Akwesasne Notes*, 1974), p. 48.

[7] William L. McCorkle, "'New Indian' Struggle Traced," *Kansas City Times*, 27 April 1976, p. 14B.

[8] Pauline J. Harris, "Support Unnecessary," *Kansas City Star*, 2 May 1976, p. 3G.

[9] Extant critiques of AIM rhetoric, therefore, appear to illustrate David Swanson's point that no criticism is theory-free because no critic confronts the simple facts of a situation in a text; rather, "all rhetorical criticism is best understood as an interpretive activity involving the application of representational/constitutive schemas to rhetorical phenomena." David L. Swanson, "A Reflective View of the Epistemology of Critical Inquiry," *Communication Monographs*, 44 (1977), 211. My claim is that extant applications have employed inappropriate schemas, and this essay suggests an alternative. For excellent related critiques of the critical schema of instrumental effects, see Edwin Black, *Rhetorical Criticism: A Study in Method* (New York: Macmillan Co., 1965), pp. 60–90, and John W. Rathbun, "The Problem of Judgment and Effect in Historical Criticism: A Proposed Solution," *Western Speech*, 33 (1969), 146–159.

[10] Not all Indians are activists, nor are Indian demands completely monolithic. There are deep cultural and political schisms in the Indian community, between urban and reservation dwellers, between traditionalists and progressives (labelled "apples" by the former for being red on the outside but white on the inside), between tribes and between various Indian rights advocacy groups. Cf. Jim Parsons, "Political, Religious Differences Divide Indian Community," *Minneapolis Tribune*, 20 November 1979, pp. 1Aff; Patrick Huyghe and David Konigsberg, "Bury My Heart at New York City," *New York*, 19 February 1979, pp. 53–57; and Howell Raines, "American Indians: Struggling for Power and Identity," *New York Times Magazine*, 11 February 1979, p. 21. Nevertheless, activist demands, as represented in AIM documents and in Native American statements and publications, are strikingly unified, as described below.

[11] Affirmation of Sovereignty of the Indigenous Peoples of the Western Hemisphere," *Akwesasne Notes*, 10 (Summer, 1978), 15.

[12] See virtually any Vine Deloria, Jr., book, but especially *Behind the Trail of Broken Treaties: An Indian Declaration of Independence* (New York: Dell Publishing Co., Inc., 1974), and *We Talk, You Listen: New Tribes, New Turf* (New York: Dell Publishing Co., Inc., 1974); also "Ganienkeh and Now Wabanaki," *Akwesasne Notes*, 8 (Early Summer, 1976), 19; Gayle High Pine, "Last Chance for Survival," *Akwesasne Notes*, 8 (Early Spring, 1976), 30–32; and "The Road Back to Our Future," *Akwesasne Notes*, 8 (Early Summer, 1976), 36.

[13] "Interview: Russell Means," *Penthouse*, April, 1981, p. 194.

[14] "Clyde Bellecourt," *Akwesasne Notes*, 10 (Summer, 1978), 8.

[15] For one inclusive statement of these demands, see "The Teton Sioux Manifesto," *Wassaja*, 1 (July, 1973), 10–12.

[16] "Our 20 Point Proposal," *Akwesasne Notes*, 5 (Early Winter, 1973), 30–31. These 20 Points are "still the most comprehensive platform of 'What Do the Indians Want' available." See "Our Own Publications," *Akwesasne Notes*, 10 (Early Spring, 1978), 33. For other expressions of the demand for land restoration, see "Affirmation of Sovereignty," p. 16; "The Dene Nation," *Akwesasne Notes*, 11 (Spring, 1979), 23–24; Gayle High Pine, "This Land Keeps Us Together," *Akwesasne Notes*, 10 (Late Spring, 1978), 23–24; and Kirke Kickingbird and Karen Ducheneaux, *One Hundred Million Acres* (New York: Macmillan Publishing Co., Inc., 1974).

[17] "Narragansett Claim Nears Settlement," *Akwesasne Notes*, 10 (Autumn, 1978), 11. Also "The 95th Congress and Indian Legislation," *Wassaja*, 6 (October/November, 1978), 3ff.

[18] Stephen Most, "Klamath Clings to Sacred Land," *Kansas City Times*, 20 May 1976, p. 20; also "Sioux Suit to Regain Black Hills Rejected," *Minneapolis Tribune*, 2 June 1981, p. 6A. However, such settlements are not always rejected; see Michael Knight, "Maine Indians Ponder Best Use of $81 Million Land Settlement," *Minneapolis Tribune*, 30 March 1980, p. 8B.

[19] Raines, p. 21.

[20] Vine Deloria, Jr., *Custer Died For Your Sins: An Indian Manifesto* (New York: Hearst Corporation, 1970), p. 179.

[21] Raines, p. 48.

[22] Expressions of ecological concern range from fears of the effects of electrical power generation on the Cheyenne in Montana, "The Northern Cheyenne: Defending the Last Retreat," *Akwesasne Notes,* 10 (Early Spring, 1978), 12–13; to arsenic pollution in Canada, "Pollution and Genocide (Northwest Territories)," *Akwesasne Notes,* 10 (Early Spring, 1978), 17; to whaling, "The Great Bowhead Controversy," *Akwesasne Notes,* 10 (Early Spring, 1978), 20–21, and "The Great Bowhead Controversy (Part II)," *Akwesasne Notes,* 10 (Winter, 1978), 28–29; to stripmining in the Four Corners region of the desert southwest, "Four Corners Stripmining Plans Spark Resistance," *Akwesasne Notes,* 10 (Early Spring, 1978), pp. 28–29; to pesticides in California, "Poison in California," *Akwesasne Notes,* 10 (Winter, 1978), 21; to Cree opposition to hydroelectric development in Canada, *Akwesasne Notes,* 5 (Early Autumn, 1973), 30. The intimate link between the land and its people is illustrated by the activists' self-description as "biosphere cultures" and "ecosystem people." Gary Snyder, "Book Review: The Old Ways," *Akwesasne Notes,* 10 (Early Spring, 1978), 31; and Ismaelillo, "Identity and Commitment," *Akwesasne Notes,* 10 (Late Spring, 1978), 20–21. The best statements of environmental degradation as genocide appear in Sotsisowah, "The Darkening Horizons," *Akwesasne Notes,* 9 (Summer, 1977), 4–6; and Howard Berman, "Resource Exploitation: The Cutting Edge of Genocide," *Akwesasne Notes,* 10 (Late Spring, 1978), 9–10.

[23] "Yellow Thunder Camp," *Crazy Horse Spirit,* Winter, 1981–82, p. 12.

[24] Stan Steiner, *The New Indians* (New York: Dell Publishing Co., Inc., 1968), pp. 39–47.

[25] "Our 20 Point Proposal," p. 30; also "Affirmation of Sovereignty," p. 16. Indian sovereignty as acknowledged by the treaty relationship was terminated by a rider to the 1871 Indian Appropriations Act. Robert W. Oliver, "The Legal Status of American Indian Tribes," *Oregon Law Review,* 38 (1959), 200. Nonetheless, Indians continually emphasize the importance of past treaties and of making the Federal government fulfill the terms of these agreements. "Treaties Made, Treaties Broken: New Legal Strategies for Subverting Indian Rights," *Akwesasne Notes,* 10 (Winter, 1978), 12–13; Vine Deloria, Jr., "The Question of the 1868 Sioux Treaty: A Crucial Element in the Wounded Knee Trials," *Akwesasne Notes,* 6 (Early Spring, 1974), 12; "Indians to Act on Broken U.S. Treaties," *Wassaja,* 1 (April/May, 1973), 1; and the special supplement in *Wassaja,* 1 (July, 1973), 1–8.

[26] A principal cause of the Wounded Knee occupation, for example, was militant frustration over the allegedly corrupt and dictatorial reign of Pine Ridge tribal chairman Richard Wilson, and an unsuccessful impeachment attempt. Cf. *Voices From Wounded Knee, 1973* (Rooseveltown, N.Y.: Akwesasne Notes, 1974), pp. 14–32, passim. Such disputes are not uncommon; a more recent incident concerned the Chippewa tribe on the Red Lake reservation in Minnesota. Cf. Patrick Marx, "BIA Drafts Withdrawal of Support From Jourdain," *Minneapolis Tribune,* 9 January 1980, p. 1B.

[27] *Voices From Wounded Knee,* p. 57; "Affirmation of Sovereignty," p. 15; and "The Poisoned Tree," *Akwesasne Notes,* 10 (Autumn, 1978), 22–23.

[28] *Voices From Wounded Knee,* p. 246.

[29] Raines, p. 23.

[30] *Trail of Broken Treaties,* p. 70. This resentment is not groundless. In 1903, the Supreme Court enshrined the missionary approach with the declaration that "Congress had plenary power to manage Indian tribal property for the benefit of the Indians, and that the decision of Congress as to what was beneficial for the Indians would not be overthrown." Felix S. Cohen, "Indian Rights and the Federal Courts," *Minnesota Law Review,* 24 (1940), 71.

[31] Felix S. Cohen, "The Erosion of Indian Rights, 1950–1953: A Case Study in Bureaucracy," *Yale Law Journal,* 62 (1953), 352.

[32] Warren H. Cohen and Philip J. Mause, "The Indian: The Forgotten American," *Harvard Law Review,* 81 (1968), 1820.

[33] "Interview: Russell Means," p. 190.

[34] "Regaining Control of Our Lives," *Akwesasne Notes,* 10 (Autumn, 1978), 6.

[35] "A.I.M.: The American Indian Movement," St. Paul: AIM National Office, undated leaflet. Concern over Church influence often focuses upon Mormon evangelism. See Beth Wood, "LDS Indian Placement Program: To Whose Advantage?" *Akwesasne Notes,* 10 (Winter, 1978), 16–17, and the related articles in this same issue, pp. 16–19. For corroborating examples of the concern over educational matters, see "The War on Our Children," *Akwesasne Notes,* 10 (Early Spring, 1978), 4–8; "Education: BIA Millions

Fail to Reach Schools," *Akwesasne Notes*, 5 (Early Autumn, 1973), 32; and "Who Will Educate Our Children?" *Akwesasne Notes*, 5 (Early Autumn, 1973), 33.

36 "'When in the Course of Human Events': An Interview With Carter Camp," *Akwesasne Notes*, 5 (Early Autumn, 1973), 11.

37 "Bellecourt Explains AIM Goals," *Wassaja*, 1 (April/May, 1973), 7.

38 Streb, p. 3. I argue below that this dilemma is false; what is important here is the notion that not all modes of discourse are equally available to Indians qua Indians.

39 For another discussion of the influence of metaphysics upon rhetorical choices, see Kathleen Jamieson, "The Rhetorical Manifestations of *Weltanschauung*," *Central States Speech Journal*, 27 (1976), 4–14. On its face, this analysis is seemingly jeopardized by the sheer multiplicity of Old Ways involved. Undeniably, Native American religious beliefs and cultural practices are wildly diverse and, hence, it may seem that to speak of *a* militant metaphysics is a critical and perhaps fatal flaw. However, this diversity exists largely on the level of detail and not of presupposition. Anthropologist Gary Witherspoon, who lived on the Navajo reservation for over a decade, suggests that apparently divergent cultures may share common metaphysical premises. Gary Witherspoon, *Language and Art in the Navajo Universe* (Ann Arbor: University of Michigan Press, 1977), pp. 4–9. Similarly, ethnographer Ruth Underhill observes that, while "American Indians have not a religion but many religions," nonetheless all possess "in common a focus on duty toward the supernatural rather than toward fellowmen." Ruth M. Underhill, *Red Man's Religion* (Chicago: University of Chicago Press, 1965), pp. 9–19. Thus, the following analysis, grounded in the general functions of the Supernatural, seems safely based. Two further considerations support this conclusion. First, Native Americans themselves clearly believe that they share certain presuppositions. Despite the "great variety of methods of worship among Indians," it is said, "there is a common background for Indian culture, tradition, and values, particularly in the areas of worship, lifestyles, and the perception of the Indian to his environment. This was and continues to be true with the Indian in his manner and style of worship, and extends into practically every facet of the Indian way, including culture, social, economic, and other areas of the Indian life." Barney Old Coyote, "The Issue is Not Feathers: Legal Attacks on Native Religious

Tradition," *Akwesasne Notes*, 9 (Summer, 1977), 21. Second, the following analysis is illustrated with the beliefs and practices of a wide variety of tribes, all pointing to the same general principles.

40 For an early account of this thesis, see George Herbert Mead, *Mind, Self, and Society*, ed. by Charles W. Morris (Chicago: University of Chicago Press, 1962), esp. pp. ix–xxxv. Numerous other good explications of this thesis exist, including Joel M. Charon, *Symbolic Interactionism: An Introduction, An Interpretation, An Integration* (Englewood Cliffs, N.J.: Prentice-Hall, Inc., 1979), esp. pp. 23–62.

41 "The IFCO Native American Consultation—A Report," *Akwesasne Notes*, 7 (Early Winter, 1975), 26.

42 J. S. Slotkin, "The Peyote Way," in *Teachings From the American Earth*, ed. by Dennis and Barbara Tedlock (New York: Liveright, 1975), p. 100. See also Carlos Castaneda, *The Teachings of Don Juan* (New York: Simon and Schuster, 1974), pp. 52–53.

43 Slotkin, p. 100.

44 Slotkin, p. 100.

45 He contrasts this way of knowing with the typical white method—revelation—in *God is Red* (New York: Dell Publishing Co., Inc., 1975), p. 80.

46 Dorothy Lee, "Linguistic Reflection of Wintu Thought," in *Teachings From the American Earth*, p. 140.

47 High Pine, "Last Chance," p. 31.

48 *Voices from Wounded Knee*, pp. 76, 170, 174.

49 Steiner, p. 26. See also Snyder, p. 30.

50 Luther Standing Bear, "Land of the Spotted Eagle," in *Chronicles of American Indian Protest*, ed. by The Council on Interracial Books for Children (Greenwich, Conn.: Fawcett Publications, Inc., 1971), p. 271. As per the discussion below Standing Bear probably refers to the *ritual* power of the spoken word.

51 Snyder, p. 30. For a different perspective on the historical relationship between speaking and writing, see Tony M. Lentz, "Writing as Sophistry: From Preservation to Persuasion," *Quarterly Journal of Speech*, 68 (1982), 60–68.

52 Pachgantschilias, quoted in *The Portable North American Indian Reader*, ed. by Frederick W. Turner, III (New York: The Viking Press, 1974), p. 245.

53 *Voices From Wounded Knee*, p. 86.

54 *Trail of Broken Treaties*, p. 13.

55 Sotsisowah, "Western Peoples, Natural Peoples," *Akwesasne Notes*, 8 (Early Spring, 1976), 34.

56 R. H. Codrington, *The Melanesians* (Oxford: Clarendon Press, 1891), pp. 118–119.

[57] Francis LaFlesche, "The Osage Tribe: Rite of Vigil," *39th Annual Report of the Bureau of American Ethnology* (Washington, D.C.: Government Printing Office, 1925), p. 186.

[58] John Neihardt, *Black Elk Speaks* (New York: Simon and Schuster, 1972), p. 27; Morris Edward Opler, *An Apache Life-Way* (Chicago: University of Chicago Press, 1941), p. 206; Willard Z. Park, *Shamanism in Western North America* (Evanston, Ill.: Northwestern University, 1938), p. 14; and *Voices From Wounded Knee*, p. 166. Power often is manifested in animation. Indians do not perceive inanimate objects to be animate, in general, any more than we do. However, they do recognize certain *a priori* potentialities for animation in certain classes of objects under certain circumstances; the crucial test is experience, the availability of personal testimony. A. Irving Hallowell, "Ojibwa Ontology, Behavior, and World View," in *Teachings From the American Earth*, p. 148.

[59] Underhill, p. 20.

[60] Opler, p. 205.

[61] Cf. Slotkin, p. 99; Castaneda, pp. 51, 53; and Bryan Wilson, *The Noble Savages: The Primitive Origins of Charisma and Its Contemporary Survival* (Berkeley: University of California Press, 1975), p. 23.

[62] Underhill, p. 16.

[63] It is significant that Indians do not consider these dreams and visions to be a fabrication of the mind or a product of the unconscious. Rather, the experience is an encounter with an external, objective entity which initiates the contact. Opler, p. 202. Generally, the "real" is not distinguished from the "imaginary," and if it were, dreams probably would be classified as the former. Opler, p. 204; also Neihardt, p. 71.

[64] Underhill, p. 16.

[65] Opler, p. 207.

[66] Castaneda, p. 69.

[67] For other useful statements of the relationship between rhetoric and magic see Kenneth Burke, *A Rhetoric of Motives* (Berkeley: University of California Press, 1969), pp. 40–46; Ernst Cassirer, *Mythical Thought*, trans. by Ralph Manheim, Vol. II of *The Philosophy of Symbolic Forms* (New Haven: Yale University Press, 1955), 24–261, passim; and Allen Scult, "Rhetoric and Magic: A Comparison of Two Types of Religious Action," in *Rhetoric 78: Proceedings of Theory of Rhetoric: An Interdisciplinary Conference*, ed. by Robert L. Brown, Jr., and Martin Steinmann, Jr. (Minneapolis: University of Minnesota Center for Advanced Studies in Language, Style, and Literary Theory, 1979), pp.

321–338. While these discussions are useful for understanding the nature of magical language, their authors would not agree that magical language is rhetorical. A thorough theoretical consideration of our respective positions on this issue is beyond the scope of this essay.

[68] Witherspoon, p. 61.

[69] Witherspoon, p. 34.

[70] Witherspoon, p. 114.

[71] Witherspoon, p. 80.

[72] Witherspoon, p. 43.

[73] Mircea Eliade provides a superb account of the way in which ritual in general enacts the archaic past in *Myth and Reality*, trans. by Willard R. Trask (New York: Harper & Row, Publishers, 1963), esp. ch. 1–3, and in *The Sacred and the Profane*, trans. by Willard R. Trask (New York: Harcourt, Brace & World, Inc., 1959), esp. ch. 1–2. In a somewhat different vein, Charles Kauffman discusses enactment as a rhetorical form in "The Reflexive Form in Rhetoric," in *Rhetoric 78*, pp. 233–240 and in "Poetic as Argument," *Quarterly Journal of Speech*, 67 (1981), 407–415, passim.

[74] High Pine, "Last Chance," p. 30.

[75] High Pine, "Last Chance," p. 32.

[76] High Pine, "Last Chance," p. 30.

[77] High Pine, "Last Chance," p. 30.

[78] High Pine, "Last Chance," p. 30.

[79] High Pine, "Last Chance," p. 30.

[80] High Pine, "Last Chance," p. 32.

[81] High Pine, "Last Chance," p. 30.

[82] Between 1,000 and 2,000 Indian languages exist in North and South America, all of which are mutually unintelligible. Gloria Levitas, Frank B. Vivelo and Jacqueline J. Vivelo, eds., *American Indian Prose and Poetry* (New York: G. P. Putnam's Sons, 1974), p. xxxiv. See also Robert F. Spencer, et al. *The Native Americans: Prehistory and Ethnology of the North American Indians* (New York: Harper & Row, Publishers, 1965), p. 2.

[83] The former description is found in Roxanne Dunbar Ortiz, "Bilingualism vs. English as a Second Language," *Wassaja*, 7 (May, 1979), 13. The latter, of course, is the title of High Pine's essay, supra, n. 13.

[84] The concept of the "representative anecdote" is discussed by Kenneth Burke in *A Grammar of Motives* (Berkeley: University of California Press, 1969), pp. 59–61, 323–325. I employ it here in the sense that the disease metaphor synecdochically represents the entire network of militant assumptions regarding the relationships between Indians, whites, and the supernatural. For exemplary uses of the metaphor, see

Gayle High Pine, "The Disease That Afflicts Creation," *Akwesasne Notes,* 7 (Early Winter, 1975), 34–35; Deloria, *Custer,* p. 188; and Sotsisowah, "Western Peoples," pp. 34–35.

[85] Park, pp. 38–135, passim.

[86] The implications of this metaphor for "preventive medicine" are noteworthy, for the metaphor seems to suggest that complete separation from the infected body is the only way to avoid contracting the contagious disease. This corroborates the observation, supra, n. 55, that many Indians choose to avoid all contacts with whites in order to preserve the purity (read: health) of their cultures.

[87] See, respectively: "An Indian Kind of Thing," *Akwesasne Notes,* 10 (Autumn, 1978), 12–14; "The Food (Food?) We Eat," *Akwesasne Notes,* 10 (Winter, 1978), 24–26, and "Native Health Could Improve By Use of Traditional Foods, Diet," *Akwesasne Notes,* 5 (Early Autumn 1973), 38; *Trail of Broken Treaties,* p. 13, and *Voices From Wounded Knee,* p. 51; *Voices From Wounded Knee,* pp. 76, 151; *Voices From Wounded Knee,* pp. 56, 109; "Sun Dance at Rosebud Revived after Sixty-Eight Years," *Akwesasne Notes,* 5 (Early Autumn, 1973), 10; and, for example, "The Hau De No Sao Nee Message to the Western World," *Akwesasne Notes,* 9 (Summer, 1977), 8–9.

[88] "Clyde Bellecourt," p. 8. My emphasis. The sweat lodge ceremony is especially significant. Its purpose is to cleanse the individual, physically and spiritually, in preparation for any attempt to approach the Great Spirit for guidance. Because white society is considered a disease, and contact with whites is contaminating, this purification ritual is able to effect a cure and is, therefore, a symbol of the native return to the Old Ways, of the rejection of white society in favor of the supernatural. Cf. "Two Warriors Die: But Struggle Goes On," *Akwesasne Notes,* 8 (Early Spring, 1976), 18.

[89] For a native record of this event, see Indians of All Tribes, *Alcatraz is Not an Island,* ed. by Peter Blue Cloud (Berkeley: Wingbow Press, 1972).

[90] For accounts of representative occupations, see: *Trail of Broken Treaties;* "21 Indians Occupying Rushmore Arrested," *Minneapolis Tribune,* 7 June 1971, pp. 1Aff; Sam Martino, "Novitiate's Future Still Cloudy," *Milwaukee Journal,* 2 January 1977, Pt. 2, pp. 1ff; "Ganienkeh's Struggle," *No More Broken Treaties,* 1 (Late Fall, 1975), p. 1; "Armed Indians Seize Wounded Knee, Hold Hostages," *New York Times,* 1 March 1973, pp. 1ff, and *Voices From Wounded Knee.*

[91] "Yellow Thunder Camp," p. 12.

[92] *Voices From Wounded Knee,* p. 9.

[93] *Voices From Wounded Knee,* p. 89.

[94] See, respectively: "The Heart of the Earth Survival School," *Akwesasne Notes,* 7 (Early Autumn, 1975), 13; "Native People in Guatemala Need Our Help!" *Akwesasne Notes,* 8 (Early Spring, 1976), 3–5; Richard Arens, "Ache: Death Camps in Paraguay," *Akwesasne Notes,* 10 (Early Spring, 1978), 23–27; "Natives of the Western Hemisphere," *Wassaja,* 1 (April/May, 1973), 11; and "The Navajo Nation: Cultivating Underdevelopment," *Akwesasne Notes,* 10 (Autumn, 1978), 7–11; *Voices From Wounded Knee,* p. 55; and "'When in the Course of Human Events,'" p. 11.

[95] This description derives in part from David Berlo's discussion of a continuum of communicative purposes, ranging from the consummatory to the instrumental, in *The Process of Communication: An Introduction to Theory and Practice* (Chicago: Holt, Rinehart and Winston, Inc., 1960), pp. 17–18.

[96] Robert L. Scott and Donald K. Smith, "The Rhetoric of Confrontation," *Quarterly Journal of Speech,* 55 (1969), 1–8. Other seminal studies include Richard B. Gregg, "The Ego-Function of the Rhetoric of Protest," *Philosophy and Rhetoric,* 4 (1971), 71–91; and the work of Robert S. Cathcart, particularly "Movements: Confrontation as Rhetorical Form," *Southern Speech Communication Journal,* 43 (1978), 233–247.

[97] For representative studies, see: Franklyn S. Haiman, "The Rhetoric of 1968: A Farewell to Rational Discourse," in *The Ethics of Controversy: Politics and Protest,* ed. by Donn W. Parson and Wil A. Linkugel (Lawrence, Ks.: House of Usher, 1968), pp. 123–142; Leland Griffin, "The Rhetorical Structure of the 'New Left' Movement: Part I," *Quarterly Journal of Speech,* 50 (1964), 113–135; Theodore Otto Windt, Jr., "The Diatribe: Last Resort for Protest," *Quarterly Journal of Speech,* 58 (1972), 1–14; James F. Klumpp, "Challenge of Radical Rhetoric: Radicalization at Columbia," *Western Speech,* 37 (173), 146–156; J. Robert Cox, "Perspectives on Rhetorical Criticism of Movements: Antiwar Dissent, 1964–1970," *Western Speech,* 38 (1974), 254–268; Richard B. Gregg, A. Jackson McCormack, and Douglas J. Pedersen, "The Rhetoric of Black Power: A Street-Level Interpretation," *Quarterly Journal of Speech,* 55 (1969), 151–160; Karlyn Kohrs Campbell, "The Rhetoric of Radical Black Nationalism: A Case Study in Self-Conscious Criticism," *Central States Speech Journal,* 22 (1971), 151–160; James W. Chesebro, John F. Cragan, and Patricia McCullough, "The Small Group Technique of

the Radical Revolutionary: A Synthetic Study of Consciousness Raising," *Speech Monographs*, 40 (1973), 136–146; Robert L. Heath, "Dialectical Confrontation: A Strategy of Black Radicalism," *Central States Speech Journal*, 24 (1973), 168–177; Brenda Robinson Hancock, "Affirmation by Negation in the Women's Liberation Movement," *Quarterly Journal of Speech*, 58 (1972), 264–271; Karlyn Kohrs Campbell, "The Rhetoric of Women's Liberation: An Oxymoron," *Quarterly Journal of Speech*, 59 (1973), 74–86; Sonja K. Foss, "Equal Rights Amendment Controversy: Two Worlds in Conflict," *Quarterly Journal of Speech*, 65 (1979), 275–288; Karlyn Kohrs Campbell, "Stanton's 'The Solitude of Self': A Rationale for Feminism," *Quarterly Journal of Speech*, 66 (1980), 304–312; and Charles Conrad, "The Transformation of the 'Old Feminist' Movement," *Quarterly Journal of Speech*, 67 (1981), 284–297.

[98] Gregg, pp. 71–91, passim.

[99] Gregg, p. 74.

[100] Aaron D. Gresson, "Minority Epistemology and the Rhetoric of Creation," *Philosophy and Rhetoric*, 10 (1977), 244–262.

[101] Cathcart, pp. 243–244.

[102] Cf. "Rainbow People," Vol. 3, in *Chronicles of American Indian Protest*, p. 317.

[103] Cathcart, p. 242.

[104] Steiner, p. 70.

[105] Andrew Ross and Stephen Most, "A.I.M. Seeking New Strength in Spiritual Roots of the Indians," *Kansas City Times*, 2 September 1976, p. 10C.

[106] Alvin Josephy, Jr., describes Indians as "the poorest of the poor," and details these problems in *Red Power: The American Indians' Fight for Freedom* (New York: McGraw-Hill Book Co., 1971), pp. 3, 159.

[107] *Voices From Wounded Knee*, p. 248.

AIDS, Perspective by Incongruity, and Gay Identity in Larry Kramer's "1,112 and Counting"

Bonnie J. Dow

On October 2, 1985, actor Rock Hudson died from complications of the AIDS virus, a little more than two months after his doctors first announced that he was being treated for the disease. In *Covering the Plague: AIDS and the American Media*, James Kinsella labels the public diagnosis and Hudson's death as "the single most important factors affecting public awareness and concern about the debate" over AIDS (1989, p. 266; see also Shilts, 1987, p. 579; Treichler, 1988, p. 205). At the time of Hudson's diagnosis, 12,067 Americans had been diagnosed with AIDS, and of that number, 6,079 had died (Shilts, 1987, p. 580).

Ironically, given that Hudson was gay, this episode somehow indicated to the media and the public that AIDS could no longer be ignored as a solely gay disease (Treichler, 1988, p. 205). Suddenly, AIDS received attention from the major television news networks, the major weekly news magazines, and newspapers throughout the country. Kinsella notes that

"AIDS reporting in print media increased by 270 percent between Hudson's diagnosis and the end of 1985" (1989, p. 144). Perhaps most significantly, the Reagan administration, which had recommended cutting the federal AIDS budget by $10 million in February of 1985, requested a $100 million boost in funding after the Hudson diagnosis (Kinsella, 1989, p. 265, 266).

The Hudson revelations forced the public, the media, and the federal government to see AIDS in a new way. Hudson's illness was particularly incongruous, as Randy Shilts notes, because "Hudson had been among the handful of screen actors who personified wholesome American masculinity; now, in one stroke, he was revealed as both gay and suffering from the affliction of pariahs" (1987, p. 578–79; see also Treichler, 1988, p. 205). The shift in orientation toward AIDS that began for the general public in mid-1985 had begun a little more than two years earlier in the gay community, when gay men began to publicly acknowledge the reality of AIDS and its implications for their lives. That earlier shift—the focus of this essay—can also be understood as arising from recognition of incongruity.

However, unlike the Hudson episode, an inadvertent cause célèbre did not occasion the shift in gays' perspective on AIDS.[1] Rather, the shift resulted from a specific campaign begun by a handful of AIDS activists and directed at the gay community, a campaign that eventually led to the formation of ACT-UP (AIDS Coalition to Unleash Power) in 1987 (Kramer, 1989). This analysis focuses on one of the significant rhetorical events early in that campaign, the publication of an article titled "1,112 and Counting" (the title refers to the number diagnosed with AIDS) in March of 1983 in the gay newspaper, *The New York Native*. The essay's author, Larry Kramer, is a well-known writer and gay activist who became one of the co-founders of ACT-UP. AIDS chroniclers credit Kramer's lengthy and vitriolic attack on the silence of the establishment and, more importantly, the New York gay community, towards the rapidly developing AIDS crisis as a key event in AIDS awareness and activism among gays (Shilts, 1987, p. 244–45; Kinsella, 1989, pp. 34–35).

In "1,112 and Counting," Kramer seeks to shock the New York gay community into an awareness of the implications of the spread of AIDS. I argue that Kramer's rhetoric exemplifies "perspective by incongruity," a technique defined by Kenneth Burke. Burke notes that perspective by incongruity works as "a process of conversion" in which a "new way of putting the character of events together is an attempt . . . to alter the nature of our responses" (1954, pp. 154fn, 86, 87). In short, Burke argues that perspective by incongruity re-describes experience through use of metaphor, analogy, and other devices that create "a shift in angle of approach . . . disclose an infinity of ways in which our former classifications can be reclassified" (1954, p. 124). However, in Kramer's rhetoric, the creation of perspective by incongruity is not an end in itself. Rather, it functions to stimulate what Maurice Natanson has termed "genuine argument," an attempt to existentially disrupt a person's world and to shock him/her into a willingness to examine fundamental beliefs and values (1965,

p. 19). Genuine argument has implications for the audience's selfhood, or identity, and is a risky and difficult goal; one that, in Kramer's case, is facilitated by the creation of perspective by incongruity. Genuine argument is a concept that allows discussion of the problems and possibilities of rhetorical action that *attempts to alter audience members' conceptions of themselves:* their identities, responsibilities, and motives.

Ultimately, with this focus on "identity" as a rhetorical process and product, this essay contributes to a line of work on rhetoric and identity articulated by Maurice Charland. Charland argues that "the development of new subject positions . . . is possible at particular historical moments" (1987, p. 141). A gay movement for AIDS activism required a new subject position for gays, one that would "resolve, or at least contain, experienced contradictions" (Charland, 1987, p. 142). In such a situation, constitutive rhetoric works to "overcome or define away the recalcitrance the world presents by providing the subject with new perspectives and motives" (Charland, 1987, p. 142).

This essay proceeds in four stages. First, I discuss the context for Kramer's rhetorical strategies, focusing on the dominant ethos of the urban gay community in the late 1970s and early 1980s and the implications of AIDS for gay identity within that community. The second section addresses the possible functions of perspective by incongruity and genuine argument, as critics have explained them, within this context. An analysis of Kramer's use of these strategies follows. The analysis focuses on his attempts to create shock, anger, and guilt among gays—emotions that motivate a radical shift in their perceptions of AIDS and of themselves. The conclusions explore the ways in which this study extends understanding of the potential for common functions of perspective by incongruity and genuine argument, particularly their role in the rhetorical de-construction and re-construction of identity.

AIDS AND GAY IDENTITY

For those now familiar with ACT-UP and other groups involved in AIDS activism, it is difficult to envision a time when the two largest gay communities in America, in New York City and San Francisco, generally denied the potential impact of the disease on their lives. In *And The Band Played On* (Shilts, 1987) and *Reports From the Holocaust* (Kramer, 1989), Randy Shilts and Larry Kramer tell riveting tales of the difficulties the gay community faced as it tried to comprehend AIDS in the early 1980s. Understanding two specific factors in American reactions to AIDS makes gay inaction comprehensible. First, many medical and political authorities dismissed the impact of AIDS, no doubt because of its invisibility as a disease of the disenfranchised. Many gay men, facing a plague, found it easier to believe the establishment than to face the frightening implications of the disease. Such a natural reaction requires little explanation. Second, and much more important and complex, the dominant urban gay culture in New York and San Francisco during the emergence of AIDS made recognition of the disease's ramifications politically and psychologically costly for many gay men.

Unlike other oppressed groups such as women or blacks, gays display no ineradicable markers of their identity. Many gays, particularly urbanized adult men who participated in the gay liberation movement of the 1970s, enacted their identity through sexual behavior. "The cornerstone of the gay movement," which generated an explosion in the gay populations of New York and San Francisco, "was sexual liberation, the freedom to have sex exactly as they liked" (Kinsella, 1989, p. 36). Shilts concurs that "promiscuity was central to the raucous gay movement of the 1970s" and "sex was part and parcel of political liberation" (1987, p. 19). The norm that developed, of creative sex with many different and often anonymous partners, had commercial as well as lifestyle implications.

An industry of sex clubs and bathhouses blossomed in the United States and Canada, providing opportunities for sexual experimentation with multiple partners. Such establishments became central to gay social and even political life, as their owners often contributed heavily to gay causes. By 1980, the negative health implications of the sex business, specifically the spread of venereal disease and parasitic infections transmitted through oral-anal intercourse,

became apparent to some. As one doctor told a gay magazine, "One effect of gay liberation is that sex has been institutionalized and franchised. Twenty years ago, there may have been a thousand men on any one night having sex in New York baths or parks. Now there are ten or twenty thousand. . . . The plethora of opportunities poses a public health problem that's growing with every new bath in town" (quoted in Shilts, 1987, p. 20).

Little attention was paid to such warnings. Generally, the gay communities in these cities were unusually healthy, reflecting the emphasis on appearance and physical fitness as sexual attractants. Sexually transmitted diseases were cured with antibiotics. The bathhouses and sex clubs, a multi-million dollar industry and a political power, had little inclination to support efforts to regulate sexual activity (Kinsella, 1989, p. 36).

For many gays, then, unrestricted sexuality was the legacy of liberation. To question such a stance, even before AIDS appeared, was to court backlash. The gay community knew Kramer primarily through his 1978 novel, *Faggots,* which chronicled gay sexual hedonism in New York and asked, in the words of the story's protagonist: "Why do faggots have to fuck so fucking much? It's as though we don't have anything else to do. . . . I'm tired of using my body as a faceless thing to lure another faceless thing, I want to love a Person!" (quoted in Shilts, 1987, p. 27). Much of the American gay press received *Faggots* negatively, some gay bookstores banned the book, and many gays accused Kramer of homophobia and anti-eroticism (Shilts, 1987, p. 26; Kramer, 1989, p. 16). Some New York gays also resented Kramer for his admiration of the more politicized San Francisco gay community, which had few closeted gays in comparison to New York. In New York, Kramer lamented, gay identity was almost exclusively sexual, rather than both sexual and political, as it was in San Francisco (Kramer, 1989, pp. 3–7; Shilts, p. 27).

By the time that Kramer published "1,112 and Counting" in 1983, many viewed him as the Cassandra of the New York gay community. The relative silence of the national gay press and the establishment media on the topic of AIDS increased Kramer's rhetorical problem.[2]

Although gay newspapers had printed scattered articles on the "gay cancer," referring to AIDS-related Kaposi's sarcoma, and "gay pneumonia," such reports were short on details and took pains to avoid alarmism (Shilts, 1987, pp. 72, 74, 107). Shilts notes that, in the last quarter of 1982, the mainstream press in the United States printed only thirty articles dealing with AIDS. Most of these reported recent cases of the disease in infants and hemophiliacs (1987, p. 213). In March 1983, when Kramer published "1,112 and Counting," the recognition by scientists and doctors that AIDS was infectious, and was being transmitted through blood and semen, was not yet widely accepted or publicized (Shilts, 1987, p. 194–95; Kinsella, 1989, Ch. 7).

Kramer did not debut as an AIDS activist or polemicist with "1,112 and Counting." In 1982, he had helped to found Gay Men's Health Crisis (GMHC), a fund-raising and informational group formed in response to the rash of deaths among gay men from the first wave of AIDS-related illnesses in New York. Kramer would clash with other members of the board of GMHC about the organization's lack of aggressiveness. When he published "1,112 and Counting" he inserted a disclaimer stating that he was not speaking for GMHC. Kramer had written on AIDS previously, in letters and short appeals in the *New York Native*, but "1,112 and Counting" introduced new strategies, new arguments, and a new level of confrontation to his rhetoric on AIDS.

PERSPECTIVE BY INCONGRUITY, GENUINE ARGUMENT, AND IDENTITY

The situation detailed above makes clear the need for genuine argument among gays on the topic of AIDS. For gay men, the message that the disease plaguing their community might be transmitted by their sexual behavior was a blow to gay identity: "Men had traveled far, geographically and personally, to come into their own sexual identities—which often meant sexual promiscuity . . . only to discover that they had to adapt to a scourge that challenged their personal and community existences" (O'Connell, 1989, p. 491). Assent to Kramer's premise in "1,112 and Counting"—that gay sex was

spreading AIDS and that gay priorities must be realigned—would require a fundamental reevaluation of gay values and the behavior that enacted those values. To open their minds to Kramer's rhetoric was, for many of them, to question their identity.

As Maurice Natanson points out, genuine philosophical argument occurs relatively rarely, for it demands much of the arguer and the audience: "What is 'genuine' is nothing more than the commitment of the self to the full implications of a philosophical dialectic, a saying, in effect, 'if you choose to open yourself to the risk of discovering that argument has a fundamental structure that has, in turn, profound implications for your own being'" (1965, p. 15). The existential disruption necessary for a person's "immediate life of feeling and sensibility [to be] made open to challenge" (Natanson, 1965, p. 19) can be an outgrowth of perspective by incongruity. As Joseph Gusfield describes Burke's concept, it "reveals the limits of a single form of thought to understand and experience reality" (1989, p. 23).

Fittingly, for the purposes of genuine argument, Gusfield views perspective by incongruity as a central element in Burke's "comic corrective," used to produce "new ways of seeing" (1989, pp. 23, 26) that allow people *to be observers of themselves while acting. Its ultimate would be not passiveness but maximum consciousness*" [emphasis in original] (Burke, 1959, p. 171). As a number of critics argue, the comic frame allows facilitation of social change; it encourages adjustment to a new order (Carlson, 1986; Murphy, 1989; Madsen, 1993). Burke notes that "it provides the *charitable* attitude toward people that is required for purposes of persuasion and cooperation" [emphasis in original] (1959, p. 166).

Perspective by incongruity contributes to the comic corrective by functioning as a species of redefinition that re-evaluates, and gives new meaning to, an existing set of circumstances. Rosteck and Leff describe perspective by incongruity as a shift between "schemes of orientation" or "frames of reference," which they, following Burke, label "pieties" (1989, p. 329). Such pieties "govern our sense of propriety" as they "direct human perception and determine our judgments about what is proper in a given circumstance" (1989, p. 329). Perspective by incongruity questions or deconstructs accepted meanings or pieties through comparison, re-classification, and re-naming.

In a process analogous to consciousness-raising, perspective by incongruity de-naturalizes a given set of meanings or values and questions their adequacy for explaining or directing experience (Rosteck and Leff, 1989, p. 331). In this sense, perspective by incongruity functions as a kind of refutation that "is at once subversive and constructive; old pieties must fall to provide space for new ones" (Rosteck and Leff, 1989, p. 330). The function of such a strategy can be transformative because it "reconstructs rather than adjusts itself to the standards of propriety accepted by an audience" (1989, p. 338). As I suggest in this analysis, perspective by incongruity can do more than test audience assumptions about their external world; it also can question fundamentally their identity in relation to that world. For example, Burke's statement that "rebirth and perspective by incongruity are thus seen to be synonymous, a process of conversion," contains a clear link to identity (1954, p. 154fn).

Previous analyses, however, use perspective by incongruity primarily to analyze redescription of issues or institutions, rather than to explore issues of identity. In a 1979 analysis, for example, Sonja Foss uses perspective by incongruity to analyze attempts by feminists Ti-Grace Atkinson and Mary Daly to re-orient their audiences toward the Catholic Church. Martha Solomon (1988) describes anarchist Emma Goldman's unsuccessful use of perspective by incongruity to critique religion, capitalism, and the state and, in fact, notes Goldman's insufficient attention to issues of identity (1988, pp. 187, 194). Rosteck and Leff (1989) examine the rhetoric of another anarchist, Voltairine de Cleyre, focusing on her efforts to redefine the significance of the Haymarket riot. Rosteck and Leff's analysis, however, divorces the rhetoric from audience and context; they argue that Burke's concept allows them "to view an oratorical text as a local achievement without dissolving it into the immediate historical context" (1989, p. 339). This approach lends little insight into how such a rhetorical strategy might interact with the interests, motivations, or character of an audience. These previous analyses attempt to illustrate the power of perspective by incongruity to "supplant a traditional view of a situation with a new and restructured one" (Foss, 1979, p. 11), but they do not explore the ways in which perspective by incongruity, and the pieties that it de-constructs and re-constructs, have profoundly personal implications for an audience—implications best explained through the concept of genuine argument.

Although a number of critics and argumentation theorists have noted the importance of the idea of genuine argument since its introduction by Natanson in 1965 (e.g., Ehninger, 1970; Brockriede, 1972; Willard, 1982, pp. xxix–xxxiii), they have done little to explore its presence in rhetorical action. Genuine argument exists as a concept—perhaps even an ideal—in the realm of theory rather than as a set of practices. This analysis suggests that critics can view genuine argument as a set of conditions, produced rhetorically, that present the possibility of engagement between rhetor and audience on questions so fundamentally important that they carry implications for the audience's identity. In this view, genuine argument is not a material product but a discursive effect; it is not the completion of a process, but the beginning of it. Ultimately, I describe genuine argument as an historical moment, initiated by rhetorical action, in which a rhetor and his/her audience become aware of the necessity of and possibility for radical transformation of themselves and their world. As Natanson argues, "'world' is in the first place the personal and immediate domain of individual experience" (1965, p. 15).

Perspective by incongruity is Kramer's primary means for facilitating that "moment" of genuine argument when, having re-conceptualized the meaning and the implications of AIDS for their community, gays confront the possibility of a radical transformation of their behavior and identity. Because of the threat posed to their sexual identity, denial and disbelief shaped the dominant frame of reference, or piety, of urban gays toward AIDS (Treichler, 1988, pp. 201–202). Kramer's purpose in "1,112 and Counting" is twofold: first, to shatter that disbelief and denial, challenging the "propriety" of gay attitudes toward AIDS; and second, to offer a new orientation around which gays can coalesce to deal more effectively with AIDS. Because of the profound implications for gay identity, these purposes place Kramer, a member of the community he addressed, and his audience in a position to engage in genuine argument, to face "existential risk" (Ehninger, 1970, p. 105), so that "the full range of affective life is shocked into openness" (Natanson, 1965, p. 17). Persuasion that occurs on such a personal level is unusual and difficult, requiring rhetoric that, as "1,112 and Counting" illustrates, is neither subtle nor painless. Indeed, echoing Burke's language describing the function of perspective by incongruity, Charland argues that "the process by which an audience member enters into a new subject position is therefore not one of persuasion. It is akin more to one of conversion that ultimately results in an act of recognition of the 'rightness' of a discourse and of one's identity with its reconfigured subject position" (1987, p. 142).

This analysis proceeds chronologically, dividing "1,112 and Counting" into three roughly equal sections, each of which builds upon previous arguments. The strategy of perspective by incongruity operates cumulatively to achieve Kramer's purposes and to create the foundation for genuine argument. In the first section, Kramer relies on statistics, examples, and strong language to shock his audience into an awareness of the breadth of the epidemic and to demonstrate the incongruity of their denial. In the second section, his purpose shifts as he details the lack of action on AIDS by medical and governmental bodies. In this section, the desired response is anger, a product of the realization that, given the gravity of the situation, the lack of action is acutely incongruous. Third, Kramer targets gays, lambasting them for their lack of action. In this section, his desired response is guilt, produced when gays are confronted with the impropriety of their own indifference. Here, Kramer begins the task of destroying the piety of gay identity based in sexuality and anonymity and constructing a new piety based in political identity and action. This new perspective, Kramer argues, is a necessary shift, given the reality of AIDS. Achieving such a perspective requires that an audience question its fundamental beliefs and values, a process that promotes genuine argument and requires attention to identity issues.

AIDS AND INCONGRUITY

The opening paragraph of "1,112 and Counting" sets a tone of confrontation that intensifies as the essay proceeds: "If this article doesn't scare the shit out of you, we're in real trouble. If this article doesn't rouse you to anger, fury, rage and action, gay men may have no future on this earth. Our continued existence depends on just how angry you can get" (p. 33).[3] With such language, Kramer begins the process of existential disruption, announcing his purpose and asserting its importance before even naming his topic. He continues: "Unless we fight for our lives, we shall die. In all the history of homosexuality we have never before been so close to death or extinction" (p. 33). Given that most gays have refused to acknowledge the gravity of AIDS, and that it has received little attention in either the gay or the mainstream press, such language appears hyperbolic. Of course, hyperbole can be a hallmark of perspective by incongruity, because it forces the mind to make connections that are "radical and new" (Solomon, 1988, p. 189). For Kramer, such connections become a first step in the formation of a new perspective.

As Kramer follows his hyperbole with equally startling statistics and examples, gay denial of AIDS, rather than Kramer's claims about death and extinction, begin to seem incongruous. All of Kramer's statistics aim at the target audience. After noting that 1,112 diagnosed cases of AIDS exist, he reveals that almost half of those cases are in New York, where 195 have died (p. 34). He underscores the speed and power of the epidemic as well: "In only twenty-eight days, from January 13th to February 9th [1983] there were 164 new cases—and 73 more dead" (p. 35). The actual numbers represent only the tip of the iceberg, because "these numbers do not include the thousands of us walking around with what is also being called AIDS: various forms of swollen lymph glands and fatigues that doctors don't know what to label or what they might portend" (p. 34).

To amplify the incongruity of denial and disbelief, Kramer invokes the testimony of doctors treating AIDS patients—doctors who admit that the disease is unmanageable:

Another [doctor] said, "The thing that upsets me the most in all of this is that at any given moment one of my patients is in the hospital and something is going on with him that I don't understand". . . . A third said to me, "I'm very depressed. A doctor's job is to make patients well. And I can't. Too many of my patients die." (p. 34)

The accumulation of evidence in this section dispels any possibility for continued denial by Kramer's audience: "After almost two years of an epidemic, there still are no answers. After almost two years of an epidemic, the cause of AIDS remains unknown. After almost two years of an epidemic, there is no cure" (p. 34). In the conclusion of this section, Kramer angrily articulates the incongruity of gay denial: "If all of this had been happening to any other community for two long years, there would have been, long ago, such an outcry from that community and all its members that the government of this city and this country would not know what had hit them" (p. 35). Here, he begins a pattern that runs throughout the essay. He contrasts "normal" behavior with behavior in the context of AIDS. This strategy, buttressed by Kramer's shocking language, shatters complacency and provides a new perspective on the crisis AIDS represents for the gay community: "Why isn't every gay man in this city so scared shitless that he is screaming for action? Does every gay man in New York *want* to die?" (p. 35).

To suggest that gays long for death suggests the ultimate in incongruity. Yet, such a strategy seeks to force awareness of implications and connections not heretofore apparent (Burke, 1954, pp. 90; Madsen, 1993, p. 174). As Solomon argues, "By yoking together items that seem contradictory (or at least incongruous) within the context of the established orientation, perspective by incongruity stimulates the receiver to resolve the contradiction, ultimately by developing a new set of meanings" (1988, p. 187).

Kramer's implication that gay silence is tantamount to consent to their eradication is precisely the kind of statement that can provoke awareness of the limits of their current orientation toward AIDS. Kramer forces gays to recognize their own impiety. Given the evidence he provides, their current approach of silence and disbelief must give way to a new orientation. Kramer lays further groundwork for that new orientation in the essay's second major section. He details the incongruity of the response of the medical establishment and the government to the spread of AIDS, an incongruity that can only be resolved through the realization that AIDS is not only a public health crisis, it also is a political issue.

In the second section, Kramer begins his discussion of each of a variety of medical and governmental institutions with "Let's talk about"; for example, "Let's talk about surveillance [of the epidemic]," "Let's talk about various forms of treatment," or "Let's talk about what gay tax dollars are buying for gay men" (pp. 36, 37, 39). Following the pattern he has set, Kramer juxtaposes the normal or expected responsibility of an institution with its incongruous, or abnormal, response to AIDS. His litany of "truly scandalous" inaction (p. 39) takes the shock and fear aroused by the first section of the essay and transforms it into anger, rather than paralysis. Such anger marks another step toward the formation of a political identity for gay men because it destroys faith that institutions will act effectively without political pressure.

He begins with a discussion of the Centers for Disease Control (CDC), an institution "charged by our government to fully monitor all epidemics and unusual diseases" (p. 36). Kramer explains that "to learn something from an epidemic, you have to keep records and statistics. Statistics come from interviewing victims and getting as much information from them as you can. Before they die" (p. 36). However, because of lack of funding, the CDC has ceased interviewing AIDS victims, meaning that "yet more information that might reveal patterns of transmissibility is not being monitored and collected and studied. We are being denied perhaps the easiest and fastest research tool available at this moment," one that, Kramer implies, would not be denied if the majority of the victims were not gay (p. 37).

In an example more specific to his audience, Kramer discusses hospitals in New York City, where "AIDS patients are often treated like lepers" because hospital workers know so little about the disease (p. 38). He points out that it is the job of the local Department of Health "to educate this city, its citizens and its hospital workers about all areas of a public health emergency. Well, they have done an appalling job" (p. 88). This failure, Kramer asserts, reflects discrimination against gays: "If three out of four AIDS cases were occurring in straights instead of in gay men, you can bet all hospitals and their staffs would know what was happening. And it would be this city's Health Department and Health and Hospitals Corporation that would be telling them" (p. 39).

In his discussion of gay tax dollars, he notes that the National Institutes of Health has waited for over a year to award $8 million of appropriated money to AIDS researchers and concludes that "there is no question that if this epidemic was happening to the straight, white, non-intravenous-drug-using middle class, that money would have been put into use almost two years ago." Kramer vivifies the incongruity of the lack of federal disbursements for AIDS research when he points out that "During the first *two weeks* of the Tylenol scare, the United States government spent $10 million to find out what was happening . . . . But then, AIDS is happening mostly to gay men, isn't it?" [emphasis in original] (p. 39, 40).

In order to resolve the contradiction that Kramer reveals between the expected responsibility of these various institutions and their response to AIDS, the audience must conclude that their political status as a marginalized, disenfranchised group explains the inaction. And, as Kramer forecast in the first lines of the essay, such a conclusion should infuriate them, particularly since "gay men pay taxes just like everyone else. . . . We desperately need something from our government to save our lives and we're not getting it" (p. 40).

Kramer's final example of public malfeasance in the face of AIDS is specific to his New York audience; he launches a sustained attack on New York City mayor Ed Koch, who has chosen, Kramer argues, "not to allow himself to be perceived by the non-gay world as visibly helping us in this emergency" (p. 41). Pointing out that Herb Rickman, Koch's liaison to the gay community, is "universally hated by virtually every gay organization in New York," Kramer details failed attempts to stimulate action from the mayor's office, where Rickman's response has been:

> to refuse our phone calls, to scream at us hysterically, to slam down telephones, to threaten us, to tease us with favors that are not delivered, to keep us waiting hours for an audience, to lie to us—in short, to humiliate us . . . He would not do this to black or Jewish leaders. And they would not take it from him for one minute. Why, why, why do we allow him to do it to us? And he, a homosexual! (p. 42)

As he does throughout the essay, Kramer highlights the incongruity of attention to AIDS by contrasting it with that accorded the concerns of other groups. In this case, however, the other groups—blacks and Jews—are also marginalized, which makes the comparison even more powerful. Kramer ends the second section of the essay with another strongly worded indictment: "With his silence on AIDS, the Mayor of New York is helping to kill us" (p. 43). Here, as earlier, Kramer uses hyperbole to illustrate the incongruity of the attitude of the mayor of the city with one of the largest gay populations in the country.

As Rosteck and Leff describe it, perspective by incongruity is the "midpoint" in the progression from "piety through an impiety to a new piety" (1989, p. 330). Perspective by incongruity is thus a "linguistic impiety" that "focuses or refocuses our encounters with the world in a way consistent with our interests" (1989, p. 331). Possible defenses of gays' former frame of reference (e.g., that AIDS is not a serious threat, that it will be cured easily, that medical and governmental institutions will do what is necessary) are revealed as impious through Kramer's demonstration of incongruity. In the first two sections of the essay, the power of Kramer's strategy is not only the result of strong language or powerful evidence, but the new connections, comparisons, and contradictions that they provoke.

However, the destruction of an old piety lays the foundation for a new one in the essay's cumulative strategy. For example, perceptions of medical or governmental response (or lack thereof) as incongruous in the second section depends upon recognition of AIDS as a public health crisis, the purpose of the first section. The third section of the essay, in which Kramer completes the progression to a new piety based in political rather than (or in addition to) sexual interests depends upon these previous moves. Building upon recognition of the political factors influencing action on AIDS, Kramer urges gays to reconstitute themselves as a political force.

This conversion, however, demands a critique of current gay identity. Thus, in this section, Kramer specifically targets New York gays' emphasis on anonymity and sexuality. He attempts to transform their anger over inaction toward AIDS into guilt produced by their recognition of their own complicity in that inaction. In this process, Kramer creates the conditions necessary for genuine argument. As Natanson notes, genuine argument requires risk because it creates "the viable possibility that the consequence of an argument may be to make me see something of the structure of my immediate world" (1965, p. 15). Arguments that challenge accepted "pieties" about identity or selfhood are rare, for they present the possibility of genuine transformation of an audience's life world. In order to fight AIDS, which Kramer presents as a threat to their ongoing existence, gays must face the necessity of such a transformation. His argument for the incongruity of gays' current stance toward AIDS is a key step in their recognition of their impiety.

In the third section of "1,112 and Counting" Kramer begins each topic with "I am sick of . . ." as he ranges across areas of gay lack of response to AIDS. Two major themes emerge: the lack of response on the part of persons, groups, or institutions that represent gays and disregard for the implications of AIDS among the gay community generally.

Just as Kramer spends the second section of the essay refuting the notion that straight authorities will rescue gays from AIDS, he begins the third section by refuting the same notion about groups that supposedly represent gays specifically. Attacking the lack of concern of New York Senator Daniel Patrick Moynihan, who, as Kramer notes "represents the city with the largest gay population in America," he lays the fault at the feet of the gay community: "I am sick of our not realizing we have enough votes to defeat these people, and I am sick of our not electing our own openly gay officials in the first place" (p. 43–44). Similarly, he castigates gay doctors: "I am sick of the passivity or nonparticipation or halfhearted protestations of all the gay medical associations . . . and particularly of our own New York Physicians for Human Rights, a group of our gay doctors who have, as a group, done nothing" [emphasis in original] (p. 44).

The gay press receives equally harsh treatment. Referring to the *Advocate,* the national gay newspaper, Kramer claims it:

> has yet to quite acknowledge that anything is going on. That newspaper's recent AIDS issue was so innocuous you'd have thought all we were going through was little worse than a rage of the latest designer flu. And their own associate editor . . . died from AIDS. Figure that one out. (p. 44)

Kramer cements the incongruity of the *Advocate*'s response with a rhetorical question: "If we can't get our own newspapers and magazines to tell us what is happening to us . . . how are we going to get the word around that we're dying?" (p. 44).

In this section, Kramer singles out those people (politicians, doctors, and journalists) who have the precise kinds of power that could make a significant difference in response to the disease, and he highlights the incongruity of their inaction. Up to this point, Kramer primarily is attacking the establishment, something from which many in his audience can distance themselves. His attacks on gay leaders and institutions serve to support his general contention that gays cannot believe that AIDS will be addressed by the status quo. In the remainder of this section, however, Kramer's arguments become more personal as he proceeds to attribute this lack of loyalty and concern to all gays, fundamentally questioning the adequacy of an orientation that overvalues anonymity, sexuality, and approval from the straight world.

Kramer begins his critique of gay identity by denouncing gays' refusal to see themselves as a community worthy of support. In another of the vehement statements typical of the essay, he declares "Go give your bucks to straight charities, fellows, while we die" (p. 44). A remarkable attack on gay hypocrisy follows:

> Gay Men's Health Crisis is going crazy trying to accomplish everything it does— printing and distributing hundreds of thousands of educational items, taking care of several hundred AIDS victims, . . . getting media attention, fighting bad hospital care, on and on, and on, fighting for you and us in two thousand ways. . . . Is the Red Cross doing this for you? Is the American Cancer Society? Your college alumni fund? . . . . The United Way? The Lenox Hill Neighborhood Association, or any of the other fancy straight charities for which faggots put on black ties and dance at the Plaza? (pp. 44–45)

The incongruity created by this image is potent, as is its capacity to create guilt in the audience. Kramer implies that, for superficial and hedonistic motives, gays' political and financial power is focused outward rather than inward, reflecting their disregard for their own community. Kramer's attack on closeted gays intensifies the impiety of activities that seek approval from the straight community:

> I am sick of closeted gays. It's 1983 already, guys, when are you going to come out? By 1984 you could be dead. Every gay man who is unable to come forward now and fight to save his own life is truly helping to kill the rest of us. . . . As more and more of my friends die, I have less and less sympathy for men who are afraid their mommies will

find out or afraid their bosses will find out or afraid their fellow doctors or professional associates will find out. (p. 45)

Echoing his earlier statements that the passivity of straight institutions and political leaders were "killing" gays, Kramer turns this hyperbole on gays, positing a stark choice between anonymity and death. This incongruous juxtaposition makes anonymity, viewed previously as a survival tactic for gays, not only counterproductive, but immoral. In Kramer's new equation, anonymity is antithetical to survival: "unless we can generate, visibly, numbers, masses, we are going to die" (p. 45).

Passivity and silence in the face of AIDS is so immoral, Kramer implies, that he equates it with voluntary genocide: "I am sick of 'men' who say 'we've got to keep quiet or *they* will do such and such. . . .['] Okay, you 'men'—be my guests: You can march off now to the gas chambers; just get right in line" [emphasis in original] (p. 46). Kramer's use of holocaust metaphors is perhaps the most vivid and consistent device for perspective by incongruity that occurs across his rhetoric on AIDS; he titles his collection of AIDS speeches and essays *Reports from the Holocaust.* On most occasions, Kramer turns such imagery on the establishment rather than on gays themselves.[4] However, in "1,112 and Counting," he wants to make the cost of inaction by gays as dire as possible, to force an awareness that is psychologically costly for his audience. This is the function of perspective by incongruity: to offer a new vocabulary or way of thinking, "exemplifying relationships between objects which our customary rational vocabulary has ignored" (Burke, 1954, p. 90), what Burke also has called "metaphorical migration" (1959, p. 173). In Kramer's case, the seemingly incongruous juxtaposition of AIDS and the Holocaust serves to foster his desired response—guilt.

Kramer unites these various attacks on anonymity and silence with his contention that such tactics reflect gays' fundamental lack of self-respect. Certainly, their misplaced priorities are incongruous given the situation surrounding AIDS, but, equally important, these priorities reflect the inadequacy of gay identity. Kramer's discussion of gay sexuality also targets this lack of self-regard among gays. Kramer expresses the incongruity of "guys who moan that giving up careless sex until this blows over is worse than death" through synecdoche: "How can they value life so little and cocks and asses so much?" (p. 46). As Kramer describes it, for those already afflicted with AIDS, the absurdity of such a position is tragically apparent: "Come with me, guys, while I visit a few of our friends in Intensive Care at NYU. Notice the looks in their eyes, guys. They'd give up sex forever if you could promise them life" (p. 46).

He concludes that to enact an identity based only on sex is not only dangerous, it reveals a lack of self-worth: "I am sick of guys who think that all being gay means is sex in the first place. I am sick of guys who can only think with their cocks.... And I am very sick and saddened by every gay man who does not get behind this issue totally and with commitment—to fight for his life" (p. 46–47). As Kramer implies here, the failure of gay activism on AIDS would indicate more than anti-gay discrimination and the failure of American institutions: it would indict gays' own identities as morally responsible and complete human beings.

At this point, Kramer has progressed from piety, through a demonstration of impiety in various forms, and is poised to begin constitution of a new piety based in political action. The shock, anger, and guilt that he has attempted to evoke thus far in "1,112 and Counting" provides the motivation for his audience to open themselves to genuine argument, to contemplate a fundamental reorientation of themselves and the structure of their lives. Such engagement is crucial to the creation of large scale membership in a movement for AIDS activism.

For Kramer to leave his audience with nothing but a scathing indictment of their institutions and life-style clearly would be counter-productive. Thus, in the final paragraphs of "1,112 and Counting," he offers a means for his audience to expunge their guilt and redefine themselves. He begins the final section with a plea: "I don't want to die. I can only assume you don't want to die. Can we fight together?" (p. 47). The striking shift in tone here indicates that

Kramer has completed the purpose of perspective by incongruity; he has established the impiety of existing frames of reference toward AIDS.

In his creation of a new perspective, which emphasizes an alternative identity for gays, he discards his earlier sarcasm and anger. Instead, he is hopeful, encouraging, and solemn as he explains the formation of the AIDS Network, a coalition of gay groups and activists engaged in lobbying Mayor Ed Koch and in training for civil disobedience. He asserts the potential of the audience to make a difference through action that will define them in a new and more powerful way: as a political force dedicated to their own survival.

Kramer describes a positive new identity that, he implies, needs only to be enacted: "Gay men are the strongest, toughest, people I know. We are perhaps shortly to get an opportunity to show it" (p. 48). In Kramer's new vision, gays will be united by their anger and by their commitment to themselves: "It is time for us to be perceived for what we truly are: an angry community and a strong community, and therefore *a threat.* Such are the realities of politics. Nationally we are 24 million strong, which is more than there are Jews or blacks or Hispanics in this country" [emphasis in original] (p. 48). In short, Kramer urges his audience to discover their "true" selves, to enact the identity that can emerge if they re-orient themselves to the demands of a new situation. Such faith in the audience is a characteristic of genuine argument.

Kramer's decision to treat his audience as rational, feeling beings capable of the change he seeks manifests his commitment to the future of the gay community and denies charges that he is homophobic and alarmist. Only a rhetor with sincere concern for the audience and a profound commitment to the issue would create such a painful polemic. As Kramer's conclusion demonstrates, he does not want to alienate his audience or to dominate them, but to move them toward a feeling of responsibility for themselves. Ehninger affirms that the person-making function of argument can entail:

> that alchemic moment of transformation
> in which the ego-centric gives way to the

alter-centric; that moment when, in the language of Buber, the *Ich-Es* is replaced by the *Ich-Du;* when the "other," no longer regarded as an object to be manipulated, is endowed with those qualities of "freedom" and "responsibility" that change the "individual" as a thing into the "person" as "not-thing" (1970, p[.] 110).

Certainly, Kramer recognizes that his audience has a choice, for without that possibility there would be no point to his argument. The care with which he constructs it demonstrates his own depth of feeling which he hopes will resonate in them. At the emotional climax of the essay, Kramer declares "I am angry and frustrated almost beyond the bound my skin and bones and body and brain can encompass. My sleep is tormented by nightmares and visions of lost friends, and my days are flooded by the tears of funerals and memorial services and seeing my sick friends. How many of us must die before *all* of us living fight back?" [emphasis in original] (p. 49). As Kramer phrases it, the answer to this question has significant moral consequences for his own selfhood and, he hopes, for the selfhood of other gays: "I know that unless I fight with every ounce of my energy I will hate myself. I hope, I pray, I implore you to feel the same" (p. 49). In a dramatic closing, Kramer lists twenty of his friends who are dead from AIDS, noting that another will be dead "by the time these words appear in print" (p. 50). This final move acts as an enthymeme, asking the audience to do the same, to count mentally their own losses. In doing so, each audience member provides his own concrete and personal proof of the toll of AIDS.

Conclusions

Randy Shilts writes that the publication of "1,112 and Counting" "threw a hand grenade into the foxhole of denial where most gay men in America had been sitting out the epidemic," and the article's impact on perceptions of AIDS created a ripple effect within the American gay community and, subsequently, the public arena (1987, p. 244; see also Kinsella, 1989, p. 35). The issue of the *New York Native* in which "1,112 and

Counting" was the cover story sold out in New York City, and the essay was reprinted in most gay newspapers in the country, largely due to Kramer's efforts (Shilts, 1987, p. 245; Kramer, 1989, p. 50). In San Francisco, a group of activists inspired by Kramer published their own manifesto in the *Bay Area Reporter,* a major gay newspaper (Kinsella, 1989, p[.] 35). Calling Kramer's article "inarguably one of the most influential works of advocacy journalism of the decade," Shilts maintains its call for change "swiftly crystallized the epidemic into a political movement for the gay community at the same time that it set off a maelstrom of controversy that polarized gay leaders" (1987, p. 245).

Kramer's essay did not complete the work of genuine argument; indeed, no one rhetorical act could accomplish such a task. However, he provoked awareness of the profound necessity for continued engagement with the issues he raised. Moreover, he conclusively altered the context in which gays viewed the disease and their own role in relation to it.

Kramer was not a hero to all. The *New York Native* fielded numerous letters accusing him of unwarranted alarmism and moralizing (Shilts, 1987, p. 245). However, the controversy that followed "1,112 and Counting" was not necessarily unhealthy; indeed, it was the outcome of the genuine argument that Kramer attempted. Regardless of some immediate negative reaction, and later disagreement over tactics in AIDS activism, Kramer realized his purpose of existential disruption.

In Kramer's case, skillful use of perspective by incongruity facilitated the engagement necessary for genuine argument to begin. Solomon's analysis of Emma Goldman's rhetorical failure highlights two necessary elements in successful uses of perspective by incongruity. First, Solomon argues, rhetors "induce impiety in their audiences because they are seeking to reorganize the listener's orientation. But with impiety comes a desire for a new orientation." Thus, to complete the process begun by perspective by incongruity, the rhetor "must point the way to a new orientation" (1988, p. 192). Second, this new orientation must build upon some retained elements of the audience's existing worldview. As Burke notes, "even when one attempts to criticize the structure, one must leave some parts of it intact in order to have a point of reference for his [or her] criticism" (1954, p. 169).

In short, as they are being asked to abandon the position they currently occupy, the audience must have a place to go and a means to get there. This is what makes perspective by incongruity a *comic* strategy for Burke; it assumes that we can learn from exposure of mistakes and that such information ultimately will benefit us. Such possibilities are even more important when an audience is being asked to revise elements of their *identity* as well as their attitudes toward institutions or issues. I suggest that incorporation of these elements, along with the personalized and risk-assuming stance of the rhetor, are the factors that move Kramer's rhetoric beyond mere harangue of his audience and into the realm of genuine argument.

At each point that he nears alienation of his audience, Kramer offers a new direction for the incongruities and the resultant powerful emotions he provokes. The fear and shock aroused by the essay's first section is channelled into anger in the second section through Kramer's exposure of the callous attitude of the establishment toward AIDS and its victims. This anger, in turn, provides the foundation for guilt as gays themselves are accused of the same callousness in the essay's third section. In the final section, Kramer offers a way out of the dissonance such guilt creates by proposing a new set of behaviors and values (indeed, a new identity), to replace those that he has debunked. This new identity, however, has roots in values that gays should find appealing: their own strength, their commitment to their own self-worth, and their dedication to their survival in the face of flagrant discrimination. Such values presumably were central to gay liberation struggles of the 1970s, and, as Kramer implies, need simply to be reasserted as the foundation for a new political identity in the age of AIDS.

In this sense, the goals of "1,112 and Counting" are ultimately reformist. Kramer builds his case on existing values within the gay community and within American society, and his rhetoric operates within a comic frame of acceptance in which "rhetors accept the social order and wish only to correct its failings" (Murphy, 1989, p. 270). Kramer is not asking for social revolution; rather, he wants gays to demand the institutional and governmental resources and attention due them as human beings and as tax-paying citizens. The kind of political activism (e.g., civil disobedience) he encourages toward that end is squarely within the American tradition of social reform.

At the most basic level, Kramer's arguments are traditional in form as well as substance; they depend upon conventional elements such as strong language and powerful evidence. However, these strategies gain new power as they come together to produce perspective by incongruity, and, ultimately, genuine argument. Natanson maintains that:

> the trouble with dichotomizing affection and cognition, feeling and thought, is that the structural features of both are darkened, as though feeling and thinking operated in different locales to be known as the private and the public. The point is that feeling is a way of meaning as much as thinking is a way of formulating. Privacy is a means of establishing a world, and what genuine argument to persuade does is to publicize that privacy. (1965, p. 16)

Kramer's rhetoric makes AIDS an issue of personal moral consequence for his audience, engaging them simultaneously at logical and emotional levels. As Natanson indicates, to ignore the intersections between logic and emotion is to overlook the powerful potential of genuine argument. In "1,112 and Counting," Kramer "publicizes the privacy" of personal identity, interweaving public and personal incongruities to "bring home" the implications of AIDS and to make them impossible to ignore.

The significance of Kramer's rhetorical strategy is linked to Maurice Charland's important insight that rhetoric can work to create its constituency rather than simply appealing to pre-existing, "transcendent subjects" (1987, p. 133). Kramer's use of perspective by incongruity encourages a revision in perspective towards AIDS that, in turn, requires a reconstitution of his audience. As critics' previous analyses of the strategy illustrate, perspective by incongruity does not always entail such a task. In some situations, however, the reorientation asked of an audience is so profound that it cannot be accomplished with a simple shift in position or attitude; instead, it requires a re-evaluation and reconstitution of *self*. This is the point, as Natanson argues, when the public and the private merge, when the lines between public deliberation and personal responsibility blur. Ultimately, genuine argument and constitutive rhetoric are not accomplishments; they are invitations. Charland maintains that "constitutive rhetorics leave the task of narrative closure up to their constituted subjects" (1987, p. 143). At key historical moments, the rhetorical power of such invitations matters a great deal, and it deserves our critical attention.

Notes

[1] Hudson had sought to keep his illness a secret as long as possible, claiming in public statements that he suffered from the flu or from liver cancer. A press spokesperson revealed that Hudson was being treated for AIDS only after hospital officials insisted (See Kinsella, 1989, p. 142–43; Shilts, 1987, pp. 573–578).

[2] The exception to this is the *New York Native*, where Kramer's piece was published. The *Native* had been fairly aggressive in AIDS coverage from the beginning, largely due to the efforts of its part time reporter, Larry Mass, who was also a medical doctor (See Kinsella, 1989, Ch. 2).

[3] The text of "1,112 and Counting" that I use here is reprinted in Kramer, *Reports from the Holocaust: The Making of an AIDS Activist* (1989). I include page numbers from this version in future references to the essay. "1,112 and Counting" originally appeared in the *New York Native*, Issue 59, March 14–27, 1983.

[4] For example, in a 1987 speech at a Boston Lesbian and Gay Town Meeting, Kramer said "AIDS is our holocaust and Reagan is our Hitler. New York City is our Auschwitz" (Kramer, 1989, p. 173).

References

Burke, K. (1954). *Permanence and change: An anatomy of purpose*. 2nd ed. Los Altos, CA: Hermes.

Burke, K. (1959). *Attitudes toward history*. Los Altos, CA: Hermes.

Brockriede, W. (1972). Arguers as lovers. *Philosophy and Rhetoric, 5*, 1–11.

Carlson, A. C. (1986). Gandhi and the comic frame: "Ad bellum purificandum." *Quarterly Journal of Speech, 72*, 446–455.

Charland, M. (1987). Constitutive rhetoric: The case of the *Peuple Québécois*. *Quarterly Journal of Speech, 73*, 133–150.

Cox, J. R. & Willard, C. A. (Eds.). (1982). *Advances in argumentation theory and research*. Carbondale, IL: Southern Illinois University Press.

Ehninger, D. (1970). Argument as method: Its nature, its limitations, and its uses. *Speech Monographs, 37*, 101–110.

Foss, S. (1979). Feminism confronts catholicism: A study of the uses of perspective by incongruity. *Women's Studies in Communication, 3*, 7–15.

Gusfield, J. (Ed.). (1989). *Kenneth Burke: On symbols and society*. Chicago: University of Chicago Press.

Kinsella, J. (1989). *Covering the plague: AIDS and the American media*. New Brunswick: Rutgers University Press.

Kramer, L. (1989). *Reports from the holocaust: The making of an AIDS activist*. New York: St. Martin's Press.

Madsen, A. J. (1993). The comic frame as a corrective to bureaucratization: A dramatistic perspective on argumentation. *Argumentation and Advocacy 29*, 164–177.

Murphy, J. M. (1989). Comic strategies and the American covenant. *Communication Studies, 40*, 266–279.

Natanson, M. (1965). Claims of Immediacy. In M. Natanson and H. W. Johnstone, Jr. (Eds.) *Philosophy, rhetoric, and argumentation* (pp. 10–19). University Park: Pennsylvania State University Press.

O'Connell, S. (1989). The big one: Literature discovers AIDS. In O'Malley, P. (Ed.). *The AIDS epidemic: Private rights and public interest* (pp. 485–506). Boston: Beacon Press.

Rosteck, T. & Leff, M. (1989). Piety, propriety, and perspective: An interpretation and application of key terms in Kenneth Burke's *Permanence and Change*. *Western Journal of Speech Communication, 53*, 327–541.

Shilts, R. (1987). *And the band played on. Politics, people, and the AIDS epidemic*. New York: Penguin.

Solomon, M. (1988). Ideology as rhetorical constraint: The anarchist agitation of "Red Emma" Goldman. *Quarterly Journal of Speech, 74*, 184–200.

Treichler, P. (1908). AIDS, Gender, and biomedical discourse: Current contests for meaning. In Fee, E. & Fox, D. (Eds.). *AIDS: The burdens of history* (pp. 190–266). Berkeley: University of California Press.

Militant Motherhood: Labor's Mary Harris "Mother" Jones
Mari Boor Tonn

There is no more unique personality in the movement. She is at once as gentle as a cooing dove and as fierce as a lioness. She is a grand combination of sweetness and gentility, strength and determination.

—Appeal to Reason, 27 March 1909[1]

From outward appearances, the tiny, white-haired widow seemed more suited to the parlor than to the political platform, to innocent altruism than to incendiary agitation. Yet for fifty years, Mary Harris Jones often spoke several times a day and under all types of adversity in her crusade to elevate the underclass: child laborers, workers in the breweries and mills, streetcar and railroad employees, and even the Mexican Revolutionaries. In 1898 and 1905, respectively, she helped found the Social Democratic Party and the International Workers of the World, industrial labor's most radical wing. But the most stable and well-known of her many associations was with the all-male United Mine Workers of America (UMWA), which first hired her as an organizer sometime before 1900 despite their *de facto* ban on women.

Remarkably, this former schoolteacher and seamstress soon became the industrial labor movement's most sought after, beloved, and effective agitator. Eugene Debs said repeatedly that she had no rival in recruiting union members, organizing walkouts, and sustaining even the most painful of strikes. The enemies of labor agreed. Desperate attempts to curb her incredible influence, however, usually backfired. Jones was most visible, for example, during bloody coal strikes in West Virginia and Colorado during 1912–1914; the repeated deportations, illegal failings, contrived murder indictment, and sexual slander of a woman past eighty further gilded her folk heroine status.

Clues to those forces that propelled Jones into labor agitation and shaped her distinctive approach lie in her tragic, albeit shadowy, past. Born into famine and rebellion in Ireland around 1830, she first lost insurgent family members to execution and exile, later lost her unionist

husband and four children to yellow fever, and finally lost her home, possessions, and dress-making shop to the Chicago fire.[2] On the heels of this last devastation, she found solace and a renewed sense of purpose at a local Knights of Labor shelter, the first labor organization to embrace women as equals. At minimum, this history of survival tempered her disarming courage and cultivated a prickly independent streak which took form in her notorious insubordination and maverick unionism.

On the platform, Jones was the classic charismatic. A spellbinding storyteller, she peopled her rhetoric with both real and folk-tale characters, punctuated it with repartee with audience members (Tonn and Kuhn), flavored it with pathos, and enlivened it with profanity, creative name-calling, and caustic wit. At times, she fashioned props, used visual aids, and orchestrated dramatic stunts for rhetorical effect. At least once, her "bloody shirt" rhetoric moved beyond the metaphorical, sparking violence as the frenzied crowd waved the blood-soaked bits of cloth she tossed them (Lee 29).

This predilection for poetic license extended even to facts about her own life. Her symbolic May 1 birthday, for example, and her accelerated aging were engineered to fit her self-cast leading roles of labor's prophet and matriarch, of which the latter is most salient. Costumed always in matronly black silk and white lace, Mary Harris Jones answered only to "Mother." She called miners her "children," her "boys."

Scholars have noted that other early women reformers at times assumed maternal roles to bolster their ethos and deflect criticism of their speaking and independent lifestyles.[3] Yet few, if any, promoted such a militant version of mother-hood, appropriated it so overtly, dramatically and consistently in every imaginable setting, and performed it for such radical purposes as did Mother Jones. Coming closest were certain other female strike leaders who surfaced after her. Symbolic motherhood as a central and constant rather than occasional strategy in the careers of labor figures such as Jones, Ella Reeve "Mother" Bloor, Leonora "Mother" O'Reilly, the lesser-known Mary "Mother" Skubitz[4] and others suggests that maternal roles had particular efficacy for women as union agitators.

This essay uses Mother Jones as a case study to explore this link between agitation in the industrial labor movement and the use of symbolic motherhood. My central claim is that maternal roles were particularly apt rhetorical strategies for female labor union agitators because agitation and mothering often share two essential dimensions: nurturing and militancy. Although the confrontational and coercive aspects of agitation may be most salient, the intensely personal and relational demands of mobilization efforts in social movements[5] bear striking resemblance to practices identified by anthropologists and feminist scholars[6] as traditionally maternal: physical preservation, fostering of emotional and intellectual growth, and development of group identity and social responsibility. The suitability of these maternal practices to agitation is reflected in the character of many movements' constituencies: individuals who may feel physically threatened, are isolated, suffer from low self-esteem and despair, and may be inexperienced in personal decision-making. In this last respect, Jones's mothering of workers supports and builds upon Bonnie J. Dow's and my argument that a nurturing persona, realized through a rhetorical form Karlyn Kohrs Campbell has termed "feminine," can empower *audiences* by "fostering the growth of the other toward the capacity for independent action" (297). While our analysis of former Texas Governor Ann Richards's nurturing role focuses on audiences who are potentially politically disaffected, Jones demonstrates that a maternal persona may be most forceful in empowering the *severely oppressed*. In this sense, maternal roles assumed by Jones and other labor leaders function similarly to a prophetic role, which can

instill hope of emancipation in seriously defeated listeners.[7]

Conversely, whereas many feminist scholars and critics have fixed upon the tender dimension of maternal nurturing,[8] far less attention has been paid to motherhood's militant face. Yet as mothers in myth, slave mothers, and even animal mothers remind us, maternal love entails the fierce protection of children, often at any cost. Indeed, the need for maternal protectiveness is most pronounced in circumstances in which physical and psychological survival of children is not guaranteed (Collins *Black;* "Shifting"; Green; Christian), conditions outside of those from which many feminists theorize about motherhood. Consequently, while a maternal persona may be warmly nurturing, it also may be confrontational, both in challenging those who threaten a rhetor's constituency and in challenging those audiences themselves to resist.

In what follows, I interpret the significance of Jones's role as "Mother" in the industrial labor movement by correlating maternal purposes with her specific goals as an agitator for coal miners. As performed by Jones, militant motherhood is grounded both in physical care and protection and in a feminine rhetorical style that is at once affirming and confrontational. Stylistically, Jones's militant maternal persona took form through her use of personal experience and personal provocation, narrative and inductive structures, intimate and familial terms of address and *ad hominem* attacks, empathy and shaming, and opportunities for audience imitation including enactment and dialogic dialectics. In concert with her physical mothering, these stylistic properties nurtured a collective "familial" identity for her audience and equipped them with skills and confidence sufficient to resist their oppression.

COAL MINING AUDIENCES

At the outset, coal miners were formidable audiences for Mother Jones in two respects. First, their hostility towards an advocate who was neither male nor a miner was initially severe. By the end of the century, allegiance to the cult of domesticity[9] was particularly strong among immigrant, uneducated, blue-collar males, who felt economically threatened by female workers (Ferguson 170). Among the most fervent opponents of woman's suffrage (Campbell, "Hearing" 42 n21), male-dominated trade unions typically forbade membership by fellow women workers (Bernard 134–136), and the majority championed the "family wage," which rewarded male workers if their wives and daughters remained unemployed (Ferguson 171). Many coal miners also doubted that a woman inexperienced in their particular pain possessed the credentials to champion their cause, an objection Jones occasionally addressed publicly (Steel, *Speeches* 6, 178). In her earliest preserved speech in 1901,[10] Jones criticized labor for its resistance towards women, both as fellow workers and union comrades (Steel, *Speeches* 6). Months later she confided to a comrade "I have come to the final conclusion that these fellows don't want a woman in the field" (Steel, *Correspondence* 16).

Second, the demographic and psychological profile of coal mining audiences made them particularly challenging to mobilize. A mix of nationalities, coal camps festered with ethnic animosity and suspicion, which language barriers intensified. Because employers controlled housing, medical care, schooling, and company stores, miners were inexperienced in making even the most ordinary personal choices. Coupled with generations of poverty, this lack of self-governance inhibited their ability to see and seek alternatives and lowered self-esteem. Furthermore, organizing entailed risks of costly reprisals: termination, blacklisting, loss of nontransferable "scrip" wages and company services, beatings, and even death through starvation or violence (Lee; Mooney). Such desperate conditions bred a deep skepticism that obstructed any outside efforts to improve their lot (Lantz 209–210).

To diffuse the cultural constraints imposed by domestic womanhood and, most importantly, to address the needs of oppressed and dependent miners, Mary Harris Jones recreated herself as the workers' "mother." An adept actress, she consciously appropriated motherhood's genteel physical trappings. Yet she infused the role she came to incarnate with the decided militancy

requisite for her mission. The dissident contours of Jones's version of motherhood were not peculiar to her, however, but reflect a long and continuing mothering tradition.

MOTHERING

Mothering is a diverse and complex practice, to be sure. Nonetheless, most mothers of all stripes appear to share three general goals: securing their children's physical survival, furthering their emotional and intellectual growth and independence, and cultivating their connection and accountability to their social group.[11]

Given these purposes, some scholars claim that mothers and women socialized into "mothering" roles have acquired distinctive cognitive patterns. Carol Gilligan, for example, argues that "maternal morality" arises from a desire "to ensure care for the dependent and unequal" (74). This "ethic of care," similar to Sara Ruddick's "maternal thinking," privileges connection, empathy, and contingent reasoning from concrete experiences over abstract, impersonal, absolute, and linear approaches to problem-solving. Despite justified criticism of their Eurocentric perspective from a number of fronts, Patricia Collins nonetheless identifies similar properties in the epistemological claims of women of color ("Social").

Moreover, this emphasis on care and relationship maintenance influences elements of the private talk and rhetorical choices of many, albeit not all, women. Whereas males often employ economic analogies to describe relationships, for example, women lean toward tending, nurturing, and growing metaphors (Spitzack and Carter 412). In addition, the maternal tasks of intellectual, emotional, and social facilitation have led some women to favor communication forms that encourage others to reason independently and to forge links between their lives and the surrounding world. For example, mother-child interaction commonly includes highly structured language games involving repetition and imitation whereby a child can develop cognitive and communication skills (Bernard 103; Bruner; Ochs). And in both primitive societies and advanced cultures, wisewomen known as "mothers" or "grandmothers" taught and teach through legends, fables, parables, and myths, which contain implied rather than explicit morals (Frye 37–38; Briffault 275; Hurtado 848). Campbell ("Rhetoric," "Femininity," *Man*) argues that many women have transferred such communication skills acquired in private to their public talk, especially if their rhetorical purposes involve personal consciousness-raising, empowerment, and forging alliances.

Despite the relative consistency of the maternal aims of preservation, growth, and socialization across cultures, context always affects which of these goals are emphasized, the ways they are conceptualized and carried out, how personal qualities associated with them become translated, and even who may perform them. Primary among any mother's concern is preserving her child's life. Yet financial and racial privilege has enabled many women to view their children's survival as ensured, minimizing the importance of maternal protection. Although Ruddick, for example, claims to have "extract[ed] the work of mothering from its context" (53), she nonetheless concedes the narrowness of the conditions from which she generalizes. "With adequate care and ... barring extreme poverty, violent racism, physical battering, and war," she writes, "children do, on the whole, survive" (71).

Consequently, dominant maternal images typically ignore mothering's militant face, a fierce otherside occasioned both by systematic oppression and isolated external threats to the welfare of children. As Collins points out, securing both physical and psychological survival of children is *the* focus of motherwork in impoverished, racist, and embattled conditions ("Shifting" 72), circumstances under which women like Jones operated. In such communities, motherhood has always included not just nurturing of children but the pronounced *resistance* against all manner of forces that threaten them.[12] Militant protective love, then, necessarily broadens the maternal "ethic of care" beyond its genteel moorings to include aggressive confrontation and occasional bodily risk. As a consequence, qualities such as self-denial and self-sacrifice traditionally expected of "good" mothers assume new meaning. For "mothers" like Jones who court imprisonment, torture, and even death to protect their "children," self-sacrifice is *literal* and becomes a means to check the excesses of *state* rather than maternal control. Such self-sacrifice, in fact, often heightens rather than contains maternal power and authority, as the sanctified mother figure in slave narratives reveals (Christian 220, 238).

Similarly, militant motherhood significantly refigures the maternal goals of socializing children and fostering their autonomy. Rather than promoting assimilation into the dominant social world, dissident mothers like Jones conceive of "citizenship" as *opposing* those social codes and mores that oppress. Furthermore, while such mothers cultivate independent decision-making skills, they eschew revered individualism that undercuts the force of collective resistance. As Collins explains, those who perform motherwork in oppressive contexts necessarily recognize that "*individual* survival, empowerment, and identity require *group* survival, empowerment, and identity["] ("Shifting" 59) [emphasis added]. This sense of collective identity is nurtured, moreover, in contexts characterized by communal motherwork. There, the collaboration of bloodmothers and various othermothers obscure biological boundaries of the nuclear family to embrace extended as well as fictive kinship networks. Like Jones's union, the substance of family transcends a physical state to become defined primarily by mutual concern and group identity.

As expected, militancy and defiance demand assertive, even aggressive, modes of presentation. Militant mothers not only confront their children's enemy, but must also train their children to do likewise if the threat they face is ongoing and systematic. As a result, the discursive and non-discursive "nurturing" by such mothers typically contains aggressive modeling cues as well as other means of facilitating resistance and survival. Most salient, perhaps, is that mothers who risk enormous danger enact resistance and resilience "for children who will imitate what they see before they can understand much of what is said to them" (Green 213). Yet while these mothers may defer their physical safety to their children's, they are not deferential in the usual sense. Because self-effacement and modesty accommodates powerlessness, dissident mothers may favor bawdy, rowdy, and irreverent personal expression to exercise and enact "a form of power" (Hurtado 848). Such mothers also may bait, tease, and otherwise provoke children in order to acclimate them to attack, to provide practice at fighting back, and to sharpen their emotional control (Miller). The result, then, is a private and public "feminine style" of communication with pronounced confrontational dimensions and contours.

NURTURING AND MILITANCY IN JONES'S MOTHERWORK

Aware of the capacity of naming to constitute, transform, and empower,[13] Mary Harris Jones christened herself "Mother" Jones. The plausibility of her chosen role, however, depended both on her proficiency and the audience's capacity and willingness to respond suitably in the "second persona" (Black 111–113). Because coal trainers were entrapped within a patently paternalistic system, they already functioned, in one sense, as "children." Moreover, by keeping miners subservient through fear, isolation, and near starvation, owners had unwittingly increased their emotional hunger, which made them particularly susceptible to maternal nurturing and protection.

Given these acute needs, Jones actually "mothered" workers: preserving them physically, fostering their personal sovereignty, and socializing them into a collective, the union. In fact, in one of her last recorded speeches, she explicitly encapsulated her agitative mission in the three maternal aims: "I have been in bullpens," she said, "and my only crime was trying to get a better citizen for this nation," one who was *"intellectually, physically, and morally developed"* (Steel, *Speeches* 221) [emphasis added].[14]

Physical Preservation

Preservative maternal love grounded Jones's philosophy. In recollections of the massive 1919 steel strike, for example, she framed the violence and the strike's loss in poetic and starkly polar images: weapons of war and the threatened "children" upon whom war feeds:

> Human flesh, warm and soft and capable of being wounded, went naked up against steel; steel that is cold as old stars, and

harder than death and incapable of pain. Bayonets and guns and steel rails and battleships, bombs and bullets are made of steel. And only babies are made of flesh. More babies to grow up and work in steel, to hurl themselves against the bayonets, to know the tempered resistance of steel (Jones 224).

Protective concern also catalyzed Jones. Her 1915 account of the treatment of imprisoned unionists, herself included, hints at partial explanation for her willingness to sacrifice self for her labor "family": allusions to the loss of her own children, the empathy she felt with other mothers caught in extreme situations, and maternal concern for physical survival of children across circumstances:

> I remember it was raining . . . Rain never means green grass to me; it always means wet babies and pneumonia. And then, again, I remember how they drove the boys out of their cell in the snow without their clothes at the point of the guns. . . .
> [B]ut worst of all, I had to watch [their mothers] that stayed behind. . . . [O]utside [my cell] Mary was calling to me, "Did you see my Johnny?" and I stood there and I knew that children are a terrible thing to have, but a more terrible thing to lose (Barnes 101–102).

On one level, Jones and other mothers here evoke the image of mater dolorosa, the "mother of sorrows." In Käthe Kollwitz's lithographs, this maternal heroine emerges from the devastation of war. Beyond weeping over her son's corpse, she scavenges food to sustain her other children, nurses survivors, and rebuilds her home, "reweaving," Ruddick writes, "the connections that war has destroyed" (142). And as the mater dolorosa "grieves her particular loss," Ruddick claims, "she mourns war itself" (142). Yet Ruddick clarifies that a maternal image confined to resignation and long[-]suffering fails as a "reliable instrument of peace" (156). Although "peace requires standing in solidarity with war's victims . . . [,] the victim's part can too easily be the part of despair and apolitical perseverance"

(157). Endurance and sacrifice must be offset by anger and active resistance of the type which had triggered Jones's imprisonment. Thus, the paradox of maternal thinking, Ruddick explains, is that while it is conducive and committed to a "politics of peace," its protective maternal goal frequently renders it "militaristic" (136). "The sturdiest suspicion of violence is of no avail to threatened peoples who do not have alternative nonviolent ways of protecting what they love . . . ." (139).[15]

Preservative love thus shaped Jones's strategic approach to agitation. Although predating Abraham Maslow, she intuitively understood that the physiological and safety needs of threatened and hungry workers had to be met before appeals to union ideology could be effective. "These men are aggravated to death at times," she told a Congressional Committee in 1914, "and it takes someone who understands the psychology of this great movement we are in to take care of them when they are annoyed and robbed and plundered and shot" (U.S. Cong. 2927). Accordingly, she fed them, tended their sick wives and children, dressed their wounds, and confronted any enemy— armed or unarmed—who threatened their safety. As James Walsh's critical studies confirm ("Approach"; "Paying"), mobilization depends as much on favorable interpersonal contact as on remote ideological appeal. And in the person of "Mother" Jones, union promises to protect, sustain, and improve the physical existence of individual workers became immediate and real.

Jones's fearless protectiveness accompanied her to the platform. An attempt on her life during one speech, in fact, caused her to pause only momentarily (Mooney 68–69). Such steeliness enacted and reinforced the militant mothering tradition she constantly invoked. "Mr. [mine] Superintendent, I am not afraid of your slimy tongue or slimy hand," she announced at a public organizing meeting. "I belong to that type of woman who stood in Boston when they said, 'If you don't stop working for the emancipation of slavery, we will shoot you dead.' The woman said, 'Shoot now. We don't believe in actual slavery'" (Steel, *Speeches* 221–222).

Like those mothers to whom she often proudly pointed, Jones bowed only to the tenets of maternal law, a code she viewed as natural, governing all species, and encompassing both tender nurturing and fierce resistance. "The brute mother," she said in 1913, "suckles and preserves her young at the cost of her own life, if need be" ("Mother Jones Mild"). In her eyes, mothers not only were justified but were obligated to defy any civil statute that violated maternal principles, especially protection of their children. In this sense, Jones and the mothers she described enacted Gilligan's contention that moral judgments of women are often based in issues of survival (74–76) or attempts to preserve significant relationships rather than in concern for following "rules" (44) they may view as arbitrary. Yet Jones's use of maternal principles as warrant for illegal acts and violent self-defense invites careful consideration of what counts as "rules," "justice," and "care." Whereas Gilligan contends that female morality is governed by an ethic of care rather than by principles, rights, and justice, Jones illustrates that care and preserving relationships themselves are principles synonymous with a maternal philosophy of genuine justice. If principled justice and statutory "justice" contradict, militant mothers act according to enduring maternal tenets, which remain tenets nonetheless.[16] For example, to justify her own defiance of court injunctions and her calls to armed retaliation, Jones occasionally used slave mothers who nobly "rose up and defied law, property rights, courts, and everything" to smuggle their children out of bondage (Steel, *Speeches* 77).

In the role of labor union agitator, Jones enacted the challenge Ruddick contends faces those dedicated to maternal principles such as preservative love. That question, she writes, is how such love "latent in maternal practice can be realized and then expressed in *public action* so that a commitment to treasure bodies and minds at risk can be transformed into resistance to the violence that threatens them" (157) [emphasis added]. And in Jones's case, that resistant goal extended beyond her own defiance to include her training of the vulnerable themselves to resist.

Personal Sovereignty

As crippling to coal miners as poverty and disease were their personal qualities: low self-esteem, general hopelessness and fear, and chronic dependency. Accordingly, Jones used communication forms conducive to achieving her maternal aim of fostering her audiences' emotional and intellectual development. Mothering is a constant negotiation among guiding children morally, connecting with them emotionally, and encouraging their self-reliance and self-sovereignty (see Dow and Tonn 289). Consequently, many mothers interact with their children in ways that mirror important aspects of what Campbell has termed "feminine" style, a rhetorical technique with similarities to consciousness-raising efforts used in many movements for purposes of mobilization.

Campbell argues that feminine rhetorical style arose as a strategy to empower female audiences inexperienced in public deliberation, a characteristic also applicable to the developmentally immature such as children and Jones's coal mining constituency. In feminine style, conclusions are based on series of examples, fictional or real-life stories, and comparisons, which encourage listeners to reason independently and act, not just in their interests but also for the welfare of their group—cardinal goals of maternal practice. Audience participation is also encouraged through rhetorical questions or question-answer patterns and by revelations of the narrator's personal reaction, which simulates or even invites dialogue. To create empathy and foster identification, rhetors may move between first, second, and third person as they simultaneously participate in and narrate the story (Donovan), a quality which mirrors much mother to child communication. Moreover, the argument and evidence forms most typically used, such as personal experience, testimony, and enactment, are those accessible to and favored by many mothers. The focus on integrating judgment with empathy and forging and maintaining relationships echoes premises underlying Gilligan's "maternal morality" and Ruddick's "maternal thinking."

The most visible hallmark of Jones's dramatic rhetoric was its intense intimacy, manifested in several features: personal terms of address; inclusive pronouns; personal experience, self-disclosure and enactment as evidence; examples and stories often drawn from the workers' own lives; simulated and even occasional dialogue with audience members; and praise and insults directed at specific individuals. Such characteristics of form, coupled with the dissident content of her talk, reinforced a nurturing persona that was at once tenderly affirming and aggressively confrontational.

Emotional Growth

As "Mother," Jones's union talk encouraged emotional strength in her audiences while maintaining her maternal authority. She always spoke directly to her "boys," often calling audience members by their given names. In so doing, she allowed miners with low self-esteem to feel noticed and cared for as individuals. In response, she would answer only to "Mother," which connected her intimately with her audiences yet strategically gave her power over them. Transcripts of Jones's public performances resonate with affectionate familial exchanges between her and audience members: her frequent reassurances that she as "Mother" would never abandon her charges and their verbalized faith that she indeed would live up to those maternal promises.

Additionally, like many mothers who use linguistic mergers to connect emotionally with their children while encouraging desired behaviors (e.g. "*I* want *us* to put on *our* hat before *you* go outside"), Jones frequently blended her own voice with those of her male listeners. Beyond creating identification, her strategic progressive movement from first, second, to third person induced miners to act: "*I* will give them a fight to the finish and all *we* have to do is to quit being moral cowards, rise up like men and let the world know that *you* are citizens of a great nation and *you* are going to make it great" (Steel, *Speeches* 146) [emphasis added]. At times, she proceeded to an exclusively male voice both to validate the personal feelings of beleaguered miners and to suggest appropriate responses: "*We* are law-abiding citizens, . . . but if a fellow comes to my home and outrages *my wife*, by the Eternal he will pay the penalty. *I* will send him to his God in the repair shop" (Steel, *Speeches* 64) [emphasis added]. This movement among voices illustrates an expressive mode Josephine Donovan claims is typical of many women who have performed mothering or have been socialized into nurturing roles. Yet equally is the militant content and contours of Jones's nurturing talk. She turned the Victorian maternal ideal of fostering "citizenship," which she had appropriated, on its head: responsible citizens obey *just* laws but also actively "fight," "rise up" against, and make others "pay the penalty" for *unjust* practices.

While Jones warmly stroked and connected with her audiences emotionally, she also continually berated miners for their cowardice, questioned their patriotism, and insulted their manhood. At times she even questioned their worthiness to live, arguing that "the bullets which should be sent into your own measly, miserable dirty carcasses, shoot down innocent men [instead]" ("Mother Jones Fiery"). On one level, her constant chiding reflects the irritation that anyone who mothers frequently experiences. Her harsh criticism, however, also may have served an important empowering function for her audiences. In many contexts, caregivers insult and tease children to foster coping skills and relationship formation (Ochs 10; Schieffelin 166), premium qualities in oppressive conditions. Some lower working-class mothers, for example, report balancing sympathy and warmth with belittlement, to cultivate "essential survival skills" in their young, including learning self-defense, self-control, awareness of when and how to speak up, and the strength to fight if necessary (Miller 199–200, 205, 210).[17] Teasing and shaming also can intensify emotional relationships (Schieffelin 166) in that feeling "safe" to tease and be teased by a particular individual indicates that a special relationship exists, is assumed, or is desired (Eisenberg 193). Jones, in fact, occasionally tacitly acknowledged these dual functions of her chidings; to miners in 1909, she couched her criticism as necessary for her union "family" to remain healthy: "No family ever succeeded very well that did not hammer one another once in a while" (Steel, *Speeches* 33).

Coupled with affirming commentary, maternal disapproval and shaming also sets parameters for children and provides a measure against which they can develop a sense of self (Bernard 103). In the process, shaming also heightens parental control by eliciting desired behaviors (Eisenberg 189; Schieffelin 165–166).

"If you are too cowardly to fight, I will fight," Jones often remarked when faced with passive audiences she wanted to act. "You ought to be ashamed of yourselves . . . just to see one old woman who is not afraid of all the bloodhounds" (Steel, *Speeches* 96).

Importantly, however, Jones's irritation and sarcasm was always mixed with a sympathetic and reassuring mercy, a blended quality Ruddick calls "compassion" and defines as "the willingness to . . . devis[e] strategies for reversing failures while forgiving or including those who fail" (99). Ruddick's description of maternal storytellers suggests the significance of compassion for a rhetor like Jones who encountered audiences paralyzed by fear, despair, lack of self-governance, and low self-worth:

> But whatever anger [a compassionate mother] includes in the plot or the telling, she also reveals that she is on her child's side—even when he seems his own enemy . . . . Children who learn about themselves through compassionate stories may . . . [learn] to appreciate the complex humanness of their plight, to forgive themselves as they have been forgiven (100).

Indeed, Jones's compassion and the affection it generated is evident in exchanges during a West Virginia appearance, which begins with Jones's criticism of her audience:

> If you would just use your brains . . . but you do not. (Cries of "Take your time, Mother.") Don't give me any advice. I will attend to you; I will stay with you. (Voice: "I believe you are right.") (Steel, *Speeches* 57).

When directed at the enemy, Jones's bawdy, razor-sharp wit fulfilled other important emotional functions for her sorely defeated audiences. First, humor enabled her to address the seriousness of their lives while providing them with sporadic psychological relief. Stenographic transcripts, punctuated by frequent applause and laughter and occasional requests for talk about familiar targets of her acid tongue, reveal the appreciation of and desire for such catharsis. Second, her humorous attacks on politicians, industrialists, and their wives connected Jones emotionally to her audiences and members to each other. Ann R. Eisenberg explains that caregivers and other family members who use humor, teasing, and sarcasm "reinforce relationships through the alignments created within the episode," such as the special personal connections invited between two persons when a third is made "the outsider" (192). Third, Jones's amusing attacks on the adversary were significant in convincing audiences with low self-esteem of their own worth and power (see Gregg). Obviously, she always depicted the opponents of labor as evil, therefore *worthy* of defeat. Yet as importantly, she also often pictured them as fools, clearly *capable of being beaten*. Humorous ridicule she tendered about a mine operator's wife evidences many of these features: cathartic release by audience members; relational alignment based in class rather than sex; and the opportunity for ego-enhancement occasioned by the enemy's buffoonery and evil:

> I saw one of [the mine owner's wives] coming down the street the other day in an automobile. She had a poodle dog sitting beside her; I looked at her and then looked at the poodle. I watched the poodle—every now and again the poodle would squint its eye at her and turn up its nose when it got a look at her. (Laughter and applause.) He seemed to say, "You corrupt, rotten, decayed piece of humanity, my royal dogship is degraded sitting beside you." She had lived off the blood of women and children.... (Steel, *Speeches* 63).

Finally, Jones's bawdy irreverence enacted powerful resistance for her audiences. Her reputation as "horrible old Mother Jones" she wore with relish rather than apology. "I am horrible, I admit," she said during a public meeting she suspected was infiltrated by the enemy, "and I want to be to you blood-sucking pirates" (Steel, *Speeches* 102). In flagrantly violating prescriptions for passive and pious womanhood, she became the type of dissident maternal role model Green (213) and Hurtado (848) contend are important to and common in oppressed communities. In fact, comments preceding make clear that

Jones intended her unorthodox behavior to serve as tangible evidence to intimidated audiences whom she wanted to purge of their fear. "How scared those villains are when one woman eighty years old, with her head gray, can come in and scare hell out of the whole bunch" (Steel, *Speeches* 96).

Intellectual Growth

The limited vision and underdeveloped problem-solving skills of her audiences propelled Jones, like many mothers, to use language patterns and structures in her public talk to facilitate their intellectual growth. Because the manner in which individuals develop intellectually depends upon the type of interactions and messages to which they are exposed (Ochs 4–6), Jones used narrative and inductive structures to free them from ingrained and oppressive social premises like social darwinism and the protestant work ethic. Many of her stories were poignant accounts of other workers' difficulties and her own extraordinary experiences; others resembled parables or myths. In general, the rhetorical power of stories is their capacity to create empathy, generate self-persuasion, and foster judgment and decisive action as listeners deduce the story's moral and draw connections between the tale and other circumstances (Bennett; Kirkwood). Multiplied, their persuasiveness was further magnified. Through example after example of industrial malfeasance, she helped audiences lay bare the lies that industriousness was invariably and fairly rewarded and only personal flaws such as sloth or sin accounted for their dismal lives. Coupled with stories of improvements won through collective action, these countless vignettes enabled audiences to generalize beyond their personal circumstances, to recognize the political basis of their poverty, and also to fashion hope from their despair.

Embedded within this inductive structure also were communicative patterns in the examples, stories, and other segments which resembled language routines used by mothers and other caregivers to foster intellectual growth. Metaphorically termed "scaffolding," these routines erect linguistic structures by which the immature can "reach" beyond their present cognitive capacity (Bruner 1–19; Ochs 5–6). (In fact, cries from Jones's audience of "Tell it, mamma, I can't" suggest their appreciation of their own limitations and her more experienced skills [see, as example, Steel, *Speeches* 98]). Scaffolding encompasses numerous verbal practices, the most common of which involve providing opportunities for imitation and modeling (Bernard 103; Pawlby 203–224; Ochs 4–6).

Two of Jones's most prominent language scaffolds entailing imitation were simulated dialogue, in which she answered her own rhetorical questions, and "reported speech" and "constructed dialogue" between characters in her stories (Tannen 98–133). The significance of both to her agitative purpose was that each models the dialectical cognitive processes severely dependent workers had to emulate to seize control of their lives. Her use of simulated dialogue in 1915 illustrates this process: "Don't blame the mine owners. I'd skin you, too. . . . if you'd let me do it. They combine, don't they? Sure. Why? Because they realize that as individuals they could not do anything" ("Mother Jones at Jop[l]in" 5). Here Jones structured and controlled the pseudo-conversation so that listeners who were participating vicariously must arrive at her desired conclusion: the powerful *become* powerful through collective action.

In virtually all of her stories, Jones cast thoughts and narrative action in the voices of characters rather than in indirect speech, which Deborah Tannen contends further increases the identification and intellectual engagement stories provide (102–104). And in the vast bulk of them, the reported dialogue occurred during a principal's encounter with an adversary. This motif, Elizabeth Stone contends, typifies stories told in any family struggling with some sort of essential survival (136). "Whatever or whoever the enemy," she writes, "the family stories offer an approach to survival . . . [with] application beyond the particular dramatic moment" (136). In "Mother's" tales, the recurring "approach to survival" offered was using one's wits. In fact, in the coda to a parable about a small boy who had exercised his "gray matter" to unmask an authority figure's dubious claims, Jones explicitly acknowledged that her agitative goal included training workers to reason independent of her, a trait all mothers encourage: "I wouldn't free

you tomorrow if I could. You would go begging. My patriotism is for this country to give to the nation in the day to come highly developed human citizens, men and women . . . [."] (Steel, *Speeches* 220).

The following two tales Jones told about her own experiences in the 1919 steel strike illustrate her usual framing and resolution of dialogic disputes between labor's antagonists and protagonists, the latter of whom was often herself. Moreover, the back-to-back positioning of the tales also suggests her appreciation for repeating structures to provide predictable patterns for cognitive involvement by listeners (Peters and Boggs 84):

> One [steel manager] says, "Now, Mother Jones, this agitation is dangerous. You know these are foreigners, mostly." "Well, that is the reason I want to talk to them. I want to organize them into the United States as a Union so as to show them what the institution stands for" . . . "But you can't do that." . . . I said, "Wait a minute, sir . . . Wasn't the first emigrant that landed on our shore an agitator?" "Who was he?" "Columbus." "Didn't he agitate to get the money from the people of Spain? . . . Wasn't Washington an agitator? Didn't the Mayflower bring over a shipful of agitators? . . . Jesus was an agitator, Mr. Manager. . . ." He never made a reply. He went away. . . .
>
> We went into Pittsburgh . . . ."Did you get permission to make a speech there, [Mother Jones]?" "Sure." "Who did you get the permit from?" "I got it a hundred and forty-three years ago from Patrick Henry, and Jefferson, and Adams, and Washington. . . . I have been using it . . . and am going to use it as long as I am here." I didn't have any lawyer; I didn't pay a penny to the court, nor a fine. . . . I had the goods on them. (Steel, *Speeches* 217–218).

As with simulated dialogue, the reported speech here between Jones and labor's opponents modeled an important cognitive process for listeners inexperienced in making even the most ordinary personal choices. Furthermore, her *effectiveness* here in dealing with establishment figures' challenges was particularly significant for persons constantly fearful of retaliation. In these and myriad other tales, Jones herself personified the archetypal survivor for her audiences, the trickster who has learned to endure through wily cunning (Stone 136).

Like all mothers, however, Jones's encouragement of her audience's self-sovereignty did not license moral anarchy. Maternal work, Ruddick claims, not only nurtures the psychic growth of others but also "disciplines [their] conscience" (148). Indeed, as Jones's talk in both the parable's coda and the interactions with steel managers reveals, personal autonomy always must be checked against more overarching principles, including "citizenship," "patriotism" and general duty to others. The nurturing of civic responsibility, social connections, and general "moral initiative" (Ruddick 108) undertaken by militant mothers, however, always includes dissident themes.

Socialization

Regardless of how effectively Jones administered her first two maternal aims, her crusade was lost if miners failed to unite and exercise their collective might. Consequently, she constantly stressed the maternal aim of forging social identity and group responsibility among her audiences. Kenneth Burke claims that the "concept of family is usually 'spiritualized' [in that] there is the notion of some founder shared in common, or some covenant or constitution or historical act from which the consubstantiality of the group is derived" (29). In Jones's rhetoric, the familial covenant obviously was the union, which the familial terms she used, the appeals she invoked, and the many stories she told helped create and sustain.

As "Mother," Mary Harris Jones helped workers, isolated by geography, ethnicity, and customs, to visualize themselves as a "family," which increased their sense of belonging and moral duty to others. In so doing, she embodied the quality of "holding" Ruddick contends is common to caretakers who must weave a sense of security and family from a life that may be frayed and threadbare. "To hold means to minimize risk and to reconcile differences rather

than to sharply accentuate them. Holding is a way of seeing with an eye toward maintaining the minimal harmony, material resources, and skills necessary for sustaining [the dependent] in safety" (78–79). These important socializing and holding functions are evident in comments Jones made in 1916 before a national UMWA convention punctuated by bickering over procedures for expenditures from the national treasury:

> Some of us are brought up in the mountains; some of us down in the hollows . . . and we cannot survey these things in the same way, and this thing of tearing each other up will have to stop. I want to say to you, Duncan McDonald, you haven't got one dollar in your treasury that belongs to Illinois.[18] It belongs to the miners of this country; every dollar of it belongs to the working men, whether they are miners, steel workers, or train men. That money belongs to us, the working class, and we are going to use it to clean hell out of the robbing class (Steel, *Speeches* 168).

Here also, Jones's union rhetoric contains properties Stone contends are common to talk in natural families: she "defines" membership in the union family, outlines its relationship to the larger world, and provides "ground rules" for its preservation, including the expectation that individual interests be subordinated to the needs of the group.

Also similar to family talk, Jones's union rhetoric always privileged certain behaviors—those she viewed as capable of creating and sustaining the union family—and certain individuals, namely herself. Mothering is not a democratic process, but necessarily hierarchical (Ruddick 72–73). And as Jones's performance demonstrates, mothering occasionally may be authoritarian. Given that internecine strife weakened solidarity and subsequent power, labor's matriarch often scolded malcontents as mothers do their miscreant children, even forcing these feuding unionists (including the national president) to shake hands publicly so as not to "give [the owners] the satisfaction of seeing you have a row . . . ." (Steel, *Speeches* 170). At times, she pulled rank as "Mother" expressly to squelch debate and democratic procedures she regarded as unproductive: "Mother don't permit the contrary [vote]" (Steel, *Speeches* 105).

Again, Jones's talk surrounding parliamentary processes indicates her preference for relational "ground rules," including pecking orders (Stone 111–145), over institutional procedures, a priority Gilligan (44, 74–76) and Ann Wilson Schaef (129) contend is characteristic of female culture. Gilligan, Schaef (113), and Nancy Chodorow (176–180) argue that developing and maintaining relationships define a large portion of identity for many females, especially mothers. Although the emphasis on connection and solidarity might seem a priority of any committed unionist, Jones constantly battled territorial attitudes of union officials and rank and file members who sought to exclude women, Mexican workers, and certain industries from both the movement and specific unions. A speech at the UMWA national convention in 1909 typifies the contrast between her view of the union as an extended, inclusive labor "family" and her audience's more exclusive perspective:

> Some of the delegates took exception to what I said here the other day, [when I] said that Joplin [Missouri] belongs to the Western Federation of Miners. There must be no line drawn. Whenever you organize a man bring him into the United Mine Workers, bring him into the Western Federation of Miners, bring him into the Carpenters' Union—bring him into any union. Whenever you do that you have taken one away from the common enemy and joined him with you to fight the common enemy . . . . I try to bring the farmers with us also, because the stronger we grow numerically the weaker the other fellow grows. I have got no pet organization. Wherever labor is in a struggle with the enemy, the name of the organization cuts no figure with me. . . . (Steel, *Speeches* 33).

Here, Jones's comments reflect characteristics Collins attributes to community othermothers whose "family" extends to embrace all manner of "fictive kin." Such women, she writes, "treat biologically unrelated children as if they were members of their own families"; their "actions demonstrate a clear rejection of separateness and individual interest as the basis of either community organization or individual self-actualization" (*Black* 129, 131). As a symbolic union othermother, Jones explicitly refused to privilege her UMWA "bloodlines" by viewing UMWA coal miners, her "own children," as "pets." The only separation she would recognize was between her working family and its "common enemy." And as always, her maternal nurturing—accomplished by emphasizing social connections and responsibilities to the union "family"—was in the service of clearly militant goals: "to clean hell out of the robbing class," "to fight the common enemy."

Jones's inclusive familial policy, however, was not absolute. A salient way in which families protect the familial institution is through stories of dealing with "black sheep" through censorship or even banishment (Stone 230–234). Because Jones recognized that disloyalty undermined union strength, she frequently shared her own refusal to tolerate the "demon incarnate" traitor, even blood brothers, and admonished audiences to follow suit. Her many tales of excluding labor Judases served a significant socializing function by conveying "not only what [family] members should do, but who they are or should be" (Stone 31).

In constantly pursuing her maternal aims of securing the physical preservation of her charges and fostering their self-sovereignty and social connections, Jones reified union ideology and empowered her audiences. And it was through this process that she also empowered herself.

Maternal Power

Mary Harris Jones's nurturing and boundless protection imbued her with affective power sufficient for hostile miners to accept her. As Raymie E. McKerrow has pointed out, power may be expressed "in nondeliberate ways, at a 'deep structure' level and may have its origins in the remoteness of our past (carried forward through a particularizing discursive formation)" (99). His contention is illustrated in an early incident Jones recounted in her autobiography: "We took [a miner badly beaten by gunmen] to the local hotel and sent for a doctor," she wrote. "I sat up all night and nursed the poor fellow.

He was out of his head and thought I was his mother" (44). In this account the affective power originating in a then absent mother-child relation was called forth, recollected, and revisited by Jones's maternal practice, helping validate her discursive sobriquet of "Mother." Moreover, because needing mothering and being mothered is a universal experience, her care on this and other occasions tapped into a phenomenon Aaron Gresson has termed "shared memory" and considers essential to coalition building for heterogenous groups. The force of shared memory is that it "acts as a springboard, a bridge and vehicle by which individuals and collectives are readied to transcend the existential and historical realities which might separate them" (19). Indeed, Jones at times intimated her acute awareness that her nurturing and protecting of miners had enabled her to overcome their initial hostility towards her and each other and lead them. "I look after them," she told a New York reporter in 1913, describing her concrete physical and emotional care of them and their families. "[A]nd I understand how to *handle* them" (Foner 494) [emphasis added].

The intense affective power that Jones's care of workers generated in turn fueled the union's political power, a phenomenon which adds another facet to the perspective that the personal and political intersect. Edwin Black has argued that audiences who accept a rhetor's chosen persona become susceptible to the ideology and arguments the role and its complementary "second persona" suggest (111–113). Consequently, those workers who accepted Jones's familial role and her claim that "every man is a duplicate of his mother" (Steel, *Speeches* 221) became compelled to match her collective care and her militant courage in enacting that concern. As a result, she frequently appealed to intense maternal allegiance to prompt acts of solidarity and resistance. "No matter what the punishment, stick to your principles, boys," she said, "and you will always be true boys of Mother Jones" (Steel, *Correspondence* 344). And always, appeals to maternal loyalty or motherly disappointment contained a militant edge as illustrated in final lines from a poem about a "clan" from which she sometimes quoted: "God grant that the woman who suffered for you, Suffered

not for a coward, but Oh, for a *fighting* man" (Steel, *Speeches* 104) [emphasis Jones's].

IMPLICATIONS

A central issue animating much public address scholarship involving female speakers is the constant negotiation between social expectations of women's roles and the competing expectations of their public missions (see, as examples, Campbell *Women*, introduction and entries; *Man*; Campbell and Jerry). Some critics have argued that invoking motherhood may help neutralize this paradox for women speakers, which on one level Mother Jones obviously confirms. Yet while symbolic motherhood may ease this reconciliation, this analysis reveals that motherhood itself may require skillful rhetorical negotiation. As Chodorow points out, women in various circumstances must constantly mediate and develop transitions between nature and culture or, put differently, between their lived experiences and social definitions of their roles (180). Because dominant maternal images often conflict with rhetorical purposes, the effectiveness of motherhood as a rhetorical strategy hinges, in part, on how successfully a speaker can both appropriate and contest those images.

As "Mother," Jones negotiated between the powerful, prevailing ideology of genteel, domestic Womanhood and her public agitative mission. To identify with male audiences most committed to sex-segregation, she appropriated the physical accoutrements, the familial and domestic language, the self-sacrificing expectations and facilitative duties, and even certain political philosophies, such as opposing woman suffrage,[19] associated with idealized, home-bound Victorian motherhood. Yet the militant mothering she practiced was far from this decorous and retiring prototype. Rather, Jones's motherhood was a necessary mix of protective fury and nurturing that involved both warm validation and aggressive confrontation. And in this sense, she incarnated a dissident mothering tradition practiced in oppressed communities around the globe, latent in many mothers of all circumstances, and impervious to time-bound classification. In fact, as evidenced in the mythic figure of Demeter, nurturing and agitation are not antithetical but fuse in archetypal mother-hood. Infuriated by the abduction of her beloved daughter, Persephone, the grieving goddess of fertility coerced her child's return by imposing famine on the world (Gilligan 22–23). Likewise, it was not just in symbolic motherhood per se, but in her caring and confrontational version of it that Jones found the admixture of warmth and dominance, accommodation and authority considered maximally effective in leadership.

Yet while this analysis acknowledges this often inescapable negotiation for women rhetors between reigning ideology and lived experiences, Jones nonetheless demonstrates that lived experiences may have power sufficient to *transcend* potent cultural constructs. Because her effectiveness resulted from her performance of the mother-child relation rather than the mere invocation of a powerful cultural symbol, she invites a fuller consideration by rhetorical and feminist critics of the sources and ends of motherhood's power. Numerous feminist scholars astutely have pointed out that motherhood since Victorian times has been a highly politicized institution constructed to control the female sex by prescribing behaviors for all women regardless of circumstance or capacity and desire to bear and rear children (see Stearney for overview). Yet McKerrow correctly cautions against limiting critiques of power to such domination theses. "It is equally the case that power is not only repressive but potentially productive," he writes, and "that its effects are pervasive throughout the social world . . . ." (101). Because Jones incarnated mothering, her maternal persona can be understood best by considering how "symbols come to possess power—what they 'do' in society as contrasted to what they 'are'" (McKerrow 104). The point is that what motherhood as a potent social symbol is (or how symbolic motherhood has come to hold power) cannot be divorced entirely from what real mothers in all sorts of circumstances *do*. The iconic status of motherhood that many rhetors have tapped for ethos purposes, after all, is not merely the result of an idealized ideological construct, but also is rooted in emotional responses to caregivers who have provided both nurturing and protection. This exploration of multiple sources of power and its various purposes requires a shift

in critical focus from what McKerrow describes as the traditional speaker-orientation of "public address" to a potentially more illuminating analysis of *"symbolism which addresses publics"* (101) [emphasis McKerrow's]. A critical rhetoric asks not just what a rhetorical strategy will do for speakers, but what discursive and non-discursive practices enable a speaker to do for audiences. In the process, such a perspective can reveal the generative, reciprocal property of power. Certainly, Jones fashioned her role as "Mother," in some measure, to combat confining sex-role expectations of her time. Yet it is doubtful that a detached symbol alone, however ideologically potent, was sufficient in persuading hardbitten coal miners to accept her and to risk starvation and even death to heed her call to join the union. Rather, the affective power engendered by Jones's nurturing and fierce protection dissolved the initial resistance to her and imbued her with authority sufficient to lead an economic revolution.

Finally, while Jones's mothering of workers strengthens the connections between "feminine" style and women's culture, it also further broadens the conceptual scope and appreciation of that style and the breadth of the female culture from which it has arisen. Jones may offer the best example to date of the declining usefulness in many distinctions between private and public communication and discursive and non-discursive practices. In important respects, Jones actually became the workers' mother and coal camps became her home. Yet this analysis of Jones's confrontational "feminine" style also builds upon earlier critical work which has pointed to differences between feminine rhetorical style and the talk specific to women's consciousness-raising groups from which Campbell generalizes. Those studies illustrated the ways in which feminine rhetorical style can involve hierarchical rather than purely egalitarian relationships between speaker and audience and can be used to advance patently programmatic rather than exclusively process-oriented goals (Dow and Tonn; Tonn and Kuhn). Likewise, Jones's militant mothering reveals that rhetorical qualities like overt confrontation and personal provocation can actually increase identification and empower audiences to think critically and act boldly rather than escalate their alienation and submissiveness as Campbell ("Rhetoric" 78) intimates. Moreover, Jones's maternal role demonstrates that hierarchy, confrontation, and the desire to change others are not properties exclusive to a "rhetoric of patriarchy" as Sonja K. Foss and Cindy L. Griffin (4) maintain but are qualities also common to "maternal" culture (see Ruddick 72–74). Nor are "efforts to change others" concurrent with a "desire" for personal "domination" or "devalu[ing] the lives and perspectives of those others" (Foss and Griffin 3).

Jones's militant mothering reveals instead that the opposite may be true; assistance with self-transformation can *value* the lives of others and can empower them to *resist domination.* To be sure, the effectiveness of confrontation and appeals to authority in achieving political ends with audiences inexperienced in deliberation depends upon how skillfully those properties are offset by other characteristics: personal affirmation, appeals to personal authority, and assurances that political changes can reap personal rewards on the most fundamental level. Indeed, Jones's embodiment of motherhood reveals that caregiving and its "ethic" is always a complex *balance* of multiple polarities: authority and independence, holding and letting go, tenderness and fierce protection, mercy and justice, emotion and intellect, expressiveness and instrumentality, tolerance and tough-mindedness, and so on (Bernard 348–365; Dow and Tonn 297; Ruddick 108). And as importantly, Jones's militant motherhood points to how context ever and always figures significantly in weighing that balance.

Notes

1 "Mother Jones Here."
2 The biographical material repeated here is that most consistently reported from various sources (Fetherling; Foner; Jones; Long; Steel, *Correspondence*). Many facts about her life remain speculation, including her age, birthday, and the circumstances surrounding the deaths of her family. Jones often altered "details" for rhetorical purposes such as to increase her authority or to build identification with all-male audiences.
3 Appeals to motherhood were common in the rhetoric of female reformers (Conway 164–177), especially suffragists like Elizabeth Cady Stanton (Griffith 195–196).
4 Skubitz was known primarily in the mining camps of southeast Kansas where she occasionally joined with Jones in organizing marches by strikers' wives.
5 Campbell "Rhetoric," "Femininity"; Walsh "Approach," "Paying"; Tonn and Kuhn; Blumer; Toch.
6 Briffault; Ryan; Ferguson; Ruddick.
7 Japp's study of Angelina Grimké's assumption of a prophet persona in her 1838 speech reveals its primary function to be ethos-building. However, when a prophet persona becomes a hallmark of an individual's rhetoric as with Marcus Garvey, Martin Luther King, Jr., and even Mother Jones, the role's more significant function is audience empowerment.
8 For example, although Ruddick acknowledges the need for militant resistance by mothers in extreme circumstances, Dow and I do not draw upon this aspect of her argument in our analysis of the nurturing function of Richards's rhetoric. Nor does Gilligan's discussion of "the ethic of care" include militant demands of maternal care.
9 The middle-class standard of purity, piety, domesticity, and submissiveness described by Barbara Welter ironically became a measure for women in all kinds of circumstances, slavery included (see Jacobs 54–56, Sells 341). Boris's analysis of debates over homework laws in 1953 not only reveal the ideal's application to working-class women but also its tenacity.
10 I have checked speech texts from UMWA minutes and various archival collections (see Tonn 238–241) against other sources, and, unless otherwise noted, use Steel (*Speeches*) to identify excerpts from the thirty-one surviving complete texts of Jones's speeches. Steel includes no congressional testimony or speech extracts from newspapers.
11 With limited exceptions, these aims appear consistent across cultures regardless of whether the mothers are slave mothers, white, middle-class mothers, or animal mothers (Bernard 69, 94, 103; Briffault; Ruddick; Shaw). I acknowledge the facts of infanticide and abandonment by women who wish to escape unwanted mothering. I also admit that a minority of mothers neglect and even physically abuse their children. Social sanctions levied against them, however, indicate such actions violate "normal" or "acceptable" behavior.
12 Collins "Shifting," *Black;* Christian; Fabj; Green.
13 (Burke 3–7; Cassirer 36, 132–134). See Steel (*Speeches* 65) for Jones's appreciation of the power of titles.
14 She made a similar remark in a speech in 1916 (Steel, *Speeches* 177).

[15] In her later life, Kollwitz herself, in fact, casts this militant dimension of motherhood in bronze. *Tower of Mothers* "depicts a circle of defiant mothers, arms outstretched, joined to protect the children massed behind them" (Ruddick 159).

[16] Celeste Condit also contends that abortion decisions by women indicate they apply moral principles that may differ from male principles (179–180).

[17] Mary Garrett argues insulting contests practiced by African-American adolescents fulfill similar functions (313).

[18] McDonald was a delegate from an Illinois district, who had co-sponsored a resolution to investigate the financial management of the national union.

[19] Jones made occasional comments that raised questions about her genuine beliefs about women's fitness for politics. Her official stance against woman's suffrage has several plausible explanations. Primary was her need to identify with male audiences. She also appeared to resent the time, money, and energy other crusades siphoned away from the labor movement. The class-stratification of the suffrage movement deepened her disaffection. Moreover, she expressed bitter disappointment that Colorado women, who had received the vote in 1893, had not used it to improve the lives of their state's workers. Finally, she often commented on the general failure of the ballot to produce necessary change.

Works Cited

Barnes, Djuna. *Interviews.* Ed. Alyce Barry. Washington, DC: Sun and Moon, 1985. (The interview with Jones included in this anthology occurred on February 7, 1915.)

Bennett, Lance. "Storytelling in Criminal Trials: A Model of Social Judgment." *Quarterly Journal of Speech* 64 (1978): 1–12.

Bernard, Jessie. *The Future of Motherhood.* New York: Dial P, 1974.

Black, Edwin. "The Second Persona." *Quarterly Journal of Speech* 65 (1970): 109–119.

Blumer, Herbert. "Social Movements." *Studies in Social Movements: A Social Psychological Perspective.* Ed. Barry McLaughlin. New York: The Free P, 1969, 8–29.

Boris, Eileen. "Mothers Are Not Workers: Homework Regulation and the Construction of Motherhood, 1948–1953." *Mothering: Ideology, Experience, and Agency.* Eds. Evelyn Nakano Glenn, Grace Chang, and Linda Rennie Forcey. New York: Routledge, 1994, 161–180.

Briffault, Robert. *The Mothers.* Abr. Ed. G. R. Taylor. New York: Macmillan, 1959.

Bruner, Jerome. "The Ontogenesis of Speech Acts." *Journal of Child Language* 2 (1975): 1–19.

Burke, Kenneth. *A Grammar of Motives.* 1945. Berkeley: U of California P, 1969.

Campbell, Karlyn Kohrs. "The Rhetoric of Women's Liberation: An Oxymoron." *Quarterly Journal of Speech* 59 (1973): 73–86

———. "Femininity and Feminism: To Be or Not to Be a Woman." *Communication Quarterly* 31 (1983): 101–108.

———. "Hearing Women's Voices." *Communication Education* 40 (1991): 33–48.

———. *Man Cannot Speak for Her: A Critical Study of Early Feminist Rhetoric,* Vol. 1. New York: Greenwood, 1989.

———. (Ed). *Women Public Speakers in the United States, 1800–1925: A Bio-Critical Sourcebook.* Westport, CT: Greenwood, 1993.

Campbell, Karlyn Kohrs and E. Claire Jerry. "Women and Speaker: A Conflict in Roles." *Seeing Female: Social Roles and Personal Lives.* Ed. Sharon Brehm. New York: Greenwood, 1988. 123–133.

Cassirer, Ernst. *An Essay on Man: An Introduction to a Philosophy of Human Culture.* New Haven, CT: Yale UP, 1944.

Chodorow, Nancy. *The Reproduction of Mothering: Psychoanalysis and the Sociology of Gender.* Berkeley: U of California P, 1978.

Christian, Barbara. *Black Feminist Criticism: Perspectives on Black Women Writers.* New York: Pergamon, 1985.

Collins, Patricia Hill. "The Social Construction of Black Feminist Thought." *Signs* 14 (Summer 1989): 745–773.

———. *Black Feminist Thought: Knowledge, Consciousness and the Politics of Empowerment.* New York: Routledge, 1991.

———. "Shifting the Center: Race, Class, and Feminist Theorizing about Motherhood." *Representations of Motherhood.* Eds. Donna Bassin, Margaret Honey, and Meryle Mahrer Kaplan. New Haven, CT: Yale UP, 1994, 56–74.

Condit, Celeste Michelle. *Decoding Abortion Rhetoric: Communicating Social Change.* Urbana and Chicago: U of Illinois P, 1990.

Conway, Jill. "Women Reformers and American Culture, 1870–1930." *Journal of Social History* 5 (Winter 1971–1972): 164–177.

Debs, Eugene V. "To the Rescue of Mother Jones!" *Appeal to Reason.* 3 May 1913, 1.

Donovan, Josephine. "Towards a Women's Poetics." *Tulsa Studies in Women's Literature in Feminist Issues in Literary Scholarship* 2 (1984): 99–111.

Dow, Bonnie J. and Mari Boor Tonn. "'Feminine Style' and Political Judgment in the Rhetoric of Ann Richards." *Quarterly Journal of Speech* 79 (1993): 286–302.

Eisenberg, Ann R. "Teasing: Verbal Play in Two Mexicano Homes." *Language Socialization Across Cultures.* Eds. Bambi B. Schieffelin and Elinor Ochs. New York: Cambridge UP, 1986, 182–212.

Fabj, Valeria. "Motherhood as Political Voice: The Rhetoric of the Mothers of Plaza De Mayo." *Communication Studies* 44 (1993): 1–18.

Ferguson, Ann. "On Conceiving Motherhood and Sexuality: A Feminist Materialist Approach." *Mothering: Essays in Feminist Theory.* Ed. Joyce Trebilcot. Towata, NJ: Rowman and Allenhead, 1984. 152–182.

Fetherling, Dale. *Mother Jones, The Miners' Angel: A Portrait.* Carbondale, IL: Southern Illinois UP, 1974.

Foner, Philip S., ed. *Mother Jones Speaks: Collected Writings and Speeches.* New York: Monad, 1983.

Foss, Sonja K. and Cindy L. Griffin. "Beyond Persuasion: A Proposal for Invitational Rhetoric." *Communication Monographs* 62 (1995): 1–18.

Frye, Northrop. *The Critical Path: An Essay on the Social Context of Literary Criticism.* Bloomington: Indiana UP, 1973.

Garrett, Mary M. "Wit, Power, and Oppositional Groups: A Case Study of 'Pure Talk.'" *Quarterly Journal of Speech* 79 (1993): 303–318.

Gilligan, Carol. *In a Different Voice: Psychological Theory and Women's Development.* Cambridge, MA: Harvard UP, 1982.

Green, Beverly. "Sturdy Bridges: The Role of African-American Mothers in the Socialization of African-American Children." *Woman-Defined Motherhood.* Eds. Jane Price Knowles and Ellen Cole. New York: Harrington Park, 1990. 205–225.

Gregg, Richard. "The Ego-function of the Rhetoric of Protest." *Philosophy and Rhetoric* 4 (1971): 71–91.

Gresson, Aaron D.[,] III. "Phenomenology and the Rhetoric of Identification—A Neglected Dimension of Coalition Communication Inquiry." *Communication Quarterly* 26 (Fall 1978): 14–23.

Griffith, Elisabeth. *In Her Own Right: The Life of Elizabeth Cady Stanton.* New York: Oxford UP, 1984.

Hurtado, Aida. "Relating to Privilege: Seduction and Rejection in the Subordination of White Women and Women of Color." *Signs* 14 (1989): 833–855.

Jacobs, Harriet A. *Incidents in the Life of a Slave Girl, Written by Herself.* Ed. L. Maria Child. Cambridge, MA: Harvard UP. 1987.

Japp, Phyllis M. "Esther or Isaiah?: The Abolitionist-Feminist Rhetoric of Angelina Grimké." *Quarterly Journal of Speech* 71 (1985): 335–348.

Jones, Mary Harris. *The Autobiography of Mother Jones.* Ed. Mary Field Parton. Chicago: Charles Kerr, 1925.

Kirkwood, William G. "Parables as Metaphors and Examples." *Quarterly Journal of Speech* 71 (1985): 422–440.

Lantz, Herman R. with J. S. McCrary. *People of Coal Town.* New York: Columbia UP, 1958.

Lee, Howard B. *Bloodletting in Appalachia.* Morgantown: West Virginia U Library, 1969.

Long, Priscilla. *Mother Jones, Woman Organizer.* Cambridge, MA: Red Sun, 1978.

Maslow, Abraham H. *Motivation and Personality.* 1954. 3rd ed. San Francisco: Harper & Row, 1987.

McKerrow, Raymie E. "Critical Rhetoric: Theory and Praxis." *Communication Monographs* 56 (1989): 91–111.

Miller, Peggy. "Teasing as Language Socialization and Verbal Play in a White Working-Class Community." *Language Socialization Across Cultures.* Eds. Bambi B. Schieffelin and Elinor Ochs. New York: Cambridge UP, 1986. 199–212.

Mooney, Fred. *Struggle in the Coal Fields: The Autobiography of Fred Mooney.* Morgantown: West Virginia U Library, 1967.

"Mother Jones at Jop[l]in." *The Workers' Chronicle* 17 Sept. 1915, 5.

"Mother Jones Here." *Appeal to Reason* 27 Mar. 1909, 4.

"Mother Jones Fiery." *The Toledo Bee* 25 Mar. 1903.

"Mother Jones, Mild Mannered, Talks Sociology." *New York Times* 1 June 1913, Sec. V, 4.

Ochs, Elinor. "From Feelings to Grammar: A Samoan Case Study." *Language Socialization Across Cultures.* Eds. Bambi B. Schieffelin and Elinor Ochs. New York: Cambridge UP, 1986. 1–13.

Pawlby, Susan J. "Imitative Interaction." *Studies in Mother-Infant Interaction: Proceedings of the Loch Lomond Symposium, Ross Priory, University of Strathclyde, September, 1975.* Ed. H. R. Schaffer. New York: Academic P, 1977. 203–224.

Peters, Ann M. and Stephen T. Boggs. "Interactional Routines as Cultural Influences upon Language Acquisition." *Language Socialization Across Cultures.* Eds. Bambi B. Schieffelin and Elinor Ochs. New York: Cambridge UP, 1986. 80–96.

Ruddick, Sara. *Maternal Thinking: Towards a Politics of Peace.* New York: Ballantine, 1989.

Ryan, Mary P. *The Empire of the Mother: American Writing About Domesticity 1830–1860.* New York: Institute for Research in History and Haworth, 1982. Harrington Park, 1985.

Schaef, Ann Wilson. *Women's Reality: An Emerging Female System in the While Male Society.* San Francisco: Harper and Row, 1981.

Schieffelin, Bambi B. "Teasing and Shaming in Kaluli Children's Interactions." *Language Socialization Across Cultures.* Eds. Bambi B. Schieffelin and Elinor Ochs. New York: Cambridge UP, 1986, 165–198.

Sells, Laura R. "Maria W. Miller Stewart (1803–1879), First African-American Woman to Lecture in Public." *Women Public Speakers in the United States, 1800–1925: A Bio-Critical Sourcebook.* Ed. Karlyn Kohrs Campbell. Westport, CT: Greenwood, 1993. 339–349.

Shaw, Stephanie J. "Mothering under Slavery in the Antebellum South." *Mothering: Ideology, Experience, and Agency.* Eds. Evelyn Nakano Glenn, Grace Chang, and Linda Rennie Forcey. New York: Routledge, 1994, 237–258.

Spitzack, Carol and Kathryn Carter. "Women in Communication Studies: A Typology for Revision." *Quarterly Journal of Speech* 73 (1987): 401–423.

Stearney, Lynn M. "Feminism, Ecofeminism, and the Maternal Archetype: Motherhood as Feminine Universal." *Communication Quarterly* 42 (1994): 145–159.

Steel, Edward, ed. *The Correspondence of Mother Jones.* Pittsburgh: U of Pittsburgh P, 1985.

———, ed. *The Speeches and Writings of Mother Jones.* Pittsburgh: U of Pittsburgh P, 1988.

Stone, Elizabeth. *Black Sheep and Kissing Cousins: How Our Family Stories Shape Us.* New York: Times Books, 1978.

Tannen, Deborah. *Talking Voices.* New York: Cambridge UP, 1989.

Toch, Hans. *The Psychology of Social Movements.* Indianapolis: Bobbs-Merrill, 1965.

Tonn, Mari Boor. "Mary Harris 'Mother' Jones." *Women Public Speakers in the United States, 1800–1925: A Bio-Critical Sourcebook.* Ed. Karlyn Kohrs Campbell. Westport, CT: Greenwood, 1993. 229–241.

Tonn, Mari Boor and Mark S. Kuhn. "Co-constructed Oratory: Speaker-Audience Interaction in the Labor Union Rhetoric of Mary Harris 'Mother' Jones." *Text and Performance Quarterly* 13 (1993): 313–330.

United States. Cong. House. Subcommittee of the Committee on Mines and Mining. *Conditions in the Coal Mines of Colorado.* 63rd Cong., 2nd sess. H. Res. 387 Washington, DC: GPO, 1914, II.

Walsh, James F., Jr. "An Approach to Dyadic Communication in Historical Social Movements: Dyadic Communication in Maoist Insurgent Mobilization." *Communication Monographs* 53 (1983): 1–15.

———. "Paying Attention to Channels: Differential Images of Recruitment in Students for a Democratic Society, 1960–1965." *Communication Studies* 44 (Spring 1993): 71–86.

Welter, Barbara. "The Cult of True Womanhood: 1820–1860." *American Quarterly* 18.2 (1966): 151–174.

Inventing Citizens, Imagining Gender Justice: The Suffrage Rhetoric of Virginia and Francis Minor

Angela G. Ray and Cindy Koenig Richards

Test cases that oppose social and institutional power have been a marked feature of U.S. legal history. Such cases have crystallized the connections between the law, political culture, and the lived experiences of citizens, and also have illuminated the abyss between expressed principles and enacted practice. During the nineteenth century, abolitionists, woman's rights activists, and civil rights advocates sought to redress grievances through the courts, offering interpretations of the law that represented fundamental challenges not only to predominant legal conceptions but also to commonly accepted practices of inclusion and exclusion. Several of these ambitious cases reached the U.S. Supreme Court. In *Scott v. Sandford, Bradwell v. Illinois, Minor v. Happersett,* and *Plessy v. Ferguson,* for example, reform-minded advocates challenged prevailing notions of citizenship—its definitions, parameters, and implications for human experience.

In all of these cases, however, the plaintiffs and their advocates were defeated in court. Amid ongoing cycles of expansion and contraction of the parameters of the polity, the judicial rulings manifested backlash. In the 1850s the Supreme Court did not validate the citizenship status of Dred Scott and Harriet Robinson Scott.[1] In the aftermath of civil war, the U.S. Congress passed the Reconstruction Amendments (the Thirteenth, Fourteenth, and Fifteenth), overturning the *Dred Scott* decision, formally defining U.S. citizens as "all persons born or naturalized in the United States," asserting greater powers for the federal government, and inaugurating what Sanford Levinson has called "at least a limited constitutional revolution."[2]

In this milieu, woman's rights activists, seeking to fulfill revolutionary promises for themselves, pressed the courts to define the privileges of citizenship as applying to all citizens regardless of sex. In Illinois Myra Bradwell sued for the right to practice law, and in Missouri Virginia Minor sued for the right to vote. Both the *Bradwell* and *Minor* cases received a hearing by the U.S. Supreme Court in the 1870s, introducing gender as an explicit category in Supreme Court decision-making and forcing previously hidden assumptions about the separate class called women into the light of jurisprudential day.[3] Yet the postwar Court did not endorse Bradwell's petition to practice the occupation for which she had prepared and did not accept the legality of Virginia Minor's effort to register to vote.[4] The *Minor* decision, which acknowledged women's status as citizens but denied that citizenship entailed voting rights, dealt a blow to women's political participation that would only be overturned after forty-five years of additional agitation, culminating in the Nineteenth Amendment.[5]

Two decades after *Minor*, when Homer Plessy sought a judicial ruling that would disallow racial segregation and restore the promise of the Reconstruction Amendments, the Court interpreted the equal protection clause of the Fourteenth Amendment to uphold segregationist practices.[6] Judicial opinions generated in these cases established pernicious precedents, committing symbolic and sometimes literal violence on large groups of people whose interests challenged the hegemonic order.[7]

Negative precedents, however, are not the only consequences of such cases. As scholars like Jules Lobel note, risky cases that contest dominant social mores can inspire political action and support social movements, can model alternative conceptions of justice, and can "nurture a culture of constitutional struggle." The goal of the test case, Lobel notes, is "broader than victory alone."[8] Activists who would employ legal action as a mechanism of social reform must confront the competing pressures of pragmatism versus idealism, of realistic assessment of outcomes versus an informed hope in legal possibility. They must find ways creatively to blend rhetorics of accommodation and audacity.[9] Furthermore, the results of such cases can be measured not only in the content of judicial opinion but also in the imagined potentials for new performative action that they can make possible for people who regularly endure inequity.

In cases such as *Scott, Bradwell, Minor*, and *Plessy*, those who sought inclusion for themselves or for others in the political, legal, and civil systems of the time engaged the Constitution to impart progressive visions of political subjectivities and actions. These test cases illustrate the potential for rhetoric that embraces traditional political texts, language, and principles to promote the imagination and enactment of new forms of political being. As they embraced the language of the law to advocate the expansion of citizenship rights, these individuals presented themselves not as rebels but as patriots, as reformers who revered the law and sought to extend its beneficence rather than as revolutionaries seeking its overthrow. They engaged the law as community members, not outsiders, and the plaintiffs' rhetorical performances enacted their capacity to be what it was argued they were or should be: free, participating members of the polity.[10] At the same time, litigators and plaintiffs alike rendered incisive critique of the community's accepted practice, and their rhetorical actions demonstrated that "the law" was not a monolith but rather a versatile resource in a rhetorical culture characterized by constitutional struggle.[11]

This essay demonstrates the ingenuity, the complexity, and the challenges of litigating a nineteenth-century test case that sought to expand the legal definition and performative parameters of citizenship. In order to illuminate the rhetorical power of legal argument developed by and on behalf of oppressed persons and to illustrate the capacity of argument that "failed" in law to promote changes in public, political cultures, we offer an in-depth analysis of the landmark case *Minor v. Happersett*. We begin with a historical narrative, showing how this test case emerged within the tumultuous political culture of organized woman's rights advocacy in the Reconstruction era. The advocacy that led to the case voiced and embodied the possibility of a new political subjectivity: that of the woman as active citizen-voter.

After examining the context in which this new role was developed and expressed, we trace the evolution of the Minor arguments more specifically, focusing on the development of a hermeneutic process as a rhetorical strategy, a strategy that offered a politically viable image of gender justice.[12] This interpretive process claimed the emancipatory power of written texts and asserted the authority of individuals rather than hierarchical institutions to read those texts correctly.[13] Although this interpretive process was vested with the capacity to reform the governing meaning of the law, it was regularly articulated as "simple" reading, as seeing the Constitution for what it was, and, most important, as a model for reading that could easily be learned and reproduced by others. In the Minor arguments, we see evidence of a hermeneutic strategy that exhibited reverence for traditional, canonical texts. It also produced interpretations contradicting dominant readings, but represented those interpretations as recognition of preexistent truth rather than as a challenge to standard precepts. This rhetorical performance actively justified changes in political behavior and implied a transformation of practice and the fundamental alterations of the political identities of millions of U.S. citizens.

The efficacy of the Minors' constitutional interpretation relied on the symbolic figure of the citizen. This role as developed in the Minors' arguments constituted a political subjectivity that women could imagine and actively perform. Therefore, following our explication of the discursive resources and hermeneutic process used by the Minors, we delineate the development of the new political subjectivity of the citizen that emerged through their rhetoric.

Specifically, we consider how the Minors articulated the categories of race and sex in relation to their universalist understanding of the citizen. Finally, we consider how the Minors' hermeneutic performance promoted political faith in the promise of the Constitution to guarantee equal rights to all citizens and in the capacity of women to engage in political meaning-making. These contributions to social change were much greater than a failed legal effort.

"WE CLAIM A RIGHT, BASED UPON CITIZENSHIP"

At St. Louis's Mercantile Library Hall on October 6, 1869, Virginia Louisa Minor, the president of the Missouri Woman Suffrage Association, rose to speak at the association's first convention. Out-of-state visitors included Susan B. Anthony and Julia Ward Howe. Minor proclaimed that the U.S. Constitution gave her, as a native-born U.S. citizen, "every right and privilege to which every other citizen was entitled." Saying that she did not come to plead for her right to the franchise—refusing to crave a "boon"—she instead demanded that her "birth-right" be recognized. "I am often jeeringly asked," she said, "'If the constitution gives you this right, why don't you take it?'" Her response to the derisive challenge was that she would do just that. Representing womanhood, she would seize her right to vote and, if necessary, would pursue the case to the U.S. Supreme Court and "ask it to make us in our rights as citizens."[14]

At the same convention, attorney Francis Minor, Virginia's husband, presented six resolutions supporting the principle that the U.S. Constitution already enfranchised women. Others, notably Massachusetts senator Charles Sumner, had long claimed that the original Constitution enfranchised the entire U.S. citizenry. The Minor Resolutions relied on the preamble and articles 1, 4, and 6 of the original Constitution, as well as the recently adopted Fourteenth Amendment, which created rhetorical resources for a decisive statement that would eventually land the question before the highest Court. Section 1 of the Fourteenth Amendment defined U.S. citizens as "all persons born or naturalized in the United States, and subject to the jurisdiction thereof," and thus Minor could resolve that the "privileges and immunities" of citizenship were "national in character and paramount to all state authority."[15]

The key to the argument—its power and its weakness—was that citizenship entailed voting rights.[16] Although most legislators and jurists denied the linkage, there was enough contrary rhetoric to make the question a contested one. On the one hand, the Constitution at this point provided for rights of individuals to vote only for members of the U.S. House of Representatives, and Reconstruction-era legislators debated the constitutional authority of the federal government to affect the voting rights of freedmen. On the other hand, in 1823 a U.S. Circuit Court judge had defined the franchise as one of the privileges of citizenship; and in congressional debates on the Fourteenth Amendment in 1866, opponents had expressed fears that section 1 would make suffrage accessible to African American men.[17] In popular public discourse, the assumption of a correlation between voting and citizenship was not uncommon; some woman's rights advocates, for example, had argued from this premise since the late 1840s.[18]

Therefore, in a rhetorical culture in which definitions of the "privileges and immunities" of citizenship were contested, the resolutions offered at the woman suffrage convention in St. Louis in 1869 proved persuasive among many activists, eliciting enthusiasm and promoting direct action. The resolutions were adopted by the convention and were circulated nationally through the pages of Elizabeth Cady Stanton and Susan B. Anthony's weekly newspaper, the *Revolution*. In a letter to the paper, Francis Minor explained the stylistic, performative consequences of such an interpretation of the Constitution. Speaking of the woman suffrage associations, he wrote of a new rhetorical style emerging from a new political subjectivity: "We no longer beat the air—no longer assume merely the attitude of petitioners. We claim a right, based upon citizenship." According to Minor, then, women, like men, were properly understood as political actors who could assertively make demands, not supplicants who timorously approached their rulers with requests. Minor called for women to act as individual

citizen-voters, testing the merits of the case in registry offices, polling places, and courtrooms.[19] Identifying the optimism and the innovation of these approaches, suffragists referred to the strategy as the New Departure, and other Reconstruction-era activists soon supplemented the Minors' work with additional legal claims of women to the ballot.[20]

Woman's rights advocates like Anthony were still reeling from the postwar betrayal of congressional Republicans, who had failed to produce expected legislation enfranchising women. Instead, while attempting to secure the political rights of freedmen, Republicans had introduced the word *male,* apparently describing the legal voter, into the Constitution for the first time, in section 2 of the Fourteenth Amendment.[21] In congressional debates on the amendment, legislators had discussed whether women could appropriately be voters, with one senator dismissing the question on the grounds that "the law of nature" prevailed over politics, keeping women and children from the polls.[22] Within the organized woman's rights movement, support for or opposition to the amendment created significant rifts. The American Equal Rights Association (AERA), founded in 1866 by former antislavery activists and woman's rights activists to agitate for universal suffrage, disbanded in 1869. Woman's rights advocates formed two associations. The New York–based National Woman Suffrage Association (NWSA) formed in May 1869, and its members included Elizabeth Cady Stanton, Susan B. Anthony, Josephine Griffing, Matilda Joslyn Gage, and Virginia Minor. The NWSA rejected male leadership and supported broad reforms, including immediate, universal suffrage. The Boston-based American Woman Suffrage Association (AWSA) first convened in November 1869. Its members included Lucy Stone, Henry Blackwell, Thomas Wentworth Higginson, and Julia Ward Howe; the AWSA consented to the leadership of men and accepted that suffrage for black men should precede woman suffrage.[23] The anger at former allies in Congress and the painful dissolution of the AERA coincided with a period of especially virulent racist and ethnocentric rhetoric on the part of a number of white women activists, including Stanton.

Amid the turmoil of Reconstruction politics and activist conflict, the advent of the New Departure presented exciting possibilities for a redirection of focus, argument, and strategy. For members of the NWSA in particular, the Minor Resolutions held out the expectation that the amendment that had seemed to be an instrument of women's oppression could become, when read aright, a catalyst for political freedom. Such a hopeful strategy echoed that of the radical constitutionalists of the 1830s and 1840s; their interpretive practices sought to convert the Constitution into an antislavery text.[24] The Minor arguments also offered the potential to reject the framing of race versus sex—a particularly dreadful forced choice for African American women activists—and instead provided a legal foundation for universal suffrage. Although some Reconstruction-era woman suffragists feared that the focus on achieving the vote through the courts would unduly remove pressure from legislators, others became avid supporters of the principles and the performative strategies that they implied. Ten thousand copies of the issue of the *Revolution* containing the resolutions were printed and circulated, dramatically expanding the scope of potential influence. Further, in 1870 the NWSA adopted the Minors' strategies as official policy, and Stanton presented the arguments to a congressional committee considering suffrage in the District of Columbia.[25]

The Minors' constitutional interpretation also precipitated a brief period of insistent rhetoric by women activists and provided a foundation for public, political action, as hundreds of disenfranchised women throughout the country demanded the right to register and vote.[26] This campaign of direct action was novel, assertive, and widespread. From Connecticut to California, Ohio to Oregon, Maine to Missouri, New Hampshire to North Carolina, women appeared at registry offices and polling places. They included Abigail Scott Duniway in Portland, Oregon; Sojourner Truth in Battle Creek, Michigan; Mary Ann Shadd Cary in Washington, DC; Isabella Beecher Hooker in Hartford, Connecticut; and Susan B. Anthony in Rochester, New York.[27] Although Anthony's 1872 vote and her subsequent arrest and trial are the events best known to today's scholars

of rhetoric—primarily because of her dramatic public speech "Is it a Crime for a U.S. Citizen to Vote?"—it would be Virginia Minor who would initiate the test case that would result in a judicial resolution by the Supreme Court in 1875.[28]

In 1872 Virginia Minor attempted to enact the citizenship for which she and Francis Minor argued. On October 15 she presented herself before St. Louis registrar Reese Happersett and requested to be registered as a voter. Happersett refused to honor her request "because she was not a 'male' citizen, but a woman." Virginia Minor, whose sex and marital status made it impossible for her to bring suit by herself in a Missouri court, joined with her husband and sued Happersett for denying her, "as a citizen of the United States and of the State of Missouri," the "elective franchise."[29] The Minors were represented by attorneys John M. Krum, John B. Henderson, and Francis Minor himself.[30] The case was heard in the St. Louis Circuit Court, the same court that had first ruled in Dred Scott and Harriet Robinson Scott's case in 1850.[31] The Circuit Court denied the Minors' petition in 1872, a decision upheld by the Missouri State Supreme Court in 1873. The case reached the docket of the U.S. Supreme Court in the October term of 1874 and was called on February 9, 1875. On March 29, the Court's unanimous decision in *Minor v. Happersett,* written by first-term Chief Justice Morrison R. Waite, accepted that women were citizens but disconnected citizenship from the franchise, supported the authority of states to deny voting rights, and ensured the necessity of a federal amendment for women's enfranchisement.[32]

The Minors' rhetoric addressed not only judicial authorities but also women citizens. The arguments that they espoused and performed asked how citizenship should be conceptualized and how it should be enacted. The message to the two audiences was the same, but the potential actions that each could take in response were profoundly different. Keeping those two audiences in mind—the one wielding the power of the violent word, the other seeking inclusion that would radically subvert existing ideologies—we delineate the contours of the Minors' arguments. Using hermeneutics as a rhetorical strategy, presenting themselves as readers—and, as such, as models inviting other readers—they engaged constitutional law and U.S. history, and they rhetorically created a symbolic citizen, offering a new political subjectivity for women to envision and enact. Reading sacred democratic texts and public history, the Minors developed a complex portrayal of citizenship as a gender-neutral, race-neutral political role that encompassed the right to full participation, expressed via the public ritual of voting.[33] Their complex interpretation, however, was presented as simple logic: Women are citizens; citizens participate in self-government; the mechanism for self-government is the franchise; women can and should vote. Suffrage, as represented through the Minors' hermeneutic practice, became a guaranteed right rather than a contested privilege.

HERMENEUTICS AND THE SOURCES OF CITIZENSHIP

Although Reconstruction-era judges who engaged in constitutional decision-making often relied on a mode of originalism—that is, a process of seeking the original intent (the presumed beliefs) of framers of the Constitution of 1787—the Minors favored a strong textualism, seeking legal meaning within the law's language itself.[34] Yet from 1869 the Minors rhetorically venerated the Founders, and, especially after the Missouri Supreme Court decision, they argued about the intentions and beliefs of the men who participated in the framing and ratifying of the Constitution of 1787. Although this engagement with originalism was a pragmatic response to opposition arguments presented by the judiciary, it created logical inconsistencies, challenging the Minors' expressed assumptions of the centrality of the constitutional text over extra-constitutional history. Still, although the exigencies of the case produced contradictory logics, the Minors' hermeneutic practice remained the same: whether the objects of their reading were legal texts or historical narratives, they offered interpretations presented in the guise of simple apprehensions of preexisting truth—change framed as conservation, subversion performed as reverence.[35] They read the Constitution as a text, and they framed historical

narrative as a text susceptible to their hermeneutic operations as well.

In their legal arguments, convention speeches, and publications, the Minors drew principally on two discursive resources in order to articulate their interpretation of citizenship in support of woman suffrage: constitutional law and historical accounts of its origins.[36] Reading the language of the law and historical narrative to mean that citizenship rendered the elective franchise a fundamental right, the Minors' constitutional hermeneutics asserted that a simple error in comprehending categories wrongly deprived women citizens of their right to vote.[37]

According to the Minors, women of the United States were excluded from the franchise owing to widespread misunderstanding of the characteristics of state and federal citizenship. In their case, a local official denied Virginia Minor the right to register to vote on the grounds that she, as a female citizen of Missouri, was subject to a state prohibition upon her participation in a federal election. Rightly understood, the Minors asserted, the dual nature of citizenship rendered such restrictions void. States had the power to regulate—but not to prohibit—the rights guaranteed to national citizens by the Constitution. Thus the practice of denying the franchise to women in federal elections illustrated a failure to comprehend the parameters of the category of federal citizen. Women citizens of the United States were properly "entitled to all the privileges and immunities of citizenship, chief among which is the elective franchise."[38]

For the Minors, citizenship could not be partial, and any exclusions from federal citizenship rights had to be made explicit in federal law. The Minors insisted that the definition of citizenship required that its privileges be applied equally and fully. In 1869 Virginia Minor told the Missouri Woman Suffrage Association that if women "are entitled to two or three privileges [of citizenship], we are entitled to all." The Minors' argument to the U.S. Supreme Court elaborated this point: "There can be no *half-way* citizenship. Woman, as a citizen of the United States, is entitled to *all* the benefits of that position, and liable to all its obligations, *or to none.*"[39] Further, they relied on the authority of venerated Founders for the precept that absence of a positive declaration of a right is not synonymous with prohibition. Virginia Minor observed in 1869 that the absence of the word *woman* in the Constitution is not proof of the exclusion of women from public life, quoting John Jay: "Silence nor blank paper, neither give nor take away anything." A few months later Francis Minor wrote to the *Revolution,* paraphrasing the Ninth Amendment: "In framing a constitution, the people are assembled in their sovereign capacity; and being possessed of all rights and all powers, what is not surrendered is retained." Francis Minor quoted John Jay and Alexander Hamilton, noting Hamilton's observation of "the wide difference between silence and abolition."[40]

In the brief to the U.S. Supreme Court, the Minors relied on this doctrine to dismiss the efficacy of the word *male* in the Fourteenth Amendment's second section. Since women, as "'citizens of the United States,' are embraced in, and protected by, the broad language of the Amendment," the use of the word *male* in a clause about proportional representation has no bearing on women's fundamental citizenship rights, they claimed.[41] The focus of section 2, on this reading, had the narrow purpose of establishing penalties for noncomplying states and did not negate the broader principle of section 1. The Minors consistently argued for and enacted a hermeneutic practice that dismissed absence. Law was a positive declaration, they said. Absent explicit categorical exclusions in federal law—which, they argued, were constitutionally illegal—citizens of all races and both sexes possessed voting rights.

When read according to a hermeneutic practice that dismissed absence, law and history disclosed what the Minors deemed to be the uncorrupted meaning of *citizenship.* Moreover, their interpretation of the Constitution and U.S. history implied that practices that categorically denied the franchise to women contravened preexisting law, the doctrine of self-government, and the principles of venerated Founders. The Minors' early arguments for woman suffrage demonstrated high regard for the words and democratic faith of the founding generation. Jay and Hamilton were invoked as revered figures who articulated well the standards to which a republic must adhere if it is to endure. However,

in the Missouri State Supreme Court ruling against their case, the Minors were met with a specific challenge to their rhetorical veneration of the framers of the Constitution of 1787. The court's opinion, by Judge Henry M. Vories, took issue with rhetoric that broadly situated constitutional authors, past or present, as supportive of woman's rights. Rather than addressing the Minors' claims about the principles of eighteenth-century framers, Vories cited the recent adoption of the Fourteenth Amendment as an example, writing:

> When we take in consideration the history of the times in which this amendment was originated, and the circumstances which in the view of its originators produced its necessity, we will have but little trouble, it seems to me, to give it its proper interpretation. . . . It was not intended that females or persons under the age of twenty-one years should have the right of suffrage conferred on them.[42]

Such an argument had rhetorical force. After all, most of the men who drafted the Reconstruction Amendments were living and capable of reporting what they had "intended." In 1871 Congressman John Bingham, a central figure in the crafting of the Fourteenth Amendment, wrote a House report rejecting New Departure arguments.[43] By invoking the intentions of congressmen who wrote, debated, and endorsed the Fourteenth Amendment, Vories challenged the Minors' emphasis on the Philadelphia framers' words and espoused principles.

In responding to the Missouri ruling in their brief for the U.S. Supreme Court, the Minors had several lines of argument open to them. They could have dismissed the relevance of the intentions of both the framers of the Constitution of 1787 and the crafters of the Reconstruction Amendments and made a strong textualist argument, relying solely on the power of the Constitution's words. In a related vein, they could have attempted to distinguish between "intended" principles recorded in legal language and the personal beliefs of constitutional authors.[44] They chose neither. Instead, working within the originalist legal milieu of their day, they applied their hermeneutic process to the subject of U.S. history, interpreting written records of past events as evidence of the eighteenth-century framers' unexpressed support of women's citizenship rights. In their argument before the U.S. Supreme Court, the Minors cited in favor of their case the history of the times in which the federal Constitution originated and the purported intentions of individuals involved in framing and ratifying the Constitution of 1787.

Beginning with the claim that "the chief difficulty in this case, is one of fact rather than of law," the Minors' Supreme Court brief identified uninformed, habitual practice, not the Constitution, as the primary obstacle to Virginia Minor's victory. The Minors thus situated their position as an argument for the correct interpretation and application of the Constitution, rather than an effort to alter the sacred law by judicial means. This opening emphasized an important aspect of the hermeneutic practice of the Minors: the assertion that their interpretation simply revealed the correct reading of the law and history. Proceeding thus to build a case for the enfranchisement of female citizens, the brief suggested that "in order to get a clearer idea of the true meaning of this term citizenship, it may be well to recur for a moment to its first introduction and use in American law."[45] The argument then turned to three elements of history in support of the Minors' case: the political circumstances in which the term *citizenship* emerged, statements by members of conventions that framed or ratified the Constitution, and voting practices in the early United States. That is, they offered not only an alternative reading of venerated texts but also an alternative interpretation of recorded history.

The Minors' political etymology of *citizenship* suggested that the term's significance was rooted in the meaning of the American Revolution. They observed that prior to independence residents of the thirteen colonies were called "subjects," a term that corresponded to their political duty to serve the sovereign of Great Britain. When the Declaration of Independence fundamentally changed the political rights, roles, and responsibilities of Americans, the term *citizen* was invoked in place of *subject*.

This, according to the Minors, was not a mere change of name but a manifestation of the radical change that Americans brought forth by revolution and the inscription of the democratic value of self-government. This political revolution meant that, in the United States, "all persons born or naturalized therein and subject to the jurisdiction thereof" would be *citizens*: not subject to the rule of a sovereign but entitled without distinction to the right and privilege of becoming "their own sovereigns or rulers in the government of their own creation."[46]

Citizenship of this nature, the Minors' brief went on to explain, was guarded and maintained by the most significant of all political rights: suffrage. Given that voting was the civic practice through which democratic self-government and the privileges of citizenship were secured, the Minors held that it was to the federal Constitution that one must look for any limitations placed upon the political rights of citizens, with the understanding that "a limitation not found there, or authorized by that instrument, cannot be legally exercised by any lesser or inferior jurisdiction."[47] Here the Minors demonstrated a consistent form of hermeneutic engagement with constitutional language and political history. Together with an insistence that exceptions and exclusions not explicitly articulated in the Constitution were irrelevant, the Minors maintained that courts must observe the statements through which authors of the law articulated democratic principles rather than attempt to intuit meaning from silence.

Challenging the state of Missouri's authority to prohibit woman suffrage, the Minors explicitly drew upon the words of revered Founders. The Minors quoted the writings of James Madison and the arguments of Madison and James Monroe from the debates in Virginia's ratification convention to show that states were granted the power merely to supervise, not to control, the franchise. Citing Madisonian language, they asserted that any course that would deny suffrage to women "violates the vital principle of free government, that those who are to be bound by laws, ought to have a voice in making them."[48] Further, they cited Luther Martin, a delegate to the Constitutional Convention of 1787, as an early advocate for equal suffrage for all citizens of the United States. Martin, they noted, took as a democratic precept

> that when . . . individuals enter into government, they have *each* a right to an *equal voice* in its first formation, and afterward have *each* a right to an equal *vote* in every matter which relates to their government; . . . *every person* has a right to an *equal vote* in choosing that representative who is entrusted to do for the whole, that which the whole, if they could assemble, might do in person.[49]

In the representation offered by the Minors' brief, individuals involved in the framing and ratifying of the Constitution described self-government as a fundamental principle of democratic republicanism in the United States, and although they did not write explicitly about gender in the passages quoted, they used inclusive terms like *individual* and *person*. The brief utilized statements such as these to evince reverence for patriots such as Madison, Monroe, and Martin, while situating these individuals as advocates for equal, participatory citizenship.

Finally, as evidence for the assertion that the individuals who framed, debated, and ratified the Constitution of 1787 understood suffrage to be a fundamental right of citizenship, the Minors' brief provided an alternative history of voting practices in the early United States. Although they observed that nothing could more clearly emphasize the necessity of equal suffrage than the authoritative words of Founders, the Minors conceded, "It may be asked: If this be so, why was not the question [of woman suffrage] sooner raised?" The Minors characterized this question as moot, based on the fact that white women in New Jersey were recognized as legal voters and cast ballots for members of the Constitutional Convention of 1787, for the ratification of the U.S. Constitution, and in the first five presidential elections. In view of this history, the Minors claimed that woman suffrage was not explicitly opposed by Founders of the United States. Noting that the framers of the Constitution were very much alive at this time—and some were residents of New Jersey—the Minors emphasized the absence of any contemporary mention

of votes for women being unconstitutional. Pointing to the constitutional authors' historical silence on the question of woman suffrage—in an age when their female neighbors were voting for or against the Constitution itself—the Minors maintained that, had the Founders been opposed to woman suffrage, they would have explicitly excluded women from the franchise.[50] This was perhaps the least credible aspect of the Minors' argument, although it offers a clear illustration of the difficulty of simultaneously advocating reverence and challenge.[51]

The Minors' rhetorical choice to conflate their assertion that courts should read constitutional language for what it makes explicit—not what it omits—with arguments about the intent of Founders regarding woman suffrage was a perilous one. Not only did the arguments about the Founders strain credulity, but the emphasis on intention deflected the import of the textualist strategy. The turn to history worked against the Minors in judicial decisions, which invoked more widely accepted political history to rule against woman suffrage. Claiming the unexpressed intentions of founding men as an argument for woman suffrage detracted from the Minors' powerful claim that the language of the Constitution, when read aright, clearly enfranchises citizens without regard to sex or race. However, this is not to suggest that the Minors were entirely misguided in their decision to venerate and invoke the Founders. Given their strategy to situate woman suffrage as a practice in line with democratic principles and necessary to self-government, seeking evidence in national heritage was a logical tactic. Indeed, there was probably much to gain—politically, rhetorically, and legally—by clearly linking the Minors' position with that of male Founders.

The Minors might have been better served by emphasizing a revolutionary spirit of equality rather than claiming that those who framed and ratified the Constitution of 1787 specifically supported gender justice, or by avoiding the issue of historical practice to focus entirely upon principles and constitutional language.[52] Nonetheless, it is important to note that they exhibited consistency in their interpretation of constitutional language and historical narrative. In each instance, their hermeneutic practice gave new meaning to venerated words while dismissing silence as a basis for legal precedent. The Minors demonstrated that, when considered without the governing, habitual assumption that women ought not to vote, neither the Constitution nor the words of its original authors excluded women from fundamental privileges of citizenship. Moreover, the Minors concluded that "the words, not lightly uttered, nor to be by us lightly considered," of the Constitution's framers revealed that

> when it comes to the practical recognition of these rights at the ballot-box, all are included. "The House of Representatives shall be composed of members chosen every second year by the PEOPLE of the several States," not by a part—not by the "males"— but simply by "the people of the several States." The same "people" who ordain and establish that Constitution as the supreme law of the land, they are to do the voting, they are to elect. There is not one word as to sex. The elector, male or female, must be one of the people or citizens, that is all.[53]

Highlighting the inclusive term *people*, the Minors demonstrated an interpretive procedure of considering possible word substitutions and ensuing variant meanings. Noting the absence of restrictive language, they invited the Court to emulate their hermeneutic process and to accept their conclusions. Furthermore, even after the demise of the case, such interpretive strategies could continue to serve as models for other woman's rights advocates.

Taken as a whole, the Minors' etymology of *citizenship*, reverential reference to the words of Madison, Monroe, and Martin, and evidence that women voted in the early United States provided a lesson in an alternative history that promoted a particular theory of legal interpretation. Specifically, their reading of historical texts and practices suggested that neither voting precedents nor state restrictions upon the franchise could legitimately deny a woman citizen her constitutionally guaranteed right to participate in self-government. Moreover, the Minors held, the federal Constitution alone could impose limitations upon the political rights of citizens of the United States. Searching the Constitution for explicit exceptions to the fundamental right to vote, they claimed, was the only legitimate basis on which the Justices could decide *Minor v. Happersett*.[54] Although the Minors represented this statement as historical fact, it was the interpretive theory upon which their case rested.

INVENTING THE WOMAN CITIZEN

The Minors' interpretive theory relied on a symbolic reformulation of the federal citizen, to one who possessed no characteristics of race, sex, regional or national origin, socioeconomic status, or religion that were relevant to the government. However, paradoxically, the Minors highlighted categories of sex and race as meaningful responses to public culture and public argument. In the Minors' rhetoric, like that of other nineteenth-century reformers who sought social change through the courts, the venerable Constitution and the revered past existed in a sacred realm. The fallen world, which needed to be made right, was the realm of assumptions and practices that failed to live up to constitutional idealism. That is, the terms of the Minors' argument required an emphasis on categories that were presumed to be irrelevant by their own premises, as a means of demonstrating the errors of practice that failed to coincide with precept.

Of course, the Minors were not the only woman suffragists to make the argument that citizenship was a gender-neutral, race-neutral status. At the 1866 formation of the AERA Elizabeth Cady Stanton had asked: "Has not the time come…to bury the black man and the woman in the citizen, and our two organizations in the broader work of reconstruction?" At a meeting the following year, she reiterated the point: "There are no special claims to propose for women and negroes.…[A]n argument for universal suffrage covers the whole question, the rights of all citizens."[55] The word *bury* has ominous connotations, especially in light of subsequent political events that created a forced choice between supporting the enfranchisement of black men only and supporting the enfranchisement of all women. Nonetheless, Stanton's legal logic was clear: in a republic, a citizen's rights to participation should not depend on personal characteristics like sex or race. The arguments of Virginia and Francis Minor resonated with the same impulses. Through interpretations of constitutional law and U.S. history, the Minors spoke of a woman citizen as an example of a person, not as a member of a separate class or as a peculiar being. They focused their arguments narrowly on woman's political relationship to her government. Concentrating on legal definitions, they deftly avoided discussions of women's biological attributes, theological status, or social circumstances.[56]

Although the Minors defined citizenship without reference to a citizen's personal characteristics, the political context of the Reconstruction era and the Minors' own focus on the political rights of women required explicit discussion of demographic groups. Indeed, the Minors offered an interpretation of the history of the adoption of the Fourteenth Amendment—and an interpretation of the amended Constitution—that made explicit analogies between black men and women (all women? white women?) that at times were based on an assumption of equivalence and, more rarely, were based on an assumption of hierarchy, with (white?) women preferred.

The precise demarcation of the category "woman" in the Minors' rhetoric is difficult to discern. White, well-to-do plaintiff Virginia Minor was presented to the courts as a representative of "all womanhood," and yet, in passages designed to resonate with Missouri law, her specific characteristics as a "native-born free white citizen" and a taxpayer were also emphasized.[57] The Minors restricted their discussion of African Americans to men, as the voters directly affected by the Reconstruction Amendments. Since they did not refer explicitly to African American women as part of their case, it is not clear whether women of color were routinely embraced under the term *woman* as it was used by the Minors. Grammatically and logically they were, but culturally and contextually this reading is less certain.[58] To the extent that the Minors' arguments represented Virginia Minor as an emblem of womanhood, her personal characteristics as a white taxpayer were elided with those of the symbolic woman citizen.[59]

The Minors' reliance on the analogy between (all? white?) women and black men increased markedly as they progressed through the courts and elicited judicial opinions about the "true meaning" of the Fourteenth Amendment. Three years before her attempt to register to vote, Virginia Minor described for the Missouri Woman Suffrage Association the history of faulty understandings about whether free African Americans were U.S. citizens, covering the period 1821–62. Citing U.S. and state attorneys-general who ruled that they were not, and finally one who ruled that they were, Minor noted: "It took forty-one years to make this simple discovery." The term *discovery* implies recognition of a preexistent truth—a coming to consciousness, not a progressive evolution in judicial practice. She made the analogy to women explicit when she said: "I have cited all these examples to show you that all rights and privileges depend merely on the acknowledgment of our right as citizens." Such rights did not depend on a revolutionary alteration of available rights but on the discovery that such rights already existed—a discovery by powerful men of the judiciary, not, Virginia Minor noted with refutative irony, by "illogical, unreasoning women, totally incapable of understanding politics."[60] Virginia Minor's analogy between free black men and "us" as women is one of simple equivalence: they were always citizens, and judicial authority took forty-one years to figure that out. We too are citizens; let us direct judicial authority to make another discovery.

The Supreme Court of Missouri decided against the Minors partly on the grounds that the Fourteenth Amendment was irrelevant to women. That amendment, Judge Vories ruled, was designed "to compel the former slave States" to ensure that the "freedmen" were "equal with other citizens before the law."[61] In response, the Minors offered to the U.S. Supreme Court an alternative interpretation, one that eclipsed race and sex and simultaneously developed more fully an analogy between black men and (all?) women. The Minors' brief stated that the Fourteenth Amendment "was designed as a limitation on the powers of the States" and hence protected "*all* the citizens of the United States . . . in the enjoyment of their privileges and immunities."[62] The link between voting and citizenship preexisted Reconstruction, according to this argument.

Although the Fifteenth Amendment, adopted in 1870, could be read as sign evidence that the Fourteenth Amendment did not enfranchise the freedmen, the Minors rejected this possibility. Its negative language ("The right of citizens of the United States to vote shall not be denied or abridged . . . on account of race, color, or previous condition of servitude") should be read, they argued, as evidence that the Fifteenth Amendment assumed a preexisting right, which it simply reinforced. The Fourteenth and Fifteenth Amendments did not make voters of black men. Rather, according to the Minors' logic, they were made voters by being encompassed under the Fourteenth Amendment's explicit definition of *citizen.* Citizenship, the Minors argued, meant voting rights even under the terms of the original Constitution, and the Fifteenth Amendment protected this right. In another example of attempting to generate an expansion of freedom from instruments of oppression, the Minors' brief cited Roger B. Taney's 1857 opinion in *Scott v. Sandford* that "if persons of the African race are citizens of a State, and of the United States, they would be entitled to all of these privileges and immunities [of citizenship]." Demonstrating again a hermeneutic practice of substitution, the Minors invited a replacement of terms: "Now, substitute in the above, for 'persons of the African race,' *women,* . . . and you have the key to the whole position." Later they connected "privileges and immunities" with voting via a powerful quotation from the Court's majority opinion in the 1873 *Slaughter-house Cases:* "The negro having, by the Fourteenth amendment, been declared a citizen of the United States, *is thus made a voter in every State of the Union.*"[63]

The Minors' brief labeled the Missouri law denying the ballot to women unconstitutional "discrimination":

> It cannot be pretended that the Constitution of the United States makes, or permits to be made any distinction between its citizens in their rights and privileges; that the negro has a right which is denied to the woman. The discrimination, therefore, made and

continued by the State of Missouri, of which we complain, is an unjustifiable act of arbitrary POWER, not of right.[64]

The argument for voting rights as a privilege of citizenship was thus built on the analogy of the black man, protected by the Fifteenth Amendment in his preexisting right to the franchise, and all women, also encompassed under the gender-neutral, race-neutral definition of *citizen* in the Fourteenth Amendment. Paradoxically, the form of the claim in the brief resonated with the pervasive ethic of white supremacy, although usually the Minors' arguments maintained the functional equivalence of white women and black men as political actors.

Moving from an analogy to a claim of equivalence permitted the Minors to identify woman's disenfranchisement as "a badge of servitude"; they argued that continued denial of voting rights to women would violate the Thirteenth Amendment, which legally abolished slavery. Under Missouri law, a married woman was unable to own property without her husband's consent; the Minors' brief adduced this fact to demonstrate "how utterly helpless and powerless her condition is without the ballot." The qualities of self-respect and self-protection, presented as reasons for extending the franchise to African American men in the aftermath of the Civil War, were emphasized by the Minors as equally applicable to women.[65]

The Minors were usually scrupulous in avoiding fruitless arguments about which classes of people suffered the greatest oppressions, although arguments for universal suffrage were occasionally transformed into assertions of the purportedly superior claims of white women to the ballot. This was more noticeable in Virginia Minor's speech to the 1869 Missouri Woman Suffrage Association than in Francis Minor's legal briefs. Although Virginia Minor implied a status of political equivalence between black men and white women, she reflected the anger and resentment common among many white, native-born woman's rights advocates of the postwar period when she spoke of foreign males. Offering a hypothetical case in a slippery-slope argument, she claimed that if women citizens could be denied the vote, then a noncitizen "Chinaman" could be elevated above her to "vote and represent her in Congress." She also questioned the status of naturalized male voters: "Is it presumable to suppose that a foreign citizen is intended to be placed higher than one born on our soil?" Similarly, she noted that in 1856 Native Americans had been deemed to be not citizens but "domestic subjects" and thus were not liable to taxation. She compared woman's legal status with that of "the savage" and found woman to be treated more unjustly, since she was unable to participate in making the laws by which she was governed but was still subject to those laws, particularly the laws of taxation.[66] Further, the Minors' Supreme Court brief included an unsubstantiated claim that "woman's condition is even more helpless" than the condition of the freedman.[67] These attributes of the Minors' rhetoric suggest the ethnocentric, racist, and classist assumptions common in much postwar woman's rights rhetoric produced by middle- and upper-class whites. Virginia Minor, a white native-born taxpayer, was figured as a representative woman citizen. The *a fortiori* argument was clear: if she is not a suitable voter, then U.S. republicanism is in trouble. Of course, specifying her characteristics as representative also undercut natural rights claims, by implying that some people deserved suffrage and thus that suffrage was earned and conferred, not possessed by right.[68] In such passages the Minors fell short of the universalist conception that they proposed elsewhere.

In the brief for the U.S. Supreme Court, Virginia Minor was represented as an example, a practical proof, a true "test case." Referring again to the infamous *Dred Scott* opinion, which denied citizenship and its privileges, the brief issued an implied warning to the Court: "The principles here laid down (as in the Dred Scott case), extend far beyond the limits of the particular suit, and embrace the rights of millions of others, who are thus represented through her."[69] The analogy to African American manhood, as well as the allusion to *Dred Scott,* a Supreme Court opinion refuted through a bloody war and overturned by recent constitutional amendments, implied the momentousness of the decision facing the Court. The category of federal citizen was race-neutral and gender-neutral by constitutional definition, the Minors argued. Citizens

of a republic participated in their government via the franchise. Would the woman citizen's privileges be recognized?

Conclusion:
The Meanings of a Citizen's Claim

The Minors' configuration of the woman citizen as a political actor failed to persuade the Court. The cultural connotations of the category "woman" proved sufficiently powerful that the Justices unanimously restricted the category "citizen" in order to accommodate conventional practice and normative assumptions of gender. Chief Justice Waite's opinion agreed with the Minors that women were citizens, but the citizen as represented by the Court did not move and speak in the world as an assertive participant. Instead, citizenship was a state of being: in the Constitution of the United States, the Court ruled, the term *citizen* meant "membership of a nation, and nothing more."[70]

The Court also took up the key question of "whether all citizens are necessarily voters." Decisively ruling that "the United States has no voters in the States of its own creation," the Court sharply constrained the federalist potentials of the Fourteenth Amendment, leaving the states to decide who would be voters. The highest courts in Missouri and the United States agreed that the "universal construction of the Constitution . . . and the almost universal practice of all of the States" (in the words of the Missouri State Supreme Court), or "uniform practice long continued" (in the words of the U.S. Supreme Court), had "settled" the question of whether the citizenship of women conferred voting rights.[71] Citing state constitutions at the time of the adoption of the U.S. Constitution, Waite's opinion noted that all but New Jersey's had limited voting to males. New states added to the original thirteen as well as the former Confederate states that had been reincorporated into the United States did not extend the right of suffrage to women, and the federal government did not construe this as a valid reason to deny admission.[72] Citizens did not necessarily possess voting rights.

Rather than swiftly securing suffrage for women citizens, then, *Minor v. Happersett* resulted in the validation of exclusionary voting practices and legally endorsed unequal citizenship on the basis of sex. In concert with the 1873 rulings in the *Slaughter-house Cases* and *Bradwell v. Illinois,* which declared that states could prohibit individuals from practicing an occupation, the 1875 *Minor* ruling further narrowed the range of legal protections offered to the federal citizen by the potentially emancipatory Fourteenth Amendment.[73] Separating citizenship from voting and authorizing state control of the federal franchise, the *Minor* decision not only affected women as potential voters but also was used as precedent for Jim Crow laws and the disenfranchisement of African American men, despite the legal protection of the Fifteenth Amendment.[74] At the same time, as legal historian Gretchen Ritter observes, the postwar judiciary made a distinction between cases involving race and those involving sex, sometimes applying the Reconstruction Amendments progressively to cases involving black men but always rejecting their application to women. [75] In addition, the glaring inconsistency between the rulings in *Slaughter-house* and *Minor,* which respectively linked and separated voting and citizenship, offers further support for the contention that the sex of the citizen proved a deciding factor for the Court of the 1870s. When the citizen was a woman, the privilege of voting was categorically denied.

Twentieth- and twenty-first-century scholars identify the *Minor* case as a stunning defeat for woman's rights and, indeed, for the democratization of U.S. political culture. W. William Hodes, for example, argues that *Minor* is comparable to the 1857 *Dred Scott* decision in its preservation of legal enslavement.[76] No historians find the decision surprising, given the political composition of the Court and the state of elite opinion on the question of woman suffrage in the 1870s.[77]

The audacity of the Minors' logic, however, routinely garners praise. Norma Basch echoes nineteenth-century activists by accentuating the ingenuity of the Minors' constitutional interpretation.[78] Ellen Carol DuBois emphasizes the "new, militant, activist stance for woman suffragists" engendered by the Minors' interpretive practices.[79] Other scholars find in the arguments of the New Departure the precursors of later modes of legal reasoning. Adam Winkler locates an origin for a "living constitutionalism"— the argument that constitutional interpretation appropriately evolves along with cultural change—in Stanton's adaptations of the Minors' logic. Sandra F. VanBurkleo finds in the Minors' Supreme Court brief evidence of a concern for voting as a form of political speech, protected by the First Amendment, that is customarily traced to the early twentieth century.[80] At the same time, Joan Hoff criticizes the New Departure strategies generally and the Minors' arguments specifically, arguing that the focus on constitutional rights enervated the radical potential of the early woman's rights movement.[81]

In scholarly assessments, as in other judgments, much depends on the framework through which the evaluation is made.[82] Our analysis has taken a generally sympathetic stance toward the Minors' advocacy. By tracing the development of their arguments over time, we have shown the strengths and the weaknesses of the evolution of their case, an evolution affected by the dialogic form of legal discourse, produced serially by advocates and judicial authorities. We have expanded the analyses of scholars like DuBois by illuminating the links between the Minors' constitutional interpretations and the new activist stance. In our view, the Minors' interpretive logic posited a key rhetorical element—the symbolic citizen—that was the basis for a new attitude, a new rhetorical style, and new performative strategies.

We agree with Hoff and other scholars that the word of the Court in *Minor* did violence to people and to progressive ideas. However, we would be loath to say that the Minors should not have pressed their case, and we read the development of the legal arguments as neither frivolous nor entirely unsuccessful. Despite logical peculiarities in the briefs and unfortunate inconsistencies in maintaining the universalist, natural rights position, the legal interpretations offered by the Minors were plausible enough to secure hearings, and, as Jack Balkin notes, the constitutionally based argument that women citizens should vote was not nearly as bizarre as the argument that corporations should be seen as "persons" in Fourteenth Amendment terms, an assertion that the Court accepted only eleven years after *Minor*.[83] The *Minor* case forced the judiciary to respond seriously to gender inequality in the public realm. In a case in which the argument for woman suffrage centered upon the interpretation of revered political discourse and constitutional language rather than the meaning of woman's physical features or maternal potential, courts were compelled to render decisions that offered rationales in legal terms for placing limitations upon women's political rights. The initiation of legal discussions of citizenship and gender in the Supreme Court of the 1870s altered the terrain of federal law and opened a new arena in which oppressed persons could make a case for inclusion. Bringing gender discrimination into the open, where it could be more directly contested, cases like *Bradwell* and *Minor* performatively defined law as a site of struggle rather than as a prescribed hegemonic order.[84]

Like many other test cases in U.S. legal history, the efforts in *Minor* promoted political action and displayed an imagined expansion of justice. The Minors' arguments, as expressed and enacted, showcased veneration for constitutional culture and also represented hope for justice—justice not to be confused with law.[85] Levinson's evaluation of Frederick Douglass's radical constitutionalist argument of 1860 applies equally well to the Minors' efforts of 1869–75:

> One cannot begin to engage in constitutional interpretation without having in mind a model of the point of the entire constitutional enterprise. That point of the American Constitution, if we are indeed to have any "faith" in its goodness, must be to achieve a political order worthy of respect, and there is a very heavy burden of proof on any analyst who would say that the Constitution *must* be interpreted in a way that brings it disrespect.[86]

In the Minors' imaginative arguments, we find a rhetorical strategy of interpretation that tends toward justice. Manifesting a belief in the possibility of a changed world, legal challenges like the Minors' created contestation over the parameters of constitutional respect. Although scholars often suggest that the Minors must have known that they would lose the case—a plausible supposition by the mid-1870s, we believe, owing to the disposition of other cases prior to their Supreme Court hearing—we see no reason to believe that the Minors began the development of their legal strategies in the late 1860s with a sense of inevitability or fatalism about the outcome. In any case, whatever their private thoughts, their rhetorical acts embodied the hope that winning was possible. In addition, the Minors' legal efforts promoted a commitment to constitutional fidelity, one that took seriously the responsibility placed upon individual citizens to support, protect, and defend the principles of U.S. law. Rather than merely assessing whether arguments for woman suffrage were likely to win the approval of a court, the Minors bound themselves to a vision of the law that was greater than a prediction of judicial behavior.[87]

Further, the Minors' efforts failed in court, but they were demonstrably persuasive in the court of opinion within the U.S. woman's rights movement, and they invigorated efforts for woman suffrage during Reconstruction. Drawing on political history and the Constitution, the Minors gave new meaning to preexisting precepts in an effort to alter political practice. In their symbolic reconstitution of the federal citizen embodied as a woman, the Minors offered an alternative vision of citizenship and imagined a new political subjectivity for women, one that many women chose to adopt, verbally and performatively. In an era when national suffrage organizations were embroiled in anger, vituperation, and frustrating debates about how best to respond to the insertion of the word *male* into the U.S. Constitution, the Minors' claim that woman suffrage was already guaranteed opened powerful new ways of thinking about the relationships between women, citizenship, and the law. At a time when decisions of the national legislature were creating painful forced choices for Northern reformers, the Minors' rhetorical constitution of the race- and gender-neutral federal citizen offered a way—albeit fragile and momentary—to salvage the call for universal suffrage. Moreover, the strategic idea articulated by the Minors—that suffrage could be aggressively pursued through legal channels—provided woman's rights advocates with a foundation for public, direct action. Before female advocates could set aside social conventions and assail registry offices and polling places throughout the nation, they had to be able to imagine that such action was feasible and justifiable. The Minors' symbolic action provided a model for such imagining. The legal arguments that they developed and promoted showcased a new, assertive political being for a woman citizen, one that others could reproduce in thought and in public action.

The Minors' arguments, publicity, and pursuit of their case to the Supreme Court established public grounds upon which women could claim to be legitimate participants in the political sphere and could act accordingly. This creative effort, which situated founding documents of U.S. republicanism as cornerstones of gender justice, thus revised the rhetorical and performative possibilities available to suffrage activists. Among activists, this line of legal argument proved resilient. Well after the Minors' defeat in the Supreme Court, Isabella Beecher Hooker, Susan B. Anthony, Virginia Minor, and Elizabeth Cady Stanton made the case that the U.S. Constitution enfranchised women, addressing their claims to woman's rights associations and to congressional committees alike.[88] Some disenfranchised women persisted in attempts to register and vote, including a group of more than fifty suffragists in New York and Brooklyn in 1885.[89] Francis Minor also persevered: he published widely circulated essays and pamphlets, and a federal suffrage bill that he authored was presented in the U.S. House of Representatives by Wyoming Republican Clarence Clark only weeks after Minor's death in 1892.[90] Suffragists continued to cite the Minors' arguments for women's constitutional right to the franchise up to the 1920 adoption of the Nineteenth Amendment.[91] The legal framework offered by the Minors' rhetoric thus attained the status of an alternative view of justice that existed alongside the authorized law as a source of resistance to its tenets.[92]

The *Minor* case demonstrates the complex intertwining of legal rhetoric and political culture, as forces of conservation and resistance alter their direction in response to each other. Furthermore, *Minor* shows how "failed" arguments in law can invigorate cultural movements, assisting in the production of new ways of imagining political selves and performing political identities. As other suffragists joined the Minors in demanding that the United States fulfill its duty to maintain a republican form of government by securing for all of its citizens the fundamental right to vote, hermeneutics presented as discovery proved to be a significant strategy for moving beyond the speech of supplication toward a demand for justice.

Notes

[1] *Scott v. Sandford,* 60 U.S. 411 (1856). For a rhetorical analysis of black abolitionists' responses to *Dred Scott,* see Todd F. McDorman, "Challenging Constitutional Authority: African American Responses to *Scott v. Sandford,*" *Quarterly Journal of Speech* 83 (1997): 192–209.

[2] Sanford Levinson, *Constitutional Faith* (Princeton, NJ: Princeton University Press, 1988), 140.

[3] Norma Basch, "Reconstitutions: History, Gender, and the Fourteenth Amendment," in *The Constitutional Bases of Political and Social Change in the United States,* ed. Shlomo Slonim (New York: Praeger, 1990), 175 (Basch's focus here is *Minor*).

[4] For an excellent history of these cases, see Ellen Carol DuBois, "Outgrowing the Compact of the Fathers: Equal Rights, Woman Suffrage, and the United States Constitution, 1820–1878," *Journal of American History* 74 (1987): 836–62; Ellen Carol DuBois, "Taking the Law into Our Own Hands: *Bradwell, Minor,* and Suffrage Militance in the 1870s," in *Visible Women: New Essays on American Activism,* ed. Nancy A. Hewitt and Suzanne Lebsock (Urbana: University of Illinois Press, 1993), 19–40.

[5] For treatments by legal scholars, see, e.g., W. William Hodes, "Women and the Constitution: Some Legal History and a New Approach to the Nineteenth Amendment," *Rutgers Law Review* 25 (1970): 26–53; Joan Hoff, *Law, Gender, and Injustice: A Legal History of U.S. Women* (New York: New York University Press, 1991), 151–91; Jules Lobel, "Losers, Fools, and Prophets: Justice as Struggle," *Cornell Law Review* 80 (1995): 1364–75; Adam Winkler, "A Revolution Too Soon: Woman Suffragists and the 'Living Constitution,'" *New York University Law Review* 76 (2001): 1456–526; Reva B. Siegel, "She the People: The Nineteenth Amendment, Sex Equality, Federalism, and the Family," *Harvard Law Review* 115 (2002): 968–77; Gretchen Ritter, "Jury Service

and Women's Citizenship before and after the Nineteenth Amendment," *Law and History Review* 20 (2002): 486–92; Sandra F. VanBurkleo, "'Words as Hard as Cannon-balls': Women's Rights Agitation and Liberty of Speech in Nineteenth-Century America," in *Constitutionalism and American Culture: Writing the New Constitutional History,* ed. Sandra F. VanBurkleo, Kermit L. Hall, and Robert J. Kaczorowski (Lawrence: University Press of Kansas, 2002), 307–48; and Jack M. Balkin, "How Social Movements Change (or Fail to Change) the Constitution: The Case of the New Departure," *Suffolk University Law Review* 39 (2005): 27–65.

6 See Marouf Hasian Jr., Celeste Michelle Condit, and John Louis Lucaites, "The Rhetorical Boundaries of 'the Law': A Consideration of the Rhetorical Culture of Legal Practice and the Case of the 'Separate but Equal' Doctrine," *Quarterly Journal of Speech* 82 (1996): 323–42.

7 See Robert M. Cover, *Narrative, Violence, and the Law: The Essays of Robert Cover,* ed. Martha Minow, Michael Ryan, and Austin Sarat (Ann Arbor: University of Michigan Press, 1993), esp. 203–38.

8 Lobel, "Losers, Fools, and Prophets," 1332–3, 1336–7. Jack Greenberg offers an alternative view, writing that lawyers "ought to try to avoid creating a new *Plessy v. Ferguson*"; Greenberg, "Litigation for Social Change: Methods, Limits, and Role in Democracy," *Record of the Association of the Bar of the City of New York* 20 (1974): 349.

9 On audacity and accommodation in prudential action, see James Jasinski, "Idioms of Prudence in Three Antebellum Controversies: Revolution, Constitution, and Slavery," in *Prudence: Classical Virtue, Postmodern Practice,* ed. Robert Hariman (University Park: Pennsylvania State University Press, 2003), 145–88.

10 This conception of enactment is drawn from Karlyn Kohrs Campbell and Kathleen Hall Jamieson, eds., *Form and Genre: Shaping Rhetorical Action* (Falls Church, VA: Speech Communication Association, 1978), 9.

11 Lobel, "Losers, Fools, and Prophets," 1333; Hasian, Condit, and Lucaites, "Rhetorical Boundaries," 323. We employ Reva B. Siegel's definition of constitutional culture as "the network of understandings and practices that structure our constitutional tradition, including those that shape law but would not be recognized as 'lawmaking' according to the legal system's own formal criteria"; Siegel, "Text in Contest: Gender and the Constitution from a Social Movement Perspective," *University of Pennsylvania Law Review 150* (2001): 303.

12 On hermeneutics and rhetorical action, see Steven Mailloux, "Rhetorical Hermeneutics," in *Interpreting Law and Literature: A Hermeneutic Reader,* ed. Sanford Levinson and Steven Mailloux (Evanston, IL: Northwestern University Press, 1988), 345–62; Steven Mailloux, *Rhetorical Power* (Ithaca, NY: Cornell University Press, 1989); Steven Mailloux, "Rhetorical Hermeneutics Revisited," *Text and Performance Quarterly* 11 (1991): 233–48; Alan G. Gross and William M. Keith, eds., *Rhetorical Hermeneutics: Invention and Interpretation in the Age of Science* (Albany: State University of New York Press, 1997); and Michael Leff, "Hermeneutical Rhetoric," in *Rhetoric and Hermeneutics in Our Time: A Reader,* ed. Walter Jost and Michael J. Hyde (New Haven, CT: Yale University Press, 1997), 196–214.

13 The Minor arguments thus exemplified a commitment to an aspect of what Levinson calls a "protestant" approach to constitutional interpretation, one that prioritizes individual rather than institutional readings. Far from ensuring "national unity," Levinson argues, a "sacred text" of a written constitution has the potential "to serve as the source of fragmentation and *dis*-integration"; Levinson, *Constitutional Faith,* 17, 27.

14 "Mrs. Francis Minor," *Revolution,* October 28, 1869, pp. 258, 259. See also "The St. Louis Convention," *Revolution,* October 21, 1869, pp. 250–1. Minor's birth name was Virginia Louisa Minor; her husband, Francis Minor, was a distant cousin. See Arnold J. Lien, "Minor, Virginia Louisa," in *Dictionary of American Biography,* ed. Dumas Malone, vol. 7, *Mills-Platner,* pt. 1, *Mills Oglesby* (New York: Charles Scribner's Sons, 1934), 29–30; and "Virginia L. Minor," *Woman's Tribune,* August 25, 1894, p. 146. For information about early woman suffrage activism in Missouri, see Elizabeth Cady Stanton, Susan B. Anthony, and Matilda Joslyn Gage, eds., *History of Woman Suffrage,* vol. 3, 1876–1885 (Rochester, NY: Susan B. Anthony, 1886), 594–611; Martha S. Kayser, "Woman-Suffrage Association of Missouri," in *Encyclopedia of the History of St. Louis,* ed. William Hyde and Howard L. Conard (New York: Southern History Co., 1899), 4: 2529–31; Christine Orrick Fordyce, "Early Beginnings," in "History of Woman Suffrage in Missouri," ed. Mary Semple Scott, *Missouri Historical Review* 14 (1920): 288–99.

15 "The St. Louis Resolutions," *Revolution,* October 28, 1869, p. 259; see also "St. Louis Convention," 250.

16 DuBois refers to this argument as "the weakest point" of the Minors' argument "but also its lynchpin"; DuBois, "Outgrowing the Compact of the Fathers," 852.

17 *Corfield v. Coryell,* 6 Fed. Cas. 546, no. 3,230 C.C.E.D.Pa. (1823); *Congressional Globe,* 39th Cong., 1st sess., 2398, 2538 (1866). See also Earl M. Maltz, *Civil Rights, the Constitution, and Congress,* 1863–1869 (Lawrence: University Press of Kansas, 1990), 96–102, 106–20.

18 In the 1850s the poet, novelist, lyceum lecturer, and woman's rights advocate Elizabeth Oakes Smith made the link explicit in her popular public lecture "Dignity of Labor": "You say that every male member of the Republic, twenty one years of age, is entitled to the rights of Citizenship, meaning the right to vote, and you call a woman a Citizen, while you deny her this right, which is a farce and an anomaly"; Elizabeth Oakes Smith, "The Dignity of Labor" (early 1850s), MS p. 16, in box 2, Papers of Elizabeth Oakes Prince Smith, Accession #38707, Special Collections, University of Virginia Library, Charlottesville.

19 "St. Louis Convention," 250; Francis Minor, "Make the Trial," *Revolution,* October 21, 1869, p. 250. The circulation of information about the Missouri Woman Suffrage Association convention and the Minor Resolutions can be traced through the *Revolution:* see "Woman's Suffrage Convention in St. Louis—Ideas to Be Fought, Not Men," October 14, 1869, p. 235; "St. Louis," October 14, 1869, p. 236; "Principles, Not Policy," October 21, 1869, pp. 248–9; Minor, "Make the Trial"; "St. Louis Convention"; "Mrs. Francis Minor"; "St. Louis Resolutions"; "A Good Determination," December 23, 1869, p. 395; Francis Minor, "Fundamental Rights," January 20, 1870, pp. 38–9. The significance of Francis Minor's claim that women could now reject the "status of petitioner" is illuminated by the work of Susan Zaeske, who examines the political roles created for women within antebellum antislavery petitions; see Susan Zaeske, "Signatures of Citizenship: The Rhetoric of Women's Antislavery Petitions," *Quarterly Journal of Speech* 88 (2002): 147–68; Susan Zaeske, *Signatures of Citizenship: Petitioning, Antislavery, and Women's Political Identity* (Chapel Hill: University of North Carolina Press, 2003).

20 Notable among these were Victoria Claflin Woodhull's 1870 Memorial to Congress and the supportive minority report issued in 1871 by House Judiciary Committee members William Loughridge and Benjamin Butler, as well as the arguments of attorneys Albert G. Riddle and Francis Miller in support of a group of women in Washington, DC, who attempted to vote in 1871. See Elizabeth Cady Stanton, Susan B. Anthony, and Matilda Joslyn Gage, eds., *History of Woman Suffrage,* vol. 2, 1861–1876 (Rochester, NY: Susan B. Anthony, 1881), 443–8, 464–82, 587–600 (hereafter *HWS* 2).

21 Section 2 reads:

> Representatives shall be apportioned among the several States according to their respective numbers, counting the whole number of persons in each State, excluding Indians not taxed. But when the right to vote at any election for the choice of Electors for President and Vice-President of the United States, Representatives in Congress, the executive and judicial officers of a State, or the members of the legislature thereof, is denied to any of the male inhabitants of such State, being twenty-one years of age and citizens of the United States, or in any way abridged, except for participation in rebellion, or other crime, the basis of representation therein shall be reduced in the proportion which the number of such male citizens shall bear to the whole number of male citizens twenty-one years of age in such State.

22 *Congressional Globe,* 39th Cong., 1st sess., 2767 (1866).

23 Eleanor Flexner and Ellen Fitzpatrick, *Century of Struggle: The Woman's Rights Movement in the United States,* enlarged ed. (Cambridge, MA: Harvard University Press, 1996), 160–3; Sara M. Evans, *Born for Liberty: A History of Women in America* (New York: Free Press, 1989), 123–4; Aileen S. Kraditor, *The Ideas of the Woman Suffrage Movement, 1890–1920* (1965; reprint, New York: Norton, 1981), 3–4; *HWS* 2: 400–1, 756–66.

24 William M. Wiecek, *The Sources of Antislavery Constitutionalism in America, 1760–1848* (Ithaca, NY: Cornell University Press, 1977), 249–75; Cover, *Narrative, Violence, and the Law,* 133–8; Lobel, "Losers, Fools, and Prophets," 1358–64; Jasinski, "Idioms of Prudence," 176–7; James Jasinski, "Intentions as Rhetorical Constraint/ Resource: The Case of Lysander Spooner's *The Unconstitutionality of Slavery* (1845)," paper presented at the biennial meeting of the Rhetoric Society of America, Memphis, May 2006.

25 Flexner and Fitzpatrick, *Century of Struggle,* 161; *HWS* 2: 313–44. Winkler identifies Stanton as an innovator of a mode of judicial reasoning in which

constitutional interpretation evolves in response to cultural change; Winkler, "Revolution Too Soon," 1473–501. The rhetoric of the Minors did not forecast this conceptual leap; instead, they argued from the text of the Constitution and from an interpretation of the framers' intent. Throughout this essay we refer to the legal arguments of "the Minors"—referring to Virginia and Francis Minor—although Francis, an attorney, drafted the legal briefs. By referring to "the Minors," we recognize their shared status as plaintiffs in the case, and we also respond to evidence that suggests a partnership in political action as well as marriage. See, e.g., Virginia Louisa Minor and Francis Minor to Susan B. Anthony, May 7, 1874, Ida (Husted) Harper Collection, Henry E. Huntington Library, San Marino, CA, in *The Papers of Elizabeth Cady Stanton and Susan B. Anthony*, ed. Patricia G. Holland and Ann D. Gordon, microfilm (Wilmington, DE: Scholarly Resources, 1991), reel 18, frames 1–3.

26 Angela G. Ray, "The Rhetorical Ritual of Citizenship: Women's Voting as Public Performance, 1869–1875," *Quarterly Journal of Speech* 93 (2007): 1–26; Lobel, "Losers, Fools, and Prophets," 1332. Not all the voting efforts postdated the Minor Resolutions, and DuBois persuasively argues that the voting campaign of 1869–75 arose from "a genuinely popular political faith"; DuBois, "Taking the Law into Our Own Hands," 23.

27 A list of known efforts by women to vote appears in Ann D. Gordon, ed., *The Selected Papers of Elizabeth Cady Stanton and Susan B. Anthony*, vol. 2, *Against an Aristocracy of Sex, 1866 to 1873* (New Brunswick, NJ: Rutgers University Press, 2000), 645–54. On Anthony, see, e.g., Gordon, *Selected Papers* 2: 524–7; *An Account of the Proceedings on the Trial of Susan B. Anthony, on the Charge of Illegal Voting, at the Presidential Election in Nov., 1872, and on the Trial of Beverly W. Jones, Edwin T. Marsh and William B. Hall, the Inspectors of Election by Whom Her Vote Was Received* (Rochester, NY: Daily Democrat and Chronicle Book Print, 1874).

28 The text of Anthony's speech appears in Karlyn Kohrs Campbell, comp., *Man Cannot Speak for Her*, vol. 2, *Key Texts of the Early Feminists* (New York: Praeger, 1989), 279–316. See also Karlyn Kohrs Campbell, "Contemporary Rhetorical Criticism: Genres, Analogs, and Susan B. Anthony," in *The Jensen Lectures: Contemporary Communication Studies*, ed. John I. Sisco (Tampa: University of South Florida, 1983), 117–32; Karlyn Kohrs Campbell, *Man Cannot Speak for Her*, vol. 1,

A Critical Study of Early Feminist Rhetoric (New York: Praeger, 1989), chap. 7. A recently edited text of Anthony's speech, reporting variations in extant versions, appears in Gordon, *Selected Papers* 2: 554–83.

29 U.S. Supreme Court, *Virginia L. Minor and Francis Minor, Her Husband, Plaintiffs in Error, vs. Reese Happersett*, Transcript of Record, no. 182, filed August 16, 1873, Petition, p. 3 (hereafter cited as *Minor*, Transcript of Record).

30 The court documents presented in Virginia Minor's favor are typically signed by all three of her attorneys. Scholars have assumed that Francis Minor authored the briefs, and the briefs' similarity to other documents written by him makes this assumption plausible.

31 The Circuit Court ruled in 1850 that the Scotts were free because of their extended residencies in Illinois and Wisconsin Territory. The Missouri State Supreme Court and the U.S. Supreme Court later overturned the lower court's decision. See *Scott v. Sandford*, 60 U.S. 393 (1856).

32 See Truman A. Post, *Reports of Cases Argued and Determined in the Supreme Court of the State of Missouri*, vol. 53 (St. Louis: W. J. Gilbert, 1873), 58–65; John William Wallace, *Cases Argued and Adjudged in the Supreme Court of the United States*, vol. 21, October Term, 1874 (Washington, DC: W. H. and O. H. Morrison, 1875), 162–78; Charles Fairman, *History of the Supreme Court of the United States*, vol. 7, *Reconstruction and Reunion, 1864–88*, pt. 2 (New York: Macmillan, 1987), 222–3; and "Woman Suffrage," *New York Times*, February 10, 1875, p. 8. On Waite and the other Justices who decided the case, see Balkin, "How Social Movements Change," 63.

33 This concept is articulated in *Minor*, Transcript of Record, Statement and Brief of Plaintiff in Error, 37.

34 See Winkler, "Revolution Too Soon," 1457; H. Jefferson Powell, "The Original Understanding of Intent," *Harvard Law Review* 98 (1995): 885–948. In addition to tracing the emergence of originalism—understood as inquiry into the expectations of individuals involved in framing and ratifying the Constitution—as an interpretive philosophy in the nineteenth century, Powell observes that "the Philadelphia framers' primary expectation regarding constitutional interpretation was that the Constitution, like any other legal document, be interpreted in accord with its express language" (903). In this sense, it would appear that the textualist reading strategies of the Minors were closer to the legal hermeneutic advocated by the

Philadelphia framers than were the nineteenth-century methods of originalism.

35 Jay Fliegelman, *Declaring Independence: Jefferson, Natural Language, and the Culture of Performance* (Stanford, CA: Stanford University Press, 1993), 186. Fliegelman uses the term "subversive reverence" to describe the invocation of a prior text in order to use it for new purposes.

36 In note 13, we observed that the Minor arguments demonstrated one aspect of what Levinson calls a "protestant" approach to constitutional interpretation: they prioritized individual rather than institutional readings. In relation to the other aspect of Levinson's conceptual approach to the Constitution—that is, what counts as the "text" to be read—the Minor arguments cannot be classified accurately as "protestant" or "catholic." By taking as their text the language of the Constitution as well as written history, the Minors embodied neither a "protestant" commitment (to reading the constitutional text alone) nor a "catholic" position (that the source of doctrine is the Constitution plus unwritten tradition). See Levinson, *Constitutional Faith*, 29.

37 *Minor*, Transcript of Record, Statement and Brief of Plaintiff in Error, 11.

38 Ibid., 4.

39 "Mrs. Francis Minor," 259; *Minor*, Transcript of Record, Statement and Brief of Plaintiff in Error, 13. Note that the brief here subtly supports women's obligations to perform military service. Women's presumed incapacity or inappropriateness for such service was a frequent aspect of arguments against their voting.

40 "Mrs. Francis Minor," 258; Minor, "Fundamental Rights," 38.

41 *HWS* 2: 729 (the microfilmed version of the Transcript of Record that we consulted is missing pp. 30–1 of the Minors' brief; the contents of those pages are reproduced in *HWS* 2: 729–30).

42 *Minor*, Transcript of Record, Opinion of Missouri State Supreme Court, 10–11.

43 *HWS* 2: 461–64; Balkin, "How Social Movements Change," 43.

44 Cf. Steven Knapp and Walter Benn Michaels, "Intention, Identity, and the Constitution: A Response to David Hoy," in *Legal Hermeneutics: History, Theory, and Practice*, ed. Gregory Leyh (Berkeley: University of California Press, 1992), 193–4.

45 *Minor*, Transcript of Record, Statement and Brief of Plaintiff in Error, 11.

46 Ibid., 12.

47 Ibid., 12.

48 Ibid., 13–14.

49 Ibid., 33.

50 Ibid., 16, 36.

51 The history of New Jersey women voters offered significant rhetorical resources for woman's rights advocates. A year before the Minors presented their arguments in St. Louis, Lucy Stone and her mother-in-law, Hannah Blackwell, attempted to vote in Roseville, New Jersey, arguing that because women in their state had never voted on their own disenfranchisement, prohibitions were illegal. See "Woman Suffrage in New Jersey," *Revolution*, November 12, 1868, p. 300; Judith Apter Klinghoffer and Lois Elkis, "'The Petticoat Electors': Women's Suffrage in New Jersey, 1776–1807," *Journal of the Early Republic* 12 (1992): 159–93.

52 In 1854, in an argument against the Kansas-Nebraska Act, Abraham Lincoln cited the Founding Fathers in order to abstract from their words a dedication to the principle of equality and to claim it in support of his argument. This strategy enabled Lincoln to invoke the Founders while shifting the focus of the debate from contentious questions regarding their silence about—and participation in—slavery and the suppression of equal self-government. Cindy Koenig Richards, "Reformulating Prudence: Conflict and Creation in Abraham Lincoln's Peoria Address," unpublished manuscript, Northwestern University, 2003. See Abraham Lincoln, "The Repeal of the Missouri Compromise and the Propriety of Its Restoration: Speech at Peoria, Illinois, in Reply to Senator Douglas," in *Abraham Lincoln: His Speeches and Writings*, ed. Roy P. Basler (1946; reprint, New York: Da Capo Press, 2001), 283–323.

53 *Minor*, Transcript of Record, Statement and Brief of Plaintiff in Error, 34, 35.

54 Ibid., 12.

55 *HWS* 2: 174, 185.

56 See Kraditor, *Ideas of the Woman Suffrage Movement*, 14–42.

57 In the Minors' argument to the Supreme Court, Virginia Minor is a representative vehicle for the enfranchisement of "all womanhood." She is identified as a "native-born free white citizen" in the petition to the St. Louis Circuit Court and in the statement to the U.S. Supreme Court. *Minor*, Transcript of Record, Statement and Brief of Plaintiff in Error, 39, Petition, 3, Statement and Brief, 3.

58 Other woman's rights activists during Reconstruction, such as Mary Ann Shadd Cary, Sojourner Truth, Frances Ellen Watkins Harper,

Frances Dana Gage, Susan B. Anthony, and Elizabeth Cady Stanton, referred specifically to African American women's need for the self-protection of the ballot. Yet vituperative debates among woman's rights activists during Reconstruction often rhetorically pitted black men against white women, questioning which group had greater need of enfranchisement or which group deserved suffrage more.

[59] For a discussion of the creation of a symbolic woman during the same period, especially in relation to class and race, see Angela G. Ray, "Representing the Working Class in Early U.S. Feminist Media: The Case of Hester Vaughn," *Women's Studies in Communication* 26 (2003): 1–26.

[60] "Mrs. Francis Minor," 259.

[61] *Minor,* Transcript of Record, Opinion of Missouri State Supreme Court, 11.

[62] *Minor,* Transcript of Record, Statement and Brief of Plaintiff in Error, 26.

[63] Ibid., 18, 28; cf. *Slaughter-house Cases,* 83 U.S. 36 (1872), 71.

[64] *Minor,* Transcript of Record, Statement and Brief of Plaintiff in Error, 28.

[65] Ibid., 32, 38–9.

[66] "Mrs. Francis Minor," 258–9.

[67] *Minor,* Transcript of Record, Statement and Brief of Plaintiff in Error, 29.

[68] See Alexander Keyssar, *The Right to Vote: The Contested History of Democracy in the United States* (New York: Basic Books, 2000).

[69] *Minor,* Transcript of Record, Statement and Brief of Plaintiff in Error, 40.

[70] *Minor v. Happersett,* 88 U.S. 162 (1874), 165, 166.

[71] *Minor,* Transcript of Record, Opinion of Missouri State Supreme Court, 10; *Minor v. Happersett,* 88 U.S. 162 (1874), 178.

[72] *Minor v. Happersett,* 88 U.S. 162 (1874), 170, 171, 176–7.

[73] See *Slaughter-house Cases,* 83 U.S. 36 (1872); *Bradwell v. Illinois,* 83 U.S. 130 (1872).

[74] Hoff, *Law, Gender, and Injustice,* 175. In 1889 Susan B. Anthony noted the evisceration of the Fourteenth Amendment by *Minor,* which directly harmed African American men as well as all women; Susan B. Anthony, "History of the Amendment," *Woman's Tribune,* February 16, 1889, p. 79. The following year, in an address to the Senate Committee on Woman Suffrage, Elizabeth Cady Stanton cited a Georgia case in which *Minor v. Happersett* was used as a precedent to argue against the voting rights of a black male citizen; Stanton, "Hearing before the Woman-Suffrage Committee," *Woman's Tribune,* February 15, 1890, p. 50.

[75] Ritter, "Jury Service and Women's Citizenship," 489.

[76] Hodes, "Women and the Constitution," 42–6.

[77] Balkin, "How Social Movements Change," 37–8.

[78] She calls the Supreme Court brief "a brilliant argument, a dazzling reconstitution of law as it ought to be, and a trenchant indictment of the way it was"; Basch, "Reconstitutions," 179. Compare suffragists' eulogizing of Francis Minor: Susan B. Anthony, "In Memoriam," *Woman's Journal,* March 5, 1892, p. 79; "Francis Minor," *Woman's Tribune,* March 5, 1892, p. 68; "Francis Minor and Benjamin F. Butler," *Woman's Tribune,* January 28, 1893, p. 28.

[79] DuBois, "Outgrowing the Compact of the Fathers," 853. See also Karlyn Kohrs Campbell and Angela G. Ray, "'No Longer by Your Leave': The Impact of the Civil War and Reconstruction Amendments on Women's Rhetoric," in *A Rhetorical History of the United States,* vol. 4, *Public Debate in the Civil War Era,* ed. David Zarefsky and Michael C. Leff (East Lansing: Michigan State University Press, forthcoming).

[80] Winkler, "Revolution Too Soon," 1473–501; VanBurkleo, "Words as Hard as Cannon-balls," 307–8, 314, 326, 347–8.

[81] Hoff, *Law, Gender, and Injustice,* 151–91.

[82] Writing of disciplinary approaches and interdisciplinary possibilities, David Zarefsky notes that "by studying important historical events from a rhetorical perspective, one can see significant aspects about those events that other perspectives miss"; Zarefsky, "Four Senses of Rhetorical History," in *Doing Rhetorical History: Concepts and Cases,* ed. Kathleen J. Turner (Tuscaloosa: University of Alabama Press, 1998), 30.

[83] Balkin, "How Social Movements Change," 53.

[84] Lobel, "Losers, Fools, and Prophets," 1333.

[85] Ibid., 1332–3, 1336–7, 1355.

[86] Levinson, *Constitutional Faith,* 77.

[87] See Levinson, *Constitutional Faith,* 46–8.

[88] Isabella Beecher Hooker, *The Constitutional Rights of the Women of the United States: An Address before the International Council of Women, Washington, D.C., March 30, 1888* (Hartford, CT: Hartford Press, 1900); "Hearing before House Committee," *Woman's Tribune,* February 9, 1889, p. 1; Stanton, "Hearing before the Woman-Suffrage Committee," 50, 52–3.

[89] "Women on the Registry List: An Organized Attempt to Secure the Privilege of Voting," *New York Times,* October 21, 1885, p. 5; "The Inspectors Were Agitated: Lillie Devereux Blake Describes

Her Visit to the Polls," *New York Times,* November 6, 1885, p. 5. See also, e.g., "As the Votes Went In," *Philadelphia Inquirer,* November 7, 1888, p. 2; "Progress of the Voting," *New York Times,* November 3, 1897, p. 4.

90 Francis Minor, "Woman's Legal Right to the Ballot," *Forum,* December 1886, pp. 351–60 (reprinted as a pamphlet: Francis Minor, *Woman's Legal Right to the Ballot, An Argument in Support Of* [New York: Forum Publishing Co., 1886]); Francis Minor, "The Right of Women to Vote at Congressional Elections," *Woman's Tribune,* January 28, 1888, p. 1; Francis Minor, *The Law of Federal Suffrage, An Argument in Support Of* ([St. Louis], 1889); Francis Minor, "Woman's Political Status," *Forum,* April 1890, pp. 150–8; Francis

Minor, "Citizenship and Suffrage: The Yarbrough Decision," *Arena,* December 1891, pp. 68–75. See Clara Bewick Colby, "Report of Federal Suffrage Committee," *National Bulletin,* January 1893, pp. 1–3; Clara Bewick Colby, "Report of Federal Suffrage Committee," *Woman's Tribune,* February 11, 1893, p. 33; *Congressional Record,* 52nd Cong., 1st sess., April 25, 1892, 3639. Clark's bill was referred to the Judiciary Committee, where it died.

91 See, e.g., "Federal Suffrage," *Woman's Tribune,* May 9, 1903, p. 53; Olympia Brown to Emma Smith DeVoe, February 18, 1913, in Emma Smith DeVoe Collection, Washington State Library, Olympia; "Are Women People?" *Woman Citizen/ Woman's Journal,* April 12, 1919, pp. 962, 966.

92 Lobel, "Losers, Fools, and Prophets," 1348.

Counter-Public Enclaves and Understanding the Function of Rhetoric in Social Movement Coalition-Building

Karma R. Chávez

New social movement and counter-public rhetoric scholars demonstrate a commitment to understanding how everyday people enact public resistance on issues such as globalization, environmental degradation, and oppressive laws (e.g., Asen & Brouwer, 2001; Blitefield, 2006; Brouwer, 1998; Foust, 2006; Mitchell, 2004; Palczewski, 2001; Pezzullo, 2001, 2003). Historically, social movement and protest scholars have explored a host of movements ranging from Black nationalism, gay liberation, feminism, and Chicano rights to abortion and conservative movements (e.g., Campbell, 1973; Darsey, 1991; Hammerback & Jensen, 1980; Jensen & Hammerback, 1980; Rosenwasser, 1972; Scott, 1968; Slagle, 1995; C. A. Smith, 1984; Stewart, 1997, 1999). Social movement and counter-public scholarship continues to center on public rhetorical actions, whether oratorical, material, visual, or performative and embodied. The emphasis on public action has been central to social movement scholarship since its inception (Griffin, 1952). As Cathcart (1972) suggested, what is essentially rhetorical in social movements are the moments of "dialectical

enjoinment" or "reciprocity" between the movement and the establishment being challenged (p. 87). This emphasis on dialectical enjoinment solidifies that only what occurs in a public and confrontational fashion is rhetorical, and it also limits exploring additional rhetoric that one might find within social movement activity. Stewart (1991) noted this deficiency in social movement studies when he quipped, "we know a great deal about the *rhetoric of the streets* when movements are at the heights of their power and visibility and are publicly challenging and confronting established institutions . . ." (p. 68). Stewart (1991) went on to point out that this focus provides only a partial picture of social movement activity, which is why he further argues that looking at "internal rhetoric" in addition to public rhetoric provides fruitful information about understanding the interworkings of movement.[1]

Despite some calls to the contrary (e.g., Gray, 2009), social movement and counter-public scholarship also concentrates on specific kinds of public action, especially those of single-issue movements (Conrad, 1981; Darsey, 1991;

Griffin, 1952, 1964; C. A. Smith, 1984; Windt, 1972). If, however, as McGee (1975) argued, "... the analysis of rhetorical documents should not turn inward to an appreciation of persuasive, manipulative techniques, but outward to *functions* of rhetoric" (p. 248), moving beyond single issues toward coalitional politics seems especially prudent. As anyone who has spent time working in or analyzing movements can attest, a significant function of rhetoric within contexts of movement activity is to generate coalitions. Yet, social movement scholars have been essentially silent on coalition-building (exceptions include Bennett, 2006; Jackson & Miller, 2009).

One explanation for the neglect of coalition-building in social movement studies is that much coalition-building occurs "behind the scenes" in places that, in referring to counter-public practice, Mansbridge (1996) called "protected enclaves," where groups can explore ideas and arguments in encouraging environments. In describing the "dual character" of counter-publics, Fraser (1992) noted they are both "spaces of withdrawal and regroupment" and "bases and training grounds for agitational activities directed toward wider publics" (p. 124). Rhetorical scholarship has been relatively limited in examining these "spaces of withdrawal," or enclaves. Although in counter-public theory, enclaves and spaces of withdrawal typically refer to groups who withdraw because they are suffering from especially harsh treatment in public (Mansbridge, 1996; Squires, 2002), I maintain that such spaces are always a necessary part of movement activity regardless of the level of oppression or crisis that groups face.

Coalition-building often involves more "behind the scenes" work than public rhetorical displays (see Albrecht & Brewer, 1990; Anzaldúa, 1990; Johnson Reagon, 1983). When working to understand coalition-building, centering enclaves as a site of rhetorical investigation proves crucial. For activists who engage in coalition-building on behalf of multiple or broad social justice and human rights causes, rhetoric functions in two primary ways within enclaves. First, activists interpret external rhetorical messages that are created about them, the constituencies they represent, or both. In the case of coalition-building, these meaning-making processes serve as the rationale to build bridges with allies. Second, activists use enclaves as the sites to invent rhetorical strategies to publicly challenge oppressive rhetoric or to create new imaginaries for the groups and issues they represent and desire to bring into coalition. It is the former function I discuss here.

In this article, I show how rhetoric functions to facilitate coalition-building between a queer rights and a migrant rights organization by demonstrating how activists interpret rhetoric that emerges from three primary sources: media, legislation and policy, and law enforcement. I define *rhetoric* both as the written and spoken messages of media reports or policy, and I also understand rhetoric to refer to the messages embedded in seemingly non-rhetorical actions of, for example, law enforcement. Although such messages may not have a persuasive intent, as I show, activists often interpret negative persuasive effects for queer and migrant communities. Using data collected during a field research project, I show how activists take up such rhetoric to create complex rationales for this coalition.

Coalition-building is also a rich site to unpack another founding assumption of rhetorical scholarship on social movements pertaining to the "ego function" in both self- and other-directed movements (Gregg, 1971; Stewart, 1999). Whereas both Gregg and Stewart examined how rhetoric in movements creates and sustains identity, the study of coalitions pushes past a preoccupation with either singular issues or identities toward what rhetoric scholar, Carrillo Rowe (2008), labeled "coalitional subjectivity" (p. 10). The adoption of a coalitional subjectivity moves away from seeing one's self in singular terms or from seeing politics in terms of single issues toward a complicated intersectional political approach that refuses to view politics and identity as anything other than always and already coalitional.

The study of coalitions, then, has much to offer toward answering perennial questions for social movement scholars, such as what is rhetorical in social movements (Cathcart, 1978; Scott, 1973; R. R. Smith & Windes, 1975; Stewart, 1980; Zarefsky, 1980) and what counts as social movement (Cathcart, 1972, 1980; Hahn

& Gonchar, 1971; Lucas, 1980; McGee, 1975, 1980; Sillars, 1980)—questions I take up in the conclusion.

RESEARCH METHODS AND QUEER AND MIGRANT POLITICS IN SOUTHERN ARIZONA

Following a robust body of performance studies scholarship that bridges textual and field approaches, Pezzullo (2001, 2003) utilized participant observation to examine the rhetorical dimensions of activists' cultural performances. Locating herself in the theoretical tradition of public and counter-public sphere theory, Pezzullo (2003) maintained the following: "Thus far, most public sphere studies have involved textual analysis of secondary sources such as newspapers, magazines, congressional transcripts, and websites to capture the arguments and implications of various public spheres" (p. 350). Because activists' cultural performances are not yet recorded, they cannot be analyzed through textual rhetorical methods, and yet, they offer a rich site for understanding the functions and uses of rhetoric. As Conquergood (1998) argued, scholars too regularly center textuality when very often cultural meanings are created orally and not via text. The same can be said for analyzing the functions of rhetoric within protected enclaves because textual methods are of little use in garnering understanding when most of the rhetorical work is oral and instantaneous. Thus, I follow Pezzullo's (2001, 2003) lead in utilizing field methods to learn about rhetoric.

For one year (June 2006–June 2007), I conducted field research with Wingspan—the lesbian, gay, bisexual, and transgender (LGBT) community center in Tucson, Arizona—and *Coalición de Derechos Humanos* (CDH)—a Tucson-based, grassroots, migrant rights, and anti–border militarization organization. For years, Wingspan and CDH have joined in coalition to confront what they have grown to understand as the related ways in which queers and migrants[2] get similarly demonized and scapegoated in the purportedly "objective" rhetoric emerging from sources such as media, legislation, and law enforcement. Throughout the past several years, at different times, migrants and queers have appeared in the public sphere as the favored subjects of scapegoating, dehumanization, and criminalization. Sometimes this targeting takes shape in legislation or ballot measures, sometimes via sensational media reports, and other times through the actions of law enforcement officials. Because both queers and migrants (always figured as separate) are favorite targets, Wingspan and CDH work together to confront these issues and offer each other helping hands when needed. Because the coalition only engages in direct acts of protest when provoked, they have produced very little public rhetoric. Yet, their complicated justifications for the necessity of engaging in coalition work provide important insight into how external rhetoric created about the two groups functions to create and sustain collective action. I sought data that centered activists' thoughts and ideas about what compels them to engage in social protest as a coalition.

CDH and Wingspan's informal coalition intensified in the early 2000s because of an increase in anti-migrant sentiment and legislation in Arizona. This anti-migrant sentiment also led to a strong recognition of some of the related ways that media reports, legislation and law enforcement represent and treat queers and migrants. Between 2004 and 2006, the rights of both queers and migrants were singled out (although not equally) through various kinds of legislation and ballot measures. Such situations prompted Wingspan and CDH to confront oppression more directly by refusing a divided approach to political activism. Through spending time listening to activists' justifications and thought processes about this coalition work, and by being involved in their enclaves, I began to understand how activists have interpreted and made use of external rhetoric about them. In the next section I explain how, in the context of their enclaves, CDH and Wingspan activists confront, and perhaps create, connections between their two communities in ways that eventually compel social movement. I accessed such data through 180hr of extensive participant observation as an activist and liaison between the two groups, where I took detailed fieldnotes on what I participated in and observed. After seven months of fieldwork, I conducted fourteen structured interviews with key activists to ask about the themes that I saw emerging from my data. Specifically, I entered the field with questions about why a queer rights and a migrant rights organization would engage in coalition-building, and I began to witness that much of activists' rationale pertained to the meaning they made from external messages received. I continued to engage in fieldwork to focus on these themes by paying specific attention to conversations that activists had when confronted with exclusionary rhetorical messages from external sources that elicited response in the Tucson public, as these seemed to be most salient to activists.

INTERPRETING RHETORIC AND BUILDING CONNECTIONS

I encountered Wingspan and CDH in 2006 at a one-day conference—"Sexuality and Homeland (In)Securities"—at the University of Arizona. During a brief talk, two leaders of the organizations, Kat, CDH's Coordinating Organizer, and Cathy, Wingspan's Director of Programs until Fall 2007,[3] unpacked some of the relations they see in the treatment of queers and the treatment of migrants. Specifically, they offered a brief analysis of the similarities between the representations of migrants and queers in the campaigns surrounding two Arizona ballot referenda. First, they discussed the 2004 voter-approved ballot initiative, Proposition 200, the Arizona Taxpayer and Citizen Protection Act, also known as "Protect Arizona Now" (PAN). PAN requires all Arizonans to provide proof that they are U.S. citizens to receive certain public benefits or to vote (Busha & Rodriguez, 2005). Premised on California's 1994 Proposition 187, PAN's Web site explains that proponents designed this initiative to protect Arizonans from "illegal aliens" who "invade" Arizona and allegedly take taxpayer benefits such as health care, welfare, and education without contributing into the system (PAN, 2004).

Next, Kat and Cathy explored the (then proposed) 2006 voter-defeated initiative (eventually labeled Proposition 107), "Protect Marriage Arizona" (PMA), which was designed to create a constitutional amendment that would ban not only same-sex marriage, but civil

unions and virtually all domestic partner benefits at all levels in the state of Arizona (Busha & Rodriguez, 2005).[4] In their brief analysis, they illustrated the similarities between the two measures. For example, both PAN and PMA were designed to make access to health care more difficult for many people. PAN requires people to prove their U.S. citizenship to receive public health care. Latino/a advocacy groups suggest that only those who are racially or linguistically suspect—primarily those who are or appear to be Latino/a—are asked to prove that they are U.S. citizens (Benson & Sherwood, 2006, p. B1). PMA would have ensured that only married, heterosexual couples were allowed to have partner benefits if they were state employees, and it would have prevented unmarried partners from having hospital visitation rights. In addition, Wingspan and CDH argued that making PAN law, and putting PMA up for a vote, "send[s] tacit state-sanctioned signals that it is acceptable to harass undocumented immigrants, people of color and/or LGBT people" (Busha, 2006).

This talk, which introduced me to these two organizations, illustrated the rhetorical constructions of migrants and queers as scapegoats for societal ills, deviants who do not deserve protections, and lawbreakers who endanger the public. The talk revealed how these images constitute some of the main ways that activists understand migrants and queers to be constructed as subjects in the state of Arizona. For many activists, making these connections from the plethora of rhetoric from sources such as media reports, legislation and policy, and law enforcement that targets the two communities provides the rationale and justification for CDH and Wingspan's coalition. Wingspan and CDH have published a small number of public texts that outline their positions, but the connections activists make between the representations of migrants and queers in Southern Arizona are more apparent through accessing their enclaves by spending time with activists in a variety of contexts such as meetings, rallies, social gatherings, and also in interviews. I now provide a discussion of the three primary sources of rhetoric about queers and migrants that activists responded to: media, legislation and policy, and law enforcement.

Media

As with many social movements (Gray, 2009), the importance of the media for both CDH and Wingspan cannot be overstated. Throughout my research, issues pertaining to media arose more than almost any other issue. Both Wingspan and CDH approach media similarly: they aggressively monitor local media outlets' reporting and slant on migrant and queer issues; and they each utilize media, both local and national outlets, as well as their own organizational outlets to promote their messages. I focus on the former function here to suggest connections between the ways that mediated rhetoric can construct migrants and queers.

Some disagreement persists within both Wingspan and CDH about the quality of the media's rhetoric relating to queer and migrant issues. For instance, one long-time CDH activist, Amelia (a pseudonym), noted that sometimes the media is adequate in coverage of migrant issues (Amelia, interview, April 7, 2007). This perspective contrasts others' thoughts. Kat, for example, explained that one of the problems with the media is that they always assume issues are black and white, and they operate under the façade of fair and balanced reporting. Kat offered the following:

> One of my biggest complaints of them like you know, say April 10th last year [2006], 18,000 people at a march [for immigrant rights in Tucson] and there were about 10 or 12 maybe, I don't even think there were that—maybe 6–10 protestors maybe in the middle of that, and we were given equal time in the media. And you know, they said, "well, we have to be fair and unbiased," and I challenged them and said do you really think 18,000 to 10 is fair, is fairly balancing it? (Interview, May 10, 2007)

Here, Kat demonstrated how the media's coverage of the march reinforces two troubling ideas. One is that their reporting suggests that the protestors at the march (many of whom are not supported by other more moderate anti-immigration groups because of their radical stances) are an appropriate counter-point to those who marched and organized the march.

This positions immigrants and their supporters as fringe groups on the left and the protestors as fringe groups on the right, thereby reducing the political significance of the marches. The other is that this kind of reporting bolsters existing anti-immigrant sentiment by suggesting that as many who support migrants also oppose them.

Many participants, such as Lupe, one of the co-presidents of CDH, suggested that the media work this way because they simply reinforce state and mainstream positions (Lupe, interview, March 27, 2007). Lupe maintained that media do not question or offer analysis, they simply report, and that reporting perpetuates troubling perceptions of migrants and migrant issues. Alexis, a CDH activist who also worked for the Pima County public defender's office, noted that the Border Patrol, for example, has an aggressive media department; and, over the last ten years, they shifted from issuing weekly press releases to releasing press statements almost daily "on the number of people they've arrested, the number of drugs they've seized, the number of smugglers they've charged" (interview, March 24, 2007). Local media regularly utilize the Border Patrol statistics and analyses and report on them as if they are unbiased truth. Thus, CDH spends a lot of time challenging the way that media report on migrant issues and migrant lives.

Wingspan also invests much energy into monitoring the media. Kent, Wingspan's Executive Director until Spring 2007, explained that having Wingspan in Tucson has greatly impacted the kind of reporting the media do in relation to queer issues because when they want a quotation, they immediately call someone at Wingspan (interview, March 27, 2007). This has led to what Kent perceived as a shift in media coverage for the better. Others generally shared Kent's assessment. Nevertheless, one of the biggest scandals in Spring 2007 pertained to media coverage. Cathy explained:

> So there's the recent Channel 9 sex in the park, sex-posé, and they do it every year when it's rating time. And you know, suddenly it was painting this picture of men, you know gay men go to parks and have sex behind bushes where little kids are playing, and it's hard to believe that that's still even

acceptable as a news story. And so I think both groups [queers and migrants] very easily and quickly can be exploited during sweeps week by the media. You know I remember a different TV station, but same time of year, doing you know, terrorists coming across the border, and showing people sneaking over in darkness at night, and its almost similar imagery you now, like what do they do at night when your children are sleeping, just really playing on fear. (Interview, April 26, 2007)

KGUN-9, an ABC-affiliated Tucson television station, featured the "sex-posé" Cathy mentioned. Although the reporter, Jennifer Waddell, assured Wingspan that the discussion of sex in the parks would not focus on gay men or reinforce stereotypes about gay men as deviants or predators, Wingspan condemned the report as both "sensationalistic" and "inflammatory" (Wingspan, 2007). Although the report also mentioned that married men (who are presumably heterosexual) use parks for sexual purposes, the story primarily featured gay men, including an interview with a gay man with his face shadowed to protect his identity, which Wingspan suggested "reinforced the stereotype of gay men as hiding in dark places..." (Wingspan, 2007, para. 5). In response to this report, the Gay and Lesbian Alliance Against Defamation[5] joined Wingspan in calling on the queer and allied community to watch the segment and express outrage at this report.

While Cathy illuminated the troubling imagery for the queer community, she also made a parallel with similar imagery used for migrants seen crossing the border at night. In highlighting the similar ways that queers and migrants can be fashioned in media reporting, Cathy supplied justification for coalition-building with migrant rights. Oscar, a Wingspan activist and bilingual educator, echoed this sentiment: " ... [T]his is my own personal pet peeve, when they show, they constantly show people running under borders" (interview, March 27, 2007). Although activists generally think queers receive fair media representation, the possibility of problematic representation always exists. As shown here, activists also note the connections between the ways sensationalistic reporting represents

migrants and queers. No one would claim that queer representation is as bad as migrant representation, but the lurking threat always exists for queers. Moreover, the overt prejudice demonstrated in the KGUN-9 report, as well as the persistent troubling representations of migrants portrayed in all kinds of media, creates a profound rationale for the two groups' coalition. As several activists mentioned to me, when media rhetoric scapegoats one group, using these instances as opportunities to build connections in community members' minds about the similarities between problematic representations of both groups helps to foster understanding between groups. As Kat explained in an interview, queer sexual relationships disgust some in the migrant community, and part of her job is to demonstrate to them how what they find deviant about queers are the same things people find deviant about them. If community members understand that they are not the only ones who are featured as shadowy lawbreakers engaging in bad behavior in the dark, then they may be more likely to challenge those representations and ideas when they see them. Coalitional partners do not always choose to publicly respond, but activists create these connections in their protected enclaves, which helps them to further justify being in coalition.

Legislation and Policy

Because a large portion of my fieldwork occurred during an election year, legislation and policy were a central concern. From the rhetorical position of migrants and queers in legislation, policy, and proposals, activists forge some of the strongest connections in building coalitions. Although there is not an equal impact on queer and migrant communities from legislation and policy, resonances exist between the ways that legislation and policy *seek* to impact both communities. Within these resonances and the commitment to seeing issues as interconnected, CDH and Wingspan use external rhetoric to justify a need for their coalition. Wingspan has only one staff member who officially devotes part of his time to policy and advocacy, although others also do so in more unofficial capacities (Fieldnote K, October 24, 2006). Volunteers do the additional policy work.[6] CDH considers at least 50% of its work to pertain to policy (Lupe, interview, March 27, 2007). Despite differences in commitment to policy, activists in both groups are centrally interested in policy matters. In this section, I discuss the ways that Wingspan and CDH activists understand policy and legislation to impact their communities in related ways.

Policies and legislation that target both queers and migrants in the same document do not exist. In these arenas, the two groups are considered completely separate to each other, and often opposed. Nonetheless, Wingspan and CDH refuse to allow these issues to remain disconnected. They make present what is absent by suggesting that what is against migrants is also against queers, and vice versa.

Having PAN on the ballot for the November 2004 election reinvigorated the coalition between Wingspan and CDH around policy and legislation, as Wingspan activists saw an important need to challenge the scapegoating of another marginalized group. Alexis explained:

> And definitely during the Prop 200 fight, they [Wingspan] were one of the first groups to sign on to the Coalition to Defeat Prop 200,[7] and they did send representatives every time we asked them to come to a press conference, an event or forum. They were there, and you know, and that was great. It was very uplifting for all of us. You know, and it pushes, we need to push the progressive community in Tucson to broaden their analysis . . . . (Interview, March 24, 2007)

Alexis implied that Wingspan's support of the anti-200 campaign in Tucson prompted other progressives to think more broadly about how policies impact multiple communities in complicated ways. Thinking broadly about the intersections of issues and impacts, as well as arguing that some queers are also migrants are central to Wingspan's rationale for supporting migrant rights; in addition, the attack on any marginalized group may signal further attacks on others. Cathy reiterated this point:

> You know the work we did with Proposition 200, it was great . . . we were called upon by the Prop 200 people to speak at every press conference. And I remember thinking that's

really cool on both ends, because they could easily not want Wingspan's support, it's like as if "why do we want the queers, they're just going to drag us down," but instead it was "no, this shows the diversity of groups against this ridiculous amendment . . . ." (Interview, April 26, 2007)

Wingspan not only supported the campaign to defeat Proposition 200 (PAN), but they also issued their own statement.[8] When it came to PAN, then, by refusing an isolated analysis of oppression, both groups were able to strengthen their own issues.

Activists in both organizations also understood PAN as a catalyst for the exacerbated anti-migrant sentiment in 2006 in Arizona. Kent described an "avalanche" of anti-migrant belief after the approval of PAN. Whereas PAN was approved by roughly 56% of Arizonans voting "yes," voters approved four 2006 anti-migrant measures with nearly 75% voting "yes." Isabel, a co-president of CDH and political personality in Southern Arizona, used the fervor over immigration, as evidenced in legislation and policy, to connect anti-migrant sentiment with anti-queer. Isabel contended:

> . . . [O]ur connections with the LGBT community now are so clear because there's open, open effort to ban us, to discriminate, to abuse, to inflict violence, to permit violence, all of that. Who have been the targets in the last 10 years? The LGBT community and migrants. Where you can openly, it's no longer, you know subtle discrimination, which we're masters at, but open, open discrimination. Look at the ballot measures. You can see it openly, it's you know, attacking who we are. (Interview, March 20, 2007)

Isabel's meaning making was strategic. She was not implying that queer and migrant struggles are literally the same, but putting the two issues in relation to each other complicates seemingly single-direction discrimination. Because activists maintain that both groups are subject to similar kinds of openly discriminatory rhetoric from legislators and voters who enact policy, strong reason exists to be in coalition.

Wingspan and CDH wrote joint statements against the proposed 2006 anti-queer and anti-migrant ballot measures, publicly creating and solidifying a connection between two seemingly disparate issues.[9]

These statements in response to a particular election, however, represent years of meaning making in which activists have engaged within protected enclaves to make it hard for either group to leave the other as the political scapegoat or for activists to be able to see the issues as unrelated. CDH activists contend that the intersections of queer issues with migration within policy and proposed policy, such as the former HIV ban on immigration to the United States and proposed laws to allow U.S. citizens or legal permanent residents to sponsor their permanent partners for immigration to the United States, provided the foundation to build coalition with Wingspan when CDH started in the early 1990s. (Lupe, interview; Isabel, interview; Amelia, interview). More recently, as Oscar explained in an interview, the rash of proposed legislation and ballot measures against the rights of queers and migrants makes the two issues, in his words, "parallel"—not the same, but similar and in perpetually close proximity.

Law Enforcement

Both Wingspan and CDH have a tense relationship with law enforcement, including the Tucson Police Department (TPD); and for CDH, the Border Patrol. Largely due to discourses of deviance and criminality that loom over migrants and queers, law enforcement is often a source of fear and intimidation for both groups. At the same time, both rely heavily on law enforcement to uphold laws when someone threatens the safety or rights of either group. As suggested earlier, migrants and queers have a contentious relationship to the state, and as arbiters of state policy, law enforcement officials often represent that relationship. Sometimes both Wingspan and CDH work together with law enforcement to achieve shared objectives, but CDH and Wingspan both also share a healthy suspicion toward law enforcement officers and institutions. Largely, this suspicion emerges from a perception among activists that law enforcement entities re-inscribe and create the connection

between migrants and queers and criminality and deviance.

The first day I spent volunteering with CDH, Alexis told me stories about the TPD's failure to protect migrants and migrant supporters, which activists understand as a rhetorical message that the TPD does not support migrant rights. She explained that one of the reasons why CDH required such a large security committee for the Community Forum at Armory Park I was attending that day was because the TPD was going to allow Roy Warden, a local vigilante, to be outside of the building (Fieldnote C, August 24, 2006). Not long before this event, Warden threatened Isabel with "blowing her head off," but the police did not consider his threat a real one. Although CDH eventually negotiated with the TPD so that Warden could not be near Armory Park, during the forum, another vigilante, Russ Dove, walked directly into the forum and began yelling at the audience. CDH security folks removed Dove long before the police arrived to help (Fieldnote C). One of the most notorious cases of more direct police abuse to migrants and supporters came during the April 10, 2006, marches. The TPD failed to separate vigilantes from the marchers, and allowed vigilantes into the center of the street during the march. When Roy Warden decided to burn the Mexican flag amidst the marchers, a high school–aged woman threw a bottle of water at the flag to put out the flames. Police tackled her and she along with several other youth was beaten (Fieldnote C). This incident not only resulted in physical abuse, but for many activists, it again communicated TPD's lack of support and perhaps even disdain for migrants and their advocates. Following the incident, members of CDH and the April 10th Coalition hosted several events calling attention to police brutality, including a play written by several high school students involved in the incident (Fieldnote G, September 23, 2006). Police abuse and harassment against migrant communities occurs in everyday situations as well, which is one of the main kinds of abuse that CDH volunteers document at regular abuse documentation sessions held at the office (Fieldnote O, November 30, 2006). Such incidents have increased as section 287(g) of the Immigration and Nationality Act allows trained local law enforcement officials to enforce federal immigration law (Archibold, 2009). Harassment and abuse of migrant and Latino/a communities has been well documented (Border Action Network, 2008; K. R. Johnson, 1995, 2000; Mirande, 2003; Romero, 2006; Romero & Serag, 2005). Abuse and harassment by law enforcement, and the messages that it sends to migrant communities about the role of law enforcement, has been a central concern for CDH since its creation (Lupe, interview, March 27, 2007).

Wingspan has also experienced abuse and harassment by the TPD, particularly in relation to public parks. At one point, the harassment was so bad that plain clothes police officers were attempting to entrap gay men at the parks and local residents hid in the bushes while wearing camouflage to catch men who they presumed were there for sex and then call the police (Fieldnote H, October 4, 2006). Police eventually stopped some of these practices under pressure from Wingspan, and they now only come to a park if a complaint is lodged. Still, Wingspan receives several calls every week, alleging police harassment. This is not surprising considering that gays (and Jews) top the list of hate crime victims in Tucson, and many report outrage at the way the police handle these incidents ("Gay and Jews," 2004). Much like with migrant communities, the harassment itself is not the only concern, but the message that such harassment sends about the worth of queers is also problematic. Of course, such association of queers with criminality is also historical, as the modern-day LGBT liberation movement in the United States was eventually spurred by responding back to police officers in New York raiding the Stonewall Inn and treating queers as criminals.

Migrants and queers often find themselves in situations where they are not protected, but criminalized. Many times the way law enforcement interacts with Wingspan and CDH constituencies is not public or a part of their official rhetoric pertaining to either group. Accessing how law enforcement officially regards migrant or queer people is, thus, not an easy task. However, by utilizing field methods to access the enclaves of these activist groups, it becomes clear how

activists interpret the rhetorical messages they perceive law enforcement to send about them and their communities. Such interpretations led to recent coalition-building after the aforementioned problem with the TPD harassing gay men in public parks. Cathy explained:

> And we were sort of shocked, and then we realized it's profiling, it's the same thing. So we held a community forum on profiling. And we were able to build an alliance with the NAACP, with *Derechos* [CDH], with Wingspan and with a student group. And we talked about how these different groups get profiled, and what does that mean for civil rights, and how do we together address that. (Interview, April 26, 2007)

Cathy noted that in bringing these groups together, several things happened. For one, although gay men having sex in public parks is controversial within and outside of the queer community, by broadening the analysis to show that the issue was not whether gay men are having sex in parks or whether they should be, it became, "this is about police who have probably better ways to spend their time, harassing people in parks . . ." (Cathy, interview, April 26, 2007). In a broader sense, it allowed all of these different groups to understand a long *shared* history of being thought of and positioned as criminal, which has material impacts for how people are able to exist.

If one considers the historical treatment of migrants, queers, and queer migrants in this country at the hands of law enforcement agencies, it should be no surprise that both Wingspan and CDH are suspicious of law enforcement practices and the messages those practices signal. In both instances, migrants and queers often find themselves in situations where they are not protected, but are rather further constructed as criminals, and it is in this juncture that activists justify the need for building coalition with each other.

Conclusion

Activists understand queers and migrants as constituted through mutually resonant and interconnected discourses, and they utilize these connections to foster coalition-building. Although the task of this article was not to detail how the coalition between CDH and Wingspan works or the type of activism they engage in together publicly, this article has demonstrated part of what it is that brings two seemingly disparate social justice organizations into a relationship with one another. By examining how activists understand mediated, political, and legal rhetoric about queer and migrant subjects, I have illustrated how we might gain a more productive understanding of the justifications that arose to build a coalition between migrant and queer rights movements. Accessing activists' interpretations of such rhetoric affords significant insight into how rhetoric functions to build coalition and eventually compel social movement. In this way, field methods supplied an important methodological resource for understanding rhetorical negotiations within counter-public enclaves.

Much like Stewart's (1991) discussion of internal rhetoric, this article has further shown the need for considering more than "rhetoric of the streets" and, one might add, the Web, to obtain a more complete picture of social movement. The notion of the "enclave" within counter-public sphere theory has largely been viewed as a protected space born of necessity, designed to safeguard a group and prevent unwanted publicity (Squires, 2002). Although there is no doubt that enclaves serve this protective function, enclaves are often a consistent component of activists' movement activity, emphasizing what Fraser (1992) called the back and forth of counter-publics. With coalition-building, in particular, enclaves function as a site of meaning production, and in the case of the particular coalitional enclaves that informed this research, those meanings were not readily accessible outside of the enclave. It is not that activists intended to construct a hidden transcript, but simply that when it comes to coalitional politics, a significant portion of the movement-building and mobilization is internally focused. With CDH and Wingspan, large segments of each group's constituency views the other group as a threat, and does not acknowledge the overlap of the two groups (as in queer migrants), or the similarity between the demonization

they experience. This means that the internal rhetorical work is especially significant to the sustenance of the coalition, as well as any public action they may take. Thus, it is necessary to expand our understanding of how enclaves function within the context of counter-publics and social movement, not only to broaden what we consider in the purview of social movements, but also so that we have a richer understanding of the many facets of rhetorical activity in these contexts.

In addition, because of the dearth of research on coalition-building within social movement studies, our theories about people's rationale for involvement in movements is limited. Gregg (1971) and Stewart (1999) explored the "ego function" within both self- and other-directed movements to suggest that the need to build one's sense of identity and self is important for activists, whether one advocates for her or his own rights or the rights of someone or something else. Examining movements where the direction is self- and other-oriented at the same time, however, challenges the "either/or" dichotomy that necessarily emerges from both Gregg and Stewart's discussions. Implicitly, coalitional politics built between mostly disparate groups are "both/and" activities. As mentioned earlier, Carrillo Rowe (2008) used the term *coalitional subjectivities* to describe the sense of self that emerges when one chooses to be in alliance with others who differ from one's self. What this study of coalitional politics has evidenced is the both/and of the self and other generated between seemingly different groups in coalition. In this study, those who are different connect issues and minimize divisions where divisions might otherwise be expected. When activists refuse to be divided, they not only evidence the development and functioning of coalitional subjectivities, but they also challenge the notion of the singular "ego" that many social movement scholars rely on to discuss motivation for involvement. Although Gregg and Stewart derived different "ego functions" depending on whether one is involved in a self- or other-directed movement, in both instances a unified and singular sense of self and orientation of the self guides the discussion. When one does not possess such an ego, as shown in activists' choices in this analysis, reasons for involvement cannot be so easily conceptualized.

More important, as argued here, it is rhetoric that has generated these complicated, coalitional subjectivities. The study of coalitions then not only adds richness to our understanding of movement activity, but it also points us in different directions pertaining to ongoing questions about what is rhetorical and how rhetoric functions in movements. The study of coalitions also calls us to question what motivates people toward social movement. An understanding of coalitional politics, how people come to develop coalitional subjectivities, and how such development disputes singular understandings of subjectivity, seem prudent directions to pursue to access the vastly changing functions of rhetoric within these precarious times.

Notes

[1] As McGee (1980) argued, approaching social movements as a phenomenon is problematic when it is the meanings of words and actions that produce social movement that should be of interest. In this way, when *social movements* is used as a noun, it suggests that a movement is a phenomenon. Using *social movement* in its verb form, as in a process of people coming together to create meanings and potentially make progress toward a particular social change, reduces the possibility of limiting social movement studies to the investigation of things. To keep the dynamism of movement alive, I typically use *social movement* as a verb and not a noun.

[2] I follow Luibhéid (2005) in primarily utilizing *migrant* and *queer* when referring to people, as opposed to other terms like *immigrant, gay,* or *lesbian.* Luibhéid argued that queer "rejects a minoritizing logic of toleration . . . ," and it suggests that "transformation needs to occur across a wide range of regimes and institutions, not just the sexual . . ." (p. x). Sedgwick (1990) also emphasized the importance of universal logics as opposed to minoritizing logics. Queer also indicates that other categories "were historically formed through specific epistemologies and social relations that upheld colonialist, xenophobic, racist, and sexist regimes" (Luibhéid, 2005, p. xi). Queer is not without its problems (e.g., see Cohen, 1997; E. P. Johnson, 2001; Rudy, 2000), but it marks some of these difficulties and histories. Moreover, I follow Luibhéid's lead in using the term *migrant.* She explained that *migrant* refers to "anyone who

has crossed an international border . . ." (p. xi). This term challenges distinctions between documented, undocumented, refugee, and asylum-seeker because such distinctions often can be relatively arbitrary as people traverse between them. For example, one might be a legal asylum-seeker one day, and then have the asylum claim denied, compelling deportation proceedings. She or he may decide it is better to risk staying in a country illegally than returning to her or his country of origin. Moreover, a vast number of undocumented immigrants in the United States simply overstayed their visitor's visas, again moving them from "legal" to "illegal" status from one day to the next. Refusing these terms draws attention "to the ways that these distinctions function as technologies of normalization, discipline, and sanctioned dispossession" (Luibhéid, 2005, p. xi). I use *migrant* strategically and politically, as I have seen firsthand how one's possession of legal documents does not necessarily lead to better treatment by others or improved material realities. Certainly, "being legal" affords opportunities otherwise unavailable, and yet often oppression that appears to target the undocumented has significant implications for those with documents. For all these reasons, I hope to minimize emphasis on legality with the use of *migrant.*

[3] All participants were offered an opportunity to select a pseudonym. Several elected not to; therefore, unless otherwise indicated, the names used are participants' actual first names.

[4] As a point of recent information, Arizonians approved a 2008 ballot referendum, Proposition 102, which created a constitutional amendment to define marriage as between one man and one woman. It did not impact civil unions or domestic partner benefits. However, in 2009, the Republican governor, Jan Brewer, signed legislation that revoked domestic partner benefits for non-married state employees, which had only been instituted 1 year earlier (see Pallack, 2009).

[5] The Gay and Lesbian Alliance Against Defamation's (GLAAD) statement was located at http://www .glaad.org/media/release_detail.php?id=3964. This URL is no longer active. GLAAD's involvement in this event is mentioned in its 2007 summary of media advocacy, *Media Advocacy: Fighting Defamation, Changing Hearts and Minds,* available at www.glaad.org/Document.Doc?id=30 (as a pdf).

[6] Wingspan has suffered from major cuts in funding throughout the budget crisis; the link to their public policy and advocacy Web page does not, as of this writing, indicate any staff member who is connected with policy at this time.

[7] The Coalition to Defeat Prop 200 was a Tucson-based collection of activists, started by members of the *Coalición de Derechos Humanos* and other local activists. As a temporal coalition, it disbanded after the 2004 election. Their Web site, www.defeat200.org, no longer exists.

[8] Wingspan's full statement against Proposition 200 reads as follows:.

> Wingspan, Southern Arizona's Lesbian, Gay, Bisexual, and Transgender [LGBT] Community Center's mission is to promote the freedom, equality, safety, and well-being of LGBT people in Southern Arizona. Because the intent of Proposition 200 is contrary to Wingspan's mission, Wingspan opposes Proposition 200. Wingspan opposes Proposition 200 because it needlessly makes voter registration more difficult, at a time when voter participation, particularly of marginalized people, is critical. Wingspan opposes Proposition 200 because we believe it will compromise our ability to provide vital social services to the community. Wingspan opposes Proposition 200 because the radical, racist, right-wing, anti-immigrant backers of Proposition 200 are many of the same individuals from fringe groups who actively work against lesbian, gay, bisexual, and transgender rights. Wingspan opposes Proposition 200 because we believe Proposition 200 wrongly scapegoats immigrants for social problems in the United States, including high rates of unemployment and underemployment, inadequate health care systems, and a failing economy. LGBT people are also often wrongly scape-goated [sic] for social problems. For these reasons, Wingspan stands together with other progressive organizations and fair-minded Arizonans against Proposition 200.

[9] Links to these statements can be found at *Coalición de Derechos Humanos and Wingspan Joint Statement: Stand Against Racism and Homophobia* (2006, October 24; http://wingspan.org/content/news_wingspan_details.php?story_id=353) and *Coalición de Derechos Humanos and Wingspan— Joint Statement: Continued Stand Against Racism and Homophobia* (2006, November 28; http://wingspan.org/content/news_wingspan _details.php?story_id=359). Elsewhere, I have conducted an analysis of these public statements in relation to queer and migrant rhetoric produced by national organizations. Chávez, K. R. (2010). Border (in)securities: Normative and differential belonging in LGBTQ and immigrant rights discourse. *Communication & Critical/Cultural Studies, 7*(2), 136–155.

References

Albrecht, L., & Brewer, R. M. (1990). Bridges of power: Women's multicultural alliances for social change. In L. Albrecht & R. M. Brewer (Eds.), *Bridges of power: Women's multicultural alliances* (pp. 2–22). Philadelphia, PA: New Society Publishers.

Anzaldúa, G. (1990). Bridge, drawbridge, sandbar or island: Lesbians-of-color *Hacienda Alianzas.* In L. Albrecht & R. M. Brewer (Eds.), *Bridges of power: Women's multicultural alliances* (pp. 216–233). Philadelphia, PA: New Society Publishers.

Archibold, R. C. (2009, February 14). Lawmakers want look at sheriff in Arizona. *The New York Times*, p. A12.

Asen, R., & Brouwer, D. C. (Eds.). (2001). *Counterpublics and the state.* Albany, NY: State University of New York Press.

Bennett, J. A. (2006). Seriality and multicultural dissent in the same-sex marriage debate. *Communication & Critical/Cultural Studies, 3*, 141–161.

Benson, M., & Sherwood, R. (2006, May 10). Lawsuit questions legality of ID rules: Election law hurts Latinos, groups say. *The Arizona Republic*, p. B1.

Blitefield, J. (2006). It's showtime! Staging public demonstrations, Alinsky-style. In L. J. Prelli (Ed.), *Rhetorics of display* (pp. 255–272). Columbia, SC: University of South Carolina Press.

Border Action Network. (2008). *Human and civil rights violations uncovered: A report from the Arizona/Sonora border.* Tucson, AZ: Author.

Brouwer, D. (1998). The precarious visibility politics of self-stigmatization: The case of HIV/AIDS tattoos. *Text and Performance Quarterly, 18*, 114–136.

Busha, C. (2006). *Sexuality and homeland (in)securities conference handout.* Tucson, AZ: Wingspan.

Busha, C., & Rodriguez, K. (2005, February 25). Guest commentary: All Arizonans should be concerned about anti-immigrant, anti-LGBT ballot initiatives. *Tucson Weekly*. Retrieved from http://www.tucsonweekly.com/gbase/opinion/Content?oid=oid:65517

Campbell, K. K. (1973). The rhetoric of women's liberation: An oxymoron. *Quarterly Journal of Speech, 59*, 74–86.

Carrillo Rowe, A. (2008). *Power lines: On the subject of feminist alliances.* Durham, NC: Duke University Press.

Cathcart, R. S. (1972). New approaches to the study of movements: Defining movements rhetorically. *Western Speech, 36,* 82–88.

Cathcart, R. S. (1978). Movements: Confrontation as rhetorical form. *Southern Speech Communication Journal, 43,* 233–247.

Cathcart, R. S. (1980). Defining social movements by their rhetorical form. *Central States Speech Journal, 31,* 267–273.

Cohen, C. J. (1997). Punks, bulldaggers, and welfare queens: The real radical potential of queer politics? *GLQ: A Journal of Lesbian and Gay Studies, 3,* 437–465.

Conquergood, D. (1998). Beyond the text: Toward a performative cultural politics. In S. J. Dailey (Ed.), *The future of performance studies: Visions and revisions* (pp. 25–36). Annandale, VA: National Communication Association.

Conrad, C. (1981). The transformation of the 'old feminist' movement. *Quarterly Journal of Speech, 67,* 284–297.

Darsey, J. (1991). From "gay is good" to the scourge of AIDS: The evolution of gay liberation rhetoric. *Communication Studies, 42,* 43–66.

Foust, C. R. (2006). Toward degrees of mediation: Revisiting the debate surrounding Hardt and Negri's. *Multitude. Review of Communication, 6,* 329–341.

Fraser, N. (1992). Rethinking the public sphere: A contribution to the critique of actually existing democracy. In C. Calhoun (Ed.), *Habermas and the public sphere* (pp. 109–142). Cambridge, MA: MIT Press.

Gays and Jews top targets of hate crimes in Tucson. (2004, February 25). *Tucson Observer,* pp. 1, 3. Retrieved from www.tucsonobserver.com/archives/pdf/2004/02/FEB%2025.pdf

Gray, M. L. (2009). "Queer Nation is dead/long live Queer Nation": The politics and poetics of social movement and media representation. *Critical Studies in Media Communication, 26,* 212–236.

Gregg, R. B. (1971). The ego-function of the rhetoric of protest. *Philosophy and Rhetoric, 4,* 71–91.

Griffin, L. M. (1952). The rhetoric of historical movements. *Quarterly Journal of Speech, 38,* 184–188.

Griffin, L. M. (1964). The rhetorical structure of the New Left movement: Part One. *Quarterly Journal of Speech, 50,* 113–135.

Hahn, D. F., & Gonchar, R. M. (1971). Studying social movements: A rhetorical methodology. *Speech Teacher, 20,* 44–52.

Hammerback, J. G., & Jensen, R. J. (1980). The rhetorical works of Cesar Chavez and Reies Tijerina. *Western Journal of Speech Communication, 44,* 166–176.

Jackson, B., & Miller, T. P. (2009). The progressive education movement: A case study in coalition politics. In S. M. Stevens & P. M. Malesh (Eds.), *Active voices: Composing a rhetoric for social movements* (pp. 93–114). Albany, NY: State University of New York Press.

Jensen, R. J., & Hammerback, J. G. (1980). Radical nationalism among Chicanos: The rhetoric of Jose Angel Gutierrez. *Western Journal of Speech Communication, 44,* 191–202.

Johnson, E. P. (2001). Quare studies, or (almost) everything I know about queer studies I learned from my grandmother. *Text and Performance Quarterly, 21,* 1–25.

Johnson, K. R. (1995). Civil rights and immigration: Challenges for the Latino community in the twenty-first century. *La Raza Law Journal, 8,* 42–89.

Johnson, K. R. (2000). The case against race profiling in immigration enforcement. *Washington University Law Review, 78,* 675–736.

Johnson Reagon, B. (1983). Coalition politics: Turning the century. In B. Smith (Ed.), *Home girls: A Black feminist anthology* (pp. 356–369). New York, NY: Kitchen Table: Woman of Color Press.

Lucas, S. E. (1980). Coming to terms with movement studies. *Central States Speech Journal, 31,* 255–266.

Luibhéid, E. (2005). Introduction: Queer migration and citizenship. In E. Luibhéid & L. Cantú, Jr. (Eds.), *Queer migrations: Sexuality, U.S. citizenship, and border crossings* (pp. ix–xlvi). Minneapolis, MN: University of Minnesota Press.

Mansbridge, J. (1996). Using power/fighting power: The polity. In S. Benhabib (Ed.), *Democracy and difference: Contesting the boundaries of the political* (pp. 46–60). Princeton, NJ: Princeton University Press.

McGee, M. C. (1975). In search of "the people": A rhetorical alternative. *Quarterly Journal of Speech, 61,* 235–249.

McGee, M. C. (1980). Social movement: Phenomenon or meaning? *Central States Speech Journal, 31,* 233–244.

Mirande, A. (2003). Is there a "Mexican exception" to the Fourth Amendment? *Florida Law Review, 55,* 365–390.

Mitchell, G. R. (2004). Public argument action research and the learning curve of new social movements. *Argumentation and Advocacy, 40,* 209–225.

Palczewski, C. H. (2001). Cyber-movements, new social movements, and counterpublics. In R. Asen & D. C. Brouwer (Eds.), *Counterpublics and the state* (pp. 161–186). Albany, NY: State University of New York Press.

Pallack, B. (2009, September 17). State drops domestic partner benefits. *Arizona Daily Star.* Retrieved from http://www.azstarnet.com/sn/ mailstory-clickthru/309409.php

Pezzullo, P. C. (2001). Performing critical interruptions: Stories, rhetorical invention, and the environmental justice movement. *Western Journal of Communication, 65,* 1–25.

Pezzullo, P. C. (2003). Resisting "National Breast Cancer Awareness Month": The rhetoric of counterpublics and their cultural performances. *Quarterly Journal of Speech, 89,* 345–365.

"Protect Arizona Now." (2004). PAN *homepage.* Scottsdale, AZ: Protect Arizona Now. Retrieved from http://www.pan2004.com

Romero, M. (2006). Racial profiling and immigration law enforcement: Rounding up of usual suspects in the Latino community. *Critical Sociology, 32,* 447–473.

Romero, M., & Serag, M. (2005). Violation of Latino civil rights resulting from INS and local police's use of race, culture, and class profiling: The case of the Chandler Roundup in Arizona. *Cleveland State Law Review, 52,* 75–95.

Rosenwasser, M. J. (1972). Rhetoric and the progress of the women's liberation movement. *Today's Speech, 20,* 45–56.

Rudy, K. (2000). Queer theory and feminism. *Women's Studies, 29,* 195–216.

Scott, R. L. (1968). Justifying violence—The rhetoric of militant Black power. *Central States Speech Journal, 19,* 96–104.

Scott, R. L. (1973). The conservative voice in radical rhetoric: A common response to division. *Speech Monographs, 40,* 123–135.

Sedgwick, E. K. (1990). *Epistemology of the closet.* Berkeley, CA: University of California Press.

Sillars, M. O. (1980). Defining social movements rhetorically: Casting the widest net. *Southern Speech Communication Journal, 46,* 17–32.

Slagle, R. A. (1995). In defense of Queer Nation: From identity politics to a politics of difference. *Western Journal of Communication, 59,* 85–103.

Smith, C. A. (1984). An organic systems analysis of persuasion and social movement: The John Birch Society, 1958–1966. *Southern Speech Communication Journal, 49,* 155–176.

Smith, R. R., & Windes, R. R. (1975). The innovational movement: A rhetorical theory. *Quarterly Journal of Speech, 61,* 140–153.

Squires, C. R. (2002). Rethinking the Black public sphere: An alternative vocabulary for multiple public spheres. *Communication Theory, 12,* 446–468.

Stewart, C. J. (1980). A functional approach to the rhetoric of social movements. *Central States Speech Journal, 31,* 298–305.

Stewart, C. J. (1991). The internal rhetoric of the Knights of Labor. *Communication Studies, 42,* 67–82.

Stewart, C. J. (1997). The evolution of a revolution: Stokely Carmichael and the rhetoric of Black power. *Quarterly Journal of Speech, 83,* 429–446.

Stewart, C. J. (1999). Championing the rights of others and challenging evil: The ego function in the rhetoric of other-directed social movements. *Southern Communication Journal, 64,* 91–105.

Windt, T. O., Jr. (1972). The diatribe: Last resort for protest. *Quarterly Journal of Speech, 58,* 1–14.

Wingspan. (2007, February 2). *Wingspan responds to Jennifer Waddell's sensationalistic journalism.* Tucson, AZ: Wingspan. Retrieved from http://www.wingspan.org/content/ news_wingspan_ details.php?story_id=371

Zarefsky, D. (1980). A skeptical view of movement studies. *Central States Speech Journal, 31,* 245–254.

Chapter 5

Tactics of Control

Thus far we have primarily considered movements that seek to transform the status quo in some significant way. This much is consistent with social movement scholarship generally. But of course to study a movement is also to study what is being moved against: that is, the forces of opposition that seek to squelch, silence, or otherwise limit the power of those in protest. The following essays are important contributions to this still emergent approach to the analysis of movement dynamics. Those with power, who are being asked to change or give up traditional ways of operating, will respond. Here rhetoric plays an equally important role.

The resources available to those with power are different from the resources available to those who seek to change the conditions of oppression. Above all, the powerful may avail themselves of certain tactics of control. Because they have greater access to political venues, media, and other means for effectively checking the claims of the insurgent movement, agents protecting the status quo will frequently seek to contain the meanings, effects, and circulation of protest rhetoric. They may appeal to traditional values of law, order, and reason; deflect, distort, and reroute protest arguments, sometimes by appearing to support or compromising with the movement; stigmatize as "radical" those voices deemed a threat to a stable society; remove or limit the emergence and growth of a social movement by laying claim to the issues that generate protest; or employ tactics that are violent rather than rhetorical, the effects of which are to shape and constrain protest rhetoric. We are thus reminded that movement rhetoric is at least a two-way street: movement activists must confront the opposition and target their rhetoric accordingly, but those to whom such rhetoric is directed must respond in a complex interplay of thrust and counterthrust. The essays that follow underscore the important lesson that protest movements cannot be understood independent of the rhetoric of those who resist challenges to established power.

In "President Johnson's War on Poverty: The Rhetoric of Three 'Establishment' Movements" (1977), David Zarefsky examines Lyndon Johnson's administrative response to poverty, called the Economic Opportunity Act, and the opposition it inspired. Zarefsky illuminates the administration's strategies to mitigate efforts by two movements that emerged in response to the policies of its Office of Economic Opportunity: in one case by means of the "symbolic defensive maneuver" of procedural "non-decision making," in the other case through face-saving and policy-sustaining compromise. Zarefsky also uses this study to challenge his predecessors, those scholars whose theories of social protest derived from minority movements of the 1960s, by claiming that not all movements are "insurgent." He argues that reform discourse is not always generated from the margins of a culture: sometimes the "establishment" seeks to challenge the existing order on behalf of the oppressed.

Not until fifteen years after Zarefsky's work did another scholar, John M. Murphy in "Domesticating Dissent: The Kennedys and the Freedom Rides" (1992), carefully consider the role of the "establishment" in social movement discourse. Skeptical of the "Establishment-Conflict" model that long favored the study of "battle" between agitators and antagonistic institutional power, Murphy reexamines the issue of "social control" in social protest. He focuses on the symbolic means by which the "establishment" attempts to "accommodate dissent while making it compatible with 'dominant systems of meaning.'" In this case, he asks, how did the Kennedy Administration and major press sources "domesticate" the Freedom Rides of the civil rights movement, which sought to test the strength of federal law regarding desegregation and to dramatize the need for federal intervention in the South? Murphy analyzes the "'extraordinary measures and routine conventions,'" through which "the hegemonic process framed the Rides such that the government could appear both to uphold the rights of the Riders and to preserve order."

Governments or corporations often have resources and therefore particular advantages in controlling strategic engagement with protestors. Jason Edward Black, in "SLAPPS and Social Activism: The *Wonderland v. Grey2K* Case" (2002/2003), discusses Strategic Lawsuits Against Public Participation (SLAPP) filed by protest targets, often on the grounds of defamation, as a means of depleting protestors' resources and energy, rerouting protestors' focus, distorting protesters' image, shifting public perception of wrongdoing onto protestors, transforming themselves into "victims," and enjoining or chilling protest speech. Although anti-SLAPP statutes exist in a majority of states, and despite the very low percentage of successful SLAPP suits, SLAPPers achieve their actual goal of diversion and subversion through manipulating a sluggish system that vindicates protestors only after the strategic damage has already been done. Thus the dynamic relations among resources, structures, rhetorical timing, framing, and silence are at the heart of this strategy of control. Black illustrates the concept through the 2000 case in which Wonderland Park in Massachusetts, accused of massive abuse against its racing greyhounds by the animal rights group Grey2K, filed a SLAPP to undermine a referendum on the November ballot, effectively stymieing Grey2K's advocacy just days before the election. Although the court threw out the injunction and restraining order on the eve of the election, Black argues that strategic timing and ground had been lost. The referendum failed by merely 2 percent of the vote.

In "Neutralizing Protest: The Construction of War, Chaos, and National Identity through US Television News on Abortion-Related Protest, 1991" (2006), Ginna Husting illuminates

mass media as complicated and often vexing "players" in movement action. Husting identifies a strong inclination in U.S. society that preserves homogenization and docility against the democratic pluralism and agonistics of protest. TV news operates, according to this analysis, as a means to thwart threats to nationalism, creating "a narrowly defined mass identity of 'good Americans' in opposition to the dangerous spectacle of protest." "War talk" is common in social movement rhetoric; it is a means of motivating activists and framing the issue and opponents at stake in the conflict. However, as Husting demonstrates, in the 1991 "abortion war" actions by pro-life and pro-choice protestors, ABC, NBC, and CBS worked against both "sides" by pitting all activism against a victimized U.S. community/family/nation. Through war tropes and accompanying narratives of "chaos vs. law and order," news coverage simplified issues and caricatured activists, framing protest as a dangerous threat to "people like us"—all the while appearing to merely report disturbing events.

Dana L. Cloud, an activist professor at the University of Texas who has been dubbed one of the "101 most dangerous intellectuals in the United States," examines the dynamism and complexity of a particular mode of disciplining counterattack she knows well, namely hate mail. In "Foiling the Intellectuals: Gender, Identity Framing, and the Rhetoric of the Kill in Conservative Hate Mail" (2009), Cloud analyzes 290 hostile conservative responses to her antiwar and other activist commitments, constructing her as a fraudulent and elitist intellectual, a national traitor, and a gender/sexual deviant who abuses her daughter. Cloud calls their function "framing by foil," the naming, diminishing, and pressure that amounts to a "symbolic kill" in Burkean terms, meant to silence the activist perpetrator and, even though it occurs under the "shield of intimacy," producing a chilling effect on similar activism. Cloud identifies hate as a rhetoric of control: the identity construction of the hater by antagonistic contrast to the recipient, or the dialectical constitution of self through the abjection of one's political adversary. Gender and sexuality, among other dimensions of power, provide rhetorical reservoirs for such attacks; moreover, such discourse reveals regimes to which author and victim are both subject, or as Cloud insightfully observes, "The personal is political not only for the recipient of hate mail but also for its authors." Cloud responded with a "pedagogy of accountability" by making those private messages public, thus shaming their authors. In some instances, the countermove produced apologies and meaningful civil dialogue.

President Johnson's War on Poverty: The Rhetoric of Three "Establishment" Movements
David Zarefsky

For over twenty years a central concern of rhetorical critics has been the study of social movements. Although Griffin's original exploration of the field included the suggestion that critics study movements which had occurred in the past,[1] a dominant pattern in recent scholarship has been the study of contemporary movements.[2] Critics of both historical and contemporary movements, however, have tacitly assumed that movements are *insurgent* forces which come into being because a minority group becomes dissatisfied with its lot and seeks through persuasion to alter the situation.[3] The development of a movement is believed necessary because those in power have an interest in perpetuating things as they are. They are motivated to act only in reaction to outside forces.

The purpose of this essay is to question the necessity of that assumption for rhetorical study, and the method will be to develop a counter-example to demonstrate that the rhetorical characteristics of movements may be replicated *within* the political power structure. Specifically, I will argue that (1) the War on Poverty during the Presidential Administration of Lyndon Johnson had a rhetorical career identical to that of a social movement, (2) little *rhetorical* significance attaches to the fact that the War on Poverty was not an insurgent effort, and (3) the counter-example should suggest the need for reassessment of rhetorical theory and criticism of movements.

President Johnson's War on Poverty, embodied in the design and implementation of the Economic Opportunity Act, is in many ways an appropriate counter-example. It was an attempt to improve both the economic condition of the poor and their status relative to the rest of society, and it was born in dissatisfaction with the existing order. It sought through collective behavior to achieve fundamental social change. But it was not an insurgent movement; it was formulated within the Executive Branch of the Federal Government and endorsed by the President of the United States. Analysis of the War on Poverty, therefore, should permit a test of whether there is something rhetorically unique about insurgent protest.

STAGES OF THE MOVEMENTS

In two essays, Griffin has described the development of movements. Movements may be *pro,* attempting to arouse public opinion to the creation or acceptance of a new idea, or *anti,* aiming for the destruction or rejection of an existing institution. In either case, a study of the movement will identify *aggressor* rhetors, who seek in the former case to establish and in the latter to destroy, and *defendant* rhetors, who seek to resist the impetus of the *pro* movement or to preserve the *status quo* against the *anti* movement. Chronologically, the movement passes through three rhetorical phases: a period of *inception,* during which the aggressor rhetors disturb *stasis* by their negation of the existing order, their conversion to an alternative, and their propagation of this alternative in search of converts; a period of *rhetorical crisis,* during which a collective audience finds it impossible to maintain the state of mental balance which formerly existed between aggressor and defendant rhetors; and a period of *consummation,* during which a decision is persevered in, whether the decision is that the movement was successful and that the aggressor rhetors may abandon their efforts or that the cause was lost and further appeals are useless.[4]

The War on Poverty fit this scheme. Essentially, it was composed of three movements. Initially, a *pro* movement sought the adoption of the Economic Opportunity Act as the embodiment of the nation's commitment to fight poverty. Upon its success, this movement was attacked simultaneously by a *pro* movement and an *anti* movement. The *pro* movement, led by militants among the poor, sought to intensify and to transform the nation's antipoverty commitment. Led by mayors and Congressmen, the *anti* movement sought to de-emphasize the commitment and to improve tighter administrative control. The simultaneous pressure of the two challenging movements eroded a middle ground and compromised the nation's willingness to continue the War on Poverty.

The Original Antipoverty Movement

The inception period of the War on Poverty occurred during the Kennedy Administration among intellectuals who had been attracted into government service.[5] During the 1950's, the nation had paid scant heed to the problems of the poor. The report of the President's Commission on National Goals made no specific mention of poverty,[6] and this apparent public unconcern was mirrored in the private sector. Although overstating the case, Sidney Lens has claimed that a generation of Americans, smugly content with military-induced prosperity, lost sight of the poor.[7] John Kenneth Galbraith's *The Affluent Society* was received widely as an encomium to American prosperity rather than as a plea for more resources to be committed to the public sector.[8]

Persistence of the old order required that people continue to believe both that the channels of vertical mobility were open and in use, and that the nation's foreign policy was of higher priority than were domestic needs. The vanguard of the War on Poverty reacted to this old order. They saw a society in which channels of mobility were closed and the poor were walled into "the other America"; they saw a nation in which the social structure denied to the poor the opportunity to achieve values which were shared with the rest of the country; they saw a situation in which the persistence of poverty at home weakened American policy abroad.

It is difficult to identify a single enactment of the negative in the inception of this struggle for a new order. Several possibilities suggest themselves. The enactment of the negative may have been John Kennedy's campaign trip through West Virginia, a trip which reportedly made him personally aware of the severity of poverty.[9] It may have been the publication of Richard Cloward and Lloyd Ohlin's book, *Delinquency and Opportunity,* which served as a manifesto for the President's Committee on Juvenile Delinquency.[10] It may have been the administrative discussions leading to the Area Redevelopment Act and the Manpower Development and Training Act. It may have been the publication of Michael Harrington's book, *The Other America,* which was thought to have a significant impact on the President.[11] Each of these specific events and documents served to increase awareness of a problem. Each identified the abolition of poverty as the "heaven"; persistent complacency, as the "hell." Each argued that redemption demanded special government policies to meet the needs of the impoverished.

Although the new program was to be an attack on poverty, poverty was not identified as the counter-movement. Nor did advocates of the program identify a specific sector of society, such as business or labor, which they believed to have a vested interest in perpetuating the poverty of others. Presumably, widening participation in prosperity was to the benefit of all. The enemy therefore was identified as unawareness, or complacency, or indifference, a generalized force which blinded the American conscience to the depth of the problem. Since men were to negate the prevailing order by negating forces within themselves, salvation was to be achieved through mortification.

Throughout the inception period, there was an increase in the quantity of discourse, although most of the expansion occurred *within* the ranks of government. Among the beliefs to which there was increasing adherence were the value of "opportunity" and the need to create an "opportunity structure," concepts derived from Cloward and Ohlin's theory that juvenile delinquency was attributable to gaps between aspirations and opportunities.[12] Another prevalent belief was the commitment to locally-based, intensive demonstration projects, derived from the experience of the President's Committee on Juvenile Delinquency. As myths, these beliefs shaped the context within which specific antipoverty proposals and ideas became meaningful.[13] They were the values to which planners of the new program appealed.

The time of rhetorical crisis occurred in the aftermath of the Kennedy assassination. The poverty program moved from an idea espoused by some officials in discussions within the government, to a formal proposal for national decision. What caused the transformation was the grafting of additional motives onto the original motives of the program's proponents. The new President needed to demonstrate that he had concern for liberal, humanitarian programs, and that his Presidency would be responsive to the underprivileged. The nation felt the need for collective self-mortification to assuage guilt resulting from the assassination. Many people's feelings of personal loss were coupled with a pervasive sense of national guilt. On December 30, 1963[,] a Louis Harris survey was published which suggested that Americans massively rejected political extremism and also that many had "an individual sense of guilt for not having worked more for tolerance toward others."[14] A belief that the late President's memory would be honored through the adoption of his program undoubtedly contributed to the acceptance of the War on Poverty. In short, the balance of forces in the mind of the collective audience was disturbed permanently by the redefinition of the poverty problem as the problem moved to the forefront of public attention. As Jones explains, ". . . new voices are added, supporting, altering, or objecting to the original formulation."[15]

The consummation phase of this movement came in the passage of the Economic Opportunity Act, ratifying a national decision that fighting poverty was an objective of high priority. Enactment of the legislation, and testimonials of faith in its prospects, were ways of persevering in that decision.[16] The testimony of Administration witnesses before the House Education and Labor Committee in 1964 contributed to the consummation phase. Chicago Congressman Roman Pucinski was moved to remark, "As far as I know, this is the first time in the history of this country that all of the Cabinet members, except the Secretary of State, have testified in support of an important measure."[17] The advocacy of Administration spokesmen, however, was of a very general sort, stressing the need for antipoverty action, assuring the committee that the bill would be compatible with ongoing programs, and occasionally discussing matters at best tangentially related to the legislation. These spokesmen were trying less to persuade Congress of the merits of a specific bill than to bear witness to the new order. Perseverance in the anti-poverty decision also was exemplified by the broad base of support for the government policy. Seldom, for example had social programs of the Democratic Party received the enthusiastic support of businessmen. By presenting the War on Poverty as a businesslike scheme offering return on an investment, however, President Johnson was able to evoke support from that quarter.[18] Similarly, by portraying the new program as fundamentally a conservative measure because of its fiscal prudence and local orientation, the President was able to garner the support of political conservatives.[19] This process of coalition-building had two functions. It made the poverty program more palatable to politicians, who saw in it a way to enlarge the ranks of their supporters. Political leaders could "shore up an existing coalition, or [develop] new and more stable alignments, *without* jeopardizing existing support," the conditions established by Cloward and Piven for government's responsiveness to a group's demands.[20] A second function of coalition-building was to enhance the prospects for continued national acceptance by enlisting in advance the support of groups who conceivably might be expected to oppose the program.

In the consummation phase, however, there were signals of danger which would prevent this movement from reaching the final *stasis* of a new order. The terms in which the program had been described, and especially the President's call for "unconditional victory," raised expectations against which later performance would be judged. If those who were caught up in a revolution of rising expectations found their expectations unmatched by the program's performance, it was likely that they would blame the program. After all, the Administration had called for total victory and had claimed that the nation had the knowledge to banish poverty.[21] Any failure, therefore, must be one of will.

Moreover, the unlikely coalition of supporters had endorsed the *abstract principle* that poverty should be eliminated. One's abstract beliefs, of course, are not always consistent with opinions or actions in specific circumstances.[22] The coalition, therefore, easily could fall apart. Disgruntled spokesmen could argue that the War on Poverty, in practice, was not what it had been claimed to be in theory. The ease with which events could facilitate this disjunction did not augur well for the survival of a national anti-poverty consensus.

The Challenging *Pro* Movement

Once the Economic Opportunity Act became law, its administrators found it necessary to defend the new order against movements like those described above. Those whose expectations were far greater than the act could satisfy criticized the new order because it did not depart enough from the old. In many cases the dissidents were local community organizers whose efforts were supported, or stimulated, by the Office of Economic Opportunity. They saw themselves as government-supported advocates for the poor, not as adjudicators of competing political needs. Seemingly unconcerned with coalition-building or with the need to change the attitudes of others entrenched within the political system, factors which dictated gradualism, the ideologues of this new movement soon decried the War on Poverty

as a sellout to established political machines.[23] They wished to return to what they regarded as the original goal of the poverty program—strengthening their power. They opposed the "power structure" of the Administration and redefined the struggle: the "power structure" embodied the counter-movement; the indigenous poor, the new *pro* movement. As Walter Miller wrote, "The Power Structure, The Poor, and their assorted rosters of heroes and villains provide for the War on Poverty a basic essential of a genuine movement—clear and concrete objects of love and hate."[24]

The inception of this new movement came in protests against specific administrative decisions of OEO—yielding to the wishes of local mayors, refusing to refund controversial projects, limiting the size of manpower programs, and so on. One example of a manifesto enacting the negative is an article by Saul Alinsky, appearing in 1965, which charged that the War on Poverty was "political pornography."[25] But a far better example is the 1966 convention of the Citizens' Crusade Against Poverty, at which OEO Director Sargent Shriver was booed and his agency's programs denounced by people who ostensibly were the programs' beneficiaries.[26] This protest revealed the key terms and equations of the new movement. The poverty program was seen as a promise without delivery; its administrators were meek apologists for the power structure.

By redefining the issues so that they involved power relationships, the leaders of the new movement enlarged the scope of conflict. They transformed the order symbolized by the Economic Opportunity Act, or[i]ginally a synthesis of the nation's antipoverty effort, from merger to division. That order was shown to be only one facet of a larger question involving the distribution of power. In making this transformation, the militants exemplified Schattschneider's dictum that the way in which an issue is defined affects its scope, and that it is the *loser* who calls for outside help by expanding the conflict.[27]

Redefining the struggle led to new alliances. Militants often allied with social workers who felt that their knowledge and skills were being ignored or denigrated by the Administration,[28] and who, like the militants, increasingly came to define their role as advocates for the poor. Supposedly, though, the Administration itself was playing that role. To justify the claim that OEO had abandoned the role of advocate, the challengers alleged that it had become the tool of the power structure. They argued that government had conspired to represent the interests of politicians who stood to gain from the largesse the poverty program would distribute, rather than representing the interests of the poor in whose behalf the war had been launched.[29] Since, as Edelman notes, the conspiracy theme personifies the source of threat, giving a person solace that "guilty leaders and their dangerous dupes are identifiable and *ad hominem* aggression is possible . . . [.]"[30] it was potent in galvanizing support for the challenging movement during the period of inception.

The rhetorical crisis for this new movement came as it engaged the political leaders of the nation's cities. No longer could politicians consider the militant poor to be only a malcontent minority. Often militants took control of what otherwise might be relatively apathetic and powerless groups. Through acts of protest they could increase their bargaining resources. To the power of their numbers they might add the power to create unpleasant and embarrassing incidents which could tarnish the power structure's image of success in responding to poverty and human misery, or even in keeping the peace.[31] Acts of local protest, such as the demonstration in Syracuse in 1965, intensified through 1966 and 1967.[32]

The consummation phase of this challenging *pro* movement saw its cause smothered by the political establishment, but without a direct encounter or defeat. Although some local leaders might have wished to do so, it would have been rhetorically unwise to repress protest. Repression would demonstrate that the poverty agency *had* indeed sold out, and that the war *was* being fought between the local politicians and the poor. Moreover, it would have revealed what the militants regarded as the true colors of the power structure. An ugly portrayal might have weakened the adherence of otherwise strong supporters of the existing order and might have radicalized the uncertain into support for the militants' cause. These results would have sustained the momentum of the new challenge and increased the chances that militancy might supplant moderation.[33]

Not wishing to endorse a transformation from an abstract War on Poverty to a concrete assault on local politicians (for fear that they and their Congressional allies might retaliate against the poverty program), and yet not wishing to attack the new movement directly (for fear of provoking confrontation), the managers of the poverty program employed a strategy which Bachrach and Baratz label "nondecision-making."[34] As they use the term, a "nondecision" is a decision which blunts a challenge to the decision-maker's interests and values. Ideally, it is a means for suffocating demands for change *before* they gain widespread public attention, thereby denying them a place on the public agenda. Perhaps the easiest means of nondecision-making is to dispense to protesting groups symbolic satisfactions, such as official recognition or publicity, as a substitute for tangible benefits, such as increased funds or a revision of policy. This distribution of rewards can be persevered in, because, as Lipsky explains, "the capacity of the political system to deny material changes to masses of people while legislating or proclaiming to the contrary is an extremely salient aspect of the political process."[35]

Among the defensive symbolic maneuvers available to politicians was postponement of a decision, especially by forming a special commission to study a problem. Another option was to make decisions on a case-by-case basis as a response to particular protest activities, but without implying a broad decision of principle, so that others who wished to make the same claim would need to begin the protest anew. Perhaps the most effective "nondecision," however, was to make procedural reforms which seemingly would respond to the protesters' demands by involving them in decision-making, but which were not accompanied by substantive changes. Lipsky and Levi explain why procedural reform may be a potent nondecision. Public agencies, they write, often are quite resilient so that the substance of policy may be unaffected by procedural changes.[36] Reforms made in response to protesters' demands might be nullified by informal controls or by controlling the flow of information so as to predetermine the action of the decision-making body by limiting the availability of options.

Although it was not introduced for this purpose, the "Quie amendment" of 1966 illustrates a procedural nondecision. To answer the criticism that the poor were excluded from decision-making in local community action programs, Congress stipulated that at least one-third of the members of local boards be representatives of the poor.[37] This guarantee of participation by the poor, however, had little impact on decisions about policy. Often other board members perceived the poor as unqualified and consequently were reluctant to cooperate with them.[38] Moreover, the role-definition of the community representatives on the boards further weakened their power. In her study of the Los Angeles antipoverty board, for instance, Marshall found that the poor on the board did not see themselves as representing an organized set of interests but instead as representing their individual consciences alone.[39] With such a view of their role, they were not likely to form coalitions or to maximize their bargaining strength. In addition, resources to implement community action programs were insufficient to permit boards to exercise much discretionary power over the purse. The result was characterized by Adam Walinsky: "The great failing of the community action program ... was that it never had very much to organize about ...."[40]

The importance attached by OEO to board membership despite the limited tangible power of the board suggests that participation was a procedural ritual rather than a means for the poor to influence substantive decisions.[41] Kenneth Clark complained that action was used "as a mere escape valve and as a displacement of energy," so that the pressure for reform was dissipated in catharsis. He charged, further, that participation became a strategy for containment of the poor, offering them the psychological benefits of control without power or access to the actual decision-making forces within the community.[42] A conspiratorial interpretation would add the charge (for which no evidence has been located) that the original proponents of participation *intended* that it so function.

The consummation of this new movement, then, was defeat. The balance of forces was disturbed and the counter-movement represented by political leaders smothered the proposals for expansion of the antipoverty effort. Eventually the aggressor rhetors ceased their efforts, apparently convinced that a struggle to persuade the government to endorse militant protest against the power structure was futile. Militant leaders of the poor, finding the implementation of the Economic Opportunity Act not up to the scale of the government's antipoverty commitment, questioned the credibility of the commitment itself. The ephemeral nature of protest helps to explain this consummation. Establishment forces, if they select appropriate maneuvers and tactics, can outlast the insurgents. Protest depends upon publicity, since it increases a group's numerical resources through the staging of public events. Publicity, in turn, requires the continuous development of new and dramatic techniques. It is difficult to sustain such a pace of innovation; eventually, in Griffin's words, "the well of invention runs dry."[43] Furthermore, if protest leaders *could* sustain the pace of innovation, they would do so only at the price of other goals. They might be unable to win any favors from public officials or the media; they might lose the support of nominal constituents who sought relief from specific conditions in their lives, who were not pacified by the drama of the struggle, and who therefore concluded that the protest leaders could not deliver on their promises. Accordingly, Lipsky concludes that if protest "is rewarded primarily by the dispensation of symbolic gestures without perceptible changes in material conditions, then rational behavior might lead to expressions of apathy and lack of interest in politics."[44]

Moreover, protest leaders had few options for responding to the symbolic defensive maneuvers of the political establishment. They might have pursued a militant course in the hope of provoking the confrontation the political leaders had sought to avoid. But, having had apparently reasonable offers spurned, the power structure need not have appeared ugly in acting finally to squelch the protesters. The uncommitted whom the militants hoped to radicalize might be repulsed instead, indignant at the stubbornness of those who would reject the government's apparent compromise. Furthermore, a potent means of governmental retaliation was available. Insofar as the militant leaders were community organizers hired by OEO, government could withdraw the funds which paid them. Such a counterattack would underscore the belief that it was not appropriate to use public funds to attack local politicians, the end which the militants believed they must accomplish in order to end poverty. Rein and Miller describe the protester's dilemma. He could not yield to the government initiatives, for to do so would be to acquiesce in a token gesture proferred [*sic*] as a substitute for reform. But neither could he persevere in his militancy, for to do so would be to invite counterattack.[45] Dependent on short-term tactics and devoid of long-term rhetorical options, he was doomed to fail.

The Challenging *Anti* Movement

Defending the poverty program against the new *pro* movement, however, was not sufficient to preserve the new order which the Economic Opportunity Act had been intended to signal. Almost simultaneously, its administrators became the target of an *anti* movement, led by people whose conviction to fight poverty stopped short of their embracing methods which threatened their self-interest and seemed to sacrifice social order and civic peace. Increasingly, local mayors and members of Congress had reservations about the new order. They were deeply disturbed by protests and demonstrations, by the apparent lack of gratitude among the poor, and by the revolution of rising expectations.[46] These aggressor rhetors, mayors and Congressmen, were not satisfied by the distinction drawn between peaceful and violent protest. Sensitive to order, they tended to see protest as all of a piece. As social judgment theory might predict, since their points of reference were far removed from those of the protesters, they accentuated the contrast.[47] Contrast effects could be observed among the aggressor rhetors of the *anti* movement—in the special sensitivity to demonstrations of any type, for example, or in the exaggerated belief that the War on Poverty challenged the very principles of local government.[48]

The *anti* movement had its inception in 1965 and 1966, and was rooted in the desire

for a return to order and decorum. What was negated was the negation of order, the anti-poverty warriors' perceived willingness to trample upon political and social traditions. For the mayors a representative enactment of the negative might be the resolution introduced at the 1965 Conference of Mayors by Sam Yorty and John F. Shelley which accused the OEO of "fostering class struggle."[49] Here was a succinct statement that fighting poverty was good but that disturbing the prevailing relationships among social classes was bad, and that the evil was of greater force than the good. For the Congressmen, the negative was enacted in hearings on the 1966 amendments to the Economic Opportunity Act, during which it became apparent that the act no longer received the broad base of support it had enjoyed the year before.[50] The amendments of 1966 themselves indicated that Congressmen were not satisfied with the poverty agency's performance. As Wilfred Rommel of the Budget Bureau advised the President, "The numerous restrictions and requirements ... do not individually present serious problems; but, taken together, they amount to 'danger signals' with respect to congressional attitudes."[51]

The rhetorical crisis for the *anti* movement came as other agencies of government responded to its concerns and pressured OEO into modifying its program. The pressure on the agency made clear that the aggressor rhetors of the *anti* movement were not isolated dissident politicians in a nation which subscribed wholeheartedly to the new order. Rather, the challengers represented influential forces to whom the poverty program's managers had the obligation to listen. Examples of the pressure on OEO include the designation of Vice President Humphrey to represent the interests of the mayors, the alleged advice of the Budget Bureau that OEO de-emphasize the controversial community action programs, and the steps taken by Congress to earmark funds for national emphasis programs, thereby limiting the administrative flexibility of OEO by reducing its discretion in the allocation of funds.[52]

The *anti* movement's consummation phase came in the Administration's decision to compromise with it, to temper its own goals and aspirations with a concern for mayoral and Congressional desires. For the mayors the consummation could be seen in 1966 in the President's appointment of Bernard Boutin as Deputy Director of OEO, in the informal veto power given to fifteen of the nation's mayors, in OEO's emphasis on funding "umbrella" agencies which represented community consensus rather than conflict, and in the decision not to renew funding for controversial projects such as the Child Development Group of Mississippi.[53] The mayors saw the consummation as a victory; the poverty program now offered funds for their cities without threats to their power. Accordingly, their support of OEO grew during 1966 and the Conference of Mayors passed a resolution endorsing the program.[54] But the agency *also* regarded its actions as a victory; it now could point to a much broader base of national support and acceptance. The fact that the base had been broadened because the nature of the program had *changed* need not be mentioned. Instead, OEO could claim that the original idea now was taking hold. William H. Crook, OEO Southwest regional director, wrote in a 1966 memorandum to Bill Moyers that "the mayors of *all* our southern cities are purring like kittens asking for another bowl of milk."[55] And, in a handwritten note to the President, Shriver took pride in the fact that Mayor Naftalin of Minneapolis, who in 1965 "was giving OEO h——" in a twelve-page letter to Hubert Humphrey, now had endorsed the OEO program, as had the U.S. Conference of Mayors. In a postscript, Shriver added, "And I don't think Dick Daley has uttered one word, or even a hint of complaint, in more than a year."[56]

For the Congressional leaders of the *anti* movement, the consummation phase came a year later, in the Economic Opportunity Amendments of 1967. These amendments required that public officials compose one-third of the membership of community action boards, and substituted Congressional mandates for agency discretion in other aspects of the program as well. In large part, however, they codified new procedures which OEO already had established. As with the mayors the consummation was a compromise. Congressional doubters could claim victory since they had "tightened up" the operation of the poverty agency and had forced the Administration to accept Congressionally-initiated reforms in order that OEO might live.[57] The Administration, though, also could claim victory. It had preserved OEO, at least as a symbol of national commitment, had secured a two-year authorization, and had garnered the largest Congressional majority in the program's history.[58]

The Cumulative Effect

Although they did not plan it this way, the *pro* and *anti* movements which challenged OEO also fortified each other. Action by one movement was likely to arouse corresponding action from the other. Militancy by aggressors of the *pro* movement angered Congressmen and mayors, convincing them that to defeat poverty would require that they abandon traditions of social order. Political pressure from the aggressors of the *anti* movement angered the militants, convincing them that the poverty agency had sold out to the power structure. OEO was caught in the crossfire between the two movements, attacked with double force. Nor would capitulation to either challenging movement have been a solution; were either the *pro* or *anti* challenging movement to establish itself as the new order, it automatically would have antagonized the other movement, which would have attacked the new order and prevented the attainment of a final *stasis*. OEO had little choice but to attempt to defend itself against both *pro* and *anti* movements, holding the middle ground between them.

OEO's response to the two movements, however, demonstrated that there was no middle ground. It defeated the *pro* movement by outlasting protest, so that protest supporters became apathetic. They were apathetic not only toward protest, however, but toward the government's antipoverty initiatives as well.[59] So in defeating the *pro* movement the agency abandoned its hopes to create a supportive constituency among the poor. Moreover, the militants of the *pro* movement, like their counterparts of the *anti* movement, exhibited contrast effects in perception. They failed to distinguish between the complete subjugation of OEO by the power structure and the type of compromise which enabled each side to claim victory. Because of the discrepancy of either capitulation or compromise from their own anchor point, they sharpened the contrast, reacting to the less extreme measure as if it were the more extreme. In so doing they reinforced their disaffection from the government. A poverty program which did not command the support of leaders of the poor was not likely to endure.

Implicit in the compromise with the *anti* movement was a lowering of the poverty program's objectives. The reduction of goals is demonstrated by a 1969 directive concerning participation by the poor. Community action agencies were advised that it was better to start with a limited goal which could be met than to pursue a more ambitious one which could require a long-term commitment of energy.[60] A program designed to answer pragmatic, short-range questions might be an appropriate means to research and develop potential antipoverty weapons for future use. But it was hardly calculated to attract or to retain the public support which the new order created by the Economic Opportunity Act was supposed to expect.

In the relationship described above lay an explanation for the stalemate in which President Johnson's War on Poverty ended. OEO continued to exist, presumably as a symbol of national commitment. By its counterattack on the *pro* and *anti* movements, though, it relinquished the substance of the commitment. It survived at the price of alienating its presumptive supporters and lowering its goals. The agency's defenders, asserting its place as a "good" order, made it faulty. Although the poverty agency would survive, the decision of 1964 would not be persevered in. A campaign against "too much government" and "social programs that have failed" soon would set it aside.

THE IMPACT OF GOVERNMENT SPONSORSHIP

Typical definitions of the term "social movement" stress collective behavior, espousal of fundamental social change, and operation outside the framework of established institutions.[61] Clearly, each of the movements comprising the War on Poverty satisfied the first two of these criteria; just as clearly, each failed to satisfy the

third. The members of the original task force which drafted the Economic Opportunity Act all were holders of high public office. From the Federal Government frequently came both the impetus and the funds for local community organizing which formed the basis of the challenging *pro* movement. And the mayors and Congressmen who led the *anti* movement to restrict OEO certainly acted in their official capacities. Nonetheless, each of these three Establishment-sponsored movements had a rhetorical career not unlike that of an insurgent persuasive campaign. Similarly, the obstacles and exigences characteristic of each stage in an insurgent movement's life also were present in the War on Poverty.

In the inception phase of the original antipoverty movement, the Federal Government became the surrogate for the poor who lacked the resources to threaten the social system with loss, harm, embarrassment, or inconvenience, so that a course of action would be changed.[62] The government supplied these resources. In sponsoring local community organizations, which became the base for later protest by the poor, the Federal Government again acted as a surrogate. Likewise, members of the U.S. Congress encouraged and became spokesmen for the *anti* movement.

There was little difference, however, between government's acting as a surrogate sponsor of a movement and government's support for a movement initiated in the private sector. For that matter, surrogate sponsorship was no different from the bestowal of legitimacy by any credible source. In each case prestige suggestion is involved. A credible source increases the credibility of a movement by associating with it. In the case of the original movement and the challenging *pro* movement, the government accelerated the process, bestowing legitimacy on the movement in the act of *chartering* it. Since the spokesmen for the *anti* movement individually enjoyed strong positive ethos, the process of prestige-suggestion did not need acceleration.

It might be expected that a movement sponsored by the government would seek salvation through mortification rather than victimage, as the original antipoverty movement did.[63] To do otherwise would set the whole against the part, pitting government against one of its current or potential constituencies. There are times, of course, when government chooses such a course, but more typically what is negated lies within the body politic as a whole—guilt, complacency, disinterest, lack of will, and so on. Symbolic national mortification, if a fiction, was a convenient one. It enabled the resulting antipoverty commitment to be viewed as a national synthesis, without a personified counter-movement to contest the claims of the antipoverty advocates.

Each of the later *pro* and *anti* movements, by contrast, identified a victim—the "power structure" in one instance, alleged revolutionaries in the other—which it could not defeat. In the first instance, the result was containment by the defendant rhetors of government. In the other, a mutually face-saving compromise was the result. This record might offer support for the claim that government-sponsored movements should seek salvation through mortification, although one should beware against overgeneralizing from one success and two failures. More to the point, mortification is not an inevitable choice even if a desirable one. Government-sponsored and insurgent movements face the same rhetorical problems in the inception phase. Both must negate the old order; both must choose a path to salvation; both may select either victimage or mortification.

Simons believes that an insurgent movement has unique problems as it approaches rhetorical crisis. He asserts that such movements, *"shorn of the controls that characterize formal organizations, yet required to perform the same internal functions, harassed from without, yet obligated to adapt to the external system,"* face uniquely severe dilemmas in response to which their rhetoric is shaped.[64] Simons' conclusion, however, is based upon a comparison of stereotyped forms. Seldom do formal organizations operate with the efficiency and effectiveness he seems to imply. In this regard the experience of the War on Poverty may be instructive. The original anti-poverty task force, though a formal structure, was hardly a close-knit organization with internal controls. Differences among its members concerning the nature of the legislation could not be contained within the group and were not resolved even by the President.[65] The task force,

however, had to perform the internal functions of a formal organization, reaching agreement on a bill and convincing Congress of its rationality and feasibility. Nor was the *anti* movement of Congressmen and mayors, though conducted within official structures, characterized by a high degree of internal control. There was no coherent attack on the direction of OEO; advocates opposed the program in different ways and for different reasons. The protest effort launched by militants among the poor also lacked effective central direction, yet had the task of building and holding a committed, cohesive constituency. These examples should suggest that officially sanctioned organizations do not always have controls to assure effectiveness. Nor, incidentally, need informal organizations always lack such controls, as the command structure of some protest movements could indicate.

The second dilemma Simons describes also was experienced by the three movements related to the War on Poverty. Harassed from without, they yet found it necessary to adapt to an external system. In the original movement the external system involved Congress, whose members were skeptical about the new program. To adapt to these pressures the Administration was forced to yield to such amendments as the requirement of a loyalty oath, and, most significantly, to consent to the removal of Adam Yarmolinsky from the staff of OEO.[66] The militant poor were harassed by the delays and the token gestures which eventually undercut their position. If they were to succeed, however, they could not reject such measures outright, since the measures seemed reasonable to political leaders on whom the militants were dependent for funds. In 1966 many mayors and Congressmen were harassed by OEO's supporters who accused them of criticizing the agency because they really wished to dismantle it and to renege on the nation's commitment. They were forced to adapt to this system, however, lest their demands for refocusing OEO appear callous and without compassion. It is noteworthy that the frontal attacks on OEO by Republicans during 1967, such as the exclusion of OEO employees from a Federal pay raise and the failure to pass a continuing resolution, engendered precisely this sort of backlash. By contrast many restrictive amendments which were tempered with a concession to the agency's symbolic existence were adopted by the Congress.[67]

What emerges from these examples is not that the dilemmas described by Simons are unrealistic. Rather, they are not unique to persuasive campaigns mounted by uninstitutionalized collectivities. Much the same conclusion could be reached concerning Simons' remaining dilemmas.[68] The War on Poverty witnessed the tension between role expectations and role definitions (in the 1964 act the OEO Director was envisioned as the coordinator of all antipoverty activities but Shriver instead became the operator and advocate of specific programs). The poverty program experienced the tension between organizational efficiency and membership needs (the desire quickly to submit applications for funding conflicted with the desire to involve the poor actively in planning). OEO found it necessary to appeal simultaneously to different audiences (the Congress and the poor, for example) and to deal with a diversity of leadership types employing a variety of moderate and militant styles. In short, the War on Poverty offers proof by example that the rhetorical dilemmas Simons describes are broader in their application than he believes. If they describe the difficulties attendant upon persuasive campaigns *generally* they do not furnish a convincing basis for marking out insurgent social movements as requiring a distinct pattern of persuasion.

With regard to the consummation phase, too, government-sponsored movements do not differ markedly from uprisings of the discontented. If the movement fails its leaders stand as false prophets. This fate befell those who advocated that the government undertake the responsibility, with Federal funds, of unseating the power structure and transferring power to the poor.[69] If the movement succeeds, the aggressor rhetors became defendants of the new order—"prophets" become "priests" in Griffin's explication of Burke.[70] Theirs becomes the job of reinforcing the belief that the new order is good, so that people will remain pious with respect to it and it will be preserved.

Joel Handler's observations about the nature of regulatory agencies might support an argument that the new order achieved through government-sponsored movements was especially likely to be unstable. In the beginning, Handler explains, government agencies are marked by administrative zeal and they "view with suspicion that which they are charged with regulating." As time passes, however, "the situation settles down. The founding reformist zealots are replaced by moderates. Those who are regulated learn how to deal with the agency, to explain their point of view, and to seek out compromise." Finally, there is a change in the general political climate. "When the reforming days that spawned the agency pass," Handler writes, "the agency usually finds itself politically alone."[71] The attention of the Executive has been diverted elsewhere, and the interests which supposedly are being regulated gain influential allies. Although Handler was writing about the prospects for welfare reform, his conclusions are historically descriptive of OEO. The activists who staffed the agency at the outset were replaced with men noted for their managerial ability such as Bernard Boutin, William P. Kelly, and Bertrand Harding. Local mayors secured allies in Congress. The interest of the President was diverted, not only to foreign affairs but also to new domestic ventures. Handler describes a progression in the *opposite* direction from that which would be required to move the new order to a final *stasis*. Rather than promoting redemption, therefore, government sponsorship of movements might make it likely that the new order will be rejected, like the old, as faulty.

This progression, however, is endemic to virtually all movements, not merely to those sponsored by government. It is the fault not of defects in administrative agencies but of human nature. As Burke has written, people by nature are divided. Therefore, while a point of final *stasis* theoretically might exist, at which rhetoric transcends itself by becoming dialectical, in practice "even the most 'universal' of dialectical manipulations will disclose partisan motives, willy nilly, whereat [*sic*] we are brought back into the realm of rhetorical partisanship."[72] The inability of movements to reach a final point of *stasis* in redemption, in other words, is an indication of human imperfection.

It has been argued that some movements sponsored by government *hasten* the deterioration of the new order if public officials play the conflicting roles of advocate and arbiter. Writers such as Haggstrom, Wildavsky, and Edelman have argued that if the challenging *pro* movement had been initiated by the aggrieved minorities themselves government would have faced fewer pressures to co-opt the movement's leaders and goals.[73] There would have been countervailing political interests for government to weigh against those urging retrenchment of the program. As it was, however, the countervailing interests were of the government's own creation. In a crunch it was easier to compromise than to defy the *anti* movement, because defiance would alienate one constituency without strengthening another.

It is difficult to evaluate this claim that government sponsorship encourages rapid deterioration of the new order. On its face the fact that the challenging *pro* movement was defeated while the challenging *anti* movement was accommodated would seem to offer support. But *both* movements were sponsored by governmental forces, so sponsorship per se does not seem to be sufficient to assure the speedy deterioration of the new order. Moreover, additional counter-evidence could be cited, such as government's sponsorship of the labor movement during the 1930's. It does not appear, then, that rapid disintegration is an *inevitable* result of government-sponsored movements. And even if it were an inevitable result the difference between insurgent and official movements would be one only of degree rather than kind. Such an incremental difference does not seem sufficient for declaring insurgent persuasive campaigns to be a unique rhetorical form.

IMPLICATIONS FOR THEORY AND CRITICISM

The experience of the War on Poverty suggests that it may be needlessly confining to limit the application of the term "movement" to insurgent campaigns. Persuasive efforts supported by the "Establishment" may not differ from revolts against the "Establishment," with respect to "the pattern of public discussion, the configuration of discourse, the physiognomy of persuasion . . . [.]"[74] Such a possibility suggests three major implications for rhetorical theory and criticism.

First, a careful distinction must be drawn between "social movements" and "rhetorical movements." The latter term may embrace behavior not covered by the former. In a recent essay, Smith and Windes lament the tendency of rhetorical critics to narrow "the concept of 'rhetorical movement' simply by restricting its referents to collective actions directed toward radical change in the social order."[75] To do so, they suggest, is to blind oneself to possible comparisons between such ventures and campaigns dedicated to other aims, such as innovation. The result is a needlessly limited theory of movements.

To assume that rhetorical movements are found where sociologists traditionally label social movements also may be to assume a perspective which emphasizes class conflict. As Paul Wilkinson explains, many views of "social movement" assume that movements are bound by social class. They are the means by which an oppressed group which seeks change prepares to confront the holders of power, who seek permanence.[76] To see in rhetorical movements the dialectical clash of opposing class interests, however, is to misread history. For sometimes the *status quo* not only is not resistant to change but may seek actively to change itself. Sometimes outside forces may desire not radical change but a return to the old order. The War on Poverty illustrates both possibilities. If the rhetorical critic employs a class-conflict view in his definition of "movement," he not only will ignore situations such as these but he will misjudge the character and motives of the actors in the system he describes.

In short, to equate "rhetorical movements" with "social movements" is to lose sight of the functions of movement rhetoric within a democratic society. The rhetorical behavior which characterizes social movements may be adopted in other persuasive campaigns for strategic purposes. Groups out of power may conceive of themselves as "movements" in order to convey a sense of destiny which sustains the adherence of the faithful. Groups in power may see themselves as "movements" in order that greater significance may be attached to their actions. Rhetors may define a given situation as merger or as division, not in reflection of social-class ideology but as definition serves the strategic purpose of widening or narrowing the scope of conflict.[77] As Paul Wilkinson summarizes, "The rhetoric of movement may almost be said to have its own momentum."[78] Hence, while it may be essential for the sociologist to distinguish between "movements" and "pressure groups," for example, the rhetorical scholar who makes the same distinction may define away interesting rhetorical behavior and distort his account of history.

The second implication for rhetorical theory and criticism should be clear: a *rhetorical* definition of "movement" is needed. Developing such a definition must begin with the recognition that the rhetorical critic of movements is not out to study some particularly rhetorical *component* of a broader social movement. Rather, movements as he studies them are in their *essence* rhetorical.[79] Hence what is needed is a definition which identifies the rhetorical situations to be called movements.

Cathcart defined rhetorical movements as responses to situations in which there is dialectical tension growing out of moral conflict.[80] In such situations aggressor rhetors describe conditions as being so bad that an immediate, drastic corrective is required. Defendant rhetors, meanwhile, interpret calls for change as challenges to the legitimacy of the system itself. Cathcart's definition either excludes or includes too much. Taken literally, "dialectical enjoinment" would exist only in situations in which conflict was so fundamental that there was *no* basic common ground between participants. Each of the competing presuppositions proclaimed and supported by adherents could be evaluated only on its own terms.[81] As a practical matter, a conflict so pervasive as to remove all common ground probably would be one between social classes, threatening revolution. If so, then Cathcart's definition of movements would exclude the same rhetorical behavior as do the traditional definitions of sociologists.

Alternatively, Cathcart's view may include virtually all persuasive campaigns. As social judgment theory would predict and as the War on Poverty illustrates, participants in a dispute may magnify the distance between their position and that of their opponents. It should not be surprising, then, that advocates interpret their opponents' position as being more fundamental a challenge than it really is, and that they may respond to the challenge with rhetorical behavior appropriate to a state of dialectical enjoinment, in order to suit their strategic purposes. Within the framework of a democratic polity, then, it may be difficult to find a persuasive campaign which does *not* satisfy Cathcart's definition of a movement. The definition seems to be either too narrow or too broad.

Recently, Charles Wilkinson has attempted to amplify Cathcart's definition. He regards movements as *"languaging strategies by which a significantly vocal part of an established society, experiencing together a sustained dialectical tension growing out of moral (ethical) conflict, agitate to induce cooperation in others, either directly or indirectly, thereby affecting the status quo."*[82] Wilkinson recognizes the difficulty in Cathcart's use of "dialectical tension," writing that the experience of such tension is "the lot of every human being."[83] But Wilkinson's qualifiers, that tension be experienced by many people over a sustained period of time, do not distinguish movements from long-term persuasive campaigns generally.

It may be, incidentally, that the inability to make such a distinction is not the fault of those who have tried. It is possible that there is no fundamental difference, that movements are a prototype for *all* long-term persuasive ventures. Indeed, a tripartite scheme similar to Griffin's has been posited to explain such diverse activities as the recognition of social problems and the conduct of psychotherapy.[84] If "rhetorical movements" and "persuasive campaigns" are synonymous, then the task of definition is a different one: to determine whether there exist rhetorically significant categories or types under the broad rubric, movements. For example, Smith and Windes distinguish between innovational movements, which customarily seek salvation through mortification, and establishment-conflict movements, which seek salvation through victimage.[85] It must be emphasized, however, that any distinctions critics draw among types of movements should enhance the ability to make rhetorical judgments or to construct rhetorical theory. Otherwise, they may be distinctions without significant differences.

The third major implication of this study is that more sophisticated rhetorical analysis of movements is needed. The need is not to study more movements simply to prove that they may be labeled as movements. The more it can be said that *any* persuasive campaign fits the rhetorical pattern of a social movement the less critically *useful* it will be simply to identify a movement, its stages, and its cast of characters. A "movement study" may not be a distinct *method* of analysis; the key terms of such a study *define* but do not *explain* elements of the discourse to be studied. They are categories, useful in enabling the critic to divide his subject into manageable units. Having made such a division, the critic still must find the appropriate method of analysis to *account for* the progression of the movement which he has described.

One attempt at such a method is the "fantasy theme analysis" of Bormann and his students.[86] In essence, Bormann argues that rhetorical visions, generated often in small-group interaction, chain out among a wider public. Hence a basic requirement of a rhetorical movement may be the sharing of common rhetorical visions. The fantasy theme analysts not only have suggested that this prerequisite exists but also have offered insight into the process by which common visions develop. Still, they do not explain why one set of fantasy themes rather than another chains out successfully, nor do they permit prediction of the rhetorical behavior of a movement.

To make such predictions, systematic and testable theories of movements are needed. Illustrative of what is involved in constructing such theories is a recent dissertation on the Equal Rights Amendment. Foss combined the descriptive method of fantasy theme analysis, to identify the rhetorical vision, with an attempt to generalize propositions about rhetorical visions in movements.[87] From her theoretical formulation she derived numerous axioms and theorems about the interrelation among rhetorical variables in a movement. The specific theorems could be tested against a wide array of movements. From this sort of testing it should be possible to develop more sophisticated judgments of the choices made by rhetors and more sophisticated theories of the rhetoric of movements.

Notes

[1] Leland M. Griffin, "The Rhetoric of Historical Movements," *QJS*, 38 (1952), 184.
[2] Illustrative of contemporary movement studies are: Parke G. Burgess, "The Rhetoric of Black Power: A Moral Demand?" *QJS*, 54 (1968), 122–133; James R. Andrews, "Confrontation at Columbia: A Case Study in Coercive Rhetoric," *QJS*, 55 (1969), 9–16; Robert L. Scott and Donald K. Smith, "The Rhetoric of Confrontation," *QJS*, 55 (1969), 1–8; Brenda Robinson Hancock, "Affirmation by Negation in the Women's Liberation Movement," *QJS*, 58 (1972), 264–71; Karlyn Kohrs Campbell, "The Rhetoric of Women's Liberation: An Oxymoron," *QJS*, 59 (1973), 74–86; Herbert W. Simons, James W. Chesebro, and C. Jack Orr, "A Movement Perspective on the 1972 Presidential Campaign," *QJS*, 59 (1973), 168–79; James W. Chesebro, John F. Cragan, and Patricia W. McCullough, "The Small Group Technique of the Radical Revolutionary: A Synthetic Study of Consciousness Raising," *SM*, 40 (1973), 136–46; James F. Klumpp, "Challenge of Radical Rhetoric: Radicalization at Columbia," *Western Speech*, 37 (1973), 146–56; and J. Robert Cox, "Perspectives on Rhetorical Criticism of Movements: Antiwar Dissent, 1964–1970," *Western Speech*, 38 (1974), 254–68.
[3] Griffin, p. 184.
[4] Ibid, pp. 184–188; Leland M. Griffin, "A Dramatistic Theory of the Rhetoric of Movements," in *Critical Responses to Kenneth Burke*, ed. William H. Rueckert (Minneapolis: Univ. of Minnesota Press, 1969), pp. 456–79. Although they employ different terms, other writers on movements identify a tripartite pattern of phases similar to those mentioned by Griffin. See, for example, C. Wendell King, *Social Movements in the United States* (New York: Random House, 1956); Eric Hoffer, *The True Believer* (New York: Harper, 1951); Erwin P. Bettinghaus, *Persuasive Communication*, 2d ed. (New York: Holt, Rinehart, and Winston, 1973).
[5] Daniel P. Moynihan, "The Professors and the Poor," *Commentary*, 46 (August, 1968), 20, for example,

attributes the War on Poverty to intellectuals in the Administration. For a fuller treatment of the inception period, see Daniel L. Knapp, "Scouting the War on Poverty: Social Reform Politics in the Kennedy Administration," Diss. Oregon 1970.

6 Cited in Byron G. Lander, "Group Theory and Individuals: The Origin of Poverty as a Political Issue in 1964," *Western Political Quarterly,* 24 (Spring, 1971), 515. The report referred to its *Goals for Americans* (Englewood Cliffs, N. J.: Prentice-Hall, 1960).

7 Sidney Lens, *Poverty: America's Enduring Paradox* (New York: Thomas Y. Crowell, 1969), pp. 296–97.

8 John Kenneth Galbraith, *The Affluent Society* (Boston: Houghton Mifflin, 1958). That few paid attention to the early scholarly studies on poverty is indicated by Sar A. Levitan, *The Great Society's Poor Law: A New Approach to Poverty* (Baltimore: Johns Hopkins Univ. Press, 1969), pp. 12–13.

9 On this point, see, for example, Theodore C. Sorensen, *The Kennedy Legacy* (New York: Macmillan, 1969), p. 64.

10 Richard A. Cloward and Lloyd E. Ohlin, *Delinquency and Opportunity* (London: Routledge and Kegan Paul, 1961), esp. pp. 13, 17, 121. The influence of this theory on the work of the President's Committee is indicated by James L. Sundquist, *Politics and Policy: The Eisenhower, Kennedy, and Johnson Years* (Washington: Brookings Institution, 1968), p. 119.

11 Michael Harrington, *The Other America* (New York: Macmillan, 1962). Harrington's book attracted the attention of Dwight Macdonald, who reviewed it in the 19 January 1963 issue of the *New Yorker.* Theodore Sorensen reportedly urged President Kennedy to read the Macdonald review; Walter Heller gave the President a copy of *The Other America,* "although it is not known whether the President read it." See Levitan, *The Great Society's Poor,* p. 13.

12 A succinct statement of the theory is in Cloward and Ohlin, esp. p. 175. The diffusion of the idea throughout the Administration was the work of David Hackett, an aide to Attorney General Robert F. Kennedy and Executive Director of the President's Committee on Juvenile Delinquency. Hackett brought Ohlin to work on the Committee staff. During 1963 he persuaded the Budget Bureau and the Council of Economic Advisers of the merit of his theory, and it served as the base for much of the original antipoverty planning. The theory also was cited as the rationale for the shifting focus of Mobilization for Youth, from juvenile delinquency to poverty, during 1968.

These events are chronicled in Knapp, pp. 132–54, 234–50, 278–98.

13 For a discussion of the context-shaping function of myth, see Murray Edelman, *Politics as Symbolic Action: Mass Arousal and Quiescence* (Chicago: Markham, 1971), p. 53. The term, "myth," refers to a concept or belief which was ne[i]ther true nor false but which was *believed* to be true.

14 Cited in Philip W. Borst, "President Johnson and the 89th Congress: A Functional Analysis of a System under Stress" (Diss. Claremont 1968), p. 24.

15 James A. Jones, "Federal Efforts to Solve Contemporary Social Problems," in *Handbook on the Study of Social Problems,* ed. Erwin O. Smigel (Chicago: Rand McNally, 1971), p. 561. See also Kenneth Burke, *A Grammar of Motives* (1945; rpt. Berkeley and Los Angeles: University of California Press, 1969), p. 421. Describing the transformation from merger to division, Burke wrote, "The moment of crisis in transcendence involves a new motive discovered en route."

16 In a recent biography of Johnson, Doris Kearns contends that the general White House strategy with respect to the Great Society was "pass the bill now, worry about its effects and implementation later." In short, the Administration saw the enactment of laws as the consummation of its domestic efforts: "The objective was to make laws, not raise problems." Doris Kearns, *Lyndon Johnson and the American Dream* (New York: Harper and Row, 1976), p. 218.

17 Roman Pucinski, in *Economic Opportunity Act of 1964* (Hearings, U.S. House Committee on Education and Labor, Subcommittee on the War on Poverty Program, 88th Cong., 2d sess., Part 2, 773.

18 Support for the poverty program from businessmen is described in Rowland Evans, Jr., and Robert D. Novak, *Lyndon B. Johnson: The Exercise of Power* (New York: New American Library, 1966), pp. 431–32. Levitan theorizes that the anticipation of cuts in the defense budget was a major factor in the support of the program by businesses seeking a new outlet for government contracts. See *The Great Society's Poor Law,* p. 83. The United States Chamber of Commerce, however, did testify in opposition to the bill during the House hearings.

19 For example, the sponsor of the 1964 bill in the House was Representative Phil Landrum of Georgia, who introduced it, saying, "This will not be an expensive program. This will be the most conservative social program I have seen presented to any legislative body. There is not anything but

conservatism in it." *U.S. Congressional Record,* 110 (August 5, 1964), 17623.

20 Richard A. Cloward and Frances Fox Piven, "The Weight of the Poor: A Strategy to End Poverty," *Nation,* 202 (May 2, 1966), 514.

21 President Johnson several times suggested that the government had knowledge of the appropriate measures to end poverty. See, for example, U.S. President, *Economic Report of the President, Together with the Annual Report of the Council of Economic Advisers* (Washington: U.S. Government Printing Office, 1964), p. 15; *Public Papers of the Presidents: Lyndon B. Johnson, 1963–64,* I, 780. A slight variation was Sargent Shriver's argument that, although all the pertinent knowledge did not yet exist, it soon would be discovered. In his commencement address at Texas Tech College, he made a comparison to the space program, saying, "We do not know how to go to the moon yet either, but we are going to get there." See Sargent Shriver, *Point of the Lance* (New York: Harper and Row, 1964), p. 61. The process of rising expectations described here is similar to that discussed in Robert M. Fogelson, *Violence as Protest: A Study of Riots and Ghettos* (Garden City, N. Y.: Doubleday, 1971), p. 136, with respect to race relations.

22 On the discrepancy between general and specific expressions of attitude, see, for example, David T. Burhans, Jr., "The Attitude-Behavior Discrepancy Problem: Revisited," *QJS,* 57 (1971), 418–28.

23 This characterization of the militants is the conclusion of Anne Austin Murphy, "Involving the Poor in the War against Poverty" (Diss. North Carolina 1970), p. 263.

24 Walter Miller, "The Elimination of the American Lower Class as National Policy: A Critique of the Ideology of the Poverty Movement of the 1960s," in *On Understanding Poverty: Perspectives from the Social Sciences,* ed. Daniel P. Moynihan (New York: Basic Books, 1968), p. 286. Miller was describing the movement, not endorsing it.

25 See Saul D. Alinsky, "The War on Poverty— Political Pornography," *Journal of Social Issues,* 21 (1965), 41–47.

26 The mood of the delegates was "mutinous"; they heckled Shriver with shouts of "You're lying!" and "He hasn't done anything for us!" and prevented him from completing his remarks. For the details of this incident, see Nan Robertson, "Reuther Asks for More Poverty Funds," *New York Times,* April 14, 1966, p. 25; Nan Robertson, "Shriver Explains Convention Boos," *New York Times,* April 19, 1966, p. 44; Louise Lander, ed., *War on Poverty* (New York: Facts on File, 1967), p. 140.

27 E. E. Schattschneider, *The Semisovereign People* (New York: Holt, Rinehart, and Winston, 1960), esp. p. 16.

28 Jones, p. 565.

29 For examples of the charges of sellout, see the testimony of Rev. Lynward Stevenson of The Woodlawn Organization (Chicago) in *Examination of War on Poverty Program* (Hearings, U.S. House Committee on Education and Labor, Subcommittee on the War on Poverty Program, 89th Cong., 1st sess., p. 360; James Ridgeway, "Poor Chicago: Down and Out with Mayor Daley," *New Republic,* 152 (May 15, 1965), 19; Rep. Augustus F. Hawkins, *1966 Amendments to Economic Opportunity Act of 1964* (Hearings, U.S. House Committee on Education and Labor, Subcommittee on the War on Poverty Program, 89th Cong., 2d sess., Part 1, 492.

30 Edelman, p. 62.

31 See Michael Lipsky, *Protest in City Politics* (Chicago: Rand McNally, 1970), pp. 2, 165.

32 For a description of the Syracuse conference, see Richard A. Cloward and Richard M. Elman, "The First Congress of the Poor," *Nation,* 202 (February 7, 1966), 148–151. On the escalation of such protest see Lander, pp. 41, 98; Daniel P. Moynihan, *Maximum Feasible Misunderstanding: Community Action in the War on Poverty* (New York: Free Press, 1969), pp. 141–42.

33 The results described here are similar to those which may occur when confrontation is attempted as a tactic to increase the resources of the alien[a]ted. See Scott and Smith, pp. 1–8, esp. p. 8.

34 Peter Bachrach and Morton Baratz, *Power and Poverty* (New York: Oxford, 1970), pp. 44–45; Peter Bachrach, "A Power Analysis: The Shaping of Antipoverty Policy in Baltimore," *Public Policy,* 18 (1970), 158.

35 Lipsky, pp. 14, 176. Lipsky cites Murray Edelman, *The Symbolic Uses of Politics* (Urbana: Univ. of Illinois Press, 1964).

36 Michael Lipsky and Margaret Levi, "Community Organization as a Political Resource," in *People and Politics in Urban Society,* ed. Harlan Hahn (Beverly Hills, Cal.: Sage Publications, 1972), p. 195.

37 The proposal was offered by Rep. Albert H. Quie in *Economic Opportunity Act Amendments 1966* (Hearings, U.S. House Committee on Rules, 89th Cong., 2d sess., Part 4, 156. This same argument, however, was advanced by many Democrats. See, for example, William Fitts Ryan, *U.S. Congressional Record,* 111 (July 21, 1965), 16993. Shriver opposed this requirement, as he indicated in a letter to Rep. Adam Clayton Powell on 26 August, 1966. See Letter from Shriver to Powell,

"The Office of Economic Opportunity during the Administration of President Lyndon B. Johnson," unpublished administrative history, Documentary Supplement, Lyndon Baines Johnson Library.

38 This challenge to the competence of the indigenous representatives illustrated what Edmund M. Burke labeled the basic dilemma of citizen participation. Both participatory democracy and expertise are to be desired, yet the desired goals may conflict. See Edmund M. Burke, "Citizen Participation Strategies," *Journal of the American Institute of Planners,* 34 (September, 1968), 287.

39 Dale Rogers Marshall, *The Politics of Participation in Poverty* (Berkeley and Los Angeles: Univ. of California Press, 1971), pp. 56–57.

40 Adam Walinsky, "Maximum Feasible Misunderstanding" [review], *New York Times,* 2 Feb. 1969, sec. VII, p. 2.

41 In a recent monograph, Charles Gilbert has argued that the net effect of widespread popular participation in government has been the opposite of that intended by the community action board: "in the context of American political organization and ideology, participation tends to work perversely from the standpoint of equalization of influence, reinforcing socioeconomic inequalities through its association with social status." Charles E. Gilbert, "Shaping Public Policy," *Annals of the American Academy of Political and Social Science,* 426 (July, 1976), 138.

42 Kenneth B. Clark, *Dark Ghetto: Dilemmas of Social Power* (New York: Harper and Row, 1965), p. 200. Although Clark was writing here about Mobilization for Youth, a federally-funded juvenile delinquency program in New York, he held the same views about the anti-poverty program generally. See Kenneth B. Clark and Jeannette Hopkins, *A Relevant War Against Poverty: A Study of Community Action Programs and Observable Social Change* (New York: Metropolitan Applied Research Center, 1968), p. 225.

43 Griffin, "The Rhetoric of Historical Movements," p. 186.

44 Lipsky, p. 202. Much of the analysis of the ephemeral nature of protest is adapted from Lipsky's work. See esp. pp. ix, 187.

45 Martin Rein and S. M. Miller, "Citizen Participation and Poverty," *Connecticut Law Review,* 1 (1968), 230. See also Martin Rein, *Social Policy: Issues of Choice and Change* (New York: Random House, 1970), pp. 210–211.

46 On dissatisfaction with protests, see Edith Green, in *Economic Opportunity Act Amendments of 1967* (Hearings, U.S. House Committee on Education and Labor, 90th Cong., 1st sess., Part 4, 3577–3578. On the reality of the "revolution of rising expectations," see, for example, Peter H. Rossi, Richard A. Berk, David P. Boesel, Bettye K. Eidson, and W. Eugene Groves, "Between White and Black: The Faces of American Institutions in the Ghetto," *Supplemental Studies for the National Advisory Commission on Civil Disorders* (New York: Praeger, 1968), p. 147.

47 See Muzafer Sherif and Carl I. Hovland, *Social Judgment* (New Haven: Yale University Press, 1961); Carolyn W. Sherif, Muzafer Sherif, and Roger E. Nebergall, *Attitude and Attitude Change* (Philadelphia: Saunders, 1965).

48 The heightened sensitivity to demonstrations is exemplified in 1968 election campaign statements attributing civil disturbances to expectations aroused by OEO. See, for instance, David R. Jones, "G.O.P. Links Riots to Johnson Policy," *New York Times,* June 3, 1968, pp. 1, 38. The same charge had been made earlier as well. See "Humphrey's Stand Criticized by Ford," *New York Times,* July 23, 1966, p. 9. That the principle of local government was thought to be under attack is indicated in the testimony of Rep. Green cited in note 46.

49 The details of this resolution may be found in Ben A. Franklin, "Mayors Challenge Antipoverty Plan," *New York Times,* June 1, 1965, p. 30; and Ben A. Franklin, "Mayors Shelve Dispute on Poor," *New York Times,* June 2, 1965, p. 20.

50 John C. Donovan, *The Politics of Poverty* (New York: Pegasus, 1967), pp. 65–68.

51 Memorandum from Wilfred H. Rommel to the President, November 3, 1966, Reports on Enrolled Legislation, P. L. 89–794, Lyndon Baines Johnson Library.

52 On the designation of Vice President Humphrey to represent the mayors, see Joseph A. Loftus, "Mayors Assured of Poverty Role," *New York Times,* June 8, 1965, p. 49. On the reported advice of the Budget Bureau, see Joseph A. Loftus, "Wide Policy Role for the Poor Opposed by Budget Bureau," *New York Times,* November 5, 1965, p. 1; "U.S. Aide Denies a Poverty Shift," *New York Times,* November 7, 1965, p. 70. On the steps to earmark funds, see "Antipoverty Funds Reduced and Earmarked," *Congressional Quarterly Almanac,* 22 (1966), 250. By 1968, sixty percent of the funds allocated for community action had been earmarked for national emphasis programs.

53 On the appointment of Bernard Boutin, see Donovan, p. 58; Barbara Carter, "Sargent Shriver and the Role of the Poor," *Reporter,* 34 (May 5, 1966), 18. On the informal veto power given

to fifteen mayors, see Sar A. Levitan, "The Community Action Program: A Strategy to Fight Poverty," *Annals of the American Academy of Political and Social Science*, 385 (September, 1969), 66. The preference for "umbrella" agencies is discussed in Warren C. Haggstrom, "On Eliminating Poverty: What We Have Learned," *Power, Poverty, and Urban Policy*, eds. Warner Bloomberg, Jr., and Henry J. Schmandt (Beverly Hills, Cal.: Sage Publications, 1968), p. 517. Concerning the Child Development Group of Mississippi, see Christopher Jencks, "Accommodating Whites: A New Look at Mississippi," *New Republic*, 154 (April 16, 1966), 22.

54 Cited by John V. Lindsay in *Amendments to the Economic Opportunity Act of 1964* (Hearings, U.S. Senate Committee on Labor and Public Welfare, Subcommittee on Employment, Manpower, and Poverty, 89th Cong., 2d sess., p. 232.

55 Memorandum from William H. Crook to Bill Moyers, May 3, 1966, Executive File WE 9, Box 27, Lyndon Baines Johnson Library. The memorandum was forwarded by Moyers to the President.

56 Letter from Sargent Shriver to the President, n. d. (stamped "Rec'd 8-30-66"), Executive File WE 9, Box 27, Lyndon Baines Johnson Library.

57 On this point, see Sar A. Levitan, "Can the War on Poverty Rise Above Partisan Politics?" *Poverty and Human Resources Abstracts*, 2, No. 5 (September–October, 1967), 20. Some members of the Administration were wary of OEO's acceptance of these amendments. In a memorandum to White House aide Barefoot Sanders, Samuel V. Merrick, a special assistant for Congressional Relations in the Labor Department, asserted that "the atmosphere has been to accommodate and this seems to me to be the road to real disaster." Memorandum from Samuel V. Merrick to Barefoot Sanders, September 29, 1967, Reports on Legislation, Box 38, Lyndon Baines Johnson Library.

58 See "Congress Clears Two-Year Antipoverty Program," *Congressional Quarterly Weekly Report*, 25 (December 15, 1967), 2546. Sargent Shriver said that the action of the House in approving the 1967 amendments was "the greatest legislative victory he has ever been associated with." U.S. Office of Economic Opportunity, *A News Summary of the War on Poverty*, 2 (November 20, 1967), 1. Shriver also referred to the 1967 Congressional action as "a notable vindication of the War on Poverty." Letter from Sargent Shriver to Charles L. Schultze, n. d. (stamped "Rec'd Dec. 15 1967"), Reports on Legislation, P. L. 90-222, Lyndon Baines Johnson Library.

59 This point is argued, for example, in Clark and Hopkins, *A Relevant War Against Poverty*, p. 125.

60 U.S. Office of Economic Opportunity, *CAP Mission Guide: Participation of the Poor in the Community Decision-Making Process* (Washington: U.S. Government Printing Office, 1969), p. 8.

61 For typical definitions of "social movement," see Joseph R. Gusfield, ed., *Protest, Reform, and Revolt: A Reader in Social Movements* (New York: Wiley, 1970), p. 2; Barry McLaughlin, *Studies in Social Movements* (New York: Free Press, 1969), p. 4; Herbert Blumer, "Elementary Collective Behavior," in *New Outline of the Principles of Sociology*, ed. Alfred McClung Lee (New York: Barnes and Noble, 1949), p. 199; Neil J. Smelser, *Theory of Collective Behavior* (New York: Free Press, 1962), pp. 110, 129–30; Ralph H. Turner and Lewis M. Killian, *Collective Behavior* (Englewood Cliffs, N.J.: Prentice-Hall, 1957), p. 308. However, Paul Wilkinson cautions that "the term 'movement' has become all things to all men." Wilkinson's own characterization of movements, though, is not fundamentally different from those cited here. See Paul Wilkinson, *Social Movement* (New York: Praeger, 1971), pp. 13, 27.

62 Bachrach and Baratz, *Power and Poverty*, p. 30; and Richard E. Walton, "Two Strategies of Social Change and Their Dilemmas," *Journal of Applied Behavioral Science*, 1 (April–June, 1965), 176, describe the needed resources.

63 "Victimage" and "mortification," of course, are terms used by Kenneth Burke. See "On Human Behavior Considered 'Dramatistically,'" *Permanence and Change* (1935; rpt. Indianapolis: Bobbs-Merrill 1965), pp. 274–94.

64 Herbert W. Simons, "Requirements, Problems, and Strategies: A Theory of Persuasion for Social Movements," *QJS*, 56 (1970), 4.

65 Sundquist, *Politics and Policy*, pp. 142–145.

66 Yarmolinsky, who had been slated to be Deputy Director of OEO, was removed from the program in a concession to secure the support of a group of North and South Carolina Congressmen whose votes were thought to be crucial to the passage of the Economic Opportunity Act of 1964. The episode is described in Rowland Evans and Robert Novak, "The Yarmolinsky Affair," *Esquire*, 63 (February, 1965), 80–82, 122–23.

67 It has been argued that such measures as the refusal to pass a rat control bill, the exclusion of OEO agencies from participation in a new juvenile

delinquency program, the exclusion of OEO workers from the 1967 Federal pay raise, and the omission of OEO from a continuing resolution permitting government agencies to operate pending approval of the budget backfired and elicited the support of such previous opponents as the *Wall Street Journal*. See "Seized by Pettiness," *Wall Street Journal*, 170 (October 23, 1967), 18. For examples of restrictive amendments which were successful, see the testimony of Joseph Montoya, *U.S. Congressional Record*, 113 (September 26, 1967), S13729; Charles S. Gubser, *U.S. Congressional Record*, 113 (November 15, 1967), H15350; John Sherman Cooper, *U.S. Congressional Record*, 113 (September 28, 1967), S13854; Paul Fino, *U.S. Congressional Record*, 113 (November 14, 1967), H15188; John N. Erlenborn, *U.S. Congressional Record*, 113 (November 15, 1967), H15344; and John J. Williams and George Murphy, *U.S. Congressional Record*, 113 (October 5, 1967), S14274, S14279.

[68] Simons, pp. 4–7.

[69] In 1965, Shriver believed that Congress had intended to *encourage* conflict at the local level. See his testimony in *Examination of the War on Poverty Program* (Hearings, U.S. House Committee on Education and Labor, Subcommittee on the War on Poverty Program, 89th Cong., 1st sess., p. 20. That the tone had changed by 1966 was evident from Sen. Joseph Clark's statement, almost as an aphorism, ". . . where you get the local power structure involved in the community action program, then you have a good chance of success. However, if the local power structure turns its back on the whole program, you are in trouble." See his statement in *Amendments to the Economic Opportunity Act of 1964* (Hearings, U.S. Senate Committee on Labor and Public Welfare, Subcommittee on Employment, Manpower, and Poverty, 89th Cong., 2d sess., pp. 158–59. And in 1967, Shriver, responding to a question about his agency's policy toward "the Alinsky theory" of social change, denied that OEO believed in or practiced it. See his testimony in *Examination of the War on Poverty* (Hearings, U.S. Senate Committee on Labor and Public Welfare, Subcommittee on Employment, Manpower, and Poverty, 90th Cong., 1st sess., Part. 9, 2823.

[70] Griffin, "A Dramatistic Theory," p. 468.

[71] Joel F. Handler, *Reforming the Poor: Welfare Policy, Federalism, and Morality* (New York: Basic Books; 1972), p. 60.

[72] Kenneth Burke and Stanley Romaine Hopper, "Mysticism as a Solution to the Poet's Dilemma," in *Spiritual Problems in Contemporary Literature*, ed. Stanley R. Hopper (New York: Institute for Religious and Social Studies, 1952), p. 109.

[73] Haggstrom, p. 515; Aaron Wildavsky, *The Politics of the Budgetary Process* (Boston: Little, Brown, 1964), p. 157; Edelman, *Politics as Symbolic Action*, p. 180.

[74] Griffin, "The Rhetoric of Historical Movements," p. 185.

[75] Ralph R. Smith and Russel R. Windes, "The Innovational Movement: A Rhetorical Theory," *QJS*, 61 (1975), 140.

[76] This conclusion is suggested by Wilkinson's survey of sociological theories of movements. See Paul Wilkinson, pp. 20–23. I am indebted to Professor Thomas Goodnight for the suggestion that this paragraph stress the oversimplification inherent in the permanence/change dichotomy.

[77] Schattschneider, pp. 16–18, discusses the scope of conflict as a strategic question.

[78] Paul Wilkinson, p. 14.

[79] The inherently rhetorical nature of movements is suggested by Charles A. Wilkinson, "A Rhetorical Definition of Movements," *Central States Speech Journal*, 27 (1976), 92.

[80] Robert S. Cathcart, "New Approaches to the Study of Movements: Defining Movements Rhetorically," *Western Speech*, 36 (1972), 87.

[81] Such a situation is defined by Henry Johnstone as requiring philosophical argumentation, since only *argumentum ad hominem* can be effective. See Henry W. Johnstone, Jr., *Philosophy and Argument* (University Park: Pennsylvania State Univ. Press, 1959), esp. chap. 5–6.

[82] Charles Wilkinson, p. 91.

[83] Ibid., pp. 92–93.

[84] See, for example, Jones, "Federal Efforts," p. 560; Jerome D. Frank, *Persuasion and Healing*, rev. ed. (Baltimore: Johns Hopkins Press, 1973), pp. 85–105.

[85] Smith and Windes, p. 144.

[86] The "fantasy theme" method is described in Ernest G. Bormann, "Fantasy and Rhetorical Vision: The Rhetorical Criticism of Social Reality," *QJS*, 58 (1972), 396–407; and exemplified by Bormann in "The Eagleton Affair: A Fantasy Theme Analysis," *QJS*, 59 (1973), 143–159.

[87] Sonja Kay Foss, "A Fantasy Theme Analysis of the Rhetoric of the Debate on the Equal Rights Amendment, 1970–1976: Toward a Theory of the Rhetoric of Movements" (Diss. Northwestern 1976), pp. 309–365.

Domesticating Dissent: The Kennedys and the Freedom Rides

John M. Murphy

On May 6, 1961, Attorney General Robert F. Kennedy told a Law Day audience at the University of Georgia, "You may ask: Will we enforce the civil rights statutes? The answer is: Yes, we will" (Kennedy, 1961a, p. 62). Unbeknownst to Kennedy, however, civil rights activists were already challenging that resolve. On May 4, white and black riders had boarded a Trailways and a Greyhound bus in Washington, D.C. with the destination of New Orleans, Louisiana for a commemoration of the *Brown* decision on school desegregation (Garrow, 1988, p. 154). They were testing compliance with a recent Supreme Court decision banning segregation in waiting rooms and restaurants serving interstate bus passengers (Branch, 1988, p. 390).[1] James Farmer, executive director of the Congress of Racial Equality (CORE), sponsor of the project, understood the difficulty the rides would cause for the Kennedys: "We put on pressure and create a crisis [for federal leaders] and then they react" (Weisbrot, 1991, p. 55).

Examination of Administration and press reactions to the crisis opens important questions concerning social control and social movements in the United States. To explore some of those questions, I shall examine the primary theoretical bases for the analysis of authority response to movements and elucidate an alternative perspective drawn from Antonio Gramsci's concept of hegemony. The case of the Freedom Rides illustrates the utility of this approach.

SOCIAL MOVEMENTS AND SOCIAL CONTROL

Traditional social movement theory offers little to help the critic interested in social control. One reason is simple: The rhetorical strategies of the movement have been the focus of attention. The rhetoric of the "establishment" is slighted.[2] As Lucas (1980) notes, "Like other scholars, rhetoricians have generally been more interested in

studying social change than social maintenance. We need to learn much more about the symbolic processes of social control" (p. 265).

The rhetoric of the establishment has also been neglected within this tradition because of its theoretical framework. These studies rely almost exclusively on the "Establishment-Conflict" theory of the development of movements (Smith & Windes, 1975). The model of agitators demanding changes from an antagonistic Establishment has remained constant since Griffin's (1952) seminal essay (see also Cathcart, 1972, 1978; Griffin, 1980). The literature on the "rhetoric of control" flows from Griffin's original assumptions (Bowers & Ochs, 1971, pp. 39–56; Windt, 1982, 1990). King (1976), for instance, uses the metaphor of war to characterize the relationship between activists and authorities, arguing that such encounters are "combat," and the rhetorical tactics he reviews are the "gladiator's blueprint for victory" (p. 134). Bowers and Ochs (1971) employ the same metaphor of war (p. 39). They continue that perspective even when they discuss the strategy of "incorporation," through which the Establishment responds to some of the agitator's demands: "The decision-makers must maintain the necessary image of strength, the establishment's membership must not perceive the change as altering in a significant way the values and goals of their institution" (p. 55). This theoretical perspective accounts for only a narrow range of confrontative rhetoric. Some critics provide excellent analysis of social movements from this perspective, but they do so in spite of their theoretical framework, not with assistance from it.

The Establishment-Conflict model also has difficulty explaining social control because, as McKerrow (1989, p. 100) suggests, it is "agent-centered." American public address studies generally assume that the individual human agent, the rhetor, freely persuades audiences, masters linguistic constraints, and creates meaningful social change. As a result, the concept of social control is philosophically antithetical to traditional social movement studies.

Stephen Lucas (1988) and David Henry (1989) argue that communication scholars have not altered the theoretical "state of the art" on social movements in the past ten years. This assertion may be true for traditional movement studies. Michael McGee (1980a; see also 1980b, 1980c, 1982; McGee & Martin, 1983), however, has articulated an alternative grounding for the study of social movements, an approach that has developed into a strikingly different theoretical framework.

McGee maintains that movement studies fail to understand the importance of human consciousness in warranting the claim of a movement (1980a, p. 243). Rather than seeing a social movement as a phenomenon, McGee claims a social movement is a "set of meanings" found in rhetorical artifacts (p. 233).[3] Critics should prove "movement" by tracing changes in the "basic vocabulary of normative terms" used to describe the environment (p. 243). Thus, McGee connects his perspective on social movements to the concept of "ideographs" (1980b), arguing that one way "we can prove 'movement' [is] by observing changes in the 'ideographic' structures of social norm-systems" (1980a, p. 243). McGee (1980b) defines an ideograph as an "ordinary-language term found in political discourse. It is a high-order abstraction representing collective commitment to a particular but equivocal and ill-defined normative goal" (p. 15). Analysis of ideographs, McGee claims, reveals "structures" of political consciousness "which have the capacity both to control 'power' and to influence (if not determine) the shape and texture of each individual's 'reality'" (p. 5). Social control is "fundamentally rhetorical" (p. 6).

Condit and Lucaites, both together and separately, have developed this approach (Condit, 1987a, 1987b; Condit & Lucaites, 1991; Lucaites, 1989; Lucaites & Condit, 1990). Their work illustrates the potential of ideographic analysis to trace alterations in the "public vocabulary" that warrant social change (Lucaites & Condit, 1990). Although their most recent work (Condit & Lucaites, 1991) focuses on the

ideograph "equality," they have examined the basic "narratives" existing in society, as well as descriptions or "characterizations" of agents, acts, scenes, and so forth that gain acceptance within a community (Condit, 1987b). Their premise is simple; they argue that rhetoric "operates simultaneously as both the figure and the ground of social movement in time" (Condit & Lucaites, 1991, p. 1). Thus, they seek to explain social change by tracing changes in ideographs, narratives, and characterizations over time. They argue that their perspective provides a history of a "collective consciousness" (1991, p. 1). Such projects are important because they outline the symbolic context within which rhetorical action takes place.

This kind of analysis, however, cannot substitute for the critique of specific episodes within the evolution of a social movement. As Lucas notes of McGee's original discussion of social movements, this approach "does not take account of the fact that although the general process of movement/change in society and the operations of specific social movements are doubtless related, they are not identical" (Lucas, 1980, p. 258). This problem plagues Condit's (1987b) analysis of the civil rights movement. She argues that alterations within the public vocabulary concerning blacks, as reflected in national magazine stories from 1939–1959, played a decisive role in the success of the movement. Given her emphasis on the public vocabulary, one wonders why the events of the 1960s proceeded so virulently. She struggles with these issues, explaining that the "riots" in the 1960s were "about economics," not politics, and noting that there are gaps between "the public realm and the private" (pp. 14–15).

The simplest explanation seems more plausible: that, while writers and editors of national magazines altered their vocabulary, material conditions did not change. Specific efforts to force white Americans to change their behavior and to acknowledge the constitutional rights of blacks were necessary. As Simons notes, "what is most conspicuous about the Condit and Lucaites [1991] study is what is absent" (1991, p. 96). The rhetor is absent. In an almost precise about-face from the assumptions of traditional movement criticism, the meaning-centered approach comes close to denying the validity of the human subject. Instead, discourse becomes supreme and the freedom of the rhetor is questioned. For that reason, Condit seems unable to understand why the material circumstances did not change as the public vocabulary altered. By focusing almost exclusively on the "collective consciousness," any critic can easily lose the feel for the concrete details of social life that reveal rhetors fighting for change.

In this essay, I sketch an alternative approach to the problem of social control, one that offers the possibility of grounding critical analysis of social control in the encounters between movement rhetors and society. I seek to develop a perspective that allows for both the ability of language to influence us as well as our potential for transforming it. Social change happens, in part, through criticism which specifies and evaluates the practices of social control that lead to the domestication or silencing of alternative voices within society (Hariman, 1989; Klumpp & Hollihan, 1989; McGee & Martin, 1983; McKerrow, 1989; Wander, 1983, 1984; Wander & Jenkins, 1972).

"Critical" Marxism is one approach that directs the attention of critics to the power of vested interests to domesticate oppositional views (Aune, 1990). Although, as Aune (1990) points out, traditional Marxism does not welcome rhetoric, critics have drawn on the work of Antonio Gramsci (1971, 1988), particularly his concept of hegemony, as a way to understand the persuasive aspects of social control. Gitlin (1980, p. 252) notes that there is "no full-blown theory of hegemony, specifying social-structural and historical conditions for its sources, strengths and weaknesses." Nonetheless, a paradigm of scholarship developed throughout the 1970s based on the fragmentary writings of Gramsci.

According to Conrad (1988), hegemony evolved from analysis of the relationship between "base" and "superstructure" in Marxist theory (Williams, 1973, 1977). Traditionally, the superstructure or culture was thought to reflect the base or modes of production. Gramsci, among others, revised that view, arguing, as Lears (1985, p. 570) states, that the "link between the two

realms is not linear causality but circular interaction within an organic whole." Dominant classes maintain their place not only through acts of coercion, but also through symbolic action which renews and recreates the social order. Gramsci developed the term "hegemony" to describe, in Gitlin's terms, "a historical process in which one picture of the world is systematically preferred over others, usually through practical routines and at times through extraordinary measures" (1980, p. 257).

Todd Gitlin (1979, 1980) is the most visible American critic within this school of thought. In fact, American media criticism has explored hegemony in a variety of ways, including Conrad's discussion of the "illusion of self" in working class songs (1988), Gray's examination of television's treatment of black Americans (1989), and Dow's feminist analysis of *The Mary Tyler Moore Show* (1990). Unlike the Establishment-Conflict model, critics of hegemony do not see society as a contest between gladiators or as a constant war. If that was the case, the country would not survive the upheaval. Instead, the genius of liberal-capitalism rests in its ability to transport "major social conflicts *into* the cultural system, where the hegemonic process frames them, form and content both, into compatibility with dominant systems of meaning" (Gitlin, 1979, p. 264).

Significantly, these theorists also do not see society as *completely* dominated by a single set of beliefs. Rather, the "normal" pictures of the world are constantly challenged and negotiated through interaction with groups who seek to develop "alternative" or "oppositional" identities (Aune, 1990, p. 163; Gitlin, 1979, pp. 263–264). What is interesting to the rhetorician are the strategies used within the negotiation. How do "established" groups maintain their hegemony? What strategies function well for oppositional groups? How are meanings negotiated between these forces in order to keep the core beliefs of the society intact while allowing for some reform? What has been of prime interest to critics of hegemony, however, are not the strategies used by opponents to establish alternative identities, but rather the symbolic means used to bring recalcitrant rhetors "into the fold." It is precisely this focus that makes hegemony attractive to scholars seeking to explain the strategies by which social movements are domesticated.

Moreover, studies based in Gramsci avoid extreme positions on the freedom of speakers. The concept of hegemony suggests that Gramsci was concerned with the ability of discourse to persuade people to act against their class interests. Nonetheless, as Lears (1985) points out, Gramsci avoided a "resolute anti-subjectivism [that] fails to account for resistance and transformation in 'discursive practice' but also threatens to degenerate into as monocausal and mechanistic a model as the economic determinism Gramsci criticized so effectively" (p. 593). Lears concludes that Gramsci saw language "as another of those structures that may appear immutable and objective but are constantly changing in fluid interaction with human subjects" (p. 593).

Unfortunately, the term "hegemony" often resembles "a sort of immutable fog that has settled over the whole public life of capitalist societies" (Gitlin, 1979, p. 252). For this concept to have meaning within social movement theory, it should be defined in terms of specific rhetorical strategies used, in Burke's words, for "dealing with situations" (1973, p. 296).[4] I argue that, in contexts such as the Freedom Rides, symbolic strategies develop to accommodate dissent while making it compatible with "dominant systems of meaning." The possibilities offered by the concept of hegemony form the basis for my approach, but I ground discussion of that idea in strategies drawn from the discourse of the Kennedy Administration and the major press organs which covered the Rides. This is a speculative inquiry designed to open discussion of strategies that operate to control dissent at critical moments in a movement's evolution. I have two purposes. First, I want to illuminate an important event within the civil rights movement, the Freedom Rides. Second, I seek to illustrate the critical power of Gramsci's theory of hegemony.

THE FREEDOM RIDES

Conrad (1981) argues that movements "can be understood most fully when critics examine origins and search for points of re-definition, for

moments when the character of the movement is altered" (p. 284). The Freedom Rides were such a moment during the civil rights movement. The Rides were the first encounter between the Administration and civil rights activists. Brauer (1977, pp. 30–60) argues that movement members developed high expectations for the Kennedys during the 1960 campaign and wanted to test the willingness of liberals to help the movement. In turn, the Kennedy brothers learned lessons from this episode that they employed in subsequent crises (Weisbrot, 1991).

After their departure from Washington, D.C., the Freedom Riders encountered little difficulty until they reached Alabama (Branch, 1988, pp. 414–415). On May 14, the two buses, about an hour apart, headed for Anniston, Alabama, with a planned stop for the night in Birmingham. The Greyhound bus arrived in Anniston first, with the Riders and two undercover Alabama state investigators on board (p. 418). A mob, warned of the arrival, attacked the bus at the station, trying to drag the Riders out onto the platform. The Alabama policemen, dropping their guise, urged the driver to leave. The tires of the bus were slashed, however, and it ground to a halt outside of Anniston. The mob caught up, threw a firebomb into the bus, and forced its occupants out to endure their version of southern hospitality. The second bus was also attacked in Anniston, but escaped to the dubious refuge of Birmingham.

After reaching Birmingham, the Riders emerged to confront a crowd armed with "baseball bats, lead pipes, and bicycle chains" (Weisbrot, 1991, p. 57). The Riders were beaten so badly that an FBI agent, carefully watching and recording the scene, said that he "couldn't see their faces through the blood" (Weisbrot, 1991, p. 57). The Riders eventually gathered at the home of Reverend Fred Shuttlesworth in Birmingham (Branch, 1988).

The abject failure of Alabama law enforcement led to federal intervention. John Seigenthaler, a Justice Department aide to Robert Kennedy, was empowered as the President's representative and sent to Birmingham to get the Riders out of the city. The initial Riders departed by plane for New Orleans, but a new group arrived in

Birmingham. They were organized by leaders of the student sit-ins at Nashville and included John Lewis, an original Rider (Weisbrot, 1991, p. 58). The new Riders, many of them members of the Student Non-Violent Coordinating Committee (SNCC), boarded a bus for Montgomery and were met by a mob at the station in that city. Seigenthaler, attempting to help some students escape, was beaten. That evening, a meeting at the church of Ralph Abernathy attracted a mob. Robert Kennedy, angered by the beating of Seigenthaler, dispatched federal marshals to protect the church and, from that point on, federal authority protected the Riders (Branch, 1988, pp. 451–464).

While a crisis is never welcome in Washington, the Freedom Rides came at an inopportune time for the new President. John Kennedy's victory in 1960 was, perhaps, the last spasm of the New Deal coalition. His narrow margin meant that every group which supported him, from civil rights organizations to southern white leaders, was convinced that they had been crucial to his success. The issue of civil rights, especially in the form of a physical confrontation, threatened Kennedy's political base.

Moreover, the Rides started as the President decided to meet with Khrus[h]chev in Vienna to defuse rising East-West tensions over Berlin and other issues (Branch, 1988, pp. 477–478). The President seemed to feel that disunity at home threatened his power to deal with Communism abroad. An angry Kennedy, preparing to leave for Vienna, called Harris Wofford, his civil rights aide in the White House, and demanded, "Tell them to call it off! Stop them!" (Wofford, 1980, p. 153). Wofford found the Riders to be unresponsive to presidential directive.

That fact revealed the more serious threat that the Freedom Rides posed to the social order. Prior to the Rides, activists used direct action to desegregate institutions from local bus service to lunch counters. Those efforts, however, took place within the framework of local and state government. If federal intervention seemed necessary, it came about through the channels of the judiciary. The Freedom Riders exploited the conflict between federal and local law and, through direct action, created dangerous fissures within the American system of government.

Walter Lippmann, possibly the most influential columnist in the country, recognized the dangers posed by the Freedom Rides. He argued that the tumult surrounding the Rides indicated that federal law "is being nullified by state laws which contradict it and by overwhelming white sentiment which does not recognize it" (1961, p. A13). The Freedom Rides represented a "nonviolent rebellion" against those state laws. The "problem of direct action" was that the federal government employed force to protect agitators "whose actions it cannot advise, guide or control" (p. A13). That power was being used against state governments and foreshadowed the creation of a national police force and a dramatic expansion of the power of the federal government at the expense of the states. Direct action as used in the Rides created a continuing, physical confrontation between levels of American government. Such protestors could not "be left unlimited and uncontrolled" (p. A13).

DOMESTICATING DISSENT

The Freedom Riders posed a threat because they struck at one of the fundamental conflicts within the American system. The order of the state is supposed to guarantee the exercise of individual rights, yet that order sometimes justifies attacks on those rights. Activists who assert their "rights" attack the system "in its own name" and seek to reveal its contradictions (Gitlin, 1979, p. 265).[5] By invoking the symbolic power of American ideology, the Freedom Riders tacitly agreed to resolve their complaint within existing channels. The Riders recognized, however, that the *form* of the protest strained the American system. As Weisbrot (1991) notes, their primary goal was desegregation of interstate travel facilities. An underlying objective: to demonstrate "the urgency of sweeping federal intervention in the Deep South" (p. 63). This was exactly what the Administration wished to avoid. They recognized that "sweeping federal intervention" would shatter Kennedy's governing coalition and alter the relationship between the state and federal branches of government (Brauer, 1977, pp. 110–112; Guthman & Shulman, 1988, pp. 98–100; Weisbrot, 1991, p. 63).[6] Thus, the reaction of the Administration and the regularities of media coverage provided the control that transported this conflict into the cultural system. Through "extraordinary measures and routine conventions," the hegemonic process framed the Rides such that the government could appear both to uphold the rights of the Riders and to preserve order.

Analysis of Administration statements on the Rides as well as coverage of the controversy in the *New York Times,* the *Washington Post,* and the three major weekly news magazines (*Time, Newsweek,* and *U.S. News and World Report*) reveals four major hegemonic strategies.[7] First, the *naming* of the major players initially favored the innocent Riders, but gradually shifted to emphasize the irresponsible nature of Riders' action. Second, the early *contextualization* of the Rides placed them within the context of the struggle for civil rights in the South, but later cast them as actions threatening America in the struggle against Communism. Third, *legal sanction,* initially given to the Riders, eventually equated them with the mobs. Finally, the Kennedy Administration used *diversion* to channel the efforts of activists away from the Rides and into voter registration, an act which supported the system. The Rides were placed in a dominant system of meaning that dismissed them as counterproductive.

Naming

Providing an audience with an orientation to a phenomenon by naming that object has been the focus of considerable critical attention (Kauffman, 1989; McKerrow, 1989; Schiappa, 1989). The labels attached to the players in the Freedom Rides controversy and the characterizations of their actions that appeared in statements of the Attorney General and in press coverage were critical in shaping the meaning of those events.[8]

Initially, the Administration and the press reacted favorably to the Riders. The *New York Times* carried sympathetic accounts of the beatings in Anniston ("Bi-Racial Buses," 1961, pp. 1, 22). The *Times* accepted the appellation of "Freedom Riders" for the group, although the paper put the phrase in quotation marks (p. 1). The paper recounted the purpose of the Rides in neutral language, indicating they were "testing

segregated facilities in bus stations" (p. 1). More important, the article accepted the accounts of the Riders regarding the attacks. The story of the mobbing of the Trailways bus was provided by "Dr. Walter Bergman, 61 years old, a former Michigan State University professor and a member of the CORE group" (p. 22). Such a characterization was inconsistent with the image of a radical. The *Times* also legitimated him by providing five paragraphs of quotation from Bergman as its sole account of the attack on the Riders in Anniston (p. 22).

The report from Birmingham bolstered the image of the Riders as well. The *Times* noted the Riders were "ambushed" (p. 1). The writing emphasized the non-violent response of the "Negroes." The account of the beatings explained that a Negro "walked" into the white waiting room, that he was "pushed," "knocked" against the wall, and "fell to the floor, bleeding from the nose. As he got up, the white man hit him again. This time, the Negro fell backward into the arms of the [other] white men. They pushed him up again. The white man struck him again" (p. 22).

This report typified the early coverage of the print media. The Riders were portrayed as courageous victims, seeking to secure their constitutional rights. As the *Washington Post* noted in a May 18 editorial: "The 'Freedom Riders' engaged in no disorderly conduct and did nothing to provoke violence—save to exercise a constitutional right. . . . That was their sole offense" ("Darkest Alabama," 1961, p. A12). Such accounts and editorials legitimated the Freedom Rides.

The Kennedy Administration, too, responded quickly to the plight of the Riders. They dispatched federal marshals to protect the Riders and the Justice Department sought an injunction against the Ku Klux Klan to prevent them from taking actions against the Riders (Lewis, 1961a). More important, the beating of Seigenthaler, the personal representative of John and Robert Kennedy, symbolically linked the Riders and the Administration. Robert Kennedy's first statement on the crisis, the text of a wire he sent to Governor John Patterson of Alabama, emphasized the attack on Seigenthaler and the betrayal of basic principles of law and order in Alabama (Lewis, 1961b). Kennedy's angry tone in the wire revealed his bias.

The portrayal of southern leaders suffered by comparison. The *Washington Post* titled the May 18 editorial "Darkest Alabama." Press coverage of the Anniston and Birmingham attacks, as indicated above, relied almost solely on the accounts of the Riders and implied that local and state officials were not worthy of the journalistic convention to include the "other side of the story." On May 20, the *Times* detailed the efforts of the Kennedys to reach Governor Patterson, noting officials felt Patterson was "deliberately refusing" the calls and implying he did not have the courage to talk to the Kennedys ("President Can't Reach Governor," 1961, p. 1). Robert Kennedy's (1961b) wire to the Governor recounted the assurances of state officials to the President, the Attorney General, and John Seigenthaler that the Riders would be protected. Kennedy's detailed recitation of the subsequent attacks left only the conclusion that Alabama officials were liars.

The tide began to turn soon after that wire was sent. The Riders wished to proceed from Montgomery to Mississippi. New Riders, including the Reverend William Sloan Coffin of Yale, sought to broaden the Rides into a massive civil disobedience campaign (Sitton, 1961b; "Yale's Chaplain," 1961). The Administration began to express impatience with the idealism of the Riders. On May 22, the *Times* signalled a change in its coverage in an editorial that noted that, while the Riders had constitutional rights, "there is an element of incitement and provocation in regions of high racial tension" ("Alabama, U.S.A.," 1961, p. 30). On May 24, Robert Kennedy (1961d) issued two statements on the crisis. In the morning, he claimed that the state officials of Alabama and Mississippi were prepared to exercise their responsibilities. He announced that federal marshals would not accompany continued bus travel. In the afternoon, reacting to the new volunteers, he differentiated between the "Freedom Riders" and the "curiosity seekers, publicity seekers and others seeking to serve their own causes." He called for a "cooling-off period" to restore "an atmosphere of reason and normalcy" (p. 25).

The legitimacy of the Freedom Rides was gradually eroding. News magazines, published after the initial coverage, reflected the change.

Time noted that the Riders claimed to be exercising their constitutional right, but "were, in fact, hunting for trouble—and last week in Alabama they found more of it than they wanted" ("Trouble in Alabama," 1961, p. 16). Such a frame of the Riders legitimized the original attacks in Alabama. Conversely, "responsible" southern leaders reached the headlines. The *Times* ran an article on May 24 titled "Alabama Militia Dislikes Its Job but Performs It With Precision" (1961, p. 23). On May 25, the *Times* noted that Alabama and Mississippi state police were providing immense protection for the Riders (Sitton, 1961a). By May 26, the paper reported that Dr. King had "spurned" the pleas of southern "liberals" to use his influence to halt the Rides. The *Times* maintained the Rides were hurting the "civil rights struggle" (Sitton, 1961b, p. 21). An editorial on the 28th claimed that the "Freedom Riders have made their point. Now is the time for restraint, relaxation of tension, and a cessation of their courageous, legal, peaceful but nonetheless provocative action in the South" ("The 'Inescapable Obligation'," 1961, p. 8E).

Throughout the last two weeks of May, the Administration, particularly the Attorney General, appeared competent and compassionate. The Administration downplayed the significance of the Rides by distancing the President. He commented only once and, instead, allowed his brother to handle the crisis. This strategy implied that the Rides could be handled through normal administrative channels. The fact that the Attorney General was the President's brother, however, assured the Riders and the civil rights organizations of the President's interest.

Other actions of the Administration also indicated a measured approach. The Kennedys sent their personal envoy to persuade state and local governments to uphold the law. Only when that measure proved inadequate did they dispatch the marshals. The *Times* and the *Post* printed the Attorney General's careful justification for that action (Kennedy, 1961c, 1961d). During the crisis, the *New York Times Magazine* published an admiring summary of Robert Kennedy's tenure at the Department of Justice, and the *Post*, with a picture of a haggard Attorney General, recounted in an almost breathless tone the "command post" in Kennedy's office (Manning,

1961; "Justice Chief's Office," 1961). In addition, the *Post* detailed Kennedy's responsible approach in a page 1 article on May 27 (Clayton, 1961). Robert Kennedy (along with Martin Luther King, Jr.[,] and Governor Patterson) appeared on the cover of the June 5 *Newsweek* with a quotation from his Law Day Address: "We stand for human liberty."

Finally, the Attorney General provided the "peg" by which the press could wind down the story. On May 29, he petitioned the Interstate Commerce Commission to put in place rules to enforce the 1960 Supreme Court decision. On the 30th, the *Times* reported the story and carried large excerpts from the petition, imposing legal phraseology and all (Kennedy, 1961e; "Robert Kennedy Asks," 1961). Kennedy's rhetoric allowed the press to frame the Rides such that they created a crisis that the government, in spite of a few problems, resolved through existing channels.

The characterizations of the major players in the Freedom Rides crisis functioned to uphold the efficiency and fairness of the American system. Initially, the Riders were positively characterized, but they gradually lost their legitimacy. Their direct action came to be viewed as provocative as a kind of "baiting," even by sympathetic observers. The people of the South were originally represented by the mobs, but later by efficient state troopers and liberal leaders who condemned the violence. The federal government, especially the Attorney General, was widely praised. His petition to the I.C.C. was regarded as the logical conclusion to the crisis, despite the fact that no action was taken until September and even then many stations remained segregated until late 1962 (Weisbrot, 1991, pp. 62–63). These characterizations undermined the status of the Riders and emphasized the system's competence to resolve racial conflict.

Contextualization

The importance of context to rhetorical action has long been a major area of emphasis (Bitzer, 1968; Miller, 1984; Vatz, 1973). Rather than viewing the "rhetorical situation" as containing "exigencies" that determine a speaker's response, theorists have recently argued that the scene for

rhetoric is socially constructed (Miller, 1984). Branham and Pearce (1987) claim that speakers "who find their rhetorical situations problematic may fashion texts that attempt to transform the contexts of interpretation in which they operate, a process we have termed 'contextual reconstruction'" (p. 425). Similarly, a hegemonic response to a social movement transforms the context from one that is favorable to the agitators to one that limits them. In the case of the Freedom Rides, the context shifted from the segregated south to the world stage.

The initial stories on the Freedom Rides, and the Administration's response, focused almost solely on segregation and racism in the South, providing the Riders with a favorable context. When foreign affairs were mentioned at all, it was noted that the mobs in Alabama caused "incalculable" harm (in the words of the *Post*) to America's standing in the world ("How the World Press Viewed the Days of Tension," 1961; "The Mob in Alabama," 1961; "Strife in Alabama Stressed in News Abroad," 1961). As the Vienna summit grew closer, the Freedom Rides were transformed. They were viewed within the context of the fight against Communism rather than the fight against racism.

On the morning of May 24th, the Attorney General introduced this theme. He concluded his statement: "We should all keep in mind that the President is about to embark on a mission of great importance. Whatever we do in the United States at this time which brings or causes discredit in our country can be harmful to this mission" (Kennedy, 1961d, p. 25). Compared to other rhetors, Kennedy was relatively restrained. *U.S. News and World Report* printed an excerpt from a speech by Senator James Eastland of Mississippi claiming that the Rides were "devised deliberately as a prelude to various high level meetings in Europe, as a propaganda method to embarrass the Government of the United States in the handling of international affairs" (1961, p. 48). The statement of the Attorney General, the events of the summit, and the attacks by men such as Eastland functioned to recontextualize the Rides. The change in the context of the Rides was not the dominant factor in limiting their effect. But, when combined with the doubts about the character of the Riders, these charges contributed to the growing sense that the Rides were not in the interest of the country.

Legal Sanction

That sense of doubt was amplified by the change in the legal status of the Riders. McKerrow (1989), drawing from Foucault, argues that, within Western democracies, there is a discourse of power that relies on the judiciary. It speaks "in terms of rights, obligations, and of the possibility of exchanging power through the legal mediation of conflicting interests" (p. 97). Citing the Supreme Court decision on interstate travel, the Freedom Riders depended on judicial sanction. By the end of May, however, the law had been turned against them.

Initial stories explained the legal basis for the Rides. The first *New York Times* story noted, "The courts have outlawed enforced segregation among interstate bus passengers" ("Bi-Racial Buses," 1961, p. 22). *Time* provided its readers with an article that elucidated the constitutional basis for the Rides ("Three Questions of Law," 1961). Moreover, the Administration took legal action in support of the Riders.

As the Attorney General sent in the marshals, he asked for a federal court injunction barring the Ku Klux Klan (which had been implicated in the earlier attacks in Birmingham) from interfering with interstate travel. The *Times* noted that the legal basis of Kennedy's suit was sound (Lewis, 1961a). District Court Judge Frank M. Johnson in Montgomery issued a temporary injunction barring the Klan from interfering in interstate travel ("Montgomery under Martial Law," 1961). Johnson earned a lasting reputation as a jurist with great integrity.

As the Riders carried their protest into the state of Mississippi, the legal basis for the protests disappeared. When the buses entered Mississippi, they picked up a state police escort. At Jackson, the Riders were let off the bus. As they entered the white waiting room, they were arrested for a breach of the peace (Sitton, 1961a). The arrests resulted from a deal between the Attorney General and Senator Eastland.

According to Robert Kennedy's oral history interviews, he was worried about the safety of the Riders. Kennedy explained, "[Eastland] told us they'd all be arrested. I said to him my primary interest was that they weren't beaten up. So I, in fact, I suppose, concurred with the fact that they were going to be arrested although I didn't have any control over it" (Guthman & Shulman, 1988, p. 97). Contrary to his assertion, he could have sought another court injunction to bar Mississippi from interference with interstate commerce. In fact, on the day the first Jackson arrests occurred, he asked for an injunction against officials in Alabama. Kennedy argued that they had known beforehand about the attacks in Birmingham and Montgomery and had done nothing to stop them. He chose not to act in Mississippi. Authorities continued to arrest, convict, and jail Freedom Riders who entered the state. Direct action was legally defined as a breach of the peace.

The legal basis of the Rides was completely overturned on June 2, 1961. When Judge Frank Johnson ruled on the government's petition to enjoin Alabama state officials, he surprised one and all by also enjoining the sponsors of the Rides. He bluntly stated, in a widely circulated quotation, "If there are any incidents such as [Montgomery] again, I am going to put some Klansmen, some city officials, some city policemen, and some Negro preachers in the Federal penitentiary" ("Tension and Justice," 1961, p. 37). Johnson's opinion made the Riders and the Klan equally responsible. The concept that the Riders had provoked their fate was endorsed. Combined with the arrests in Mississippi, this injunction turned legal presumption against direct action.[9]

Diversion

From the perspective of hegemony, conflicts are not necessarily eliminated. Instead, they are domesticated within the culture's dominant system of meaning. The three strategies detailed functioned to bring the Riders under control. Their grievances remained. It was difficult for the Administration to deny the justice of the case against segregation. In fact, it is clear that this Administration sought to help the movement; the Kennedys wanted a form of action they could support. Thus, they diverted the energy of the agitators into activities which avoided the issue of state nullification. Even as the Freedom Rides continued, a variety of forces pressed civil rights organizations to embrace voter registration.

Voter registration was mentioned occasionally during the coverage of the Rides. Roscoe Drummond of the *Washington Post* concluded a column on the Rides by asking, "For example, if these young men and women had organized to get all qualified Negroes on the registration rolls of these states they have been riding through, would this not be of more service to the people they are trying to help?" (Drummond, 1961, p. A7). Voter registration would bring about *real* change, Drummond argued, while direct action only disturbed the peace.

The Justice Department quickly mobilized to convince civil rights organizations of the advantages of voter registration. Assistant Attorney General Burke Marshall accompanied the director of a new organization, the Voter Registration Project, to a meeting with the IRS commissioner to secure a tax exemption for the group. In early June, Marshall met with leaders of the Freedom Rides to push voter registration. On June 16, Robert Kennedy told the Freedom Ride Coordinating Committee that they were not productive. Kennedy argued that the law was clear: The federal government had more authority to protect people registering to vote than it did to protect the Freedom Riders. By late July, the leaders of all major civil rights organizations met in New York to formulate voter registration strategy with Burke Marshall and Harris Wofford. On June 26, Marshall and Kennedy generated a page 1, "above the fold," article in the *New York Times* that asserted that all major civil rights leaders agreed "the vote is the key" (Lewis, 1961b, pp. 1, 9). The Freedom Rides ended (Branch, 1988).

Conclusion

The Freedom Rides posed the first domestic test for the Administration, and it responded well. Robert Kennedy's cooperation with Eastland in Mississippi told white southern Democrats that the Administration was not happy with the Riders. After the Rides, Burke Marshall repeatedly insisted that the regular use of marshals was highly impractical (Weisbrot, 1991). On the other hand, even the limited intervention of the federal government raised the credibility of the Administration with civil rights organizations. Most prominent black leaders, including King, were pleased with the petition to the I.C.C. and with the support the Kennedys offered for voter registration campaigns (Garrow, 1988, pp. 160–164). By the time the Freedom Rides ended, John Kennedy's governing coalition was still intact.

More important, the "nonviolent rebellion" was brought under control. Protest of the kind practiced by the Freedom Riders was dangerous because it forced the national government to use force to coerce states to obey the law. Such a transfer of power to activists was intolerable, and they were diverted into the voter registration campaign. As Brauer (1977) points out, "They [Robert Kennedy, Burke Marshall, and Harris Wofford] would have been reluctant to admit it, but the channeling of civil rights activists into voter registration work offered a much lower risk of the kind of violence that had accompanied the Freedom Rides—violence that almost necessitated federal military intervention" (p. 112). Certainly, neither the Kennedys nor most civil rights workers foresaw the vicious campaign of terror that states such as Mississippi would eventually wage against voting rights activists, but, for the Administration, even those problems paled next to the ones caused by the Rides. Branch (1988) concludes, "The Voter Education Project was created essentially by a forced march in the opposite direction from the Freedom Rides, in spirit if not in purpose" (p. 482).

The pragmatic success of the Administration, however, should not obscure a critical assessment (in McKerrow's sense) of its discourse. The "baiting" argument, used so often in major media outlets and in the rhetoric of the Administration, resembles nothing so much as the "blame the victim" calumny that plagues rape victims. Just as women are accused of "asking for it" by walking alone on dark streets, so the Freedom Riders were "looking for trouble" by exercising their constitutional rights. While this argument was not new to southern black activists (see Campbell's 1989, pp. 145–150, analysis of Ida B. Wells' opposition to lynching), its presence in the discourse of an Administration which had committed itself to the campaign for civil rights was noteworthy. The racist mobs could not help it; they were "provoked" into action. One result of the Freedom Rides was to turn legal and moral presumption against direct action.[10]

The second result of the Rides was the diversion of the energies of the movement into voter registration. The Freedom Rides demonstrated that state governments had "nullified" federal civil rights laws. The national government had difficulty responding to this challenge without changing the system by expanding its own police power. Voting rights campaigns, however, symbolically reaffirmed the political system by asking for participation. Concerns about state "nullification" were dropped in favor of efforts to change state governments through the electoral process. The hope that the federal government would intervene immediately on the basis of existing law was dashed; instead, activists had to hope that increasing numbers of black votes would someday create change by electing new legislators. While the eventual success of this campaign in electing black officials throughout the nation cannot be doubted, its limitations are clear. The Constitution is supposed to guarantee each individual's civil rights. For the federal government to tell oppressed individuals to seek those rights through the electoral process undermines that constitutional guarantee. A minority in a democracy should not have to secure its rights by winning them in an election. Rather, a dissenter's rights should be "self-evident" in order to avoid a tyranny of the majority. That was not the view of the Kennedy Administration regarding black Americans.

HEGEMONY AND SOCIAL MOVEMENTS

This analysis has sought to reveal the complex nature of social control as an element in evaluation of social movement rhetoric. A traditional critique of the Freedom Rides controversy would focus on the statements of the Riders and the reactions of southerners such as Governor Patterson.[11] The "dialectical enjoinment" between the two positions would be noted, the success of the Riders in pressuring the Attorney General into action would be explained, and the Freedom Rides would be counted as a triumph of the civil rights movement. Such an agent-centered approach would have the advantage of producing close analysis of the rhetorical strategies used by the movement rhetors to create change. The compromises made by the movement and the strategies of social control used by the Administration, however, would be neglected. The "Establishment-Conflict" model does not explain the domestication of the movement at this critical juncture.

Conversely, the "meaning-centered" approach has much to recommend it in terms of understanding the "public vocabulary" available in specific situations. The "terministic screens" of this research, however, focus attention on the "big picture" to the neglect of specific moments in a movement's evolution. Analyses offered by Condit (1987a, 1987b) and Lucaites and Condit (1990) trace the integration of blacks into the mainstream of American public discourse, but they do not examine the process which occurred as the norms represented by ideographs were grappled with by rhetors in their historical context.

The perspective offered here seeks to provide an alternative framework for the analysis of social movements, one that incorporates an understanding of the language of social control, but also retains the traditional emphasis on specific rhetorical action within a movement's evolution. Gramsci's theory of hegemony focuses attention on the strategies used to accommodate dissent within dominant systems of meaning. My critique, then, seeks understanding of "the discourse of power which creates and sustains the social practices which control the dominated" (McKerrow, 1989, p. 92).

Understanding oppressive practices, however, is not enough. As McKerrow points out, a critical rhetoric seeks to "have consequences" (p. 92). Unfortunately, like the "meaning-centered" approach to movements, McKerrow's discussion of critical rhetoric tends to diminish the role of the human subject (Charland, 1991). Increasingly, more critics, including McGee in his latest work (1991), have argued that "texts" are not created by speakers at all, but by "inventive" audiences. Their view has consequences for the ability of a critical rhetoric to make a difference and points up the contributions an analysis of hegemony can make not only to the critique of movements, but also to an understanding of broader issues in critical theory.

As Aune (1990, p. 163) points out, "neo-Gramscians" argue the "task of the intellectual class at the present time is to construct a counter-hegemony" that can lead to greater freedom for oppressed people. Such work is either unnecessary or impossible from within the current prism of critical theory in communication. It is unnecessary if audiences possess the ability to "re-construct" texts to their own advantage. Unfortunately, there is no evidence that people have improved their material circumstances by doing so (Evans, 1990). A "counter-hegemony" is impossible if all human rhetors are hopelessly enmeshed in a "collective consciousness." No class or political interests exist because they are all circumscribed by language. No one is responsible for oppression and no action can alter inequities because language is beyond the control of people. Critique can only be against language itself and, as Charland (1991) argues, this position offers no real hope for social change.

A perspective based upon hegemony, however, creates the possibility of meaningful critique leading to change. This approach not only reveals oppressive practices, but also holds those who engage in such discourse responsible for their choices. As Lears (1985) argues, a critique based on hegemony directs the critic to "discover what was left out of the public debate and to account historically for those silences" (p. 586). Gramsci's theory of hegemony provides the critic with a "place to take a stand" (Charland, 1991) without resorting to transcendental norms of conduct or values. The political and rhetorical alternatives are often to be found in the silenced discourse of rhetors in their historical situations. Alternative or oppositional identities can provide a base from which to challenge oppressive social practices (Aune, 1990). The concept of hegemony has much to offer to rhetorical theories of social control.

Notes

1 A 1947 Supreme Court decision prohibited segregation in interstate travel and a number of activists, including Bayard Rustin, undertook a nonviolent journey of Reconciliation throughout the South to test compliance with that ruling. The riders were arrested with no publicity. In December of 1960, the Supreme Court (*Boynton v. Virginia*) reaffirmed and extended the earlier decision to include facilities at interstate travel stations such as restaurants, rest rooms, etc. The Congress of Racial Equality (CORE), under the direction of new leader James Farmer, decided the time was right to try again, although Farmer changed the name of the project to the Freedom Rides (Branch, 1988, pp. 171–172, p. 390).

2 The "Establishment" or the "social order" are flexible terms that encompass a variety of meanings. With many of the previous social movement articles under review, I take the "Establishment" to mean those "defenders of the established order" (Smith & Windes, 1975, p. 140). Authorities, as well as countermovements, defend the status quo. I am concerned with the former. When I use the terms "Establishment" or "social order," I mean what James Q. Wilson (1990, p. 33) has recently defined as the "American Way" of structuring society. Americans have developed traditions, such as the separation of powers, etc., which define how we act in the political arena. The *Webster's* definition of "an established order of society" or "the group of social, economic and political leaders who form a ruling class" also seems clear. Later in the essay, I narrow my focus to the specific issue of separation of powers. In the "American Way" of structuring society, states are given a great deal of discretion and most of the police power for enforcing the law. This particular aspect of the "Establishment" is the concept under attack during the Freedom Rides.

3 I am not sure McGee is completely accurate in his assessment that the traditional paradigm for movements sees them as "phenomena." See Lucas' (1980) response to that argument. At the same time, it is true that such studies undervalue "human consciousness" and neglect issues of social control.

4 Both Gusfield (1989) and Tompkins (1985) note the continuities between the work of Gramsci and Burke. Tompkins, in particular, argues that Burke offered "original insights into the hegemonic process" (p. 125).

5 Northrop Frye develops a similar analysis when he discusses the myths of freedom and concern (1971).

6 In his 1964 oral history interviews concerning the Freedom Rides, Robert Kennedy recognized the threat posed by the Rides and placed the need to maintain the separation of powers between the levels of government far above any other consideration: "In my judgment, Mississippi is going to work itself out, and Alabama is. Now,

maybe it's going to take a decade and maybe a lot of people are going to be killed in the meantime. And that's unfortunate. But in the long run I think it's for the health of the country and the stability of the system. It's the best way to proceed" (Guthman & Shulman, 1988, p. 100)[.] Attorney General Kennedy clearly saw that the "stability of the system" was at stake and responded accordingly.

[7] This analysis has not examined television coverage of the Freedom Rides. Newscasts in 1961 were only fifteen minutes long. Television had not yet attained the power that accrued to it during the Kennedy Administration and, particularly, with Kennedy's funeral. In addition, none of the histories of the Rides mention television coverage at all, in stark contrast to Birmingham in 1963 and Selma in 1964. In the case of the Rides, television was not as significant a player as the major press organs. Finally, I do not argue that the Kennedys and the press were in a conspiracy to deprive the Freedom Riders of their rights. Rather, as Gitlin (1980) notes, major press organs also have a stake in the continuance of the social system and tend to see the world in those terms. Just as important, a great deal of recent research on the Presidency (see, for instance, Windt, 1990) emphasizes the ability of the modern, "rhetorical" President to define issues for the public and set the ground for the public debate. The press is subject to such influence.

[8] This concept of "naming" is similar to Condit's (1987b) discussion of characterization. Condit, however, defines characterization as creating "universalized" definitions that turn into "character-types" (Condit, 1987b, p. 4). I am not making such a claim for the labels attached to the Freedom Riders; the naming was specific to the situation and time.

[9] In April of 1965, the Mississippi convictions were overturned by the Supreme Court (Brauer, 1977, p. 108). Until that time, Johnson's opinion and the Mississippi cases formed a legal foundation defining direct action as a breach of the peace.

[10] In addition to direct action, the movement made use of the legal system to bring about court orders and movement activists lobbied legislators. Yet the new laws and the court decisions were generally ignored in the South until direct action campaigns forced compliance. The loss of this weapon was devastating. The tactics of the Mississippi officials paved the way for successful resistance to the SCLC campaign for integration in Albany, Georgia. It took the ineptitude of "Bull" Connor

and the rhetorical masterpiece of King's "Letter from a Birmingham Jail" to regain the presumption lost in the Freedom Rides (Branch, 1988, pp. 524–562, 708–805; Weisbrot, 1991, pp. 63–67).

[11] The analysis that has been done of the rhetoric of the Administration during the Freedom Rides is embedded within Goldzwig and Dionisopoulos's (1989) examination of John Kennedy's civil rights discourse. They discuss the rhetorical constraints that bounded Kennedy's action and conclude that his rhetoric evolved as a result of outside pressures. Their analysis underestimates the freedom of action enjoyed by a President to define events (Hart, 1984, 1987) and ignores the important role played by Attorney General Robert Kennedy. While the Administration operated under constraints, the Kennedys were active in creating views favorable to their position.

References

Alabama, U.S.A. (1961, May 22). *New York Times*, p. 30.

Alabama militia dislikes its job but performs it with precision. (1961, May 24). *New York Times*, p. 23.

Aune, J. A. (1990). Cultures of discourse: Marxism and rhetorical theory. In D. C. Williams and M. D. Hazen (Eds.), *Argumentation: Theory and the rhetoric of assent* (pp. 157–172). Tuscaloosa: University of Alabama Press.

Bi-racial buses attacked, riders beaten in Alabama. (1961, May 15). *New York Times*, pp. 1, 22.

Bitzer, L. (1968). The rhetorical situation. *Philosophy and Rhetoric, 1*, 1–14.

Bowers, J. W., & Ochs, D. J. (1971). *The rhetoric of agitation and control*. Menlo Park, CA: Addison-Wesley.

Branch, T. (1988). *Parting the waters: America in the King years 1954–1963*. New York: Touchstone.

Branham, R. J., & Pearce, W. B. (1987). A contract for civility: Edward Kennedy's Lynchburg address. *Quarterly Journal of Speech, 73*, 424–443.

Brauer, C. M. (1977). *John F. Kennedy and the second reconstruction*. New York: Columbia University Press.

Burke, K. (1973). Literature as equipment for living. In *The philosophy of literary form* (pp. 293–304).

Campbell, K. K. (1989). *Man cannot speak for her: A critical study of early feminist rhetoric*. New York: Greenwood Press.

Cathcart, R. S. (1972). New approaches to the study of movements: Defining movements rhetorically. *Western Speech, 36*, 82–88.

Cathcart, R. S. (1978). Movements: Confrontation as rhetorical form. *Southern Speech Communication Journal*, 43, 233–247.

Charland, M. (1991). Finding a horizon and telos: The challenge to critical rhetoric. *Quarterly Journal of Speech*, 77, 71–74.

Clayton, J. E. (1961, May 27). Robert Kennedy's aim in south: To uphold laws but take no sides. *Washington Post*, pp. A1, A4.

Condit, C. M. (1987a). Crafting virtue: The rhetorical construction of public morality. *Quarterly Journal of Speech*, 73, 79–97.

Condit, C. M. (1987b). Democracy and civil rights: The universalizing influence of public argumentation. *Communication Monographs*, 54, 1–18.

Condit, C. M., & Lucaites, J. L. (1991). The rhetoric of equality and the expatriation of African-Americans, 1771–1826. *Communication Studies*, 42, 1–21.

Conrad, C. (1981). The transformation of the "Old Feminist" movement. *Quarterly Journal of Speech*, 67, 284–297.

Conrad, C. (1988). Work songs, hegemony, and illusions of self. *Critical Studies in Mass Communication*, 5, 179–201.

Darkest Alabama. (1961, May 18). *Washington Post*, p. A12.

Dow, B. J. (1990). Hegemony, feminist criticism, and *The Mary Tyler Moore Show*. *Critical Studies in Mass Communication*, 7, 261–274.

Drummond, R. (1961, May 24). Alabama rioting. *Washington Post*, p. A7.

Eastland, J. E. (1961, June 5). Senator Eastland on the "Freedom Riders." *U.S. News and World Report*, p. 48.

Evans, W. A. (1990). The interpretive turn in media research: Innovation, iteration, or illusion. *Critical Studies in Mass Communication*, 7, 147–168.

Frye, N. (1971). *The critical path*. Bloomington: Indiana University Press.

Garrow, D. (1988). *Bearing the cross: Martin Luther King, Jr., and the Southern Christian Leadership Conference*. New York: Vintage Books.

Gitlin, T. (1979). Prime time ideology: The hegemonic process in television entertainment. *Social Problems*, 26, 251–266.

Gitlin, T. (1980). *The whole world is watching*. Berkeley: University of California Press.

Goldzwig, S. R., & Dionisopoulos, G. N. (1989). John F. Kennedy's civil rights discourse: The evolution from "Principled Bystander" to public advocate. *Communication Monographs*, 56, 179–198.

Gramsci, A. (1971). *Selections from the prison notebook*. (Q. Hoare & G. Nowell Smith, Trans.) New York: Lawrence & Wishart.

Gramsci, A. (1988). *An Antonio Gramsci reader*. (David Forgacs, Ed.) New York: Schocken Books.

Gray, H. (1989). Television, black Americans, and the American dream. *Critical Studies in Mass Communication*, 6, 376–386.

Griffin, L. (1952). The rhetoric of historical movements. *Quarterly Journal of Speech*, 38, 184–188.

Griffin, L. (1980). On studying movements. *Central States Speech Journal*, 31, 225–232.

Gusfield, J. (1989). Introduction. In J. Gusfield (Ed.). *Kenneth Burke: On symbols and society*. (pp. 1–52). Chicago: University of Chicago Press.

Guthman, E. O. & Shulman, J. (Eds.) (1988). *Robert Kennedy in his own words*. New York: Bantam.

Hariman, R. (1989). Time and the reconstitution of gradualism in King's address: A response to Cox. In *Texts in context: Critical dialogues on significant episodes in American political rhetoric* (pp. 205–218). Davis, CA: Hermagoras Press.

Hart, R. (1984). *Verbal style and the Presidency*. New York: Academic Press.

Hart, R. (1987). *The sound of leadership*. Chicago: University of Chicago Press.

Henry, D. (1989). Recalling the 1960's: The new left and social movement criticism. *Quarterly Journal of Speech*, 75, 97–112.

How the world press viewed the days of tension. (1961, June 5). *Newsweek*, p. 22.

The "Inescapable Obligation." (1961, May 28). *New York Times*, p. 8E.

Justice chief's office like a command post. (1961, May 23). *Washington Post*, p. A8.

Kauffman, C. (1989). Names and weapons. *Communication Monographs*, 56, 273–285.

Kennedy, R. (1961a, May 7). Text of Attorney General Kennedy's civil rights speech at University of Georgia. *New York Times*, p. 62.

Kennedy, R. (1961b, May 18). Attorney General's wire. *New York Times*, p. 78.

Kennedy, R. (1961c, May 18). Text of Attorney General's wire. *Washington Post*, p. A7.

Kennedy, R. (1961d, May 25). Attorney General's pleas. *New York Times*, p. 25.

Kennedy, R. (1961e, May 30). Excerpts from bus petition to *I.C.C. New York Times*, p. 7.

King, A. A. (1976). The rhetoric of power maintenance: Elites at the precipice. *Quarterly Journal of Speech*, 62, 127–134.

Klumpp, J. F., & Hollihan, T. A. (1989). Rhetorical criticism as moral action. *Quarterly Journal of Speech, 75,* 84–96.

Lears, T. J. J. (1985). The concept of cultural hegemony: Problems and possibilities. *American Historical Review, 90,* 567–593.

Lewis, A. (1961a, May 21). 400 U.S. marshals sent to Alabama. *New York Times,* pp. 1, 78.

Lippmann, W. (1961, May 23). Tragedy in Alabama. *Washington Post,* p. A13.

Lucaites, J. L. (1989). Rhetorical legitimacy, <public trust> and the presidential debates. *Journal of the American Forensic Association, 25,* 231–238.

Lucaites, J. L., & Condit, C. M. (1990). Reconstructing <equality>: Culturetypal and counter-cultural rhetorics in the martyred black vision. *Communication Monographs, 57,* 5–24.

Lucas, S. E. (1980). Coming to terms with movement studies. *Central States Speech Journal, 31,* 255–266.

Lucas, S. E. (1988). The renaissance of American public address: Text and context in rhetorical criticism. *Quarterly Journal of Speech, 74,* 241–260.

Manning, R. (1961, May 28). Someone the President can talk to. *New York Times Magazine,* pp. 22–29.

McGee, M. (1980a). "Social Movement": Phenomenon or meaning? *Central States Speech Journal, 31,* 233–244.

McGee, M. (1980b). The "Ideograph": A link between rhetoric and ideology. *Quarterly Journal of Speech, 66,* 1–16.

McGee, M. (1980c). The origins of "Liberty": A feminization of power. *Communication Monographs, 47,* 23–45.

McGee, M. (1982). A materialist's conception of rhetoric. In R. E. McKerrow (Ed.), *Explorations in rhetoric: Studies in honor of Douglas Ehninger* (pp. 23–48). Glenview, IL: Scott, Foresman.

McGee, M. (1991). Text, context, and the fragmentation of contemporary culture. *Western Journal of Speech Communication, 54,* 274–289.

McGee, M., & Martin, M. A. (1983). Public knowledge and ideological argumentation. *Communication Monographs, 50,* 47–65.

McKerrow, R. E. (1989). Critical rhetoric: Theory and praxis. *Communication Monographs, 56,* 91–111.

Miller, C. R. (1984). Genre as social action. *Quarterly Journal of Speech, 70,* 151–167.

The mob in Alabama. (1961, May 23). *Washington Post,* p. A12.

Montgomery under martial law. (1961, May 22). *New York Times,* pp. 1, 26.

President can't reach Governor. (1961, May 20). *New York Times,* pp. 1, 18.

Robert Kennedy asks I.C.C. to end bus segregation. (1961, May 30). *New York Times,* pp. 1, 7.

Schiappa, E. (1989). The rhetoric of nukespeak. *Communication Monographs, 56,* 253–272.

Simons, H. W. (1991). On the rhetoric of social movements, historical movements, and "top-down" movements: A commentary. *Communication Studies, 42,* 94–101.

Sitton, C. (1961a, May 25). Bi-racial bus riders jailed in Jackson, Miss.[,] as they widen campaign. *New York Times,* pp. 1, 24.

Sitton, C. (1961b, May 26). Dr. King refuses to end bus test. *New York Times,* pp. 1, 21.

Smith, R. R., & Windes, R. R. (1975). The innovational movement: A rhetorical theory. *Quarterly Journal of Speech, 61,* 140–153.

Strife in Alabama stressed in news abroad. (1961, May 24). *New York Times,* p. 23.

Tension and justice. (1961, June 12). *Newsweek,* pp. 37–38.

Three questions of law. (1961, June 2). *Time,* p. 16.

Tompkins, P. K. (1985). On hegemony—"He Gave It No Name"—and critical structuralism in the work of Kenneth Burke. *Quarterly Journal of Speech, 71,* 119–131.

Trouble in Alabama. (1961, May 26). *Time,* pp. 16–17.

Vatz, R. E. (1973). The myth of the rhetorical situation. *Philosophy and Rhetoric, 6,* 154–161.

Wander, P. (1983). The ideological turn in modern criticism. *Central States Speech Journal, 34,* 1–18.

Wander, P. (1984). The rhetoric of American foreign policy. *Quarterly Journal of Speech, 70,* 339–361.

Wander, P., & Jenkins, S. (1972). Rhetoric, society, and the critical response. *Quarterly Journal of Speech, 58,* 441–449.

Weisbrot, R. (1991). *Freedom bound: A history of America's civil rights movement.* New York: Plume Books.

Williams, R. (1973). Base and superstructure in Marxist cultural theory. *New Left Review, 82,* 3–16.

Williams, R. (1977). *Marxism and literature.* New York: Oxford University Press.

Wilson, J. Q. (1990, July 2). The newer deal. *New Republic,* p. 33.

Windt, T. O. (1982). Administrative rhetoric: An undemocratic response to protest. *Communication Quarterly, 30,* 245–250.

Windt, T. O. (1990). *Presidents and protesters.* Tuscaloosa: University of Alabama Press.

Wofford, H. (1980). *Of Kennedys and Kings.* New York: Farrar, Straus, Giroux.

Yale's chaplain among 11 seized in Montgomery. (1961, May 26). *New York Times,* pp. 1, 20.

SLAPPS and Social Activism: The *Wonderland v. Grey2K* Case

Jason Edward Black

The early morning hours of November 8, 2000, marked the unsuccessful end of a two-year campaign to ban greyhound racing in Massachusetts. The referendum movement was led by Greyhound Racing Ends Year 2000 (Grey2K) and was opposed by the racetrack corporation Wonderland Park (Eidinger 1). After the campaign advertisements ceased, the votes were tallied and the political smoke had cleared, it turned out that Grey2K's initiative, Question 3, failed by less than 2% of the voting population—a narrow margin for a referendum (Eidinger 2). What remains vital for academic study is not the loss itself, but how Wonderland Park was able to silence Grey2K. Though marred by a host of legal issues, accusations of defamation, and finger pointing, Grey2K's grassroots campaign failed—not on its merits or due to its legal ills—but by a strategy employed to chill the free speech of ordinary citizens participating in activities for social change.

Wonderland Park used the Strategic Lawsuit Against Public Participation (SLAPP) to stifle Grey2K's voice from a communicative and public relations standpoint, though not through legal standing. In fact, Grey2K fought successfully for dismissal of the SLAPP, but by the time the court turned its attention to the motion to dismiss, the publicity of the SLAPP charges had already left a mark on the campaign to end the plight of racing greyhounds; most significantly, the 2000 election was over.

The SLAPP arose with the advent of increased public activism during the 1960s and gained academic attention in the late 1980s when legal scholars George Pring and Penelope Canan began combating this genre of cases designed to limit the public's right to free speech (see Beder). According to Pring and Canan, SLAPPs remain one of the most vicious and devious ways that governmental agencies and corporations squelch the individual or social movement voice. They write, "A new breed of lawsuits is stalking America. Like some new strain of virus, these court cases carry dire consequences for individuals, communities, and the body politic. Americans by the thousands are being sued, simply for exercising one of our most cherished rights: the right to communicate our views to our government officials, to 'speak out' on public issues" (Pring and Canan 23). The implications of this litigious strategy are disastrous for individual expression and the public's right to involve itself in civic affairs and political change. Mark Jackson concurs, noting "these suits are aimed not at rectifying truly defamatory statements made by defendants, but rather, at intimidating them from voicing their public concerns. Moreover, corporations use SLAPPs to discourage involvement not only by the named defendants, but also by their neighbors and the remaining community" (Jackson 493).

Oftentimes, SLAPPs are issued against individuals or grassroots groups who can barely afford to pay non-profit registry fees, let alone engage in lengthy legal battles over false claims (California Anti-SLAPP Project). Indeed, as Frederick Rowe argues, "for (the establishment) hiring lawyers and financing such a lawsuit is a tax-deductible business expense. But for victims of SLAPP suits, typically neighborhood associations or private citizens, the high costs of defending inflict heavy financial burdens that may deter further opposition to the proposed development" (Rowe 220). The companies and governmental agencies that employ SLAPPs ensure a number of consequences for the public voice, namely that it will be stopped, punished and brought to court. This often prevents people from speaking out against a policy, politician, corporation or industry.

There remains another factor of SLAPP litigation not addressed in the anti-SLAPP statutes currently gaining popularity in 27 states across the nation. This consequence involves limiting free speech while communicatively shutting down a protesting group through perfectly timed assaults designed to poison the public well regarding electoral campaigns for social change. The SLAPP is not so much legally grounded as it is legally strategic. Most SLAPPs lose, according to Sharon Beder, but are filed for the advantage of tainting the opposition and shifting the filer (object/agency of change) from corporate monster to victim:

> Such cases never win in the courts . . . but companies and organizations taking this legal action are not doing so to win compensation. Their aim is to harass, intimidate and distract their opponents. They "win" the court cases when the (activists) are no longer able to find the financial, emotional or mental wherewithal to sustain their defense. They win the political battle, even if they lose the court case if the (activists) and those associated with them stop speaking out against them (Beder 64).

This type of maneuver is highly disadvantageous for movements that are not time sensitive and seek reform as a general goal. For those movements that have advanced their goals into the electoral process and remain time dependent, however, the SLAPP is lethal as it simultaneously taints a campaign and drains its funds on the eve of an election (see Blackwelder; Lum; Saccuzzo; and Tate). Campaigns and movements that involve referendums and policy changes particularly find a harrowing demise at the hands of SLAPP filers.

This article examines the case study of *Grey2K v. Wonderland Park* and assesses the use of the SLAPP as a definitive challenge to free speech. I argue that anti-SLAPP statutes, while often allowing for gradual dismissal of legal claims and monetary damages, do not protect a movement or individual from a disparaging public image or loss of capital prior to a referendum for reform or abolition. The SLAPP is examined as a genre of legal action; then the failure to protect free speech through anti-SLAPP legislation is explored. Grey2K's anti-racing measure and subsequent opposition led by Wonderland Park

is used as a case study leading to suggestions for preventing the damage that SLAPPs create in the public arena.

SLAPP USES AND ANTI-SLAPP FAILURES

The California Anti-SLAPP Project defines SLAPPs as "civil complaints or counterclaims filed against individuals or organizations arising from their communications to government, or speech on an issue of public interest or concern" (California Anti-SLAPP Project). Typically, government agencies, corporations and industries shroud SLAPPs in the language and arguments of legitimate legal claims. Common lawsuits include defamation, invasion of privacy, malicious prosecution, abuse of process, conspiracy, interference with contract, intentional infliction of emotional stress, nuisance and injunction. Overall, these lawsuits take the common form of (1) a civil complaint or counterclaim (for monetary damages and/or injunction) (2) filed against non-governmental individuals and/or groups (3) because of their communications to a government body, official, or the electorate (4) on an issue of some public interest or concern (Lum 411). While all of these "false" claims could potentially limit free speech, the most applicable area to the communication field is the defamation charge. Inherent in a defamation claim is "the intentional false communication which is either published in a written form (libel) or publicly spoken (slander) that injures one's reputation" (California Anti-SLAPP Project).

Legal scholar Mark Jackson posited that since *New York Times v. Sullivan* corporations have been making greater use of the defamation strategy. He clarified that ". . . intimidation lawsuits have become a major weapon in the corporate arsenal. Using defamation suits against civic-minded citizens, groups, and publishers, corporations have drastically squelched citizen and news media involvement. In this way, the defamation suit has become a tool to ward off public criticism and oversight" (Jackson 492). According to *New York Times v. Sullivan*, defamation demands that two primary factors remain in place in order to become actionable.

For one, the defamation claim must typically come from a private citizen. Public officials must prove a higher threshold of malice in order to gain success through a defamation claim. As Justice Brennan noted in *Sullivan:* "in a democratic society, one who assumes to act for the citizens in an executive, legislative, or judicial capacity must expect that his official acts will be commented upon and criticized" (*New York Times v. Sullivan*). A correlate of the public-private distinction involves the insertion of a private citizen into a public debate. Upon entering a public debate, one's "private" status falls away (*Materia v. Huff*).

Secondly, the defamation claimant must prove malice or "intentional harm without truth" of the statements, either written or spoken (*Materia v. Huff*). Ostensibly, this means that the individual claiming defamation must be able to prove that the accused acted without regard to the truth. This is a difficult veil to pierce. The court, especially in the case of possible SLAPP suits, demands that claimants prove malice through a high level of propensity (Beder 65). When the alleged defamatory expression cannot be deemed malicious, the court generally rules on the side of the defendant.

SLAPPers who file under the guise of "defamation" understand fully that their claims of libel and slander will most likely suffer dismissal. Beder reports that most SLAPPs are dismissed, and of those that go on to court, 77% are won by the defendant. Interestingly, less than ten percent are won by the claimants (Beder 64). Time becomes the enemy of citizens and movements employing their free speech in the public sphere. By the time the "filers lose (typically years later if there is no effective anti-SLAPP statute in force, or if it is not invoked) or settle (ordinarily after the opposition has run out of money, or energy, or activists), their objectives of intimidation and of shifting the forum and issues to ones of their choosing have usually been accomplished" (Braun 968). So, why do SLAPP filers spend the time and money to submit these claims to the court? The answer is more subversive and strategic than dependent on some recovery of "face" sacrificed by alleged defamation of character. California Anti-SLAPP argues that "while most

SLAPPs are legally meritless, they effectively achieve their principal purpose: to chill public debate on specific issues" (California Anti-SLAPP Project). The chilling effect of SLAPPs is manifested in several ways.

SLAPP Uses

First, SLAPPs seek to stop the action—be it a protest, an issue campaign, a referendum or a simple letter to the editor—through economic means. The cost to a filer is part of doing business; stopping opposition and squashing a minority voice remains typical of everyday corporate dealings. "The object is to quell opposition by fear of large recoveries and legal costs, by diverting energy and resources from opposing the project into defending the lawsuit," argues Jerome Braun (967). "Usually the filers have considerably more resources than their targets, who are typically (although not always) citizen activists without significant corporate or government backing ... The financial and human costs of litigation, which pose serious threats to the targets, are simply another cost of doing business for filers well positioned to absorb them" (ibid.). On the other hand, a court case—replete with legal fees and litigation costs—can spell disaster for a grassroots organization. Beder claims that "in this way the legal system best serves those who have large financial resources at their disposal, particularly corporations" (Beder 65). What better way to stop free speech than by taking away the mechanisms that allow its flow? Regardless of the lawsuit's outcome, activists and protesters will certainly be out the funds needed to defend such a suit (see McCarthy).

Second, SLAPPs attempt to stop free speech by threatening others who may be tempted to speak their minds. One telltale sign of a SLAPP shrouded in a defamation suit is the listing of "John and Jane Doe's" as defendants. The threat is manifest because "most actions are initiated by large, deep-pocketed corporations against individuals without sufficient resources to satisfy a substantial judgment ... In situations where the John Doe's criticism has merit, a corporation that sues for defamation is simply using the lawsuit as a scare or intimidation tactic to prevent individuals from speaking out" (Scileppi 333). This allows the SLAPP filer to fill in any individual or group's name, pending the protester or grassroots organization's continued practice of speaking against the filer. As a result, SLAPPs "scare off potential opponents" (Beder 66). Hence, the free speech of others suffers limitations due to the threat of legal action.

Third, SLAPP cases shift the balance of public opinion and power. One such shift involves the movement of free speech from the public forum to the legal realm. At the point that an organization's voice gets remanded to a courtroom, that voice diminishes in the public eye. If a protester's funds, energy and time are spent in a courtroom, the issue of reform or abolition loses resources and begins to fade from public memory (Beder 66). Another shift involves the public's sympathy for the corporation or government and the transference of "evils." According to Beder, Americans are suspicious of those named "defendant" in lawsuits, particularly when those accused of defamation comprise a minority public going up against an established institution or industry (Beder 66). By filing a lawsuit, a SLAPPer moves the finger pointing away from itself and toward the protesting group. So, whereas in the debate's inception stage reformers place the "evil" on the industry's shoulders, the final phase concludes with the industry SLAPPing back in an attempt to pin the ill on the reformers. Wonderland track was characterized as the murderer of some 9,000 greyhounds per year. Evidence of the track's abuse and illegal euthanization of these dogs constituted an evil that needed remedying (Emily Jackson 47). Grey2K illuminated Wonderland as injurious to society.

The faux lawsuit that Wonderland filed merely five days before the election, however, transformed the issue from greyhound killing to defamation, naming as perpetrator the Grey2K campaigners. Pring and Canan deem this "issue transformation," defined as shifting "the emphasis from citizen's perceived injuries to the (SLAPP) filer's claimed injuries" (Pring and Canan 10). They go on to posit that "these transformations serve to suppress the issue of who is right in the underlying dispute; they block solution" (10). The public is distracted by such a transformation, and the issue becomes not what arises on the ballot, but rather how "evil" social

reformers are for having defamed an industry merely trying to defend itself.

Anti-SLAPP and Its Failure

Theoretically, anti-SLAPP statutes arose to protect free speech. A common feature of anti-SLAPP statutes is the protection of free speech during the petition or protest stage of a campaign for social reform. Essentially, the communicative tactics of activists and movements are fully protected from SLAPPs; squashing free speech under petition is viewed as infringement and becomes just cause for dismissal of a defamation case. Drawing from what Pring and Canan call a "standard" anti-SLAPP law (Pring & Canan 199), Massachusetts's §59H ("Special Motion to Dismiss Claim Based on Exercise of Constitutional Right of Petition") should be examined here. The Massachusetts anti-SLAPP states that "in any case in which a party asserts that the civil claims, counterclaims, or cross-claims against said party are based on said party's exercise of its right of petition under the constitution of the United States or of the Commonwealth, said party may bring a special motion to dismiss" (Massachusetts Annotated Laws ch. 231, §59H 2001). Petitioning includes written and oral statements reasonably likely to encourage reform.[1] This particular clause allows activists to bring forth a motion to dismiss, though not necessarily guaranteeing such a dismissal.

Interestingly, the onus for providing evidence of the motion to dismiss falls to the SLAPPer. In fact, if the plaintiff does not proffer evidence of falsity or harm, its entire case loses at the hearing stages of the suit. This remains another characteristic of anti-SLAPP statutes. Referring to Massachusetts once again, "the court shall grant such a motion unless the party against whom such special motion is made shows that (a) the moving party's exercise of its right to petition was devoid of any reasonable factual support or any arguable basis in law and (b) the moving party's acts caused actual injury to the responding part" (Massachusetts Annotated Laws ch. 231, §59H 2001). This reversed type of proof protects the public activist by placing a burden on the SLAPPer to prove its case.

The right of citizen participants to petition retains importance as a vital pillar of American participatory democracy and civic engagement. The Constitution enshrined this right, which dates back centuries and precedes the Bill of Rights. The First Amendment's assurances of expression and petitioning "immunize a broad range of citizens' conduct to promote or oppose official action by government at all levels" (Rowe 224). Petitioning, as a civil liberty, gained increased and codified protection through the Supreme Court's Noerr-Pennington doctrine conceptualized at the turn of the 20th century (*Eastern Railroad Presidents Conference v. Noerr Motor Freight, Inc.; United Mine Workers v. Pennington*). Erin Lum argues that the doctrine powerfully influenced the way citizens could express their free speech. Mainly, the decision allowed the public the right to participate and counter-campaign during public debates, government policy drives, and corporate activities.[2] Noerr-Pennington blocked laws such as the Sherman Act (and now RICO laws) from interfering with an individual's right to free speech. The Noerr-Pennington also applies to defamation cases.[3]

Where anti-SLAPP legislation fails is the stage between the SLAPP's filing and the almost certain granting of the defendant's motion to dismiss. I argue when free speech is associated with an election, specifically when an issue of reform will be decided by ballot, that SLAPPs win despite anti-SLAPP protection. When the order on a motion to dismiss a SLAPP occurs five months after an election (due to the legal system's snail-like pace) the damage to free speech has been done. Namely, fair debate regarding the issue-at-ballot becomes clouded by negative public relations resulting from the establishment's use of the SLAPP. It is this piece of the anti-SLAPP puzzle that remains missing.

Nearly 30 U.S. states possess anti-SLAPP measures, but none accounts for this type of image distortion. When the SLAPP is filed on the eve of an election—wherein a protest organization has attained referendum status for its issue—a shift in "evils" can result in a loss by only 2% of the vote, as was the case with Grey2K. Hence, even when the SLAPP is dismissed and free speech is "theoretically" protected it is too

late to recover from the 11th hour finagling on the part of the SLAPPer. Though a raw, empirical number of cases filed during the "11th hour" does not exist in the literature, Beder's review of SLAPPs between 1996 and 1998 indicates that a majority of cases filed against "campaigns" or "referendum movements" occurred within two days of the election day (Beder 66).

For instance, the last thing the public remembers about Grey2K before the Question 3 ballot is the lawsuit filed by Wonderland Park claiming Grey2K to be liars, phonies, legally deficient and defamatory. The 9,000 exterminated greyhounds, often found starved and riddled with bullet holes, fall to the wayside (see Emily Jackson). The racing industry, in Grey2K's case, gains exoneration in the public eye because it arises as the victim of a harsh case of defamation.

Subversive strategies to counter movements are certainly not new, and much rhetorical scholarship has been dedicated to identifying the success and unfairness of such tactics. In *The Rhetoric of Agitation and Control*, Bowers, Ochs and Jensen detail the features of quelling the free speech of movements. SLAPPs would fall under their category of control deemed *suppression:* "Suppression demands not only an understanding of the opposing ideology (or idea) but a firm resolve and commitment on the part of the decision makers to stop the spread of that ideology by hindering the goals . . . of the agitative movement." (Bowers, et al. 54). Following suit, Stewart, Smith and Denton identify several counter-movements in American history, such as the Sedition Law of 1798, the Espionage Act of 1917 and the activities of the U.S. Office of Censorship that have sought to shut down movements from a public relations standpoint. They claim, despite the importance of free speech, that legalized suppression of the public voice continues: "There is probably no concept more important to the theory of democratic government than free speech. Freedom of expression is a First Amendment right guaranteed in our Constitution. Historically, however, institutions have made many attempts to limit, to control, or to suppress freedom of expression by the press and individuals" (Stewart, et al. 147).

The counter strategy of SLAPPs allows the same species of suppression. There is no stopping the SLAPPer from damaging the image or saliency of a protester's free speech. Even the threat of paying legal fees and relatively heavy fines gets shrugged off by SLAPPers, mostly because the victory guaranteed in defeating their grassroots adversary in an election is well worth the investment of time and money (Pring and Canan 191). Filing a false claim of defamation and other SLAPPs is just a business expense to plaintiffs.

Interestingly, current legal research indicates that corporate entities, in particular, cannot technically sue for defamation. This is so, argues Mark Jackson, because the reputation of a corporation is not the same type of reputation as that of a natural person; defamation law is not well served by treating personal and corporate reputations as equivalent. As corporations cannot suffer personal reputation injury, "corporations as a class are less deserving of reputational protection than individual" (Mark Jackson 495). In a hypocritical showing, corporate leaders support laws that separate their "private lives" from the company in the case of a lawsuit against the company. After all, such leaders do not want their personal wealth touched; this being said, statutes of incorporation and legal insurances protect a leader from monetary harm. At the same time, though, when a so-called issue of defamation arises, these leaders desire their private lives to be associated with the corporation. Blights against the corporation, then, come to be blights against individuals. Hence these individuals, along with their respective companies, argue that they can sue for defamation. Institutional figures cannot have this private-public dialectic both ways.

CASE STUDY: GREY2K AND CAMPAIGN 2000

The argument that anti-SLAPPs fail to protect free speech during an election manifested through the case of *Grey2K v. Wonderland Park*. In November 2000, Wonderland and its owner Charles Sarkis filed a defamation suit against Grey2K for advertisements the anti-racing group ran in support of Question 3, the public referendum to end the cruelty of greyhound racing in Massachusetts. This portion of the essay details

the battling parties' proceedings and demonstrates how despite the free speech victory of dismissing a SLAPP claim, an activist group found itself in jeopardy when a strategic lawsuit was filed on the eve of an election. In this way, the Massachusetts anti-SLAPP statute failed to protect Grey2K.

Grey2K began in July 1999 when president David Vaughn filed the organization as an "initiative petition" agency under Article 48 of the Massachusetts Constitution (Considine "Plaintiff's Memorandum"). The state required Vaughn and others to collect a requisite number of public signatures in order to advance the racing ban onto the November 7, 2000 ballot. Indeed, Grey2K along with its backers succeeded in moving Question 3 to the Massachusetts state ballot. The group began advertising the ban on greyhound racing, citing several instances of abuse and illegal euthanization. The evidence came from credible sources such as officials from the Massachusetts Society for the Prevention of Cruelty to Animals, Greysland Adoption Agency, Greyhound Adoption Project, veterinarians and, perhaps most scathingly, from former employees of the Wonderland Park itself (Cronin and Tierney). Additionally, Grey2K provided the Commonwealth of Massachusetts State Racing Commission's own annual report from 1999 to account for a number of missing and exploited greyhound dogs (Cronin and Tierney).

The cornerstone of Grey2K's campaign, and the undoubted reason behind Wonderland Park's defamation suit, was a 30-second television spot run from October 11 to Election Day on November 7. Primarily, Sarkis argued that the images of dead and dying greyhounds in the advertisement were neither from Wonderland Park nor Massachusetts. He also argued that the use of his image and his quotes about the Grey2K campaign in the advertisement linked Wonderland Park to the images of dead and dying greyhounds from across the nation. Grey2K conceded this, but claimed the greyhound racing industry to be a nationally based network of tracks, breeders, dumping farms, laboratory disposal areas and second-rate tracks, often set up in more rural areas where regulation barely exists (see Cronin). The advertisement ran as follows:

Client: Grey2K Production: 30 sec. TV Title: No Abuse Code: G2k-01-00	Voiceover: Font: Last Updated: 10/11/2000
VIDEO	**AUDIO**
Greyhounds Racing (Tape 6) **WOS: "Over 9,000 Greyhounds Are Killed Every Year . . . For Not Being Fast Enough"** Carcasses being thrown into a truck (tape 6)	Exciting music Silence
Track owner (Sarkis) claiming "No abuse" (tape 6)	"They are not abused, they are not neglected, and they are not killed. It's an absolute lie and they have no proof to substantiate it" [6 sees] (Charles Sarkis, Wonderland Greyhound Park Owner)
Starved greyhound drinking (tape 7) Greyhound in cage Carcasses being thrown into a truck (tape 6) **WOS: 2 out of 3 greyhounds that race will not survive beyond their fourth birthday.**	Sad, depressing music
Greyhound still looking at camera	VO: "It's no way to treat a dog. Ban greyhound racing in Massachusetts. Vote 'Yes' on Question 3"

Sarkis and Wonderland filed their Verified Complaint merely five days before the election claiming that: "acting in concert to achieve their common goal, (Grey2K) has demonstrated a willingness to deploy any tactic necessary, including the use of false and misleading representations of fact" (Considine "Verified Complaint"). Calling the advertisements a "smear" campaign, Wonderland went on to request (1) $10 million in damages said to have occurred as a result of Grey2K's alleged defamation through slander, (2) an injunction placed on the Grey2K campaign, and (3) a restraining order on running the advertisements. Again, the claims of defamation were all predicated upon Grey2K's use of non-Wonderland greyhounds in conjunction with Sarkis' image and words included in the television advertisement (Considine "Verified Complaint").

On November 6, Grey2K filed a motion to dismiss the injunction and restraining order, arguing that they indeed qualified for protection from SLAPP through their engagement of petition. Additionally, attorneys for the organization posited Wonderland's lack of evidence to show malice: "Plaintiffs fail to show any legitimate reason why Grey2K should be enjoined from exercising its constitutionally protected right to free speech . . . the plaintiffs cannot succeed on the merits of its case."[4] Grey2K further discussed the implications of enjoining and restraining a public's free speech on the veritable eve of a referendum vote: "Indeed, the issuance of the requested preliminary injunction would severely interfere with the operation of a fair election and would inflict irreparable harm upon Grey2K by silencing its voice in this most crucial of moments, immediately before election day" (Cronin).

Finally, Grey2K challenged Wonderland to provide evidence—which had been missing from its complaint and supporting brief—concerning the false accusations, alleged defamation, and resulting damages. In a typical, sloppily drafted

SLAPP response Sarkis and Wonderland asked to block the injunction's dismissal due to a loophole: that Grey2K was a Political Action Committee (PAC) and not an organization, and thus could not dismiss based on the anti-SLAPP statute (Considine "Plaintiff's Memorandum"). Judge J. Botsford ruled on November 6 to dismiss the injunction and restraining order due to lack of evidence on Wonderland's part. Grey2K's SLAPP accusations, however, would wait several months before attracting the judge's attention. The actual dismissal of the defamation case would not be decided on until April 13, 2001; and Grey2K would find neither the time nor the resources to file a full dismissal of Wonderland's case until November 15, eight days following the election.

The time between the SLAPP filing and the election proved deadly for Grey2K. News of the faux defamation lawsuit spread quickly and infiltrated local sections and front pages of the *Boston Globe* and *Boston Herald* (Eidinger 1). Rick Klein of the *Herald* wrote that "track owners have repeatedly blasted (Grey2K) for using what they contend are misleading images of abused dogs from other states in its crusade to ban greyhound racing in Massachusetts" (Klein "Track Owner Sues" B1). Nowhere in the article are positions in defense of Grey2K offered. Several more articles came out in favor of Wonderland's feigned legal and reputational plight (Gaines B6). To be fair, the Boston area media had not been receptive to Grey2K's plight and subsequent referendum campaign. In a sense, then, the media did not change its valence with the onslaught of Sarkis's legal filings. Certainly, though, the media played some role in dismissing Grey2K as a tactically unethical group both before and after Wonderland's lawsuit. It was the SLAPP suit, however, that brought such negative public opinion to bear. According to Eidinger, none of the Boston newspapers and television stations supported Question 3, and many required editing of the dead greyhound footage before airing due to the SLAPP suit (1). This meant that Wonderland's SLAPP indeed halted Grey2K's full and intended freedom of expression, at least via the press.

The well had been poisoned on the eve of the election and Massachusetts's anti-SLAPP statute did not protect Grey2K. On the morning of November 8 the results were finalized. Question 3 had lost by less than 2% of those voting in the election. Of the 2,733,831 votes cast, 1,276,708 voted "yes," 1,327,123 voted "no," and nearly 130,000 did not vote at all on the issue of banning greyhound racing.

Five months following Grey2K's defeat, Judge Maria Lopez ruled to dismiss Wonderland's suit based upon, in part, Sarkis's and Wonderland's anti-SLAPP violations. Lopez argued in the order that Wonderland had intentionally filed the defamation suit on the eve of the election, and that the injunctions attached to the complaint attempted to chill Grey2K's free speech:

> . . . This suit is suspect as a SLAPP suit given the fact that plaintiffs filed the present action against the defendants during the campaign and immediately sought a preliminary injunction which would have prevented the defendants from broadcasting their campaign advertisements, thereby undermining their ability to petition for new legislation . . . the defendant's pleadings, affidavits and exhibits demonstrate that they had reasonable factual support for their message that greyhounds are needlessly killed and abused in Massachusetts (Lopez).

The ruling suggested that Sarkis became a public official when he began running counter-campaigns and that Grey2K argued from an "unknown truth" with regard to the killing and abuse of greyhounds at Wonderland Park and at Massachusetts's greyhound racetracks generally. Malice, therefore, was not established by Wonderland Park. Overall, the defamation charges held no weight. The case, according to Lopez, was a veritable public relations ploy from the start.

For Grey2K's troubles, Lopez awarded full attorneys' fees and costs (the maximum allowance under Massachusetts law), but she could not reverse the 2% loss indicated by the November polls. In fact, the only remuneration and relief Grey2K received were the fees and costs—which had already been paid up front during the election when they truly needed the funds—and the satisfaction of knowing they had successfully defended a SLAPP case. The victory, however, was pyrrhic. Beder reports that 20% of all SLAPPs come against animal welfare or animal rights organizations (Beder 66). In 2000 Grey2K became a statistic, and lost in the process their battle to ban greyhound racing.

Grey2K's referendum debacle deals with the limitations of anti-SLAPP legislation in preventing negative publicity from entering an election issue. Perhaps through more timely hearings and speedy procedures the problem can be corrected; or maybe legislation should amend U.S. anti-SLAPP laws to require a certain time period in which a SLAPP filer must file prior to the actual election date. This essay's conclusion points toward ways social activists seeking reform can combat SLAPPs.

IMPLICATIONS

Anti-SLAPPs protect free speech to a point, but fail when a movement or activist's reputation is at stake prior to an election. The failure occurs when the industry, governmental agency or politician opposing a reform or abolition measure, by way of ballot, files false allegations on the eve of the election, thus shifting the campaign focus away from the issue at hand. When this occurs, the petitioning group retains characteristics as ethically and legally unsound, and the plaintiff comes away as the victim (Beder 64). Knowing definitively that it will lose the lawsuit, such SLAPPers only file to stifle free speech and end the public campaign for issue reform. The lawsuit, as I have discussed, poses negative implications for the public image of the movement or activist, resulting in a poor result at the polls.

To protect against the damages incurred by SLAPPs—to both reputation and pocketbook—movements should first be prepared with defensive legal strategies. This involves, at a minimum, understanding their respective state's anti-SLAPP statutes (if they exist) and seeking an individual versed in state law and dedicated to the cause to act as an *ad hoc* campaign organizer. Also, though, legal strategies should be planned in advance should a SLAPP arise.

One such strategy involves petitioning the judge to have the SLAPP filer pay up front for the defamation cases. That is, filers would pay court costs—not attorneys' fees—for both sides of the suit. Should the social activists' communication actually be deemed "malicious" and "defamatory," such groups would then later be ordered to repay the corporate filers. This motion remains advantageous as "the filer typically has the means to finance the litigation and regards it simply as a business expense, and the target rarely has such resources, and litigation costs can be burdensome or even overwhelming" (Braun 978). This tactic involves a bit of turnaround and fair play. According to Braun, "because the costs of litigation are one of the principal weapons filers use to intimidate targets, removing this threat leaves the target less threatened and freer to resist" (978). Such motions have been ordered in California's SLAPP cases.

Second, a movement or petitioning public might consider asking the judge to punish individual attorneys should the cases they help bring before the court turn out to be SLAPPs. As Braun explains, "The filer may be sufficiently wealthy not to care about losing or even about monetary sanctions, but the attorney presumably cares about being sanctioned, both in terms of the money and in terms of his or her ethical obligations, reputation, and professional standing. Sanctioning the attorney in this situation could have a major impact on this kind of litigation."[5] With legal and business ethics being challenged in the wake of the Enron, Tyco, Martha Stewart and Haliburton cases, attorneys for corporations might find that the cost of allowing citizens the right to free speech pales in comparison to litigating a SLAPP case and losing their credibility and livelihood.

A third strategy entails employing a bevy of affirmative defenses. Brion Blackwelder, an environmental action attorney, suggests attacking indistinguishable claims. "When counterclaims, usually as tort actions for defamation or interference, are brought, take a deep breath, read the pleading and outline it carefully, and then work to kill it off with a Motion to Dismiss, or a Motion for Summary Judgment. Immediately attack pleadings that are too vague to state a cause of action. Enough attempts to state a cause of action will result in dismissal with prejudice" (Blackwelder 85). He continues that the time, place, and nature requirements of defamation claims are often bypassed in a sloppily drafted SLAPP. As such, activists might point out the absence of "substance with sufficient particularity" within the SLAPP claim. Certainly, when defending the "time and place" of its campaigning, a movement can rely successfully on the Noerr-Pennington doctrine for protection within the "petition" stage of its activism. Such *prima facie* affirmative defenses are typically heard, if not out rightly affirmed by courts.[6]

But what if these courtroom strategies fail? How can activists plug the hole glaringly present in current anti-SLAPP statutes? In this age of preemptive rhetoric and strategy, is there a way a movement can undercut the SLAPP before it commences? Here is where proactive communicative tactics come to the fore; hence I suggest a bit of rhetorical counter-strategy. Activists should always and unconditionally expect its governmental or institutional adversary to come forth with a SLAPP suit. A group should never be caught off-guard when a SLAPP suit arises.

Bearing this in mind, when appealing to the media, movements should disseminate the problems with SLAPPs and explain fully that the opposition will likely employ this tactic to squash free speech. Such communication to the general public via the media should come early in a movement's campaign. If a movement can link the evils of SLAPP with adversaries of free speech, then two results occur. First, in the case that SLAPPs come forward, the media and public know exactly why the lawsuits are being filed: to block free speech, intimidate the movement, stop the public's right to learn all it can about an issue and shift the issue away from the institution or industry's ills. Or, as Lum puts it, to place citizens at risk of personal liability for their petitioning activity, to threaten a citizen's constitutional rights and to "chill" citizen activism (Lum 413). Second, if SLAPPers do not employ a false lawsuit, they still appear villainous because they are associated historically with the side of a debate typically willing and capable of filing SLAPPs. In either scenario the movement halts the negative effects a SLAPP generates between the time of its filing and the election for reform.

Such a strategy might have helped Grey2K in its quest to end greyhound exploitation in

Massachusetts, and it might assist others in future battles to inject one's voice into the dominant public. Ultimately, it is the goal of this essay to stimulate further inquiry into ways to bolster free speech by severely limiting the repressive power of SLAPPs.

Notes

[1] The Massachusetts anti-SLAPP statute states fully: "As used in this section, the words 'a party's exercise of its right to petition' shall mean any written or oral statement made before or submitted to a legislative, executive, or judicial body, or any other governmental proceeding; any written or oral statement made in connection with an issue under consideration or review by a legislative, executive, or judicial body, or any other governmental proceeding; any statement reasonably likely to encourage consideration or review of an issue by a legislative, executive, or judicial body, or any other governmental proceeding; any statement reasonably likely to enlist public participation in an effort to effect such consideration; or any other statement falling within constitutional protection of the right to petition government" (Massachusetts Annotated Laws ch. 231, §59H 2001).

[2] The context of the Noerr-Pennington doctrine is as follows: the doctrine, which emerged from two important anti-trust cases, established the principle that petitioning activity aimed at procuring government action cannot be subject to liability. In *Eastern Railroad Presidents Conference v. Noerr Motor Freight, Inc.* members of the trucking industry sued a group of railroads for waging an anti-competitive publicity campaign against the truckers, alleging a violation of the Sherman Act. In their complaint, the truckers claimed the railroads' publicity campaign was designed to promote laws that would destroy the trucking industry, tarnish the industry's reputation, and deter customers from continuing to employ truckers. Furthermore, the truckers argued that the publicity campaign caused the Pennsylvania governor to veto a pro-trucking law, resulting in direct injury to the industry. Although the truckers' cause of action was for violation of the Sherman Act, the U.S. Supreme Court held that the railroads' campaign, despite being initiated for anti-competitive purposes, was protected by the Petition Clause. The Court found the railroads' campaign constituted "political activity" aimed at influencing the passage of laws, and that no violation of the

Sherman Act can be predicated on "solicitation of government action with respect to the passage and enforcement of laws" (See Lum 415).

In the later case of *United Mine Workers of America v. Pennington,* a miner's union sued a coal producer to recover royalty payments it alleged were due under a collective bargaining agreement. The coal producer filed a counterclaim against the union, alleging the union violated the Sherman Act by conspiring to restrain and monopolize interstate commerce. Citing the decision in Noerr, the Court held that the trial judge improperly allowed the jury to consider facts showing that the union and its alleged co-conspirators made joint efforts to influence the Secretary of Labor and the Tennessee Valley Authority. In remanding the case for a new trial, the Court directed the lower court to instruct the jury that the union's petitioning activities were protected under the Noerr precedent, thus shielding the union from Sherman Act liability. As in Noerr, the Court held that "joint efforts to influence public officials do not violate the antitrust laws even though intended to eliminate competition" (*United Mine Workers v. Pennington,* 381 U.S. 657, 14 L. Ed. 2d 626, 85 S. Ct.. 1585 [1965]).

[3] For more information, see *Eastern Railroad Presidents Conference v. Noerr Motor Freight, Inc.,* 365 U.S. 127, 5 L. Ed. 2d 464, 81 S. Ct. 523 (1961); *United Mine Workers v. Pennington,* 381 U.S. 657, 14 L. Ed. 2d 626, 85 S. Ct. 1585 (1965). The doctrine arises from the combination of both cases into a joint precedent for free speech protection.

[4] See Cronin.

[5] Attorneys are already subject to an ethical obligation not to bring baseless actions or to sue for purposes of harassment. Bringing a legal action for purposes of retaliation or intimidation, based on constitutionally privileged speech or conduct, violates subsections (A) and (B) of the California Rules of Professional Conduct section 3-200, because of the action's purpose and because the attorney knows (or should know) of an impregnable constitutional defense. An attorney may be able to claim ignorance (however disingenuously) of her client's purpose in bringing an action. But it would be difficult to argue that a complaint for tort damages, based for example on a comment made to a zoning board in the course of a hearing, either presents probable cause or is warranted under existing law or a good faith argument for law reform. Any attorney may reasonably be held to a basic awareness of the civil

protections of the First Amendment (see Braun 980).

[6] See Beder; Lum; and Tate.

Works Cited

Beder, Sharon. *Global Spin: The Corporate Assault on Environmentalism.* White River Junction, VT: Chelsea Green Publishing, 1998.

Blackwelder, Brion. "Traits and Tools for Ethical Environmental Advocates in Florida." *Florida State University Journal of Land Use & Environmental Law* 17 (Fall 2001): 67–84.

Bowers, John W., Donovan J. Ochs, and Richard J. Jensen. *The Rhetoric of Agitation and Control.* Prospect Heights, IL: Waveland Press, 1993.

Braun, Jerome I. "Increasing SLAPP Protection: Unburdening the Right of Petition in California." *University of California–Davis Law Review* 32 (Summer 1999): 965–1035.

California Anti-SLAPP Project, "Introduction," 1996, found at http://www.casp.net/intro.html (24 August 2001).

Considine, Kevin N. *Plaintiffs' Memorandum of Law in Opposition to the Defendants' Emergency Special Motion to Dismiss Under G.L c. 231 §59H* in Commonwealth of Massachusetts, Superior Court Civil Action #00-4891E, Sarkis and Wonderland Greyhound Park, *plaintiffs* v. Grey2K, et. al., *defendants* (5 December 2000).

———. *Verified Complaint* in Commonwealth of Massachusetts, Superior Court Civil Action #00-489IE, Sarkis and Wonderland Greyhound Park, *plaintiffs* v. Grey2K, et. al., *defendants* (2 November 2000).

Cronin, Cheryl M. *Defendant's Opposition to Plaintiffs' Motion for Preliminary Injunction* in Commonwealth of Massachusetts, Superior Court Civil Action #00-489IE, Sarkis and Wonderland Greyhound Park, *plaintiffs* v. Grey2K, et. al., *defendants* (6 November 2000).

Cronin, Cheryl M., and James Tierney. *Defendant's Special Motion for Dismissal Under G.L c. 231 §59H and Request for Hearing* in Commonwealth of Massachusetts, Superior Court Civil Action #00-489IE, Sarkis and Wonderland Greyhound Park, *plaintiffs* v. Grey2K, et. al., *defendants* (15 November 2000).

Eastern Railroad Presidents Conference v. Noerr Motor Freight, Inc. 365 U.S. 127 (1961).

Eidinger, Joan. "Bay State Ballot Initiative to Ban Dog Racing Fails by Narrow Margin." *Greyhound Network News* 9:4 (Winter 2000–2001): 1–4.

Gaines, Judith. "Down to the Wire: The World of Greyhound Racing, a Fixture in Massachusetts for 65 Years, Awaits a Life or Death Decision in Tuesday's Ballot Referendum." *The Boston Globe* (5 November 2000): B2.

Jackson, Emily. "Dead Dog Running: The Cruelty of Greyhound Racing and the Bases for its Abolition in Massachusetts." *Animal Law* 7 (2000): 47–92.

Jackson, Mark D. "The Corporate Defamation Plaintiff in the Eras of SLAPP: Revisiting *New York Times v. Sullivan*." *William and Mary Bill of Rights Journal* 9 (February 2001): 491–522.

Klein, Rick. "Wonderland in Jeopardy as Question 3 Looms," *The Boston Globe* (7 November 2000): B1.

———. "Track Owner Sues Backers of Dog Question." *The Boston Globe* (4 November 2000): B1.

Lopez, Maria (Judge). *Memorandum of Decision and Order on Defendants' Special Motion for Dismissal* in Commonwealth of Massachusetts, Superior Court Civil Action #00-4891E, Sarkis and Wonderland Greyhound Park, *plaintiffs* v. Grey2K, et. al., *defendants* (13 April 2001).

Lum, Erin Malia. "Hawai'i's Response to Strategic Litigation Against Public Participation and the Protection of Citizens' Right to Petition the Government." *Hawaii Law Review* 24 (Winter 2001): 411–439.

Massachusetts Annotated Laws ch. 231, §59H (2001).

Materia v. Huff. 394 Mass. 328 (1985).

McCarthy, Carlotta E. "Citizens Cannot Be SLAPPed for Exercising First Amendment Right to Petition the Government—*Hometown Properties. Inc. v. Fleming,* 680 A.2d 56 (R.I. 1996)." *Suffolk University Law Review* 31 (1998): 759–770.

New York. Times v. Sullivan. 376 U.S. 254 (1964).

Pfeiffer, Sacha. "Judge Refuses to Block Greyhound Ads." *The Boston Globe* (7 November 2000): B6.

Pring, George W., and Penelope Canan. *SLAPPs: Getting Sued for Speaking Out.* Philadelphia: Temple University Press, 1996.

Rowe, Frederick M. "Resolving Land Disputes by Intimidation: SLAPP Suits in New Mexico." *New Mexico Law Review* 32 (Spring 2002): 217–238.

Saccuzzo, Jason Paul. "Bankrupting the First Amendment: Using Tort Litigation to Silence Hate Groups." *California Western Law Review* 37 (Spring 2001): 395–425.

Scileppi, David C. "Anonymous Corporate Defamation Plaintiffs: Trampling the First Amendment or Protecting the Rights of Litigants." *Florida Law Review* 54 (April 2002): 333–360.

Stewart, Charles J., Craig Allen Smith, and Robert E. Denton. *Persuasion and Social Movements,* 3d Ed. Prospect Heights, IL: Waveland Press, 1994.

Tate, Kathryn W. "California's Anti-SLAPP Legislation: A Summary of and Commentary on its Operation and Scope." *Loyola of Los Angeles Law Journal* 33 (April 2000): 801–834.

United Mine Workers v. Pennington. 381 U.S. 657 (1965).

Neutralizing Protest:
The Construction of War, Chaos, and National Identity through US Television News on Abortion-Related Protest, 1991
Ginna Husting

Using a particularly "hot" instance of the US abortion war in 1991 as a case study, this paper analyzes a dominant trope for reporting abortion-related protest: protest as chaotic, violent war. In August 1991, Operation Rescue led its first massive, two-month clinic blockade in Wichita, Kansas (it had organized others, but none remotely this large). The 1991 blockade and its counter-protests garnered more network news time than abortion-related activism before or since. Coverage of abortion-related activism in 1991 became saturated with discourses of war. Wichita became the "beachhead in the Heartland," the "front lines" of the violent war between pro-choice and anti-abortion activists. The conflict was, according to the news, "tearing this nation apart."

While descriptions of protest as war did not begin in 1991, war tropes have since become a commonplace in media coverage of activism of all kinds in the United States (the "Battle for Seattle" is a clear example). In relation to abortion-related protest, it has become a stock phrase. The 2004 "March for Women's Lives" was routinely described in print and TV news as a battle or war despite organizers' and participants' more comprehensive agenda.[1] The banality of the phrase "abortion war" helps to obscure that something politically significant is being achieved with its utterance. The cliché, like most, has become so common that we fail to hear both its resonances and the dangerous discursive work it does to deaden democracy. This paper is precisely about that work and its political significance. What happens when a bit of commonsense—"protest is war"—becomes a master narrative in television news?

Answering this question is a difficult, fraught project given the complexity of issues and passionate engagement on all sides. Thus, let me clarify at the outset: my politics are pro-choice. My analytical goal, though, is not evaluation of abortion politics. It is instead analysis of anti-democratic, interpretive/discursive news strategies and the mediated knowledge they produce about the "abortion war." I use 1991 coverage to show how television news, redolent with discourses of war and violence, betrays no simple bias toward pro-choice or anti-abortion agendas. Instead, the "war over abortion" as a discursive theme serves to discredit activists on all sides. News stories, through continual, simplistic invocations of the war trope, construct a narrowly defined drama of abortion-related activism as war and chaos. The news likewise offers two major subject positions in the war: activists on both sides of the issue versus the imagined community of people like you and me. Thus, the war trope works to delegitimize collective action, and to sustain a national identity in opposition to protesters on all sides of the issue.

Although it may seem to be a truism that abortion-related protest is in fact a war, the present analysis requires suspension of that assumption. While activists themselves have framed conflict over abortion as a war, the news frame narrates a very different kind of conflict: instead of a "holy war" or a "terrorist assault on women's right to choose," the news in 1991 narrated a civil war between two clearly defined

extreme militaristic groups (feminists vs. fundamentalists) whose violence poses a deep threat to decent politics and American community. The fact of activism itself, rather than abusive or violent behaviors of certain activists, threatens to destroy the "home territory."[2]

THEORIZING THE NATION: ARENDTIAN THEORY AND TELEVISION NEWS

Analyzing the means by which news marginalizes activism is hardly new. Cultural analysis of journalism has illuminated how news purveys meaning as it conveys "facts."[3] Journalists, in representing reality, produce it for viewers. Newscasts use consistent villains, victims, and heroes in conventionalized story structures.[4] News stories, crafted through codes of balance, objectivity,[5] and deep populist sentiment,[6] reify "mainstream society" through opposition to the deviants of the news frame.[7] This construction of "people like us" in opposition to an "other" is especially common in news coverage of social movements.[8] In this paper, I link these concerns to burgeoning scholarship on agonistic democracy and democratic contention.[9] Proponents of agonistic democracy eschew normative models of consensual politics, holding that ideals of unanimity create the dangerous or evil Other and destroy public spheres where actors can "address the 'other' as a legitimate adversary rather than as an evil enemy. . . ."[10] Construction of a homogeneous, harmonious nation is a politics of elimination, of erasure and censorship, and is antithetical to a vibrant democratic process.

Combining cultural analysis of news and its "others" with theoretical models of "rowdy" rhetorical deliberation, then, this paper contextualizes protest packages through Hannah Arendt's theory of political action and Mary Douglas's work on ritual pollution.[11] I use both theories to show how televisual themes like war and chaos ritually secure an imperiled national identity and foreclose the public sphere.[12] My analysis has three parts: a brief discussion of Arendtian theory relevant to analyzing media and the public sphere, an empirical analysis of news texts, and a contextualization of the foregoing analysis using Arendt's and Douglas's theories.

One of Arendt's foremost concerns is political action and those processes and structures that encourage and constrain it. Her approach shares much with symbolic interaction and poststructuralist models of selfhood. For Arendt, the public sphere emerges whenever individuals come together to create a common world, "... to bring something into being which did not exist before."[13] Only within this public sphere can we create the opportunities for resistance and change.[14]

Political action requires the condition of plurality in which people with differing backgrounds, perspectives, and abilities come together: "being seen and heard by others derive their significance from the fact that everybody sees and hears from a different position. This is the meaning of public life."[15] The public realm, then, is constructed through expression of and contest between identities, backgrounds, and opinions. The public sphere arises whenever people engage each other in this way. A common world must be constituted from a plurality of perspectives.

Moreover, political action exemplifies natality—our capacity to continually refound or renegotiate our world in concert with others who may be in political contest with us. The political—which comprises contest between ideas and views—challenges spaces of conformism or non-thought, and creates places of disclosure where individuals can come to know themselves through their action and interaction with others.

On this account, it is through the process of interaction that we can achieve a coherent identity. When we act, we do not reflect a prior selfhood. Rather, through political action we continually reconstitute who we are. As Calhoun aptly summarizes, "It is in public that we come fully into ourselves, that we achieve a fullness of personality, that we disclose our personal identities."[16] The enemy of political action is closure, or "constatation," the ways that identities and aspects of the world become understood as given or unassailable.[17] When we define our identity as a way we are, rather than an emergent, contingent process, we begin to lose the possibility for political action.

Arendt contends that the political realm, where together we constitute the world and its meaning, has been eclipsed by the rise of the social, which erodes plurality. The precise nature of the social is elusive.[18] At various times in her work, it is a sphere of limitation, public opinion, bureaucratic institutions, "mass culture," habit, and conformist behavior and more.[19] Yet, this concept provides a framework for analyzing links between the public sphere and the news. It points to diverse practices and strategies that encourage and maintain thoughtlessness, or homogeneity of behavior, identity, and opinion. A variety of institutions, practices, and norms for behavior can steer individuals from thinking and acting independently, toward behaving in socially prescribed, expected, acceptable ways. In Arendt's terms, such practices inhibit authentic, unique identities.[20] Arendt sees evidence for the social in forms of nationalism that induce citizens to display unanimity of opinion and perspective. In such a vision of the social, difference becomes deviance. Arendt criticizes the notion of a national family, in which difference and contest are suppressed in favor of a fictive familial unity. The social, through its emphasis on conformity and unity among a nation's citizens, eliminates difference, silencing a diversity of political perspectives and expressions.[21] Action, thought, and opinion become normalized through the creation of the "average" or appropriate citizen and marginalization of those who violate norms.[22] A panoply of perspectives and locations in the world collapse into simple unified categories of "normal" (the patriotic, democratic, reasonable center) and "off-center" (that is, extreme and therefore unreasonable). The rise of the social is the process of standardizing and naturalizing identities.

Although Arendt seldom discussed media, her model suggests certain qualities of televisual news inimical to political action. News coverage contributing to the rise of the social collapses distinctions within and between activist movements and tactics. Oversimplification forces a duality of perspectives on what should be a plurality of conflicting issues, practices, and opinions. Likewise, such news substitutes constative or naturalized, pejorative group identities (e.g., radical feminists) for meaningful coverage of issues, words, and deeds. In the present case, such news creates a narrowly defined mass identity of "good Americans" in opposition to the dangerous spectacle of protest. Thus, the news participates in nation-building rhetoric through the discursive construction of national identity.

DATA AND METHOD

This study's data include all 52 nightly network news segments on American abortion-related protest in 1991, totaling 1580 seconds of broadcast. I chose 1991, since it was a hot year for the abortion war. The first Bush White House was ardently pro-life, and during that administration, many legal impediments to abortion at the federal, state, and international level were proposed or enacted. Moreover, although the President and pro-life organizers shared similar perspectives, frustration that abortion was still legal in the United States was growing among anti-abortion activists. Operation Rescue's development of their new technique, clinic blockades ("rescues"), was in part a response to a rising feeling of dissatisfaction with the pace of legal challenges to Roe vs. Wade.[23]

The use of television news in particular was strategic for two reasons. First, most Americans get their news from television rather than newspapers.[24] Second, televisual narratives and visuals provide a rich set of data for analyzing meaning construction. I used the Vanderbilt Television News Archive to locate all abortion-related protest segments on NBC, ABC, and CBS, using their segment-by-segment index of broadcasts. I created narrative and visual (shot-by-shot) transcriptions of segments and identified recurring visual and narrative themes or codes in the coverage. Selecting war and chaos vs. law and order—the most frequent and prominent of these themes—I analyzed in detail how these codes work in the coverage.

Network news coverage of abortion-related protest in 1991 follows a simple chronology. Coverage started to increase as Operation Rescue initiated its blockade in Wichita, Kansas. The year's coverage began in January with segments on the annual Right to Life March in Washington, DC. These were followed by segments on various state bills whose goal was to restrict access to abortion (in, for example, Utah, Louisiana, Mississippi, and North Dakota). In May, NBC and CBS aired three-minute stories on pro-choice protest against the Supreme Court's decision to uphold the federal gag rule. In July, all three networks had two-minute segments on a large rally organized by the National Organization for Women. The networks began to have weekly segments on abortion war in August, when Operation Rescue began its two-month blockade of abortion clinics in Wichita. These stories comprised 40 of 52 total segments in 1991 on abortion-related protest.

The abortion war is narrated both by news staff and through sound bites from sources. The number of pro-choice and anti-abortion sources is roughly equal for CBS (29-26) and ABC (8-9), but NBC seemed to favor pro-choice sources (20-12). The equitable number of sources and time devoted to protesters suggests balanced, neutral, or objective reporting. This is not to say, of course, that the news is therefore an accurate mirror of or window on the world; it is precisely through illuminating the trope of war that the news's political engagement becomes apparent.

THE THREE WARS

Of course, pro-life and pro-choice activists themselves understand protest as war.[25] Strategic use of war talk can discredit opposition, mobilize adherents, and frame the conflict as a just or holy war. It may seem, then, that describing protest as war simply reflects the nature of the conflict. Anti-abortion protests are violent; often, Operation Rescue works precisely through creating chaos; police must keep law and order in such situations to ensure women's access to clinics. Such narratives may originate in protesters' descriptions of their work, but once appropriated by the news, they disallow for social protest as legitimate, productive political activity. Analyzing how the war trope works at the level of the news text thus uncovers a surprising discrepancy between activists' and news frames: neither of the wars fought by Operation Rescue and pro-choice counter demonstrators is the war narrated by the news.

Operation Rescue's battle is part of a holy war against the enemy—abortion providers and pro-choice activists. The pre-born are its primary victims. Alternatively, pro-choice advocates' use of war language tends to describe clinic bombings, murder of providers, and clinic blockades. The victims are pregnant women, unwanted children, and clinic staff. But for TV news, the abortion war is a civil conflict between unreasonable extremist activists on both sides of the issue. In this vision of war, liberal feminists stand for the entire "anti-abortion" movement. Operation Rescue members in turn stand for the entire pro-life and anti-abortion movements. Liberal pro-choice activists become parallel to Operation Rescue participants as they harm the nation through their battles. "People like us" are caught in the "crossfire"; police and politicians attempt to restore law and order.

Thus, a whole array of activists and positions is collapsed into a caricature of conflict, while the main victim becomes the nation/community/family. Protest destroys the nation's unity. This news narrative, far from the activists' own characterizations, offers a vision of war that marginalizes activism as the source of the problem. In Arendtian terms, the news frame substitutes closed group identities for a plurality of opinions, positions, and activities of political and social actors.

ACTIVISM AS WAR: BESIEGING AMERICA

The equation of protest and war is almost ubiquitous in this coverage. All segments over 20 seconds in length (41 of 52) describe protest as military conflict. The discourse of war often occurs at the beginning and end of segments, where "battle" becomes shorthand that elides the complexities of struggle over abortion. Examples include introductions such as "This is the front line in the war over abortion";[26] "A battle cry from the other side of the abortion debate";[27] "The National Organization for Women is drawing up its battle plan";[28] "When pro-life supporters declared holy war on this clinic, they did it with a vengeance";[29] and "OR has targeted Wichita with virtually all of its resources, hoping to establish an anti-abortion beachhead in the Heartland."[30] None of these segments then justifies why the conflict should be considered a war. Continual repetition of the trope replaces any

sustained examination of the history of the "war" and of the arguments from a variety of perspectives. Thus, battle becomes shorthand, eliding the complexity and specificity of public activism over abortion.

One of the most relentlessly militarized segments begins, "The battle over abortion is not only being fought in the courts and in the state houses all over the country, but in the street as well. The weapons are protest and counter-protest, psychological pressure, and sometimes even physical violence" (which is never elucidated).[31] The correspondent concurs: "This kind of demonstration may look spontaneous, but the battle has become a sophisticated game of spies and counter-spies, secret meetings, and the rush to set up lines of defense."

These introductions constitute an interpretive schema through which everything shown afterward becomes evidence of the initial claim, reinforcing the warlike character of protest. The consistent referral to "the war" in the rest of the segment can then stabilize otherwise competing or contradictory elements of the story within a pre-fabricated vision of war. The use of war talk as introduction also renders the trope itself invisible. Visuals and narrative suggest that the conflict really *is* war: reported activities are inscribed as militaristic before the audience hears/sees what happened.

Indeed, the trope's invisibility may be the very condition of its potency.[32] Their very banality makes them seem transparent, as though they are merely description rather than interpretation grounded in a specific set of interests (for example, those of corporate news in securing audiences for advertisers). In this case, as in most invocations of war for social problems, the frame dramatizes the issue, making it newsworthy.[33]

In dramatizing abortion-related activism, the news portrays protest on both sides as a violent, chaotic war, neither side of which is reasonable. A clear example of this is a segment CBS aired on 23 August 1991. In this segment, references to war and violence situate news staff firmly within the realm of the objective and encourage viewers to identify with a national identity in contrast to the spectacle of the protesters. This segment appeared on CBS during the sixth week of the OR campaign. OR's primary focus was a clinic performing third trimester abortions (in 1991, it was one of three in the United States to do so). Protesters combined rallies and prayer vigils with efforts to block the road and entrance to the clinic; they stood arm in arm or sat in dense groups to prevent cars and people from entering. Daily, large numbers of people were arrested, released, and rearrested. This segment covers the first concerted response from national abortion rights activists to the campaign.

In this segment, which counts as truly awful news by Langer's estimation, the fragmentation of a family metonymically attests to the fragmentation of the nation through protest.[34] CBS's anchor introduces the segment in terms which, while disarticulating "anti-abortion" and "pro-life," clearly invoke the news's version of the battle over abortion: "At least 80 more anti-abortion demonstrators who call themselves pro-life were arrested in Wichita, Kansas today for blocking a clinic. In tonight's Eye On America, a different perspective on this issue." The rest of the segment contrasts the perspectives of a pro-choice sister, Linda Barber, and her brother, Rick Middleton. Linda Barber and Rick Middleton are given equal time in the segment, and both express their frustrations and beliefs in extremely small (27 second) sound bytes. Their constative identities are given by their designation as "anti-abortion" and "pro-choice" rather than through anything they might say or do. The segment displays a point/counterpoint structure that balances statements by the family; shortly after the first sibling speaks, the other discusses the same issue. For example, in lines 22-24, Barber says "I don't see why my brother hasn't looked to see who is surrounding him on his side." Correspondent MacNamara then interjects, "For these two, brother and sister, this is not a political debate, it's a moral and emotional war." Whether or not MacNamara accurately summarizes the siblings' views, he is ironically testifying to the news frame itself: in these segments, protest is not a part of legitimate political debate. It is a moral and emotional war on reasonable politics. The segment next cuts to a clip of Rick Middleton, who says "She's escorting people in and out of here to have their babies killed, and I feel like she shares in that responsibility and I wouldn't want that on my conscience. I don't

want it on hers." In fact, most of the rest of the segment alternates between the siblings' (and a few others') statements, with the correspondent interjecting between each, establishing balance. Repeatedly these interjections assure us that this is, in fact, a war simply through repetition of the claim (Appendix, lines 7, 9, 11, 23, 28, 38).

The siblings' father, Jack Middleton, supplies the story's significance. He appears, saying: "It's really sort of a gut-wrenching experience if you want to know the truth." Then the correspondent deepens the sense of melodrama with framing statements such as: "Caught in the crossfire in this family feud is their father, Jack Middleton"; "Which side are you on?" and "How do you feel about it dividing the family?" Father Middleton responds to these questions as follows: "I don't know that I can say I'm on either side." And "I don't like it. It, ah, I could probably thank Randy Terry for that." Although the elder Middleton refuses to "pick sides," he is acknowledging the "war" and attributing responsibility to (OR's) activist leaders. The correspondent then immediately reframes Middleton's statement, saying: "For those whose objectives are political power and issue celebrity, Wichita is one more skirmish in the nation's abortion war. But for the foot soldiers on both sides, for the families divided by the fight, the wounds of this war may linger lifetimes." The correspondent thus alters Middleton's assessment, as he supplies "both sides" with a vocabulary of motive—the desire for "political power and issue celebrity." The correspondent is suggesting that activist leaders *as* activist leaders are demagogues. "They" prey upon our family members, or sucker us into pernicious forms of activism. Ultimately, we, the potential foot soldiers or rank and file activists, will be wounded if we enter the battlefield. The segment thus finishes by holding out a closed, constative subject position through Jack Middleton, "the father." He provides the voice of America, the reasonable middle ground in this war, threatened by and opposed to activism. A metonymic shift occurs by which brother and sister become representative of two movements, and father is the bearer of a safe and reasonable space far from the fevered pitch of activist conflict. The family stands in for community and nation, which should be united (under father) rather than divided. Possibilities for Arendtian political action are eliminated through the tight, balanced structure of this segment, as "reasonable" positions are constructed through opposition to protest. The abortion war is a civil war, and activist leaders foment trouble, conning our family members and disrupting the harmony of community.

CBS on 24 August provides another example of how the news levels distinctions between different kinds of abortion-related protest, this time in coverage of a pro-choice counterdemonstration in Wichita. In this segment, the anchor introduces the rally in terms that equate abortion rights groups and OR as they become enemies fighting a war: "Wichita was once again the scene of a huge demonstration today in the battle over abortion, but this time it was the abortion rights activists leading the charge." The anchor situates himself and the correspondent as objective commentators on the war, imparting the newest information on the battle. Bellicosity resonates in the correspondent's opening statement as he explains that the protest was "ringed in tight security," after which the narrative and visuals cut to footage of the abortion rights rally. This mention of security, combined with the abrupt cut to the protest, dramatizes the rally and conveys a sense of immediacy. One is never told why security ringed the rally, but the open-ended statement evokes numerous possibilities; for example, to avoid violent confrontation between anti-abortion and abortion rights protesters, or to ensure that abortion rights protesters would not "turn violent." The segment situates OR protesters as deviants; a man on the street says, "I'm a little bit upset with the lunatic fringe that we've had in town." Directly afterward, a woman in the street says, "This is my town. I want 'em out"—a line worthy of Gary Cooper in *High Noon*. Both of these lines, uttered by people in the street, offer what seems to be common-sense truth; *they* are clearly deviant, marginal, and unwelcome in Wichita. Thus is difference collapsed into a normalizing vision of a homogeneous political center. The use of townspeople to voice these reactions also holds out an imagined community, identified as "this town," and the people in it who find themselves upset, disrupted, endangered by invasion.

The next line juxtaposes the two enemies, OR and abortion rights activists, as the correspondent explains that the abortion rights rally "was a pep talk and a chance to counter the political attention that 3,000 arrests have given OR and its jailed leaders." Notably, when the correspondent acknowledges the public attention OR has gained from the campaign, he describes it as *political* attention. This underscores OR's activities as strategies or tactics to garner public attention without acknowledging the role that news media play in enabling OR to become publicly visible. The correspondent's elision of the fact of *media* attention—and what organizers need to do to get it—preserves the frame of television news as window on the world; the news as medium remains invisible in this narrative. The implicit understanding that it takes two to make a war is reinforced by the following juxtaposition. After we hear that "the warning today was 'the battle's not over'," the camera cuts to the abortion rights rally where Patricia Ireland of the National Organization for Women condemns OR as "storm troopers [who] leave behind emboldened local vigilantes." While Ireland attempts to narrate *her* perspective on the war, her rhetoric is rearticulated in the segment's master frame to illustrate the bellicosity of *all* protest. Equalization of conflicting protesters continues as MacNamara narrates: "While OR kept its distance from this rally, one who did venture in drew the crowd's wrath." The accompanying visual shows ten to fifteen abortion rights protesters tightly clustered around a pro-life counter demonstrator, vigorously yelling and screaming at him.

Both segments frame abortion-related protest as a threat to imagined community by situating "people like us" as victims of this war. Both tend to read pro-choice activism somewhat more sympathetically than anti-abortion activism. In addition, the news makes a clear distinction between anti-abortion activists and OR leaders, presenting the former as victims—those who were people like us but were pulled in to "America's battle" by scheming, power-hungry leaders. Nevertheless, ultimately all activists are positioned as participants in a war that threatens to consume American viewers. To reiterate, a battlefield cannot also be a democracy, and the potential for political action is foreclosed in these segments.

The question of why the network news constructs the middle ground both as apolitical (so that the middle ground or center becomes conflated with *not taking* a stand) and as "the nation" is a complex one. Several theoretical and empirical points become important in relation to this mediated nationality. First, the news's abortion war is a civil war rather than a foreign one. Some cultural wars (e.g., the war on poverty, the war on drugs), though, have a clearly delineated "us" and an equally clear enemy (personalized or not). The difference partly lies in public opinion on these issues. Although public opinion is created and produced, a clear "majority" stance on an issue can be articulated to the favored side of a culture war, which serves to justify the war itself.[35] On abortion, though, public opinion is complex and avoids a whole-hearted embrace of either abortion rights or anti-abortion arguments. Polls suggest that most Americans believe abortion is acceptable in some cases but not in others.[36]

Strange alliances among activists also make endorsement of a particular side in this "civil war" difficult. For example, the anti-abortion movement arose primarily from political conservatism and fundamentalism in the United States. While fundamentalism and conservatism are often disparaged when embodied by ethnic/racial/national/religious constellations that are "other" in the American national imaginary (e.g., Muslims and Jews), white American conservatism and Christian fundamentalism have been extremely popular and powerful cultural and political forces for centuries. The Great Awakenings, for example, mobilized adherents around a fusion of conservatism and a particular brand of Calvinist fundamentalism in the US.[37] These tensions, along with the news code of objectivity, encourage dissociation from any particular side or perspective (unlike Gulf War coverage).[38] Indeed, news texts periodically embrace both anti-abortion and abortion-rights perspectives (implicitly or explicitly): the anchor's disarticulation of "anti-abortion" and "pro-life" in CBS's segment on 23 August is a clear example of such an implicitly critical perspective. The rest of the segment, however, marginalizes both sides as it resituates "the mainstream" in opposition to protesters. Thus, what the news offers overall is not so much a dominant ideology biased against pro-life or pro-choice as a discursive field rife with contradictions, disturbances, and often silences. This uncertainty facilitates a discourse that moves viewers into a fictive centrist position radically dissociated from activism.

CHAOS VERSUS LAW AND ORDER

An associated discourse, "chaos vs. law and order," recurs throughout the coverage to intensify the presentation of abortion-related protest as war. Over half of the long segments use chaos as a trope; two-thirds use chaos or law and order. Most of the segments focusing primarily on protest invoke chaos as well as law and order, while most of the segments in which the primary focus is on political events invoke law and order exclusively. Clearly, these discourses are empirically prominent in the coverage. The question thus becomes *how* they work and what they signify. As I will show, they work in concert with war discourses, though less dynamically, to marginalize protest and distance it from, or place it exterior to, the national community of Americans.

Television news often invokes chaos by means of narrative and through language expressing either a sudden and abrupt disruption or a situation ready to explode or spin out of control. These tropes in turn allow the nation or community to be personified as an innocent victim of activist aggression. For example, on 24 May 1991, an NBC correspondent introduces a story on abortion-rights demonstrations as follows: "The decision lighted a fuse under pro-choice activists around the country" ("around the country" describes two protests in Boston and New York City over the Gag Rule). In one sense, the phrase "lighted a fuse" is banal, a common figure of speech. In the context of a discursive war, though, use of this kind of talk to describe both OR actions and abortion-rights activism works to portray protest as a simmering problem, an unpredictable threat to the well-being of the community or country.

A detailed example of the interaction between chaos, law and order, and violent destruction of community can be found in ABC's 13 July 1991 segment on a three-year OR campaign to close a Dobbs Ferry, New York clinic. The anchor introduces the segment by saying "the pro-life movement's three-year campaign to make an example of Dobbs Ferry is tearing that community apart." The correspondent follows with: "Suddenly this peaceful town was under siege" (note the suggestion of immediacy, unexpected drama and danger). "People in this community . . . have tried their own tactics to regain a semblance of order. But three years later, the demonstrators remain." This narrative alternates between the chaos of the demonstrations and the peaceful, idyllic town of Dobbs Ferry. The visuals ironically bolster the trope of violence and chaos by depicting the serenity of the town. Most of the visual track of the segment comprises the following shots: two men fishing off a jetty; an uncrowded local swimming pool with someone swimming underwater; two children lazily swinging; a park. The one visual that represents chaos is an old clip of protesters locked together inside the clinic; it runs in slow motion and is quite unsteady in focus and view (*cinema verité* camerawork). This sort of shot gives the impression of chaos and instability at the clinic, despite the fact that there is virtually no action. The protesters sit or lie on the floor, immobile and locked together. My point is emphatically not that clinic blockades are orderly and nonviolent; rather, the problem is that the news's frame of chaos and violence is established through innuendo and bald assertion rather than through evidence of chaos or violence.

Chaos can be invoked directly as well and usually precedes talk of law and order. The latter contains or bounds the former through sympathetic portrayals of the forces of sane, responsible government. For example, on 5 August 1991, ABC's anchor begins a story on "the nation's building *debate* over abortion" (emphasis mine). The correspondent then says, "After four weeks of chaos outside Wichita clinics, a federal judge vowed today to restore order and launched a blistering attack against OR" (so now the community itself goes to war). In the first two lines of this coverage, *debate* over a controversial issue is equated with warfare and chaos. Later in the segment, the correspondent declares that "the

month of protest is wrenching the city. More than a quarter of the police force is assigned to clinic duty." The forces of law and order are threatened by the chaos wrought by OR. In addition, with this narrative, the city is personified; it is "wrenched."

The narrative is supported by visuals representing chaotic protest in front of a clinic. People sit on the road leading to the clinic's front door, crowded together, facing different directions. We hear the loud buzz of indistinguishable voices talking simultaneously as we see a policewoman elbowing a white male. The protest looks disordered and chaotic, and the police stand trapped in the middle of seated protesters by whom they cannot pass. The next shot shows a line of about fifteen abortion-rights protesters, arms linked, advancing toward a line of OR protesters with arms similarly linked to form a barrier to the clinic entrance. The pro-choice escorts then rush the OR line, as people push against one another, jostled and sandwiched by the second line of linked protesters.

Most of the segments focusing on political rather than protest-related events tend to omit chaos. Instead, the segments typically invoke law and order to describe the police or juridical activity. For example, "law and order" is invoked on 7 August 1991 as the correspondent declares that "the added security [of police at the protests] has cost Wichita more than 300,000 dollars at a time when the budget is already strapped." The law-and-order frame is heightened with a clip of President Bush asserting that "everybody has the right to protest, and it oughta be done within the law. My view is you ought to ah, ought to, obey the law." The anchor closes the segment by saying that "only one thing seems clear tonight; this didn't happen the way it was planned because it's hard to imagine anybody planning this" (referring to the OR campaign and the controversy it engendered). The anchor's statement may seem quite strange; in fact, Operation Rescue spent much time and money planning the clinic blockade and controversy. The trope of chaos is a more immediate and dramatic story that allows correspondent and anchor to avoid direct assertions or accusations of Operation Rescue's plans (which would work against the superficial news code of balance in this coverage).

Moreover, this segment introduces another trope—the Western outlaw. During OR's campaign in Wichita, Judge Kelly authorized federal marshals to guard clinic entrances. The Justice Department contested Kelly's use of federal marshals at clinics. After the introduction of federal marshals on the news, segments repeatedly refer to protests and legal issues as "showdowns" and other language evocative of Western films' law-versus-order trope. For example, on 17 August, NBC's anchor discusses challenges to Roe vs. Wade as threats to "the Supreme Court decision that made women's choice the *law of the land*." Bruce Morton then declares that "today a federal judge ruled that law [a Louisiana bill outlawing abortion] unconstitutional, which simply brings the court *showdown* over abortion that much closer" (emphasis mine).

Visuals can amplify the Western motif. For example, on 6 August, ABC uses a powerful set of shots (worthy of Sergio Leone) to convey law and order vs. the forces of chaos: ten federal marshals, shot from below at a distance (one wearing a ten-gallon cowboy hat), gather in pre-dawn darkness in front of clinic gates. This echoes the Western genre in which sheriff and marshals ride in at dawn to save the city. The frame is particularly effective since all three networks on previous days describe pro-choice and pro-life protest and counter-protest as chaos, which local forces of order (Wichita police) could not control. All three networks echo this theme later in the week, showing stark lines of federal marshals in dark sunglasses and dark jackets, legs apart, in front of clinic gates. One segment begins with a medium shot of the road in front of the clinic gate, revealing the shadow of four federal marshals who stand in front of a high spiked gate with legs apart, arms crossed at the chest. The shot slowly pans upward to show the marshals themselves, protecting the gate from the forces of violence. This segment works by visualizing order to invoke the specter of chaos. Both chaos and law-and-order are discursive mechanisms that resonate through the master discourse of war to show us the uncontrollability, unpredictability, and harm of protest within the nation. All three codes articulate to marginalize activism as acceptable, necessary political activity.

ARENDT, DOUGLAS, AND TELEVISION NEWS

On this formulation, news on abortion-related protest becomes an apparatus of the Arendtian social par excellence. Dispute over abortion is presented as a war between two equally dangerous sets of activists. Failing to distinguish between violent and non-violent protest, the news proclaims all forms of protest to be violent, disruptive, war-like and dangerous. In this way, pro-choice is equated with pro-life, and it is precisely the ensemble of the two that threatens the public good.

While differences between groups of protesters are erased through television news coverage, the most important erasure of Arendtian plurality occurs with the construction of "community" or "nation." Family/nation/community becomes a master trope in this coverage, displacing the issue of abortion, its history, its uses in the United States, and its relationship to the condition of women, class, and race. The exclusions are telling. The "we" of community, family and nation is simply asserted or anchored against the existence of "them"—protesters and activists. Pluralism replaces plurality; "we" are part of a homogeneous family/community/nation, as in the coverage of the Middletons and Barbers. This echoes Arendt's assertion that "society always demands that its members act as though they were members of one enormous family which has only one opinion and one interest."[39] In the coverage examined above, this demand is textually imposed both on activists and viewers. Whether they refuse or accede to this demand, of course, is a different matter—but the text does encourage such a reading. "We" are a family/community/nation beset by unruly protesters who threaten the social order and calm of our public spaces.

Hence, news stories performatively construct that which they purport simply to reflect or describe. They make the act of protest itself violent, collapsing distinctions between kinds of activism and activists as they cover all protesters with the language of war. Ironically, the effect is to displace or trivialize harassment, bombings and threats perpetrated by specific people. Violence did occur that year. According to the National Abortion Federation (NAF), for example, law-enforcement agencies reported eight arson attempts, one bombing, and one attempted bomb/arson. Likewise, NAF received reports on twenty-nine incidents of invasion of clinics, forty-four incidents of vandalism, three death threats, six assaults, 142 instances of harassing calls and hate mail, and fifteen bomb threats. Yet, none of this violence was referred to in news coverage of abortion-related protest as war, perhaps because this kind of violence is difficult to account for in terms of two sets of bellicose enemies using military tactics against one another. It suggests another kind of violent conflict altogether. Instead, to preserve an epiphenomenal veneer of objectivity and balance, news texts constructed the docile, inactive body as true citizen in contrast to the unpredictable, violently active bodies and deeds of protesters.

The performativity of the news text can be understood in another way as well: as an enactment of a ritual of purification. Mary Douglas theorized that social systems work according to a classification system that orders the world and people, things, and acts within it.[40] Such classification systems are necessary, since they give meaning and sense to the world. Elements that resist classification, however, present a problem, since they threaten the classification system or the "order of things." These elements are, in effect, matter out of place, and as such become dangerously dirty or polluting elements. They threaten to disturb or pollute the systems of meaning necessary to maintenance of a social system. Douglas contended that such liminal elements are subject to rituals of purification that draw on the opposition of nature/culture and clean/dirty. Douglas's famous examples include food and earth. The earth, for example, is not in itself dirty, but on shoes or a kitchen table it is matter out of place and becomes dirty. On this formulation, hybrid elements, or those that straddle or mix categorical features, become especially dangerous categories, since they threaten the stability of the categorical system. Protesters straddle categories. They are elements within a social system that challenge the social order and trouble its boundaries. The coverage works to resituate them outside the borders of reasonable political claims and action.

In the news coverage analyzed above, codes of war and protest work as rituals of purification. Protesters in the war on abortion become bodies out of place. They are continually represented as outsiders, as threats to the space of family/community/nation. Through these representations, the news maps a narrative of pollution onto those who threaten to dislodge the myth of homogeneity, of nation as a unified "people like us." Descombes's description of homeland as a "rhetorical territory" applies:

> The character is at home when he is at ease in the rhetoric of the people with whom he shares life. The sign of being at home is the ability to make oneself understood without too much difficulty.... A disturbance of rhetorical communication marks the crossing of a frontier.[41]

Activists of all kinds represent a disturbance of this rhetorical territory, this imagined community. They threaten to make the spaces of nation and home *unheimlich* (unhomelike/uncanny), riven with contest and disagreement. Discourses of chaos work in much the same way, situating protesters as bodies/selves that disrupt the cultural order of the nation/community/homeland. Chaos, after all, is the disordering of a system. In this case, chaos disorders both physical space—through the presence of unruly bodies on city streets, outside of clinics—and the political routines of law and order. Activists are *outsiders* whose objectives are "political power and issue celebrity," in opposition to locals (for example, those "people on the street" who declare that "This is my town. I want 'em out," or "I'm a little bit upset with the lunatic fringe that we've had in town."). Protesters, then, ritually pollute the national imagined community. Little wonder, then, that protesters of any sort seem to invoke sheer fury on the part of non-protesters. While perhaps it is the case that street activism has lost its utility, we need to understand why it causes rage and seems so ineffectual.

Conclusion

Critiques of the news often leave us asking where we go from here, and how the news can be different. Drawing on Arendt, one arrives at an increasingly common conclusion: we need active, engaged coverage from a multiplicity of perspectives that can historicize issues and create spaces for differences.[42] Such coverage could create informative, agonistic, and exciting news on public abortion discourse and civic journalism.[43] If we take the Arendtian critique seriously, though, the simple creation of alternative media is insufficient to create space for political action because the news serves normalizing functions— it constitutes a disciplinary technology for the production of certain kinds of identity. While creating alternative sources of news (such as public access television) is useful, that alone does not destabilize the kinds of identity currently created by news (and other) practices. Any effective counter-news will require re-shaping identity in profound ways. Perhaps it can arise within—as an essential part of—a new form of transforming social movements that intervenes in the kind of nation building above.

Alternatives to the coverage analyzed above are critical, since the use of chaos, violence, and war to discredit social protest is not limited to news on abortion-related activism. Even casual attention to media coverage of the 2004 Democratic National Convention protests or the 2000 WTO protests, or the 2001 FTAA protests, for example, reveals the same kind of techniques opposing good citizenship to activism. Such codes are constative in an insidious way. As they close off possibilities for activism and stabilize or anchor protest as inherently dangerous, they make the logic of war, violence, and chaos ineluctable and difficult to question. Representing activists as warriors dissolves their humanity; warring parties proceed with brutality rather than reason. Moreover, since perspectives, histories, personal concerns and the like are irrelevant in battle, they become irrelevant in representations of activism.

The news constructs a social body based on sameness, where difference becomes deviant. It promotes the social by erasing the plurality of activists' positions and perspectives. In this erasure, the possibility for a public sphere, a space for meaningful political action through agonistic politics, is destroyed. This, then, is the significance of televisual news tropes that demonize

or marginalize activism in the name of a mythic "us"; the very possibility of shared creation and alteration of the world is at stake.

Notes

[1] On representation as "war," see, for example, CBS Evening News, 24 April 2004; CNN Saturday Night, 24 April 2004; CNN Live Sunday, 24 April 2004; NPR Weekend Edition Saturday, 24 April 2004; on more comprehensive agenda, see, for example, NBC Sunday Today, 24 April 2004; CNN Late Edition with Wolf Blitzer, 25 April 2004; CNN Sunday Morning, 25 April 2004.

[2] David Morley, *Home Territories: Media, Mobility, and Identity* (London: Routledge, 2000).

[3] James W. Carey, *Communication as Culture: Essays on Media and Society* (New York: Routledge, 1988); Barbie Zelizer, "When Facts, Truth, and Reality Are God-Terms: On Journalism's Uneasy Place in Cultural Studies," *Communication and Critical/Cultural Studies* 1 (2004): 100–19.

[4] Marion Meyers, "African American Women and Violence: Gender, Race, and Class in the News," *Critical Studies in Media Communication* 21 (2004): 95–118.

[5] See, for example, Edward Jay Epstein, *News from Nowhere: Television and the News* (New York: Random House, 1973); Todd Gitlin, *The Whole World is Watching: Mass Media in the Making and Unmaking of the New Left* (Berkeley: University of California Press, 1980); and Gaye Tuchman, *Making News: A Study in the Construction of Reality* (New York: Free Press, 1978).

[6] Daniel C. Hallin, "Network News: We Keep America on Top of the World," *Watching Television: A Pantheon Guide to Popular Culture*, ed. Todd Gitlin (New York, Pantheon Books, 1986).

[7] Jimmy L. Reeves and Richard Campbell, *Cracked Coverage: Television News, the Anti-Cocaine Crusade, and the Reagan Legacy* (Chicago: University of Chicago Press, 1994).

[8] Gitlin, *The Whole World Is Watching*; William A. Gamson, *Talking Politics* (Cambridge, UK: Cambridge University Press, 1992); Andrew Rojecki, *Silencing the Opposition: Antinuclear Movements and the Media in the Cold War* (Urbana, IL: University of Illinois Press, 1999); Lauren Danner and Susan Walsh, "'Radical' Feminists and 'Bickering' Women: Backlash in U.S. Media Coverage of the United Nation's Fourth World Conference on Women," *Critical Studies in Media Communication* 16 (1999): 63–94.

[9] See for example, Chantal Mouffe, *The Return of the Political* (London: Verso, 1993); Robert L. Ivie,

"Evil Enemy Versus Agonistic Other: Rhetorical Constructions of Terrorism," *The Review of Education, Pedagogy, and Cultural Studies* 25 (2003): 181–200; Gerard A. Hauser and Amy Grim, ed., *Rhetorical Democracy: Discursive Practices of Civic Engagement: Selected Papers from the 2002 Conference of the Rhetoric Society of America* (Mahwah, NJ: Erlbaum, 2004).

10 Ivie, "Evil Enemy Versus Agonistic Other," 187.

11 Robert L. Ivie, "Rhetorical Deliberation and Democratic Politics in the Here and Now," *Rhetoric and Public Affairs* 5 (2002): 277–85.

12 Morley, *Home Territories.*

13 Hannah Arendt, *The Human Condition* (Chicago: University of Chicago Press, 1958), 79.

14 Lisa King, "A Politics of the Everyday: Identity and Normalizing Power," PhD dissertation, University of Illinois, 2001.

15 Arendt, *The Human Condition,* 57.

16 Craig Calhoun, "Plurality, Promises, and Public Spaces," *Hannah Arendt and the Meaning of Politics,* ed. Craig Calhoun and John McGowan (Minneapolis: University of Minnesota Press, 1997), 237.

17 Bonnie Honig, "Toward an Agonistic Feminism: Hannah Arendt and the Politics of Identity," *Feminist Interpretations of Hannah Arendt,* ed. Bonnie Honig (University Park, PA: Penn State University Press, 1995).

18 Hanna F. Pitkin, *The Attack of the Blob: Hannah Arendt's Concept of the Social* (Chicago: University of Chicago Press, 1998).

19 For example, Arendt, *The Human Condition;* Hannah Arendt, *The Origins of Totalitarianism* (New York: Harcourt, Brace, and World, 1966).

20 "Authentic" and "unique" may be misleading; despite her use of such terms, identity arises from action for Arendt. Identity is not 'given'—rather, it arises from certain kinds of practices.

21 Nancy Fraser, "Communication, Transformation and Consciousness Raising," in Calhoun and McGowan, *Hannah Arendt and the Meaning of Politics,* 166–75; Honig, "Toward an Agonistic Feminism."

22 For example, Faye Ginsburg, "Saving America's Souls: Operation Rescue's Crusade Against Abortion," *Fundamentalisms and the State: Remaking Polities, Economies, and Militance,* ed. M. E. Marty and R. S. Appleby (Chicago: University of Chicago Press, 1993), 557–88; David Meyer and Suzanne Staggenborg, "Movements, Countermovements and the Structure of Political Opportunity," *American Journal of Sociology* 101 (1996), 1647.

23 James Risen and Judy L. Thomas, *Wrath of Angels: The American Abortion War* (New York: Basic Books, 1998).

24 Shanto Iyengar, *News That Matters: Television and American Opinion* (Chicago: University of Chicago Press, 1987).

25 For analyses of public discourses on abortion, see Celeste M. Condit, *Decoding Abortion Rhetoric: Communicating Social Change* (Urbana: University of Illinois Press, 1990); Faye D. Ginsburg, *Contested Lives: The Abortion Debate in an American Community* (Berkeley: University of California Press, 1989); and Marsha Vanderford, "Vilification and Social Movements: A Case Study of Pro-Life and Pro-Choice Rhetoric," *Quarterly Journal of Speech* 75 (1989): 166–82.

26 NBC, 30 March 1991.

27 NBC, 24 August 1991.

28 CBS, 6 July 1991.

29 ABC, 13 July 1991.

30 CBS, 5 August 1991.

31 NBC, 30 March 1991.

32 George Lakoff and Mark Johnson, *Metaphors We Live By* (Chicago: University of Chicago Press, 1980).

33 For example, Michael Billig, *Banal Nationalism* (Thousand Oaks, CA: Sage Press, 1995); on banal nationalism, see Danner and Walsh, "'Radical' Feminists and 'Bickering' Women."

34 John Langer, "Truly Awful News on Television," *Journalism and Popular Culture,* ed. P. Dahlgren and C. Sparks (London: Sage, 1992).

35 Reeves and Campbell, *Cracked Coverage.*

36 Maggie J. Patterson and Megan W. Hall, "Abortion, Moral Maturity and Civic Journalism," *Critical Studies in Mass Communication* 15 (1999), 91–115.

37 Mary P. Ryan, *Cradle of the Middle Class: The Family in Oneida County, New York, 1790–1865* (Cambridge: Cambridge University Press, 1981).

38 Epstein, *News from Nowhere: Television and the News;* Gitlin, *The Whole World is Watching;* Tuchman, *Making News.*

39 Arendt, *The Human Condition,* 39.

40 Mary Douglas, *Purity and Danger: An Analysis of Concepts of Pollution and Taboo* (New York: Praeger Press, 1966).

41 Descombes quoted in Morley, *Home Territories,* 17.

42 David Barsamian, "Listening In: An Interview with Susan Douglas," *Z Magazine* 14 (January 2001): 36–42.

43 Patterson and Hall, "Abortion, Moral Maturity and Civic Journalism."

APPENDIX

23 August CBS

1. Anchor: At least 80 more antiabortion demonstrators who call themselves pro-life were arrested in Wichita, Kansas, today for blocking a clinic. In tonight's Eye on America, a different perspective on this divisive issue.

2. Policeman-megaphone: You have five minutes to leave this location . . . .

3. Pro-life protester sobs.

4. Policeman-megaphone: You are all under arrest at this time. Begin arresting them.

5. Correspondent Bob MacNamara: The streets of Wichita. The frontlines in America's battle over abortion.

6. Protesters: Don't do it!

7. Correspondent: A war waged with rhetoric, rosaries, and righteousness.

8. Protesters: Let us do what God has called us to do.

9. Correspondent: While the scores of daily arrests are the body count in this conflict . . . .

10. White middle-aged male protester: Praise the Lord!

11. Correspondent: Its most lasting casualties may be the families it divided . . . . Rick Middleton, father of five, has been arrested twice this month.

. . . .

14. Rick Middleton: I was just going to come watch, initially. But ah when I saw those girls, six months or more pregnant, waiting to get in to have that baby killed I just couldn't stand aside.

15. Correspondent: Still, someone else he saw upset him even more.

16. Rick Middleton: It breaks my heart to see my little sister over there.

17. Linda Barber: Someone needs to be here. Someone has to let the patients know that there are people out there who are with them. No, I don't think peace and harmony in the family is worth sacrificing these patients.

18. Correspondent: For a month now, Linda Barber has helped patients keep their appointments at the besieged woman's clinics.

. . . .

20. Linda Barber: Oh my God, what—look at 'em. [camera pans to 30 protesters who are scaling a large fence surrounding the clinic]

21. Linda Barber: I look out at the crowd out there and it's anything but peaceful. Some of them were vicious, hateful. . . .

22. Linda Barber: I don't see why my brother hasn't looked to see who is surrounding him on his side.

23. Correspondent: For these two, brother and sister, this is not a political debate, it's a moral and emotional war.

24. Rick Middleton: She's escorting people in and out of here to have their babies killed, and I feel like she shares in that responsibility, I wouldn't want that on my conscience. I don't want it on hers.

25. Correspondent: So you're accusing her of helping and abetting a murderer.

26. Linda Barber: I don't think I can forget the look on my brother's face when he confronted me about aiding and abetting murderers. Um at some point in time I may forgive it but I don't think I'll ever forget it.

27. Jack Middleton: It's really a sort of gut-wrenching experience if you want to know the truth.

28. Correspondent: Caught in the crossfire in this family feud is their father, Jack Middleton. A twenty-five year Wichita police chaplain.

29. Jack Middleton: They're trying to each help in their own way what they see as an injustice. One is concerned with the unborn, the other is concerned with the living.

30. Correspondent: Which side are you on?

31. Jack Middleton: I don't know that I can say that I'm on either side.

32. Rick Middleton: My parents raised me to follow my convictions, and I know that they wouldn't want me to do any less.

33. Linda Barber: When you have an issue that's this personal, that's this emotional, I don't see any way it can keep from splitting families.

34. Correspondent: How do you feel about it dividing the family?

35. Jack Middleton: I don't like it. It ah, I could probably thank Randy Terry for that.

36. Randy Terry: We just say "God please be merciful to us."

37. Randy Terry: This is America's second Civil War. Our activities give us political firepower.

38. Correspondent: For those whose objectives are political power and issue celebrity, Wichita is one more skirmish in the nation's abortion war. But for the foot soldiers on both sides, for the families divided by the fight, the wounds of this war may linger lifetimes. Bob MacNamara, Wichita.

Foiling the Intellectuals: Gender, Identity Framing, and the Rhetoric of the Kill in Conservative Hate Mail

Dana L. Cloud

I was deluged with so much hate mail, but none of it was political . . . . It was like, "Gook, chink, cunt. Go back to your country, go back to your country where you came from, you fat pig. Go back to your country you fat pig, you fat dyke. Go back to your country, fat dyke. Fat dyke fat dyke fat dyke—Jesus saves."

—Margaret Cho, "Hate Mail From Bush Supporters" (2004)

My question to you. If you was [sic] a professor in Saudi Arabia, North Korea, Palestinian university or even in Russia. etc. How long do you think you would last as a living person regarding your anti government rhetoric in those countries? We have a saying referring to people like you. Only in America. My advice to you since I think you lack sex or engage in lesbian sex, is to get laid with a good wholesome thick cock.

—Albert, an example of the author's hate mail (March 7, 2007)[1,2]

After commenting in a 2004 comedy sketch that Bush was not Hitler—but could be if he applied himself—comedian Margaret Cho was deluged with racist, sexist, and homophobic hate mail (DeC, 2004). Even though Cho (2005) was able to incorporate the content of some of her mail into her comedy routines, a contributor to the *American Politics Journal* online described how serious the phenomenon was: "It is obvious to the most obtuse observer that the reservoir of misogyny which overflows here—in this type of hate mail directed at any woman who 'steps out of line'—is the self-same reservoir which fuels the stoning, mutilation, rape, and multifarious other abuses of women worldwide" (DeC, 2004).

Because sexist speech is constant and mundane and sexism diffuse and under-recognized, Lillian (2007) observes how difficult it was for her in her research to find a concentrated, coherent sample of neoconservative sexist speech (p. 737). Here, I offer analysis of one such sample: the hate mail I received from readers of conservative publications and listeners to right-wing talk radio (especially the top 10 talk-radio programs, which include Rush Limbaugh, Laura Ingraham, and Michael Medved; see "Top Talk Radio Audiences," 2008). In order to understand the strategies and consequences of hate mail targeting politically outspoken women, I conduct an analysis of my archive of hate mail, containing approximately 290 messages, most of them from

2002, 2007, and 2008 following my participation in antiwar controversies, inclusion on pundit David Horowitz's list of "dangerous" professors, and interviews on right-wing talk radio.

Employing the methods of social movement frame analysis, rhetorical criticism, and autoethnography, I identify three key adversarial identity frames attributed to me in the correspondence: the scholar as elitist intellectual, the Leftist as national traitor, and the feminist/lesbian as gender/sex traitor. These identity frames serve as *foils* against which the authors of the letters articulate their identities as real men and patriots. These examples demonstrate how *foiling* one's adversary relies on the power of naming; applies tremendous pressure to the target through the identification and invocation of psychological, economic, and physical vulnerabilities; is amplified in its impact by an intimate mode of address; and employs the resources of tone and verbal aggression in what Burke identified as "the kill": the definition of self through the symbolic purgation and/or negation of another. Even so, engaging correspondents in dialogue points to the possibility of a solidaristic discourse that interrupts the foiling process. In contrast to the image of an elitist, traitorous, transgressive woman, the correspondents secure their symbolic identities as real men and patriots. I call this process *framing by foil,* a concept that may contribute to the literature in critical media studies, rhetorical theories of identification, and social movement studies on collective identity frames.

I argue that a threatening foil enables the constitution of a conservative ideological and masculine subject position. As Judith Butler explains in *Excitable Speech* (1997), hate speech, as a performative event, constitutes its subjects and its objects in opposition to one another. I turn then to an analysis of the identity frames exhibited in my e-mail messages and examine how the alignment of my interlocutors takes the form of what Kenneth Burke calls the symbolic kill in the conflation of the categories of woman and traitor. I conclude the essay with a discussion of how forcing a return to the dialectical moment of engagement between Self and Other by making this e-mail public creates a culture of accountability for engaging mail/male authors in productive dialogue.

WHY AUTOETHNOGRAPHY?

Investigating my own hate mail affords an opportunity to understand conservative subjectivity formation in mass-mediated social movements. Although I have long been skeptical of autoethnographic methods as licensing and cultivating solipsistic work, I believe that good autoethnography "offers a way of giving voice to personal experience to advance sociological understanding" (Wall, 2008, p. 39; see also Denzin, 2000; Holman Jones, 2005). In making sense of a victimizing experience (as does Valentine, 1998), autoethnography offers insights akin to what in the women's movement is called consciousness-raising: conversation allowing one to see that her experience is not peculiar to herself but rather is part of a larger sociopolitical picture in which inequality and injustice condition interaction. Autoethnography is thus the practice of renewed discovery that "the personal is political" (Hanisch, 2006/1970; Holman Jones, 2005). Hate mail originates not in the minds of ordinary people but rather in the political conflicts among contending groups in society. Judith Butler (1997) notes that the process of linguistic subject formation is not under the control of any individual subject who is, rather, "compelled by authoritative interpellations" (p. 160). The personal is political not only for the recipient of hate mail but also for its authors.

IDENTITY FRAMES AND THE SYMBOLIC KILL

My approach to hate mail as rhetorical text encompasses movement frame analysis and rhetorical criticism. First, I employ identity frame analysis, a method emphasizing how individuals and groups manage their identities in communication. In the present case, hate mail is not the random expression of deviant individuals; rather, the authors are agents of a mixed neoconservative/populist social movement (discussed at more length below) organized around key radio programs and Internet sites (Brock, 2004).

Therefore, literature on identity framing in social movements helps to explain the formation of group ideology and belonging and identify how hate mail serves this purpose.

A concept that may describe the process of identity construction in any social movement (not just conservative ones), a frame is "an interpretive schema that simplifies and condenses the world out there by selectively punctuating and encoding objects, situations, events, experiences, and sequences of actions within one's present or past environments" (Snow & Benford, 1988, p. 137). Framing serves three functions for movements regardless of particular ideology: the crafting of identity and maintaining solidarity, providing members of a group with a frame for their grievances and explanation of the problem's source, and providing members a sense of potential efficacy in addressing their grievances (Adams & Roscigno, 2005, p. 761). Zald (1996) describes how movements use cultural repertoires (e.g., attitudes about gender) to construct frames and deploy them strategically to advance personal and collective aims (p. 261). Melucci (1996) also calls our attention to how antagonism operates in the formation of identities:

> [T]he unity of collective action . . . rests on the ability of a collective actor to locate itself within a system of relations [which] cannot construct [the actor's] identity independently of its recognition (which can also mean denial or opposition) by other social and political actors. . . . Social actors enter a conflict to affirm the identity that their opponent has denied them (pp. 73–74; see also Benford & Snow, 2000; Gamson, 1992; Snow & Benford, 1988).

As McCaffrey and Keys (2000) have noted, it is important to understand not only the self-frames of individuals and groups but also how the sense of self often is the product of defining oneself against the characteristics of an antagonist. Authors of political hate mail construct their own identities by framing themselves in terms of their opposite in communication denigrating perceived enemies and threats. This pattern holds for movements across the political spectrum (see also Shibutani, 1997; for a study of this process

in white supremacist organizations, see Adams & Roscigno, 2005).

Rhetorical theory has also accounted for the process of self-definition through the negation of the Other. Burke (1969) argues that not only do individuals and groups define themselves in opposition to others, they *necessarily* do so in a social field organized in terms of hierarchy. Burke describes how there can be no such thing as a purely positive self-definition; rather, self-definition is a process undertaken in dialectical relationship with others. The firmer the identity one seeks, the more polarizing the discourse of self-definition becomes, resulting in what Burke calls *ultimate terms* that glorify oneself and vilify the Other (pp. 183–197). Urging rhetoricians to notice the dangers in this process of naming: "Consubstantiality is established by common involvement in a killing," he writes (p. 265).

Burke tells the story of a group of young boys who "stirred up a rattlesnake," which was then killed by one of the boys' fathers. Then the boys "had their pictures taken, dangling the dead snake. Immediately after, they organized the Rattlesnake Club. Their members were made consubstantial by the sacrifice of this victim, representing dangers and triumphs they had shared in common. The snake was a sacred offering; by its death it provided the spirit for this magically united band" (p. 266). Like the boys with the snake, movement groups consolidate their identities and purposes around the figure of a threatening but ultimately vanquished foe.

McCaffrey and Keys (2000) point out that social movement scholars have not exhausted the exploration of movement-countermovement dynamics in identity framing, and understanding the role of the personification of the adversary. I believe that Burke's insight about the dialectical nature of the production of the self may be a useful supplement to that literature. Out of this combination, I propose to label the exclusive definition of self in terms of an adversary Other *framing by foil*, or *foiling*.

According to the *Oxford English Dictionary Online* (2008), a "foil" (derived from both the Latin *folium*, or leaf, and the French *fouler*, to trample, and *feuille*, leaf ["foil," 2008]) is either (a) that which sets something else off by contrast;

(b) that which is crushed or trampled; or (c) that which is thwarted. "To foil" something is in a literal sense to press a thin sheet (or leaf) of metal around a shape so that the shape appears in relief. There is potential violence done to one thing or person in the interest of establishing the identity of another; words can make foils that establish a sense of identity by warping and flattening the features of another (thus "foiling," i.e., impeding or blocking, the target's agentive momentum).

In the present case, the dominant foils constructed in my hate mail are threefold: the fraudulent intellectual, the national traitor, and the gender/sex traitor. Around these threats, the identities of the authors appear in relief: patriots and *men* of the people. This process of identity framing can occur across an array of media and settings, from public political oratory to internal movement communication in reports and newsletters, news commentary and coverage, traditional (hand- or typewritten and mailed correspondence), and, of course, electronic mail.[3]

Such correspondence must be viewed in structural context, in which hate mail addressed to women is a formulaic manifestation of gender discipline experienced by outspoken women in various occupations (see Barnes, 2002; Friedman, 2007; Hanson, 2002; "Hate Mail for Nurse Insisting on Respect," 2008; Richardson & McGlynn, 2007; Valentine, 1998; Wilkinson, 2004). However, the fact that woman hating has a formula does not mitigate its misogyny; indeed, the near universally available repertoire of sexist tropes is cause for more, not less, alarm. More than the generic or modal characteristics of hate mail, the crafting of identity frames for the author in the condemnation of the target is the primary object of my analysis, which demonstrates hate mail to be a political and ideological intervention on contested terrain. In the present case, the contestation has been over the politics of the academy.

IN THE COMPANY OF DANGEROUS INTELLECTUALS

In 2006, David Horowitz listed me among the "101 most dangerous" intellectuals in the United States in his book *The Professors* (Horowitz,

2006). My placement in his book and its sequel (2007), two letters to the editor of the student newspaper (one reworking the Pledge of Allegiance in 2002, the other a group letter protesting the Israeli invasion of Lebanon in 2007; see Adams, 2006), my two appearances on conservative radio programs (Michael Medved, July 11, 2002; Laura Ingraham, March 6, 2007), and my public protests of Horowitz's lectures seem to be the major prompts for large volumes of right-wing mail addressed to me. My e-mail address is provided in every article published about me on the Internet and in David Horowitz's books. The timing of waves of e-mail with specific events suggests that public expression of my ideas is the prompt for conservative discussion and reaction.[4]

Conservatism is a complex political movement encompassing several tendencies united primarily by aversion to abrupt social change and to socialism, along with faith in established traditions and cultural norms that provide social stability (Dunn & Woodard, 1991, p. 31). The versions of conservatism articulated by Horowitz, Ingraham, and others prominent in conservative talk radio and online forums only partially represent the politics of neoconservatism, a tendency emerging in the 1980s among intellectuals, disillusioned with the New Left (Boot, 2004; Gottfried, 1993, p. 79; Kristol, 2004, p. 33; Muravchik, 2004, p. 244). These leaders aimed to "create a counterestablishment" including publications and think tanks (like the American Enterprise Institute; Gottfried, 1993, p. 85; Kristol, 2004, pp. 34–37) that could, in turn, inform the development of a state buttressed by the family and capable of spreading market-based democracy around the world (Gottfried, 1993, p. 87; Stelzer, 2004). Significantly, Jeane Kirkpatrick (2004) defined neoconservatism as a response to the Left counterculture, which, she argues, constituted "a sweeping rejection of traditional American attitudes, values, and goals" (p. 236).[5]

In addition to giving expression to this critique of New Left, Ingraham and Horowitz also espouse the ideology of the New Right and its social (rather than strictly economic or intellectual) conservatism in favor of nationalism, conservative heteronormative family values,

Christian faith, states' rights; and against movements for and federal redress supporting racial justice and women's rights, including and especially abortion rights (see Gottfried, 1993, p. 98). The discourse of conservative media celebrities like Horowitz and Ingraham is, then, a strategic amalgam that aims to discredit the intellectual Left on a basis that finds favor among traditionally conservative media audiences. The primary consequence of this circulation is the mobilization and coaching of a confident conservative base rather than outreach to mainstream media and politicians (see Brock, 2004).[6]

I first came to the attention of conservatives in September and October of 2001, when I defended my colleague Robert Jensen, also among the 101, in print after he published an antiwar editorial opinion column and the President of the University publicly rebuked him (sources and details withheld pending review). Many of us among the progressive faculty found the President's emotional, anti-intellectual, public denunciation of a member of his own faculty to be quite chilling. Then, in the summer after the September 11, 2001, attacks, I published a controversial antiwar editorial (citation withheld). This attempt at critical-rational intervention into public discussion was met almost univocally by angry responses by fax, e-mail, and phone. For example, under the heading "Eat a Bag of Shit," Mark (July 8, 2002) wrote, "How about I print this out and shove it up your ass when I visit (your town) in August?" Tim (July 8, 2002) engaged in name-calling: "Wow, you are a typical liberal jackass."[7]

In 2005, I raised the ire of David Horowitz when I took part in a disruptive protest of his appearance on my campus. Far from an exercise in mere hyperbole, Horowitz's (2006) book, subtitled *The 101 Most Dangerous Academics in America,* serves to identify in clear terms the threat against which conservatives in his orbit are to mobilize (see Jaschik, 2008). The book itself grew out of his website DiscovertheNetwork.org (2006), an elaborate map of scholars, celebrities, and alleged terrorists and their ostensible links to one another. As Adams and Rosigno (2005) point out, this careful definition of an enemy is a movement resource that aids recruitment, motivates action, and sustains solidarity among those aligned with Horowitz's views.

Furthermore, Horowitz (wrongly regarded by some as a "crackpot") has been increasingly successful in garnering publicity for his legislative attempts to pass the Orwellian misnamed "Academic Bill of Rights." He has national influence as well; Karl Rove and Congressman Tom DeLay helped to distribute copies of Horowitz's political primer *The Art of Political War: How Republicans Can Fight to Win* (Horowitz's, 1999) to all Republican members of Congress (Jones, 2006). Rove has referred to Horowitz's pamphlet as "a perfect pocket guide to winning on the political battlefield."

Horowitz's representation of Left intellectuals as "dangerous" provokes movement toward the symbolic kill described by Burke. In this way, the concepts of "danger" and "threat" are the master frames of this discourse (see Landzelius, 2006). Frames of identification and division extend dialectically between public collective self-definition into the interpersonal repertoires of movement participants in their daily lives (Bormann, 1972). In order to discern the unfolding of these frames, I turn now to an examination of my correspondence, attending first to the ways in which it constructs a foil of the elitist Ivory Tower intellectual.

FOILING "DANGEROUS" INTELLECTUALS: ANALYSIS OF GENDER-NEUTRAL MAIL

In this section, I analyze the first main category of the intimidating private messages I have received, demonstrating how such messages strategically extend the public campaign against public intellectuals into the private realm. The hundreds of messages many critical intellectuals receive causes disruption and inconvenience (by the sheer volume and disturbing character of the mail); in its attempt to provoke insecurity and self-doubt, this form of harassment also cultivates fear of continuing to speak out. Centrally, hate mail *names and pressures* its targets in ways that bring into sharp relief the author's subject position in the process.

Initially, I sorted my 290 messages (of which nearly all are overtly hostile) into "gender-neutral" (without significant reference to sexual acts or the gender or sex of sender or recipient) and "gender-specific" (referencing sex or gender of sender and/or recipient and/or explicitly sexual references) somewhat overlapping categories, and then performed a content analysis of each piece of correspondence looking for themes (e.g., antiacademic and patriotic) and strategies (e.g., invective, satire, and threat). It is worth noting that, with only one or two exceptions, all of the letter writers are (or identify themselves as) men. Of the 290 messages, about 150 were both adversarial in tone and sufficiently developed for more detailed consideration as examples of identity framing by foil. The majority of these (120) were more or less gender-neutral; the 30 examples of gender-specific mail represent a minority of my hostile correspondence.

Gender-neutral examples call into question my intelligence, right to teach, patriotism, and national belonging. In language that could be addressed to either men or women, I have been asked to leave the country. I have been called an anti-Semite and the equivalent of Hitler and Stalin; some writers threaten to take action against me. Close analysis of these texts revealed the foiling strategies of my interlocutors as falling into three broad characterizations of me: as a fraudulent Left intellectual, national traitor, and gender traitor. Against these figures, the writers' identities take shape as those of ordinary people defending the nation and the young against fraudulent, traitorous, and elitist intellectuals.

In accusing scholars of elitism, fraud, and indoctrination, hate-mailers exploit the state of perpetual insecurity and self-doubt common to young scholars. For example, a correspondent in 2007 wrote, "You're an absurd, fucking fraud! You'd starve in the real world, which is why you've fled to the comfort of a college campus."[8] Often, Horowitz, Ingraham, Ann Coulter, and other conservative voices on the air and on the Internet deride academics as unqualified, out of touch with reality, hypocritical, opportunistic, and threatening to students' free thought and expression. For example, in a July 9, 2002 online column on (Horowitz's) FrontPageMag.com, Tammy Bruce charged me with hypocrisy, intellectual dishonesty, incompetence, and membership in a latté-sipping "Academic Elite" out of touch with the sentiments of the honest, hardworking, patriotic, and grateful public at large. Her derision echoes throughout the

subsequent letters from her readers. For any critical professor who ever feared not reaching "real people" with their work, this is a stinging rebuke.

There is a powerful populist appeal in this discourse. As Laclau (2007) has argued, movement leaders may crystallize the desires and ambitions of ordinary people and focus them on a scapegoat. In the context of economic crisis, increasing representation in the workforce of women, minorities, and immigrants, heightened nationalism, and the decline of traditional class-based forms of organizing, these appeals offer attractive scapegoats for working class anxieties (see Fine et al., 1997; Turl, 2008). Bruce's (2002) caricature taps into and focuses these anxieties, coaching her audience to jab at the qualifications and probe the insecurities of faculty members, especially women and persons of color in what is often a racist and sexist institutional environment. In contrast to the "academic pretender," the foiling discourse here positions Bruce, her colleagues, and her readers as "real people" with "common sense."

Some writers escalate this argument by advancing actual threats to my employment. For example, in a letter threatening to petition his church members, the University of Texas Chancellor, and Board of Regents against my continued employment, Gabriel wrote, "Laura made you sound stupid this morning. I would say you need to go back to school and get a bit more 'edumicated' before tangling with a woman like her" (March 9, 2007). In equally threatening manner, a retired infantry colonel wrote (to my Dean):

> Just from a communications standpoint, Dana Cloud was crushed by Laura. For someone who is in a Department of Communication, she was a failure in the debate . . . I would hope you will take the same approach to removing her as did the University of Colorado when they removed the tenured Prof Churchill. Just because Cloud is tenured, does not mean that she cannot be removed. Do it!!! (March 7, 2007).

Dan, in a March 29, 2007 letter, crowed that I had been thoroughly rebutted on the radio, adding pointedly, "Let's just say it was quite surprising that someone who teaches courses on 'persuasion' was so unpersuasive in responses. Maybe you should add a course in 'how to dodge even the most straightforward questions'." In the same vein, Lance (March 6, 2007) wrote,

> Hey there, Dana, heard you on the Laura Ingram program, gotta say, you have guts to go against her . . . Although you lost. . . . Face it . . . Laura Ingram buried you! What were you thinking? It sounded like you were dodging all the questions she was asking you, which doesn't surprise me as all of 'you people' dodge questions. . . .

This writer begins his letter with an act of symbolic demotion, referring to me familiarly by my first name, then crows about Ingraham and Horowitz's success in stumping me with an unanswerable question. Interestingly, his letter also uses the language of "dodging questions," as do many others, again suggesting that listeners to conservative radio take cues from hosts regarding the best ways to ridicule Ph.Ds.

The strain of populist anti-intellectualism in my mail is prominent, but contradictory when correspondents go out of their way not only to impugn *my* intellect but also to demonstrate their own alleged erudition. Indeed, a number of the critiques of the "Ivory Tower" are quite eloquent and witty. Vrooman (2007) notes that some rants "make high art of hostility" (p. 55), creating witty and curmudgeonly political, and pedantic personae (see Carroll, 1979). For example, Lawrence (July 2, 2002), wrote that I myself must be a parody, for I was "such an egregious jackass" to actually exist; he concludes that I must be "the Jonathan Swift for our age." Thus, against my position as a fraudulent intellectual, the author emerges from the foiling process as a lay intellectual with a rapier wit.

Writers comparing me to Hitler, Stalin, or other totalitarians also made use of the parodic style: "Dear Comrade in Arms, I admire and respect your use of intolerance in the name of tolerance. . . . I could have used people like you. Sincerely, Adolf" (Don, March 6, 2007). Of course, the point of such satire is that the writer is *not* like me, or more accurately, like the persona he has constructed of me. Rather, using me as a foil, writers in this vein establish themselves

as ordinary intellectuals: sharp-witted but uncorrupted by the elitism and arcane discourses of the academy, which are identified as the source of my foolishness. My persona emerges as one that is ridiculous rather than threatening.

Other messages, however, construct me as an earnest threat to students. Typical was that of N.: "I hate that you and your like are indoctrinating young minds at OUR universities and getting subsidized with OUR tax dollars" (July 3, 2002). In the few instances where I have responded to challenges to the accuracy of my evidence, I have received long rants in reply. The identities of the letter writers emerge by contrast: If I am an elitist, intellectual fraud engaged in the indoctrination of youth, then the letter writers appear as the grassroots guardians and protectors of youth from the "leftist animal" (as one letter put it) and its ideology of treason. That I am an outspoken woman compounds the offense, arranging womanhood, incompetence, and treason as the foils, and producing authors characterized by masculinity, judgment, and fidelity.

SLEEPING WITH THE ENEMY: GENDER, SEX, AND TREASON

The explicitly gendered and sexualized letters are fewer in number than the anti-intellectual letters. However, I remember these with striking clarity. They deployed fear, shame, and disgust in ways that resonate with my, and perhaps many women's, experiences of sexism, abuse, and gender-related trauma of various kinds. More than any others, these letters were invasions of my private space and self. They also demonstrate that to be a woman critical of the nation is to be both a bad woman and a bad citizen.

The gender-specific mail equates *woman* with *traitor* or *alien/enemy*: "Face it, Dana, you are anti-American," wrote Lance (March 6, 2007), who continues,

> My suggestion for you . . . . Move to another country, maybe England . . . Or better yet the middle east where as a woman, you will be treated like a dog! Sound fun?

Another writer offered to buy me an airline ticket and $500,000 if I would renounce my U.S. citizenship "and promise never to come back to

America. She doesn't need you anymore. You sleep with her enemy" (March 6, 2007).

Ironically, the phrase "sleeping with the enemy" echoes feminists of the late 1960s, some of whom found sleeping with men incongruent with the radical critique of the sex/gender system. Interestingly, the description of treason as "sleeping with *her* enemy" underscores how criticizing the nation violates the norms of womanhood. Female dissenters are treated and represented differently both in public life and private correspondence than male dissenters because of the complex interconnections among gender ideology, national identity, the division of labor, and justifications for war in the modern nation state. In prerevolutionary America, the ideology of republican motherhood "attempted to integrate domesticity and politics" (Kerber, 1976, p. 203). "Republican motherhood preserved traditional gender roles at the same time that it carved out a new, political role for women" (Zagarri, 1992, p. 192). Grayzel et al. (1999) explain that nationalist discourses figure national geography in terms of the virginal or maternal body, represent the ideal woman as one dedicated to national service and sacrifice, and render women's capacity to respond to war in almost exclusively emotional terms (see also Gould, 2008; Hansen, 2001; Kaplan, Alarcon, & Moallem, 1999; Ranchod-Nisson, 2000; Rose & Hatfield, 2007; Stoler-Liss, 2003; Werbner & Yuval Davis, 1999; Yuval Davis, 1997).

In summary, national identity is often articulated through gender. McClintock (1997) explains that nationalism constitutes identities in social conflicts that are always gendered; thus, national power "depends on the prior construction of *gender* difference" (p. 89). McClintock's analysis helps to explain how it becomes paradoxical and dissonant (for an audience of conservatives) in this frame for "actual" women to mount a critique of nationalism and imperialism, or for any assertive and effective critic of nationalism and war to be, in fact, a woman. A "good" woman defends the nation and reproduces and nurtures its warriors and workers. As a result, women who speak out against nationalism and war pose a dual threat to conventional gender roles and the sanctity of the nation state—and to the potent amalgam that works to secure allegiance to both regimes. In the context of

this literature, outspoken women who also reject standard definitions of heterosexual womanhood are doubly traitors to the national order.

A 2002 example exemplifies these interconnections:

> You are a scary woman. Scary in the sense that you might reach one student with pro terrorist and communist leanings. A heads up to you, comrade, liberalism and communism died on 9/11. Your email was posted on a very popular website; expect major backlash over your manifesto of America hatred. If you hate America so much, why not move to Indonesia, Palestine or one of the other countries you listed? It would be a good first start, covering your face with a burka. You should be ashamed of yourself. (signed) Patrick: Pro-God, pro family, pro America, and anti communist/terrorist/islam. (July 5, 2002)

This writer explicitly identifies himself by foiling me when he signs off; in contrast with him I am anti-God, antifamily, anti-American, procommunist, and proterrorist. This example figures the female critic of the American nation as "scary" and then aligns the critic with "Third World" nationalism, as if the only way a woman could critique one nation is to become conventionally feminine and obedient to the norms of another country. Thus, the theme of treason intersects vulgar gendered and sexualized language as if for me to criticize the nation is to violate the norms of womanhood is to become monstrous: a "scary woman."

A second characteristic of the gender-specific mail is the labeling of queer gender identity and/or sexual orientation as threatening, deviant, and disgusting. A letter that opens, "Dear Butch" (2002), combines gender-neutral themes with heavily gendered attacks. The letter reads: "I feel sorry for you. What a warped view of things you have. But I'm sure you think you are 'enlightened.' If you hate America so much, hike up your skirts and head for the border." Here, "Butch" is clearly an insult. The command to "hike up my skirts" is contradictory in this note, at odds with defining me as a "butch," a category of lesbians rarely found in skirts. However, hiking up one's skirts puts one in a position of sexual vulnerability; the image is an attempt at symbolic diminishing through the invocation of the feminine, when all of the other terms in the letter are blunt and, contrary to the author's statement that he felt sorry for me, agentive ("go," "head," "start," "marxist," "atheist," "lesbo-feminist," and "commune"). Such exclusionary discourse symbolically expels bad women/critics from the national fold. The identity of the conservative writer then emerges as the counterpart to the dangerous, deviant, improper, alien woman. The letter-writer's masculinity is defined in extreme opposition to the transgressive feminine, again demonstrating the workings of the foil. He is the icon of agentive personhood and arbiter of gender norms and relations.

The third category of gendered hate mail features expressions of pity and prayer for my mental and spiritual health. As Ehrenreich and English (1978) have argued, advice giving to women primarily by men has always been a gendered form of social discipline from the fields of psychiatry to self-help literature. Foucault (1988) likewise describes the history of madness as a social construct that defines disruptive subjects in manageable ways. Similarly, Cloud (1998) calls attention to how the language of healing dislocates political response into the intimate realm. In this context, to say (even sincerely), "I feel sorry for you," "you need help," or "I will pray for you" is an exertion of power over the pitiful. I received several letters in which writers, ostensibly perplexed by my attitudes and behavior, have concluded that I am mentally ill or bereft in my godlessness. In addition, these letters often mentioned concern for my daughter. For example, Kathy (July 1, 2002) told me that it was "very sad that you don't know God, but what's even sadder is that you aren't allowing your daughter to know God. My prayers are with you and your daughter." The mention of my family in such letters suggests that the category of republican womanhood is operative in defining the identity of conservative women like Kathy; she expects me to limit my influence to the spiritual education of my daughter. By addressing me from the stance of a Godly woman, Kathy foils me as adopting a public persona too far removed from the republican vision of influence through maternal care.

A more hostile letter stated, "I pledge to pray for your poor daughter. How sad it must be to live with such an angry, confused person" (Robert, July 2, 2002). "What is your major malfunction lady?" begins another of my letters. "Where does your bitterness come from?" (Jon, July 5, 2002).

C. (March 6, 2007) also believes that my problem is emotional, a diagnosis somehow extrapolated from my photograph:

> I have come to the conclusion (especially after looking at your picture on the U of T web site) that only someone who was deeply hurt or humiliated (probably early in life) could be bitter towards the country and society that gave you so much. The truth is I am sorry for you. I will pray that your eyes will be opened to the displaced anger or hurt that resides inside you.

This passage is a gendered and paternalistic insult that dismisses bitterness toward one's country as a product of pathology. For those conservatives who experience cognitive dissonance (see Festinger, 1957; Cooper, 2004) when an educated person makes arguments that are significantly contradictory to their beliefs, it is important to frame their criticism of the United States as something other than a rational, evidence-driven discourse. If an argument constitutes the rantings of a "bitter," "hurt," "angry," or "confused" person, the political threat of a contrary point of view is neutralized in a clear example of denigration of the source of unwelcome information. Beyond serving this dissonance-relieving function, the pathologizing discourse foils me as irrational, not only to discredit my point of view but also to give shape to the writer's own identity as a rational citizen.

A fourth suggestion of the gendered e-mails is that a proper woman should discipline her public voice and behavior as well as her private behavior and appearance. I believe that condemnation of indecorum is strongly gendered. The best example from my correspondence of this tendency came from a woman, Wendy (March 6, 2007): "I think it is rude and crude to demonstrate when someone is trying to give 'another opinion' on campus. Shame on you . . . . Where are your manners?" For men, it is less of an offense to engage in public demonstration of outrage (even belligerence) than it is for women. It is difficult to imagine a letter addressed to an adult male asking him, "Where are your manners?" Here, the foil is clear: That I lack propriety positions this writer as the arbiter of appropriate gender performance.

The fifth category of gendered mail is composed of dehumanizing messages, which include pronounced appearance-oriented and otherwise aggressive and dehumanizing insults. For example, Peter wrote,

> Hello you disgusting pig . . . I feel bad for you that you are such an angry and hateful person, your ugly daughter will end up failing in life like you. . . . How vapid you are to even have a web page, do you really think anybody cares if you live or die outside of your ugly kids and dogs. . . . Lots of love you piece of garbage. God bless. (July 8, 2002)

Another letter called me pathetic, and "an incomprehensible human being" (Frank, date unavailable). To be incomprehensible is to be alien, something less than fully human. Disgusted correspondence also attempts to dehumanize its target by calling them garbage and animals, especially pigs. However, the logic of the foil would suggest that if I am ugly, the author is good-looking, which does not seem to be the point at all. Rather, I believe that this category establishes its target as monstrous, rendering the letter author as a human pitted against an inhuman enemy, thus warranting violence against the monstrous.[9] Attacks on personal appearance and sexual orientation are also particularly gendered, given the ways in which U.S. culture encourages women to discipline their hair, faces, and bodies in accordance with stringent norms, cultivating a sense of inadequacy and insecurity around these issues that men do not share (Wolff, 2002). That Peter's letter mentions my family life makes this insulting in private, invasive terms. Calling my daughter ugly extends the violation of the personal address into domestic space in a very concrete way and invokes my subversion of the role of the republican mother in both ideology and identity.

Thus, the sixth and threatening gendered mail category deployed accusations of child abuse—both sexual and ideological. The most pronounced example of this is from S., who wrote, "You're a sexual deviant with a daughter?!! You should be arrested for child abuse!" (March 6, 2007). On the ideological side, Tim wrote, "I ache for your daughter; what life she has in store after years of being spoon fed your distorted, relativist, socialist rhetoric" (July 8, 2002). These writers constitute their identities in relief from mine; if I am a deviant, indoctrinating pedophile (equated with any minority sexuality), they are "normal" people who guard their children from malign influences. Ironically, they insist on their point of view while criticizing my alleged attempts to indoctrinate others. Conservatism is regarded as extraideological in all of this discourse.

The ultimate message of a series of letters in which mostly male authors presume to dehumanize and discipline women in both political and sexual contexts is one that warrants violence. Violence is a sanctioned dimension of hegemonic masculinity in U.S. culture (see Fine et al., 1997); the logical culmination of the adversarial framing strategies in these letters is to mark women like me as violations of the natural order, and such violations may be punished. If outspoken, critical women are the targets of this mail, then its authors become its very masculine weapons, wielding sexual violation as the ultimate correction to female insurrection. Thus, the letter from "Albert" (March 7, 2007) quoted in my epigraph suggests that raping a lesbian (advising her to "get laid with a good wholesome thick cock") will both restore her to her proper place in the arrangement between the sexes *and* cure her of her deviant beliefs. The mechanism of foiling reaches its ultimate expression in the logic of the kill, when, in opposition to the target as inhuman and deviant, the authors become the symbolic weapon launched from afar by neoconservative culture warriors.

My outspoken criticism of U.S. wars abroad has been met with a number of sexualized bodily threats. After asking, "Want to see how they treat women over in those countries?" L. appended a URL for a news story about women being gang raped in Pakistan. (An irony of his letter is that his support for war is based on condemnation of the practices of Muslims, yet he would relish the sort of punishment such a regime might levy against someone like me.) K. wrote in a March 18, 2008, obscene, personal, and political rant that he was glad that "it is dangerous for you to speak . . . you love immigrants from the third worlds GO FUCKING LIVE WITH THEM, YOU DUMBASS CUNT DRINK THE WATER" (March 18, 2008).

Ominously, Abu warned me, "My own allegiance is to those who are brave enough to deal with the likes of you, in ways that you richly deserve. Fortunately, they are coming. Look into the camera and say after me: 'I am an academic.' My mother was an academic . . . We are truly the daughters of hate" (July 5, 2002). Strangely, this writer invokes my maternal line as parallel to my academic hubris and my belief system, suggesting that the danger I represent is characteristic of all women and passed down from generation to generation, perhaps since Eve. As Kenneth Burke pointed out, the unchecked impulse to define oneself by purging what one is not—or, as argued in the present article, foiling them—escalates to the contest between absolutes: good and evil, human and inhuman, male and female.

The patterns in my mail reveal how, in the minds and psyches of some conservatives, to be a female critic of the nation is to be doubly traitorous. The line between sexual deviance and ideological treason is very blurry in the letters I have examined, so that the denigration of my gender, my sexuality, my body, my family, and my psyche become interchangeable with condemnation of my beliefs. Because I am a woman, to discipline my appearance and behavior are necessary correlatives of falling into line ideologically.

I believe that the impact of such mail on its female recipients—who may have internalized gender-based insecurity about professional qualifications and physical appearance, and who may have real reason to fear workplace discrimination or physical/sexual assault—is compounded in ways that my male colleagues do not experience. One of these colleagues once advised me to ignore my hate mail, saying that he never gave a thought to his own. I found myself starkly reminded that (generally) men and women, by virtue of living in sexist society, experience the world very differently from one another.

From my standpoint, not only could I *not* avoid my e-mail, it was also *very important* to attend to it as a person, a citizen, a woman, an activist, and an intellectual. Such messages address their target not as a political antagonist in an ideological conflict but rather as a private person in an intimate domain. The privacy of the inbox shields these writers from public view and broader accountability. Although I would not equate symbolic violation or the threat of sexual assault with physical sexual assault itself, both threat and act depend on the shield of intimacy. When one strips the shield away, the power of private intimidation is lessened.

FOILING INTIMIDATION IN THE PUBLIC SPHERE

Cho (2005) describes what happened when she posted her hate mail on her website, including senders' e-mail addresses and names: After receiving hundreds of messages from Cho's supporters, the senders began to apologize to her.

> I was getting apology emails flooding in so fast, I couldn't believe it. (In whining voice): "I'm sorry I called you a gook chink cunt. I didn't mean it. I'm very sorry. Now please make these gay people leave me alone!"

Like Cho, I too realized that I had a great deal of support, and I began sharing my hate mail in public forums, including my blog. Turning the tables on cyberintimidators and bringing their violations into the light of day has had some unforeseen consequences. Most importantly, many chagrined writers backpedaled on their original positions and/or apologized for the tone of their letters. With two, I engaged in productive, civil correspondence. One is Don, who over the course of three e-mail exchanges, went from comparing me to Hitler to appreciating my point of view and wishing me luck. Similarly, Greg (March 27, 2007) had warned me that I should take the "new McCarthyism" very seriously. On my blog, I posted the complete version of this e-mail under the title "Horowitz minion admits to being a new McCarthyist." After two more exchanges, I received something like an apology:

> Admitting fault is a huge soul reliever. Trust me, I admit fault quite frequently . . . I won't postulate that you and I can ever see eye to eye but perhaps we can learn from each other. You are obviously an intelligent individual . . . Let's keep these lines open.

I found these conversations to be remarkable "teaching moments," examples of what I call "the pedagogy of accountability." When people's words are dragged into the light of day, those persons become accountable to a larger community. In spite of the conservatism of commercial mass media and the paucity of real public debate in our society (see Calhoun, 1993; Habermas, 1988; Warner, 2005/2001) one can, if only in a minority of cases, shift personal attacks that attempt to locate power in the intimate realm to a humanizing arena of public dialogue and accountability. Such dialogue is evidence for the possibility of solidarity with fellow citizens whose ideas are necessarily influenced by the partisan rhetorical resources available to explain their uneasiness with the state of the world.

These exchanges show that women assailed in private regarding public matters can reverse the vector of that relationship by going public with their hate mail. It bears saying, however, that this transformation is not the product of reasoned dialogue alone. The pedagogy of public accountability is also the pedagogy of public shaming. My correspondents were deeply embarrassed to find words that they had assumed to be private on public display. Shame can be a powerful motivator, and in deploying it I forced these writers to become accountable to an imagined community of civilized people. In Butler's (1997) terms, publicity brings the authors-as-agents into relief as part and parcel of a broader sociopolitical context and its relations of power.

The discovery that publicity can be disarming in a culture war may bear upon how we act in public and teach in the traditional classroom. The demands for transparency and accountability are fundamental to the causes of justice and freedom.

Asking students to "own up" to the implications of their own common sense in a dialogic process may cultivate democratic habits out of the muck of racism, sexism, nationalism, and homophobia.

Conclusion: Foiling the Foils, or, toward Solidaristic Dialogue

I have argued in this essay that conservative hate mail, particularly that aimed at transgressive women, articulates the identities of its authors against the foils, or constructed personae, of their targets. The mail renders me and other outspoken women as fraudulent, treasonous, and deviant threats to not only the conservative ideology and war efforts, but also to the very self-concept of those efforts' defenders. Defined in contrast to the dangerous intellectual woman, the authors of my hate mail stand as righteous representatives of the "people" and the arbiters of acceptable masculine and feminine roles and behavior.

My analysis has established the workings of the strategy of identity framing by foil, or foiling. From my analysis we can draw out some of the characteristics of this strategy: First, it is closely tied to naming; the ability to name one's enemy in political or scatological terms (fraud, traitor, and cunt) focuses self-definition acutely. Second, identity framing by foil applies tremendous pressure to the target through the identification and invocation of psychological, economic, and physical vulnerabilities: self-doubt, internalized oppression, fear of job loss, loss of children, and sexual assault. These vulnerabilities are amplified by the intimate medium of address, in which the writers employ the resources of tone (parodic, belligerent, threatening) and verbal aggression (insult and rant). Third, in the process of establishing the shape of the foil, the rhetor brings him/herself into sharp relief as the antitarget, in other words, as the weapon. This strategy enacts what Burke identified as "the kill": the definition of self through the total symbolic purgation and/or negation of another.

Finally, although messages are individually authored, they are generated out of an organized political antagonism. That is, Tammy Bruce knows she is arming her readers with the language of anti-intellectualism and patriotism, and misogyny is unfortunately a deep cultural well. Both the political language of mediated conservative ideology and the reservoir of culturally available identities and attitudes are resources for the individual author. Conservatives like Horowitz and Ingraham attempt to put adversarial, irrational demagoguery in place of a real public sphere. As Brock (2004) explains, from their posts behind keyboards and microphones, they marshal spokespersons for impoverished—but effective—ways of talking and thinking about the clash of ideas in U.S. culture.

Further research could explore how the strategy of foiling might be discovered at work in other social movement and political discourse, from Presidential campaign advertising to military training documents, from the anticorporate rhetoric of radical environmentalism to the union steward's flyer distributed on the shop floor, from the racial exclusionism of far-right discourse to the class antagonism articulated by those on the left, from the pulpits of the Baptists to the mosques of ordinary Muslims, or from the family member of a murder victim to the family member of the criminal awaiting execution. In such contexts, an examination of the texts' strategies of naming, pressure, identification of the foil, and establishment of the self in relief may produce new insights about the rhetorical production of identity frames.

But are all identity frames and their corresponding foils equally fictive, or are some more faithful to existing social relations than others? Employers and agents of the state (and of their attendant ideologies) do actually threaten and constrain the life chances of many ordinary people around the world. Movements casting oppressive persons and exploitative institutions as foils, then, would find some warrant in the correspondence of the frame to power relations in the material world. In contrast, pointing out when a foiling frame is unwarranted (i.e., when there is no relation of actual enmity or material antagonism) may promote solidarity among people previously at odds.

This solidarity depends upon recognizing that many of my vitriolic correspondents may not even be hardened culture warriors. There can be productive dialogue across ideological positions

about what makes a good society. Shifting perspective from the personal to the political—from the interpersonal to the movement and from the self to the society—is a source of agency for the isolated targets of identity framing by foil and for critics working to understand how ideological and political commitments grip us bodily and emotionally, pressing us one against the other in someone else's fight.

Notes

1 Please go to https://webspace.utexas.edu/clouddl/ CloudHateMailTables.doc for a holistic summary in tabular form of all of my hate mail.
2 All spelling, grammar, and punctuation errors are original to the emails from which I quote.
3 Space prohibits a complete discussion of the particularities of electronic mail. Some authors argue that the medium influences the content and impact of hate mail directed at women (see Herring, 2008; Kelley & Savicki, 2000; McGarty & Douglas, 2001; Miller & Durndell, 2004; Monberg, 2005; Morahan-Martin, 2004; Vrooman 2001, 2007).
4 Hits on my blog (withheld) also indicate a pattern of responsiveness to my public activity. Visits peaked on August 30, 2007, in the wake of the letter to the editor against the Israeli invasion of Lebanon. As an example of conservative discussion of my activities, see the FreeRepublic.com thread about my revised pledge of allegiance: http://www .freerepublic.com/focus/f-news/714618/posts.
5 On the culture war as a strategy of the neoconservative movement, see Dunn & Woodard (1991, p. 6); Bloom (1987).
6 Numbers of other scholars on Horowitz's list received hate mail after such appearances in conservative media. Querying them, I found that frequency and intensity of hate mail depended, with some exceptions, on various factors including overt opposition to Horowitz's efforts, criticism of Israel, minority race or sexuality, and espousal of militant tactics and revolutionary ideologies.
7 Suggesting the circulation of a form letter, other professors also received letters beginning with the word "Wow," and containing the epithet "liberal jackass."
8 Unfortunately, despite repeated queries to Ingraham's producers, I have been unable to acquire a recording of the program on which I appeared.
9 In rhetorical, film, and media studies, the category of the monstrous includes characters whose

nature runs against conventional expectations or who embody deep contradictions in popular consciousness from school shooters to lesbian mothers (see Creed, 1993; Gil, 2002; Goc, 2007; Gubrium, 2008; Hoerl, 2002; Wall, 1997; Williams, 1992). Such narratives render those cast as monsters as deserving of death.

References

Adams, M. (2006, August 16). Professors against Israel. *FrontPageMag.com.* Retrieved October 17, 2008, from http://www.frontpagemag.com/Articles/Read.aspx?GUID=A5DD82DA-83B2-421C-BA36-1B4391EDC2F2.

Adams, J., & Roscigno, V. J. (2005). White Supremacists, oppositional culture, and the World Wide Web. *Social Forces, 84,* 759–778.

Benford, R. D., & Snow, D. A. (2000). Framing processes and social movements: An overview and assessment. *Annual Review of Sociology, 26,* 611–639.

Bloom, A. (1987). *The closing of the American mind.* New York: Simon & Schuster.

Boot, M. (2004). Myths about neoconservatism. In I. Stelzer (Ed.), *The neoconservative reader* (pp. 43–51). New York: Grove.

Bormann, E. (1972). Fantasy and rhetorical vision: The rhetorical construction of reality. *Quarterly Journal of Speech, 26,* 396–408.

Brock, D. (2004). *The republican noise machine.* New York: Random House.

Bruce, T. (2002, July 9). A scrap of cloth. *FrontPageMag.com.* Retrieved April 10, 2008, from http://www.frontpagemag.com/Articles/Read.aspx?GUID=9F7B510E-F1E6-4657-878F3E896C3114A2.

Burke, K. (1969). *Rhetoric of motives.* Berkeley: University of California Press.

Butler, J. (1997). *Excitable speech.* London: Routledge.

Calhoun, C. T. (Ed.). (1993). *Habermas and the public sphere.* Cambridge, MA: MIT Press.

Carroll, D. (1979). *Dear sir, drop dead! Hate mail through the ages.* New York: Collier.

Cho, M. (Speaker). (2005). Hate mail from Bush supporters. *Assassin* [CD]. Nettwerk American.

Cloud, D. L. (1998). *Control and consolation in American culture and politics: Rhetorics of therapy.* Thousand Oaks, CA: Sage.

Cooper, J. (2004). *Cognitive dissonance: 50 years of a classic theory.* London, New York: Sage.

Creed, B. (1993). *The monstrous-feminine: Film, feminism, and psychoanalysis.* London, New York: Routledge.

DeC. (2004, January 15). The Cho Hate mail archive project. Retrieved April 15, 2008, from http://www.americanpolitics.com/20040114CroMag.html.

Denzin, N. (2000). Aesthetics and practices of qualitative inquiry. *Qualitative Inquiry, 6,* 256–265.

DiscovertheNetworks.org. (2006). Retrieved May 28, 2008, from http://www.discoverthenetworks.org.

Dunn, C. W., & Woodard, J. D. (1991). *American conservatism from Burke to Bush.* Lanham: Madison Books.

Ehrenreich, B., & English, D. (1978). *For her own good: 150 years of the experts' advice to women.* New York: Anchor-Doubleday.

Festinger, L. (1957). *A theory of cognitive dissonance.* Los Angeles: Stanford University Press.

Fine, M., Weis, L., Addleston, J., Carlson, D., & Apple, M. (1997). (In)secure times: Constructing white working-class masculinities in the late 20th century. *Gender & Society, 11,* 52–68.

"Foil." (2008, June 5). *Oxford English Dictionary Online.*

Foucault, M. (1988). *Madness and civilization.* New York: Vintage (Original work published 1965).

Friedman, J. (2007, Summer). Blogging while female. *Bitch,* (36), 17.

Gamson, W. A. (1992). The social psychology of collective action. In A. D. Morris, & C. McClurg (Eds.), *Frontiers in social movement theory* (pp. 53–76). Ithaca: Yale University Press.

Gil, P. (2002). The monstrous years: Teens, slasher films, and the family. *Journal of Film and Video, 54,* 16–30.

Goc, N. (2007). "Monstrous mothers" and the media. In N. Scott (Ed.), *Monsters and the monstrous: Myths and metaphors of enduring evil* (pp. 149–165). Amsterdam, Netherlands: Rodopi.

Gottfried, P. (1993). *The conservative movement.* New York: Twayne.

Gould, P. (2007). Civil society and the public woman. *Journal of the Early Republic, 28,* 29–46.

Grayzel, S. R., Keene, J. D., Schultheiss, K., Cooper, S. E., Jacobs, E., Doan, L., et al. (1999). *Women's identities at war: Gender, motherhood, and politics in Britain and France during the First World War.* Chapel Hill: University of North Carolina Press.

Gubrium, A. (2008). Writing against the image of the monstrous crack mother. *Journal of Contemporary Ethnography, 37,* 511–527.

Habermas, J. (1988). *Structural transformation of the public sphere.* Cambridge, MA: MIT Press.

Hanisch, C. (2006). The personal is political. In S. Barnes, J. Ezekiel, & S. Gilmore (Eds.), *Women and social movements in the United States: The second wave and beyond.* Retrieved May 2, 2008, from

http://scholar.alexanderstret.com/pages/viewpage
.action?pageId=2259 (Work originally published
1970).

Hansen, L. (2001). Gender, nation, rape: Bosnia and
the construction of security. *International Feminist
Journal of Politics, 3*, 55–75.

Hanson, C. (2002, May/June). Women warriors: How
the press has helped and hurt in the battle for
equality. *CJR: Columbia Journalism Review*, 46–49.

"Hate Mail for Nurse Insisting on Respect." (2008,
January 30). *Nursing Standard, 22*(21), 5.

Herring, S. C. (2008, January). The rhetorical
dynamics of gender harassment online. *Nursing
Standard, 22*(21), 5.

Hoerl, K. (2002). Monstrous youth in suburbia:
Disruption and recovery of the American Dream.
Southern Communication Journal, 67, 259–276.

Holman Jones, S. (2005). Autoethnography: Making
the personal political. In N. K. Denzin, & Y. S.
Lincoln (Eds.), *The Sage handbook of qualitative
research* (pp. 763–792). London: Sage.

Horowitz, D. (1999). *The art of political war: How
Republicans can fight to win.* Washington, DC:
Committee for a Non-Left Majority.

Horowitz, D. (2006). *The professors: The 101 most
dangerous academics in America.* Washington, DC:
Regnery (Original work published 2006).

Horowitz, D. (2007). *Indoctrination U.* New York:
Encounter Books.

Hunt, S. A., Benford, R., & Snow, D. A. (1994).
Identity fields: Framing processes and the social
construction of movement identities. In E. Laraña,
H. Johnston, & J. R. Gusfield (Eds.), *New social
movements* (pp. 185–208). Philadelphia: Temple
University Press.

Jaschik, S. (2008, February 19). Communicating about
David Horowitz. *Inside Higher Ed.* Retrieved
April 10, 2008, from http://insidehighered.com/
news/2008/02/19/horowitz.

Jones, A. (2006, June 16). Connecting the dots. *Inside
Higher Ed.* Retrieved April 10, 2008, from http://
www.insidehighered.com/views/2006/06/16/jones.

Kaplan, C., Alarcon, N., & Moallem, M. (Eds.).
(1999). *Between woman and nation: Nationalisms,
transnational feminisms, and the state.* Durham:
Duke University Press.

Kelley, M., & Savicki, V. (2000). Computer mediated
communication: Gender and group composition.
CyberPsychology and Behavior, 3, 817–826.

Kerber, L. (1976). The republican mother. *American
Quarterly, 28*, 187–205.

Kirkpatrick, J. (2004). Neoconservatism as a response
to the counterculture. In I. Stelzer (Ed.), *The
neoconservative reader* (pp. 213–232). New York:
Grove.

Kristol, I. (2004). The neoconservative persuasion. In
I. Stelzer (Ed.), *The neoconservative reader*
(pp. 31–38). New York: Grove.

Laclau, E. (2007). *On populist reason.* London: Verso.

Landzelius, M. (2006). "Homo Sacer" out of left
field: Communist 'slime' as bare life in 1930s
and Second World War Sweden. *Human
Geography* (Geografiska Annaler Series B ser.),
88, 453–475.

Lillian, D. L. (2007). A thorn by any other name:
Sexist discourse as hate speech. *Discourse and
Society, 18*, 719–740.

McCaffrey, D., & Keys, J. (2000). Competitive
framing processes in the abortion debate:
Polarization-vilification, frame saving, and frame
debunking. *Sociological Quarterly, 41*, 41–62.

McClintock, A. (1997). No longer in a future heaven:
Gender, race, and nationalism. In A. McClintock,
A. Mufti, & E. Shohat (Eds.), *Dangerous liaisons:
Gender, nation, and postcolonial perspectives*
(pp. 89–113). Minneapolis: University of
Minnesota Press.

McClintock, A., Mufti, A., & Shohat, E. (Eds.).
(1997). *Dangerous liaisons: Gender, nation, and
postcolonial perspectives.* Minneapolis: University
of Minnesota Press.

McGarty, C., & Douglas, K. (2001). Identifiability
and self-presentation: Computer-mediated
communication and intergroup interaction. *British
Journal of Social Psychology, 40*, 399–416.

Melucci, A. (1996). *Challenging codes.* Cambridge, UK:
Cambridge University Press.

Miller, J., & Durndell, A. (2004). Gender, language,
and computer-mediated communication. In
K. Morgan, C. A. Brebbia, J. Sanchez, &
A. Voiskounsky (Eds.), *Human perspectives in
the Internet society: Culture, psychology, and gender*
(pp. 235–244). South Hampton, Boston: Wessex
Institute of Technology Press.

Monberg, J. (Ed.). (2005). Trajectories of computer-
mediated communication. *Special issue of Southern
Communication Journal, 70*(3).

Morahan-Martin, J. (2004). Paradoxes on the impact
of the Internet on women. In K. Morgan, C. A.
Brebbia, J. Sanchez, & A. Voiskounsky (Eds.),
*Human perspectives in the Internet society: Culture,
psychology, and gender* (pp. 275–286). South
Hampton, Boston: Wessex Institute of Technology
Press.

Muravchik, J. (2004). The neoconservative cabal. In
I. Stelzer (Ed.), *The neoconservative reader* (pp.
241–258). New York: Grove.

Ranchod-Nelson, S., & Tetreault, M. (Eds.). (2000).
*Women, states, and nationalism: At home in the
nation?* New York: Routledge.

Richardson, B. K., & McGlynn, J. (2007, May 28). Gendered retaliation, irrationality, and structured isolation: Whistle-blowing in the collegiate sports industry as gendered process. Paper presented at the 57th Annual Conference of the International Communication Association, San Francisco, CA. Retrieved 10 April, 2008, from Academic Search Premier database.

Rose, M., & Hatfield, M. O. (2007). Republican motherhood redux?: Women as contingent citizens in 21st century America. *Journal of Women, Politics, and Policy, 29*, 5–30.

Shibutani, T. (1997). On the personification of adversaries. In T. Shibutani (Ed.), *Human nature and collective behavior: Papers in honor of Herbert Blumer.* Englewood Cliffs, NJ: Prentice-Hall.

Snow, D. A., & Benford, R. D. (1988). Ideology, frame resonance, and participant mobilization. In B. Klandermans, H. Kriesi, & S. S. Tarrows (Eds.), *International social movements from structure to action. Comparing social movement research across cultures* (pp. 197–218). Greenwich, CT: JAI Press.

Stelzer, I. (Ed.). (2004). *The neoconservative reader.* New York: Grove.

Stoler-Liss, S. (2003, Fall). Mothers birth the nation: The social construction of Zionist motherhood in wartime in Israeli parents' manuals. *Nashim: A Journal of Jewish Women's Studies and Gender Issues, 6*, 104–118.

Top Talk Radio Audiences. (2008, October). *Talkers Magazine.* Retrieved October 17, 2008, from http://www.talkers.com/main/index.php?option =com_content&task=view&id=17&Itemid=34.

Turl, A. (2008, May 9). The myth of the reactionary working class. *Socialist Worker.* Retrieved July 17, 2008, from http://socialistworker.org/2008/05/09/ myth-reactionary-working-class.

Valentine, G. (1998). "Sticks and stones may break my bones": A geography of personal harassment. *Antipode, 30*(4), 305–332. Retrieved April 10, 2008, from Academic Search Premier database.

Vrooman, S. S. (2001, Spring). Flamethrowers, slashers, and witches: Gendered communication in a virtual community. *Qualitative Research Reports in Communication, 2*, 33–41.

Vrooman, S. S. (2007). The art of invective: Performing identity in cyberspace. *New Media & Society, 4*, 51–70.

Wall, A. (1997, September/October). Monstrous mothers: Media representations of post-menopausal pregnancy. *Afterimage, 25*(2), 14–17.

Wall, S. (2008). Easier said than done: Writing an autoethnography. *International Journal of Qualitative Methods, 7*, 38–52.

Warner, M. (2005). *Publics and counterpublics* (New ed.). New York: Zone Books (Work originally published 2001).

Werbner, P., & Yuval Davis, N. (Eds.) (1999). *Women, citizenship, and difference.* London: Zed Books.

Wilkinson, S. (2004, Winter). Where the girls aren't. *Nieman Reports, 30*.

Williams, T. (1996). *Hearths of darkness: The family in the American horror film.* Madison: Fairleigh-Dickinson.

Yuval Davis, N. (1997). *Gender and nation.* London: Sage.

Zagarri, R. (1992). Morals, manners, and the Republican mother. *American Quarterly, 44*, 192–215.

Zald, M. N. (1996). Culture, ideology, and strategic framing. In D. McAdam, J. D. McCarthy, & M. N. Zald (Eds.), *Comparative perspectives on social movements* (pp. 275–290). Cambridge, UK: Cambridge University Press.

Chapter 6

Tactical Modifications

Movements take place in time. They are not fixed or momentary, but historical processes that must evince signs of change and modification. As circumstances change so too does the rhetoric that responds to and recreates them. The sheer historical sweep of the struggle for racial justice or against sexism and misogyny ensured that significant transformations and unforeseen developments would perforce alter their characteristic rhetorical practices. Early studies suggest that movements unfold in time and may be marked by inception, crisis, and consummation. That view has been seriously challenged in recent years, not least because it presents a rather too tidy schema for such diverse and complicated phenomena. How do we account for the complex contingencies that emerge during the unfolding life of a movement and the various transformations those contingencies elicit?

In the following essays, we see rhetorical critics attempting to account for such transformations. The forces of influence are many: changes in political opportunities or cultural meanings, shifts in international relations, the exhaustion of certain arguments or frames and the need for fresh approaches, the advent of unsuspected but decisive problems, the emergence of a new generation, and other factors alter the course of movement rhetoric in fundamental ways. Again, the lesson is clear: movements are by nature fluid, turning now this way and now that, counting small victories against small losses, adapting, retrenching, and seeking new means to effect their ends. A movement that did not adapt and modify in response to such changes, we may be certain, would not remain a movement for long.

In "The Contemporary American Abortion Controversy: Stages in the Argument" (1984), Celeste Condit Railsback draws our attention away from a focus on movement events and actors by examining language strategies in the abortion controversy across time. Charting abortion arguments through seven successive stages between 1960 and 1980, Railsback identifies key ideological terms— or "ideographs"—as well as strategic patterns and relationships that emerge and change with the debate. This approach emphasizes the "responsive" nature of the evolving positions, rather than treating "the rhetoric of an organization as one static unit." In other words, abortion arguments constitute a "social text," a broad constellation of discourse that is forged by the interaction of movements, countermovements, and the public at large.

In "From 'Gay is Good' to the Scourge of AIDS: The Evolution of Gay Liberation Rhetoric, 1977–1990" (1991), James Darsey also studies a movement's strategic discourses over time, but stresses a different relationship between rhetoric and history. Key to his conceptualization are "catalytic events" that create conditions ripe for certain protest discourse and constrain protest discourse— thus marking the boundaries of "rhetorical eras" within the lifespan of a movement.

The final essay in this chapter, Charles J. Stewart's "The Evolution of a Revolution: Stokely Carmichael and the Rhetoric of Black Power" (1997), explores the emergence of increasingly radical rhetoric within the civil rights movement. Stewart too is interested in the transformations of protest rhetoric over time. Where earlier work focused on *external* factors that influenced strategy modifications, Stewart suggests evolution also occurs as a result of *internal* influences. As a social movement ages, he observes, new generations of activists are born. Younger activists often become disillusioned with the established movement, finding it too slow, too timid, too accommodating. The resulting internal strife these activists create serves a transformative function, "intended to perfect the movement through purges of the movement's failed leadership, organizations, strategies, and principles." Stokely Carmichael's explosive call for black power, Stewart argues, typifies this "evolutionary struggle" within the civil rights movement. Carmichael did not intend to create a new movement, but instead to reconfigure the old movement to meet the urgent demands of its new generation of activists.

The Contemporary American Abortion Controversy: Stages in the Argument
Celeste Condit Railsback

Most Americans are tired of hearing about the painful and apparently irresolvable issue of abortion.[1] They feel that they have heard all the arguments, have seen all the ghastly pictures, and have been offered no happy answers. The current public debate about abortion seems to be stalemated, but this is a relatively recent stage in the controversy. A tracing of arguments about abortion during the crucial decades of the sixties and seventies shows major changes in the public arguments used to discuss the topic.[2] The controversy has evolved through seven identifiable stages, from emotional narrative to squabbling implementation and stalemate.

A close examination of these stages accomplishes several objectives.[3] It helps to explain how and why the current American assessments of abortion have come to be as they are. It also fills research gaps cited by Robert S. Cathcart, James R. Andrews, and Leland Griffin, because it provides a "social movement" study that is detailed, that focuses on language strategies rather than on events and actors, and that takes into account the interaction between "movement" and "counter-movement," rather than viewing a movement in isolation.[4] Finally, the study also provides more general hypotheses about patterns of rhetoric in the process of social change.

PRELUDE— PROFESSIONAL ARGUMENTS

When the argument over abortion became public in the early sixties, it was not the first time. In the 19th century, a similar violent and vigorous argument over abortion had raged.[5] This argument was settled when the various state legislatures outlawed almost all abortions. Gradually, a dominant ideology solidified which held that abortion constituted the taking of human life and was an assault on the primary social values of "family" and "motherhood." As described by Barbara Plant, however, that settlement did not provide a congenial solution for all, and it produced small-scale, but persistent resistance.[6] Advocates in the sixties made little reference to these earlier arguments. Indeed, most of them seemed oblivious to the existence of such argumentation.[7]

Of more direct importance to the eventual formulation of the public argument in the sixties were the abortion arguments in the professional fields that occurred in the fifties.[8] Professionals gave focus to the early public arguments and also recruited abortion reform advocates—many from the ranks of the physicians. Thus, the first stage of the contemporary American abortion controversy was the professional stage.

The professional debate appeared in scholarly forums.[9] The controversy involved psychiatrists, doctors, social workers, population analysts, and lawyers who were faced with ever-increasing tensions because their roles required them to provide assistance of various kinds to women who desired abortions and who often sought illegal abortions.[10] The issues of their arguments were narrow and related primarily to the specific concerns of the various professions. For example, one of the first "solutions" to the abortion "problem" was the decision among physicians to create hospital committees to decide which women could have "legal" abortions. This solution eased only the emotional burden felt by individual physicians.[11] The growing pressures that had led professionals to experience a "problem" with abortion, however, soon led nonprofessionals to similar experiences.[12] Once nonprofessionals became involved, the professionally oriented and limited issues were rapidly found to be inadequate; they did not cover the full range of concerns in vocabulary appropriate to the public.

THE EARLY SIXTIES

Public argument in the early sixties centered on legal reforms and consisted largely of the retelling of the tale of illegal abortion. The second stage of the argument, therefore, was dominated by a narrative form. The tale consisted of powerful descriptions of the traumas many women faced when having illegal abortions. In these mini-dramas, the rhetors described the agents, purposes, scenes, and agencies in "typical" illegal abortions.

The women in these dramatic horror stories were depicted quite sympathetically. For example, Marguerite Clark referred to the "wan nervous girl [who] could see only one way out of her dilemma."[13] Later, Sherri Finkbine, who had unknowingly taken thalidomide and had gone to Sweden to abort a deformed fetus, was portrayed as "a healthy and happily married Arizona woman, mother of four" and host of *Romper Room*.[14]

The reasons cited for these abortions were also dramatic. The women were emotionally ill, they had been raped, they carried deformed fetuses, or they were young girls of fourteen or fifteen who had been seduced by older men (even their fathers) and had been deserted.[15] Even the stories that cited socio-economic reasons portrayed the most drastic possible cases of destitution—women who were "unwilling and unable to face a future with another mouth to feed."[16]

The portrayals of the means used in these illegal abortions were often ghastly. In contrast to references to "safe and simple" legal operations in which the doctor simply "scrapes the products of conception out of the uterus,"[17] the articles graphically detailed the instruments of illegal abortions. One author indicated that the "bizarre items doctors have found include turkey quills, knitting needles, hairpins, rattail combs, plastic bottles and even elastic bandages," as well as "the most favored 'instrument' of the amateur"—"a straightened out wire coat hanger inserted into a catheter" used for a "pack job."[18]

Recountings of these instruments were often accompanied by gory descriptions of the techniques of an entire abortion. One story of a young woman, who had an engineering student abort her, told that

> he bought an ordinary flashlight; removed the batteries and cut the bottom off with a can opener. He used the flashlight as a speculum. . . . through this "speculum" he pushed a catheter into which he had threaded a wire. He then forced air through the contraption, which unknown to him, had penetrated a blood vessel in the girl's womb. An air bubble entered the blood stream and in seconds reached her brain. Today this young woman is totally paralyzed.[19]

Other grisly methods—falling down stairs or injecting caustic soap solutions into the womb—were also frequently described, and the most shocking details possible were included. One such story told of an abortionist who thought he did not have all the fetal matter out and ended up pulling out a woman's intestines.[20] These horrific descriptions of the methods used in illegal abortions added great impact to the emotional rejection of illegal abortion sought by the Pro-reform authors.

As Kenneth Burke has noted, the container and the thing contained must suit each other, and in this case, the arguers generally provided a suitable scene for the grotesque operations.[21] The "back alley" became the common term for the illegal abortion scene, but detailed depictions of dirty kitchens (some even with photographs) or back car seats were also plentiful in this period.[22] In addition, the involvement of the "underworld" was related in stories of women who met strangers on street corners or in front of sleazy hotels, to be blindfolded and driven to temporary, hidden destinations. Direct references to other "rackets," such as prostitution and gambling, were also included.[23]

Restatements of such stories aroused strong emotion, but they did not present a case for the desirability of abortion, only for the undesirability of illegal abortion.[24] Moreover, the audience, as well as many of the advocates themselves, believed that abortion was murder and a challenge both to God and patriarchal authority.[25] Consequently, activists urged only that abortions be permitted in limited and extreme circumstances. When five states modified their laws in the mid-sixties, the reforms reflected these limitations: abortions were legalized in the special cases of rape, incest, fetal deformity, or threat to the pregnant woman's physical or mental health.[26]

Resistance to these changes can be discovered in anti-reform arguments, which were infrequent. In contrast to the Pro-reform argument, which would eventually go through several significant ideographic shifts, the anti-legalization argument remained focused on one ideograph throughout—"life." Pro-life advocates stated simply that abortion was the taking of life, and hence *all* abortions had to remain illegal.[27] Pro-life advocates also argued for positive alternatives to abortion, such as adoptions or more rigid sexual standards.[28] This strategy allowed the dominant ideology to maintain its key values intact, while still responding to the tale of illegal abortion.

Thus, in the early sixties, the argument about abortion did not present a direct challenge to the prevailing beliefs about abortion, family, and motherhood. Instead, through an emotionally powerful narrative, it argued for minor concessions for extreme circumstances. Advocates of the dominant ideology answered that such exceptions could not be made because they would amount to murder. Both sides gained many adherents, but the Pro-reform side gained ground, because, for the first time in roughly a century, legal abortions were sanctioned in situations beyond the protection of the pregnant woman's life.

THE LATE SIXTIES

It was unlikely that the abortion argument would rest at this point, however. Advocates of reform had, intentionally or not, made a forceful emotional claim against the horrors of all illegal abortions.[29] If knitting needles and back alleys were repugnant for "good women with good reasons," they were also gruesome for women with more "selfish" purposes. Moreover, the increased expectations of access to abortions outran the increased availability of abortions. Few additional abortions were performed under the new laws.[30] More central perhaps, the continued repetition of the tale of illegal abortion, and the Pro-life advocates' response to it, put a great deal of pressure on the narrative. If there were contradictions in the ideology and social conditions the tale bridged, the narrative would reveal them. The contradictions disclosed by the tale were many.[31]

The most blatant inconsistencies appear in the depictions of the agents involved—both the women having abortions and the men (frequently) performing the abortions. On the one hand, the women so vividly and fully characterized as aborters were generally young, single "victims." On the other hand, the Pro-reform advocates noted in passing that illegal abortion really affected married women more frequently: "not the wanton teenager . . . not the naive girl in the big city . . . but the young (between 21 and 25 years) married woman is most likely to undergo an abortion," they warned.[32] A Pro-reform article might describe two or three "typical cases" of young victims, often having already declared that such cases were not typical at all.[33]

This contradiction arose because of the need to appeal to two ideological components. In the first instance, the tale worked best to generate sympathy within the "old" ideology if it told of the unfortunates who, through no fault of their own, were forced into an abortion. The entrenched ideology held that the only women who should have sex were those who were married, and if sex in marriage resulted in pregnancy, then every wife would want to carry through that pregnancy to enact or reenact the joys of motherhood.[34] Women were held generally responsible for their pregnancies and only youth, rape, or catastrophe could excuse them.

Despite the rhetorical strength of this tale of illegal abortion, the motivating forces that led to many illegal abortions were quite different—the desire or economic need to control one's family, life style, and status through abortion.[35] Yet, because the women's liberation ideology had not been fully and publicly articulated, there were no salient arguments readily available to express the need or desire for abortion as a demand, and no advocates expressed the political "rights" of women.[36] Therefore, until the late sixties, the reality remained incongruously juxtaposed against the tale built by the arguers.[37]

A contradiction also existed in the descriptions of the abortionists. On the one hand, abortionists were described as "hacks" and "incompetents." They were men who

> lead disorganized lives—numerous divorces, alcoholism, drifting from job to job and place to place. Police sometimes find pornographic literature in their possession. Sometimes abortionists have sexual relations with their patients before aborting them.[38]

However, the reformers emphasized that, in fact, "90% of all the illegal abortions are performed by physicians using sterile procedures."[39] Sympathetic portraits described "a genial, graying family doctor who had served them (the community) for thirty years . . . founder of the Grove Public Library, former city councilman and the PTA's choice for Father of the Year in 1960."[40]

This contradiction arose from two sources. At the surface level, two different arguments for liberalizing abortion laws conflicted. The fear of disease and death from illegal abortion was a major impetus for reform, and painting a dirty and incompetent abortionist was necessary to generate that fear. Simultaneously, however, to placate the reigning ideology, advocates wished to argue that changing abortion laws would not bring about a change in the moral climate, and would not lead to more abortions. Therefore, they argued that legal changes would only legalize existing practices; illegal operations already conducted by physicians would merely become legal.

More importantly, there was a dramatic difference between the types of abortionists available to different classes. Upper middle class women were often able to get safe abortions from competent physicians. They had long been travelling to Cuba, Mexico, and Puerto Rico for abortions that might not have been completely legal, but that were fairly routine.[41] More frequently, perhaps, their close contact with a private physician allowed them to get abortions at home as well. Poorer women turned to the abortionist quack.

Again, however, the ideological structure that would allow the clear expression of this discrepancy was not firmly in place in the early sixties. It was not until the later sixties that the term "discrimination" became general enough to be applied to abortion and the third stage of the argument, the ideographic stage, occurred.

By the late sixties, the Civil Rights movement's key terms—"freedom," "equality" (or "discrimination"), and "rights"—had gained strong salience.[42] The broad exposure and general acceptance of these terms provided a way to explain publicly the contradictions in the tale of illegal abortion.[43] The ideographs sorted out the confusion between tales of married and single women, competent physicians and incompetent hacks, by arguing that illegal abortion resulted from "discrimination." Affluent, married women were able to flaunt the poorly enforced law and gain safe abortions from well-qualified doctors. Their abortions constituted the statistics. The horror stories were created by the poor, single women who received "hatchet jobs" from untrained criminals.[44] The poor were being treated "unequally" and their "rights" violated. The heightened salience of the ideographs thus allowed advocates to do more than lament the sad stories of illegal abortion; the ideographs allowed the expression of a legal and social demand.

This shift from narrative toward ideographic argument also required that a new policy be offered. If existing laws were objectionable because they caused discrimination, the inequity could not be remedied by changes in laws to allow a few of the more pitiable abortions, but only by elimination of the entire discriminatory system. Instead of arguing for reform laws, the new demand was for repeal of virtually all abortion laws.

During the late sixties, arguments about abortion also became tied with another growing "discrimination" issue, that of women's rights in general. If women were "free to choose" not to have children, their lifestyles would be quite different than if their only role was as "mother." Consequently, "control of our own bodies" began, in this period[,] to become a major claim about "rights" in support of legalization of all abortions.[45] This line was not yet firmly instantiated as an ideographic argument for "choice," but clearly the foundations of that claim were laid at this point.

The appearance of this argument was the first major challenge to the dominant ideology. Although the auxiliary ideograph "discrimination" made total legalization of abortion necessary,[46] that argument still worked within the key value terms of the status quo (e.g. "equality"). In contrast, the claim for "control of our own bodies," and the consequent implied repudiation of the role of "motherhood," would, in the seventies, come to represent a major challenge to the dominant ideology, which portrayed woman's highest (and virtually sole) calling as that of bearing children.[47] That break would generate the feminist stage of the argument and result in the key ideograph of the movement—"choice."

One final argument was of major importance in the late sixties—concern about "the unwanted child."[48] Before the 1960's, advocates had used eugenic arguments to condemn abortion. Eugenicists had argued that abortion led to the decrease of the upper classes and the increase of the lower classes.[49] This argument was reversed in a benign form in the "no unwanted children" argument in the later 1960's. Especially in 1967, Pro-reform advocates contended that unwanted children were a serious social problem. They linked unwanted children to delinquency and the cycle of poverty and child abuse. Abortion, they argued, was preferable to bearing a child who would be unwanted, for the sake both of the child and the society.[50]

The late sixties thus saw major shifts from narrative based argument to ideographic argument, from a reform argument to a repeal argument, and from an argument based on the dominant ideology to a feminist argument which would challenge the dominant ideology.

THE EARLY SEVENTIES

Some temporary legislative successes for the advocates of repeal signalled that America at least was tempted by these new arguments to endorse legalized abortion and to accept a more tolerant general understanding of abortion.[51] New York, for example, legalized virtually all abortions in 1970, and the number of abortions performed there sky-rocketed.[52] The success of the reform laws and the resultant demand for repeal, however, were correlated with other changes as well. Reform advocacy was not conducted in a vacuum, and during this period there were major changes in the argument against legalized abortion which were advanced by those who called themselves "Pro-life." Those opposed to liberal abortion laws consistently had argued from the dominant ideology that the fetus must be protected as a human life.[53] In the late sixties they seemed to realize that the ideograph "life" was not protecting the fetus because the public did not unconditionally characterize a fetus as a human life. Then, and increasingly in the early seventies, they began to mobilize and to advance strong arguments linking the fetus and "life."

Several material grounds were available to establish this discursive link. First, scientific references to genetic development were frequently cited.[54] Second, the distribution of photographs of fetuses seemed to have the effect of representing the fetus as human.[55] Third, the liberalizing of abortion laws by some states added highly visible, material grounds for this linkage; there were a few highly-publicized late-term abortions where the fetus struggled to survive for a pathetically short period. These added force to characterizations of the fetus as human.[56] Finally, reform and repeal laws allowed massive numbers of legal abortions for wide-ranging purposes in the repeal states.[57] These conditions were widely successful in challenging the Pro-reform narrative, which had suggested that women sought abortions only for "good" reasons.

Overall, the reaffirmation of the fetus as human seemed to make great headway in undermining the "choice" ideology. Both a strong voter reaction and a shift in tone in the popular magazines signalled rejection of repeal laws in 1971 and 1972.[58]

Meanwhile, the rationale for supporting legal abortion was also evolving. The focus on "discrimination" led to a belief in the "right" to abortion. This belief interacted with the earlier depictions of illegal abortions to produce a new ideographic argument. A combination of the ideograph "right" and the narrative depiction of the disastrous consequences of a lack of "choice" resulted in the generation of the ideograph "choice." The term gradually gained strength from the late sixties into the mid-seventies.[59] It was not until the seventies, however, that the "Pro-choice" argument became dominant and replaced the ideograph "discrimination."

Development of this fourth stage of the argument was tightly interwoven with the rise of the feminist movement. The abortion controversy both fueled the development of the feminist ideology and fed on feminism's development. The ideograph "choice" had particularly important implications for the woman's role in the traditional family. It was a crucial factor in the right to select non-traditional lifestyles for women. The right to choice and new concepts of "family" eventually were accepted by many.[60] It was at this fourth stage, the feminist stage, that the argument from the legal arena impinged on the public controversy.

In its January 1973 ruling on *Roe v. Wade*, the Supreme Court avoided resolving the issues in the abortion controversy at an ideographic level.[61] The Court accepted the Pro-choice characterization of motherhood as an occasionally negative state, accepted the Pro-life characterization of the fetus as human potential, but it rejected both the claim to absolute choice and the claim for the absolute humanity of the fetus.[62] Although the policy implications outlined by the Court were more extreme than any the public consciousness might then have felt comfortable with, the general characterization

of abortion as an occasionally necessary, if distasteful, element of community and legal life was quite consistent with the evolving popular opinion, according to the polls.[63]

Pro-life reaction to this decision was virulent. Pro-life advocates always had characterized legalized abortion as a journey down a "slippery slope" to destruction.[64] When the Supreme Court rendered its decision on *Roe v. Wade,* the lamentations were vehement. At that point, the Pro-life advocates believed that they had established undeniably the full humanity of the fetus. Therefore, they viewed the Supreme Court's ruling not as a rejection of the humanity of the fetus, but as a rejection of the principle of human life in general. Such a rejection produced a major reaction, apocalyptic in tone.[65] Legal abortion was now a fact, however, and that made a major difference in the discussion of abortion in the public arena.

THE MID-SEVENTIES

The fifth stage of the debate, the normalization struggle, was characterized by two competing tendencies: (1) attempts to normalize abortion by working it into the daily understandings of Americans and (2) an escalation of the opposition to such normalization, focusing on a constitutional amendment. In addition to relatively minor issues such as the propriety of television portrayals of abortion, fetal research, and the beliefs of church members, the major questions of fetal viability and funding for abortions provided the battle grounds for this struggle.[66]

The fetal viability issue was pointed up by the manslaughter trial of Dr. Kenneth Edelin. This sensational trial, arising from Edelin's performance of an abortion by hysterotomy, revealed the inadequacies of the Supreme Court's decision; in actual cases, "choice" and "life" were brought into bloody conflict. But the Court had not ranked one ideograph over the other; consequently, public understanding of abortion remained confused. Individuals such as Maria Pitchford and Drs. Edelin and William Waddill were caught in these definitional conflicts.[67]

The issue of public funding of abortions was equally tortuous. At the narrative level, public funding of abortions was as desirable for preventing back alley abortions as had been legalizing abortions in the first place. However, on this issue the Pro-choice advocates faced their own ideology as a limiting condition. Disputants who opposed public funding of abortions used the Pro-choice group's own ideograph, "choice," as an argument against requiring those who believed abortion to be immoral to pay for abortions through their taxes.[68] Congressional adoption of the Hyde Amendment, which cut off most federal funds for abortions, the Court's support of that amendment, and the general tenor of public advocacy all indicated that the limitation of public abortion funding on grounds of "choice" was the view most popularly held at that time.[69]

During the seventies, therefore, the rhetorical process of working the new ideographs, narratives, and characterizations of abortion into the public ideology went forward in piecemeal fashion. Although abortion was legal, and although the tale of illegal abortion was widely recognized, the fundamental conflict between the ideographs "life" and "choice" was not resolved and a continuing adherence to a positive characterization of the family and motherhood was not disturbed.[70] In addition, Pro-life advocates maintained a steady effort to limit the times, places, finances, and conditions under which an abortion could be performed. Thus, by 1977, the sixth stage of the argument, the stalemate, had occurred.

THE LATE SEVENTIES

New argumentative strategies based on comparison arose from the standoff. Advocates on both sides attempted to assert a superior claim to their opponents' ideographs, narratives, and characterizations. For example, Pro-choice advocates claimed legal abortions protected "life"—the lives of adult women. Meanwhile Pro-life advocates claimed that "choice" was exercised in the decision to have sexual intercourse, and that one did not have a right to choose to kill.[71]

This stalemate was actually the first step in a public reconciliation of the two ideographic clusters. The standoff led to a reaching for new audiences. Pro-life advocates attempted to convert liberals on the humanistic, ideographic grounds of "life." Pro-choice advocates attempted to convert conservatives on the practical and ideographic grounds of costs and "no government interference."[72]

These attempts to gain new adherents led rapidly, in the late seventies, to a seventh stage, fragmentation. As the ideologies became less and less univocal, the Pro-life argument took three major forms.[73] First, Catholics and liberals argued on the basis of the ideographs "life" and "humanity."[74] Second, fundamentalists and the Right argued from the ideograph "family" and from characterizations of women, home, and children.[75] Finally, all parties used the argument based on "love," which asked for sacrifice for the sake of the fetus.[76]

The Pro-choice ideology also showed some signs of differentiation.[77] A demand for "control" and rejection of male "oppression" remained, but it was not complete. The request for "control" was rooted in a negative characterization of the traditional family. That was generally effective as a demand for eliminating the old order, but because "choice" and "individual freedom" were the bases of the new order, there were no concrete narratives and no clear, positive characterizations supplied by the Pro-choice advocates to indicate what should replace the old order. It seemed that any image or characterization that was suggested to fill the void might imply a denial of the freedom to choose an alternative image or characterization.

In addition, fundamental disagreements and uncertainties existed among the advocates.[78] Some wished to celebrate motherhood as a special feminine strength; others wished to deny uniqueness to motherhood.[79] One possibility in rejecting the old order of female second-class status was to promote the female to first-class status ahead of males. To many, however, that sounded too much like the Phyllis Schlafly–style claim that women already were "put on a pedestal."[80] Moreover, the previous emphasis on equal rights from the Civil Rights movement led to a focus on equal treatment of women and men. Even the equality solution was problematic. Whether because of natural causes or socialization, many women did not want to give up the positive values of child-bearing, motherhood, and customs of deference to males. Thus, although the Pro-choice advocates generally agreed that they wanted to replace the "traditional" family, many wanted to celebrate a new concept of "family," and others rejected family altogether.

This stage of fragmentation signalled a form of public reconciliation. In spite of continued vociferous argument from advocates on all sides, the poll data, legislative outcomes, and public characterizations of abortion indicate that the public had begun to accept key values from both sides. This does not mean that "public agreement" of any permanent and clear form had been achieved. Nonetheless, the controversy had reoriented our national understanding of abortion in a manner that more fully recognized both the undesirability and desirability of abortion for its roles in protecting women, fetal life, and social family structures.[81] In other words, the material forces of the various sides had been balanced precariously through a long and difficult rhetorical process.

The material forces involved (working women, churches, doctors, patriarchs, etc.) could not "negotiate" with each other directly. An individual woman could only have or not have an abortion. She could only be forced or not forced into motherhood. However, on the social level, rhetoric could mediate these material forces to engender a social consensus about abortion which expressed all of the relevant forces. Such a consensus allowed the continued existence of these social forces in some form or another, and determined the nature of the *experience* of abortion for all Americans.[82]

Even in a callously quantitative way, in fact, a compromise had been reached. Many abortions were conducted legally each year, but social attitudes against abortion and in favor of nurturing had been retained, so that abortion had not generally become the birth control method of choice (as it had in Eastern countries where no such public mediation of values took place every time abortion policy was altered).[83] The rhetorical balance thus materially protected women from hundreds of thousands of dangerous illegal abortions, while discouraging many hundreds of thousands of preventable fetus killings. It did not satisfy all participants, but it met some of the needs of all.

After twenty years of vitriolic debate an important plateau in the public argument about abortion was reached in 1980. The argument had passed through seven identifiable stages. First, a *professional* stage of argument conducted in non-public arenas had shaped and encouraged a public argument. Then, the early public argument began with a *narrative* phase, in which stories of the horrors of illegal abortion were recounted. Third, in interaction with the Civil Rights issue and as a result of weaknesses in the narrative argument, the *auxiliary ideographic* stage focusing on "discrimination" developed. Fourth, feminist concerns spurred the stage of *intrinsic ideographic* argument, as the ideograph "choice" became central. Then, in the mid-seventies came the complicated stage of *normalization* following legal intervention. Some parties attempted to work out the details of legal abortion, while others escalated the arguments against it. In the sixth stage came the *stalemate;* two mature ideological components presented themselves to the public and compared their values and practices to each other. Finally, the arguments on each side began to reach out for new audiences, and in so doing, to fracture, becoming multi-vocal. The seventh stage, *fragmentation,* signalled that elements of a new ideological structure had become widely accepted by the public—abortion was legal, a majority favored a "woman's choice," and millions of women were exercising the option of legal abortion. However, this structure was tightly hedged by other values, and "choice" was thus limited by "life" and "family."[84]

The American process of public argument led to a reaffirmation of the core of each of these values and interests by broadening the vocabulary and altering legal and medical conditions. Even though the rhetorical war had been vicious and even violent at times, the resulting stasis was exactly what the heralds of public argument (Milton, Locke, Mill, etc.) proclaimed open public argument would bring—a rational moderation (though not an ideal or necessarily equitable one) of the conflicting interests of arguing groups.

IMPLICATIONS

This study indicates the need for several lines of further research. For example, the relationship between the patterns described here and Aileen Kraditor's distinction between arguments from "expediency" and from "justice" in the suffrage movement need to be explored.[85] A fuller explanation of the relationship between the arguments of the women's movement and the abortion controversy is also worthy of examination.[86] On the theoretical level, the seven-stage pattern of argument that arose in the abortion argument may prove to underlie, at least in part, some set of social movements. An investigation of the generalizability of the pattern seems desirable.

Finally, this essay demonstrates a viable method for rhetorical analyses of social change. First, it indicates the value of diachronic, rather than synchronic investigation. Too many movement studies treat the rhetoric of an organization as one static unit, rather than as a responsive, developing set of arguments.[87] Second, instead of focusing on the advocacy of only one side of a controversy, it analyzes the social text created by the advocates of various sides of the controversy, interacting with each other and the public.[88] Third, in contrast to Burkean and other studies, which prescribe a pattern to be found in discourse (e.g. order, guilt, victimage, or inception, crisis, and consummation), this study argues that if we purposefully and systematically follow specific units of discourse throughout the course of a movement, we may discover a variety of patterns and relationships.[89] We may note ideographs, narratives, and characterizations; or fantasy themes, personae, and scenarios; or metaphors, culturetypes, and images. A systematic tracing of a specific set of features can tell us a good deal about both the content and structure of the movement. In the process of collecting several such systematic, diachronic studies of the discourse produced in our "social text," we may add significantly to our theoretical understanding of the fascinating processes of human social change.

Notes

[1] See, for example, Robert N. Lynch, "Abortion and 1976 Politics," *America*, 6 March 1976, p. 177. The exhaustion of the issue was also noted in the legislature; see, Susan Fraker et al., "Abortion Under Attack," *Reader's Digest*, September 1978, p. 42. Since there can be no "neutral position" on a moral issue such as abortion, I wish to admit my biases from the outset. I believe that abortion, especially after the first eight weeks of pregnancy, is highly undesirable because it takes the life of a potential human and submits a woman to an unpleasant (or worse) medical procedure. I do not believe, however, that the most effective means to reduce the number of abortions (especially late-term abortions) is to outlaw all abortions.

[2] This analysis is based on a systematic reading of all the articles indexed under the heading "abortion" in the *Reader's Guide to Periodical Literature* from 1960 to 1980. In addition, a non-systematic analysis was made of newspaper articles and editorials, pamphlets, books, and broadcast items. The major differences between the magazine sample and the other sources are these: the newspapers are more particularized, dealing with specific subsets of issues; the broadcast media tend to be vastly abbreviated, except in Public Broadcast debates; and pamphlets tend to be extremist.

[3] The method involved counting and analyzing what some theorists consider to be the two main elements of argumentative discourse—the ideographs and the pentadic elements. An ideograph is a condensed social normative term which serves as a warrant for public behavior (e.g. "liberty"). See Michael Calvin McGee, "The 'Ideograph': A Link Between Rhetoric and Ideology," *Quarterly Journal of Speech*, 66 (1980), 1–17. A "pentadic analysis" charts the grammar of the motive structure in a discourse. The grammar consists of the relationships among the agents, acts, agencies, scenes, and purposes which are "characterized" concretely by the rhetors. See Kenneth Burke, *A Grammar of Motives* (1945; rpt. Berkeley: University of California Press, 1969).

[4] See Robert S. Cathcart, "Defining Social Movements by Their Rhetorical Form," *Central States Speech Journal*, 31 (1980), 267; and in the same number, James R. Andrews, "History and Theory in the Study of the Rhetoric of Social Movements," 274–81; and Leland Griffin, "On Studying Movements," 226; see also Leland Griffin, "The Rhetoric of Historical Movements," *Quarterly Journal of Speech*, 38 (1952), 184–88.

[5] James C. Mohr, *Abortion in America: The Origins and Evolution of National Policy, 1800–1900* (New York: Oxford [University] Press, 1978).

[6] Barbara Plant, "Abortion as a Secondary Birth Control Measure: A Functional Approach," M.A. Thesis, University of Windsor, April 1971.

[7] Authors may cite pre–18th century roots of abortion policy, but they pay little attention to later periods, especially to the 20th century. See John T. Noonan, Jr., *The Morality of Abortion: Legal and Historical Perspectives* (Cambridge, Massachusetts: Harvard

University Press, 1970), pp. xi–xvii; Lawrence Lader, *Abortion II: Making the Revolution* (Boston: Beacon Press, 1973), p. xi; for a slight exception, see Betty Sarvis and Hyman Rodman, *The Abortion Controversy* (New York: Columbia University Press, 1974).

8 I borrow the distinction among "fields" of argument from Stephen Toulmin, *The Uses of Argument* (Cambridge: The University Press, 1958). For elaborations of the concept, see Bruce E. Gronbeck, "Sociocultural Notions of Argument Fields: A Primer," in *Dimensions of Argument: Proceedings of the Second Summer Conference on Argumentation,* ed. George Ziegelmueller and Jack Rhodes (Annandale, Va: Speech Communication Association, 1981), pp. 1–21. In the same volume, see also David Zarefsky, "'Reasonableness' in Public Policy Argument: Fields as Institutions," pp. 88–100; and "Historical Reason: Field as Consciousness," pp. 101–13; and Walter R. Fisher, "Good Reasons: Fields and Genre," pp. 114–26.

9 See, for example, Harold Rosen, ed., *Therapeutic Abortion* (New York: Julian Press, 1964). For a discussion of early conferences, see Sarvis and Rodman.

10 I am making no attempt to speculate on the "causes" of this alteration in pressure. It does not matter whether the increased tension was caused by an increase in the numbers of illegal abortions, the number of legal abortions sought, or merely changes in attitudes. The rhetorical effect was "tension" among the physicians and they expressed that through discourse and behavior changes. Doctors with opinions ranging from Guttmacher's liberalism to Nathanson's eventual conservativism on the issue testified to these "tensions." See Bernard Nathanson with Richard Ostling, *Aborting America* (Garden City, New York: Doubleday and Company, Inc., 1979); Alan Guttmacher, *The Case for Legalized Abortion Now* (Berkeley: Diablo Press, 1967).

11 See Lawrence Lader, *Abortion* (Boston: Beacon Press, 1966), pp. 24–41, for a Pro-choice view. Throughout, I use the terms "Pro-reform," "Pro-life," and "Pro-choice" as indications of what the advocates call themselves, not as labels of endorsement.

12 It also led some professionals to enter the public arena as well (e.g. Guttmacher and Nathanson).

13 Marguerite Clark, "Abortion Racket, What Should Be Done?" *Newsweek,* 15 August 1960, pp. 50–2, or Muriel Davidson, "Deadly Favor," *Ladies Home Journal,* November 1963, pp. 53–7. When citing arguments, I will generally refer to only one or two representative examples. It would be too unwieldy to list all of the articles that use a particular argument.

14 "Abortion and the Law," *Time,* 3 August 1962, p. 30.

15 For example, Marguerite Clark; James Ridgeway, "One Million Abortions," *New Republic,* 9 February 1963, pp. 14–17; "Why Did You Do It? France's Biggest Postwar Mass Abortion Trial," *Newsweek,* 10 June 1963, p. 54.

16 Clark, p. 51; Allan F. Guttmacher, "Law that Doctors Often Break," *Reader's Digest,* January 1960, pp. 51–4.

17 John Bartlow Martin, "Abortion," *Saturday Evening Post,* 20 May 1961, pp. 19–21; "Abortion Facts Reported," p. 86; Faye Marley, "Legal Abortion Safer," *Science News Letter,* 2 March 1963, p. 134.

18 Davidson, pp. 53–4.

19 Davidson.

20 Martin, p. 21.

21 Burke, p. 3.

22 Martin, pp. 19–20; Walter Goodman, "Abortion and Sterilization: The Search for the Answers," *Redbook,* October, 1965, pp. 70–1; Jack Starr, "Growing Tragedy of Illegal Abortion," *Look,* 19 October 1962, pp. 52–3.

23 Martin, pp. 19–20; Lader, *Abortion,* pp. 65–6.

24 Other arguments were also widely used in this period. The most important of these was the largely anti-Catholic argument that no religion should be allowed to impose its morality on others. In addition, physicians made the argument that they should be able to assess their patients' treatment based on medical expertise. A wide array of specific, refutative arguments were also used; for example, there were charges and counter-charges with regard to the Finkbine thalidomide case. Throughout, I will make generalizations about the major strands of argument in each period, but when I claim that an argument was made in a certain period, I mean it was most dominant then, not that the argument was not made at any other time, or that no other arguments were made at that time.

25 This ideology was expressed most vocally in the Catholic magazines during the early period. Other magazines did not carry the Pro-life argument until the late sixties (even conservative magazines like the *National Review*). For more elaboration, see Celeste Condit Railsback, "The Contemporary American Abortion Controversy: A Study of Public Argumentation," Diss., University of Iowa, 1982. This ideology and interest was not, of course, exclusively Catholic, but they were the most vocal group. This changed later in the controversy as

conservative and fundamentalist organizations became involved: In the early sixties, the argument was based on God's gift of life. In later periods it was based on other foundations for "life" and on the importance of the family.

26 Legal changes occurred in 1967, as Colorado, North Carolina, and California all modified their statutes more or less after the American Legal Institute's Model Code. In 1968 Georgia and Maryland also made changes. In 1969, Kansas, Delaware, Arkansas, New Mexico, and Oregon modified their laws. A list of the dates of reform and repeal bills can be found in Sarvis and Rodman, pp. 30–33.

27 See "Is Abortion Ever Justified? Two Church Views," *U.S. News and World Report,* 3 September 1962, p. 89; "Candle in a Dark World: West German Protestant Consultation Centers to Check Abortions," *America,* 19 October 1963, p. 445; R. A. McCormick, "Abortion," *America,* 19 June 1965, pp. 1241–44.

28 "Candle in a Dark World," and McCormick.

29 From early in the sixties, advocates publicly argued for total repeal of abortion laws. Their views were generally not given much public and legislative attention until the late sixties. Other advocates argued only for reform.

30 "Abortion and the Law," *Newsweek,* 2 December 1968; Lawrence Lader, "First Exclusive Survey of Non-Hospital Abortions," *Look,* 21 January 1969, pp. 63–65.

31 To indicate that the narratives contained contradictions is not to indict them. The contradictions are a result of the rhetorical situation, not the ineptitude or error of the speakers.

32 Clark, "Abortion Racket: What Should Be Done?", p. 51.

33 Clark; Goodman, pp. 70–1.

34 For example, Richard P. Vaughn notes that "the immature side of her nature rebels against the prospect of being a mother," but at another level she craves "the experience of fulfillment and creativity that accompanies motherhood," in "Psychotherapeutic Abortion: Bill under Consideration in California," *America,* 16 October 1965, pp. 436–8. See also, "Abortion by Consent?" *Christian Century,* 1 February 1967, p. 132[,] which seems to view abortion as a temporary whim. The dramatic "fetus talking to its mother" articles draw on these stereotypes as well: "Slaughter of the Innocent," trans. L. F. Chrobot, *America,* 2 June 1962, p. 39. In addition, the contrast between articles about women who desperately want children but miscarry and the women who desperately want abortions speaks to the tensions here.

35 The actual number of illegal abortions is uncertain. Most estimates range from 200,000 to two million. In any case, the number had to be substantial (especially given 350,000 hospital admissions for complications from abortion). For "real causes," see Walter Goodman, and also, "Abortion Sought Abroad," *Science News Letter,* 24 July 1965, p. 63; *Health,* April, 1965, pp. 24–25.

36 I refer here to the date the "women's movement" was brought into the public consciousness, not the academic or aesthetic circles. Gallup polls and popular magazine coverage indicate that this did not occur until the late sixties.

37 This is, of course, a reflexive relationship; the material conditions surrounding the act of abortion help to generate the ideographs, but then are affected by interpretations produced by the ideology once it is developed.

38 Martin, p. 52.

39 Estimates range from "many" to 75% to 90%. "Abortion Facts Reported," *Science News Letter,* Andre E. Hellegers, "Law and the Common Good," *Commonweal,* 30 June 1967, p. 418ff.; Ridgeway, p. 14.

40 "Doc Henrie's Farewell," *Newsweek,* 30 June 1962, pp. 22ff.

41 Goodman, p. 71; Lader, *Abortion,* pp. 56–7; Davidson, p. 54.

42 I am not arguing that changes in economics or social structure had taken place, merely that the terms were prevalent in popular discourse at the time. Even the somewhat negative polls showing that "racial harmony" was a major concern in the presidential elections of the period establish this point. See "Most Important Problems during Election Campaigns," *Gallup Opinion Index,* No. 181, September 1980, p. 11.

43 A shift in attitudes can be traced, for example, in the desirability of black neighbors to whites. From 1958 to 1963 the primary position changes occurred in the South. From 1963–1965 there were also important attitude changes of about ten percent in the North. George H. Gallup, *Public Opinion: 1935–1971* (New York: Random House, 1972), pp. 1572–73, 1824, 1941.

44 See as examples, Lader, *Abortion;* P. Kerby, "Abortion: Laws and Attitudes," *Nation,* 12 June 1967, pp. 754–56; "Abortion and the Law," *Newsweek,* 2 December 1968, pp. 82–83.

45 See as examples, "Protecting Civil Liberties: The Right to Have an Abortion," *Current*, May 1968, pp. 26–28, or Robert E. Hall in *Saturday Review*, 7 December 1968, pp. 78–9.

46 Discrimination, the argument went, was caused by the rich having the resources to circumvent a law that was not supported by public experience, whereas the poor did not have such resources. Reform laws did not ameliorate that discrepancy.

47 See n. 34. The concept "choice" arose as much from this demand to have motherhood be an option, as from any other source.

48 "Desperate Dilemma of Abortion," *Time*, 13 October 1967, pp. 32–3; "Coping with Abortion: Panel Discussion," *Mademoiselle*, October 1967, pp. 211–212. Further reflections of the argument can be found in Carl Reiterman, ed., *Abortion and the Unwanted Child* (New York: Springer Publishing Co., 1971). This issue was also tied to the argument over the population "explosion" and the role of abortion in containing that growth.

49 Mohr, p. 167.

50 "Coping with Abortion."

51 Alaska and Hawaii adopted very liberal laws, and New York adopted a virtual repeal law. However, in 1971 and 1972 there was a strong counter-reaction as referenda in North Dakota and Michigan were vigorously rejected and New York's repeal law was almost overturned, while Pennsylvania, Connecticut, and even the federal courts rejected abortion repeal. Actual changes in attitudes are difficult to document. Judith Blake, in "The Abortion Decisions: Judicial Review and Public Opinion," in Edward Manier, William Liu and David Solomon, eds., *Abortion: New Directions for Policy Studies* (Notre Dame, Indiana: University of Notre Dame Press, 1977), pp. 51–81, concluded that there was relatively little change from 1964 to 1971. At that time, the laws were merely "catching up" with public attitudes. However, there was a fair amount of change reported after this period by Eric M. Ulsaner and Ronald E. Weber in "Public Support for Pro-Choice Abortion Policies in the Nation and States: Changes and Stability after the Roe and Doe Decisions," in Carl E. Schneider and Maris A. Vinovskis, eds., *The Law and Politics of Abortion* (Lexington, Massachusetts: D. C. Heath and Company, 1980), pp. 206–23.

52 Over 200,000 abortions were performed in New York in a single year; see Lader, *Abortion II*, pp. 166–67.

53 See as examples Norman St. John-Stevas, "Abortion, Catholics, and the Law," *Catholic World*, January 1968, pp. 149–52; Eunice Kennedy Shriver, "When Pregnancy Means Heartbreak: Is Abortion the Answer?" *McCalls*, April 1968, p. 139.

54 Brendon F. Brown, "Criminal Abortion," *Vital Speeches of the Day*, 1 July 1970, pp. 549–53; Harold B. Kuhn, "Now Generation Churchmen and the Unborn," *Christianity Today*, 29 January 1971, p. 38; Virgil C. Blum, "Public Policy Making: Why the Churches Strike Out," *America*, 6 March 1971, pp. 224–28; Rev. James Fisher, letter to the editor, *National Review*, 9 February 1971, p. 116.

55 Kirk, p. 1407; "Twisted Logic: Propositions to Legalize Abortion," *Christianity Today*, 22 December 1972, pp. 24–5. In addition to the testimony of these Pro-life sources, it is telling evidence to the effectiveness of the picture campaigns that Lader is silent about the defeat of the referenda on abortion in Michigan. He indicates a good bit of organization and effort by Pro-choice forces in Michigan, and does not attempt to account for the loss. Lader, *Abortion II*, pp. 182–84.

56 Blum; Irene Fischl, "Why Are Nurses Shook Up Over Abortion?" *Look*, 9 February 1971, p. 66; J. O. Douglas, "Abortion Problems in Britain," *Christianity Today*, 17 March 1972, p. 47.

57 Lader, *Abortion II*; Paul Marx, "On Not Changing Womb into Tomb," *Catholic World*, January 1972, p. 218.

58 On the counter-reaction, see Russell Kirk, "The Sudden Death of Feticide," *National Review*, 22 December 1972, p. 1407 or "Twisted Logic: Propositions to Legalize Abortion," *Christianity Today*, 22 December 1972, pp. 24–5.

59 Ramifications of the still-developing ideograph "choice" have not yet been fully appreciated. Applications to euthanasia, the draft, suicide, work, and even travel become increasingly important as the persuasive power of the term grows. Examples of the "choice" rhetoric can be seen in John D. Rockefeller III, "No Retreat on Abortion," *Newsweek*, 21 June 1976, p. 11; and Francis Baudry and Alfred Wiener, "Women's Choice: Pregnancy or Abortion," *Mademoiselle*, April 1974, p. 34.

60 Gallup poll data show that a majority of the people adopted the ideographs of the "women's movement" while maintaining the concrete characterizations of the dominant ideology. For a more detailed analysis, see Railsback, pp. 113–18.

61 *Roe v. Wade*, 410 U.S. 113 (October 1972), 70–1B, pp. 154, 163.

62 *Roe v. Wade*, pp. 153, 163.

63 To describe public opinion adequately would require more space than is available. I have argued, however, that Judith Blake's interpretation is oversimplified. The public accepted the ideographs of both sets of advocates, but viewed their application as a weighting based on two factors: stage of fetal development and goodness of purpose as defined by the dominant ideology. See Railsback, pp. 167–75.

64 Robert M. Byrn, "Goodbye to the Judeo-Christian Era in Law," *America,* 2 June 1973, p. 511; Eunice Kennedy Shriver, "When Pregnancy Means Heartbreak: Is Abortion the Answer?" *McCalls,* April 1968, p. 139.

65 Byrn; Russell Shaw, "Alienation of American Catholics," *America,* 8 September 1973, pp. 138–40; John A. Miles, Jr., "Wife of Onan and the Sons of Cain," *National Review,* 17 August 1973, pp. 891–94; Timothy O'Connell, "For American Catholics: End of an Illusion," *America,* 2 June 1973, p. 514; John T. Noonan, Jr., "Right to Life: Raw Judicial Power," *National Review,* 2 March 1973, pp. 16–64.

66 Mrs. Theodore Wedel, "Maude Case: Pressure or Persuasion," *America,* 15 December 1973, p. 465; "That's Entertainment," *Time,* 27 August 1973, p. 630; Robert R. Beusse and Russell Shaw, "Maude's Abortion: Spontaneous or Induced?" *America,* 3 November 1973; "When to Baptise . . . When to Dismiss," *America,* 21 September 1974, p. 123; Tony Fuller, "Baptism of Ire," *Newsweek,* 2 September 1974, p. 75; "Fight Over Fetuses," *Time,* 31 March 1975, p. 82; J. Robert Nelson, "New Protection for the Unborn Child," *Christian Century,* 20 August 1975, p. 725.

67 Dr. Kenneth Edelin was tried and convicted for killing a fetus when he conducted a second term abortion, but his conviction was eventually overturned. Dr. William Waddill was brought to trial three times in a similar case that bridged the abortion-murder linguistic ambiguity. Maria Pitchford was tried for attempting to abort herself when she was unable to obtain a late-term medical abortion from legal sources. David M. Alpern, "Abortion and the Law," *Newsweek,* 3 March 1975, pp. 18–29; Carol Altekruse Berger and Patrick F. Berger, "The Edelin Decision," *Commonweal,* 25 August 1975, p. 77; "Abortion: The Edelin Schock Wave," *Time,* 3 March 1975, p. 54; Eileen Keerdoja and Ying Yilng Wu, "Dr. Wadill: Triple Jeopardy?" *Newsweek,* 7 January 1980, p. 10; "The Scarlet A," *Time,* 11 September 1978, p. 22.

68 "Abortion and the Poor," *America,* 2 February 1980, p: 73; "Hyde Amendment," *America,* 8 March 1980, p. 181; Peter Steinfels, "Politics of Abortion," *Commonweal,* 22 July 1977, p. 45.

69 The Hyde Amendment withdrew government funding of abortion through sources such as Medicaid. Other amendments eliminated funding for military and other government personnel. In the legislature, the most frequent argument for elimination of government funding remained the claim that abortion was the murder of the unborn. However, this was not the most effective argument because it appealed primarily to the solid anti-abortion constituency. The argument that federal funding of abortions was a "choice" and that it took away the choice of some taxpayers was more crucial because it appealed to the "swing vote." Although no polls of legislators are available to indicate the reasons for their choices (and such polls would probably be inaccurate), the fact that the argument for "taxpayers choice" gradually gained in frequency of presentation throughout the several years of hearings indicates that it came to be viewed as one of the most persuasive arguments. See Rep. (Mrs.) Lloyd, *Congressional Record,* 124, pt 13, 13 June 1978, (Washington, D.C.: The U.S. Government Printing Office), p. 17261. See also Mr. Quie of Minn.[,] same publication, vol. 122, pt 2, 10 August 1976, p. 26788, or Mr. Guyer, 24 June 1976, p. 20411.

70 The acceptance of these disparate factors is evident in poll data which show that majorities favored positions which gave women the choice in abortion, but, when asked about which abortions should be legal, they were most lenient with the "hard case" abortions and scaled their leniency to the stage of pregnancy and whether or not birth control had been used. Poll data also support continued reliance on traditional sex role stereotypes. See Railsback, pp. 114–18, 167–72.

71 As examples see Thomas A. Prentice, "Letters from Readers," *Progressive,* December 1980, p. 37; James Jason Kilpatrick, "A Comment," *National Review,* 25 May 1979, p. 679; "Fight Over Abortions," *U.S. News and World Report,* 19 December 1977, p. 68. For a more detailed discussion, see Railsback, pp. 237–44.

72 As examples of such "reaching out" arguments, see Richard John Neuhaus, "Hyde and Hysteria," *Christian Century,* September 10–17, 1980, p. 852; Susan Fraker, "Abortion Under Attack," *Newsweek,* 5 June 1978, pp. 36–7; "Unborn and the Born Again," *New Republic,* 2 July 1977, p. 5.

[73] Compare the leftist tone of Juli Loesch, "Pro-Life, Pro-ERA," *America,* 9 December 1978, p. 435 to the conservative tone of Basile J. Uddo, "Inquiry on Abortion: View of J. T. Noonan," *America,* 7 July 1979, p. 14. For further detail, see Railsback, pp. 259–71.

[74] For examples of such rhetoric, see Mary Meehan, "Abortion: the Left Has Betrayed the Sanctity of Life," *Progressive,* September 1980, p. 34; Juli Loesch, "Pro-Life, Pro-ERA," *America,* 9 December 1978, p. 435; Anne Bernard, "Born and the Unborn Alike," *America,* 26 March 1977, p. 272; Francis X. Meehan, "Social Justice and Abortion," *America,* 17 June 1978, p. 478.

[75] For example, see Basile J. Uddo, "Inquiry on Abortion: View of J. T. Noonan," *America,* 7 July 1979, p. 14; Dale Vree, "Bourgeois Abortions," *National Review,* 27 October 1978, p. 1351; John Warwick Montgomery, "Abortion: Courting Severe Judgment," *Christianity Today,* 25 January 1980, p. 54.

[76] Thomas Ashford, "Countdown to an Abortion," *America,* 12 February 1977, p. 128; Peter Steinfels, "Politics of Abortion," *Commonweal,* 22 July 1977, p. 45.

[77] Compare Gloria Steinem, "Update: Abortion Alert," *Ms.,* November 1977, p. 118 and Ellen Willis, "Abortion Backlash: Women Lose," *Rolling Stone,* 3 November 1977, p. 65 to Linda Birde Francke, quoted by Elaine Fein, "The Facts about Abortion," *Harper's Bazaar,* May 1980, p. 76. See also, Railsback, pp. 271–280.

[78] See the ambivalence indicated in Alice Lake, "Abortion Repeaters," *McCalls,* September 1980, p. 58.

[79] Compare Mary Scott Welch and Dorothy Hermann, "Why Miscarriage Is So Misunderstood," *Ms.,* February 1980, p. 14, to Gloria Steinem, "Nazi Connection," *Ms.,* November 1980, p. 14; October 1980, pp. 88–90.

[80] These are the same arguments described in feminist philosophy; see Alison Jagger, "Political Philosophies of Women's Liberation," in *Feminism and Philosophy,* ed. Mary Vetterling-Braggin, Frederick A. Elliston, and Jane English (Totowa, NJ: Littlefield, Adams, and Company, 1981).

[81] This does not rule out further legal change. However, major shifts in attitudes and experience seem unlikely, and even further legal change will probably provide exceptions for some legal abortions.

[82] This is not to suggest that serious legal and material conflicts or "irrationalities" do not remain. For example, the current number of late-term abortions, current funding conditions, and squabbles over "informed consent" laws show important residual problem areas that desperately need further negotiation.

[83] Henry P. David, ed., *Abortion Research: International Experience* (Lexington, Massachusetts: Lexington Books, 1974); Daniel Callahan, *Abortion: Law, Choice, and Morality* (New York: The MacMillan Co., 1970), pp. 219–66; Lader, *Abortion,* pp. 116–131; Robert Blumstock, "Hungary," *Attitudes in Eastern Europe and the Soviet Union,* ed. William A. Welsh (New York: Pergamon Press, 1981), 330–31.

[84] As described in notes 60 and 63, the polls provide proof of such an interpretation. In addition, admission by Pro-choice advocates of the negative aspects of abortion, and continued rejection of those who used abortion as their primary birth control method, further suggested the hedgings around the legalization of abortion. See Railsback, pp. 278–79.

[85] Aileen S. Kraditor, *Ideas of the Woman Suffrage Movement, 1890–1920* (New York: Columbia University Press, 1965), pp. 43–74.

[86] Jagger.

[87] For an argument in favor of the historical approach, see Andrews. For a good example of his method, see James R. Andrews, "Piety and Pragmatism: Rhetorical Aspects of the Early British Peace Movement," *Communication Monographs,* 34 (1967), 423–36.

[88] See Griffin and compare to Simons, who describes first, reform strategies, and then status quo strategies without viewing the interaction of the two. See Herbert Simons, Elizabeth Mechling, and Howard N. Schr[e]ier, "Mobilizing for Collective Action from the Bottom Up: The Rhetoric of Social Movements," *Handbook of Rhetoric and Communication,* ed. John W. Bowers and Carroll C. Arnold, in press, 1984.

[89] Leland Griffin, "A Dramatistic Theory of the Rhetoric of Movements," *Critical Responses to Kenneth Burke,* ed. William H. Rueckert, (Minneapolis, Minnesota: University of Minnesota Press, 1969). Other patterns are described in Ralph Turner and Lewis Killian, *Collective Behavior* (Englewood Cliffs, NJ: Prentice-Hall, Inc., 1972). They note two phase sets—mass excitement, popular involvement, formal phase[,] and institutional phase, and the problem, proposal, policy, program, and appraisal phases.

From "Gay is Good" to the Scourge of AIDS:
The Evolution of Gay Liberation Rhetoric, 1977–1990

James Darsey

The capacity to get free is nothing; the capacity to be free, that is the task.

Andre Gide, *The Immoralist*

These words of Gide are given voice by Michel, who is beginning a narrative describing his awakening to his homoerotic desires and, more generally, to the joys of life and sensuality. Though the statement evinces a universal wisdom that places it beyond the claim of any single group, it is very nearly prophetic as a description of the course of gay liberation efforts in the United States over the last two decades. What began in the early 1970s in the giddy rush by a newly radicalized movement to *get free* is now absorbed in the unglamorous and often disheartening struggle to *be free* in a hostile environment. The rhetoric of gay liberation in the United States from 1977, the beginning of Anita Bryant's Save Our Children campaign, to its current concerns over AIDS is an important source of data in our efforts to understand rhetorical movements dealing with sociopolitical and rhetorical constraints. It forms a critical and as yet unchronicled chapter in the rhetorical history of a significant American social movement.

CONCEPTUAL FRAMEWORK FOR THE STUDY

As Suzanne Riches and Malcolm Sillars suggest, students of rhetoric and related studies widely agree that the longitudinal, comprehensive study of a social movement is the paradigmatic ideal.[1] Such studies have the potential to provide fundamental insights into relationships between rhetoric and history, between rhetoric and its antecedents, among competing rhetorics within a movement, and among opposing rhetorics. The perspective is evolutionary; it emphasizes rhetorical change, an element that is essential to the very definition of movement.

For all these advantages, though, and for all our commitment to such a model, we have few studies of the kind described.[2] They are, as Judson Crandell noted in proposing them more than forty years ago, "cumbersome."[3] The undertaking of the comprehensive study of a rhetorical movement may be the scholarly equivalent of triathletic training, an act of overall stamina as much as skill in any particular event. The critic must sift through discourses that may span years or even decades, that may emanate from a staggering array of organizations and individual rhetors, resulting in a polyglot that somehow must be represented adequately and typified. For historical movements, those that have run their course, the critic must decide when they began and when they ended. To what extent must the antislavery rhetoric of the American Revolution be comprehended in a study of abolitionism or abolitionism in a study of the modern black civil rights movement? Does women's liberation begin in the 1960s, or is it continuous with the suffrage movement of the nineteenth century? Which, if any, among these movements might be said to have ended? Ongoing movements demand the critic's continuing attentions, at least periodically; they refuse to be fossilized and retired to the display case.

And for all this effort, the rewards may be unsatisfying, especially if we take the view represented by those such as Hart who believe the primary goal of our scholarship should be theory building. Many of these studies will be part of the slow, steady accretion of confirming evidence for some large hypothesis, a journeyman's labors.[4] Yet while the emphasis may be on those who create the hypotheses and those who fail to find confirmation, meaningful generalization in this decidedly social-scientific model is not the product of any single study, no matter how competent or careful. The researcher's effort is interpretable only as part of the aggregate.

Removed from the requirements of theory building, the energy required merely to characterize the data for these studies may force their authors to content themselves with achieving accurate and precise description, a kind of rhetorical chapter to a book someone else will edit.

This case study is offered as a kind of second chapter in a continuing rhetorical chronicle of the gay liberation movement in the United States. This chapter, which examines gay liberation rhetoric from 1977 to 1990, is an addition to an earlier study that examined the rhetoric of this movement from its 1948 inception as a sustained movement for social reform in the United States to 1977 when the study was completed.[5] This ongoing effort might be justified by the uniqueness and inherent worthiness of the body of discourse,[6] and I have argued elsewhere that the rhetoric of gay liberation is unique in being perhaps the most thoroughly postmodern of reform discourses.[7]

Conversely, this effort might be justified, as suggested above, by its potential contribution to our understanding of the rhetorical behavior of social movements and of rhetoric in general: The gay liberation movement in the United States may be especially useful for theory-building studies. It has no confusing antecedents; it has a well-defined point of origin; it is of short enough duration that we can make a relatively complete inventory of its organizations, publications, and spokespeople; and there are significant archives containing rich rhetorical records. It is, in short, like Sprague-Dawley or Whistar rats, possessed of a kind of purity that allows researchers to discount confounding variables in explaining observed interactions and effects.

On the basis of the characteristics of the movement and of data that represent coverage of more than forty years of rhetorical history (a combination of this study with the earlier study that ended in 1977), the final section of this essay presents some tentative conclusions with respect to what Andrews has identified as the "real questions" confronting the student of rhetorical movements: "What circumstances *stimulate* rhetorical behaviors? And what

rhetorical behaviors are *chosen* within the range of behavioral possibilities?"[8] Even tentative answers to these questions may seem to argue against the uniqueness of any one movement. Still, definitive conclusions about what might be extrapolated from the discourse to social movements in general and conclusions regarding the unique features of this rhetoric depend equally on an accumulation of studies "examining in detail the *rhetorical progression* of particular historical movements."[9] For the moment, we must content ourselves with a modest contribution to rhetorical history, a necessary building block in the "foundation for mature, empirically grounded theory,"[10] an investment whose theoretical dividend awaits the accumulation of case studies such as this one.[11]

CATALYTIC EVENTS AND RHETORICAL MOVEMENTS

The rhetorician who studies social movements diachronically must find grounds for talking about rhetorical periods or eras, that is, eras in which discourses exhibit both significant distinctiveness from others occurring in adjacent periods and some central defining concerns within. In a too-little-appreciated essay, Joe Munshaw offers a helpful starting point for articulating relationships between time and discourse. "To succeed in adopting a process viewpoint for structuring his studies," writes Munshaw, "the rhetorical historian must develop a clear conceptualization of the relationship of time to history and rhetoric."[12] Munshaw's enterprise involves looking at history as change in public discourse instead of as a series of events punctuated by wars, changes of government, and technological innovations.

> The rhetorical historian's unique contribution lies in the development of structures that treat history as rhetoric. Sometimes structures borrowed from other types of historians adequately serve his purposes of analysis and explanation. Often, however, the rhetorical historian will need to develop his own structures because the questions he hopes to ask are different from those of other historians.[13]

The Cold War era, for example, would be a useful designator for a large-scale rhetorical analysis of the evolution of U.S. foreign policy. Its usefulness would be determined not by its conformity to divisions that historians have used to divide time, but by its ability to define a distinct era in the history of American foreign policy discourse. Again citing Munshaw: "Events belong in a period because of their similarity. When events change drastically, usually the historian perceives that a new period different from the older period is created."[14] In many, perhaps most, cases, there will be no predetermined categories for the rhetorical scholar, and the problem becomes one of isolating natural divisions in the unfolding of discourse over time.[15]

Clearly, one key to identifying natural divisions in discourse is when situations and exigencies change dramatically. Toward that end, I have developed a methodology around *catalytic events* as useful markers of rhetorical eras and partitions for rhetorical sampling. Catalytic events are moments in the life of a movement that provide the appropriate conditions for discourse. As such, they are events that (1) are historical rather than rhetorical, (2) are nontactical (either extraneous to the movement in origin, spontaneous in origin, or both), (3) achieve tremendous significance for the movement, and (4) precede rhetorical responses that constitute demonstrably discrete, internally homogeneous rhetorical eras.[16] There can be little doubt, for example, that colonial rhetoric changed substantially after the Boston massacre. Similarly, abolitionist rhetoric changed after the passage of the Kansas-Nebraska act, labor rhetoric after the outbreak of the two world wars, black rights rhetoric after Rosa Parks refused to give up her seat on a Montgomery bus, women's liberation rhetoric after the publication of Betty Friedan's *The Feminine Mystique*, and gay liberation rhetoric as a result of AIDS. Each of these is only one example within its respective movement.

The complete rhetorical study of a movement would chart its entire history with respect to such events. Even when considering *social movement* as meaning rather than a phenomenon, there must be some sense of stages in the progression of meaning, and those stages must be marked by some conceptual device.

CATALYTIC EVENTS AND THE RHETORIC OF GAY LIBERATION, 1977–1990

The identification of catalytic events is a problem in criticism in the same way that the identification of relevant features of discourse is a problem in criticism. The critic must bring all he or she knows about rhetoric, social movements, and the movement being considered to the problem of identifying catalytic events. In this case, and in its antecedent, the hypothesis was forwarded that particular events provided meaningful divisions in the discourse. That hypothesis was tested statistically, and the results were supportive.

As a conceptual device, catalytic events (in this case the ones isolated) provide meaningful divisions that aid the critical task. As Lucien Goldmann puts it, though structures are realities, they also are concepts of research; structure "originates from the solution of practical problems encountered by living beings."[17] In the final analysis, the evaluation of any particular structure and of all criticism must be pragmatic. "Is this understanding helpful and useful?" That is the proper question. As Goldmann goes on to remark, with each problem we solve through the imposition of structure, the structures themselves are adapted a little, and we thus renounce the possibility of an ideal solution.[18]

In the forerunner of this study, seven catalytic events and five significant rhetorical periods were identified in the gay liberation movement in the United States.[19] The first period in the life of the movement, which followed the publication by Alfred Kinsey and his colleagues of *Sexual Behavior in the Human Male* in 1948, was primarily organizational. Whatever discourses may have been produced were likely for in-group consumption, were primarily social in content, and had few vehicles for preservation. Consequently, there is little evidence of rhetorical activity in this earliest period of the movement's history. The first significant rhetorical period for the U.S. gay liberation movement, characterized as *establishing groundwork*, corresponded roughly to the time of Joe McCarthy's political prominence from 1950 to 1954. This was followed by a period characterized as *educating and encouraging* in the aftermath of the censure and decline of McCarthy and the near simultaneous publication of a model penal code in which, among other reforms, homosexual acts between consenting adults were decriminalized. In 1961, Illinois became the first state in the United States to adopt, essentially unchanged, the American Law Institute's Model Penal Code and Franklin Kameny, after losing a discrimination case that went to the Supreme Court, was inspired to create the Mattachine Society of Washington, D.C. In the wake of these catalytic events, the gay liberation movement achieved a period characterized as a move *toward strength and independence.* This third rhetorical era lasted until 1969 when a New York City riot now known as the Stonewall rebellion ushered in a period of *aggressive self-identity,* a rhetorical stance characterized by offensive strategies and activism that, in about 1973, gave way to a period characterized as *uncertain maturity.* The original study ended at the point at which discourse began in response to a 1977 Dade County, Florida, referendum. In that referendum, voters rescinded an ordinance passed by the county board prohibiting discrimination against gay people in housing, employment, and public accommodations. Anita Bryant was the key opposition figure, and in retrospect, it seems clear that for several years thereafter the gay rights movement was put in a defensive position as it focused on referendum battles over similar ordinances across the country.[20]

The current study, then, begins with the era catalyzed by Anita Bryant and posits two additional catalytic events and corresponding rhetorical eras. The referendum campaigns inspired by Bryant held public attention and were the primary preoccupation of the gay rights movement from 1977 to 1980. By 1980 and the inauguration of Ronald Reagan, the intensity of combat had lessened, and the movement's devil figures became more diverse and amorphous. Anita Bryant was replaced by Jerry Falwell, the Moral Majority, neoconservatism, and right-wing evangelicalism in general. Many of the concerns remained the same, but the style changed considerably. Finally, by 1983, two years after the *New York Times* reported the original story on a rare form of cancer being found in homosexual men, AIDS and the medical, political, and social threats it poses had come to color all gay discourse. Indeed, the underlying thesis

of more than one text (including the recent and acclaimed film "Longtime Companion") has been that AIDS, in essential ways, has changed the meaning of what it is to be gay in the United States. As one figure in Rosa von Praunheim's film trilogy "AIDS Update" says when asked about the impact of AIDS on gay life, "Everything has changed."

As in the original study, discussion is focused by the findings of a value analysis of selected samples of discourse with attention usually limited to the five most frequently coded value appeals in each period.[21]

Period VI: Defending Fragile Achievements

By 1977, *homophile liberation* had been a presence in America for thirty years, the visible and activist post-Stonewall wing of the movement for nearly a decade. In the congenially liberal afterglow of an era in which popular political action had ended American involvement in an unpopular war and brought down two U.S. presidents, gay liberationists began to talk with pride of their achievements and of the increasing social and legal acceptance of homosexuality. Everything seemed positive for the movement, but then Dade County, Florida, passed an ordinance prohibiting discrimination against homosexuals in housing, employment, and public accommodations. In this environment of sunny tolerance, the surprise was the vocal, religiously fueled popular reaction against the ordinance led by singer Anita Bryant, a reaction that resulted in a referendum battle that reached far beyond Dade County.

Bryant's successful campaign against the Dade County ordinance and its expansion into the nationwide Save Our Children movement served notice on the gay community that history did not have an immutable, liberal-progressive direction, that it could not be trusted simply to run its course. From 1973 until Bryant's emergence, the gay liberation movement had been in a stage characterized as uncertain maturity. The dramatic gains of the early seventies had given way to quiet lobbying such as letter writing, the mundane processes of conventional political influence carried out by groups like the National Gay Task Force. Many gay people had lost interest; organizations atrophied; no credible devils existed to threaten the peace; and the *movement* was threatened with dissolution. Then a series of events beginning with the battle in Dade County served as a sobering antidote to complacency.

Unity is the most prominent value appeal in this period. Gay rights supporters had to regroup and regather those who had wandered away from the party when it had begun to get dull. Beyond this most general and perennial sense, unity is as difficult for the gay rights movement as it is for any movement where the constituency is a national rather than a regional or local community. Issues that may be defined geographically, a local ordinance for instance, must be ideologically transformed into a common cause. It is a problem that has plagued social movements in America from the Revolution onward. Gay liberation in the United States has an advantage here in that it historically has been the political facet of a subcultural milieu, and that subculture has been defined nationally. It is a largely urban subculture in which there are certain centers widely recognized as the province of gay people wherever they may live. Gays in Idaho and gays in Kentucky may share, as a part of their common cultural currency, a knowledge of bars in Greenwich Village or a repertoire of experiences from "the Castro." Newspapers in the gay community encourage this identification. In the papers surveyed for this study, the best example was a lengthy feature in the New York *Native* on California's Russian River resort area, a favorite vacationing spot for gays. Gay publications, though identified with their places of origin, often have a national circulation and provide national and international coverage.[22] This kind of transgeographical consciousness encourages references to the gay community as a national phenomenon and a corresponding mentality in which any threat is a threat to the whole.[23]

An editorial from the Philadelphia *Gay News* is illustrative. "Bryant Threatens All GAYS!" read the headline. Referring to the anti-Bryant forces in Dade County, the editorial admonished the reader: "Florida gays are doing all they can, but that is not enough. We must all help. Otherwise, Anita Bryant and friends might show up in your town."[24]

Unity also became a concern in the crisis posed by the Save Our Children movement as the debate over proper strategies of response intensified. The period preceding the uproar over Bryant and her following had been a period of quiet respectability, gay lesbian lobbyists in suits carrying leather attachés. Indeed, this presentation has been much more typical of the gay rights movement throughout its history than the colorful glimpses of gay counterculture provided each June as evening news programs cover Pride Day marches.[25] Many in the gay community encouraged continuation of moderate and reasoned tactics in 1977. David Goodstein of the generally conservative *Advocate* couched his preferred strategies in the mantle of professionalism, and he praised this virtue at every opportunity. Peter Goodman, then newly appointed director of the Human Rights Foundation, led a "most professional" organization, and the successful fight against a referendum to overturn gay rights protections in Seattle was "a tribute to professionalism."[26]

Bryant's national tours, though, also were met with angry scenes of near violence and at least one pie-throwing incident, suggesting that not everyone in the gay community was of the same mind as Goodstein. As "Angry as Hell" put it in the *Gay Community News:* "Let's not feel awful about bustin' Anita's chops . . . We can try to be cheap Christ imitators or we can be real."[27] *Gay Community News* later found itself part of "A House Divided" over its role in organizing a rally against Bryant in Boston. In the face of threats and recriminations from within the gay community, the editors at *GCN* responded: "Instead of a much needed coming together and a necessary supportive effort, many politicians and gay businesses retreated to a stance of fear and nonactivism masquerading as 'respectability.'"[28]

Again, the problem itself is not unique to the gay movement. The battle over tactics, especially violence and civil disobedience, has been an important feature of almost every significant social movement in U.S. history.

A combination of appeals to **work, determination,** and **strength** constitute the second most prominent value cluster in Period VI. The dominant member of this cluster is determination (26 appeals compared to 16 for work and

4 for strength). The ratio suggests the defensive state of a movement working against the odds. So many appeals to determination give the discourse the tone of things spoken through clenched teeth. "Strong people, led by the indomitable Nancy Roth . . . were determined to make SOHR a viable organization," editorialized the *Advocate*.[29] Gays talked of themselves as living in a climate where simple viability required the combined forces of strength, indomitability, and determination. The *Gay Community News* began to sound melodramatic when the editors proclaimed the strength of their determination:

> In the face of economic blackmail from within the community, lack of commitment from political allies, and violent homophobic terrorism, we must reiterate our mandate and the principles by which we abide. *Gay Community News* is committed to providing a forum for all of the diverse and opposed elements and perspectives within the gay community, and to maintaining open lines of communication between us all.[30]

Achievement is the third most prominent appeal in this period, and there is a sense in which it is at the center of this discourse. If it can be characterized by any one thing, the rhetoric of gay liberation in the period spawned by the Dade County campaign can be characterized as defending fragile achievements; it was about the recognition that gains, once made, are not guaranteed for permanence, a painful iteration of the hoary saw "The price of liberty is eternal vigilance." In some of the referendum campaigns that followed Dade County, gays saw rights taken away. At the same time, a demoralized constituency made for an ineffective movement, and the gay community wrestled with maintaining an awareness of what good had been wrought in the years since Stonewall. An editorial in the Philadelphia *Gay News* presented one formula in its title, "One step back, two steps forward."[31]

It became important to the movement to stress what achievements it could find in this period. One editorial from Boston's *Gay Community News* congratulating the National Gay Task Force for its role in the historic White House meeting with Carter staffer Midge Costanza, heavy on achievement appeals, was reprinted in an issue of the Philadelphia *Gay News* that also happened to be in the current sample.[32] If there were not enough achievements to go around, we obviously would have to share.

Combined appeals to **safety** and **security** constitute the fourth group in Period VI. What gay rhetoric was acknowledging was that the times were turbulent and uncertain, that what had been achieved could become unachieved quickly, that the climate was changing from one in which liberalism had a certain presumption to one in which conservatism did. These developments threatened not just the social and legal security of gays, but also their physical safety. "Kill a Queer for Christ" bumper stickers were no joke. The sampled editorials contain reports of fire-bombed automobiles, threats to life, vandalization of property, and physical attacks on gay men.[33] Editorial cartoons, though not coded, were obsessed with the theme of violence being done to gays by Anita Bryant and right-wing and religious extremists.[34] The most ominous editorial in this sample probably is the one that features a reproduction of a Ku Klux Klan calling card that reportedly had been left at the newspaper office. "You have been paid a **Friendly Visit** by the Ku Klux Klan," it said. "Should we pay you A REAL VISIT?"[35] Compared to earlier periods, there is a high number of aggression appeals in Periods VI and VII. Most of these are contained in descriptions of aggression against gay people rather than acts of aggression by gay people. The influence of this hostile climate was pervasive, and it manifests itself in a preponderance of metaphors of war and violence in gay rhetoric. The radical right was accused of "murdering" the ERA, for example, and all political actions became "battles."[36]

Finally, **tolerance,** which had been a major concern in each of the first four rhetorical periods of the gay liberation movement but which had received only incidental attention in Period V (1973–1977) reemerges here as a predominant appeal.

Period VII: Fortifying against a Conservative Tide

Anita Bryant gradually faded from prominence, her contract with the Florida Citrus Growers unrenewed, her marriage in disarray. But unlike

McCarthy's fall in 1955, Bryant's decline did not remove what seemed to be the single stubborn barrier to enlightenment. Bryant was the forward-running crest of a wave of conservatism that, as it declined in intensity, also became more pernicious in its apparent ubiquity. In 1980, Ronald Reagan was elected President of the United States with the vocal and much publicized support of the Moral Majority and other groups loosely allied under that umbrella. Conservatives were in the White House and in the Congress; they were in Lynchburg, Virginia; and they were in a renascent Klan and an increasingly visible Nazi party. If it had lost its poniard, the political right had gained in its ability to conquer the opposition by division.

Talking out of both sides of his mouth, a talent normally reserved for politicians, David Goodstein provided a perfect example of the confusion in the gay community in an editorial in which he provided reasons, for every candidate running for president in 1980, that gays should become involved in their campaigns. Ronald Reagan, for example, was to be "rewarded" by the gay community for his statement against California's Proposition 6 in 1978. "Our best chance for success after this next election," wrote Goodstein, "is to be known to *whoever* [sic] [emphasis Goodstein's] wins, Republican or Democrat."[37] The example admittedly is extreme, but it exposes a movement without unifying principle or direction, a movement simply hedging its bets.

In this setting, it seems predictable that **unity** would be a primary appeal in Period VII, this time sharing the number one spot with the combined appeals of **work, determination,** and **strength.** Most movement leaders, unlike Goodstein, recognized that gay power did not have sufficient reserves to survive diffusion. Among the editorials sampled for this period, three dealt with specific political races. Only Goodstein's failed to urge unified gay support of specific candidates.[38]

In fairness to Goodstein's position (or lack thereof), unity is a special problem for a movement based on its own right to diverge from the norm. The gay rights movement constantly courts the embarrassing charge that it does not really advocate diversity, but only a wider circle of conformity. In asking for tolerance from the surrounding straight culture, the movement is forced to exercise it within its own ranks. The perennial debates over the place of *leathermen* and *drag queens* in Pride Day parades is one example of this tension between the value of tolerance and that of practicality. Responding to an article by novelist John Rechy in which he argued, in the editor's words, that "sadomasochism is a blight on our community and an impediment to the political action we so desperately need," the editors of *Gay News* came down on the side of tolerance and diversity: "We applaud the differences in our community because that diversity is our basic strength."[39] Similarly, the Christopher Street Liberation Day Committee of New York City seemed almost proud of its "turbulent, often tumultuous, 13 year history characterized by much internecine strife" as it noted of its endeavors: "Unanimity was never expected as a goal but a diverse representation of many individuals and groups from the New York gay and lesbian community who would work together to ensure a successful March and Rally was hoped for."[40]

Throughout the gay movement's history, and indeed throughout the history of social movements in the United States, one debate that centers on the value of unity is the question of coalition building. Virtually every major movement for social change in this country, at some point in its career, has fought fierce internal battles over the increase in strength and resources gained by coalition building versus the dilution of identity, program, and purpose. Within the gay movement, the calls for coalition building usually come from the left, Marxist groups whose vision of a union of the oppressed stems from a unitary idea of the root of oppression. In the present sample, the call to build coalitions was represented in two editorials, one dealing with gay response to the Ku Klux Klan, the other with gay response to the Nazis. Sara Bennett and Joan Gibbs argued for "strong autonomous movements . . . which take up the struggles of *all* issues which affect women, lesbians and gay men whether or not they affect *only* women, lesbians and gay men. This means not only fighting sexism and heterosexism but also fighting racism and classism—all the institutions that maintain the patriarchy, capitalism and imperialism."[41] Writing for the Spartacist League, Tom Dowling, a self-identified former member of the Red Flag Union, dismissed as "suicidal" "a strategy for a narrowly gay-centered mobilization against the Nazis, as put forward by the 'Stonewall Committee,' a hodge-podge of feminists, reformists, and liberals stage-managed by the Revolutionary Socialist League." Expressing his confidence in the basic decency of Chicago's heavily minority population (which obviously he had never had the practical experience of trying to coordinate), Dowling claimed that what was needed was "the will to forge a labor/minorities mobilization to bring out thousands of militant protestors to stop the Nazis."[42]

For all the talk about a common cause, even for the far left, as reflected in the titles of their essays, what truly is common is the enemy. It is an old rhetorical dictum that it is easier to get people to agree on what they are against than on what they are for, and it is confirmed in these examples. John Rowberry recognized it when he noted, "there are no differences between leatherman and the clone that matter when both are threatened by the same enemy, [sic] there are no differences between gay men and gay women that matter when both face annihilation."[43] It is not that there are no differences; it is that there are none that matter in the face of a grave and common threat. The qualifying phrases are critical.

As mentioned already, the combined appeals of work, strength, and determination became entwined with appeals to unity as the primary concern of Period VII. The profile would appear to look little different from Period VI, but a difference in distribution does reflect a difference in tone. While the combined work-determination-strength appeals in Period VI were dominated by determination, suggesting a sharply defensive rhetoric, work and determination are almost equal in Period VII, with work barely edging out determination.

Social movement theory implies that groups struggling against oppression tend to assume the character of the oppressor. The revelation began to emerge that life would not continue to improve as a natural operation of history, that there were competing interests in the world (not all of which shared the same vision of the ideal future), and that the vision of the future that we, in fact, would institute would have much to do with the concerted efforts of self-interested groups. This revelation, stemming from the successes of Bryant's followers, inspired an almost neo-Puritan ethic among gay rights activists. One of the features of White's value-coding scheme is the ability to code certain equations of value, and one of the most prominent equations of this period is some variant of D-A or "determination leads to achievement." Some of the variations include "lack of determination (work) leads to lack of achievement (failure)." And "work (determination) has in the past led to achievement." In many cases the debt to the religious right for this lesson is explicit.

John Rowberry revealed an awareness of the difference between battling Anita Bryant and battling the New Right when he wrote:

> We have recently seen our greatest enemy, the religious fundamentalists, rise to unprecedented [sic] levels of power. The seemingly overwhelming immediacy of an Anita Bryant pales by comparison to a grassroots movement that is as well organized and financed as these new harbingers of social temperance. They have brought into their self-proclaimed moral battle not only their hatred for all things gay, but their equal dislike for the liberal and progressive politics and policies that were our allies during the past decades.[44]

This paragraph captures most of the rhetorical characteristics of this period: the insecurity, the understanding of the fragility of achievement, the realization that the New Right may be less dramatic than Anita Bryant but more insidious. There is a lesson here for organizing as Rowberry makes clear later in his article:

> Part of the problem that we face today is that we have never done enough for our own good. We greeted each local law-change as a major political victory, while the new right collected another million signatures and another million dollars for their war chest. We celebrated each political endorsement

as the crown that would guarantee the kings [sic] reign, and the new right gathered another million names and got another million pledges.[45]

For several paragraphs, Rowberry continues in this vein, a long series of anaphora and epistrophe. To defeat the right, he is saying, gays must become more like them. That requires hard work, persistence, stamina, doggedness—all the dull, Protestant qualities that seem so antithetical to gay culture.

Rowberry was not alone in preaching this minatory tale. When Philadelphia was the only major American city that did not have a Pride Day celebration in 1980, the Philadelphia *Gay News* blamed it on the fact that "people in our community just didn't want to put in the time and effort, or figured that others would do it." David Goodstein's ever-avuncular voice counseled that continued progress "depends on all of you: if all of you sit out the 1980 campaign, those who have mobilized against gays could cause Congress to pass antigay legislation, could prompt the next president to rescind the minimal federal gains we've made, and could encourage state legislatures to pass civil and criminal sanctions."[46]

As it had in Period VI, **achievement** follows unity and work-determination-strength as a frequently invoked value in Period VII. The period from 1980 to 1982 consolidated a change in the way gay people looked at the achievements that began with the Dade County battle. Achievements had been looked upon as permanent fixtures, as monuments to be housed in the gay pride museum and celebrated each Pride Day, as the irrevocable work of history. As Rowberry admonished: "We treated the defeat of the Briggs Initiative as proof that justice would always prevail," but now we had even the indomitably melioristic Goodstein writing about the possibility of rescission. Others, including Rowberry, were less charitable still. "We can start over, because we are, in 1981, at ground zero," Rowberry wrote, making twenty to thirty years of movement activity a surreal joke.[47]

Of course, it was as erroneous to say that nothing had been achieved as it was to think about what had been achieved as being in a class with the Roman viaducts. Peter Frisch, David Goodstein's colleague at the *Advocate*, put a materialistic, decidedly eighties yuppie twist on gay achievement when he wrote of the skyrocketing number of gay-owned or gay-identified businesses around the country and the consequent increase in gay economic muscle.[48] Frisch, in keeping with the commercial concerns of his publication (a BMW ad appears on the same page as Frisch's editorial) and the values of his time, saw money as the route to influence and thought gay men had achieved recognition as an economic force larger than their numbers would suggest.

The appeals to **truthfulness, justice,** and **safety-security,** the three categories that tied for third place as concerns of Period VII, already are apparent in the concerns over unity, achievement, and work-strength-determination. The three-way tie perhaps was predictable since these groups of appeals often occur in various combinations. In an equation straight from classical liberalism, truth is thought to be the guarantor of justice and security, and when justice is threatened, security often is threatened along with it.

That the appeal is to truthfulness rather than to knowledge is a manifestly nonpositivistic, rhetorical stance and reflects some of those postmodern tendencies in the gay rights movement alluded to earlier. Every oppressed group, in significant ways, is alien to its oppressors, unknown, mysterious, exotic; that is a primary vehicle to oppression. We find it difficult to oppress ourselves or those in whom we recognize ourselves. It is in the interstices abandoned to ignorance that fear and loathing fester, and it is a concomitant burden of the alien group to make themselves familiar. For gays and lesbians this is the significance of the banners and placards reading "We are your children" that are staples at Pride Day marches. But as long as the alien is represented by an oppressive other or through the other's media, the truth is a political battleground. Gays, as others before them, have struggled against damaging, sometimes incendiary misconceptions spread knowingly or unknowingly on network television, in magazines, in films, and in newspapers. It was during Period VII, in fact, that there was prolonged and often bitter debate within the gay community on the proper response to the film "Cruising[,]" starring Al Pacino. Though no editorials on this subject were included in the coded sample, a number of articles and letters to the editor were noticed in different publications. Notice also was taken of a lot of *media watch* material in gay publications, including a regular column by that title in the New York *Native.*

Of the materials included in this sample, the most poignant instance of the struggle against unfair representation by major media concerned coverage of the 1981 Atlanta murders in which the disappearance and murder of young children, especially black boys, was rumored to have homosexual overtones. The coverage was poignant because the movement has had to fight the same battle so many times before, as the editorial acknowledges in its opening line: "It's like so many similar stories in the past."[49] The editorial cites several instances of conflicting evidence and criticisms of coverage from nongay sources.

Related to the unity appeal, a major form of the truthfulness appeal in this sample was the unattractive result of internecine squabbles, one group or faction charging another with all manner of mendacities.[50]

Justice historically has been defined by gay rights advocates in narrow legal terms.[51] This is one of the primary reasons the movement never has emerged as a genuinely radical force in American politics; it never has challenged root assumptions underlying the law.[52] This tendency continues in Period VII, where the courts are looked to as the last bastion against conservative popular sentiment and mounting legislative and physical attacks on gay people. "This year," expostulated the *Gay News,* "we'll be voting for judges of the various courts in the city and commonwealth. The winners will be the people who will preside over courts which decide cases affecting lesbians and gays, as well as non-gays." The editorial went on to counsel that votes should be decided based, first, on qualifications and, second, on whether or not a candidate's view of the law was "in our best interests."[53] John Rowberry, basing his arguments largely on the Bill of Rights, warned that the "new christian [sic] right" supports "racism ... tax exemption for the church without following the separation of church and state doctrines that *are* clearly in the constitution," at the same time opposing "equal rights for racial and cultural minorities." It had expressed a willingness, Rowberry wrote, to violate "rights of privacy in one's home" and "the rights to lawful public assembly."[54] Other editorials expressed concerns regarding either the judiciary or the police.[55]

The appeals to security and safety in Period VII represent a continuation of the siege mentality developed in Period VI. Assaults continued on the precarious gains made by gay people in the previous decade, a halt to further progress was a threat, and antigay violence rose, part of the rise of what now has been federally recognized as a special type of crime, the hate crime. Sara Bennett and Joan Gibbs warned that "the current growing size and boldness of the Klan is a direct outgrowth of a more widespread and visible rise in racism and other reactionary stances as evidenced by the attacks on the limited gains of Third World people, women and lesbians and gay men."[56] The editors of *Gay News,* finding a common root beneath anti-Semitism and homophobia, found a lesson in Jewish history regarding the fragile nature of "surface tolerance."[57] In 1977, when the previous study ended and this case study began, the polling firm of Yankelovich, Skelley, and White reported that 56% of those polled said they would vote for legislation guaranteeing the civil rights of homosexuals.[58] Half a decade later, gay rights advocates were fortifying the fortress walls against the possibility of all-out attack.

Period VIII: AIDS—Battling the Hydra

Just before the Independence Day holiday in 1981, the *New York Times* announced the occurrence of a rare cancer among gay men. The following week, the New York *Native,* on its cover and as its page eight headline, heralded "Cancer Hits the Gay Community." Though worrisome, the cancer could not be recognized in 1981 as the devastating epidemic that we all would come to know as AIDS. Over the course of the next two years, as death tolls rose and the multifarious forms of the disease were identified as having a common provenance, AIDS became the obsessive concern of gay rights activists, coloring all activity concerning the welfare of gay men and lesbians in the United States. AIDS presented the gay community with not only a public health crisis, but crises in the social, legal, and psychological spheres as well. AIDS catalyzed a shift in the rhetoric of the gay movement.

The shift is reflected in the coverage by papers like the New York *Native* whose readership included large numbers of those directly affected. Almost a year after the breaking of the original story, the *Native*'s coverage still was restricted largely to newsbrief items like the one in the June 7–20, 1982, issue regarding the establishment of a health hotline in New York City through which "Questions about the year-old outbreak of diseases linked to a mysterious collapse of immune defense among urban gay men will be referred to members of GMHC [Gay Men's Health Crisis]."[59] A year later, 15 of 40 news pages (ads, classifieds, and arts and entertainment excluded) featured AIDS in a significant way.[60]

Combined appeals to **work-strength-determination** again share the top rank for the most frequently appealed to values, though this time it is **justice** consuming equal attention rather than **unity**. The form of many of the work-strength-determination appeals is familiar from earlier periods. Gays often urge each other to exercise their influence in the political arena by voting, lobbying, and writing to elected representatives. Period VIII provides continuing evidence of this approach. "'I'm not political.' Will this be heard while candidates for public office are being asked to swear allegiance to the Bible (as interpreted by the fundamentalists), rather than to the Constitution?" asked David Steward of California writing in *Gay Community News*.[61] Steward's implicit faith in the power of the vote and the Constitution reflects the same basic respect for the process of American politics that we have seen as a recurrent characteristic of gay rights rhetoric.

At the same time, there is a healthy and well-earned suspicion of government. There is little faith that government, left to its own devices, will look after the best interests of gay people. A number of the work-strength-determination appeals in this period reflect this cynicism in their assertion that the government is not working, is not doing all it could

and should, especially with respect to AIDS.[62] In fact, 1987 saw gay men, lesbians, and their supporters march on Washington, D.C., in numbers that some have estimated to be as high as 500,000, more than the number who gathered to hear Martin Luther King, Jr., deliver the "I Have a Dream" speech in 1963. The march was inspired largely by what the *Windy City Times* called "the Reagan government's shameful and callous nonresponsiveness" to the AIDS crisis.[63] Consequently, many of the work-strength-determination appeals in this period reflect the gay community's determination to take care of its own in the face of AIDS.[64]

The government role in the AIDS crisis is one of the major foci of the justice appeals in this period. Rep. Henry Waxman is quoted as saying, "It is clear that if this disease were hitting members of the American Legion or Chamber of Commerce, Ronald Reagan couldn't ask for money fast enough."[65] Waxman was not the only one suggesting that the government's response to AIDS was shaped by the fact that gay men and intravenous drug users were the population hardest hit. The editors of the *Windy City Times* expressed their belief "firmly and unequivocally, that if AIDS were a disease that struck primarily white, heterosexual men, these and other solutions would long ago have been implemented."[66]

Again connected with the work-strength-determination appeals, there also are a number of warnings of the injustices that will occur if gays do not involve themselves in the political process and elect candidates who will be sympathetic to gay issues.[67] Even in the face of AIDS, justice continues to have a narrow legalistic coloring for gay activists rather than the broader moral coloring given it by other radical and reform movements in the United States.[68]

The reemergence of **truthfulness** as a major concern reflected in the rhetoric of the movement in Periods VII and VIII is peculiar given the long hiatus since it had last been a major factor. In Periods II and III (1955–1960 and 1961–1968), as gays were becoming increasingly visible while still shrouded in misconception due to lack of accurate knowledge, there was a great premium in the gay press on finding the truth about homosexuality and on using the truth to combat senseless discrimination and fear. Periods VII and VIII provide a parallel as gays were forced into the public consciousness by AIDS, a mysterious and frightening disease for which it was difficult to find the cause, the cure for which eludes us still. There is a renewed emphasis in the rhetoric of Period VIII on correcting general misconceptions about gays perpetuated by the mainstream media, but most of the truthfulness appeals in this period are connected to AIDS specifically.[69]

That gays always have had the option of passing, that they, unlike women or blacks, for example, do not wear their stigma on the surface has made the question of gay identity itself a matter of truthfulness. One editorial in this sample called the remonstrance to "come out" "the oldest message of the lesbian and gay movement" and "the most basic."[70] The appeal is double-edged. It asks gays to be truthful with themselves and in their relationships with others about who they really are, and it rests its political agenda on the sanguine assumption that direct knowledge of gay people effectively will combat harmful myths and misconceptions: To know us is to love us. In Period VIII, an unusual but significant variation on this theme appeared as presumably nongay political figures, including Roy Cohn and Terry Dolan, began to die of AIDS. The present sample contained a meditation on the intestate mess left by Rep. Stewart McKinney (R-CT).[71]

AIDS also accounts for the rank order and the tenor of the **safety-security** appeals in Period VIII. For the first time in the period coded for this study, safety (a concern for one's physical well being) appears more often than security (a concern for one's psychological or economic well being) in the combined appeal. And, for the first time across all eight periods, health, though not ranked in the top five appeals even here, makes a more than incidental appearance in the discourse. The most common form for these appeals was the recitation of statistics. By 1983, the numbers affected by AIDS had begun to rise geometrically. "The City Health Department reports 16 city residents with AIDS since September 1981," reported the Philadelphia *Gay News,* continuing "EIGHT OF THEM HAVING BEEN REPORTED IN THE LAST FOUR MONTHS."[72] By 1988, it was

the number of panels in "the Quilt" that were being counted, and those numbers made the numbers reported from Philadelphia in 1981 seem innocuously small.[73]

Finally, **tolerance** rounds out the roster of top-ranked value appeals for Period VIII. It always is one of the in-group functions of social movement discourse to provide an outlet for commiseration over the sorry state of the world and the particular group's poor place in it. From its beginnings, the rhetoric of gay liberation in the United States has featured indictments of the lack of tolerance shown for gays by straight society and warnings that the situation will get worse unless gays act. Period VIII continues this tradition. There is one account of a gay man fired from his job, and the Roman Catholic church received more than incidental recognition in the three periods coded here as a bastion of bigotry.[74] But intolerance, though Lenny Giteck was correct in pointing out that it did not begin with AIDS, did achieve a new intensity and a new focus as the result of AIDS.[75] As one writer put it, "the conservative right has launched a new cold war, with a new cast of demonized 'others,'" a play in which gay men become "diseased-ridden infectious carriers."[76] In a sense, AIDS and the heightened intolerance that accompanied it pervade Period VIII, so much so that the intolerance often seems to exist beyond the individual coding unit or even the individual piece of discourse. Understood this way, it illustrates something of the text-context relationship that it has been the burden of this study to illustrate: the relationship between catalytic events and the resultant discourse.

Conclusion

This detailing of key value appeals in gay rights rhetoric for the thirteen-year period from 1977 to 1990, coupled with the results of my earlier analysis of gay rights rhetoric from 1948 to 1977, allows us to make some observations about changes in this discourse over more than four decades. In addition, it allows us to speculate as to how the nature of these changes might apply to social movements generally. Moreover, since historical events are integral to the method employed here, we have the opportunity to raise hypotheses about the ways in which history and rhetoric interact.

Social progress, often expressed as an appeal to justice as it is in the current case, is the self-professed but elusive goal of all social movements. By that measure, the one clear picture that emerges from careful study of a movement in the interim stages between inception and success is that progress is neither clear nor unidimensional.

If progress may be defined rhetorically as rendering unnecessary the expenditure of argumentative energy or attention on certain claims, then the gay rights movement indisputably has progressed in some areas, primarily those areas that are internal, addressed to movement members themselves. Concerns with naturalness, adjustment, and self-regard, for example, which were prominent in the early rhetoric, have all but disappeared in the later periods. The abatement of those appeals suggests that the movement has enjoyed some success in convincing its constituency that they are not inherently abnormal in some pejorative sense, maladjusted, or sick. To borrow from Richard Gregg's work, the movement appears to have been most effective in fulfilling "ego-functions."[77] This reconstruction of the components of gay self-identification was a necessary propaedeutic to vigorous political action. From 1977 to 1990, as the emerging prominence of work-determination-strength appeals suggests, there is little of the old hesitation among gays in asserting that better and more equitable treatment is deserved from society.

Ego-functions, though, are not wholly an internal matter subject to adjudication within the group. It was only when the American Psychiatric Association officially removed the stigma of sickness from homosexuality in its 1973 revision of the *Diagnostic and Statistical Manual* that the gay rights movement finally could claim clear presumption on the question. The event indicates the degree to which sub-cultures are dependent on the cultures of which they are a part, even on matters essential to defining the lines of demarcation between them. No amount of self-persuasion regarding, in this case, the essential health of gay people could withstand widescale criticism as long as

that criticism appeared to have the blessing of the psychological and psychiatric establishment. Dominant cultures have ultimate control over vehicles for legitimation, one of the key factors in defining dominance. The dominant culture also controls agenda setting, which makes any movement of social reform that falls short of complete revolution reactive. This point is acknowledged in the definition of *catalytic event* forwarded here as "something that arises outside the bounds of movement strategy but that shapes the subsequent discourse of the movement."

Still cultures, perhaps especially the culture of the United States in [the] late twentieth century, are not homogeneous, univocal entities. For everything given by the liberal left, something may be taken away by the reactionary right. There are paradoxes of progress in the lives of social movements. Gay rights activists, from the beginning, have struggled against the invisibility that has been both a curse and a blessing. One editorial characterized the imperative to "come out" as "the oldest message of the lesbian and gay movement," and "the most basic."[78] Early appeals to knowledge and truthfulness often concerned the representation of gays to the surrounding straight culture, and, in Period IV (1969–1972), recognition emerged as a major value in itself.[79] The achievement of recognition and visibility has been viewed by the gay rights movement both as an end in itself and as a vehicle for further gains.

It has been the movement's success in this arena, though, that has helped to create a backlash that is signaled by increased appeals to safety and security. That trend becomes obvious only when the data for 1977–1990 are combined with the data for 1948–1977. There are no significant appeals to safety or security until Period V (1973–1977), when safety appeals were ranked second. From that time to the present, combined appeals to safety and security are prominent in gay rights rhetoric as increasing concerns are expressed over antigay violence and discrimination. This analysis of the discourse suggests that as a result of their "success" gays may be subject to more overt forms of hostility than when, as one writer describes it, "They crouched in their closets, took girls to company parties, and waited, hoping that if only we'd be good and do as we were told, they'd get tired of persecuting us and leave us alone to lead our quiet little respectable lives."[80]

If progress has been a tradeoff in some areas, in other areas, there seems to have been no progress at all. Though the overwhelming number of child molestation cases involve heterosexual men, gays still suffer under the public conviction that they pose a special threat in this area. Nothing serves better than a highly sensationalized sex crime with homosexual overtones to draw forth from the gay press fervent professions of gay solidarity with straight society against heinous behaviors. Such displays would be unremarkable except that the intensity of their self-righteous indignation is susurrous with a synecdochal urge for extermination that has been evident in gay rights rhetoric throughout its history in the United States. The apparent urge spans time from San Francisco Mattachine's 1954 announcement that it shared with straight society the goal of "reducing the high incidence of sex variation in future generations"[81] to Michael's query in "The Boys in the Band," "Who was it that used to say, 'You show me a happy homosexual, and I'll show you a gay corpse'?"

In the current sample, the editors of the Philadelphia *Gay News* in 1981, regarding the murders then being investigated in Atlanta, rhetorically posed the question, "What should the response of the community be?" Among their suggestions, the one deemed most important was that the gay community *should make* no excuses for the killings "if there is a homosexual aspect."

> Let us join with others in calling for sure punishment for the guilty. Taking a life is the most vile of deeds. There should be no mollycoddling of the guilty, no matter what the circumstances, and no matter what his or her sexual orientation may be.[82]

Here is the overeager and bloodthirsty language of the lynch mob—the platitudinous moralizing, the disregard for circumstances, the ancient equation of vengeance with justice, the desire for resolution with at least the illusion of certitude—all with the understanding that it may be against some part of the self that it is turned.

More than the gay community's failure to dispel the myths of rampant child molestation and murder among gays, this reaction reflects how thoroughly gays have been inculcated with the values of straight society. The inculcation includes not only such questions as murder, but also, more subtly and insidiously, those values by which gay people comprehend themselves. It is not the murder of children that accounts for the severity of the above quotation; it is the desire to purify the self, to make amends for what one has been taught is odious in one's nature, to extirpate the sordidness within. There is no evidence in the clamorous statement just quoted that the standards for purity themselves have been scrutinized and questioned. In recent years gays may have come to feel better about themselves as individuals than they did in the 1950s, but it appears that this may be tied to their ability to eschew stereotypes in their own lives and to emulate the surrounding straight culture; it appears that there remain very real reservations about homosexuality in general precisely in the degree that it fails to share the values of the larger society. One article in the current sample treats these issues under the title "Reflections on Internalized Homophobia."[83]

It is still the exceptional voice that attempts, as John Rowberry does in his eulogy to John Wayne, to make "God-fearing, patriotic, [and] fundamental" "seem like nefarious qualities." Rowberry, writing in a magazine devoted to gay sado-masochism, thus already violating many taboos, wrote of Wayne that he "represented and will represent for some time to come a particular image of the American male that at least 10 million other American men think to be the height of admirable masculine sensibility." When Rowberry noted near the conclusion, "While he lived, not one breath of scandal was ever uttered about the Duke. Now, months after his final roundup or shoot-out, or whatever it is you want to call it; not one breath of scandal emerges," it seemed almost perverse.

Perhaps this is the fundamental question for any movement for social reform, the question of how to define success. How much do *we* become like *them* in order to enjoy the fruits of what they call success, and how much do *we* make *them* acknowledge that there are alternatives that must be respected? Bowers and Ochs use the terminology of "vertical" versus "lateral" deviance to describe this broad distinction between orientations to the dominant value system.[84] The present example makes clear that this cannot be separated from how thoroughly *we* have learned the lessons *they* have taught about *us*. I may feel that I deserve rights as an individual, but I may have difficulty demanding those rights as a gay person. In fact, I may feel more deserving of rights the more distance I can place between myself and constructs I have absorbed about gay people.[85]

Although our study of the gay rights movement may help to clarify this rhetorical dynamic, it is, again, not unique. That movements for social reform are hindered or thwarted by the constructs members have absorbed about themselves is evident in the black rights movement's self-affirmation and in the women's movement. In this latter case, nineteenth-century women were so convinced of the inappropriateness of their activity that Abby Foster's husband, Stephen, was called upon to chair the Seneca Falls convention, and twentieth-century women have struggled to redefine *woman* in ways that simultaneously allow for both opportunities in a male-dominated world and the reassessing, revaluing, and potential remaking that world.

Of the findings of this study, one of the most important concerns the interplay of catalytic events and discourse. The danger is that the findings, because they comport with the dictates of common sense or seem to have face validity, should be deemed less valuable for that reason, that they may suffer from an excess of what one reviewer of the material from 1948 to 1977 identified as plausibility.[86] Given the contexts as described, the shape of each rhetorical period seems eminently reasonable, even predictable. Yet the model of interaction suggested here is not narrowly deterministic or materialistic. To say that the rhetorical choices that were made are consonant with surrounding events is not to say that other choices, equally consonant, were impossible. I think, rather, that catalytic events operate on the discourse on three levels: First, they operate to constrain the range of rhetorical action in the same ways Kenneth Burke talks about the place of "scene" in his account of

motive; they form part of a "rhetorical situation," which, if it does not demand *a* response, certainly allows for a certain range of responses at the same time it limits the sheer numbers of possibilities for response. An event without the existence of those for whom it may be rhetorically made significant is only an event. It is not, in itself, a rhetorical situation. Ongoing social movements provide those interested constituencies. Gay people certainly could not ignore AIDS; it had to be addressed in some way, but not necessarily in these particular ways. American Legionnaires, on the other hand, were not obligated in the same ways by the mysterious deaths in Philadelphia in 1976. Events invite the imputation of meaning; they call out for narrative frames, for stories. The stories or acts, as Burke suggests in his account of the dramatistic pentad, are shaped by the ideologies and beliefs held by the various storytellers, the vehicles of dissemination they have available to them, and so on through the other two or three elements, as well as by the events themselves. AIDS has been represented as God's curse against those who have transgressed holy ordinance, as a CIA-sponsored attempt at genocide, and as the terrifying consequence of implacable nature operating according to its own laws. Competing stories metamorphose from act to scenic element and, as much as the event itself, define the exigence.

In addition to operating scenically, catalytic events serve to punctuate the progress of movement discourse. A catalyst is a chemical that is used to speed up a reaction, a reaction that would have occurred anyway, only much more slowly. With slow reactions, as with evolutionary trends, the gradual quality of change often makes it difficult to distinguish discrete phases. Use of a catalyst, however, reduces transitory periods and thus dramatically juxtaposes changed states that otherwise would have been indiscernible. The analogy, of course, has limits. Social activity is not reducible to scientific laws, and it is impossible to say what would have happened if some significant historical event had not occurred. The argument easily could be made in many specific cases that an event hastened the realization of nascent trends, though it also seems likely that the event colors the outcome in ways that a true catalyst does not. If catalytic events tend to forward existing trends rather than define entirely new directions, it probably is because they occur in the context of an ongoing agenda, and they are interpreted within that context. In addition to this qualification, it should be obvious that a catalytic event is not a manipulable variable in the way that the catalyst is for the chemist; the student of social movements cannot selectively apply such events to meet his or her needs; he or she only can look for them in the history of the movement and use them as they are found.

Finally, and most crudely, some catalytic events become incorporated into movement discourse, what Aristotle called "inartistic proofs." As inartistic proofs, certain claims that were problematic rhetorically may be transformed into warrants for further claims. One of the central issues for gay activists, for example, has been establishing the existence of significant discrimination against gays. Even after decades of visibility and activity, gays still struggle to make antigay discrimination understood. In 1982, Lenny Giteck found "a silver lining in the dark cloud of AIDS." That silver lining was that AIDS had done what gay rhetoric had failed to do: "shown the world that we gays actually exist." That Giteck includes the condition of oppression in gay existence is made clear when he constructs a dialogue with fictitious Irving Schmertz, head of Plagues, Epidemics, and Famines at NBC news:

> "Listen, Mr. Schmertz," I began, "Doesn't Tom Brokaw know that homosexuals have been discriminated against for years? No, for *centuries*. It didn't start with AIDS!"

> "Are you sure about that?" Schmertz asked. "I don't remember our doing any documentaries on it. What kind of discrimination are you referring to?"[87]

History has an irrefragable quality. It happened; all of us saw it; therefore, it is fact.

Yet even history's assertions are not absolute. The events of history may be suppressed, or they may be forgotten. One might have thought, for example, that in the wake of the Dade County referendum battle when Robert Hillsborough was stabbed to death by four teenagers screaming "Faggot, faggot, faggot! This one's for you, Anita!" the case for antigay discrimination would have been established once and for all. Or even earlier, that the chronicle of ruined lives and spoiled careers left behind by the innuendo of McCarthyism would have given the point to gay activists. Most frightening, the events of history may be warped beyond recognition. Current projects dedicated to denying the Holocaust, an event that recent historical study has revealed to be as important to gay history as to Jewish history, are only the most egregious examples.

The urge to recover history is never entirely innocent; it contains not only the passionate desire to control or to liberate, to reveal the genetic code, to know who we are now by knowing who we have been, but also the yearning to know history itself, the precise nature of the past's claim on the present. The historical perspective is inescapable whenever the object of attention has a temporal dimension, five minutes or five hundred years. Rhetorical history is a variety of history, and it shares in these same motives as reflected in this installment in an ongoing account of the rhetoric of gay liberation in the United States. There are specific insights here into the rhetoric of the gay liberation movement; a large body of discourse has been characterized broadly to allow the making of summary statements. There also are tentative statements about the larger issues, statements that can be made with confidence only when we have enough comparable studies to allow generalization. Certainly an aggregation of such studies could provide fresh ammunition for theoretical debates that currently seem to have more gun powder than shells, providing us with a great show of fire and smoke but few reasons for surrender, compromise, or resolution and little direction for the future.

Notes

1 Suzanne Volmar Riches and Malcolm O. Sillars, "The Status of Movement Criticism," *Western Journal of Speech Communication* 44 (1980): 281. See also Stephen E. Lucas, "Coming to Terms with Movement Studies," *Central States Speech Journal* 31 (1980): 264.

2 In addition to Sillars' and Riches' assessment, see Charles J. Stewart, "A Functional Perspective on

the Study of Social Movements," *Central States Speech Journal* 34 (1983): 77.

[3] S. Judson Crandell, "The Beginnings of a Methodology for Social Control Studies in Public Address," *Quarterly Journal of Speech* 33 (1947): 36.

[4] Roderick P. Hart, "Theory Building and Rhetorical Criticism: An Informal Statement of Opinion," *Central States Speech Journal* 27 (1976): 71, and "Contemporary Scholarship in Public Address: A Research Editorial," *Western Journal of Speech Communication* 50 (1986): 283–295.

[5] James F. Darsey, "Catalytic Events and Rhetorical Movements: A Methodological Inquiry" (unpublished master's thesis, Purdue University, 1978). The bulk of the rhetorical analysis from this study was published as James Darsey, "From 'Commies' and 'Queers' to 'Gay is Good,'" in *Gayspeak: Gay Male and Lesbian Communication*, ed. James W. Chesebro (New York: Pilgrim Press, 1981), 224–247. Though published with the imprimatur of SCA and at a time when books from the discipline were more scarce than they are today, *Gayspeak* failed to garner a single review in any SCA-affiliated journal even though some contributors, myself included, made personal appeals to book review editors and secured review copies for them. Nor was the book included in an otherwise outstanding bibliography in the first edition of Stewart, Smith, and Denton's *Persuasion and Social Movements* (Prospect Heights, IL: Waveland Press, 1984), an oversight corrected, again after a personal appeal, in the recently published second edition of that work. Outside SCA circles, in contrast, the volume received more than 200 reviews in places as diverse as academic journals like *Signs* and popular sources like the *Los Angeles Times,* and though many of those reviews contained sharp criticisms, citations in many places suggest that the volume continues to enjoy wide use. *Gayspeak* also has the distinction of being one of the few works published under the auspices of SCA that could be found on the shelves of local bookstores across the country. A recent trip to a new bookstore in Columbus, Ohio, revealed, much to my surprise, that this still is true nearly ten years after the book's original publication.

[6] Karlyn Kohrs Campbell, "The Rhetoric of Women's Liberation: An Oxymoron," *Quarterly Journal of Speech* 59 (1973): 74–86.

[7] James Darsey, "Die Non: Gay Liberation and the Rhetoric of Tolerance," in *Gayspeak II,* ed. R. Jeffrey Ringer (forthcoming); James Darsey, *Vessels of the Word: Studies of the Prophetic Voice in American Public Address* (unpublished Ph.D. dissertation, University of Wisconsin, 1985).

[8] James R. Andrews, "An Historical Perspective on the Study of Social Movements," *Central States Speech Journal* 34 (1983): 68.

[9] Andrews, 68.

[10] Lucas, 264. See also James R. Andrews, "History and Theory in the Study of the Rhetoric of Social Movements," *Central States Speech Journal* 31 (1980): 274–281, and Ralph R. Smith, "The Historical Criticism of Social Movements," *Central States Speech Journal* 31 (1980): 290–297.

[11] See James Andrews' call for such studies in the symposium that was, in part, responsible for the case study focus of this special issue: "An Historical Perspective on the Study of Social Movements."

[12] "The Structures of History: Dividing Phenomena for Rhetorical Understanding," *Central States Speech Journal* 24 (1973): 33. Perhaps a clue to the relative obscurity of Munshaw's essay is my belief that the time in which it appeared was concerned with theory as opposed to method. Compare Munshaw's essay with the essays from the first SCA seminar on social movements published in *Central States Speech Journal* 31 (1980). I recognize that these are not independent considerations. Methods often are theoretically laden, and empirically based theories, to a significant degree, are defined by the methods that have been used to gather the data upon which the theories are based. Nonetheless, one can make distinctions based on where the primary focus of discussion lies, and there is considerable difference between a Judson Crandell or a Leland Griffin or a Joe Munshaw engaged in an attempt to figure out how to go about the rhetorical study of a social movement and a Michael McGee and a Robert Cathcart facing off over whether social movements are phenomena or meaning.

[13] Munshaw, 30.

[14] Munshaw, 35.

[15] John Bowers and Donovan Ochs in their enormously popular text, *The Rhetoric of Agitation and Control* (Reading, MA: Addison Wesley, 1971), have provided the most visible effort in this direction, but their schema is heavily theory-laden, assuming *a priori* the sequence of a number of specific strategies. In addition to presuming specific strategies, the claims for sequencing is susceptible to criticisms for what Sillars has identified as a problematic characteristic of contemporary theories, the assumption of linearity. In fact, at least one test case using Bowers and Ochs' schema revealed problems in precisely this area.

James Darsey, "Escalation of Agitative Rhetoric: A Case Study of Mattachine Midwest, 1967–1970" (paper presented to the convention of the Central States Speech Association, Southfield, MI, April 1977, included in ERIC as ED 140 358).

[16] Like most other ideas that make claims at innovation, catalytic events as an analytical tool have a number of antecedents and historical analogs, both in practice and in theory. C. Wendell King has discussed "accidental influences" and their relationship to social movements, *Social Movements in the United States* (New York: Random House, 1956), 108–111. In discussing the inception of revolutions, Crane Brinton suggests the importance of events that escape the controlled parameters of tactics and achieve spontaneity, *The Anatomy of Revolution,* revised edition (New York: Vintage Books, 1965), 77–86. Rhetorical scholars Charles Stewart, Craig Smith, and Robert Denton also have made suggestive allusions to the importance of events in the life of a movement. They note that, in addition to "skilled leaders, dedicated followers, satisfactory organization, a social system that tolerates protest, and a climate conducive to change," "[e]vents such as Three Mile Island, Kent State, and *Brown v. Board of Education* are essential for the progress of social movements," *Persuasion and Social Movements* 13. Later the authors refer to a "triggering event" that the social movement looks to "give birth to a new phase of enthusiastic mobilization" (p. 45). Most recently in rhetorical studies, David Proctor has proposed "dynamic spectacles," fusions of material events and symbolic constructions, as focal points for the discourse of communities in conflict. Reflecting concerns similar to those driving this study, Proctor writes: "Methodologically, then, the dynamic event provides a frame for studying the dynamic phenomenon of community. The frame functions not as a template to be pressed over the rhetoric, but rather works as a boundary for data collection and analysis." David E. Proctor, "The Dynamic Spectacle: Transforming Experience into Social Forms of Community," *Quarterly Journal of Speech* 76 (1990): 130.

[17] "Structure: Human Reality and Methodological Concept," in *The Structuralist Controversy: The Language of Criticism and the Sciences of Man*, eds. Richard Macksey and Eugenio Donat (Baltimore: Johns Hopkins University Press, 1972), 98.

[18] Goldmann, 98.

[19] Darsey, "Catalytic Events and Rhetorical Movements." It was primarily the substantive conclusions of this study, concerned with the rhetoric of gay liberation rather than with methodological questions, that was published as "From 'Commies' and 'Queers' to 'Gay is Good,'" in *Gayspeak,* 224–247.

[20] See Darsey, "Catalytic Events and Rhetorical Movements," or "From 'Commies' and 'Queers' to 'Gay is Good.'"

[21] Because this study is an extension of an earlier study, the decision was made to stick as closely as possible to choices regarding treatment of the discourse made in the first study. This includes choices regarding coding rules, statistical tests, and other matters. Value analysis, a content-analytic coding scheme developed in the 1940s by Ralph White, was used as a method of quantifying significant characteristics of the discourse. In the application of the value analysis itself, there is one important deviation from the original study that is worthy of note. Health, a value in White's schema not generally considered among the most useful for propaganda studies, was coded in the current study though it was not in the original study. In reviewing the discourse samples from the original study, only one editorial was found in which the value health was featured, an editorial on venereal diseases. The contrast between the relative lack of concern with health issues in the first seven rhetorical eras and the significant concern with such issues in the final era studied here, an era dominated by AIDS, is as dramatic as it was predictable.

Another alteration of the original research design that was made in the interest of improving the study without inhibiting comparability was doubling the sample size for each period from approximately 5,000 words in the first study to approximately 10,000 words in this follow up. The samples, as in the original study, are newspaper editorials and opinion pieces from gay presses, and a rudimentary form of stratified sampling was used in their selection in order to ensure representation geographically, organizationally, temporally, and ideologically. While lesbian voices were not systematically excluded from this sample and in fact there are a number of editorials by lesbians included, neither was there any attempt to include publications specifically addressed to the lesbian community. Given the rift that often surfaces between the gay male and lesbian communities and given that lesbians often have found the women's movement a more congenial home than the gay liberation movement, this study, as with the original one, should be taken as more representative of the gay liberation movement as it has been associated primarily with gay men than of gay male and lesbian interests. For examples of the debate over gay male and lesbian relations, see Jeffrey Escoffier, "Can Gay Men and Lesbians Work Together?" *Out/Look* 2 (Fall 1989): 1, and "Community Voices," [Letter to the editors] *Gay Community News,* 6 (April 28, 1979), 4. Within each stratum, the sampling was as random as it could be practically made without resorting to the formal apparatus of generating random numbers, etc.

More information on the method and its application can be found in Darsey, "Catalytic Events and Rhetorical Movements: A Methodological Inquiry," or in Darsey, "Catalytic Events and Rhetorical Movements: A Methodological Proposal" (paper prepared for the SCA seminar in social movements, November 1989).

22 See, for example, Peter Frisch's November 15, 1979, editorial (p. 5) in the *Advocate* in which he reflects on the national nature of both the publication and the gay rights struggle. See also Bruce Voeller and Jean O'Leary, "In Praise of Lyn," [Community Voices] *Gay Community News* (April 2, 1977), 4.

23 It also is true that the existence of gay centers of leadership and cultural definition contributes to the kind of condescension and snobbery that Rome exhibited toward the provinces. The provinces, in return, threaten the unity of the whole by becoming resentful and uncooperative. See Dennis Melbatson, "NGTF, the March and the Hinterlands," *Gay Community News* (April 21, 1979), 5. For some general and tentative thoughts on how the subcultural nature of gay liberation influences identification, both in the Burkean, rhetorical sense and in the more common sense, see James Darsey, "Gayspeak: A Response," in Chesebro, ed., 58–67.

24 [Philadelphia] *Gay News* (April 1977), 22.

25 See Darsey, "Die Non . . . ," in *Vessels of the Word.*

26 "Opening Space," *Advocate* (July 26, 1978), 5; (December 27, 1978), 5.

27 "Community Voice," *Gay Community News* (April 2, 1977), 4.

28 "A House Divided," *Gay Community News* (September 16, 1978), 4.

29 David Goodstein, "Opening Space," *Advocate* (July 26, 1978), 5.

30 "A House Divided," 4.

31 (January 1978), 22.

32 "On to Washington," *Gay Community News* (March 26, 1977), 4; "Guest Editorial: On to Washington," (April 1977), 22.

33 "Bryant Threatens all GAYS!" [Philadelphia] *Gay News* (April 1977), 22; "A House Divided," *Gay Community News* (September 16, 1978), 4; "Speak for Yourself," *Gay News* (May 18, 1979), 15.

34 See [Philadelphia] *Gay News* (April 1977), 22; [Cleveland] *Gay News* (February 1977), 24; and *Southern Gay News* (February 1978), 22.

35 "The right-wing threat: It's very real and dangerous," *Gay News* (April 20, 1979), 13.

36 "The right-wing threat: It's very real and dangerous," 13; "Opening Space," *Advocate* (December 27, 1978), 5.

37 "Opening Space," *Advocate* (February 7, 1980), 5.

38 "A Secondary Primary? No," *Gay News* (May 1–14, 1981), 21; "Not Representative," *Gay News* (March 19–April 1, 1982).

39 "S&M: Actually, an asset," *Gay News* (May 1–14, 1981), 21.

40 "CSLDC Responds," *Gay Community News* (June 26, 1982), 5.

41 "Liberation is Not in a Vacuum: Fighting the Klan," *Gay Community News* (March 15, 1980), 5. Though not officially part of the sample and not coded, a letter on the same page, "Unite to Fight," also is illustrative.

42 "Gays and Nazis," *Gay Community News* (July 3, 1982), 4.

43 "1984: The Countdown Begins," *Drummer,* Issue 42 (1981), 6. Issue numbers rather than dates are fairly common for gay publications, especially those in a magazine format. These publications often are unable to maintain a regular publication schedule because of financial and legal problems.

44 "1984: The Countdown Begins," 6.

45 "1984: The Countdown Begins," 6.

46 "Gay Pride '81," [Philadelphia] *Gay News* (May 1–14, 1981), 21; "Opening Space," *Advocate* (February 7, 1980), 5.

47 "1984: The Countdown Begins," 6.

48 "Opening Space," *Advocate* (October 15, 1981), 6.

49 "Thinking about Atlanta," *Gay News* (April 17–30, 1981), 19. In the study this one extends, there was a 1957 editorial regarding the Stephen Nash murders and their effect on perceptions of the gay community. See "From 'Commies' and 'Queers' to 'Gay is Good,'" 234. Another notorious case was that of John Wayne Gacy. There have been others of more strictly local interest.

50 See "Not Representative," *Gay News* (March 19–April 1, 1982), and "CSLDC Responds," 5.

51 Darsey, "From 'Commies' and 'Queers,'" p. 233, *passim.*

52 Darsey, "Die Non . . . ."

53 "A Secondary Primary? No," 21.

54 "1984: The Countdown Begins," 6.

55 "Gays and Nazis," *Gay Community News* (July 3, 1982), 4; D. B. Goodstein, "Opening Space," *Advocate* (February 7, 1980), 5; "The Wisdom of Solomon," *Gay News* (June 27–July 10, 1980), 15.

56 "Liberation is not in a Vacuum: Fighting the Klan," 5.

57 "Anti-Semitism, homophobia have same root," *Gay News* (April 17–30, 1981), 19.

58 As reported in *Time* (November 21, 1977), 44.

59 New York *Native* (June 7–20, 1982), 6.

60 New York *Native* (October 24–November 6, 1983). By 1985, in one typical issue the ratio was 20 of 28 pages. New York *Native* (September 30–October 6, 1985).

61 "Gay Health and Well Being," *Gay Community News* (November 30–December 6, 1986), 5. See also "NATIVE Endorsements" and "Important Voter Information," New York *Native* (November 5–18, 1984), 5.

62 See, for example, "Axelrod's Pig Blood," New York *Native* (October 7–13, 1986). The editorial in the present sample most suspicious of government is the one that insinuates that AIDS might be caused by a chemical agent unleashed by the Army or the CIA. The editorial, aware of the skeptical reaction it would receive, concludes: "For years, the U.S. Army has been trying to come up with a chemical that could destroy the immune system. That's not paranoia. That's the CONGRESSIONAL RECORD." "Acquired Industrial Dioxin Syndrome?" New York *Native* (September 12–25, 1983), 3.

63 "Keep the March on Washington Alive," *Windy City Times* (October 15, 1987), 13.

64 See, for example, "AIDS Update," *Gay News* (March 25–31, 1983), 13.

65 "AIDS Update," 13.

66 "FDA Protestors Combine Courage and Wisdom," *Windy City Times* (October 20, 1988), 11.

67 For example, see "Ray Flynn and Lesbian/Gay Liberation," *Gay Community News* (September 29, 1984), 4, and "NATIVE Endorsements" and "Important Voter Information," 5.

68 See, for example, Jackie Goldsby, "'O, Say Can You See' . . . As Far as We Tell You to Look," *Out/Look* (Winter 1990): 1. The entire editorial is devoted to examining the potential impact of upcoming Supreme Court decisions on the gay community.

69 See Lenny Giteck, "Lenny," *Advocate* (December 24, 1985), 5, and "The Gay Press," New York *Native* (January 16, 1989), 13.

70 "There is No Substitute for the Quilt and No Substitute for Coming Out," *Windy City Times* (October 13, 1988), 11.

71 Dave Walter, "Tales of Congress," *Advocate* (September 26, 1989), 27. In the same commentary, Walter dealt with the fact that Barney Frank was advantaged by having "come out" before the revelations regarding his relationship with Steve Gobie surfaced.

72 "AIDS Update," *Gay News* (March 25–31, 1983), 13. See also Cliff Amesen, "Veterans and AIDS," *Gay Community News* (February 25–March 3, 1990), 5.

73 "There is No Substitute for the Quilt and No Substitute for Coming Out," 11.

74 Lenny Giteck, "No Hope for the Pope," *Advocate* (December 23, 1986), 5; "Keep the March on Washington Alive," *Windy City Times* (October 15, 1987), 13.

75 Lenny Giteck, "Lenny," 5.

76 "'O, Say Can You See' . . . As Far as We Tell You to Look," 1.

77 Richard B. Gregg, "The Ego-Function of the Rhetoric of Protest," *Philosophy and Rhetoric* 4 (1971): 71–91.

78 "There is No Substitute for the Quilt and No Substitute for Coming Out," 11.

79 In addition, recognition was the fifth ranked value for Period VIII.

80 Phillip Bockman, "The New Respectability," New York *Native* (September 24–October 7, 1984), 14. Bockman's indiscriminate switching of person in his use of pronouns is confusing, but the careful reader will discern that those who are initially "they" become "we" (gay men) in order that straights may become "they."

81 "The Mattachine Program," San Francisco Mattachine Newsletter (June 25, 1954), n.p., quoted in Darsey, "From 'Commies' and 'Queers' to 'Gay is Good,'" 230.

82 "Thinking About Atlanta," [Philadelphia] *Gay News* (April 17–30, 1981), 19.

83 Maryanne deGoede, *Gay Community News* (July 12–18, 1987), 5.

84 Bowers and Ochs, 7.

85 For some preliminary empirical evidence on how gay men and lesbians may separate their self-concepts from constructs they may have about homosexuals, gays, or lesbians, see Fred E. Jandt and James Darsey, "Coming Out as a Communicative Process," in Chesebro, ed., 12–27.

86 Stephen O. Murray, "Review of Gayspeak: Gay Male and Lesbian Communication," *Advocate* (January 7, 1982).

87 Lenny Giteck, "Lenny," 5.

The Evolution of a Revolution:
Stokely Carmichael and the Rhetoric of Black Power

Charles J. Stewart

During the past twenty years, a growing number of researchers have focused on how the rhetoric of social movements and social movement organizations changes over time in response to temporal changes, changing social values, challenges from within and without, and ideological refocusing. For instance, Charles Conrad studied the transformation of the "Old Feminist" movement from 1850 to 1878 by tracing changes in argument and identifying "a watershed moment" at the 1860 Woman's Rights Convention "when feminism started to become suffragism."[1] James Darsey studied how the Anita Bryant–inspired referendum against gay rights, the inauguration of Ronald Reagan, the rise of the Moral Majority, and the "scourge of AIDS" served as "catalytic events" that altered the rhetoric of the gay liberation movement from 1977 to 1990.[2] My study of the changes in the internal rhetoric of the Knights of Labor from 1879 to 1913 revealed how its leaders attempted to adjust to enormous increases and then decreases in membership, identification with the Haymarket Riot and anarchists, failure of its linchpin cooperatives, the rise of the American Federation of Labor, and the depression of the 1890s.[3]

While all social movements evolve and adapt to societal changes, significant departures from established movement norms and procedures seldom take place without internal conflict. If a movement evolves gradually over time—from woman's rights to suffrage, from temperance to prohibition of alcoholic beverages, or from the humane treatment of animals to animal rights, internal conflict may be minimal. On the other hand, the emergence of new organizations, leaders, ideologies, or strategies may generate considerable internal conflict. Fred Powledge chronicles the jealousies, competition, and in-fighting within the civil rights movement.[4] The rise of a young Martin Luther King, Jr.,

his leadership of the successful Montgomery bus boycott, creation of the Southern Christian Leadership Conference (SCLC) in 1957, and enormous popularity threatened the status of older civil rights leaders and the principles and strategies of their long-established organizations such as the National Association for the Advancement of Colored People (NAACP) founded in 1909, the National Urban League founded in 1910, and the Congress of Racial Equality (CORE) founded in 1942. Similarly, the sit-ins that black college students conducted in South Carolina and the creation of the Student Nonviolent Coordinating Committee (SNCC) in 1960 challenged King's leadership and increased his commitment to nonviolent, civil disobedience as the primary means to achieve integration. Most social movements not only survive internal conflicts but find them nourishing and rejuvenating. For example, fragile coalitions among competing organizations, leaders, and ideologies may be critical for successful campaigns or to fend off outside assaults.

There are times, however, when internal conflicts differ fundamentally from gradual and peaceful evolutionary changes over time and squabbles over strategies, leadership, organizational policies, turf, or ideological purity. They are struggles from within that reject all that a movement has been, is, and promises to become in its moral crusade to end oppression, exploitation, and injustice. For example, Samuel Gompers led such a struggle within the labor movement when he and his infant American Federation of Labor challenged and eventually replaced the mighty Knights of Labor and its fundamental principle of industrial unionism that admitted all workers to membership, regardless of skill level or trade.[5] Dave Foreman was the chief lobbyist for the Wilderness Society before becoming disillusioned with the slow pace, failures, tactics, and penchant for compromise of the environmental movement. He became a cofounder and leader of Earth First! that rejected the established movement and its principle of lobbying through institutions for acceptable environmental compromises.[6] Abbie Hoffman and Jerry Rubin founded and led the Youth International Party (Yippies) that radicalized and transformed the peace and counter-culture movements of the 1960s.[7] And Stokely Carmichael, the chairman of SNCC, championed a "black power" ideology within the civil rights movement that repudiated the movement's leaders, organizations, strategies, and emphasis on integration as the means to end oppression and injustice.[8]

I believe Conrad identifies a fundamental cause of evolutionary struggles within social movements when he writes that "Implicit in the origin of a movement are the dynamics of its development and its possible transformation."[9] Just as societal elements create social movements because of frustration and disillusionment with the failure of *institutional establishments* to meet needs and rising expectations, so do elements within movements—particularly new generations of activists—become frustrated and disillusioned with the failure of *social movement establishments* to satisfy urgent needs and rising expectations. The resulting internal conflict is intended to perfect the movement through purges of the movement's failed leadership, organizations, strategies, and principles. We can understand such rhetorical conflicts best if we see them as evolutionary struggles from within rather than conflicts with external institutions, gradual evolutions from one central principle or goal to another, or new social movements.

The unrealistic dreams of perfect social orders that permeate social movement rhetoric heighten expectations and demands that remain only dreams after years of struggle and suffering. Frustration builds within new generations of activists who become increasingly disaffected with social movement establishments which preach messages of patience and gradualism, the rhetorical staple of the institutional opposition. An evolutionary struggle awaits events that provoke a significant number of movement members to cry "Enough!" and leaders who appreciate the importance of timing, address members' frustrations, recreate and redefine social reality, offer new dreams, and identify with a new generation of true believers. Stokely Carmichael's rhetoric of black power can best be understood as such an evolutionary struggle within the civil rights movement that grew out of increasing disaffection with established civil rights movement organizations and leaders, the philosophy of integration, and passive, nonviolent, civil disobedience that had produced little apparent change after a decade of hope, struggle, and suffering. Black power was not a new social movement but an effort to transform the civil rights revolution to make it more effective and acceptable to a new generation of protestors.

This study provides insights into the evolutionary nature of social movement rhetoric as new generations of leaders strive to adjust ideologies to members' rising expectations and demands for the long-promised, perfect social orders.[10] It is based on histories of the civil rights movement, essays that have analyzed the rhetoric of black power, accounts of people who were associated with Carmichael or attended his speeches, essays Carmichael wrote to explain black power, his co-authored book with Charles V. Hamilton entitled *Black Power: The Politics of Liberation,* and six of Carmichael's speeches delivered to both predominantly white and predominantly black audiences during 1966 and 1967. Part one reviews the growing disillusionment within the civil rights movement during the mid-1960s that set the stage for major evolutionary change. Part two reveals how Carmichael and others seized the moment to instigate evolutionary changes within the movement that had struggled so long to end the oppression of black Americans and attain the justice denied them. Part three describes the emergence of Stokely Carmichael as the charismatic champion of black power. Part four analyzes the conflicting visions of reality presented in the rhetoric of traditional movement rhetors and Carmichael. And part five discusses the dialectical tension that erupted between Carmichael and black power advocates on the one hand and institutional and movement establishments on the other.

GROWING DISILLUSIONMENT WITHIN THE CIVIL RIGHTS MOVEMENT

More than 250,000 leaders, members, and sympathizers of the civil rights movement gathered in Washington, D.C. on August 28, 1963 both to celebrate the movement's achievements and to demand "Freedom Now!" They applauded and cheered Martin Luther King, Jr.'s "I Have a Dream" speech and speeches of several other leaders. They cheered and shouted "We demand!" as Bayard Rustin, a founder of CORE and SCLC, challenged them to "carry the demands of this revolution forward," proclaimed this was a "time for you to act," and recited a list of movement demands.[11] And they shouted "I do pledge" to the pledge A. Phillip Randolph, a black labor leader, introduced with the words, "I pledge that I will not relax until victory is won."[12] The quarter of a million marchers went home with renewed hope and imbued with a new zeal to achieve final victory.

The euphoria of the massive gathering in Washington was to be short-lived, however. Three weeks after the march, racists bombed the Sixteenth Street Baptist Church in Birmingham, a center of movement activity, during Sunday services and killed four young girls. Observers began to detect a "new militance" and disillusionment within the movement after this tragedy and the continuing terror campaign against civil rights workers and supporters throughout the south. During the Freedom Summer of 1964, there were six murders, thirty-five shootings, sixty-five bombings and burnings of homes, businesses, and churches, and at least eighty recorded beatings.[13] The murder of three civil rights workers in Mississippi, two of them white, outraged the nation. In Malcolm X's words, the dream had become a nightmare.[14] Malcolm X toured the country during the spring and summer of 1964 giving differing versions of "The Ballot or the Bullet" speech in which he addressed the growing frustrations of black Americans with the failure of government, white liberals, the civil rights movement, and integration to bring about meaningful changes for black Americans. A favorite target was the march of the previous summer that he referred to as the "circus" or the "Farce on Washington."[15] In a speech in Detroit, he ridiculed the march and addressed a new generation of activists:

> What can the white man use, now, to fool us, after he put down that march on Washington, and you see all through that now. He tricked you, had you marching down to Washington. Yes, had you marching back and forth between the feet of a dead man named Lincoln and another dead man named George Washington, singing "We shall overcome." He made a chump out of you. He made a fool out of you. He made you think you were going somewhere and you ended up going nowhere but between Lincoln and Washington. So today our people are disillusioned. They have become disenchanted. They have become dissatisfied. And in their frustrations they want action. You see this young black man, this new generation, asking for the ballot or the bullet. That old Uncle Tom action is outdated.[16]

As the movement spread to northern states and the ghettoes of large northern cities, riots and demonstrations in nine northern cities between July 18 and September 7, 1964 revealed a growing militancy, anger, and despair within black communities and the movement. In August 1964, the Democratic Party convened in Atlantic City and outraged members of the movement when the regular Mississippi delegation was seated in spite of evidence of massive discrimination against black voters in Mississippi and an interracial slate presented by activists. Fred Powledge writes that "The experience of political reality at Atlantic City showed the younger Movement activists, who saw the challenge outcome as a defeat and an insult, just how weary they had become."[17] Disillusionment with movement leaders and their white liberal allies escalated in March 1965 when participants in the Selma to Montgomery march were beaten and Martin Luther King, Jr. turned the march around a few days later rather than risk bloodshed from heavily armed police waiting for the marchers. Many members of SNCC, who were mostly young and militant, felt betrayed by a movement leadership believed to have made a deal with the Justice Department not to proceed. To them, it was "a sellout."[18] Malcolm X, who had relatively few followers but a powerful message, was assassinated on February 21 while speaking in New York City. The Watts riot of August 11 to 16 shocked the nation and widened the fissures in the civil rights movement, particularly its relationship with white liberals in the north.

In early 1966, CORE and SNCC deepened the fissures within the movement when they advocated armed self-defense and SNCC became an all black organization. There was growing disillusionment with integration as the way to attain freedom and equality for black Americans. Stokely Carmichael became chairman of SNCC and shifted the organization from nonviolent, civil disobedience to more militant and separatist stances, tactics, and demands.[19] In many ways, Carmichael was a mirror image of the young, angry, militant leaders in the student rights, peace, and counter-culture movements of the time. These movements had considerable influences upon one another and were led and populated heavily by young activists who were becoming, in Wilson's words, "tired of being sick and tired."[20] For instance, Mario Savio has been credited with starting the Free Speech Movement at the University of California at Berkeley, the beginning of the student rights movement, following a summer in the south conducting voter registration campaigns and freedom schools. Martin Luther King, Jr. was finding it increasingly difficult to convince other movement leaders and members that nonviolent, civil disobedience, and alliance with white Americans were the most effective methods of attaining freedom and justice.[21] Growing numbers of militants questioned both the tactics and the goals of the movement. Orde Coombs, a contributing editor of *Essence,* wrote that:

> Its members (SNCC) were young, idealistic, brave and very dissatisfied with the older civil-rights leaders. Those men had grown up when lynching was a spectator sport, and they knew the resiliency of American racism. The young thought that commitment, passion and courage were enough to transform their land, and when it

did not turn out that way a bitterness began to congeal among them.[22]

SEIZING THE MOMENT

In June 1966 James Meredith, a civil rights legend who had desegregated the University of Mississippi and was now a law student at Columbia University, began a 220-mile pilgrimage across Mississippi to urge black citizens to register to vote and to demonstrate that blacks no longer had to fear white violence. On the second day of his march, Meredith was shot from ambush by a white racist. Although he was not seriously injured, Meredith could not continue, and several civil rights leaders, including Martin Luther King, Jr. of the SCLC, Floyd McKissick of CORE, Roy Wilkins of the NAACP, Whitney Young of the Nation Urban League, and Stokely Carmichael of SNCC, met to discuss continuing Meredith's march for him. Immediate divisions resulted from differences over white participation and the involvement of the Louisiana-based Deacons of Defense who carried guns. In the end, Wilkins and Young refused to take part in the march, and less than 200 people, including King and Carmichael, took up the march.[23]

Each evening the leaders of the renewed march spoke at rallies, with most in attendance wanting to see and hear King and Carmichael. The press noted that Willie Ricks, the field secretary of SNCC, was heard to shout a catchy new phrase, "Black Power!"[24] The controversial U.S. Representative Adam Clayton Powell had reportedly used the phrase on earlier occasions. Carmichael later admitted that he had intended to introduce the nation to "black power" during the march and was biding "my time till the moment was ripe."[25] That moment arrived on June 17 in Greenwood, Mississippi—the heart of SNCC country—when state troopers decided that marchers could not put up their sleeping tent on the grounds of a black high school, even though they had permission to do so, and arrested Stokely Carmichael when he ignored their order. That night's rally attracted some 3,000 people, five times the usual number, and Carmichael was released minutes before the rally began. The pressures for change that had been building for years within the civil rights movement were about to culminate in a significant evolution of the struggle for black rights. According to Cleveland Sellers, a participant that evening and program secretary for SNCC, speeches by King, McKissick, and Ricks "were particularly militant" and set the tone for what followed:

> When Stokely moved forward to speak, the crowd greeted him with a huge roar.
>
> He acknowledged his reception with a raised arm and clenched fist.
>
> Realizing that he was in his element, with his people, Stokely let it all hang out.
>
> "This is the twenty-seventh time I have been arrested—and I ain't going to jail no more!" The crowd exploded into cheers and clapping.
>
> "The only way we gonna stop them white men from whuppin us is to take over.
>
> We have been saying freedom for six years and we ain't got nothin. What we gonna start saying now is BLACK POWER!" The crowd was right with him. They picked up his thoughts immediately. "BLACK POWER!" they roared in unison.
>
> Willie Ricks, who was as good at orchestrating the emotions of a crowd as anyone I have ever seen, sprang into action. Jumping to the platform with Stokely, he yelled to the crowd, "What do you want?"
>
> "BLACK POWER!"
>
> "What do you want?"
>
> "BLACK POWER!"
>
> "What do you want?"
>
> "BLACK POWER!! BLACK POWER!!! BLACK POWER!!!!"
>
> Everything that happened afterward was a response to that moment. More than anything, it assured that the Meredith March Against Fear would go down in history as one of the major turning points in the black liberation struggle.[26]

The civil rights movement would never be the same in tone, demands, tactics, and relationships.

A new generation of activists, goaded by frustration with the lack of progress for black Americans in the rural south and the urban north and the perceived failure of established movement organizations and leaders to bring about real and lasting changes, was taking center stage and challenging the heart and soul of the movement. As Lerone Bennett writes, "Black power, in essence, is his [Stokely Carmichael] attempt—and the attempt of many who share his vision—to change the dimensions and direction of the civil rights movement and restructure it around new axes and new power bases."[27] No single catalytic or triggering event brought about the evolution of the civil rights movement, but a long series of events, crises, and failures to meet rising expectations fostered by movement rhetoric resulted in widespread disaffection with both institutional and movement establishments. Stokely Carmichael was not the first black leader to advocate separatism, the notions of black power, or the slogan itself. Marcus Garvey, W. E. B. Du Bois, Adam Clayton Powell, Eldridge Cleaver, and Malcolm X preceded him, but neither the country nor the movement was ready for their militancy, ideas, and language.[28] However, Carmichael was the right person, at the right place, at the right time. He sensed the mood of the movement, seized the moment, and mounted the stage set by others to launch major evolutionary changes in the movement.

THE EMERGENCE OF A CHARISMATIC LEADER

Stokely Carmichael was the ideal charismatic leader of the black power struggle within the civil rights movement. He was not an outsider like Malcolm X of the Black Muslims or Eldridge Cleaver of the Black Panthers, but an insider as a member and chairman of SNCC who had paid his dues literally and figuratively. He had been active in the mainstream of the civil rights movement for six years, since he was a high school student, and had been in the front lines of sit-ins, marches, freedom rides, and demonstrations, including the Summer Project in Mississippi and the Democratic National Convention in 1964. He was often seen in the presence of Martin Luther King, Jr. He had exhibited bravery and heroism during numerous arrests, beatings, and threats, witnessed the murder of friends, and expected to be killed before he turned thirty.[29] When he attacked the old movement to which he had been committed, including its leaders, methods, goals, and achievements, his audiences listened in part because he was a respected veteran of their age speaking from his war experiences and advocating urgent changes that would bring meaningful results and end their frustrations and disappointments. He had tried the old ways and found them wanting.

Stokely Carmichael's appearance and dress, in contrast to older movement leaders, exuded charisma with the young audiences he spoke to most often. He was young, tall at six-foot-one, built like a basketball guard, dark, handsome, and virile.[30] SNCC associates dubbed him the "Magnificent Barbarian," and a writer noted that he was the sculptor's ideal model for "a statue of a Nubian god."[31] Unlike the older, more conservative leaders, Carmichael dressed to suit the occasion, sometimes in tee shirt and jeans, sometimes in bib overalls, and when he was giving formal speeches, a blue-gray or dark suit, blue shirt, striped tie, Italian boots, and sun glasses. Carmichael, like many young leaders of the 1960s, understood what his youthful audiences wanted and was skilled at adaptation and identification. Others, such as Willie Ricks and Floyd McKissick, could set the stage, but he was the star performer.

Carmichael's speaking style differed markedly from the "preacher style" of the older leaders of the civil rights movement. He and others like him were "secularizing" the movement. He was an actor-showman with a gift for histrionics. At one moment he was a sophisticated and soft-spoken academic explaining the economics or philosophy of black power; at another he was a poor old southern boy with a southern drawl; at another he was a shouting, threatening militant; and at another he was "imitating the sound of horses' hoofs, straddling an imaginary steed, bouncing up and down in a simulated gallop" to set the scene of historic conflicts between red men and white men.[32] His audiences cheered, shouted, laughed, clapped, and danced. Larry Richardson compared Carmichael's style and interaction with his audience to jazz artists, "I think Jazz men perform better when interaction is strong; they will always go 'one more time' when the crowd is 'digging.' Stokely Carmichael, in my view, similarly elicits overt audience response in the form of applause, laughter, or audience comment, and then he reacts to the response, thereby generating more response."[33] He brought life, excitement, optimism, and a feeling of involvement into the aging civil rights movement. Expectations could rise again.

Carmichael was a master of adapting language and materials to each audience.[34] Before predominantly white, college student audiences, he might read one of his essays from the *Massachusetts Review* or the *New York Review of Books*. Both language and manner would be sophisticated and scholarly and, as a university graduate, he was one of them. Before predominantly black, non-college student audiences, he would employ a hip style of the in-group, speak with a southern accent, and select materials well-suited to their experiences. As a member of SNCC and a resident of Harlem and the Bronx, he was one of them. He identified with the youthfulness of both audiences by attacking the war in Vietnam and all establishments. He pulled no rhetorical punches when discussing the situation facing young black and white Americans and was cheered for "telling it like it is."

Stokely Carmichael did not create the mood for change within the civil rights movement, nor did he create the phrase "black power." He did serve as the charismatic catalyst to commence the black power phase of the evolution of the movement. Bennett writes that:

> Black Power did not spring full-blown from the head of Stokely Carmichael. It was in the air; it was in the heads and hearts of long-suffering men who had paid an enormous price for minuscule gains. Although other men had used the words Black Power (notably Adam Powell), it was the genius of Stokely Carmichael to sense the mood gestating in the depths of the black psyche and to give tongue to it.[35]

Rebellion had been brewing for some time within the civil rights movement, but

Carmichael had the movement credentials, charisma, following, skills, and determination necessary to make the rebellion happen. And the timing was right.

CONFLICTING VISIONS OF REALITY

Social movements must persuade a significant number of people that the generally accepted view of reality—past, present, and future—is erroneous and that major changes are warranted to bring about a more perfect society, a reality that matches expectations.[36] Rhetors who foster the evolution of a social movement, then, must define and construct a social reality that (1) differs markedly from that maintained by both established institutions and established social movement organizations and leaders and (2) "rings true" with audiences. Stokely Carmichael's messages provided this redefinition and reconstruction of social reality for his audiences in terms and experiences they understood well.

The Past and Present

Carmichael's rhetoric struck at the foundations of the social reality prevalent in the civil rights movement and much of society during the mid-1960s, that the United States was evolving into a color blind society through integration of the races with steady and substantial gains for black Americans. On the contrary, he claimed, a thoroughly racist society existed after years of struggle and suffering to gain freedom and equality, and the black community was the "victim of white imperialism and colonial exploitation."[37] American society remained an exclusive rather than inclusive society and continued to value property rights over human rights. More than a century after the Emancipation Proclamation he was still regarded as 3/5ths of a man, Carmichael would exclaim, and then feign difficulty in saying the word "constitution," asking audiences to help him because he could enunciate only 3/5ths of the word.[38] White institutions and individuals continued to control everything in black communities, including resources, political decisions, law enforcement, housing standards, and ownership of land, housing, and stores. How could black people

"make it" in this racist society? "The majority view is a lie," he argued, because it is "based on a premise of an upward mobility that doesn't exist for most Americans."[39] Of the five traditional means that had allowed past immigrants to make it in America—unskilled jobs, small shops, having money, knowing people, and being highly educated—the first four did not exist for black Americans and the fifth was a false panacea because it was getting harder for the poor to get an education. "For the Negro, there is an additional problem," Carmichael noted, "He is not psychologically attuned to think of college as a goal. Society has taught him to set short sights for himself, and so he does."[40] America was now offering a sixth alternative, however, Vietnam. "This country has reduced us, black people, to such a state," he exclaimed in Detroit, "that the only way our black youths can have a decent life is to become a hired killer in the army."[41]

The gains made through the old ways and coalitions were too little for too few. Carmichael characterized the prevailing vision of social justice through integration as an "insidious subterfuge" dreamed up by a "tiny group of Negroes who had middle class aspirations," "were already just a little ahead," never wanted to be black in the first place, and were interested in merely loosening "up the restrictions barring the entry of Black people into the white community."[42] The goals of old civil rights leaders—open accommodations, housing, education, and job opportunities at the executive level, Carmichael charged, were meaningful only to a "small chosen class" of black Americans, the occasional black who had made it.[43] Such goals were irrelevant to the black masses in the rural south and the ghettos of the north. The "dream street" offered under the guise of integration, Carmichael argued, "siphoned off" only the few most acceptable and qualified "individuals" from the black community. You "had to be the best" to enter the white community, the five or six best from each black school, a "tokenism" that amounted to only 6 percent nationwide and 15 percent in the south, while "they leave the rest of our children to stay in the filthy ghettos that they took the money from."[44] After more than a decade of struggling for integration, he concluded, "Civil rights protest has not materially benefited the masses" of black people, only "those who were already just a little ahead."[45]

The Future

For Stokely Carmichael, black power was a new day, a new awakening, and a time for a new militancy. "We know what's happening," he exclaimed in Detroit, "Brother, it's 1966 and we been here for years and our eyes are open wide. And we seeing you clear through, and you're nothing but a racist country . . . ."[46] "The posture of the civil rights movement was that of the dependent, the suppliant," he wrote in *The Massachusetts Review.*[47] White America would give nothing away, so black people had to stop begging, stand tall, fight back, stop singing "We Shall Overcome," and "take what belongs to us."[48] It was time to tell whites to "move on over, or we're going to move on over you."[49] In Detroit he exclaimed, "Baby, it's time we stayed here and fight it out here" rather than become a hired killer in Vietnam.[50] "It's time to get some black power," he shouted again and again.[51] To the delight of his audiences at Tougaloo Southern Christian College and Morgan State College, Carmichael declared that we are "going to right wrongs in this generation" and, "Following in Mr. [Frederick] Douglass's footsteps we intend to strike our first blow for our liberation, and we will let the chips fall where they may."[52]

The "liberation" of black Americans and creation of a more perfect social order would come about in several ways. First, blacks had to take control of language and definitions. "It is very, very important," he said, "because people who can define are the masters"; "The power to define is the most important power that we have."[53] White people had used definitions and words to contain the black community. "If we allow white people to define us by calling us Negroes, which means apathetic, lazy, stupid, and all those other things," he warned, "then we accept those definitions."[54] Echoing other movements of the time, Carmichael told his audience at the University of Wisconsin at Whitewater that we "shall have to struggle for the right to create our own terms through which to define ourselves and our relationship to the society, and to have these terms recognized. This is the first necessity of a free people, and the first right

that any oppressor must suspend."[55] Carmichael admonished audiences, "don't you ever call those things riots," as white liberals and civil rights leaders did, "because they are rebellions, that's what they are."[56]

Second, it was "time for the black freedom movement to stop pandering to the fears and anxieties of the white middle class . . . and return to the ghetto to organize these communities to control themselves."[57] Carmichael challenged black physicians and lawyers to abandon the big money and prestige they had achieved among whites "uptown" and come back into their communities and use their skills to help the masses of black people.[58] He challenged Morgan State students to "stop being ashamed of being black and come on home" because their parents had not worked hard for years so they "could scrub floors and be Uncle Toms." "Can you be aggressive," he asked, "Or are you afraid?" He tried to shame students into action: "You came here to learn how to help your people of Baltimore in the ghettos, and then you turn your backs on them as soon as you get a chance."[59]

Third, the only way to achieve meaningful and lasting change was for black people to take care of and control their own communities. "Black people must be in positions of power, doing and articulating for themselves," Carmichael declared; they needed to understand that they would have to "go it alone" because that is what they had been "doing for lo these four hundred years."[60] "That's not reverse racism," he argued, "it is moving onto healthy ground."[61] Once black people had gained control of their communities and a power base, they could move to better their schools, "tell everyone in this country that we're not going to your damn war [Vietnam] period," and "if they touch one black man in California . . . we will move to disrupt this whole damn country."[62] Power and control would come through organizing the ghettos. "Can the ghettos in fact be organized," Carmichael asked? "The answer is that this organization must be successful, because there are no viable alternatives . . . And 'Integration' is meaningful only to a small chosen class within the community."[63]

Fourth, unlike integration, black power would not abolish the black community but retain its rich heritage. "The racial and cultural personality of the black community must be preserved," Carmichael exclaimed, "and the community must win its freedom while preserving its cultural integrity. This is the essential difference between integration as it is currently being practiced and the concept of Black Power."[64] Carmichael objected to the phrase "culturally deprived" common at the time. Since culture is anything man-made, "How the hell can I be culturally deprived?" he asked. "You deny my very existence, to use that term."[65] He castigated "Negroes" for imitating white society, and explained that "Our concern for Black Power addresses itself directly to this problem, the necessity to reclaim our history and our identity from the cultural terrorism and depredation of self-justifying white-guilt."[66] White society, he exclaimed at UCLA and Morgan State, had censored history and maintained control by making "us ashamed of being black."[67] Carmichael often introduced a syllogism to raise black consciousness and enhance a new self-identity and pride. The syllogism went this way in his Detroit speech:

> Sounds a bit absurd; I'm disturbed by a lot of black people going around saying, "Oh, man, anything all black, it ain't no good." I want to talk to that man. . . . There's a thing called a syllogism. And it says like, if you're born in Detroit, you're beautiful; that's the major premise. The minor premise is—I am born in Detroit. Therefore, I am beautiful. Anything all black is bad—major premise. Minor premise—I am all black. Therefore [long pause] yeah, yeah, yeah. You're all out there, and the man telling you that anything all black is bad, and you talking about yourself, and you don't even know it. You ain't never heard no white people say that anything all white is bad. You ain't never heard them say it.[68]

Carmichael's audiences would laugh and applaud with a new awareness and perhaps a new self-image.

If a major criterion for reconstructing and redefining social reality is believability, that the alternative reality "rings true" to audiences and strikes a "responsive chord," Carmichael was masterful.[69] He targeted a new generation of civil rights activists who were frustrated with the lack of meaningful social change and disillusioned with the timidity and passivity of older movement leaders who preached patience, caution, and gradualism. He tapped into growing cynicism of audiences by labeling integration as both a failure and a fraud perpetrated upon the black masses by the movement itself. His messages mirrored audience experiences with token integration, white-flight to the suburbs, cautious leaders, growth of the ghettos, poor schools, violence in black communities, low self-respect, political powerlessness, stifled expectations, and the escalating brutality of the war in Vietnam in which black Americans were represented disproportionately.

Carmichael created a symbolic realignment within the movement by replacing words such as Negro, Negro people, ghetto, segregation, and integration with black, black masses, colony, colonialism, and liberation that altered how audiences saw the ghettos of large American cities and American institutions and linked the civil rights movement with the African movements for independence from colonial powers.[70] A minority in this country became part of a worldwide majority. Like other young leaders of social movements in the 1960s, Carmichael understood the importance and power of words, that whoever controls language controls the world. His attacks on the Vietnam War and the cultural imperialism of white society linked black power with the anti–Vietnam War, student, and counter-culture movements. Carmichael understood that the struggle was moving from the rural south to the ever-growing ghettos of northern cities and filled a void long ignored or ineffectively addressed by older civil rights leaders. Black Americans might achieve the perfect society sought for so long if they remained where they were. Carmichael spoke to the black masses in cities such as Detroit, Los Angeles, San Francisco, and Baltimore rather than black individuals in the rural south and tapped into two slogans prevalent in movements at the time, "all power to the people" and "all power to black people." He associated "integration" with failure, apathy, shame, begging, tokenism, and subservience and "black power" with real change, commitment, pride, taking, and self-determination—all mainline American values. Above all, Carmichael's militant black power rhetoric provided his generation with a new dream of a more perfect order (even if an ambiguous one), new hope, a new self-identity, and pride in being black.

DIALECTICAL TENSION IN THE MORAL ARENA

Carmichael's rhetoric polarized society into enlightened, young, black militants and everyone else. Unlike traditional civil rights leaders who emphasized the inherent goodness of most white Americans and the essential coalition with white liberals, Carmichael asserted that white Americans see themselves as a "master race," as "masters of the world," and "think they're God."[71] This white supremacist attitude was readily apparent in actions within the United States, Africa, and Asia, particularly in Vietnam.

But Carmichael's rhetoric was not aimed primarily at white racists and espousers of segregation, the traditional targets of civil rights activists. His main targets were within the civil rights movement. His harshest rhetoric rained down on the movement's white allies, the white liberals and modern day missionaries who were allowed to say "only through me shall you have better things."[72] "That's what is called integration," he said, "You do what I tell you to do and we'll let you sit at the table with us."[73] If these whites were really interested in integration, Carmichael declared, they would move out of their white suburbs into the ghettos such as Watts, send their "lily-white" children to overcrowded schools, enroll blacks in labor unions, and "share their salaries with the economically insecure black people they so much love."[74] Even young, northern whites who had risked their lives working for integration and voter registration in the South were butts of his wrath. Carmichael told listeners in Detroit they had "to examine our white liberal friends," the adults who could afford to come to Mississippi to work for integration because black mothers were cleaning their houses and taking care of their children, and the white, liberal students who could come south because they had plenty of money and were fighting to smoke pot and wear beards rather than for their

lives.[75] At University of California at Berkeley he asked, "Can the white activist stop trying to be a Pepsi generation who comes alive in the black community, and be a man who's willing to move into the white community and start organizing where the organization is needed?"[76] Well-known, white civil rights supporters were special targets. In Detroit, he called labor leader Walter Reuther "the great white father of Detroit" and the "master-captain-bossman."[77] At UCLA Carmichael called President Lyndon Johnson a "buffoon" and Vice President Hubert Humphrey a "handkerchief head," a yes-man worse than an Uncle Tom.[78]

Carmichael's polarization was not only black versus white but "black" versus "Negro." He referred to all integrationists and older leaders as "Negroes," a code name for Uncle Toms who were passive, self-centered, greedy, and ashamed of being black. They were a tiny minority wanting desperately to make it in the white community, to be accepted by whites. They cared little about the black masses. Carmichael noted, for instance, that the president of the black college from which he had graduated was trying so hard to become white that he was now in favor of the Vietnam War: "he's made it in this society, he's integrated fully. Let him stay there."[79] Famous black Americans such as Ralph Bunch, Carl Rowan, and George Schyler were now indistinguishable from whites. He often declared "I'm no Negro leader," even though he was chairman of SNCC until mid-1967, to disassociate himself from "Negro leaders." He accused these leaders of allowing whites to define integration as wanting to marry white girls, jumping to deplore violence whenever there was a black "rebellion" (but not white violence), and being more responsible to white political machines than black communities.[80] Carmichael and Hamilton wrote in *Black Power: The Politics of Liberation* that "None of its [civil rights movement] so-called leaders could go into a rioting community and be listened to. In a sense, the blame must be shared—along with the mass media—by those leaders for what happened in Watts, Harlem, Chicago, Cleveland and other places . . . . We had nothing to offer that they could see, except to go out and be beaten again. We helped to build their frustration."[81]

What Robert Cathcart calls a "dialectical enjoinment in the moral arena" erupted immediately after Carmichael's speech in Greenwood, Mississippi[,] and escalated as he wrote essays and spoke throughout the country. Cathcart argues that:

> The enactment of confrontation gives a movement its identity, its substance and its form. No movement for radical change can be taken seriously without acts of confrontation. . . . Confrontational rhetoric shouts "Stop!" at the system, saying, "You cannot go on assuming you are the true and correct order; you must see yourself as the evil thing you are."[82]

Carmichael was confronting two systems at once with little rhetorical restraint, the established order and the established social movement. As might be expected, segregationists and the press reacted in kind to Stokely Carmichael and the militancy of black power advocates. When he spoke in Nashville, Tennessee, for example, American Legion Post 5 denounced him as one of the "warped idiots" who "reek with scum." The Tennessee State Senate passed a resolution condemning Carmichael for spreading "race hate and incitement to violence," while the Tennessee House of Representatives adopted a resolution demanding "deportation proceedings against Mr. Stokely Carmichael, who seems to hate this country so much." When riots broke out in Nashville a few hours after a Carmichael speech, the *Nashville Banner* declared they were the result of "Carmichael's devised deviltry" and his speeches of "sedition, insurrection, anarchy, murder, and arson."[83] The announcer of radio station WKNR's documentary series "Project Detroit" reflected widespread reaction to Carmichael and black power when he introduced a replay of Carmichael's July 30, 1966 speech in Detroit with these words:

> Much has been said and written of late concerning the term black power. Originally thrust upon the head of American idiom during the Meredith march in Mississippi, black power has been damned by most, praised by few if any. . . . Most have interpreted Carmichael's term in basic

ways: "the greatest setback for the cause of the Negro and civil rights in this century." Others, and they are few, argue that all Carmichael means is economic and political power—the Negro population uniting. The controversy continues.[84]

The media highlighted Carmichael's attacks on white liberals, Negro leaders, honkey cops, the "thalidomide drug of integration," and apparent threats of retaliatory violence such as "if you touch us with your hand, we're going to break your arm" and "if you play like Nazis, we're not going to play Jew this time around."[85] A study of media interpretations and published reactions to Carmichael and black power led Wayne Brockriede and Robert Scott to conclude that "one meaning and one image thoroughly has engulfed the public mind and has dominated the attitudes of most white liberals: Black Power is violent racism in reverse, and Stokely Carmichael is a monster."[86]

Carmichael achieved the moral confrontation essential for social movements because he threatened white supremacy, institutional control, and the moderate civil rights movement with which many institutional leaders and members of the media had become comfortable, if not supportive. But this rhetorical conflict was not the typical struggle between institutions and movement; it was a major conflict in the moral arena between established social movement leaders and black power advocates, most notably Stokely Carmichael. He did not try to convert older leaders and followers but to delegitimize them and provoke their retaliation in words and actions.

Established civil rights leaders and supporters could not tolerate Carmichael's attacks on their integrity and everything they had strived for and attained since the mid-1950s. He was challenging their legitimacy as movement leaders, particularly their abilities to control identification, communication channels, language, and moral suasion. Roy Wilkins, in his keynote address at the NAACP convention, declared: "No matter how endlessly they try to explain it, the term 'black power' means antiwhite power. . . . It has to mean 'going it alone.' It has to mean separatism. . . . We of the NAACP will have none of this. We have fought it too long. It is the ranging of race against race on the irrelevant basis of skin color."[87] Vice President Hubert Humphrey, an outspoken proponent of civil rights for decades, exclaimed at the same convention:

> It seems to me fundamental that we cannot embrace the dogma of the oppressor—the notion that somehow a person's skin color determines his worthiness or unworthiness. Yes, racism is racism—and there is no room in America for racism of any color. We must reject calls for racism, whether they come from a throat that is white or one that is black.[88]

Even the great conciliator and coalition builder Martin Luther King, Jr. had difficulties with what he saw as a dangerous new slogan for the civil rights movement, even though he understood the growing disillusionment from within. He wrote, "But revolution, though born of despair, cannot be long sustained by despair. This is the ultimate contradiction of the Black Power movement."[89] And in his presidential address at the 1967 convention of the Southern Christian Leadership Conference, King proclaimed, "Let us be dissatisfied until that day when nobody will shout 'White Power!'—when nobody will shout 'Black Power!'—but everybody will talk about God's power and human power."[90]

Racism was the moral ground over which this evolutionary challenge was being fought, and both established institutions and movement leaders painted black power as nothing less than racism in reverse, one evil attacking another evil from which nothing good could emerge. Black power was a dangerous, radical doctrine that would tear the nation and the movement apart. Carmichael and Hamilton rejected the racism in reverse charge as a "deliberate and absurd lie." They argued, "There is no analogy—by any stretch of definition or imagination—between the advocates of Black Power and white racists. Racism is not merely exclusion on the basis of race but exclusion for the purpose of subjugating or maintaining subjugation."[91] "The black people of this country,["] Carmichael and Hamilton wrote, "have not lynched whites, bombed their churches, murdered their children and manipulated laws and institutions to maintain oppression."[92] The charge of racism in reverse was offered as further evidence of how out of step older movement leaders were with the needs and aspirations of black Americans.

Thus, Carmichael's charisma with militant, young audiences and his confrontational rhetoric provoked the conflict necessary for evolutionary change within the civil rights movement. If as Simons, Mechling, and Sch[r]eier claim, a "partial explanation for the success of many social movements" is the opposition they encounter, then Carmichael's rhetoric was doubly successful because it provoked opposition from two establishments, institutional and social movement.[93] Undoubtedly Carmichael gained legitimacy with militant audience members because the movement establishment appeared to be siding with institutions and racists in attacking this articulate, young fighter who was telling it like it was. Simons's observation, that "Whereas the moderate might regard authority figures as 'misguided' though 'legitimate,' the militant would tend to regard these figures as 'willfully self-serving' and 'illegitimate',," is an accurate description of Carmichael's rhetoric.[94] He succeeded in raising a critical question within the minds of his young, militant audiences: were established civil rights leaders and white liberals, including the President and Vice President of the United States, attacking Carmichael and black power because it was racism in reverse, or were they trying to maintain legitimacy, control of the movement, and put down a dangerous rebellion appealing to a new generation of activists disillusioned with the old?

Conclusion

If Stokely Carmichael's rhetoric of black power struck a highly responsive chord within his targeted young, militant audiences, what happened to the evolutionary struggle preached with such revolutionary zeal? The rhetorical situation that made his message possible and attractive also mitigated against the massive evolutionary change he sought within the movement. First, the civil rights movement was exhausted and splintered, but in the sweep of history, the struggle for social justice was just beginning. The Meredith march marked the last time movement organizations and leaders united in a demonstration or campaign. Second, the nation's preoccupation with the war in Vietnam soon engulfed all movements of the time and drained them of energy and support. Third, Carmichael provided abundant symbolic satisfactions but few tangible ideas and no tangible plans for accomplishing societal perfection through black power. What was to replace integration efforts in housing, education, employment, and government? Fourth, Carmichael refused to take on the role of leader, to use SNCC as an organizational and power base, or to create a new organization to carry out campaigns for black power. Like an old fashioned tent meeting revivalist, Carmichael came to town, stirred up a great deal of excitement and enthusiasm, made conversions, and then left for the next town. In his absence and with no leadership or structure left behind, the newly energized and converted soon returned to life as usual. And fifth, Carmichael changed his name to Kwame Ture (after Kwame Nkrumah and Sekou Toure of Guinea), chose a larger stage by organizing the All African People Revolutionary Party in 1967, and moved to the People's Republic of Guinea in 1968. Without a charismatic leader to replace him, the black power struggle within the civil rights movement failed to reach its potential.

The rhetoric of black power was not without evolutionary influences, however. It forever replaced "Negro" with black and African-American. Blacks were more determined than ever to stand up, stop begging, and take what was rightfully theirs. A new militancy replaced passivity and creative suffering as strategies and rhetorical stances. The conflict over black power helped to instill a feeling of pride in being black and in black culture and heritage. The civil rights movement evolved into a struggle of, by, and for black Americans. And the movement became a national rather than a southern phenomenon.

Stokely Carmichael and his rhetoric of black power illustrate that a dynamic similar to that which gives rise to social movements may also instigate conflict within social movements and transform them in significant ways while sustaining the fundamental goals that brought the movement into existence. Years of suffering, crises, and unmet expectations—not a single catalytic event or Stokely Carmichael—created feelings of frustration, disillusionment, and cynicism within movement members and a growing disaffection with older civil rights organizations, leaders, strategies, and principles. Stokely Carmichael was the right person, at the right time, and in the right place to foment an evolution of the civil rights movement. Little in his rhetoric was original, and many of his speeches seem to borrow heavily from those of Malcolm X. But while Garvey, Du Bois, Powell, Malcolm X, and Cleaver, among others, had employed similar ideas, language, arguments, and attacks on both institutional and movement establishments, they were ahead of their time, were not in the mainstream of the movement, lacked an organizational base, or were unable to identify with a new generation of activists.

Carmichael was a master of expressing the frustrations and demands of a younger generation of civil rights activists with whom he identified in age, appearance, manner, language, and ideas. He was one of them and a mainstream civil rights leader who dared to tell it like it was and attack all elements that had formed alliances to espouse integration and passive, civil disobedience as the paths to a more perfect social order. Carmichael, like many young movement leaders of the 1960s, understood the need for terministic control to achieve a symbolic realignment within both the movement and society. The word black instilled a new identity, pride, and cultural association among black Americans while the word Negro vanished from the American lexicon. The phrase "black power" communicated effectively with young audiences who were demanding "power to the people," while Malcolm X's "black nationalism" had failed to excite a significant following. Perhaps it sounded foreign or extreme to many. Carmichael understood and appealed to the symbolic back to Africa movement, not the literal one espoused by Garvey, among young black Americans who were adopting African names, dress, hairstyles, jewelry, dance, music, sculpture, and language. He offered his generation new hopes and dreams and confidence that they could do what the older generation had failed to do. Black power was not a new social movement but an attempt to achieve an evolution of the civil rights revolution to make it both more effective and palatable to a new generation of activists.

Notes

1 Charles Conrad, "The Transformation of the 'Old Feminist' Movement," *Quarterly Journal of Speech* 67 (1981): 290.

2 James Darsey, "From 'Gay Is Good' to the Scourge of AIDS: The Evolution of Gay Liberation Rhetoric, 1977–1990," *Communication Studies* 42 (1991): 46–58.

3 Charles J. Stewart, "The Internal Rhetoric of the Knights of Labor," *Communication Studies* 42 (1991): 67–82.

4 Fred Powledge, *Free at Last? The Civil Rights Movement and the People Who Made It* (Boston: Little, Brown and Company, 1991).

5 Stewart, *Internal Rhetoric* 72–73; Charles J. Stewart, Craig Allen Smith, and Robert E. Denton, Jr., *Persuasion and Social Movements*, 3rd ed. (Prospects Heights, IL: Waveland Press, 1994): 100; Charles J. Stewart, "Labor Agitation in America: 1865–1915," *America in Controversy: History of American Public Address*, ed. DeWitte Holland (Dubuque, IA: William C. Brown Company, 1973): 153–170.

6 Jonathan I. Lange, "Refusal to Compromise: The Case of Earth First!" *Western Journal of Speech Communication* 54 (1990): 473–494; Brant Short, "Earth First! and the Rhetoric of Moral Confrontation," *Communication Studies* (1991): 172–188.

7 John W. Bowers, Donovan J. Ochs, and Richard J. Jensen, *The Rhetoric of Agitation and Control,* 2nd ed. (Prospect Heights, IL: Waveland Press, 1993): 65–83; Theodore O. Windt, "The Diatribe: Last Resort for Protest," *Quarterly Journal of Speech* 58 (1972): 1–14; The Walker Report, *Rights in Conflict: The Violent Confrontation of Demonstrators and Police in the Parks and Streets of Chicago During the Week of the Democratic National Convention of 1968* (New York: Bantam Books, 1968).

8 Robert L. Scott and Wayne Brockriede, *The Rhetoric of Black Power* (New York: Harper & Row, 1969); Kwame Ture (Stokely Carmichael) and Charles V. Hamilton, *Black Power: The Politics of Liberation in America* (New York: Vintage Edition, 1992).

9 Conrad 297.

10 This study also adds to our understanding of Stokely Carmichael's rhetoric in three important ways. First, it reveals that his rhetoric of black power was not original with him but evolved from decades of protest from leaders such as Marcus Garvey, W. E. B. Du Bois, and Malcolm X. Second, it locates Carmichael as an evolutionary leader within the civil rights movement rather than as a creator of a competing social movement. And third, it supports the claims of Brockriede and Scott that the establishment assumed black power meant violence, that the media presented a partial and distorted picture of Carmichael and his message, and that white liberals and civil rights leaders reacted too quickly and thoughtlessly to the distortions of his speeches and writings. See Wayne Brockriede and Robert L. Scott, "Stokely Carmichael: Two Speeches on Black Power," *Central States Speech Journal* 19 (1968): 3–13.

11 Bayard Rustin, audiotape rec. 28 Aug. 1963, Washington, D.C.

12 A. Phillip Randolph, audiotape rec. 28 Aug. 1963, Washington, D.C. 1.

13 Powledge 583.

14 Malcolm X, *The Autobiography of Malcolm X* (New York: Ballantine Books, 1973): 281.

15 Malcolm X 280–281.

16 Malcolm X, "The Ballot or the Bullet," audiotape rec. 3 April 1964, Detroit.

17 Powledge 607.

18 Powledge 624.

19 Adam Fairclough, *To Redeem the Soul of America: The Southern Christian Leadership Conference and Martin Luther King, Jr.* (Athens, GA: University of Georgia Press, 1987): 311–313.

20 John Wilson, *Introduction to Social Movements* (New York: Basic Books, 1973): 90.

21 Fairclough 253–331; Parke G. Burgess, "The Rhetoric of Black Power: A Moral Demand?" *Quarterly Journal of Speech* 54 (1968): 128–129.

22 Orde Coombs, "Stokely Carmichael: Ready for the Revolution," *Essence* November 1982: 141.

23 Fairclough 314–315.

24 Powledge 633.

25 Lerone Bennett, Jr., "Stokely Carmichael: Architect of Black Power," *Ebony* September 1966: 32.

26 Cleveland Sellers, "From Black Consciousness to Black Power," *Southern Exposure* September 1981: 67.

27 Bennett 27.

28 Arthur L. Smith (Molefi Kete Asante), *Rhetoric of Black Revolution* (Boston: Allyn and Bacon, 1969).

29 Robert Penn Warren, "Two for SNCC," *Commentary* April 1965: 46–47; Gordon Parks, "Carmichael," *Life* 19 May 1967: 82.

30 Pat Jefferson, "The Magnificent Barbarian at Nashville," *The Southern Speech Journal* 33 (1967): 79; Coombs 87.

31 Bennett 26.

32 Jefferson 81; Dencil R. Taylor, "Carmichael in Tallahassee," *Southern Speech Journal* 38 (1967): 92.

33 Larry S. Richardson, "Stokely Carmichael: Jazz Artist," *Western Speech* 34 (1970): 217–218.

34 Pat Jefferson, "'Stokely's Cool' Style," *Today's Speech* 16 (1968): 19–24; Brockriede and Scott 3–13.

35 Bennett 32.

36 Stewart, Smith, and Denton 45.

37 Stokely Carmichael, audiotape rec. 24 May 1967, U. of California, Los Angeles; Brockriede and Scott 103.

38 Stokely Carmichael, *Stokely Speaks* (New York: Random House, 1971): 72.

39 Stokely Carmichael, "Who Is Qualified?" *New Republic* 8 January 1966 as reprinted in *Stokely Speaks* 16.

40 Carmichael, *Stokely Speaks* 10.

41 Stokely Carmichael, audiotape rec. 30 July 1966, Detroit.

42 Carmichael, *Stokely Speaks* 47; Carmichael, U. of California, Los Angeles; Ture and Hamilton 53–54.

43 Carmichael, U. of California, Los Angeles; Scott and Brockriede 107.

44 Carmichael, Detroit.

45 Carmichael, *Stokely Speaks* 11.

46 Carmichael, Detroit.

47 Stokely Carmichael, "Toward Black Liberation," *The Massachusetts Review* 7 (1966): 646.

48 Carmichael, Detroit.

49 Carmichael, *Stokely Speaks* 60.

50 Carmichael, Detroit.

51 Carmichael, Detroit.

52 Stokely Carmichael, video rec. 12 April 1967, Tougaloo Southern Christian College, Tougaloo, Mississippi, The Educational Video Group, 1992; Carmichael, *Stokely Speaks* 63.

53 Carmichael, *Stokely Speaks* 64, 66; Ture and Hamilton 36.

54 Carmichael, *Stokely Speaks* 65.

55 Scott and Brockriede 99.

56 Carmichael, Detroit.

57 Scott and Brockriede 108.

58 Carmichael, Detroit.

59 Carmichael, *Stokely Speaks* 62–63, 75, 70.

60 Carmichael, *Stokely Speaks* 52; Carmichael, Detroit.

61 Carmichael, *Stokely Speaks* 52.

62 Carmichael, Detroit.

63 Scott and Brockriede 110–111.

64 Scott and Brockriede 107; Ture and Hamilton 55–56.

65 Carmichael, *Stokely Speaks* 73.

66 Scott and Brockriede 99.

67 Carmichael, U. of California, Los Angeles; Carmichael, *Stokely Speaks* 62.

68 Carmichael, Detroit.

69 David A. Snow and Robert D. Benford, "Master Frames and Cycles of Protest," *Frontiers in Social Movement Theory*, ed. Aldon D. Morris and Carol McClurg Mueller (New Haven, CT: Yale University Press, 1992): 141.

70 Steven R. Goldzwig, "A Social Movement Perspective on Demagoguery: Achieving Symbolic Realignment," *Communication Studies* 40 (1989): 208; Karlyn Kohrs Campbell, "The Rhetoric of Radical Black Nationalism: A Case Study of Self-Conscious Criticism," *Central States Speech Journal* 22 (1971): 151–160.

71 Carmichael, Detroit; Carmichael, Tougaloo.

72 Carmichael, Detroit.

73 Carmichael, *Stokely Speaks* 50.

74 Carmichael, Detroit; Carmichael, *Stokely Speaks* 54.

75 Carmichael, Detroit.

76 Carmichael, *Stokely Speaks* 51.

77 Carmichael, Detroit.

78 Carmichael, U. of California, Los Angeles.

79 Carmichael, Detroit.

80 Carmichael, *Stokely Speaks* 72, 65, 70–71; Carmichael, Tougaloo.

81 Ture and Hamilton 50.

82 Robert S. Cathcart, "Movements: Confrontation as Rhetorical Form," *Southern Speech Communication Journal* 43 (1978): 243.

83 Jefferson, "The Magnificent Barbarian" 78, 86, 87.

84 WKNR Radio, "An Interpretation of Black Power," audiotape rec. 7 Aug. 1966, Detroit.

85 Carmichael, Tougaloo; Carmichael, *Stokely Speaks* 47, 51.

86 Brockriede and Scott 4.

87 Robert L. Scott and Wayne Brockriede, "Hubert Humphrey Faces the Black Power Issue," *Speaker and Gavel* 4 (1966): 13.

88 Hubert H. Humphrey, "Address to the NAACP Convention, July 6, 1966," *Congressional Record* 12 July 1966: 15596.

89 Martin Luther King, Jr., *Where Do We Go From Here: Chaos or Community?* (New York: Harper & Row, 1967): 45.

90 Martin Luther King, Jr., "The President's Address to the Tenth Anniversary Convention of the Southern Christian Leadership Conference, Atlanta, Georgia, August 16, 1967," reprinted in Scott and Brockriede, "Stokely Carmichael" 164.

91 Ture and Hamilton 47.

92 Ture and Hamilton 47.

93 Herbert W. Simons, Elizabeth W. Mechling, and Howard N. Schreier, "The Functions of Human Communication in Mobilizing for Action from the Bottom Up: The Rhetoric of Social Movements," *Handbook of Rhetorical and Communication Theory*, ed. Carroll C. Arnold and John Waite Bowers (Boston: Allyn and Bacon, 1984): 836.

94 Herbert W. Simons, *Persuasion: Understanding, Practice, and Analysis* (Reading, MA: Addison-Wesley, 1976): 280.

SELECTED BIBLIOGRAPHY

MOVEMENTS

AIDS

Andriote, John-Manuel. *Victory Deferred: How AIDS Changed Gay Life in America.* Chicago: University of Chicago Press, 1999.

Brier, Jennifer. *Infectious Ideas: U.S. Political Responses to the AIDS Crisis.* Chapel Hill: University of North Carolina Press, 2009.

Brown, Michael P. *Replacing Citizenship: AIDS Activism and Radical Democracy.* New York: Guilford, 1997.

Bull, Chris, ed. *While the World Sleeps: Writing from the First Twenty Years of the Global AIDS Plague.* New York: Thunder's Mouth, 2003.

Cohen, Cathy J. *The Boundaries of Blackness: AIDS and the Breakdown of Black Politics.* Chicago: University of Chicago Press, 1999.

Crimp, Douglas. *Melancholia and Moralism: Essays on AIDS and Queer Politics.* Cambridge, MA: MIT Press, 2004.

Crimp, Douglas, and Adam Rolston. *AIDS Demo Graphics.* Seattle: Bay, 1990.

Epstein, Stephen. *Impure Science: AIDS, Activism, and the Politics of Knowledge.* Berkeley: University of California Press, 1998.

Fabj, Valeria, and Matthew J. Sobnosky. "AIDS Activism and the Rejuvenation of the Public Sphere." *Argumentation & Advocacy* 31 (Spring 1995): 163–184.

Gould, Deborah. *Moving Politics: Emotion and ACT UP's Fight against AIDS.* Chicago: University of Chicago Press, 2009.

Hallas, Roger. *Reframing Bodies: AIDS, Bearing Witness, and the Queer Moving Image.* Durham, NC.: Duke University Press, 2009.

Juhasz, Alexandra. *AIDS TV: Identity, Community, and Alternative Video.* Durham, NC: Duke University Press, 1995.

Kramer, Larry. *Reports from the Holocaust: The Making of an AIDS Activist.* New York: Cassell, 1997.

Morris, Charles E., III, ed. *Remembering the AIDS Quilt.* East Lansing: Michigan State University Press, 2011.

Patton, Cindy. *Globalizing AIDS.* Minneapolis: University of Minnesota Press, 2002.

Ramirez-Valles, Jesus. *Compañeros: Latino Activists in the Face of AIDS.* Urbana: University of Illinois Press, 2011.

Stockdill, Brett C. *Activism against AIDS: At the Intersections of Sexuality, Race, Gender, and Class.* Boulder, CO: Rienner, 2003.

American Indian / Red Power

Banks, Dennis. *Ojibwa Warrior: Dennis Banks and the Rise of the American Indian Movement.* Norman: University of Oklahoma Press, 2004.

Black, Jason Edward. "Native Resistive Rhetoric and the Decolonization of American Indian Removal Discourse." *Quarterly Journal of Speech* 95 (February 2009): 66–88.

Deloria, Vine, Jr. *Custer Died for Your Sins: An Indian Manifesto.* New York: Macmillan, 1969.

Garroutte, Eva Marie. *Real Indians: Identity and the Survival of Native America.* Berkeley: University of California Press, 2003.

Hoxie, Frederick E., ed. *Talking Back to Civilization: Indian Voices from the Progressive Era.* Boston: Bedford/St. Martin's, 2001.

Kelly, Casey Ryan. "Orwellian Language and the Politics of Tribal Termination (1953–1960)." *Western Journal of Communication* 74 (July–September 2010): 351–371.

Konkle, Maureen. *Writing Indian Nations: Native Intellectuals and the Politics of Historiography.* Chapel Hill: University of North Carolina Press, 2004.

Means, Russell, with Marvin J. Wolf. *Where White Men Fear to Tread: The Autobiography of Russell Means.* New York: St. Martin's, 1995.

Morris, Richard, and Philip Wander. "Native American Rhetoric: Dancing in the Shadows of the Ghost Dance." *Quarterly Journal of Speech* 76 (May 1990): 164–191.

Nabokov, Peter. *Native American Testimony: A Chronicle of Indian-White Relations from Prophecy to the Present, 1492–2000.* New York: Penguin, 1999.

Nagel, Joane. *American Indian Ethnic Renewal: Red Power and the Resurgence of Identity and Culture.* New York: Oxford University Press, 1997.

Peltier, Leonard. *Prison Writings: My Life Is My Sundance,* edited by Harvey Arden. New York: St. Martin's, 2000.

Sanchez, John, and Mary E. Stuckey, "The Rhetoric of American Indian Activism in the 1960s and 1970s." *Communication Quarterly* 48 (Spring 2000): 120–136.

Smith, Paul Chaat, and Robert Allen Warrior. *Like a Hurricane: The Indian Movement from Alcatraz to Wounded Knee.* New York: New Press, 1996.

Stromberg, Ernest, ed. *American Indian Rhetorics of Survivance: Word Medicine, Word Magic.* Pittsburgh, PA: University of Pittsburgh Press, 2006.

Animal Rights

Adams, Carol J. *The Sexual Politics of Meat: A Feminist-Vegetarian Critical Theory,* 2nd ed. New York: Continuum, 2010.

Armstrong, Susan J., and Richard G. Botzler. *The Animal Ethics Reader,* 2nd ed. New York: Routledge, 2008.

Atkins-Sayre, Wendy. "Articulating Identity: People for the Ethical Treatment of Animals and the Animal/Human Divide." *Western Journal of Communication* 74 (May–June 2010): 309–328.

Ball, Matt, and Friedrich, Bruce. *The Animal Activist's Handbook: Maximizing Our Positive Impact on Today's World.* New York: Lantern, 2009.

Bekoff, Mark. *The Animal Manifesto: Six Reasons for Expanding Our Compassion Footprint.* Novato, CA: New World Library, 2010.

Goodale, Greg, and Jason Edward Black, eds. *Arguments about Animal Ethics.* New York: Lexington, 2010.

Grandin, Temple. *Animals Make Us Human: Creating the Best Life for Animals.* Boston: Mariner, 2009.

Jasper, James M., and Scott Saunders. "Recruiting Strangers and Friends: Moral Shocks and Social Networks in Animal Rights and Animal Protest." *Social Problems* 42 (1995): 493–512.

Linzey, Andrew. *Animal Gospel.* Louisville, KY: Westminster John Knox, 2000.

Mechling, Elizabeth Walker, and Jay Mechling. "Kind and Cruel America: The Rhetoric of Animal Rights." *Rhetorical Dimensions in Media: A Critical Casebook,* 2nd ed., edited by Martin J. Medhurst and Thomas W. Benson. Dubuque, IA: Kendall/Hunt, 1991.

Pacelle, Wayne. *The Bond: Our Kinship with Animals, Our Call to Defend Them.* New York: Morrow, 2011.

Scully, Matthew. *Dominion: The Power of Man, the Suffering of Animals, and the Call to Mercy.* New York: St. Martin's, 2002.

Simonson, Peter. "Social Noise and Segmented Rhythms: News, Entertainment and Celebrity in the Crusade for Rights." *The Communication Review* 4 (2001): 399–420.

Singer, Peter. *Animal Liberation: The Definitive Classic of the Animal Rights Movement,* 3rd ed. New York: Harper Perennial, 2009.

Sunstein, Cass R., and Martha C. Nussbaum. *Animal Rights: Current Debates and New Directions.* New York: Oxford University Press, 2004.

Anti-Globalization / Global Justice

Amoore, Louise, ed. *The Global Resistance Reader.* New York: Routledge, 2004.

Bennett, W. Lance. "Communicating Global Activism." *Information, Communication & Society* 6 (2003): 143–169.

Cockburn, Alexander, Jeffrey St. Clair, and Allan Sekula. *Five Days That Shook the World: The Battle for Seattle and Beyond.* New York: Verso, 2000.

Danaher, Kevin, and Jason Mark. *Insurrection: Citizen Challenges to Corporate Power.* New York: Routledge, 2003.

Demarais, Annette Aurelie. *La Via Campesina: Globalization and the Power of Peasants.* London: Pluto, 2007.

Eschle, Catherine. *Global Democracy, Social Movements, and Feminism.* Boulder, CO: Westview, 2001.

Fernandez, Luis A. *Policing Dissent: Social Control and the Anti-Globalization Movement.* New Brunswick, NJ: Rutgers University Press, 2008.

Juris, Jeffrey S. "The New Digital Media and Activist Networking within Anti–Corporate Globalization Movements." *Annals of AAPSS* 597 (2007): 189–208.

Mahuya, Pal. "Theorizing Resistance in a Global Context: Processes, Strategies, and Tactics in Communication Scholarship." *Communication Yearbook* 32 (2008): 41–87.

Mertes, Tom, ed. *A Movement of Movements: Is Another World Really Possible?* New York: Verso, 2004.

Moghadam, Valentine M. *Globalization and Social Movements: Islamism, Feminism, and the Global Justice Movement.* Lanham, MD: Rowman & Littlefield, 2008.

O'Brien, Robert, Anne Marie Goetz, Jan Aart Scholte, and Marc Williams. *Contesting Global Governance: Multilateral Economic Institutions and Global Social Movements.* New York: Cambridge University Press, 2000.

Opel, Andy, and Donnalyn Pompper, eds. *Representing Resistance: Media, Civil Disobedience, and the Global Justice Movement.* Westport, CT: Praeger, 2003.

Sanjeev, Khagram, Kathryn Sikkink, and James V. Riker, eds. *Restructuring World Politics: Transnational Social Movements, Networks, and Norms.* Minneapolis: University of Minnesota Press, 2002.

Welton, Neva, and Linda Wolf. *Global Uprising: Confronting the Tyrannies of the 21st Century: Stories from a New Generation of Activists.* Gabriola Island, BC: New Society, 2001.

Antilynching

Allen, James, Hilton Als, John Lewis, and Leon F. Litwack. *Without Sanctuary: Lynching Photography in America.* Santa Fe, NM: Twin Palms, 2000.

Cameron, James. *From the Inside Out: A Lynching in the North.* Honolulu, HI: That New Publishing Co., 1980.

Dray, Philip. *At the Hands of Persons Unknown: The Lynching of Black America.* New York: Modern Library, 2003.

Ehrenhaus, Peter, and A. Susan Owen. "Race Lynching and Christian Evangelicalism: Performances of Faith." *Text and Performance Quarterly* 24 (July/October 2004): 276–301.

Fuoss, Kirk W. "Lynching Performances, Theatres of Violence." *Text and Performance Quarterly* 19 (January 1999): 1–37.

Ginzburg, Ralph. *100 Years of Lynchings.* Baltimore: Black Classic, 1988.

Hall, Jacquelyn Dowd. *Revolt against Chivalry: Jessie Daniel Ames and the Women's Campaign against Lynching.* New York: Columbia University Press, 1993.

Kirschke, Amy Helene. *Art in Crisis: W. E. B. Du Bois and the Struggle for African American Identity and Memory.* Bloomington: Indiana University Press, 2007.

Madison, James H. *A Lynching in the Heartland: Race and Memory in America.* New York: Palgrave Macmillan, 2003.

Margolick, David. *Strange Fruit: The Biography of a Song.* New York: Ecco, 2001.

Miller, Erica M. *The Other Reconstruction: Where Violence and Womanhood Meet in the Writings of Wells-Barnett, Grimké, and Larsen.* New York: Garland, 2000.

Pfeifer, Michael J. *Rough Justice: Lynching and American Society, 1874–1947.* Urbana: University of Illinois Press, 2004.

Royster, Jacqueline Jones, ed. *Southern Horrors and Other Writings: The Anti-Lynching Campaign of Ida B. Wells, 1892–1900.* New York: Bedford/St. Martin's, 1996.

Schechter, Patricia A. *Ida B. Wells-Barnett and American Reform, 1880–1930.* Chapel Hill: University of North Carolina Press, 2001.

Zangrando, Robert L. *The NAACP Crusade against Lynching, 1909–1950.* Philadelphia: Temple University Press, 1980.

Antinuclear

Benford, Robert D. "'You Could Be the Hundredth Monkey': Collective Action Frames and Vocabularies of Motive within the Nuclear Disarmament Movement." *Social Forces* 71 (1993): 677–701.

Boyer, Paul S. *By the Bomb's Early Light: American Thought and Culture at the Dawn of the Atomic Age.* New York: Pantheon, 1985.

Hogan, J. Michael. *The Nuclear Freeze Campaign: Rhetoric and Foreign Policy in the Telepolitical Age.* East Lansing: Michigan State University Press, 1994.

Keyes, Ken, Jr. *The Hundreth Monkey.* Coos Bay, OR: Vision, 1983.

Knopf, Jeffrey W. *Domestic Society and International Cooperation: The Impact of Protest on U. S. Arms Control Policy.* New York: Cambridge University Press, 1998.

Laffin, Arthur J., and Anne Montgomery, eds. *Swords into Plowshares: Nonviolent Direct Action for Disarmament.* San Francisco: Perennial Library, 1987.

Mannix, Patrick. *The Rhetoric of Antinuclear Fiction: Persuasive Strategies in Novels and*

Film. Lewisburg, PA: Bucknell University Press, 1992.

Mayer, David S. *A Winter of Discontent: The Nuclear Freeze and American Politics.* New York: Praeger, 1990.

Mitchell, Gordon R. *Strategic Deception: Rhetoric, Science, and Politics in Missile Defense Advocacy.* East Lansing: Michigan State University Press, 2000.

Norman, Liane Ellison. *Hammer of Justice: Molly Rush and the Plowshares Eight.* Pittsburgh, PA: Pittsburgh Peace Institute, 1989.

Rochon, Thomas R., and David S. Meyer, eds. *Coalitions and Political Movements: The Lessons of the Nuclear Freeze.* Boulder, CO: Rienner, 1997.

Rojecki, Andrew. *Silencing the Opposition: Antinuclear Movements and the Media in the Cold War.* Urbana: University of Illinois Press, 1999.

Schell, Jonathan. *The Fate of the Earth.* New York: Knopf, 1982.

Sklar, Morty, ed. *Nuke-Rebuke: Writers and Artists against Nuclear Energy and Weapons.* Iowa City: Spirit That Moves Us, 1984.

Taylor, Bryan C., William J. Kinsella, Stephen P. Depoe, and Maribeth S. Metzler, eds. *Nuclear Legacies: Communication, Controversy and the U.S. Nuclear Weapons Complex.* Lanham, MD: Lexington, 2007.

Antislavery / Abolition

Bacon, Jacqueline. *The Humblest May Stand Forth: Rhetoric, Empowerment, and Abolition.* Columbia: University of South Carolina Press, 2002.

Browne, Stephen H. *Angelina Grimké: Rhetoric, Identity, and the Radical Imagination.* East Lansing: Michigan State University Press, 1999.

Friedman, Lawrence J. *Gregarious Saints: Self and Community in Antebellum American Abolitionism, 1830–1870.* New York: Cambridge University Press, 1982.

Glaude, Eddie S., Jr. *Exodus!: Religion, Race, and Nation in Early Nineteenth-Century Black America.* Chicago: University of Chicago Press, 2000.

Kraditor, Aileen. *Means and Ends in American Abolitionism: Garrison and His Critics on Strategy and Tactics, 1834–1850.* New York: Pantheon, 1969.

Lampe, Gregory. *Frederick Douglass: Freedom's Voice, 1818–1845.* East Lansing: Michigan State University Press, 1998.

Mayer, Henry. *All on Fire: William Lloyd Garrison and the Abolition of Slavery.* New York: St. Martin's, 1998.

McBride, Dwight A. *Impossible Witnesses: Truth, Abolitionism, and Slave Testimony.* New York: New York University Press, 2001.

McGlone, Robert E. *John Brown's War against Slavery.* Cambridge, UK: Cambridge University Press, 2009.

Morris, Charles E., III. "'Our Capital Aversion': Abigail Folsom, Madness, & Radical Antislavery Praxis." *Women's Studies in Communication* 24 (Spring 2001): 62–89.

Painter, Nell Irvin. *Sojourner Truth: A Life, A Symbol.* New York: Norton, 1997.

Ruchames, Louis. *The Abolitionists: A Collection of Their Writings.* New York: Putnam's, 1963.

Stauffer, John. *The Black Hearts of Men: Radical Abolitionists and the Transformation of Race.* Cambridge, MA: Harvard University Press, 2002.

Yellin, Jean Fagan, and John C. Van Horne, eds. *The Abolitionist Sisterhood: Women's Political Culture in Antebellum America.* Ithaca: Cornell University Press, 1994.

Zaeske, Susan. *Signatures of Citizenship: Petitioning, Antislavery, and Women's Political Identity.* Chapel Hill: University of North Carolina Press, 2003.

Arab Spring / Arab Awakening

Ahmari, Sohrab, and Nasser Weddady, eds. *Arab Spring Dreams: The Next Generation Speaks Out for Freedom and Justice from North Africa to Iran.* New York: Palgrave Macmillan, 2012.

Benmamoun, Mamoun, Morris Kalliny, and Robert A. Cropf. "The Arab Spring, MNEs, and Virtual Public Spheres." *Multinational Business Review* 20 (2012): 26–43.

Bradley, John R. *The Arab Spring: How Islamists Hijacked the Middle East Revolts.* New York: Palgrave Macmillan, 2012.

Dabashi, Hamid. *The Arab Spring: Delayed Defiance and the End of Postcolonialism.* London: Zed, 2012.

Feiler, Bruce. *Generation Freedom: The Middle East Uprisings and the Remaking of the Modern World.* New York: Harper Perennial, 2011.

Ghonim, Wael. *Revolution 2.0: The Power of the People Is Greater Than the People in Power: A Memoir.* Boston: Houghton Mifflin, 2012.

Manhire, Toby. *The Arab Spring: Rebellion, Revolution, and the New World Order.* New York: Random House, 2012.

Nanabhay, Mohamed. "From Spectacle to Spectacular: How Physical Space, Social Media and Mainstream Broadcast Amplified the Public Sphere in Egypt's 'Revolution.'" *Journal of North African Studies* 16 (2011): 573–603.

Noueihed, Lin, and Alex Warren. *The Battle for the Arab Spring: Revolution, Counter-Revolution and the Making of a New Era.* New Haven, CT: Yale University Press, 2012.

Pollack, Kenneth M., et al. *The Arab Awakening: America and the Transformation of the Middle East.* Washington, DC: Brookings, 2011.

Civil Rights / Black Power

Bond, Julian, and Andrew Lewis. *Gonna Sit at the Welcome Table.* Boston: Cengage, 2000.

Branch, Taylor. *Parting the Waters: America in the King Years, 1954–63.* New York: Simon & Schuster, 1988.

Breitman, George, ed. *By Any Means Necessary: Speeches, Interviews, and a Letter, by Malcolm X.* New York: Pathfinder, 1970.

Condit, Celeste Michelle, and John Louis Lucaites. *Crafting Equality: America's Anglo-African Word.* Chicago: University of Chicago Press, 1993.

DeLaure, Marilyn Bordwell. "Planting Seeds of Change: Ella Baker's Radical Rhetoric." *Women's Studies in Communication* 31 (Spring 2008): 1–28.

Harold, Christine, and Kevin DeLuca. "Behold the Corpse: Violent Images and the Case of Emmett Till." *Rhetoric and Public Affairs* 8 (Summer 2005): 263–286.

Hoerl, Kristen. "Burning Mississippi into Memory? Cinematic Amnesia as Resource for Remembering Civil Rights." *Critical Studies in Media Communication* 26 (March 2009): 54–79.

Houck, Davis W., and David E. Dixon, eds. *Rhetoric, Religion, and the Civil Rights Movement, 1954–1965.* Waco, TX: Baylor University Press, 2006.

King, Martin Luther, Jr. *I Have a Dream: Writings and Speeches That Changed the World,* edited by James Melvin Washington. San Francisco: HarperSanFrancisco, 1992.

Olson, Lynne. *Freedom's Daughters: The Unsung Heroines of the Civil Rights Movement from 1830 to 1970.* New York: Scribner's, 2001.

Pauley, Garth E. "John Lewis's 'Serious Revolution': Rhetoric, Resistance, and Revision at the March on Washington." *Quarterly Journal of Speech* 84 (August 1998): 320–340.

Scott, Robert L., and Wayne Brockriede. *The Rhetoric of Black Power.* New York: Harper and Row, 1969.

Singh, Nikhil Pal. *Black Is a Country: Race and the Unfinished Struggle for Democracy.* Cambridge, MA: Harvard University Press, 2004.

Terrill, Robert E. *Malcolm X: Inventing Radical Judgment.* East Lansing: Michigan State University Press, 2004.

VanDeburg, William. *New Day in Babylon: The Black Power Movement and American Culture, 1965–1975.* Chicago: University of Chicago Press, 1992.

Conservative and Right Wing

Ansell, Amy E., ed. *Unraveling the Right: The New Conservatism in American Thought and Politics.* Boulder, CO: Westview, 1998.

Bennett, David Harry. *The Party of Fear: From Nativist Movements to the New Right in American History.* Chapel Hill: University of North Carolina Press, 1988.

Berlet, Chip, and Matthew N. Lyons. *Right-Wing Populism in America: Too Close for Comfort.* New York: Guilford, 2000.

Brummett, Barry. "A Pendatic Analysis of Ideologies in Two Gay Rights Controversies." *Central States Speech Journal* 30 (Fall 1979): 250–261.

Dobratz, Betty, and Stephanie L. Shanks-Meile. *The White Separatist Movement in the United States: White Power White Pride.* Baltimore: Johns Hopkins University Press, 2000.

Diamond, Sara. *Roads to Dominion: Right-Wing Movements and Political Power in the United States.* New York: Guilford, 1995.

George, John, and Laird Wilcox. *American Extremists: Militias, Supremacists, Klansmen, Communists & Others.* Amherst, NY: Prometheus, 1996.

Hardisty, Jean. *Mobilizing Resentment: Conservative Resurgence from the John Birch Society to the Promise Keepers.* Boston: Beacon, 2000.

Helvarg, David. *The War against the Greens: The "Wise-Use" Movement, the New Right, and the Browning of America,* rev. ed. Boulder, CO: Johnson, 2004.

Klatch, Rebecca E. *A Generation Divided: The New Left, the New Right, and the 1960s.* Berkeley: University of California Press, 1999.

Medhurst, Martin J. "The First Amendment vs. Human Rights: A Case Study in Community Sentiment and Argument from Definition." *Western Journal of Speech Communication* 46 (Winter 1982): 1–19.

Solomon, Martha. "The 'Positive Woman's' Journey: A Mythic Analysis of the Rhetoric of STOP ERA." *Quarterly Journal of Speech* 65 (October 1979): 262–274.

Stern, Kenneth S. *A Force upon the Plain: The American Militia Movement and the Politics of Hate.* New York: Simon & Schuster, 1996.

Swain, Carol M., and Russ Nieli, Eds. *Contemporary Voices of White Nationalism in America.* New York: Cambridge University Press, 2003.

Warnick, Barbara. "The Rhetoric of Conservative Resistance." *Southern Speech Communication Journal* 42 (Spring 1977): 256–273.

Disability Rights

Charlton, James I. *Nothing about Us without Us: Disability Oppression and Empowerment.* Berkeley: University of California Press, 2000.

Cherney, James L. "Deaf Culture and the Cochlear Implant Debate: Cyborg Politics and the Identity of People with Disabilities." *Argumentation & Advocacy* 36 (Summer 1999): 22–34.

Christiansen, John B., and Sharon N. Barnhartt. *Deaf President Now! The 1988 Revolution at Gallaudet University.* Washington, DC: Gallaudet University Press, 1995.

Davis, Lennard J. *Enforcing Normalcy: Disability, Deafness, and the Body.* New York: Verso, 1995.

Fleischer, Doris Zames, and Frieda Zames. *The Disability Rights Movement: From Charity to Confrontation.* Philadelphia: Temple University Press, 2001.

Jankowski, Katherine A. *Deaf Empowerment: Emergence, Struggle, and Rhetoric.* Washington, DC: Gallaudet University Press, 1997.

Johnson, Mary. *Make Them Go Away: Clint Eastwood, Christopher Reeve, and the Case against Disability Rights.* Louisville, KY: Advocado, 2003.

Johnson, Mary, and Barrett Shaw. *To Ride the Public's Buses: The Fight That Built a Movement.* Louisville, KY: Advocado, 2001.

Linton, Simi. *Claiming Disability: Knowledge and Identity.* New York: New York University Press, 1998.

Longmore, Paul K. *Why I Burned My Book and Other Essays on Disability.* Philadelphia: Temple University Press, 2003.

Longmore, Paul K., and Lauri Umansky, eds. *The New Disability History: American Perspectives.* New York: New York University Press, 2001.

McRuer, Robert. *Crip Theory: Cultural Signs of Queerness and Disability.* New York: New York University Press, 2006.

Shapiro, Joseph P. *No Pity: People with Disabilities Forging a New Civil Rights Movement.* New York: Three Rivers, 1994.

Switzer, Jacqueline Vaughn. *Disabled Rights: American Disability Policy and the Fight for Equality.* Washington, DC: Georgetown University Press, 2003.

Wilson, James C., and Cynthia Lewiecki-Wilson, eds. *Embodied Rhetorics: Disability in Language and Culture.* Carbondale: Southern Illinois University Press, 2001.

Environmental Justice

Brown, Stuart C., and Carl G. Herndl, eds. *Green Culture: Environmental Rhetoric in Contemporary America.* Madison: University of Wisconsin Press, 1996.

Bullard, Robert D. *Confronting Environmental Racism: Voices from the Grassroots.* Cambridge, MA: South End, 1993.

Cox, Robert. *Environmental Communication and the Public Sphere,* 2nd ed. (London: Sage, 2009).

DeLuca, Kevin Michael. *Image Politics: The New Rhetoric of Environmental Activism.* New York: Guilford, 1999.

Endres, Danielle, Leah Sprain, and Tarla Rai Peterson, eds. *Social Movement for Climate Change: Local Action for Global Change.* Amherst, NY: Cambria, 2009.

Hendry, Judith. *Communication in the Natural World.* State College, PA: Strata, 2010.

Killingsworth, M. Jimmie, and Jacqueline S. Palmer. *Ecospeak: Rhetoric and Environmental Politics.* Carbondale: Southern Illinois University Press, 1992.

Luhmann, Niklas. *Ecological Communication.* Chicago: University of Chicago Press, 1989.

Nash, Roderick. *Wilderness and the American Mind,* 4th ed. New Haven, CT: Yale University Press, 2001.

Peterson, Tarla Rai. *Sharing the Earth: The Rhetoric of Sustainable Development.* Columbia: University of South Carolina Press, 1992.

Pezzullo, Phaedra C. "Performing Critical Interruptions: Stories, Rhetorical Invention, and the Environmental Justice Movement." *Western Journal of Communication* 65 (Winter 2001): 1–25.

Pezzullo, Phaedra C. *Toxic Tourism: Rhetorics of Pollution, Travel, and Environmental Justice.* Tuscaloosa: University of Alabama Press, 2009.

Slawter, Lisa D. "TreeHugger TV: Re-Visualizing Environmental Activism in the Post-Network Era." *Environmental Communication* 2 (July 2008): 212–228.

Szasz, Andrew. *Shopping Our Way to Safety: How We Changed from Protecting Our Environment to Protecting Ourselves.* Minneapolis: University of Minnesota Press, 2009.

Waddell, Craig, ed. *And No Birds Sing: Rhetorical Analyses of Rachel Carson's Silent Spring.* Carbondale: Southern Illinois University Press, 2000.

Wolfe, Dylan. "The Video Rhizome: Taking Technology Seriously in *The Meatrix.*" *Environmental Communication: A Journal of Nature and Culture* 3 (November 2009): 317–334.

Feminist / Women's Liberation

Baxandall, Rosalyn, and Linda Gordon, eds. *Dear Sisters: Dispatches from the Women's Liberation Movement.* New York: Basic, 2001.

Borda, Jennifer L. "Negotiating Feminist Politics in the Third Wave: Labor Struggles and Solidarity in *Live Nude Girls Unite!*" *Communication Quarterly* 57.2 (April–June 2009): 117–135.

Chávez, Karma R., and Cindy L. Griffin, eds. Special Issue on Power Feminism. *Women's Studies in Communication* 32 (2009): 1–127.

Collins, Patricia Hill. *Black Feminist Thought: Knowledge, Consciousness, and the Politics of Empowerment.* New York: Routledge, 2000.

Dever, Carolyn. *Skeptical Feminism: Activist Theory, Activist Practice.* Minneapolis: University of Minnesota Press, 2003.

Dow, Bonnie J. *Prime Time Feminism: Television, Media Culture, and the Women's Movement since 1970.* Philadelphia: University of Pennsylvania Press, 1996.

Echols, Alice. *Daring to Be Bad: Radical Feminism in America, 1967–1975.* Minneapolis: University of Minnesota Press, 1989.

Evans, Sara. *Tidal Wave: How Women Changed America at Century's End.* New York: Free Press, 2003.

Fixmer, Natalie, and Julia T. Wood. "The Personal is *Still* Political: Embodied Politics in Third Wave Feminism." *Women's Studies in Communication* 28 (Fall 2005): 235–257.

Heywood, Leslie L. *The Women's Movement Today: An Encyclopedia of Third-Wave Feminism.* Westport, CT: Greenwood, 2006.

Moraga, Cherríe, and Gloria Anzaldúa, *This Bridge Called My Back: Writings by Radical Women of Color.* New York: Kitchen Table, Women of Color Press, 1983.

Morgan, Robin. *Sisterhood Is Powerful: An Anthology of Writings from the Women's Liberation Movement.* New York: Random House, 1970.

Pearson, Kyra. "Mapping Rhetorical Interventions in 'National' Feminist Histories: Second Wave Feminism and *Ain't I a Woman.*" *Communication Studies* 50 (Summer 1999): 158–173.

Rowe, Aimee Carrillo. *Power Lines: On the Subject of Feminist Alliances.* Durham, NC: Duke University Press, 2008.

Steinem, Gloria. *Outrageous Acts and Everyday Rebellions.* New York: New American Library, 1983.

GLBTQ
(Gay / Lesbian / Bisexual / Transgender / Queer)

Bennett, Jeffrey A. *Banning Queer Blood: Rhetorics of Citizenship, Contagion, and Resistance.* Tuscaloosa: University of Alabama Press, 2009.

Blasius, Mark, and Shane Phelan, eds. *We Are Everywhere: A Historical Sourcebook of Gay and Lesbian Politics.* New York: Routledge, 1997.

Bornstein, Kate, and S. Bear Bergman. *Gender Outlaws: The Next Generation.* Berkeley, CA: Seal, 2010.

Carter, David. *Stonewall: The Riots that Sparked the Gay Revolution.* New York: St. Martin's, 2004.

Clendinen, Dudley, and Adam Nagourney. *Out for Good: The Struggle to Build a Gay Rights Movement in America.* New York: Simon & Schuster, 1999.

Cohen, Cathy J. "Punks, Bulldaggers, and Welfare Queens: The Radical Potential of Queer Politics?" *GLQ* 3 (1997): 437–465.

Conrad, Ryan, ed. *Against Equality: Queer Critiques of Gay Marriage.* Oakland, CA: AK Press, 2010.

D'Emilio, John. *Sexual Politics, Sexual Communities: The Making of a Homosexual Minority in the United States, 1940–1970.* Chicago: University of Chicago Press, 1983.

Ghaziani, Amin. *The Dividends of Success: How Conflict and Culture Work in Gay and Lesbian Marches on Washington.* Chicago: University of Chicago Press, 2008.

Gray, Mary L. "'Queer Nation Is Dead/Long Live Queer Nation': The Politics and Poetics of Social Movement and Media Representation." *Critical Studies in Media Communication* 26 (August 2009): 212–236.

Phelan, Shane. *Identity Politics: Lesbian Feminism and the Limits of Community.* Philadelphia: Temple University Press, 1991.

Pinello, Daniel R. *America's Struggle for Same-Sex Marriage.* New York: Cambridge University Press, 2007.

Rand, Erin J. "A Disunited Nation and a Legacy of Contradiction: Queer Nation's Construction of Identity." *Journal of Communication Inquiry* 28.4 (2004): 288–306.

Shilts, Randy. *The Mayor of Castro Street: The Life and Times of Harvey Milk.* New York: St. Martin's, 1982.

Smith, Ralph R., and Russel R. Windes. *Progay/Antigay: The Rhetorical War over Sexuality.* Thousand Oaks, CA: Sage, 2000.

Sycamore, Mattilda Bernstein. *That's Revolting: Queer Strategies for Resisting Assimilation.* New York: Soft Skull, 2008.

Labor

Cloud, Dana L. *We Are the Union: Democratic Unionism and Dissent at Boeing.* Urbana: University of Illinois Press, 2011.

Darsey, James. "Prophet's Call and Burden: The Passion of Eugene V. Debs." *The Prophetic Tradition and Radical Rhetoric in America.* New York: New York University Press, 1997.

Dubofsky, Melvyn, and Joseph A. McCartin. *American Labor: A Documentary Collection.* New York: Palgrave Macmillan, 2004.

Foner, Philip S. *History of the Labor Movement in the United States.* 7 Vols. New York: International, 1987.

Foner, Philip S. *Mother Jones Speaks: Collected Writings and Speeches.* New York: Monad, 1983.

Foner, Philip S. *Women and the American Labor Movement: From Colonial Times to the Eve of World War I.* New York: Free Press, 1979.

Gompers, Samuel. *Seventy Years of Life and Labor: An Autobiography,* ed. Philip Taft and John A. Sessions. New York: Dutton, 1957.

Hammerback, John C., and Richard J. Jensen. *The Rhetorical Career of César Chávez.* College Station: Texas A & M University Press, 1998.

May, Matthew S. "Hobo Orator Union: Class Composition and the Spokane Free Speech Fight of the Industrial Workers of the World." *Quarterly Journal of Speech* 97 (2011): 155–177.

Nelson, David. *Shifting Fortunes: The Rise and Decline of American Labor, from the 1820s to the Present.* Chicago: Dee, 1998.

Parsons, Lucy E. *Famous Speeches of the Eight Chicago Anarchists.* New York: Arno, 1969.

Roediger, David. *The Wages of Whiteness: Race and the Making of the American Working Class.* New York: Verso, 2000.

Schlesinger, Arthur M., Jr. *Writings and Speeches of Eugene V. Debs.* New York: Hermitage, 1948.

Stewart, Charles J. "The Internal Rhetoric of the Knights of Labor." *Communication Studies* 42 (Spring 1991): 67–82.

Triece, Mary Eleanor. *Protest and Popular Culture: Women in the U.S. Labor Movement, 1894–1917.* Boulder, CO: Westview, 2001.

Latina/o

Blackwell, Maylei. *¡Chicana Power!: Contested Histories of Feminism in the Chicano Movement.* Austin: University of Texas Press, 2011.

Chávez, Karma R. "Border (In)Securities: Normative and Differential Belonging in LGBTQ and Immigrant Rights Discourse." *Communication and Critical/Cultural Studies* 7 (June 2010): 136–155.

Cisneros, Josue David. "(Re)Bordering the Civic Imaginary: Rhetoric, Hybridity, and Citizenship in La Gran Marcha." *Quarterly Journal of Speech* 97 (February 2011): 26–49.

Delgado, Fernando Pedro. "Chicano Movement Rhetoric: An Ideographic Interpretation." *Communication Quarterly* 43 (Fall 1995): 446–454.

Enck-Wanzer, Darrel, ed. *The Young Lords: A Reader.* New York: New York University Press, 2010.

Flores, Lisa A. "Creating Discursive Space through a Rhetoric of Difference: Chicana Feminists Craft a Homeland." *Quarterly Journal of Speech* 82 (May 1996): 142–156.

Grosfoguel, Ramón, Nelson Maldonado-Torres, and José David Saldívar, eds. *Latin@s in the World-System: Decolonization Struggles in the 21st Century U.S. Empire.* Boulder, CO: Paradigm, 2005.

Hammerback, John C., Richard J. Jensen, and Jose Angel Gutierrez. *A War of Words: Chicano Protest in the 1960s and 1970s.* Westport, CT: Greenwood, 1985.

Holling, Michelle A., and Bernadette M. Calafell, eds. *Latina/o Discourse in Vernacular Spaces: Somos De Una Voz?* Lanham, MD: Lexington, 2011.

Jiménez Román, Miriam, and Juan Flores. *The Afro-Latin@ Reader: History and Culture in the United States.* Durham, NC: Duke University Press, 2010.

Muñoz, Carlos. *Youth, Identity, Power: The Chicano Movement,* rev. ed. London: Verso, 2007.

Pineda, Richard D., and Stacey K. Sowards. "Flag Waving as Visual Argument: 2006 Immigration Demonstrations and Cultural Citizenship." *Argumentation & Advocacy* 43 (Winter–Spring 2007): 164–174.

Sowards, Stacey. "Rhetorical Agency as *Haciendo Caras* and Differential Consciousness through Lens of Gender, Race, Ethnicity, and Class: An Examination of Dolores Huerta's Rhetoric." *Communication Theory* 20 (May 2010): 223–247.

Torres, Andrés, and José E. Velázquez. *The Puerto Rican Movement: Voices from the Diaspora.* Philadelphia: Temple University Press, 1998.

Torres, Rodolfo D., and George Katsiaficas. *Latino Social Movements: Historical and Theoretical Perspectives.* New York: Routledge, 1999.

Occupy

Blumenkranz, Carla, et al. *Occupy!: Scenes from Occupied America.* London: Verso, 2011.

Chomsky, Noam. *Occupy.* Brooklyn, NY: Zuccotti Park, 2012.

Dean, Jodi, James Martel, and Davide Panagia, eds. Special Issue on Occupy Wall Street. *Theory & Event* 14, no. 4 Supplement (2011).

DeLuca, Kevin M., Sean Lawson, and Ye Sun. "Occupy Wall Street on the Public Screens of Social Media: The Many Framings of the Birth of a Protest Movement." *Communication, Culture, & Critique* 5 (December 2012): 483–509.

Faraone, Chris. *99 Nights with the 99 Percent: Dispatches from the First Three Months of the Revolution.* Boston: Write to Power, 2012.

Flank, Lenny, ed. *Voices from the 99 Percent: An Oral History of the Occupy Wall Street Movement.* St. Petersburg, FL: Red and Black, 2011.

Nichols, John. *Uprising: How Wisconsin Renewed the Politics of Protest from Madison to Wall Street.* New York: Nation, 2012.

Rebick, Judy. *Occupy This!* Toronto: Penguin Canada, 2012.

Shepard, Benjamin Heim. "Labor and Occupy Wall Street: Common Causes and Uneasy Alliances." *WorkingUSA* 15 (March 2012): 121–134.

Van Gelder, Sarah, ed. *This Changes Everything: Occupy Wall Street and the 99% Movement.* San Francisco: Berrett Koehler, 2011.

Peace / Antiwar / New Left

Albert, Judith Clavir, and Stewart Edward Albert, eds. *The Sixties Papers: Documents of a Rebellious Decade.* New York: Praeger, 1984.

Andrews, James R. "Confrontation at Columbia: A Case Study in Coercive Rhetoric." *Quarterly Journal of Speech* 55 (1969): 9–16.

Berg, Rick, and John Rowe. *The Vietnam War and American Culture.* New York: Columbia University Press, 1993.

Breines, Wini. *Community and Organization in the New Left, 1962–1968: The Great Refusal.* New Brunswick, NJ: Rutgers University Press, 1989.

Cohen, Robert, and Reginald E. Zelnik, eds. *The Free Speech Movement: Reflections on Berkeley in the 1960s.* Berkeley: University of California Press, 2002.

Gitlin, Todd. *The Whole World Is Watching: Mass Media in the Making and Unmaking of the New Left.* Berkeley: University of California Press, 1980.

Griffin, Leland M. "The Rhetorical Structure of the 'New Left' Movement: Part I." *The Quarterly Journal of Speech* 50 (April 1964): 113–135.

Heineman, Kenneth J. *Campus Wars: The Peace Movement at American State Universities in the Vietnam Era.* New York: New York University Press, 1993.

Miller, Jim. *Democracy Is in the Streets: From Port Huron to the Siege of Chicago.* New York: Simon & Schuster, 1987.

Morgan, Edward P. *What Really Happened to the 1960s: How Mass Media Culture Failed American Democracy.* Lawrence: University Press of Kansas, 2010.

Myers, R. David, ed. *Toward a History of the New Left: Essays from within the Movement.* Brooklyn: Carlson, 1989.

Rorabaugh, W. J. *Berkeley at War: The 1960s.* New York: Oxford University Press, 1989.

Swerdlow, Amy. *Women Strike for Peace: Traditional Motherhood and Radical Politics in the 1960s.* Chicago: University of Chicago Press, 1993.

Unger, Irwin. *The Movement: A History of the American New Left, 1959–72.* New York: Dodd, Mead, 1974.

Varon, Jeremy. *Bringing the War Home: The Weather Underground, the Red Army Faction, and Revolutionary Violence in the Sixties and Seventies.* Berkeley: University of California Press, 2004.

Prison Reform and Death Penalty Abolitionist

Abu-Jamal, Mumia. *Live from Death Row.* New York: Perennial, 2002.

Davis, Angela Y. *Are Prisons Obsolete?* New York: Seven Stories, 2003.

Haines, Herbert H. *Against Capital Punishment: The Anti-Death Penalty Movement in America, 1972–1994.* New York: Oxford University Press, 1996.

Hames-Garcia, Michael. *Fugitive Thought: Prison Movements, Race, and the Meaning of Justice.* Minneapolis: University of Minnesota Press, 2004.

Hartnett, Stephen John, ed. *Challenging the Prison-Industrial Complex: Activism, Arts, & Educational Alternatives.* Urbana: University of Illinois Press, 2011.

Jackson, George. *Soledad Brother: The Prison Letters of George Jackson.* Chicago: Lawrence Hill, 1994.

James, Joy, ed. *Imprisoned Intellectuals: America's Political Prisoners Write on Life, Liberation, and Rebellion.* Lanham, MD: Rowman & Littlefield, 2003.

Linebaugh, Peter. *The London Hanged: Crime and Civil Society in the Eighteenth Century.* Cambridge, UK: Cambridge University Press, 1992.

Lynd, Staughton. *Lucasville: The Untold Story of a Prison Uprising,* 2nd ed. Oakland, CA: PM, 2004.

McCann, Bryan J. "Genocide as Representative Anecdote: Crack Cocaine, the CIA, and the Nation of Islam in Gary Webb's 'Dark Alliance.'" *Western Journal of*

Communication 74 (July–September 2010): 396–416.

McCann, Bryan J. "Therapeutic and Material <Victim>hood: Ideology and the Struggle for Meaning in the Illinois Death Penalty Controversy." *Communication and Critical/Cultural Studies* 4 (December 2007): 382–401.

Meiners, Erica R. *Right To Be Hostile: Schools, Prisons, and the Making of Public Enemies.* New York: Routledge, 2007.

PCARE. "Fighting the Prison-Industrial Complex: A Call to Communication and Cultural Studies Scholars to Change the World." *Communication and Critical/Cultural Studies* 4 (December 2007): 401–420.

Peltier, Leonard. *Prison Writings: My Life Is My Sun Dance.* New York: St. Martin's, 1999.

Rodríguez, Dylan. *Forced Passages: Imprisoned Radical Intellectuals and the U.S. Prison Regime.* Minneapolis: University of Minnesota Press, 2006.

Pro-Life / Pro-Choice

Black, Jason Edward. "Extending the Rights of Personhood, Voice, and Life to Sensate Others: A Homology of Right to Life and Animal Rights Rhetoric." *Communication Quarterly* 51 (Summer 2003): 312–331.

Blanchard, Dallas. *Religious Violence and Abortion.* Gainesville: University Press of Florida, 1993.

Branham, Robert James. "The Role of the Convert in 'Eclipse of Reason' and 'Silent Scream.'" *Quarterly Journal of Speech* 77 (November 1991): 407–426.

Condit, Celeste. *Decoding Abortion Rhetoric: Communicating Social Change.* Urbana: University of Illinois Press, 1990.

Dubriwny, Tasha. "Consciousness Raising as Collective Rhetoric: The Redstockings' Abortion Speak-Out of 1969." *Quarterly Journal of Speech* 91 (November 2005): 395–422.

Feldt, Gloria. *The War on Choice: The Right-Wing Attack on Women's Rights and How to Fight Back.* New York: Bantam, 2004.

Ginsburg, Faye D. *Contested Lives: The Abortion Debate in an American Community.* Berkeley: University of California Press, 1989.

Lake, Randall. "Order and Disorder in Anti-Abortion Rhetoric: A Logological View." *Quarterly Journal of Speech* 70 (November 1984): 425–43.

Luker, Kristin. *Abortion and the Politics of Motherhood.* Berkeley: University of California Press, 1984.

Mason, Carol. *Killing for Life: The Apocalyptic Narrative of Pro-Life Politics.* Ithaca, NY: Cornell University Press, 2002.

Maxwell, Carol J. C. *Pro-Life Activists in America: Meaning, Motivation, and Direct Action.* New York: Cambridge University Press, 2002.

Nelson, Jennifer. *Women of Color and the Reproductive Rights Movement.* New York: New York University Press, 2003.

Rose, Melody. "Pro-Life, Pro-Woman? Frame Extension in the American Antiabortion Movement." *Journal of Women, Politics and Policy* 32 (2011): 1–27.

Solinger, Rickie, ed. *Abortion Wars: A Half-Century of Struggles, 1950–2000.* Berkeley: University of California Press, 1998.

Staggenborg, Suzanne. *The Pro-Choice Movement: Organization and Activism in the Abortion Conflict.* New York: Oxford University Press, 1991.

Tea Party

Berlet, Chip. "Taking Tea Parties Seriously: Corporate Globalization, Populism, and Resentment." *Perspectives on Global Development and Technology* 10 (2011): 11–29.

DiMaggio, Anthony R. *The Rise of the Tea Party: Political Discontent and Corporate Media in the Age of Obama.* New York: Monthly Review, 2011.

Foley, Elizabeth Price. *The Tea Party: Three Principles.* New York: Cambridge University Press, 2012.

Gatchet, Amanda Davis. "Preserving America: The Tea Party Movement and the Cultivation of Revolutionary Conservatism." In *The Politics of Style and the Style of Politics,* edited by Barry Brummett. Lanham, MD: Lexington, 2011.

Leahy, Michael Patrick. *Covenant of Liberty: The Ideological Origins of the Tea Party Movement.* New York: Broadside, 2012.

Lepore, Jill. *The Whites of Their Eyes: The Tea Party's Revolution and the Battle over American History.* Princeton, NJ: Princeton University Press, 2010.

Huebert, Jacob H., and Yuri N. Maltsev. *The Tea Party Movement.* Westport, CT: Greenwood, 2012.

Meckler, Mark, and Jenny Beth Martin. *Tea Party Patriots: The Second American Revolution.* New York: Holt, 2012.

O'Hara, John M. *A New American Tea Party: The Counterrevolution against Bailouts, Handouts, Reckless Spending, and More Taxes.* Hoboken, NJ: Wiley, 2010.

Skocpol, Theda, and Vanessa Williamson. *The Tea Party and the Remaking of Republican Conservatism.* New York: Oxford University Press, 2012.

Temperance

Blocker, Jack S., Jr. *Retreat from Reform: The Prohibition Movement in the United States, 1890–1913.* Westport, CT: Greenwood, 1976.

Blumberg, Leonard U., with William L. Pittman. *Beware the First Drink!: The Washington Temperance Movement and Alcoholics Anonymous.* Seattle: Glen Abbey, 1991.

Bordin, Ruth. *Frances Willard: A Biography.* Chapel Hill: University of North Carolina Press, 1986.

Bordin, Ruth. *Women and Temperance: The Quest for Power and Liberty, 1873–1900.* Philadelphia: Temple University Press, 1981.

Frick, John W., and Don B. Wilmeth, eds. *Theatre, Culture and Temperance Reform in Nineteenth-Century America.* New York: Cambridge University Press, 2003.

Griffin, Charles J. G. "The 'Washingtonian Revival': Narrative and the Moral Transformation of Temperance Reform in Antebellum America." *Southern Communication Journal* 66 (Fall 2000): 67–78.

Gough, John B. *Platform Echoes: Living Truths for Head and Heart.* Hartford, CT: Worthington, 1890.

Gusfield, Joseph R. *Symbolic Crusade: Status Politics and the American Temperance Movement.* Urbana: University of Illinois Press, 1963.

Levine, Harry Gene. "The Discovery of Addiction: Changing Conceptions of Habitual Drunkenness in America." *Journal of Studies on Alcohol* 39 (January 1978): 143–74.

Pegram, Thomas R. *Battling Demon Rum: The Struggle for a Dry America, 1800–1933.* Chicago: Dee, 1998.

Reynolds, David S., and Debra J. Rosenthal, eds. *The Serpent in the Cup: Temperance in American Literature.* Amherst: University of Massachusetts Press, 1997.

Tyrrell, Ian R. *Sobering Up: From Temperance to Prohibition in Antebellum America, 1800–1860.* Westport, CT: Greenwood, 1979.

Tyrrell, Ian R. *Woman's World/Woman's Empire: The Woman's Christian Temperance Union in International Perspective, 1880–1930.* Chapel Hill: University of North Carolina Press, 1991.

Warner, Michael. "Whitman Drunk." In *Breaking Bounds: Whitman and American Cultural Studies,* edited by Betsy Erkkila and Jay Grossman. New York: Oxford University Press, 1996: 30–43.

Willard, Frances. *A White Life for Two.* Chicago: Woman's Temperance, 1890.

Woman Suffrage

Borda, Jennifer L. "The Woman Suffrage Parades of 1910–1913: Possibilities and Limitations of an Early Feminist Rhetorical Strategy." *Western Journal of Communication* 66 (Winter 2002): 25–52.

Campbell, Karlyn Kohrs. *Man Cannot Speak for Her.* 2 Vols. New York: Praeger, 1989.

Catt, Carrie Chapman, and Nettie Rogers Shulman. *Woman Suffrage and Politics: The Inner Story of the Suffrage Movement.* New York: Scribner's, 1926.

Conrad, Charles. "The Transformation of the 'Old Feminist' Movement." *Quarterly Journal of Speech* 67 (August 1981): 284–297.

DuBois, Ellen Carol. *Women's Suffrage—Women's Rights.* New York: New York University Press, 1998.

Flexner, Eleanor. *Century of Struggle: The Women's Rights Movement in the United States.* Cambridge, MA: Belknap/Harvard University Press, 1975.

Gifford, Carolyn DeSwarte, and Amy R. Slagell. *Let Something Good Be Said: Speeches and Writings of Frances E. Willard.* Urbana: University of Illinois Press, 2007.

Kraditor, Aileen S. *The Ideas of the Woman Suffrage Movement, 1890–1920.* New York: Norton, 1981.

Lundarin, Christine A. *From Equal Suffrage to Equal Rights: Alice Paul and the National Woman's Party, 1910–1928.* New York: New York University Press, 1986.

Solomon, Martha, ed. *A Voice of Their Own: The Woman Suffrage Press, 1840–1910.* Tuscaloosa: University of Alabama Press, 1991.

Stanton, Elizabeth Cady, Susan B. Anthony, and Matilda Joslyn Gage, eds. *History of Woman Suffrage.* 6 Vols. Rochester, NY: Mann, 1881–1922.

Stillion Southard, Belinda A. *Militant Citizenship: Rhetorical Strategies of the National Women's Party, 1913–1920.* College Station: Texas A & M University Press, 2011.

Terborg-Penn, Rosalyn. *African American Women in the Struggle for the Vote, 1850–1920.* Bloomington: Indiana University Press, 1998.

Wheeler, Marjorie Spruill, ed. *One Woman, One Vote: Rediscovering the Woman Suffrage Movement.* Troutdale, OR: NewSage, 1995.

Wood, Maude. *Front Door Lobby,* edited by Edna Lampey Stantial. Boston: Beacon, 1960.

INTERDISCIPLINARY PERSPECTIVES

Agamben, Giorgio. *The Coming Community,* translated by Michael Hardt. Minneapolis: University of Minnesota Press, 1993.

Aronowitz, Stanley, and Heather Gautney, eds. *Implicating Empire: Globalization and Resistance in the 21st Century World Order.* New York: Basic, 2003.

Asen, Robert, and Daniel C. Brouwer, eds. *Counterpublics and the State.* Albany: State University of New York Press, 2001.

Butler, Judith. *The Psychic Life of Power: Theories in Subjection.* Palo Alto, CA: Stanford University Press, 1997.

Chenoweth, Erica, and Maria Stephan. *Why Civil Resistance Works: The Strategic Logic of Nonviolent Conflict.* New York: Columbia University Press, 2011.

Chesters, Graeme, and Ian Welsh. *Social Movements: The Key Concepts.* New York: Routledge, 2010.

Day, Richard J. F. *Gramsci is Dead: Anarchist Currents in the Newest Social Movements.* London: Pluto, 2005.

Del Gandio, Jason. *Rhetoric for Radicals: A Handbook for 21st Century Activists.* Gabriola Island, BC: New Society, 2008.

Foust, Christina R. *Transgression as a Mode of Resistance: Rethinking Social Movement in an Era of Corporate Globalization.* Lanham, MD: Lexington, 2010.

Goodwin, Jeff, James M. Jasper, and Francesca Polletta, eds. *Passionate Politics: Emotions and Social Movements.* Chicago: University of Chicago Press, 2001.

Hardt, Michael, and Antonio Negri. *Multitude: War and Democracy in the Age of Empire.* (New York: Penguin, 2004).

Jasper, James M. *The Art of Moral Protest: Culture, Biography, and Creativity in Social Movements.* Chicago: University of Chicago Press, 1997.

Kahn, Seth, and Jonghwa Lee, eds. *Activism and Rhetoric: Theories and Contexts for Political Engagement.* New York: Routledge, 2011.

Laclau, Ernesto, and Chantal Mouffe. *Hegemony and Socialist Strategy: Towards a Radical Democratic Politics,* 2nd ed. London: Verso, 2001.

Mansbridge, Jane, and Aldon Morris, eds. *Oppositional Consciousness: The Subjective Roots of Social Protest.* Chicago: University of Chicago Press, 2001.

McAdam, Doug, Sidney Tarrow, and Charles Tilly. *Dynamics of Contention.* New York: Cambridge University Press, 2001.

Melucci, Alberto. *Nomads of the Present: Social Movements and Individual Needs in Contemporary Society.* Philadelphia: Temple University Press, 1989.

Terranova, Tiziana. *Network Culture: Politics for the Information Age.* London: Pluto, 2004.

Tilly, Charles, and Lesley Wood. *Social Movements, 1768–2008,* 2nd ed. Boulder, CO: Paradigm, 2009.

Warner, Michael. *Publics and Counterpublics.* New York: Zone, 2002.

MEDIA AND SOCIAL MOVEMENTS

Cottle, Simon, and Libby Lester, eds. *Transnational Protest and the Media.* New York: Peter Lang, 2011.

Donk, Wim van de, Brian D. Loader, Paul G. Nixon, and Dieter Rucht, eds. *Cyberprotest: New Media, Citizens and Social Movements.* New York: Routledge, 2004.

Downing, John D. H. *Radical Media: Rebellious Communication and Social Movements.* Thousand Oaks, CA: Sage, 2001.

Eyerman, Ron, and Andrew Jamison. *Music and Social Movements: Mobilizing Traditions in the Twentieth Century.* New York: Cambridge University Press, 1998.

Frey, Lawrence R., and Kevin M. Carragee, eds. *Media and Performance Activism.* Vol. 2 of *Communication Activism.* Cresskill, NJ: Hampton, 2007.

Gamson, William, and Gadi Wolfsfeld. "Movements and Media as Interacting Systems." *Annals of the American Academy of Political and Social Science* 528 (1993): 114–125.

Hands, Joss. *@ Is for Activism: Dissent, Resistance, and Rebellion in a Digital Culture.* London: Pluto, 2011.

Harold, Christine. *Our Space: Resisting the Corporate Control of Culture.* Minneapolis: University of Minnesota Press, 2007.

Lievrouw, Leah. *Alternative and Activist New Media.* Malden, MA: Polity, 2011.

McChesney, Robert W. *The Problem of the Media: U.S. Communication Politics in the Twenty-First Century.* New York: Monthly Review, 2004.

Ryan, Charlotte. *Prime Time Activism: Media Strategies for Grassroots Organizing.* Boston: South End, 1991.

Ryan, Charlotte. "Successful Collaboration: Movement Building in the Media Arena." In *Rhyming Hope and History: Activists, Academics, and Social Movement Scholarship,* eds. David Croteau, William Hoynes, and Charlotte Ryan. Minneapolis: University of Minnesota Press, 2005: 115–136.

Strietmatter, Rodger. *Voices of Revolution: The Dissident Press in America.* New York: Columbia University Press, 2001.

Watson, Tom. *CauseWired: Plugging In, Getting Involved, Changing the World.* Hoboken, NJ: Wiley, 2008.

Whiteman, David. "Out of the Theaters and into the Streets: A Coalition Model of the Political Impact of Documentary Film and Video." *Political Communication* 21 (January/March 2004): 51–69.

INDEX

ABOUT THE EDITORS

Charles E. Morris III is Professor of Communication and Rhetorical Studies and of LGBT Studies at Syracuse University. He has a B.A. from Boston College. He received his M.A. and Ph.D. from The Pennsylvania State University. He is the cofounding editor of *QED: A Journal in GLBTQ Worldmaking*. His books include *Queering Public Address: Sexualities in American Historical Discourse* (2007), *Remembering the AIDS Quilt* (2011), and *An Archive of Hope: Harvey Milk's Selected Speeches and Writings* (2013). His essays have appeared in the *Quarterly Journal of Speech, Communication and Critical/Cultural Studies, Rhetoric & Public Affairs,* and elsewhere. For his work as an archival queer, Professor Morris has received two Golden Monograph Awards, the Karl Wallace Memorial Award, and the Randy Majors Memorial Award from the National Communication Association.

Stephen Howard Browne is Professor of Speech Communication at The Pennsylvania State University, where he teaches courses in rhetorical theory and criticism. He received his B.S. from the University of Oregon, his M.A. from Colorado State University, and his Ph.D. from the University of Wisconsin. He is the author of *Edmund Burke and the Discourse of Virtue* (1993), *Angelina Grimke, Rhetoric, Identity, and the Radical Imagination* (1999), and *Jefferson's Call for Nationhood: The First Inaugural Address* (2003). He has published more than thirty essays in the history and criticism of rhetoric in the *Quarterly Journal of Speech, Communication Monographs, Rhetoric and Public Affairs,* and other journals. Professor Browne has received the National Communication Association's Diamond Anniversary Book Award and the Karl Wallace Memorial Award.